The Inter-Asia Cultural Studies Reader

Asian Cultural Studies or Cultural Studies in Asia is a new and burgeoning field, and the *Inter-Asia Cultural Studies Journal* is at its cutting edge. Committed to bringing Asian Cultural Studies scholarship to the international English-speaking world and constantly challenging existing conceptions of cultural studies, the journal has emerged as the leading publication in Cultural Studies in Asia.

The Inter-Asia Cultural Studies Reader brings together the best of the ground-breaking papers published in the journal and includes a new introduction by the editors, Kuan-Hsing Chen and Chua Beng Huat. Essays are grouped in thematic sections, identifying issues which are important across the region, such as state violence and social movements, as well as work produced by *IACS* sub-groups, covering topics such as feminism, queer studies, cinema studies and popular culture studies.

The *Reader* provides useful alternative case studies and challenging perspectives, which will be invaluable for both students and scholars in media and cultural studies.

Essays by: Firdous Azim, Melani Budianta, Partha Chatterjee, Hee-Yeon Cho, Cho Han Hae-joang, Chua Beng Huat, Ding Naifei, Hilmar Farid, Hanasaki Kohei, Josephine Ho, Kelly Hu, Hans Tao-Ming Huang, Po-keung Hui, Kim Hyun Mee, Kim Seong-nae, Kim Soyoung, Liu Jen-peng, Eric Ma, Meaghan Morris, Muto Ichiyo, Tejaswini Niranjana, Ashish Rajadhyaksha, A. B. Shamsul, Sun Ge, Toriyama Atsushi, Eva Tsai, Wang Hui, Paul Willemen, Yoo Sun-Young, Shunya Yoshimi.

Kuan-Hsing Chen is Professor in the Center for Asia-Pacific/Cultural Studies at the National Tsing-Hua University in Taiwan. He is founding co-executive editor of *Inter-Asia Cultural Studies*. His previous publications, in English and Chinese, include *Towards De-Imperialization – Asia as Method* (2006), *Trajectories: Cultural Studies Inter-Asia* (1998) and *Stuart Hall: Critical Dialogues in Cultural Studies*, edited with Dave Morley (1996).

Chua Beng Huat is Professor in the Asia Research Institute and the Department of Sociology, National University of Singapore. He is founding co-executive editor of *Inter-Asia Cultural Studies*. His previous publications include *Life is Not Complete Without Shopping* (2003) and *Consumption in Asia: Lifestyles and Identities* (2000).

The Inter-Asia Cultural Studies Reader

Edited by
Kuan-Hsing Chen and
Chua Beng Huat

Routledge
Taylor & Francis Group

LONDON AND NEW YORK

First published 2007
by Routledge
2 Park Square, Milton Park, Abingdon, Oxon OX14 4RN

Simultaneously published in the USA and Canada
by Routledge
270 Madison Ave, New York, NY 10016

Routledge is an imprint of the Taylor & Francis Group, an informa business

Editorial selection and material © 2007 Kuan-Hsing Chen and Chua Beng
Huat; chapters © 2007 the contributors

Typeset in Garamond 3 and Gill Sans by
Florence Production Ltd, Stoodleigh, Devon
Printed and bound in Great Britain by
The Cromwell Press, Trowbridge, Wiltshire

British Library Cataloguing in Publication Data
A catalogue record for this book is available from the British Library

Library of Congress Cataloging in Publication Data
A catalog record for this book has been requested

ISBN10: 0–415–43134–4 (hbk)
ISBN10: 0–415–43135–2 (pbk)
ISBN10: 0–203–96098–X (ebk)

ISBN13: 978–0–415–43134–7 (hbk)
ISBN13: 978–0–415–43135–4 (pbk)
ISBN13: 978–0–203–96098–1 (ebk)

Contents

Notes on contributors and translators

1 **Sun Ge** 孫歌 was born in 1955 and received her BA degree in Chinese Literature at Jilin University, China. She is currently an Associate Researcher in the Institute of Literature at the Chinese Academy of Social Sciences. She has written several works in Chinese including *Seeking Alternative Frame of Reference* (*Qiu Cuo Ji* 求錯集) (Sanlian Bookstore 三聯書店), and 'Position of Literature' 文學的位置 (in *Intellectual Inquiry* 3, 4 學術思想評論 3 期、4 期) 1/4 etc.
   Translators: **Hui Shiu-lun** 許兆麟 is finishing his dissertation in Comparative Literature at Hong Kong University. Lau Kinchi 劉健芝 teaches in the Cultural Studies Program at Lingnan in Hong Kong.

2 **Wang Hui** is Professor in the College of Humanities and Social Sciences, Tsing Hua University, Beijing, where he also heads the Institute for Advanced Studies in Humanities and Social Sciences. An executive editor of the most important monthly journal, *Du-Shu*, Wang Hui is a leading intellectual in China. His major research areas include Chinese intellectual history and modern Chinese literatue. His books include *The Rise of Modern Chinese Thought* (现代中国思想的兴起) (2004), *China's New Order* (2003), *For a New Asia* (为了新的亚洲) (2003). He serves on the board of *Positions: East Asian Cultural Critique, Critical Asian Studies, Post-Colonial Studies, The Traces, Twenty First Century* (二十一世纪), *China's Scholarship* (中国学术).
   Translator: **Matthew Allen Hale** is a student of anthropology at the University of Washington in Seattle, USA. His dissertation research concerns agrarian issues and the emerging New Rural Reconstruction movement in China. He has translated several works by Chinese scholars.

3 **Tejaswini Niranjana** is Senior Fellow at the Centre for the Study of Culture and Society, Bangalore, India. She is the author of *Siting Translation: History, Post-structuralism and the Colonial Context*, and co-editor of *Interrogating Modernity: Culture and Colonialism in India*. She was one of the organizers of the workshop on Rethinking the Third World held in Jamaica in 1996. At present, she is coordinating a project on gender and media for CSCS, and preparing a monograph based on her comparative research in Trinidad and South Africa.

4 **Chua Beng Huat** is Professor in the Asia Research Institute and the Department of Sociology, National University of Singapore. He is co-executive editor of *Inter-Asia Cultural Studies*. His most recent publication on consumption culture is *Life is Not Complete without Shopping* (Singapore, 2003).

5 **A. B. Shamsul** researches, teaches and writes on politics, culture and economic development in Southeast Asia. He is Professor of Social Anthropology and, currently, Director, Institute of the Malay World & Civilization, Universiti Kebangsaan Malaysia, Bangi, Malaysia.

6 **Partha Chatterjee** was born in 1947. After getting his BA degree in Political Science at the University of Calcutta, India, he went on to earn his Ph.D. degree in Political Science at University of Rochester in 1971. After teaching there for a year, he went back to India and worked at the Center for Studies in Social Sciences, Calcutta. He became a professor in 1979 and has headed the Centre from 1997 until 2006. He was also Visiting Professor at Columbia University, New York; Oxford University, England; New School, New York; and Leiden University, the Netherlands.

7 **Hanasaki Kohei**, an independent scholar and freelance writer on philosophy and social thought, studied at Tokyo University. A former associate professor at Hokkaido University, Hanasaki Kohei has, since the 1970s, engaged in solidarity works with indigenous Ainu people's movement claiming their own ethnic rights. Author of many books on philosophy and social thought. *The Wind Blows as it Likes* (1976), *An Essay on Philosophy of Liberation* (1986), *Calm Land – Mastuura Takeshiro and the Ainu People* (1989), *Philosophy of Identity and Co-viviality (Living Together Keeping Differences)* (1993), *Individual and Transcendence* (1996). Currently co-president of the People's Plan Study Group based in Tokyo, and a resident of Otaru City, Hokkaido.

Translator: **Muto Ichiyo**, born in 1931, is a writer on political and social affairs, and has been engaged actively in the anti-war movement and other social movements since the 1950s. Author of 10 books including *Critique of the Dominant Structure* (1970), *Base and Culture* (1975), *Unmasking the Japanese State* (1984), *Reinstating Political Thought* (1988), *Visions and Realities* (1998), and *Problematizing the Postwar Japanese State* (1999). Has taught in the Sociology Department of the State University of New York at Binghamton since 1983. The founder of the Pacific Asia Resource Center and currently Co-President of the People's Plan Study Group based in Tokyo.

8 **Kim Seong-nae** 김성례 is an Associate Professor of cultural anthropology at the Department of Religious Studies, Sogang University, Seoul. She has written several articles about the Cheju April Third Incident in English, including 'Sexual politics of state violence: on Cheju April Third Massacre of 1948' (*Traces*, Spring 2001). Her current research interests are narrative analysis of historical trauma and healing process, and modernity and popular religiosity in Korea.

9 **Hilmar Farid** is a writer-activist, living in Jakarta. He is a founding member of Jaringan Kerja Budaya, a collective of artists, researchers and cultural workers, and a researcher at the Indonesian Institute for Social History in Jakarta.

10 **Yoo Sun-Young** 유선영 received a Ph.D. from Korea University in Seoul, Korea, and has given lectures on cultural studies and history of Korean journalism at Korea University and Sogang University, Seoul, Korea. She now is working for

the Korea Press Foundation as a research fellow. Her research interest has been in cultural studies, especially concentrating on the modern formation of Korean popular culture as guided by the problematics of (post-)colonial modernity.

Translator: **Francis Lee Dae-Hoon** 이대훈 is now doing a doctoral thesis on security politics in Northeast Asia in the Department of Peace Studies of the University of Bradford in Britain.

11 **Shunya Yoshimi** 吉見俊哉 is Professor in the Institute of Socio-Information and Communication Studies at the University of Tokyo. His research focuses on issues of power related to popular culture and daily life in a modernizing society. His recent books have included studies of the social history of popular entertainment in Tokyo, the role of telecommunications in society, and the politics of Tokyo Disneyland. He is the author of such works as *Urban Dramaturgy* (1987) and *Cultural Sociology in the Age of Media* (1994).

Translator: **David Buist** graduated from the University of London in 1985 with a degree in anthropology. He went on to study in the graduate schools of Duke University and the University of Tokyo. He currently holds the position of research associate in the Institute of Socio-Information and Communication Studies at the University of Tokyo. Besides translating academic works, he also has research interests in nationalism and modern thought in Japan, the politics of culture, and hermeneutics.

12 **Toriyama Atsushi** 鳥山淳 was born in 1971. He is now researcher of the Institute of Regional Study of Okinawa University and also editor in chief of the quarterly journal *Keshi Kaze*, which is published in Okinawa.

Translator: **David Buist** (see above).

13 **Cho Han Hae-joang** is Professor of Cultural Anthropology at the Department of Sociology, Yonsei University, Seoul. Cho's major publications include *Women and Men in South Korea* (1988), *Reading Texts, Reading Lives in the Post-Colonial Era* vols 1, 2, 3 (1992, 1994, 1994), *Children Refusing School, Society Refusing Children* (1996), and *Introspective Modernity and Feminism* (1998). Her current cultural studies work includes youth, gender, class, education, nationalism, consumer culture, and popular culture. A founding member of the feminist activist group, Alternative Culture (Ttohana ui Munwha), Cho implements her research in youth issues with her directorships at the Yonsei University-based Center for Youth and Cultural Studies, and at the Youth Factory for Alternative Culture (which is sponsored by Seoul City Government).

Translator: **Michael Shin** is a Ph.D. candidate in the History Department at the University of Chicago.

14 **Firdous Azim** is Professor of English and now teaches at BRAC University in Dhaka, Bangladesh. She is the author of *The Colonial Rise of the Novel* (Routledge, 1993), and has edited a number of books including *Infinite Variety: Women in Society and Literature* (University Press, Dhaka, 1996). Her interests include post-colonial and feminist theory. She is a member of Naripokkho, a women's activist group in

Bangladesh and is actively involved in women's liberation issues. She has been a Commonwealth Scholar and Fellow based at the University of Sussex and at SOAS, University of London. She is a member of IACS and is also a contributing editor for *Interventions* and *Feminist Review*, both published from London. Her present research is on Toru Dutt, and English and women's writing in nineteenth-century Bengal. She is a regular contributor to literary columns in Bangladesh and is interested in popularizing theoretical post-colonial concerns.

15 **Eva Tsai** is currently Assistant Professor at the Graduate Institute of Mass Communication, National Taiwan Normal University. Her past research work has appeared in the anthology, *Feeling Asian Modernities* (Hong Kong University Press, 2004), *Modern Chinese Literature and Culture*, and *Inter-Asia Cultural Studies*. She has a forthcoming article on Japanese scriptwriter Nozawa Hisashi in *Japan Forum* and a forthcoming chapter on stars and televisual culture in the anthology, *Television, Japan, and Globalization* (University of Michigan Press). She is researching stationery culture and writing a book about Japanese television drama writers.

16 **Josephine Ho** 何春蕤 has been writing both extensively and provocatively to open up new discursive space for gender/sexuality issues. Her books, all written in Chinese as timely interventions into local gender/sexuality politics, include *The Gallant Woman – Feminism and Sexual Emancipation* 豪爽女人 (1994), *Gendered Nations – Sexuality, Capital and Culture* 不同國女人 (1994), *Sexual Moods: A Therapeutic and Liberatory Report on Female Sexuality* 性心情 (1996), *Radical Sexuality Education: Gender/Sexuality Education for the 'New Generation'* 性／別校園 (1998), and *The Admirable/Amorous Woman* 好色女人 (1998). She then turned to the editing of a number of ground-breaking anthologies of local gender/sexuality research as well as the organization of international conferences on cutting-edge gender/sexuality topics. Describing herself as a feminist sex radical, she now serves as Chair of the English Department and the Coordinator for the Center for the Study of Sexualities at National Central University 中央大學性／別研究室, Taiwan, well-known for both its activism and its intellectual stamina. Website at http://sex.ncu.edu.tw.

17 **Hans Tao-Ming Huang** 黃道明 is currently Post Doctoral Research Fellow at the English Department, National Central University, Taiwan. He received his Ph.D. in Media Studies, University of Sussex, UK in 2003. He is currently working on a book project on the state regulation of sexualities in Taiwanese society since 1949.

18 **Liu Jen-peng** 劉人鵬 is Professor of Chinese Literature at National Tsing Hua University in Taiwan. She is the author of *Jindai Zhongguo Nuquan Lunshu: Guozu, Fanyi yu Xingbie Zhengzhi (Modern Chinese Discourses on Women's Rights: The Politics of Nationalism, Translation and Gender/Sexuality)* (Taipei: Xueshengshuju, 2000).

Ding Naifei 丁乃非 is Professor of English and a member of the Center for the Study of Sexualities at National Central University, Chung-li, Taiwan. She is the author of *Obscene Things: Sexual Politics in Jin Ping Mei* (Durham: Duke University Press, 2003).

19 **Meaghan Morris** is Chair Professor of Cultural Studies, Lingnan University, Hong Kong. She has written widely on popular historiography, cultural studies, and

feminist cultural theory. Her books include *'Race' Panic and the Memory of Migration*, co-edited with Brett de Bary (Hong Kong University Press with Iwanami Shoten, Tokyo, Jiangsu Education Press, Nanjing, and Moonhwa Kwahaksa, Seoul, 2001); *Too Soon, Too Late: History in Popular Culture* (Indiana University Press, 1998); *Australian Cultural Studies: A Reader*, co-edited with John Frow (Allen & Unwin, 1993); and *The Pirate's Fiancée: Feminism, Reading, Postmodernism* (Verso, 1988). She is currently completing a study of action cinema as popular historiography (*White Panic: History in Action Cinema*) and a biography of the Australian journalist and travel writer Ernestine Hill.

20 **Ashish Rajadhyaksha** is a film and cultural studies theorist in India and the co-editor of *The Encyclopedia of Indian Cinema*. He is a Senior Fellow at the Centre for the Study of Culture and Society.

21 **Paul Willemen** was part of the editorial group of *Screen* in the 1970s; he edited *Framework* in the 1980s and is the author of many books on cinema, including *Questions of Third Cinema* (with Jim Pines, 1987), *The Encyclopaedia of Indian Cinema* (with Ashish Rajadhyaksha, 1995) and *Looks and Frictions* (1994). He is currently Research Professor at the University of Ulster.

22 **Kim Soyoung** 김소영 is Professor of Cinema Studies at Korean National University of Arts. She has published several books on modernity, cinema and gender including *Specters of Modernity: Fantastic Korean Cinema* (2000). Her essays appeared in journals in Japanese, English and Korean. She is also a filmmaker, tracing women's history in Korea. Her filmography includes *Koryu: Southern Women/South Korea* (an opening film for Seoul Women's Film Festival 2001).

23 **Melani Budianta** is Professor at the Faculty of Cultural Studies, University of Indonesia, presently teaching at the Department of English, Literary Studies Program, and American Studies Program. She has completed a number of researches in post-colonial theory, gender and cultural studies, published in Indonesia as well as in international scholarly journals. She received her Ph.D. in English Language and Literature from Cornell University in 1992.

24 **Eric Ma** 馬傑偉 is Associate Professor of Communication at the Chinese University of Hong Kong and the author of *Culture, Politics and Television in Hong Kong* (Routledge, 1999).

25 **Kim Hyun Mee** 김현미 is Associate Professor at the Department of Sociology and also teaches in the Graduate programme in Culture and Gender Studies at Yonsei University, Seoul, Korea. As a cultural anthropologist, her areas of interest lie in the political economy of gender, feminist cultural studies, post-colonialism. Her current research includes the Korean pop culture wave in the Asian regions and the women migrant workers employed in the entertainment sector of Korea.

Translator: **Hong Sung Hee** 홍성희 is a graduate student of Tisch School of the Arts Maurice Kanbar Institute of Film and Television, New York University.

26 **Kelly Hu** 胡綺珍 is currently Associate Professor at the Department of Communication & Institute of Telecommunications, National Chung Cheng University. Her
research interests include digital technology, cultural production/consumption,
Chinese transnationalism, and globalization.

27 **Muto Ichiyo** 武藤一羊 , born in 1931 in Tokyo, is a writer on political and social
affairs, and has been engaged actively in the anti-war movement and other social
movements since the 1950s. Author of books including *Subject and Front*, (1967),
Critique of the Dominant Structure, (1970), *Base and Culture* (1975), *Unmasking the
Japanese State* (1984), *Reinstating Political Thoughts* (1988), *Visions and Realities* (1998),
Problematizing the Postwar Japanese State (1999), and *Empire vs. People's Alliance* (2003).
Muto Ichiyo has taught in the Sociology Department of the State University of
New York at Binghamton from 1983 through 1999, and is the founder of English
political journal AMPO and the Pacific-Asia Resource Center and is currently Co-
President of the People's Plan Study Group based in Tokyo. A board member of
Focus on the Global South until 2002. Muto Ichiyo has written numerous English
articles on global democracy and its agencies, alternative perspectives, the Japanese
state and social movements, such as 'For an Alliance of Hope' in J. Brecher (ed.),
Global Visions (1993); 'Alliance of Hope and Challenges of Global Democracy'
(1994); 'The Birth of the Women's Movement in the 1970s', 1997; 'Redefine and
Practice our Peace, our Security, if they do theirs' (2000); 'Some Thoughts on
Empire' (2002).

28 **Hee-Yeon Cho** is Professor at the Department of Sociology and NGO Graduate
School at Sungkonghoe University. He is also one of the co-representatives of
Korea Progressive Academy Council, which is an umbrella united organization of
22 progressive studies associations. He has been involved in the anti-dictatorship
movement and progressive academic movement as a part of it in the 1980s and
1990s. He is also one of the founding members of People's Solidarity for
Participatory Democracy, one of the most influential social movement organizations
in South Korea. He has written lots of books such as *Social Movement and Organizations
in South Korea, Class and Poverty, The State, Democracy and Political Change, Opposition
against from Abnormality to Normality* and so on.

29 **Po-keung Hui** 許寶強 received his Ph.D. in Sociology from the State University
of New York at Binghamton in 1995. He is now teaching at the Cultural Studies
Department of Lingnan University in Hong Kong. His main research interests are
cultural economy, history of capitalism, and alternative development. He has co-
edited the *Cultural and Social Studies Translation Series* 文化社會研究譯叢 , jointly
published by Oxford University Press (Hong Kong) and Bianyi Chubanshe (Beijing).
He is the author of *What Capitalism is Not* 資本主義不是什麼 (Hong Kong Oxford
University Press, 2002).

Acknowledgements

The *Inter-Asia Cultural Studies: Movements* project has been an inspiring, exciting and rewarding experience. We would like to take this opportunity to thank all those who have contributed to and assisted with a project still in a very early phase of its intellectual journey. We are grateful to all the writers who have contributed to the past issues of the journal, particularly those who have agreed to be included in this volume, and to members of the editorial collective and the advisory board for their unfailing support; without this, the project as a whole, and the present *Reader* in particular, would not have been possible. Generous funding for the initial phase of the project was provided by the Japan Foundation; National Science Council (ROC) and National Tsing Hua University (Hsinchu, Taiwan) continues to provide ongoing support. Finally, a two-year visiting research fellowship provided by the Asia Research Institute at National University of Singapore enabled the two editors to work on this *Reader* under the same institutional roof. We would like to thank Grace Hui-Chuan Wu and Emma Chun-Yu Liu for their assistance on the production of this *Reader*.

When we started the project in late 1990s, there were not many intellectual groups working together across the national boundaries in Asia. Limited and small as the Inter-Asia Cultural Studies project was, and is, it has demonstrated that solidarity across borders is possible. This thread has broken the ice. Over the past decade, we have been very happy to witness more groupings emerging, though the process is still very slow. We hope that regional interactions and integration will soon be more widely perceived as an urgent intellectual responsibility in Asia. What we will continue to do for the moment is to open more spaces and build more mechanisms, bringing in new members from the generation of intellectuals that follows us, so that when the momentum arrives, networks of trust and friendship will be in place and will be able to be mobilized. The present volume marks only a beginning of the next and subsequent stages of the project: a greater and greater production of knowledge, beyond the journal and associated books, can follow.

Introduction

The *Inter-Asia Cultural Studies: Movements* project

Throughout the twentieth century, the West has been the inspiration for Asian intellectuals. The West has mediated and shaped the mode of knowledge production in the analyses of Asian societies, politics and cultures, and in self-understanding. The hegemony of 'the West as method' blocks the possibility of us looking towards relatively similar historical experiences shared in Asia, Latin America and Africa. The formulation of 'Asia/Third World as method' is to open up the West-oriented singularity and to multiply frames of reference and sites for identification.[1] The *Inter-Asia Cultural Studies: Movements* project is a small attempt to search for alternatives.

In early 1997, Rebecca Barden, then the senior editor of Cultural Studies within Routledge, approached us to start an Asia-based journal. Having organized the two Trajectories Conferences in Taipei in 1992 and 1995,[2] some of us thought that there was a sufficient basis to take up this challenge. We recognized the simple fact that no 'Asian' publishers had built up distribution networks enabling the circulation of critical materials throughout Asia and beyond, only transnational publishers such as Routledge.[3] In order to establish connections and to produce knowledge within Asia, accepting this invitation could mean being able to bring about a fundamental change: acting to tilt the unbalanced direction of the flow of knowledge through the existing infrastructure. So we decided to form an editorial collective and respond to the call.

Since the inception of the project, we have been conscious that there is no unity to the imaginary entity called 'Asia', hence the term 'Inter-Asia'. In 1998, the first Inter-Asia Cultural Studies Conference was held in Taipei to prepare the first issues of the journal. The name *Inter-Asia Cultural Studies: Movements* was agreed upon by the editorial board during the meeting, and the journal was inaugurated in 2000. It started with three issues a year and, since 2005, has published four issues a year.

Our agenda has been simple: to contribute to the integration of an imagined Asia at the level of knowledge production. More specifically, we set out to: (1) generate and circulate critical work in and out of Asia and beyond; (2) slowly link and facilitate dialogues between the disconnected critical circles within Asia and beyond; and (3) provide a platform on which academic and movement intellectual work can intersect. Only later did we realize our own naivety: these aims were far easier said than done. Nonetheless, to a limited extent, we are achieving some of these ends.

Hitherto, English publications about cultures in Asia have been published mainly outside Asia and international publications in English from Asia have been minimal. Difficulties in 'translating' scholarly work based on Asian languages into English has resulted in intellectual production in Asia being somewhat disconnected from the global circuit. As one of the first pan-Asian international journals in Humanities and Social Sciences to publish and circulate quality interdisciplinary scholarly work in Cultural Studies-related fields generated directly out of Asia, the journal fills a critical gap in making intellectual work produced in Asia available in English. Stemming from our objective to publish works produced in Asian languages, we have also made a special commitment to translation work. And, further, to facilitate mutual translation, the journal has been building alliances with locally-based leading journals in Asia. By 2007, essays previously published in the journal have been translated from and into several Asian languages – for example, Korean, Japanese, Chinese and Indonesian.

In the past, having Asian intellectuals 'looking West' has left intellectual circles in Asia disconnected from each other. One of the tasks of the journal is to build a platform for an 'Inter-Asia' intellectual community by creating links between and across local circles. Therefore, the journal performs a double function: (1) linking together communities in Asia; and (2) linking Asia to the global community. As elsewhere, journals in Asia have played important roles in intellectual and political processes, partly because a journal is always a space where groups of intellectuals congregate. Though a journal is the material product circulating in social space, other networks of event and activity are always generated through the intellectual groupings around the journals. Through the strategy of building a list of affiliated journals, so that translation copyrights between the *IACS* journal and other Asian-language journals can be waived, we are able to link some circles together.[4] Further, although Asia-based, the Inter-Asia Cultural Studies project is not self-enclosed. We have published essays from Europe, North America and Latin America. We have been actively linking with, and will continue to link with, global intellectual communities. We have, therefore, managed to initiate some of these dialogues, though it is still early days.

The title of the journal, *Inter-Asia Cultural Studies: Movements*, positions the project as a part of the larger Asian intellectual movement. One central mission is to construct a space of intellectual activism between critical scholars and movement organizers. We see this space as a product of our own history of struggles in Asia, in various forms of democratic social and political movements, and it is the journal's responsibility to continue that line of critical intellectual work beyond academic institutions. Given our recognition that there is no cultural and/or historical unity, but in fact very significant regional and sub-regional differences throughout 'Asia', including the effects of globalization on regionalization, there is an urgent demand to move beyond nation-state boundaries to intersect the regional and sub-regional. In this work, the journal is providing space to the intellectual communities in Asia, for long overdue voices.

As the journal's mission is to link across the Asian continent, an editorial collective was constituted with 24 scholars (who are both leaders within their own national contexts and are also internationally known), located in 20 cities spread through 15 countries across the Asia-Pacific. Such a wide geographical spread of the editorial board members is rare in the Humanities and Social Sciences and it has only become possible with the emergence of the Internet. Because of the interdisciplinary nature of Cultural Studies, the academic backgrounds of the board members include: Sociology, Anthropology, English Literature, Film Studies, Communication and Media Studies, Comparative Literature, Political Theory, Translation Studies, Intellectual History, Political Economy, Political Sociology, Social History, Gender Studies, Queer Studies and Urban Studies. Since 1998, the editorial collective has met twice a year in different Asian cities. Besides charting important editorial policies, in each of these instances work-shops and seminars were organized to meet local intellectuals. The editorial collective has also organized four larger-scale conferences so that different circles and networks could converge, and materials for publication could be further generated. The first conference was held in Taipei in 1998, the second in Fukuoka, Japan in 2000, and the third in Bangalore, India, in January 2004. The fourth conference took place in Seoul, in July 2005.

Over the years, *IACS* has been gradually indexed in the following: the Bibliography of Social Science; Cambridge Scientific Abstracts; Current Contents/Arts and Human-ities; Current Contents/Social and Behavioral Sciences; the International Bibliography of Social Sciences; Sociological Abstracts; and Worldwide Political Science Abstracts. From 2005, it has been included in the Social Science Citation Index (SSCI) and the Arts and Humanities Citation Index (A&HCI). Inclusion in the major indexes means that the *IACS* project has effectively created a space where scholars from the next generation, who are forced to deal with such mechanical 'recognition' by their employers in the securing of their academic careers, can find a space for their intellectual work.

In 2004, during the editorial collective meeting at the Bangalore Conference, it was decided that an Inter-Asia Cultural Studies Society be established. We deemed that the project was ready to make the next move to expand the network, beyond individuals and into institutions, with the focus of the *IACS* project shifting from journal production to wider intellectual activities. After two years of preparation, the IACS Society was formally established in Seoul, with Kim Soyoung, film director and Professor of Screen Studies in the Korean National University of Arts, as director and Shin Hyunjoon, Head of East Asian Studies Center at Sungungheo Unversity, as executive director.

The two major items on the agenda of the Society are to organize biannual conferences and also graduate student summer camps. The first open-call conference in 2007 was hosted by the Center for Contemporary Cultural Studies at Shanghai University, directed by Professor Wang Xiaoming. A pre-conference for postgraduate students was held. The theme of the main conference was 'Conditions of Knowledge and Cultural Pro-duction'. To fill a major gap in Cultural Studies, one focus of the conference was on three dimensions of peasantry, namely agriculture, village and peasant; the dominant population in Asia is the peasantry, yet the field of Cultural Studies has been completely silent on this complex and urgent issue. The inaugural postgraduate student summer camp was planned for South Korea in 2008.

Besides the IACS Society, the project is advancing to form an Inter-Asia Cultural Studies Institute, as a coordinating body to initiate a deeper and larger scale of Inter-Asia interaction. An Inter-Asia publisher is also being considered so that greater intellectual resources can be made available directly out of Asia.

In all these endeavours, the IACS project is of course confronting problems that have to be overcome. First, as a regional journal, it remains limited by both the bias and basis of its origination in East Asia. Though the editorial policy is to maintain a balance in the publication to include materials outside of East Asia and Southeast Asia, the interaction between sub-regions has not yet fully unfolded, nor has the building of contacts with critical circles in West and Central Asia. How to link with the not-yet-connected parts of Asia needs to be a major objective for the future.

Second, in comparison with other English journals, *IACS* has done relatively more translation work, so as to include the writings of non-English-speaking intellectuals.

Translators capable of rendering difficult intellectual materials from Asian languages into English are few. The project will have to cultivate more networks of translators in order to perform the function of trans-local linkages.

Third, already mentioned, the *IACS* project is an initiative bringing intellectual circles in different parts of Asia to recognize each other's concerns and understand the research being carried out. Far from becoming each other's reference point, there is a long way to go to evolve a critical mode of knowledge. We will need to work hard to make subsequent generations of intellectuals conscious of the different historical conditions in Asia, in order to transform problems generated from an over-reliance on knowledge of or from the West. We envisage that the opportunity for such transformation will take place on the level of collaborative work across borders among postgraduate students and younger faculty members.

Fourth, interaction between critical circles in Asia is indeed occurring, though its speed is slow and the intensity could be stronger. The most productive way of interaction is still being sought. Due to the past experiences, *IACS* must transcend its current limit of communication through written language: visual and audio forms of expressions have to be incorporated.

Fifth, the agenda to link intellectuals in academic and social movements, with the slogan 'to movementize scholarship, to theorize movement', has not yet been fully carried out. Though there is systematic participation from the movement circle, the dominant forces in the project are still located in the academic institutions. How to widen *IACS*'s links is an issue that is constantly addressed. Past practices have made those of us involved in the transnational dialogue realize that we can no longer conceive of the interactive field in a stable and rigid form. We will need to reconceptualize the meaning of 'movement' and 'scholarship'. In the context of neo-liberal globalization, academic institutions proved to have relatively stable resources and have become major sites for the reproduction of 'movement'. In the process of becoming an integral part of the 'movement', the meaning of the academy itself is redefined. In short, 'to movementize scholarship, to theorize movement' needs to be pushed further.

It should be clear from the above discussion that the *Inter-Asia Cultural Studies* project has yet to achieve all its intended aims.

Those who have been involved come from very diverse intellectual and academic backgrounds, not to mention the immensely different local histories in the regions in which each of us has been immersed. At this point, our networks are limited to the South, Southeast and Northeast Asias; further links will hopefully be extended in the future. Even though the network is still small, we already know and feel that the living conditions of the network members are far from being the same. To understand the critical works generated, we need to look beyond the surface of discursive production to reach the material living conditions within which the intellectual works are produced. We have learnt not to use a set of fixed criteria to quickly give judgements on works produced in very different places. We have learnt to see each other's strengths and weaknesses, and to work within these limits and differences. Our, unpronounced, hope has been that, at some point in the future, when different sites in Asia become reference points to one another and different intellectual circles begin to interact, new and alternative modes of knowledge production might be able to emerge from this experiment. We are now only at an early stage of discovering what intellectual concerns exist in our own localities. We need to work longer, further and deeper.

We do nevertheless have some measures of success. In the past, it was difficult to locate materials directly produced in non-English-speaking parts of Asia. Even if one could find them, they were likely to be found in Anglo-American publications, in which authors living in Asia often had to compromise on addressing their own local concerns to cater to the issues and concerns presupposed in the Anglo-American local contexts.[5] Now, the journal has opened a space for problematics grounded in different localities in Asia to emerge. In the past, to develop a reading list for a graduate seminar on Cultural Studies in Asia, it would have been hard to know where to begin. Now, gradually, the journal has made it possible to meet some of these concrete demands. In the process of being 'forced' to produce each issue on schedule, critical materials have emerged and accumulated. A rigorous referee system, seriously applied, has enabled the journal to maintain a strong academic standard, and hence to establish itself as a major publication in the international field of Cultural Studies. The journal now makes a modicum of material available in English for interested readers who want to read pan-Asian, locally-based intellectual work coming directly out of Asia.

For the past ten years or so, we have attempted to put some of these highly motivating ideas into practice. We all feel there is something important and worthwhile emerging in these intense dialogues among ourselves and beyond. The *Inter-Asia Cultural Studies Reader* is our first attempt to share what we have achieved in this initial stage with those who are concerned with the project.

Kuan-Hsing Chen and Chua Beng Huat

Notes

1 See Kuan-Hsing Chen (2005), 'Asia as method', *Taiwan: A Radical Quarterly in Social Studies*, no. 57: 139–218 (in Chinese).

2 See Kuan-Hsing Chen (1998), ed. *Trajectories: Inter-Asia Cultural Studies*, London: Routledge.

3 There are now trans-border bookstores, such as Kinokunia, and the Singapore-based Page One, which have emerged in various Asian cities, but not publishing houses. None of the American university presses, which have had huge intellectual impact in Asia, have solid global distribution networks.

4 A more obvious example is the big 'journal alliance' panel organized in the 2000 Inter-Asia Cultural Studies Conference, held in Fukuoka, where a number of journal editors were invited to reflect on the history and problems of the journals they have edited. See *Inter-Asia Cultural Studies* (2001), Journal Alliance section.

5 In the field of Cultural Studies, the problematic is always locally grounded. The editorial process has taught us that most of the original and creative papers are indeed those addressing local issues and concerns. Therefore, whether a problematic has local bearing has become one of our editorial principles.

Part I

Setting the agenda

Chapter 1

How does Asia mean?

Sun Ge
(Translated by Hui Shiu-Lun and Lau Kinchi)

Introduction

The question of Asia, like the question of modernity, resists any attempt to provide a clear explanation partly because it is loaded with interconnected issues from many facets. Asia is not only a political concept, but also a cultural concept; it is not only a geographical location, but also a measure of value judgement. The Asia question itself does not bear any necessary relation to the question of hegemony and counter-hegemony, although the attempts to tackle this question have brought into play considerations of hegemony of the East and the West. The question itself does not entail nationalism, although the theme of nationalism has been conjured in the course of discussing this question. Another reason why the question of Asia is difficult to explicate is that it is hardly a question of substantialization, namely, by way of ascribing to it unequivocal geographical attributes. Quite contrarily, it is often invoked in the discussion of questions that bear no direct relation, or are even in stark opposition, to any geographical considerations. For a long historical period, Asia has not been treated as a self-contained geographical concept, but has only been put forward ideologically in opposition to Europe. The discussion of Asia involved not only the question of Eurocentrism, but also the question of hegemony within the East. As difficult as it is to sort out the question of Asia, it remains an underlying thread running through the intellectual history in the modern world. Hence, we still have to grapple with the question of Asia as one that constitutes a totality in itself.

The fact that, in the history of the academic world, 'Asia' as a singular term has emerged to name collectively a plurality of countries and regions deserves our attention. As Edward Said has pointed out in his book *Orientalism*: 'To speak of scholarly specialization as a geographical "field" is, in the case of Orientalism, fairly revealing since no one is likely to imagine a field symmetrical to it called Occidentalism. Already the special, perhaps even eccentric attitude of Orientalism becomes apparent. For there is no real analogy for taking a fixed, more or less total geographical position towards a wide variety of social, linguistic, political, and historical realities.' (Said 1985: 50) However, what Said fails to understand is that there is another side to this problem. That is, for the Asians engaged in the discussion of the Asia question, though one cannot say there is precisely something called 'Occidentalism' worked out by them, there indeed exists, and not without reason, in abstraction an ambiguous single entity named the 'West'. Although it is no longer meaningful today to consider the 'West' as a single entity, Occidentalism had, at least in the modern history of East Asia, once played a key role in mediating the self-knowledge of the nations within the East with important questions being stirred up in the process.[1] Said's study has shown us the political and ideological nature of the object of Orientalism. He has also shown us the Eurocentrism concealed in Orientalism. Thanks to this understanding, we can begin our discussion on a higher level. In view of the recent efforts of the Western intellectuals in deconstructing the myth of colonialism, we do not need to pursue any specialist research before we can accept as common knowledge the question of 'the right to discourse' of the West over the East, implicit in both Orientalism and the Asia question. At the same time, if we turn our attention to the history of the East, we can also find that its question of Asia is involved in similarly complicated ideological positions. However, in the hands of the Asians, Orientalism becomes different from that which Said criticizes, for it is directed against the Asian Occidentalism. To a large extent, it is not positioned against the Western world from the perspective of the East, but rather against an image of the West constructed in Asia. Therefore, it not only involves the question of reclaiming the right from the West, but importantly, it reveals complicated historical relations within the Asian nations. Thus, the question of Asia must not merely be pursued within the framework defined by the dichotomy of East versus West, but also should be considered as dealing with internal problems in the Asian region. In turn, the contextual exploration of the Asia question will echo, and respond to, the Saidian question posed by Western intellectuals.

This paper will inquire into the question of Asia within the historical context of East Asia. I will mainly deal with materials from the intellectual history of modern Japan. This focus is the result of my personal acquaintance with this particular field, and is also taken because the question of Asia does not assume a similar importance, and hence position, equally in the intellectual histories in East Asia. In other words, the awareness of the Asia question as being problematic was only sensed by those countries situated on the peripheries, as opposed to in the centre, which had undergone both struggles for survival and cultural crises. Hence, it is not at all a coincidence that we can learn more about the question of Asia from Japanese intellectual history than from China's, and this basic fact prompts me to take a different perspective from that of Western intellectuals on the question of Asia – a question that deserves greater attention from intellectuals in both the East and West. In the course of thinking about this question, it occurs to me that the reflection on the Asia question has brought about a variegated process leading us to confront our own history. In the end, in thinking about the Asia question, we are not led to being absorbed in the question 'What is Asia?', but rather to reflect on 'What sort of issues in fact are set forth in discussions with regard to Asia?' In other words, Asia is merely a medium, through which we are effectively led to our history, and it is precisely because of this historical significance that it is important we keep asking 'How does Asia mean?'

Two approaches: does Asia exist?

The question of Asia is tricky, simply because, as a subject matter, it carries a different content in different times, without any inherent connections between them. Therefore, if the question of Asia is pursued in terms of causal relations, we shall not be able to gain much from it. Yet there is indeed continuity with regard to a certain sense of direction underlying the question of Asia. Without a good grip on the historical contexts of the discourse on Asia, we would not be able to understand the mode of existence of the Asia question. In the context of Japanese intellectual history, the question of Asia is often associated with the following 'accepted observation': after the Meiji Ishin (Restoration), there are two lines of thinking among intellectuals in Japan regarding the question of Asia; one is represented by Fukuzawa Yukichi's (1960) idea of 'Disassociating from Asia and integrating with Europe' (*Datsu-A ron*); and the other is represented by Okakura Tenshin's advocation of 'Asia is one'. The former upholds that Japan should forsake the 'unmanageable allies' in Asia so as quickly to join the ranks of the European and American powers. The latter stresses the commonality of Asia civilizations in the embodiment of the value of 'love' and 'beauty' which cannot be offered and superseded by the European civilizations.

The publication date of 1885 for Fukuzawa's *Datsu-A ron* is important in understanding the work's context. Okakura's (1976a) 'Ideals of the East with Special Reference to the Art of Japan', written in English, was published in 1903, and is also a work of its time. The two ways of thinking embodied in these works were not intended to oppose each other. It was only when the Japanese intellectuals of later generations reconstructed Japan's intellectual history that Fukuzawa and Okakura were turned into representatives of two opposing views of culture, both according with the need of later generations to position Japan *vis-à-vis* Western civilization in modern Japanese history.

At the turn of the century, Meiji Japan was confronted by a seemingly simple, and yet complicated, problem. On the one hand, Japan was keen to shake off its centuries-long subordination to the centrality of Chinese culture, and also the traditional competition with Korea for a place closer to the centre, by becoming part of the Western and world civilization, and re-ordering the international relations in East Asia. Yet on the other hand, it had to face racial opposition in which the West had the upper hand. Being coloured, Japan could not really become the ally of Europe and America; it could not but present itself to the world theatre with its Asian face. Long before the founding of the modern state, the Japanese had already begun to challenge China as a cultural centre. And as Japan had to open itself to the West even before the Meiji Ishin, it became impossible merely to confine oneself to the region of East Asia when dealing with the relationships between the three East Asian countries. We must rethink the whole in the global context or, to be more precise, in the context of the international political configuration among Europe, America and East Asia. Hence, in the field of intellectual history, Fukuzawa's (1995) *Bummeiron no gairyaku* (*An Outline of a Theory of Civilization*) formulated a unilinear evolutionary perspective on the progression of history to justify predatory states of affairs in the process and the Western civilization as the culmination of that particular evolutionary process. On the other hand, scepticism was also incurred about the evolutionary view of history. Intellectuals with a different mindset from those clinging to evolutionary views were committed to developing a critique of the material civilization of the West, while digging at the same time into the tradition of the East so as to uncover principles that transcend the predatory logic. The cultural positions of the latter are more aesthetic. However, no matter how different the two approaches were, in the context of the Meiji era, the apparent opposition between them was derived from the same sense of crisis, with regard to the question of confronting the Western civilization. Both sides were aware that, in order to fight and prevail over the encroaching Western powers, it was necessary to count on Asia as the counterpoising sphere against Europe and America, and to count on building an alliance among the three East Asian countries, and even among other coloured races. It was only after the Second World War, after Japan had seen the pernicious extension of pan-Asianism into the Greater East Asia Coprosperity Sphere, that reflections on history constructed Fukuzawa and Okakura as representatives of two different views of civilization. Postwar Japan was left with the twin legacies of identification with, and criticism of, the Western civilization. It was in the attempt to reconcile these tensions that Fukuzawa and Okakura were turned into two pivotal points on which the essential structure of pan-Asianism hinges.

Before writing *Datsu-A ron*, Fukuzawa, in fact, advocated 'The solidarity of East Asia' (*Toyo rentai ron*). For him, this idea had a double structure, i.e. it stresses that each East Asian country must push for revolutionary reform of the old regime and overthrow the power of the conservatives within the country, and only then can it be rid of the pressure from the Western powers. In other words, Fukuzawa's conception of 'solidarity' does not regard national boundaries as its precondition, but rather predicates upon the criterion of 'civilization'. He does not believe that the coloured races can join hands to resist the Western powers simply because they are coloured. He also, therefore, advocates that actual support should be given to the progressives of neighbouring countries in helping them with their coup to overthrow their own conservative regimes, so as to export 'civilization'.

During Fukuzawa's time, the so-called 'pan-Asianism' was not a theoretical proposition, but a cry for action, for which the vehicle could be roughly grouped together under the title 'aspiring activists' (*ronin* or *shishi*) – radical elements engaged in subversive activities in neighbouring East Asian countries. The Japanese *ronins* were deeply involved in the 1884 coup in Korea. Similarly, for the 1911 revolution of China, persons with Japanese names were also intensely implicated.[2] At the turn of the 20th century, Japan's Asianism contained, in a paradoxical relationship, both a sense of solidarity and a desire to expand. It also harboured a genuine sense of crisis and an antagonism against the presence of the European and American powers. In connection with this, we can list a number of political activists and intellectuals connected to pan-Asianism: Konoe Atsumaro (the chairman of the House of Peers and the founder of the East Asia Common Culture Society) advocated strongly, on the grounds of racial differentiation, intervention into the affairs of China to save it from the fate of colonization by the white people. Tarui Tokichi (a frustrated political activist of the popular movement), in the first edition of *Daito gapporon* (*The Great East Federation*) published in 1893, strongly proposed the integration of Japan and Korea in the struggle against the European powers. Miyazaki Toten (1970) (an activist who gave life-long support to the revolution in China) wrote *Sanjusannen no yume* (*My Thirty-three Years' Dream*), which expressed his aspirations for and feelings about the Chinese revolution. Kita Ikki (an activist holding ultra-nationalist views, who was very influential with young generals and colonels in the Showa period) was preoccupied, as a nationalist, with pan-Asianism.

In fact, Fukuzawa can doubtlessly be included in this list, for his idea of disassociating Asia is based on the idea of East Asia as one. In addition, of course, the *Datsu-A ron* (*Disassociating Asia*) was the outcome of Fukuzawa's emotional involvement in the politics of the time. Many scholars have pointed out that Fukuzawa's *Datsu-A ron* is outspokenly opposed to the national mood at the time of its publication. Therefore, rather than seeing it as the result of his theoretical thinking, it should be understood as a reflection of Fukuzawa's individual way of reacting to particular affairs.[3] Fukuzawa had, in fact, in this short piece, lucidly demonstrated to us the theoretical part of his thinking, which is his principle of relativism with regard to understanding the question of civilization. *Datsu-A ron* is only a short article, but it is highly charged throughout with Fukuzawa's particular sense of urgency. It starts with: 'Communication in the world is becoming more and more convenient and time-saving, and the influence of the Western civilization is looming over the East, sweeping everything along with it on its way.' (Fukuzawa 1960: 238) However, for Fukuzawa, the influence spreading from the West could not be simply taken as the coming of an angel. Beneath the facade of its fascination was concealed its potential for destruction. He wrote, 'Civilization is like the spread of measles and we do not have any means to stop (cure) it. We cannot even withhold an epidemic that is harmful, let alone civilization that comes double-edged with both advantageous and disadvantageous effects, while the advantages often overshadow the disadvantages!' (Fukuzawa 1960: 238) The comparison of civilization to measles, and the belief that the wise should choose to 'help it spread' and enable the people 'to sooner bathe in the atmosphere of its ways', embodied Fukuzawa's opinion of the main trend of the world of his times: it was an ineluctable trend that Western civilization would dominate the whole world, and nations of the East were incapable of resisting it, just as the Tokyoites were defenceless in the face of measles spread from Nagasaki. However, since the advantages of civilization outweigh its disadvantages, it seems that the only choice is to accept it. Whilst it is true that Fukuzawa's theory of civilization is not without its own detailed contents, and *Datsu-A ron* only suggests the perspective from which he sees modern civilization, the measles metaphor he employs separates him from later generations who uncritically admire Western civilization, unable to sense the inherent tensions. Our reading of the intellectual history in question must begin with this understanding.

After he had stated his fundamental judgement on Western civilization, Fukuzawa expressed his disappointment with the immediate East Asian neighbours, and urged Japan to break off with its neighbours in the East, for he thought they were doomed to fall. Fukuzawa's greatest fear was that the West would regard Japan as a barbaric country, like its doomed neighbours. What is primarily conveyed in *Datsu-A ron* is Fukuzawa's sense of doom for the survival of the Japanese nation; his disappointment with the neighbouring Asian countries; and, as a consequence of this disappointment, his evaluation of Asia as barbaric. There may be different interpretations of his 'break-off statement', but the undeniable fact is that Fukuzawa, Japan's most remarkable modern thinker, is completely committed to the 'Survival of the Fittest' way of thinking in his reflection on Asia's value. Fukuzawa has even gone to the extreme of ignoring Japan's geographical location in order to ideologically cut Japan off from Asia. This shows that Fukuzawa had already begun to consider the question of relativity with regard to the geographical conception of Japan. In relativizing the geographical conception of Japan, Fukuzawa is obviously relativizing the conception of civilization at the same time. Although Fukuzawa emphasizes 'integrating into Europe', he is certainly not handing over to the Europeans the sole claim to civilization, for he believes that Japan is also eligible to join Europe in the march of civilization.

Anyone who understands a little of Japan's modern intellectual history would know that at the time of Edo, there was an idea of the 'Hua Yi Order' among the Japanese Confucianists. This comes from ancient China's way of geographical thinking, supplemented by some cultural evaluation. It is thought that the Di (the uncouth northern tribes in ancient China) can be raised to become the 'Di humans' through mercy. This reflects the functional disposition of the kind of thinking in the differentiation between the Hua (the Han Chinese) on the one hand, and the Yi (Eastern tribes in ancient China) and the Di on the other. As the territory of China was being expanded throughout history, it became possible to view the assimilation of 'outer fringes of civilization' as China's 'internal affairs' (although the processes of intermarriage between the Hua and the Yi-Di in the history of China were greater than could be covered by the term 'assimilation'), and this way of thinking continued even until the times of the Qing Dynasty in the face of unequal demands from the Western powers. When Hong Kong was ceded, it was understood to be an act of pacification towards the Yi by the Hua. Hence, in China, in view of the flexible sense of territorial boundary, the categories Hua and Yi were basically that of substantial political geography, where the position of 'Hua' as the centre was irreplaceable. However, in Japan, Hua and Yi were taken to be the two measures of political culture, marking the presence or absence of 'mercy', 'virtue' and 'ethical governance', and were no longer merely understood geographically as the relation between the centre and its peripheries. For example, the well-known Confucianist Ogyu Sorai argued in his *Ten Essays in Ken-en* that: if the Yi can elevate themselves and become like the Xia (the name the ancient Han people called themselves), then they should be regarded as Hua; if the Xia regresses to become like the Yi, they should be looked down upon as the Yi. The main criterion for distinguishing Hua from Yi is whether both adhere to the rites and teachings of the sage kings of the ancient times (quoted from Koike 1985). Dazai Shundai also said in his *Keizai roku* (*Discussion of Economics*) that, etiquette, the people of Yi are no more different than the people of Hua. Conversely, for the people of Hua the centre could become the Yi and the Di once they lose their etiquette (quoted from Koike 1985). Therefore, for the Japanese, 'Hua' and 'Yi' are interchangeable; it is only the hierarchical order of the ethical governance that must be preserved.

Since the beginning of a new era with the fall of the Ming dynasty and its replacement by the Qing dynasty, the upper class of Japanese society gradually arrived at the view of the so-called 'Hua-Yi metamorphosis'. In this view, the Japanese refuted the ortho-doxy of the China of the Qing Dynasty as the representative of 'Hua', and hence claimed to replace China as the representative of 'Hua'. This move contained Japan's first ideological reaction against the previously unchallenged position of China as its esteemed teacher. However, there is another, similarly important, point about this event that must not be ignored. What these modern Japanese did in their ideological reaction was to separate the sign from its physical referent, so that 'Zhong Hua' (Hua the Centre, referring to China) could become a sign for any arbitrary entity, freed from any relation to the territorial boundary of China. Thus, a premise foreign to Chinese thinking was instituted, i.e. the so-called cultural identification and the provenance of that culture can obtain a relation of relative autonomy from one another. In the last phase of the Shogunate, as the Japanese were applying the perspective of the Hua-Yi order in dealing with the world, a related slogan also emerged: 'Revere the Emperor, expel the barbarians' (*Sonno joi*). This was a reaction to the demand from the West for Japan to open its door, and this slogan also carried the message of the symbolization of Japan. Later history showed that the two 'hans' (domains) with the loudest cry against the barbarians were pushing the hardest for Japan to open its door.[4] From the Meiji era, the Japanese had been thinking along such lines, in the face of world civilization, and opened themselves fully to the world. During the Meiji era, the Japanese calmly accepted the Western civilization as 'Zhong Hua'.[5] They regarded the more advanced West as a more orthodox representative of 'Zhong Hua' than themselves, thus stretching 'the Hua-Yi metamorphosis' even further, even to a global context.

Fukuzawa has undoubtedly adopted this line of thinking, although in the opposite direction. In fact, the so-called 'Disassociating Asia and integrating into Europe' is to abstract Japan from its Asian geographical context by turning it into a symbol of transferable cultural carrier, hence making it possible for Japan to proclaim its integration with other powerful modern states at the other end of Eurasia. Under these circumstances, the geographical location of Japan becomes irrelevant. This new set-up of the 'world' rearranges 'the Hua-Yi metamorphosis' order as they had tried to arrange it before, when the relationship between 'Zhong Hua' and 'Yamato' constituted the axis for them.

'Disassociating Asia and integrating into Europe' and the 'Zhong Hua-ization' of the Western world prevailed together, reflecting the sense of cultural crisis and national crisis of the intelligentsia and the upper circles of the Japanese society in the 1880s. This was very different in orientation from the similar sense of crisis in China at about the same time. For the Chinese, their sense of crisis was directed towards a reshaping of their culture from within, while for the Japanese, it prompted them to seek, outside Japan, new world connections that may help them to shake off the crisis. Since Fukuzawa turned Japan into a symbol, where it could be relatively abstracted from its geographical location, he had to, then, re-allocate it a new position. However, he knew better than anyone that the position could not be in Europe. Thus, Fukuzawa's situation was even more precarious than that during the times of Edo when the idea of 'the Hua-Yi metamorphosis' was put forward. The latter merely tried to convert the relation between Japan and China. Furthermore, it was mainly 'Zhong Hua' that was subjected to symbolization, without depriving Japan of the anchor of a home. However, when Fukuzawa subjected Japan to symbolization and attempted to break it free from Asia, it became more difficult to maintain one's wishful thinking: You want to integrate into Europe, but are you welcome? You want to break away from Asia, but is Asia agreeable?

In the 1880s, the situation was already too difficult for Fukuzawa to deal with. The imminent question was, with two opium wars ushering in the invasion of China by the European powers, Japan too was confronted with the danger of a life and death situation on the one hand, and the possibility of extending its influence into China on the other. This was an absolutely concrete situation, leaving no room for the play of symbolization. The dilemma of Fukuzawa's relativism could not become the primary concern of today, because it cannot be abstracted from its specific context. However, it is understandable that at the time when Fukuzawa's idea of 'Disassociating Asia' merged with the consciousness of crisis, particularly under the sway of the outcomes of the Sino-Japanese and the Russo-Japanese Wars, which gave Japan an illusion of being a powerful state, not having the anchor of a home could hardly present itself as a problem.

However, Fukuzawa has left a chronic problem to future generations, i.e. the recurrence of alternative trends of thoughts of 'Disassociating Asia' and 'Reviving Asia'. Right up to the present day, the argument over whether Japan is an Asian country continues to be voiced, and Fukuzawa's symbolization of Japan must be held partly responsible for this. Fukuzawa has made the symbolization of Japan into such a binding force that only an alternative symbolization can replace it, leaving later generations no other choice than to look for a different view of civilization to counter that of Fukuzawa, in order that Japan can have a place in Asia.

About two decades after Fukuzawa, Okakura (1976a) published 'The Ideals of the East with Special Reference to the Art of Japan', which proposed a view of civilization that stressed the integral nature of Asia, and its context was completely different from Fukuzawa's. Its concern was no longer how Japan could survive in the predatory modern world, but rather how Japan could offer the modern world values for a new understanding of civilization. Okakura's thinking on the civilizations of the East and the West is wholly confined to 'the activities of the Spirit'. His conception of Asia as an integral whole is founded on his reservations about the civilization of the West. He is different from Fukuzawa in this respect because, unlike Fukuzawa, he does not see the development of the world in terms of victory and defeat, with victory as the measure of the hero. At the time when Okakura published his work in London, he was confronted with the same problems that Said would face more than half a century later, i.e. Occidentals only understand the Orient by way of self-centering and making easy assumptions, therefore the civilization of the East is only admitted into the world picture through the projection of Western civilization, but never as an autonomous value system. As Okakura said in another article: 'If the Orient must overcome their ignorance about the Occident, then need not the Occident abandon what they have already known about the Orient? The Occident possesses an extensive system of learning, yet they are also deeply biased!' (Okakura 1976b: 97) In this respect, Okakura's conception of Asia as an integral whole reflects the tension inherent in the relation between the East and the West, which is totally different from Fukuzawa's, even though both are the products of attempts to respond to the intrusion of the West.

'The Ideals of the East' begins with a famous paragraph. It includes a statement that contains the underlying perspective of Okakura's discourse:

> Asia is one. The Himalayas divide, only to accentuate, two mighty civilizations, the Chinese with its communism of Confucius, and the Indian with its individualism of the Vedas. But not even the snowy barriers can interrupt for one moment that broad expanse of love for the ultimate and universal, which is the common thought of inheritance of every Asiatic Race, enabling them to produce all the great religions of the world, and distinguishing them from those maritime people of the Mediterranean and the Baltic, who love to dwell on the Particular, and to search out the means, not the end, of life.
>
> (Okakura 1976a)

As all the peoples of Asia embrace a love for the Ultimate and the Universal, which is lacking in the civilization of Western Europe, as those peoples are obsessed with the technical, the civilization of Asia is far superior to the civilization of Western Europe. Okakura did not forget to stress the specific function of Japan as he expounded on the civilization of Asia. For him, Japan was fulfilling the function of a museum for the civilization of Asia. However, if compared to Fukuzawa, Okakura's complex about Japan was more flexible, although his discourse was later appropriated to support the proposition of the Greater East Asia Coprosperity Sphere, despite this proposition never being Okakura's concern. If 'The Ideals of the East' was taken to be a narrative of history or art history, the way it approaches knowledge and the knowledge in question would become dubious. However, in the context of Okakura's confronting the West, his position provides his narrative with an extremely important value, i.e. Okakura has, at the beginning of this century, made the Occidentals see that the Orient have their own way of knowing and evaluating themselves, totally different from the Occidentals' idea of Asia. Furthermore, the Orient's view of Asia indeed constitutes culturally a challenge to the Eurocentric view of civilization.

Okakura had led a legendary life. He was sent to Europe and America in his early years to study the history of art in the West, which only made him believe more strongly in Asian art. Okakura was also interested in real politics at this time: however, his personality caused his official career to be beset with frustrations, but he was not at all deterred, and continued throughout his life to concern himself with the fundamental problems of political thinking and culture in the field of art. This enabled him to put forward propositions in opposition to those of the prevailing concern in a Japan that was increasingly absorbed in the values of the West. What he proposed was the values of Asia. He concluded that the fundamental problems of the world should be judged on the basis of standards derived from Asia and not from the West. This way of thinking was not, in fact, against the current of its times, for it coincided with the desire, harboured by the Japanese government and the upper circles, to place Japan in a superior position within the newly interpreted Hua-Yi order. In fact it would be more appropriate to view Okakura's idea of 'Asia is one' as a variation of Japan's construction of a new world order.

If we contrast what is said above with Fukuzawa's exposition of the idea of 'Disassociating Asia', the two are in opposition to each other with respect to the cultural values propounded by them. Yet this is not all. In fact, deep down we can see something in common between the two. Whereas Fukuzawa sees Western civilization as a kind of epidemic, although having greater benefits than measles, Okakura sees it as inferior, as totally absorbed in the consideration of means rather than ends. Both of them were confronted with the opposing relation of East and West, and an existing Asia. More importantly, each had, in his own way, subjected Asia to symbolization. For Fukuzawa, the existing Asia became the symbol of a doomed barbarity, while for Okakura, Asia was the symbol of Love, out of which the world's three great religions were born. With regard to the question of whether to break off from Asia or to revive it, Fukuzawa and Okakura can indeed be seen as the two foci in history; around them, the elliptical trajectory of Japan's modern history can be traced.[6] The question of whether to 'Disassociate Asia' or to 'Revive Asia' is, in other words, asking whether Japan is an Asian country – whether Japan bears any responsibility and obligation to Asia. These two poles have always been the variations in a duet that refuses to go away in the intellectual history of modern Japan. They indeed constitute the foci of an ellipse and, what is more, unspent energy is still radiating from these two foci even to this day. However, if we allow ourselves to be confined merely to this ellipse in our consideration of the question of Asia in the modern history of Japan, another equally important thread of Japan's modern thought would be omitted. In order to examine comprehensively the meaning of the question of Asia, we have to go beyond the picture provided for us by Takeuchi Yoshimi and Hashikawa Bunzo, and temporarily bracket together the opposing positions of Fukuzawa and Okakura. This will allow us to see an overview of their similarities, and to locate further a different thread of thought, which is in contrast to that of Fukuzawa and Okakura. We would, in this way, discover that both Fukuzawa's and Okakura's discourses have a highly ideological function, and similarly neglect consciously the deficiency in the divide between Asia and the West.[7] In contrast to this practice, later in the intellectual history of modern Japan there emerged a different thread of thinking that, objectively speaking, is directed against their practice of symbolization and the way the divide between East and West is constructed. This thread points to a different approach that began with Watsuji Tetsuro.

Watsuji Tetsuro (1889–1960) was a philosopher of equal standing with another philosopher, Nishida Kitaro (1870–1945), in the modern history of Japan. His writing activities mainly lasted from the early 20th century to the postwar era. He was actively involved in the academia in matters of grave political significance in the Showa period for issues such as the construction of Japanese nationalism and the debates around Tennoism. In this regard, Watsuji Tetsuro was basically taking the stand of the rightist intellectuals. However, it is still not quite right to view him as an intellectual concerned with praxis, for his concerns were from beginning to end confined within the academia, and the question he pursued insistently concerned the limitation and the effectiveness of the central value system based on individualism in the modern West. Proceeding from this basic thinking, he repeatedly explored the relation between subjectivity and objectivity, questioning whether it is possible to isolate each term as an object of knowledge, and also the question regarding the mode of relation between an individual and the collective to which the individual belongs.[8] Watsuji (1935) wrote *Fudo: ningengakuteki kosatsu* (*Local Conditions and Customs: Studies of the Human Sphere*) in the 1920s, and published it in 1935, at a time when Japanese fascism was growing in influence. Ideologically, Watsuji supported Tennoism and upheld Japan to be the centre of the conception of the world. This dimension of Watsuji's thought overshadows the productive aspects of his conception of the world; however, we must not throw away the baby with the bath water and turn our back on the task of reflecting on the positioning of Watsuji's *Fudo* in history. This work put forward the theme of the organic relation between forms of human society and the natural conditions for discussion, against the background of Watsuji's dissatisfaction with the philosophical thinking of the West, and the modern conception of values. Watsuji was motivated by the critique of philosophical thought, of which Descartes is the representative, that postulated that the subjective mind was the substance of the existential conditions of being human. He was also sceptical about the contemporary orientation in the values of his time. Thus, he undertook to rethink the connotations of 'human'.[9] In Japanese, 'human' usually denotes a particular individual as well as someone being among others. Additionally, 'human sphere' adds to the notion of 'human' the connotations of one's sense of being part of a group and interpersonal relationships, hence it can be employed to indicate the state of being of an individual, and of being part of a whole, at the same time, without differentiating the one from the other. In other words, the concept of 'human sphere' already comprises the notion of self and the notion of others, while the term in Chinese does not carry these connotations. Watsuji believed that it was the contribution of modernity to establish the ways for an individual qua an individual to approach the world. However, individualism wanted to suppress the fact that 'an individual was only a conjuncture in the web of the human sphere' by substituting the individual, which is the part, for the human sphere, which is the whole. Therefore, he saw it as his task to rectify the mistake committed by the abstract approach of individualism in modern Western thought through dedicating himself to establishing 'the ethics of the study of the human sphere'.[10] Watsuji's *Fudo* can be regarded as an extension of *Ningengaku toshiteno rinrigaku* (*The Ethics of the Study of the Human Sphere*), and also as the preparatory step for his later work *Rinrigaku* (*Ethics*) (Watsuji 1937). Although Watsuji revised his perspectives in the course of his movement from one work to the other, he was consistent in his criticism of the modern Western individualistic way of thinking, in which the subjective is opposed to the objective and its unilinear perspective of historical progress. Besides directing against individualism, Watsuji was also motivated by his desire to correct the deficiency in Heidegger's (1987) *Being and Time*, where Heidegger paid more attention to the temporal dimension than to the spatial dimension; hence the deliberate stress of the significance of spatial difference to the human civilizations. In his *Fudo*, Watsuji repeatedly states that the history of mankind and the natural conditions in which humans resided could not be treated in isolation from one another. History is the history of 'local conditions and customs', and 'local conditions and customs' is the 'local conditions and customs' of history. In other words, the static differentiation between human as the subject and nature as the object is senseless, and the specificity of natural conditions is the constraint of fate which mankind cannot surmount.

Watsuji Tetsuro distinguished the local conditions and customs of mankind (by mankind Watsuji did not mean to include every human being on Earth, but only that part of the human race needed for the demonstration of his arguments, which meant only the region covered by this question of Asia) into three types: monsoon, desert and pasture. (In his later work *Rinrigaku*, he added two more types to the three already given: the human sphere of the pioneer, and the human sphere of the steppe, so as to include in his consideration types such as America and Russia; however, the former three divisions remained his primary concern.) The first two types include East Asia (or 'Asia', as Okakura refers to it in his discussion), South Asia and West Asian Islamic countries. The last type refers to the Mediterranean and the Baltic regions, regions regarded by Okakura as being disposed to the pursuit of means and not the end of life. Simply by considering the way in which the divisions were made, we can tell that in Watsuji's discussion of the question of local conditions and customs, the binary opposition set up between Asia and Western Europe by ignoring the natural division of geography is meaningless to him.

According to Watsuji, the national conditions of monsoon bring about the cultures of India, Southeast Asia, Japan and China. The basic feature of monsoon is 'moist'. Moisture is the fountain from which all things flourish and grow, notwithstanding the threat it poses to the existence of mankind. Hence, it is the symbol of 'life', and the people living in the monsoon regions, therefore, must not pit themselves against the root of life, but instead must acquire tolerance and passivity, which in turn accounts for the cultural characteristics found in these regions. The national conditions of desert produce the cultures of Egypt and Arabia and, therefore, Christianity, Judaism and Islam. 'Dry' is the feature of the desert's natural condition, and as it threatens the existence of mankind and all living things, it is the symbol of 'death'. Peoples living in the desert regions are thus made to confront nature, forging combative relations to it. Furthermore, they also tend to relate to other tribes in the form of confrontation. The personified God is the contribution of the desert peoples to mankind, only counterpoised by the depersonified Absolute Being of India. Europe is the region that has the natural conditions of pasture. Being endowed with both moist and dry characteristics, nature in the pasture region accords well with the desires of mankind, enabling mankind easily to discover the laws of nature for it to follow. This is the foundation of science. Furthermore, the ability to manipulate nature also makes it easier for mankind to free itself from the shackles of nature, and consequently produces the spirit from competition to rivalry, as represented by the Greeks. This is not only the source of the expansionist character of Europe, but also the root of the formation of slavery, in the services of the liberation of a few from nature, at the expense of many, by reducing them to the raw existence of livestock. This is the soil from which the flowers of the European civilizations blossom.

As an elaboration of his position propounded in his treatment of *Ethics*, Watsuji's *Fudo* cannot be said to be a successful work. First, he failed to provide a comprehensive theoretical model to deal with the relation between the individual and society, and the relation between the subjectivity of humans and the objectivity of nature. Consequently, he can hardly avoid being misread as a 'natural determinist'. Although he repeatedly stated in his work that 'natural conditions is not the cause of culture', and 'the historicality and the conditionality of nature are the two moments of culture', his narrative mode appears to be that of natural determinism as it unfolds. Therefore, in order to grasp properly the *Fudo* perspective, it is necessary to take into consideration Watsuji's basic approach in his treatment of ethics. This will enable us to discover that, notwithstanding the contradictions in *Fudo* and Watsuji's theoretical inadequacies, it has, in fact, concealed within it a very important thought.

In *Ningengaku toshite rinrigaku*, Watsuji, borrowing from Heidegger's phenomenological studies, differentiates between 'beings' and 'Being'. He stresses that a being, according to the popular sense, is a phenomenon, an Other to Being, and Being manifests itself through a being. Only when we subject the popular sense of phenomenon to the hermeneutical method of phenomenology can it be liberated from the 'given' (i.e. transforming the phenomenon into Kantian intuition), and acquire the structure of a phenomenological object, thereby disclosing the 'dynamic structure of the Being of the Human Sphere' contained in the everydayness of the phenomenon. In connection with this, the return to 'Being' from 'beings' is to proceed from 'beings'; that is to say, the point of departure is confined by the range of possibility of actual experiences. It is not possible that beings can be present at all times, and can be equally accessible to everyone in the same way. Hence, the Being of human is historical, and a change in the historical situation means that the possibility of approaching a being, and the ways to interpret it, will be different and may even be transformed (Watsuji 1963: 122–128).

The philosophical elaboration by Watsuji Tetsuro shows that he basically adopts the position of phenomenology and the hermeneutical method, particularly in approaching history. This cannot be ascribed to him as his invention. His invention rather lies within this: he does not merely confine himself to elaborating on the theoretical level, but tries to translate the philosophical understanding to history itself.

In *Fudo*, Watsuji carried out what he declares in *Ningengaku toshite rinrigaku* as 'the destruction of hermeneutics'. This is what is proposed by Heidegger – that 'destruction is a critical process in which the traditional concepts, which at first must be employed, are de-constructed (*Kritische Abbau*) down to the source from which they were drawn'. But Watsuji considers that Heidegger's idea of man remains abstract and unhistorical, for he can only think in terms of an individual, distanced from the double structure that binds an individual and society. In other words, Heidegger fails to get close enough to the founding praxis of the Being of the human sphere. What Watsuji wants to accomplish is to trace back to the roots of the traditional concepts of relation between man and nature, and relation between history and natural conditions, so as to re-open them and shake off the abstraction imposed on them by Heidegger, retrieving the foundational Being of the 'everyday reality'. Therefore, when Watsuji studies the influence of natural conditions on human activities, he is not occupied mainly by the human activities themselves. His main concern is, rather, the relation between a particular human activity and the natural conditions. Again and again he calls attention to the historicality of natural conditions and the conditionality of nature in history, out of a desire to dissolve the subject–object binary oppositional thinking of modern Western philosophy that is centred on the subject, and replace it with the relation between subject and object as the point of departure. (It is undeniable that the intelligentsia of the East has also participated in the aggravation of the polarization of this binary thinking.) Closely read, we will find that every piece of his treatment of natural conditions and customs is focused on the formative processes of the relation between human and nature, rather than the results of established culture. This is his practice of prying open the traditional concepts.

When *Fudo* appeared in the 1930s, its most important significance was not the world history it provided in the sketch, which was actually so problematic that it was more or less ignored by later Watsuji scholars, but rather the way the sketch was outlined. It provided a refreshing opportunity for a new approach to history. Watsuji's determination to dissolve the subjectivity made him take up the position of a bystander as he sketched the forms of civilizations of Eurasia, and strived to introduce a deterministic perspective of natural conditions into the discourses on the cultural specificities for every civilization he undertook to sketch, thereby trying to construct a configuration of pluralistic spheres, coexisting with one another. Within such a configuration, no single culture was in a hegemonic position over the others. Neither could there be any culture deemed to possess universal values. With such a specificity given, Watsuji's argument for viewing Japan as the centre of world history and his ideological support for Tennoism were deconstructed under the weight of his own theoretical understanding.[11] More importantly, in the 1930s, Watsuji unwittingly provided the clue to a different approach to the question of Asia from that of Fukuzawa and Okakura. His approach starts with everyday reality, and not with concepts and ideologies in the pursuit of knowledge about the world, thus moving away from the model of the symbolization of Asia produced by Fukuzawa and Okakura. In fact, only by resorting more to everyday experience can an investigation of the question of Asia really be carried out. Although the question of Asia was never a question for Watsuji, as almost all Watsuji scholars have pointed out that Asia never figured as a fundamental fact in Watsuji's mind, Watsuji did, without knowing it himself, bring forth a critical question: does Asia really exist? And his work *Fudo* shows us a path different from that framed by the East–West binary opposition. Thus Asia is being dislodged from its position of being a given, allowing it to be open to interrogation.

It is beyond my ability to provide an overall assessment of Watsuji's thinking on ethics. However, I can say that it is important that a different line of thinking be retrieved from Watsuji's position on the question of Asia, otherwise our understanding of the Asia question in the Japanese intellectual history would be based, in a limited way, on those trails blazed by Fukuzawa and Okakura, and the chance for considering Asia differently would be lost. Subsequently, we would be led to an unnecessary disjunction between intellectual history and the other social sciences, and be unable to discern the limitation of each discipline hence this would leave the Asia question to be tackled solely in the domain of intellectual history. In fact, if we go beyond the confines of the 'ellipse' defined by Takeuchi Yoshimi and Hashikawa Bunzo, we can discover that the important moment for the discussion of the Asia question may not be located within the intellectual history demarcated from other disciplines, but rather at the point of convergence between it and other disciplines. The later development of the Asia question, on the one hand, had continued to be constituted along the paths prescribed by idealization and symbolization, which were leading to the proposition of the Greater East Asia Coprosperity Sphere; on the other hand, it had also begun to follow Watsuji's suggestion by considering the pursuit of the close connection to natural conditions and geography which suggested the notion of 'the actually existing Asia'. When these two approaches, one geared toward ideas and the other reality, find their point of encounter, their actions upon each other would bring forth new issues, ones which had not happened in Watsuji's time but some decades later.

Convergence of the two approaches

As two different responses out of a sense of crisis about their own time, Fukuzawa's and Okakura's views of Asia have virtually defined the direction of thinking for Japanese intellectuals of later generations. However, there is an enormous blind spot concealed in this line of thinking: from the very beginning, Asia is approached as a symbol, making it possible for Asia to be detached from its actual geographical location; this in turn leads to the restriction of the West, which is set in contrast to Japan, as an abstract background, expressed only vaguely. As a consequence, it becomes possible to discuss the matter in extremely abstract and ideological ways. As Meiji Japan managed to push rapidly through the modernization process and became a power among the modern states of the world, the formation of fascistic nationalism was escalating during the Taisho period and the early Showa period, in which the question of Asia, instead of bearing a sense of the national crisis during the Meiji period, was metamorphosed into an instrument of public opinion for the legitimization of Japan's desire to become the overlord in East Asia. The height of this development was the projection of the Greater East Asia Coprosperity Sphere, a project disdained by all other Asian countries. To the postwar Japanese intelligentsia, the most important event was the Tokyo Trial convened by the Allies. The 'Europe' that Fukuzawa had wanted Japan to join refused to accept Japan into their company as a member of the United Nations, while its Asian neighbours would not accept Japan as a possible ally due to its wartime aggression. Thus, the postwar Japan was left truly homeless, being separated from Asia without succeeding in integrating with Europe. The ambition of the Greater East Asia Coprosperity Sphere fell to the ground. However, after the 1950s, the duet of 'Disassociating Asia' and 'Reviving Asia' re-emerged, and by the time of the mid-1960s, there was again the cry of 'the affirmation of the Greater East Asia War', casting once more a shadow over the question of Asia. Fukuzawa and Okakura should certainly not be held responsible for such an outcome, yet the duet of 'Disassociating Asia' and 'Reviving Asia' in the intellectual history of modern Japan did begin with them. As the pressing antagonism between the East and the West during the Meiji period faded, the question of Asia slid gradually towards aggression and expansion, driving into obscurity its possibility for introducing into the history of civilization a turning point. This is why the question remains undecided today and why, whenever opinions regarding the question of Asia are put forward, the aggression committed by Japan is always raised.

For Asians, the Asia question is primarily a question of the sense of solidarity, a sense that arises in the midst of the aggression and expansion perpetrated by the West. Thus, the sense of solidarity is articulated with a sense of national crisis, which distinguishes the question of Asia from the Orientalism and even the criticism of Orientalism in the West. In 1924, Sun Yat-sen (1986) made a speech in Japan on 'pan-Asianism', focusing on the question of race. In reference to the Russo-Japanese War, Sun stressed that the coloured races were excited by this war for 'it was the first time in the recent several centuries that the Asians had beaten the Europeans'. By 'Asia', Sun meant to include all the coloured races of the Asian region. He further argued from the above assertion that the culture of the Rule by Benevolence in Asia would necessarily win out over the European rule by Force, and went on to warn Japan to make a prudent choice between the two positions. Sun Yat-sen did his utmost to stress the necessity of a sense of solidarity for Asia. 'In treating pan-Asianism, what sort of problems do we want to solve with the fruits of our study? It is none other than finding out how the suffering peoples of Asia can resist the European powers. In a word, it is to defend the oppressed peoples against injustices perpetrated on them.' Sun Yat-sen's view of Asia contains something that is lacking in Japanese views of Asia – a fundamental concern for weaker peoples. For the early Japanese thinkers, the question of weaker peoples did not constitute their primary concern. Even so, there was still a certain consistency between Sun Yat-sen and the early Japanese thinkers, and this consistency was even stronger than that found between the current and the earlier generations of the Japanese thinkers. Indeed, among Sun Yat-sen or Fukuzawa and Okakura, the question of the Asian solidarity was provoked by the white race and, for that matter, even when Fukuzawa would like to seek the termination of the connection, while Sun and Okakura viewed building solidarity within Asia as their means, they were all confronted by the problem of 'how to react to the European powers'. But, after the Second World War ended, this problem no longer claimed priority in people's minds. On the contrary, what had been relegated to a secondary question now came to the fore – this is the question concerning the factuality of the sense of Asian solidarity. The Greater East Asia Coprosperity Sphere not only destroyed the dream of 'restoring the status of the Asian peoples' as Sun Yat-sen saw it then, it also tore apart the Japanese intellectuals' illusion of solidarity. Notwithstanding that the chant of pan-Asianism was at its loudest during that period, it had turned into a mere ideological war cry, where it had once been an ideal and a way of thinking, for it was not in any way prepared to face and deal with the fact of its aggression against its Asian neighbours.

After Sun Yat-sen, the soil for the cultivation of discussion of the question of Asia disappeared in China, but Japan was haunted by this question all along. In postwar Japan, the intellectual arena had to rethink its position in the global setting, finding it impossible to go beyond Asia to face the world directly. The most crucial question was whether Japan, after its defeat in the war, was under any obligation to Asia. As for pan-Asianism, which was always bound up with the aggression of imperialism in the 20th century, the question was how the shadow cast by this history could be made to disappear.

Under such circumstances, 'Asia', together with 'nationalism', became words so engulfed in ambiguity in modern Japanese language that progressive intellectuals of postwar Japan basically avoided the question of Asia altogether. Takeuchi Yoshimi, however, was an exception. He was the one with the audacity to be 'a cat's paw', and traced the provenance of the terms that were marked by the imprint of an ignominious historical memory, so as to uncover the principle underlying them.

The journey that Takeuchi Yoshimi's thinking has gone through will not be discussed here.[12] The important point here is that his way of thinking basically proceeds by delving into the object he undertakes to criticize or even reject, so as to differentiate his position from it from within. Before he tackles the question of Asia, he has already, in this manner, dealt with two symposiums for youth: 'Overcoming the Modern' and 'The World History Position and Japan', which aimed to incite young people to take to a war of aggression. In his treatment of these two symposiums, Takeuchi Yoshimi tries to differentiate three aspects: thinking, ideology and the user of thinking. By doing this, he hopes he can abstract from the intertwining aspects the tradition of Japanese thinking. Of most of the controversies provoked by him, it is important to note that their activities can be characterized as 'differentiating between the baby and the bath water'. Takeuchi's peculiar approach enables him to feel no qualms in digging up for examination those events and thoughts in the history of modern Japan that are imbued with rightist characteristics. Among these is the question of Asia.

Takeuchi is prompted by his postwar pursuit of the question of nationalism. When he provoked the debate on 'national literature' in 1951, Asia constituted for him an essential perspective from which to reconfigure nationalism. The situation of postwar Japan was of a defeated nation occupied by America and made to act as America's Asian ally in the cold war setting. Such extreme complexity pushed Japan into a new round of discussions around 'Disassociating Asia and integrating into Europe'. Among the highly critical, progressive intellectuals, quite a number devoted themselves to searching for weapons in the modern European and American thought, and hence left behind the question of Asia. As for the leftist intellectuals related to the Japanese Communist Party, they were faced with the double-bind problems of internationalism and nationalism against the cold war background, and they too did not give a place to the question of Asia. Still haunted by echoes of the Greater East Asia Coprosperity Sphere, progressive intellectuals also stayed away from this subject which is redolent of unpleasant historical memories. Thus, the question of Asia was basically shelved in the vein of the rightist view of history. Takeuchi's insistence in such circumstances on broaching the question of Asia and the question of pan-Asianism deserves particular attention, for he explicitly stated that bypassing Asianism and the rightist nationalist thoughts in the sorting out of the tradition of Japanese thought would only lead to something fictitious and conceptual. Takeuchi came to this particular understanding on the basis of his observation about the cultural movement of Japan's proletariat and the internationalist stand of the leftist intellectuals from the Communist Party network. He thought that this movement neglected the right-wing 'trend of native thought', and simply refuted it from the outside, and hence could not constitute any genuine criticism of it. Therefore, when Umesawa Tadao published his ecological view of history in the 1950s, and effectively set off a flush of talks about 'Disassociating Asia' and 'the uniqueness of Japan', Takeuchi Yoshimi realized that it was a crucial moment in the modern history of Japan. As his most forceful response, he compiled the book *Asianism* and published it in 1963 with the long introduction 'The Prospect of Asianism'. Takeuchi is almost the only one in Japan's intellectual history to pursue the question of Asianism, and to abstract principles from it. Although the limitation of his thinking is very obvious, through him we can search relatively deeper into the vein of Japan's Asianism.

'The Prospect of Asianism' is a reading guide for the book, *Asianism* (Takeuchi 1963). The latter was published by Chikuma Shobo, as Volume 9 of the *Collected Works of Modern Japanese Thinking* (*Gendai Nihon shiso taikei*). Writings representative of Asianists since the Meiji period were collected in the book. Takeuchi selected the historical material himself, composed a chronology, and even separated the material into categories according to the ways he saw them. Takeuchi's basic understanding is: Asianism is simply a disposition, not a substantial body of thinking that can be objectively defined. Hence, it is different from thinkings that are organically related to reality, and can be receptive of nationalism, statism, expansionism and even left-wing internationalism without coinciding completely with any of them. At the same time, Asianism is not an established thinking such as democratism, socialism or fascism, hence it cannot stand on its own and must depend on other ways of thinking for its being. For that matter, Asianism by itself is not capable of being 'narrativized' into a history of a single trend of thought.

Why, then, does one still want to broach a subject that cannot constitute a historical proposition in its own right? Takeuchi points out that in Japan's modern history, Asianism is a 'mood' present all around, and the ideas that run through Japan's modern history are founded on this 'mood'. Since the left-wing thinking in Japan avoids the question of nationalism, thereby alienating itself from the actual social life of Japan, they basically have not sorted out and carried forward the legacies of thoughts since the Meiji period, leaving them solely to be remoulded by the ultra-nationalism of the right-wing ways of thinking. In fact, what we see in the fate of Asianism is exactly the epitome of the fate of the intellectual history of modern Japan. Takeuchi Yoshimi thus took it upon himself to sort out this intellectual legacy encoded by the right-wing thinking, seeking to draw out the Japanese intellectual tradition that defies being reduced to ideologies.

Takeuchi Yoshimi arranges the selected material into four parts: (I) Prototype; (II) Mood; (III) Logic; (IV) Transmigration (tensei). In Prototype, Takeuchi includes Okakura's 'The Ideals of the East' and Tarui Tokichi's 'The Great East Federation'.

These two articles are of different orientations. Takeuchi puts them together in Part I, Prototype, for he recognizes the sense of solidarity contained in Japan's Asianism, as does Okakura in his idea of an integral culture and Tarui Tokichi in his notion of strategic alliance. The former lays down the foundation for Asianism culturally, while the latter provides the scenarios for an Asia in union on the practical level. Tarui's federalist idea differs from the cry for aggression in that it does not aim to occupy Korea, but rather stresses that the binding in federation between Japan and Korea is made on the basis of an equal footing. Takeuchi regards them as the prototype of Asianism, for he sees in them a highly idealistic nature that is founded on a sense of crisis about the actuality. For the parts Mood and Logic, Takeuchi includes articles from Miyazaki Toten, Uchida Ryohei, Okawa Shumei and others – in total, the work of seven people. These people either had had direct involvement in the internal affairs of other Asian countries or even had taken part in the aggression. Takeuchi intends to abstract from the writings of these active agents the shape of the mood of Asianism and the line of development of the logic. Takeuchi observes that, if for these people Asianism and expansion since Meiji are almost indistinguishable, it makes no sense to rigidly define the two as distinct from each other. On the contrary, what needs to be differentiated is, rather, whether the thinking in question would generate discursive potential and consistency. On the basis of this consideration, Takeuchi chooses papers from Miyazaki and Okawa, while rejecting those that agitated for the Greater East Asia Coprosperity Sphere. He sees the latter as only 'pseud' thinking, that establishes itself through the suppression and destruction of all thinkings around Asianism; he considers them as 'the extreme form of thoughtlessness of Asianism'.

At the same time, Takeuchi tries to extract from the interstice between these two parts (Mood and Logic) a question: How to come to the understanding that Mood and Logic became separated when Japan's pan-Asianism turned to imperialism, as Logic turned into the logic of aggression and Mood failed to become principle? Takeuchi pursued this question in his collection of three papers in the fourth part. The papers are 'Nationalism in Asia' by the geographer Iizuka Koji, 'Kotoku Shusui and China' by the historian Yishimoda Sho, and 'The intellectuals of Japan' by the writer Hotta Yoshie. Among these three intellectuals' conceptions of Asia, the sense of urgency that Takeuchi characterized the question of Asia with at the Prototype state dissolved, together with the romantic sentiment of pan-Asianism that once instigated a zeal for assassination campaigns and inspired imperialistic ideologies in a time of political turmoil. They represent the most objective analyses of all the papers in the book, complementing well Takeuchi's reading guide. The naming of the part Transmigration (tensei) reveals that, to a large extent, Takeuchi intends to make sense of the questions raised in these texts by his contemporary intellectuals within the historical context of Asianism.

'The Prospect of Asianism' is not concerned with the question of Asia, and not even how the Japanese see Asia. It is concerned with the fundamental problems implicated in the modernization of Japan, i.e. the inherent connection between expansion and the modernization of Japan, which the trajectories of Asianism can help to reveal. During the Meiji period, Asianism was concerned with principles and ideals. By the advent of the 20th century, this side of Asianism's concern gradually disappeared and, finally, turned into the extreme form of thoughtlessness, and hence the tragic fate of Asianism.

Takeuchi Yoshimi has sharply noted that although it is difficult to sum up Asianism for the different shapes it takes, it remains as a mood throughout and fails to rise above itself and develop into a 'thinking'. Consequently, the development led to its appropriation by the rightist groups with strong inclination towards expansion. Kokuryukai (Black Dragon Society) and Genyosha (Black Ocean Society) are two such groups, and they became the principal agents in the translation of Asianism into practice. Logic, in turn, is gradually reduced to the logic of imperialism, leading finally to the idea of the Greater East Asia Coprosperity Sphere. Takeuchi further points out that the separation of Mood and Logic began with Kotoku Shusui and Uchida Ryohei, disciples of the civil liberty thinkers Nakae Chomin and Toyama Mitsuru of Genyosha respectively. The two disciples were, from the very beginning, unable to build up among themselves the kind of understanding and friendship found between their teachers. Thus, Kotoku Shusui approached the question of imperialism on an abstract level, while Uchida Ryohei took the practical level, which led to a path that took the rightist turn. Leftist intellectuals, in giving up nationalism for internationalism, were left with 'importing socialism' from the start, thus turning thinking into pure abstraction. Kotoku is a typical example. On the other hand, the ideology for aggression of the Amur River Society succeeded in monopolizing the question of Asia. All this was due to a sense of reality induced in them by nationalism. Takeuchi points out that, because the left failed to carry forward the intellectual legacy of nationalism of the Meiji period, the legacy could only pass on through forms of right-wing thinking. Thus, the left must also be held responsible as an 'accomplice' in the development of Asianism into imperialism.

Asianism, compiled by Takeuchi, is a masterpiece and probably the only one of its kind in the intellectual history of postwar Japan. In this particular work, Takeuchi displays the whole complex configuration of the question of Asia: the relation between Japan's modernization and expansionism; the relation between Japanese nationalism and internationalism; and the blind spots between the leftist and rightist approaches to the question of nationalism. It was not until Takeuchi elaborated on the discourses on Asianism since the Meiji period that the question of Asia could be located at the intersection of a complicated system of trends. And as Takeuchi sees it, the question of Asia does not constitute a centre of significance by itself; it only acquires its significance as a thread, articulating the different trends mentioned above. In this way, Takeuchi problematizes Asia directly, and thereby aggression and Tennoism – the thorniest problem to deal with in the intellectual history of modern Japan.

However, as he himself clarifies in *Asianism,* Takeuchi's view of Asia remains only a Mood. This is particularly clear if we look at his other writings concerning Asia, in which the question of Asia is discussed together with the question of modernization. He not only deliberately turns Asia into an abstract idea in opposition to Western Europe, but also turns Europe into an abstract entity. This certainly has to do with the inherent reference to principles of the problems Takeuchi directly confronts and the problems he insists on formulating. However, there is another side to this problem: Mood alone is not enough to raise the idealization of Asia to the level of principle underlying the sphere of world history. Perhaps Takeuchi's idea of Asia is effective in countering Orientalism criticized by Said, and in sketching the uniqueness of Japan. Despite the fact that in his idea of Asia, Takeuchi overly stresses both 'Asia' and 'the

West' as a monolithic whole, integral in itself, the problems confronted directly in Takeuchi's idea are real and intense. Yet this is not enough to enable Takeuchi's idea of Asia to face an Asia that is a composite of economic, cultural, political and social strands. Its limitations immediately reveal themselves once it is taken beyond the field of ideas. This limitation of Takeuchi can only be made apparent by placing it side by side with an alternative idea of Asia that is similarly concerned with principles and yet not merely restricted to idealistic exposition. Just as is the case with Watsuji Tetsuro in relation to Fukuzawa and Okakura, the frame of reference for Takeuchi's idea of Asia can only be found outside the field of intellectual history in Japan. Fortunately, at the end of the 1950s, such a frame of reference existed among the works of the intellectuals of Japan: it is Umesawa Tadao's ecological historiography of civilization.

Umesawa Tadao is a layman with regard to intellectual history, but he is able to turn his speciality in zoology at the Science Faculty of Tokyo University into a richly inventive thinking, namely, a habit of judging matters according to one's sense of things without simplistic acceptance of any established premise and conclusion. In 1955, Umesawa joined an expedition to Afghanistan, Pakistan and India. After the trip, he began to question the concept of Asia as an integral whole and the holistic mode of thinking of Asia versus Europe. He started to construct a world picture of his own to counter the Marxist historical materialism in Japan. In 1956, he published *Between East and West* and, in 1957, his representative work *An Ecological Historiography of Civilization*. Umesawa's basic view is that the understanding of Asia as an integral whole is that of the West. For the Asians, Asia is a composite of multifarious cultures. Additionally, Japan occupies a peculiar place in Asia; it cannot be the representative of Asia, let alone set itself up as an example for other Asian countries. In contrast, Japan bears more affinities with Western Europe and, therefore, it makes no sense to contrast Japan with Western Europe in order to ascertain Japan's characteristics. In order to do that, Japan should be compared with other Asian countries. Just around that time, Toynbee was visiting Japan, so Umesawa's work was being publicized as a response to Toynbee's challenge, contrary to Umesawa's own intentions. Umesawa's whole range of works throws doubt on, in an ironic way, the function of ideology. The value of his works is not to be sought in its conclusion, but rather in his firm approach to ecological history in his discussion of cultural differences, and in his stress on the significance of personal experience. This approach reminds one of *Local Conditions and Customs* by Watsuji Tesuro, and further suggests the possibility of a line of thinking in contrast with the humanistic approach of intellectual history.

By ecology, Umesawa means the ways of life of humans. From colour designs and behavioural characteristics, to clothing, food, shelter and transportation, all are for him crucial criteria for differentiating cultures. He tries to establish a theory of 'cultural function' in contrast with a 'genealogy of culture'. In a genealogy of culture, the essence of each culture is stressed; but for a theory of cultural function, cultural form is stressed. Take architecture as an example. With genealogy, its starting point is the material and the sort of wood used, etc, but the starting point of cultural forms would be the style and the use of a work of architecture. Umesawa, borrowing from the theoretical approach of biology, tries to sketch the variations in the ways of life of human communities, while variation is being understood along the line of parallel and pluralistic relations. In this connection, another pair of contrasting categories is necessarily invoked.

In addition to the contradiction between the genealogy and the cultural forms, we also have the opposition between the biological theory of evolution and the ecological study of metamorphism. Umesawa points out that in the history of human understanding, these two pairs of opposites are internally related: evolution is necessarily a theory of genealogy or pedigree, which stresses that human beings ultimately reach the same *telos*, and differences existing between different regions are only differences in different stages before the final stage. On the other hand, metamorphism in ecology recognizes that the subject and the environment are in a dialectical relation. It also admits that each way of life has its own *raison d'être*. Umesawa, in his attempt to sort out the law of history by means of the ecological historiographical approach, formulates a theory of 'subject-environmental system of self-movement'. No judgement of cultural values is involved in this formulation and, more importantly, the way of understanding things in terms of their 'essence' as the fundamental attributes is being challenged here.

On the basis of understanding such 'non-essential' attributes in ways of life as the criterion for the study of the law of history, Umesawa redraws the division within Eurasia. He names the two ends of this continent, i.e. Western Europe and Japan, 'the first region', characterized by the highly modernized ways of life found in them. He names areas outside this region as 'the second region', characterized by non-modernized ways of life. Then Umesawa compares each of the characteristics of one region to a corresponding characteristic in the other region,[13] and stresses along a line of thinking in close proximity to that of Watsuji Tetsuro, the relation of natural conditions to the making of history. On the historical geometrical map drawn by Umesawa, Eurasia is divided into a wet region, an arid region and a subarid region. He further asserts that: 'From the ecological point of view, history is the traces left by the process of interaction between humans and land. In other words, they are the traces left by the subject-environmental system of self-movement. Among those key factors that determine the pattern of this process, nature is the most important factor. The display of natural factors is not random, but rather in the form of a geometric distribution' (Umesawa 1967: 169).

In the landscape of the world history from the view of ecological history, the meaning of Asia is being questioned. Umesawa said that he heard a certain intellectual in Pakistan tell him that, 'We are all Asians', and was shocked, for he felt that the identity claim was merely a conceptual play, lacking in either substantial content or affective support. He asserted that this could only be a certain 'diplomatic fiction' (Umesawa 1967: 178).

Umesawa Tadao went a stride further than Watsuji Tetsuro. Though the latter brings in 'local conditions and customs' to the question of Asia, and ignores the ideological aspect of the question, he is not prepared to challenge the concept of Asia itself. As for Umesawa Tadao, the truthfulness of the concept of Asia itself becomes doubtful. Moreover, the assumption of an objective approach by Watsuji Tatsuro is, after all, a form of representation corresponding to his inner humanistic attitude, which leads to his affinity to thinking with right-wing inclinations. Umesawa Tadao, on the other hand, being formed in, and through, a natural science discipline, adopts a stronger epistemological attitude towards his object of study. However, as Umesawa Tadao pursued his study in 1957, he found he was situated at a time when the intellectuals in Japan were preoccupied with thinking over nationalism and Japan's position in Asia, whether it should be responsible for Asia, and whether it was a special nation in

Asia. This situation presented Umesawa Tadao with an unexpected difficulty, preventing his ecological approach in the study of history from becoming a 'knowledge', for it was inevitably appropriated along the lines of ideological thinking that necessarily led to arguing for the superiority of Japan and the breaking away from any obligation to Asia.

But even so, the ecological approach to the study of history has, after all, provided another possibility for rethinking since Watsuji Tatsuro. For the accepted mode of thinking in terms of the binary opposition between East and West, the so-called Oriental culture and the Occidental culture are each characterized by their own particularities, which in turn are to be understood in terms of constitution of unchanging essence. When Okakura put forward the idea of Asia as an integral whole, his assumptions about the civilization of Asia are based on a genealogical view of culture. Therefore, even though he has noticed evidence of cultural differences between Asian countries, and even within the same country, when he is dealing with the difference within the Asian civilization itself, Asia for him is still regarded as possessing the value of an independent entity, serving to counterpoint Europe, rather than becoming a fluid concept in terms of cultural functions. Fukuzawa's 'Disassociating Asia' is also a cultural genealogy with a different starting point. When Fukuzawa discusses the question of the positioning of Japan, he bases it on a presupposition of the unchanging essence of civilization, rather than proceeding from the consideration of the functions of civilization. Thus, even though it is possible for Japan to join the West in Fukuzawa's thinking on the question of modernity, the value of civilization represented by the 'West' is absolute. The starting point that Okakura and Fukuzawa have determined for Japanese intellectual history is basically a starting point within the frame of cultural genealogy yet, in their thinking, there are elements of a cultural functional perspective that fail to develop under the weight of the tension of their times. Regrettably, later scholars of Japanese intellectual history fail to take up this side of their thinking, and even help push the essentialist view of culture towards the extreme, as Takeuchi Yoshimi, in his reworking of the question of Asia, does when he calls to our attention the transformation into fascistic nationalism of the earlier sense of solidarity that guided the thinking of Asia. Notwithstanding the shrewd thinking of Takeuchi Yoshimi, the taking up of the question of Asia again fails to break away from cultural essentialism in the postwar era. Although Takeuchi has noticed the genealogical perspective in the thinking of the question of Asia, his confinement within the mode of thinking of intellectual history makes it impossible for him to disrupt the essentialist thinking on culture.

Given such a situation, Umesawa Tadao was met with misreading that gave him headaches each time he published his work. In the summer of 1957, he was invited to give a talk at a regular meeting of the Society for the Study of the Science of Thinking. He was asked to speak on the topic 'Japan seen from the Ecological Historical Perspective'. Umesawa Tadao took this opportunity to clear up misreading of his works, and made a sharply critical speech. He pointed out that *An Ecological Historiography of Civilization* was regarded as a discourse on Japanism by its readers, which was not what he had expected, and contrary to suggestions for revision in the theoretical framework and the examples in the text. Umesawa Tadao regards Japan as belonging to the first region, taking Japan as having a structure of modernization similar to that of Europe. This has the effect of boosting the spirits of some of those agitating for 'Japanism' and making those who are against 'Japanism' scowl. Umesawa said, 'While I am dealing with the constitution of the world, the reception only focuses on a very small region, leaving the systemic approach to a totality, the most important theoretical considera- tion, or rather that which I am most proud of myself in the book, untouched by any in-depth criticism.' 'I am really shocked by the indifference of Japanese intellectuals toward the state of the world outside Japan.'

Despite Umesawa Tadao's effort to invite academic discussion in a purely epistem- ological manner, he had provoked a new round of debate about the ideas of 'Dis- associating Asia' and 'Reviving Asia'. There were those who demanded that the ecological approach to history be applied directly to, or extended to solving, the problems Japan, in reality, was facing. After rebuking such demands, Umesawa Tadao sharply criticized the prevailing state of learning in Japan: '"the ecological approach to history" is not concerned with the question of "ought" in its inquiry, but with the approaches to finding out about the structure of the world and the formative processes involved, hence it cannot be an evaluation of the existing situation and certainly not the guiding principles for transformation . . . I find the predilection for the question "ought" of the Japanese intellectuals really overwhelming.' (Umesawa 1967: 128–146)

Among the various misreadings, Takeyama Michio's (1958) 'The Positioning of Japan's Culture' is the most representative. This is a speech made at the group discussion of Japanese Culture Conference, an organization of anti-communist liberal intellectuals. In the speech, Takeyama quoted, out of context, Umesawa's idea of Japan, together with Western Europe, as belonging to the first region, in order to support his argument for the superiority of the Japanese nation in Asia. On the one hand, Takeyama flagrantly spoke discriminatingly against other Asian countries as he stressed that Japan was not one of the Asian countries and did not bear any obligation to Asia. On the other hand, he also stressed that Japan was the example in modernization for other Asian countries. Although both start with the same proposition that Japan is not part of Asia, Takeyama and Umesawa think in opposition to one another: Umesawa opposes all ideological efforts to serve the demands of reality and attempts to dissolve this 'diplomatic' fiction of 'Asianism' through a recontextualization within the framework of world history, while Takeyama turns Umesawa's ecological approach to history into a new fiction, serving the ideology of the superiority of Japan.

The claim of Japanese superiority represented by Takeyama's view of Japanese culture is a continuous line of thinking running throughout the intellectual history of modern Japan. During the Meiji period, such a frame of mind is accompanied by a sense of national crisis, which fosters the emergence of eminent thinkers.[14] However, after the Second World War, this particular frame of mind has gravely debilitated the substance of thought, metamorphosing into the loud brawls of ideological assertions, causing great detriment to the tradition of thought in Japan, and leading astray elements of thinking which otherwise are capable of being deepened. The violent appropriation of Umesawa Tadao by Takeyama profoundly reveals the detrimental power of such a frame of mind. At the end of the 1950s, the thinking of Asianism and the anti-Asianism thinking of the ecological approach to history, or the theory of local conditions and customs, cross paths for the first time in the midst of the new round of 'Disassociating Asia' debates. This intellectual convergence is made possible through the effort of Takeuchi Yoshimi and, in a different way, from that of the appropriation of Umesawa by Takeyama.

In August 1958, Takeuchi Yoshimi wrote a series of articles on 'Two Conceptions of the History of Asia' for Tokyo Shimbun. In the articles, he deals with Umesawa Tadao's and Takeyama Michio's ideas of 'Disassociating Asia' from a historical perspective. Takeuchi ploughs through the ostensible similarity between the two conceptions and explores the central difference between the two: in Umesawa's ecological approach, what is stressed is the interaction and counteraction taking place between the human subject and the natural environment. It is neither a geographical determinism nor a determinism of energy resources. Takeyama, however, twists such an ecological approach into a unidirectional determinism in the service of his anti-communist political agenda. While Umesawa bases his understanding on the experiences and observations acquired in the field of ecology, and his functional perspective does not involve questions of values, Takeyama bases his understanding on the established ideology of Eurocentrism, leaning towards the values of a monistic view of civilization. Umesawa multi-spatializes history, i.e. while history is normally regarded as a self-contained development of a unidimensional nature, Umesawa, in his ecological approach, treats this common conception of history as a record of the 'traces' of the ecological metamorphism which, Umesawa stresses, is of a pluralistic nature, thus rendering history impossible to be maintained as a self-sufficient subject. Takeuchi Yoshimi calls this 'the annihilation of history'. As for Takeyama, history becomes omnipotent, turning into a heavy 'being'. For Umesawa, all things are, in the final analysis, constituted by elements horizontally related to one another. But for Takeyama, the only system of values he can understand is that which can be hierarchically arranged. To establish the order of each value or, more precisely, to arrange the values according to a certain established order, is the spring of his enthusiasm in the pursuit of knowledge. This explains why, even though both Umesawa and Takeyama idealize history and the world in an image of their own, one takes as his principle actual evidence, while the other, dogmas.

Having offered the above succinct analysis, Takeuchi Yoshimi further points out that: 'In trying to find out the principle of Asia from the subjective perspective of Japan, one must confront the reality of Japan's ignorance about Asia, as Umesawa has pointed out. But what Takeyama is doing is that, instead of confronting one's own ignorance, he takes advantage of it.' (Takeuchi 1958: 90–91)

The above conclusion of Takeuchi Yoshimi reveals to us the whole complexity of the question of Asia. First, he unveils that the basic position of Japan's intellectual history lies in the assumption of Japan as the subject in the search for an understanding of the principle of Asia, a position shared by Japanese thinkers through the ages. Furthermore, he points out that the search for the principle of Asia must be based on the understanding of Asia, and this is just what Japanese thinkers, through the ages, have not done thus far. Thirdly, he discloses that advocates of 'Japanism', like Takeyama, are taking advantage of the ignorance and the blind belief in the superiority of the Japanese for their own ideological or political purposes. In fact, Takeyama is only a typical example of 'self-consolation' in the increasingly fevent new movement for self-isolation from the world since the Second World War. The ignorance of the intellectuals and the ordinary folk in Japan about their Asian neighbours, not to mention the whole of the rest of Asia, is a blind spot not to be overlooked in the Japanese views of Asia, from the time of Fukuzawa to that of Umesawa Tadao.

In such a situation, it is very difficult to build up Japan's intellectual tradition. This inherent deficiency of Japan's intellectual history with regard to the question of Asianism makes it impossible for thinkers in Japan not to move beyond the horizon of intellectual history. The frame of reference provided by Umesawa Tadao is unique in its 'annihilation' of history and value judgement, and also in its corresponding epistemological approach to Asia. Because of this uniqueness, it not only makes the blind spot of intellectual history visible, it also finds a point of juncture with the latter.

In 1961, just after Umesawa Tadao published his work on the ecological approach to history, and before Takeuchi Yoshimi (1970) wrote his article on Asianism in Japan, the two had a very interesting conversation with one another. Judging by information available at this time, this seems to have been the only cooperation between intellectual history and ecological history with regard to the question of Asia. The questions brought about in this conversation precisely suggest the direction, and the differences, in the thinking about the question of Asia by Japanese intellectuals, since that time.

Their basic common position in this dialogue is the criticism of the monistic view of civilization. Takeuchi has committed his life to the destruction of the Eurocentric monistic conception of civilization, so as to work towards a pluralistic conception of civilization. It is precisely because Umesawa holds a similar position to Takeuchi that Takeuchi can respond to Umesawa's writing in an accurate way, thus clearing up serious misreadings of Umesawa's work. Umesawa expresses his agreement with the ideas in Takeuchi's 'Two conceptions of Asia' as soon as the dialogue began, and acknowledges Takeuchi Yoshimi for having expressed, in a concise manner, what he wanted to articulate but failed to, showing that Umesawa is also aware of his sharing of a common position with Takeuchi Yoshimi.

However, between the two, there lies a chasm of difference. While Takeuchi Yoshimi grants that Asia does exist, Umesawa thinks that the defining line is meaningless. To go further, the former's assertion about Asia is made within the realm of ideas, a pure realm that the latter is seeking to dismantle. The latter negates Asia precisely because he is aware of the overly optimistic and wishful thinking of the former's working with pure ideas. To Takeuchi, Asia is an idea, a method, and the instrument he can use to refute the use of evolutionary theory to explain history. But whether this Asia exists substantially or not, is not the crucial question for Takeuchi. In fact, he is doing his utmost not to substantialize Asia. To Umesawa Tadao, the symbolization of Asia ignores the multifarious facets of Asia, which is not acceptable to his academic training. For him, the pluralistic nature of civilization does not need to be articulated through setting up the binary opposition of Asia versus Europe. Just dissolving the presupposition of a unifying Asia will do the job. However, on a higher level, they were both confronted with a real problem: the government of postwar Japan claimed itself to be the example of modernization in Asia, disguising its intention to dominate Asia. The political situation is so severe that they are able to transcend their theoretical differences and work together, on the basis of a shared sense of responsibility as intellectuals. It is this severe political situation that enables them to attempt to transcend their theoretical difference to work together, grounded on their sense of responsibility as intellectuals.

In the dialogue, Takeuchi Yoshimi offers the following definition for Asia: 'I think Asia is produced in response to Western powers in the course of modern history. That is to say, after the invasion of Western powers, the various ancient and medieval regimes are being destroyed from within. This destructive power perhaps may be called the productive power; or the spirit. In short, this is a movement that begins with the establishment of modernization or of capitalism.' (Takeuchi 1970: 146) Accordingly, those countries understood as lacking such an inherent power of self-negation are not to be counted as Asian countries. Takeuchi Yoshimi cites Israel as being one of those countries that cannot be called Asian, while Cuba is to be included as an Asian country. Japan, since it does not possess the power of self-negation, cannot be counted as an Asian country either.[15]

Umesawa Tadao cannot agree with such an idealized and symbolized definition of Asia, for it is impossible for him to imagine a region such as Asia as being detached from its geographical attributes and turned into an object constructed by intellectual history. But he agrees with Takeuchi Yoshimi regarding the positioning of Israel and Cuba, and he even adds that 'Central and South America can be regarded as the Asia of the New Continent' (Takeuchi 1970: 146). But this is as far as the compromise goes, for Umesawa is fundamentally dubious about the effectiveness of treating Asia as an idea. When Takeuchi Yoshimi imposes the definition of inherent self-negation on Asia, the regional structures and the endogenous uneven relations defining the Asian region itself are all being covered up. Therefore, after having gone along with Takeuchi Yoshimi's suggestion of treating Asia as an idea, Umesawa immediately directs the discussion to the aspect that he is concerned with and which Takeuchi Yoshimi neglects. This is the structural problem of a collective of large and small states peculiar to Asia.

Beginning from his earliest published work, *An Ecological Historiography of Civilization*, Umesawa is very much concerned with Asia's system of civilization. He points out that, in the second region, there is the large central state with its ancient civilization, defying disintegration even as it enters into the modern world, while at its fringes there may develop the modern form of the first region. Thus, Umesawa is the first to raise the question concerning the relation between large states and surrounding small states within the regional structure of Asia. As mentioned above, he points out that in 'the second region' there are four traditional empires, namely, the Chinese Empire, the Turkish Empire, the Russian Empire and India. The small states surrounding them are under the shade of the cultures of the empires, and cannot be the centre of civilization, although it is possible for them to develop technologies.

Notwithstanding his inability to perfect his supposition, in contrast to Takeuchi Yoshimi's blindness to the dynamics of relations of forces between large states and small states throughout history, Umesawa's thinking is obviously more illuminating to later studies of Asia. In the dialogue, Umesawa Tadao points out, 'the size of a state is a crucial factor that must be taken into consideration in the discussion of Asia . . . The ways large states and small states exist should be very different. Furthermore, their historical backgrounds are in reality also different.' 'Therefore, in dealing with actual problems and problems of the future, the question of the motive power operating through the interrelation of these materially inscribed states must also be considered. That is to say, the sediments from history are an integral part of their interrelationships. I think all this cannot be made to disappear simply by reacting against the West. The troubles of Asia are far more complicated.' (Takeuchi 1970: 147–148)

Takeuchi frankly admits that he is not concerned with the relation between large states and small states, for he is more concerned with how the civilization of Asia can be revised to the level of universal principles so as to counter the might of the principle of Western Europe. Umesawa believes that this is only an optimistic ideal, and to those

Asians with similar ideas this is an act of good intention. As to whether such a presupposed state can really gain the upper hand, this is very doubtful. 'Inside Asia itself, one cannot say that there does not exist key elements detrimental to universal values of humans.' (Takeuchi 1970: 150)

After Umesawa cites India as an example, reminding us of the danger of alienating ideas from actuality, Takeuchi Yoshimi makes the following conclusion: 'I hope such a realism can be respected, so that ideas can be prevented from being formed in opposite directions.' (Takeuchi 1970: 154) Obviously, Takeuchi recognizes the tension between idea and reality. It also shows that the position he takes in intellectual history can work with the position of the ecological approach to history to rid themselves of the influence of ideological assumptions.

Regrettably, such cooperation has not persisted between Takeuchi and Umesawa. They continue to reflect on the question of Asia along their own lines of thinking, with no sign of further opening themselves up. Takeuchi still adheres strictly to the level of ideas in the discussions of the ideals of Asia and the question of the possibility of a different course of history for Asia in the book *Asianism*, compiled in 1963. By 1975, when he edited the book *The Unfolding of Asian Studies*, he had already done away with any consideration of the complexities implied in the question of Asia and had reverted to the state in which he wrote *Modern China and Modern Japan*. He proclaimed, 'Asia is the concept of defiance with regard to modern Europe'.[16] On the other hand, Umesawa persists in his reflection on civilization along the line of his ecological approach to history. However, he too seems to have given up the intention to work with intellectual history scholars. In the 1980s, he was committed to developing a new area of research – civilization studies – and he mainly worked with ethnologists and cultural anthropologists, many of whom are from the faculty of science and engineering.

From 1984, Umesawa convened the annual international conference on civilization studies, in the name of the National Museum – the institution to which he belonged. The products of these conferences are compiled into anthologies of papers such as *Civilization Studies on Modern Japan*, *Civilization Studies on Urbanization* and *Civilization Studies on Ruling Regimes*. In these discussions, the suppositions Umesawa raised at the end of the 1950s in his *An Ecological Historiography of Civilization* are elaborated upon, allowing him to put forward, in a more distinct manner, his understanding of the history of civilization and the comparative study of the history of civilization.

In the keynote speech collected in the *Civilization Studies on Modern Japan*, Umesawa offers an account of his overall understanding of the system of relations between the subject and the environment:

> Even when dealing with history, I think it is always necessary to approach history from the perspective of our understanding of civilization. That is to say, the most important understanding of the historical perspective of civilization is that it is not simply the successive relations that are our concern; the synchronic relations must also always be taken into consideration. For any given period, there simultaneously coexist various cultural elements, all kinds of institutions and media, constituting a whole system. Therefore, history can be regarded as the changes in time undergone synchronically in these coexisting features. Hence, if one confines oneself to only a part of the whole system and studies its diachronic profile, the possibility

for solving any problem is next to nil. I do not mean to criticize historians, but in the past, all kinds of history are often treated as the diachronic process of change occurring to a part of the features in an extremely over-simplified way. The situation would be changed immensely by the introduction of the historical perspective of civilization, i.e. all things that are contemporary are related to one another in a certain way, and this system of relations is moving all together.

(Umesawa 1984: 23–24)

Umesawa Tadao's civilization studies may not be of much originality as far as its contents are concerned, particularly in the section on the question of Asia, where he puts forward the differentiation between the first region and the second region, a division basically not accepted by people after him. However, his work in bringing forth the civilization studies, and his decades-long endeavours, deserve particular attention. He brings in new thrusts to the study of the question of Asia, whereas it has always been conducted before within the field of intellectual history, which is drowned in ideas, thus making it inevitable that the question is confined to a narrow view. Furthermore, Japanese scholars in intellectual history turn out to be unable to make a necessary reflection on the narrowness of their views. The appearance of Watsuji Tetsuro could have provided a pivotal change of horizons in the intellectual histories, from remaining within the state of 'mood' in Asian studies towards opening up a much wider perspective of regional structure. This kind of pivotal change, however, did not take place then. Umesawa is again another such pivot, and thanks to Takeyama Michio's deliberate appropriation and Takeuchi Yoshimi's prompt correction, Umesawa's works are being taken to the most productive level, thereby enabling them to bring about a truly open view for the Asian studies scholars in contemporary Japan.

However, after he had abandoned the attempt in the early 1960s to engage Takeuchi Yoshimi in dialogue, Umesawa Tadao also gradually loses the edge of tension in his thinking. Today, 40 years after the publicity of *An Ecological Historiography of Civilization*, he is not so vigilant about the reproduction of the discourse of Japan-centrism. On the contrary, his perspective begins to turn from 'the Structure of the World' to 'the Culture of Japan'. Ironically, he is now falling back to the position he criticized 40 years ago of 'the inclination to be framed by the question "ought" of the Japanese', and turning his ecological approach to the evaluation of the existing state of affairs, or even to a guiding principle for the contemporary reforms, as an attempt to identify the path that Japan should take into the 21st century.[17] The destiny of Umesawa's ecological approach to history, in turn, has demonstrated the difficulty for social science and humanist thinking in maintaining a dialogue; it also suggests that it is not possible to remain solely within a single discipline in dealing with the question of Asia.

At the beginning of the 1960s, Japan and Asia were in a turbulent situation, presenting a solid and intense context for intellectuals to cross boundaries and engage in interdisciplinary dialogue. After the 1970s, the interdisciplinary dialogue gradually lost the edge, not only among the intellectuals of Asia, but also within the intelligentsia of Japan itself. Although the discussions on the question of Asia during this period, compared to the 1960s, were richer and more systematic, it was becoming more and more an academic exercise and intellectually oriented. It is questionable whether the accumulation of knowledge obtained in such a way can really help the Japanese understand Asia. When the grave fact that Takeuchi Yoshimi and Umesawa Tadao were confronted with is pushed under the carpet, the Japanese knowledge of Asia can only amount to the extremely biased orientalism as criticized by Said.

The concealed fact of the ongoing duet of 'Disassociating Asia' and 'Reviving Asia' in Japan implies the lack of a sense of responsibility towards Asia on the part of Japan. It also indicates that Japan is lacking in the area of self-identification. Takeuchi Yoshimi endeavoured to establish such a sense of responsibility within the realm of intellectual history because he was aware of an opening for self-identification concealed in the knowledge of Asia of modern Japan. None of the political discourse of the Greater East Asia Coprosperity Sphere, in the earlier years or the later academic discussion, could hide this fundamental truth: Japan fails to constitute its subjectivity sufficiently in the process of knowing Asia because it fails to turn the question into an opportunity for self-identity.

In fact, it can be considered an act of violence to put Watsuji Tetsuro and Umesawa Tadao together in the discussion as if they were tracking the same line of thinking. The positions of their thinking and their ways of learning differ so obviously that we are discouraged from doing just that. Furthermore, there is no sufficient evidence to show that Umesawa Tadao has been essentially influenced by Watsuji Tetsuro. However, the reason I still venture to put them together is out of a consideration that we are too used to discussing a problem within the boundary of one discipline, and so neglect the complexity and the many-sidedness of the problem. We tend easily to criticize our predecessors for the limitations of their thinking while neglecting the rationale peculiar to the historical context against which the thinking takes its form, hence we also fail to see the possibility of the growth of knowledge. All this makes it too easy to delude ourselves into thinking that we are breaking new paths. Take Watsuji Tetsuro's *Local Conditions and Customs* as an example. If it is only read as an ethical treatise within the field of ethics, then it is not clear where to locate it in the later intellectual tradition. With the help of critiques from people like Sakai Naoki,[18] we can see more clearly now that the idea of local conditions and customs in Watsuji is different from Umesawa Tadao's ecological approach to history: the former obliterates subjectivity on the basis of genealogical cultural essentialism in genealogy in modern Western thought, while the latter tries to resist such cultural essentialism with the standpoint of functionalism.

But if we confine our consideration only to this level, we will not be able to confront the following more complicated facts: Asianism is such a problem because it involves different fields and intellectuals of varying positions at the same time, thus what we see here is not merely the complicity between universality and particularity. Not even the complicity between imperialism and colonialism in its Eastern version is enough to constitute the full horizon for the study of Asianism. Besides this perspective, we can see an even richer constitution through the process of the persistent construction of Asianism by the Japanese throughout the modern period. It is in this connection that I think we can, in fact, locate a position for Watsuji Tatsuro's local conditions and customs perspective in a much wider horizon, which is a different horizon standing in opposition to that of Asianism as an ideal, suggesting a different approach to Asia. Through the civilization studies of Umesawa Tadao, I see a growth of this possibility, that is, to question afresh the Asian question by taking Asia as a region rather than as an idea. With Watsuji Tatsuro, such a way of questioning is unwitting and indistinct and is premised on the absence of Asia. With Umesawa Tadao, the questioning becomes conscious and unambiguous, taking the idealism and the cultural essentialism on Asia as objects to be deconstructed. But, at the bottom line, the concern with local conditions and customs must be recognized as the contribution of Watsuji Tetsuro. No matter what sort of ideological effect *Local Conditions and Customs* had, it has, after all, provided a pivotal point for the discussion of Asianism to steer away from Fukuzawa's and Okakura's idealistic approach, towards a different dimension of thinking.

The positioning of *Asian perspectives* and the problems it reveals

Almost at the same time as Watsuji Tetsuro's ethical study, there existed an unnoticed line of thinking that problematized Asia. As it is more theoretically inclined and lacking in the inherent tension of thinking, it therefore did not arouse as much interest as the discussions of the Asian question. However, the possibility for a new turn implicit in this line of thinking is becoming more discernible half a century later.

This is the thinking on Asia of the historians associated with the Kyoto School of thought. The founder of this tradition of historiography was Naito Konan, and as I have not done any systematic study on this school, I cannot offer an overall evaluation. Here, I offer only preliminary thoughts on two historians and their thinking on Asia.

The first is Suzuki Naritaka (1907–1988). He took part in the two symposia, 'The Standpoint of World History and Japan' and 'Overcoming the Modern', in the early 1940s. He specialized in Western medieval history. His teacher, Karaki Junzo, was labelled as 'anti-modern'. As a scholar of the Kyoto School, it is symbolically significant for Suzuki to have taken part in these symposia which, on the one hand, indirectly supported the propagation of fascist ideologies and, on the other, earnestly pursued theoretical discussion. To Suzuki and other Kyoto School scholars, theoretical pursuits were a more important concern than pursuing thinking that confronted reality and political responsibility. It is precisely this attitude of judging from aloft matters of politics that caused them to be used by political forces.

Suzuki does not directly engage in the historical study of Asia. His concern is the pattern of 'world history'. He thinks that one of the fundamental problems for modern history is 'the becoming one of the world'. The becoming-one process is not brought about through 'a natural process of thousands of years of mutual relations between the various parts of the world that eventually give birth to an integrated world. Rather, this occurs through a sudden and drastic process of incorporation into one entity, with the history of long periods of isolation shared by various parts of the world that had not been broken by exchanges among them interrupted as if overnight' (Suzuki 1990: 14–15). Suzuki stresses that the world becomes one not through the sharing of common ideals and orders consistent with one another. It is rather the consequence of Europe's unilateral expansion, the Europeanization of non-European regions. Suzuki also points out, in a similar vein, that 'Europe began to emerge in an all-pervading context from ancient times, and also took shape in an all-pervading context in medieval times. While, for Asia, tracing back to the dawn of the history of mankind, we find several distinct cultures taking shape separately and developing autogenously and independently of one another. These distinct origins then developed into autonomous, self-contained cultures, churning out histories that are closed to and autonomous from one another. Unlike to Europe, whether politically or culturally, Asia has never been a unified whole. While the unifying nature of Europe is real, it is unreal for Asia to be ascribed a unifying nature. If Asia can be attributed a common Asian consciousness, this is only possible for the last hundred years. And that is only made to emerge as a reaction to Western European imperialism.' (Suzuki 1990: 33)

Suzuki's way of thinking is representative of the dominant notion in the modern period and understanding of the world within intellectual circles. Such thinking not only coincides with Toynbee's 'challenge and response' model of historical explanation, it also coincides with the track of thinking among modern Japanese intellectuals on the question of the substantialization of Asia. Interestingly, such a way of thinking is that of intellectuals in the West in relation to the discussions on the process of the globalization of modernity, except that it is appropriated by Suzuki so to counter Eurocentric ways of thinking. Undeniably, the mindset for posing questions in this way possesses the paradoxical character peculiar to Westernized intellectuals of the East. This enables Suzuki to identify more easily with the idea of 'Japan's uniqueness' on the theoretical level. It is certainly not coincidental that he and Takeyama Michio engaged in conversation many times.[19]

Certainly, the question of Asia cannot be tackled directly through people like Suzuki, whose expertise lies rather in the field of European history. Among scholars of Japan studies, Miyazaki Ichisada (1901–1998) directly dealt with the study of Asia in its entirety, and echoed Suzuki's world history perspective from the perspective of Asian Studies. Even though there is nothing in common between Miyazaki and Suzuki in terms of specific conclusions, the pivotal point of Miyazaki's thinking and that of Suzuki are in agreement. Both are motivated by a will to resist the hegemony of Western Europe and endeavour to construct a new idea of world history.

In 1942, Miyazaki was instructed by the Ministry of Education to take part in compiling and writing *The Outline of the History of the Greater East Asia*. This was, of course, scholarship commissioned by the authorities and was meant to serve aggression. However, Miyazaki dealt with this thorny problem according to the Kyoto School's ways of understanding. 'Of course, in terms of scholarship, such things should not be written. But we can neither turn a blind eye to the Asian history according to the vision of Europeans looking down from a commanding position in which Asia is represented as stagnant without progress and development.' (Miyazaki 1975: 2) It is with the will to challenge Eurocentrism that Miyazaki, together with others, undertook to 'rewrite' the ideological objective of the Ministry of Education's attempt to produce a reader for the people of the Greater East Asia Coprosperity Sphere. They broadened the history of Asia by including West Asia, as well as East Asia. The rewriting also transposes the provenance of civilization from East Asia to West Asia, describing the process of the gradual movement towards the East of civilization, until it finally reaches Japan. In this portrait of the flowing of civilization into the East, Miyazaki showed a contradictory attitude towards the positioning of Japan. Ideologically, he is inclined to echo the idea of regarding Japan as the centre, but he is so rigorously trained in his scholarship that he cannot allow himself to do that. Consequently, he adopted an objectivistic attitude with regard to the historical positioning of Japan.

It is, however, not true that Miyazaki's concept of Asia is directed against Japan's militarism. In fact, like most other scholars of the Kyoto School, Miyazaki does not have a clear understanding of the current political situation. As a result, in a simplistic manner, he identified politically with the ideologies of militarism. But the political stand of Miyazaki does not occupy a significant position in his scholarly activities. Beyond theoretical considerations, he does not show any interest in questions of thinking and ideologies.[20] His theoretical concern is the problem of the constitution of world history. And the question of the unity of Asia can become an object for his thinking because, like Suzuki, he also wants to depict a picture of world history different from that framed by Eurocentrism. Therefore, even though his thinking assumes Japan to be representative of Asia in the struggle against Western Europe, which leads to the justification of Japan's aggression beginning from the Sino-Japanese War of 1894–1895, he does not simplistically take the ideologies of Japanese nationalism and militarism as his basic position. The view he establishes through his study of Asia implicitly contains in it quite rich productive elements.

An Outline of the History of the Greater East Asia had not been finished by the time of Japan's defeat, saving Miyazaki from leaving a taint on his record. But this did not significantly affect him. Even when the Ministry of Education gave the order, shortly after Japan's defeat, to erase all traces of evidence of such a project, he managed to publish the work in 1947 under a different title, *An Outline of the History of Asia*. The basic characteristic of Miyazaki's study can be seen in this work, and it is particularly remarkable that *An Outline of the History of Asia* contains significant elements from the legacy of Asianism while reworking them into a new direction.

As *An Outline of the History of Asia* takes the entire Asia as its object of study, theoretically it must deal with the fundamental fact that the region of Asia is characterized by cultural differences, a fact leading Umesawa Tadao to deny the existence of Asia. While Suzuki invokes a unifying Asia to confront the challenges from Europe, Miyazaki does not put forward an integrated Asia as a countering force. He thinks that the history of Europe has been studied quite comprehensively, and has become part of world history. But the study of the history of Asia remains far behind, inadequate for assuming a position in world history. In view of this, Miyazaki wants to move the study of Asia forward so that the history of Asia, seen by the West as stagnant, can become a part of world history. As for the cultural differences in Asia, Miyazaki believes that this cannot be cause enough to keep them isolated from one another, for 'the ties of communication link them closely together.' (Miyazaki 1987: 20) But Miyazaki is also inclined, like Umesawa, to confront the regional differences within Asia. Thus, in *An Outline of the History of Asia*, he differentiates between three main civilizations in Asia: the Indian, the Chinese and the Persian Islamic civilizations. All other Asian cultures are regarded as variations of the three main types. On the basis of this, Miyazaki directs his attention to the discussion of 'communications' between these civilizations from ancient times until today, focusing particularly on the disintegration and mutation of civilization due to the inherent mobility of the civilization in question.[21]

Miyazaki discusses, from a completely different direction than that of Umesawa, the interconnections between the different areas in Asia, without framing it within the opposition of Europe and Asia. On the contrary, Miyazaki translates his mode of analysis on the interconnections between different cultures within Asia to the relation between Europe and Asia. He thereby dissolves the simple model of the opposition between Asia and Europe in analysing their relations. In attending to the interconnection between Asia and Europe historically, he moves forward one step further than did Suzuki. His conceptions of the history of Asia are described as 'a history of communications' and 'a history of contacts'.

According to Miyazaki, historical studies must begin from 'tangible facts' that are well known to people, but 'the phenomena of facts are not all there is, for they are only the results produced by the encounters between immense powers. The power includes not merely the whole of the people's and the state's intellectual and will power, but also the potential of the economic resources of the land activated by this power. In fact, the regions that exist in history are produced as the field of the actions of such power. The power that shapes a region is also the power that shapes an age.' (Miyazaki 1987: 224) This reminds one of the unresolved difficulty in Watsuji's thinking of the relation between local conditions and history, the fundamental proposition concerning Umesawa in his ecological approach to history, and the studies of regional histories in today's Japan. And the way Miyazaki thinks about regions suggests that it is possible for the study of regional history and the study of intellectual history to converge.

Miyazaki has consistently opposed the kind of Asian studies that treat the distinct cultures of different regions as an isolated object of study, and then compiles the non-related isolated studies into a book. In his discussion of the 'contest' between different peoples and cultures, he tries to show the inherent organic connections that history allows us to see. To do that, Miyazaki follows the study of European history and divides the history of Asia into ancient, medieval and modern, and further extends this framework to the discussion of the continuation of the modern period into 'the most recent modern period'. He then argues that the 'Renaissance' occurs in West Asia, East Asia, and then Europe, denoting the respective beginnings of the modern age in each area. Such a process occurred around the ninth century in West Asia, the eleventh century in East Asia, and between the fourteenth and fifteenth centuries in Europe. Miyazaki thinks that this process follows a temporal sequence, with the phases in the sequence mutually influencing one another. The European Renaissance is the latest to occur and, with the greatest achievements, provides Europe with the foundation to engage in the most powerful projects of expansion in the modern period.[22] The most problematic point in Miyazaki's narration of history is his taking for granted the mode in which history is narrated in modern Europe. He believes that this can be regarded as a universal mode of narration, even though such a representation of history is derived from the need to explain history in Europe. Thus, he thinks that one can employ such a mode of narration to deal with various situations in different areas of Asia. Therefore, the explanations he offers of the Renaissance in different areas cannot but be a semblance of truth, and his account of the formation of nationalism as well as the modern state in modern China is strained.

However, what Miyazaki does should not be compared with the simplistic appropriation of Western theoretical frameworks. He thinks hard on his methodology for studying history, one which aims towards the establishment of world history as an organic whole, and it is on the basis of the assumption of the inherent organic connections of world history that he employs the Western model. Thus, Miyazaki does not appropriate Western theoretical frameworks of history statically.

He is concerned throughout with the dynamic relations linking Asia and Europe as the content for demonstrating his theoretical model. For example, Miyazaki thinks that the motive power of the Industrial Revolution in England comes from India. As England had, very early on, laid the ground for wool production and processing, the beginning of the importation of raw cotton from India stimulated the development of the textile industry at home. However, as wool processing was originally performed as a cottage industry, the massive importation of cotton posed new demands on this mode of processing, leading to the standardization of production and the establishment of specialized factories. Efficient and low-cost machinery was then invented, with the steam engine representing the revolution in motive power, giving rise to the Industrial Revolution. 'Without the supply of raw materials and the markets for the exportation of products produced with them, the newly invented machines perhaps would have lain idle until they were destroyed by the reactionary forces of the medieval period, leaving behind for the later generations only a nostalgic topic for conversation. In fact, even the spirit of the Industrial Revolution itself was aroused as a response to the impact of the active trade with the East.' (Miyazaki 1987: 350–51) Miyazaki deals with the relationship between the East and the French Revolution in similar ways, stressing particularly the influence of the Chinese and the Japanese Confucian social forms on the Christian societies of Western Europe, which were in opposition to Islam. He believes that the non-religious form of Confucianism helps break the binary thinking in the demarcation between the 'us and them' of religious thought, thereby providing those arguing for the elimination of religion in Europe with powerful intellectual weapons (Miyazaki 1987: 354–55).

For Miyazaki, England's Industrial Revolution and the French Revolution were the beginning of what he calls 'the most modern era', that is, what normally is called the beginning of modernity. When Miyazaki considers these two historical events by relating them to Asia, the significance of this gesture is not that his argument is convincing, but rather that his idea, written 40 years ago, brings up a subject which has become the focus of a series of discussions for later generations. Above all, it even subtly echoes the expositions of Wallerstein and Braudel on the globalization of capitalism.

There are, however, still other problems. Miyazaki and Suzuki, being from the same generation, were confronted with the urgency of their times, which was intimately connected to the nourishment sustaining their scholarship. The relationships between the Kyoto School and the Second World War require a separate paper, but I will simply note that the objectivity of the Kyoto School was maintained through very turbulent times. Many scholars personally took part in the war of aggression. Such a contrast between scholarship and the times in which it is conducted deserves study, rather than being dealt with reductively. The problem of the elimination of subjectivity in Watsuji should also be discussed within such a context. I believe that within this particular historical context, some very interesting questions may be drawn from an examination of the so-called objectivity of scholarship.

The intellectual tradition created by the Kyoto School has left a complicated legacy for intellectuals of later generations engaged with the question of Asianism. Between the idealistic approach to, and the symbolization of, Asia in the question of Asia, on the one hand, and the rejection of treating Asia purely on the level of ideas, on the other, is a different approach – that of searching for an understanding of historical structure out of materiality. Even though Kyoto School scholars fail to sort out the relation between thinking and scholarship and put scholarship in the service of ideologies, their writings suggest the possibility of understanding Asia differently. That is, they offer the possibility of bringing the idea of Asia and the material Asia together, allowing the two approaches to integrate through the perspective of a fluid 'history of communications'.

Regrettably, although many works on the question of Asia have appeared since the 1980s, most are merely, as Miyazaki has already criticized, isolated studies of different areas of Asia then compiled into a book without bothering even to ask whether the chapters are in anyway related. These studies may have made some contribution and furnished further details. However, they fail to reach the level achieved by their predecessors with regard to an overall picture. Dynamics and a sense of crisis are missing. So too are a boldness of vision and an aspiring spirit in scholarship.

It is only in the early 1990s that a new trend of discussion on the question of Asia, aroused by the publication of a seven-volume series, emerged among intellectuals in Japan. That series is *Asian Perspectives*[23] published in 1993 and 1994 by the Tokyo University Press. The chief editor was Mizoguchi Yuzo, Emeritus Professor of the Tokyo University, in collaboration with other professors of the Tokyo University, Hamashita Takeshi, Miyajima Hiroshi and Hiraishi Naoaki.[24] This series has gone further in its questioning than any discussions of the issue of Asia in postwar Japan. The contributors reflect on the 'unfolding of the historicity of knowing as regards Asia in Japan'. They also approach the question of Asia in terms of the history of the questioning, and re-examine both the meaning of the relations between Japan and Asia and the relationship between the question of Asia and the question of modernity. Although it is inevitable that the collection contains both good and bad work and diverse themes, the series nevertheless has achieved once again the problematization of 'Asia'. However, the most remarkable thing about the series is the collaboration between Mizoguchi Yuzo and Hamashita Takeshi that symbolizes the joining of intellectual history and regional studies, the most important of its kind since the short conversation between Takeuchi Yoshimi and Umesawa in the early 1960s.

Mizoguchi Yuzo specializes in Chinese intellectual history. The most distinctive characteristic of his studies is his approach to an object of study from within. That is, he is attentive to the texture of the object of study without assuming any presupposition to be true. In his study of Chinese intellectual history, particularly of the period when the Ming Dynasty is collapsing and the Qing Dynasty is emerging, he grasps the complex context specific to this critical historical transition, and follows close to the internal tensions of that period in posing his questions. As an intellectual historian, he displays an internal intensity much stronger than what we find with other historians. The intensity manifests itself in the way Mizoguchi conducts his interrogation, which always unfolds along the line of 'moments of tension' in history.[25] The primary motive of Mizoguchi's study of Chinese intellectual history is to search for principles that are understood by him in ways similar to that of Takeuchi Yoshimi. He is not concerned with the interpretation of anything outside the concrete historical process; the principles he discusses reside in unrepeatable historical events.

Mizoguchi began his academic career by critically examining postwar intellectual historians, such as Takeuchi Yoshimi and Maruyama Masao. However, he carries on the tradition of Japan's modern intellectual history in his pursuit of principles. His own studies only concern the question of Asia indirectly; Chinese intellectual history is always his primary preoccupation. But as he proceeds with his study, he manages to dissolve all established premises and ideas in his field, particularly the premise defining the so-called modern thinking produced by the 'occidentalists' in the East. This makes him very different from Miyazaki. Although Miyazaki also attends to the turbulences and transformations in Chinese history, his entrance into Chinese history is always guided by the periodization of European history. In addition, although Miyazaki does uncover important questions in his study of Chinese history, he is bound to neglect whatever cannot fit into that periodization. And the part Miyazaki neglects is precisely those problems Mizoguchi is concerned with and prepared to deal with. What Mizoguchi has displayed is a historical picture very different from that derived from modern European narrative. What Mizoguchi manages to portray in his remarkable analysis in historical case studies is beyond the reach of the presumed Western mode of thinking, which is the engraved texture of China's modernity. The tracing of the engraved texture in Mizoguchi's historical studies leads to the study of history over a long period, and this characteristic distinguishes his historical study from those of historians who only deal with periodized history. In this respect, the case studies of Mizoguchi are deeply imbued with a sense of history. On the basis of scholarship over long periods of time, Mizoguchi tries to forward a conception of the principles of China's modernity and, hence, to theorize it. Mizoguchi's approach to the history of China from within reveals to us the limitations of concepts from the modern West, making the series he edits something that must not be neglected.

Hamashita Takeshi's specialty is modern and contemporary Chinese history, particularly economic history. He pursues the inherent structure of the object he sets out to study, and tries to construct it as a rule-governed structure. His concern for structure prompts him to reconfigure the organic connections in the Asian region, which resulted in his famous study of the tribute system. Hamashita reveals through an analysis of the tribute system in East Asia, with China as the centre, a very important fact: for East Asia at the transformational period of modernization, there was no nation-state in the Western sense. The region's history formed in and through the trans-border grid of the tribute system, and its inherent dynamics are also subject to the excitation of the tribute system. Even in Japan's conception of severance from Asia and endeavours in modernizing itself, these events occurred in reaction to the historical constraint of tributary relationships; that is, as merely the means rather than as the ends, to free Japan from the position of a tributary state. Hamashita's regional study is a direct response to the question of Asia. He discusses not only the relations existing in the East Asian region, but also the limitation of the externally defined 'modernity' for East Asia in the comparison between Asia and Europe. But there is a fundamental contradiction in his discussion of the question of Asia. For Hamashita, East Asia is conflated with Asia. Furthermore, he is not interested in the question of the relation between an abstract idea of Asia and the understanding of East Asia in terms of the existing network of the tribute system. As a result, he is forced to apply the network of the tribute system to discussions of the regional structures of other Asian areas.

Both Mizoguchi and Hamashita are surprisingly in harmony in their interrogation of the limitations and even ineffectiveness of the employment of the modern concept of the European nation-state in the understanding of the history of East Asia. Notwithstanding that, Mizuguchi broaches the questions within the framework of the country 'China', while Hamashita considers matters within the framework of a region with China as the centre. It is precisely in this respect that the series engages with the problems provoked by the impact of the encounter between the internal dynamics of the non-European world and the European world from very different perspectives.

Regrettably, perhaps because of a paucity of likeminded historians, the series lacks an overall examination of the conceptions of Asia formed in Japan since the beginning of the modern period. Originally, volume five was to be dedicated to discussions of 'modern Japan's understanding of Asia' by the four editors, but in the end only one chapter, by Hiraishi Naoaki, was published. Hiraishi's chapter, 'Modern Japan on "Asianism"', is the only article in the volume that seeks to sort out Asianism, but it is unable to provide the essential points for guiding relevant discussions. Furthermore, the article is restricted by the demarcations made within Japan's intellectual history. Thus, it is unable to consider the rich contents covered in the series. In addition, the scholars who contributed to this volume also lack a sense of placing their studies in the historiography on intellectual history and the social sciences since the Meiji period. Furthermore, it is the series' obvious intention to break away from the practice of restricting contributions only to scholars from one nation, as represented in the habitual conceptions of 'Japanese on Asia'. Consequently, one-fifth of the writers are from other East Asian nations and the United States. Therefore, with regard to its relationship to the carrying forward of Japan's intellectual tradition and the tradition of scholarship, the position of the series is not clear. Interestingly, however, the scholars of intellectual history as represented by Mizoguchi and the scholars of the social sciences, as represented by Hamashita, display their connections to the traditions of scholarship and thinking of earlier generations in their fields of research. This makes it possible to explore the thread of Japan's Asianism through their studies. We can discover that, as people today have already moved beyond the simplistic binary frame of the opposition between East and West, and are confronted with the complicated problem of globalization, the Japanese today are still primarily engrossed in the question of Japan's self-identification. If, while reading this series, we remove the contexts of an entire century of thinking on Asianism in Japan from our consideration, we will be unable to find entry deep into this Asianism.

After skimming the history of thinking on Asianism, beginning with Fukuzawa Yukichi, we may now understand a hidden contradiction in the modern Japanese person's Asian complex. Since ancient times, Japan and China were in an unequal relationship. With that background, Japan, upon entering the modern era, attempted to take the place of China and become the main agent confronting the West through the 'Hua-Yi metamorphosis'. Thus, the contradiction is developed by at least three constituents: Japan, China and the West. Whether the West is an abstract fabrication is not a key question here. What is crucial is how Japan locates its position in the dynamics of such a configuration. One can say, unlike as for China, the problem of self-identification for modern Japan can only be solved through the medium of Asia. The complexity of the problem is because Japan's reflection on Asianism is all but unable to free itself from the determination of such a non-academic factor of actuality. Thus, it constitutes almost all along a theme for right-wing intellectuals, forcing Takeuchi to adopt the 'cat's paw' method as he tries to uncover reflections on Japanese intellectuals' responsibility to Asia and on the modernity of Asia. And it is precisely along such a thread that the various transpositions in Asianism can occur in history. How can the series *Asian Perspectives* differentiate itself from this historical thread that recalls such unhappy memories?

No matter how the editors of *Asian Perspectives* defined their tasks, it is not possible for them to initiate totally new discussions. In fact, the intellectual tradition that they cannot but confront poses many very different problems to them. How to settle the problem of the symbolization of Asia raised by the elliptic trajectory defined by Fukuzawa and Okakura Tenshin? How to tackle the visualization by Watsuji of replacing the conception of Asia versus Europe with the conception of three distinct modes of local conditions and customs? How to deal with the efforts of Miyazaki in the reconstruction of world history through the reconstruction of the relationship between Asia and Europe via the history of communications? How to take up the reflection of Umesawa with regard to the deconstruction of the conceptual framework of Asia and the substantialization of the Asian region through the breaking of its symbolization? How to confront the 'ideology of Japanism' from Watsuji to the Kyoto School? And how to treat the goal of Japan's cultural identification that Takeuchi seeks to achieve through the examination of Asianism?

It is true that *Asian Perspectives* expands the horizon of reflection beyond Japan to cover the entire Asia, but what the scholars face is first and foremost the problem of Japan. And today, after the relationship between Japan and Asia is being objectified and turned into an object of academic study, it is not for scholars of intellectual history such as Mizoguchi Yuzo, who are adept at dealing with the internal entanglements in history, to respond to such a situation. It is for fine scholars of economic history such as Hamashita Takeshi, Kawakatsu Heita and Miyajima Hiroshi to respond. This, to a certain extent, displaces the direction of the questioning from the elliptic trajectory delineated by Takeuchi with regard to the question of Asia, making it closer to the field of Umesawa and even Miyazaki. At the same time, it also weakens the ideological problem that Asianism faces historically, but it also, in turn, clouds its own positioning.

Hamashita (1986) participated in the conference 'Civilization Studies', which was hosted by Umesawa. His article 'Tribute and migrants' was included in the collection *Civilization Studies on Ruling Institutions*. Of course, this cannot be proof that Hamashita identifies with Umesawa, for he holds a basic understanding of Asia opposite to Umesawa. He not only acknowledges the necessity of the independent existence of the Asian region, he further stresses the relativization of the concept of nation-state through geopolitics. Compared to Umesawa's denial of the existence of Asia and his adoption of the state as the basic unit in the discussion of the question of civilization, Hamashita's approach is very different. Yet, on a deeper level, Hamashita can be considered as representative of those scholars in Japan who study an area in the broad sense of a sphere, as in Umesawa's ecological approach to history, providing it another chance to be reactivated.

Umesawa noticed very early the question of differentiating in the Asian region between large states of civilization and small states on the fringes of the large states.

Watsuji only touched upon this question lightly. As a result, he failed to draw the attention of scholars of intellectual history. Umesawa, too, is not able to develop the notion of the difference between a central civilized state and the small states around its fringes into 'relations studies'. Miyazaki tries to discuss the question of trade relations in the Asian region, but he cannot deal with the historical material for such a study and remains merely at the stage of envisioning. Moreover, Miyazaki cannot free himself from the discursive framework of a nation-state, and does not reach even the extent of Umesawa's argument for differentiating between large states and small states. However, for scholars such as Hamashita, in their studies, the question of the relations between a civilized large state and the small states bordering it constitutes the main line of research. Furthermore, unlike Umesawa and Miyazaki, they do not take the state as a unit of research, but go beyond the boundaries of states and turn their attention to the study of the relations between trans-border social structures and the world. They also, through their practice, provide the foundation for communication between economic history and intellectual history, thereby turning Umesawa's 'annihilation of history' into the task of rewriting history. Thus, we find in Hamashita's works, the attempt at reinterpretations of the Greater East Asia Coprosperity Sphere and 'Disassociating Asia and integrating into Europe'.[26] This is the problem that Umesawa tries to evade and that Miyazaki simplifies and rationalizes. Hamashita neglects the strong inertia of the logic of intellectual history and does not bring his own research and the fruits of the study of corresponding intellectual history together. For this reason, his interpretation of the Greater East Asia Coprosperity sphere and of 'Disassociating Asia' has not resulted in anything positive except in ideological misreading. But this is not a reason to reject Hamashita's scholarship; rather, it reveals the predicament of regional studies without intellectual history. More important than this predicament is the opening that Hamashita's works are able to create. The nation-state framework is radically questioned in his studies, and this leads to a reinterpretation of modern Asia (East Asia to be more exact), thereby creating a possibility for communications between intellectuals of East and West and also an effective frame of reference for scholars of intellectual history. In this connection, Hamashita, Kawakatsu and Miyajima complement one another. Kawakatsu's (1994) 'The establishment and development of the East Asian economic sphere' and Miyajima's (1994) 'The formation of small peasant society' discuss the question of the East Asian regional system from a perspective 'outside China'. Kawakatsu's paper particularly deserves our attention. This is not because he has briefly sorted out the economic history viewpoint of the historians of the Kyoto School represented by Kuwabara Jitsuzo, or because he has worked on and added to Umesawa's ecological approach to history. It is because he has attempted to put forward his own view of 'the system of countries that are closed to the outside' within this intellectual tradition, and has further developed some key questions in the discourses on Asia in Japan.

Kawakatsu's study of economic history and Miyazaki's of Asian history have very similar perspectives in that both focus on the trade relationships among the different countries of East Asia rather than on factors of ideology, and the mutual impacts and contacts that come with these relationships. They also focus on the interaction as a result of trade relationships between Asia and Europe in the midst of the modernization process. Interestingly, although Kawakatsu does not cite Miyazaki, he too pays attention to the relationship between the Industrial Revolution in England and the cotton from India, and arrives at a conclusion completely consistent with Miyazaki on the basis of a richer data analysis than what Miyazaki could have had:

> Before the Industrial Revolution, England needed a century for the reproduction of products produced in India. Only with the arrival of the Industrial Revolution could a reproduction even better than the original product be successfully produced. It is generally believed that England's Industrial Revolution was not caused by anything outside England. But rather, it was the strong external pressure exerted on England by the region with the original product that made the Industrial Revolution inevitable. The Industrial Revolution is by definition accompanied by a radical revolution of the economy and society. If generally it is said that the impact of the West is the international conditions of Japan's industrial revolution, the international conditions of the Industrial Revolution of England must then be the impact from the East, or rather Asia.
>
> (Kawakatsu 1996: 61)

However, Kawakatsu discusses the Asian background of England's Industrial Revolution in a completely different context from that of Miyazaki. And that context was Kawakatsu's effective questioning of the use of schemas from the historiography of Western Europe in the study of the economic history of Asia. The questioning of the Industrial Revolution in England as autogenous is directed against the postwar Japanese historian Otsuka Hisao, who argued that England's Industrial Revolution was autogenous. Kawakatsu not only calls into question such a conclusion, he also questions the comparative method Otsuka employs in his historical studies by taking the mode of the modernity of Western Europe as the criterion for the judging and the comparing of Japan's modernity. Undeniably, this is also the schema employed even by Japanese historians such as Miyazaki who were blessed with insight from their study of Chinese history and attempted to go beyond Eurocentrism. Therefore, in view of such a situation, Kawakatsu appeals for 'the search for a perspective for Asia'. On a deeper level, then, Kawakatsu's Asian studies have revealed the vulnerability of historians of China, such as Miyazaki, who initiated 'the communications history' approach, bringing the existing studies of relations between Asia and Western Europe to an even more complicated dimension. And it is in this dimension that Kawakatsu proposes his view of the system of 'closing Japan to the outside world'.

This is his response to the 'world system' of Wallerstein.[27] However, if we pursue Kawakatsu's thinking further, we are led necessarily to another problem. Running through the trajectories of thinking from the discourse of a world system of self-isolated states to the discourse on the perspective of wartime history is the subtext of a shifting of the focus of the narrative of the East Asian history from the mainland countries. This implies the dissipation of the question raised by Hamashita's conception of the tribute system with regard to the structural relations between large and small. Even more important, however, than the difference between Kawakatsu and Hamashita, is that Kawakatsu is now confronted with the same problem as that which confronted Umesawa. Their theories are unable to dissolve the ideological posing of the idea of 'Disassociating Asia'. Similar to Umesawa's eventual move towards surrendering himself to the ideological formulation of 'Disassociating Asia', Kawakatsu faces the same trap. When he puts forward the idea of the loose union of 'Nichidoneraria',[28] he neglects the very important problem that the turning of the focus of the Asian perspective from the mainland to the sea does not make the centuries of relations between Japan and the mainland disappear. If Kawakatsu were unable to face squarely the history of Japan's relation to East Asia, then it would be the fate of his theory of the marine states to be ideologized. Umesawa's theory was used for the support of the claim of Japan's superiority during his time, and it is possible now for Kawakatsu's theory to be appropriated for the justification of the liberal historical view, while he remains a marginal figure among the liberal group.

Umesawa had at least gestured toward entering into a dialogue with Takeuchi. But the desire for such an engagement is missing in Kawakatsu's study. I would suggest to set up, other than an engagement in dialogue, a frame of reference for studies like that of Kawakatsu, by putting their seemingly unrelated studies together and reconstructing their relations of correspondence, and thereby grasping more accurately the complexity of the discourse of Asia. That both Kawakatsu and Umesawa discussed the question of Japan as a marine state in the same conference suggests significantly that their neglect of tension in the intellectual history lead both scholars to follow the same direction in their scholarship.

Perhaps this is the positioning of Chinese intellectual history as represented by Mizoguchi in the series. The editors of the series do not seem to have reached consensus on the point where intellectual history and economic history cross. But Mizoguchi's (1994a) 'The founding of the theory of the principle and Qi in China', Kojima's (1993) 'The intellectual history proceeding from regional consideration', and Terada's (1994) 'The nature of 'agreement' in the legal order of the Ming and Qing Dynasties' form a distinct point of contrast. Through them it is revealed that, for a century, the thinking of the Japanese on 'Asianism' was at its weakest on the question of 'China in Asia'.

Beginning from the time of Fukuzawa and Okakura until the time of Umesawa and Miyazaki, China has always been an extremely difficult subject for discursive representation. Just as Hamashita, Kawakatsu and others have shown, the difficulty lies in the fact that the process of modernization and severing from Asia for Japan was forged out of its struggle for autonomy from the domination of China. As the characteristics of Japan as a modern nation-state took shape, and as Japan perpetrated aggression against China time and again since it entered the modern age, the self-identification of Japan throughout intensified around its relation of tension to China. Takeuchi comes closest to facing this vulnerability of Japan. He stresses in the intellectual history written throughout his life the significance for Japanese of understanding China. But even he could only transform China into a symbol for the modernity of East Asia for Japan, and he does not really manage to get near to the complexity of China itself. The academic intellectuals of the Kyoto School, led by Chinese historians, started establishing China studies at the beginning of this century, but due to the obvious limitation of their thinking their academic work is confined to an extremely narrow range. Moreover, their oversimplified reaction to questions of ideologies also hampers their ability to tackle intellectual questions. One can say in the intellectual tradition that *Asian Perspectives* confronts, there is always a thorny question deferred. How can Japanese intellectuals be made actually to face China, so that China not only becomes the object of academic discourse, but also the resource for modern thinking? The Japanese intellectuals who had undergone again the movement for 'Disassociating Asia and integrating into Europe' were still unable to make the question of China part of their cultural and intellectual resources when they tackled the series of questions of Asianism first raised by Fukuzawa.

Undeniably, the outstanding contributions to *Asian Perspectives* of the scholars of economic history make them the 'selected representative' of the series. However, their success is partly due to finding a point of contact with international concern, particularly the countering relation to Wallerstein's 'world system'. And their pioneering work in researching the economic history of East Asia also provides new perspectives and resources for discussions of the globalization of capitalism. Yet, they are, at the same time, very limited in their achievement of writing the history of China. For in their academic concern, the field of vision is determined by the discourse of globalization among Western scholars, and the complexity of the modernity of China is only significant to the extent that the responses to the Western scholars allow. As the nation-state framework is being taken apart by working in the field of regional studies, the necessity for the in-depth study of the particularities of the history of China is thus pushed out of sight. By contrast, pursuers of Chinese intellectual history, and even pursuers of Japanese intellectual history, are confronted with a more serious difficulty. As they attempt to probe deep into the inherent complexity of intellectual history, they cannot but discover that very limited methodological resources are available in academic and intellectual arenas. Furthermore, the area in which they can maintain a dialogue with the world is also far smaller than that enjoyed by scholars of economic history. To a certain extent, one can say that scholars of intellectual history are pursuing the production of discourses with regard to 'regional concerns', while scholars of economic history are globalized through their regional discourses. Yet it is precisely the scholars of intellectual history who have problematized 'China', a term ambiguously defined in the context of modern Japan and remains unclear even in the context of the contemporary world. As Mizoguchi points out in his Preface to the fourth volume in the series: 'The opposition between the Asian world and the European world is a product of the Asian process in becoming a modern state. This artificially produced divide in turn jeopardizes the natural course of the Asian world' (Mizoguchi 1994b: 7). It is obviously Mizoguchi's study in Chinese intellectual history that leads him to such an observation, which is clearly explained in his 'China as method'. Just as his paper in the series shows, he is actually probing not only for the so-called internal 'matrix' of Chinese history through his study of Chinese history, but also for a system of thinking radically different from the mode of thinking in Western historiography (particularly its modern form). This enables the probing of Mizoguchi and similar scholars such as Kojima and Terada to point towards a direction different from that of Miyazaki and other scholars of China studies of the Kyoto School. This suggests that, in the field of Chinese intellectual history, a similar challenge to the study of economic history was being raised. But as the object of its study, China is not admitted into prevailing discourses of Japan's intellectual circles, and the challenge stresses that one must try to uncover the principles from within China itself. China studies becomes inevitably a marginal concern in the discourse of Asia.

It is a pity that *Asian Perspectives* cannot go further in turning 'Asia' into a symbol for cooperation between scholars of intellectual history and economic history, as well as regional studies. The main reason for such a failure is that the series is ineluctably confronted with the history of Japan's Asianism, which has already lasted for almost a century and the history of the duet in 'Disassociating Asia' and 'Reviving Asia'. Yet it is unable to bring itself to look squarely at the question. In other words, in this series we cannot find a point where the two thinkings represented by Takeuchi and Umesawa of the earlier generation come into contact with one another. The study of regional history, wittingly and unwittingly, weakens the historical context of the question of Asia in Japan. As a consequence, it is forced to face questioning again as to whether the schema of the centre and periphery would not lead to another attempt to justify the idea of the Greater East Asia Coprosperity Sphere. Or, whether it would lead to an oversimplified notion of 'breaking ties with Europe and integrating with Asia' in contrast to 'Disassociating Asia and integrating with Europe'.

If we briefly examine the question of Asia running in Japan for nearly a century, a very interesting phenomenon can be observed. The conception of Asia in Fukuzawa and Okakura contained undeveloped possibilities for a different turn, but the situation of the war destroyed all possibilities of productive re-appropriation of their thinking. With Watsuji's theory of local conditions and customs, the reflection on Asia begins to suggest ways in which genuine development in thinking can be realized: clear the question of Asia of its idealistic character and turn it into the learning of the actualities. From Watsuji's local conditions, through Umesawa's ecological approach to history, to Hamashita's regional studies and Kawakatsu's system of closed countries, the disciplines involved are very different, and the discourses on Asia coming from them are also very different. Yet the underlying thread of 'departing from the idealistic treatment of the question of Asia' runs consistently through them. The two threads of thinking on Asianism for almost a century in modern Japan came into contact in the 1960s. And today in the series, they are brought together for the second time, yet no matter whether it is the first or the second time, no real convergence of the two threads can be observed. It is this keeping of distance from the idealism of the Asian question that makes the discussion of the question of Asia today evade, to some extent, the history of Asianism and evade the inherent tension of the question of Asia faced by earlier generations. This, in turn, deprives it of the capacity for responding forcefully to the various questions emerging from the background of the reflection on Asia by intellectuals in today's Japan.

Hamashita discusses three questions in the prefaces to the first three volumes of *Asian Perspectives*. One question regards the multifaceted nature of the question of Asia. Bringing together scholars from different disciplines in different sketches of the spatial Asia, Hamashita treats concepts through a wide range of fields. He tries to question the limitation of employing concepts according to the prevailing methodologies of the social sciences, which synthesize and generalize concepts in order to grasp the ever splitting and mutating of the social space and the semantic space. He shows the question of Asia to be comprised of multifarious angles and to be approached by many available cognitive methods. Second, on the basis of having shown the multifaceted nature of the question of Asia, he seeks to sketch the 'regional system' of the Asian region as an integral whole. Hamashita's representative study of the tribute system and similar studies in economic history and international relations pursue just this objective. In these studies, Asia is depicted as an organic whole with inherent machineries. In this whole, Chinese civilization is the centre of a tributary network, with Southeast Asia,

East Asia, South Asia and West Asia maintaining relations to it either in the form of paying tribute or in the form of trading. The tribute system constitutes an ordered region with an inherent logic completely different from modern Europe. That is, in contrast to the 'state' as a unit, there is the regional mechanism of 'the centre to its periphery' and the corresponding relationships of paying tributes and conferring titles. And third is a reflection on Asia from the perspective of the periphery. As the periphery is fluid and complex, it effectively reveals the actual conditions of communications and negotiations among the internal differentiating factors of the Asian region. The periphery alters the prevailing situation in the study of history that takes as its object of study the centre of things under consideration. It breaks the usual approach of relating one centre to another centre in studying, and replaces it with the centre versus periphery perspective that enables the internally complex relations to be revealed. This not only points out for us the 'centre to centre' blind spot in the East versus West shaping of questions and reveals the peculiarity of the internal fluidity of the Asian region, it is also greatly illuminating in establishing new perspectives in research.

It is obvious that the three questions raised by Hamashita cannot be underestimated in their inspiring power to affect the study of intellectual history and history. Mizoguchi has also drawn on this thinking of Hamashita, showing that it is possible for intellectual history and regional history to come together in research. Hamashita's approach to Asia certainly requires the support of a great amount of concrete research, and the papers collected in the series serve witness to just this function. However most of these papers are in the field of social sciences, such as economic history and intellectual relations history, and papers in the field of intellectual history that echo Hamashita are few. Hence, the aspiration to outline the problem of modernity in Asia with regional history becomes easily questioned. Hamashita is, after all, only an expert in the study of the relations of tribute and trade in East Asia and Southeast Asia. Can the mode of study derived from examining this region be extended in a simple and direct fashion to cover the whole of the Asian region? As Miyazaki has considered working out the organic connections of 'the communications history' between Asia and Europe, how could the tribute system of Asia proposed by Hamashita deal with such a legacy?

In his article 'Tribute and treaties', Hamashita (1997) discusses the relationship between tribute and treaties. But this is only a question of the internal structure of modern East Asia, and does not involve trading as conducted in Europe. It is true that the internal fluidity of East Asia is being established, but in such a model, the fluid relationships and the tension of opposition between East Asia and Western Europe, between Asia and Europe, can hardly be revealed. I am certainly not making excessive demands of Hamashita's study of economic history, asking him to bring everything together and offer a comprehensive picture. But is it possible that the perspective geared to the study of economic matters in regional studies may have removed the question of conflictual relations, such as intellectual history seeks to confront? Has this then resulted in the erasure of the tension of conflicts in political thought and cultures in history, just as Miyazaki did? Might this lead further to justifying all forms of violence in history? If the vision of Hamashita's writing can consider more fully the fruits of intellectual history, and if scholars of intellectual history can work more closely with Hamashita, then it may be possible for the task of reconstructing Miyazaki's 'history of communications' to be taken further. If the failure between Takeuchi and Umesawa to cooperate could turn into a new starting point, then upon what kinds of questions would *Asian Perspectives* reflect?

Kishimoto Mio wrote an excellent review of *Asian Perspectives*. She notices this internal problem of the series, but she represents it from a totally different angle:

> Within the same 'Asian Perspectives' there exists two orientations with regard to two different attitudes towards 'the inherent culture of a region' which still have not converged with one another. One is concerned with the lasting, inherent cultural forms, and tries to think within that culture the orientation of one's questioning. The other questions the concept of inherent culture itself, and is concerned with the tendencies of the encounters between trends that are moving and changing all the time. For researchers of Asia, no matter who the person is, he or she cannot but face this double character contained in the concept of a region, and the attraction and danger of each side of this dual nature.
>
> (Kishimoto 1995: 40)

Let us consider Kishimoto's question from a different angle. The difference that refuses to be resolved does not lie in whether the culture of a region is inherent or mobile, but rather in its being a succession of the tradition in which the question of Asianism has been discussed for almost 100 years. In concrete terms, there are two traditions within the discussion of Asianism. One is represented by scholars of intellectual history, with the question of Asia taken to be concerning Asia as an idea of opposition to Western Europe. This tradition appears in different forms in different periods, nonetheless it is always there with regard to the 'idealistic nature' of this tradition. ('Idea' here does not denote a concept, but the mental activity in contrast to the economic and social activities.) The study of intellectual history today must at least also take as one's object of study the ideal content of the question of Asia, and more or less face the inherent tension in history, even if one does not, as Takeuchi did, 'put oneself into' the question under consideration. The tradition was initiated by Watsuji and carried forward by scholars of social sciences. This tradition to a large extent excludes the influence of the humanistic spirit and stresses that the question of Asia should only be concerned with the actual. And the ecological approach to history represented by Umesawa typically reflects the 'de-idealizing ' and the 'de-ideologizing' nature of the approach to the question of Asia by this tradition. Even Miyazaki, being the historian most deeply imbued with the humanistic spirit, has to an extremely large extent eliminated the inherent tension in history in accordance with the 'scientificity' peculiar to the Kyoto School.

Hamashita and others carry on this de-idealizing tradition from the perspective of economic history. His unsuccessful exposition of the Greater East Asia Coprosperity Sphere and 'Disassociating Asia' reflects his efforts in the pursuit of 'de-idealization'. It may be said that intellectual history deals with subjective ideas and activities of the mind; it is appropriate for revealing the intensity of history. On the other hand, economic history and regional studies deal with abstract laws, and often dissolve the tension of the intricacy of the historical moments, excluding it from consideration. *Asian Perspectives* has carried in it the basic strands of the tradition of Asianism, lasting for almost a century. But the awareness for sorting out the strands is not there. Yet, this century is, more than any other period in history, equipped to bring the two traditions of thinking on Asianism together, which, however, it fails to achieve. It is precisely with respect to that, that we cannot but say that a necessary step is missing from *Asian Perspectives*. Before 'setting off from Asia', 'reflection on Asia' must be done. In other words, the series, the most representative collection on the question of Asia in the 1990s in Japan, fails to take up 'Asia' and fully interrogate and sort out this name with regard to its complicated history and tendencies that this name connotes at a given time. The problem is this: as early as Fukuzawa's time, the questioning had already begun and reached its high point at the time of Takeuchi and Umesawa, but it has not been completed. While the questioning continues to take place alongside debates with regard to breaking away from Asia on the one hand, and embracing Asia again on the other, the questioning is now turning into a latent thread, framing the thinking of today. It would be wrong to avoid facing this and take regional studies in an oversimplified manner as a completely new study.

In order to locate its position, Asia must be considered not only in contrast to Umesawa's ecological approach to history and civilization and the studies of economic history of the Kyoto School. It must also be considered against another thread of thinking on Asia – Asianism in which Asia is idealized. It is in this connection that the criticism of Ueda Makoto quoted by Kishimoto seems to be too rash. Like 'Disassociating Asia and integrating into Europe', the gesture of 'breaking away from Europe to embrace Asia' expressed in the expression 'Asia as the starting point of thinking' has become obsolete. For scholars of Japan today, it is in fact necessary to sort out both 'breaking away from Europe to embrace Asia' and 'Disassociating Asia and integrating into Europe' with regard to theoretical as well as actual concerns. Furthermore, in a sense, if thinking on the margin is to possess originality, it is necessary for it to probe for the points where one is tied to tradition.

In the epilogue to *Asian Perspectives*, a crucial question is touched upon:

> It can be said that this series is an attempt to look for the paradigms of Asian history for the discussion of the changes occurring in modern Asia. To consider this from a different angle, it can also be said that the series can locate itself in a different order of discussion, that is, new discourses of Japan and Japanese are explored in and through the changes that the modern world has undergone. In other words, this is a link in the exploration for the characteristics of Japan. The characteristics being explored should not be understood as a cultural identification pursued since the Meiji period that took the West as its model. It should neither be understood as the emphasis on Japan in itself. It means that the series lays out what is involved in the commitment to think through Japan's cultural identification in Asia through the contextualization of Japan in Asia. This is a task that requires attention in the pursuit of continuity over the long period of history. We have recognized that the starting point of our discussions are peculiarities in the nature of being a region, a region in the unfolding of processes of assimilation and dissimilation that take place within and between the homogeneity and the heterogeneity that co-determine a region. In this process, it is necessary, on the one hand, to set out on the study of regional history in order to restore an idealized 'west' to the West as a region for Japan's 'return to Asia.' That return would

require the efforts of several generations if it is to be completed. It is also necessary to take the Asian region, which has always been particularized and regionalized, as partaking of an idea in our discussions on the other hand.

(Asian Perspectives, Vol. 7 1993: 289–90)

As the quote from Edward Said at the beginning of this paper suggests, Asia in fact exists throughout in the form of an idea for Western intellectuals, even though it is an idea serving the needs of Eurocentrism. Similarly, for intellectuals of the East, the West also becomes like a symbol, an idealized 'principle'. When *Asian Perspectives* directly lays out its intention to achieve a deconstruction of the idea of the West and to lift Asia as a principle into the context of world history, it does not show a simple desire for 'breaking away from Europe to embrace Asia'. On the contrary, what it has in fact shown is the prospect of a possibility that can only be realized through cooperation between intellectuals of the East and intellectuals of the West. It should be said that the ideality of Asia as a region is the most valid precondition for the establishment of Asia as a category. In the narratives of the Asian intellectuals, the West – an idealistic category with almost no significance to intellectuals of the West – is there already. Historically speaking, this idealistic category functions as the medium that pushes Asians into forming self-recognition.

However, just as an idealistic West cannot become a universal principle, neither can an idealistic 'Asia' historically constituted by the Japanese gain admission to the world of principle. *Asian Perspectives* has discussed in a reserved manner the possibility of taking the idea of Asia as a world history principle with universal validity, but the series does not make a distinction between such an idea and the idea of Asia formulated by people from Fukuzawa to Takeuchi. In fact, the 'idea' pursued in the series goes far beyond the level of 'mood' or 'symbol' reached by Fukuzawa and Takeuchi, and possesses a depth that the Kyoto School could not have hoped to achieve. The pursuit in the series of an idea of Asia is predicated upon two different orientations, that of the study of regional history and that of intellectual history, in their attempts to arrive at the formulation of a principle. Undeniably, in the narration of globalization carried out from the perspectives of the West today, the idealistic nature narrating Asia is being concealed, and its position in world history is not clear. Furthermore, it is far from having enough weight to become pressing for the self-recognition by the intellectuals of Europe and America. On the contrary, whether it is in the East or in the West, Asia, the idea, is still basically only a cause for confirming or criticizing the West as universal principle. At the same time, the Orientalism criticized by Said has produced a different idea of Asia, which has subtly influenced Asian intellectuals. This makes us easily feel contented with Takeuchi's reflection on Asia. Discussions on Asia are often neglected because the limitations of Western ideas are not experienced by us with such an urgency, or we are often complacent about the employment of the simple binary opposition between East and West to explain the complexity of history. In doing this, we cannot, in fact, notice the regional historical tension inherent in Asia contained in the idea of Asia. If the above understanding quoted from the Afterword of *Asian Perspectives* could be realized, if the intellectuals of Asia could make the idealized West regionalized, and the regionalized Asia idealized, what kind of changes could come about for scholarship in the world?

However, the understanding from the series has not really been put into practice. The main reason for this could be that the regional studies of scholars of economic history and the study of ideas by scholars of intellectual history have not converged. Although both have felt strongly the limitations of the ideas of the West, it takes trans-disciplinary cooperation to establish the ideas of Asia. Neither economic history nor intellectual history alone can accomplish such a task. Moreover, the context of Japan's Asianism contains such rich resources and profound lessons that the failure to sort them out creates the largest obstacle to the formation of the ideas of Asia in contradistinction to that of Orientalism.

What does Asia imply? As a member of Asia, it is not merely due to the need to respond to the voices of the post-colonial intellectuals in the West that we reflect on Asia. On the contrary, whether Asia should be taken as a perspective of instrumental value, and on which level the question of Asia should be broached, is of concern to our own history. On the basis of this, we would ask: is Asia merely a question for the Japanese or other neighbouring East Asian countries? To the Chinese who, for a century, have not established any relation of partnership with the Japanese, what does Asia mean?

Notes

1 It is necessary to distinguish between 'Occidentalism' as used here and 'modernism' as used in Japanese, for these two positions have different effects in the history of East Asia. In the modern history of Japan, there is a long succession of 'Occidentalism', including almost all modern thinkers beginning with Fukuzawa. With regard to the Showa period, Maruyama Masao and Takeuchi suggested in their different ways the presence of Occidentalism and out of these suggestions formulated their own questions. Their formulations of questions are different from that of the 'modernists', who lack a sense of crisis.

2 We can see in this list, Japanese activists of very different inclinations. There are aspirants like Miyazaki Toten with a certain flavour of 'internationalism' who do not consider the interests of Japan to be the basis. There are also activists with obvious expansionist ambitions, such as Uchida Ryohei

3 In *Modernity in China and Japan*, Hashikawa Bunzo (1974) wrote an article, 'Fukuzawa and Okakura', saying that 'On Disassociating Asia' shows that there are real reasons for Fukuzawa's strong posture. The immediate cause in the series of those scholars for taking such a hard-line posture is to do with the failure of the Kapsin Coup in Korea, in which Fukuzawa almost certainly participated in its plotting, and the modernization he expected of Korea seemed to recede almost out of sight. Furthermore, it was also due to the intervention of the Qing government that the coup collapsed. This made Fukuzawa turn his aggravated vengeance and reproach towards the Qing court. In 'On Disassociating Asia', extremely disdainful words were used against the China of the Qing Dynasty and Korea, stressing that their barbarism made it impossible for them to become modernized and civilized. Hiraishi Naoaki (1994) quoted in his *Asianism in Modern Japan* the studies of people like Sakano Junji as showing that when Fukuzawa wrote the article above, Ito Hirobumi was negotiating in Tianjin with Li Hongzhang for the resolution of the Kapsin Coup. Thus, the possibility that Fukuzawa wrote this article in order to make his position clear to Ito cannot be ruled out. Okamoto Koji (1998) in an article 'Japan and Asia, or Japan in Asia?' quoted the research of Tomita Masahumi and others as showing that 'On Disassociating Asia' did not catch people's attention before the war, and only came under consideration after the war. This has to do with the effects of the Tokyo trial, which drove intellectuals to probe the thinkers of the Meiji period for the roots of Japan's aggression against Asia.

4 In 1866, Satsuma-han and Choshu-han, the two staunchest proponents of 'Revere the Emperor, expel the barbarians', allied to topple the Tokugawa Shogunate. England immediately displayed a stance closely related to that of overthrowing the Shogunate so as to establish a coalition

government by the daimyo under direct imperial rule with the emperor as the head of the national government vested with supreme authority. This won the favourable impression of daimyo and their consent to buy arms from England. In the meantime, the Shogunate turned to France for support to maintain its position. Thus, the basic contradiction playing out in Edo became hinged upon the movement for the toppling of the Shogunate and carrying out reform, leading to the agitation for the restoration of Imperial Rule and 'Radical Innovation' in 1867. This paved the way for the beginning of the transformation of Japan into a modern state. After the Meiji Restoration, Japan took to the path of Meiji Enlightenment.

5 Though there have not been any instances observed yet of the term 'Zhong Hua' to refer to Western civilization, some scholars have pointed to the actual existence of such a way of thinking. For example, Watanabe Hiroshi pointed out in 'Progress' and 'Zhong Hua' that since the beginning of the advocacy of the 'Meiji Enlightenment' during the last phase of the Edo period, Meiji Enlightenment was understood by the Japanese as Zhong Hua-ization, while real China was treated in low esteem. By the Meiji period, the Japanese took the civilization of the West as the true 'Zhong Hua' and refused to refer again to China as 'Zhong Hua', except as China. Yet the fundamental values of Confucian thinking in China were taken to be the essence of the Western civilization. This enabled them to feel an affinity with Western civilization, beyond the simple utilitarian attitude of the Japanese spirit, Western knowledge. According to Watanabe, during the Meiji period, Japanese Confucians played a key role in the advancement of Meiji Enlightenment. In their understanding, civilization was the embodiment of Confucian values, and the modern West was the one to realize this.

6 Takeuchi first presented this view in 'Prospects on Asianism'. In this article, Fukuzawa was portrayed in contrast to Okakura. Takeuchi thought that there might be many and various intellectuals and activists of the Meiji period who were concerned with the question of Asia, but with regard to civilization, only Fukuzawa and Okakura could be regarded as representing the two opposing positions determining people's horizon of civilization. Later, in 'Fukuzawa and Okakura', Hashikawa Bunzo (1974) explicitly formulated such a pattern of contrasting relations in the intellectual history of Japan as 'a centrifugal longing for the civilization of Western Europe on the one hand, and a centripetal "attachment" to Asia (original "nostalgia")'. Hashikawa said further, 'In a certain sense, it can be said that Japan's modern history is an elliptical movement spinning around these two foci, which can be looked upon as two statements of declaration or prophecy.'

7 In discussing the question of Asia, both Fukuzawa and Okakura knowingly stressed the sense of Asia and Europe as a whole. This is not due to the crudeness of their thinking, but rather the demand of the sense of crisis of their times. It is true that Fukuzawa clearly has a sense of the nation or state as the basic unit while Okakura clearly distinguishes between different cultures and even regional differences within the same culture, but these are not the gist of their discourses.

8 *The Ethics of the Study of the Human Sphere* is an important work in this respect. This is a philosophical work that inquires into ethics, the human sphere, the world and Being. Through the study of these four concepts Watsuji Tetsuro develops his discussion of the relation between subject and object in modern Western philosophy. Watsuji had also taken from hermeneutics a basic position adopted for his later work, *Local Conditions and Customs*. His position is that the fundamental perspectives of the relations of the human sphere include the possibility of the objectification of the self, taking 'showing' (that is, beings) as the medium for the search for the fundamental 'phenomenon' (that is, Being). Later, he elaborated the basic thinking in this work in three volumes, called *Ethics* (Watsuji 1937) and expounded the basic position of his studies of the human sphere.

9 In *The Ethics of the Studies of the Human Sphere*, Watsuji distinguishes between 'human' and 'human sphere' in Japanese, pointing out that the significance of the latter lies in its insistence on defining the meaning of human in terms of the relations among humans. That is, humans do not exist in isolation from one another. In his treatment of ethics, 'human sphere' is conceptualized in contrast to the values of Western individualism, hence the superiority of the collective character of the human sphere over the individual is stressed. As he engaged himself with the reality of Japanese society during his time with such a perspective, he was led to the formulation of his stance of 'Japanism'. One can say that Watsuji is the creator of the doctrine

on the Japanese that takes the Japanese nation as a unified whole, strengthening the sense of integratedness of the modern nation-state. After the Second World War, Watsuji in close relation to this way of thinking pushed hard for the justification of the imperial institution. Therefore, even during Watsuji's time, there were criticisms directed against his 'Japanism' (e.g. Tosaka Jun). To this day, there still are critical intellectuals questioning the role Watsuji's *Ethics* played in the production of the doctrine of the specialness of Japan, such as Sakai Naoki.

10 With regard to Watsuji's concepts of the 'human sphere' and 'human relationships', Sakai Naoki (1997a) offered his criticism both theoretically and on the level of their functions in reality. The crux of the doctrine is its substitution of the concept of the human sphere as an integral whole for the actual existence of the individual, thereby dissolving the existing contradiction between an individual and a group, enabling the so-called commonality of the collectivity-nation to be justified in the absence of contradictions.

11 Limitations of space make it necessary to save the discussion of this problem for another occasion. Watsuji was a complicated philosopher. The limitations we find in him reflect the limitations of Japan at his time. His deliberate dissolution of subjectivity and construction of cultural nationalism reflect the dilemma confronting Japanese intellectuals both before and after the Second World War. In fact, there is no genuine contradiction between Watsuji Tetsuro's attitude of placing himself above the matters of the world and his later involvement in politics. This is exactly the field of tension underlying Japanese intellectual history during the Showa period. But it is also obvious that the so-called 'objectivity' stressed by Watsuji is actually non-existent. When Watsuji reduced the content of 'human sphere' to simply an integral entity, what could the assertion of his absence from it mean? I think, besides the theoretical contradiction (that is, the effective cancellation of the spatial occurrence of actual experience stressed by Watsuji), there is also a hidden question that should be addressed. This is the paradoxical relation between the characteristic of the position of the modern academism of Japan in direct connection to the academic posture of the Kyoto School on the one hand and the historical social reality on the other. The crucial question is how later generations are to deal critically with such a complicated intellectual legacy. I am in basic agreement with Sakai Naoki's criticism of Watsuji's *Ethics* in his *Problematic in the So-called Japanese Thoughts*, which points sharply to the negative role *Ethics* has played in the construction of a united Japanese imagination, and offers an extremely remarkable exposition of the process of the construction of such an imagination. But I think Sakai's criticism must be supplemented by a more complicated historical analysis. If Sakai is read together with studies done in Japan by Japanese, like Yuasa Yasuo's (1995) *Watsuji Tetsuro*, it will be very helpful to the understanding of the complexity of Watsuji as well as the complexity of the history of the Showa period. In Yuasa's discussion, the limitation of Watsuji is understood as the fate of modern Japanese philosophy, thereby bringing forth the question of the epochal character implicit in Watsuji's thinking.

12 The trajectory of Takeuchi's thinking is itself an extremely complicated subject, too difficult to be accounted for in a simple manner. Interested readers can consult my paper 'The Positioning of Literature – Takeuchi Yoshimi's Paradox' (Sun 1998).

13 *An Ecological Historiography of Civilization* has this to say of the characteristics of the two regions: the first region does not have revolution while the second region gained its independence through revolutions. The first region possesses an advanced capitalistic economy in the modern period while the second region establishes authoritarian systems. The first region is situated around the fringes of ancient civilizations while the second region is the birthplace of ancient civilizations. The first region depends upon spontaneous inherent forces in effecting historical changes while the second region depends upon external forces for historical changes (Umesawa 1967: 67–103).

14 As the sense of national superiority of Fukuzawa and Okakura was a response to their sense of national crisis, rather than based on value judgements, it could still serve as healthy nourishment for thought. Many of the Asianists contemporary with them also had a sense of superiority and, to different extents, also shared such a characteristic. Later, by the Taisho period, in the hands of Tsuda Sokichi and many Japanese orientalists, the sense of Japan's superiority underlying their thinking had turned into a motive force for the pursuit of knowledge. In the meantime, a group of Japanese intellectuals, echoing the official ideology, began to ideologize the sense of national

superiority of Japan itself. Consequently, the nationalist disposition in thinking during the Meiji period lost its intellectual potential. It must be pointed out that such a thoughtless sense of national superiority is still being stirred up like dregs from time to time and continually arousing substandard controversies. The debate around the liberalistic historical view at the end of 1996 is a case in point. The debate was hinged upon Japan's national confidence. The level from which the debates started and the level they managed to reach were low. Yet the re-emergence of this fundamental proposition in the intellectual history of Japan should not be shrugged off.

15 Takeuchi avoided raising directly the question of whether Japan is an Asian country or not, for he believed that Japan should be responsible for the development of Asia. And yet, he could not agree with the elitism Japan had assumed since the beginning of modern Japan. Therefore, he criticized Japan's 'non-Asianism' in an implicit manner in many articles. Among these, 'The modern age of China and the modern age of Japan' is representative. This piece also is his representative work in directly advocating multiculturalism. In it, he thoroughly deconstructs the definition of modernity according to the model of Western Europe, and redefines its meaning with his Asian principle, while at the same time directing his sharp criticism against Japan's elitist culture.

16 In the preface to *The Perspective of Asian Study*, Takeuchi (1975) stresses: 'If Asian studies is to be established, it can only be as a reconstruction of the conception of civilization. That is, as learning, it is only possible as a process of the self-transformation of the gesture of an incessant probing, as a scholarship that seeks to transform itself from within, taking modern Europe as its blueprint. For, according to my assumption, Asia is the concept of opposition to modern Europe, that is, Asia can only come to be through the heralding of the future of civilization.'

17 See Asahi Shimbun, 9 August 1999, p. 13, for the coverage of the International Conference on Marine Science and Umesawa's 'commemoration speech'. He said, 'Japan is after all a maritime state, and has never been rewarded for reaching out to mankind', and suggested that Japan 'should look for its fortune southward, towards the ocean, and link with the many islands of the Pacific Ocean'.

18 Sakai (1997) points out that Watsuji's *Local Conditions and Customs* is a duplicate of the cultural essentialism of the West and that he did not hide this. What is interesting is that when Watsuji's work was translated into English, the part where he talked about the relation of his studies of cultural types to studies before him was deleted. In this deleted part, Watsuji included himself in the genealogy of Western studies of local conditions. Obviously, the English translation wanted to suppress this for Watsuji's idea of local conditions would only arouse the interest of the West as a non-Western work. Yet, Watsuji's idea of local conditions does share similar characteristics of his Western counterparts. When he stresses the relations between local conditions and culture, he also stresses the unchanging constant of each culture, thus turning the discussion into an exposition according to the principle of particularity. Sakai points out, 'The reduction of the uniqueness of cultural difference to the difference of particulars is to be framed by the movement of universalism (generality) of imperialism/colonialism.' That is to say, Watsuji is in fact in complicity with the narratives of the universalism of imperialism and colonialism when he stresses the particularity of each type of local conditions.

19 According to the bibliography of Suzuki's works in *Modernity in World History*, Suzuki and Takeyama Michio attended together 22 small symposia. Takeyama is one of the few regular participants at symposia in which Suzuki also took part. Takeyama is not a historian of the West. Therefore, he cannot really be regarded as a partner to Suzuki. Thus, the frequent working together of the two suggests that their basic positions were in agreement.

20 Miyazaki in the Introduction of his *Study of the History of Asia*, Vol. I, explained that he did not publish papers during the war as an act of defiance against the government and the military: 'Since the war began, I thought Japan would be in a very difficult situation if it is defeated, thus I was willing to do anything to boost the combative power of Japan. However, my papers were not written for this purpose. I knew very well that publishing these papers would not in any way help boost the fighting spirit and the combative power.' (Miyazaki 1975:2–3).

21 Territorial boundary has scarcely any meaning in Miyazaki's historical studies. He might be limited by the horizon of the knowledge system that formed him and could not directly conduct cross-cultural historical studies. But even in his studies of Chinese history, his concern was

always with the conflicts among ethnic groups and the consequence of those conflicts. This characteristic was reflected not only in his study of the modern history of China. In his study of the history of Asia, the same perspective was also consistently present. In *An Outline of the History of Asia*, the first chapter is entitled 'The establishment of the various cultures of Asia and their development', the second 'The negotiations among the various Asian peoples', and the third 'Communications between the various Asian cultures and their development'. These titles show clearly the characteristics of his thinking. Although the data used in these chapters are too crude, they show the characteristic of his cross-cultural study. He has, for example, brought together in his discussion the peculiarities of local conditions and the mythic legends of the founding of states, summing up the mythic legends into variations spun from three main types of state-founding legends from the Chinese civilization, the Indian civilization and the Persian civilization, respectively. He has also conducted studies on the role played by nomadic peoples in the transmission of culture, and pointed out that the nomadic peoples have acted as the media for communications between different cultures, while they themselves are characterized by the relatively weak accumulation of culture. What is particularly remarkable is that Miyazaki knowingly positions various civilizations from the point of view of world history. Particularly with regard to the Islamic civilization, which has significantly influenced the civilization of Europe, he highly appraises it for its significance to world history, thinking that the civilization of the Arabic Empire has inherited the legacies of the ancient civilizations of Persia, Mesopotamia, Egypt, India and Greece, paving the ground for the development of modern world history.

22   Here, Miyazaki (1940) revises the traditional distinction between the East and the West into the differentiation among 'three worlds': West Asia, East Asia and Europe. He proposes the mode of historical differentiation of 'three worlds and three periods'. He then concludes that, in these three worlds, ancient history was characterized by unity from above in the empire and the medieval period was characterized by the tendency of decentralization with the devolution of powers to local or regional administration, whereas the Renaissance characterized the modern period. In West Asia, the occurrence of the 'Renaissance' after the religious reformation heralded the arrival of the modern age; the 'Renaissance' here consists of the revival of the Persian civilization of the Abbassid, as well as the Greek civilization. As for East Asia, the modern period began with the revival of Confucianism during the Northern Song Dynasty in China, about two centuries later than East Asia's Renaissance. Miyazaki focuses his discussion on the influence of 'Renaissance' on one another among the three worlds.

He holds that the significant influence of the 'Renaissance' that began in West Asia or East Asia was in painting, and the Song painting that developed later in turn influenced the Islamic world, and proceeded further to provide inspiration for the Italian Renaissance. He devotes much space to demonstrating the role painting played in the linking of the three worlds in the development of the modern spirit. He even appends to his paper as many as nine photos of paintings. However, one cannot but admit that the relation between the relevance of painting to the processes of Renaissance in the three worlds on the one hand, and the positioning of painting in their respective traditions on the other hand, are far more complicated than the wishful depiction Miyazaki offers. Furthermore, the other arguments with regard to transformation in philosophy, science, literary style and other areas fail to go further than superficial description. However, in Miyazaki's discussion of the Renaissance in the three worlds, there is a basic line of thinking that deserves our attention: spatially, he stresses the horizontal relations of the Renaissance, while temporally he denies the possibility of contemporaneity for the three worlds. That is, Miyazaki has noticed the existence of the inherent thread of cultural development in each region, even though he is forced to entrap himself within the evolutionary discourse of linear historical progress by his emphasis on consistency in the mode of history of Asia and Europe.

23   The original Japanese means 'Asia as the starting point of reflection'. The intention is to break through the confinement to Asia in established thinking. Here it is rendered as 'Asian Perspectives', for a literal translation would violate the habit of titling in Chinese.

24   In 1989, Tokyo University Press published Mizoguchi Yuzo's (1989) *China as Method*. By way of discussing the studies of history, the book raises straightforwardly the challenging question of how Asia and modern China in Asia become world principles, providing a new way of

thinking with regard to the question of relativizing modern values of the West. In fact, this book is an elaboration of *The Turning and Development of Chinese Pre-modern Thinking* (Mizoguchi 1980). As the former is written in an easier manner than the expert treatment in the latter, and the questions are raised more directly, it has aroused quite a stir in Japanese academia. This interest prompted the Tokyo University Press to entertain the idea of probing further into the questions raised by the book. Thus, the preparation for *Asian Perspectives* was launched.

25 In 'The Modern Age of China and the Modern Age of Japan', Takeuchi Yoshimi offers an extremely interesting definition of history. 'Rather than regarding it as a point in history, a limiting condition with no possibility of extension, the moment is the site for the production of history (not a pointless point).' (Takeuchi 1993: 21) Needless to say, the above passage is amazingly consistent with Walter Benjamin's 'Theses on the Philosophy of History'. More importantly, the way of grasping history revealed by Takeuchi in fact brings out in relief the 'a-historicality' of today's historians in their inability to grasp the moment. Mizoguchi has most brilliantly shown his ability to take up history in just this way in his representative work *The Transformation and Development of Chinese Pre-modern Thinking*. In the explanation Mizoguchi offers of Li Zhuo Wu's naming of 'the natural state of being human beyond the reach of any established given premises', he developed his grasp of the transformational period between the disintegrating phase of the Ming Dynasty and the beginning of the formation of the Qing Dynasty. This was not the consequence of conceptual deduction and given premises, but rather was made possible by his remarkably perceptive sensitivity to the inherent tensions in history.

26 For details, see Hamashita Takeshi's (1997) *Tributary Systems and Modern Asia*. This specialized study is a collection of his papers on tribute systems his 'Tribute and treaties', originally published in *Modernity in World History*, is also included in this volume. In this book, Hamashita Takeshi establishes his basic perspective with regard to the trans-border tribute system of East Asia, directly constituting a challenge to the modern sense of nation-state. He queries in the Preface in a quite abstract way the question of the historical possibility of 'Asianism' and the Greater East Asia Coprosperity Sphere: 'Geopolitics as a discipline starts from the state as the premise of its consideration and its field of vision is completely confined within the area of the state. Hence, the object of study of geopolitics and the object the state seeks to gain control are historically different, and this is a point that has instead been neglected.' (Hamashita 1997: 13) Obviously, Hamashita hopes to redefine geopolitics: 'In this book, the concept of geopolitics is used in the fundamental and broad sense. It refers to the totality of politics taking place on the basis of geographical conditions. Thus it is different from the geopolitics of the early twentieth century, whose analytic frame reflects the perspective of the concern for centralization of the sovereign state. But in order also to probe into the historical positioning of discussions that occurred in the history of East Asia with regard to 'Asianism', 'Greater Asianism', and the 'Greater East Asia Coprosperity Sphere', I believe we must also respond to the demands raised by geopolitics. That is to say, we must re-examine the political analysis together with its methodology of the geopolitics proposed then.' (Hamashita 1997: 13)

In the chapter 'The East Asian international system', he points out that the proposition of severing from Asia is a similar gesture to that of the claim of the Choson Dynasty of Korea to be the legitimate inheritor of Zhong Hua. It seems to be displaying its national characteristic in front of the Chinese Empire on the one hand, and also suggesting that both the periphery and the centre share the conception of 'the extension of the ruling power of the centre across the land within its reach'. In the third part, 'Japan and Asia in the modern East Asian international system', he continues to argue that the ideas of disassociating Asia and of the Greater East Asia Coprosperity Sphere were reactions against the underlying frame of mind formed in the 'Hua-Yi' order. In this order, China was the centre of the tributary system. But the reaction does not aim to destroy this order, rather to occupy the centre of this order. Thus, 'Westernization' of Japan is not the end, but rather Japan's means to rejoin Asia.

27 Kawakatsu Heita's idea of 'a system of self-isolated states' was forwarded to complement Wallerstein's idea of the 'world system'. He argues that it is not correct for Wallerstein to take his 'world system' as the only system, built around the economy as the centre, in the history of mankind. It is only one form of modern economic society. In contrast to this, in the same historical period, a system of self-isolated states of the three East Asian countries was formed between

1600–1850. China, Japan and Korea developed one after the other into self-contained economic systems, and assumed attitudes that rejected free trade. That these countries also banned or maintained trade with foreign countries, as well as closing to foreign influence, were part and parcel of the tribute system. Kawakatsu stresses that, from after the seventeenth century until the founding of the states by the East Asian countries, a worldview and international order completely different from that of Western Europe was formed in this region.

28 See Asahi Shimbun, 9 August 1999, for coverage of the 'International Conference on Marine Studies'. Kawakatsu suggested the conference to set up a united body between Japan (Nippon), Indonesia and Australia and named it 'Nichidoneraria'. He further stressed building loose social networks so as to avoid being dominated by power politics.

References

Fukuzawa, Yukichi 福澤諭吉 (1995) *An Outline of a Theory of Civilization* 文明論の概略, Iwanami Shoten 岩波書店.

Fukuzawa, Yukichi (1885/1960) 'On Disassociating Asia' 脱亞論 in *Complete Collection of Fukuzawa Yukichi Vol. 10* 福澤諭吉全集. Iwanami Shoten 岩波書店, 238–240. (First published in 1885).

Hamashita, Takeshi 濱下武志 (1986) 'Tribute and migrants' 朝貢と移民. In Umesawa Tadao and Matubara Masaki (eds) 梅棹忠夫・松原正毅編 *Civilization Studies on Ruling Institutions* 統治機構の文明学. Chuokoronsha 中央公論社.

Hamashita, Takeshi (1997) 'Tribute and treaties' 朝貢と條約, *Tributary Systems and Modern Asia* 朝貢システムと近代アジア, Iwanami Shoten 岩波書店: 141–227.

Hashikawa, Bunzo 橋川文三 (1974) 'Fukuzawa Yukichi and Okakura Tenshin' 福澤諭吉と岡倉天心 in Takeushi Yoshimi and Hashikawa Bunzo (eds) 竹内好・橋川文三編 *Modernity in China and Japan Vol. 1*, 近代日本と中國（上）, Tokyo: Asahi Shimbunsha 朝日新聞社, 18–35.

Heidegger, Martin (1987) *Being and Time* 存在與時間, Chen, Jia Ying and Wang, Qing Jie 陳嘉映、王慶節 (trans.), Beijing: Sanlian Books 北京三聯書店.

Hiraishi, Naoaki 平石直昭 (1994) 'Asianism in Modern Japan' 近代日本のアジア主義 in *Asian Perspectives* アジアから考える, Tokyo: Tokyo University Press 東京大学出版会.

Kawakatsu, Heita 川勝平太 (1994) 'The establishment and development of the East Asian economic sphere' アジア経済圏の成立と展開, *Asian Perspectives* Vol. 6 アジアから考える Vol. 6 長期社会変動: 13–65.

Kawakatsu, Heita (1996) *Japanese Civilization and the Modern West* 日本文明と近代西洋, NHK Publishing 日本放送出版協会.

Kishimoto, Mio 岸本美緒 (1995) 'The various perspectives that take Asia as the starting point – "crossing" and "dialogue" アジアからの諸視角 －＜交錯＞と＜對話＞ *Historiography Studies* 歴史学研究 676: 36–47.

Koike, Yoshiaki 小池喜明 (1985) 'The tradition of driving off the barbarians' 攘夷と傳統 Pelican Publishing ぺりかん社.

Kojima, Tsuyoshi 小島毅 (1993) 'The intellectual history proceeding from regional consideration' 地域からの思想史, *Asian Perspectives* Vol. 1 アジアから考える Vol. 1: 33–51.

Miyajima, Hiroshi 宮島博史 (1994) 'The formation of small peasant society' 東アジア小農社会の成立, *Asian Perspectives* Vol. 6 アジアから考える, Vol. 6: 67–96.

Miyazaki, Ichisada 宮崎市定 (1940) 'Renaissance in the East and Renaissance in the West' 東洋のルネッサンスと西洋のルネッサンス, *Asian History Studies* No. 2 アジア史研究 No. 2: 336–87.

Miyazaki, Ichisada (1975) *Study of the History of Asia* アジア史研究, Vol. II., Dohosha 同朋会.

Miyazaki, Ichisada (1987) *An Outline of the History of Asia* アジア史概説 Chuokoronsha 中央公論社.

Miyazaki, Toten 宮崎滔天 (1970) *My Thirty-three Years' Dream* 三十三年の夢, Heibonsha 平凡社.

Mizoguchi, Yuzo 溝口雄三 (1994a) 'The founding of the theory of the principle and Qi in China' 中国における理気論の成立, *Asian Perspectives* Vol. 7 アジアから考える, Vol. 7: 77–130.

Mizoguchi, Yuzo (1994b) 'The formation of Asian societies and states' アジアの社会と国家の形成, *Asian Perspectives* Vol. 4 アジアから考える Vol. 4: 1–11.

Mizoguchi, Yuzo (1989) 'China as method' 方法としての中国, *Asian Perspectives* Vol. 4 アジアから考える Vol. 4: 1–11.

Mizoguchi, Yuzo (1980) *The Turning and Development of Chinese Pre-modern Thinking* 中國前近代思想 の曲折と展開 Tokyo University Press 東京大学出版会.

Okakura, Tenshin (1976a) 'The ideals of the East with special reference to the art of Japan' 東洋の理想, *Modern Japanese Thought Series: A Collection of Okakura Tenshin's Works* 近代日本思想大系： 岡倉天心集, Chikuma Shobo Publishing 筑摩書房, 9–96.

Okakura, Tenshin 岡倉天心 (1976b) 'The wakening of Japan' 日本の覺醒, in *Modern Japanese Thought Series: A Collection of Okakura Tenshin's Works* 近代日本思想 大系：岡倉天心集. Chikuma Shobo Publishing 筑摩書房, 97–155.

Okamoto, Koji 岡本幸治 (1998) 'Japan and Asia, or Japan in Asia?' 「日本とアジア」か「アジアの日本」か in *The Asianist View in Modern Japan*, Minerva Shobo 近代日本のアジア観.

Said, Edward (1985) *Orientalism*, London: Penguin.

Sakai, Naoki 酒井直樹 (1997a) 'Return to the West/Return to the East' 西洋への回歸/東洋への回歸 in *Problematics in the So-called Japanese Thoughts* 日本思想という問題, Iwanami Shoten 岩波書店, 79–142.

Sakai, Naoki (1997b) 'An Analytical Theory of Cultural Difference and the Internality of Japan' 文化的差異の分析論と日本という内部性 in *Problematics in the So-called Japanese Thoughts* 日本思想と いう問題, Iwanami Shoten 岩波書店, 145–205.

Sun, Ge 孫歌 (1998) 'The positioning of literature – Takeuchi Yoshimi's Paradox' 文學的位置－ 竹内好的悖論, *Intellectual Inquiry Vol 4 學術思想評論 第四輯*, Liaoning University Press 遼寧大學 出版社.

Sun, Yat-sen 孫中山 (1986) 'Speech to Commercial Chamber etc of Edo' 對神戶商業會議所等團體 的演說, *The Complete Collected Works of Sun Zhong-shan, V.11* 孫中山全集第十一卷, Zhong Hua Brook Co. 中華書局, 401–409.

Suzuki, Naritaka 鈴木成高 (1990) *The Modernity of World History* 世界史における現代, Sobunsha 創文社.

Takeuchi, Yoshimi (1958) 'Two Conceptions of the History of Asia' つのアジア史觀, in *Japan and Asia* 日本アジア, 83–91.

Takeuchi, Yoshimi (1963) 'The Prospect of Asianism' アジア主義の展望 in *Asianism* of *Modern Japanese Thought Series* Vol. 9 近代日本思想大, Chikuma Shobo Publishing.

Takeuchi, Yoshimi 竹内好 (1970) 'The idea of Asia' アジアの理念. Originally published in *The Science of Thinking* 思想の科学, now quoted from *In Concrete Context: Dialogues of Takeuchi Yoshimi*: 状況的・竹内好對談集, Godo Publishing 合同出版社, 141–154.

Takeuchi, Yoshimi 竹内好 (1975) 'The Perspective of Asian study' 亞洲学の視點. Preface to *For the Furthering of Asian Study* アジア学の展開のために, Sojusha 創樹社.

Takeuchi, Yoshimi 竹内好 (1993) 'The modern age of China and the modern age of Japan' 中国の近代と日本の近代, *Japan and Asia* 日本とアジア, Chikuma Shobo Publishing 筑摩書房, 11–57.

Takeyama, Michio 竹山道雄 (1958) 'The positioning of Japan's culture' 日本文化の位置, *The Transformation of the Culture and Tradition of Japan* 日本文化の傳統と變遷, Shinchosha 新潮社.

Terada, Hiroaki 寺田浩明 (1994) 'The nature of 'agreement' in the legal order of the Ming and Qing Dynasties' 明清法秩序における[約]の性格, *Asian Perspectives* Vol. 4 アジアから考える Vol. 4: 69–130.

Umesawa, Tadao (1967) *An Ecological Historiography of Civilization* 文明の生態史觀, Chuokoronsha Inc. 中央公論社.

Umesawa, Tadao 梅棹忠夫 (1984) *Civilization Studies on Modern Japan* 近代日本の文明学, Chuokoronsha, Inc. 中央公論社.

Watsuji, Tetsuro 和辻哲郎 (1963) 'The ethics of the studies of the human sphere' 人間学としての 倫理学, in *The Thinking of Modern Japan Series: Watsuji Tetsuro* 現代日本思想大系・和辻哲郎, Chikuma Shobo Publishing 筑摩書房, 55–128.

Watsuji, Tetsuro (1937, 1942, 1949) *Ethics Vol. 1–3* 倫理学（上・中、下）Iwanami Shoten 岩波書店.

Watsuji, Tetsuro (1935) *Local Conditions and Customs: Studies of the Human Sphere* 風土--人間学的
　　考察, Iwanami Shoten 岩波書店.

Yuasa Yasuo 湯淺泰雄 (1995) *Watsuji Tetsuro* 和辻哲郎, Chikuma Gakugei Bunko ちくま学藝文庫.

Appendix: Names and special terms

Names

Dazai Shundai 太宰春台

Fukuzawa Yukichi 福澤諭吉

Hamashita Takeshi 濱下武志

Hashikawa Bunzo 橋川文三

Hiraishi Naoaki 平石直昭

Hotta Yoshie 堀田善衞

Iizuka Koji 飯塚浩二

Itoh Hirobumi 伊藤博文

Karaki Junzo 唐木順三

Kawakatsu Heita 川勝平太

Kishimoto Mio 岸本美緒

Kita Ikki 北一輝

Kojima Tsuyoshi 小島毅

Konoe Atsumaro 近節篤麿

Kotoku Shusui 幸德秋水

Kuwabara Jitsuzo 桑原騭藏

Li Zhuo Wu 李卓吾

Maruyama Masao 丸山真男

Miyajima Hiroshi 宮島博史

Miyazaki Ichisada 宮崎市定

Miyazaki Toten 宮崎滔天

Mizoguchi Yuzo 溝口雄三

Naito Konan 內藤湖南

Nakae Chomin 中江兆民

Nishida Kitaro 西田幾多郎

Ogyu Sorai 荻生徂徠

Okakura Tenshin 岡倉天心

Okamoto Koji 彭澤周

Okawa Shumei 大川周明

Otsuka Hisao 大塚久雄

Sakai Naoki 酒井直樹

Sakano Junji 坂野潤治

Suzuki Naritaka 鈴木成高

Takeuchi Yoshimi 竹內好

Takeyama Michio 竹山道雄

Tarui Tokichi 樽井藤吉

Terada Hiroaki's 寺田浩明

Tomita Masahumi 富田正文

Tosaka Jun 戸坂潤

Toyama Mitsuro 頭山滿

Tsuda Sokichi 津田左右吉

Uchida Ryohei 內田良平

Ueda Makoto 上田信

Umesawa Tadao 梅棹忠夫

Watanabe Hiroshi 渡邊浩

Watsuji Tetsuro 和辻哲郎

Yishimoda Sho 石母田下

Yuasa Yasuo 湯淺泰雄

Special terms

Amur River Society (Black Dragon Society) 黑龍會

Asahi Shimbun 朝日新聞

Aspiring activists 志士 or 浪人

Breaking ties with Europe and integrating with Asia 脫歐入亞

Chikuma Sobo Publishing 筑摩書房

Closing Japan to the outside world 鎖国

Datsu-A ron 脫亞論

Di 狄

Disassociating Asia 脫亞

Disassociating Asia and integrating with Europe 脫亞入歐

Fudo 風土

Gen'yosha (Black Ocean Society) 玄洋社

Greater East Asia Coprosperity Sphere 大東亞共榮圈

Hua-Yi Metamorphosis 華夷變態

Hua-Yi Order 華夷秩序

Human sphere 人間
Kyoto School of thought 京都学派
Meiji Ishin 明治維新
Revere the Emperor, expel barbarians 尊王攘夷
Reviving Asia 興亞
Solidarity of East Asia 東洋連帶論
Theory of local conditions and customs 風土論
Xia 夏
Zhong Hua 中華

Editor's note

We wish to thank Yue-Tsen Chung 鍾月岑 (Ph.D. in History at the University of Chicago, currently an Assistant Professor in the Institute of History, National Tsing Hua University) for her detailed editorial work, and Hashimoto Kyoko 橋本恭子 (graduate student at National Tsing Hua University, Taiwan) for her final touches.

Chapter 2

The politics of imagining Asia
A genealogical analysis

Wang Hui
(Translated by Matthew A. Hale)

The 'new empire' that has re-emerged in the 'war on terror' follows naturally upon the heels of neoliberal globalization. The latter seeks to restructure various social traditions according to neoliberal marketist principles such as the legal protection of private property, the state's withdrawal from the economic sphere, and the transnationalization of productive, commercial, and financial systems. The former uses the violence, crises, and social disintegration caused by the processes of neoliberal globalization as pretenses to reconstruct a military and political 'new empire'. These two apparently different discourses cooperate to knit together military alliances, economic associations, and international political institutions in the construction of a total order at all levels – political, economic, cultural, and military. That new order may, therefore, be called a 'neoliberal empire/imperialism'.

In his article 'Why Europe Needs a Constitution,' Habermas argues that it is necessary to organize nation-states into a unified political community in order to uphold the European social model and its modern achievements (Habermas 2001). In order to defend the European way of life in terms of welfare, security, democracy and freedom, Habermas proposes three major tasks in the construction of a 'post-national democracy': to form a European civil society, to build a Europe-wide political public sphere, and to create a political culture in which all citizens of the European Union would be able to share. He recommends that Europe apply to itself 'as a whole, "the logic of the circular creation of state and society that shaped the modern history of European countries"' so as to establish a unified constitution by popular referendum. A Europe formed according to these three main tasks resembles a super state or empire: its component societies retain their own characteristics and autonomy to a certain degree, but on the other hand it has unified standing institutions that carry out governmental functions, including a unified parliamentary and legal system, and it is supported and safeguarded by a historically formed civil political culture and social system.

Mirroring the progress and crisis of Europe's unification is a two-fold process taking place in Asia. On the one hand are the concentration and expansion of a new kind of power network with the USA as its center. For instance, in the Afghanistan War, each Asian country actively participated in the US-centered war alliance for its own particular economic or political reasons. On the other hand is the advance of Asian regional cooperation following the 1997 financial crisis. In June 2001, China, Russia, Kazakhstan, Tajikistan, Kyrgyzstan, and Uzbekistan founded the 'Shanghai Cooperation Organization,' and in November 2001 China came to an agreement with the ten countries of ASEAN that in ten years China would sign a free trade agreement with ASEAN. This plan rapidly expanded from '10 plus 1' to '10 plus 3' (ASEAN plus China, Japan and Korea), eventually to '10 plus 6' (ASEAN plus China, Japan, Korea, India, Australia, and New Zealand). A Japanese news agency published an article saying that 'If the unification of Asia accelerates [. . .] the sense of distance between Japan and China will disappear naturally in the process of regional unification; eventually, based on the first occasion of regional negotiation excluding the United States – a conference that joins ASEAN and the summit of Japan, China, and Korea, [. . .] Japan and China may achieve an "Asian version of the reconciliation between France and Germany"' (Nishikyo 2002). Since the views of China, Japan, and the ASEAN countries on regional progress is not entirely consistent, what the expansion of this regional plan (the addition of India, Australia and New Zealand brings the membership up to 16) indicates is not so much the spread of the idea of Asia as the product of the power dynamics among the region's various nation-states.

The course of Asian regional integration includes many complex, contradictory features. On the one hand, in the name of the region or 'Asia' it appeals to supra-national interests, but on the other hand, it incorporates nation-states into a larger, protective community. On the one hand, this regionalism includes the intent to challenge global hegemony through constructing regional autonomy, but on the other hand, it is the product of global market relations under 'new imperial' dominance. From a historical perspective, the discussion of 'Asia' is not an entirely new phenomenon. In the early modern wave of nationalism we encountered two sharply opposed visions of Asia: the colonialist vision developed from Japan's 'continental policy,' and the Asian social revolution vision centered on national liberation and socialist movements. The former constructed the idea of Asia (ya zhou) or Tōyō based on the binary between East and West, whereas the latter discussed the issue of nation from an internationalist perspective. Discussion of Asia, therefore, cannot avoid reviewing the early modern colonialist and nationalist movements.

Asia and Tōyō: questions of derivation

Historically speaking, the idea of Asia is not Asian but, rather, European. In 1948, Takeuchi Yoshimi wrote in an article called 'What is Modernity?': '[If we want to] understand East Asia (Jpn. Tōyō), [we must appreciate that] what constitute Asia are European factors existing in Europe. Asia is Asia by dint of its European context' (Takeuchi 2005: 188). This view can also help us to explain Fukuzawa Yukichi's negative way of defining Asia, i.e. through his call to 'shed Asia' (tuo ya) (Maruyama 1997: 9–11). Scholars have various opinions about the role of 'On Shedding Asia' (tuo ya lun) (published on 16 March 1885) in the development of Fukuzawa's thought. As I see it, however, the important question is why the slogan developed from this article, 'shed Asia and join Europe' (tuo ya ru ou) (although Fukuzawa never actually used the words 'join Europe'), became a recurring theme of modern Japanese thought. In the frame-work of 'On Shedding Asia,' the notion of Asia included two levels. First, Asia referred to a region with a high degree of cultural homogenization, i.e. Confucian Asia. Second, the political meaning of 'shedding Confucianism' was dissociation from China-centered imperial relations and construction of a European-style nation-state oriented towards 'freedom,' 'human rights,' 'national sovereignty,' 'civilization,' and 'independent spirit.' In the context of the continuous expansion of 'the state,' this new political form and its power relations, 'Asia' was fundamentally negated as a cultural and political model opposed to the nationalist vision of modernization. According to the logic of Takeuchi's comment that 'Asia is Asia by dint of its European context,' the notion of Asia's essence implied by Fukuzawa's proposal to 'shed Asia,' i.e. Confucianism and its social system, is actually internal to European thought. If 'what constitute Asia are European factors existing in Europe,' the birth of 'Asia' must result from Asia's negation of itself. In this sense, Fukuzawa's proposal to 'shed Asia' and Takeuchi's proposal both derive from the nineteenth-century European conception of 'world history.'

Just as European self-consciousness required knowledge of its 'outside,' 'shedding Asia' was a way of forming self-consciousness through differentiating Japan from Asia. From this perspective, 'shedding Asia,' this proposal of early modern Japanese particularism, in fact derived from early modern European historical consciousness. In other words, Japanese particularism derived from European universalism. In the words of Karl Jaspers, 'Dissociation from Asia was part of a universal historical process, not a particularist European gesture towards Asia. It took place within Asia itself. It was the path of humanity and the true path of history.' He continues:

> Greek culture seems to be a phenomenon of the Asian periphery. Europe disengaged from its Asian mother when it was not yet mature. A problem emerges: at which step, which time, and which place did this rupture occur? Could Europe get lost in Asia again? Is there a lack of consciousness in the depths of Asia? Does its degradation equal a lack of consciousness?
>
> If the West emerged from the Asian matrix, its emergence appears to be a bold movement in the liberation of human potential. This movement entails two risks: first, Europe could lose its spiritual basis; second, as soon as the West becomes conscious, it continually risks falling back into Asia.
>
> However, if the risk of falling back into Asia were actualized today, this risk would be actualized under the conditions of new industrial technology that would transform and destroy Asia. Western freedom, individualism, many Western categories, and enlightened consciousness would be abandoned, and they would be replaced by Asia's eternal characteristics: its existing forms of despotism, its fatalistic tranquility, its lack of history or volition. Asia would be the enduring world influencing the totality. It is older than Europe and, moreover, it includes Europe. All that derives from Asia and must return to Asia is temporary. [. . .]
>
> Asia has become a principle of depth. When we objectively analyze it as a historical phenomenon, it disintegrates. We cannot treat its opposing term, Europe, as a transcendental entity, so Eurasia becomes a dreadful specter. Only when we treat them as the epitome of certain historically specific, ideationally coherent things, rather than as a perception of the whole, then they become a determinate language of depth, and a code representing truth. Eurasia, however, is a code coexisting with the whole of Western history.
>
> (Jaspers 1989: 82–83)

If 'shedding Asia' is not the premise for Japanese particularism but rather a particular step in Europe's universal progress, what kind of European thought gave rise to this 'universal progress'?

In the eighteenth and nineteenth centuries, the European Enlightenment and colonial expansion provided conditions for the development of a new system of knowledge.

Historical linguistics, race theory, modern geography, political economy, theories of state, legal philosophy, the study of religion, and historiography all rapidly developed hand in hand with the natural sciences and constructed a new worldview in every aspect. The notions of Europe and Asia were both products of this process of knowledge construction. In the works of European writers such as Montesquieu, Adam Smith, Hegel, and Marx,[1] the core of the construction of this European notion of Asia had the following characteristics: multi-national empires as opposed to European modern or monarchical states; political despotism as opposed to European modern legal and political systems; and nomadic and agrarian modes of production completely different from European urban and commercial life. Since the European nation-state and the expansion of the capitalist market system were considered an advanced stage or *telos* of world history, Asia and its aforementioned characteristics were consequently relegated to a lower stage. In this context, Asia was not only a geographic category, but also a form of civilization: Asia represented a political form defined in opposition to the European nation-state, a social form defined in opposition to European capitalism, and a transitional stage between prehistory and history proper. Throughout most of the nineteenth and twentieth centuries, discourse on Asia was embedded within a universalist narrative about European modernity that defined the apparently opposed historical blueprints of both colonists and revolutionaries. The three central themes and keywords of this narrative were empire, nation-state and capitalism (or market economy).

In many nineteenth-century European texts on history, philosophy, law, state, and religion, Asia was presented as the 'center' of all nations in the world and the 'starting point' of world history. But in the framework of 'shedding Asia', the Confucianism of China was regarded as the 'source of history'. This view about 'source' or 'starting point' arose from a double need that required both connection and breaking away. From the discovery by historical linguists of the connection between European languages and Sanskrit, we could examine how a political economist like Hegel would connect this linguistic discovery with nineteenth-century European racial theories and state theories so as to define 'Asia as the starting point of history':

> It is a great discovery in history – as of a new world – which has been made within rather more than the last twenty years, respecting the Sanskrit and the connection of the European languages with it. In particular, the connection of the German and Indian peoples has been demonstrated, with as much certainty as such subjects allow of. Even at the present time we know of peoples which scarcely form a society, much less a State, but that have been long known as existing. . . . In the connection just referred to, between the languages of nations so widely separated, we have a result before us, which proves the diffusion of those nations from Asia as a center, and the so dissimilar development of what had been originally related, as an incontestable fact.
>
> (Hegel 1899: 60)

Asia must, therefore, meet two conditions in order to constitute the 'starting point' of world history. First, Asia and Europe must be two correlated organic parts of the same historical process. Second, Asia and Europe must occupy two drastically different stages of this historical continuum, and the main standard for evaluating these stages must be 'the state.' The reason Asia marked the 'starting point' or prehistorical stage was that it still lacked states and had not yet formed historical subjects. In this sense, when Asian regions complete the transition from traditional empires to 'states,' from agrarian or pastoral to industrial or commercial modes of production, from village to urban or 'civil society' forms of organization, then Asia would no longer be Asia.

Because his account of civil society, market, and commerce derives from the Scottish school of political economy, Hegel's notion of a despotic Asia is linked to a certain economic system. If we contrast Hegel's historical philosophical account of the four stages – the Orient, Greece, Rome and the Teutonic peoples, with Adam Smith's delineation, from the perspective of economic history, of four historical stages – hunting, pastoral, agricultural, and commercial, it is not difficult to discover internal relations between Hegel's historical description centered on political forms and Smith's historical stages centered on productive forms. Smith treats the development from agricultural society to commercial society as the transition from European feudal society to modern market society. Thereby, he internally connects the ideas of modern era, commercial era and European society in the form of a historical narrative. The model of market movement that he describes is an abstract process: the discovery of the Americas, colonialism and class differentiation are all presented as an economic process of endless market expansion, labor division, technology advancement, rise of tax and wealth. A kind of narrative on the circulative movement of world markets is thus established through this formalist narrative method. This method regards the market mode as both the result of historical development and the inner law of history; here the concrete spatial relationship of colonialism and social differentiation is transformed into a temporal process of production, circulation, and consumption. In *The Wealth of Nations*, Smith's division of four historical stages corresponds to a taxonomy of specific regions and peoples. When describing the 'nations of hunters, the lowest and rudest state of society,' for example, he mentions 'the native tribes of North America'; when discussing 'nations of shepherds, a more advanced state of society,' he names his contemporary Tartars and Arabs as examples; when describing '[nations of husbandmen,] a yet more advanced state of society,' he turns backwards to ancient Greece and Rome (in a previous chapter he also mentions Chinese agriculture). As for what commercial society, he refers to Europe which he calls 'civilized states' (Smith 1976: 689–92). In Hegel's vision, all these issues were incorporated into a political framework concerning the state. The reason 'nations of hunters' were 'the lowest and rudest' form of society was that the scale of their communities was too small to produce the political division of labor necessary for state formation. In Gellner's words, 'for them, the question of the state, of a stable specialized order-enforcing institution, does not really arise' (Gellner 1983: 5). Hegel's narrative of world history therefore explicitly excludes North America (characterized by hunting and gathering) and situates the Orient at the starting point of history. If Smith divides history into various economic or productive modes, then Hegel nominates historical stages according to region, civilization, and state structure, but both correlate mode of production or political form with specific places (Asia, the Americas, Africa, and Europe), and both organize these places within a chronological narrative.

The notions of Asia or China articulated by Montesquieu, Hegel, Marx, and Fukuyama all developed through comparative description of civilizations. In order to construct Asia as this particular type of civilization in contrast with European civilization, it was necessary to elide its internal development and change; even the history of conflicts between northern and southern Chinese ethnic groups (i.e. what European writers called the conquering of China by the 'Tartars' and vice versa) was not regarded as changes in 'historical forms'. In the words of Montesquieu: '[T]he laws of China are not destroyed by conquest. Their customs, manners, laws, and religion [were] the same thing' (Montesquieu 1914). In this culturalist horizon, Asia does not have history or the historical conditions or impetus for producing modernity. The heart of this modernity is the 'state' and its legal system, its urban and commercial way of life, or its mechanism for economic and military competition based on nation-states. Perry Anderson wrote in his critique of European notions of the 'Asiatic mode of production' and its 'despotism':

> The concept of 'despotism' has from its origins been an outsider's appraisal of 'the Orient.' As far back as ancient Greece, Aristotle famously claimed that 'Barbarians are more servile by nature than Greeks, and Asians are more servile than Europeans; hence they endure despotic rule without protest . . . But they obey established rules and pass them on from generation to generation, so they are secure'.
> (Anderson 1974: 463)[2]

Early modern European notions of Asian state structures were produced through the long history of the conflict of European states with the Ottoman Empire. Machiavelli's *The Prince* first pitted the Ottoman state with European monarchies, and argued that the Ottoman monarchical bureaucratic system was categorically different from all European state systems. Similarly, Bodin, often regarded as the first European theorist of sovereignty, also contrasted European 'royal sovereignty' with Ottoman 'lordly power' (Anderson 1974: 397). With the nineteenth-century expansion of European colonialism, this contrast eventually mutated into the contrast between European nation-states and Asian empires, to such an extent that today it is difficult to recognize that the 'despotism' or 'absolutism' we associate with Asia in fact derives from European generalization about the Ottoman Empire (Anderson 1974: 493). In this perspective, especially typical of Western Europe, early modern capitalism is the product of Western Europe's unique social structure, and there is a necessary or natural relation between capitalist development and the system of nation-states, with feudal states as their historical precondition. Under the influence of this conception of history, imperial systems (vast, multi-ethnic empires such as the Ottoman, Chinese, Mughal, and Russian systems) are viewed as the political form of Oriental despotism incapable of producing the political structure necessary for the development of capitalism (Anderson 1974: 400, 412). It was this notion of despotism derived from descriptions of empire that made it possible for later generations to contrast Europe with Asia in terms of political categories (democratic Europe vs. authoritarian Asia), and which made it possible for Fukuzawa and his successors to contrast Japan with Confucian China through the theory of 'shedding Asia.'

The idea of Asia in early modern European thought was always closely connected with the vast territory and the complex ethnicity of an empire, as contrasted with the republican system of Greece and European monarchy – in the wave of nationalist movements in the nineteenth century, republican system or feudal monarchy existed both as predecessors of nation-state and as political forms distinct from that of any other region. In other words, despotism became closely associated with the idea of vast empire in the transition from feudal state to nation-state. The category of 'state', opposed to empire, therefore acquired its superiority in value and in history. European thinkers such as Montesquieu firmly negated some relatively positive descriptions of politics, law, customs, and culture in China by some priests (such descriptions had been the base of the European Enlightenment pictures of China, particularly those by Voltaire and by Leibniz). They proceeded to summarize the political culture of China by 'despotism' and 'empire'. According to the classic description since Montesquieu, the major characteristics of an empire are: the sovereign monopolizes the distribution of property with his military power, thereby eliminating aristocracy that could balance the sovereign's power and blocking the growth of nation-state (Montesquieu 1914: 126–9). If we analyze this European notion of despotic empire of mixed ethnicity and vast territory by contextual-izing it in the self-understanding of early modern Japan, we would be able to discern the foundation of two ideas – the contrast between a single-ethnicity Japan, mutating from feudalism to a modern state, and a multi-ethnicity China, trapped in Confucian empire systems; and the proposition of so-called 'turning down the friends of Asia'.

The early modern Japanese idea of 'Asia' was also founded on this sort of European-style culturalism. In Maruyama Masao's words, 'it reflected Japan's rapid process of westernization following the Meiji period, for the cultural and political path formed through the confluence of statism and post-Meiji westernization was so obviously different from those of all the other Asian countries' (Maruyama 1998: 8). In explain-ing the formation of early modern Japanese 'state rationality' Maruyama points out that the sovereign states of early modern Europe were born through the disintegration of the Christian world-community symbolized by the (Holy) Roman Empire, and their international society was an agglomeration of all independent states, whereas 'Japan was the opposite; it began to develop a nation-state only after it had been forced into this international society' (Maruyama 1997: 146). This is why the early modern Japanese notion of 'equality among states' developed through a struggle against the hierarchical Confucian notions of 'differentiating between barbarian and civilized' (yi xia zhi bian) and 'expelling barbarians' (rang yi lun). According to this contrast between the principle of formal equality in European international law and the Confucian idea of 'expelling barbarians,' early modern Japanese expansionism can be explained as a result of lacking European-style 'state rationality' or as a product of Confucianist 'expelling barbarians'. Maruyama argues that in Fukuzawa:

> Internal liberation and external independence were understood as a single problem. According to this logic, individualism and statism, statism and internationalism achieved a splendid balance – this was indeed a fortunate moment. However, the harsh realities of the international context soon shattered this balance.
>
> (Maruyama 1997: 157)

The notion of 'expelling barbarians' paved the way for the modern state's expansion and exclusion, but if that is all, then the tragedy of early modern Japan is a tragedy of 'incomplete westernization' or 'incomplete modernization' rather than a tragedy of Japanese modernity itself.

In a later article explaining the notion of 'state rationality,' Maruyama wrote:

> 'State rationality' goes beyond the stage of absolute sovereignty to an age of co-existence among all modern sovereign states. According to the principles of inter-national law, these modern sovereign states establish diplomatic relations and pursue

their state interests through means such as treaties, alliances, and war. This sort of 'international community' seems to have already taken shape in seventeenth-century Europe, where it was called the Western State System. 'State rationality' developed under the twin pillars of the principle of equality among sovereign states and the balance of powers.

(Maruyama 1997: 160)

Japan's 1874 invasion of Taiwan, however, and its 1894 invasion of Korea both appealed to European international law and its notion of formal equality among sovereign states. Should we interpret these actions within a framework of 'the decadence of state rationality,' or should we interpret them within a process of seeking or forming this European 'state rationality'? There is no real contradiction between such imperialist actions and the embrace of the notion of sovereign equality in order to cast off the imperial Chinese tribute system or hierarchical relations. Rather than explaining this problem through a binary opposition between tradition and modernity or xenophobia ('barbarian-expulsionism') and international equality, we would do better to consider the derivativeness of Japan's early modern nationalism, colonialism, and Asianism. That is, we should examine early modern Japanese expansionism within its 'European context.'

According to the classic model of nationalism forged in the French Revolution, the nation-state is the basic precondition for the individual as unit of power (i.e. the citizen). Without this political community, without the precondition of national uniformity, it would be impossible to establish the individual as a juridical subject. As European writers have asked over and again:

Will a free Europe take the place of monarchical Europe? The wars against other monarchies undertaken to defend the fruits of the [French] Revolution quickly became a liberatory mission involving annexation of other countries' territories. [. . .] The revolution and the empire tried to incite other nations to overthrow their monarchs in the name of liberty, but this expansionism eventually drove these peoples to unite with their traditional monarchies in opposition to France.

(Gerbet 1989: 12)

Here the key issue is that, on the one hand, the bourgeois nation-state and its individualist notion of citizenship were political paths to abandon the hierarchy of aristocratic systems and ancient empires, but, on the other hand, they were the best political forms for the expansion of capitalism (especially the formation of national markets, the expansion of overseas markets, and the system of private property), and this expansion was never limited to borders of nation-states. So even if they could have actualized the system of 'rights' awaited by Fukuzawa, there was not necessarily any guarantee that this 'system' would not possess expansive or invasive features. In this sense, there is not a real contradiction between his theory of 'shedding Asia' and the reality of 'invading Asia' – both can find grounds in the 'European context' from which they derive. Pointing this out does not mean denying the historical connection between early modern Japanese imperialist expansion and the political tradition of 'respecting the emperor and expelling the barbarians'; my aim is to highlight how the use of this political tradition was produced under new historical conditions and relations, and that reflections on this political tradition should therefore become an organic part of reconsidering such new historical conditions and relations.

Narodism (from Russian: 'populism') and the dual meaning of 'Asia'

Twenty-six years after Fukuzawa published 'On Shedding Asia,' the Chinese Revolution of 1911 broke out. Shortly after the Provisional Government of the Republic of China was founded, Lenin published a series of articles applauding that '[today] China is a land of seething political activity, the scene of a virile social movement and of a democratic upsurge,' and condemning the civilized and advanced Europe, which, 'with its highly developed machine industry, its rich multiform culture and its constitutions,' had nevertheless remained 'in support of everything backward, moribund, and medieval' under the command of the bourgeoisie (Lenin 1977a, 1977b). These observations constitute part of Lenin's theory of imperialism and proletarian revolution, where he argued that, as capitalism entered the imperialist phase, the various social struggles of oppressed peoples around the world would be integrated into the category of world proletarian revolution. This method of connecting European and Asian revolutions in analysis can be traced back to Marx's article 'Revolution in China and in Europe,' written for the *New York Daily Tribune* in 1853 (Marx 1853). Lenin and Fukuzawa's opposing views are based on a common basic understanding, that is, that Asian modernity was the outcome of European modernity, and regardless of Asia's status and fate, the significance of its modernity manifested itself only in its relationship with the more advanced Europe. Lenin regards Russia as an Asian country, but this orientation is defined not from the perspective of geography but from the degree of capitalist development and the process of Russian history. In 'Democracy and Narodism in China,' he wrote that 'Russia is undoubtedly an Asian country and, what is more, one of the most benighted, medieval, and shamefully backward of Asian countries' (Lenin 1975). Although he was warmly sympathetic to the Chinese revolution, Lenin's position was 'Western European' when the issue switched from Asian revolution to the changes within Russian society. In the nineteenth and twentieth centuries, Russian intellectuals regarded the spirit of Russia as the struggle and collision of two forces: the Eastern and the Western, the Asian and the European. In the quotation above, Asia is a category connected with notions such as barbarity, medievalness and backwardness. It is for this reason that the Russian revolution had a prominently Asian character – that is, because it was directed against Russia's benighted, medieval, and shamefully backward social relations – and at the same time, had a global significance.[3]

The special position of Asia in the rhetoric of world history determined how the socialists understood the task and direction of modern revolution in Asia. After he read Sun Yat-sen's 'The Significance of Chinese Revolution', Lenin criticized the democratic and socialist programs proposed by this Chinese revolutionary that transcended capitalism. He noted that they were utopian and populist. Lenin observed, 'The chief representative, or the chief social bulwark, of this Asian bourgeoisie that is still capable of supporting a historically progressive cause, is the peasant' (Lenin 1975). Before the Asian bourgeoisie accomplished the revolutionary task that the European bourgeoisie had accomplished, therefore, socialism was out of the question. He adroitly used historical dialectics to assert that Sun Yat-sen's 'Land Reform Outline' was 'reactionary' because it went against or beyond the present historical stage. He also pointed out that because of the 'Asian' character of Chinese society, it was exactly this 'reactionary outline' that could accomplish the task of capitalism in China: '[populism], under the disguise of "combating capitalism" in agriculture, champions an agrarian program that, if fully carried out, would mean the most rapid development of capitalism in agriculture.'

Lenin's impressions of the Chinese revolution were based on his reflection on the Russian reforms of 1861, and especially the failure of the 1905 revolution. In 1861, after the failure of the Crimean War with Great Britain and France over control of the Balkans and the Black Sea, Alexander II initiated reforms to abolish serfdom. Two points about these reforms should be highlighted. First, these reforms originated from pressures external to Russian society. Second, the 'Decree of Emancipation' announced on 19 February 1861 was carried out under the premise of full protection of landlord interests, and the Russian peasants paid a heavy cost for Russia's top-down process of industrialization. This is why Lenin argued that 1861 led to 1905 (Lenin 1973). From the reforms of 1861 to the revolution of 1905, the concentration of land did not give rise to capitalist agriculture; instead it led peasants of agrarian communes to demand vehemently the appropriation and redistribution of landlord lands (Lü 2004).[4] It was against this background that Lenin linked his thoughts on the 1905 revolution to Russia's land question. In 'The Agrarian Program of Social-Democracy in the First Russian Revolution, 1905–1907,' focusing on the Russian land question, Lenin described two models of agricultural capitalism as 'the Prussian path' and 'the American path': in the former case state and feudal landlords allied to deprive the peasants of communes and their land ownerships with violence, turning feudal economy into Junker bourgeois economy; whereas the latter 'might be better for the peasants instead of a small number of landlords',[5] 'which confiscates and splits up the feudal estates'. It took all land into state ownership in order to abolish the serf system in the countryside. It was exactly such economic necessity that led the Russian peasants to support the nationalization of land. In considering the relation between the Russian land reform and the failure of the 1905 revolution, Lenin concludes that under Russia's social conditions, 'Nationalization of land is not only the only way to thoroughly abolish the medieval agricultural system, it is also the best land system possible under capitalism' (Lenin 1972a).

Lenin believed that the Russian Populist (Narodnik) agrarian program was bound to lead Russia to return to a small peasant economy in which village land was divided up into small plots, and this kind of economic system could not provide the impetus for capitalist development. He endorsed the 'American path' first because only abolition of medieval agrarian relations through nationalization of land could provide the possibility to develop agricultural capitalism, and second because Russia had large volumes of virgin land and other conditions for the American path as opposed to the paths of European countries. The development of capitalist agriculture must involve the coercive reshaping of earlier social relations, but this could happen in various ways:

> In England this reshaping proceeded in a revolutionary, violent way; but the violence was practised for the benefit of the landlords, it was practised on the masses of the peasants, who were taxed to exhaustion, driven from the villages, evicted, and who died out, or emigrated. In America this reshaping went on in a violent way as regards the slave farms in the Southern States. There violence was applied against the slaveowning landlords. Their estates were broken up, and the large feudal estates were transformed into small bourgeois farms. As regards the mass of 'unappropriated' American lands, this role of creating the new agrarian relationships to suit

the new mode of production (i.e., capitalism) was played by the 'American General Redistribution', by the Anti-Rent movement [. . .] of the forties, the Homestead Act, etc.

(Lenin 1972a)

It was from this perspective that Lenin saw the truly revolutionary potential of Sun Yat-sen's program. He marveled at this 'advanced Chinese democrat' who knew nothing of Russia but still argued like a Russian and posed 'purely Russian questions':

Land nationalisation makes it possible to abolish absolute rent, leaving only differential rent. According to Marx's theory, land nationalisation means a maximum elimination of medieval monopolies and medieval relations in agriculture, maximum freedom in buying and selling land, and maximum facilities for agriculture to adapt itself to the market.

(Lenin 1975)

In contrast, 'Our vulgar Marxists, however, in criticising "equalised redistribution," "socialisation of the land," and "equal right to the land," confine themselves to repudiating the doctrine, and thus reveal their own obtuse doctrinairism, which prevents them from seeing the vital life of the peasant revolution beneath the lifeless doctrine of Narodnik theory.' Through examining Sun Yat-sen's revolutionary program against Russia's particular historical background, Lenin concluded that 'The Russian revolution can succeed only as a peasants' agrarian revolution, and the agrarian revolution cannot complete its historical mission without carrying out nationalization.' If the main characteristic defining the 'American path' in contrast to the Prussian and English paths was the nationalization of land, the 'Chinese path' represented a bottom-up 'peasants' agrarian revolution.'

The Russian reforms took place against the background of the Crimean War, the 1905 Russo-Japanese War, and the First World War, so Lenin's reflections on the path of Russia's reforms could not avoid addressing the international relations created by European imperialism. If Russia's land question must be solved through 'nationalization' (i.e. transferring ownership to the state), what kind of 'state' could bear this responsibility? Lenin wrote that:

[T]he national state is the rule and the 'norm' of capitalism; the multi-national state represents backwardness, or is an exception. [. . .] This does not mean, of course, that such a state, which is based on bourgeois relations, can eliminate the exploitation and oppression of nations. It only means that Marxists cannot lose sight of the powerful *economic* factors that give rise to the urge to create national states. It means that 'self-determination of nations' in the Marxists' Programme *cannot*, from a historico-economic point of view, have any other meaning than political self-determination, state independence, and the formation of a national state.

(Lenin 1972b)

So when Lenin discussed 'the awakening of Asia,' his concern was not with socialism but with how to create the political conditions for the development of capitalism, that is, the question of national self-determination. Two points are worth noting here. First, the 'national state' and the 'multi-national state' (i.e. 'empire') are opposed, the former being the 'norm' of capitalist development, the latter forming its antithesis. Secondly, national self-determination is 'political self-determination,' and under the conditions of Russia and China, the necessary form of 'political self-determination' was to use socialist methods to form the political conditions for capitalist development, i.e. the political structures of the nation-state: '[C]apitalism, having awakened Asia, has called forth national movements everywhere in that continent, too; [. . .] the tendency of these movements is towards the creation of national states in Asia; [. . .] it is such states that ensure the best conditions for the development of capitalism.' Under the particular conditions of 'Asia,' only peasant-led agrarian revolution and socialist state-building could create the preconditions for capitalist development, so all reform programs opposed to peasant liberation and redistribution of land must be rejected.

There is no need to exaggerate the influence of the 1911 Revolution in China on Lenin or on the Russian Revolution. In contrast, the October Revolution in 1917 arose against the background of European wars and influenced the Chinese Revolution profoundly in more visible ways. Lenin paid special attention to the 1911 Revolution in the context of his prolonged reflection on the problems of state, socialist movement, and people's democratic dictatorship. Yet two facts are seldom remembered. First, the October Revolution took place after China's Republican Revolution of 1911. The method of socialist construction after the October Revolution can, to a great extent, be regarded as a response to the revolutionary situation in Asia. Lenin's theory of national self-determination and his interpretation of the significance of revolution in backwards countries in the era of imperialism were both introduced after the Chinese Revolution and were theoretically connected with his analysis of this revolution. Second, the Russian Revolution greatly shocked and profoundly influenced Europe, and it can be regarded as the historical event that separated Russia from Europe. There is no fundamental difference between Lenin's revolutionary assessment and the notions of Asia in the writings of Smith or Hegel. All perceived the history of capitalism as an evolutionary process beginning in the ancient Orient and flowering in modern Europe, and moving through the stages of hunting and agriculture to modern industry and commerce. For Lenin, however, this world-historical framework had two meanings from the start. First, the global expansion of capitalism and the Russian uprising of 1905 that it stimulated were the main forces that would awaken Asia – a land that had been 'standing still for centuries' and had no history (Lenin 1977a). Second, since the Chinese Revolution represented the most advanced power in world history, it clearly indicated the point at which the imperialist world system would be broken through. In the protracted debate between Slavophiles and Westernizers among Russian intellectuals and revolutionaries, Lenin developed a new sort of logic that could be called 'shed Europe and join Asia' (tuo ou ru ya). It was within this logic that the Chinese revolution provided a unique path combining national liberation with socialism. This unique path provided the precondition for a new kind of revolutionary subject: the alliance between workers and peasants with the Chinese peasant as the principal component.

'Great Asianism' in the perspective of social revolution

Lenin's theory gives us a clue for understanding the relation between early modern Chinese nationalism and the question of Asia. It is worth noting that early modern

Japanese Asianism was first directed at 'reviving' or 'stimulating' Asia (xing ya; zhen ya), but soon it became intertwined with expansionist 'continental policy' and the imperialist vision of 'Greater East Asia.' Beneath this shadow, the intellectuals and revolutionaries of China, Korea, and other Asian countries could not express any interest in any variations of such an 'Asianism.'

A few limited writings on this topic by Chinese revolutionaries such as Zhang Taiyan, Li Dazhao, and Sun Yat-sen were produced in a context associated with Japan. For them, the question of Asia was directly related to the Chinese revolution, social movement, and national self-determination. At the end of 1901, Sun Yat-sen published 'On the Theories of Preserving and Partitioning China' (zhi na bao quan fen ge he lun) in the *Toho Society Journal*. Addressing two theories then prevalent in Japan – that of preserving China and that of partitioning China, Sun pointed out that 'From the perspective of state power (guo shi), there is no reason to preserve [China]; from the perspective of national sentiment (min qing), there is no need to partition [China].' There was no reason to 'preserve' China because, from the perspective of revolutionary politics, the Qing state and the people stood opposed to one another, and there was no need to 'partition' China because one of the aims of the revolution was precisely to implement national self-determination (Wang 2004: 65–7).

In 1924, during his last visit to Kobe, upon invitation, Sun again articulated his views on the Asia question in a speech, which was his famous 'Great Asianism' (da ya zhou zhu yi) (Sun 1986a). He delineated two visions of Asia with ambiguity: one was the 'birthplace of the most ancient culture,' but which lacked 'a completely independent state'; the other was the Asia about to be rejuvenated. The former had inherent connections with the 'multinational states' in Lenin's account, but what was the starting point of this Asian rejuvenation or rejuvenated Asia? Sun said that the starting point was Japan, since Japan had abolished a number of unequal treaties and become the first independent state in Asia. In other words, we could say this starting point is the nation-state rather than Japan in particular. He also applauded the Japanese victory in the Russo-Japanese war of 1904:

> The Japanese triumph over Russia was the first triumph of an Asian over a European nation in the past several centuries. [. . .] All Asian nations are exhilarated and start to hold a great hope. [. . .] They therefore hope to defeat Europe and start movements for independence. [. . .] The great hope of national independence in Asia is born.
>
> (Sun 1986a: 402)

Sun called attention to a subtle notion – 'all Asian nations.' This notion is not only Asia as the origin of the most ancient civilization, but also an Asia that contains independent nation-states; it is not only East Asia within the Confucian cultural sphere, but also a multicultural Asia. The unity of Asia was based on the independence of sovereign states. 'All Asian nations' is the outcome of national independence movements and not an awkward imitation of European nation-states. Sun insisted that Asia had its own culture and principles – what he called 'the culture of the kingly way' (wang dao) as opposed to 'the culture of the hegemonic way' (ba dao) of European nation-states. He titled his speech 'Great Asianism' partly because he connected the idea of Asia with the notion of 'the kingly way.' If we compare his speech with the imperialist idea of Asia, it becomes clear that although it preserves its association with Confucian ideas such as 'the kingly way' or 'virtue and morality' (ren yi dao de), Sun's notion of Asia is not an Asia with a core of cultural homogeneity. It is instead an Asia consisting of equal nation-states. According to this notion of Asia, the inherent unity of Asia is not Confucianism or any other homogeneous culture, but a political culture that accommodates different religions, beliefs, nations, and societies. Within this category of political culture, Sun discussed China, Japan, India, Persia, Afghanistan, Arabia, Turkey, Bhutan, and Nepal, and the tributary system of the Chinese empire. Cultural heterogeneity was one of the main characteristics of this idea of Asia, and the category of nation provides the vehicle for the heterogeneity inherent in the idea of Asia. In Sun Yat-sen's usage, cultural heterogeneity provided the historical basis for a nation-state's internal unity and resistance against external interference.[6]

Although Sun's speech mentioned the tributary system of China, he did not intend to affirm the hegemonic or central status of China in relation to surrounding areas. It was used to prove the necessity of the kingly way. In the context of 'Great Asianism', Sun's idea of the 'kingly way' was opposed to the 'hegemonic' logic of colonialism. He believed that the tributary model contained mutual recognition of the multiplicity of culture, ethnicity and religion, in which modern states would be able to discover the cultural resource for surpassing imperialist politics. When he referred to the tribute paid by Naples to China, he did not intend to relive the dream of great China. It was because he firmly believed the tributary relation contained equality based on mutual recognition and mutual respect. Sun supported the national liberation and independence movements in Southeast Asia. His ideas of Asia and national independence deeply influenced this region.[7] He hoped that the pluralism of empire culture could be united with new relations among nation-states so as to obviate the imperialist colonization and the tendency toward high cultural homogenization. His vision of Asia consisted of Japan in the East, Turkey in the West, and nation-states founded on Hinduism, Buddhism, Islam, Confucianism, and other cultures in the inner areas. He said, 'We must insist on Great Asianism and recover the status of Asian nations. If we use only virtue and morality [ren yi dao de] as the basis to unite all nations, all nations of Asia, [when united,] will become powerful' (Sun 1986a: 408–9). According to Sun, the culture of the kingly way defends the oppressed nations, rebels against the hegemonic way, and pursues the equality and liberation of all peoples. Sun discerned the relationship between nationalism and the concept of race, and recognized that nationalism's logic of resistance also contained a logic that could lead to its opposite, that is, the logic of oppression and hegemony. When he appealed to the notion of race to legitimize national independence, therefore, he proposed 'Great Asianism.' Great Asianism, or 'Pan-Asianism' (fan ya zhou zhu yi), is antithetical to the Japanese proposal of 'Greater East Asianism' (da dong ya zhu yi). As a form of multiculturalism, it criticizes the Japanese notion of 'East Asia' (or tōhō) which is highly homogenized. This notion is therefore not only a vision to transcend imperialism through self-determination, but also a multi-nationalism that surpasses the homogeneity of ethnicity, culture, religion and belief.

This self-deconstructive logic is the very basis of the close connection between 'Great Asianism' and internationalism. Sun on the one hand defined Asia from an ethnic perspective, but on the other hand defined the Russian liberation movement as allied with Great Asianism so as to surpass the demarcations of ethinicity. He said:

There is a new state in Europe which is discriminated against by all white Europeans. The European regards it as a venomous snake or a violent beast and dares not approach it. Some people in Asia hold the same view. Which state is this? Russia. Russia is parting ways with the white Europeans. Why does it do so? Because Russia advocates the kingly way and not the hegemonic way; it insists on virtue and morality rather than talking about right and might. It upholds justice to the utmost, and objects to the oppression of the majority by the few. Hence the new culture of Russia is entirely compatible with the old culture of the East. Russia will therefore come to join hands with the East, and part ways with the West.

(Sun 1986a: 409)

Here skin color is not the yardstick but rather the socialist 'new culture' after the 'October Revolution,' with which 'Great Asianism,' as a 'mass liberation movement' of oppressed nations, resonates. If we compare Sun's words with Li Dazhao's 'Great Asianism and New Asianism' and 'New Asianism Revisited,' both published in 1919, we notice that all of these texts describe a vision of Asia centered on national self-determination and internationalism, defined against the background of Japan's 'Twenty-one Demands' to China, and catalyzed by Russia's October Revolution. Li Dazhao argues that Japanese 'Great Asianism' is really a 'Great Japanism' similar to the USA's Monroe Doctrine. Li regards the 'Great Asianism' of Japan as a 'Great Japanism' carried out as a form of 'Asian Monroe Doctrine'. Its substance is 'not peace, but invasion; not national self-determination, but imperialist annexation of weaker nations; not Asian democracy, but Japanese militarism; not organization befitting the world's organization, but organization deleterious to the world's organization' (Li 1919/1999a). His 'New Asianism' involved two points: 'One is that, before Japan's Great Asian-ism has [been] destroyed, we weaker Asian nations should unite to destroy this Great Asianism; the other is that, after Japan's Great Asianism has [been] destroyed, the Asian masses as a whole should unite and join the organization of the world – [only] then will it be possible to join the organization of the world' (Li 1919/1999b). What they valued was not alliance among states but rather an alliance among 'the masses as a whole' (quan ti min zhong), and regional or world organization must be a 'great alliance of the masses' premised on social revolution and social movements.

The understandings of 'Asia' by Lenin, Sun Yat-sen, and Li Dazhao were closely related to their understandings of the task and direction of China's revolution. As for Lenin's Asia, we can clearly see a synthesis between revolutionary logic and the special definition of Asia in Hegel's conception of world history (a medieval, barbarous, ahistorical Asia). This Hegelian + revolutionary conception of Asia not only includes ancient (feudal), medieval (capitalist), and modern (socialist) modes of historical development; it also stresses the unique position defined for 'Asia' (especially Russia and China) in the age of world capitalism and imperialism, emphasizing the unique path of capitalist development within a society with a peasant economy as its main component. The state question is addressed in a double sense: on the one hand, national self-determination is sought within an imperialist international order; on the other hand, the state and its violence must be directed toward peasant interests and capitalist development. These two aspects together comprise a revolutionary perspective on Asia's social characteristics. In this perspective, what makes Asia Asia is not any cultural essence abstracted from Confucianism or any other type of civilization, but rather the special position of Asian countries in the capitalist world-system. This special position is not produced by a structural narrative of world capitalism, but by a dynamic analysis of the class composition and historical traditions internal to Asian society.

It is for this reason that there are extreme differences between the 'Asia' defined by social revolutionary perspectives, on the one hand, and by the various culturalisms, statisms, and theories of civilization that emerged from early modern history. The former focuses on investigating social forces and their relations. The question pursued by social revolutionaries is: taking agrarian relations as the center, what kind of relations exist between the peasantry, the gentry, the emerging bourgeoisie, warlords, and urban workers? Just as Mao Zedong demonstrated in his 'Report on an Investigation of the Peasant Movement in Hunan' and 'Analysis of the Classes in Chinese Society,' these analyses of class composition are not structural, but rather political analyses made from the perspective of social revolution and social movements. These participants in revolutionary movements are not seeking the usual ownership ratios of determinate social groups, but rather the attitude and potential of various groups regarding social revolution and social movements. So this sort of 'class analysis' is really more of a dynamic political analysis within the framework of class analysis. Political analysis is characterized by attention to the agency of subjects. Ignoring this, it is impossible to understand why, in the class transformations of early modern China, members from the middle and upper social strata could become the main forces of revolutionary movements, or why intellectuals from imperialist countries could become steadfast friends and comrades of the oppressed nations. If we analyze 'Asia' from this kind of social revolutionary perspective, those generalized and static descriptions of 'Asia' or 'Tōyō' lose their validity, because the perspective of 'political analysis' requires a dynamic analysis of international relations and relations internal to different societies. From the perspective of social revolution it asks: in this historical movement, who are our enemies, and who are our friends? And this question of friendship or enmity pertains to relations both among and internal to nations.

According to Machiavelli's ancient explanation, 'politics' is related to an active subjectivity (neng dong de zhu ti xing) or a subjective agency (zhu ti de neng dong xing). A political perspective requires both the placement of conscious subjects within this perspective and the discernment of various active subjects – discernment of friends and enemies, and assessment of the direction of social movements. A 'political perspective' is always an 'internal' perspective, a perspective that places oneself in dynamic relations of friend and enemy, a perspective that puts the political actions of thinkers or revolutionaries into intimate relations with the cognition (ren shi) of Asia, China, Japan, and Russia. The strongest part of this perspective is that it can overcome the framework of statism and international relations among nation-states by discerning different political forces within and among societies. In this perspective, questions of opposition or alliance are founded not on stable frameworks of relations among states or nations, but on forces internal to each society and their possible dynamic relations. In order to illustrate the characteristics of this kind of political perspective or analysis, we may contrast it with the notion of 'state rationality' (perhaps including its opposite, 'state irrationality') that Maruyama Masao used to discuss Fukuzawa Yukichi. According to Maruyama, one of Fukuzawa's contributions to the history of thought was that he articulated a 'state rationality' appropriate to the needs of his day. From the perspective of this rationality, modern Japan's exclusionism and expansionism can be seen as results of lacking or betraying this state rationality. In other words, for Fukuzawa no politics is more important than the establishment of 'state rationality' (Maruyama 1997). Carl Schmitt opened his now widely quoted *The Concept of the Political* with the words 'The concept of the state presupposes the concept of the political.' '"[P]olitical" is usually juxtaposed to "state," or at least brought in relation to it,' but 'equating the state with the political' cannot represent the true form of the political: 'The equation state = political becomes erroneous and deceptive at exactly the moment when the state and society penetrate each other' (Schmitt 1996: 19, 20, 22). His purpose was to illustrate that this situation 'must necessarily occur in a democratically organized unit.' My purpose here in differentiating the political and the state is not to delineate the characteristics of a 'democratically organized unit,' but to understand political practice during the era of the Russian and Chinese revolutions. In the context of social revolution, 'the political' exists among various active subjects and in the self-conscious will of classes, class fractions, and political parties. These forces attempt to influence, dominate, transform, or control state power, but the state does not have an absolute capacity to encapsulate 'the political' within its 'structural-functional' operations. From this perspective, the equation state = political (i.e. active subjects having already become 'structural-functional' factors of state power) describes not the normal situation but rather the result of a process of depoliticization.

In contrast to the analytical perspective of 'state rationality,' 'political cognition' during a period of social revolution is not the mode of action of political subjects (e.g. states) in a normative sense, but rather the reality and direction of carrying out a historical movement from the perspective of 'active political subjects and their mutual movement.' This requires the cognizant (ren shi zhe) to transform themselves into 'active subjects,' that is, to place themselves or the interests they represent within a field of political analysis, giving rise to a political summons (zhao huan). Lenin perceived in Sun Yat-sen's program a link between the Chinese revolution and 'purely Russian questions,' so he proposed a program of national self-determination, launching an inquiry into on whom revolutionary forces must rely, whom they must oppose, and which kind of state must but established in order for capitalism to develop in 'Asia.' The political decision to combine socialism with the state was the product of this political analysis. Similarly, Japanese intellectuals such as Miyazaki Toten and Kita Ikki, based on their cognizance that China's independence and liberation was a necessary step in the liberation of Asia, and even in the liberation of humankind, either took part in the practice of China's revolution or undertook direct investigation into the movements of Chinese society, and in this way they produced profound political analyses and energies. After the 1911 Revolution, 'What Kita Ikki saw was the wretched obeisance to Great Britain in Japan's foreign policy.' His analysis of the 'theory of preserving China' (zhi na bao quan lun) was truly political: if Japan entered the group of six lending countries, 'learning from the European countries' [methods] of economic partitioning,' would that not be 'to play the running dog, [helping to] partition [China] in the name of preserving [China]'? If one really wanted to 'preserve' China, one must work towards China's independence and national awakening, and that required drawing clear lines between traitorous warlords and the 'emerging revolutionary classes.' The lending of money to warlords in the name of 'preserving China' in fact demonstrated the relationship between state politics and the expansive aspirations of Japanese plutocrats (Nomura 1999: 32–7). Kita supported and participated in Sun Yat-sen's revolution, but he sharply criticized Sun's acceptance of loans from Japanese plutocrats and his excessive reliance on foreign aid, saying that Sun failed to discriminate between 'war and revolution' (Wang 2004: 174–5). Here the ideal of 'liberating Asia' (Sun's 'Great Asianism') and the problems of 'Chinese revolution' and 'remaking Japan' generated intimate ties, and in this political perspective, not only did the abstractness of the idea of 'Asia' disappear, but also China and Japan were no longer monolithic, unanalyzable concepts.

Another example is Yoshino's June 1919 article published in the *Chūō kōron* 'Do Not Vituperate the Activities of Beijing Student Groups,' where he cut through the superficial appearance of the 'pro-Japan faction' (Cao Rulin, Zhang Zongxiang *et al.*) and the 'anti-Japanese voices' of the student movement, proposing that: 'If we want to get rid of the jinx of anti-Japanese [sentiment], the way is not to fund unrest among the people by supporting messieurs Cao and Zhang, but to [address] our own government's policy of supporting [Chinese] warlords and plutocrats' (Nomura 1999: 68–9). As I see it, this perspective is a 'political perspective.' During the second year of the War of Resistance against Japan, when the Nanjing government was forced to move to Chongqing, Ozaki Hotsumi perceived the deepening of the Communist Party's influence and the weakening of the influence of the Zhejiang plutocrats, and he concluded that: 'This has accelerated the desire for national liberation, and the national liberation movement has already become a force that is difficult for the Republican Government to control'; 'China's "reddening" is determined by China's particular complexities and its complex content; I think it should be understood as something quite different from the situation in Russia' (Nomura 1999: 176, 184). As I see it, this interpretation is a 'political interpretation.' After the Marco Polo Bridge Incident, Tachibana Shiraki questioned his own cognition of China, saying: 'My vision has been fixed on China's objective aspects in an effort scientifically to grasp its various conditions, but my consideration of the crucial subjective conditions has been too shallow. How could this relation be established under these conditions? I must begin anew' (Nomura 1999: 206). As I see it, this way of cognizing China through going back to 'subjective conditions' is also a 'political mode of cognition.'

In terms of the history of thought, these cognitions of China or conceptions of Asia eventually strayed from their initial course in various ways and to various degrees. This was mainly because, in the face of powerful state politics, they could not fully implement these modes of analysis. That is, in the face of 'the state,' the 'active subject,' the heart of the political perspective, disappeared. This tragedy reminds me of a thesis proposed by a European historian: if we want to determine a central theme of world history since the nineteenth century, that theme would have to be the nation-state. While reading Professor Namura's research on the thought and activities of Miyazaki Toten, I noticed that his analysis began with 'Miyazaki's two major regrets': 'First, why did he take part in this revolution as a Japanese person and not as a Chinese person?' And 'Second, before devoting his life to the Chinese revolution, why did he not commit himself to bettering Japan?' Namura then makes an insightful analysis: 'We can say that these two questions of Miyazaki's regret were deeply influenced by the political situation during the Meiji and Taisho periods. [. . .] [T]he basic source of this regret was the tragic sense of being "torn in two" by the relations between the countries' (Nomura 1999: 117). After quoting Miyazaki's words in honor of the Japanese emperor and state, Namura comments: 'As a man of the Meiji era, Miyazaki never managed to break free from the shackles of this curse: the state's emperor system [tian huang zhi guo jia]' (Nomura 1999: 165). Kita Ikki went much further than Miyazaki: on the one hand he regarded Japan's internal revolutionary transformation as a precondition to the liberation of Asia, but, on the other, he also claimed that 'Our seven hundred million compatriots in China and India could not stand up on their own without our support. [. . .] While the authorities of Euro-American revolutionary theory all take this superficial philosophical position and cannot grasp the "gospel of the sword," the farseeing Greece of Asian civilization has already constructed its own spirit. [. . .] People who eschew armed states have the views of children' (Kita n.d.: 292). Here, rather than carrying his political ideas about 'remaking Japan' over into Sino-Japanese relations during the imperialist period, Kita instead uncritically imagined Japan as the armed liberator of Asia. As in his 1903 description of the Russo-Japanese War as a 'decisive battle between the Yellow and White races' (Kita n.d.: 78–96), notions such as 'state' and 'race' prevent him from making a political analysis of his own society, so that today it is easy to notice 'an immense inconsistency between his ideal image of Japan as a "proletarian," "revolutionary" state and its colonialist reality' (Wang 2004: 171). When Ozaki Hotsumi trumpeted an 'East Asian Cooperative Community' in the late 1930s against the background of Japanese invasions throughout Asia, or when Tachibana Shiraki applied his analysis of Chinese society to his construction of Manchukuo as a 'decentralized autonomous state,' what we see in their mode of analysis is precisely the equation 'state = political,' and the deviation from the political mode of analysis that they insisted on for a long time. Political analysis halted at the gate of the 'Japan Empire' for different reasons. From a perspective of social revolution, this is 'the statification [guo jia hua] of politics,' a moment at which the shadows of thinkers overlap with that of the very object – the 'Japan Empire' that they had earlier sought to transform.

In the visions of Lenin and Sun Yat-sen, national self-determination is a synthesis of nationalism and socialism. On the one hand, it requires the establishment of nation-states as the predetermined condition for capitalist development. On the other hand, it emphasizes that this process of state-building at the same time transforms traditional imperial relations through social revolution. Socialists believe that weaker nations' demands for self-determination always include demands for a certain degree of democracy, and, moreover, their support for national independence movements is always linked to support for democratic forces. In this synthesis of internationalism and national self-determination, not much room is left for a category like 'Asia' – Asia is only a marginalized part of the capitalist system, a geographical region that can enter the world capitalist system and the struggle against the world capitalist system only through national revolution. If we want to discuss how socialist thought relates to Great Asianism, then [we should recognize that], in the early modern context, they both have historical ties to certain forms of nationalism. The socialist idea of national self-determination is founded on the early modern European binary between 'empire' and 'state.' Those efforts to found 'colonialist autonomous governments' such as Manchukuo under the banner of 'Great Asianism' similarly employ the ideas of sovereignty, independence, and autonomy in order to incorporate Japan's imperialist policies into a narrative of progress. The Japanese intellectuals mentioned above expressed sincere sympathy for China's revolution and profound insight into China's social movements, so why did even someone as insightful as Kita Ikki eventually convert to the very state system he had once criticized, even to the point of supporting policies of imperialist invasion? I cannot discuss these issues in greater detail, but two factors may provide certain explanatory possibilities: first, early modern Japan lacked the conditions for social revolution, so these keen intellectuals could not carry out within Japanese society the political perspective they had developed through their observation of China's revolution. Second, lacking these social conditions, socialist thought could not constitute the forces necessary to overcome nationalism and statism.

With the ebb of Asia's national liberation movements and the Chinese revolution, that political perspective of social revolution and movement, that political mode of analysis capable of linking the social movements of Russia, China, Japan, and other Asian countries, eventually receded from consciousness as well. Since the late 1970s, following the decline of the 1960s social movements and the end of the national liberation movements, we entered an era of 'depoliticization,' a process in which state mechanisms have gradually appropriated active subjectivity or subjective agency into 'state rationality' and the tracks of the global market. As the question of 'Asia' again becomes a concern of many intellectuals, we seem incapable of finding the political mode of analysis through linking different societies that last century's revolutionaries adeptly developed through placing themselves within revolutionary history. In the present era, discussions of the question of Asia center on regional markets and regionalism that is centered on alliances against terrorism and linked by financial security, and so forth.

Asia in narratives of modernity: land and sea, state and network

Today's intellectual discussions of 'Asia' take place under the conditions of neoliberal globalization. Above, I mentioned two discourses of 'empire.' One is the discourse of global empire with the US as its center and global organizations such as the World Bank, the WTO, and the IMF as its mechanism. According to Sebastian Mallaby, the formation of this global empire 'would not amount to an imperial revival. But it would fill the security void that empires left – much as the system of mandates did after World War I ended the Ottoman Empire' (Mallaby 2002: 2). The other is the discourse of regional empires, with the European Union as model, aimed at resisting the monopolized domination of the global empire. UK Prime Minister Blair's foreign policy advisor Robert Cooper calls this vision of empire a 'cooperative empire.' In his classification, the two types of 'postmodern states' are the EU as a 'cooperative empire,' and the International Monetary Fund and World Bank as (agents of) 'voluntary global economic imperialism.' Both types operate according to a set of laws and regulations, as opposed to traditional empires' reliance on centralized power. Cooper's vision of 'cooperative empire' and 'the imperialism of neighbors' were proposed in the shadow of the Balkan and Afghanistan wars. He associated 'humanitarian intervention' with this new kind of imperialism, making 'humanitarianism' the theoretical premise for 'empire' (Cooper 2002a, 2002b).

Against the background of colonialism and imperialist wars, Asian intellectuals have generally taken the East/West binary for granted in their conceptions of history. Early modern ideas of Asia, moreover, often had strong culturalist overtones, inevitably tending toward essentialist perspectives in understanding and constructing 'Asian' identity. Not only are ideas of Asia formed in this way unconvincing in practice; even if successful, do we really want to establish the kind of 'cooperative empire' or 'imperialism of neighbors' that can carry out violent intervention in the name of humanitarianism? How can such a politically, economically, and culturally complex Asian society form a 'linking mechanism' (lian dai ji zhi) to provide a form of regional organization different from both the early modern nationalist state model and the two 'imperial' models described above? Having experienced both the cruel history of colonialism and the powerful movements for national liberation, can we find a flexible kind of mechanism that can avoid the traps of both 'imperial' and statist models?

Let us begin our search with the various historical narratives of an 'East Asian world.' The construction of such a world as a relatively self-sufficient 'cultural sphere' (wen hua quan) is the invention of early modern Japanese thought, but there are different ways in which this world has been sketched. Nishijima Sadao described 'the East Asian world' as a self-contained cultural sphere: geographically, China formed a center surrounded by Korea, Japan, Vietnam, and the area between the Mongolian and the Tibetan plateaus. Culturally, it was characterized by the Chinese writing system, Confucianism, Buddhism, and a system of laws and decrees (Nishijima 1993: 89). The effort to establish a connection between geographic region and culture aimed to construct East Asia as an organic whole, but how did this idea of 'Asian Organism' come into being? According to Maeda Naonori, the traditional view of Japanese scholars did not include Japan in the East Asian world:

> It is generally believed that before modern times, before the history of different regions in the world attained commonality, China was a world, and India was yet another world. From the perspective of cultural history, the world of China can be regarded as the world of East Asia, including Manchuria, Korea, Annam, etc. This is what people used to believe. Although we considered the possibility, we were hesitant to include Japan in this world. But this is only a question of cultural history. We know almost nothing about whether the inner development of Korean or Manchurian societies, not to mention Japan, were connected or parallel to China. We know that in the European world, for instance, the developments of British society were parallel to and interrelated with those of the European continent. But whether a similar phenomenon existed in East Asia, especially between Japan and China, was still not clear until modern times. Moreover, the question itself has not yet been taken seriously. The received idea has been that the development of Japan's social structure, from ancient times to the medieval and modern periods, has been completely unrelated to those on the continent.
>
> (Maeda 1993: 135)

The view that set Japan apart from Asia was closely associated with the unique historical circumstances before Japan opened its ports and with the notion of Japan's particularity that arose after the ports were opened. Connection and distinction, shedding Asia and joining Asia: these antitheses formed the opposing and coordinated characteristics of the early modern Japanese nationalist narrative of Asia.

The impetus for constructing the organic wholeness or self-containment of the East Asian world has always been the idea of a nationalistic, industrial, and capitalistic 'West'. The notion of a 'sphere of East Asian civilization' (dong ya wen ming quan) was an organic constituent of early modern Asian nationalist knowledge, and people sought behind it not only cultural particularity but also an 'inherent' and 'universal' dynamic of nationalism, industrialism, and capitalism appropriate to this cultural particularity. Hence the effort to search for modernity in Asia deconstructed the Hegelian framework of world history, but the inherent standards of the Hegelian world order were not questioned but reproduced: nationalism, capitalism (industry and trade etc.), and theories of state organized a meta-historical narrative about East Asian history.

Miyazaki Ichisada, a representative historian of the Kyoto school, proposed a new definition of 'East Asia' (Tōyō) (Miyazaki 1993). On the one hand, this account no longer regarded the 'East Asian world' as part of the 'Chinese world,' instead locating China and its history within a category of 'East Asian history' (Tōyō shi). On the other hand, through analyzing changes in transportation and commerce during the Sui, Tang, and Five Dynasties period (581–960 CE), Miyazaki argued that 'one could perceive in Song society obviously capitalistic tendencies and phenomena that differed drastically from those of medieval society.' From this basis he developed a set of narratives about an East Asian modernity comparable to Western modernity (Miyazaki 1993: 168). Miyazaki wove together the history of various regions through a notion of 'communication and transportation' (jiao tong), and from this perspective he elaborated on 'Song Dynasty capitalism,' 'East Asian early modernity' (Tōyō de jin shi), and 'nationalism' (guo min zhu yi). In a chapter on 'nationalism in early modern East Asia,' he analyzed ethnic relations from the Qin unification all the way to the Qing Dynasty. He argued that during the Song Dynasty, 'nationalist upsurges' appeared, national contacts went beyond tributary relations, and the Dayue and Dali kingdoms, although nominally tributaries to the Song court, actually were 'independent and unrestrained nation-states' (Miyazaki 1993: 195–211). Although the (Mongolian) Yuan Dynasty interrupted this process, it later stimulated 'Han-Chinese-centered nationalism.' In this sense, the development of nationalism in Asia is treated as parallel to that in the West. Miyazaki boldly employs various European concepts. His understanding of the Tang-Song transition and especially of the Song Dynasty is based on the notions of capitalism and nation-state. Such a search for history in East Asia is inevitably characterized by teleology. We can perceive the European binary of 'state' vs. 'empire' in the link of 'East Asian modernity' and nation-state.

In this regard, Hamashita Takeshi's discussion of the Asian tributary system is a criticism of both 'shedding Asia' and particularism. In the field of economic history, he reconstructs an East Asian world order centered in China and woven together through a tributary system (chao gong ti xi), and in this way he affirms a set of historical ties within Asia (including those between Japan and China). Although he similarly emphasizes the modern forces internal to Asia, unlike Miyazaki, whose notion of 'East Asian early modernity' is based on European-style nationalism, Hamashita founds the inner organicity of Asia on this distinctive tributary network (Hamashita 1999). At the center of his theory are three hypotheses: first, Asia forms an organic whole, not only culturally but also economically and politically. Second, this organism is centered in Chinese civilization and organized according to the trans-state tributary network. Third, coupled with this tributary network is a set of 'center/periphery' relations constituted through practices of tribute and imperial bestowal (ce feng), to be distinguished from European-style relations among 'states.' If Miyazaki's account is grounded in Eurocentric assumptions, then Hamashita deconstructs the link between the nation-state and modernity, constructing an alternative narrative of regional and world history. In his view, moreover, the Asian tributary network was not completely destroyed by Western capitalist expansion; 'Asia as world-system' continues to exist in the early modern age.

Hamashita's account is inspiring. He discovers an inner theme to connect Asian states and uses it as a starting point for envisioning the contemporary world. He also uses a 'peripheral' perspective to expose the continent-centrism and the principles of dynastic orthodoxy in official Chinese historiography. This is a forceful criticism of advocates of particuliarism who refuse to recognize the historical relations between Japan and the rest of Asia. For Chinese scholars who are accustomed to considering China from within, this theory provides a perspective for viewing China from its periphery. This effort to search for East Asian modernity based on a tributary imperial system also challenges the Eurocentric binaries of empire vs. state and tribute vs. commerce.

The so-called 'unity of East Asia' is a construct premised on the category of Asia, while Hamashita's study (in order to define the 'unity of Asia') stresses commercial aspects of the tributary system, especially the maritime commercial relations which overlapped with relations internal to Asia. Here I attempt to supplement, balance, and develop Hamashita's work. First, the practice of tribute was a historical result of the interaction among agents participating in this system and not a self-contained or complete structure. In this sense, the tributary system was a constantly shifting process of how multiple centers of power gave birth to each other. Whenever a new power took shape or entered the picture, the internal power relations would change. Hamashita defined six types of tributary relations: (1) tribute from local chiefs (tu si) and local officials (tu guan); (2) tribute under relations of vassalage (ji mi); (3) tributary states with the closest ties (to the imperial court); (4) tributary states with two-way relations (with the imperial court); (5) tributary states on the outer edge of the periphery; (6) states in primarily commercial (hu shi) relations (with the imperial court) (Hamashita 1999: 35–6). But this narrative relies excessively on the static 'center/periphery' framework, so it cannot account for the constant changes in the historical connotations of tributary practices. From a strictly economic perspective, Miyazaki had already divided Chinese history into different periods based on major routes of transportation and communication: from ancient to medieval times was the inland-centered period; from the Song to the Qing Dynasty was the Grand Canal-centered period; and with the late Qing began the coast-centered period – a new circumstance that took place under European influence (Miyazaki 1993: 168, 170). If center/periphery relations within China were constantly shifting, so was the tributary system. For example, the tributary relations that the Song court established under conditions of war with northern peoples could not at all be described by Hamashita's framework of 'center/periphery' relations, nor could the Qing court's relations with Russia since the seventeenth century.

The instability of center/periphery relations is one of the most important charac-teristics that distinguish the modern capitalist world. The theory of center/periphery relations with China as the center, therefore, cannot entirely explain the changes in power relations within Asia since the nineteenth century. As Hamashita pointed out in an essay written in his early career, the intensification of the Western capitalist powers' financial permeation into Asia and especially China was closely related to the international financial market's expansion following the discovery of gold in the USA and Australia (Hamashita 1995). Financially speaking, the history of the modern Chinese economy can be regarded as the process through which the Chinese economy was woven into the fabric of a unified international accounting structure centered in London. In this sense, the modern age of Asia is the process in which Asia has been gradually incorporated economically into modern world history, an incorporation characterized by financial subordination-domination relations. If we apply the framework of center/periphery to nineteenth- and twentieth-century power relations within Asia, it will inevitably conceal the actually central status in the new world-system of traditionally peripheral categories. For example, if Japan's shedding Asia and modernization (including the first invasion into Taiwan and the first Sino-Japanese war of 1894–5) is explained in the framework of 'shaking off the status of a tributary state' (i.e. the center/periphery framework), great changes in the center/periphery relations that have been taking place since the Opium Wars will be obscured. The binaries of 'center/periphery' and the empire of China vs. the tributary state actually reproduces the binary of empire-state in modern European thoughts. As Maruyama says, European state rationality came into being in the struggle against trans-state authorities such as the Sacred Roman Empire and the Roman pope, and in the struggle against the request for autonomy by medieval social powers such as feudal lords, autonomous cities, and local churches (Maruyama 1997: 160). This framework cannot explain the role of Japan in early modern Asia, or exactly why the periphery (Japan, Korea, Hong Kong, Taiwan, Singapore, etc.) became the center or sub-center of nineteenth- and twentieth-century Asian capitalism, while continental areas such as mainland China, India, and Inner Asia declined and became 'peripheral' or colonized.

Hamashita's innovative research also makes it possible for a regional study that is not centered on states but on networks, but it is exactly in the widened perspective of networks that the excessively static structure of tributary trade or center/periphery relations is challenged. As Hamashita himself has noticed, at the beginning of the nineteenth century, the overseas Chinese private trade network successfully transformed the official tribute system into a private trade system, and this was the result of long-term processes. Po-keung Hui argues:

> When the Europeans arrived in East Asia at the beginning of the sixteenth century, they tried to connect with the official tribute system so as to promote the development of trade. But they realized that they increasingly relied on the extensive overseas Chinese trade networks. Especially since the beginning of the nineteenth century, the official tribute system centered in China was merely a fantasy of the government concerning control that had never been actualized because China was confronted with the growing hegemony and invasion of imperialist powers. To a large degree, therefore, it was not the official tribute system but private overseas Chinese trade networks that integrated the East Asian regions into a single system.[8]

According to Hui, it was not tribute but rather private overseas trade, including smuggling, which constructed a more important connection between the East and Southeast Asian trade networks. Under the conditions of European imperialism in the nineteenth century, the development of the Southeast Asian market was less a result of tributary commerce than a result of breaking out of that system. The important characteristics of the commercial form in Southeast Asia from the eighteenth to the nineteenth century were smuggling, arms trafficking, and European monopolies.[9] Here, the historical development of networks is precisely the result of shifts in the existing relations between center and periphery.

Second, in the vision of 'maritime East Asia' woven together by the tributary network, historical routes of communication and transportation within the Asian continent and their changes over time were reduced to a subordinate and marginal status. If we compare Nishijima's 'East Asian world' with Hamashita's, the latter centered on the east coasts, peninsulars and islands of the Eurasia continent, including Northeast Asia and Southeast Asia, approximately the same as the category of the 'maritime world' in which the contemporary Japanese academia is interested. Hamashita developed his idea of Asia in opposition to Eurocentrism. His description focused on aspects such as commerce and the circulation of silver and stressed the historical communications between China and East and Southeast Asia – i.e. exchanges enabled mainly through marine transportation. This narrative, therefore, responded to the economistic logic and framework of maritime theory in the European narrative of capitalism. In his account, the maritime theory, as a theory of modernity, became increasingly the central methodology to observe the question of Asia, because this theory dealt with politico-economic relations that corresponded with the modern treaty system. Although he used the tribute system as his narrative framework, he specifically pointed out that the basic rules of this world system must be modified. The modification should aim to establish a new East Asian system that is centered on the sea and different from the Western commerce system. For the same reason, this 'historical world with its own inner unity' centered on East and Southeast Asia stressed the importance of culture, political structure, and the sea in the formation of regional relations, especially regional trade relations. But this idea of Asia that emphasizes unity lacks a thorough analysis of continental transportation and communication – between China and Inner, West, and South Asia, and Russia – that dominated the tribute system for many centuries, and it seldom addresses the relation between the formation of maritime trade spheres and continental dynamics. Nor does it provide a sufficient account of the West's role in these processes. The so-called maritime age came into being under conditions of European industrialization, development in maritime military technology, and the formation of the nation-state system in Europe. It belittled the historical connections and social relations within the continent and subordinated it to maritime hegemonies and economic relations connected by maritime passages.

Throughout Chinese history, the relations among the Northwest, the Northeast, and the Central Plains have been the fundamental force driving the changes in China's social system, population, and mode of production. Even in the so-called maritime age, inland transportation routes and relations played a vital role. Chen Yinke has traced the origins of Sui and Tang policies and regulations to, first, the Northern Wei Dynasty, and, second, the Northern Qi, Liang, and Chen dynasties, and third, the Western Wei and Northern Zhou dynasties. He points out: 'Sui and Tang artifacts and systems spread widely to the desert in the North, Hanoi in the South, Japan in the East, and Inner Asia in the West, but monographs on their origins and transformations are rare; it is a regrettable lacuna in Chinese historiography' (Chen 1992: 515). His studies on Tang political and military history argue that Chinese policies, population, and culture since the Sui and Tang dynasties were already the product of multiple Eurasian cultures, policies, and regulations. Owen Lattimore similarly describes an 'Asian continent' with the Great Wall as its center, which transcended political and ethnic borders. This idea of a 'center' meant that on both sides of the Great Wall were two parallel social formations, agricultural and pastoral. These two social formations maintained longlasting contacts along the Great Wall, and their interaction deeply affected both societies. Lattimore's alternative account of a 'center' counterbalances the previous insistence on the central status of agriculture in the South and draws our attention to how China's frontiers and frontier peoples took shape. The Central Plains pastoral society and the southern agricultural society developed at the same time, and the area in between developed a 'frontier condition' (Lattimore 1962: 55). The Great Wall-centered, Yellow River-centered, and Grand Canal-centered narratives of Chinese history contrast sharply with one another. The shifting of the center of historical narratives was related to the shifting of the 'heartland' from dynasty to dynasty. Moreover, it was also related to how one observes historical change, and especially the forces driving historical change. According to Lattimore, the internal route of expansion in Chinese history was originally from North to South. The pressures of European colonialism and industrialization forced the expansion to move from southern to northern China. He therefore uses the terms pre- and post-West to describe the transformation of internal relations on the Asian continent.

The differentiation between pre- and post-West, however, also becomes too simplistic when we study inland movements. After the Manchu controlled the central plain, large scale migration of population, economy, commerce and other cultural relations from the central plain to the north became an important phenomenon. In the seventeenth and eighteenth centuries, this South-to-North movement originated mainly in the internal movements of the Qing Empire, and had little to do with the Western powers. In 1857, when Marx considered Chinese attitudes toward maritime hegemonies, he noticed that while Western states used military force to expand their trade with China, Russia spent less but gained more than any of the belligerent states (Marx 1857). Although Russia had no maritime trade with China, it enjoyed an overland trade centered in Kiakhta. The value of goods bought and sold in 1852 amounted to US$150 million, and, since the goods were relatively inexpensive, the quantity of goods involved was striking. Because of this increase in trade, Kiakhta grew up from an ordinary fortress and marketplace into a major city, and direct and regular postal communication was established between it and Beijing, which is about 900 miles away. Marx and Engels both pointed out how the Sino-British and Sino-French coastal conflicts created the possibility for Russia to obtain vast territory and great profit in the inland Amur River basin (Marx 1980a, 1980b; Engels 1980). Engels predicted that Russia was 'fast coming to be the first Asiatic Power, and putting England into the shade very rapidly on that continent,' and he criticized British media and the British Ministry for suppressing information on how Russia gained a greater profit in China, Afghanistan, and other Inner Asian regions when they publicized the Anglo-Chinese treaty (Engels 1980: 82–6). If we understand the 1905 Russo-Japanese War's impact on the course of Japanese modernization, or China's later alliance and subsequent split with the Soviet Union, within a dialectic of continental and maritime relations, then it becomes clear that continental relations between Asia and Europe have indeed played a large role in shaping East Asian modernity.

Theories of Asia centered on the tributary system tend to emphasize the aspect of economic relations (especially maritime commercial networks) at the expense of events such as wars and revolutions. Sun Yat-sen's description of overseas Chinese as 'mothers of the Chinese revolution' illustrates the influence of overseas networks (especially in Japan and Southeast Asia) on China's modern revolutionary history, networks which overlapped with tributary routes. After the failure of the Hundred Days' Reform in 1898, Japan became not only a refuge for exiled reformers and the first generation of Chinese revolutionaries, but also the cradle of the Chinese Enlightenment. It was at this time that a number of Japanese intellectuals became direct participants in China's revolutionary and reform movements. Chinese communities in Southeast Asian countries such as Vietnam, Malaya, the Philippines, and Myanmar not only provided material resources for China's reform and revolution; they also injected a special vitality into the wave of nationalism that eventually swept the entire region, forming a transnational network of social movements. Following the 1911 Revolution, this revolutionary movement based in overseas coastal areas took root on the Chinese mainland and provided the initial impetus for the political revolution, the agrarian revolution, and the military struggles that soon developed. The interaction between coastal networks and inland areas thus manifested itself during the revolution era.

Similarly, the ties and differences between land and sea also influenced the characteristics of Asian wars to a certain extent. In an appendix to *The Concept of the Political* entitled 'Theory of the Partisan,' Carl Schmitt puts the guerrilla or 'partisan' of 'irregular warfare' at the center of political thought, regarding the partisan as an 'irregular force' in contrast with 'this regularity of the state and the military':

> There is no place in the classical martial law of the existing European international law for the partisan, in the modern sense of the word. He is either [. . .] a sort of light, especially mobile, but regular troop; or he represents an especially abhorrent criminal, who stands outside the law [. . .] The partisan is [. . .] different not only from the pirate, but also from the corsair in the way that land and sea are distinguished as (two different) elemental spaces of human activity and martial engagement between peoples. Land and sea have developed not only different vehicles of warfare, and not only distinctive theaters of war, but they have also developed separate concepts of war, peace, and spoils. The partisan will present a specifically terrestrial type of active fighter for at least as long as anticolonial wars are possible on our planet.
>
> (Schmitt 2005: 3, 6, 13–14)

'Through comparison with typical figures of maritime law and a discussion of the aspect of space', Schmitt further elaborated on the 'tellurian character of the partisan'. Beginning with the Opium Wars, the external pressures facing China switched from inland to coastal areas, and the traditional forms of warfare likewise changed. During the First Sino-Japanese War (1894), the Japanese navy thoroughly destroyed the Qing's Northern Navy and took control of the East Asian waters. But from the invasion of northeastern China in 1931 to the full-scale outbreak of the War of Resistance in 1937, the mighty Japanese army nevertheless failed to subjugate poor and militarily-backwards China. Of course the war's outcome was determined by many complex political, economic, and military factors, so it is hard to analyze from a single perspective, but the failure of Japan's military victories on regular battlefields to secure a final victory in the war is clearly related to the special form of this war, that is, the interweaving of regular and partisan warfare, and of inter-state and 'people's war.' Acting in concert with the regular army were the flexible, irregular partisan forces dependent upon the character of the land and the general population's support, political consciousness, and clear cognition of friend and enemy.

In this ethnically complex, geographically vast inland region mainly populated by peasants, China's revolutionaries synthesized military and revolutionary mobilization, using unique military forms to break through the concepts of regular warfare (war among states) as defined by European international law, and laying a foundation for postwar political and military forms completely different from those prior to the war. China's revolution unfolded throughout China's inland mountain ranges, waterways, jungles, and prairies, and through the intensification of agrarian revolution, modern China's political forces, especially the revolutionary party, turned several generations of peasants and their descendants into revolutionary and military subjects. Through military experience and revolutionary mobilization, that agrarian society which, from a European perspective, was the symbol of backwardness and conservativism, could become an active political force, and the forging of revolutionary state-building, industrial planning, urban development, and new urban–rural relations was intimately linked to the emergence of this new political subject. If reviewed from the perspective of Mao Zedong's discussions of guerrilla strategy during the War of Resistance, his theory of protracted war and the question of the role of peasants and villages in warfare, and his concept of New Democracy, perhaps we can develop a new understanding of China's revolution.

From each of these perspectives, how to relate Asia's continental and maritime eras, how to relate Asia's organic wholeness with its internal cultural and historical complexity: these questions await further research. Simple maritime theory cannot explain the profound polarization currently underway between China's coastal and interior (especially northwestern) areas, and the coastal economy's domination over the inland economy. Nor can it explain the forces driving China's (and Russia's) modern revolution centered on agrarian revolution, or the special characteristics of the Second Sino-Japanese War. More importantly, the tributary system is not a simple economic relation; it encompasses ritual and political relations among various social groups with differing cultures and beliefs. In the course of long historical processes, networks formed through tribute, commerce, and migration still provide the means for revolutions, wars, and other social interactions. In this sense, the complex meanings and uses of tributary relations, and especially their points of overlap or conflict with modern capitalist relations, is a topic worth further exploration.

Third, the theory of the tributary system is defined in opposition to European nation-states and their treaty system. It overcame the earlier idea that regarded the nation-state as the only force capable of propelling modernization, but the dichotomy between tributary and treaty systems is also derived from that between empire and state. As early as the seventeenth century, the Qing state was already using the treaty form to define borders in certain frontier regions (such as the Sino-Russian border), to create regular frontier patrols, to determine custom-duty rates and trade mechanisms, to exert sovereign rights over residents within its administrative sphere, and to establish tributary and treaty relations with European countries. Hence the Qing was not only an empire of mixed national composition, but also a political entity with advanced state systems as well. Its well developed tributary network included treaty relations. If we interpret Qing society through the simple opposition between state and empire, treaty and tribute, we will not be able to see how empire construction and state construction were two overlapping processes, and we will not be able to understand the basic characteristics of modern Chinese nationalism. It is because of the composite relations between the tributary and state systems that we cannot describe the tributary system simply as a hierarchical relation between center and periphery.[10] Here the question whether East Asia or China is state-centered or tributary is not significant. The pivotal question is to clarify various notions and types of political body, and various notions of state, so as not to obscure the notion of state with the history of modern capitalism and nation-state. Research on the tribute system and network emphasize economy and commerce, which is an alternative type of study on the form of capitalism. But it should not be ignored that the tribute system is linked with ritual, politics, culture, internal and external relations and economics, embodying a peculiar political culture.

If the tributary system is a product of a different type of state than modern European sovereign states, then we need to reinterpret the relation between tribute and states by comparing different types of both categories. In Chinese history, tributary and treaty relations are not completely opposite categories. For example, when the Qing government began to develop commercial, political, and military relations with European countries, tributary relations were a form of inter-state relations. The Qing court's relations with countries such as Russia, Portugal, Spain, Holland, and Great Britain were called tributary relations, but they were also in fact diplomatic and treaty relations. Hamashita, when classifying types of tribute, points out that one he calls 'mutual market' (hu shi) relations is very similar to what would later be called 'diplomatic' or 'foreign trade' relations. Within the tributary sphere, there also existed a relation involving tribute and imperial gift-returning (hui ci). Sometimes the two gifts were of equal value, and sometime the return gift was worth more than the tribute. Tributary relations, therefore, involved both economic and ritual forms of interaction. The ritual inequality and actual reciprocity, the ritual character of the tributary relation and the actual substance of tributary trade, overlapped. If it is an inherent characteristic of the tributary practice that state and tributary relations overlapped, why not consider European states' domestic and international relations from another perspective, that is, why not regard the treaty system not as a structural form but as a product of historical interactions among various forms and forces? For example, we can ask: was Great Britain's nineteenth-century commercial relationship with India and North America defined by treaty or tributary relations? Was the USA's (or the USSR's) twentieth-century relationship with its 'strategic partners' in the Cold War a relation among sovereign states or between center and periphery, or lord and vassal? During the Opium Wars, [the Qing scholar and official] Wei Yuan already recognized that the main difference between China and Britain in commercial affairs was not a difference between a system based on tribute and a system based on treaties, but rather another kind of difference: tribute was not the mainstay of China's economy, so there was no internal impetus for linking the imperial government and military directly to foreign trade, whereas Britain's domestic economy extensively relied on tributary and commercial relations with its colonies, and this forced the British state to take an active role in supporting overseas commercial activities, including with military force. If, as Wang Gungwu argues, China's overseas commerce was a 'commerce without empire,' then British commerce was the opposite: an organized alliance of military and business under state auspices (Wang 1990). It was only in order to force China to sign unequal treaties that the Western powers recognized the Qing state as a formally equal legal subject, thus applying to a non-European entity the notion of sovereignty previously reserved for international law among Christian or 'civilized' states. If one explains the Qing conflicts with Japan over the Korean peninsular and the First Sino-Japanese War according to a normative framework of either 'tributary' or 'treaty' relations (i.e. sovereignty based on formal equality), then the major changes in Asian power relations during the nineteenth century are obscured. It will thereby lead to the justification of the expansionism of European international law with a universalist 'rationality'. If one bases one's argument on a binary of tribute vs. treaty, or empire vs. state, and then attacks such Eurocentric ideas by inverting the relations between the two terms, the complexity of historical relations within Asia will probably be oversimplified. We need to consider carefully how to define the relationship between Asia's 'center/periphery' mechanisms and Europe's 'state' mechanisms, which have both overlapping and opposed aspects.

The question of Asia's modernity must eventually deal with the relationship between Asia, on the one hand, and European colonialism and modern capitalism, on the other. As early as the 1940s, Miyazaki began to explore the 'beginning of Song capitalism' by studying the history of wide-ranging communication and transportation among various regions. He argued that those 'who regard history since the Song as the growth of modernity have arrived at the time to reflect on Western modern history in light of the developments in early modern East Asian history' (Miyazaki 1993: 240). That his theory of 'East Asian early modernity' overlapped with the Japanese idea of a 'Greater East Asian Sphere' does not obscure Miyazaki's insightful observations. He observed that in a kind of world-historical framework, the digging of the Grand Canal, migration to metropolises, and the circulation of commodities such as spices and tea connected the European and Asian trade networks, and the expansion of the Mongolian Empire promoted artistic and cultural exchange between Europe and Asia, not only changing the internal relations in Chinese and Asian societies, but also connecting Europe and Asia by land and sea. If the political, economic, and cultural features of 'Asian modernity' appeared as early as the tenth to eleventh century, were the historical development of these two worlds parallel or associated? Andre Gunder Frank responded to this question by demonstrating that Asia and Europe had already established important ties by the thirteenth or fourteenth century, and moreover that any discussion of the birth of modernity must begin with an appreciation of a world-system composed of such long-standing relations (Frank 1998).[11] The significance of communication and transportation is not the stiff bundling together of two worlds; it is more like two gears connected with a belt: when one turns, the other must turn as well. So a logical conclusion is that:

> The European Industrial Revolution was definitely not an independent European historical sequence, because it was not only a problem of machinery but also an issue of the whole social structure. For the Industrial Revolution to take place, the prosperity of the bourgeoisie was necessary, and moreover, the capital accumulation from trading with East Asia was indispensable. To make the machines work required not only power but also cotton as raw material. East Asia provided the necessary raw materials and markets. If there had not been interaction with East Asia, the Industrial Revolution might not have taken place.
>
> (Miyazaki 1993: 236–8)

Miyazaki's research mainly focuses on China's internal history; his writings on the interactions between Asia and Europe are thin. Frank's research, on the other hand, is economistic and commerce-centered; he seems to have little to say about historical forces internal to European society and their relation to the birth of capitalism. In their maricentric and structuralist narratives, war, contingent events, and other historical factors are pushed into the background. But these narratives, from different perspectives, do provide important tools to help us re-narrate 'world history.'

Hence, in such an interactive narrative of history, the validity of the idea of Asia diminishes, since it is neither a self-contained entity nor a set of self-contained relations. It is neither the beginning of a linear world history nor its end. This idea of Asia, which is neither starting point nor end, neither self-sufficient subject nor subordinate object, provides an opportunity to reconstruct 'world history.' If we need to rectify mistakes in the theories of Asia, we must re-examine the notion of Europe too. As we correct the errors in the idea of Asia, we must also re-examine the idea of Europe. In Lenin's style, we should ask: where does this advanced Europe come from, after all? What sort of historical relations have resulted in Asia's backwardness? Historical relations internal to societies are also important, but in the long run, how should we appraise the effects of continually extending inter-regional relations on a society's internal situation? If theories of Asia continue to be based on taken-for-granted notions of Europe, and the forces that gave rise to the concept of Europe are not thoroughly re-examined in the context of European historical development, these theories will not be able to overcome their ambiguity.

Conclusion: a problem of 'world history' – Asia, empire, and nation-state

What the accounts of Asia that we have discussed above reveal is not so much Asia's autonomy as the ambiguity and contradictions in the idea of Asia. This idea is at the same time colonialist and anti-colonialist, conservative and revolutionary, nationalist and internationalist, originating in Europe and shaping Europe's image of itself, closely related to visions of both nation-state and empire, a notion of non-European civilization, and a geographic category established through geopolitical relations. We must take seriously the derivativeness, ambiguity, and inconsistency of how the idea of Asia emerged as we explore the political, economic, and cultural independence of Asia. The keys to transcend or overcome such derivativeness, ambiguity, and inconsistency can be discovered only in the specific historical relations that gave rise to them.

First, the idea of Asia was created in close relation to the issues of modernity and capitalism, and the core of the modernity issue was the development of the relationship between nation-state and market. The tension between nationalism and supranationalism is closely related to the dual reliance of capitalist markets on state and inter-state relations. Such discussions often focus on issues such as nation-state and capitalism, the diverse historical relations, policies and governance, customs, and cultural structure of Asian societies nested in the narrative of modernity. Values, policies, and rituals independent of this narrative of modernity have been suppressed or marginalized. One important step in reflecting on European 'world history' is to challenge Eurocentric historical narratives and to redefine these suppressed historical legacies – values, policies, rituals, and economic relations, etc.

Second, at this point, the nation-state is still the main force behind regional relations within Asia. Its main manifestations are that: (1) regional relations are the extension of state relations: whether we are talking about the Asian Forum promoted by Malaysia, or the East Asian Network advocated by South Korea, or regional organizations such as ASEAN or the Shanghai Six, all are inter-state relationships formed to develop economic relations or state security collaboration. (2) The construction of Asian sovereignty has never been complete: the standoffs on the Korean peninsula and the Taiwan Strait and the incomplete sovereignty of postwar Japan all illustrate that the nationalist processes begun in the nineteenth century still play a major role in shaping relations in East Asia. (3) Since the new discourse on Asia is directed at forming protective and constructive regional networks against the domination and turbulence caused by globalization, the question of the state still occupies a central place in the question of Asia. The imagining of Asia often appeals to a sort of ambiguous Asian identity, but if we pursue the preconditions for this idea's system and principles, then the nation-state will emerge as the political structure trying to be overcome. So, however we deal with the legacy of national liberation movements (respect for sovereignty, equality and mutual trust etc.) and traditional regional relations under the present conditions, this is still an important question.

Third, the dominance of the nation-state in Asian imaginaries arose from the binary of empire/nation-state created in modern Europe. The historical implication of this binary is that the nation-state has become the single modern political form and the principal precondition for the development of capitalism. This binary, however, underestimates the diversity of political and economic relations that were summarized as belonging to the category of empire, and underestimated the diversity of internal relations within nation-states. Modern Asian imaginaries are based mainly on inter-state relations, seldom dealing with Asia's complex ethnicity, regions and modes of interaction that are overshadowed by the category of empire – e.g. trans-state tribute system, migration network etc. The question is: as the nation-state has become the dominant political structure, will the traditional experiences of communication, coexistence, and policies and regulations in Asia provide ways and opportunities to overcome the internal and external dilemmas brought about by the nation-state system?

Fourth, the unity of Asia as a category was established in opposition to Europe. It encompasses heterogeneous cultures, religions, and other social elements. Whether we base our judgment on historical traditions or current policies, one does not see the possibility or conditions in Asia for creating a European Union-style super-state. Buddhism, Judaism, Christianity, Hinduism, Islam, Sikhism, Zoroastrianism, Daoism, and Confucianism all originated in this continent we call Asia, on which three-fifths of the world's landmass lie and over half of the world's population live. Any attempt to summarize the characteristics of Asia with one unitary culture will fail. The idea of Confucian Asia cannot fully represent the characteristics of even China alone. Even if the idea of Asia is reduced to the idea of East Asia, its own internal cultural heterogeneity cannot be escaped. New imaginings of Asia must combine cultural and political plurality with regional political and economic structures. A high degree of cultural heterogeneity does not mean that Asia cannot form certain regional structures; it merely reminds us that this kind of structure must have a high degree of flexibility and plurality. So two possible directions for imagining Asia are: (1) glean from the institutional experiences common to Asian cultures in order to develop new models allowing different cultures, religions, and peoples to interact on equal terms within and among states;

and (2) form multilayered, open social organizations and networks linked through regional connections to coordinate economic development, mitigate conflicts of interest, and alleviate the dangers posed by the nation-state system.

Fifth, Asia has longstanding religious, commercial, cultural, military, and political ties to Europe, Africa, and the Americas, so it is inappropriate to describe Asia as something like an enlarged nation-state. The idea of Asia has never been purely self-defined; it is the product of relations among these various regions. The critique of Euro-centrism is not an affirmation of Asiacentrism, but rather a rejection of that sort of egocentric, exclusivist, and expansionist logic of domination. In this sense, revealing the disorder and plurality within the 'new empire,' breaking open the taken-for-granted notion of Europe, is not only one of the preconditions for reconstructing the ideas of Asia and Europe, but also the necessary path for breaking out of the 'new imperial logic.'

Sixth, if the excavation of Asia's cultural potential is also the critique of West-centrism, then the reconstruction of the idea of Asia is also a resistance to the colonial interference and domineering forces dividing Asia. The commonality of Asian imaginaries partly derives from the imaginers' common subordinate status under European colonialism, the Cold War, and the present global order, and the trends of national self-determination, socialist and democratization movements. We will not be able to understand the modern significance of Asia or the origin of disunion and war in Asia if we forget these historical conditions and movements. People regard the fall of the Berlin Wall and the dissolution of the Soviet Union and the Eastern European socialist bloc as the end of the Cold War, but in Asia, the Cold War has to a large extent continued and developed new derivative forms under new historical conditions. Today's discussions of the question of Asia, however, are carried out either by intellectual elites, or by states, and the various social movements in Asia – workers' movements, student movements, peasant movements, women's movements, etc. – are indifferent to this question. This phenomenon contrasts sharply with the powerful wave of Asian national liberation in the twentieth century. If the national liberation and socialist movements of the twentieth century have ended, at least their remains are still an important source for the stimulation of new ways of imagining Asia.

By way of conclusion, let me emphasize again what I have conveyed: the issue of Asia is not simply an issue *in* Asia, but an issue of 'world history.' To reconsider 'Asian history' is to attempt to reconstruct nineteenth-century European 'world history,' and to attempt to break out of the twenty-first-century 'new imperial' order and its logic.

Notes

1 Here a special note on Marx's theory should be added. In the preface to *A Contribution to the Critique of Political Economy*, he described the 'Asiatic, ancient, feudal and modern bourgeois modes of production' as 'epochs marking progress in the economic development of society' (Marx 1977). After 1859, however, this preface was never reprinted during Marx's lifetime. In 1877, Russian scholar Nicolai K. Mikhailovski used Marxism to argue that Russia should establish capitalism in order to abolish feudalism. Marx commented that his work merely attempted to describe the path that Western capitalism developed from within feudalism, and that one should not 'transform his historical sketch of the development of Western European capitalism into historical-philosophical theory of universal development predetermined by fate for all nations, whatever their historic circumstances in which they find themselves may be. [. . .that view] does me at the same time too much honor and too much insult' (Pandover 1979: 321).
2 Translator's paraphrase of Wang's Chinese translation of Anderson's text.

3 Russian intellectuals' ideas of Europe and Asia were obviously influenced by political developments in Western Europe and the Enlightenment conception of history. On the debate between Slavophiles and Westernizers, see Berdyaev (1995: 1–70).

4 I am grateful to Professor Lü Xinyu for introducing me to the Russian debate on agrarian reform and Lenin's theory of 'Prussian' and 'American' paths. My discussion here is largely based on her research (Lü 2004).

5 Translator's paraphrase of Wang's quotation of Lenin's text in Chinese.

6 Sun said in his conversation with journalists in Kobe: 'Unification is the hope of all Chinese citizens. If China is unified, people all over the country can live in ease and comfort, and if not, they will suffer. If the Japanese people cannot do business in China, they will also suffer indirectly. We Chinese believe that the Japanese people sincerely hope China be united. But the possibility of China's unification is not determined by China's domestic affairs. Since the outbreak of the Chinese revolution, violent upheavals have continued to arise for years. China cannot be unified not because of Chinese forces but completely because of foreign forces. Why can't China unify? The foreigners are the sole cause. The reason is that China and foreign countries have signed unequal treaties, and every foreigner uses those treaties to enjoy special privileges in China. Recent people from the West are not only using unequal treaties to enjoy special privileges but also to abuse those treaties in outrageous ways' (Sun 1986b: 373–4). Because Asia had not undergone a complete transition to the nation-state form, 'Great Asianism' could not design a complete apparatus for such regional groups. Sun's idea of Asia is closely related to his respect for the sovereignty of nation-states. His 'Great Asianism' is somewhat analogous to what Coudenhove-Kalergi proposed in *Pan-Europe* (the thesis of a Pan-Europe based on the sovereignty of nation-states), and to the Pan-American organizations that came into existence earlier. This type of regional construction can be regarded as a regional organization within the League of Nations, whose function was to adjudicate over conflicts between regional groups such as 'Pan-Europe,' 'Pan-America,' North America, South America, the UK, the USSR, and the Far East (Gerbet 1989: 34; Coudenhove-Kalergi 1926).

7 For instance, Sun participated in the Philippines Revolution from 1908 to 1900, sending two batches of weapons to Philippines revolutionaries. He believed that the Philippines revolution would help the Chinese revolution to succeed. The revolutions of Indonesia and other Southeast Asian countries were in fact influenced by Sun's nationalism and by the Chinese revolution, but they tended to emphasize the nationalist quality of Sun and the Chinese revolution, while somewhat eliding their socialist characteristics.

8 The quotation is from Po-keung Hui's Ph.D. dissertation. I appreciate Mr Hui's kindness for letting me read and cite his manuscript.

9 Such unofficial connections between China and Southeast Asia, in particular the Southeast Asian Chinese communities formed in smuggling, trading and migration and their peculiar means of connecting with China, provided an overseas base for late Qing Chinese revolutions. The particular connection of contemporary China and overseas Chinese economy is also based on such earlier connections. In other words, the unofficial connection between China and Southeast Asia (nan yang) supplied modern Chinese revolutions with a particular Asian dynamic.

10 For example, the Russian and Qing courts established tributary relations, but, to a certain extent, neither ever placed itself lower than the other to define a hierarchical relation. Each regarded the other as its own tributary state. Tributary ritual practice itself is the product of interaction among complex forces, and hierarchical ritual includes principles of equality and possibilities for various interpretations from different perspectives. Fletcher (1995) addresses this in his research on the history of Chinese imperial relations with Central Asian polities.

11 Frank points out that that European capitalism has steadily grown in the worldwide economy and population since 1400, and that this process is consistent with the East's decline since around 1800. European countries used the silver they acquired from their colonies in the Americas to buy their way into the Asian markets that just happened to be expanding at that time. For Europe, the commercial and political mechanisms for this Asian market were unique and effective for the worldwide economy. Just as Asia entered decline, the Western countries became industrial economies through the mechanisms of import and export. In this sense, modern European capitalism is the result both of changes in productive relations within European societies, and of relations with Asia (Frank 1998).

References

Anderson, Perry (1974) *Lineages of the Absolute State*, London: Verso.

Berdyaev, Nikolai (1995) *Russian Thought* 俄罗斯思想, Lei Yongsheng 雷永生 and Qiu Shoujuan 邱守娟 (trans.), Beijing: Sanlian 三联书店.

Chen, Yinke 陈寅恪 (1992) 'Origins of the Sui-Tang System' '隋唐制度渊源略论稿' *Selected Historical Papers by Chen Yinke* 陈寅恪史学论文选集 Shanghai guji chubanshe 上海古籍出版社.

Cooper, Robert (2002a) 'Why We Still Need Empires', *Guardian Unlimited*, 7 April, http://observer.guardian.co.uk/worldview/story/0,11581,680117,00.html

Cooper, Robert (2002b) 'The New Liberal Imperialism', *Guardian Unlimited*, 7 April, http://observer.guardian.co.uk/worldview/story/0,11581,680095,00.html.

Coudenhove-Kalergi, Richard N. (1926) *Pan-Europe*, New York: Knopf.

Engels, Frederick (1980) 'Russia's Successes in the Far East', *The Collected Works of Karl Marx and Frederick Engels*, Moscow: Progress Publishers, 82–6.

Fletcher, Joseph F. (1995) *Studies on Chinese and Islamic Inner Asia*, Aldershot, Hampshire: Variorum.

Frank, Andre Gunder (1998) *ReOrient: Global Economy in the Asian Age*, Berkeley: University of California Press.

Gellner, Ernest (1983) *Nations and Nationalism*, Oxford: Basil Blackwell.

Gerbet, Pierre (1989) *La construction de l'Europe* 欧洲统一的历史与现实, Beijing: Chinese Academy of Social Sciences Press 中国社会科学出版社.

Habermas, Jürgen (2001) 'Why Europe Needs a Constitution', *New Left Review* 11: 5–26.

Hamashita, Takeshi 浜下武志 (1995) 'Asia and the Formation of the Capitalist Colonial System: British Banking Capital's Permeation into China in the 1850s' '资本主义殖民地体制的形成与亚洲：十九世纪五十年代英国银行资本对华 渗入的过程' *Young Japanese Scholars on Chinese History: Song, Yuan, Ming, and Qing Dynasties Volume* 日本中青年学者论中国史·宋元明清卷 Beijing: Zhonghua shuju 中华书局, 612–50.

Hamashita, Takeshi 浜下武志 (1999) *Early Modern China's International Moment: The Tributary Trade System and the Early Modern Asian Economic Sphere* 近代中国的国际契机：朝贡贸易体系与近代亚洲经济圈, Zhu Yingui 朱荫贵 and Ou Yangfei 欧阳菲 (trans.), Beijing: CASS 中国社会科学出版社.

Hegel, G. W. F. (1899) *The Philosophy of History*, J. Sibree (trans.), New York: Colonial Press.

Jaspers, Karl (1989) *The Origin and Goal of History* 历史的起源与目标, Beijing: Huaxia chubanshe 华夏出版社.

Kita, Ikki 北一辉 (n.d.) *The Collected Works of Kita Ikki* 北一辉著作集 Vol. 2, みすず书房.

Lattimore, Owen (1962) *Inner Asian Frontiers of China*, Boston: Beacon Press.

Lenin, V. I. (1972a) 'The Agrarian Program of Social-Democracy in the First Russian Revolution, 1905–1907,' *Collected Works* Vol. 13, Moscow: Progress Publishers, Marxists Internet Archive, http://marxists.nigilist.ru/archive/lenin/works/1907/agrprogr/index.htm.

Lenin, V. I. (1972b) 'The Right of Nations to Self-Determination,' *Collected Works* Vol. 20, Moscow: Progress Publishers, Marxists Internet Archive, http://www.marxists.org/archive/lenin/works/1914/self-det/ ch01.htm.

Lenin, V. I. (1973) 'The Agrarian Question in Russia Towards the Close of the Nineteenth Century,' *Collected Works* Vol. 15, Moscow: Progress Publishers, Marxists Internet Archive, http://www2.cddc.vt.edu/marxists//archive/lenin/works/1908/agrquest/index.htm.

Lenin, V. I. (1975) 'Democracy and Narodism in China', *Collected Works* Vol. 18, Moscow: Progress Publishers, Marxists Internet Archive, http://marxists.architexturez.net/archive/lenin/works/1912/jul/ 15.htm.

Lenin, V. I. (1977a) 'The Awakening of Asia,' *Collected Works* Vol. 19, Moscow: Progress Publishers, Marxists Internet Archive, http://www.marxists.org.uk/archive/lenin/works/1913/may/07b.htm.

Lenin, V. I. (1977b) 'Backward Europe and Advanced Asia,' *Collected Works* Vol. 19, Moscow: Progress Publishers, Marxists Internet Archive, http://www.marxists.org/archive/lenin/works/1913/may/ 18.htm.

Li, Dazhao 李大钊 (1919/1999a) 'Great Asianism and New Asianism' '大亚细亚主义与新 亚细亚主义' (*The Whole Works of Li Dazhao*), Vol. 3, Shijiazhuang: Hebei Education Publishing House, 354–9.

Li, Dazhao 李大钊 (1919/1999b) 'New Asianism Revisited' '再论新亚细亚主义' (*The Whole Works of Li Dazhao*), Vol. 3, Shijiazhuang: Hebei Education Publishing House, 146–8.

Lü, Xinyu 吕新雨 (2004) 'Agricultural Capitalism and the Modernization Path of the Nation-State' '农业资本主义与民族国家的现代化道路', Horizon 视界 13: 143–215.

Maeda, Naonori 前田直典 (1993) 'The End of Antiquity in East Asia' '古代东亚的终结' *Selected Translations of Japanese Scholars' Research on Chinese History* 日本学者研究中国史论著选译 Vol. 1, Beijing: Zhonghua shuju 中华书局.

Mallaby, Sebastian (2002) 'The Reluctant Imperialist,' *Foreign Affairs* 81(2): 2–7.

Maruyama, Masao 丸山真男 (1997) *The Early Modern Japanese Thinker Fukuzawa Yukichi* 日本近代思想家福泽谕吉, Qu Jianying 区建英 (trans.), Beijing: Shijie zhishi chubanshe 世界知识出版社.

Maruyama, Masao 丸山真男 (1998) *History of Japanese Political Thought* 日本政治思想史, Tokyo University Press, 东京大学出版会.

Marx, Karl (1853) 'Revolution in China and Europe', *New York Daily Tribune*, 14 June, Marxists Internet Archive, http://www.marxists.org/archive/marx/works/1853/06/14.htm.

Marx, Karl (1857) 'Russian Trade with China', *New York Daily Tribune*, 7 April, Marxists Internet Archive, http://www.marxists.org/archive/marx/works/1857/04/07.htm.

Marx, Karl (1977) 'Preface', *A Contribution to the Critique of Political Economy*, Moscow: Progress Publishers, Marxists Internet Archive, http://www.marxists.org/archive/marx/works/1859/critique-pol-econ-omy/preface.htm.

Marx, Karl (1980a) 'The British and Chinese Treaty', *The Collected Works of Karl Marx and Frederick Engels*, Moscow: Progress Publishers, Marxists Internet Archive, http://marxists.org/archive/marx/works/ 1858/10/15.htm.

Marx, Karl (1980b) 'The New Chinese War', *The Collected Works of Karl Marx and Frederick Engels*, Moscow: Progress Publishers, Marxists Internet Archive, http://www.marxists.org/archive/marx/works/1859/ 10/01.htm.

Miyazaki, Ichisada 宫崎市定 (1993) 'East Asian Early Modernity' '东洋的近世', *Selected Translations of Japanese Scholars' Research on Chinese History* 日本学者研究中国史论著选译 Vol. 1, Beijing: Zhonghua shuju 中华书局.

Montesquieu, Baron de, Charles de Secondat (1914) 'Book XIX', *The Spirit of Laws* 论法的精神, Thomas Nugent (trans.), London: Bell and Sons. http://www.constitution.org/cm/sol_19.htm.

Nishijima, Sadao 西嶋定生 (1993) 'The Formation of the East Asian World' '东亚世界的形成', *Selected Translations of Japanese Scholars' Research on Chinese History* 日本学者研究中国史论著选译 Vol. 2, Beijing: Zhonghua shuju 中华书局.

Nishikyo, Bunso 西协文昭 (2002) 'The Relationship between Japan, the US, China, and Russia from the Perspective of China's Twenty-first Century Strategy' '从中国的二十一世纪战略看日美中俄关系', *Seikai Shupo* 世界周报, 12 February.

Nomura, Koichi 野村浩 (1999) *Early Modern Japanese Cognizance of China* 近代日本的中国认识, Zhang Xuefeng 张学锋 (trans.), Beijing: Central Translation Press 中央编译出版社.

Pandover, Saul K. (ed.) (1979) *The Letters of Karl Marx*, Englewood Cliffs, NJ: Prentice-Hall.

Schmitt, Carl (1996) *The Concept of the Political*, George Schwab (trans.), University of Chicago Press.

Schmitt, Carl (2005) 'The Theory of the Partisan', A. C. Goodson (trans.) *The New Centennial Review* 4(3), http://msupress.msu.edu/journals/cr/schmitt.pdf, 1–78.

Smith, Adam (1976) *An Inquiry into the Nature and Causes of the Wealth of Nations.* A. S. Skinner, R. H. Campbell, and W. B. Todd (eds.), London: Oxford University Press.

Sun, Yat-sen 孙中山 (1986a) 'Talk to Organizations Including the Kobe Chamber of Commerce' '对神户商业会议所等团体的演说', *Complete Works* 孙中山全集 Vol. 11, Beijing: Zhonghua shuju 中华书局, 401–9.

Sun, Yat-sen 孙中山 (1986b) 'Conversation with Japanese Journalists in Kobe' '在神户与日本新闻记者的谈话' *Complete Works* 孙中山全集 Vol. 11, Beijing: Zhonghua shuju 中华书局, 373–4.

Takeuchi, Yoshimi 竹内好 (2005) *Overcoming Modernity* 近代的超克 , Sun Ge 孙歌 (ed. and trans.), Beijing: Sanlian shudian 三联书店 .

Wang, Gungwu (1990) 'Merchants without Empire'. In James Tracy (ed.) *The Rise of Merchant Empires*, Cambridge University Press, 400–21.

Wang, Ping 王屏 (2004) *Early Modern Japanese Asianism* 近代日本的亚细亚主义 , Beijing: Shangwu yinshuguan 商务印书馆 .

Special terms

ba dao 霸道

ce feng 册封

chao gong ti xi 朝贡体系

da ya zhou zhu yi 大亚洲主义

da dong ya zhu yi 大东亚主义

differentiating between barbarian and civilized 夷夏之辨

dong ya wen ming quan 东亚文明圈

expelling barbarians 攘夷论

fan ya zhou zhu yi 泛亚洲主义

guo jia hua 国家化

guo min zhu yi 国民主义

guo shi 国势

hui ci 回赐

hu shi 互市

ji mi 羁縻

jiao tong 交通

lian dai ji zhi 连带机制

min qing 民情

nan yang 南洋

neng dong de zhu ti xing 能动的主体性

On Shedding Asia 脱亚论

quan ti min zhong 全体民众

ren shi 认识

ren shi zhe 认识者

ren yi dao de 仁义道德

shed Asia 脱亚

shed Asia and join Europe 脱亚入欧

tian huang zhi guo jia 天皇制国家

Tōyō 东洋

Tōyō de jin shin 东洋的近世

Tōyō shi 东洋史

tu guan 土官

tu si 土司

tuo ou ru ya 脱欧入亚

wang dao 王道

wen hua quan 文化圈

xing ya; zhen ya 兴亚 ; 振亚

zhao huan 召唤

zhi na bao quan lun 支那保全论

zhi na bao quan fen ge he lun 支那保全分割合论

zhu ti de neng dong xing 主体的能动性

Chapter 3

Alternative frames?

Questions for comparative research in the third world

Tejaswini Niranjana

[Edouard] Glissant said to me: 'I have never met you in Barbados, and you have never met me in Martinique. Why?' And I replied, 'Because those journeys were not on our agenda'.
(George Lamming, *Conversations*)

This paper is dedicated to the possibility of creating a critical space for ongoing conversations between intellectuals in different third-world locations. Prompted in part by my own journeys to the West Indies, these reflections will focus on the need for such conversations in our contemporary historical–political context, where the old boundaries are being erased and redrawn, and where the traversing of geographical distance has become, in a sense, both easier and more difficult depending on where one is going.

The project some of my friends and I embarked upon in the late 1980s found immediate resonance in the *Inter-Asia Cultural Studies* field. When I first met Kuan-Hsing Chen and other members of the IACS journal collective, I realized that their questions, although shaped by very different contexts, were uncannily similar to those of myself and my friends in their conceptual and political charge. Therefore, while this paper was not primarily written with this journal's potential audience in mind, there seemed to be a certain appropriateness in placing here the story of 'those journeys' that provided the provocations for my questions. In addition, while the IACS collective has chosen to 'problematize' even as it 'thematizes' the notion of 'Asia', my own earlier project considered, in very similar ways, the question of the 'third world'.[1]

This said, I am not unaware of the many difficulties we may encounter in using the term 'third world' today, when it is no longer charged with the positive task of forging solidarities based on our common experience of colonialism and our common struggles for self-determination and sovereignty. Clearly, our post Cold War present is configured differently from the 1950s and 1960s the age of decolonization and the Non-Aligned Movement when it was possible for the term 'third world' to function as an active political category, even though the term itself was coined in the metropolis after the Second World War to endorse the aid and development programmes that took the place of the old imperialism (Singham and Hune 1986). To invoke the term today in an unproblematic anti-imperialist sense might well put one on the side of the ruling elite in one's own nation-state, an elite which has sought to establish connections with other non-metropolitan elites in order to claim back market-space from the Western transnational corporations that are increasingly infiltrating formerly 'closed' economies.

The usage I propose, as I hope to demonstrate, is meant to suggest the possibilities of different kinds of solidarities and exchange (than those between ruling groups), both for intellectuals as well as others engaged in the critique of dominance within their own societies. For my purposes, I shall use the term 'third world'[2] to refer to a location formed by the 'Bandung project' (the NAM) and its subsequent dismantling. In addition, it will describe a post-colonial political subject formed by Marxisms and nationalisms of various kinds who has had to address her/himself in recent years to questions of caste, race, community and gender that had not (indeed could not have) centrally figured in the decolonization debates, and which today seriously undermine the projects of elite nationalism.

To sketch quickly the immediate historical–political context of the contemporary critique of 'nation' in the case of India, one might recall that, for radical politics in the 1970s and 1980s (especially those of the Marxist–Leninist groups and the women's movement), the nation-state was a significant addressee. While the critique of the nation was central to radical politics, this critique was, in many ways, still part of the political and cultural logic of the national-modern. The secularism and modernity of the politics depended, as we can now see, on the disavowal of caste, religious identity, ethnicity, regional and linguistic difference. Indeed, the energy and reach of feminism or the Marxist–Leninist (M-L) movement seemed to be made possible by these very disavowals. In the 1990s, however, political events such as the 'anti-Mandal agitation', the rise of the Bharatiya Janata Party, the formation of successful regional parties, etc, combined with the drive to privatize and liberalize the Indian economy, have disrupted the narratives of the national-modern, a disruption within which the work of many of us today is situated. For someone like myself, affiliated with the critique of the languages of dominance in her society, a reworking and redeployment of the concept of the 'third world' may suggest yet another entry-point into the problem of the universal-modern.

I would want to argue, then, for a 'reworlding' of the Third World; for the renewal of our attempt to address seriously the dependency (cultural, political, economic) and the 'underdevelopment' of our societies. Given that the nation is still a viable unit for many of us, and given the past use of the term 'third world' by ruling elites to claim victimization and 'aid', I suggest we reconsider the critical-political uses to which the term can be put within each nation-state. By insistently posing the question as to what being 'third world' actually means, and which sections of a society this situation affects most (i.e. for whom is 'underdevelopment' a problem?), we can pressurize our ruling groups to clarify their anti-imperialist rhetoric, and force them into political choices that are more accountable and more representative. The assumption of commonality between rulers and ruled underlying the invocation of 'third world' in international forums must be called to account, and those who govern made to accept the implications of this assumption. Diverse claims to egality and justice could be strengthened by the availability of successful examples from similarly 'third-worlded' regions. What we might want to call for is the deployment of the term 'third world' in expanding the theories of what Partha Chatterjee calls 'democracy' (his term for a political society, the realm in which political claims are articulated today by various (subaltern) groups), a notion which may well be seen as opposed to 'modernity' (a reference to civil society in the third world: a realm that is the exclusive preserve of a few who are eligible to become 'citizens') (Chatterjee 1996).

The renewed attention paid to 'democracy'[3] should lead also to the revitalization, and democratization, of the academic disciplines in which we work. My own discipline, English Studies, has, for some time now, been subject to various strands of political questioning. Looking back on what has come to be called 'the critique of English Studies in India', one observes certain impasses we have come to recognize, in particular around the problem of relevance. The post-Independence generation of English teachers (R. B. Patankar, Ayyappa Panikkar and U. R. Ananthamurthy, to name just a few figures who were teaching in the 1970s) seemed to resolve the question of the relevance of its profession by doing business as usual in the classroom but engaging actively in the intellectual life of its community primarily in Marathi or Malayalam or Kannada. In the 1980s, however, a few teachers in Hyderabad, Delhi and Calcutta for example were beginning to raise different sorts of questions in the English classroom, largely due to their involvement in feminism. In the 1990s, the sharpening of conflicts around issues of nation, community, caste as well as gender, appeared to bring the dissatisfaction and unease of both students and teachers more directly into the classroom, leading to a sustained questioning of received curricula, pedagogical practices and research emphases. Putting it somewhat schematically, we might say that two kinds of work have begun to receive increased attention within English departments: (a) research that seeks to examine Indian languages, literatures and cultural practices, to investigate different kinds of writing (such as writing by women or dalits), or to enlarge the discipline by studying hitherto devalued cultural forms such as popular cinema or children's literature; and (b) research into 'commonwealth' or even third-world cultures and literatures. Although the first kind of agenda does seem to require major reorientations in terms of methodologies and politics, the Indian student/teacher is, all said and done, not particularly handicapped in the study of what is in some sense 'theirs'. (Given the burden of nationalism clearly visible in their curricula that the post-Independence social sciences carry in India, and given the necessarily belated relay of this burden to English Studies, the most predictable response I get when I say I teach Caribbean and African texts is: 'But why not *Indian* texts?' There are several possible answers to this question, which for reasons of space I will not go into here.) The second sort of agenda, that of teaching 'third-world' literature, is handicapped from the start. Scarce institutional resources can barely be stretched to acquire conventional materials required by the discipline, let alone diverted to the purchase of little-known texts from non-metropolitan places. The teacher's woes are magnified in comparison to those of the researcher, whose access to primary and secondary material is severely limited. Since, in spite of these problems, both teaching and research in these areas continue, I would like to argue here for a re-examination of the implicit premises with which we in India set out to teach and study other third-world contexts, and suggest that the current times call for a critical fashioning of new research agendas that might rethink the assumptions even as they emphasize the importance of comparative work.

Indians, Indians everywhere

One of the signs of our times is the spectacular international visibility of the 'Indian' (not just beauty queens but also technologists, scientists, artists, economists, historians, or even literary theorists!). As a self-congratulatory cultural nationalism overcomes us, we seldom stop to think about the formation of this 'Indian' and his/her deployment by the political economy of global capitalism. An economy that we do not need to emphasize is also an economy of academia and the production of knowledge. In the middle of the 20th century, in the age of Nehruvian socialism and the Non-Aligned Movement, and in the aftermath of the worldwide anti-imperialist struggle, Indians claimed solidarity with other formerly colonized peoples and extended various kinds of support to nations less privileged than they were. At the end of the millennium, however, the Indian is not simply another postcolonial but one who would claim to have attained exceptionality, or special status, an achievement that increasingly sets him or her off from other inhabitants of other postcolonies. Earlier axes of identification are transformed and old solidarities are disavowed as the middle-class Indian, even as she vociferously asserts her cultural difference, becomes a relay in the circuits of multinational capital. Although a good deal of recent critical scholarship has focused on the formation of the Indian citizen–subject and analysed the exclusions (of caste, community and gender, for instance) that underwrite it, the subtle changes occurring in the composition of the 'Indian' in transnational spaces have yet to be seriously investigated.

I mention this as a concern arising from my visits to the Caribbean, where I encountered in Jamaica and Trinidad a variety of perceptions regarding 'Indians', perceptions often actively fostered, especially by newly immigrant Indian groups, international organizations such as the Vishwa Hindu Parishad (part of the Sangh Parivar 'family' which includes the Bharatiya Janata Party) and even the Indian nation-state through its High Commissions. Safe in an Indian university, one can simply read the West Indian text as one among other literary artefacts in a continuum of 'newer English' writings; but the Indian researcher working in a Caribbean or African location might well be called upon to make explicit his or her alignments with people of Indian origin who live in those spaces, and explain his or her motives for undertaking comparative research. This demand may be related to the deployment of the notion of 'culture' by Indians from India as well as people of Indian origin in the West Indies, their invocation of an ancient past and a glorious civilization as proof of racial superiority. As a Guyanese friend put it, 'Indians always say culture is what *they* have and the black people don't'.[4] As I have discussed elsewhere, there is a complex politics to the invocation of Indianness in the Caribbean, the details of which often elude the visiting Indian researcher, partly because of his/her own unexamined notions of what 'Indian culture' means (Niranjana 1995).

Teaching the Caribbean

Another profound disorientation I experienced in the Caribbean was that of being in a west that was not the West. Earlier visits outside India had always been to first world spaces, and however different each might have been from the other they were, for me, collectively that which was not Indian, not third world. My encounters with the Caribbean forced me to begin asking other questions about sameness and difference whether in the realm of the political (with regard to notions of nation and region), the economic (questions of 'dependency' and 'development') or the cultural (the tradition versus modernity debate) than those I was accustomed to asking, in relation to India and the West, for example. Not only this, but the encounters had a crucial impact on the questions I addressed in the classroom, the teaching strategies I adopted, and the texts that I taught.[5]

Some years ago, I wrote a paper based on a course I had taught in 1989 on Africa and the Caribbean in which I attempted to explore the implications of teaching non-Western literary texts in Indian Departments of English.[6] For me as well as my students, it had been a first-time exposure to these texts, contexts and histories. Given the dearth of material in our largely Eurocentric libraries, the task of teaching the course was a difficult one, and the engagement with the texts had to be carefully negotiated and re-negotiated at every step.

Clearly our concern was not just one about 'content', using new texts in place of the old. I had suggested in the paper that this kind of easy substitution does not question the need for a canon of great texts, a need which brings with it the imperative to teach the canon in particular ways. My argument was that the demand to be included or accommodated within the existing paradigm did not pose a threat to the paradigm itself, 'since it never questions the criteria which determine exclusion in the first place' (Niranjana 1995: 249). Instead, I had suggested, we must look at *how* we teach/read and examine the expectations we bring to our reading of African and Caribbean texts. I had emphasized the importance of teaching non-metropolitan texts while at the same time resisting 'their incorporation into the canon' by not employing 'customary ways of reading' (Niranjana 1995: 249).

My contention then was that the non-metropolitan texts posed a radical challenge to the discipline and to conventional literary critical approaches, not because of any intrinsic quality they possessed but because embedded as they were in histories similar in some ways to that of India our questions or interests coincided, or came into a conjuncture with, these Caribbean and African works. The risk, of course, was that in stressing similarities we might ignore real differences between specific third-world societies. All the same, our engagement with these texts 'forced our attention away from the aesthetic to the political dimension', 'making us seek assonance and dissonance not in poetic form but in the realm of culture, politics and history' (Niranjana 1995: 250). What we managed to accomplish to a certain extent was 'to place the text more firmly amidst material and social practices instead of in a purely literary tradition' (Niranjana 1995: 250).

Looking back at these concerns, it seems to me that the emphasis was still on the *literary text*, with not enough attention being paid either to the discursive networks from which it had emerged, or to other kinds of cultural artefacts. Perhaps this was a problem, simply, of inadequate information. Perhaps it was also the formulation of the question itself as one of text plus context that was getting in the way, for in this formulation the text can ultimately be detached from the context, which is imaged as simply surrounding it. The question of how to decide the demarcations of a text's boundaries (or of what constituted a 'text' in the first place) was not addressed, except in passing, and consequently one ended up displaying as texts in the classroom precisely those sorts of pieces (a Walcott play, an early Brathwaite poem, a Lamming novel) that the discipline of English Studies would have no difficulty accepting, omitting entirely for example the popular music of the Caribbean, an understanding of which is so central to any attempt at studying West Indian cultural politics.[7]

It seems to me now that the problem was related to our third-worldist attempt to discover cultural artefacts of 'our own', which were, to use Kwame Anthony Appiah's words, deserving of dignity. In addition, concepts like the 'political' and the 'aesthetic' appear in hindsight to have been invoked as though their meanings were 'given', and the distinction between them too quickly posed, although at the time the terms did perhaps serve as a kind of shorthand for entire methodologies. In 1990, the need for disciplinary transformation was certainly being expressed in different quarters, but for me at least the larger significance of this proposed transformation was, as yet, not adequately thought through. It was only after the dramatic national events of late 1990 (I refer in particular to the anti-Mandal agitation of upper-caste youth seeking to deny affirmative action for the lower castes) that the question of what it meant to challenge 'English' in India could be asked in a different form, and the whole terrain on which the dominant 'aesthetic' was constructed could be investigated from a different critical perspective. 'Mandal', as an event, drew the attention of many middle-class left-oriented secular Indians to the 'invisibilizing' of caste in the composition of the citizen–subject. In literary studies, dominated by a modernism congruent in many ways with the secularism of the post-Independence era, it became possible, sometimes by consolidating earlier dalit and feminist initiatives, to confront directly the exclusions that helped form the realm of the aesthetic. Investigating the historical formation of the aesthetic realm, it seems to me, can have important implications for comparative third-world cultural studies, in terms of what we set out to compare and how we go about our task.

The problem of ethnography

One of the tasks of the third-world comparativist is the reconceptualization of third-world spaces that are not her own. Such a task might involve working against the conventional metropolitan characterizations of these spaces, which necessarily presuppose the ethnographic eye, the anthropological attitude.

Although the literary/cultural comparativist often has no formal training in the discipline of anthropology, its modes of argument and its habits of thought are bound to infect any enterprise, like the comparativist's, which undertakes the study of cultural formations other than the one inhabited by the investigator. Predictably, the question of anthropology would never come up when Indian students, for example, study British or American literature. The frameworks and locations that endorse the production of 'modern' knowledge ensure that the question only applies to the study of non-Western or perhaps we should say 'Southern' cultures.[8] However, in the years after decolonization, anthropology has come under a sustained interrogation of its originating impulses and procedures from several different quarters, noteworthy among them for our purposes is the postcolonial-turned-anthropologist (Asad 1973; Scott 1989). Since the project of classical anthropology is to produce a self-understanding of the West through a study of 'other' cultures, the anthropological investigator tends to assume the centrality of Western civilization. Given this location provided by the discipline for the investigator, how can the third-world 'anthropologist' begin to question this centrality?

When such an anthropologist (and clearly I use this description to name a set of subject-positions, no matter what the disciplinary training of the investigator) ventures into another third-world space, the normalization of her/his location and thereby subject-position is opened up to questioning, and the possibility for a critique of the dominant episteme, I would argue, begins to emerge. Such a critique would, of necessity, involve the third-world intellectual – in particular, the Indian intellectual, often by definition upper-class and upper-caste – in an unlearning of his or her privilege (different from the unlearning that takes place in a 'national' context) and a recognition of his or her complicity with the institutions and disciplinary frameworks of metropolitan knowledge production.

By now it is fairly well established that the modern academic disciplines, including of course anthropology, were born simultaneously with a new phase in European expansion, underwriting as well as underwritten by the project of colonial governance (Said 1978; Asad 1973). Whether scholars in the colonial period helped produce stereotypes about the colonized or detailed information about customs and practices, in either case they were constructing a world variously described as non-modern, traditional or primitive, a world thereby rendered amenable to domination by a more 'advanced' civilization. It is the scholar's professed expertise (what James Clifford (1983), has so aptly called 'ethnographic authority'), certified by metropolitan academic institutions, that continues to endorse the 'truth' and factuality of this knowledge.

The ethnographer functions like a *translator* – indeed, the project of anthropology has been seen as that of translating one culture into terms intelligible to another (Asad 1986; Niranjana 1992). What has only recently come to be addressed within the discipline is the question of how relations of power, such as those under colonial or neo-colonial domination, determine the direction and nature of translation, often simplifying, as Talal Asad has pointed out, towards the stronger language/culture (Asad 1986; Fabian 1986). This also raises once again the question of audience and of the ethnographer's subject-position. Who writes, and for whom? What might be the possible differences between metropolitan and third-world representations of third world contexts?

Bases of comparative research

Hitherto, the often undeclared bases of comparative study have been a humanism and a universalism that presumed a common human nature: in spite of their superficial differences, all people in the world were thought to be ultimately the same, or in the process of becoming like one another. This was, however, an argument made from above, as it were. The 'liberal' Western ethnographer, for instance, could claim the common humanity of the investigator and the objects of study, even if it was on the part of these 'objects', that a humanity was to be uncovered through the labour of the ethnographer's translation of their words and deeds into his/her Euro-American language. What could then be compared was the non-Western context with the anthropologist's Western one. Implicit in this kind of comparison, despite the protestations of human commonality, is what Achille Mbembe, writing about the African context, has called 'the perspective of a failed universality':

> The common unit, the ultimate foundation, *even the intrinsic finality of the comparative project is Western modernity*, understood either as the standard against which one measures other societies, or as the final destination toward which they are to move. And each time 'African' is introduced into the operation, the comparative act is reduced to an arithmetic relation of 'superiority' and 'inferiority'. Hierarchical figures slip in between these three chimeras of similitude, resemblance, and similarity, establishing orders of value defined in an arbitrary manner, the function of which is to legitimate discrimination and, too often, violence.
>
> (Mbembe 1992: 142–143, emphasis added)

As I have argued in my work on the politics of translation, the very premise of a universal history on which, in comparative study, the unity of human consciousness is predicated allows as for example in the Hegelian model of world history the formation of an inner hierarchy that situates third-world cultures below the Euro-American (Niranjana 1992: 69–70).

Consequently, even when third-world intellectuals themselves undertake comparative work, their task becomes one of comparing *their* cultural products with metropolitan ones – Kalidasa becomes the Shakespeare of India, Tutuola the African Fielding. This is part of the urge to find something in our colonized cultures that, as Kwame Appiah puts it, 'lives up to [the label]' (whether it is that of Philosophy or Literature), to find something that is ours which '*deserves* the dignity' (Appiah 1992: 148, emphasis in original). The fact is, says Appiah, taking the case of Africa, that 'intellectuals educated in the shadow of the West' are bound 'to adopt an essentially comparative perspective' (Appiah 1992: 151). The inherent asymmetry of the comparativist project framed in these terms would be at least displaced (since it cannot simply be done away with) when two different third-world contexts are being compared or studied together by one whose subject-positions and location are *in* the third world.

Outside metropolitan circuits?

This, then, is an argument about the formation of perspective, about how one's location helps critique one's complicity with metropolitan systems of knowledge and representation. Although it is now acknowledged that the space from which one is speaking, its histories, its questions, crucially configure the perspective of the investigator, the implications of such a configuration for comparative research in the third world have not yet been mapped out. If ethnographic work – always comparativist by definition – has hitherto been embedded both literally as well as figuratively in structures of dominance, we might speculate as to what might happen when the founding impulse is no longer one of greater and more efficient control. If one is not representing, or producing knowledge, in order to govern and regulate, what could be the alternative impulses?

If one of those impulses is the conscious formulation of the political project of dismantling Eurocentrism, where would one look for resources (besides of course in one's own local context, which for various reasons may not be adequate) but in other third-world spaces? The project cannot be an isolated one, located only in a single postcolony. While I would certainly not want to deny that colonial and postcolonial trajectories of various regions have been different from each other, arguments for exceptionality in the contemporary context can only weaken the possibilities for the emergence of urgently needed new solidarities.[9] The silence about our common histories mirrors the silence about the possibility of a shared future. There is perhaps, then, some purchase to be gained by positing shared histories at a certain level, since the colonies as well as the disciplinary networks in which they are produced and held have been part of the global enterprise of colonialism/neo-colonialism. As to what the 'gain' might be, only the outcome of comparative projects may be able to suggest. Only by risking the formulation of problems in which more than one nationality has similar kinds of stakes can we push for a reconfiguration of our research paradigms.

Just as work on culture in India needs to take into consideration Orientalist structures of representation (Niranjana 1993; Niranjana 1992b), one should undertake similar ground-clearing tasks for other third-world contexts with which one is attempting to engage. As I discovered during my sojourn in the West Indies, my awareness of the ways in which 'India' had been produced, in colonialist discourse for example, did not provide a guarantee that I could perceive similar, if different, structures of representation in relation to the Caribbean. Third-world intellectuals who are beginning to think about third-world spaces other than their own, need to address the question of how these different regions have been discursively constructed as objects of knowledge, to examine closely the technologies and theories that have enabled their emergence, and to understand the extent to which our readings of each other in the present are informed by those discursive grids.[10]

Alternative frames

If the disciplines have so far been caught up in these paradigms of domination, what kind of representations of the third world might be produced when this agenda is disrupted? What happens, we may ask, when a West Indian reads the Nigerian Chinua Achebe? When a South Asian reads the West Indian Kamau Brathwaite? When Lucky Dube in South Africa sings Jamaican-style reggae? What is the significance of these new representations? What sorts of cultural transformations do they signal? Would they function differently from metropolitan cultural products in third-world circuits? What new critical spaces might they help open up in the new locations where they begin to circulate?

More questions: why indeed should we speak to each other across the South? Why should we engage in comparative research across third-world locations? Perhaps the 'ends' of the new comparative work are oblique. Perhaps what this kind of work can do is to contribute to the development of *alternative frames of reference*, so that Western modernity is no longer seen as the sole point of legitimization or comparison. Let me emphasize that I do not intend to suggest that we can eliminate first-world knowledge structures or produce subjectivities entirely unmediated by the 'West'. My argument is simply that the norming of the comparative axis needs to be questioned. In much of our critical work, as well as our popular cultural conceptions, the two poles that make themselves manifest are 'India' and 'the West'. To recognize that there exist outside our everyday sphere geographical and political spaces other than the West, spaces that have always intersected with our history but by the very logic of colonialism cannot be acknowledged in their mutual imbrication with our past, to arrive at this recognition is a first step towards rewriting our histories as well as envisioning, and enlarging, our futures: together, and anew.[11]

Critical engagements with other third-world spaces might help inaugurate for, and in the South, a new internationalism, different (in its motivations, its desires, its imagined futures) from the aggressive globalization set in motion by the first world. Woven into this paper is an argument about perspective and intellectual/political location. *In* the third world, how do we *read* one another so that we do not appear simply as footnotes to Western history (Mukherjee 1995)? How do we learn to question the epistemological structures through which knowledge about third-world peoples are produced? I quote here the Guyanese scholar-activist Walter Rodney:

> When an African abuses an Indian he repeats all that the white men said about Indian indentured 'coolies'; and in turn the Indian has borrowed from the whites the stereotype of the 'lazy nigger' to apply to the African beside him. It is as though no black man can see another black man except by looking through a white person. It is time we started seeing through our own eyes.
>
> (Rodney 1969: 33–34)

What kind of critical awareness ought we bring to our teaching and writing so as to avoid reproducing the stereotypes about black/brown/yellow people that exist in what V. Y. Mudimbe calls the 'colonial library' (Mbembe 1992: 142)? How do we learn to ask questions that resonate with the actual concerns of people in other third-world places? What sort of library or archive do *we* need to construct? What new kinds of literacy do we need to acquire? How can we learn to overcome our multiple amnesia?

This paper has expressed some anxiety about the emergence of the new cosmopolitan Indian who might actively seek identification with the first world rather than the third. In addition, I have tried to suggest why this identification was problematic by focusing on the *common* problems faced by third-world comparativists, pointing implicitly to the dangers of Indian researchers replicating in relation to other third-world contexts the very manoeuvres and representational modes that had negated and 'dehistoricized' their own spaces. In so doing, my intention was not to argue for a simple return to our international politics of the Nehru era, but to urge a rethinking of present possibilities by pointing to forms of solidarity obscured by the growth of the globalized economy.

With the new globalization, the paths to the first world will be more clearly defined than ever before, rendered easier to traverse. Other locations on the map will appear all the more blurred, all the more difficult to reach. Now more than ever a critical perspective on our contemporary political–cultural identities requires that we place those other journeys on our agenda.

Acknowledgements

This paper owes its origins to ongoing conversations in different locations with David Scott, Mary John, Nadi Edwards, Satish Deshpande, Susie Tharu and Vivek Dhareshwar. For comments on an earlier draft of this paper, I am grateful to Uma Maheshwari, Anita Cherian, Rekha Pappu and K. Srilata. My thanks also to the following for critical engagements that have provoked me into reshaping some of my arguments: Craig Calhoun, Ernesto Laclau, Chantal Mouffe, Kumi Naidoo, Luiz Soares and Otavio Velho.

Notes

1   The editorial statement of the journal attempts to interrogate these two terms in conjunction with one another. However, this is not a task I have taken up in the present paper.
2   'Third' also because not first, not even second. In addition, 'third' in the historical postwar sense of the term, refers (although in a limited sense, remembering important exceptions like China and Cuba) to 'non-aligned' nations with a 'mixed' economy, not quite socialist, not quite capitalist.
3   It should be clear by now that Chatterjee' s use of the term, which I follow here, is quite different from what is meant by the enforcers of the New World Order.

4 The situation is further complicated when we have Indians from India studying 'East Indian West Indians'. The cultural forms of these diasporic communities are often imaged by Indians as fragmented, deficient or derivative.

5 I postpone a detailed discussion of these changes to a later date, only indicating for example that I have had to find ways of introducing students at least aurally to the popular culture of the West Indies, simultaneously attempting to initiate a discussion on the politics of language in the Caribbean.

6 This paper, titled 'History, really beginning: compulsions of postcolonial pedagogy', has been subsequently published in Rajan (1992).

7 The Walcott, Brathwaite and Lamming texts often become assimilated into literature courses in such a way that their links both formal and thematic to popular culture are obscured, leading to their being read like any other modernist text.

8 Interestingly, it is not just the reading of the cultural artefacts of the South that is seen as an anthropological activity. The ethnographic question 'sticks' to the production of the artefacts too. For example, a standard literary critical dismissal of African writers like Chinua Achebe is that they are 'too anthropological'. The same question might sometimes stick to minority literatures in the first world (African–American writing immediately comes to mind) or to Indian dalit writing or women's writing.

9 Indians and Brazilians, to give just two examples, often claim such exceptionality in different contexts. Such a claim can only be complicit in the production of the category of the universal.

10 Writing about the African context and using the term 'colonial library' coined by V. Y. Mudimbe, Achille Mbembe (1992: 141) contends that prior to any contemporary discourse on Africa, there is a 'library' an inaugural prejudice that destroys all foundations for valid comparisons.

11 As David Scott has remarked, 'The issue, of course, is not to erase the West as though to restore to its others some ancient pre-colonial unity, as though, indeed, the West were erasable. The issue . . . is rather to establish a reflexively marked practice of dialogical exchange that might enable the postcolonial intellectual to speak to postcolonials elsewhere . . . . through these shared-but-different histories and shared-but-different identities' (Scott 1989: 83–84).

References

Appiah, Kwame Anthony (1992) 'Ethnophilosophy and its critics'. In *In My Father's House: Africa in the Philosophy of Culture*, Methuen.

Asad, Talal (ed.) (1973) *Anthropology and the Colonial Encounter*, Humanities Press.

Asad, Talal (1986) 'The concept of cultural translation in British social anthropology'. In J. Clifford and G. Marcus (eds) *Writing Culture: The Poetics and Politics of Ethnography*, University of California Press.

Chatterjee, Partha (1996) 'Two poets and death: on civil and political society in the non-Christian world', unpublished paper.

Clifford, James (1983) 'On ethnographic authority', *Representations*, 1, 118–146.

Fabian, Johannes (1986) *Language and Colonial Power: The Appropriation of Swahili in the Former Belgian Congo, 1880–1938*, Cambridge University Press.

Mbembe, Achille (1992) 'Prosaics of servitude and authoritarian civilities', *Public Culture* 5(10): 123–145.

Mukherjee, Meenakshi (1995) A phrase in a talk on 'The Caribbean and Us', *IACLALS Annual Conference*, Mysore: January.

Niranjana, Tejaswini (1992a) *Siting Translation: History, Post-structuralism and the Colonial Context*, University of California Press.

Niranjana, Tejaswini (1992b) 'History, really beginning: compulsions of postcolonial pedagogy' in Rajeswari, S. R. (ed.) *The Lie of the Land: English Literary Studies in India*, Oxford University Press.

Niranjana, Tejaswini (ed.) (1993) *Interrogating Modernity*, with P. Sudhir and V. Dhareshwar, Seagull Books.

Niranjana, Tejaswini (1995) 'The Indian in me: gender, identity and cultural politics in Trinidad'. Paper presented at the International Conference on the Indian Diaspora, Trinidad: University of the West Indies, St. Augustine.

Rajan, Rajeswari Sunder (ed.) (1992) *The Lie of the Land: English Literary Studies in India*, Oxford University Press.

Rodney, Walter (1969) *The Groundings with my Brothers*, Bogle-l'Ouverture.

Said, Edward (1978) *Orientalism*, Vintage.

Scott, David (1989) 'Locating the anthropological subject: postcolonial anthropologists in other places'. In J. Clifford and V. Dhareshwar (eds) *Traveling Theories, Traveling Theorists.* Special Issue of *Inscriptions* (No.5).

Singham, A. W. and Hune, Shirley (1986) *Non-Alignment in an Age of Alignments*, Zed Books.

Chapter 4

Conceptualizing an East Asian popular culture[1]

Chua Beng Huat

No one would ever suggest conceptualizing Asia as a culturally homogeneous space. The adjective 'Asian' is complicated by a multitude of possible cultural references, from relatively culturally homogeneous countries in East Asian, such as Japan and Korea[2] to multiethnic/multiracial/multicultural/multireligious/multilingual postcolonial nations in Southeast and South Asia. For this occasion, I would risk this complexity and talk about East Asia plus one, namely Singapore, because of its overwhelming majority population of ethnic Chinese. The imaginary coherence of this grouping lies in the relatively imaginable possibility of constructing an 'East Asian' identity. Such a project of constructing a coherent and stable East Asian identity is a project that has a rather long standing. Most recently, in the early 1990s, in the triumphant days of the rise of capital in these countries, this group of countries was designated as a relatively coherent 'cultural' unit under the label of the 'dragon' economies. The symbol of the 'dragon', the sign of imperial China, obviously refers to their allegedly common Confucian heritage, which points beyond the Chinese population and enabled the inclusion of Japanese and Korean populations. This alleged presence of Confucianism in the ways of life of the huge, aggregated population of these countries provided for both the reason and its 'discovery' of Confucianism as an explanation for the rise of capitalism in East Asia, parallel to the affinity of Protestantism in the emergence of capitalism in the West (Tu 1991a). After the 1997 Asian financial crisis, this Confucian project has been displaced. Against this displacement, I am attempting to delineate an object of analysis, calling it 'East Asia Popular Culture', to designate the development, production, exchange, flow and consumption of popular cultural products between the People's Republic of China (PRC), Japan, South Korea, Taiwan, Hong Kong and Singapore.

Confucian East Asia displaced

First, let me briefly review the idea of a Confucian East Asia. During those triumphal days, from about the mid-1980s till 1997, continuous domestic economic growth in Korea, Taiwan, Hong Kong and Singapore, with Japan as the forerunner and model, coupled with the economic opening-up of the PRC, spawned several ideologically significant gestures in East Asia. The economic condition had spawned the search for an explanation of the rapid expansion of capitalism in East Asia in Confucian philosophy as everyday life (MacFarquar 1980).[3] More specifically, the visible expansion of overseas Chinese capital in Asia finessed a new confidence in the so-called Chinese 'culture', which supposedly unites and provides cultural continuities exemplified by, among other allegedly 'ethnic-cultural' characters, the apparent positive disposition to engage in business activities, among the overseas Chinese across their geographical dispersion; a suggestion that disregards the historical colonial economic social structure that left the immigrant Chinese with few opportunities other than to trade.[4] Nevertheless, the diasporic ethnic Chinese business communities and their intellectual promoters, perhaps the most euphoric about what appeared to be sustainable miraculous economic growth, convened international conferences on Chinese businesses, Chinese communities and Chinese identities.

The new confidence gave rise to the idea of a 'cultural China', spearheaded by the neo-Confucianist, Tu Weiming, and circulated through his editorial introduction, 'Cultural China: the periphery as the center', in the special issue of *Daedelus*, *The Living Tree: the Changing Meaning of being Chinese Today* (Tu 1991b). With the rise of the ethnic Chinese economies in Asia outside the PRC, Tu surmised that these 'peripheral' locations 'will come to set the economic and cultural agenda for the center [PRC]'. The desire behind the concept of 'cultural China' was not the political displacement of the Communist Party in the now marketized PRC, but more importantly, the possibility of a resurrection of a neo-Confucianism that will unite not only the dispersed Chinese population, but by extension the larger population of East Asia.

In this construction of a Confucian East Asia, the countries included are organized in a relatively fixed configuration: the ethnic Chinese dominant locations, such as Hong Kong, Taiwan and Singapore are the exemplary 'periphery' and the PRC as the economic laggard because of its very recent entry into global market capitalism but it is also the economic future of the grouping because of its massive consumption power. Beyond the immediate Chinese dominant locations, Japan is the economic leader and often the model, although culturally suspect because of memories of the Second World War and, finally, South Korea is economically at a similar structural level as Hong Kong, Taiwan and Singapore but culturally, arguably, formally more Confucian than these locations.

Even before the 1997 Asian regional financial crisis cast a pall on the euphoria and the Cultural China project, sceptics abounded. Detractors saw the search for Confucian values as no more than an ideological gloss over political authoritarianism in the less than democratic nations in the region. The actual might and reach of the economic power of the overseas Chinese communities in the region had also been a constant source of disagreements. The 'uniqueness' of the Chinese family firm has been frequently exposed as, among other things, an institution of exploitation of family, particularly women and child labour (Yao 2002). However, critics were kept baying at the margins until the financial crisis. With the crisis, half-hearted espousers of things 'Confucian' had quickly scurried off the stage. Only the staunchly ideologically committed are willing to continue to fly the flag, such as the Senior Minister of Singapore, Lee Kuan Yew. Pestered by international journalists for his view on the so-called 'Asian values' in the face of the economic crisis, he suggests,

> [There] has been a debasement of what I call Confucian value; I mean duty to friends and family. You're supposed to look after your family and your extended family, and to be loyal and supportive of your friends. And you should do it from your private purse and not from the public treasury. Now when you have weak governments and corruption seeps in, then this private obligation is often fulfilled at the public expense, and that's wrong.
>
> (*Straits Times*, 28 May 1998)

The ideological and emotional desire for a Confucian East Asia lives off a simple assumption that Confucianism constitutes the foundational culture of everyday life of East Asians. Empirically, any cursory observation of the Southeast Asian ethnic Chinese population will suggest that this is a flimsy assumption. Take, for example, Singapore, where the learning of Mandarin is compulsory for all primary and secondary ethnic Chinese students. Here, few individuals below the age of 30, or even 40, have ever read any Confucian texts. The shallowness of Confucianism in the everyday life of Singaporeans was further reflected in the failure to institute it as a part of the curriculum in moral education among the Chinese students. In the late 1980s, in an attempt to supposedly shore-up moral values against the supposedly corrupting cultural influences from the West, religious education, without God, was introduced as compulsory moral education to primary and secondary school students. Confucian ethics were offered as an option for Chinese students who professed no religion; the teaching material was developed by foreign experts, including Tu. The moral education curriculum, including Confucian ethics, was quickly abandoned when local social scientists discovered that students were becoming more religious as a result of the lessons and this may potentially give rise to greater divisiveness among the multiracial and multireligious population. The evidence would suggest that any presumption of cultural 'depth' in the grand Chinese philosophical traditions among Singaporean Chinese is dubious.[5] This shallowness in Singapore is at one extreme of the highly uneven inscription of Confucianism in the everyday life among the six East Asian locations with, perhaps, the Korean society at the other end of the continuum; indeed, Korean scholars are among the most active East Asian intellects who are engaged in the ongoing attempt to square Confucianism with contemporary social theories and contemporary democratic politics.

The idea of an East Asian pop culture

In contrast to the very uneven and abstract presence of Confucianism, since the 1980s popular cultural products have criss-crossed the national borders of the East Asian countries and constituted part of the culture of consumption that defines a very large part of everyday life of the population throughout the region. This empirically highly visible cultural traffic allows for the discursive construction of an 'East Asian Popular Culture' as an object of analysis.

American music, movie and television industries loom large globally, penetrating all locations where local income levels have reached a standard that can pay the price. Consequently, in economically developed parts of Asia, the predominant cultural/moral interests in popular culture and its consumption are often focused on American imports. Public discussions are often ideologically directed at the generalized liberal attitudes that are portrayed in American popular cultural products. This cultural liberalism is seen by some people as pushing the conservatism of Asians and is thus desired. Others cast it as culturally and morally 'corrosive' of 'wholesome' Asian values.[6] Significantly, side by side with the American popular culture, in every major urban centre in East Asia – Hong Kong, Taipei, Singapore, Shanghai, Seoul and Tokyo – there are dense flows of cultural products from the same centres into one another, albeit the directions and volumes of flows vary unevenly between them.

Popular cultural products and personalities from these East Asian urban centres criss-cross as daily features of all major newspapers in these cities. The trials and tribulations of the pop stars and celebrities make up part of the daily gossip by fans in different locations. Music, movies and television reviewers often face barrages of complaints from fans of the stars – singers and actors of big and small screens – if they penned negative reviews of the fans' pop 'idols'; the term 'idols' has become an adjective that characterizes a specific segment of the popular culture products, as in 'idol-drama'. Some of the artists, such as the so-called 'fifth generation' of the PRC film directors or individual Hong Kong directors, such as Wong Kai Wai, have received focused analysis because they have reached international 'artiste' status. So too, have the Japanese 'trendy dramas' whose popularity has declined since the end of the 1990s. They are but part of a larger regional phenomenon.

As popular culture is unavoidably a sphere of capitalist activities, the economics of this larger phenomenon are most concretely observable. Marketing, distribution, promotion and circulation of popular cultural products throughout the geographic East Asia are now part of the planning of all product producers, from financiers to directors, producers and the artistes, wherever these individuals might be located geographically. For example, a space like Singapore is inundated with television shows, movies, popular music, fashion and food from all parts of East Asia. At the same time, Singaporean television companies are cooperating in joint ventures with production companies and/or engaging artistes from elsewhere in East Asia in local productions, so as to expand their own market and enterprise. These flows of finance, production personnel and consumers across linguistic and national boundaries in East Asian locations give substance to the concept of East Asia Popular Culture.[7] This thick and intensifying traffic between locations – the economics of this trans-location cultural industry, the boundary crossings of pop cultural products, of artistes and the variable modes of consumption of audiences of different median different locations – as a cultural phenomenon in its own right has received relatively scant analytic interest.

Nevertheless, there is some pioneering work and more is coming on stream. The most notable is Iwabuchi's (2002) analysis of the penetration of Japanese popular cultural products in East and Southeast Asia, although he is well aware of the larger East Asian regional context for the production, circulation and consumption of popular culture as an 'underdeveloped area in the study of cultural globalization' (Iwabuchi 2002: 50). This work provides important insights into the industrial strategies adopted by Japanese popular cultural industries in their attempts to penetrate the Asian regional market since the early 1990s. He came to the conclusion that, at least for the popular music industry, 'Japanese ventures for cultivating pan-Asian pop idols have only been, at best, partially successful' (Iwabuchi 2002: 107); and since the record company, Pony Canyon, 'retreated from Asian markets in late 1997' (Iwabuchi 2002: 107), even 'partially successful' may be an overly optimistic conclusion. In contrast, Japanese television dramas of romance among urban young were very popularly received by young audiences throughout the region during the later half of the 1990s.[8] Iwabuchi found that popular reception in Taiwan was based on a sense of 'coevalness' between the Taiwanese audience and the Japanese represented in the dramas – 'the feeling that Taiwanese share a modern temporality with the Japanese'. This 'coevalness' constitutes the dynamic vector in generating and sustaining 'cultural proximity' between the audience and the drama-mediated representation of the Japanese (Iwabuchi 2002: 122). Finally, Iwabuchi also examined Japanese audiences' reception of popular culture products imported from elsewhere in Asia. Here, he found that, diametrically opposite the Taiwanese reception of Japanese television dramas, the Japanese audience's reception of imported Asian popular culture was based on a 'refusal to accept that it [Japan] shares the same temporality as other Asian nations' (Iwabuchi 2002: 159) and that reception of the imported products was mediated by a sense of nostalgia of Japan's own past that is the present of elsewhere in Asia.[9] The analysis of these two empirical instances and their explanations provides us with insights into the differences between local audiences watching imported popular culture products; insights that have implications on methodological issues in cross-cultural reception research.

Although Japanese television dramas constituted the bulk of the total export of Japanese television programmes, the success of these dramas in the region was somewhat serendipitous because the television industry was not very interested in the export market as the financial returns were paltry relative to the costs of production. By the early 2000s, the regional space of Japanese television drama faced increased competition from the aggressive export of similar products from Korea, where the government had targeted the export of Korean popular culture as a new economic initiative, after the 1997 Asian regional financial crisis. In the popular music industry, the opening up of the People's Republic of China as a huge consumer market provided a much needed infusion of motivation energy in reviving the Chinese popular music industry in the 1990s. The ailing Cantonese pop music (Cantopop) became progressively displaced by Mandarin popular music, which in turn created a space for Taiwan as a centre for Mandarin–Chinese music production. Thus, at the beginning of the 21st century, the above mentioned dense traffic of popular culture products across the national/cultural boundaries in East Asia has far exceeded the analytic boundaries that are determined by any focus on a specific location. It is this empirical reality's conceptual and analytic shape and contour that cultural studies in Asia must now work out, and the present attempt is a preliminary step.[10]

Methodological note

As I have suggested elsewhere,

> The life of a consumer product is very short. It is meant to be so in order to keep the factory that produces it working, the workers employed, its consumers happy but not for long, and the economy moving. This brevity of existence is a constraint on critical analysis of any consumer object, singularly or in constellation as a trend or a lifestyle. The problem is that by the time the analyst figures out the critical angle for commentary, the object in question would have already been consumed and committed to the trash-heap. Consumed and rejected, or unsold and rejected, either way it is discarded . . . the brevity of life of a consumer object and of a consumer trend makes it unavoidable that all published materials on consumer products and trends are by definition 'historical'.
>
> (Chua, 2003: vii)

The same is true of popular culture products of course. Film, television programmes, popular music and musicians – in short, the data one is working with – are often already off the screen way before any analysis is completed. Secondly, many of the readers/ audiences have not seen the films nor heard the music; that is, they are not familiar with the products the analyst is engaged with. For these reasons, analytic interest should not be in the products themselves, although as they constitute the empirical material of the analysis it is unavoidable to analyse and comment on them. The larger analytic interest should be oriented towards the structures and modalities through which the products partake in the social and economic material relations within the different locations where the products are produced, circulated and consumed.

The most generalized outline of East Asian popular culture as an object of analysis may be delineated by its three constitutive elements: production, distribution and consumption. Each East Asian location participates in different and unequal levels in the production and consumption of the circulating popular cultural materials. Here, the structural configuration that was noted in the displaced Confucian East Asia project appears to be serviceable: Japan as the financial leader is also a production site that leads and indeed, shows the way in many aspects of the popular culture. Ethnic-Chinese dominant locations constitute a subset that produces and consumes cultural products of different Chinese languages – Mandarin, Cantonese and Minan, also known as Hokkien (*Fujian*) which, for the Taiwan independentists, is Taiwanese – with a written script that is comprehensible to most individuals literate in any Chinese language, in spite of the two different written scripts and local innovations, such as Cantonese or *Fujian* words. The written script enables access to material across different spoken Chinese languages, which explains the curious phenomenon that Chinese audiences are often found watching Chinese movies and television programmes with Chinese subtitles. In this ethnic Chinese subset, the PRC remains at the margin of production because of the lingering effects of its socialist ideology and politics, which I will discuss in greater detail later. There is an emergent popular cultural traffic between South Korea and Japan, after 1989, when the very porous 'ban' on the importation of the Japanese cultural products into Korea was formally lifted (Han 2000). Meanwhile, South Korea is beginning to export its own products into all the other East Asian locations, creating a so-called 'Korean Wave' in these locations. Given the uneven presence of the different locations in production, distribution and consumption, these processes need to be examined at every East Asian location. Collaborative research efforts are therefore essential to comprehensively analyse the object, East Asian Popular Culture. The following are tentative steps in teasing out the constituent elements of both the production, distribution and consumption processes to facilitate comparative studies across the region.

Production and export/distribution

The production of a popular cultural product – writings, all technical skills from acting, singing, filming and recording, and financing arrangements – can either be entirely located in a single geographic location or, alternatively, with contemporary technology and globalized economy, each of the necessary constituent processes can be executed from different locations. In the case of the East Asian popular culture industry, preference for either arrangement tends to reflect the relative dominance of the production location in exporting its finished products. At one end of the dominance is the case of Japan in television drama and popular music. The ability to finance expensive television drama productions and stage expensive concerts and promotions has given the Japanese popular culture industry a dominant exporting position, giving rise to an ubiquitous impression that there is a 'Japanese invasion' or 'Japanization' of popular culture throughout the region, in spite of, according to Iwabuchi (2002: 85–120), the Japanese popular culture industry's tentativeness about expanding into the rest of Asia.

The high quality of Japanese television is captured, in a rather essentialist manner, by an American critique:

> The most positive aspect of the primacy of form and the perfection of role is the creation of excellent images. The Japanese concern with the visual, in combination with their advanced technology, ensures that Japanese television is often very pleasing to the eye. Sets are technically well designed and the photography is excellent . . . If television is used as a means of relaxation and escape, as opposed to education and enlightenment, it may be very enjoyable to lose oneself among the images without having to bother with the search for ideas.
>
> (Stronach 1989: 155)

The most illustrative examples are Japanese television urban drama series. These series are also known as 'trendy drama' for obvious reasons: the story line is generally about romance among urban young professionals. The visual pleasure comes from the fact that, on the set and scenes, the characters, major and minor, are very well dressed in designer clothes, live in cosy small apartments, eat in expensive – usually Western – restaurants in the entertainment districts of the city but, above all, all the actors and actresses are beautiful men and women; of this last element, more will be discussed later. According to the producer of the very first of these dramas, *Tokyo Love Story*, when he was given the task as a producer, at age 28, Japanese television was filled with programmes for middle-aged individuals and he would not watch any of them. He asked himself, and people like him, what would he/they like to watch on television and came up with a simple list: beautiful people, beautiful clothes, good food and good entertainment, the plot is secondary.[11] Although the production cost per episode was phenomenally expensive, with about 50% going to pay the beautiful cast, the local Japanese market, in the euphoric days of the bubble economy, was able to support the cost. No considerations were given to a potential export market. The subsequent popularity of these series was possibly a surprise to the Japanese producers and came as surplus profit when it happened.

Successes throughout East Asia did not go unnoticed; they spawned an explicit ambition to address directly the enlarged audience population in order to consolidate it. In 2000, the drama series, *Romance 2000*, was simultaneously broadcast in Tokyo, Taiwan, Hong Kong and Singapore. Conceptually, with the desire to capture directly the expanded audience, the plot of the series incorporated elements of generalized 'pan Asian' interest. It went beyond the formulaic simple story line of such dramas to include Cold War politics, which is still very much alive in East Asia today. The plot understandably became very complex, with the beautiful lovers cursed by political ideologies. Briefly summarized: as an unnamed government had kidnapped and threatened to kill his mother and sister if he did not carry out its orders, a young Korean was forced to become an assassin in Japan. As fate would have it, a young Japanese woman found him when he was hurt, she harboured and nursed him back to health and, of course, fell in love with him. She became involved in his affairs, leading eventually to her own death – she sacrificed her life to safe a multitude of people in an amusement park from a bomb explosion. One could say the complex plot, incorporating a generalized regional political anxiety, ultimately destroyed the fantasy that sustained such a drama of romance. In addition, it sank the series. In contrast to the serendipitous success of the drama created for a Japanese audience, ironically, this conscious attempt to transnationalize the content, presumably to be 'more relevant' to the enlarged East Asian audience, failed. Conceptually, this 'noble' failure poses some interesting issues. Are the audiences of the East Asian popular culture ready for the mixing of cultural and political themes that are hewed from different locations? Does the failure suggest the absence of a possibility of an emergence of what might be called an 'East Asian identity' from emerging through popular culture, in this instance television drama? The answers to these and other questions will, of course, have serious implications on the development of the contents of the products and on any idea of an East Asia as a culturally, relatively coherent entity.

Such failures aside, the popularity of the Japanese 'trendy dramas' across East Asia from the mid to late 1990s was without doubt. This was reflected not only in media attention but also attracted much academic analysis, both in Japan and elsewhere in East Asia.[12] An international conference on such dramas, held at the International Christian University in Tokyo, drew participants from every location in East Asia, including young East Asian scholars studying in the US.[13] Within the television drama industry, the quality of Japanese production clearly sets the industry standard; producers elsewhere in East Asia tend to take the Japanese as industry leader. Perhaps, the very high standard of production, and thus the elevated demands of a Japanese audience, has contributed to the relative absence of imports from other East Asian locations into the Japanese market. Iwabuchi, however, provides an ideological explanation for the unequal flow of products in and out of Japan; he argues that this is the result of 'Japan's refusal to accept that it shares the same temporality as other Asian nations' (Iwabuchi 2002: 159). Nevertheless, some breaks in the boundaries are taking place; for example, Japanese pop singers have sung duets with those from the region, partly in efforts to expand their market reach into the huge Chinese audience, and even globally, through singing in English.[14] In any case, the relative impermeability of the Japanese pop cultural sphere to imports from other East Asian locations is a question that requires further research.

The Korean popular culture industry appears to be the most influenced by the standards of Japanese production. Dare one suggest that this is part of the postcolonial connection? At the political level, there was a formal ban on Japanese cultural products since its decolonization from Japanese imperialism, immediately after the Second World War. This formal ban was not lifted until October 1998, with the Joint Declaration of the New 21st Century Korea–Japan Partnership. However, the ban did not make Korea impermeable to Japanese popular cultural products; even the government-owned Korean Broadcasting Station was guilty of illegal importation (Han 2000: 14–15). In the words of one Korean cultural commentator: 'We firmly lock and bar front doors but leave our back doors wide open. With our left hands we indignantly slap away any offers but we are busy snatching at any opportunities with our right. This has been our society's attitude toward popular Japanese culture during the last 30 years' (Do Jung Il quoted in Kim Hyun-Mee 2002: 1).[15] In addition to this constant stream of underground importation, Japanese popular cultural products have also been 'copied', 'partially integrated', 'plagiarized', 'mixed' and 'reproduced' into Korean products. Little wonder that Korean fans of Japanese popular music suggest, 'When we listened to

Korean songs it is easy to recognize similar or same parts from Japanese songs' (quoted in Kim Hyun-Mee 2002: 4). Kim further concludes that 'in the case of TV animations and comics, most [Korean products] are adaptations of Japanese products so Japanese culture in Korea has already set its roots deep into the emotional structure of Koreans' (Kim Hyun-Mee 2002: 4). After the lifting of the ban, Japanese cultural products now flow smoothly into Korean popular cultural spaces. And in 2002, the first Japanese and South Korean co-produced television drama series, *Friends* – a drama series about the relationship between a Korean man and a Japanese woman – was broadcast in both locations simultaneously, marking not only a pop culture event but also a 'political' event in Korean–Japanese relations.

Significantly, production of Japanese 'trendy drama' has lapsed and the exports slowed by late 1990s. The media space in Hong Kong, Taiwan and Singapore has been, in a sense, replaced and occupied by Korean imports; the influence of Japanese trendy drama on the Korean product is unmistakable. The importance of Korean export can be seen from its effects in Singapore. In 1999, the local monopoly that publishes all the major newspapers in all four official languages of the city-state ventured into commercial television with two free-to-air stations, one in English (I Channel) and the other in Mandarin (U Channel), under a new company called *Mediawork*. Of the two channels, the English-channel local programmes have been an abject failure and the studio effectively shut down within less than two years of its establishment. The local English programming is reduced to daily news programmes; all the other programmes are imported, largely from the US. On the other hand, the Mandarin channel was able to carve out and take away a significant size of the audience population from the already established state-owned station, *MediaCorp*, through a combination of broadcasting Korean drama series and local variety shows which look and feel like the similar shows in Taiwan, which in turn are very similar to those in Japan. MediaCorp has since also imported Korean drama series; such that, by late 2003, there is at least one Korean drama series on Singaporean television stations every night, after the daily news. The drama series has brought Korean artistes not only onto Singaporean television screens but also into the entertainment pages of the print media, particularly Mandarin publications. Korean drama series have thus become a site for local media competition, which perhaps justifies these exports as part of the so-called 'Korean Wave', which includes Korean movies and Korean popular music exports.

Korean movies made their debut in East Asia, as perhaps elsewhere, through the Hollywood style blockbuster *Shiri*, followed by *Joint Security Area*, in late 1990s. Both films translated the Cold War tension of North–South Korea into personalized relations. The first is a romance between secret agents from both side of the divide, a female agent from the North being involved with a male counterpart from the South. The second film thematized 'illicit' friendship and camaraderie between North and South Korean soldiers who police the demilitarized zones. A second category of Korean films that were popular in their time is what may be labelled 'gangster comedies', where criminals are let off all accusations, guilt and punishment and humanized by their ineptness or goofiness in other aspects of their daily lives.[16] Since then Korean films have had a constant but not particularly dense presence in the East Asian market. Again, it should be noted that this Korean presence came at a time when Japanese films had been all but absent in the export market. However, the success of the Japanese horror movie, *The Ring*, in late 1990s, sparked off a string of 'horror/ghost' movies from Korea, Hong Kong, Singapore and Thailand, which is still coming on stream in 2003.

In terms of production and export capacity, Hong Kong and Taiwan may be said to occupy the same in-between position as the South Korean popular cultural industry. However, they occupy prominent, if not dominating, positions in the pan ethnic-Chinese segment of East Asian Popular Culture. In addition to their own domestic audiences, which still constitute the first market, television programmes, films and music from Hong Kong and Taiwan have always had a constant presence in the other locations where there are significant ethnic Chinese populations, such as Singapore and Malaysia and, of course, the PRC, especially after its economic liberalization. Hong Kong had been the major production site of Chinese movies from the 1950s to the late 1980s, and although the production rate slowed down considerably in the 1990s, it remains the major production location of Chinese movies, predominantly in Cantonese and increasingly also in Mandarin. However, its television drama programmes have grown as a result of film producers, such as the Shaw Brothers, switching to the small screen. Taiwan has a continuing presence in exporting 'traditional' family dramas in which the much maligned and oppressed daughter-in-law eventually triumphs when her moral righteousness survives her long suffering. However, since the success of the young adult romance drama, *Meteor Garden* (discussed below), it has also begun to export contemporary drama series, including the 'updating' of traditional family dramas by dressing the characters in contemporary clothes, without altering the plots and themes.

In popular music, Hong Kong was without rival in the 1970s and 1980s, with the invention of Cantopop. However, in the 1990s, with the impending and final 'incorporation' as a Special Authority Region of the People's Republic of China, Cantopop has waned and all major popular music performers have switched over to singing in Mandarin in order to catch the huge mainland market. This switch in language has enabled Taiwan to emerge as a major recording location for Mandarin-pop. It features much more prominently as a place to train, record and market music for all ethnic-Chinese singers who are not hewn from Hong Kong, particularly those from Southeast Asia, especially Singapore and Malaysia.[17]

The presence of the PRC as a production location for East Asian popular culture can be said to be very marginal, in contrast to its huge consumer market for imports from other East Asia locations. (Since the absorption of HK as an SAR, HK television companies have been quick to capitalize on the huge market by making television series that are directed specifically at the mainland audience.[18]) This is due in part to the underdevelopment of such industries under socialism, and economic marketization is still in its early days. As consumerism is a new phenomenon in PRC, its mass cultural products are still far behind in quality and style for them to be picked up by the more advanced consumers in the other affluent Asian locations; there is a sense of what is commonly labelled 'country feel' (*tu qi*).

However, there are two divergent, deeper 'cultural' problems that constrain its cultural products for the export market. First, ironically, the PRC is tied to being the root-site of 'traditional' Chinese culture. Secondly, the popular cultural products from the PRC, from rock music to television, films and other visual art forms, are deeply inscribed and haunted by the revolutionary politics of the past, particularly the Communist revolution, and its antagonists, 'tradition' and authoritarianism, both traditional and contemporary. As the origin of Chinese history, PRC producers are often compelled to translate into screen historical dramas and/or transform literary classics of either historical or mythic pasts, such as the famous historical/mythical huge novels, *Water Margin* and the *Three Kingdoms*, which were very well produced long-running television drama series. As long narratives of heroic acts of mythic figures in ancient Chinese history, these series speak little to the young consumers of popular culture; the length of the series only emphasizes its tedium. In terms of contemporary popular culture, the deep inscription of revolutionary politics and its discontents is most observable in the case of rock music from PRC. The lyrics are so heavily laden with local politics (De Kloet 2000) that they are difficult to understand by consumers who are not part of the local scene; consequently, their presence in the other ethnic-Chinese predominant locations in East Asia is limited to the margins of 'alternative' music. Similarly, PRC television programmes are ideologically overdetermined and regularly play up the themes of involuntary exile or voluntary migration against the social and political conditions in the mainland itself (Sun 2002).

These two divergent ideological constraints are reflected in the works of no less an internationally acclaimed director than Zhang Yimou. Along with his critique of the oppressiveness of the 'Chinese traditions' in such films as *Raise the Red Lantern* and his depiction of the rural poverty of contemporary China in films such as *Not One Less*, he also did the monumental film *Hero*, which narrates a version of the failed assassination of the brutal Emperor Qin, the first man to unify what was then China.

Zhang's movies, like those of the other directors from the PRC, are unable to avoid political inscription and reading by foreign audiences. The reading by audiences in the West or West-educated in East Asia is very succinctly put by Chen Xiaoming:

> once his films enter the world film market, politics inevitably captures the spotlight. Hence, in the eyes of a Western beholder, Zhang Yimou's *Judou* (1991) is interpreted as an innuendo against the gerontocracy, and *Raise the Red Lantern* (1992) is seen as a political power struggle. Political readings of these Chinese films are not necessarily farfetched misreadings insofar as the cultural imaginary of Oriental culture has always already inculcated an invisible, but omnipresent, nexus of absolute power and totalitarianism, which overshadows Zhang Yimou's, and others', films. It does not matter whether such a power nexus refers to ancient feudalism or despotism, or to the 'proletariat dictatorship' of modern China, for the cultural imaginary of Oriental culture is fundamentally timeless – the present is all but a reappearance of the past. Politics is thus a determinant situation in the cultural imaginary of China.
>
> (Chen 2000: 229)

Such complex political inscriptions are too taxing for mass audiences of popular culture and the films are, consequently, delegated to the international, art-house and film festival circuits with their sophisticated audiences.[19]

The other essentially consumer location is Singapore. With its very limited domestic market, Singapore has no film and music industries and a relatively new television industry.[20] However, it is cash rich. Here, the decomposition of the production process, with each input coming from different locations, is most observable. From its very beginning (and it continues to be true), the Singaporean television industry depended on imports of professionals from Hong Kong. Until recently, the Hong Kong professionals worked behind the screen. However, since early 2000, Hong Kong television actors and actresses have been appearing in leading roles in situation comedies and other productions; two notable examples are Lydia Sum who leads in *Living with Lydia* and Carol Cheng in *Oh! Carol*, both programmes have survived the first season and have become weekly features. In these instances, the 'lesser' position of Singapore is clearly reflected, as Singaporean actors are placed in supporting roles, one might say as 'apprentices' to the Hong Kong stars.[21] A similar arrangement is also found in Singapore financed movies.[22] The other television company, Mediawork, has also launched, in 2004, its first collaborative productions with Taiwan company, *Sanlih e-tv*, in a teenage drama series featuring the members of an all-male singers/actors group, 5566, entitled *Westside Story*, making reference to Taipei's teenage shopping area, Simenting (West Gate Square), with one of the popular Singaporean female actresses in its stable acting as the mother of the lead character. At this point in the development of Singapore's television industry, such joint productions must be seen as a way of introducing Singaporean artistes into the ethnic-Chinese segment of the East Asia Popular Culture, as the products are often sold to Taiwan and PRC stations.[23]

In recent years, joint ventures, co-productions or direct financing of films have picked up pace. Reflecting the government's ambition in establishing a 'creative industry' in the knowledge-based economy, the government has set up a film commission to help finance film projects. As part of this industrial strategy, the film company, *Raintree Pictures*, was established within the state-owned television company, *MediaCorp*. So far, interests in production financing are restricted to collaboration with participants in the pan-ethnic Chinese segment, particularly with Hong Kong; in addition, there are collaborations with individual artistes in other Southeast Asian countries. A successful co-production effort is the three-part film series, *Infernal Affairs*, in 2003–2004, a detective story set entirely in Hong Kong with Hong Kong actors, where Singapore does not feature at all, either in setting or actors on screen. A central non-Hong Kong character was played by the Mainland Chinese actor, Chen Daoming. And, it must be mentioned that the producer of this film series is a Hong Kong person working in Singapore for *Raintree*.

From a methodological angle, a location like Singapore, being at the other extreme end of the production continuum and an essentially consumption location, is very advantageous in observing and researching the relative placing of all these production locations. Singapore's radio waves, television screens and movies theatres constitute sites in which Japanese, Korean, Hong Kong and Taiwanese films, television drama and variety shows and popular music compete for space, reflecting their relative market position in the different media and genres. This will be discussed in the next section.

Obviously, the linearity of the written text and its reading on this occasion is a clumsy structure for the depiction of the complexity of flows of popular cultural products, and thus the porosity of the 'national' boundaries, throughout East Asia. These flows take place routinely on a synchronous plane within these spaces through a variety of media, including *manga*, films, television, music and fashion. To give a sense of the fluidity of these flows, I will take the example of the latest sensation in East Asian popular culture, the F4 phenomenon.

In 2000, a Taiwanese producer reproduced a Japanese *manga* story into a television series, *Meteor Gardens*. The college-students drama series featured four completely unknown young men (of the same height) as the principal actors, collectively introduced to the media world as F4. The series was an instant success throughout East Asia. It was screened in Hong Kong and Singapore and subsequently in Korea in 2002, whereas in the PRC they were watched on DVDs.[24] It transformed F4 from complete obscurity to the hottest boy-band in the past two years; their television appearance had finessed their entry into popular music, although their singing skills are noticeably limited. Every public appearance by F4 throughout the region draws huge crowds of screaming fans; for example, their appearance in a Shanghai shopping centre had to be cut to 10 minutes because of the crushing crowd, and their scheduled concert was cancelled by the local government. Their success in East Asia has, of course, spawned other Taiwanese boy bands and individual male singers who are marketed throughout an especially ethnic-Chinese predominant East Asia, usurping popular attention at a time when Hong Kong singers and Cantopop are in relative decline.

Before proceeding with consumption issues, the current structural arrangement of the production and export of East Asian cultural products can be summarized thus: Japan is the leader that sets the industry quality standard and is the prime production and export location, with relatively little importation from the rest of the constituent regional locations. South Korea has made a very conscious effort to export its popular culture products as part of its export-oriented economy, especially after the 1997 Asian regional financial crisis. Hong Kong and Taiwan play central roles in the production of Chinese language popular culture products, with an apparently skewed division of labour, movies and television programmes in Hong Kong and popular music in Taiwan. PRC and Singapore remain largely locations of consumption of East Asian popular culture, each with its own problems of trying to elevate itself into a serious production location. The PRC appears unable at this point to shake off its ideological baggage, both traditional/historical and contemporary/political, for its popular culture products to have mass appeal, while Singapore is trying to get into the business through its investment power, without apparently any other ideological interests.

Audience position as methodological constraint

If the production processes of popular cultural products can be disaggregated and organized transnationally, consumption is, however, thoroughly grounded in specific locations. Consumers are geographically located within cultural spaces in which they are embedded and meanings and viewing pleasures are generated within the local cultures of a specific audience. Of course, the 'local' cultural space is not to be conceived as a hermetically sealed entity but one that is porous and actively engaged, appropriating and absorbing cultural elements and fragments from all the directions with which the 'local' has contact. Without this openness, there would be no such discursive object as East Asian Popular Culture. Nevertheless, local cultural proclivities continue to work their effects in the ongoing movements and boundary shaping of the local cultural sphere.

Conceptually, there are three possible audience or consumption positions in consuming popular culture programmes. The first and least complicated position is an audience watching a locally produced programme. Here, the audience is embedded in the very culture of the location of production as his/her own. Identification with the themes and characters may be said to come 'naturally' – as in phenomenologically the 'natural attitude of everyday life' – and references can be readily made to events, individuals and other activities that are 'similar' to those on screen. The audience may be said to 'know' the filmic or lyrical representations of events, issues and characters from the 'inside'. There is an excess of knowledge that is then used to judge the 'accuracy', 'truth' and 'critical reflections' of the content of the cultural programme. In this sense, the program may be used as a 'critical' mirror to one's own life and community. An exemplary instance is Kim Soyoung's analysis of the eclipse of 'Korean women' in recent big budget Korean films, such as *Joint Security Area*, as indicative of a generalized shrinking of the 'women's sphere' and the elevation of male-bonding in post 1997 financial crisis Korea (Kim Soyoung 2003).

Second, the audience could be a diasporic subject watching or listening to a programme that is thematically concerned with one's homeland. The programme may be produced either by homeland or foreign producers. Here, the audience position and relation with the content is once removed, that is, less immediate than the first position. Nevertheless, the audience is still being interpellated, voluntarily or otherwise, into the programme. The same knowingness as the first position will be brought to bear on the content. However, the judgements made are likely to be with hesitancy, due to, and dependent on, the distance of both space and time away from home. An additional 'nationalist' element may arise if the programme is foreign produced; the audience may protest and charge the foreign producer with politically motivated misrepresentation or, if one were in political exile, affirm the representation as a reasonable critique of conditions in the 'homeland'; a critique or misrepresentation lays obviously not in the substance of the content but in the viewing position of the audience. For detailed analysis of the diasporic subject position on East Asian popular culture, see Sun's (2002) insightful analysis of various films and television programmes, produced for the PRC audience, with either local or foreign or co-funding.

The third position is an audience watching an imported programme. Here, the audience is not embedded in the culture of the production location. The audience is thus distanced from the detailed knowledge of the first and second position; what knowledge he or she has is derived from outside the programme itself. It is in this viewing position that the differences between the cultures of the location of consumption and that of the production location become most apparent. The 'meaningfulness' of the programme is now relocated into the horizon of relevance of the audience's own cultural context. The audience has now brought his or her own cultural context to bear on the content and to read accordingly; here, the earlier mentioned empirical studies, by Iwabuchi (2002), of Taiwanese audiences of Japanese dramas and Japanese consumers of popular culture products imported from elsewhere in Asia are illustrative and instructive. It is in this sense that the cultural product may be said to have crossed a 'cultural' boundary, beyond the simple fact of having it means it has been exported/imported into a different location as an economic activity.

Each of these stances may involve different investment of the self in identification with the characters and themes on screen or in music. The effects of the consumption of the imported cultural products will, of course, differ from those derived from consuming a product which represents the culture in which one is embedded. The intensity of self-investment is likely to decrease in proportion to the immediacy of 'home/national' self-identification, with the third viewing position coming closest to an idea of 'mere' entertainment. Each of these positions is, of course, a field of analysis in its own right and each would illuminate different aspects of audience-ship.

In this particular instance, in the delineation of the discursive concept and object of an East Asian Popular Culture, the central analytic focus is on how products criss-cross the cultural boundaries within the region to reach non-home audiences. Consequently, the analytic starting point would have to be that of the third audience or consumption position of a local audience watching foreign imports. This is a necessary methodological constraint in the analysis of cultural border crossing of popular culture material. The East Asian Popular Culture must therefore be conceptualized as a complex discursive object that incorporates, and is constituted by, the popular culture of each regional location as both culture of production and culture of consumption. The ever-changing contours, shapes and substance of this discursive object are, therefore, necessarily a collaborative collective enterprise of analysts across the region.

Being a Singaporean and living in Singapore, I am therefore methodologically constrained to confine myself to sketching out some, by no means exhaustive, characteristics of a Singaporean audience as part of this East Asian popular cultural sphere.[25] This exercise is therefore largely an illustrative instance, as the same constraint would apply to local analysts elsewhere throughout the region with different outcomes. Furthermore, I shall restrict myself to the discussion of television and film products rather than music, both for ease of presentation and reception, because they are much less abstract than music.[26]

How a Singaporean watches imported television

Urban stories

Singapore as a city-state has no rural hinterland. Singaporeans in general have little or no contact with things and sentiments rural. 'Rural' is ideologically often reduced to 'backward', 'underdeveloped' and lacking in urban amenities, thus inconvenient; at its most generous, 'rural' appears as nostalgia, a place to escape the urban stress. Consequently, imported drama series that are popularly received are almost all urban romance stories featuring young, single professionals, either living on their own or with their families of origin; in general, the Japanese series tend to have young professionals in their own well-appointed apartments, while the Korean series appear yet to have shaken off the yoke of family. Historical period dramas of work from Japan and Korea – and there are plenty of such drama series in both countries – do not travel well to Singapore and thus are never seen on local television. However, programmes that are set in imperial Chinese dynasties are common because there is a vague (fake) sense among the ethnic-Chinese Singaporean audience of knowing Chinese history.

The trials and tribulations of urban living are of course intimately familiar to Singaporeans. Familiarity makes the urban stories accessible, audience friendly. A Singapore consumer can readily identify with the themes and characters as representations of 'urban' people and phenomena that are familiar, if not similar, to themselves; that is, if desired, a Singapore audience can allow itself to identify completely with the representation of the urban characters on screen. However, 'foreignness', nevertheless, remains a feature desired by the same audience. First, local programmes generally deal with issues of Singaporean everyday life, with messages that are relevant and didactic but, precisely because of these features, can become 'tiresome' rather than 'entertaining'. So, foreignness, and the 'exoticism', of imported products are part of the local audience's desire and viewing pleasure. However, of greater conceptual significance is that the 'imported' status of the programme can be used by a Singapore audience to limit the degree of identification, that is the degree of interpellation of self, with the themes and characters on screen. That the product is a foreign import enables a Singaporean audience to maintain a stance of 'watching', in a voyeuristic manner, the lives of others, elsewhere in East Asia. It enables a difference between self and other East Asians to be maintained, in spite of sharing similar urban and familial dispositions. Thus, foreignness must remain recognizably foreign in the programme. The most immediately foreign difference should be, of course, language; however, as discussed below, this is most easily erased through dubbing. Two other markers are retained, background music and outdoor scenery.

Background music, particularly the programme's theme songs, is generally left un-touched, preserving the foreignness. However, this is increasingly unreliable as a marker of the location of production. First, the visual and the audio contents of a programme can be produced separately at the point of production. The importing location is free to supply both dialogue and music to the video material; the 'imported/foreign' features are thus suppressed for the local audience. Second, the background music can be intentionally foreign at the point of production; for example, Taiwan drama series often come with background music sung in Japanese – in the interest of 'exoticizing' local products and/or exporting the product to foreign locations. In a location such as Singa-pore, where both Taiwan and Japan are foreign, such mixing leaves the 'foreignness' undisrupted but locating the 'origin' of the product is made problematic.

Scenery is a more stable marker of foreignness as it is built into the visuals of the story. Scenery transports a localized audience into a foreign space and place; it constitutes a mode of visual tourism. Thus, avid fans of television dramas can become so enamoured by the sceneries that the locations become 'must visit' places when the fan gets a chance to be an actual tourist to the country in question and, upon arrival, feel completely familiar with the environment, with a sense of *deja vu*. Screened sights have become tourist sites. At their peak of popularity, Singaporean tour promoters did organize tours of the 'trendy drama' sites in Tokyo for the fans; similarly for Singaporean fans of Korean television drama.[27]

An extension of scenery and a marker of foreignness to the Singapore audience is the seasons. Seasons are completely foreign to Singaporeans who live permanently in hot tropical weather. Autumn, with its changing colours of the trees, and winter, with its cold and snow, are quintessentially romantic – enhancing the romantic themes intrinsic to the programmes – for Singaporeans.[28] Along with cold weather is fashion. The hot, humid tropical climate is a bane of the fashionable because it denies them the seasonal changes of fashion. The fashionable Singaporean is thus jealous of the layers upon layers of warm clothes that enables the making of fashion statements; (s)he is denied the 'layering' effects of fashion.

Chinese languages

There are four 'official' languages in Singapore; of which English and Mandarin are two that are used in dubbing and subtitling of imported television programmes and films from East Asia.[29] All imported films and television programmes, no matter whether the products are in Korean, Japanese or other Chinese languages, such as Cantonese from Hong Kong and *Minan* from Taiwan, are dubbed into Mandarin; as we will see, this practice has great significance in the consumption of East Asian popular culture. English subtitles are often provided, reflecting the primacy of the language in Singapore. There have been instances when a television series was particularly popular and English subtitles were not provided, which led to public complaints from those Chinese who do not understand Mandarin that they were being denied the pleasure of watching the series.[30] Obviously, dubbing of foreign languages makes the cultural products accessible to a Singaporean audience. Japanese and Korean popular music have a far lesser presence in Singapore than popular television programmes and films, largely because of the language barrier. However, with duo-sound technology in television, a Singapore audience can watch Korean and Japanese programmes in the original languages if they so choose.

Elsewhere in Chinese-dominant East Asian locations, Mandarin is not always the official or even the primary language of the Chinese. In Hong Kong, the official language is Cantonese, with Mandarin making an increasing appearance. In Taiwan, a mixture of Mandarin and *Minan* or *Fujian* language is the common practice. All these Chinese languages and more were, until not too long ago, living languages among the Singaporean Chinese population. In the early 1970s, they were labelled derogatorily as 'dialects' and since then banned from all mass media. In their place, the government, ostensibly with the desire to unify the multi-tongued Chinese population through a single, standard, formal language, adopted Mandarin as the one language – both phonologically and written – for all Singaporean-Chinese; thus, there is dubbing of Chinese programmes other than those in Mandarin.

Technically, Chinese languages can be phonologically strange to each other, although a relatively common written language facilitates communications among all literate Chinese. Consequently, Chinese films and television programmes will very often have the dialogue and lyrics of songs in one of the Chinese languages, with Chinese written scripts as subtitles. These subtitles are different from conventional subtitles that translate the film's language into a completely different language, such as from Japanese to English. Although the Chinese subtitles may have the same translation function, they translate from one Chinese language to another Chinese language.

Although it is often assumed that the written script provides the common language for all literate Chinese, the meaning of a written word is nevertheless not always assured. This is because a written word may be used only phonologically as a transliteration of spoken sound, with the meaning of the word completely discarded; then, it would be completely meaningless if read literally. For example, in Cantonese, the common sound for 'yes' is 'hai' and a Chinese character with similar sound is used in the written script of Cantonese newspapers or Cantonese subtitles. The written word means 'category' in Mandarin, which is completely different from 'yes', which in Mandarin, would be written as 'si'. The multiple Chinese languages situation sometimes creates an interesting disjuncture when a Chinese audience is watching a film or a television programme that is dubbed in one Chinese language while carrying scripted Chinese subtitles in another, when one simultaneously listens to and reads the dialogue.

One disjuncture that significantly reflects the localness of consumption is illustrative. As noted earlier, the ethnic Chinese population in Singapore was, before the 1970s, very Chinese-multilingual. However, this multilingualism has been progressively reduced by the official policy of banning the use of all Chinese 'dialects' except Mandarin. Nevertheless, the presence of the suppressed languages was never entirely erased. A socially and culturally severe consequence is that, other than Mandarin, all Chinese languages have come to mark their users as the poorly educated, the uncouth and the rude – generally, the lower social class. These other Chinese languages can no longer be entrusted with carrying a serious communicative substance. The appearances of speakers of non-Mandarin Chinese languages on television programmes and films have thus become 'laughable' and are, accordingly, used by local producers to get the desired 'comedy' effects (Chua and Yeo 2003). Significantly, this 'comedy' effect has been put to critical use recently in locally produced films, in which dialect-speaking Chinese characters use their self-deprecation as a mode of marking their marginalization in Singapore society, particularly English-speaking Singapore society, thus raising indirectly the marginalization of 'Chineseness' in spite of being a demographically Chinese predominant society.

The marginalization of other Chinese languages also has its effect on the boundary crossing of films and television programmes from other Chinese–East Asian locations. For example, in Taiwan, for those who are politically committed to independence from the PRC, there is a preference to speak exclusively *Fujian*; this language has been politically elevated to the status of 'Taiwanese' and is spoken with pride. The mismatch of the political status of the *Fujian* in Singapore and Taiwan results in a Singaporean audience laughing at the wrong nuances in the dialogue, and it completely misses the political intention of the insistence of the use of the language in Taiwan television, films and music.[31] The result is not only a miscommunication but also a political misreading when a Singaporean who still knows the remnants of *Fujian* watches a Taiwanese film (Chua and Yeo 2003). A similar effect often holds in the way Chinese-Singaporeans watch Cantonese programmes from Hong Kong.

Beyond the specificity of one Chinese language other than Mandarin, a different kind of disjuncture occurs when two Chinese languages are used simultaneously, one in dialogue and in subtitles. On one occasion, I was watching a Korean gangster comedy in which the dialogue was in Mandarin and the subtitles in Cantonese.[32] Questions of the migratory path of the film arose: given the Chinese linguistic conditions, the film was likely subtitled in Hong Kong and re-dubbed in Singapore, otherwise the dialogue would be in Cantonese.[33] If this was so, then the film is first exported from Korea to Hong Kong and then re-exported to Singapore. Or could it have been dubbed and subtitled in Hong Kong in two different languages in the first place, in order to capture both Mandarin and Cantonese-speaking audiences in Hong Kong itself, since there is a significant, and increasing, size of only Mandarin-speaking audiences? And was the film then re-exported to Singapore? Finally, could it have first been imported to Singapore and intentionally dubbed and subtitled in the two languages with the view of re-exporting it to Hong Kong? The path of circulation of this particular film is an interesting puzzle. This latter issue is, perhaps, not specific to a Singapore–Chinese audience but all Chinese audiences as such.

The above elements are constitutive of the audience position of Singaporean consumers of East Asian popular culture. They may or may not be shared by audiences elsewhere in the region. Indeed, it is conceivable the localized audience of each of the constituent locations of East Asia will have its own set of specific characteristics grounded and derived from their respective everyday life. However, it is not inconceivable that the audiences of all the constituent locations would also share certain characters by virtue of being consumers of the same products in circulation. These questions remain empirical issues that can be answered only through collaborative comparative analysis across the region. The possibility of a set of shared features raises, perhaps, the most contested question that underlies this conceptual exercise and its implied research programme.

Effects of viewing: a pan East Asian identity?

Finally, to the most controversial issue that needs to be considered in the conceptualization of East Asian Popular Culture, the question of an East Asian identity as an ideological effect of the production and consumption of the popular culture. This is, no doubt, the most elusive and the most contentious question. An initial step must be to identify how the cultural products may work in unison to create a discursive and imaginative space for the emergence of such an identity.

First, it should be noted that the border-crossing popular urban television dramas and films have displaced, if not erased, references to East Asia as a space of 'traditional' in relation to a sense of the 'rural'. The struggle of rural migrants into urban areas in search of better living is a theme that is almost exclusively still used because of its continuing social relevance for PRC products (Sun 2002). The image of the rest of East Asia is urban and modern. Occasionally, the 'rural' will be evoked as a nostalgic reference to a mythic time and place when life was simpler and people less cunning than the urban present, an imaginary escape but not a place to live in the present.[34] The emphasis of the urban facilitates culture-border crossing; in contrast to the idea of 'tradition' that specifies the 'uniqueness' and 'boundedness' of a culture, the urban increasingly lacks specificity, it is 'anywhere', 'anyplace' and 'anyone'; the urban thus passes through cultural boundaries through its insistence on 'sameness' – the most extreme of this urban sameness is, of course, the banking district of every city, and then come the shopping complexes of imported goods, each differentiated only by landmark buildings of famous designer-architects, that is if one even knows who these star-architects are in the first place.

Second, the focus on the urban, young and single professionals has a tendency to displace the central place of the family; an urban consumer-oriented culture is evoked to displace the tradition-soaked Confucianism. However, unlike the American series – such as *Friends* and *Sex and the City* – in which the family has all but disappeared, in East Asian urban television dramas and films, the family still has a presence. The family appears to alternate between an obstacle and a refuge to romance and the city. The presence of family and its influence varies across the locations of production and is accordingly inscribed into the culture products. As noted earlier, references to family as an institution have largely disappeared in Japanese 'trendy' drama, but continue to have a very significant presence in Korean urban drama series, and strong versions of Confucian filial piety are still often scripted into such series. The presence/absence of the traditional family is, in part, determined by the 'age' of the screen characters; it can be completely absent in series that feature urban, adult professionals in their late 20s or older but has to be present in teenage or school drama series, even if vaguely.

For example, in a number of recent Taiwanese series centred on college youth, the family is referred to in dialogue but parents are distinctively absent, enabling the children to do things contrary to parental desires.[35] Furthermore, in these instances, the screen characters have sympathy and form coalitions with each other against their parents. Within the context of the popular culture programmes, Confucian familialism appears to be largely a working-class ideology in contemporary East Asia. Dramas with working-class themes and characters continue to be inclined to use the family as the foil to dramatize its members' struggle for upward mobility, while the middle class turns increasingly urban, inscribed with competitive consumer-based individualism dictated by global capitalism.

Third, the emphasis on urban lifestyles enables the screen-visual images of middle-classness to transcend the relativities of real incomes in different East Asian locations. Although the income of an accountant, for example, in Taiwan and Korea is much lower than in Tokyo and Singapore, so too are the relative costs of living in these cities; consequently, while each urban middle-class stratum is embedded in their different spatial locations, a comparable level of lifestyle consumption is available to most, if not all. With the emphasis on lifestyles, urban middle-class Asians are given inter-changeable bodies on screen, despite income differences and geographical location dispersion. Young professionals throughout East Asia will be able to identify with their screen representations in a 'clear, direct, and seemingly transparent' manner, through the 'immediate and efficacious' media that is television and films (Chow 1995: 10). To put it more categorically, urban dramas are imaginable, realistic, and foster identification among those who are willing to interpellate themselves into the screen, by temporarily or permanently suppressing their national/ethnic identities; again, Iwabuchi's empirical study of the Taiwanese audience's reception of Japanese trendy dramas and his conceptualization of this reception as based on 'coevalness' testifies to this (Iwabuchi 2002: 85–120).

Fourth, East Asian popular culture, following the lead of Japanese popular culture, consciously cultivates a genre of 'beautiful' youth; particularly noticeable are the leading men who are boyish, have brown-tinted, full, fluffed-up long hair and are earnest, if not innocent – a mode of 'beautiful masculinity'.[36] The lead women are beautiful, of course, self-confident with very non-revealing clothing, commonly in formal office wear, showing very little explicit sexuality. The packaging is so similar that only the trained eyes of aficionados who can recognize the actors and actresses are able to distinguish one country's product from that of another, particularly television drama, on screen; an indoor shot of a Korean drama looks very much like one from Taiwan or Japan or, increasingly, from Hong Kong.[37] The beautiful look is arguably more important than acting or other performing talents, including singing. The similarity of packaging and the indistinguishable sameness creates visual and discursive room for the insertion and projection of an idea of 'Asian-ness', with nationalities suppressed.

Finally, unlike the Confucian identity that is supposed to seep quietly, through years of implicit socialization, into the identity formation of East Asians, the construction of a pan-East Asian identity is a conscious ideological project for the producers of East Asian cultural products, based on the commercial desire of capturing a larger audience and market. Apart from co-financing, producers increasingly feature and mix artistes from different East Asian locations in the same television programmes and films, in the hope that audiences from the different locations will identify with the artistes that are hewn from their own space and place, thus expanding aggregate consumption. At its most extreme, a film may even be divided into 'filmlets', each coming from a different location, with its own directors and artistes.[38]

Obviously, there are no linear effects of consumption of popular culture on such a film's audience, ranging from completely without resonance to a strong sense of identification. However, the displacement of the 'traditional', the emphasis on the similarities of young, urban, middle-class consumer lifestyles and a projection of 'Asianness' are the building blocks to facilitate audience identification across East Asia with the personas on screens, large and small. One could say that the discursive and conceptual spaces for the possible emergence and formation of a pan-East Asian identity have been laid. It is here that the strategic methodological insistence of the audience position is consequential. It has to be a local audience, watching imported products, which is potentially able to transcend their grounded nationalities to forge abstract identification with the foreign characters on screen, a foreignness that is in turn potentially reabsorbed into an idea of (East) 'Asia'.

The expansion of East Asian popular culture is still a nascent phenomenon. It is also a new phenomenon in generational terms, for it has emerged in the current generation of youth below 30 years, who can or have moved beyond, or embrace only much diluted emotions towards the histories of the Japanese colonization of Korea and Taiwan, Japanese incursions in China before the Second World War and Japanese occupation of Singapore during the War. The place of this nascent phenomenon in the process of East Asian identity formation will obviously be long and circuitous. Although there are signs of its emergence, they come, ironically, from instances of attempts to suppress it by national political interest. A good example is the case of Chang Huei Mei, more popularly known as 'Ah Mei'. The Taiwanese popular singer was banned from concert appearances in the PRC, and all her appearances in screen and print ads selling soft drinks were removed from the media, after she performed at the inauguration ceremony that celebrated Chen Shui Bian's election to the Presidency of Taiwan. Nevertheless, Chang's popularity among her PRC fans continued unabated and she was finally allowed to return to perform in the PRC after having performed during the 2001 government supported trade union May Day celebration in Singapore and a charity show in Hong Kong in August the same year. The singer, buoyed by her fans across the ethnic Chinese dominant locations in East Asia, appeared to be beyond the clutches of the state and, in fact, able to bring the latter to capitulation. Whatever may be one's political sentiment about the desirability of such an emergent identity, its possibility is nevertheless an issue that cannot be analytically avoided, without intellectual dishonesty.

Conclusion

Popular cultural products criss-cross cultural borders everyday in East Asia. East Asian popular culture has been able to carve out a significant segment of the regional consumption economy, although the US popular culture industry still dominates the airwaves and the large and small screens, and is unlikely to be displaced anytime soon. Furthermore, players in the US media industry are not sitting by waiting to lose part of their global empire but have formed a partnership with East Asian producers to produce East Asian popular culture.[39] There are, of course, many worthy researches to be done on the economies of these transnational product chains and product flows; similarly for researches into the organizations of the media industries in different specific locations and transnationally. The possibility and realization of a transnational East Asian identity, facilitated by the production and consumption of popular culture, remain empirical questions in each of the East Asian locations. The mapping of the manifest forms and contents of the pan-East Asian identities will require the collaboration of researchers in different locations, as the identities take shape and change. I only hope that I have delineated here a conceptual boundary within which such empirical research may find a starting point.

Notes

1 An earlier version of this essay, entitled 'The making of an East Asia popular culture', was delivered as the Inaugural Distinguished Visiting Scholar Lecture, Carolina Asia Center, University of North Carolina, Chapel Hill, 28 February 2003.
2 Throughout this essay, Korea refers only to South Korea.
3 This later morphed into the search for 'Asian Values' in multiracial societies in Southeast Asia, such as Singapore and Malaysia.
4 The literature on diasporic Chinese businesses abound, covering the entire range of praises and critiques; a selection of which is Redding (1990), Ong and Nonini (1997), Ong (1999) and Yao (2002). Similarly for the issue of pan-Chinese identities, see Ang (2001); Chun (1996).
5 This attempted inscription of Confucianism to the ethnic Chinese Singaporeans further ignored the historical fact that the local Chinese educated community was heavily influenced by the May Fourth Cultural Movements of the early 1920s and had since then adopted the use of the so-called 'common language' rather than classical texts in the local Chinese school curriculum.
6 While the generalized term of 'Western' influence is often evoked, Europe is largely absent in the popular cultural sphere.
7 In a consumption space like Singapore, where there are substantive quantities of South Asian population and Malays, Bollywood products also feature prominently in the popular cultural sphere.
8 The popularity of Japanese television drama led Iwabuchi to organize the International Conference on Japanese Drama, International Christian University, Tokyo, 2001. The book of edited essays is to be published by Hong Kong University Press.
9 This finding about the Japanese audience's reception of other Asian popular culture as 'nostalgia' for Japan's past is, as noted by Chin (2000: 250) also found in another Japanese critic's, Tsubouchi Takahiko's, 'explanation' of the popularity of the television drama Oshin, in Asia during the 1980s. Chin himself, instead of criticizing such a simplistic reductionist reading of the reception by Asian audiences, proceeded to use these Japanese readings as the evidence for the presence of 'Asian regionalism', 'Asianism' or 'Asian consciousness'. Without empirical evidence of the basis for a popular reception of audiences in different locations in Asia, the best that could be said of Takahiko's reading is the critic's own desire 'to Japanize Asia' and 'Asianize Japan', 'a desire both to see Japan as the embodiment of Asia and to construct Asia as a reflection of Japan's past' (Chin 2002: 254). Such Japanese 'superiority' is, if anything, a sure way of alienating other Asians rather than a basis for an Asian regionalism.
10 The very sketchy and preliminary manner of this unfinished piece of conceptual work is presented as the inaugural lecture of the Carolina Asia Center, and is, I hope, consistent with the spirit of the opening of the new research centre where the definition of its character lies in the work that has yet to be done.
11 This was a statement given by the producer of *Tokyo Love Story* in a talk given at the International Conference on Japanese Drama, International Christian University, Tokyo, 2001. Up until that time, and in contrast to the 'trendy dramas' that feature urban, beautiful, independent and unmarried working youth, the Japanese television series were largely about family problems (Gossmann 2000).

12 Eva Tsai (2003) gives a fascinating reflective biographical account as a researcher of such dramas.

13 International Conference, 'Feeling "Asian" Modernities: TV drama consumption in East and Southeast Asia', International Christian University, Tokyo, 2001. During this conference, analysts from Southeast Asia countries, with the exception of the paper from Singapore, worked on non-Japanese drama series.

14 During a trip to Kyoto in February 2004, I saw a Korean television drama being broadcast in two languages. This and one news event channel were the only non-Japanese programmes in 12 channels.

15 As the Japanese pop cultural products were 'illegal', this generated additional pleasures of illicit consumption, see Kim Hyun-Mee (2002).

16 The first category includes the films *Shiri* and *Joint Security Area*, the second includes the films *My Wife is a Gangster* and *Guns and Talk*. In the last film, mid to late 20s assassins who could design elaborate plots of murder are shown to be completely at the mercy of women, as clients and as potential victims.

17 The most outstanding example of a Singaporean singer who had achieved star status is Stefanie Sun Yanzi. The Taiwanese, I am told, claim her as one of their own.

18 Eric Ma of the Chinese University of Hong Kong reported research on such productions during the 'Feeling Asia' conference at ICU, 2000.

19 For example, the most recent US financed *wuxia* blockbuster film, *Hero* by Zhang Yimou, was immediately subjected to debates of whether the director, known for having his films banned in the PRC because of their critical political stance, has 'sold out' to the Party when his film was released without event, and was a huge commercial success.

20 In the 1950s, there were two film studios that produced Malay films

21 The latest joint production television series, for 2002–2003, is *'Innocently Guilty'*, an oxymoronic translation of the Chinese title *'There Are Fair Weather Days in the Law'* (*Fa nei you qiang tian*), a reference to the generalized Chinese belief that the court is to be avoided at all cost. It stars the Hong Kong actress, Anita Yuen.

22 One such instance is the 'ghost story', *The Tree*, which features Singaporean leading actress, Zoe Tay, next to Hong Kong actor, Wu Zhenyu (Francis Ng).

23 One Singaporean actress that has achieved some success through this mode of entry is Fann Wong, who played the Little Dragon Girl in a popular *wuxia* series and, in 2003, starred in Jackie Chan's blockbuster, Hollywood produced movie, *Shanghai Knights*.

24 It was also the very first popular Mandarin television series to be screened in Indonesia after the lifting of the official ban on Chinese culture. It was alleged that the *'Meteor Gardens* has turned many Indonesians on to anything Chinese' (*Straits Times*, 21 July 2002).

25 Significantly, if the idea of 'Asian-ness' is absent, identification is also absent. For example, Sun (2002: 100) notes that PRC audiences consistently report that they do not identify (*rentong*) with Taiwanese or Hong Kong televisual cultural products.

26 I am concerned in this essay with only the ethnic-Chinese audience. The two other constituent racial groups in the population, Indians and Malays, have their own viewing preferences in Hindi movies, and thus, in spite of geographic and national location, do not partake significantly in the East Asian popular cultural sphere.

27 Tour companies in Singapore organize tours to these televised sites for the fans. In a recent instance (December 2002), a group of Singapore tourists to Korea for winter holidays were persuaded by one of the members of the tour to change their designated ski resort to one that was featured in the popular drama series, *Winter Sonata* (*Straits Times*, 4 January 2003).

28 Singaporeans never fail to mention their first encounter with snow in their correspondence and memories. For example, a friend who is a foreign correspondent wrote this in January 2003: 'It is very cold here in New York and temperatures fall below zero daily. But I was lucky enough to see amazing snow fall in the city, which drives New Yorkers crazy but had me with a big smile on my face for the entire day.'

29 The other two are Malay and Tamil, a southern Indian language of the majority of the resident Indian population.

30 English subtitles make it, in principle, accessible to South Asian and Malay audiences, although as noted in note 25, Malays and Indians seldom consume East Asian popular culture, preferring Hindi films and locally produced Malay programmes.

31 The association of low social class status with *Fujian* language is most pronounced in popular music, where popular songs imported from Taiwan *Fujian* are sung almost exclusively by working-class men in karaoke lounges.

32 In the late 1990s and early 2000s, there was a spate of Korean movies that were well received in Singapore, that featured 'emotionally sensitive' male or female gangsters who may be social misfits or inept, but deadly sophisticated in their execution of murder and other violence. This mismatch of character is used as the foil for comedy; such as *Guns and Talks* and *My Wife is a Gangster* in contrast to the more serious gangster film, *Friends*.

33 For a Singaporean Chinese who does not realize that Cantonese can be phonologically transcribed with Chinese written words, the subtitle would be incomprehensible. Nevertheless, he or she would still understand the dialogue.

34 In most newly industrialized countries that have undergone very rapid urbanization, nostalgic imagination of the simplicity of pre-industrialized and urbanized life is often evoked as a lament and a criticism of the high stresses of life in the city in pursuit of better material life (Chua 1995).

35 This is especially true in the depiction of absent parents who are fabulously successful entrepreneurs but thoroughly negligent of their families, especially teenage children; for example, the series *MVP Lover* and the earlier mentioned *Westend Youth*.

36 For example, the four members of Taiwanese F4 (*Meteor Gardens*), the Taiwan-born Japanese actor, Takashi Kaneshiro, and Korean actors Bae yong Jun (*Winter Sonata*) and Won Bin (*Friends*).

37 In one instance, in Hanoi, I was not able to identify where in East Asia the on-screen drama programme was from until Mandarin could be heard beneath the local quality voiceover of Vietnamese narration; in Vietnam, due to lack of funds, there is a tendency for a narrator to tell the story that is unfolding in a voiceover rather than dubbing the original dialogue.

38 The most recent offering in this 'filmlet' structure is a film called 'Three', which contains three ghost stories, one each from South Korea, Thailand and Hong Kong, produced by a company that is consciously aiming to be pan-Asia.

39 Indeed, all the major record companies – Polymer, EMI, Bertelsmann, Warner and Sony – are already here, with East Asia accounting for up to a quarter of their global earnings since the mid 1990s. In addition, Warner Brothers have entered into joint production, with Singapore's Raintree Pictures and Hong Kong's Milkway Image, of a new film adaptation of popular Taiwan romance novel, *Turn Left, Turn Right*, in 2003 (*Straits Times*, 17 December 2002).

References

Ang, Ien (2001) *On Not Speaking Chinese*, London: Routledge.

Chen, Xiaoming (2000) 'The mysterious other: postpolitics in Chinese films'. In Arif Dirlik and Xudog Zhang (eds) *Postmodernism and China*, Durham, US: Duke University Press, 222–238.

Chin, Leo (2000) 'Globalizing the regional, regionalizing the global: mass culture and Asianism in the age of late capitalism', *Public Culture* 12(1): 233–258.

Chow, Rey (1995) *Primitive Passions: Visuality, Sexuality, Ethnography and Contemporary Chinese Cinema*, New York: Columbia University Press.

Chua, Beng Huat (2003) *Life is not complete without shopping*. Singapore: Singapore University Press.

Chua, Beng Huat and Yeo Wei Wei (2003) 'Singapore cinema: Eric Khoo and Jack Neo – critique from the margin and mainstream', *Inter-Asia Cultural Studies* 4(1): 117–125.

Chua, Beng Huat (1995) 'That imagined space: nostalgia for the *kampungs*' in Brenda S.A. Yeoh and Lily Kong (eds) *Portrait of Places: History, Community and Identity in Singapore*, Singapore: Times Editions, 222–241.

Chun, Allen (1996) 'Fuck Chineseness: on the ambiguities of ethnicity as culture as identity', *Boundary 2* 23: 111–138.

De Kloet, Jeroen (2000) '"Let him fucking see the green smoke beneath my groin": the mythology of Chinese rock'. In Arif Dirlik and Xudong Zhang (eds) *Postmodernism and China*, Durham, US: Duke University Press, 239–274.

Gossmann, Hilaria M. (2000) 'New role models for men and women? Gender in Japanese TV drama' in Timothy J. Graig (ed.) *Japan Pop: Inside the World of Japanese Pop Culture*, Armonk, New York: M. E. Sharpe, 207–221.

Han, Seung-Mi (2000) 'Consuming the modern: globalization, things Japanese, and the politics of cultural identity in Korea', *Journal of Pacific Asia* 6: 7–26.

Iwabuchi, Koichi (2002) *Recentering Globalization: Popular Culture and Japanese Transnationalism*, Durham, North Carolina: Duke University Press.

Kim, Hyun-Mee (2002) 'The inflow of Japanese culture and the historical construction of "Fandom" in South Korea'. Paper presented at the International Conference on Culture in the Age of Informatization: East Asia into the 21st Century, Institute of East and West Studies, Yonsei University, 16 November.

Kim, Soyoung (2003) 'The birth of the local feminist sphere in the global era: trans-cinema and Yosongjang', *Inter-Asia Cultural Studies* 4(1): 10–24.

MacFarquar, Roderick (1980) 'The Post-Confucian challenge', *Economist*, 9 February.

Ong, Aihwa and Nonini, Donald M. (1997) *Ungrounded Empires: the Cultural Politics of Modern Chinese Transnationalism*, London: Routledge.

Ong, Aihwa (1999) *Flexible Citizenship: the Cultural Logic of Transnationalism*, Durham, North Carolina: Duke University Press.

Redding, S.G. (1990) *The Spirit of Chinese Capitalism*, Berlin/New York: W. de Gruyter.

Stronach, Bruce (1989) 'Japanese television' in Richard G. Powers and Hidetoshi Kato (eds) *Handbook of Japanese Popular Culture*, New York: Greenwood Press, 127–166.

Sun, Wanning (2002) *Leaving China: Media, Migration and Transnational Imagination*, Lanham, Maryland: Rowan and Littlefield Publishers.

Tsai, Eva (2003) 'Decolonizing Japanese TV drama: syncopated notes from a "sixth grader" researcher relocated in Taiwan', *Inter-Asia Cultural Studies* 4(3): 503–512.

Tu, Wei-Ming (1991a) *The Triadic Chord: Confucian Ethics, Industrial East Asia and Max Weber*, Singapore: Institute of East Asia Philosophy.

Tu, Wei-Ming (1991b) *The Living Tree: the Changing Meaning of Being Chinese Today*, Special issue, *Daedelus, Annals of the American Academy of Arts and Science*.

Tu, Wei-Ming (1991c) 'The search for roots in East Asia: the case of the Confucian revival' in Martin E. Marty and R. Scott Appleby (eds) *Fundamentalism Observed*, Chicago: Chicago University Press.

Yao, Souchou (2002) *Confucian Capitalism*, London: Routledge.

Chapter 5

Producing knowledge of Southeast Asia

A Malaysian view

A. B. Shamsul

Introduction

For a long time, students and scholars from Southeast Asia studied and learnt about the region not from one another directly but rather in an indirect manner, from the experts located at the various Centres of Southeast Asian Studies in the United States of America, the United Kingdom and Australia. Very rarely, a Malaysian would enrol as a graduate student at Universitas Indonesia to study about Indonesian history, or at Chulalongkorn University to study Thailand's bureaucracy, or at the University of the Philippines to study Philippine society and culture. The Malaysian would usually end up either at Cornell University, or the School of Oriental and African Studies, University of London or Monash University in Australia as a graduate student.

The question is why don't Southeast Asians learn and study about Southeast Asia from one another? There are a number of interconnected circumstances and reasons for this to have happened.

Historically, the region was divided up into spheres of influence by European colonial powers, namely, the Dutch, British, French and the Americans. Each of the divided colonized components, or colonial states, became modern nation-states after independence. Although independent, each of these nations still has strong, especially economic, ties with its former colonizers. The less emphasized tie, nevertheless significant, is in the educational sphere. For instance, until now, high school examinations in Malaysia are still conducted by, or franchised from, the Cambridge Examinations Syndicate, UK. It means that those who have finished high school in Malaysia are eligible to enter any tertiary institution in the UK, provided they have the right qualification and, most importantly, funds. Similarly, Indonesians who could afford to study abroad after high school would choose to go to the Netherlands, the Filifinos to the USA, the Vietnamese, Cambodians and Loatians to France, the Bruneians and Singaporeans, as well as Malaysians, to Canada, New Zealand and Australia.

As a result, there exists not only different educational systems in Southeast Asia but, more importantly, different knowledge acquisition and production systems, or traditions, informed by the specific needs of nation-building in each of the newly independent nation-states. This gives rise to what I would call 'methodological nationalism', a way of constructing knowledge based mainly on the 'territoriality' of the nation-state and not on the notion that social life is a universal and borderless phenomenon, hence the creation of 'Indonesian studies', 'Malaysian studies', 'Philippine studies', 'Thai studies' and the like. In spite of this, these knowledges in the epistemological sense, one that is based on European schema and social theories deeply rooted in, and informed by, Cartesian principles.

Therefore, the nationalist project of each of the new independent nation-states of Southeast Asia, especially in the educational sphere, remains grounded and framed within an educational framework established by colonial administrations that, in turn, continues to sustain its colonizing functions, even after independence. The production of knowledge in each of the new nation-states in the region has been shaped within that colonial knowledge frame and epistemology. It also shaped the way individuals within the nation-states perceive and make choices about 'what good education is', 'who the experts are' and 'where to go' to pursue further education, both at the undergraduate and graduate level. The colonizer–colonized nexus in knowledge production was not only sustained but also strengthened by specific programmes such as the Colombo Plan scholarship.

Kratons, or the 'exalted centres', of Southeast Asian studies were then established in three major locations: first, the Commonwealth centres in the UK (SOAS), Australia (ANU, Monash), Canada (UBC) and New Zealand (Auckland), second, the Dutch centres (Leiden and Amsterdam), and in the USA (Ithaca and Berkeley). Hundreds of Malaysians, Bruneians, Singaporeans and Burmese would rush to the Commonwealth centres, Indonesians to the Dutch centres, and the Filifino to the USA, to learn about their own history, politics, economy, society and culture from the experts at these centres.

In 1993, a group of Southeast Asian scholars, all graduates from these centres, convened in Jakarta and agreed to put forward a proposal to promote 'Southeast Asian studies for Southeast Asians' (Taufik and Yeti 1994, Nordholt and Visser 1995). The proposal eventually became an exchange programme for Southeast Asian scholars and institutions with the main aim of making it possible, for the first time, in an organized manner, for Malaysians to learn about Filifino history directly from Filifino historians, about Thai society and culture from Thai professors and so on. That was the beginning of the project that came to be called the 'Southeast Asian Research Exchange Program' (SEASREP), generously funded, initially, by the Toyota Foundation and, later, together with the Japan Foundation through its Asia Center established in October 1995.

This new endeavour could be viewed as an attempt to decolonize social science in Southeast Asia. However, it is an illusion that the existence of such a project has transformed the old ways, so to speak. The old colonial-based knowledge production tradition and orientation still dominate the institutional development of academic institutions in the region. At the same time, a variety of local forces determines the forms and functions of the knowledge, both in the academic and the larger political, cultural and public context. This essay presents an observation and elaboration on the construction of the colonial-based knowledge production system in present-day Southeast Asia, and it also highlights the kind of internal and external challenges it has to come to terms with. I shall draw empirical examples from the Malaysian experience, the one that I am presenting as a case study.

The production of social scientific knowledge: a paradigmatic framework

It is useful to begin any attempt to analyse the state of the art of a particular form of knowledge with a clear picture of the general position of the knowledge itself. This is especially important if we are trying to examine the articulation of a particular form or variant of that knowledge, in our case the production of social scientific knowledge not only about Southeast Asia but also the development of social science and its set of academic disciplines within Southeast Asia. We must also not forget that both 'Southeast Asia' and 'Malaysia' are, in themselves, accepted geo-political units as well as analytical units.

I therefore contend that any explanation regarding the development and production of social scientific knowledge within Southeast Asia cannot be separated from the development of social scientific studies about 'Southeast Asia'. In other words, I am arguing that there has been a symbiotic relationship between the growth of social science as an 'ideal academic endeavour' in Southeast Asia and the growth of 'area studies' called 'Southeast Asian studies'. This has been the case because the social science that arrived at the shores of the Malay archipelago, in the form of an ideal academic endeavour or area studies, came together, as part of the whole baggage, with European imperialism and domination that began about six centuries ago. Since no knowledge exists outside history, it could be said that the history of Southeast Asian studies is the history of the growth of social science in Southeast Asia. What is more significant is the fact that, in recent times, with the commodification of education, the post-colonial states in Southeast Asia have played a direct role in shaping the development of both the 'academic endeavour' and the 'area studies' aspects of social science in Southeast Asia.

I would suggest that the production of social science, as a corpus of knowledge, can be divided, for analytical purposes, into three main components which are, however, always interrelated.[1] Each of these components can be best seen as a process, thus recognizing not only its dynamic internal features but also the external factors that shape it. The three processes we are concerned with here are: (i) the construction of knowledge; (ii) the bureaucratization of knowledge; and (iii) the consumption of knowledge.

Briefly, the construction process essentially involves an exercise of theorizing and conceptualizing about a subject, employing a variety of analytical tools and perspectives in order finally to accumulate and create a form of knowledge on that subject matter. The bureaucratic process involves the way in which the acquisition, accumulation and dissemination of the knowledge is organized and financed in accordance with the contemporary interests of the organizers. The consumption process involves the audience or end-user of the knowledge, which usually shapes the way the knowledge is to be contextualized and packaged, which in turn influences the construction process as well as the bureaucratization process.

Based on this paradigmatic framework, I would like to put forward the following arguments that could serve as a backdrop to our understanding of the development of social science and social scientific knowledge about and within Southeast Asia.[2]

First, I wish to suggest that there exists, for want of a better term, a knowledge baseline or continuum of social science in Southeast Asia, which I call the 'plurality to plural society continuum', which inspires the construction of knowledge about and within Southeast Asia. Secondly, within this continuum, at both concrete and abstract levels, there seem to be a number of axes upon which the creation, maintenance and practice of social science and social scientific knowledge about, and within, Southeast Asia have been approached. We shall now examine them in turn.

The 'knowledge baseline': the plurality to plural society continuum

Social scientific knowledge on and in Southeast Asia has a clear knowledge baseline, meaning a continuous and interrelated intellectual-cum-conceptual basis, which emerged from its own history and has, in turn, inspired the construction, bureaucratization and consumption process of this knowledge. The two popular concepts that have been used frequently to characterize Southeast Asia are 'plurality' and 'plural society', both of which are social scientific constructs that emerged from empirical studies conducted within Southeast Asia by scholars from outside the region.

In historical terms, 'plurality' characterizes Southeast Asia before the Europeans came and divided the region into a community of 'plural societies'. Plurality here signifies a free-flowing, natural process not only articulated through the process of migration but also through cultural borrowings and adaptations. Politically speaking, polity was the society's political order of the day, a relaxed non-bureaucratic style of management focusing on management and ceremony by a demonstrative ruler.[3] States, governments and nation-states, which constitute an elaborate system of bureaucratic institutions, did not really exist until Europeans came and dismantled the traditional polities of Southeast Asia and subsequently installed their systems of governance, using, to borrow Bernard Cohn's[4] concept, 'colonial knowledge', which gave rise to the plural society complex.

Historically, therefore, plural society signifies both coercion, mainly through colonialism, and an externally-initiated project. It also signifies the introduction of knowledge, social constructs, vocabulary, idioms and institutions hitherto unknown to the indigenous population (such as maps, censuses, museums and ethnic categories), the introduction of market-oriented economies and systematized hegemonic politics. 'Nation-states' or 'state-nations' emerged from this plural society context.

It is not difficult to show that the production of social scientific knowledge on and within Southeast Asia has moved along this plurality–plural society continuum. When we do research and write about Southeast Asia during the period before the advent of European influence we are forced to respond to the reality of that period, a period that saw the region as the meeting place of world civilizations and cultures, where different winds and currents converged, bringing together people from all over the world who were interested in 'Gospel, gold, and glory', and where groups of indigenes moved in various circuits within the region to seek their fortunes.[5] As a result, we have had, in Java, a Hindu king with an Arabic name entertaining European traders. In Champa, we had a Malay raja ruling a predominantly Buddhist populace trading with India, China and the Malay archipelago. Whether we employ the orientalist approach or not, we cannot avoid writing about that period within a plurality framework, thus emphasizing the region's rich diversity and colourful traditions. In other words, the social reality of the region to a large extent dictates our analytical framework.

However, once colonial rule was established and the plural society was installed in the region, followed later by the formation of nation-states, our analytical frame, too, changed. Not only did we have to address the reality of the plural society but also the subsequent developments engendered by the existence of a community of plural societies in the region. We began to narrow our analytical frame to nation-state, ethnic group, inter-nation-state relations, intra-nation-state problems, nationalism and so on. This gave rise to what I have called 'methodological nationalism', a way of constructing and using knowledge based mainly on the 'territoriality' of the nation-state and not on the notion that social life is a universal and borderless phenomenon, hence the creation of 'Indonesian studies', 'Malaysian studies', 'Thai studies' and so on.

With the advent of the Cold War and the modernization effort we became narrower in our frame of reference. We began to talk of poverty and basic needs in the rural areas of a particular nation, also focusing on resistance and warfare, slums in urban areas, and economic growth of small-holder farmers. The interests of particular disciplines further narrowed our focus to various communities in remote areas, a particular war in a mountain area, a failed irrigation project in a delta, or gender identity in a market town.

In fact, in numerical terms, the number of studies produced on Southeast Asia in the plural society context supersedes many times those produced on Southeast Asia in the plurality context. Admittedly, social scientific studies about and within Southeast Asia developed much more rapidly after the Second World War. However, the focus became increasingly narrow and compartmentalized not only by discipline but, more importantly, by plural-society produced nation-state boundaries, hence the '*kratonization*' of social scientific knowledge in Southeast Asia.

It is inevitable that a substantial amount of social scientific knowledge about, and in, Southeast Asia itself, paradigmatically, has been engendered and contextualized within the plural society framework, because 'nation-state' as an analytical category matters more than, say, the plurality perception of the Penans of Central Borneo, who, like their ancestors centuries ago, move freely between Indonesia and Malaysia to eke out a living, along with other tribal groups and outside traders, ignoring the existence of the political boundaries. In fact, anthropologists seem to have found it convenient, for analytical, scientific and academic expedience, to separate the Indonesian Penans from those of Malaysia when, in reality, they are one and the same people (King 1999, Shamsul 1996).

Therefore, the plurality–plural society continuum is not only a 'knowledge baseline' but also a real-life social construct that was endowed with a set of ideas and vocabulary, within which people exist day-to-day. It could be argued that it is both abstract or academic and also real in the everyday life of Southeast Asians.

To complicate matters, at the abstract level, and as a subset of the knowledge baseline, the social scientific study of Southeast Asia has been approached along a number of axes, at least four in the construction-cum-bureaucratization process. The consumption process axis has been motivated by at least three central motivations. Let us now briefly examine these axes.

The construction and bureaucratization axes: the four major axes

There are at least four major axes along which the construction and bureaucratization of social scientific knowledge about Southeast Asia have taken place. These axes are my own construction and abstraction based on my observations on the numerous debates on: (i) what constitutes not only social science but also 'Southeast Asian studies' in Southeast Asia and Malaysia; (ii) how to approach, describe and study Southeast Asia; (iii) why social science is combined with humanities (or arts) in most Southeast Asian countries; (iv) how to organize teaching, research and funding relating to social science and area studies; and (v) how social scientific findings and reports, based on basic and applied research, are written. Of course, the validity and applicability of these constructions could be contested, modified, improved and refined. I admit that these axes are closely connected and, in many cases, overlap. The overlapping could emphasize differences and/or similarities.

The first axis is that of discipline versus area studies. There is an ongoing debate between those who prefer to approach the study of Southeast Asia from a disciplinary perspective, on the one hand, and those who believe that it should be approached from an area studies angle employing an inter-disciplinary approach, on the other.

The former prefer to start clearly on a disciplinary footing and treat Southeast Asia, or Malaysia, as a case study or the site for the application of a particular set of theories that could also be applied elsewhere globally. The aim of such an approach is to understand social phenomena found in Southeast Asia and to make comparisons with similar phenomena elsewhere. Those preferring the latter approach see Southeast Asia as possessing particular characteristics and internal dynamics that have to be examined in detail using all available disciplinary approaches with the intention of unravelling and recognizing the indigenous knowledge without necessarily making any comparison.

The bureaucratic implications of these two approaches can perhaps be clearly discerned in the way social science, in general, and social scientific knowledge about Southeast Asia, in particular, is taught, gathered and disseminated. This brings us to the next axis, namely undergraduate versus postgraduate studies.

Those who favour area studies often believe that Southeast Asian studies can be taught at the undergraduate level to obtain a university degree specializing in Southeast Asian studies through the establishment of Southeast Asian studies departments or programmes, combining the basic skills of various disciplines to examine social phenomena particular to the region. Acquiring proficiency in one or two languages of the region is a must in this case. The problem with this bureaucratic strategy is that these departments have to be located in a particular faculty, say, in the arts, humanities or social science faculty. This denies those with a background in the natural sciences the opportunity to learn about and understand Southeast Asia.

Therefore, the discipline-inclined people would argue that Southeast Asian studies should be taught at the graduate level to allow those grounded in the various disciplines, whether in the social or natural sciences or in other fields of study, to have an opportunity to specialize in Southeast Asian studies. Therefore, a geologist or an engineer who, for instance, is interested in the soil and irrigation systems of Southeast Asia could examine not only the physical make-up of Southeast Asia but also the human–environment relationship. This is particularly relevant at the present time since environmental and ecological issues have become global concerns.

As such, this has forced many individuals, institutions and governments to think carefully about how they should invest their precious time and money when they are requested to support the setting up of, say, a programme, centre or institute of Southeast Asian studies. They often ask whether universities should continue to have the prerogative on the teaching, research and dissemination of knowledge about anything connected with Southeast Asia. Why not in non-university institutions?

This brings us to the third axis; university versus non-university. For many years, we imagined that only at university could we acquire knowledge about Southeast Asia, whether approached from the disciplinary or area studies angle. We know that large sums of money have already been invested in developing Southeast Asian studies programmes and institutes in the context of the university bureaucratic framework. This is the accepted tradition even today.

However, many governments and other funding bodies feel that to obtain knowledge about Southeast Asia one need not go to university, but could acquire it through non-academic but research-oriented institutions established outside the university structure to serve particular purposes. Historically, the intelligence units within various governments have adopted this strategy. At present, with the mushrooming of 'think tanks' and national research bodies such as LIPI (Indonesian Institute of the Sciences) in Jakarta and ISEAS (Institute of Southeast Asian Studies) in Singapore, the acquisition of competent knowledge about Southeast Asia for special purposes outside the university framework has been possible.

It seems that the underlying rationale for such a pluralistic-bureaucratic approach in the pursuit and acquisition of knowledge about Southeast Asia is that a university is the home of basic research while non-university organizations should be the home of applied research. This brings us to the final axis, academic versus policy-oriented research.

While academic endeavours pursued within the context of Southeast Asian studies in the universities are motivated by interest in basic research, which is by definition scholarly, those pursued outside the universities are often perceived as not being scholarly enough because they are essentially applied or policy-oriented in nature and serving rather narrow, often political, interests.

It is argued that the critical difference between these two approaches is that the academic one is always open to stringent peer-group evaluation as a form of quality control, but that the applied one is not always assessed academically. In fact, the latter is often highly confidential and political in nature, thus denying it to be vetted by the peer group, hence its perceived inferior scholarly quality. The basic research-based academic endeavours are therefore seen as highly scholarly, whereas the non-academic ones are perceived as highly suspect as scholarly works and not considered to contribute to the accumulation of knowledge on Southeast Asia.

However, research institutes such as ISEAS in Singapore would argue that, even though it is essentially a policy-oriented research institute mainly serving the interests of the Singapore government, it still produces scholarly work of high quality and encourages basic research to be conducted by its research fellows either on an individual or a group basis. In other words, a non-university research institute of Southeast Asian studies, such as ISEAS, could simultaneously conduct applied and basic research without sacrificing the academic and scholarly qualities of its final product; or put in another way, it is 'policy-oriented yet scholarly'.

It should be clear by now that the arguments found in each of the discussions regarding these axes are guided by specific contextual and 'consumer' demands for, or 'the demand curve' of, Southeast Asian studies. In other words, more often than not, the construction as well as the bureaucratization process of knowledge on Southeast Asian or Malaysian studies has been framed to answer one basic question, 'knowledge of 'Southeast Asian studies' for whom and for what?' and this we shall examine next.

The consumption axis: the three motivations

The consumption axis is about serving the needs of the audience and end-user. In this context it could be argued that social scientific knowledge in and about Southeast Asia is a commodity with a market value. Often the 'market rationale' and not the 'intellectual rationale' prevails in matters such as the setting-up of a Southeast Asian programme, centre or institute. In fact, the funding of research on Southeast Asian studies has often been dictated not by idealistic, philanthropic motives but by quite crass utilitarian desires, mainly political or economic ones. There are at least three important motives found in the consumption of the knowledge process about Southeast Asia.

The first of these concerns basic, applied and strategic research. As funding for education often becomes the victim of national government budgets, especially in market-driven economies of the developed and developing world, research in general has been defined in terms of national research and development (R&D) objectives. Since funding from non-governmental bodies, local or international, is relatively small compared with that offered by national governments, the latter often set the agenda for research in a particular nation-state. Social science research often has to abide by such a 'nationalist' agenda.

The unfortunate thing is that more often than not the allocation for social science research is relatively small compared with that for the natural sciences. The latter are seen as crucial to the 'scientific and technological' development of the nation in its pursuit of industrialization. The former is often seen, for want of a better term, as some kind of 'supporting and service science'. In fact, in many circumstances, social science and social scientists are often viewed with suspicion for their alleged 'subversive potential'; hence they need to be controlled or 'sanitized of negative elements'. This usually leads to the emergence of government-sponsored, and hence favoured and preferred social science on the one hand, and a less-favoured social science on the other. The latter is said to be found in universities and the former within government bureaucratic organizations.

With such a divide, universities often emphasize the importance of basic research in social science, while government agencies concentrate on applied social scientific research serving national interests, such as evaluating the implementation of particular government economic programmes for the poor. However, recent trends show that even universities have begun to be actively involved in applied research, such as consultancy tasks.

In Southeast Asia, social science research has therefore become more nation-based and rarely crosses national boundaries, whether in the field of basic or applied research. Findings from this research have become the integral component of what is now known as Southeast Asian studies.

Neither must one ignore the role and contribution of non-governmental bodies, or the NGOs, in the construction and expansion of the corpus of knowledge called Southeast Asian studies or Malaysian studies. Bodies such as think-tanks, environmental groups, human rights organizations and consumer associations have recently contributed enormously to the process of producing this knowledge; we can no longer ignore their contributions. They help to reshape the agenda of social scientific research in universities and government agencies. Some of these groups are locally based, while others are international organizations with political clout. It is well known that the International Monetary Fund (IMF), the United Nations (UN) and the World Bank (WB) are equally involved, either directly or indirectly, in the whole exercise of setting the agenda of basic and applied research on nations in Southeast Asia and the rest of the world.

From the perspective of individual researchers, wearing many hats has become the fashion of the day. Very rarely can academic social scientists avoid the attraction of becoming consultants, whether for government, international bodies or local private firms, for market survey exercises or policy evaluation projects. It is therefore hard for individual social scientists to remain interested simply in basic research. Many have, in fact, decided to devote their careers solely to applied research, particularly for institutions in the private sector.

It could therefore be argued that the line that divides basic and applied research is becoming increasingly blurred. In this context, it is relevant to see the basic-applied research axis as sited in a continuum rather than framed in a dichotomy.

The second motive relates to the teaching of social science, both at the undergraduate and postgraduate level, which, especially pertaining to Southeast Asian and Malaysian studies, is still largely the concern of universities. A university is essentially academic in nature but not without an interest in policy orientation. It is organized along the undergraduate–graduate axis mentioned above; that is, within a bureaucratic frame of discipline or area studies. The decision as to which way the arrangement should be shaped is often influenced by market forces beyond the university, namely the job market.

However, what is interesting here is the unequal treatment given to different social science disciplines. For instance, economics and political science are always given top priority for their visible returns unlike, say, anthropology and sociology. Interestingly, the latter disciplines are often viewed as dangerous or subversive because of their views, which are perceived as critical and often anti-establishment.

As a consequence, there have always been attempts to domesticate the teaching of social science within the university context by organizing it into area studies or even ethnically motivated anthropological studies (Malay studies?). Such an exercise is often rationalized ideologically; namely, to fulfil the national interest. So the teaching of social scientific knowledge on Southeast Asia or on a particular nation within the region has been organized within the context of an institute of, for instance, Malay language and culture, Brunei studies or Thai studies.

However, this way of organizing social scientific instruction on Southeast Asia is not recent in origin. In Malaysia, the British, for example, pioneered the establishment of Malay studies, Chinese studies, Indian studies, and Islamic studies departments in Malaysia and Singapore, all in the orientalist mould modelled on the School of Oriental and African Studies (SOAS) in London. As such, one could argue that the domestication of social science is part of a colonial legacy and its orientalist projects as much as it is motivated by recent ethnicized national interests. Both, in many ways, are responding to plural society circumstances or concepts mentioned above.

Another important dimension of the teaching of social science and Southeast Asian studies within Southeast Asia is related to what could be termed the 'fractioning' of the bureaucratization process. From economics emerged business or public administration studies, which have been developed into full-fledged degree-awarding academic faculties. Prompted by pragmatic and contemporary concerns, multidisciplinary academic faculties, such as development studies, communication studies, extension studies and human ecology, have also been set up, dealing with important 'thematic areas' considered critical to the countries' development and progress. These faculties seem to serve specific, real and imagined, market demands.

However, we rarely examine the state of the teaching of social science subjects within the primary and secondary school system. Here, the choice of which discipline and empirical focus is very highly selective and again dictated by the so-called national interest. It is indeed a novelty at this level to study countries other than one's own, as school textbooks and curricula have shown.

On the whole, teaching needs are often organized around a broad philosophy of education embraced by the nation-state and inspired by two major orientations: to fulfil intellectual objectives and vocational needs. These imperatives will ultimately order the teaching of social science and Southeast Asian studies in the region.

The third motive comes under the heading of public interest or general education. It is important to recognize how public interest has shaped aspects of social science teaching, research and knowledge dissemination within a nation-state. For instance, we know of the existence of museums (research and exhibition types), public libraries, national cultural centres, botanical and medical research institutes, zoos, academies of the arts and so on, which have been established with public and private funds to meet the public's perceived general education needs.

In this context, linkages with commercial interests are often very strong. Many of these organizations fulfil national touristic needs, fostering national identity objectives or supporting 'national awareness' campaigns. Of course, what is offered and disseminated for such purposes is a kind of 'social scientific knowledge made easy' for immediate public consumption. However, the conceptual basis of such efforts is serious, indeed involving well-trained social scientists in a number of fields, either as academic resource persons or professional consultants. This is the public fact of social science, made up of a combination of academic and popular knowledge.

In the private sector, the importance of social scientific knowledge about Southeast Asia must not be underrated. Market survey research, for instance, is crucial for commercial purposes, within which social science, in various guises, is utilized in a number of creative ways for advertising purposes. After all, in some sense, marketing is about the manipulation and reshaping of public habits or the peddling of cultures, particularly stereotypes, for profit motivation. In this context, social science graduates are in great demand for their general knowledge of the society, but they are subsequently retrained professionally to suit particular markets or commodity-specific contexts, whether it is *jamu* (herbal medicine) or computers. We can say that public interests vary according to national economies and societal needs. Social scientific knowledge is then processed and packaged in accordance with these circumstances.

In other words, the unwritten, underlying and ever-present motive that drives the consumption axis, and its 'three motives', is the market, which, in turn, presents itself in various forms fulfilling not only public but also private sector needs and imperatives. It is in this context that we could say that the growth of social science in the last few decades or so in Malaysia and elsewhere has involved the interaction of not only academic analyses and public advocacy but also commercial imperatives.

Postwar social science in Southeast Asia: a brief survey

It is important to examine closely the political history and political economy within which social science developed and grew in Southeast Asian nations after the Second World War, namely, during the Cold War era.

The postwar period could be seen as the decolonization era. However, many of the newly independent nations retained much of the economy and political structure established by their former colonial masters. In other words, the colonial states were the precursors to most of the new nations. As such, the new nations also inherited the colonially created plural societies that have engendered endless internal problems from their inceptions during colonial rule to the present day.

While the decolonization process was taking place, the western world was increasingly polarized along an East–West divide based on ideological grounds, namely communist against non-communist. The Cold War became a chilling reality to many, including those in Southeast Asia, where the threat of 'red devils from the North' and the hegemony of the domino theory combined to create fear and bloodshed amongst inhabitants of many communities and provided justification for foreign powers to intervene and dictate their lives.

These political circumstances made the governments of western nations, in particular the United States, the biggest consumer and promoter of social science, especially in the form of social scientific knowledge about Southeast Asia. National security and international peace and stability interests were the main motivating factors in the development of social science on Southeast Asia, or Southeast Asian studies, extensively supported by the United States and other western nations, which professed that the fall of Southeast Asia into the hands of the communist bloc would mean that half of the world would be communist. The general mood was that, in order to maintain a 'free' Southeast Asia, the region had to be protected and defended at any cost. To defend Southeast Asia was considered not only a strategic demand but almost the salvation for the West. And the best way to save Southeast Asia, the major powers decided, was to modernize it.

One must not forget, however, that the United States was, and still is, the largest arms-producing nation in the world. It is not too far-fetched to suggest that the United States has much interest in testing its weapons in 'local wars' and demonstrating their effectiveness to potential buyers. As we all now know, this is what happened in Vietnam. It was obvious that the Vietnam War became the testing ground not only for the various American-produced weapons but also those produced by the Chinese and Russians. In the end, this war became the human-inflicted ecological disaster of the century.[6]

The academic dimension of Cold War political developments was integrated into and articulated through the activities of various institutions, both governmental, such the US State Department, or non-governmental, such as the Ford Foundation.[7] The whole process was inspired by the modernization approach, which eventually gave rise to numerous multi-disciplinary theme-oriented studies, such as policy studies, development studies, population and demographic studies, public administration and policy studies and communication and media studies. These are, in fact, the precursors of present-day 'think-tanks'.

By the late 1950s, we began to see in the countries of Southeast Asia the emergence of a demarcation between intellectually-based and policy-based social science, the former supposedly focusing its interest on basic research and the latter on applied research. Each seems to be a domain of its own, almost like different '*kratons*', co-existing in the same era on the same island, hence the '*kratonization*' of social science in Southeast Asia. It was not a coincidence that intellectually-based social science was taught in the universities or tertiary institutions, while the latter was taught in government funded professional institutions.

By the 1960s, national governments in Southeast Asia began to introduce policy-oriented, national-development-inclined social science institutions in Indonesia (LIPI), Singapore (ISEAS), Thailand (NIPA) and Malaysia (INTAN). Since these governments had allocated much funding for this purpose, sometimes with strong financial support from countries such as the United States and Australia, they began to send large numbers of local social scientists, including senior government officials, to be trained abroad under various types of graduate studies programmes. Many went to universities in the United States and Australia, where special degree-awarding programmes were created, mostly in well-known universities, primarily for citizens of developing countries.

By the 1970s, there was a substantial group of qualified bureaucrats, each with an MA or Ph.D. in social science, within government services, statutory bodies and semi-governmental agencies in Southeast Asia. They played a central role in the national development exercise or planned change process in Southeast Asia. As expected, economists led the way, followed by political scientists and other disciplines. If the economist was playing the 'prima donna' role, the political scientist played the 'guardian angel', having their own research institutes specially built by the respective governments. While the former served as 'meteorologists' of the national economies, the latter had the role of the nation's 'political clairvoyants', predicting where trouble would come from next, how to resolve it, which groups were to be banned and which individuals were to be detained.

By the 1980s, there was a proliferation of private think-tanks and research institutes, all manned by social scientists of various types and different theoretical persuasions, advising each government what was good or bad for the country. Some of these institutions were stooges for foreign bodies, others were puppets of the governments they served and a few catered for a handful of high-powered politicians. One must not forget that the army and police force have played a crucial role in supporting some governments in Southeast Asia, even to this day. These 'national security' personnel attended specially created armed forces staff colleges to be trained in 'soft' and 'hard' social sciences.

One could say that social science in Southeast Asia began to move from a stage of being 'nationalized', or serving the interests of national development, in the 1960s and 1970s, to being 'professionalized', or serving the interests of the state and capital as well the international community, in the 1980s and 1990s. The latest development has been the rise of the bureaucratic intellectual class within Southeast Asian countries. This class is largely made up of academics and corporate executives who move in and out of universities, government bodies and private institutions as economic advisors, policy risk consultants and various sorts of expert analysts.

One must understand the political economic contexts of these countries: the faster their economies grow, the more foreign investors rush in and the more analysts and experts are needed to ensure healthy profits are made, losses are reduced and capital flight can be speedily arranged. Expert advice from social scientists of all kinds plays a crucial role in serving the interests of local and foreign capital as well as state interests.

During these years, especially from the 1970s onwards, the so-called academic or intellectually based social science taught in the universities of Southeast Asia continued to be dwarfed, almost subjugated, as a result of the dominance of the nationalized (read policy-oriented) and professionalized social science. As a compromise, more and more social scientists from the universities were being drawn into the professional arena purely for financial gains. Many began to wear at least two hats: the academic and the consultant. They were often joined by their counterparts from abroad.

Within universities, the professionalization tendencies continued to result in the further bureaucratic fractioning of social science, especially in the teaching of social science-oriented subjects, with the rise of faculties, centres, institutes, schools and departments of business studies, strategic and security studies or policy studies. One could argue that, since most of these universities are funded by the government and even more by private money, they were merely, as it were, responding to market demand. Therefore, the 'vocationalization' of university education began in earnest in Southeast Asia in the 1980s.

In short, by the 1980s and 1990s, academic social science and the social scientists themselves began to be disempowered. In fact, the social scientists were often seen as anti-development, ungrateful critics of the government, rabid radicals and so on. Many of them became activists and joined either local NGOs or, to give a greater feeling of security, internationally based NGOs. Universities were infiltrated by spies and informers mainly to defuse student power and to reduce the influence of the so-called overly theoretical academics. This situation, in some countries in the region, created tension between the university-based and non-university-based social scientists, only to the disadvantage of a healthy development of social science in Southeast Asia in general. The university-based social scientists remained the weaker group.

Inevitably, the political and economic circumstances that influenced the development, growth and *kratonization* of social science in Southeast Asia not only set the priorities of the social science research agenda but also dictated the kind of 'relevant' genre to be popularized in the social scientific sphere. Non-university social science concentrated on policy oriented matters or profit-motivated business issues. The university social scientists, as a group, were divided. Some, driven by idealism of the highest order, preferred to concentrate on theoretical debate with their counterparts abroad. Others, seeing academic jobs purely from a careerist point of view, put much effort into basic teaching and consultancy jobs outside. However, it must be noted that not all universities in Southeast Asia pay their academic staff as well as those of the Singapore or Brunei governments. We know that in Indonesia, for instance, academicians have to seek other income-generating activities because their salaries are simply not enough to survive or support their lifestyle.

As a result of this pattern of development, libraries around the world began to be flooded with a massive amount of knowledge and literature on economic development and growth in Southeast Asia, its political stability, religious tolerance and ethnic cooperation. These papers were produced mainly by non-university organizations and the private sector. Poverty came to be, and still is, seen as a statistical problem; trees and political detainees now occupy centre stage. However, one has to admit that a healthy development has occurred, especially in the context of environmental studies, in that more and more social scientists and natural scientists are getting together to examine the problems in detail, both in basic and applied research terms.

As universities in Southeast Asia become 'corporatized', basic research within social science is seriously undermined. This is despite the fact that everyone concerned with education in Southeast Asia is in agreement with Allan Bloom's (1988) celebrated book *The Closing of the American Mind*, which proposes the need to intellectually liberalize the US education system to produce more intellectuals and inventors, instead of vocationalizing education and producing in droves certificate-holders for the market.

We shall now turn to a more concrete case, namely the Malaysian one, to understand how social science got rooted, consolidated and deepened over a century.

A case study: Malaysia

During the colonial era, social science was essentially fulfilling the needs of colonial administrative science. Malaysian colonial administrator–scholars contributed tremendously to shaping the way we see, understand and study our societies. The academic social scientists such as Firth (1948), Leach (1951) and Freeman (1950) were instrumental in preparing a series of reports for the British colonial government in its second forward movement after the War.

The establishment of tertiary educational institutions, and hence the teaching of social science in Malaysia, could also be said to fulfil colonial interests. For instance, the University of Malaya was established to attract the local Chinese populace into the English-medium education system with the intention of diluting the influence of the Chinese-medium education system in Malaya that was seen as the propagator of communist ideology (Ong 1992). The setting-up of academic departments such as Malay studies, Indian studies and Chinese studies was very much in line with the needs of colonial science fashioned by a set of investigative modalities that begets the 'colonial knowledge'.

However, it is also necessary to recognize the fact that not all of the social scientific studies conducted in the colonial era were simply fulfilling colonial needs. Some, such as Firth's (1946) classic work, *Malay Fishermen*, have generated debates and new research and have become classics in their fields.

It is interesting to note that the writings that resulted from social scientific research on Malaysia during the colonial period centred on the relationship between three popular themes: culture, economics and political action. The theoretical roots of this inquiry can be traced back to the contributions of well-known pre-war scholars such as Boeke (1910) and Furnivall (1939) on social change in the societies of Southeast Asia during the colonial period. Postwar scholars such as Wertheim (1965), Geertz (1963) and their younger colleagues in the 1980s and 1990s examined similar social change-related issues, namely the transformation of Southeast Asian societies in the wake of nation-state formation and the increased integration of local communities into a global economy (King 1999, Evers 1980).

For instance, a study by the anthropologist Geertz (1973) on the culture of power influenced numerous political scientists and historians in the 1980s and 1990s to conduct a detailed study on the articulation of the culture of power both at the national level, such as the important work of Anderson (1983), and the local level, such as the contribution of James Scott (1976, 1985). These works, like Geertz's, have had a much wider theoretical impact. Anderson's 'imagined community' and Scott's 'moral economy' stimulated debates amongst scholars from all disciplines, inside and outside Southeast Asia, not only about the phenomenology of nationalist and peasant politics respectively, but also about the importance of comparative political studies.

Another popular area of social science inquiry is about multiethnic Malaysia that continues to fascinate social scientists, local and foreign. Its main focus has been on the study of the notion of identity, particularly ethnic identity and ethnic group relations. Malaysian specialists, since the days of Furnivall up to the present era of Donald Horowitz (1985), have made significant contributions in this field, which many Europeanists have currently found to be important and helpful in their re-examination of the issues of identity and ethnicity in the present troubled Europe.

Another increasingly important topic that has attracted Malaysianists from outside and within these countries is related to religion, in particular religious revivalism. There is a deep-seated international concern over the rise of fundamentalist activities in some of the economically more successful countries of Southeast Asia, such as Malaysia and Indonesia. Quite a number of books and conference proceedings have been published recently on this issue (Hefner and Horvatisch 1997). Research on this subject has increased, too, as a result of the availability of funds from outside Southeast Asia, particularly from countries with large economic investments in the region.

Of late, many excellent works on Malaysia, mainly by anthropologists, have initiated the questioning of prevailing theories about gender identity. Those who have conducted empirical research amongst peasants and factory workers have been the main contributors to this trend. Besides, 'women and Islam in Southeast Asia' has also become a major research topic. A recent popular topic is, of course, on the economic crisis.

The rise of a number of Southeast Asian countries, including Malaysia, as 'little economic tigers' or 'dragons' has increased research on Southeast Asian political economic systems, not only amongst social scientists but also in business schools around the world. Therefore, political economy has been a major growth area in Malaysian studies, especially in the last six years or so. Much of the analysis within this field has focused on the pace and socio-political features of the region's economic growth, thus challenging the statist emphasis or previous works in political economy.

Most of the contributions by non-academic bodies interested in Southeast Asia or Malaysia, such as international think-tanks, could also be categorized as political economic studies, although mostly applied in nature. Many scholars of Malaysia, mainly economists and political scientists, have been engaged as consultants or resource persons by such institutions, thus blurring further the academic and non-academic divide that has existed in Malaysia. Besides fulfilling the traditional demands of government agencies involved in formulating trade policies, one could argue that one of the new demands, in the 1980s and 1990s, on Malaysian social studies, as well as on Southeast Asian studies in general, comes from large corporations with investments in Southeast Asia. Indeed, more so now in the present economic crisis that seems to be easing, at least as observed from the recent set of statistics in the financial sector.

Here we can clearly see the criss-crossings of the construction-cum-bureaucratic axis and the consumption axis outlined above. This can also be seen in the context of the development of social science for national development purposes within Malaysia.

In Malaysia, no such body has been established. In Indonesia, for instance, there is LIPI and in Thailand NIDA. Bodies such as INTAN (*Institut Tadbiran Awam Negara,* or the National Institute of Public Administration) does play a similar role but INTAN's coverage is not as extensive as that of LIPI. In fact, the effort is currently more decentralized in Malaysia, in the sense that institutions such as MIER (Malaysian Institute of Economic Research) and ISIS Malaysia (Institute of Strategic and International Studies) were established to fulfil specific governmental social scientific needs.

The role of NGOs such as ALIRAN, *Sahabat Alam Malaysia* and the Consumer Association of Penang should not be underrated in the production of social scientific knowledge about Malaysia, not only in terms of academic consumption but also public interest. The Museum Sarawak plays a double role: as a world-class research museum on Borneo society and environment and as an excellent public museum.

At the personal experience level, I was introduced to social science when I registered in the first batch of university students to enrol in the newly established Social Science Programme at the University of Malaya in 1970. The Programme was introduced as part of a national policy on 'National Unity' that the Malaysian government launched in the aftermath of the racial riot of May 1969 in Kuala Lumpur. Although the idea was mooted long before, the government then thought that it was timely for subjects, such as anthropology, sociology, psychology and political science, officially categorized as social science disciplines, to be introduced and taught as fully fledged disciplines within proper academic departments. The government thought that social science subjects at the university would provide some Malaysians with the analytical tools to understand deeper ethnic problems in Malaysia and perhaps solve some of them. Such an opinion was indeed suggested by a group of American scholars, funded by the Ford Foundation, who submitted a report on the racial riot as well as how to prevent future ones.

This was by no means the first time Americans have been involved in social science related activities in Malaysia. In fact, they had been involved since the mid-1960s, at the invitation of the then Deputy Prime Minister, Tun Razak, who was the Minister of Rural Development and personally keen to introduce a new system of development administration to replace the old British one (Shamsul 1986). This was the context within which Milton Esman (of University of Pittsburgh, and later of Cornell University) and John Montgomery (Harvard University) came to Malaysia in 1965 to prepare a detailed report, called the Montgomery Report (Shamsul 1986: 6) on how to set up an effective development administrative machinery in Malaysia. It was the most crucial document in that it almost single-handedly 'nationalized' social science in Malaysia. It made a number of recommendations, such as the setting up of a National Institute of Public Administration (INTAN), the sending of civil servants for graduate studies in the United States with support from Malaysian and American governments and funding agencies, and the importation of American social scientists to work in various government departments to streamline research activities, such as in the Statistics and Census departments.

The Americans and their version of social science had never had such direct access to the government prior to this, for the British colonial government and its officers had always preferred the gentle way of dealing with the 'natives', rather than the 'fast-food' style of the Americans. Scholars such as Professor Milton Barnett of Cornell University (with whom I had the opportunity to work as a research assistant in 1971), who represented the Agricultural Development Council (ADC), New York in Southeast Asia, had a room next door to Tun Razak, the then Prime Minister of Malaysia, to advise him on matters relating to large-scale land development programmes and to secure R&D funds and generous support from bodies such as the Agricultural Development Council, New York.

I would argue that the development of non-university social science has received a tremendous boost with the involvement of the Americans since the mid-1960s. Since universities in Malaysia are fully funded by the government, their development has been very much dictated by civil servants and politicians, who are mostly social science-trained. The government's social science *kraton* was definitely bigger and more powerful than the university one. As a result, up to the present day the government has refused to set up a National Social Science Research Council, hence Malaysia is not represented in UNESCO's Social Science Research Councils of Asia. The government continues to send civil servants with degrees in social science to represent Malaysia in international social science meetings.

Politically, the university social science has been perceived as a source of problems for the government. From the mid-1960s to the mid-1970s, university students majoring in social science formed the most powerful pressure group in Malaysia, often forcing the government to change its domestic and international policies. The student leaders were students of social science, who received tremendous support from their lecturers. In short, the social science students and teachers at the local universities were, at the same time, social activists. However, the government imposed a draconian law to reduce university students and lecturers to second-class citizens in Malaysia, through 'The University and the University College Act 1974' (UUCA). This, among other things, banned university lecturers and students from becoming committee members of associations, societies and trade unions outside the campus. The 1974 Act also demanded that every academic manuscript produced by the academic staff had to be vetted by their heads of department – fortunately this ruling has not been enforced.

In December 1974, when the biggest student riot in Malaysian history occurred, about 1500 students were temporarily detained and a further 100 student leaders and lecturers were detained without trial, some for up to six years. Since then there has been an all-out effort by the government to 'sanitize' university social science. But this effort has had limited success.

In 1977, as a result of the initiative of a group of concerned university lecturers, a protem committee was set up to organize the establishment of a Malaysian Social Science Association (MSSA). This was the direct result of the first ever Conference on the 'State of Social Science in Malaysia' organized by the Department of Anthropology and Sociology, UKM, in 1974. MSSA managed to attract some 300 members, academics and non-academics. Very few social scientists from the government bureaucracy enrolled as members of the association. Today, it remains predominantly an organization of university-based social scientists. Very rarely has the association been consulted by the government on matters pertaining to social issues and problems within the nation, nor have its members been invited in their official capacity to represent Malaysia in UNESCO social science meetings and so on. Lately, serious attempts have been made by the government, through the Ministry of National Unity and Social Development, to set up a Permanent Social Science Committee, chaired by a senior civil servant.

The MSSA has been active in publishing and has organized talks, seminars and conferences, but has had little nationwide impact, except that it is often perceived as representing the 'opposition voice'. Due to the fact that, individually, the leaders of the association have been associated with what the authority perceived as anti-establishment movements in the country, some having been detained without trial after the student riot of 1974, and it is therefore easy for the government and, to a certain extent, the public, to perceive the association as anti-establishment-inclined, too. We must also take note that there are other 'social science' associations operating in Malaysia before MSSA, such as the Malaysian Economic Association, based at the Faculty of Economics and Administration, University of Malaya.

Recently, it has been reported that the government is very concerned about international criticism on Malaysia and is considering how to curb this criticism, for example on issues relating to labour, ecology and human rights. The critics have been recognized as foreign social scientists who work closely with local ones. To arrest this perceived problem, the government has recently decided to monitor applications for research permits by foreign and local researchers, particularly social scientists, more directly through the Prime Minister's Economic Planning Unit.

Social scientific writing in Malaysia can therefore be broadly divided into two types: first, that produced by the non-university group (government bodies, private firms, NGOs, etc), ranging from consultant reports and evaluation studies to propagandistic material for public consumption; and, secondly, those produced by the university group. The former has certainly been flooding the market. The latter has been produced in dribs and drabs, most of which are read by a small specialised audience.

The theoretical approach of each of these groups can generally be divided into pro-establishment and critical of the establishment. It must be emphasized that within each approach there exist a number of schisms, often based on ethnic lines and sometimes on ideological ones (Shamsul 1998). For instance, amongst the so-called radical academics, or those critical of the establishment in Malaysia, it is quite common to use some form of Marxism to advance chauvinistic ethnic arguments, hiding behind pseudonyms, often using names of a different ethnic group, say a Chinese using a Malay name as a pseudonym or vice versa (Shamsul 1996: 491–494).

There is also a tendency amongst social scientists who study Malaysia, irrespective of their theoretical orientation, to view Malaysia either from an alarmist or a consensus point of view (Shamsul 1998). In the former, Malaysia is perceived as society waiting for doomsday, when a massive racial conflict will destroy it. In the latter, Malaysia is seen as a society continuously struggling to find a fulcrum and, since it has to contend with a moving one, it is experiencing an almost perpetual state of 'stable tension'.

Conclusions

There are a number of observations that we could make based upon the above discussion, pertaining to the state of social science and social scientific knowledge within and on Southeast Asia and its development as well as its practice within the said region.

First, in order to present a useful analysis regarding social science in Southeast Asia, we have to locate its origin, development and practice in a longitudinal perspective, reaching back historically over a number of centuries well into the pre-colonial period. Secondly, we have to recognize the significant transformative impact of the colonial era upon the construction and organization of social scientific knowledge in the region; in particular, the major orientation shift from that of plurality to plural society-based, the latter being a consequence of a conscious divisive politico-economic policy of European colonial masters in Southeast Asia. The central role of colonial investigative modality and the resultant 'colonial knowledge' is recognized. With decolonization, the newly emerging nation-states inherited most of the colonial structures of economy and governance, including the knowledge construction structure.

Thirdly, driven by the Cold-War-initiated modernization programme, social science and the construction of social scientific knowledge within Southeast Asia were generally shaped by external forces and dominated by the ideological needs of major Western powers, especially the United States. As a result, the development and practice of social science in Southeast Asia have been dichotomized, to a great extent, by the policy-versus-academic divide. However, the push towards modernization became the prime national agenda item for most of the independent Southeast Asian nations. As a result, Southeast Asian social science was further divided into government versus academic versus private sector types of social science, resulting in the reorientation and reorganization of the knowledge construction process within the region's social science. The proliferation of heavily social-science-based private and government-sponsored think-tanks and research institutes has been the result of this development. Nonetheless, it is also important to note that despite this centrifugal tendency, most of the social scientists who run the different institutions in the three above-mentioned '*kratons*' were drawn mainly from one important pool, namely, academia. In other words, there was an active movement of social scientists to and from the government, the academic and the private-sector-funded institutions. It is also commonplace for an academic to play a double role; as an academic social scientist and, at the same time, as a professional consultant to a private agency. Quite often some have ended up in politics and become cabinet ministers. The Malaysian case provided an interesting example of the divide between 'academic social science' and 'civil servant social science'.

It could therefore be argued that such a development saw the rise and expansion of what could be called the bureaucratic intellectual class within each of the Southeast Asian nations. This class is made up of highly qualified and experienced local social scientists who, directly and indirectly, define and shape not only the content of government policies and the trajectory of corporate activities, but also the survival of social science in academia.

However, this is not an unexpected trend if we re-examine the experience of the development of European capitalism. It was the alliances of intellectuals and commercial groups advancing their respective causes that first brought together the agents, ideas and interests necessary to set the European industrial capitalism-based modernization project in motion. With the race towards becoming a Newly Industrialized Country (NIC) taking central stage in most Southeast Asian countries, the importance of social science and social scientific knowledge, in its various forms and colours, has increased tremendously, further consolidating the *kratonization* process.

The pluralized existence, nature and pattern of present-day social science and social scientific knowledge in Southeast Asia will persist, especially within the context of the phenomenon of highly integrated markets and culture, popularly known as globalization.

Finally, through this brief and schematic essay, I hope I have shown the following: first, it is important for us to see social science, both the knowledge and the practice, beyond the state versus society dichotomy; second, its development has many trajectories each shaped by history, political economy and the sheer weight of contemporary events; third, there are individuals who matter in the shaping of social science into what it is within a nation, be it a nationalized or professionalized one; fourth, social scientists are not a homogeneous lot, commonly being divided into factions by ideologies and social realities of nations; and, finally, I am not sure that social science outside Southeast

Asia, especially in the developed western nations and Japan, is really free from the nationalized and professionalized or, for that matter, ethnocentric, influences alluded to in this essay, especially those described in the Malaysian case.

It shall take at least another generation of social scientists for the present 'Southeast Asian studies for Southeast Asians' programme to take root and consolidate, because the challenges to it being fully realized would come not only from national governments but also from the academic community in the developed countries.

Notes

1   Of course, there exists an enormous literature on the construction of knowledge in general. However, what is more relevant for the present discussion is that relating directly to the field of social sciences and humanities and also to the area of studies called 'Southeast Asian Studies'. For the former, a must read is Edward Said's (1978) *Orientalism*, and its later edition published by Penguin in 1995, which has a postscript by Said that contains a reply to his critics. It is also useful to read Nandy (1983). For an interesting analysis on the construction of knowledge in anthropology see Nencel and Pels (1991). For a useful summary of the development of Southeast Asian studies as an area of studies, in this case in the USA, see Hirschman (1992). See also, *Southeast Asian Journal of Social Science* (1999).
2   On the present state-of-play of global social science, it is useful to refer to the series of volumes by Wallerstein (1991, 1996, 1999).
3   Perhaps we should re-examine some of the salient points on this matter made by Wolters (1982) and the works of some of his students, particularly Milner's (1982, 1995).
4   See the two famous contributions of Cohn (1987, 1996) on 'colonial knowledge'. Perhaps it is also useful to take an intellectual excursion into the theoretical realm of 'post-colonial studies' where the debate on colonial knowledge and its impact on knowledge construction in the decolonized world is indeed fascinating, see, for instance, Moore-Gilbert (1997) and Smith (1999).
5   See Davies' (1997) brilliant account of European history.
6   It is interesting to note how politicized are discussion and discourse on ecological issues thus far, be they by academicians and others, especially on the issues of the destruction of tropical forests and the social life of the forest dwellers in Southeast Asia. None seems to remember that the USA during the Vietnam War inflicted the worst man-made ecological disaster in the world, see Lewallen (1971). The 'greenies' seems unable to see the 'reds'.
7   The first detailed investigative account on the USA special 'culture and freedom' project launched and conducted worldwide as a covert activity, including in Southeast Asia, during the Cold War era has been written by Saunders (1999).

References

Anderson, Benedict (1983) *Imagined Communities*, London: Verso.

Bloom, Allan (1988) *The Closing of the American Mind*, Harmondsworth: Penguin Books.

Boeke, Julius H. (1910) *Tropisch-Koloniale Staathuishoudkunde: Het Probleem*, [Tropical Colonial Economics: The Problem] Ph.D. thesis, Leiden University, The Netherlands.

Cohn, Bernard (1987) *An Anthropologist among the Historians*, New Delhi: Oxford University Press.

Cohn, Bernard (1996) *Colonialism and its Forms of Knowledge*, Princeton, New Jersey: Princeton University Press.

Davies, Norman (1997) *Europe: A History*, London: Pimlico.

Evers, Hans-Dieter (1980) *The Sociology of Southeast Asia*, Kuala Lumpur: Oxford University Press.

Firth, Raymond (1946) *Malay Fishermen*, London: Athlone.

Firth, Raymond (1948) *A Report on Social Science in Malaya*, London: Her Majesty's Stationary Office (HMSO).

Freeman, Derek (1950) *Report on the Iban Agriculture*, London: HMSO.

Furnivall, John S (1939) *Netherlands India: A Study of Plural Economy*, Cambridge, UK: Cambridge University Press.

Geertz, Clifford (1963) *Agricultural Involution*, Berkeley, CA: University of California Press.

Geertz, Clifford (1973) *Interpretation of Cultures*, Chicago: Chicago University Press.

Hefner, Robert & Horvatisch, Patricia (eds) (1997) *Islam in an Era of Nation-States: Politics and Religious Renewal in Muslim Southeast Asia*, Honolulu: University of Hawaii Press.

Hirschman, Charles (ed.) (1992) *Southeast Asian Studies in the Balance: Reflections from America*, Ann Arbor, Michigan: Association for Asian Studies Inc.

Horowitz, Donald (1985) *Ethnic Groups in Conflict*, Berkeley, CA: University of California Press.

King, Victor (1999) *Anthropology and Development in Southeast Asia*, Singapore: Oxford University Press.

Leach, Edmund (1951) *Social Science Research in Sarawak*, London: HMSO.

Lewallen, John (1971) *Ecology of Devastation: Indochina*, Baltimore, Maryland: Penguin.

Milner, Anthony (1982) *Kerajaan*, Tucson: University of Texas.

Milner, Anthony (1995) *The Invention of Politics in Colonial Malaya*, Melbourne: Cambridge University Press.

Moore-Gilbert, Bart (1997) *Post-Colonial Theory: Contexts, Practices, Politics*, London: Verso.

Ong, Hak Ching (1982) British policy and Chinese politics in Malaya. Ph.D. thesis, University of Hull, UK.

Nandy, Ashis (1983) *The Intimate Enemy: Loss and Recovery of Self under Colonialism*, New Delhi: Oxford University Press.

Nencel, L. and Pels, P. (eds) (1991), *Constructing Knowledge*, London: Sage.

Nordholt, Nico S, & Visser, Leontine (eds) (1995) *Social Science in Southeast Asia: From Particularism to Universalism,* Amsterdam: VU University Press.

Said, Edward (1978) *Orientalism*, New York: Pantheon.

Saunders, Frances S. (1999) *Who Paid the Piper? The CIA and the Cultural Cold War*, London: Granta.

Scott, James (1976) *Moral Economy of the Peasant*, New Haven, CT: Yale University Press.

Scott, James (1985) *Weapons of the Weak*, New Haven: Yale University Press.

Shamsul A.B. (1986) *From British to Bumiputera Rule: Local Politics and Rural Development in Peninsular Malaysia*, Singapore: Institute of Southeast Asian Studies.

Shamsul A.B. (1996) 'Debating about identity in Malaysia', *Southeast Asian Studies* (Kyoto), 34(3): 476–499.

Shamsul A.B. (1998) 'Ethnicity, Class Culture or Identity? Competing Paradigms in Malaysian Studies', *Akademika*, 53, July: 33–59.

Smith, Linda Tuhiwai (1999) *Decolonizing Methodologies: Research and Indigenous Peoples*, London: Zed.

Southeast Asian Journal of Social Science (1999) Special Issue on 'Southeast Asian Studies', Vol XX.

Taufik, Abdullah and Yeti, Maunati (eds) (1994) *Towards the Promotion of Southeast Asian Studies in Southeast Asia*, Jakarta: Indonesian Institute of Sciences.

Wallerstein, Immanuel (1991) *Unthinking Social Science: The Limits of Nineteenth Century Paradigms*, London: Blackwell.

Wallerstein, Immanuel (1996) *The Social Sciences: Report of the Gulbenkian Commission on the Restructuring of the Social Sciences (Mestizo Spaces)*, Stanford: Stanford University Press.

Wallerstein, Immanuel (1999) *The End of the World as we Know it: Social Science for the Twenty-first Century,* Minnesota: University of Minnesota Press.

Wertheim, Willem (1965) *East–West Parallels: Sociological Approaches to Modern Asia,* Chicago: Quadrangle Books.

Wolters, Oliver W. (1982) *History, Culture and Region in Southeast Asian Perspective*, Singapore: Institute of Southeast Asian Studies.

Part II

State violence

Chapter 6

Democracy and the violence of the state

A political negotiation of death

Partha Chatterjee

I begin with a word on Saadat Hasan Manto whose Urdu short story 'Toba Tek Singh' will feature in the final section of this paper on the violence of the state. Like most Bengalis of my generation, I was brought up to believe that there did not exist, in any other language of India, any semblance of a literature that could even be vaguely construed as representing a modern aesthetic sensibility. However, to the credit of my embarrassingly narrow-minded and chauvinistic compatriots, I have to confess that I first came across Manto in the late 1970s in a Bengali translation of 'Toba Tek Singh'. I distinctly remember the experience of reading those eight or ten pages of sparse, unornamented, newsreport-like prose. It shook me up, and as I began to absorb the full impact of Manto's deadly irony, I knew I was in the presence of a great craftsman of words. Since that time, I have read a fair amount of his works in Bengali and English translations, have followed some of the critical literature on him that has appeared in recent years, and have come to accept, without the slightest sense of contradiction with my incurable Bengaliness, that Manto is arguably the greatest modernist prose writer of our subcontinent.

It is modernity that I will talk about. And also violence, which is a theme that etches itself so strongly on Manto's stories. In some ways, I will talk about the violence of modernity. But since I do not have the facility to draw large conclusions from the singular familiarity of fictional narratives, I need a different site to ground my thoughts. I will do so in the much-talked about field of Indian democracy. I will speak about state and society in India as they come together in the democratic process. On that ground, I will talk about modernity, religion and the violence of the state.

There is now a large literature examining the relation between state institutions and society in India. Rudolph and Rudolph (1987) have suggested that the balance has shifted periodically from a 'demand polity', in which societal demands expressed as electoral pressure dominate over the state, and a 'command polity', where state hegemony prevails over society. The late M. S. A. Rao, in his last work done jointly with Francine Frankel, had suggested that public institutions such as the bureaucracy and organized industry, which had previously been the centres of dominance, were now under pressure from the rising power, especially of the lower castes, in political institutions such as the legislatures and the political parties (Rao and Frankel 1990). From the periodic swings of the Rudolphs' model, the narrative here has become one of the decline of a political order. Further underscoring the theme of decline, Atul Kohli (1991) has described the recent history of Indian politics as one in which, by surrendering to the immediate electoral pressures exercised by various social groups, democratic state institutions have been allowed to decay, leading to an all-round crisis of governability.

One problem I have had with the existing literature, framed as it is largely within the confines of a modernization narrative, whether of a Weberian or a Marxian type, is that the conceptual domains of state and society have either had to be sharply distinguished, with the central state institutions carrying the burden of an interventionist project of modernizing traditional social institutions and practices, or collapsed entirely so that state practices become completely moulded by the pulls and pressures of prevailing social institutions. With the unquestioned spread and deepening of electoral politics in India in the last three decades, it has become difficult to locate the sites, if any, of an interventionist project of changing society, or indeed of the transformations that have been brought about by the expansion of democracy itself.

In a series of recent papers, I have attempted to sketch out a conceptual field where some of these questions could be tackled (Chatterjee 1998a, b, c, forthcoming). One move I have suggested is to think of a field of practices mediating between state institutions and civil society. I have favoured retaining the old idea of civil society as bourgeois society, in the sense used by Hegel and Marx, and of using it in the Indian context as an actually existing arena of institutions and practices inhabited by a relatively small section of the people whose social locations can be identified with a fair degree of clarity. In terms of the *formal* structure of the state as given by the constitution and the laws, all of society is civil society; everyone is a citizen with equal rights and therefore to be regarded as a member of civil society; the political process is one where the organs of the state interact with members of civil society in their individual capacities or as members of associations. In actual fact, this is not how things work. Most of the inhabitants of India are only tenuously, and even then ambiguously and contextually, rights-bearing citizens in the sense imagined by the constitution. They are not, therefore, proper members of civil society and are not regarded as such by the institutions of the state. However, it is not as though they are outside the reach of the state or even excluded from the domain of politics. As populations within the territorial jurisdiction of the state, they have to be both looked after and controlled by various governmental agencies. These activities bring these populations into a certain *political* relationship with the state. But this relationship does not always conform to what is envisaged in the constitutional depiction of the relation between the state and members of civil society. Yet these are without doubt political relations that may have acquired, in specific historically defined contexts, a widely recognized systematic character, and perhaps even certain conventionally recognized ethical norms, even if subject to varying degrees of contestation. How are we to begin to understand these processes?

It is to tackle questions of this kind that I proposed the idea of a *political society* occupying a zone between the state on the one hand and civil society as bourgeois society on the other. Faced with similar problems, some analysts have favoured expanding the idea of civil society to include virtually all existing social institutions that lie outside the strict domain of the state.[1] This practice has become rampant in the recent rhetoric of international financial institutions, aid agencies and non-governmental organizations, among whom the spread of a neo-liberal ideology has authorized the consecration of every non-state organization as the precious flower of the associative endeavours of free members of civil society. I have preferred to resist these unscrupulously charitable theoretical gestures, principally because I feel it important not to lose sight of the vital and continually active project that still informs many of the state institutions in India to transform traditional social authorities and practices into the modular forms of bourgeois civil society. That civil society as an *ideal* continues to energize an interventionist political project, and that as an *actually existing form* it is demographically limited, are both facts that I think must be borne in mind when considering the relation between modernity and democracy in India.

Some of you may recall a framework used in the early phase of the Subaltern Studies project in which we talked about a split in the domain of politics between an organized elite domain and an unorganized subaltern domain. The idea of the split, of course, was intended to mark a faultline in the arena of nationalist politics in the three decades before independence during which the Indian masses, especially the peasantry, were drawn into organized political movements and yet remained distanced from the evolving forms of the postcolonial state. To say that there was a split in the domain of politics was to reject the notion, common in both liberal and Marxist historiographies, that the peasantry lived in some 'pre-political' stage of collective action. It was to say that peasants in their collective actions were also being political, except that they were political in a way different from that of the elites. Since those early experiences of the imbrication of elite and subaltern politics in the context of the anticolonial movements, the democratic process in India has come a long way in bringing under its influence the lives of the subaltern classes. It is to understand these relatively recent forms of the entanglement of elite and subaltern politics that I am proposing the notion of a political society.

In illustrating what I mean by political society and how it works, I have earlier used the example of a squatter settlement in the city of Calcutta and the efforts of the members of this settlement to assert their presence in urban life.[2] This they do through a body that has the form of a voluntary association but which uses a moral rhetoric of kinship and family loyalty. Since the settlement is premised on the illegal occupation of public land and therefore on the collective violation of property laws and civic regulations, the state authorities cannot treat it on the same footing as other civic associations following more legitimate social and cultural pursuits. Yet state agencies and non-governmental organizations cannot ignore it either, since it is but one of hundreds of similar bodies representing groups of population whose very livelihood or habitation involve violation of the law. These agencies therefore deal with the settlers' association not as a body of citizens but as a convenient instrument for the administration of welfare to a marginal and underprivileged population group.

The squatters on their part accept that their occupation of public land is both illegal and contrary to good civic behaviour, but they make a claim to a habitation and a livelihood as a matter of right. They profess a readiness to move out if they are given suitable alternative sites for resettlement. The state agencies recognize that these population groups do have some claim on the welfare programmes of the government, but those claims could not be regarded as justiciable rights since the state did not have the means to deliver those benefits to the entire population of the country. To treat those claims as rights would only invite further violation of public property and civic laws.

What happens then is a negotiation of these claims on a political terrain where, on the one hand, governmental agencies have a public obligation to look after the poor and the underprivileged and, on the other, particular population groups receive attention from those agencies according to calculations of political expediency. The squatter community I talked about has to pick its way through this uncertain terrain by making a large array of connections outside the group with other groups in similar situations, with more privileged and influential groups, with government functionaries, with political parties and leaders, etc. In the course of its struggles over almost five decades, the squatters have managed to hold on to their settlement, but it is an extremely insecure hold since it is entirely dependent on their ability to operate within a field of strategic politics. I make the claim that this is the stuff of democratic politics as it takes place on the ground in India. It involves what appears to be a constantly shifting compromise between the normative values of modernity and the moral assertion of popular demands.

Civil society then, restricted to a small section of culturally equipped citizens, represents in countries like India the high ground of modernity. So does the constitutional model of the state. However, in practice, governmental agencies must descend from that high ground to the terrain of political society in order to renew their legitimacy as providers of well-being and there to confront whatever is the current configuration of politically mobilized demands. In the process, one is liable to hear complaints from the protagonists of civil society and the constitutional state that modernity is facing an unexpected rival in the form of democracy.

I further explore this theme by giving you one more example from the domain of popular politics in the Indian city.[3] On 5 May 1993, in the early hours of dawn, a man died in a Calcutta hospital. He had been admitted a few days before and was being treated for diabetes molutus, renal failure and cerebro-vascular accident. His condition had deteriorated rapidly in the previous 24 hours and, although the doctors attending him struggled through the night, their efforts were in vain. A senior doctor of the hospital signed the death certificate.

The name of the man who died was Birendra Chakrabarti, but he was better known as Balak Brahmachari, leader of the Santan Dal, a religious sect with a large following in the southern and central districts of West Bengal. The sect itself is no more than 50 years old, although it probably has its antecedents in earlier sectarian movements among the lower-caste, especially Namasudra, peasants of central Bengal. Its religious doctrines are highly eclectic, consisting entirely of the views of Balak Brahmachari himself as expressed in his sayings, but they are characterized in particular by a curious involvement in political matters. The sect's mouthpiece, *Kara Chabuk* [The Strong Whip], regularly published its leader's comments on current political subjects in which there was the recurrent theme of 'revolution', a cataclysmic churning that would surgically cleanse a corrupt and putrid social order. The sect, in fact, first came into the public spotlight in the period 1967–1971 when it participated in political demonstrations in support of the Left parties and against Congress rule. The Santan Dal activists, with many women in their ranks, some in saffron clothes, holding aloft their tridents and shouting their slogan 'Ram Narayan Ram', were an incongruous element in Leftist demonstrations in Calcutta at the time, and could not but attract attention. But no one accused the sect of opportunistic political ambitions, because it made no claims to electoral representation or recognition as a political party. Since then, many of the followers of the sect have been known to be sympathizers and even activists of the Left, especially of the Communist Party of India (Marxist) – CPI(M) – the leading partner in the Left Front that has ruled West Bengal since 1977.

On this particular morning in May 1993, the followers of Balak Brahmachari refused to accept that their spiritual leader was dead. They recalled that, several years ago, in 1967, he had gone into *samadhi* for 22 days during which, from all outward appearances, he was dead. But he had woken up from his trance and returned to normal life. Now once more, they said, their Baba had gone into *nirvikalpa samadhi*, a state of suspension of bodily functions that could be achieved only by those with the highest spiritual powers. The members of Santal Dal took the body of Balak Brahmachari from hospital to their ashram in Sukhchar, a northern suburb of Calcutta, and began to keep what they said would be a long vigil.

Soon the matter became a *cause celebre* in Calcutta. The press picked it up, publishing reports of how the body was being kept on slabs of ice under heavy air-conditioning and of the defensiveness of the Dal spokesmen against hostile criticism. One Bengali daily, *Ajkal*, pursued the story with particular vigour, turning it into a fight for rational values in public life and against obscurantist beliefs and practices. It accused the local authorities and the health department of the West Bengal government of failing to implement their own rules regarding the disposal of dead bodies and of conniving in the making of a serious public hazard. Soon the authorities were forced to respond. On the 13th day of the vigil, the Panihati municipality clarified that it had served the Santal Dal leaders with a notice asking them to cremate the body immediately, but that under the municipal laws it had no powers to carry out a forcible cremation (*Ajkal*, 18 May 1993). On behalf of the Santal Dal, Chitta Sikdar, the secretary, kept up a regular defensive campaign in the press, maintaining that the spiritual phenomenon of *nirvikalpa samadhi* was beyond the understanding of medical science and that Balak Brahmachari would soon resume his normal bodily life.

The standoff continued. *Ajkal* raised the tempo of its campaign, opening its columns to prominent intellectuals and public figures who deplored the persistence of such superstitious and unscientific beliefs among the people. Groups of activists from progressive cultural organizations, the popular science movement and the rationalist society, began to hold demonstrations in front of the Santan Dal headquarters in Sukhchar. *Ajkal* spared no efforts to provoke the spokesmen of the Dal and to ridicule their statements, refusing to refer to the dead leader by his sectarian name of Balak Brahmachari and instead calling him 'Balak Babu' – a nonsensical 'Mr. Balak'. There were some heated confrontations at the gate of the Santan Dal ashram, with the Dal activists reportedly stocking arms and preparing for a showdown. One night, some crackers and handmade bombs exploded outside the ashram and a group of Dal activists came out and shouted over their loudspeakers: 'The revolution has begun' (*Ajkal*, 21 June 1993).

Nearly a month after the official death of Balak Brahmachari, his body still lay on ice slabs in an air-conditioned room with his followers waiting for him to break his *samadhi*. *Ajkal* claimed that there was an unbearable stench in the entire neighbourhood of Sukhchar and that the residents of the area had had enough. Now it began to be openly alleged that it was because of electoral reasons that the government was reluctant to intervene. The elections to the local government bodies in rural West Bengal, the crucial panchayats, which had become the backbone of Left Front support, were scheduled for the last week of May. Any action against the Dal could antagonize a lot of Left Front supporters in at least four districts of West Bengal. It was also suggested that some important leaders of the CPI(M) were sympathetic to the Santan Dal and that one minister in particular, Subhas Chakrabarti, the minister in charge of tourism and sports, was regarded by Dal members as a fraternal supporter.

On 25 June 1993, 51 days after the official death of Balak Brahmachari, the health minister of West Bengal announced that a medical team consisting of leading specialists in medicine, neurology and forensic medicine would examine the body of Balak Brahmachari and submit a report to the government. The Indian Medical Association, the apex professional body of medical practitioners, immediately protested saying that to call for a new examination implied a lack of confidence in the death certificate issued from the hospital. It pointed out that no scientific grounds had been furnished to question the original judgement of the hospital doctors. The government doctors went ahead nevertheless and returned from Sukhchar to say that they had not been allowed to touch the body. They reported that the body had been putrefied and carried signs of mummification and that it had not decayed completely because of the extremely low temperature at which it had been kept (*Ajkal*, 26 June 1993).

By this time, Subhas Chakrabarti had been given charge by the CPI(M) leadership to devise a solution to the impasse. Accompanied by the local CPI(M) leaders, he visited the Sukhchar ashram and later told journalists that he was trying to persuade the followers of the Baba to cremate the body. He agreed that there was no scientific reason for doctors to re-examine a body that had been certified as dead, but insisted that this was a necessary part of the process of persuasion. He pointed out that 'Babadom' was still prevalent in the country and that thousands of people were followers of these religious leaders. He warned that it was dangerous to take religious fanaticism lightly. It was the government's view, he said, that applying force could provoke fanaticism. When asked if he was aware of the health hazard that had been created in the neighbourhood of Sukhchar, he claimed that he had smelt nothing, but that was probably because he was a habitual inhaler of snuff (*Ajkal*, 26 June 1993).

On 30 June, in a four-hour operation beginning at two in the morning, a force consisting of 5000 policemen stormed the Santan Dal headquarters, took charge of the body and removed it to a nearby crematorium. *The Telegraph* reported that the last rites were performed by the guru's brother

> as the security cordon pushed back wailing women who still believed their departed cult leader would be resurrected. The state government, severely criticised for soft-pedalling the issue, heaved a sigh of relief.

The police force, which was attacked by Dal activists with acid bulbs, knives, tridents, glass bottles and chilli powder, used tear gas shells to immobilize the defenders and gas cutters to make its way through window grilles and collapsible gates into the heavily fortified headquarters. But it did not resort to shooting. Many Dal activists as well as policemen were hurt, but, as the official press release put it, 'there were no casualties' (*The Telegraph*, 1 July 1993; *The Statesman*, 1 July 1993).

The minister Subhas Chakrabarti congratulated the police and the local administration for carrying out a very difficult and sensitive operation. He referred to the popular Hindi film *Jugnu* and said the job was more difficult than what the actor Dharmendra had faced in that film. 'Of course,' he said to journalists, 'you think all that is lumpen culture, but I think it is an apt example.' The following day, *Ajkal* in its editorial announced: 'We have come to the end of that age in West Bengal when lumpen culture could be called lumpen culture. Progressive West Bengal has seen the end of the age of reason. Now begins the age of *Jugnu*' (*Ajkal*, 2 July 1993).

Despite the relatively smooth and successful conclusion of the matter, the controversy did not die down. Chitta Sikdar, the secretary of the Santan Dal, protested to the chief minister against what he described as an authoritarian and undemocratic action of the government. He said the treatment received by Balak Brahmachari at the hands of the rulers of society would be remembered in history in the same way as the trials of Jesus Christ, Galileo and Socrates. On the other hand, opinions such as that of *Ajkal* condemned as opportunistic the attempt by sections of the government and the ruling party to target the second-rank leaders of the sect for misleading their innocent followers and profiting from their overexcited religious sentiments but not criticizing the sects and the so-called 'godmen' themselves for spreading unreason and superstition. Twelve days after the cremation of Balak Brahmachari, the secretary of the Santan Dal and 82 others were arrested and charged with rioting, assault, obstruction of justice and other offences (*Ajkal*, 13 July 1993).

Members of the Santan Dal continued for several months to write letters to newspapers portraying themselves as victims of an undemocratic and illegal police action. They asked what laws of the land the Baba's followers had broken by believing that he would come back to them. Did a religious belief in extraordinary spiritual powers deserve blows from the policeman's truncheon? And was it not the case that the Dal followers were finally subjected to police action because most of them were low-caste peasants whose marginal political value had evaporated after the local government elections were over? While public memory might be short, one letter warned, the memory of victimhood was merciless. The perpetrators of injustice would one day meet their day of judgement (*Dainik Pratibedan*, 5 February 1994). The case illustrates, I think, several of the points I have raised so far about the relation between modernity and democracy in a country like India. Modernity is a project that is located in the historical desires of certain elite sections of Indians. The specific story of the emergence and flowering of those desires and their sources in colonial projects has been much discussed. There was a time when the country was under colonial rule, when it was believed by these elites that the crucial transformative processes that would change the traditional beliefs and practices of the people and fashion a new modern national self must be kept out of the reach of the colonial state apparatus. With the end of colonial rule and the coming to power of these classes in the postcolonial state, that transformative project became firmly located in the dynamic potential of the organs of the new national state. That those organs were now part of a constitutional system of representative democracy made the modernizing project an expression of the will of the people and thus gloriously consistent with the legitimizing norms of modernity itself.

Religion came under the sway of this transformative project in a major way. In the colonial period, the transformation was carried out through a variety of social institutions, including new sectarian movements of reformed religion, both Hindu and Islamic, using all of the new cultural technologies of print and pedagogy. In the process, a certain cultural consensus emerged among the elite sections of Indians on the norms of religious practice in modern life. These norms made it possible for the leading groups in society to make distinctions between acceptable ritual behaviour or doctrinal belief and unacceptable superstition and irrationality. Following independence, the normalizing of religious practice was carried out most ambitiously through the legal organs of the state in the constitution itself and also in the set of legislations known as the Hindu Code Bill. The minority religious practices were left largely untouched by this exercise, not because they were not thought to be in need of reform but because of the uncertainty as to whether the will of the people, as expressed by a parliamentary majority, carried an adequate measure of legitimacy for the minority communities. In other words, there was already a nuanced and differentiated notion of representation built into the idea of democratic legitimacy, even though the idea of separate representation of minorities was anathema.

This project of cultural transformation through the powers of a democratically constituted state has become considerably muted in the last two decades. A crucial experience that, I think, defined the new limits of state action in Indian democracy was that of Indira Gandhi's emergency regime in 1975–77. That brought home to India's elites the fact that modernizing agendas could be made the political pretext for setting up an authoritarian regime that was little more than a perversion of the so-called will of the people. Such a regime put at risk all of the legal-political guarantees for a large, complex and differentiated bourgeois civic life, even if it did not directly threaten the well-being of the bourgeoisie as a class. Moreover, the emergency regime also failed to prove that it could sustain itself as a self-reproducing structure, as in other authoritarian systems in the postcolonial world, in the face of the various impediments it faced from both within and outside the country. Following the collapse of the emergency regime in 1977, a consensus emerged among modernizers of both the Left and the Right that it was unwise to push through projects of social change by means of state intervention unless these were first negotiated through certain mediating processes between state and society.

Although many of the sites and activities characteristic of the arena I have called political society can be shown to have emerged within the spectrum of nationalist political mobilizations in the colonial period, I would say that it has taken on something like a distinct form only since the 1980s. Two conditions have facilitated this process. One is the rise to dominance of a notion of governmental performance that emphasizes the welfare and protection of populations the 'pastoral' functions of government, as Michel Foucault called it, using similar governmental technologies all over the world but largely independent of considerations of active participation by citizens in the sovereignty of the state. This has enabled the mutual recognition by state agencies and population groups that governments are obliged to deliver certain benefits even to people who are not proper members of civil society or of the republican body of true citizens. The second condition is the widening of the arena of political mobilization, even if only for electoral ends, from formally organized structures, such as political parties with well-ordered internal constitutions and coherent doctrines and programmes, to loose and often transient mobilizations, building on communication structures that would not ordinarily be recognized as political (for instance, religious assemblies or cultural festivals, or more curiously, even associations of cinema fans, as in many of the southern states).

The proliferation of activities in this arena of political society has caused much discomfort and apprehension in progressive elite circles in India in recent years. The comment about 'lumpen culture' in the *Ajkal* editorial I cited earlier is typical. The complaint is widespread in middle-class circles today that politics has been taken over by mobs and criminals. The result is the abandonment or so the complaint goes of the mission of the modernizing state to change a backward society. Instead, what we see is the importation of the disorderly, corrupt and irrational practices of un-reformed popular culture into the very hallways and chambers of civic life, all because of the calculations of electoral expediency. The noble pursuit of modernity appears to have been seriously compromised because of the compulsions of parliamentary democracy.

Given a history in India of more than 100 years of modern representative institutions, we can now see a pattern of evolution of this familiar Tocquevillian problem.[4] Early liberals, such as Dadabhai Naoroji or Gopal Krishna Gokhale, or even Muhammad Ali Jinnah in the early phase of his political life, were entirely convinced of the inherent value of those institutions, but they were also hugely circumspect about the conditions in which they could function. As good 19th-century liberals, they would have been the first to specify requirements such as education and a proved commitment to civic life that would have to be met before a people could be considered fit, in their language, 'to receive parliamentary institutions'. If we look at it from another angle, we might say that for men such as Naoroji or Gokhale, democracy was a good form of government only when it could be adequately controlled by men of status and wisdom. With the rise of the so-called Extremists in nationalist politics, especially with the Khilafat and Non-cooperation movements, there came into organized political life in India many forces and many ideas that did not care too much about the niceties of parliamentary politics. It was Gandhi, of course, who in this period, intervened decisively in the political arena created by the new representative institutions of the late colonial order. Even as he claimed to reject parliamentary institutions along with all of the other trappings of modern civilization, he was more instrumental than anyone else in bringing about the mobilization that would, in the end, make the Indian National Congress the ruling political organization of independent India. As has been shown in many studies, Gandhi's words and actions are shot through by the parallel themes of unleashing popular initiative and controlling it at the same time.[5] With the formalization of Congress rule in the first decade and a half after independence, control became the dominant motif in the close interweaving of state initiative and electoral approval in the so-called Congress system of the Nehru period.

The journey from the Nehru period to the crisis of the mid-1960s to the re-establishment of Congress dominance in the state populism of the first Indira Gandhi regime is a trajectory that is not unfamiliar to the historical experience of many third-world countries. What was distinctive in the life of Indian democracy is, I think, the defeat of Indira Gandhi's emergency regime in a parliamentary election. It brought about a decisive shift in all subsequent discussion about the essence and appearance of democracy, its form and content, its inner nature and outward appearance. Whatever may be the judgement of historians on the 'real' causes of the collapse of the emergency regime, the 1977 elections established in the arena of popular mobilizations in India the capacity of the vote and of representative bodies of government to give voice to popular demands of a kind that had never before been allowed to disturb the order and tranquillity of the proverbial corridors of power. One cannot but wonder if this is not the momentous experience that separates the popular understanding of democracy in India from that in Pakistan, where it is possible today for both elites and subalterns to say in unison that electoral democracy is a fake and that the path to true democracy may have to pass through a spell of military dictatorship.

However, before we in India are too quick to congratulate ourselves, let me restate what I have been arguing so far in this paper. The contrary themes of popular legitimacy and elite control remained embedded in the conception of Indian democracy from the very beginning. They have not gone away, nor have they been resolved or superseded. They have only taken new forms as a result of the ongoing struggles between elite and popular conceptions of democracy. They are being played out once again in the recent debates over democratic modernization in India. On the one hand, the uncertain demands of popular ratification have led committed modernizers to throw up their hands and lament that the age of reason had been brought to an end by the political surrender to the forces of disorder and irrationality. They read the many compromises with electoral compulsions as signs of the abandonment of enlightened politics. Generally less noticed are the transformative effects of these contrary mobilizations among the supposedly unenlightened sections of the population. Since this is an area that is only beginning to be studied, I can only make certain preliminary remarks on it. However, this constitutes, I believe, the most profound and significant set of social changes that are being produced by the democratic process in India today.

In one of my recent writings, dealing with the question of minority rights and the secular state in India, I suggested that the more democratic strategy would be to promote representative processes *within* the minority communities themselves (Chatterjee 1997: 228–262). It has been objected that this is 'too strong' a requirement, that it is a concession to religious-communitarian politics itself, and that it smacks of the 'separate electorates' system in British India or even (some have said) to the *millet* system in Ottoman Turkey. I could give a range of answers to these objections, but the one that will be most pertinent here is the following. All of these objections spring from the inability to recognize a domain of politics that is located neither within the constitutional limits of the state nor in the orderly transactions of bourgeois civil society, even though it is *about* both. The encounter with the constitutional state and the normative requirements of civil society has engendered a certain demand for representativeness within the various communities that *are* the social forms of populations in India. This is the most tangible effect of democratization in this country. Even as population groups both engage with and resist the agencies of the state, they give rise to an internal process in which community leaderships are criticized, new voices are heard, other examples of other communities are cited, and the demand raised for greater representativeness within the community. These processes have occurred most visibly in recent years in the mobilizations among the dalits and the so-called other backward castes. However, they have also occurred among tribal populations and indeed among the religious minorities. In addition, if one looks to the immensely rich and productive debate coming out of the women's movement in India, one cannot fail to notice the importance of the strategic question: legal reform through state initiative from the top or mobilization of initiatives within the relatively unmobilized spaces of the communities themselves? To choose the former is to underscore the moral primacy of the modernizing state. To advocate the latter is to accept the risks of walking through a normatively uncertain political terrain. If my critics demand that I state my preference between the two, I would say that while the former strategy has not necessarily exhausted itself, I believe that the real challenge lies in exploring the possibilities of the latter.

Let me also say that there has already evolved among the governing classes in India one response to this strategic choice. I see this as a variant of the colonial strategy of indirect rule. This involves a suspension of the modernization project, walling in the protected zones of bourgeois civil society and dispensing the governmental functions of law and order and welfare through the 'natural leaders' of the governed populations. The strategy, in other words, seeks to preserve the civil virtues of bourgeois life from the potential excesses of electoral democracy. I am convinced that this was the attitude taken by the economically dominant groups in Bombay, the industrial and financial capital of India and the apex of its urban cosmopolitan culture, towards the political leadership of the Shiv Sena, the most overtly fascist element in the Hindu right-wing formation that, until two years ago, ruled the state of Maharashtra.

The other response is less cynical, even as it is more pragmatic. It does not abandon the project of enlightenment, but attempts to steer it through the thicket of contestations in what I have called *political society*. It takes seriously the functions of direction and leadership of a vanguard, but accepts that the legal arm of the state in a country like India cannot reach into a vast range of social practices that continue to be regulated by other beliefs and administered by other authorities. However, it also knows that those dark zones are being penetrated by the welfare functions of modern governmental practices, producing those effects on claims and representation that I have called the urge for democratization. This is the zone in which the project of democratic modernity has to operate – slowly, painfully, unsurely.

In bringing up the example of the negotiations over the disposal of a dead body in Calcutta, I was not trying to provide a narrative of the correct handling of contradictions among the people. Nor am I saying that the specific form in which a local crisis of modernity-versus-democracy was resolved on that occasion flowed out of a conscious political project of social transformation in which the ruling parties in West Bengal are engaged. Rather, my intention was to point out the possibilities that exist in that normatively nebulous zone that I have called political society. When I use that term, I am always reminded that in the *Prison Notebooks*, Antonio Gramsci begins by equating political society with the state, but soon slides into a whole range of social and cultural interventions that must take place well beyond the domain of the state. I have tried here to emphasize that even in resisting the modernizing project that is imposed on them, the subaltern classes embark on a path of internal transformation. At the same time, in carrying out their pedagogical mission in political society, the educators – enlightened people like us – might also succeed in educating themselves. That, I submit, will be the most enriching and historically significant result of the encounter between modernity and democracy in a country like India.

Finally, I come to the subject of violence. Manto's distinctness, as has been pointed out many times, lies in his merciless, sometimes brutally unsentimental, handling of the theme of violence. His English translator Khalid Hasan (1987: 8) has remarked: 'He alone of the writers of his time was able to turn the bloody events of 1947 into great literature'. Few will quarrel with this judgement. But it is worth asking why others did not even try to do what Manto did. Is there some mystery here about the nature of the violence of 1947 that defied representation? I think it is useful to consider this question in the context of the complicated relationship of modernity to democracy and of the role of the violence of the modern state.

In August 1954, seven years after partition and a year before his death, Manto is supposed to have written an epitaph for himself. 'Here lies Saadat Hasan Manto,' it said. 'With him lie buried all the arts and mysteries of short story writing. Under tons of earth he lies, wondering if he is a greater story writer than God' (Hasan 1987: 9–10).[6] Some may read these lines as one more example of Manto's penchant for shocking his readers by an exaggerated display of his bloated ego. What vulgar insolence, they might say, to compare the creativity of a story writer with that of god! But others, an unfortunate few, perhaps, will recognize here the condition of the modern secular mind, trapped under tons of political doubt. If ever there was poignancy in irony, I think it is here. It expresses the predicament of a creative human spirit that must continue the work of creation in a world which, it believes, has been permanently abandoned by god. How does it do its work?

Let us note, first of all, that the condition we are talking about here is not one that belongs to the world of the popular. The latter is suffused with the idea that the act of making the world requires powers that are much larger than what belongs to ordinary humans. The violence of human life is also made sense of, more often than not, as the violence of the gods, sometimes transparent, sometimes inscrutable. I once spent many months scouring the archives for eyewitness accounts of communal riots in Bengal. I came away with the lasting impression that even as ordinary people often described in vivid detail the disastrous things that happened to them, they tended to attribute the reasons to some externalized cause, something that was purposive but beyond themselves. In one of his many famous disagreements with rationalists, Gandhi insisted after the Bihar earthquakes of 1934 that these were a 'divine chastisement' for the sin of untouchability. Deliberately taking up a position located in popular beliefs, he said, in effect, that this was a violence of god. When asked why god should inflict a punishment that did not distinguish between upper castes and untouchables, Gandhi (1958: 87) said, 'I am not God. Therefore I have but a limited knowledge of his purpose'. On the basis of what I know about the subject, I am not persuaded that there exists in popular consciousness a notion of violence that is fundamentally without reason. Violence may be committed for vengeance, for punishment, for justice, for practising an occupation, for a host of other reasons including possession by spirits, demons, gods, but rarely, perhaps never, as a senseless act without deliberate cause.

It is the modern secular consciousness, for whom – famously – the world has become a disenchanted place, that faces this peculiar problem of making sense of violence in human life. At the risk of grossly oversimplifying a huge history to which the greatest minds of the modern world have devoted their attention, let me say that at least as far as the world of modern political life is concerned, there have been two strategies that have been followed to bring reason and order to the facts of violence. One is to create a transcendental umbrella of ethics under which to shelter and domesticate the use of violence. This produces certain notions of goodness and justice that are believed to be true and, in the appropriate conditions, the use of violence is considered a legitimate instrument to achieve those transcendentally established moral goals. Justice, punishment, discipline, progress, science – there have been many notions of the just and the good that have legitimized violence in the modern world. The other strategy is to devise an economy of violence. The question here is not whether to use violence, but how much? Of what kind? To what purpose? With what results? It is not an ethical imperative that works here, but one of costs and benefits, of matching causes to effects, of efficiency.

Modern political life makes sense of violence either by measuring it against an ethical imperative or by reducing it to the grid of an economy. We can see both moves being made in the story I narrated earlier about the death of Balak Brahmachari. The protagonists of rationality were complaining about the squeamishness of the government, hemmed in by electoral pressures, in imposing its own rules of public order and morality. If the government had to use force, the rationalists were saying, it should have used it, because it would have been justified. The government, in the end, did use violence, but within a carefully deployed economy of forces and effects so that it could say that no more violence was used than was necessary to produce the desired results: 'there were no casualties', it declared. The members of the Santan Dal, to the extent that they participated in this discourse of modern politics, protested against what they believed was an illegitimate use of force that violated their right to hold and practise their religious beliefs. Everyone participated in making sense of the violence of the modern state.

To the extent that I know the history and literature of the violence of 1947 in India, I believe there is a similar eagerness on all sides to make sense of it in terms of the logic of the modern nation-state. There are considerations of ethics – and of praise or blame – in the demands and concessions of different parties – the Congress, the Muslim League, and the British. What is the loss of partition for Indians is the success of independence for Pakistanis. And then there are the considerations of economy. Was the violence inevitable? Could it have been avoided? Were the British too hasty in wanting to get out? Could a little more state violence at the right time have avoided the uncontrolled explosion of communal violence? It is not that nothing has been said about 1947. In fact, a great deal has been said, and is still being said. It has been said within the twin parameters of ethics and economy.

Manto's uniqueness lies in the fact that he refused to accept the parameters of either ethics or economy in talking about the violence of 1947. He had no recourse to a morality that was given to him either by god or by transcendental reason. Nor would he allow himself to be seduced by the economic calculations of governmental violence. For him, the violence of partition called for a response that was, if I may put it this way, an act of pure politics, where morality and economy had to be created all at once, all by oneself, *de novo*, from the bare elements of human interaction. It was at such a moment of pure politics that Bishan Singh 'stood in no man's land on his swollen legs like a colossus' – pure politics, grounded in nothing other than its own domain. But this moment of pure politics cannot be sustained. The scope of its creative promise is too enormous, the burden of its responsibility too great. Bishan Singh, also known as Toba Tek Singh, screamed and then collapsed to the ground.

> There, behind barbed wire, on one side, lay India and behind more barbed wire, on the other side, lay Pakistan. In between, on a bit of earth which had no name, lay Toba Tek Singh.
>
> (Manto 1987: 18)

Perhaps, it is only after the fact of life itself buried under tons of earth, that one can contemplate if, at that moment of pure politics, one was a greater story writer than god. But it is not a risk many will take. In fact, my hunch is that this is the reason why no one other than Manto has even tried doing what he did. To embrace politics in its pure uncertainty, its unrelieved dangerousness, without the security of an anchor in some pre-given idea of the good, without the technical instruments of measuring costs and benefits, is terrifying. To seek refuge in history and statecraft is to return to the comfort of the familiar. That is what most of us prefer to do. We are not great storywriters.

The discomfort that many feel with the goings-on in what I have called political society is, I think, because it raises the spectre of pure politics. This is a zone where, I have said, the certainties of civil–social norms and constitutional proprieties are put under challenge. Rights and rules have to be, seemingly, negotiated afresh. Only those voices are heard that can make the loudest noise and can speak on behalf of the largest numbers. There is violence in the air. Not everything that happens here is desirable or worthy of approval. But then, how can we be sure that what we desire or approve is what is truly good? Who can decide that except those who go through the dangerously creative process of politics itself? I think Manto would have recognized these people. Those who dream of building the new democratic society must aspire to be greater storywriters than god.

I do not know if in those fervid, disorderly zones of what I have called political society, the foundations of a new democratic order are being laid today. That is for historians of a future generation to analyse and describe. What I do know is that the practices of democracy have changed in India in the last four decades, that the project of state-led modernization has been drastically modified, and that the forms of involvement of the subaltern classes with governmental activities as well as with representative institutions have both expanded and deepened. There are new efforts to garner popular legitimacy in favour of elite dominance, such as the political formation that goes under the sign of Hindutva, which has sought to demonstrate to the ruling classes of the country that it can create an alternative and more viable structure of class rule than the decrepit Congress. On the side of those who are governed, they have succeeded, in the teeth of severe opposition from the dominant sections, to bend and stretch the rules of bourgeois politics and rational bureaucracy to create forms of democratic practice that, even as they retain the names given to them by Western sociology and political theory, have become unrecognizably different. These are the creations of the Indian people. Perhaps some day a great storywriter will appear to give them new names and a new language.

Notes

1 For arguments of this kind, see Cohen and Arato (1992).
2 This example is discussed in Chatterjee (1998b).
3 I am grateful to Ashok Dasgupta and Debashis Bhattacharya of *Ajkal* for their generous help in researching the story of Balak Brahmachari's death.
4 Sudipta Kaviraj (1998) has explicitly formulated this as a Tocquevillian problem in 'The Culture of Representative Democracy'.
5 The writings of the *Subaltern Studies* group of historians have explored these themes most elaborately. See in particular Guha (1998).
6 I was drawn to this epitaph by Aamir R. Mufti's (2000) reflections on it.

References

Chatterjee, Partha (1997) 'Secularism and toleration', *A Possible India: Essays in Political Criticism*, Delhi: Oxford University Press.
Chatterjee, Partha (1998a) 'Beyond the nation? Or within?' *Social Text*, Autumn.
Chatterjee, Partha (1998b) 'Community in the East', *Economic and Political Weekly*, January.
Chatterjee, Partha (1998c) 'The wages of freedom'. In Partha Chatterjee (ed.) *The Wages of Freedom: Fifty Years of the Indian Nation-state*, Delhi: Oxford University Press.

Chatterjee, Partha (2000) 'Two poets and death: on civil and political society in the non-Christian world'. In Tim Mitchell and Lila Abu-Lughod (eds) *Questions of Modernity*, Minneapolis: University of Minnesota Press.

Cohen, Jean L. and Arato, Andrew (1992) *Civil Society and Political Theory*, Cambridge, MA: The MIT Press.

Gandhi, M. K. (1958) 'Bihar and untouchability', *Collected Works*, New Delhi: Publications Division, vol. 57.

Guha, Ranajit (1998) *Dominance Without Hegemony,* Cambridge, MA: Harvard University Press.

Hasan, Khalid (1987) 'Introduction' to Saadat Hasan Manto. In Khalid Hasan (trans.) *Kingdom's End and Other Stories*, London: Verso.

Kaviraj, Sudipta (1998) 'The culture of representative democracy', in Partha Chatterjee (ed.) *The Wages of Freedom: Fifty Years of the Indian Nation-State*, Delhi: Oxford University Press.

Kohli, Atul (1991) *Democracy and Discontent: India's Growing Crisis of Governability*, Cambridge: Cambridge University Press.

Manto, Saadat Hasan (1987) 'Toba Tek Singh'. In Khalid Hasan (trans.) *Kingdom's End and Other Stories*, London: Verso.

Mufti, Aamir R. (2000) 'A greater story writer than god: gender, genre and minority in late colonial India'. In Partha Chatterjee and Pradeep Jeganathan (eds) *Subaltern Studies XI*, Delhi: Oxford University Press.

Rao, M. S. A. and Frankel, Francine (1990) *Dominance and State Power in India: Decline of a Social Order*, 2 vols, Delhi: Oxford University Press.

Rudolph, Lloyd, I. and Rudolph, Susanne Hoeber (1987) *In Pursuit of Lakshmi: The Political Economy of the Indian State*, Chicago: University of Chicago Press.

Editors' note

Delivered as the Saadat Hasan Manto Lecture at the Centre for the Study of Developing Societies, Delhi, in January 2000.

Chapter 7

Decolonialization and assumption of war responsibility

Hanasaki Kohei
(Translated by Muto Ichiyo)

Kato Norihiro's discussion of post-defeat Japan

One book that earned journalistic acclaim and triggered a controversy in Japanese intellectual fora from 1997 to 1998 was *Discussing Post-Defeat Japan* by literary critic Kato Norihiro (1998). In problematizing the basic mode of being of postwar Japan, Kato uses the idea of 'twistedness' as the key to understanding what he calls 'post-defeat' Japanese society. While war-defeated Japan has had this 'twistedness' built into its core, he argues, the Japanese society has ignored it and been behaving as though it did not exist.

Kato observes that since the Asian-Pacific war, which Japan fought, was condemned as an unjust war of aggression, those Japanese who sacrificed their lives, believing in the cause of the state, died meaningless deaths. With the meaning of the war thus denied by external circumstances, those who survived could not maintain the continuity of their wartime identity, nor could they deny it and break from it by their own choice. Kato calls this suspended identity a 'twist'. Here he uses 'twistedness' in personal terms to describe the ambivalent state of mind of many Japanese individuals.

However, he uses the same word to characterize postwar Japanese state and society. The postwar Japanese state is plagued by a twist because it has avoided consistent and responsible evaluation of the war. On the one hand, the Japanese government has time and again apologized to its Asian neighbours for 'acts of aggression'. But, on the other, government leaders and politicians periodically came out with blatant statements justifying what Japan did to its neighbours. Kato finds in this double-talk a 'twistedness' embedded in Japanese state and society. Kato's logic, which mixes up the personal and state levels, is extremely confusing.

In the context of state and society, Kato argues that Japanese society has perpetuated its schizophrenic duality as it has refused to admit the presence of this twistedness. Japan is, as it were, Dr Jekyll when it apologizes to its Asian neighbours for aggression, but it is at once Mr Hyde when it justifies and glorifies its past and makes excuses for its conduct.

Given this, he suggests, the priority task for the Japanese is first to admit the presence of the 'twistedness' and, on that basis, overcome this split personality by absorbing Mr Hyde into Dr Jekyll. Only then can 'we' re-emerge as a single nation that can qualify as a body able to apologize to others.

As a necessary step toward the reconstruction of this 'we', Kato proposes that Japan proceed through a particular national procedure the mourning of the three million

Japanese war dead. We will be constituted as a 'we' only after we, as a nation, have paid tribute to our war dead. Only then can we apologize as Japanese to our Asian neighbours for having killed twenty million of them.

Anticipating the criticism that his proposal is but another attempt to revive Japanese nationalism, Kato disavows nationalism. He is simply proposing that 'we take upon ourselves' a 'national frame', rather than the constitution of a nationalistic Japanese community. If we abandon the task of becoming a nation, he reasons, we cannot make ourselves 'more open' to others, nor can we dream of going beyond the nation state.

Disavowals notwithstanding, Kato's reasoning follows a typical nationalist pattern; he proposes to reconstitute a nation with a single identity analogous to an individual. When Kato expresses his eagerness to let the 'we' stand up, he no doubt has in mind a single national community that subsumes individuals – an imagined community filled with shared national emotions that will be crystallized in national mourning rituals.

Until some time ago, I used to think that it would be necessary for us to recover our national consciousness as Japanese nationals in order to constitute a body that could fulfil the unsettled colonial and war responsibilities of the Japanese Empire. Japan as a nation, I thought, should be the body to apologize to, and compensate, the Asian people who were invaded and colonized by Japan. In this essay, I will re-examine my position by critical reference to Kato's proposition.

In connection with this, I would like to emphasize that Japan, in the postwar state reconstruction process, has ignored the settlement of its historical legacies of colonialism. I mean the decolonialization proper, including, but not reduced to, the settlement of war responsibilities in the narrow sense. This essay is intended to discuss the two related topics in a single context – the question of subjects for the assumption of war responsibility and the problem of decolonialization in postwar Japan.

The problem of decolonialization

Kang Sanjun (1998), who teaches social and cultural studies at Tokyo University, points out that Japan's official postwar national history has excluded, and made invisible, the colonized people who were once subjects of the Japanese Empire. Worse still, it has forgotten the process that led to their exclusion from its society in the postwar period. In this context, he quotes the following passage from historian Mitani Taichiro, who teaches political and diplomatic history of modern Japan at Tokyo University.

In the Japanese case, the decolonialization process as such, as distinguished from demilitarization, had a relatively small impact on the domestic course of affairs. To put it in another way, decolonialization was reduced to demilitarization. Moreover, the Cold War deepened at the very moment when decolonialization was supposed to be carried out. With the shift in the occupation policy, the political and economic reconstruction of postwar Japan became reoriented toward satisfying the requirement of the Cold War. The Cold War also influenced the decolonialization processes of Japan's former colonies. Decolonialization there was frozen at a level that would not hamper Japan's role in the Cold War. Now that the Cold War is over, the unfulfilled task of Japan's decolonialization has re-surfaced for settlement. Mitani understands this as the second stage, so to speak, of Japan's decolonialization process (Mitani 1997).

Decolonialization primarily means the liberation and independence of former colonies, but it also refers to the corresponding process of decolonialization of the colonial powers.

Mitani mainly discusses this latter process, the process of Japan 'liquidating its empire and Japan freeing itself of its empire' (Mitani 1993). These are the tasks Japan ought to have carried out as its own responsibility. In reality, however, by accepting the Potsdam Declaration that unilaterally set Japan's new territorial boundaries, the defeated Japan accepted decolonialization passively 'as a given and as the obvious'. With its colonial empire 'automatically disappearing' as the result of its defeat, Japan proper 'did not engage itself in decolonialization processes'. The Japanese people accordingly failed to take decolonialization seriously. Decolonialization, Mitani observes, was considered 'synonymous with, or a mere extension of, demilitarization and democratization'.

Granted these objective circumstances that left Japan insensitive to the issue of decolonialization, Mitani should have paid more attention to the fact that precisely because of this insensitivity, the pre-war imperial consciousness was not liquidated, but survived in postwar Japanese society.

Generally, Mitani's account is merely descriptive, and fails to problematize precisely who should carry out the process of decolonialization. I am not satisfied with the third-person stance that permeates Mitani's discourse. By attributing the decolonialization process in the 1990s solely to the end of the Cold War, Mitani totally misses the significance of people's movements in bringing it into focus. He fails to appreciate the people's movements which, since the 1970s, have ignited decolonialization processes everywhere. I have in mind, for instance, the indigenous peoples who raised voices of condemnation against their conquest and colonial domination, and the worldwide women's movement that identified the common roots of patriarchal and colonial domination. He also fails to mention the responsibility the Japanese government must fulfil for decolonialization.

It is true, as Mitani points out, that in the early postwar period there were no people's movements, nor serious social thinking, that pursued the task of decolonialization itself, as distinguished from demilitarization. There certainly were serious schools of thought and movements that sought to eradicate militarism and criticized the emperor system as the root of Japanese fascism, but they developed solely in the context of demili-tarization. The central policy choice of the postwar Japanese state was to allow itself to be fully integrated with the postwar US hegemonic system, with a view to securing impunity for Emperor Hirohito for his war responsibilities and preventing Japanese people from being attracted to communism. The Cold War soon broke out, effectively and conveniently helping postwar Japan to bury the tasks of decolonialization. In this setting, not only did Japan not apologize to the peoples it had colonized, it also failed to assume responsibility for the damage done.

The Japanese people's understanding of Japan changed in the postwar period. Before 1945 the self-image of Japan was one of a vast, outstretched Empire. After 1945, it shrank, along with Japan's territory. The new understanding is that, since antiquity, Japan has been a natural community, integral to the Japanese archipelago. With their eyes bandaged by this myth of 'we, the natural historical community' and by their consciousness as war victims, the postwar Japanese struck their imperial past from their mind. By the same token, they could not imagine that they had to settle the consequences of modern Japan with other peoples – peoples Japan colonized and otherwise victimized. This is why Koreans frequently become frustrated and upset when they discuss history with Japanese, finding in them little sense of national responsibility for what Japan did to the Koreans in the past. This lack of a sense of national responsibility can be attributed to the postwar construction of Japanese national history, where Japan's modern past was never properly grasped as a history of empire building and the eventual failure of this project and where, as Kang points out, the exclusion of Koreans and other former subjects of the Japanese Empire has been totally obliterated.[1]

Rise of neo-nationalism

In the 1990s, following the end of the Cold War, the Gulf War, and the subsequent demise of the Soviet Union, strands of neo-nationalism sprang up and made considerable headway in Japanese society. Their ideological positions are wide-ranging, from the soft-pedalling style of Kato Norihiro, who advocates a guilt-free Japanese nation, to the extreme position of Ishihara Shintaro (now governor of Tokyo), who spouts anti-American rhetoric in a bid to attain Japanese hegemony in Asia. In spite of their differences, they are all historical revisionists who attack the 'postwar view of history' in one way or another.

The most eye-catching group of neo-nationalist intellectuals launched a campaign around 1996 against the 'postwar view of history'. They argue that the 'postwar view of history', which they claim dominates school textbooks, is a 'masochistic view of history' which sees only the vices and not the virtues of the Japanese nation (Fujioka 1996). They propose viewing modern Japanese history as a narrative of the state, with the people gallantly and assiduously working together to face the severe national ordeal. Proselytizing this view, they hold mass rallies and lobby local assemblies to pass petitions calling upon the Ministry of Education to erase from school textbooks any mention of the 'comfort women'. The dark side of history should not be taught, they claim, because children should be inspired with national pride. These campaigns have attracted signficant numbers of the younger generation. In 1998, Kobayashi Yoshinori (1998), a popular cartoonist and one of the most conspicuous spokespersons of this campaign, published *Discussing the War* – a comic book! In this book, Kobayashi glorifies patriotism and attempts to justify Japan's imperialist wars, using this crude message, 'Will you go to war? Or do you stop being a Japanese?' The book has sold half a million copies, the majority to young people, showing an ominous rise of nationalist feelings among the younger generation.

Alarmed by this historical revisionism, concerned intellectuals and activists have developed counter-arguments. Verbal battles first erupted between the neo-nationalists and critics over the 'comfort women' issue. It soon developed, however, into a broader debate on the Japanese government's attitude and policy toward the official system of sexual slavery. After repeated negations, the Japanese government was finally forced to admit the state involvement in organizing and running the system of military sexual slavery and, accordingly, had to admit its 'moral responsibility'. However it was, and still is, adamant in refusing to take legal responsibility for this, and on these grounds refuses to pay state reparations to the survivors. In an attempt to avoid taking legal state responsibility, it improvised an ambiguous scheme, the Asian Women's Fund (AWF), which would collect donations from citizens and pay the survivors 'atonement money' out of this non-governmental fund. Survivors from Korea, the Philippines and elsewhere denounced the AWF as a gimmick, designed by the state to evade responsibility, and refused to receive this 'atonement money'. Groups and individuals working on the sexual slavery issue were split over whether the AWF should be seen as a deceptive government manoeuvre to evade state responsibility, or as a step forward, however small, toward redress for the survivors. Intense debate continues.

This debate soon developed from the pros and cons of the Asian Women's Fund to broader themes of what shouldering 'national war responsibility' meant. This debate was triggered by Ueno Chizuko (1997, 1998), who teaches sociology at Tokyo University. In her article 'Politics of memories' and book *Nationalism and Gender*, she offered a major challenge to the nationalistic discourse which she believed prevailed in the Japanese and Korean movements seeking redress for the 'comfort women'. In these writings, she criticized the notion that Japanese people, as members of the Japanese nation state, should assume responsibility for colonialism. At a symposium held by the Resource Center on Japan's War Responsibilities, Ueno was criticized by historian Yoshimi Yoshiaki, philosopher Takahashi Tetsuya, and two resident Korean intellectuals, writer/thinker Soh Kyonshik and historian Kim Puja. The proceedings of this symposium were published in a book, *Nationalism and the 'Comfort Women' Issue* (The Resource Center on Japan's War Responsibilities 1998).

Nationalism and feminism

In *Nationalism and Gender*, Ueno (1998) developed an interesting argument on the points we are discussing. Chapter 1, 'The nation state and gender', is a critique of the categories of the modern nation state and the nation from a gender perspective. The nation, Ueno argues, being defined right from its inception as a male association, is unable by definition to achieve gender equality within its framework. Since the modern nation state is constituted as a patriarchal one, women's participation riding on the state's strategy of nationalizing women can never lead to the liberation of women. Such participation only traps the women's liberation movement and leads it to compromise and failure. Exclusivity is ingrained in the category of the nation in the sense that a person at any point in time can belong to only one nation and no other. This category, forcing an individual either to be a member or a non-member, carries oppressive implications. To evade this trap of absorption into a single category of collectivity, a multiplicity of categories of affiliation, corresponding to the multiplicity of the individual identity, should be recognized.

I agree that the notion of monolithic collectivity should be rejected. Nevertheless, we have to live within it. Totally rejecting collectivity would mean relating to others only by difference and constantly fleeing from any involvement in relationships. This might be conceptually possible but, in practice, could lead to evasions of rightful responsibilities. It must be admitted, however, that any collectivity entails exclusivity. This is because any collectivity has to have its inside and outside. Recognizing this, it is necessary for us, in the context of social practice, to constitute a collectivity such as 'we', on an ad hoc basis, take it upon ourselves, and get it to interact with other collectivities which we also take upon ourselves.

But let me quote Ueno as she discusses the 'comfort women' issue (Chapter 2 of her book). In December 1991, Kim Haksun and two other Korean former 'comfort women' led a lawsuit in Japan, demanding an official apology and compensation from the Japanese government. This was a landmark event that brought the 'comfort women' issue to the attention of the Japanese public. Ueno sees in this a drastic paradigm shift. This shift occurred, Ueno argues, as the 'comfort women' issue, for the first time, came to be recognized as a case of a sexual crime committed by the Japanese military. 'This shift was brought about by the Korean women's movement as well as the democratization movement in the 1980s. Behind the Korean women's movement was the upsurge of the feminist movement throughout the world.'

It is true that the feminist movement was a major factor that brought the 'comfort women' issue to the front of stage. But I am afraid that by reducing the complex factors at work to one, she misses others that also worked to bring that issue to the surface. In particular, she misses the factor of renewed decolonialization processes in the 1990s.

Kim Puja (1988), who studies Korean modern history of education and gender, criticizes Ueno's discourse for having 'little concern for colonialism and a poor awareness that she herself is a concerned party, rather than an outsider'. Generalizing this point, she remarks that not only Ueno, but also Japanese women in general, 'have a tendency to construct the "comfort women" issue within the confines of a feminist discourse that is indifferent to national problems'. As evidence of this, she points out that although the 'comfort women' issue was already widely known in Japan in the 1970s, Japanese women did not make it an issue until the Korean women raised it in the 1990s. On this ground she urges the Japanese women's movement to re-examine its postwar history, reflecting on whether or not it was indifferent to Japan's colonialism and national issues. She wonders whether Japanese feminists, having lived as members of a ruling nation, have felt no need to face national issues seriously.

What is Ueno's position *vis-à-vis* criticisms along the lines of Kim Puja's argument? Ueno examines several existing paradigms that situate the 'comfort women' issue differently, and then criticizes and rejects each of them as one-sided.[2] Having done so, she proposes to 'place this issue in the context of comparative history and thereby make it understandable and resolvable'.

By comparative history, she no doubt means international comparative studies on the issues of sexual violence against women at war and in armed conflict situations. But I am not satisfied with this conclusion, as she is proposing merely to make academic this highly practical issue. While she admits that the 'comfort women' issue requires a comprehensive understanding of 'gender, class and nation', she in fact does not positively integrate the 'nation' aspect into her discourse. Rather, she carefully shuns the national factor, apparently wary of being dragged into nationalist discourses.

Ueno defines nationalism as the 'identification of the individual with the nation state'. According to her, expressions like 'I as a member of a nation that victimized other people' or simply the use of 'we' would in itself commit us to nationalism. Accordingly, when other people retrogressively condemn Japan for what it did to them, Ueno would say that she is not answerable. For by being answerable to what the Japanese state did, she would be identifying herself with the Japanese state or nation. The 'comfort women' issue involves only personal relationships between Ueno as an individual and the former 'comfort women', also as individuals.

Ueno herself is not making a plea for an abstraction of the individual. On the contrary, in her book's conclusion, she opposes recourse to 'such abstract universal agents like the "global citizen", "the individual", or "humanity" as a way of overcoming the exclusivity of the nation'. She points to the temptation of 'the concept of universal, cosmopolitan citizenship', saying that succumbing to it would lead to the fallacy that the individual can be free from any belonging and be allowed to behave as though the burdens of history did not exist. What constitutes 'me', she argues, is 'the diverse relationships in concert – gender, nationality, occupation, status, race, culture, ethnicity and so on – none of which I can flee from but none of which I can be reduced to'. What she refuses to accept is the privileging and essentializing of one over the others, and the logic of representation, allowing someone else to speak on behalf of 'me proper'.

Stating that 'me proper' cannot and should not be reduced to a single category is a declaration of the right to self-definition and self-representation. This is a feminist manifesto of refusal to be defined by others and of struggle against the oppression that forces women into the male-created discursive space. I support this position. But I am disappointed when she refers to the various relationships constituting 'me' only in negative terms, that is, merely as something 'I cannot flee from but cannot be reduced to'.

Ueno admits that as part of her historical and social relationships, she is involved in the relationships that make her 'a member of the Japanese nation'. Given her agreement on this, she should have positively defined what it means to her to shoulder responsibility as a member of the nation.

Subjectivity as 'Japanese'

In a forum on the theme of 'What did post-colonial thinking mean in Japan', carried by the journal *Space of Criticism* in 1996, Tomiyama Ichiro (1996), who teaches sociology at Osaka University, observes that 'before discussing post-coloniality, we must problematize the absence of any basic discussion about the processes of decolonialization and the abandonment of the responsibility for decolonialization in Japan'. Therefore, 'if belatedly, we need to discuss decolonialization processes now'. But to discuss the colonial responsibility, he pointed out, 'it is unavoidable that we call to the stage a certain very rigid body to assume the responsibility'. Here he has to ask how such a rigid body and the more open and flexible subjectivity discussed in the post-colonial discourse can be compatible. 'Here we face a very difficult problematic.' Tomiyama himself does not have an answer to this dilemma.

At the same symposium, Soh Kyonshik (1998), a writer teaching at Hosei University discussing the Japanese state's responsibility for reparation, names 'you, the Japanese' as the ones who bear the primary responsibility for changing the Japanese state. He points out that most of the former Zaibatsu corporations and major construction companies raked in enormous profits from the colonial rule and war, and that in the postwar period they rebuilt themselves on this basis. Japan's postwar prosperity was made possible by this fact. The tripartite complicity established in the past among the Japanese state, companies and people, has been carried over into the postwar period, and each Japanese is a beneficiary from this inherited structure of privilege. This being the case, conniving at the state's evasion of responsibility for reparations to the victims is in itself a criminal act. He asks:

> Isn't it the case that the Japanese have been clinging to their comfortable lives, more or less aware of this crime? Aren't the Japanese, as they live in this historical and current relationship as members of the Japanese state and nation, already responsible (for this crime)? When I urge you to take responsibility as Japanese, I mean exactly this.

(Soh 1998: 68)

In the face of the accusation that the Japanese as a whole are an accessory to this crime of cover-up, I take the stand that as long as I was born as a member of the colonizer nation state, and am still positioned in a historical situation where the decolonialization of Japan is not complete, I would provisionally take upon myself the definition of being a 'Japanese', the definition that is given to me by other people and that puts me into the national Japanese collective. I say 'provisionally' because I do not think I should remain forever passively defined and bound by this given relationality. Japanese colonial rule as viewed from the colonized peoples presents itself as nothing other than national oppression by the Japanese as a race. The colonized peoples thus take the Japanese race to task for their colonial responsibility. In the context of decolonialization, this identification of the nation state with the race is grounded in both imagery and reality.

Even so, it would be wrong for us to jump from an awareness of our historical colonizer state responsibility to identification with the Japanese nation. If we did so, we would be constructing ourselves in the image of the racially constituted Japanese as projected by the accusers. In that event, we would fall into the trap of the essentialist nationalist paradigm.

How far can individuals be responsible for the conduct of the nation state of which they are members? This should not be uniformly and sweepingly determined. The notion that every person who belongs to a nation state carries an exactly equal share of responsibility for what the state has done should be criticized as nationalistic, in the sense that the national identity is singled out as the essential category, overshadowing other categories of identities that individuals also take.

Moving back to Ueno, she sees in Soh Kyonshik's discourse a nationalist paradigm that fails to problematize sexual violence beyond national boundaries. Her concern centres on how feminism can be set free from the nationalist paradigm. But this has the potential of carrying her to the other extreme, by dismissing the national factor.

Oka Mari (1998), who teaches contemporary Arab Literature at Osaka Women's College, reacts to Ueno precisely on this weakness. Oka makes the point that feminism can overcome nationalism only when it is committed to the practice of squarely facing and disintegrating the national relationships people are already enmeshed in. But Ueno does not do so. In defending her right to select her own identity, Ueno refuses to respond to the question raised by others about her responsibility as a Japanese. Oka argues that the 'me' that is constituted and projected by others is to her an 'other' and, as such, is something that she cannot freely choose. 'I' therefore must encounter the 'me' as perceived by the eyes of others and try to answer the questions posed to that 'me'. This is the first step, she says, toward disintegrating the asymmetrical colonial power relationships in which she enjoys a privileged position (Oka 1998: 236).

Oka's argument is fully correct as a normative one. But essentialism can easily penetrate Oka's 'me as other' as caught in the eyesight of others, and can fix the 'me' there. If I totally accept this categorical image of me projected by others and internalize it, this 'me as other' will force me to negate my life itself, because it will be structurally guilty of the exploitation of third-world people. We must free ourselves from the essentialist paradigm that posits a homogeneous collectivity. But on the other hand, the rejection of essentialism merely by opposing a 'me proper' (Ueno), which relates to others only by differences would erase the entire instance of responsibility, the instance at which an individual places a certain moral obligation upon him/herself in response to the calls of others. To the side asking for a response, this act of erasure would signify an exercise of privilege.

How then should this responsible subject be constructed?

First, the essentialized notion of the racially constructed Japanese should be turned down. It would leave little space for individuals who refuse to absolutize the state, endeavour to create relationships beyond national boundaries, and carry out decolonialization as the manifestation of their inner urge to be free and live a meaningful life. Any person exposed to the injustices of the Japanese state naturally feels righteous anger at the neglect of redress for the victims and the cover-up of the crimes by the Japanese state, and feels pain for the sufferings of the victims. Although this ethical feeling does not choose nationality, if the person is Japanese, the ethical pains felt must be more intense. This is a special, ethical feeling felt as a member of the collective that committed the crime. The 'comfort women' debate concerns precisely this point, the responsibility of being a member of a collective called the nation state.

It should be clear that the Japanese people have allowed the Japanese state and corporations to evade settlement of their colonial past for more than half a century. This is why the former 'comfort women' have to demand redress now. This fact defines the postwar responsibility which falls on the shoulders of those Japanese who had no direct war or colonial responsibility, including younger generations. If it is a crime, it is a crime of cover-up and concealment. Political theorist Muto Ichiyo (1998) discusses this matter in the light of the nature of the postwar Japanese state, which integrates within itself three mutually contradictory principles: the unbroken line of continuity from Japan's imperial past (most notably in the form of the retention of Hirohito as emperor), American free worldism and constitutional pacifism. Because of this peculiar formation (a twistedness in the statehood), the postwar Japanese state has been unable to break from its past, nor has it been able to openly justify it.

Now that this postwar state has entered into a historical process of disintegration and metamorphosis, the direction of reorganization of the postwar statehood is being contested. This is the most pressing task facing the residents and their communities on this archipelago. As Muto says, we will only be able to cease to be an accomplice to the crimes committed by the state – war, colonialization and cover-ups – when we have overcome the postwar Japanese state and transformed it into a political formation based on alternative principles. However, we take on this task not because we are named and urged to do so, but because we have an inner urge and sense of obligation to do so.

Tasks of Kyosei

Post-Second World War Asia, with the rise of national liberation movements, turned into an arena of West–East confrontation. In territories suffering from splits of nations, in particular, brute violence was exercised by the military and police against the opposition forces. Much blood was shed in the process. It is now time to recall these memories, to ask why the nation states, built through vast sacrifices of the people, came to betray the ideals they originally held high. In fact, it is time to call into question the state-centred paradigm of politics. As a concept for a new political philosophy, I have been talking about 'co-viviality', an English word coined from the Japanese word 'kyosei', literally 'living together'.

The concept originated in Japanese movements against industrial pollution towards the end of the 1960s. At the beginning, it was used in slogans like 'For a civilization where human beings and nature can "live together" (co-vive)'. In the 1970s, 'the logic of co-viviality' came into use in various movements against social discrimination, such as the women's liberation movement and those of the Buraku people, disabled persons and ethnic minorities. Within these movements, the logic of co-viviality was used as a guideline to end discrimination against specific social groups. Co-vivial relationships meant relationships in which differences do not generate discrimination. From these specific usages came a broader meaning of co-viviality as the guiding principle of alternative political and social formation. Co-viviality was also introduced as a means of transforming the unequal relationships between people in the core and periphery, because under the existing structure which perpetuates inequality, differently positioned people in the world system are pushed into antagonistic positions and are prevented from living together in positive interaction and solidarity.

I have been engaged since the 1970s in activities for the recognition of the Ainu as an indigenous people, for the recovery of their indigenous rights. I have also participated in activities to overcome discrimination against Koreans in Japan. I discovered through this process that the movement for the resolution of these issues necessitated two lines of logic. One regards the responsibility of the nation and the state in the decolonialization process, a topic I have discussed earlier. The other concerns a new multi-ethnic and multi-cultural democracy. At first, activists did not clearly perceive the importance of the logic of new democracy, but this idea earned their recognition as the movement developed and as international solidarity deepened. International solidarity increasingly demonstrated the effectiveness of the strategy of criticizing and reforming the state policies and institutions of a country, through the combined mobilization of forces inside and outside the country. Conversely, the importance of decolonialization as the disintegration of the imperial consciousness and the liquidation of the negative legacies of colonialism began to be increasingly perceived in the midst of the move toward a co-vivial democracy, in which people could come together in solidarity beyond state and national borders.

I am aware, however, that people who are condemning the colonizer state and nation may immediately find themselves alarmed, and even upset, by my mention of co-viviality. Their wariness is legitimate. In fact, 'Let us live together!' has been a mainstream slogan in Japanese society since the mid-1980s, appropriated in advertisements or as official catchphrases in order to cover up existing social antagonisms. Underneath this sleek phrase, we often find, tucked away, continuing, and even strengthened, discrimination, in new forms, against ethnic and other minorities.

Under these circumstances, it is important for people who have been discriminated against to keep guard against the easy use of the term. It is only in the midst of practices that actually transform the existing relationships that the idea of co-viviality can prove itself relevant. Conditions, or in fact procedures, that transform the existing antagonistic relationships into conditions of freedom should therefore be seriously sought.

This is exactly what Ri Takanori (1998), who teaches cultural studies at Tokyo University, seeks to do in his essay, 'Beyond the representation of a "better Japanese"'. Taking the 'comfort women' issue as a touchstone, Ri examines the common procedures that would be required to create a co-vivial relationship over this issue. Ri says that the notion of 'better Japanese' would not lead to such a relationship. Kato Norihiro's contention, according to Ri, is favourably received in Japan because Japanese people perceive in it the plausible message that 'we are capable of taking war responsibility, and so let us, Japanese, build a better Japan for ourselves'. The wish to be 'better Japanese' represents an emotional sharing exclusively among Japanese for the sake of the Japanese alone. This emotion, Ri points out, functions as a shield which prevents Japanese from reacting to others, and as a frame within which Japanese can be content with themselves to the exclusion of others. What then is the basis for co-vivial relationality? Ri's answers are implicit in a series of questions he asks:

> Why are the former 'comfort women' accusing the Japanese of what was done to them more than 50 years ago? Is it not because they want to unlive the past at present, however imperfect an unliving it may be? Are not they demanding redress in clear and acceptable procedures, in the form of apology and compensation? Is it not because the procedural settlement is a kind of joint work (by them and the Japanese) in which their past relationship with the Japanese, which was simply abominable, could somehow be mediated to a present that is clearly distinct from the past? Isn't this the way they wish to be saved and healed? Even though they can never forget the past, are they not anxious to be able to relativize or even forgive it by building a new relationship (with Japanese) so that they can be saved? Is it not true that responding to this call will not only save their past but save their future by overcoming the absolute barrier between the assailant and the victim?
>
> (Ri 1998)

At the earlier mentioned symposium, Soh Kyunshik urged Japanese to develop a plan to create 'another Japan, a Japan different from the past Japan with its family-like cohesiveness with the Emperor at the top, and a Japan also different from the postwar Japan whose symbolic image was the family organized around the father working assiduously for company interests'. It is in the nuclear family image that Soh sees the core of postwar Japanese nationalism. Anxious to have another Korea, Soh invites those Japanese and Koreans who have plans for another Japan and another Korea to come together in solidarity. I fully support this idea.

Since 1989, I have joined like-minded people in a movement to envision and actuate another Japan and an alternative world. This movement is called the People's Plan 21. We felt that changing Japan could not be a task isolated from the regional and global context. It is a task integral to the transformation of the global system. I wish that efforts to create 'another Japan' will be increasingly oriented toward deconstructing Japanese nationalism and will join forces with the people's movements in Asia and elsewhere, particularly with decolonialization movements in East Asia. Together, hopefully, we will see the emergence of a new paradigm that goes beyond the constraints of the nation state and nationalism everywhere.

Notes

1 Grasping the present as a new decolonialization stage in the historical context leads us to the task of critiquing and reorganizing the historical knowledge about pre-war and postwar Japan. As Tessa Morris-Suzuki (1998) points out, this problem has much in common with the issues

debated on the global level about history and memory. Criticizing resurgence of nationalism on a global scale as a backlash against the collapse of the old paradigm that histories are automatically national histories, she emphasizes the need to go beyond histories centred on nation states and proposes that history be constituted as 'an ongoing dialogue between many memories and material traces of the past.'

Takashi Fujitani observes that, since the mid-1980s, the modes of being of the memories of the Holocaust, Hiroshima, the Battle of Okinawa, colonialism, slavery, Vietnam, the Conquest, the Nanking massacre, 'comfort women' and so on, have been highlighted. Public memories, he remarks, have been formed as plausible and value–laden memories as the result of conspiracies between various differential indicators such as nation, race, class, gender, and sex (retranslated from the Japanese text). Fujitani cautions all who do work in the area of memories to be fully aware of this. Arlette Farge self-critically observes that historians have not paid attention to the 'narrative of suffering' as the 'living abode of history'. She commends a new historiography that can bear the task of accepting the intruder called 'evoked sufferings'. This is an attempt to retell the histories by making public the suppressed memories – memories, for instance, of the women victimized by sexual violence at war (Farge 1998).

2 Ueno (1998: 104) identifies five paradigms that she says are used to discuss the 'comfort women' issue: the national shame (patriarchal) paradigm, wartime rape paradigm, prostitution paradigm, sexual slavery paradigm, and the emperor system paradigm.

References

Farge, Arlette (1998) 'On suffering', *Shiso* 思想 No. 890.

Fujioka, Nobukatsu 藤岡信勝 (1996) *Modern and Contemporary Japanese History Told as a Disgrace* 汚辱の近現代史 , Tokuma Shoten 徳間書店 .

Kang, Sanjun 姜 尚中 (1998) 'Geography of psychical images of the nation and de-nationalizing narratives' 国民の心象地理と脱-国民的語り. In Komori Yoichi and Takahashi Tetsuya (eds) 小森陽一・高橋哲哉編 *Beyond National Histories* ナショナル・ヒストリーを越えて , Tokyo University Press 東京大学出版会 .

Kato, Norihiro 加藤典洋 (1998) *Discussing Post-Defeat Japan* 敗戦後論 , Kodansha 講談社 .

Kim, Puja 朝鮮人 (1988) 'How to view the Korean "comfort women" issue' 金富子 慰安婦」問題 への視座. In Resource Center on Japan's War Responsibilities (ed.) 日本の戦争責任資料センター編 *Nationalism and the 'Comfort Women' Issue* シンポジウム ナショナリズムと 「慰安婦」問題 , Aoki Shoten 青木書店 .

Kobayashi, Yoshinori 小林よしのり (1998) *Discussing the War* 戦争論 , Shogakukan 小学館 .

Mitani, Taichiro 三谷太一郎 (1993) 'Preface to "Cold War in Asia and Decolonialization"' アジアの冷戦と 脱 植民地化 序文 , *Iwanami series, Modern Japan and Its Colonies, Vol. 8* 近代日本と植民地 第8巻 .

Mitani, Taichiro 三谷太一郎 (1997) *Wars and Politics in Modern Japan* 近代日本 の戦争と政治 , Iwanami Shoten 岩波書店 .

Morris-Suzuki, Tessa テッサ・モーリス-鈴木 (1998) 'Global memories, national accounts' グローバルな 記憶・ナショナルな記述 , *Shiso* 思想 No. 890.

Muto, Ichiyo 武藤一羊 (1998) 'Unwinding the twist: How do we overcome the postwar Japanese state?' ねじれを解く一戦後国家をどう越えるか , *Revision No. 1* 雑誌『再審 (レヴィジオン)』 第1号 , Shakai-hyoronsha 社会評論社 .

Oka, Mari 岡真理 (1998) 'Why can we define us as ourselves?' 私たちは、なぜ自ら名のることができる のか. In Resource Center on Japan's War Responsibilities (ed.) 日本の戦争責任資料センター編 *Nationalism and the 'Comfort Women' Issue* ナショナリズムと 「慰安婦」問題 , Aoki Shoten 青木書店 .

The Resource Center on Japan's War Responsibilities (ed.) (1998) 日本の戦争責任資 料センター編 *Nationalism and the 'Comfort Women' Issue* ナショナリズムと 「慰 安婦」問題 , Aoki Shoten 青木書店 .

Ri, Takanori 李孝徳 (1998) 'Beyond the representation of a "better Japanese"' よりよ い日本人という 形象を超えて in Komori Yoichi and Takahashi Tetsuya (eds) 小森 陽一・高橋哲哉編 *Beyond National Histories* ナショナル・ヒストリーを越えて , Tokyo University Press 東京大学出版会 .

Soh, Kyonshik 徐京植 (1998) Remarks at a symposium held by the Resource Center on Japan's War Responsibilities (ed.) 日本の戦争責任資料センター編 *Nationalism and the 'Comfort Women' Issue* ナショナリズムと「慰安婦」問題 , Aoki Shoten 青木書店 .

Tomiyama, Ichiro 冨山一郎 (1996) Remarks in panel discussion 'What does the post-colonial thinking mean?' 座談会「ポストコロニアルの思想とはなにか」, *Space of Criticism 批評空間 II–II*.

Ueno, Chizuko 上野千鶴子 (1997) 'Politics of memories' 記憶の政治学 , *Impaction No. 103 雑誌『インパクション』* , Impact Publishing インパクト出版会 .

Ueno, Chizuko 上野千鶴子 (1998) *Nationalism and Gender ナショナリズムとジェンダー* , Seidosha 青土社 .

Chapter 8

Mourning Korean modernity in the memory of the Cheju April Third Incident

Kim Seong-nae

Introduction: the Cheju April Third Incident[1]

This paper concerns the politics of representation involving political violence and the memory of a violent event in modern Korean history. In particular, I focus on the legacy of the 1948 Cheju April Third Incident, which took place on Cheju Island located off the southwestern coast of the Korean peninsula. This incident is known in Korea as *sasam sakon* or the 4.3 Incident (often called simply '4.3,' after the date of its occurrence). The 4.3 Incident started when a few hundred communist guerrillas attacked police and 'rightists' all around the Cheju Island on 3 April 1948.[2] When counter-insurgency operations were launched to suppress the insurgency, the situation turned into a bloody mass massacre of civilians, who formed the majority of victims. The 4.3 Incident and its violent conclusion in mass massacre prefigured the Korean War in 1950, the better known ideological battle that ended in stalemate and the loss of millions of lives. Although the suppression resulted in a massive death toll of 80,000, or nearly one third of the entire island population, the event has been largely overlooked in historical texts and virtually forgotten in everyday life.[3] As far as anti-communist ideology continues to dominate state politics in South Korea, and the legacy of the 4.3 Incident remains officially as a communist insurgency, much of the memory of the civilian massacres has been effectively silenced.

This paper attempts to offer a timely examination of a little known tragic event in Korean modern history.[4] Like the words 'Auschwitz' and 'Hiroshima/Nagasaki', the words 'Cheju April Third Incident' were a taboo in the public discourse on Korean modernity due to its apocalyptic irrationality (cf. Haver 1996). More than a mere violent event, the Cheju April Third Incident poses an essential threat to the conceptualization of Korean modern history and modernity altogether. This paper argues the essential limit and insufficiency of historical consciousness and representations of this most violent yet little known event.

However, as testimonies of the 4.3 Incident began to be published and memorial activities organized starting in the late 1980s, there has been a new examination of the historical meaning of the 4.3 Incident. Was it, in fact, a communist insurgency as the state has defined it or a popular uprising against a foreign occupation? Or was it a nationalist movement for complete independence and national unification as local dissident intellectuals contend? Or was it mainly a civilian massacre? Such a debate about the historical character of the 4.3 Incident relocates the local event of 50 years ago on the plane of contemporary national politics. The peripheral memories of political violence and recurrent debates on the Cold War ideology demand the Korean nation rewrite its modern history.

After 50 years of near silence, the historical facts of the 4.3 Incident are being reconfigured in various representations. In this paper, I inquire into the representational forms of the 4.3 Incident and the political consequence of these representations, how the memory of massacre is refigured in public commemoration ceremonies, official documents, victims' testimonies, survivors' memoirs, historians' investigative works, newspaper articles, art exhibitions, and also shamanic rituals. Moreover, I show these representations are contested and negotiated in claiming the historical truth of the 4.3 Incident, in the new arena of late 1990s/early 2000s postcolonial politics where the old ideological struggle of the Cold War is reframed as the discursive struggles between local memory and national history.

Remembrance fractured

Here, I approach memory not as retrieval but as a reconfiguration of the past, for memory selects from the flux of images of the past those that best fit its present needs. The very structure of memory of the 4.3 Incident is contingent upon the social and political dynamics of forgetting and remembering that produces it in both everyday and public life.

Scene 1

'It must be a wonderful world that even the red guerrillas (*p'algaengee*) receive a memorial ceremony!' said a survivor of the 4.3 Incident at its 47th anniversary ceremony in 1995. The honeymoon couples disinterestedly taking memorable pictures in the bright yellow flower garden, which was at the back of the ceremonial place, indeed decorated that wonderful world.[5]

As the 4.3 Incident is staged in a public commemoration, the tourists go sightseeing. Even the survivors' painful memories at the ceremony would satisfy their innocent and yet irresponsible curiosity. Let us look at the tourist billboard with a sign of 'Beautiful Cheju' standing in front of Cheju City Hall. Between the two poles the placards of different messages are hung in order: cherry blossom festival on the top; seven celestial maidens festival; tourism photograph contest; then, at the bottom, the memorial ceremony for the victims of the 4.3 Incident at its 47th anniversary. It tells precisely where the memory of the 4.3 Incident is staged in the current public sphere of Cheju society: at the bottom.

Such a low positioning of the memory of the 4.3 Incident in the public consciousness illustrates its subterranean reality. The memory has been kept underneath the glory of nation-building and the economic miracle in the last half-century of modern Korean history. Nevertheless, the memory of the 4.3 Incident has persisted by hanging at the bottom of daily affairs for the last 47 years between 1948 and 1995.

Scene 2

Inside the van taking the mourners back home after the Buddhist memorial ceremony at Kwan-um Temple, a young woman spoke of receiving a survivor's pension after her father-in-law, then the village militia (*minbodan*) during the 4.3 Incident, died grandly in the fight.[6] Fully dressed up as if going to a feast, she boasted about his war medal. She was the only person among the interviewed mourners who spoke up loudly about the dead. As if disagreeing with the young woman, however, an old woman in her late 60s, whose face was hidden under the shade of a cloth wide-brim hat on the back seat whispered in my ear that usually the surviving pensioner did not come to this ceremony, and only relatives of the dead who died unjustly and could not benefit from such a pension came. She herself had come to attend this memorial ceremony in order to pay respects to the memory of her two stepsons, who died during the 4.3 Incident. Her pity for these dead made the young woman ashamed of her father-in-law's war medal. The old woman whispered further that it might be somewhat *immoral* to receive the war pension. Her cautious criticism had a point since the young woman had come to commemorate her father-in-law's participation in a counter-insurgency raid. Kwan-um Temple had served then as the headquarters of the guerrilla army during the 4.3 Incident, where more than 200 guerrillas were killed by the Korean army in March 1949. The place was then burnt to ground in a military counter-insurgency raid, and rebuilt later.

Scene 3

Among the 2000 surviving families who attended the unified memorial ceremony at Tapdong Plaza, there were some survivors who did not have the dead relatives' tablets on the altar. The altar was shaped in a makeshift oval resembling Cheju Island, and was located in the centre of the ceremonial ground. They had dared not report the victim to the Cheju Provincial Parliament's 4.3 Special Committee, for fear that they should be suspected of 'being the families of insurgents' of the 4.3 Incident.

Scene 4

Yet there were men in their 70s who complained about the way the tablets of the dead police and military men were mixed with those of the insurgents under the same village name. They insisted that the spirits of the dead insurgents could not sit together with those of the war dead at the same altar table.

Modernity and the politics of memorial representation

The public commemoration of the 47th anniversary of the 4.3 Incident in 1995 was an unusual event in the context of Korean modern history. Chejudo Province Governor Shin Ku pom present at the ceremony 'officially' promised to construct a commemorative monument for the victims of the 4.3 Incident with governmental finance for the sake of 'reconciliation with the past'. His promise was an adoption of the rhetoric of the state policy of 'straightening-up of history' (*yoksa paro seuki*), which was launched then by the civilian government President Kim Young sam, whose central motto was 'the second nation-building'. At that time, South Korea had undergone an overall restructuring of state policy after 30 years of military rule was taken over. Although it seems that national and local projects conjoin under the urgent command of a new history making, in practice the two projects cannot be easily reconciled. Such a public act of remembering the 4.3 Incident may well transgress the official version of the 4.3 Incident as a 'communist insurgency', meaning an anti-national, anti-state event.

The public commemoration of the 4.3 Incident is a peripheral form of history making, yet it can be a contested form of remembrance. The memorialization of an anti-state event such as the 4.3 Incident contests 'the peculiar form of acceleration which characterizes [the] modernity' of the Korean nation, paraphrasing Koselleck (1985: 5). This modernity I identify with the legacy of national unification, the ideal of which has been deferred for the last 50 years. The ideal of national unification was, in fact, imminent in the first 8 years of Korean modern history from 1945 to 1953 until the Korean War ended, which is generally termed '*haebang konggan*' meaning literally 'the Space of Liberation', when Korea was neither colonized nor fully independent (Choi and Chong 1989). Nevertheless, the project of Korean modernity remains 'incomplete,' due to the national partition implemented by the US and Soviet foreign forces. The two Korean governments in the south and north were established in August 1948. Two Koreas are indeed the modern states without a nation. Ever since then, the 'impaired' project of Korean modernity has indeed accelerated under the quest for national reunification and constantly been renewed in the practices of remembering the purportedly 'unified nation' of the pre-colonial era. I would call this peculiar form of remembrance on behalf of national unity a 'monumental contemplation of the past,' in the sense that the national past is re-constructed through memorial practices of the nation-states (Nietzsche 1957).

It could be said that Koreans have lived under 'a state of emergency' for national unity and identity. This profound sense of emergency has served to justify state violence in the separate regimes of South and North Koreas. The 4.3 Incident broke out before such a state of emergency became 'naturalized' through the formal establishment of the two states. 'A microscope on the politics of postwar Korea' (Cumings 1990: 251), the 4.3 Incident remains stigmatized as a primal scene in the procession of Korean modernity that is closely related to the political violence of the state. Regarding genocide in Nazi Germany, Bauman (1989) and Fritzsche (1996) argue that far from an aberration, political violence is a central event of modern history in which mass death was facilitated by the rationalization process of nation rebuilding. In the recent history of mass deaths, such as the cases of Argentina (Robben 1995), Venezuela (Coronil 1997), and also Ireland (Feldman 1991), the political violence of the state appears to be a 'constitutive' element of the modern state system.[7]

In a similar line of argument, it must be understood that the civilian massacre during the 4.3 Incident was a planned act of state terrorism (Park 1999). When the initial communist guerrillas' insurgency broke out on Cheju Island on 3 April 1948, the US military government and right-wing political leader Rhee Syung Man, who later became the president of the First Republic of Korea, branded Cheju as 'a red communist island' and an enemy of the state. In the process of overturning this crisis moment, the Republic of Korea was established on 15 August 1948. The birth of the anti-communist state in South Korea in the midst of intense suppression of guerrilla insurgency makes the repressive state apparatus an ironic offspring of the 'emancipatory' function of Korean modernity. The South Korean state drive of modernity for the sake of a communist-free unified nation has kept out those enemies of the state for nearly 50 years and effectively justified political violence on its own people.

In this context, the public commemoration of the anti-state event, such as the 4.3 Incident, is given a particular position as an anti-state peripheral memorial. Such a peripheral memory that confronts the anti-communism ideology of South Korea destabilizes the homogeneous time of the imaginary unified nation and inscribes the violence and historical trauma of Korean modernity.

The peripheral memories of the 4.3 Incident consist of *memorial representations* or 'figurative representations of real events' that bear a motive of commemoration (White 1992: 37). Commemoration is a mnemonic technique for localizing collective memory in particular images of space and time (Hallbwacks 1992). By 'figurative representation,' I presume the linguistic function of memory and commemoration as it is written or read in the textual mode. On the plane of memorial representation, the historically real event becomes the literal event, which is 'an artifact that is textual in nature,' and thus verbally constructed (White 1987: 209).

Addressing the question of whether it is 'appropriate' to write about the Holocaust, White contends that, depending on the ethical stance the writer chooses, the truthfulness or impropriety of any representation is assessed in terms of the truth of fictions, not that of the historical facts (White 1992). According to him, the ethics of writing about events is predicated on the very procedure of historical representation, and also 'its effectiveness in justifying current political policies that are crucial to the security' of the state (White 1987: 80).

In short, memorial representation is the historical plotting of effective ideology, whether it is true or not. To be effective, the ideology of the truth lends itself to the construction of meaning of memory as text in context – a context of experiences. As the scenes of the 47th commemoration ceremonies illustrate, in the fractured forms of memory, the 4.3 Incident takes on a new life and is reconstructed as historical fact, awaiting new, yet fractured, meanings. If the 4.3 Incident means the family honour of war dead to the young woman, it also means family secrecy of insurgents to the old woman. If the 4.3 Incident means communist guerrilla insurgency for some survivors, it means popular uprising for others. These fractured meanings contest the fact that the conceptions of the 4.3 Incident are never coherent or candidly identifiable with a single imagery.

Nevertheless, the very discordance of meanings of the 4.3 Incident tends to conjure up the spectre of a past ideological struggle among the survivors. To salvage the memory silenced over 50 years, the people and community again go through recurrent violence in remembering the Incident. We are now witnessing a moment in which fractured memories compete to establish a new regime of truth on the 4.3 Incident. There are multiple truths and ideologies as far as there exist multiple fractured memorial representations of the 4.3 Incident. The politics of memorial representations of the 4.3 Incident, opposing or contending for the truth, are typically seen in the controversy over the naming of the 4.3 Incident.

Naming positions

There are two dominant naming positions in the representations of the 4.3 Incident. The problem of naming is concerned with the question of the political subject as name-giving actor and the subject's relationship with the circumstantial structure.

(1)   Communist guerrilla insurgency (*kongsan chui pan'lan* or *kongsan pok'dong*)
This definition represents the official account of the 4.3 Incident. The 4.3 Civilian Victims' Survivors Association (Sasam Minkanin Huisaengja Yujokwhoe, or Yujokwhoe

for short), which was originally organized in 1989 as the anti-communist survivors' association, takes up this naming position. This name for the 4.3 Incident has not been corrected in historiography. The reason for this is that this definition represents the state ideology of the South Korean Government: anti-communism.

(2)   People's uprising (*minjung hangjaeng*)
This naming position is represented by the Cheju local progressive intellectuals' social action groups, such as the 4.3 Institute, which was established in 1989 in memory of the 40th anniversary of the 4.3 Incident. This position interprets the 4.3 Incident as the Cheju people's resistance against national partition and against the American imperialism that caused it. Accordingly, the 4.3 Incident was a movement of national independence and anti-colonial and anti-imperial resistance (Koh 1989). This naming position disavows the label 'communist' attached to the armed insurgents who initiated the 4.3 Incident; instead the guerrillas are honoured as popular rebel heroes who tried to build a new fully independent unified nation. In this sense, they are claimed as the 'authentic' nationalists (cf. The 4.3 Institute 1989–1995).

Through the publication of testimonials and the rewriting of pre-4.3 history, the 4.3 Institute has striven to establish an honourable place in history for the 4.3 Incident by inserting it into the legacy of popular resistance against foreign forces that have opposed Cheju indigenous autonomy and national unity. In doing so, the 4.3 Institute has projected the historical meaning of the 4.3 Incident into the domain of current political issues, such as democratization, national autonomy, and South–North reunification.

According to this naming position, the Cheju people appear to be political *actors* who consciously acted on their beliefs. Although the position is grounded on different aims, the naming position of the 4.3 Institute shares with the official naming position, the premise that the subjects involved in the 4.3 Incident were ideologically wilful. Here, these two opposing narratives of popular resistance and counter-insurgency converge onto a single historical truth: the 4.3 Incident as an ideological struggle. In spite of the nobility of objectives, the progressive intellectuals' political over-determination betrays their ethical stance against their will. In practice, it was the mere people taking no ideological side who the 4.3 Institute named as rebels but who died mostly during the Incident. They were *innocents* for no causes or claims.

Remaining innocent without a name: 4.3 (*sasam*)

In the case of the 4.3 Incident, the problem of naming is so ideologically charged that it could bring about further misunderstanding and confusion. In due consideration of this intricate problem, the Chejudo Provincial Parliament 4.3 Special Committee's (1995) First Report of 4.3 Casualties and the Chemin Ilbo 4.3 Special Assignment Reporter Team's (1994) serial articles '4.3 Speaks' that appeared once or twice a week for ten years from 1989 to 1999, blot out ideologically coloured words such as 'insurgents,' 'communist guerrilla,' and 'resistant people.' Instead they have specified neutral terms to distinguish two different agents of the 4.3 Incident: 'armed force' (*mujangdae*) and 'punitive force' (*t'oboldae*). These new terms are intended to erase the trace of ideological confrontation. In the refusal to name, they shift the focus away from the ideological struggle between the two opposite forces to its political effect, that of *mass massacre*.

This kind of disclaiming the naming position is manifested in the common use of the term '4.3' (*sasam*), indicating simply the date of the occurrence of the 4.3 Incident, April 3 1948, when the mujangdae attacked the police and extreme right-wing paramilitary forces, such as the Northwest Youth Group (Merrill 1980). However, the initial incident was only the trigger for the mass massacre, whose problems were much more cumulative and intricate. The aftermath of this event, which stretched on for over a year, until the guerrilla head was killed in June 1949, was a civilian mass massacre by the punitive forces of the newly established South Korean state. The constabulary considered the mid-mountain area ranging within 5 km from the seashore 'the enemy region' (*choksong chiyok*). All the villagers in that region were forcibly removed to the coastal villages. The punitive forces burnt down all villages and massacred whoever remained there, most of them peasants who hesitated to leave their cattle-raising and their field harvesting. It was mid October 1948, the harvest season for barley and millet. The survivors of this massacre fled to the mountains and hid in caverns. Some young men of this 'mountain people' joined the guerrillas out of rage against this unprecedented massacre. In searching out those cavern hideaways and sites of guerrillas, fifty thousand militia members were recruited from the people who were dislocated from mid-mountain villages and were now kept in refugee camps at coastal villages. These militia and the hideaways could have been family members, relatives, or village neighbours. In the actual scene of the mass massacre, there was no clear distinction between enemies and allies. The same people had to play the double role of both (Han 1989, 1991).

This moment of the 4.3 Incident was characterized by internal warfare among the islanders who were made to perform the double role of perpetrator and victim in this '*theatre of massacre*.' This kind of mimetic duplication of violence illustrates a critical understanding of the arbitrariness of power and the ambivalent meaning of violence, the legacy of which complicates the search for the historical truth of the 4.3 Incident. The double indemnity borne by the Cheju people during the 4.3 Incident has affected a seemingly involuntary silence concerning the 4.3 Incident in an everyday context for fifty years (Hyon 1993).

In this context, when the '4.3 Speaks' and the Cheju Parliament Report referred to '4.3 victims,' it does not specify the identity of the perpetrators, as if they were innocents who were sacrificed for something they did not know, perhaps for history itself. This suggests an implicit agreement on the fact that the 4.3 Incident was an unnecessary violence to Cheju people. This method of evasion of the naming position seems to be cautiously devised to diffuse perspectives or opinions concerning the event. By referring to the event just as '4.3', the speaker can avoid taking a side on the event.

The five serials of journalistic documentary on the 4.3 Incident, '4.3 Speaks', which were published from 1994 to 1999, and the Chejudo Provincial Parliament 4.3 Special Committee's First Report of the 4.3 Casualties, contend that we move beyond the current preoccupation with the question of the direct cause of the initial outbreak on 3 April 1948, whether it was a communist insurgency or people's uprising; and instead that we approach the incident from its traumatic experience of mass death.

How then do we get at 'the historical truth of the 4.3 Incident'? Next, by reading the Chejudo Parliament Report, I will explore how the local ideology of 'the historical truth of the 4.3 Incident' is effectively reconfigured enough to set up a paradigmatic truth for other memorial representations.

In the conclusion of this report, the Report states 'the tragedy of 4.3 lies in the fact that it resulted in an enormous death toll' (14,125 persons). For corroboration of this claim, the Report points to a secret document of the US Military Occupational Forces on 1 April 1949: 'Over 80% of the dead were shot to death by the punitive force', a death toll that approximates the findings (84.2%) of the Parliament Committee's preliminary research. According to the report, the deaths caused by the mujangdae cover only 10% of the total casualties. However, other than these statistics, the report omits the identity of the perpetrators in the list. It testifies to public fear of the danger to specify it, owing to ongoing surveillance of politically impure and pro-communist elements.

While establishing the justifiable aspect of its research on the basis of the approximate truthfulness of the statistics, the Cheju Provincial Parliament 4.3 Special Committee appeals to government and national assembly to take the initiative for clarifying the historical truth of the 4.3 Incident and the recovery of the Cheju people's honour, which has remained officially as red insurgents, or *p'okto*. The first step in getting at the truth of the 4.3 Incident, the Report suggests, is in seeking '*the* historical fact'.

The Report suggests an answer: the 4.3 Incident was *not* a communist insurgency. Then what else could the 4.3 Incident be? This question has incited controversy over the primacy of factuality in representations of the 4.3 Incident. This controversy touches on the ethical issue of truthfulness of all memorial representations. Related to this question of the historical fact of the 4.3 Incident, this report could be read as the testament (will) of Korean modernity and the testimony to the subterranean legacy of state terror. The Report was itself a memorial representation in commemoration of *the innocent dead*.

Peripheral memory in national history

The paradigm of local memory of innocent deaths to which the Chejudo Parliament Report has urgently committed itself, has not yet taken in national history because the state has not taken the initiative to clarify the historical truth of the 4.3 Incident.

However, every truth of the 4.3 Incident is a narrative artefact. The question is where the truth is situated. Pierre Nora's notion of the *sites of memory* is useful for delineating the intricate relationships between history, memory, and the nation (Nora 1989). According to Nora, the sites of memory are the places 'where memory crystallizes and secretes itself': these include monuments, commemoration rites, symbols, activities, manuals, mottoes (Nora 1989: 9). His insight into the 'conquest and eradication of memory by history' in the case of the French Revolution is useful for thinking through the legacy of the modern Korean nation-state, which has ceaselessly reinvented the past through the work of a dictatorial memory of a unified nation – a kind of modern memory – characteristic of a post-colonial state.

President Kim Young sam's official motto promulgated in his 1996 new year state policy address, 'the straightening-up of history,' means to construct the future of Korea – a first-class nation in the world – upon a 'making straight' of the corrupt past. Most obviously this refers to the immorality and injustice of the three previous military regimes. Purging two ex-presidents for their criminal involvement in the Kwangju Massacre in 1980, Kim equates the task of 'straightening-up of history' with 'the second building of the nation-state'. This kind of equating the nation and the history into a single frame of fate is not a new phenomenon in the most recent present; it has been pervasive throughout Korea's modern history of national development.

However, the different course of modern Korean history, beginning from the 4.3 Incident to the 5.18 Kwangju Uprising, consists of the multiple subnational memories of suppression and massacre of dissidents and enemies of the state. A genealogy of these memories, which is a kind of counter-memory in Foucault's (1977) term, has become a moral and psychological burden of South Korean modernity. The morality of self-purgation as it is manifested in the new nation-building project of President Kim Young sam is 'the other side of history that no cunning of reason can ever justify and that, instead, reveals the scandal of every theodicy of history.' (Ricoeur 1992).[8] The memory of Korean nationhood continues to rest upon a sacred theodicy of anti-communist national unification. Predicated on a negative and reactionary principle, the national memory of anti-communism has been used in a defensive manoeuvre to suppress any new secularizing force. During the late 1980s' democratization movements, the holy unification of memory and history in the nation was shattered when popular protest successfully overturned Chun Tu-whan's military regime in 1987. With the advent of civil society in place of military dictatorship, the modern Korean history was able to highlight various modes of popular memory, disclaiming its articulation to national identity.

Public commemorations of the 4.3 Incident started exactly around this period. Memorial activity groups, including the Anti-Communist 4.3 Survivor's Association, the 4.3 Institute, the 4.3 Special Assignment Reporter Team, and the Chejudo Parliament 4.3 Special Committee, emerged in public and began to engage in the politics of the 4.3 memory, in competition and negotiation with each other. Their activities can be understood as 'the work of mourning,' which laments the statist legacy of anti-communism and at the same time makes possible the remembering of state terror and violence founded on that sacred ideology. In this context, the memory of the 4.3 Incident functions as a counter-memory that 'designates the residual or resistant strains that withstand official versions of historical continuity'; counter-memory is the history of discontinuity' (cf. Davis and Starn 1989: 4).

In the face of this repercussion of popular memory, however, the state has managed to recreate its identity as another victim of its own historical failure. The language of 'reconciliation and forgiveness' appears the central motto of public commemoration ceremonies of the 4.3 Incident, which were financed by the provincial government. The prime purpose of this kind of intricate inversion of the vocation of mourner lies in the closure of debates on the truth of the 4.3 Incident. Here, the motto of reconciliation and forgiveness disguised as the work of mourning is indeed a kind of *'forgetful forgiveness'* that could not do justice to the pain of memory (Ricoeur 1995). Next, we will witness the state's script of 'forgetful forgiveness' that attempts to erase popular memory of the 4.3 Incident in national history.

Displaced monuments

The memorial of 'the Tomb of One Hundred Ancestors for One Descendant' (Paekcho Ilson Chimyo) attests to this state script. Three times since 1993, memorial ceremonies have been organized by delegates of the 4.3 Civilian Surviving Families Association in the company of governmental officials, national assembly members, and provincial parliament members. In the memorial ceremony, the actual surviving families of the victims have taken second place.

There is a background story for this belated commemoration. Since the massacre of 132 civilians under the charge of a communist conspiracy during the Korean War in 1950, the surviving families' memorial ceremonies were banned, and the memorial tombstones erected by them were destroyed. The civilian massacre of the 4.3 Incident had been executed continually during the Korean War. After the massacre, their access to the site of the massacre was prohibited for 8 years. When survivors went to the massacre site in 1958, they found a mass of corpses whose bones were intermingled and unidentifiable. So they divided a mass of bones among the descendants of victims and buried a set of bones representing one person at the collective graveyard. They erected a memorial cenotaph in commemoration of the collective deaths of 132 people. They named themselves 'one descendant of one hundred ancestors' because they could not identify and distinguish the group remains. Survivors then took advantage of the brief democratic milieu between the successful 4.19 Student Uprising in 1960 and the 5.16 military *coup d'etat* in 1961. However, after the military *coup d'etat*, they were interrogated for their burial act and also for their erection of the memorial cenotaph. During subsequent moments of democratic flowing, such as in 1980 and in 1987, the survivors have tried to erect the memorial again and again. Their persistent attempts at commemoration have been thwarted by the two consecutive military regimes in the 1980s.

The memorial cenotaph that was erected in 1994 by official delegates actually belongs to the state, although the survivors themselves also participated in the project. For this reason, the memorial has inscribed on it the names of those official delegates as the chief mourners. Their memorial addresses take three of four sides of the memorial. The names of the dead are squeezed onto just one side of it. The memorial writings inscribed specify the reason for erecting the memorial: 'forgetting of violence in the past and reconciliation with the future.' While this official discourse recalls the tragedy of an ideological struggle between the left and the right some 40 years ago, it calls for forgiveness and reconciliation between the two opposing positions regarding the 4.3 Incident – communist insurgency and people's uprising. However, this move for reconciliation blames the Cheju people in both camps for the collective violence and allows the state to evade its own moral responsibility for it.[9]

In short, the erection of 'the Tomb of One Hundred Ancestors for One Descendant' is a memorial to national loss – the loss of state control – rather than a memorial for the dead. The rectangular top marble of the memorial bearing the design of the South Korean national flag wreathed with the national hibiscus flower looks overwhelmingly oppressive in its environment of the landscape of round-shaped and grass-covered 'tombs of one hundred ancestors for one descendant.' The stark contrast of shapes and materials between the two memorials attests to the domineering posture of the state power. This overwhelming posture of a marble memorial betrays the true meaning of mourning. It serves to mask the secret operation of state terror, focusing more on the forgetting of national loss than on the remembering of the victim.[10] This attempt is bound more to a nation's quest rather than to the suffering of the dead. The memorial tombstone of 'One Hundred Ancestors for One Descendant' is indeed a monument to the unshaken progress of Korean modernity in successfully displacing the violent past of the state with a deceptive rhetoric of reconciliatory national unity.

The limits of representation

The 'successful verbalization' of the 4.3 Incident in the official discourse of 'reconciliation and forgiveness' blurs the moral agency of mourning by turning the agent of violence into a moral agent. While the language of pain is suppressed, the language of agency is professed. Veena Das describes precisely this kind of language of agency as an 'invisible and mute violence' (Das 1987: 12). On the language of violence that is used by the agencies of the state, Elaine Scarry (1985) contends that 'the language of agency of violence' alienates the experience of suffering and pain of the victims. When the historical fact of violence is emphasized and the felt-experience of pain is transferred beyond the sentient distress of the person, the objectification of pain into a verbal sign can have different effects for opposite purposes.

In the language of agency such as 'forgiveness and reconciliation', the experience of real pain is converted into a regime's fiction of power and is thus pushed into further invisibility and deeper obscurity. The aura of realness and certainty emanating from the official discourse of reconciliation is even self-deceptive to the extent that the inventiveness the state practices makes it possible to create the narcissistic victimhood in which the agent identifies himself with the victim of its violence (cf. Santner 1990).[11]

However, there are limits to representations of the violent past (cf. Friedlander 1992). The voices of the perpetrators and those of the victims are indeed mutually exclusive. The obsessive endeavour to hold on to the totality and singularity of the 4.3 Incident as an ideological struggle could serve only to verify the permanent truth of anti-communism as a state-ruling ideology.

At this point we need to 'de-totalize' or decentralize the working-through of mourning so as to let the peripheral memory of painful experience challenge the self-sufficiency of national history. We need to cultivate the capacity to perceive and feel grief for the suffering of the real victim of violence (cf. Das 1990).[12] The first published documentary novel about the 4.3 Incident, *Twilight of Mt. Halla* (Han 1991), testifies to the peripheral memory of the painful experience of the 4.3 Incident and portrays an effective ideology of 'survival' among people who have never lost their struggle for life. This novel consists of stories of personal experiences of village dwellers who had to hide away in deep mountain caves. The hideaways survived there, courageously, by forming an autonomous cave community while waiting for the end of punitive measures of the army. These cave dwellers' endurance in the stark uncertainty constitutes the hidden script of resistance to the modern Korean state's apocalyptic capability for mass death.

Conclusions: inconsolable memory in the body of this death

In this paper, I have illuminated how multiple memories, configured in narrative representations, dominate, oppose, compete and negotiate with each other in order to produce truths of the Cheju April Third Incident on the plane of commemorations. However, the ultimate purpose, in which I am here engaged, is not just a full description of the politics of representational forms of local and national memory, but a standing on a new truth against the conventionally established certainty of truths and meanings.

I suggest further that we must look at fragmented forms of memory that are conserved in a diffuse consciousness of violence and also the violence of representation (cf. Ortner

1995; Scott 1992). We must find the site of memory that evades the wholesale manipulation and appropriation by hegemonic memory of the state. The fragmented memories survive in 'the body of this death', a corpse who could speak only in ghostly image and in murky and subliminal spaces such as dreams and possession illnesses. These are the spaces where the spirits of the dead lament and testify 'this death' of 'that time' – the 4.3 Incident – and where the dead can speak without being co-opted by the language of agency and the agency of violence (Kim 1989; cf. Haver 1996). However, 'the body of this death' that could be revitalized only in such a subliminal space remains *inconsolable* due to the impossibility of its historicization in the real world. Here it is precisely the impoverished ordinariness of 'this death' that is important.

Let us listen to a Cheju shaman's ritual rendering of the ordinary condition of mass death during the 4.3 Incident. Mijo, a Cheju shaman and 35 year old woman, retells the story of the 4.3 Incident from the perspective of a dead soul returning to the present to 'speak out' during a shamanic ritual. In practice, the shaman Mijo's story is a testimony, a memorial act, and also an event of remembering.

> *People died as if wild reeds were mowed.* When the shaman performs the *youngkye ullim*, the lamentations of the dead soul in the ritual, it is not me, the shaman, but the dead soul who cries, telling the story of how he or she died. Sometimes the dead soul appears in a dream as a human figure. Or a sudden thought flashes instantly. But mostly a particular feeling touches my heart as if I have something to say. If the dead soul died by getting stabbed, I feel a sharp hurt in my chest and an urge to speak up about something. Then I ask the client if the person died by sword or by an accident. The client would reply that he or she died by sword during the 4.3 Incident.
>
> If it is the case that a woman of the surname Kim died of stab wounds, I would tell her story in the lamentation as follows: 'She was born in the Kim family, lived for a while, and married. Once encountering the 4.3 Incident, no one would see again in the evening the person seen in the morning. As if wild reeds were mowed, she died of stab wounds. She ate the breakfast for the meal of the other world. She went to the other world without saying goodbye to her parents, leaving behind orphaned children. Even in the other world, she has not been able to rest until now due to worrying about her children who would grow up alone. But if one longs for a mother, how can one get away from this longing? Even if one has not looked at the face of a mother for thousand years, one would not forget the face of a mother.'
>
> Like this, the shaman has to make up a whole life story of the dead soul. If the daughter offers up a ritual for the mother because the dead soul of the mother cries, the shaman would speak to the daughter: 'how much hardship should you have gone through because you did not have this mother around? As you remembered me the mother and offered up a ritual for me, I hastened to come to you and your house. But the wall of your house is too high to go over. When can I meet my child, tell her my sorrow, and then go back to the other world?'
>
> In this way, through the shaman's voice, the dead soul and the daughter keep speaking their pent-up words. In doing so, the shaman consoles the repressed hearts of both the dead soul and the living daughter.'
>
> (my interview, November 1993)

Retold and enacted in the ritual, Shaman Mijo's story does justice to the dialogical reconstruction of death and memory; it puts together the ghostly words of the dead and the live testimony of the survivor, the ritual laments of the dead and the personal history of the survivor. In the mode of dialogue between victim mother and witness daughter, this ritual narrative makes a counter-statement against the repressive force of history that has 'mowed' the unfulfilled desires of the ordinary people who died during the 4.3 Incident. In this imaginative dialogue between the living and the dead, the popular ethics of life and death is constructed, and the 'effective ideology' of inconsolable memory is produced.

This shamanistic memorialization of the 4.3 Incident illustrates how political violence has become submerged in the popular memory, and has been re-inscribed in the inconsolable memory of 'mowed' bodies of 'this death'. Together with the mute corpse in bare reality, the lamenting ghost in the imaginary realm constitutes 'the microcosm of violent space and time that s/he inhabits', which is indeed 'a reflection of the macrocosm of the violent modern state' (Das 1990: 32). This body of 'this death' at 'that time' bears witness to the counter-memory of the innocent death during the 4.3 Incident. It could be the task of ethnography to listen attentively to the fragmented yet ordinary stories and memories of 'this death', while writing in the struggle against mere political consolation and the present imperative for reconciliation with the past. This task may help reveal a new truth of the Cheju April Third Incident and conduct a proper work of mourning on the Korean modernity.

Notes

1 The historical status of the Cheju April Third Incident has been changed drastically following the 50th anniversary of this event in 1998, when the main arguments of this article were initially formulated. In December 1999, a broad alliance of various non-governmental organizations on the initiative of the 4.3 Institute bore fruit in the legislation of a Special Act for Inquiring into Suspicious Deaths and Recovering Honour to the Victims of the Cheju April Third Incident. On the basis of this law, a National Commission on the Cheju 4.3 Incident directly accountable to the Prime Minister was set up on 28 August 2000. The Act conferred on the Commission the following functions: investigation of the events; accepting and examining petitions from the victims or surviving relatives; restoration of the honour of the victims and surviving relatives; erection of commemorative shrines. On 1 May 2003, the Commission published its report on the investigation. This first official report dealt mainly with the human rights violations committed against the civilian population by the police and the military.

2 American military sources give much smaller numbers of guerrillas, of the order of 200 (Merrill 1980: 159).

3 Here the number 'eighty thousand' is not a definite estimation. It varies from 14,000 to 80,000 depending on the sources. But taking into account the cases of unreported deaths, such as those of the disappeared, it is generally surmised that at least more than 30,000 people died during the 4.3 Incident.

4 A similar kind of reframing of the meaning of the violent event in the past has occurred in the case of the Taiwan Uprising of 28 February 1947 (Lai et al. 1991).

5 The numbered scenes present episodic snapshots of the 47th anniversary ceremony of the 4.3 Incident in 1995, which was held at several places for, respectively, different purposes.

6 The village militia or minbodan, which was organized among the few survivors after the initial phase of the 4.3 damages, in fact, functioned as a paramilitary force against guerrilla attacks. Like regular soldiers, the militia, who were mostly recruited from the old (over 65) or the youth (under 17), stood sentinel at the stone fortress built along the outskirts of the village. The surviving families of the militia who died on duties received pensions just like those of the soldiers who died in the war (Kim 1995).

7   These rather recent cases of mass deaths and state violence suggest the dignifying and moralizing effects of coercive authority of the state that allow for the co-operation of victims in their victimization under the rubric of 'modernization,' 'democracy' or 'peace.'

8   In discussing the mimetic function of narrative and its relation to narrative identity, Ricoeur suggests the moral rule of faithfulness which, in turn, makes possible praxis, that is, mimesis praxis (Ricoeur 1992: 153–160). His insight into the relations between narrative theory and ethical theory could extend to the historian's quest for the ethical implications of history as writing. Debating on the historical place of Nazism and Auschwitz, Friedlander and other historians, such as Hayden White, indicate the danger and limits of representations that establish a master narrative on history and build a theodicy of history for itself (Friedlander 1992; White 1992). There are opposing views on the nature of historical truth of the Holocaust. In response to critics on his rather neutral position on Auschwitz, White suggests various modes of employment of the historical events in historical writing – comic, pastoral or ironic employment – and emphasizes the significance of a 'middle-voice' position of rhetorical writing, to which he relates as the ethical position of historical narrative. This paper takes up White's middle-voice position for a narrative strategy so as not to fall into oppositional discourses on the 4.3 Incident.

9   Under the rubric of 'total healing of the 4.3,' the ceremony organizer proposed to expand the surviving families' rite to the whole provincial scale for the sake of the prosperity of society and the state. As printed in pamphlets, in gratitude, the representative of surviving families pledged allegiance to the policies of both provincial and central government. This episode suggests the absurdity of the situation.

10 This kind of government-financed commemoration purports to suppress the popular memories of the victims, so that it deepens what Taussig (1984) calls the 'culture of terror'.

11 In his reflections on the discourses of mourning and allegories of grieving in postwar Germany, with the text analysis of films and popular materials, Santner focuses on 'the work of mourning' in a Freudian sense as an attempt to come to terms with a traumatic experience. He sees Germany in general as marked by an inability to mourn, which fosters a tendency to deny what is painful and disorienting in the past. He asserts one has to regain ethical values in postwar German culture and society in order to confront its fascist past. In the case of South Korea, perhaps it is time to confront its fascist past–present for the sake of posterity, which will be ultimately national reunification.

12 In her anthropological studies of ethnic riots in India and Sri Lanka, Veena Das asks us to get engaged in the moral action to transform a victim and survivor's status into a historical writer. The experience of suffering may become a mark of special status. Having suffered, one has acquired a right to impose suffering upon others for the sake of redeeming suffering itself. She insists that the right of final pronouncement over the nature of this violence must rest with the survivor, who is the real mourner. She emphasizes the task of mourners, who happen to be mainly women, to articulate the two worlds of ordinary life and critical events, and the worlds of family and politics.

References

The 4.3 (sasam) Institute 4.3 연구소 (1989–1995) *The 4.3 Institute Newsletters 4.3 연구소 소식*, Chejudo 제주도.

Bauman, Zygmunt (1989) *Modernity and the Holocaust*, Ithaca: Cornell University Press.

Chejudo Provincial Parliament 4.3 Special Committee 제주도의회 4.3 특별위원회 (1995) *The First Report of the 4.3 Casualties in Cheju Province 제주도 4.3 피해1차보고서*, Chejudo Parliament. 제주도 의회.

Chemin Ilbo 4.3 Special Reporter Team 제민일보 4.3 특별취재반 (1994) *The 4.3 Speaks 4.3 은 말한다 1 권*, Seoul: Chunyewon. 서울: 전예원.

Choi, Chang-jip and Chong Hae-ku 최장집/정해구 (1989) 'Total understanding of 8 years of emancipatory space' 해방공간8년의 총체적 이해, *Understanding of the History Before and After Liberation 4 해방전후사의 인식4집*, Seoul: Hankilsa. 서울: 한길사.

Coronil, Fernande (1997) *The Magical State*, Chicago: The University of Chicago Press.

Cumings, Bruce (1990) *The Origins of the Korean War Volume II: The Roaring of the Cataract: 1947–1950*, Princeton: Princeton University Press.

Das, Veena (1987) 'The anthropology of violence and the speech of victims', *Anthropology Today* 3(4): 11–13.

Das, Veena (1990) 'Introduction: communities, riots, survivors – the South Asian Experience'. In Veena Das (ed.) *Mirrors of Violence*, Delhi: Oxford University Press, 1–36.

Davis, Natalie and Starn, Randolph (1989) 'Introduction,' *Representations*, 26, Spring, 1–6.

Feldman, Allen (1991) *Formations of Violence: The Narrative of the Body and Political Terror in Northern Ireland.* Chicago: University of Chicago Press.

Foucault, Michel (1977) 'Nietzsche, genealogy, history'. In Donald F. Bouchard (ed.) *Language, Counter-Memory, Practice: Selected Essays and Interviews/Michel Foucault*, Ithaca: Cornell University Press.

Fridlander, Saul (ed.) (1992) 'Introduction', *Probing the Limits of Representation: Nazism and the 'Final Solution',* Cambridge: Harvard University Press.

Fritzsche, Peter (1996) 'Nazi modern', *Modernism/modernity* 3(1), 1–22

Hallbwacks, Maurice (1992) *On Collective Memory*, Lewis Coser (ed. and trans.), Chicago: University of Chicago Press.

Han Rim-hwa 한림화 (1989) 'Resentment and rage of the Yongkang village people' 용강마을 사람들의 한과 분노, *Society and Thought* 사회와 사상 Jan, Seoul 서울.

Han Rim-hwa 한림화 (1991) *Twilight of Mt. Halla* 한라산의 노을, Seoul: Hangil sa. 서울: 한길사.

Haver, William (1996) *The Body of this Death: Historicity and Sociality in the Time of AIDS*, Stanford: Stanford University Press.

Hyon Ki-young 현기영 (1993) 'Thirsty gods' 목마른 신들, *Last Herdsman* 마지막 테우리, Seoul: Changchak kwa Pipyong sa. 서울: 창작과 비평사.

Kim Seong Nae 김성례 (1989) 'Lamentations of the dead: historical imagery of violence,' *Journal of Ritual Studies* 3(2), 251–285.

Kim Seong Nae 김성례 (1995) 'The iconic power of modernity: reading a Cheju shaman's life history and initiation dream.' In Kenneth M. Wells (ed.) *South Korea's Minjung Movement: The Culture and Politics of Dissidence*, Honolulu: University of Hawaii, 155–165.

Koh Chang-h'un 고창훈 (1989) 'The development and the character of the April Third People's Uprising' 4.3 민중항쟁의 전개와 성격, *Understanding of the History Before and After Liberation 4* 해방전후사의 인식 4집, Seoul: Hankilsa 서울: 한길사.

Koselleck, Reinhart (1985) *Futures Past: On the Semantics of Historical Time*, Keith Tribe (trans.), Cambridge: The MIT Press.

Lai, Tse-Han, Ramon H. Hyers and Wei Wou (1991) *A Tragic Beginning: The Taiwan Uprising of February 28, 1947*, Stanford: Stanford University Press.

Merrill, John (1980) 'The Cheju-do rebellion', *Journal of Korean Studies* 2: 139–197.

Nietzsche, Friedrich (1957) *The Use and Abuse of History*, Adrian Collins (trans.), Indianapolis: Library of Liberal Arts.

Nora, Pierre (1989) 'Between Memory and History: Les Lieus de Memoire', *Representations* 26, Spring: 7–25.

Ortner, Sherry (1995) 'Resistance and the problem of ethnographic refusal', *Comparative Studies in Society and History* 37(1): 173–193.

Park Myung-rim 박명림 (1999) 'Democracy, reason, and historical studies: Cheju 4.3 and Korean Modern History' 민주주의, 이성, 그리고 역사연구: 제주 4.3 과한국현대사. In Institute of Historical Problem *et al.* 역사문제연구소 외 편 (eds) *Cheju 4.3 Studies* 제주 4.3 연구, Seoul: Yoksa Pipyongsa. 서울: 역사비평사: 425–460.

Ricoeur, Paul (1992) *Oneself as Another*, Kathleen Blamey (trans.), Chicago: University of Chicago Press.

Ricoeur, Paul (1995) 'Reflections on a new ethos for Europe', *Philosophy & Social Criticism* 21(5/6).

Robben, Antonius C. G. M. (1995) 'The politics of truth and emotion among victims and perpetrators of violence'. In Carolyn Nordstrom and Antonius C. G. M. Robben (eds) *Fieldwork Under Fire*, Berkeley: University of California Press, 81–104.

Santner, Eric L. (1990) *Stranded Objects: Mourning, Memory and Film in Postwar Germany*, Ithaca: Cornell University Press.

Scarry, Elaine (1985) *The Body in Pain: The Making and Unmaking of the World*, Oxford: Oxford University Press.

Scott, James (1992) 'Domination, acting, and fantasy,' In Carolyn Nordstrom and J. Martin (eds) *The Paths to Domination, Resistance, and Terror*, Berkeley: University of California Press.

Taussig, Michael (1984) 'Culture of terror-space of death. Roger Casement's Putomayo Report and the explanation of torture', *Comparative Studies in Society and History* 26(4): 467–497.

White, Hayden (1987) *The Content of the Form: Narrative Discourse and Historical Representation*, Baltimore: The Johns Hopkins University Press.

White, Hayden (1992) 'Historical emplotment and the problem of truth'. In Saul Friedlander (ed.) *Probing the Limits of Representation*, Cambridge: Harvard University Press.

Special terms in Korean in Romanization–Korean–Chinese–English

haebang konggan 해방공간 解放空間 the Space of Liberation (1945–1953)
kongsan p'okdong 공산폭동 共産暴動 communist insurgency
minbodan 민보단 民保團 village militia
minjung hangjaeng 민중항쟁 民衆抗爭 people's uprising
mujangdae 무장대 武裝隊 civilian armed force
p'okto 폭도 暴徒 riots, insurgents
t'oboldae 토벌대 討伐隊 punitive force
youngkye ullim 영계울림 lamentation of the dead in the shamanic ritual

Editor's note

This essay is the newly revised version of a paper presented at the Cheju April Third Uprising 50th Anniversary Symposium, Seoul, 28 March 1998. Various versions of the original paper were translated and published in *Gendai Shiso* 26–7 (June, 1998) in Japan and *Cheju 4.3 Studies* (1999), a collection of symposium papers, in Korea.

Chapter 9

Indonesia's original sin

Mass killings and capitalist expansion, 1965–66

Hilmar Farid

> This primitive accumulation plays in Political Economy about the same part as original sin in theology.
>
> (Karl Marx, 1867)

Introduction

In the history books of the Suharto regime, the killings of half a million members and sympathizers of the Communist Party of Indonesia and other leftist organizations in 1965–66 were non-events. The only significant killing that occurred at that time was supposedly the killing of six army generals and a lieutenant in Lubang Buaya, a small village on the outskirts of Jakarta, on 1 October 1965. The regime commemorated the killing every year with a national day of remembrance and a ceremony called 'Sacredness of Pancasila Day' (*Hari Kesaktian Pancasila*). With textbooks, films, and field trips to the Museum of the Extreme Left at the site where the killings of the army generals took place, the regime tried to make school children feel repulsed and horrified by this violence, and to feel thankful that Suharto had taken power to save the country from any further treasonous and treacherous acts. If many Indonesians were killed at that time, then it was a matter far removed from Suharto's rise to power. It was only a matter of old feuds among civilians surfacing at a time of anarchy. The regime's most comprehensive propaganda book, authored by the army historian Nugroho Notosusanto and the prosecutor Ismail Saleh (Notosusanto and Saleh 1989), devoted all of two paragraphs to the mass killing, or 'clash' in their terminology, and concluded that 'the bloodbath among members of the society was directly related to events in the past'. The authors suggested that civilians who had been previously maligned or harmed by the PKI took their revenge in 1965–66. The military itself had no relation to the killings.

Surprisingly enough, many scholars with no particular stake in supporting the regime have endorsed its claim that the killing was due to long-standing conflicts among civilians. Iwan Gardono Sujatmiko (1992), probably the first Indonesian to write a dissertation about the killing, fatalistically concluded that the mass killing was inevitable since the PKI was on the 'losing and wrong' side; it was a party that had become the enemy of the people. Clifford Geertz, an anthropologist noted for his subtle hermeneutics, similarly argued in his memoir that the killings were not the result of state violence (Geertz 1995). The fall of Suharto in 1998 and the subsequent flood of new history books has not led to a serious weakening of this explanation of the killings. Hermawan Sulistyo, in his recently published book on the killings in East Java, reverts to the Suharto regime line: they were a 'logical consequence' of a bitter, pre-existing conflict between the communist party and its political rivals (Sulistyo 2000).

In the first section of this essay I argue that the killings represented a case of vertical, bureaucratic violence. I must admit there is nothing intellectually challenging in asserting this: the evidence is fairly clear and some scholars have already made the argument (Southwood and Flanagan 1983, Fein 1993, Robinson 1995). I feel compelled, however, to outline briefly the case since so many prominent Indonesian scholars, even those associated with the anti-Suharto 'reformasi', absurdly persist in explaining the killings as horizontal, spontaneous violence and in believing that Indonesians are a volatile, primitive people prone to violence. The first section of this essay is thus an unwanted necessity. Perhaps the novelty that the first section contains, apart from the quoting of oral interviews with former PKI members, is some analysis of the killings as a case of bureaucratic violence *made to look like spontaneous violence*.[1]

The argument that I would like to focus upon is the one I make in the second section. It concerns the killings as the foundation for the growth of capitalism in Indonesia. Certainly Indonesia is not a unique case in the world. There were many *coups d'état* accompanied by bloodshed in the South (Latin America, Africa, and Asia) between 1960 and 1975. Chomsky and Herman (1979) have noted that many military officers or cliques of officers who seized power in coups subsequently implemented pro-US economic policies and committed gross human rights violations. These coups resulted in new phases of capital accumulation in the affected countries. The case of the economic transformation of Chile after General Pinochet's coup of 1973 is well known.

For the case of Indonesia, I would like to shift the narration of the mass killings from one of primitive people to primitive accumulation. The mass killings and arrests, the expropriation of people from their houses and lands, and the elimination of working-class political formations, were integral parts of an economic strategy of the clique of army officers who were seizing state power. With the repression of workers at mining and plantation enterprises, the connection between the political repression and the economic strategy is perfectly clear. But the connection holds true for other more indirect cases as well. In general, Suharto and his allied army officers orchestrated the repression and pushed aside President Sukarno with an economic strategy already in mind. They usurped power with a pre-existing plan to promote capitalist growth and tie the Indonesian economy to the West, and thereby end Sukarno's anti-imperialist programme. They planned on receiving foreign aid, loans, and investment from Western countries and to gain access to Western markets for Indonesian exports.[2] The army-directed mass violence resulted in the separation of a large number of people from their means of production and subsistence.

The military state that resulted from this generalized terror campaign devoted itself over the following years to promoting the interests of domestic and foreign capital. It expropriated people for development projects and maintained a docile populace, thus repeating the same sort of violence that it committed in its early years. The army certainly did not simply serve as a kind of loyal attack dog for foreign and domestic capital – it dominated the state and most definitely had its own institutional interests. However, since Suharto's military state was entirely dependent upon foreign aid and loans (until it finally overdosed in the late 1990s) and upon economic growth for its domestic legitimacy, it had to find ways of harmonizing its own interests with those of capital.

It is widely understood in the literature on the political economy of Indonesia that the mid-1960s represents a dramatic historical break, that the economy under the New Order was radically different from the pre-1965 economy. A noted scholar on Indonesian contemporary politics, Richard Robison, for instance, noted that the expansion of capitalism after the mid-1960s was possible 'only after the political victory of the military over the PKI and the Sukarno regime, which in turn secured a victory at the social level for the propertied classes over the threat posed by the landless and the urban workers' (Robison 1986: 109). Yet the focus in Robison's studies, as in so many others, is on the capitalist development itself, not on those pre-conditions for the development, and pays little attention to how the army's continuing use of violence helped to create those landless workers. I do not view capitalism as solely a matter of the bourgeoisie, as Robison's studies of Indonesia's 'business class' imply. Nor do I view the working class as only those people who are today working in a factory for a wage. Rather, following Marx himself, I see capital as a social relation which involves the formation of a working class and its reproduction year-in year-out as a populace willing to work under the command of those who control the capital.

The army's masks and myths

It has become a kind of cheap thrill in the post-Suharto era to declare that Suharto was the mastermind of the 30 September Movement (*Gerakan 30 September* or G-30-S), that he engineered a coup attempt precisely so that it could provide him with the pretext for repressing it. I have my doubts about this theory and, more generally, about this tendency to keep speculating about the existence of a mastermind. No new hard evidence has emerged that would allow us to determine who was actually behind G-30-S, even if the official version is hopelessly unreliable. Several new books, including testimonies from a number of figures directly involved in the movement, have merely become the mirror image of the government version in their groundless assertions concerning the identity of the mastermind (Latief 2000, Subandrio 2001, Sembiring 2004). This preoccupation with conspiracy theories has led many scholars, victims and human rights activists to overlook the specifics of Suharto's creeping coup and the terror campaign that followed the coup attempt.

In the weeks immediately after G-30-S, Suharto and his colleagues in the army were capable of organizing an effective, nationwide terror campaign because they had control over the army and material support from foreign governments, particularly the United States (which provided Suharto with equipment for radio communications). One of Suharto's first steps after receiving the mandate from President Soekarno on 1 October, to 'carry out restoration of security and order', was to replace almost all the top leaders of the army and the military commanders outside Jakarta. He set up an investigation team at every level of military command to arrest and detain military personnel suspected of being involved in G-30-S.[3] The first targets were two army battalions and the palace guard troops that had been directly involved in the G-30-S, and then the members of the Navy and the Air Force who were suspected of being Sukarno loyalists. Using his existing power base in the Army Strategic Reserves Command (Kostrad) and his new position as the commander of the Command for Restoration of Security and Order (Kopkamtib n.d.), he established the power of his own clique over the entire armed forces.

Suharto's control over the media considerably determined the political developments. Within a short time his troops took over the national radio station and closed down all newspapers and printing houses, except for two newspapers published by the military.[4] At Antara, the state news agency, hundreds of journalists were fired and jailed. In mid-October its central office and branches were put under the authority of Suharto himself as the Kopkamtib commander. The army's information centre and officers under Suharto's command became the only official sources of information about the country's condition for several weeks after the G-30-S incident. President Sukarno, who tried to calm the public and demanded that violence against those suspected of being involved in G-30-S be stopped, was silenced. Once the military took control of the mass media, the president's speeches were not broadcast anymore on the radio and were not accurately or fully reported in the newspapers.

Suharto's clique used its control over the media to promote an image of the PKI as a kind of wild beast of larger-than-life proportions. The media circulated stories about sadistic violence committed on the generals in Lubang Buaya – eye gouging, genital mutilation, orgiastic pleasure in inflicting pain.[5] Suharto's terror campaign was designed not just to make the public hate the PKI but also to feel directly threatened by it. The army made near daily announcements about new 'evidence' it uncovered in raiding PKI buildings and homes. In many regions of Indonesia, the army declared that it had discovered a PKI hit list of people to be executed, such as religious leaders and non-communist politicians. All those on the list were encouraged to feel that the PKI was out to murder them. These lists too were probably part of the same intelligence operation since they included fanciful lists of the weapons to be used, such as instruments for gouging out eyes (which in many cases were actually tools for tapping rubber trees), as well as ditches or holes in the earth, like the well in Lubang Buaya, for throwing away the corpses. Newspapers reported sensational discoveries, such as containers filled with firearms upon which had been carved Chinese characters and slogans such as 'Long Live PKI!'

Most of the stories were complete fabrications. Instead of consolidating their forces to seize power, as the army propaganda contended, the leaders and members of PKI and other left-wing mass organizations were usually passive and confused. When attacked by the army and its allied civilian militias, they were not even aware of what had actually taken place in Jakarta on 1 October. Rusyana, one of the high-ranking leaders of the party in West Java, heard about the kidnapping of the generals and the G-30-S movement from a radio broadcast:

> Then I went out of the house. It so happened that some CC [Central Committee of the PKI] officials were visiting the locals. So I contacted [him]. . . . I asked, 'What is going on?' 'Well, for the time being we have to evade [this situation] . . . in case something happens.' Yeah, it's better if we contact the people whom we can possibly help, right? It so happened that there was a nice *khotib* (Islamic preacher) [laughing]. Yeah, some of them [Muslim preachers] supported it [the PKI]. . . . in the Pandeglang area they [pro-G-30-S army officers] gathered the political parties to declare their support for the Council of Revolution, led by Lieut. Col. Pratomo, who headed the Kodim [District Military Command] in Pandeglang. Yeah, it was after only 12 hours, in the evening Suharto made a speech about G-30-S being

counter revolutionary. Well, then, it collapsed all of a sudden. It went in reverse, didn't it? [. . .] We heard [about it] at nine, oh my God it was a real bungle. So, I didn't come home [laughing].

Regular members and supporters of leftist organizations were even more uncertain. A former member of a communist youth organization recalls,

We were confused. The leaders of the organization didn't know what to do. There was a curfew, so I didn't stay at home. I slept in the backyard along with other friends. We didn't know anything. After a few nights we went our different ways, trying to save ourselves. Some returned to their villages, some stayed. There was no instructions or briefings from the organization. I don't know, and then . . . it was a mess. In November I lost contact with my friends. In fact it was in prison where I met many friends. It was there where I actually learned what was going on [laughing].

Whatever the real intentions of the party leaders at that time, it was clear that none of the cadres or members of leftist organizations were prepared for an open confrontation with the military. Gunawan, an artist belonging to the progressive cultural organization, Lekra, then setting up the decorations for the Asian Games in Jakarta, recalled,

In the morning, I woke up, that was October 1st. [My] friends woke up, listened to the radio, [to] that announcement. What happened? They all crowded [around the radio], right. Everybody was, yeah, how could it be this way? But, we didn't feel that we were involved in anything. I didn't even know about the incident. If we didn't know and weren't involved, nothing would happen to us, right? So we were quite calm, we didn't go anywhere. It was only later, day by day, we wondered how did it become like this? Why were the Gerwani [women's organization] office, CC-PKI office, BTI [peasant union] office destroyed? Aidit's house [Chairman of PKI]. Whoa, the problem spread. Well then, once Lekra office was occupied, the books ransacked, my, my, this couldn't get any worse. We realized that we could also become targets.

The movement in Jakarta had virtually no support outside the city except from several groups in Central Java led by middle-rank military officers. In Jogjakarta, some students and members of the youth organization took to the streets in support of the movement. A former student activist involved in the demonstration said,

We knew nothing about the killings of generals in Jakarta. Friends from CGMI [a leftist student organization] briefed us about a coup attempt by 'rightwing generals' in Jakarta that was forestalled by Untung. So we went out for a demon-stration on October 2, 1965 to support the Revolutionary Council. At the KOREM [military headquarters] Major Kartawi gave a speech. He was a KOREM officer in charge of military operations. So, I didn't know what the G-30-S was about, I knew nothing. We truly believed that the rightwing Council of Generals was real. We had no chance to discuss these things thoroughly. Only later, in prison, we tried to reconstruct what actually happened by asking friends who seem to know more about the role of the Special Bureau [of the PKI], Aidit [the party's chairman], and whether the *Politbiro* knew anything about it. So, in prison we learned more about what happened. We didn't know that some generals were killed in Jakarta and we never dug any holes [in which to dump corpses]. There was no plan to kill reactionary leaders or landlords. There was nothing like that.

It is often noted that every large-scale killing is preceded by a dehumanization of the victims. This is a global pattern. The communists of Indonesia were dehumanized so that the public would not see the communists as fellow citizens but only as demons bent on spreading atheism and sadism. Those civilians who approved of the killings of the communists often argue today that it was a time when 'you either kill or be killed', as if the PKI members were dangerous killers ready and determined to kill all their enemies. But what needs to be recognized is that this atmosphere was intentionally manufactured by the army. After all, if it were really a conflict between two sides, one would expect the PKI to have committed its share of the violence. Despite all the media hype at the time and the subsequent thirty-plus years of state-sponsored anti-Communist propaganda, there is little evidence of any large-scale killings by the PKI either immediately before or after 1965.[6] The so-called 'social conflict' actually consisted of unilateral attacks. Members of the party and other leftist organizations offered virtually no resistance to attacks on their offices and homes. In many places the military rounded up alleged communists with ease and carried out mass executions.

Following another aspect of this global pattern, which we have seen elsewhere – such as in Rwanda – the Indonesian army organized paramilitary, civilian groups to participate in the terror campaign. In the first week of October, anti-communist mass organizations were created out of existing organizations and individuals who had long-standing ties to the army. The army mobilized non-communist youth groups all over Indonesia to carry out the violence against people associated with the PKI. Three days after the kidnapping and killing of the generals the 'Action Unity for the Destruction of the September 30 Movement' (KAP-Gestapu) was formed by civilians who enjoyed the support of the army (Nasution 1985: 272–74). Civilian public figures, especially from Muslim organizations such as Ansor, a youth wing of Nahdlatul Ulama (NU), were staged to minimize the impression of a direct confrontation between PKI and the Army.[7] The US embassy in Jakarta reported back to the State Department in a cable of 4 November 1965:

> In Central Java, Army (RPKAD) is training Moslem Youth [probably either Banser or HMI] and supplying them with weapons and will keep them out in front against the PKI. Army will try to avoid as much it can safely do so, direct confrontation with the PKI . . . Army is letting groups other than Army discredit them [the PKI] and demand their punishment.
>
> (Cited by Robinson 1995)

The involvement of these paramilitary and civilian organizations in the violence has confused some scholars into thinking that the violence represented a conflict between these organizations, such as NU, and the PKI. The chain of their argumentation, however, lacks a crucial link, that between largely non-violent political rivalry and large-scale killing. How did a long-standing political rivalry turn into mass murder? Why was the conflict resolved through a bloodbath? The implicit, sometimes explicit assumption widely shared by academics and state officials alike is an ahistorical essential-ism, that Indonesians are a naturally violent and temperamental people who are accus-tomed to resolving their conflicts through violence. Such an explanation is not only false, but also misleading because it distracts our view from the most important actor in the 1965–66 wave of violence, i.e. the military.

If we actually examine the events of 1965–66, we find that the long-standing political conflict cannot account for the killings. In Bali, the PNI and the PKI had been bitter rivals since the late 1950s. After G-30-S and the anti-PKI hype from the army, the PNI did not by itself go out and kill communists. The PNI militia did launch some attacks on PKI homes and buildings but it appears not to have killed anyone during the months of October and November 1965. It was only in December, once the RPKAD troops arrived, that the mass killing began. The same pattern can be seen in North Sumatra where the military began by provoking non-communist youth groups into attacking PKI supporters by saying that the PKI would kill them all if G-30-S was successful. In Central Java, the notorious special forces actively armed youth groups and developed 'cooperation' to purge PKI because the unit did not have enough troops (Sundhaussen 1982). On many occasions those who did not join the violence against the PKI were considered PKI supporters themselves and thus became victims themselves.

From discussions that my colleagues and I have had with ex-political prisoners, eyewitnesses, and political figures, we have found that many victims were executed after they had been taken into custody. The victims were taken out from prisons, military buildings, and makeshift detention centres and trucked to remote locations for execution and burial in mass graves. The bureaucratic nature of the killing is indicated by the term used at the time: '*dibon*', which could be translated as 'ticketed'. A 'bon' is a receipt, indicating in this case that the army had lists of names which they used to call people out of prison. There was some paperwork involved in this mass killing. One survivor in Bali recalled how a list of PKI members was prepared in his village:

> Before that, in November 1965, we were taken to the *pura* [village temple] by the village head to take an oath and register. We were told to take an oath condemning the PKI in return for our lives. The oath went like this, 'I condemn PKI's doing and I no longer want to be a member of that party.' The oath was in Balinese. At that time I didn't want to do it. Why should I take an oath? In the past Lekra was allowed to exist by the government. Why should I condemn it now? I didn't even understand what mistake should be condemned. Later I found out that that list was used to look for people to be killed. Now I begin to think, well because we ourselves condemned the party, we admitted that we're wrong, it's only natural that we would be killed, that's how it worked. See, that's indeed my thinking, and I didn't want that to happen. After the killing happened maybe people in the village also knew that the list was going to be used for killing. In fact the list still exists in village offices. In this place alone there were 40 people written on the list including old people. The archive is still with the village head.

Admittedly, it is difficult at this stage to construct a detailed description of the various processes by which people were killed. There is, however, enough information to know that the army played a dominant role in instigating, organizing, and carrying out the killings. One can see the same pattern of bureaucratic violence masquerading as spontaneous violence in many of the later army operations, most dramatically and unconvincingly in the mobilization of the East Timorese militias during the referendum in 1999.

Primitive people or primitive accumulation?

A framework often used for understanding the extermination campaign of 1965–66 is the discourse of human rights. Using international human rights instruments and laws as parameters, the focus of analysis is the kind of violations committed, the number of violations, and the identity of the perpetrators and the victims. Human rights discourse is no doubt valuable for affirming the dignity of the victims, that they were indeed humans who had rights and were not animals or demons who should have been killed, tortured, and raped. There is, however, a certain blindspot to this discourse since it fails to connect state or military violence to economic struggles over property and wealth. Violations remain understood at the level of state politics, and not in the context of the dynamics of the existing capitalist order. The killing of trade union activists and workers in the plantations of North Sumatra, for example, signifies more than just a violation of human rights. It signifies a defeat for the workers and a reduction of the remaining workers' will and capacity to resist the plantation owners. Conventional human rights research does not include within its scope the profound effects that such an event can have on the hopes, expectations, self-organization, and cultural life of a community of workers.

The discourse of political economy, at least in its present form, on the other hand does not remedy these limitations for it suffers from the same blindspot: it fails to connect economic processes to state violence. There are many studies about the shifting orientation of economic policy, the change of structure and technology in production, and the growth of domestic capital after 1965 (Robison 1986; Booth 1992; Hill 1996), but all appear to be disconnected from the mass killing which took place at the same time. The market just seems to move like an automaton with a will of its own, following laws of its own, divorced from state violence. One may note that this is a long-standing failure of classical political economy, wherein most theorists took it for granted that workers work for a wage without inquiring into how a labour market is formed in the first place, much less how it is continually composed and recomposed by state violence. Such social facts just seem to exist from time immemorial. Marx criticized their work by arguing that 'in actual history, conquest, enslavement, robbery, murder, in sum force' is responsible for the creation of a large propertyless population. As is well known, Marx termed this historical process 'primitive accumulation', a process 'whereby the social means of subsistence and production are turned into capital, and the immediate producers are turned into wage-labourers' (Marx 1867: 874).

I suggest we think of the great upheaval of 1965–66 as one of those epoch-making moments when, to quote Marx, 'great masses of people are suddenly and forcibly torn from their means of subsistence'. I do not wish to suggest that capitalism in Indonesia began in 1965. One should understand primitive accumulation as something which, besides forming the starting point of capitalism, returns again and again, as the basis or basic precondition which is necessary for further phases of capital accumulation.[8]

It recurs particularly in a time of crisis when it becomes an obstacle to the reproduction of the system. The separation of producers from their means of production and subsistence, the most important feature of primitive accumulation, is imposed through 'direct extra-economic force', particularly the state (Marx 1867: 899–900). This can be seen in Java during colonial times when land and natural resources were removed from the control of the rural inhabitants and made to serve the growth of capital in the Netherlands. Taxes, forced cultivation of export crops, and indebtedness helped create an army of landless persons. *Pax Neerlandica*, which was built by the dispatch of troops throughout Nusantara during the second half of the 19th century, did not merely integrate the archipelago into one administrative system, but also forced the colonized into the logic of capital accumulation. The importance of this process for capital formation was marked by the notorious proverb that Java at that time was the 'cork upon which the Netherlands floats'.

Here, I do not want to delve into the question on the origins of capitalism in Indonesia and the creation of a proletariat. I only wish to contend that the extermination of 1965–66 represents one specific, epochal moment in the history of capitalism in Indonesia, a moment that is written in 'letters of blood and fire'. Mass killing, as will be shown below, has considerable influence on the balance of class power, reflected in the increase of inequality at the workplace and the freedom for capital to implement work schemes that disadvantage workers. It was also violence that allowed the New Order rulers to implement economic policies that reversed the anti-imperialist and democratic ideals of an entire generation of nationalists.

Suharto's terror campaign, his 'creeping coup', destroyed the economic livelihood of millions of families. An estimated half million persons were killed and a million and a half persons were indefinitely detained as political prisoners. The families of such prisoners lived with the constant threat of harassment from state officials. It is impossible to determine just how many hectares of land and how many houses were seized by the army and its allies. According to one writer, about half a million hectares of agricultural land that had been redistributed during the land reform programme of the early 1960s were either retaken by the former owners or the local army officers (Utrecht 1970). In some areas, the army's seizures of land and murdering of peasant activists became the basis for the rapid expansion of cash-cropping. The radical peasant organization, the BTI, challenged the pattern of production, which according to them only gave high incomes to the landlords and, in turn, deepened the inequalities in the village.

The destruction of popular organizations meant the ending of grassroots efforts at alternative development. An ex-activist of Pemuda Rakyat (People's Youth), described his activities before he was detained,

> As a teacher I also provided guidance to the society to make them progress in all fields. For example, for the elderly people in that era who were illiterate, we taught them reading, writing, etc. We gave direction how to plant crops as well, although they actually had more experience. In my case, my theory was perfected by the practice I did myself. For example at that time, we showed them the technique *telo mukibat*, then the technique *telo pendem* was also successful, for example by eating whatever was available but nutritious. I think at that time what was called *turba* (*turun ke bawah* or going down with the people) really meant to be united with the people, to eat what was called *tiwul* and *sanggreng*.

At the time he was arrested, his knowledge and ability to work collectively for managing subsistence agricultural production were robbed as well. The New Order supplanted these types of people with the programme Bimas/Inmas, which carried the agenda of the Green Revolution and was supported by international financial institutions (Palmer 1977). This programme changed agriculture from that oriented toward fulfilling the peasants' own needs to that oriented toward commodity production. This programme encouraged peasants to leave their traditional patterns and 'rationalize' production by decreasing the use of human labour in the fields. This encouraged more people to leave the villages. Violence was often used to force peasants to get involved in such programmes. In West Java, the army repeatedly visited community leaders and urged the peasants to use the new seeds, fertilizers, and pesticides. Peasants who refused the programme were accused of being members of BTI.

On the one hand, the result of this Green Revolution was indeed astounding in terms of the increase of agricultural output. On the other hand, inequality and poverty also increased (Hüsken and White 1989, Booth 1992). The use of new technology and production processes required large investments that could only be made by wealthier landlords. Many peasants thus lost their land, which had been their means of subsistence because of this kind of competition. In Java, the number of landless peasants increased by five times in the period of 1973–80 (*Sinar Harapan*, 8 July 1981). One of the government's boasts in the 1980s was that Indonesia was able to be self-sufficient in rice because of that programme, but that success was very short-lived. By the late-1990s Indonesia returned to importing 9% of its rice needs, exactly the same amount as it did in 1965.

Workers were specifically targeted in the violence of 1965–66. The 'cleansing operation' from October 1965 onwards included industries, especially those industries where, according to their intelligence, leftist unions were dominant. As noted by a scholar, the repressive measures were basically a 'political response by a newly consolidating political coalition . . . to the possibility of the re-emergence of a left-wing dominated, militant labor movement' (Hadiz 1997). The destruction of workers' power was an important part of post-1965 government economic policy. In meetings to formulate steps for improving the economy, government ministers formulated repressive labour policies that had been advocated by foreign investors and lenders (Winters 1996). Obviously, such organized repression was only possible once the workers had been robbed of their unions and their knowledge of resistance.

The arrests and killings dramatically altered the relations of power between capital and labour at the workplace. In the plantations of North Sumatra, it has been estimated that 16% of the workers disappeared; some were killed and some ran away. With the union crushed and the workers anxious of further army attacks, the plantation owners reorganized production by using more casual labourers – a system the plantation workers union had prevented from being implemented in the past. The owners were also able to drive down wages and keep the workers disorganized (Stoler 1985: 164–69). In several industries, businessmen with military support made use of the wave of violence to revive forced labour. A report by the American TV network NBC in 1967 revealed that workers at rubber plantations in Sumatra were prisoners working at gunpoint. An excerpt from the narration to the film footage:

Indonesia has a fabulous potential wealth in natural resources and the New Order wants it exploited. So they are returning the private properties expropriated by Sukarno's regime. Goodyear's Sumatran rubber empire is an example. It was seized [by the rubber workers] in retaliation for US aggression in Vietnam in 1965. The rubber workers union was Communist-run, so after the coup many of them were killed or imprisoned. Some of the survivors, you see them here, still work the rubber – but this time as prisoners, and at gunpoint.

(Quoted in Griswold 1975)

The number of unions and the number of workers joining the unions decreased dramatically after 1965. The government closed down all independent unions and formed a single government-controlled union. The destruction of the workers' capacity for resistance was an important outcome of the mass murders of 1965–66. When conducting labour education training classes in various cities of Java in the late 1980s, I realized that many workers were very worried that a repeat of the 1965–66 violence could occur. One major obstacle for the growth of labour unions was the fear among the workers themselves; they were unwilling to join a union for fear they would be abducted, tortured, or killed.[9] State violence in this case played a crucial role in creating a cheap and submissive labour force – Indonesia's selling point for attracting foreign capital during the New Order period.

One fact often overlooked is that the army reinvented slave labour after 1965. The public roads and buildings in many regions of Indonesia were built by political prisoners who were forced to work on such projects without a wage (Razif 2004). A tapol in Palu, Central Sulawesi, explained how hundreds of political prisoners in his city were mobilized to construct buildings and houses, including the local military headquarters.[10] In the morning they were packed in a truck and then taken to the construction sites spreading all over the city. Half were taken to abandoned fields to work on the land that was to be turned into plantations. Many of them died, generally because of sickness as a result of hard work with insufficient food. Bloated bellies were an epidemic in the detention centre and medicine was limited. There were also those who had to struggle to find their own food in the fields while listening to the mockery from the guards who reminded them that Sukarno had suggested people cope with the pre-1965 economic shortages by eating rats from the rice fields. The largest slave labour project was Buru Island, where political prisoners, confined to barracks from sundown to sunup, were forced to turn arid grassland into arable fields. After ten years of unpaid labour, the political prisoners managed to turn the island into the most important rice producer and food staple in the Maluku islands.

The survivors of the terror lost their jobs, their houses, their land, their pensions, and their belongings. Many families lost their sole income earner. Even after a political prisoner, a *tapol*, was released from prison, he or she could neither obtain a job in the public sector nor in many private sector firms. The government issued a set of regulations that forbade political prisoners from working in occupations where they could influence public opinion, such as writers, performing artists (e.g. puppet master), and government officials. A child of a tapol in central Java recounts the difficulties her father faced after being released from prison:

But it's true that the surveillance of my father was a bit too tight. If he was sick for three days and didn't appear [in public], he'd be summoned again. The point is he was not allowed to get out, [he] remained under city detention. Once we planned to open an English course so that father had some activity, but [we] didn't get the permit. The KORAMIL didn't dare to give permission, [we] had to go to KODIM and the Office of Social and Political Affairs they said. Father himself felt uneasy, what could he say? He didn't have any job and was dependent on my mother. I myself regretted the government's attitude at that time for not giving freedom for father to do something. Whatever business he was trying to do was not permitted. So, in the end his activity was only at home, reading, writing, that's it. Because he couldn't do anything else. Maybe that's what sped up his death in 1985. He felt frustrated as a man who had to depend on my mother when he wasn't that old. He was only in his 60s. He was still fresh. While here many were still working, his friends were still working.

Family members of the tapols too were denied eligibility for employment in the government and strategic industries, and if somehow they did manage to get hired they could be summarily fired if their identity was discovered in the course of the screening tests routinely conducted by Kopkamtib and its successor, Bakorstanas (Coordinating Body for National Stability). After the mass release of political prisoners at the end of the 1970s, the New Order issued numerous laws and regulations to discriminate against ex-political prisoners and their families. Local community leaders, factory owners and schools were constantly alerted about the 'latent danger of communism'. The discourse of potential threats of communists, fundamental to the legitimacy of Suharto's regime, shaped industrial relations.[11] Potential employees were obliged to show a letter declaring that they were not involved in the G-30-S or related in any way to the PKI or a leftist organization, and have no familial relations with ex-political prisoners. One option to avoid this kind of problem with the government was not to admit that the victims were part of one's family. Jaelam from Tasikmalaya told his story:

> [In order] to be able to become a government official [one] had to severe familial ties. My child who worked as a high school teacher died not as my child. That relationship was broken, as if she was not my child. Although in our hearts that was not the case, but administratively, as it was determined by 'law', guaranteed by law, she was forced not to become my daughter. It's better if I'm considered dead, that I'm not considered child's father at all. That was very painful, wasn't it? Then, the second thing, my elder brother worked at Pertamina [state gas and petroleum company]. There was a kind of screening for the sake of 'clean environment'. He said that he didn't have any sibling who was involved in G-30-S. Yet, I was his younger brother. He even cried at our father's lap. [Father said to me] 'Sorry that your brother did this. It was only to save [our] stomachs.' It went to that extent.

To avoid the repression, families of political prisoners and those killed or disappeared tended to avoid problems at work. They were not confident to engage in struggles to improve their livelihood at the workplace. The fact that they were able to get jobs in such precarious conditions was considered a 'blessing', even if the wage was low. For decades the families of political prisoners denied themselves as 'subjective beings' (Marx 1867: 724). This made the reproduction of the capital relation much easier. If the estimates of the number of political prisoners and those killed are reliable, the total amount of people affected by the 'clean environment' laws would reach more than three million all over Indonesia.

The importance of repression on the workers and forced labour certainly does not rely on the nominal amount of money this labour contributed to the New Order. Buru Island and other detention camps were not the 'cork upon which Indonesian capitalism floated'. They are important to consider in their role as formative moments in the capital–worker social relation. Approaches that solely focus on the penetration of money in production processes do not understand the most fundamental problem of capitalism, that is imposition of work through the commodity form, which is achieved both through the silent compulsion of economic relations and physical repression. Repression on the workers, including the employment of forced labour, became crucial to determine the conditions of wage labour. As has been noted by many experts, capitalism in Indonesia had not been fully developed by the mid-1960s, not only because of a scarcity of money capital, but also because of the existence of widespread non-capitalist and anti-capitalist social practices, especially outside Java, which were deemed 'anti-development' practices by the government.

Systematic violence against women during this period is important to consider in this context. The separation of the producers from their means of production and subsistence also meant a separation from their control over the process of social reproduction (Mies 1986). One of the main targets in the anti-Communist campaign launched by the military was a left-wing women's organization, Gerwani. Its members were accused of torturing the kidnapped generals on 1 October 1965 by mutilating their bodies and cutting off their genitals while dancing naked. Such a lurid and demonstrably false story became part of New Order political culture by symbolizing the danger of politically strong and sexual women (Wieringa 2003). It was this story that served as the reference point for the New Order restrictions on women's political activities.

The Suharto government tried to restrict women's sexual lives and thus control the demographic rates. Contrary to the previous government, the Suharto regime followed the doctrine that a large population was an obstacle to economic development (Hull and Hull 1992). While the family planning programme implemented nationwide since the 1960s was intended to control population growth, government officials, intellectuals as well as military officers began to involve themselves in regulating the family. In many areas it was conducted by physical force and went practically unchallenged.

The mass violence of 1965–66 played an important role in diminishing women's will to resist patriarchal ideologies. The steady stream of propaganda about the fictitious sexual tortures of the generals served as a constant reminder of the dangers of assertive women. Gender relations were altered under the New Order to create new norms; instead of women active in both the family and society, the militarized government under Suharto imposed the paradigm of the income-earning male and the domesticated wife.

Conclusion

The lesson that many Indonesians learned from the violence of 1965–66 was to avoid having anything to do with politics. The New Order's conception of the public as a 'floating mass' – a mindless mass of people that easily flows in whatever direction it is told to flow – was a reflection of a very real situation: the public followed those in power, mouthing the propaganda, going through all the rituals and ceremonies, such as the elections every five years. The military state was subconsciously imagined as a beast around which one must tiptoe and whisper. It was such fear that made people acquiesce to mistreatment, from forced labour to unequal work relations, from land grabbings to military violence against women. The story of primitive accumulation is still being written in the annals of world history 'with letters of blood and fire'.

Notes

1 In this connection, one topic that merits further research is Suharto's self-fashioning as a meticulous follower of legal procedure. He never terrorised people by boasting of how many people he killed. Instead, the efficacy of his image worked the opposite way: much of the public knew he had killed many people (it was an open secret) and felt terror in seeing the 'smiling general' behave as if he had not (Ayu Ratih 1997).

2 This point became clear when reading documents of the US embassy in Jakarta from 1965 to 1966. See *Foreign Relations of the United States, 1964–1968, vol. 26, Indonesia: Malaysia-Singapore; Philippines* (Washington: US Government Printing Office, 2001).

3 This operation was designed more to bring the troops under the command of Suharto and put the pro-Sukarno officers on the defensive. Many officers and troops were detained for months and even years on the flimsiest of evidence, often just the suspicion that they were not sufficiently supportive of Suharto. This kind of cleaning operation was continuously employed by Suharto in the following period to destroy every form of resistance towards his rule, including the one from the officers who used to be his close allies during 1965–66.

4 The ban was lifted on 6 October 1965 but the newspapers considered leftist were never published again and, in effect, remained under a ban.

5 We now know for certain that these stories were lies (Anderson 1987). We do not know exactly who invented them but we can reasonably assume the authors were army intelligence officers engaged in psychological warfare. There are many indications that there was a psychological warfare operation underway in October. The US ambassador, Marshall Green, suggested on 5 October that there should be a covert operation to 'spread the story of the PKI's guilt, treachery, and brutality' (US embassy to Department of State, 5 October 1965, cited by Brands 1989). The CIA was extensively involved in many other anti-Communist propaganda campaigns in the world (McGehee 1990).

6 In 1968, NU wrote a report about 60 cases of murder and assault against its members and sympathizers (Feillard 1999: 76–77). In the same year, a number of PKI leaders and members organized an armed resistance that appeared more as an attempt to save themselves rather than a movement to seize power (Liem 2004). It is possible that the 60 cases mentioned above were part of the activities of this group. Nevertheless, it has to be remembered that, at the same time, the Army was conducting a 'second cleaning operation' against its allies who were demanding compensation for their 'services'.

7 In Central and East Java, Nahdlatul Ulama was directly involved in the mass murder. In Bali, a similar role was played by Tameng Marhaen, an organization under the PNI (Indonesian National Party), while in Flores and Timor it was Catholic Youth. All of these organizations were closely connected to the military in launching their actions. Some of them even congregated in 'laskar' (troops) under direct supervision from the military.

8 Karl Polanyi developed this thought by highlighting various social processes and strategies that are intended to remove the arrangement protecting the society from the market (Polanyi 1944).

That process did not occur only once in history but keeps repeating, along with the dynamics of capital expansion on the one hand and various forms of social resistance on the other.

9 Businessmen often used the allegation 'PKI' to hinder the activities of worker activists at the workplace or industrial site. Among the workers themselves there was a bitter joke about willingness 'to be PKI-ed' (treated as PKI) if they join the activities of a workers' union.

10 The logic of forced labour was extended to imprisoned artists as well; painters, especially the well-known ones, were forced to produce paintings for free, paintings that their army masters sold on the market.

11 In 1986–87 when Indonesia went through a crisis, tens of thousands of government officials from various departments were laid off due to 'unclean environment' violations, that is, they were related to a political prisoner. But according to several interviews, this mass dismissal was a pre-planned effort to minimize the number of state workers. The 'unclean environment' justification freed the government from its responsibility to provide compensation for the workers and ensured they would not be confident to resist. A similar strategy was often employed in the private sector towards workers who were involved in political activities.

References

Anderson, Benedict R. O'G (1987) 'How did the generals die?', *Indonesia* 43(April): 109–34.

Ayu Ratih (1997) 'Suharto's New Order State: imposed illusions and invented legitimations', unpublished paper.

Booth, Anne (ed.) (1992) *The Oil Boom and After: Indonesian Economic Policy and Performance in the Suharto Era*, Singapore: Oxford University Press.

Brands, H. W. (1989) 'The limits of manipulation: how the United States didn't topple Sukarno', *The Journal of American History* 76(3): 785–808.

Chomsky, Noam and Herman, Edward (1979) *Washington Connection and Third World Fascism*, Cambridge: South End Press.

Feillard, André (1999) *NU vis-à-vis Negara: Pencarian Isi, Bentuk dan Makna*, Yogyakarta: LKiS.

Fein, Helen (1993) 'Revolutionary and antirevolutionary genocides: a comparison of state murders in democratic Kampuchea, 1975 to 1979, and in Indonesia, 1965 to 1966', *Comparative Studies in Society and History* 35(4): 796–823.

Geertz, Clifford (1995) *After the Fact: Two Countries, Four Decades, One Anthropologist*, Cambridge: Harvard University Press.

Griswold, Deirdre (1975) *Indonesia: The Bloodbath That Was*, New York: World View Publishers.

Hadiz, Vedi R. (1997) *Workers and the State in New Order Indonesia*, London and New York: Routledge.

Hill, Hal (1996) *The Indonesian Economy since 1966: Southeast Asia's Emerging Giant*, Cambridge: Cambridge University Press.

Hull, Terence and Hull, Valerie (1992) 'Population and health policies'. In Anne Booth (ed.) *The Oil Boom and After: Indonesian Economic Policy and Performance in the Suharto Era*, Singapore: Oxford University Press, 411–436.

Hüsken, Frans and White, Benjamin (1989) 'Java: social differentiation, food production, and agrarian control'. In Gillian Hart *et al.* (eds) *Agrarian Transformation: Local Processes and the State in Southeast Asia*, Berkeley: University of California Press, 234–265.

Kopkamtib (n.d.). *Himpunan Surat-Surat Keputusan/Perintah jang Berhubungan dengan Kopkamtib 1965 s/d 1969*, Sekretariat Kopkamtib.

Latief, Abdul (2000) *Pleidoi Kolonel A Latief: Soeharto terlibat G30S*, Jakarta: Institut Studi Arus Informasi.

Liem, Andre (2004) 'Perjuangan Bersenjata PKI di Blitar Selatan dan Operasi Trisula'. In John Roosa, Ayu Ratih dan Hilmar Farid (eds) *Tahun yang tak Pernah Berakhir: Memahami Pengalaman Korban '65*, Jakarta: ELSAM, 163–200.

Marx, Karl (1867/1976) *Capital* Vol. 1, New York: Penguin.

McGehee, Ralph (1990) 'The Indonesian massacres and the CIA', *Covert Action Quarterly*(Fall): 56–59

Mies, Maria (1986) *Patriarchy and Accumulation on a World Scale*, London: Zed Books.

Nasution, Abdul Haris (1985) *Memenuhi Panggilan Tugas. Jilid 6: Masa Kebangkitan Orde Baru*, Jakarta: Gunung Agung.

Notosusanto, Nugroho dan Ismail Saleh (1989) *Tragedi Nasional Percobaan Kup G-30-S/PKI di Indonesia*, Jakarta: Intermasa.

Palmer, Ingrid (1977) *The New Rice in Indonesia*, Geneva: United Nations Research Institute for Social Development.

Polanyi, Karl (1944) *The Great Transformation: The Political and Economic Origins of our Time*, Boston: Beacon Press.

Razif (2004) 'Romusha dan Pembangunan: Sumbangan Tahanan Politik untuk Rezim Soeharto'. In dalam John Roosa, Ayu Ratih dan Hilmar Farid (eds) *Tahun yang tak Pernah Berakhir: Memahami Pengalaman Korban '65,* Jakarta: ELSAM.

Robinson, Geoffrey (1995) *The Dark Side of Paradise: Political Violence in Bali*, Ithaca: Cornell University Press.

Robison, Richard (1986) *Indonesia: The Rise of Capital*, Sydney: Allen and Unwin.

Sembiring, Garda dan Harsono Sutedjo (eds) (2004) *Gerakan 30 September1965: Kesaksian Letkol (Pnb) Heru Atmodjo*, Jakarta: Hasta Mitra.

Southwood, Julie and Flanagan, Patrick (1983) *Indonesian: Law, Propaganda and Terror*, London: Zed Books.

Stoler, Ann Laura (1985) *Capitalism and Confrontation in Sumatra's Plantation Belt, 1870–1979*, New Haven: Yale University Press.

Subandrio, Hajj (2001), *Kesaksianku tentang G-30-S*, Jakarta: Forum Pendukung Reformasi Total.

Sujatmiko, Iwan Gardono (1992) 'The destruction of the Indonesian Communist Party (PKI): a comparative analysis of East Java and Bali', Ph.D. Thesis, Harvard University.

Sulistyo, Hermawan (2000) *Palu Arit di Ladang Tebu: Sejarah Pembantaian Massal yang Terlupakan*, Jakarta: Kepustakaan Populer Gramedia.

Sundhaussen, Ulf (1982) *The Road to Power: Indonesian Military Politics 1945–67*, Kuala Lumpur: Oxford University Press.

Utrecht, Ernst (1970) *Indonesië's Nieuwe Orde: Ontbinding en Neokolonisatie*, Amsterdam: Van Gennep.

Wieringa, Saskia (2003) 'The birth of the new order state in Indonesia: sexual politics and nationalism', *Journal of Women's History* 15(1): 70–91

Winters, Jeffrey (1996) *Power in Motion: Capital Mobility and the Indonesian State*, Ithaca: Cornell University Press.

Part III

Americanism

Chapter 10

Embodiment of American modernity in colonial Korea

Yoo Sun-Young
(Translated by Francis Lee Dae Hoon)

Introduction: modernization of 'individual' and 'body' in colonial conditions

In the early 1930s, Korean intellectuals began to use the term *Americanism* to point out the newly emerging social and cultural phenomena of the time.[1] This Americanism under Japanese Occupation was a neglected area of study for the modernization in Korea, and raised two topics of research for colonial Korea. One is that apart from institutional modernization taking place under the colonial conditions, there was another important process that deserves due attention, the modernization of the individual. The individual modernization under colonial circumstance was confined to, and carried on, the body level. In other words, individual modernization under Japanese Occupation was getting reduced to bodily modernization, as strongly suggested by the usage of the term 'Americanism'. The discussions then were always about bodily senses and experiences, such as heterosexual relationships, individual speech manners, walking style and bodily movements (Oh 1931: 29, Chung 1930, Kim 1933, Paikaksanin 1941).[2] Such observations bring us to the other problem that modernization of the individual/body was quite a different process from that of institutional modernization in its orientation and working mechanism – a process of inscribing American modernity on the colonial body of Korea.

In Korea during the colonial period, modernization meant an aspiration for the wealth and power of nation and was hence identified with westernization itself. The desired change was to create a new life-world that included, on an individual level, copying and mimicking new 'modern' bodily gestures, ways of speech, facial expressions, languages and outlooks. In a colonial situation, however, models of mimicking or the significant other had to come from the West, the authentic origin of modernity, and secondly it had to continuously provide such ideal types or models for mimicking. The two conditions were best met with American modernity during that time in Korea. With its unprecedented and miraculous success of Protestant evangelism in Korea, with its well-known prosperous 'New World' image, with its modern sense of jazz music, and with its compelling and most favoured entertainment of Hollywood movies to the colonized Koreans, America continuously provided, although it was fragmented, the way to visualize the modern – gestures, expressions, body movements, and poises and accents – as well as how to express it with new terms, human relations and values.

This paper attempts to give an analysis and interpretation of the modernization of body aesthetics and techniques, or the first array of bodily movements modelled after

American modernity.[3] At the same time, this paper tries to pay attention to a particular modernity of colonial Korea through tracing back to the beginning the modernization of the individual and then bodily modernization.

Conditions of Americanization in colonial Korea

Expansion of the private realm

The end of the nineteenth century was a time when the imperialistic ambitions of powerful nations were growing. Affected by the tide of imperialism and the subsequent colonization by Japan, the traditional Korean identity was in crisis. This crisis of Korean identity occurred on two levels – nation and culture. The fissure of national identity was created by the colonization of the nation-state and the sudden disappearance of its own public realm, and both of these events had played crucial roles in confirming the communal identity of the Korean people. The highly centralized monarchic state of Korea that had maintained the unity of the nation until it was forced to open to the outside world by Japan, lost its reign with the colonization. As the state authority waned, the state-centred communal epistemology and ethics provided by Confucianism also lost their hegemonic power. Instead, private desire and interest began to shape much of the values and morals of the individual who was to be driven to disconnect him/herself from the primary order of traditions due to the loss of the nation-state (Hwang 1984: 62–64).

The vacillation of cultural identity was a by-product of both imperial forces preventing its continuity, and domestic forces, i.e. individuals, voluntarily abandoning it. The yearning for modernization was so imperative that Koreans who blamed themselves for losing the nation were fully motivated to sever themselves from their own cultural heritages and legacies. The Korean (Chosun, then) society was defined and criticized by themselves as well as others as stagnant, powerless and semi-barbarian, to the extent that, eventually, Korea fell into Japanese Occupation. Denouncing one's own history and tradition in order to start again also led to a confused self-perception and self-identity, and created room for the western modernity to occupy the place of seemingly the only solution. (Cho *et al.* 1969: 5–6, Pukyodonggok 1922: 83, *Kaebyog* June 1923: 6–11; *Dong-A Ilbo* 2 November 1925). In this context, signifiers and images of Western modernity, which were circulated in the forms of commodity, discourse, fashion and knowledge, began to work for Koreans as a sort of guiding light that indicated to where they should go and what they should do in this rapidly changing world.

It is from here that my current enquiry starts. This article attempts to understand the particulars inherent in the history of colonial modernization of Korea when the colonized people had lost their traditional, communal space of the past and, therefore, had to create a new self-identity according to their private interests and desires, and when Hollywood-style senses and practices stood as important references to that end.

Emergence of western modernity as a new regime of value

Colonization drives the colonized to seek a new self-identity. The colonized individual tries to find it, outside of both the dysfunctional state and the mutilated tradition as well as from outside the colonial laws and rules that command an identity of a subaltern, that is, inside the world of an individual's private desires, needs and interests. In particular, the past social caste being the most important institutional source of self-identity was also on the way out. What this situation implies to the colonized is that they are compelled to find a new regime of value that will work as a leading axis in constituting a new identity in a colonized social space.

It was western modernity and western modernization that rose in this situation as an alternative regime of value.[4] Modernity became a criterion for differentiating and positioning an individual, thus creating a new order in society. Individual identity was formed along this new value, and the degree of individual modernization became a token of differentiating oneself from the others. As soon as modern education became the royal road to modernization, the body was rapidly reconstituted as a stage of surfacing specific forms that indicated the individual status of enlightenment.

Western-style modern education was itself a determining cultural capital that one should attain in order to reinstate his/her vacillating social caste. In the 1910s, an earlier period under Japanese rule, many Koreans hesitated to receive the colonial education as a way of national resistance. However, when they saw their hope for independence shattered by the failure of the March 1 Movement in 1919, they became eager to send their children to schools, suddenly raising the entrance competition, which had never been lowered during the colonial era, to a quite high level. Modern education was like an official certificate of social recognition towards individual modernization. The colonial system, however, not only fundamentally restricted shifts in social status but also produced modern-educated, unemployed intellectuals en masse (Oh 2000).

Hyper-sensitization of the body

A ritual that draws our attention is that modernization of the mind through education and enlightenment demanded, and in fact went in hand in hand with, a different outlook of the body. Students were distinguished from others because, once enrolled in the modern education system, they were required to have short hair, formerly a strong taboo in Korea,[5] as well as to replace traditional clothing and footwear with western-style uniforms, hats and shoes. In this context, bodily changes either preceded or concurred with changes in consciousness, rather than the other way round. The western modernity, however, was injected into Korea as a ready-made good regardless of Korea's domestic development. Modernity as a ready-made good could only be deciphered on an individual level by how many and how well a person possessed and consumed modern end-products. Thus, the body became an exhibition space for modernity's ready-made products. During a transitional period that sees modernity becoming the central value, the body is used to exhibit or parade an embodiment of this modernity to others so that they can evaluate the person. Therefore, the process by which a colonized individual reintegrates his identity to the core of a new regime of value, i.e. modernity, is a process of transforming his/her public self by constantly reacting to others' gaze and by drawing a positive reaction from them.

The colonized individual who gets obsessed with exhibiting oneself in modernity is thus reconstituted as a corporeal being rather than a spiritual one. The colonized become sensitized to the daily gaze of others towards themselves because they are bound to two exterior gazes, i.e. the gaze of surveillance and contempt of the colonizer and the gaze of other compatriots measuring the level of individual modernization. The body in this regard is a space of ambivalence. The body is both an undeniable stigma of derision and inferiority of the colonized subject under the gaze of the colonizer, and a material or medium that the person can cover with modernity in order to temporally hide the stigma.

Modern appearances became an object of desire and compensation, stronger in effect than what Franz Fanon called the 'white masks' desired by coloured people. It gives twofold compensation. One was vis-à-vis the Japanese colonizers – Japanese and Koreans are not mutually discernible, at least in skin colour, and Japanese people, in their desire to attain western modernity, were not free from the inferiority complex of the non-white, non-western and late-modernized status. What was at stake, therefore, was who was to become more western and modern faster, fulfilling an imagined comparative advantage. The other compensation was vis-à-vis Korean neighbourhood compatriots. The modern appearance as a goal of collective desire was what Fanon called the 'white mask', which rendered a difference from other Koreans, rather than from the colonizers, transforming the inferiority feeling of the colonized into a feeling of ontological stability in transition. However, this was, at the same time, a process of constituting fragmented subjectivity that was obsessed with comparisons (Fanon 1967). The Body of the colonial was getting sensitized by the look of (O)thers and, in consequence, was putting priority on bodily existence.

The modernization project of bodily existence was carried out on three levels. On the first level, this project was to replace traditional aesthetics of the body with modern Western ones. The Western-type body emerged as 'the absolute state of flesh' (Barthes 1981: 56–57) that realizes the absolute and fundamental ideal, which Barthes once found in the face of Greta Garbo. By the same mechanism as the way that the veiled Garbo was worshiped for her ambiguous and partially exposed body, the western body was worshiped as the externalization of modernity. The second level of modernization was to make one's appearance Western, that is, modern. The reconfiguration of bodily appearance demanded consuming or possessing Western-style goods, mostly imported from Japan and the Western countries. This means that those people who transformed their appearance did so by following Western-style fashion in short hairstyle, cosmetics, cigar-case and cane. Because Koreans of the time were bound by long-standing ethics concerning their body,[6] changing bodily appearance meant as much liberation as denial of, and resistance to, the tradition, history and norms of their parent generation. The third level of modernization is related to body movements. In a Confucian society, where immobility and quietness had been valued, the standards and proper manners of bodily movements were regulated by rules and conventions. Social changes let people opt for gestures, facial expressions, walking styles, etc in a new faster and larger scale, as such styles were taken as the newly informed representation of modernity. These modern movements of body were perceived as expressions of a liberated body and enlightened soul, a bodily statement representing an upgraded liberation from the hierarchical and oppressive tradition, the past.

Spatial and class limitation of colonial modernity

The current discussion about the colonial modernity of Korea under the Japanese Occupation is limited by a few conditions of the time. One is that the space of modernity was confined to cities. Although rapid urbanization occurred during the colonial period, the gaps and lags between Kyongsong and other regions in terms of economic, social and cultural modernization were so great that Kyongsong was the only city in the process of modernization in Korea. The collective desire for modern things and images, therefore, took its shape mostly in the streets of Kyongsong. It was a city of 180,000 population at the time of the Japanese takeover, but grew to a city of nearly one million population by 1945.

Secondly, there is a limitation in who 'intellectuals and modern boys and girls who roamed the asphalt streets' were that composed the urban scenery of Kyongsong. Once named as 'flaneurs', wandering the city streets from cafes to tea rooms and cinemas and from departments to theatres, like Walter Benjamin who strolled the streets of Berlin and Paris in the early twentieth century dreaming of a nineteenth-century modernism, they were mostly jobless bourgeois, intellectuals, cafe waitresses[7], *kisaengs*, students and upper-middle-class youths (Shin 1998: 23–31).

Thirdly, as modernity came by consuming western ready-made goods, those who pursued it were confined to those who could afford it. They had to be above middle-class in order to consume the western modernity being displayed in modern city space.[8] They were the ones who lost privileges of their past caste, but had had higher education, and those who knew more about the west, and therefore felt more lacking than others. They were the ones called *Modern Boys* (*Mobo* or *Mob*) and *Modern Girls* (*Moge* or *Mogel*), or *Ultra-modern girls* as the latest fashion-name in the 1910s (*Dong-A Ilbo*, 5 May 1920), and then common nouns since the mid-1920s.[9] These *modern* men and women made their distinction from others in their language, behaviour, style, fashion, hobbies and other activities.

One problem for them was the level of knowledge needed to appropriate modern standards in gestures and consumption. Two restrictions are placed on modernity when it becomes an object that is collectively desired and consumed in a society. One is the restriction that modernity can only be 'appropriately' consumed with a certain level of knowledge and information, and the other is the restriction of scarcity becoming a luxury. These restrictions were the driving forces that make modernity come to acquire the classificatory power of differentiating social classes – by becoming a cultural article deluxe.

American modernity and its prevalence

America fantasy

Colonized Koreans needed an ideal type for the modern representation of their body in its appearance as well as in its technique, and America provided that ideal. In order to understand Americanism in colonial Korea, one needs to contemplate upon all dimensions of America's impact upon the daily lives of Koreans. First, there was America as what Fanon called a governing fiction, America in the imaginary and fantastic dimension. Secondly, there was America as its missionaries, who paved the way to modernization of the daily, real lives of Korean people. And lastly, there was America as Hollywood movies and the jazz sound and the beat that both stood as, and provided, symbolic and visual images of modernity.

In the imaginary/fantastic dimension, America was conceived as the richest nation in the world as well as a gentleman-like brotherly nation that had no intention to occupy, but rather help weak countries to achieve independence (*Tokrib Shinmun*, 27 February 1899), as the most powerful nation in the capitalist world (*Hwangsong Shinmun*, 16 September 1898), as the birthplace of Modernism,[10] and as a benefactor to Chosun.[11]

Even after Occupation, it was not difficult to find writings by intellectuals, bureaucrats, and journalists that praised the positive influence of the America in raising moral standards among Koreans.[12] Of all nations, America was the western nation to which Koreans felt most friendly. There is one unpublished newspaper cartoon by an anonymous reader, censored by the Japanese authority at the time of publication, because it exaggerated the size of two nations, by depicting Japan as so tiny while America is giant (Chong 1998). It shows us how deeply a fantasy of America had been immersed in the colonial Korean's mind.

In the cartoon, an American soldier wrapped in the Stars and Stripes is threatening by pointing his gun at undersized Japanese. To the colonized subjects of Korea, America as such existed as a collectively constructed, governing fiction (Fanon 1967: 215–216). There is one more episode that shows what America meant to Koreans. Sakau Moriya, who was a director of the general affairs department of the Government-General of Chosun, delivered a speech to a group of school principals of various levels. His point was that, in spite of Japan achieving a great development in Chosun, Koreans have still kept a deep hatred toward Japan. Therefore, he suggested, Japan should try to enlighten Koreans' minds and souls, the spiritual realm of which has been taken charge of by Americans and Europeans. And he despised some Koreans for the reason that they expected America would help them to achieve independence from Japan (Moriya 1924: 29–36).[13] That many protagonists chose America as their final destination at the end of the novels written by famous pro-Japan novelists in the 1920s shows how deeply, as if it were the unfulfilled dream of modernization, America existed in the mind of the colonized subjects (Paik 1985: 244–249).

Thanks to this governing fiction, the missionary work by American churches recorded an unprecedented success in colonial Korea, which further promoted the image of America as a benefactor and contributor of Korea's modernization. This observation is illustrated, for example, by the fact that a *shinyosong*, a new woman, was usually depicted as one who could speak English, read the Bible and chanted hymns (Hwang 1937). Such new-type women would often call themselves Aster, Marry, Maria, or Melitha,[14] wrote for women's enlightenment in journals and newspapers or spoke on radio programmes. It was also a fashion in the 1920s and 1930s that so-called modernized young couples would avoid a traditional marriage ceremony and instead go to church for a *Yesookyo-sik*, a Christian-style marriage, dressed in western suits and white dresses, following an English-dominated service officiated by a western minister, and were then carried away to a party by riding in a car usually manufactured by Ford.[15] The term 'Yesookyo-sik' for marriage came into usage in the 1920s to designate modern-style marriage (*Dong-A Ilbo*, 3 April 1930).

In addition, it was the images of Hollywood movies, and melodies and rhythms of the accompanying jazz music, that added distinctive patterns, appearances and rhythmic touches to the body and senses. Motion pictures and jazz music captured the fantasy of young people as well as intellectuals and students in cities until the mid-1930s (Yoo 1997).

American modernity set

American modernity was not the only type of modernity in Korea. Japan's colonial capital in Korea, Kyongsong was a cosmopolitan city from the beginning of Japanese Occupation. Along with Japan came, at the same time, Britain, France, Germany, Italy, Holland, Canada and America. They came as fragmented information on contemporary form and in a discontinuous, sporadic way from places such as Paris and Hollywood or Tokyo and Osaka.[16] A performance programme by the Baeguja Dance Company[17] at a Koreans-only theatre in Kyongsong in November, 1929, is a good example of how different forms of modernity were mixed in the city in a cosmopolitan fashion. The three-day show included, among others, American-style dances, an English-style doll-bride dance, Swiss dances with a Swiss pastoral scene in the background, Latin American dances, Gypsy dances, traditional Chosun folk-songs with dance, African hudahuda dances, facial comedy and movies. The advertising copy read 'A Grand, Fantastic-ally Modern Symphony in Fascinating Curves' (*Dong-A Ilbo*, 19 November 1929). The kinematographies were also about 'sceneries in France and England, whale fishing in the ocean, the Alps covered in snow, Russian youths, farces by cute western actresses in swimming suits, etc' (Payongsaeng 1929: 39–40).

Modernists understood Kyongsong through Tokyo and rarely compared it with Paris. What was modern to them came as fragments or scraps, hardly forming any coherent entity. Its relevance to reality was temporary and transient. Among such unstable sources of modernity, the made-in-America modernity had the highest authority in its authenticity, and thus provided most bits for a mosaic image of modernness.

Countries such as France, Germany or Italy were unable to provide such a set, having its components and operational styles, in a continuous and sufficient way. Jazz was the background music to American modernity just as it was to American movies. For individuals who were then disconnected from the guidance of state and tradition, the experiences in the media came as a source of fascination, shock and delusion because they seldom happened in reality and the reality had a different context. (Thompson 1995: 225–232). American senses and images that filled the soundscape and ocularscape of colonized cities reacted with the fantasy and shock of the colonized to give a multiplied effect. With its sounds, visual images and illusions, American modernity formed the basis for transforming, producing and spreading the aesthetics and the movements of the body.

American sense and sensibility: Hollywood modernity

In 1906, movies were introduced to Korea for the first time in the form of kinematog-raphy. After that, they became one of the regular features of city life in Korea: Kyongsong had 3000 regular moviegoers by the mid-1920s (*Dong-A Ilbo*, 1 January 1925), for example. Since 1924/5, western movies became the most loved cultural genre for Koreans. This was reflected in the daily reportage of Hollywood movies with pictures in most newspapers, a rare practice at that time.[18] The spectators were mostly teenage secondary school pupils at the beginning, but by late 1920s they were mostly adult intellectuals (*Chunang* April 1936). Those moviegoers were called 'advanced modern people' at that time (*Dong-A Ilbo* 6 April 1930). Even though most films were so worn out after one or two years of showing in Japan that some characters were unrecognisable

(*Dong-A Ilbo* 18 November 1925, *Dong-A Ilbo* 10 May 1927, *Maeil Shinbo* 4 May 1927), movies were generally called 'the only source of pleasure' in the colonial period (Payongsaeng 1929). As movie fans were regarded as modernists and up-to-date intellectuals, there appeared a few fanatics passionately devoted to an expertise in film news and information (*Pyolgeongon* 1930).

Most of the movies imported in the 1920s were American, approximately 95%. From France and Germany, only about ten films were introduced every year (*Dong-A Ilbo* 1 January 1925, 10 May 1927, 6 April 1930). Even in the 1930s, when the Japanese and Korean film industry achieved some development, American movies took 60–70% of the movie market in Korea (Yoo 1997: 110). However, there were also criticisms of them as well. Many film critics argued that most of the imported movies were of low quality (*Dong-A Ilbo* 4 January 1926), while some intellectuals attracted to Russian socialism condemned American movies as being 'just reactionary movies where Yankees want to disseminate American spirit with some sweet spices such as cheap triangular love affairs and mechanical tricks'.[19]

For students, intellectuals and the male and female upper-middle class, however, American movies were something more than a low-quality entertainment. They played 'a role of social agency of enlightenment and education' so intensely as to be characterized as an immoral influence towards 'sexual anarchism' (*Dong-A Ilbo* 10 October 1925). The public used to perceive movies as a 'textbook of modernity' in the colonial situation (Park 1939), and some critiques saw it as a problem that Korean-only schools allowed students to watch movies while Japanese-only schools prohibited them (*Dong-A Ilbo* 10 October 1925). Movies were certainly beyond the boundary of arts, and became a 'reference of fashions' and a 'map of customs' by their influence over 'cultural life in general'. In this respect, Japanese and Korean movies were no match to foreign (American) movies (*Dong-A Ilbo* 2 October 1937). A prolific film critique, Lee Oon-Kok was one of those who understood how movies affected the formation of modern sensibility, styles and body. It was in his understanding of the relationship between movies and modern senses that he once commented: 'positive was the role of movies in making people take the pleasure of opening up their intellect and sensibility, but negative was it to make them carry on such pleasure to real life' (Lee, *Dong-A Ilbo* 5 October 1937). Such a perception was, however, well shared by the public at that time.

Jazz as a symbol of modernity

When jazz bands and jazz dance arrived in Korea through China and Japan, they were received as a new symbol of modernity. Lee Seo-Koo, who worked as a writer, theatre person, journalist and literary critique throughout the colonial period, saw the mood of the 1920s as inseparable from jazz. He scorned that there were few pupils or modern boys or girls who had not enjoyed jazz while even *kisaeng*s (similar to *geisha*) resorted to jazz expertise in order to become *modern kisaeng*s. Very critical of the then popular 'Korean Jazz Band', he described the band's performances as players trying to create a 'great power' to arouse the audience by their sensational movements of head, shoulder, waist and hips (Lee 1929).

Along with the western house, piano, solo singing, radio antenna and western food, it became a vital part of the so-called *munhwasaenhwal*, cultural lifestyle[20] to listen to jazz music from a gramophone, and the 'pretty demonic city of the twentieth century',

Kyongsong, became an attraction to youths for its 'daytime symphonies and nightly jazz' (Park 1934: 41; Choi 1929; Choo 1929). Shops ranging from tailors to barbers and from public baths to restaurants and pubs in cities began to attract customers by playing music and songs from a radio or gramophone (*Pyolgeongon* March 1927: 107). Jazz as the modern sound created a soundscape that characterized modern Kyongsong's nightlife.

'From "Yankees" land', jazz came to Kyongsong with 'erotic dances, which spread gestures of moving the upper body backward and the lower body forward' and 'turned the city streets into a playground for *eros*, *gros* (*grotesque*), and bodies' (Oh 1931: 32). Moreover, it produced *modern boys* who 'felt an ecstasy of hugging and kissing when they walked the paved streets of the colonised city with their lovers, wearing double-button overcoats and doing jazz steps' (*Maeil Shinbo* 1 January 1937). This was the jazz modernism of the colonial city of Kyongsong. Like sound effects for eroticism and hedonism as well as for desires to ride on the newest trend, jazz infused itself into modern bodily movements. Senses in colonial Kyongsong were changing such that one cafe-goer regretted in 1929 that the city was becoming too Americanized, doing away with the city's European taste prevailing 10 years before (*Cheongsaegji* 1938: 46–47).

Embodiment of American modernity

Modern body aesthetics

In 1925, an American all-women baseball team visited Korea to play a goodwill match with a Korean men's team in front of 3000 spectators. The match was arranged by an American mission and widely reported in full pages in newspapers (*Dong-A Ilbo* 25 November 1925). Baseball was introduced to Korea before 1920 by American missionaries, and soon became a popular sport. All the technical terms were borrowed from English without translation, and football, basketball and tennis were similarly introduced (Avison 1921: 27).

In 1923, *Dong-A Ilbo*, the most prominent daily of the time, hosted its first women's tennis tournament, where students from Christian schools participated. This event drew a great public attention. Through the sports introduced by American churches as one of their missionary works, Korean women began to accept 'sports' as normal activities and familiarized themselves with partial exposure of their body by wearing short skirts, sport shoes and sport socks. In effect, the introduction of western sports contributed to the spread of a modern concept that a 'healthy' body was a very important part of a person's life and required exercise to keep it up.

Interest in a healthy body soon led to a new concept for a beautiful body and bodily style. Criteria for a beautiful face, 'wide forehead, short lashes and moderate nose' before, now became those of a western beauty, 'shallow forehead, double eyelid, long lashes and high nose'. For a beautiful body, too, while it was 'slender waist, small feet and small hands' that counted in the past, it was now 'large hands and feet, tall height and sporty body' (*Dong-A Ilbo* 11 April 1926). This was how a newspaper came to run an article on medical surgery for creating double eyelids, under the title, 'Ways to make ugly eyes beautiful' (*Dong-A Ilbo* 25 February 1927).

This was a rapid change of perception compared with the 1890s when westerners' 'big bright eyes, high nose, large ears and thick lips' were a cause of fear to Koreans and which brought about rumours of their being cannibals (Naw 1898). In the late 1920s, young people emotionally attached to film heroes and heroines such as John Gilbert, Ronald Coleman, Ramon Navaro, Lilian Gish, Dianna Dervine, Collin More, John Barrymore, Rudolf Valentino, Robert Taylor, Cary Grant, Marlene Dietrich and Greta Garbo, often mentioned those stars' names and body parts in describing the physical shape of their friends and lovers in terms of similarities (Choi 1929, Lee 1929: 34). Moreover, their ideal type, changing from Valentino to John Barrymore, followed the changing fashion in screen heroes (*Shinyosong* 1933a: 119). The ideal spouse type for highly educated young women also became a man with a large chest and a height far taller than the average Korean (*Yosong* 1938).

At the centre of these western aesthetics were Hollywood movies and their beautiful heroes and heroines. Young Koreans, both men and women, 'envied the body line and slim legs of the western actresses on screen' (*Yesool* 1934: 58). A devoted socialist, Huh Heon, was no exception: he lamented being too old to approach a beautiful woman after being fascinated by the 'marble legs' of western women that he saw for the first time on his sea route to the US (Huh 1929: 9). Even inside the minds of the intellectuals of the time, who were in Tokyo to study – for example, Yom Sang-Sub[21] and Kim Dong-In[22] who fell in love with half-American half-Japanese girls named *Mary* – 'genuine modernity' had to be the West and Christianity, and 'Ms. Mary Brown playing organ' was the personified god of modernity in sensual mood (Kim 1989: 24–26).

People learned standards for beauty from the media, such as cinema, magazines, newspapers and photography (*Yesool* April 1935: 75–77). Under the colonial conditions, it was the voyeuristic gaze that gave the most accessible sense of beauty, now predominantly aligned towards western beauty, physique and style. But, this also triggered an inevitable inferiority complex in Koreans, whose beauty standards looked lacking and low compared with those of the Westerner, the White. A rare beautician in the mid-1930s, Lee Hyun-Bae, even claimed that she was determined to create Korean beauties by her beauty treatment, which included shaving, massage, permanent wave and make-up, because 'people from abroad say that, and even in my standards, there is no real beauty in Korea' (Lee 1937: 70–71).

Modernization of appearance

The terms, *modern boy* and *modern girl* appeared first in the mid-1920s and became popular and fashionable words from around 1927.[23] Even though some intellectuals targeted their fashion, behaviour and lifestyles in their criticism of the contemporary youngsters of the idle rich for their senseless imitation of the latest fashion of the west, there was frequent newspaper and magazine coverage on these modern boys and girls that took their modern 'appearances' as a new cultural phenomenon detached from the tradition. For newspapers and popular magazines, the latest fashion among youths, such as hairstyle, make-up, gestures, manners of speaking, sports and films, were always good topics for news and stories.

In the early 1920s, those women in 'swept-back' hairstyles with the chignon who were educated in the modern style and involved in social activities were called '*tremori* (swept-back)', and in the mid 1920s, there appeared short haircut women who were called '*danbal meein* (short-cut styled beauty)' or '*danbal rang* (short-cut styled girl)' or '*danbal yosong* (short-cut styled woman)' as a way of indicating their distinctiveness as more modern than others in different hair-styles. Until then, western dress was not predominant. But after 1927, people began to name those as 'modern' who wore westernized clothes and shoes, and had their hair short or swept-back or permanent-waved and had their faces made-up. However, such modern girls were not so numerous until the early years of the 1930s. For example, a magazine article in 1930 estimated that there were about 20 short-hair new women in Kyongsong among *kisaeng*s, writers, actresses, doctors and socialists (*Pyolgeongon*, March 1930).

It seems the short-cut style for women could only become popular in the mid-1930s. In other words, it used to be that 'those wearing long hair, long skirts and rubber shoes were *Ku Yosong*, old-style women and those wearing short hair, short skirts and western shoes were *Shin Yosong*, new-style women', but now modern girls were 'those liberated women in western dress equipped with mind-blowing beauty rather than political views' (*Pyolgeongon*, December 1927), or 'those who wore thin socks, western shoes, a coat, short hair and heavy cosmetics' (Choi 1927, You 1927). At the same time, for modern boys, a western suit was a must and 'a walking stick, horn-rimmed glasses, a hat and a pair of point-toe shoes' were standard (Choi 1927, You 1927), while a modern girl was now identified by 'a western dress in splendidly light or seductive colours, silk stockings, short hair, pointed shoes and dark red lips' (Park 1927b: 116), or by 'permanent hair, dress with pattern design, pointed shoes, sensual make-up and mysterious gestures' (Yun 1937: 48–49).

Modern girls and *modern boys* were those considered to be more modernized, who frequented theatres, concert halls and cafes, idling away times with shopping, strolling, doing make-up or gossiping, or those cafe waitresses, *kisaeng*s and girl students. They were socially recognized as new bearers of modernity, but unlike previous *shin yosong* (new women) and *shinsa* (gentlemen), they were not socially respected. Nevertheless, modern boys and modern girls were certainly an extension of their predecessors in that they constructed their identity from a modernized appearance and behaviour as well as in upgrading their personal modernity and public self by appearance alone. What they did more was to imprint a western modernity on their body much more clearly than the compromising *shin yosong* and *shinsa* generation who were caught between the traditional past and the transitional present.

Because these people were the ones who were leading the street fashion, they were eager to stay up-to-date in their appearance by obtaining necessary knowledge and commodities, the ideals of which always came from Hollywood movies. America was 'the producer of "modern girls" not only for the Orient but for everywhere' (*Maeil Shinbo* 14 May 1927). It also provided 90% of the latest clothes, food and even beer, so much wanted by these modern boys and girls (Choi 1927: 120). This was why, to some observers of those days, modern-looking guys used the same kind of neckties, chest-pocket handkerchiefs, and belts of the same colour and design (*Maeil Shinbo* 12 August 1927). It was also this perception of America that made English the most favourite language to learn in order to read and understand advertisements, signboards, imported food products and daily goods, as well as to enjoy foreign culture and books, or even to make life successful (*Bae-Hwa* 1929: 105–106).

Moreover, the theme music of movies became the most popular among popular songs, and the dances in movies spread quickly to social dancing. New customs that appeared in American movies, sometimes criticized as the source of 'lowbrow customs of the time', were copied into dresses, behaviours and desires of modern boys and girls

(Paikaksanin 1941). By the late 1930s, most city men turned to western suits for daily use, but their designs and styles, for example short trousers and walking with hands in pockets, were then already known to be imitations from the movies they saw. However, such imitations gave a performance of failed actors because of physical and other differences (*Shinsegi* 1939: 24). Coming into the 1930s, some women began to pour hydrogen peroxide liquid over their hair in order to turn the black colour into yellow, like the western blond (Yun 1937: 49), and some girl students tried to make their hair stylish by a variety of methods, including ironing in order to look more like western girls (*Maeil Shinbo* 11 November 1937).

Modernization of body techniques: Korean flapper

If a body is to represent modernity, it requires modernization of bodily movements. The transition from quiet, slow and reserved to large, speedy and demonstrative movements signalled the liberation of the body from the shackles of tradition, which in turn meant liberation of the person. Once equipped with western appearance, *shin yosong* and *modern girls* were bound to complete their modernity by modern gestures. There coexisted in Kyongsong in the mid-1920s, on the one hand, the aesthetics for a traditional oriental lady favouring expressionless face, fear of night travel and obedience to husband and parents, and, on the other hand, the aesthetics for new style or western women with 'expressive' emotions, travelling long distances alone, revolting against parental admonitions, and arguing for oneself: and the two imaginations clashed with each other, with much ensuing debate (*Dong-A Ilbo* 11 April 1926).

Almost every article that compared new and old style women in 1925 raised the cheerful and active attitudes of new style women and recognized the bouncy walking style, rudeness towards men and show of femininity as their characteristics (*Shinyosong* 1925). *Modern women* were supposed to keep their eyes wide open and fixed forward (Yun 1931), and to learn 'new skills of expression' such as 'actively swinging all four limbs while walking and running, and expressing one's opinions with both face and body, while utilising fingers, shoulder, chest, legs and lips more than words in doing so' (Kwanaksanin 1933: 30–32). In the early 1930s, the queen of modernism was the woman who could 'walk bouncy-bouncy while giving a wink to every guy on her way and wearing thin eye brows and red lips': she was supposed to conquer the streets like a daughter of that city (Lee 1934). Some viewed such vigour of the new women as an imitation of men's behaviour and appearance (*Pyolgeongon* 1928). When a woman shook hands with men in big gestures or made bursting laughs with men, she was definitely a *modern woman* (Rimyunja 1926). Such modern women were described as 'women permeating a smell of electricity' or praised as bright, accurate, speedy and busy women 'just like Anglo-Saxon tennis players' (*Maeil Shinbo* 4 April 1928).

'*Flapper*' was another name for those women. In the 1920s and 1930s, *modern girls* in Korea were called by several names, the most popular of which was flappers. According to a definition in the dictionary of new terms published by a women's magazine in 1931, a flapper was 'the type of personality played by Clara Bow, Aris White and Nancy Carol in western movies'. It was a name for 'women both highly modern and as virgin-like as inexperienced of social life' or 'lively charming ladies fluttering their skirts and flashing their leg-beauty' (*Shinyosong* 1931a: 90). The 1933 version of that dictionary described flappers as 'women walking down the streets waving their blue skirts like a flag of a French warship' and defined its meaning as 'tomboys like Clara Bow or Nancy Carol' (*Shinyosong* 1933b).

Thus, flappers in Korea were identified with Clara Bow, the 'President of the world's modern girls' (*Dong-A Ilbo* 29 March 1928) and also with symbols ranging from a blue skirt and big stride to tomboy acts, animated spirit and virginity. Such a characterization was associated with the symbol of the jazz era of the 1920s and 1930s, the American flappers, who were also known for their man-like vivacity, youthfulness, vigour, impulsive behaviour, drinking and petting. The flapper image of new women, for being a component of their hedonistic lifestyle, was also a product of the images of sex, love and crime in Hollywood movies at that time (Higashi 1978: 110–114, Turim 1994: 140–141, 151–152). Blue skirts became highly popular among flappers in Korea sometime in the early 1930s. The blue colour of skirts, originally symbolizing freedom, but acting as a signifier for sexual freedom, was for 'poor Korean daughters who run on the streets in flickering blue *sarumada* (skirt in Japanese)', who were also labelled as 'toys of the bourgeois' just like a 'commodity' (Ahn 1932, Yun 1937).

While American flappers were able to enjoy a bourgeois consumerist lifestyle with their income, the majority of Korean flappers in the colonial period were too poor to fulfil their desires. They could only fulfil their desire to consume through relating to their lovers or boyfriends, substituting just-liberated body acts with sex appeal and converting their body into an object of heterosexual desires.[24] For example, in admiration for Marlene Dietrich's beautiful legs, innocent Korean girls favoured black stockings that were avoided by ordinary women in the West for its link with the prostitute image (*Yesool* 1934). This and other similar examples show why we should be aware of another process of 'particular modernization' within the process of modernization of a colonial society.

In any account, for Korea intellectuals, modern colonial girls did not look different from the previous modern *jazz kisaeng* or *modern kisaeng*. The liveliness of their lip and eye movements as well as their hand gestures came from every corresponding gesture of movie actresses, and the revolutionary walking (with the whole leg rather than just from the knee down) also came from watching movies. In addition, the whole rhythm in these modern movements and gestures came from that of jazz music that they heard from movies and gramophones. In this way, modern girls had the same fashion of walking and shaking their hips as *jazz kisaeng* (Lee 1929: 33–35).

They were often criticized as symbols of the end of civilization who were obsessed with the prostitute culture (Kim 1940: 46). A socialist writer, Kim Ki-Jin,[25] did not hesitate to call *modern girls* and *new women* of the Kyongsong streets as 'near-prostitutes in red lips' (Kim 1925a), and this was an expression of the socialists of the time who refused what they saw as the vulgarity of Yankee culture and sensual Americanism that were carried by new-style urban women in colonial Korea.

Colonial modernity: eroticism and possession by distinction

If we assume the body is something that is constructed, repressed and transformed in a particular, cultural framework of a society or in a particular regime of discourse and power, the body is a space where mundane events are imprinted. On a body is imprinted the culture of society at a particular time through a process of construction of a cultural identity. As such, history writes its own story on the body (Butler 1998). If one calls this the imprinting of culture on a body, this paper is about rewriting the history of how the momentary, sensual, visual, fragmented experiences of modernity that came along with a particular idea of America were inscribed on the people's body of the colonial under Japanese Occupation. In that sense, the modern city of Kyongsong was an exhibition hall of western styles, modes and end products. Kyongsong was a city of 'tailors, trams, cars and theatres as well as cafes, near-prostitute new-style women, extravagance and buzzing fashions' (Kim 1925a: 22–23), and also a spectacular site for such things ranging from 'jazz, sound, cars, trams, rickshaws, speed, styles, and the Salvation Army bands' (*Shindonga* 1931), to '*fin-de-siecle* cafes, bars, fashionable dresses, show-windows, pubs, cubic buildings, tea-rooms, theatres, cinemas, department stores, delicate neon lights and mah-jong' (*Maeil Shinbo* 1 January 1937). In short, it was a city of ecstatic modernity as spectacular.

It was in this modernity's exhibition space that the colonial subjects experienced modernity. However, their experiences were both stimulating and shocking, much based on discontinuous impressions and on swift, sliding by and fragmented images. In such a situation, one's reaction to the world experiences hypersensitivity, distraction and visual excess (Charney 1995, Donald 1995, Benjamin 1969, Singer 1995). But all this was too much of an excessive stimulus for the colonized modernists who dreamed of the modern regardless of their history and tradition.[26] Walter Benjamin saw neuropsychic aspects in such experiences about the modern, which he explained as a shock-experience that disappears from consciousness as soon as it occurs. While in the consciousness, such fragments of discontinuous images of a snapshot presence get lost, they reside in the body, senses and preconsciousness as feelings, reactions and trauma; on the whole, as a shocked experience (Benjamin 1969: 155–165, Charney 1995: 281–283). Moreover, this experience is fundamentally similar to that of watching a movie, because both are essentially sensual and shocking in nature (Charney 1995: 279–285).

Such an experience escapes the hold of the consciousness and the reason, but gets imprinted onto the body and senses: it stays as a sort of trauma. Benjamin described this shock trauma as self-defensive anxiety syndrome following Freud. When shock experiences become routine, one develops an anxiety syndrome, which is the unconscious expression of sensual attention towards likely dangers from the outside, accompanied by a high level of tension in bodily movements (Benjamin 1969: 160–162, Singer 1995: 94, Freud 1992: 476–477). In other words, those living with the history of colonization always pay more attention to the trends and stimuli of the exterior and the other than to what comes from their own interior. However, the other that one's self is gazing at, or the *object*, is not always the whole.

In a colonial situation, the colonial subjects, who could imitate and consume the information, images, knowledge and sounds only in ambiguity, with inaccuracy, in delay, in fragments, in superficiality, and in discontinuity, could not be free from anxiety and feelings of deficiency given that what they had access to was not the sound whole. Such deficient and ambiguous modernity can itself become a source of its own mystification, easily acquiring the status of a fetish. Fetishistic modernity brings about an excessive development of the visual among the colonial and directs voyeurism and scopophilia as ways towards visual pleasure, as Mulvey (1989) noted. For colonial Koreans, pleasure has two trajectories crossing at one point, the subjectivity. One trajectory goes towards orgasmic pleasure that one gets by letting sexual desires go off after making one's bodily senses highly sensitised. This is why hedonism and eroticism were always at stake whenever one raised the harms of Americanism in relation to the modernity of colonial Korea.

When the colonized body is put under surveillance, it becomes sensitive to and frustrated by exterior stimuli while its internal tensions wait for a let-out in the form of an aggressive attitude, or ferocity. According to Fanon's clinical analysis, this aggressiveness, which resides on the skin, leads to fits of hysterical sensitivity, but may be temporarily soothed with eroticism (Fanon 1963: 50–58). Koreans of that time were deprived of the chances to release their energy through bodily labour, and thus, needed to compensate their internalized sensitivity and ferocity, even momentarily, by bodily pleasures. It was then the Hollywood movies and jazz tunes of the 1920s and 1930s, full of images of pleasures such as love, love affairs and bourgeois consumption, that provided a moment for the repressed colonial body to seize and justify the pleasure of eroticism in the name of modernity and liberation. In other words, the eroticism in colonial Korea can be interpreted as a juxtaposition of American modernity over Korea's colonial situation.

The other trajectory goes towards the pleasure of making a distinction achieved through a fantasy that embodiment of modernity guarantees superiority over other fellow subjects or even over the colonizers of the same skin colour. Because this form of narcissism demands continual fulfilment of desires, it arouses boundless desires and consumption towards the latest, the original and the most genuine 'westernness'. Having disposed of a stable and centred self-ego, the depersonalized body is reconstituted as a plastic that can transform into any type of materiality in reaction to exterior fashions and stimuli (Bordo 1998). This desire for self-transformation is nothing but a schizophrenic subjectivity entrapped in a fantasy of body show-off. As Fanon aptly pointed out, one who imitates the body techniques of the master does so not like a habit but in an unconfident way, for they come from implicit knowledge: he cannot develop a normal bodily schema. Instead, it is often the case that he denounces his own body according to the gaze of a third person (Fanon 1967: 110–111). Body transformation, therefore, is another outlet for denouncing one's own indeterminate body. At the same time, such mimicry of the other can only be schizophrenic because it always ends up being a partial and incomplete representation of the other, only to remind oneself of what is not of him. Then, formation of self-identity through identifying oneself with the other is trapped in a restless oscillation. The subjectivity thus formed carries the pair of narcissism and paranoia (Bhabha 1994).

It is difficult to demonstrate the Americanized modernity that was inscribed on the body of colonized Koreans during the Japanese rule with lucid evidence and facts. It is because it was imprinted as a modern *habitus*, as an ambiguous, invisible and collective orientation, and also as a desire to be compensated for collective trauma. This is why Koreans felt closer to American culture than to the traditional culture right after the Liberation (1945) and why this was regarded as an 'odd phenomenon' (Lim 1984: 23). Moreover, in spite of such a phenomenon, this is also why little attention has been paid to the Americanization of the Korean society and the meaning of the American presence in Korea since then (while a nationalistic reading of history has underestimated foreign influence in an effort to do away with colonial views): this is also another 'odd phenomenon' (Paik 1985: 248–252). In this context, we need to render a new focus on those instances that are undetectable when discussions about Korean modernization during the Japanese Occupation are confined to the institutional dimension of colonization and early de-colonization – the instances where modernity was conceived, experienced and embodied onto the mind and body of individuals. The modernization of the individual as such was different from the institutional and public modernization in terms of logic, orientation and values. With a close look at such instances, we may grasp the conjuncture of Americanization and colonial modernity in the realm of individual/body and make it rise to the surface of history.

Notes

1 This article is a collection of traces of Americanisms that appeared in magazines and newspapers published in Korea in the 1920s and 1930s. The publishing business in the colonial time lingered due to a small market and poor investment in the country. Except for two larger newspapers, *Dong-A Ilbo* and *Chosun Ilbo*, and one contemporary affairs magazine, *Kaebyug*, most of the printed media did not survive beyond their first issue or first year. A few exceptions were popular magazines such as *Pyolgeongon*, *Yosong* and *Shinyosong* that lasted for a while. Such popular magazines had articles such as personal autobiographical stories, gossips, essays, critiques, and reports on new fashions and thoughts, written mostly by young intellectuals and journalists of the time. This article approaches the reality of Americanisms of that time through such magazine and newspaper articles.

2 Jung In-Ig's article was entitled 'Addiction to Americanism'. He expressed his worry that Americanism was definitely prevalent in directing how two sexes relate each other, even though there were two major tendencies in Korea at that time, Americanism and Russianism. Russianism in this case referred to the tide of socialism among some intellectuals.

3 Discussions and debates on modernity range from those about new human relations and organizing principles emerging from the eighteenth-century enlightenment and industrialization, to those from post-structuralist and post-modernist critiques. This paper does not intend to add any more to these familiar discussions. Rather than taking modernity as a discourse of knowledge, I focus on the 'modernness' that non-western peoples and colonized subjects under the nineteenth-century imperialism perceived and admired. Modernity as such was an ambiguous, fragmented and sensitized perception. For example, if one indicator of modernity, individualism, meant freedom from the tradition and if free love was tantamount to practising modernness for the youth of colonized society, colonial modernity is better described as free-love-ism perceived, realized and expressed by those who did, than defined by individualism.

4 An incident of two journalists of *Kaebyog* in 1921 symbolizes how modernity was becoming daily values in that period. The two forgot to bring their invitation tickets to a school literary event and asked the ticket examiner to pass them in for reporting. However, only the one wearing the western suit was allowed in while the other (the author of the article) was turned down because he was wearing *hanbok*, traditional clothing (Chunpa 1921).

5 In those years, wearing short-cut hair was highly symbolic. In Confucian norms, every part of one's body comes from his parents and ancestors and cannot be subject to voluntary change. At the same time, loyalty to the king and devotion to parents were the most important criteria for an individual's quality and characteristic. Because parents and king formed an identical supreme, short-cut hair meant what it sounded; severance with the tradition and immoral betrayal towards parents and king. This context attaches a significant meaning to the individual act of cutting hair short as the first ritual of modernizing oneself. In other words, a short haircut was as much an embodiment of foreign values in denouncing tradition as a sort of self-destruction by accepting the social stigma of immorality. The self-destructive aspect strongly demanded a deserving

compensation for the person, who turned to representing his new identity by more signs of modernity.

6 From a Confucian ethics that all parts of a body do not belong to its owner because they are inherited from one's parents, the real owner of them.

7 Even though they served in cafes, many of them had been regarded as modernized new women. For example, they were often enlisted in the rolls of famous alumni of middle schools. Those figures were usually chosen by magazines that put a high news value on new modernized women. Nowadays, working in the amusement industry, including as a cafe waitress, is considered to be unrespectful.

8 Sun Woo Chon made an analysis of household income distribution in Kyongsong in 1921, from the governmental statistics of 'Household School Fee Rating System' (household school fee was a tax added to either land and/or house tax, to fund public schools). Sun classified those with a yearly income higher than 1000 won as the middle and upper classes, and divided household income groups into the top, upper, middle and lower groups. According to this classification for the total 38,978 households in the city, the top income group consisted of 0.49% (192 households), the upper, 1.99% (775) and the middle, 8.31% (3,239). Or, the middle and upper class were only 10.79% of the total city population (Sun 1922: 45–55). As the monthly income of newspaper contributor-writers and school teachers ranged from 50 to 60 won and was considered to be just about enough for living costs of the time, a yearly income of 1000 won should have guaranteed middle-class consumption for modernity commodities.

9 The capitalized English pronoun 'It' came from the film *It* (1927) starring Clara Bow and designated 'sexual charm'. In an article introducing fashionable expressions of the time, a women's magazine, *Shinyosong*, explained; 'Now that Koreans have come out of a long tradition, they began to call sexual charm or sometimes *decadent* women of the street as 'It' (*Shinyosong* 1931). People began to call new modern experiences like love relations, sex and other private senses, 'It' for they were tabooed from being mentioned under the shadow of tradition. This was a part of a more general pattern of the time in which a representation of modernity, such as free love, created cracks in the traditional norms, in this case, under the protection of an unfamiliar foreign expression in the form of a pronoun.

10 Understanding modernism as a mechanism and urbanism as a product of Americanism was also a way of criticizing pleasure consumerism. Many socialists of the time held a critical view towards America as a civilization in relation to their stance against capitalism (Im 1930).

11 The number of American-run schools in Korea in 1933 was 217, and which had 775 classes and 26,000 registered pupils. Christian schools, the founders of which were mostly Americans, numbered some 230 and educated some 40,000 pupils. Their education facilities saw no match in quality except public schools established by the colonial regime. Protestant Christians were as many as 300,000 and the hospitals run by them treated altogether as many as one million leprous patients free of charge. Moreover, they set up institutions leading petroleum, mining and electricity industries as well as welfare services and youth programmes. Therefore, there were many in Korea at that time who pointed out that pro-American sentiment was growing strong because of such social works by American churches in Korea (*Samchonri* 1933).

12 In 1912 and 1913, soon after the Japanese Occupation, the official newspaper of the colonial government, *Maeil Shinbo*, ran an editorial criticizing the Koreans who went to Christian churches, foreign missionaries and mission schools and heartlessly abandoned their own culture and tradition in order to realize their dream of becoming westerners, as well as strongly protesting against the American missionary congregations for how they exerted influence over Koreans. In other words, the colonial government wanted to advocate that even Christianity should be *Japanized* in colonial Korea, doing away with its original ideas and values. *Maeil Shinbo* ran five editorials from 4 to 8 March 1913 on 'Christian Mission Schools' and also, in the editorial of 5 September 1912, it condemned 'Christian Believers'.

13 This citation is from a pamphlet of 41 pages, which was written in English and published by the Government-General of Chosun in 1924.

14 Hwang Aster, Hwang Marry, Park Aster, Kim Melitha, and Kim Maria all studied in the US and later became key figures in the education field, such as a professor in Ehwa Women's College and an education supervisor.

15 Like other public events in western style, new-style marriage ceremonies in the church used many English terms instead of Korean ones, such as bride, bridegroom, veil and wedding ring as well as frock coat, morning coat, collar, and neck-tie. It was often said that the only Korean words used were the names of the bride and bridegroom. Sometimes, even those names were called Maria, Yoseb (Joseph), Yohan (John), Ro-s (Rose) or Heren (Helen). Such marriage style and language, it was observed, started from 1919, as new a import from America (*Pyolgeongon* 1926 November: 79; 1926 December).

16 Tokyo and Osaka were the forefront bases of Japan's Americanism in the 1920s. As Japan also pursued its own Americanism through consumption of American movies, fashions and jazz (Yoshimi 2000: 202–209), it is not so different from other Asian countries in cultivating Americanism. However, if one ignores the particular historical situation and context of the place where Americanism took place and just considers the question of consumption, one may fall into the fallacy of over-generalizing Americanism as a global, universal phenomenon around the 1920s.

17 Baeguja Dance Company was composed of 20 dancers who were all young girls. Baeguja herself was a topical dancer in the later period of the 1920s, by her popular dances that were different in style from Choi Seng-Hee's, safely the top star dances in Korea during the occupation period. Bae was known as a former member of Tengatsu Kasuyuki's dance company of Japan, and to have performed with the company in various countries of the West. In 1929, she set up a dance institute in Korea. The November performance in 1929 was her second one in the country with her newly trained students (*Samchonri* 1929).

18 Almost daily or in a special series in newspapers was the news from Hollywood, such as its new movies, popularity rating of movie stars, their goings-on and new fashions as well as the news of new movies in Tokyo and Kyongsong. For example, *Dong-A Ilbo* introduced to its readers cinema-related facilities in Hollywood in six daily articles from 11 to 17 November 1925, with the title 'Cinema City Hollywood', and later the same year, reported the recent life of Charlie Chaplin, in four articles from 26 to 29 November.

19 The author was the enlightenment novelist Shim Hoon and the American movie he criticized here was 'Wings' (1927) starring Clara Bow (*Chosun Ilbo* 17 November 1928).

20 *Munhwasanghwal*, or cultural lifestyle meant a civilized lifestyle, which was nothing other than a westernized and modernized one (*Pyolgeongon* 1929: 106).

21 Yom Sang-Sub (1897–1963) was one of the prominent novelists in the history of modern literary Korea. He had worked for a couple of newspapers during the colonial period. He had advocated the newly emerging middle class's conservative attitude to the world and emphasized the realization of individual self and personality through his works.

22 Kim Dong-In (1900–1951) was also one of famous novelists in the history of Korean modern literature. He organized and published the first Korean literary coterie magazine *The Creation, Changjo* in 1919 and had written novels mainly attached to Naturalism and Romanticism.

23 A special collection of articles appeared in the popular magazine, *Pyolgeongon*'s December issue in 1927, entitled 'Full Review of Modern Girls and Modern Boys'. One author recorded, 'since half a year ago, we can easily hear of "Modern Girls" in Seoul' (Park 1927b: 4 November). There was also a newspaper article commenting 'these days (in *Kyongsong*) words like *Mobo* and *Moge* have become fashionable, while *Mobos* in Tokyo were . . .' (*Maeil Shinbo* 24 December 1927).

24 Most of the words in fashion in the early 1930s were French or German or English ones, and those referring to women were mostly foreign expressions for sexy, seductive style women. What was then comparable to a *Madonna* was a *portable* from portable gramophone, but denoting 'an easy-going woman friend suitable as a promenade partner', and the French word *coquettish* was used for a 'sensual and coquettish woman'. *Vamp* from *vampire* was for actresses in a treacherous woman's role in plays or movies. The French word *grue* was another name for Korea's modern girls of the time, once defined as a 'woman standing on the street with one leg folding over the other like a crane, looking for erotic places' (*Shinyosong* April 1933: 76–77; *Pyolgeongon* 1930b: 87; *Shinyosong*, November 1932: 69; *Shinyosong*, June 1931c: 66–67).

25 Kim Ki-Jin (1903–1985) is a central protagonist initiating the organization of KAPF, the Korea Artista Proleta Federatio (1925–1935) and contributed to the socialist movement in colonial Korea.

26 A socialist poet, Park Pal-Yang (1905–1946), who frequented cafes with his literary friends always wearing a worn-down Russian rubashka jacket, once scorned that even though the modern city of Kyongsong exhausted people's senses with its sensual and momentary intoxications, it would be too cruel to modern petty bourgeois men if the city had not had such sensual comforts of modern lifestyle (Park 1927a: 116).

References

Ahn, Sokyong 안석영 (1932) 'Sky blue: while listening to a song of Miss K who is getting closer to her grave' 스카이불유-분묘로 가는 K양의 노래를 듣고 , *The Nyuin* 女人 1(June): 81–82.

Avison, O. R. (1921) 'The influence of Christianity in Korea since its introduction', *Chosun* 朝鮮 (June) 77: 22–27.

Barthes, R. (1981) 'The face of Garbo' (Translated by A. Lavers), *Mythologies*, New York: Hill & Wang, 56–57.

Benjamin, W (1969) 'On some motifs on Baudelaire'. In H. Arendt (ed.) *Illuminations* (Translated by H. Zohn), New York: Schoken Books, 155–200.

Bhabha, H. (1994) 'Of mimicry and man: the ambivalence of colonial discourse'. In H. Bhabha *The Location of Culture*, London: Routledge, 85–92.

Bordo, S. (1998) 'Material girl: the effacement of postmodern culture'. In D. Welton (ed.) *Body and Flesh: A Philosophical Reader*, London: Routledge, 85–92.

Butler, J (1998) 'Foucault and paradox of bodily inscription'. In D. Welton (ed.) *Body and Flesh: A Philosophical Reader*, London: Routledge, 307–313.

Charney, L (1995) 'In a moment: film and the philosophy of modernity'. In L. Charney and V. R. Schwartz, (eds) *Cinema and the Invention of Modern Life*, Berkeley: University of California Press, 279–294.

Cho, Yongman, Song, Minho and Park, Byungchae 조용만.송민호.박병채 (1969) *New Culture Movement under Japanese Occupation* 일제하의 신문화운동 , Seoul: Minjunsokwan 민중서관 .

Choi, Haksong 최학송 (1927) 'A symbol of decadence' 데카단의 상징, *Pyolgeongon* 별건곤 10: 118–120, Seoul.

Choi, Seungil 최승일 (1929) 'The great city Kyongsong panorama' 대경성 파노라마 , *Chosun Literary* 조선문예 1(1): 85–87, Seoul.

Chong, Jinsok 정진석 (ed.) (1998) *The Collection of Censored Newspaper Articles Under Japanese Occupation* 일제시대 민족지 압수기사 모음 , Seoul: LG Press Foundation LG 상남언론재단 .

Chung, Inik 정인익 (1930) 'Addiction to Americanism' 아메리카니즘 중독 , *Pyolgeongon* 별건곤 5(7): 73–75, Seoul.

Chunpa 春波 (1921) 'The Western suit is allowed while those who wear traditional clothing are kicked out' 洋服者는 들이고 韓服者는 내몰아, *Kaebyok*, 개벽 No. 17, November: 83–84

Choo, Ilsoo 주일수 (1929) 'Review on Kyongsong of High Speed from Morning through Late Night' 고속도 대경성 레뷰-아침부터 밤중까지 , *Chosun Literary* 조선문예 1(1): 88–91, Seoul.

Donald, J. (1995) 'The city, the cinema: modern spaces'. In C. Jenks (ed.) *Visual Culture*, London: Routledge, 77–95.

Fanon, F. (1963) *The Wretched of the Earth* (Translated by C. Farrington), New York: Grove Press.

Fanon, F. (1967) *Black Skin, White Masks*, New York Grove Press.

Freud, G. (1992) *The Introduction of Psychiatry* (Translated by Lee Kyu–hwan), Seoul: Yookmoon.

Higashi, Sumiko (1978) *Virgins, Vamps, and Flappers: The American Silent Movie Heroine, Monographs in Women's Studies*, Montreal Canada, Eden Press.

Huh, Heon 허헌 (1929) 'A travel essay: crossing over the Pacific Ocean toward America, the country of gold' – 세계일주기행-태평양의 노도차고 황금의 *나라 미국으로* , *Samchonri* 삼천리 , 1 (June): 6–9, Kyongsong.

Hwang, Sindok 황신덕 (1937) 'Historical review on women's movement of Korea 조선부인운동의 사적 고찰 , *Hakhae* 학해 Seoul: Hakhae 학해사 .

Hwang, Sungmo 황성모 (1984) 'Continuity and discontinuity of Korean culture: 1910–1960' 한국문화의 연속성과 단절성, *Social History of Korea* 한국사회사론, Seoul: Simsoldang 심설당, 50–88.

Im, Insaeng 임인생 (1930) 'Modernism' 모더니즘, *Pyolgeongon* 별건곤 January.

Kim, Kijin 김기진 (1925a) 'The middle school student, intelligentsia from local province' 향당 의 지식계급 중학생, *Kaebyog* 개벽 58: 22–23, Seoul.

Kim, Kijin 김기진 (1925b) 'Difference between new women and old styled women' 구식여 자와 다른 점, *Shinyosong* 신여성 3(6): 38–40, Kyongsong.

Kim, Yunsik 김윤식 (1989) *Study on Yom Sangsup* 염상섭연구, Seoul: Seoul National University Press. 서울대학교출판부.

Kim, Jinsong 김진송 (1999) *Permit Dance Hall in Seoul* 서울에 딴스홀을 허하라, Seoul: Hyunsilmunhwayonku 현실문화연구, 57–61.

Kwanaksanin, 冠岳山人 (1933) 'Textbook for modern courtesy' 모던 修身 敎科書, *Kumkang* 金剛 1: 30–32, Kyongsong.

Lee, Soekoo 이서구 (1929) 'Pleasure and sentiments of Kyongsong: jazz' 서울맛 서울 정조-경성의 짜즈, *Pyolgeongon* 별건곤 4 (December): 32–36, Seoul.

Lee, Sunhee (1934) 'A woman of tearoom' 茶黨여인, *Pyolgeongon* 별건곤 8(3): 34–36, Seoul.

Lee, Hyunbae 이현배 (1937) 'The reason why Korea has no beauty' 조선에 미인없는 원인은 무엇, *Yosong* 여성 2(6): 70–71, Seoul.

Lim, Heesup 임희섭 (1984) *Social Transformation and Cultural Change in Korea* 한국 의 사회변동과 문화변동, Seoul: Hyunamsa 현암사.

Moriya, Sakau (1924) 'Development of chosen and necessity of spiritual enlightenment', *Government-General of Chosen*, September, Pamphlet.

Mulvey, L. (1989) 'Visual pleasure and narrative cinema'. In L. Mulvey (ed.) *Visual and Other Pleasures*, Bloomington, Indiana University Press, pp. 14–26.

Naw (1898) 'The Foreigner' *The Korean Repository*, June, 207–211.

Oh, Sokchon 오석천 (1931) 'Farce on modernism' 모더니즘 戲論, *New People* 新民 67: 29–32.

Oh, Songchol 오성철 (2000) *The Formation of Elementary Education of Colonial Korea* 식민지초등교육의 형성, Seoul: Kyoyukkwahaksa 교육과학사.

Paikaksanin 백악산인 (1941) 'Harms from American movies' 미국영화의 해독, *Samchonri* 삼천리 13(6): 193–195. Kyongsong.

Paik, Nakchung 백낙청 (1985) 'Meaning of America in Korea' 한국에 있어서 미국 의 의미. In Paik Nakchung *National Literature and World Literature* II, 민족문학 과 세계문학 II, Seoul: Changjakkwabipyung sa 창작과비평사.

Park, Palyang 박팔양 (1927a) 'Brief comment on modern boy' 모던보이 寸感, *Pyolgeongon* 별건곤 10: 116. Kyongsong.

Park, Yonghee 박영희 (1927b) 'Characteristics of so-called modern boy and modern girl in bourgeois society' 유산자사회의 소위 '근대녀'근대남'의 특징, *Pyolgeongon* 별건곤 10: 114–116. Kyongsong.

Park, Nochun 박노춘 (1939) 'Cinema & student girls' 영화와 여학생, *Cinema/Theatre* 영화연극 1: 38–41, Kyongsong.

Park, Seyoung 박세영 (1934) 'Toward a city' 도시를 향하여, *Figure* 形象 1: 41, Kyongsong: Shinheungmunhwasa 신흥문화사.

Payongsaeng 파영생 (1929) 'Screen of consolation' 스크린의 위안, *Pyolgeongon* 별건곤 4 (September): 39–40, Seoul.

Pyolgeongon (1926) November: 79; December.

Pyolgeongon (1927) December, 2(10): 117–118.

Pyolgeongon (1928) February, 11: 104–105.

Pyolgeongon (1929) September: 106–113.

Pyolgeongon (1930a) March, 5(3): 74–77.

Pyolgeongon (1930b) June, 5(5): 108–111.

Pukyodonggok, 北旅東谷 (1922) 'On our cultural movement through critic of Eastern and Western Culture' 동서의 문화를 비판하여 우리의 문화운동을 논함, *Kaebyog* 개벽 29, Seoul.

Rimyunja, 履面子 (1926) 'On the trail of modern woman, short-haired beauty of reputation' 경성명물녀-단발랑미행기, *Pyolgeongon* 별건곤 1(2), Seoul.

Samchonri (1929) September: 43–45.

Samchonri (1933) September: 22–25.

Shin Bomsoon 신범순 (1998) 'A little feast in streets of a city: an approach to 'decadence' in 1930s' 1930 도시거리의 작은 축제–1930 년대 데카당스에 관한 접 근, in Shin Bomsoon *Decadence and 'subject petit a' in Modern Poems of Korea* 한국 현대시의 퇴폐와 작은 주체, Seoul: Shinkumuhhwasa 신구문화사, 13–31.

Shindonga (1931) November: 102–103

Shinsegi (1939) September, 1(7): 24.

Shinyosong (1925) June–July, 3(6): 38–40.

Shinyosong (1931a) October, 5(9): 90.

Shinyosong (1931b) May, 5(4): 52.

Shinyosong (1931c) June, 5(5): 66–67.

Shinyosong (1932) November, 6(11): 69.

Shinyosong (1933a) October, 7(10): 119.

Shinyosong (1933b) April 7(4): 76–77.

Singer, B (1995) 'Modernity, hyperstimulus and the rise of popular sensationalism'. In L. Charney *et al.* (eds) *Cinema and the Invention of Modern Life*, Berkeley: University of California Press, 72–99.

Sun, Woochon 선우전 (1922) 'A study on the livelihood of Chosun populace (1)' *Kaebyog* 개벽 3(2): 45–55, Kyongsong.

Thompson, J. B (1995) 'Tradition and self in a mediated world'. In P. Heelas *et al.* (eds) *Detraditionalization*, Cambridge: Blackwell, 89–108.

Turim, Maureen (1994) 'Seduction and elegance: the new woman of fashion in silent cinema'. In S. Benstock and S. Ferriss (eds) *On Fashion*, New Brunswick, NJ: Rutgers University Press, 140–158.

Yesool (1934) December: 58

Yosong (1938) March, 3(3): 30–35.

Yoo, Sunyoung 유선영 (1997) 'Cultural identity of the yellow colony: Americanized modernity' 황색식민지의 문화정체성 아메리카나이즈드 모더니티, *Media & Society* 언론과사회 18: 81–122. Seoul: Nanam 나남.

Yoshimi, Shunya 吉見俊哉 (2000) 'Consuming "America": from symbol to system'. In Chua Beng-Huat (ed.) *Consumption in Asia: Lifestyles and Identities*, London & New York: Routledge, 202–224.

You, Kwangyol 유광열 (1927) 'Commentaries on modern girl & modern boy' 모던걸 모던보이 대평론, *Pyolgeongon* 별건곤 10: 112–113, Seoul.

Yun, Jihoon 윤지훈 (1931) 'Ten commandments for modern women', *Shinyosong* 신여성 5(4): 70–73, Seoul.

Yun, Songsang 윤성상 (1937) 'Modern women in fashion' 유행에 나타난 현대여성, *Yosong* 여성 2(1): 48–49, Seoul.

Chapter 11

'America' as desire and violence

Americanization in postwar Japan and Asia during the Cold War

Shunya Yoshimi
(Translated by David Buist)

The self as 'America' in East Asia

What has 'America' meant in everyday terms for the people of East Asia since the end of the Second World War? What indeed does it continue to mean for us in the present day? Would it not be possible to review the relationship with America, built up especially during the period of the Cold War, from a comprehensive regional perspective, taking into account the level of people's everyday consciousness and culture besides military and politico-economic aspects? At least as concerns such countries as Japan, South Korea, Taiwan, the Philippines, Vietnam and Indonesia, 'America' has had a uniquely strong and significant presence, which it has not had in quite the same way in any other region, whether South Asia, West Asia, Europe or South America. Most of these countries of the Pacific Rim were once under either temporary or long-term Japanese military occupation. They have since been incorporated into the American sphere of influence as bases for the activity of the American military and multinational corporations. As seen from the perspective of American Cold-War strategy, there can be no doubt that the Pacific Rim area, extending from Japan to Indonesia, formed a continuous space for the establishment of hegemony in Asia. Looking at the everyday consciousness and cultural practices among the people living in this region, does one find a similarly distinctive presence of 'America'? Is there also a spatial continuity whereby the cultural responses to 'America' are similar throughout the region?

Despite the evident importance of research on such a wide-ranging and complex phenomenon, hardly any attempt has been made until very recently to study the significance of 'America' in a region-wide context from the perspective of everyday consciousness and culture while also considering political and military issues. Some work has recently begun on international political relations and strategies involving America and the East Asian region as a whole. However, such work remains largely restricted to politics in the narrow sense. Very little has yet been done in order to analyse international political relations in the broader sense of the politics of everyday culture. For example, no concerted international comparative research has yet been undertaken on the influence of American military bases on urban musical culture and sexuality in Japan, South Korea, Taiwan and the Philippines, despite the fact that this issue has been proposed as an interesting research topic by a number of commentators. Whenever the influence of postwar American culture in Asia has been adopted as a research topic, it has almost always been confined within the national perspective of a single country.

To illustrate my point, let us consider a three-volume publication in dictionary form published in Japan at the beginning of the 1980s with the title 'American Culture'. This was a very valuable attempt to examine from various perspectives how 'America' had penetrated into Japanese culture and customs since the end of the Second World War. It divides the postwar era until the 1970s into three periods. The first period, from 1945 to 1960, is called the 'Period of Love/Hate towards America'. This was an age in which the wartime feeling of unease towards 'America' turned into yearning, and people lived their daily lives according the American model, even while sympathizing politically with the anti-base protests. The cultural products and fashions cited by this book as characteristic of this period are such things as 'chewing gum', 'English conversation', 'Readers' Digest', 'Jazz', 'Blondie', 'Pro Wrestling', 'Westerns', 'Disney' and 'Popeye', all of which carry a heavy scent of 'Americanism'. The second period, the 1960s, is called the 'Period of American Penetration'. Against the backdrop of rapid economic growth during this period, American lifestyle penetrated deeply into the lives of average Japanese. The items selected for special attention at this stage are 'Coca-Cola', 'home drama', 'supermarket', 'kitchen revolution', 'mini-skirt', 'jeans', 'folk song', and 'hippie', amongst others. The things considered in the third stage, the 1970s, such as 'outdoor life', 'diet', 'sneakers', and the TV 'ratings battle', indicate that 'America' had ceased so much to be an object of desire, and had instead become a source of information about the latest world trends (Ishikawa *et al.* 1981). In this series, the postwar phenomenon of 'Americanism' in Japan was seen not just as the result of American military and political imposition, but as a process of deep structural change involving the emotions and desires of Japanese people. 'America' provided a convincing answer to the void left in the collective consciousness by war defeat. During the course of postwar history, Japanese people reconstructed their own sense of national identity through the medium of desire and antipathy towards 'America'.

Whilst recognizing the importance of this work, I wish to point out two limitations in its approach. First, it focuses too narrowly on the principal theme of culture and customs. For instance, one could have included among the items for analysis such things as the 'emperor', 'MacArthur', 'censorship', 'military bases', 'violence', or 'Okinawa'. However, none of these is included. The concept of 'culture' is depoliticized and treated as something entirely separate from political or military matters. It is emphasized that 'America' became a symbol of wealth and freedom onto which Japanese people themselves pinned their hopes. Placing the issues of unequal power relations and domination outside the sphere of analysis obscures the ideological and political processes that operate precisely by projecting 'America' as an object of desire. For example, postwar musical culture developed through the employment of Japanese musicians on American bases, and was decisively influenced by contact with American military personnel. The book reviewed here fails to give adequate attention to this. Its account of the development of postwar music focuses instead on the enthusiastic reception given to leading American Jazzmen by Japanese fans, and how this led eventually to the establishment of jazz in Japanese musical culture. The happenings in and around the American bases are left in parentheses, and the focus is instead on American culture in the wider world outside the perimeter fence.

The second limitation of this attempt at cultural history is that it confines its account to the Japanese mainland, whereas a full analysis of the phenomena concerned must necessarily look beyond to the contemporaneous situation in Okinawa, and even further afield, such as Korea, Taiwan, and the Philippines. For instance, the musical culture developed on the American bases during the occupation, like Okinawan music in a later period, was influenced in no small degree by contemporaneous Philippine bands. One could also consider cultural relations between Japan and the Philippines up to the 1950s from the perspective of personnel interchange within the military base network in the region, which had an effect on the development of music and sexuality during that period. There is also a need to examine how, in Korea and Taiwan, 'America' was incorporated into peoples' consciousness just as the previously dominant presence of 'Japan' was being negated. Another important theme for consideration is the cultural history relating to the role of 'America' in East Asia during the Korean and Vietnamese wars. The various forms of social consciousness and cultural consumption that have arisen in Southeast Asia following Japan's economic expansion into that region, including the so-called phenomenon of 'Japanization', must also be considered in the context of their continuity with postwar 'Americanization'. Such a wide-ranging domain of research comes into view as soon as one links the issue of 'America' in postwar Japan with the issue of 'America' in East Asia during the Cold War.

This kind of approach relates to the field of post-colonial studies (which has seen rapid recent growth in the East Asian region). The postwar dominance of America in East Asia is, in a certain sense, a reconstruction of the Japanese imperial order that existed until the end of the war. In accordance with the China-containment policy first set out by George F. Kennan, Japan's industrial power was linked to the natural resources and markets of Southeast Asia. Meanwhile, Korea, Taiwan and Okinawa were to act as military buffers for the co-prosperity sphere thus formed. Within such a global strategy, the decolonization movements in the various Asian regions were ultimately subverted into the Cold War order and became part of the structure of American hegemony. There has recently been much re-examination of the continuity of colonial consciousness and practice in the areas once under Japanese colonization. This includes a growing body of work on mass culture, media, urban culture and intellectual practice in Okinawa, Korea, Taiwan, Manchuria and Micronesia. It is essential that the mediating role of 'America' be considered in these investigations of the further postwar development of colonial consciousness and practice in Asia under the Cold War order. As has been stressed by Kuan Hsing Chen, analysis of the Cold War order and Americanism must be pursued in relation to the horizon of contemporary decolonization (Chen 2002: 77–83).

America prohibits – military occupation and the censorship system

Let us first consider how Japan's defeat in 1945 and subsequent occupation by US forces influenced the development of postwar mass culture in that country. According to one perspective, it would seem that the cultural policies pursued mainly by the American Civil Information and Education Bureau (CIE) during the occupation had the effect of spreading Americanism from its earlier prewar base among the urban middle classes to the nation as a whole. Indeed, only one month after Japan's unconditional surrender on 15 August 1945, an English conversation guide book (called *Nichibei Eikaiwa Techou* – 'Japanese–American English Conversation Booklet') became a bestseller with over four million copies in circulation. In 1947, NHK began broadcasting a radio programme (called *Amerika Tayori*– 'Letter from America') simply consisting of current affairs reports from Washington. This too gained great popularity. In 1949, the morning edition of the Asahi Newspaper began carrying the comic strip 'Blondie', which provided a comical illustration of the American lifestyle and prosperity. This continued to enjoy wide popularity right up to its replacement in 1951 with 'Sazae-san'. Although the scenes portrayed in 'Blondie' did not directly show such things as electric appliances and automobiles, the postwar Japanese who had already acquired the desire for 'American prosperity' read into the vague designs of the cartoons the symbols of such prosperity (Iwamoto 1997: 155–166, 1998: 147–158). In 1950, the Asahi Newspaper sponsored an 'American Exposition' on the outskirts of Osaka, which proved to be far more popular than had been expected. Large crowds came to see the exhibits, which included a 'White House hall' recounting American history from the Mayflower to Roosevelt, a main exhibition hall with displays of American prosperity, a television hall, and panoramas providing a virtual scenic tour of America with pictures of New York skyscrapers, the statue of liberty, the newly developed West, and the Golden Gate Bridge. Thus, speaking in general terms, it was certainly not the case that the explosion of mass desire towards 'America' was simply a result of brute force by the military occupation or the civil policies it promulgated.

However, the complexity of the postwar Japanese encounter with 'America' cannot be understood simply as an extension of the already existing prewar trend towards 'Americanization'. Needless to say, throughout the occupation, Japan was in no position to determine its own future without negotiating with an overwhelmingly powerful 'other'. This was true of all the spheres of life, from economics and politics to culture and lifestyle. As demonstrated by John Dower, American domination was not entirely one-way, and did not always have the effect intended. Nevertheless, as far as concerns the experience of those directly involved, 'America' presented itself as an overwhelming source of authority, against which it was very difficult to mount any challenge. 'America' was more than just an image of new lifestyles and culture. It was an ever-present force intervening in people's daily lives, whose word could not be challenged. It was a directly present 'other' with which people had to deal on an everyday basis. These direct effects of the American occupation can be considered in two categories: effects consciously pursued as a part of occupation policy, and effects that arose unconsciously through the interaction of occupier and occupied. The principal element in the former category of conscious effects was, of course, the system of censorship, and the various accompanying cultural policies that were pursued. These related mainly to the mass media, including cinema, broadcasting, newspapers and publishing, all of which were powerful forces in the culture of America itself.

Censorship during the occupation has already been quite extensively studied by historical researchers in the fields of journalism, cinema, and literature. Such research has focused mainly on the censorship activities of the Civil Censorship Detachment (CCD), which was an organization within the Counter Intelligence Section (CIS) of the American Pacific Army. As indicated by Ariyama Teruo, the censorship activities of this detachment began originally as part of American military strategy in territories re-conquered from the Japanese military, such as the Philippines. It was conducted mainly from the perspective of military intelligence, and was therefore somewhat at odds with the policies pursued in the occupation of the Japanese mainland (which was planned mostly under the auspices of the State Department). Initially the strategy of the allied powers had been to proceed towards a land invasion of Japan following the conquest of the Philippines and Okinawa. According to this plan, the CCD's role was to be a military one, collecting information on resistance to the invading forces. Therefore, its focus was on 'censorship' of the communications media, such as telegraph and telephone. It had not been organized with the intention of dealing with newspapers, broadcasting, magazines, and other mass media. However, in the event, the occupation of Japan began without a land invasion of the mainland. In the absence of any other suitable organization to fulfil the role, responsibility for censorship of the mass media fell into the hands of the CCD. It thus came to exert an influence far out of proportion to its organizational status. In the early stages of the occupation, the CCD's censorship activities were extremely wide-ranging, covering the various forms of mass media (films, radio, newspapers and magazines), as well as textbooks and books in general, the theatre, letters, telegrams, and telephone (Ariyama 1996: 41–61).

A remarkable feature of the CCD's organizational expansion was that it came to employ large numbers of Japanese personnel. Despite its extremely wide remit, it lacked sufficient numbers of suitably qualified American staff to carry out its duties. It was therefore forced to rely on Japanese personnel in order to accomplish its mission. According to Yamamoto Taketoshi, most of the lower ranking censors who dealt directly with representatives of the media were Japanese. Japanese also fulfilled the role of translating newspaper and magazine articles into English for inspection by American officers. As the media subject to censorship expanded, the proportion of Japanese employees grew steadily larger. What had initially been recognized only as an emergency measure eventually became standard practice. By 1947, there were more than 8000 Japanese conducting censorship activities for the CCD (Yamamoto 1996: 298–299). This number is remarkable when compared to any of the other organizational divisions of the occupation. Although this cannot be conclusively verified, Matsuura Souzou surmises that not a few of these Japanese employees had previously worked as censors in the disbanded wartime Interior Ministry (Matsuura 1969: 50). Matsuura refers here to an episode recorded in the diary of Mark Gain while he was staying in the town of Sakata. According to this, it appears that many of the people who lost their jobs as a result of the disbanding of the Special Police Force (*Tokko Keisatsu*) were re-employed as 'liaison officers' between the Japanese and the American military. Three out of the six *Tokko Keisatsu* officers in Sakata were re-employed as such 'liaison officers' (Gain 1998).

No documents have survived clearly showing the subsequent careers of those who had worked for the disbanded wartime Cabinet Information Bureau or the Interior Ministry Public Order Bureau. However, there can be no doubt that the occupation forces faced a serious shortage of personnel with sufficient command of the Japanese language, and resorted to the employment of whatever Japanese personnel they could find to carry out the work of censorship. According to Monica Braw, in 1946, the number of people employed by the CCD had grown to 8743, of whom as many as 8084 were Japanese or Korean. Most of these had been recruited from within Japan. These new staff members were provided with basic training in censorship, but 'the training program was not very thorough, consisting of only one hour a day for six days'. In the event, each censor carried out his task individually, following the guidelines set out in 'various textbooks, catalogs, and lists of commands'. These documents were frequently amended and supplemented. As a result, acts of censorship were often very arbitrary (Braw 1988: 84–89). Furthermore, as clearly stated by Brigadier Thorpe of the CIS (of which the CCD was a subdivision), the CCD and CIS to a considerable extent inherited the role of the wartime Cabinet Information Bureau. This was done in the name of 're-educating' the Japanese people. In fact, irrespective of their very different ideological stances, the work of the CCD had much in common with that of the disbanded Information Bureau and the Interior Ministry Public Order Bureau.

In addition, the organizational structure of the Cabinet Information Bureau did not simply disappear with its formal abolition. Many of its activities were continued within the government in organizations with new names. For instance, according to Kawashima Takane, in November 1945, just before being disbanded, the Information Bureau set up a new Public Opinion Survey Section. This was moved to the Interior Ministry Regional Bureau when the abolition of the Information Bureau was decided in December. In January 1946, it was moved to the Cabinet Office as the Public Opinion Research Unit. At the time of its establishment, two thirds of the staff of this new section were former personnel of the Information Bureau. In the process of being moved from the Information Bureau to the Interior Ministry and then to Cabinet Office, its size grew considerably to a total of 32 personnel. It inherited some the duties of the old Information Bureau, including soliciting opinions at public gatherings, analysis of newspapers and publications, and public opinion surveys. Similar moves to secure organizational continuity were made in the Interior Ministry Public Order Bureau. Although the Special Police Force was officially abolished and its members banned from holding public office, attempts continued to establish an organization for collecting information relating to the maintenance of public order. In December 1945, security sections were set up in the head offices of prefectures, and a Public Safety Section was established in the Interior Ministry Public Order Bureau. These eventually developed into public security police forces established in police stations throughout the country. Thus, in some parts of the Cabinet Information Bureau and the Interior Ministry Public Order Bureau, 'a skilful attempt at postwar organizational survival was mounted, effectively closing the gap between the Japanese government's aim of sabotaging the process of democratization in order to achieve an 'orderly surrender', and GHQ's goal of an 'orderly occupation' (Kawashima 1995: 54–62).

The far-reaching censorship operation carried out by the occupation forces exposed a fundamental contradiction of the whole occupation system: it attempted to impose 'democracy' using almost identical techniques to the wartime system of thought control. While emphasizing the importance of freedom of expression in all the media, General MacArthur imposed a severe regime of censorship extending to the furthest corners of cultural and expressive activity. What is more, one of the explicit prohibitions of this system was to forbid any public recognition that censorship was taking place. Publishers were ordered to remove from their publications all indications that they had been subject to censorship. No articles about censorship personnel or the censorship process were allowed to be published. Indeed, reference in the media to the presence of the 'occupation army' itself was suppressed. The media were required to make as if the occupiers were no longer present in the country. Hirano Kyouko mentions an interesting anecdote recounted by the film historian Joseph L. Anderson, who spent his youth in occupied Japan while his father was working there. When he saw the film *Children of the Honey Nest* by the director Shimizu Hiroshi, Anderson was surprised at the earnest effort to 'expunge any trace of the presence of the occupying military . . . At that time [during the occupation] large railroad stations were crowded with occupation army soldiers. Nevertheless, in the railroad scene in the film, there was not the slightest sign of any soldiers. The RTO (military Railroad Transportation Office) signs seen all over the place at the time were not shown in the film' (Hirano 1998: 87–88). Thus, the fact of censorship itself was censored, and an 'Orwellian' (Dower 1999) discursive space was created within the postwar Japanese media, as a result of the occupiers' suppression of their own presence.

Another aspect of the occupation's censorship policy was its inconsistency, even arbitrariness. Until it was disbanded in 1949, the function of the CCD remained consistent throughout the occupation period. However, the content of its censorship criteria was in a state of constant flux depending on the situation of the moment. There was a general rightward drift from an earlier focus on the exclusion of militarist discourse, to a later concern with the suppression of leftist discourse. This entailed a complete change in what was censored and what was forbidden. In the absence of any consistency of content, it is doubtful whether censorship actually achieved any consistent ideological effect. Nevertheless, precisely as a result of this inconsistency, media producers came ultimately to exercise a certain degree of 'self-constraint' or 'self-censorship', since they had no idea what kind of expressions were liable to fall foul of the censors. In the words of John Dower, this was

> a system of secret censorship and thought control that operated under the name of 'free expression' – indeed, waved this banner from the rooftops – and yet drastically curbed any criticism of General MacArthur, SCAP authorities, the entire huge army of occupation, occupation policy in general, the United States and other victorious Allied powers, the prosecution's case as well as the verdicts in the war-crimes tribunals, and the emperor's personal war responsibility once the victors pragmatically decided that he had none.

Thus, instead of bringing liberation, as it claimed to be doing, America ('the land of freedom') provided Japan with further 'lessons about acquiescing to overweening power and conforming to a dictated consensus concerning permissible behavior' (Dower 1999: 439).

America seduces – the army of occupation in the urban space of Tokyo

During the occupation, 'America' did not, however, remain simply an external presence in the postwar culture of Japan, a proscribing and controlling 'other'. Despite the frantic attempt by the censors to conceal its presence from film and print, the army of occupation was itself very much a part of the mass-cultural scenery of postwar Japan. When one considers this other unconscious level, 'America' appears not so much as a 'prohibiting' presence, but as a 'seducing' presence in the everyday consciousness of the times. As an illustration of this, let us consider the link between American military bases and postwar popular music. Many young Japanese singers suddenly found employment entertaining American soldiers on the bases and in recreation facilities, where life went on largely in isolation from the surrounding society and working conditions were relatively good. There were many young popular singers who began their singing careers entertaining American troops. Ito Yukari began singing on American bases from her father's back at the age of six. Eri Chiemi also began singing to American soldiers while she was still in the fourth grade of primary school. Matsuo Kazuko took the stage at Kita Fuji Base at the age of 15. Meanwhile, Mori Mitsuko was making a living touring bases singing the jazz she had learnt. Several hundred musicians used to gather daily at the northern Marunouchi exit of Tokyo Station, where they were 'auctioned off' as band players before the American military trucks. From this developed the postwar system of talent recruitment by brokers, which later dominated mass entertainment in the age of television (Kuwabara 1981: 48–54). Numerous powerful cultural influences – jazz, fashion, sexual culture – spread out from the American bases and took root very soon after the beginning of the occupation.

This type of cultural influence spreading from American military bases is far from being a phenomenon restricted to Japan. It can found throughout the Asian area where American bases were established during the Cold War, including Japan, Okinawa, South Korea, and the Philippines. Kang Nobuko provides a vivid account of how rock music developed in Korea through links with the American bases set up after the Korean War. In this is recounted the story of Shin Jung Hyo, later to become known as the 'godfather' of Korean Rock. As a youth, having lost both his parents in the Korean War, he listened to the American forces radio station (AFKN) on an American military communications wireless he had bought. He then learnt to play the guitar by himself, and wondered the streets of Seoul playing it. After studying with a guitar teacher, he then became a musician in the American Eighth Army's show. In Korea during the 1950s, 'playing at the Eighth Army's show was the only way of making a living as a musician. At their height, there were as many as 264 stages where such shows were held, and those appearing in the Eighth Army's show could earn a guaranteed yearly income of $1,200,000, at a time when the total value of South Korea's yearly exports was no more than about $1,000,000' (Kang 1998: 149–154). One can see clear parallels here with the process that produced Japan's postwar singers and entertainers during the occupation. Likewise, in the 1960s, Okinawan Rock music was born as a result of interaction with the American bases during the Vietnam War.

However, the linkage between popular culture and the American bases in postwar Japan cannot be reduced to a simple relation of influence. Although it was through a direct connection with the occupying power that many aspects of popular culture regained their footing after the war, popular culture itself adopted a rhetoric of negating this connection. In other words, as the occupation drew to its close, Japanese popular culture attempted to forget its links with the occupier. Underground images associated with the occupation, such as the 'black market' and 'pan-pan girl', became increasingly marginalized. As the violent America of the occupation was obscured, 'America' instead became a model of lifestyle consumption. The link between these two aspects of 'America' is a highly convoluted one. I would like to explore this here on the level of urban space. There were very different ways of relating to 'America'. At one extreme there was a direct encounter with the violence of the bases in such places as Okinawa, Tachikawa, and Yokosuka. At the other extreme there was a hidden relation with 'America' in the centres of consumer culture, like Roppongi, Harajuku and Ginza. Although the latter are today not typically thought of in connection with the American military, the reason why they became such special places for Japanese youth after the war cannot be understood unless one takes into account their relation to the American military facilities that once existed within them.

Before the war, Roppongi had been a 'soldiers' town'. Numerous military facilities were concentrated there, including those of the territorial army, Konoe Shidan and Kempeitai. The area was devastated by air raids during the war, and the remaining facilities were inherited by the American military after the surrender. Military headquarters, barracks, and housing for military personnel came to be located there. Since these facilities were not returned to Japan until around 1960, Roppongi remained in the shadow of the American military throughout the 1950s. Unlike Yokota, Tachikawa and Yokosuka, however, there was no airbase or any very large number of troops housed there. There was, therefore, little sense of 'America as the source of violence'. It was here that the young people who came to be known as the *Roppongi-zoku* ('Roppongi tribe') came to gather. TV personnel, rockabilly singers and their associates began gathering in Roppongi, and thus it gradually developed its present image as a place for fashionable and colonial-style night life.

Likewise, the development of Harajuku into a 'young people's town' cannot be explained without reference to Washington Heights, which was once a residential facility for American officers. The construction of the Heights began immediately after the end of the war. It was fully equipped with a hospital, school, fire station, church, department store, theatre, tennis courts, and golf course. It thus became a symbol of 'American affluence' appearing suddenly like a mirage amid the surrounding burnt out ruins, barracks and black markets. In the 1950s, shops targeted at officers' families, such as Kiddy Land and Oriental Bazaar, came to line the streets in the area. It was amid this new townscape that Central Apartments was built. This was known as the most luxurious residence in Tokyo, and came to be a symbol of the district. In the words of Kobayashi Nobuhiko, who lived in Harajuku in the early 1960s, those who lived in this building mostly worked for trading companies or in other occupations connected with the American military – 'people who were above the clouds to "ordinary Japs"' (Kobayashi 1984). At that time, Harajuku still had the sense of being 'off limits' as a place reserved largely for the American military. Eventually the American military presence contracted, and the Apartments' residents changed from people connected with the American military to people working in fashion-leading professions, such as cameramen, designers, and copy writers.

As for the Ginza district, meanwhile, 'the main buildings were requisitioned for use as occupation army facilities . . . stars and stripes were seen fluttering all over the area, giving an impression just like that of an American town. There was great activity around the PX set up in Matsuya Department Store, since it was frequented by officers and troops from all branches of the Allied forces. War orphans thronged around the entrance selling things or offering their services as shoeshine boys.' (Harada 1994: 176) Even before the war, Ginza had already provided a flavour of Americanism, but during the occupation it was 'Americanised' in the more direct sense of becoming a foreign concession. Even the streets acquired names invoking a colonial landscape, such as 'New Broadway', 'X Avenue', 'Embassy Street', 'Saint Peters Street', 'Poker Street', and 'Hold Up Avenue'. This naming of streets in the American style was not restricted to Ginza. The occupation forces called the main roads radiating outwards from the imperial palace 'avenues', while the roads running in irregular circles around the centre were called 'streets'. The 'avenues' were labelled A to Z in a clockwise order, and about 60 different names were given respectively to the streets. The official names were used mostly for functional purposes, but in Ginza, where the central command headquarters was located, it seems that some of the names were also popularly used.

References to the Ginza district in popular songs of the time give some indication of the heavy presence of the occupation army, combined with sexual images of the ruined and burnt out city. For example, in one hit song from 1946, entitled *Tokyo no Hana Uri Musume* ('Tokyo Flower Girl'), the contemporary landscape of Ginza was represented as follows: 'Jazz is playing, the lamplight shadow of the hall/Buy my flowers, buy my flowers/An American soldier in a chic jumper/A sweet fragrance chases after his shadow'. Given the already mentioned strict censorship by CCD, it is somewhat strange that such a song should have been heard, drawing so direct a connection between the Ginza and American soldiers. Later songs show a growing tendency to a more oblique mode of reference. The 1949 hit, *Ginza Kankan Musume* ('Ginza Kankan Girl') has the following words: 'That girl is cute, that kankan girl/Wearing a red blouse and sandals/Waiting for someone on a street corner of Ginza/Looking at the time, grinning nervously/This is the Ginza kankan girl'. In 1951, a song called *Tokyo Shoeshine Boy* came out with these words: 'That girl in red shoes/Today still walking the Ginza/With presents of chocolate/Chewing gum and castella'.

A discontinuity of historical memory now obscures this process whereby places once occupied by American military facilities became centres for the consumer culture of youth. So far I have mentioned the appearance of the 'Roppongi tribe' beginning in the late 1950s, and the curious changes in the lyrics of songs about Ginza. In 1957, the 'Western Carnival' was held at the Nissei Theatre in Ginza, starring Yamashita Keijiro, Hirao Masaaki, and Mickey Curtis. This achieved enormous popularity and, along with the influence of Elvis Presley, spurred the fashion for rockabilly. However, by this time the connection with the occupation forces was no longer obvious. Whereas Japanese musicians in the 1940s had polished their skills playing for American soldiers, the musical trends of the 1960s onwards were supported by an audience of Japanese youth. Already at the beginning of the 1950s, as the American military pulled out of the Japanese mainland, the Japanese jazz bands that had played for the troops were leaving the bases and starting to play for Japanese singers instead. At that time, there were as many as 150 jazz bands in Tokyo, and more than 3000 band players (Komota 1970: 143). Eri Chiemi and Yukimura Izumi both debuted with jazz numbers. Together with Misora Hibari these two singers attained stardom as part of the same trend. It was against this background that the TV entertainment world took shape by the beginning of the 1960s. By this time, the link with 'America' had become indirect.

America fragments – between 'desire' and 'oblivion'

However, let us not forget that the period from the late 1950s to the 1960s, which saw the development of the youth culture described above, was also a period of intense struggle over the military bases. This began in 1953 with protests against the American army test-firing range in Ishikawa. The first anti-base movement in Tokyo began in the same year with a large rally of residents opposed to the Setagaya Base. In 1955, protest erupted over the enlargement of the American military airbase in Tachikawa (in the outskirts of Tokyo). In October of the following year, farmers, trade unionists and students staging a sit-in to prevent surveying of the land clashed with police, giving rise to about 1000 casualties. At roughly the same time, large protests were taking place in Okinawa in response to repeated rapes and killings of Okinawan women by American soldiers and against an occupation policy generally at odds with residents' wishes.

Thus, in the Japan of the late 1950s, two 'Americas' had begun to appear. On the one hand, there was an 'America' that was an object of consumption, whether through material goods or as media images. This 'America' had gradually lost its associations with military violence, despite having been born on the American bases and in the military recreation facilities. On the other hand, there was also an 'America' that was literally embodied in violence, and became the object of anti-base protest. These were nevertheless different aspects of the same 'America'. A relation with American military bases lay behind the formation of the fashionable postwar images of all the places mentioned above. To this extent, it is possible to trace a continuous cultural geo-political horizon between Ginza, Roppongi and Harajuku, on the one hand, and Yokosuka and Okinawa, on the other. Nevertheless, at about the time Japan entered the era of high economic growth in the late 1950s, a fault line opened up between the two 'Americas'. The 'America' embodied in such places as Ginza, Roppongi and Harajuku, and the 'America' of Yokosuka and Okinawa came to seem like entirely different things. The former 'America' came to be understood as if it had existed from the very beginning entirely on the level of consumer culture. In the case of the latter 'America', the cultural dimension was erased from the picture, and overwhelming attention was drawn to the problems of pollution, violence and prostitution emanating from the bases.

This division between the two 'Americas' was reflected in, and reinforced by, the division in roles between the Japanese mainland and Okinawa. One remarkable expression of this is seen in the currency exchange rate policy. In the mainland, the rate was fixed at one dollar to 360 yen, in accordance with the 'Dodge Line'. Thus, the yen was deliberately undervalued in order to give a boost to economic recovery by encouraging exports. In the case of Okinawa, however, America's main goal was not economic recovery, but to provide a stable environment for the construction of military bases. Local labour, construction companies and service industries were mobilized to construct the bases. The money thus earned was used to import goods and recycled into the local economy. In order to encourage imports, the exchange rate was set at 120 'B-yen' to the dollar. The extreme difference in exchange rate between the mainland and Okinawa lead to the development of very different economic structures. In the mainland, an export-led growth economy developed, while in Okinawa the economy became heavily dependent on the bases. These were two sides of the same coin. The policy adopted in Okinawa encouraged the development of a subordinate economic structure, with a very weak manufacturing sector and an inordinately large tertiary sector centred on import trading. In the mainland, export industries grew steadily, nurturing the formation of a mass consumer society (Makino 1996, Minamura 1995).

The separation of the mainland from Okinawa clearly reflected the great change in America's policy towards Asia that occurred around 1947. With the beginning of the Cold War, the focus shifted from the earlier goal of democratization and the decentralization of power, to a policy designed to make Japan into the leading member of the Western camp in Asia. This policy turnaround became definitive after the Chinese revolution. Japan would have been far less important to American policy if there was still a pro-American government in mainland China to act as a block against the southward spread of Soviet power. However, with the formation of a communist government in China, Japan ended up becoming the cornerstone in America's Asia policy. It became necessary to construct a military bulwark against communism in East Asia, and to stabilize the Japanese economy as the centre for economic growth in the region. In the absence of any immediate prospect for the expansion of economic relations between Japan and China, the idea of reviving the Japanese economy by linking it to the markets of Southeast Asia had already been proposed to the Truman administration by George F. Kennan. This was a plan for an 'East Asian Co-prosperity Sphere' under an American military aegis. However, this was not a sufficient condition to make Japan into the centre of an anticommunist economic sphere in Asia. It would also be necessary to reduce Japan's military burden in order to avoid any drag on the speed of its economic recovery. To solve this dilemma, the military burden was placed mainly on Okinawa, while the Japanese mainland was allowed to concentrate its energy on economic growth. General MacArthur was a particularly enthusiastic proponent of this strategy. By making Okinawa into a fortress, military stabilization in East Asia could be attained while the Japanese mainland was demilitarized.

The American strategy of dividing economic and military functions among the countries of East Asia can be discerned even more clearly when one considers the case of South Korea. Lee Jong Wong provides a very convincing account of how both Japan and Korea were drawn into a system of divided roles as a result of America's Asian policy in the 1950s. The Eisenhower administration sought a way of simultaneously both reducing government budget deficits and maintaining global military hegemony. This required a trade-off, which was achieved by a division of labour between Japan, on the one hand, and countries such as Korea, Taiwan, and the Philippines on the other. Thus, in the 1950s, 'while Asia policy in general became increasingly military centered, policy toward Japan turned in the direction of an economic emphasis. In parallel with this, policy toward "front-line countries", like South Korea, stressed even more the military aspect, thus restricting the potential for economic growth' (Lee 1996).

Of course, this system of a division of labour between economic and military roles was not followed consistently throughout the early Cold War period. In the early stages of the Eisenhower administration, Japan was expected to become not just an economic centre for East Asia, but also a military one. Lee reveals a 1954 memorandum of the American joint chiefs of staff in which it is stated that Japan's recovery of military strength was 'of fundamental importance to the construction of a position of strength against communism in the Far East'. Indeed, in 1953, against the background of a worsening situation in East Asia, the mainstream opinion in American military circles was in favour of a large-scale remilitarization of Japan. However, such plans for Japan to become a major military centre were blocked on one side by the growing anti-base peace movement in Japan, and on the another side by Asian countries fearing the revival of Japanese imperialism. In the event, the military element in Japan was peripheralized, and support was given to the concentration on economic growth. The military burden of defence against China and North Korea was shifted instead to South Korea and Taiwan. Thus, the United States gave its backing to the dictatorial regimes of Chiang Kai Shek and Syngman Rhee, whose authoritarian power enabled these countries to build armed forces far out of proportion to their economic strength.

In this way, from the mid-1950s onwards, the role of military defence against the socialist block in the Far East was assigned to South Korea and Taiwan – and Okinawa too – while mainland Japan took on the role of a centre for economic growth. The year 1955, of course, marked the beginning of the so-called '1955 system' in Japan. This year also saw the beginning of the period of postwar rapid economic growth, later symbolized by such events as the Crown Prince's wedding, the domestic appliance boom, the Tokyo Olympics, and the Osaka Exposition. In the context of the theme of this paper, one could say that the image of 'America' in Japan underwent a process of structural transformation and concealment after the mid-1950s. In other words, there was a shift from an Americanism modelled directly on America, to an Americanism more deeply embedded in a particularistic national consciousness and more focused on the images of consumer lifestyles.

From the end of the 1950s, American military facilities became almost invisible in the urban areas of the Japanese mainland. This was in stark contrast to the situation in Okinawa, where the worsening situation in Indochina was making the presence of the bases even more prominent. In 1953, there were 733 American military facilities located in Japan, covering a total land area of about 1000 square kilometres. These facilities were found in every region of the country, and included 44 air bases, 79 training ranges, 30 naval port facilities, 220 barracks, and 51 residential complexes. The American military presence was thus a fact of daily life clearly visible to anyone. However, this presence was gradually reduced during the course of the late 1950s and 1960s until, in 1968, there were only seven air bases, 16 training ranges, nine port facilities, four barracks, and 17 residential complexes. The number of troops also gradually decreased, from 260,000 in 1952, to 150,000 in 1955, then down to 77,000 in 1957, and 46,000 in 1960. The greatest reduction was in land forces, so that the emphasis of the American military presence shifted to the navy and airforce. By the end of the 1960s, there were only relatively few facilities left in the Tokyo area, including the bases at Yokota, Tachikawa, Yokosuka and Zama. The presence of American military personnel ceased to be a part of people's everyday lives. 'Base culture' became contained in a few centres well isolated from the surrounding society.

Thus it was that the image of 'America' in Japan came to be divorced from the experience and memory of a direct encounter with the bases and their associated violence, in contrast to the entirely different situation in other parts of East Asia, such as Okinawa, South Korea and Taiwan. 'America' was sanitized as an image consumed through the media, and thus spread its seductive power uniformly among the whole population. In the late 1940s and early 1950s, 'America' had held very different meanings for different groups of Japanese. For some people, 'America' was a 'liberator', while for others it was a 'conqueror'. 'America' was simultaneously an object of desire and a source of fear. It represented both wealth and decadence. There were many different 'Americas', depending on the variables of class, generation, gender, region, and individual circumstances. This was because America was no mere image but a reality encountered in everyday life. People's notions of 'America' were shaped by their direct experience of particular American soldiers, systems or changes.

However, from the late 1950s onwards, 'America the occupier' ceased to be part of most people's everyday experience. By becoming a problem confined to 'certain regions' (i.e. those still hosting bases), 'America' was distilled as a uniform image with even greater power than before to gain people's hearts. This can be illustrated by the depictions of America in advertising at the time. Whereas, until the early 1950s, the word 'America' was simply invoked as a *model* to be emulated, from the late 1950s, Japanese families – above all housewives – performing the 'American lifestyle' were presented as the *ideals* to be emulated. 'America' also came to be associated with the 'pop-culture' of Japanese youth. So long as 'America' was simply presented as the ideal, the meanings people attributed to it could be diverse. However, just as 'America' ceased to be a matter of direct and concrete daily experience, its image became inscribed in the identities of Japanese people. As 'America' became less direct, more mediated, and increasingly confined to images, it conversely became more interiorized and its effect on people's consciousness and identity became deeper.

'America' in South Korea, Taiwan, and the Philippines

What has 'America' meant to the people of other East Asian countries in the postwar era? In the case of South Korea during the Cold War, the position of 'America' in people's consciousness has been largely determined by the state of relations with North Korea. At the end of the Second World War, 'America' was welcomed with open arms as the liberator from hated Japanese colonial rule. At this stage, closeness to America was associated with opposition to Japan. However, this changed with the outbreak of the Korean War. With the emergence of the North/South division as an overwhelming fact of life, 'America' became associated in everyday consciousness more with 'anti-communism'. The emphasis of America's policy toward Asia shifted from democratization and the elimination of Japanese imperialism to the construction of an 'anti-communist' stronghold in Asia. Conservative political forces in Japan were revived as a mechanism towards this goal. South Korean identity came to focus on self-preservation from the threat posed by the divided self of the 'Northern enemy'. Thus, people's psychological dependency on 'America' deepened. In the words of Mung Bu Shuk, 'through the process of the Korean War, pro-Americanism and anti-communism were raised from the level of mere principals to the level of a "civil religion"'. Indeed, when protest erupted in 1982 against the Gwangju incident and the American military's backing of the authoritarian regime, followed by an arson attack on the American cultural centre in Pusan, all this was denounced as the work of North Korean spies (Mung 2001). Within a thought structure that equated 'anti-Americanism' with the North Korean insurgency, it was impossible even to conceptualize 'America' as an 'other'. At that time in South Korea, the mere act of questioning 'America' was seditious and beyond the pale of possibility. All events were interpreted according to a highly simplified code in which protection against the deadly contagion of communism was paramount.

This reception of 'America' in South Korea mediated by the menacing image of the enemy to the north underwent great change through the process of the democratization movement. Mung speaks of this as follows: 'The American government's implicit consent (even active support) for the military's bloody suppression of the Gwangju protests came as a profound shock to the South Korean people, and led to the revival of a critical perspective toward America which had disappeared during the long period since the Korean War in the 1950s.' Similarly, Kwang Hyok Bom tells us that South Korea in the 1980s was 'transformed into a major center of anti-Americanism' following the assassination of Park Chung Hee and the Gwangju protests. The policy of economic growth followed up to that time by the Park government was an expression of 'a collective desire to become a developed country and live prosperously like America', and was thus similar to the policy being pursued in Japan. However, in the 1980s, 'through the movement for democratization and unification, long entrenched taboos were broken, and previously unheard words, such as 'Yankee Go Home!' and 'American imperialism' became everyday currency. For the first time since the Korean War, the American embassy and other facilities became the target of occupation and siege. Ritual burnings of the stars and stripes became frequent. America came to be seen as an 'evil' standing in the way of South Korean independence, unity and peace' (Kwang 2001: 31). The old structure of thought, in which pro-Americanism was associated with modernization and anti-Americanism with the acceptance of communism, was replaced by a new structure linking pro-Americanism with dictatorship and disunity, and anti-Americanism with democracy and unification.

Despite this, as Mung astutely points out,

> our understanding of America has until now been focused on the America that gave its support to authoritarianism. Consciously or unconsciously, the 'desiring masses' have nevertheless internalized American values. In reality, both anti-Americanism and pro-Americanism have basically amounted to the same thing in South Korean society, in so far as they both reflect a dependency on America. Extreme yearning and extreme hatred both derive from a subordination of the self to the other. There can be no escape from 'America-centeredness' so long as we continue to think that all problems will be solved just by defeating America.
>
> (Mung 2001)

Mung stresses the need to re-examine the Gwangju incident, and all the other incidents of the Cold War in South Korea, as issues pertaining to the desires of South Korean people, rather than just seeing them in terms of a thought structure of 'America versus the South Korean masses'. The important point here is not so much to expose America's unjustified intervention in the incidents concerned, but rather to show how a colonial structure centred on America has become embedded in the desires of South Korean people. In fact, according to Mung, 'America' is now an even more gigantic presence in South Korean daily life than it was at the time of the Gwangju incident. Since the end of the Cold War, America has attained overwhelming world dominance, and was the only possible source of salvation for South Korea during its period of deep economic crisis.

The significance of 'America' in South Korea has been profoundly mediated by two historical facts: Japanese colonial domination and the division of the peninsula into two states. The desire and dependency towards 'America' in the consciousness of South Koreans moves in step with their complex feelings with respect to 'Japan' on the one hand, and the 'North' on the other. This is not all. Along the way to the realization of the dream of economic development and a consumer society, desire toward 'America' has become deeply entrenched. 'America' may not have come to structure self-consciousness in so direct a sense as it has in the case of Japan, but it has, nevertheless, found a way into South Korean everyday consciousness via the complex mediation of its relations with 'Japan' and the 'North'.

Some of the same complexity is found in the case of Taiwan, which also experienced a long period of Japanese colonial rule. The key factor in both Korea and Taiwan is the process whereby Japanese prewar colonial domination was replaced by postwar

American hegemony. In neither case was America the first external power to intervene. There had been a previous encounter with Japan as the 'Other'. America skilfully inherited this imperial relation between Japan and East Asia during the Cold War. To this extent, 'America' usurped Japan's role as the model of modernization in the region. 'America' provided the scenario for a new lifestyle through the medium of the English language, films, television, and advertising. In this sense, 'America' may have acted as the model of consumerist modernity for Japan, South Korea and Taiwan. However, let us consider exactly what kind of relations 'America' had with its former bases in Taiwan, its economic aid to the country, and to the Nationalist Party (KMT). Having previously been invaded by Holland and China, the island of Taiwan fell prey in the modern era to Japanese imperialism. It was then re-colonized by the KMT, and received military and economic aid from America as part of the Cold War policy of anti-communism. In the present day, however, Taiwan is in the process of becoming a 'semi-imperial' power expanding into overseas markets within its own minor sphere of influence. This expansion relies not on military force as a means to extract profits, but instead uses economic and political advantage to intervene indirectly in other countries, influencing their policies and manipulating their markets (Chen 1996: 167–169). Having itself been multiply subjected to domination, Taiwan has now attained a 'semi-imperial' status of its own, and subjects more peripheral areas to economic, political and cultural subordination. One might ask what role 'America' has played in this rise from colonial to 'semi-imperial' status.

It should at least be clear that any consideration of the issue of 'America' in countries such as South Korea and Taiwan must take into account the manner in which identities are formed in the context of the cultural geopolitics of East Asia, including the roles of Japan, North Korea and China. The Philippines, however, present a somewhat contrasting case where the issue of 'America' has been very direct and all-embracing. This is well illustrated in an ethnographic study by Fenella Cannell conducted in the Bicol district of south-east Luzon. This study examines how impoverished young people have internalized 'America' through an analysis of their daily conversations and various types of cultural performance, such as amateur singing contests and beauty pageants. The subjects of this study are poor young peasants, who have neither the opportunity to go and work in America nor to buy American goods. Cannell sees a connection between these people's desire to be 'beautiful', as expressed in the various cultural performances in which they participate, and the imitation of 'America' as an imagined 'other'. However, this 'imitation' goes beyond merely incorporating elements of American culture as a subsidiary part of their lives. The imitation of 'America' becomes a means of self-transformation for these impoverished Philippine youths. This cultural practice of self-transformation is now an integral part of the culture of the Bicol district.

The period of Spanish colonialism has left its mark on the urban landscapes of Bicol with its grandiose churches. However, in the everyday lives and consciousness of present day Filipinos, by far the greatest influence is that of an imagined 'America'. Throughout the Philippines, luxury goods, public buildings, the clothing and cuisine consumed in the cities, and films are all looked upon as 'American things', even if they were in fact produced in Asian countries. 'America' is imagined as the source of all power, wealth, cleanliness, beauty, joy and attractiveness. People in the Philippines conceive their own cultural identity always in relation to this imagined 'other'. Thus, Hollywood films are treated as high-class items, and are shown in the well air-conditioned cinemas on the main street of Naga, the central town of Bicol. Tagalog-language films are seen as inferior in comparison. However, even the latter are typically set in the capital Manila, which is most closely associated with the image of 'America'. Even in the rural villages, 'America' is placed at the pinnacle of the symbolic order and, overseas, the entire textual production of the Philippine cultural industry.

The 'American' facilities lining the main street in Naga are beyond the reach of the region's rural poor. When women from the villages go to the town with baskets of fish to sell, they illegally occupy space on the roof of the market place to carry out their trade. They barely even glance at the department stores, restaurants and fast-food joints on the main street. If they need to eat while in town, they will go to a small shop on a side street to buy food. The stores lining the main street belong to a completely different world to that of such rural women. Nevertheless, even for these impoverished people, the imagined exterior world of 'America' remains an indispensable path to empowerment. Even those who have no contact with American products in their daily lives will serve foreign canned goods on special occasions, such as festivals. Furthermore, going to work in America is seen as the only way for Philippine people to escape poverty. A person's fate is determined not by his/her relation to the country in which he/she lives, but in relation to an external place, America. Recently, it is true, increasing numbers of Filipinos have gone to work in Japan or the Middle East. Nonetheless, 'America' remains the supreme model of what a 'prosperous foreign country' is imagined to be (Cannell 1995: 224–228).

However, according to Cannell, when people in the Philippines imitate 'America', they are not simply expressing subordination to American culture. Rather, they are attempting to acquire the power of the imagined 'America' through a process of self-transformation. For example, when women in Bicol get drunk at neighbourhood wedding parties, they prefer to sing American pop songs, even if they are well versed in local songs and would never sing American songs when sober. Their spirits fortified by drunkenness, they adopt bold postures and become more self-aware, while singing carefully memorized English lyrics whose meaning they may not clearly understand (for example, the song may deal with unfamiliar scenes such as leaves falling in autumn). By displaying their ability to sing these songs belonging to the 'high culture', they symbolically take on something of the power of 'America'. Through such symbolic action, those unable to purchase American items of consumption gain a means of acquiring proximity to 'America'. Of course, the person singing, and those around her, know full well that she is neither an American, nor even a professional Philippine singer, but no more than a scruffily dressed village woman. The gap between reality and image is nonetheless overcome by the imagination. This imagination sometimes extends to caricature. Cannell mentions a woman she met whose nickname was 'wealthy Marie' because her house was reputed to be full of radios, refrigerators, and electric fans, which, 'just like an American', she would throw out as soon as they became only slightly old. This was despite the fact that she belonged to the poorest tribe in the village, and her house had an earthen floor and leaky roof. Likewise, holes in house walls caused by typhoon damage are sarcastically called 'air conditioners'. When feet get covered in mud as a result of labour in the paddy fields, this is referred to as 'my manicure'. When food served at a celebration in someone's house meets with approval, it is likened to the cuisine in an American restaurant.

This study of daily cultural practice in Bicol addresses issues that have always been at the centre of cultural studies, such as the struggle over hegemony and the dynamics of subjectivity. Cannell sees the reproduction of the 'self as America' in the Philippines not as a process of subordination to the American 'other', but rather as a matter relating to the empowerment of the disadvantaged within a structure of subordination, through a process of self-transformation by Filipinos themselves. However, this also shows the extent to which Filipinos' self-construction has been mediated by 'America'. As Arjun Appadurai states at the beginning of his now classic excursus on globalization, 'American popular music interpreted in Filipino style has even greater currency in the Philippines than do the original songs in the United States. What is more, it surpasses the United States in faithfulness to the original' (Appadurai 1996). Far more people in the Philippines can perform complete renditions of American songs than in the United States. Through this music, Filipinos sing nostalgically about a world that they have never lost. However, to repeat the main point once again, it is precisely such an identification with 'America' that provides the impoverished masses of the Philippines with one of their few means of gaining a form of cultural capital, be it only temporary and confined to the imagination.

This structuring of the Filipino identity through the medium of 'America' can be traced back to the time of mass emigration to the United States just after the First World War. This migration gained impetus thanks to the fact that the Philippines at the time was not regarded as a 'foreign country', whilst migration from Japan and China was being restricted under the policy of exclusion. In his autobiography entitled *The America of my Heart*, Carlos Bronsan provides eloquent testimony of how Filipinos internalized 'America' through the experience of many hardships in the period between the First World War and the Japanese occupation. Bronsan was born into a poor peasant family in the Ilocano region at the beginning of the twentieth century. This was precisely at the historical moment when the independence movement failed and the government fell into the hands of a privileged pro-American elite. At that time, 'the Philippines was being driven slowly but surely into economic collapse. . . . An Americanized younger generation had become completely incomprehensible to adults. Even in the countryside, where poor peasants toiled flat out for the landlords, young people were caught up in the trend and rebelled against tradition'. They took it upon themselves to learn English, and thought seriously about going to America. However, having gone to America in search of 'freedom', what they found there was blatant and violent racism, exploitation, corruption, and acts of horrendous barbarism the like of which they had never encountered in the Philippines. Faced with such a situation, Bronsan himself gradually became inured to violence and cruelty, 'confined in a corrupt corner of America seeing only violence and hatred'. Nevertheless, he did not completely lose his faith in 'America the land of freedom'. After a period of frequenting gambling dens, he finally discovered a way of regaining himself through writing. For a while, he worked as an editor of a newspaper for Filipino agricultural labourers. He rediscovered 'America' through literature. However full of corruption the real America, 'whether one is born here or a foreigner, whether one is educated or not, first and foremost we ourselves are America' (Bronsan 1984: 208–210). When the Philippines was invaded by the Japanese military, Filipinos in the United States volunteered in droves for the American army. Thus, it was precisely through an identification with 'America' that they acquired their sense of unity as compatriots and a collective desire for independence.

The Japanese occupation of the Philippines reinforced the convoluted path by which Filipinos came to acquire a national identity of their own mediated by the higher identity of 'America'. Having already absorbed the notion of 'America' as the 'land of freedom and civilization', Filipinos could only view the invading Japanese military as 'barbarians'. Tsuno Kaitaro's account of the Japanese occupation of the Philippines includes the following illustrative anecdote. Before the Japanese invasion, vaudeville had already become a highly popular form of mass entertainment in the Philippines. The performers of this genre were known by such names as 'the Filipino Fred Astair', 'the Filipino Clark Gable' and 'the Filipino Charlie Chaplin' on account of their apparently close resemblance to the originals. During the occupation, many cinemas were forced to close, and when they were later allowed to reopen, strict censorship prevented many films from being shown. To fill the gap caused by the lack of permitted films, cinemas put on stage shows performed by movie actors. These shows often featured skits ridiculing the Japanese occupiers. One such skit portrayed a Japanese soldier with numerous wrist watches attached to both arms frantically searching for more watches to confiscate (Tsuno 1999: 73–86). To the extent that watches were viewed as a symbol of modernity, the Japanese were seen as pillagers of the 'modernity' that already existed in the Philippines. Filipinos were under no illusions whatsoever about the 'empire' of the Far East. They saw the Japanese as barbarous, wicked and cheap. This further reinforced Filipinos' fantasies about 'America'. Ikehata Yukisuke describes the situation as follows:

> The greatest irony of the Japanese occupation of the Philippines was that it reinforced the dependency of Filipinos on America. This was entirely contrary to the Japanese invaders' pretext of liberating the Philippines from American colonial domination. The expectations and loyalty of Filipinos towards the United States grew even stronger during the period of Japanese occupation. They looked forward eagerly to reoccupation by America as a means of liberation from the cruel Japanese military. The pro-American sentiment built up among the people of the Philippines during the Japanese occupation cannot be overlooked when considering the deep sense of dependency on America that developed after the war in all fields of life, including politics, the economy and military. (Ikehata 1996: 18–19)

The obvious failure of the Japanese occupation of the Philippines demonstrates that classical methods of colonial domination are no match, either militarily or culturally, for the American mode of domination that incorporates democratic elements. To the extent that Filipinos had a special sense of dependency on 'America', this dependency had its origins in the peculiar characteristics of American colonial policy. It is true that America's colonization of the Philippines at the turn of the twentieth century had involved the thorough suppression of opposing forces and the imposition of a unitary government on the entire archipelago. However, as Benedict Anderson points out, there was little enthusiasm for the formation of a strong colonial administrative apparatus in the Wilsonian America of the early twentieth century. Through the enactment of a tariff law in 1909, the Philippines was drawn entirely into the sphere of the American consumer economy. A highly dependent industrial structure based on agricultural commodities such as sugar and coconuts was created. However, there was no strong presence of a colonial administration. Only a weak administrative organization linked to the power of local landowners (caciques) was formed (Anderson 1995: 10–13). American domination was largely limited to the military and economic realms. Mass emigration to the United States also prevented the emergence of any overt conflict between the colonial government and the independence movement. America's prewar domination of the Philippines, focusing on the acquisition of economic power and military bases rather than political and administrative colonization, provided a model for its postwar domination in Asia as a whole.

As I have attempted to show in the above discussion, there is more to the analysis of the role of 'America' in postwar Japanese mass culture than simply the dimension of cultural consumption. It is necessary to clarify the manifold ways in which 'America' has been consumed in other parts of Asia, and in the continuum of history since the prewar era. To the extent that Japanese people's desire towards 'America' has become sedimented in the unconscious and obscured by oblivion, the cultural geopolitics that made such an unconscious possible must be examined in its historical context. The resulting discontinuity is also the discontinuity that spatially divides Japan from Okinawa, South Korea and Taiwan, in the same way as the wartime and postwar eras have been divided temporally within Japan. The same temporal discontinuity was not experienced in places such as Okinawa, Korea and Taiwan, where the postwar military dictatorships, and the Korean and Vietnamese Wars created a sense of continuity with the wartime era. In light of this, the Japanese 'postwar' must be subject to ongoing questioning. In the Japanese mainland, since the 1950s, the consumption of Americanism has reached levels unprecedented anywhere else in the world. This differs from the Philippines, where American songs are sung more faithfully than in the United States, and differs also from Latin America, which has been exposed frequently to violent interventions from its high-handed northern neighbour. After the Second World War, America discovered in the former 'semi-imperial' power of Japan the conditions for becoming a subordinate mirror of itself. Japan, meanwhile, found the means to reconstruct its own identity by looking in the superior mirror of 'America'. It is therefore necessary to conduct further analysis on how the former regions of the Japanese empire accepted American hegemony after the war, and how they transformed their subject positions in that process.

References

Anderson, Benedict (1995) 'Cacique democracy in the Philippines: origins and dreams'. In Vincente L. Rafael (ed.) *Discrepant Histories*, Manila: Anvil Publishing, 10–13.

Appadurai, Arjun (1996) *Modernity at Large: Cultural Dimensions of Globalization*, University of Minnesota Press.

Ariyama, Teruo 有山輝雄 (1996) *Study of Media History During Occupation* 占領期メディア史研究 , Kashiwa Shobo 柏書房 .

Braw, Monica (1988) *Inspection: 1945–1949* 検閲 1945–1949, Jiji Tsushin Sha 時事通信社 .

Bronsan, Carlos (1984) *America in Our Hearts* 我が心のアメリカ , Imura Bunka Jigyo Sha 井村文化事業社 .

Cannell, Fenella (1995) 'The power of appearances: beauty, mimicry, and transformation in Bicol'. In Vincente L. Rafael (ed.) *Discrepant Histories*, Manila: Anvil Publishing, 224–228.

Chen, Kuan Hsing 陳光興 (1996) 'Eyes of the empire' 帝国の眼差し, *Thought 'Cultural Studies'* 思想「カルチュラル・スタディーズ」: 176–169.

Chen, Kuan Hsing (2002) 'Why is "great reconciliation" impossible? De-Cold War/decolonization, or modernity and its tears (Part I)', *Inter-Asian Cultural Studies* 3(1): 77–99.

Dower, John (1999) *Embracing Defeat*, W.W. Norton & Co.

Gain, Mark (1998) *Japanese Diary* ニッポン日記 , Chikuma Gakugei Bunko 筑摩書房 .

Harada, Hiroshi 原田弘 (1994) *Tokyo Under Occupation As Seen From MP Jeep* の ジープから見た占領下の東京 , Soshisha 草思社 .

Hirano, Kyouko 平野共余子 (1998) *Emperor and Kiss* 天皇と接吻 , Soushisha 草思社 .

Ikehata, Yukisuke 池端雪浦編 (ed.) (1996) *Philippine Under Japanese Occupation* 日本 占領下のフィリピン , Iwanami Shoten 岩波書店 .

Ishikawa Hiroyoshi, Fujitake Akira & Ono Kousei 石川弘義・藤竹暁・小野耕生 (eds) (1981) *American Culture* アメリカン・カルチャー 1–3, Sanseidou 三省堂 .

Iwamoto Shigeki 岩本茂樹 (1997) 'Blondie' ブロンディ , *Sociology Department Journal, Kansai College No. 78* 関西学院大学社会学部紀要 No. 78: 155–166.

Iwamoto Shigeki 岩本茂樹 (1998) 'Blondie' ブロンディ *Sociology Department Journal, Kansai College No. 79* 関西学院大学社会学部紀要 No. 79.

Kang, Nobuko 姜信子 (1998) *Japanese and Korean Musical Note* 日韓音楽ノート , Iwanami Shinsho 岩波新書 .

Kawashima, Takane 川島高峰 (1995) 'Investigation on post-war theories', *Study of Media History* メディア史研究 No. 2.

Kobayashi, Nobuhiko 小林信彦 (1984) *Personal Account of Tokyo's Prosperity* 私説東 京繁昌記 , Chuo Koron Sha 中央公論社 .

Komota, Nobuo 古茂田信男 (1970) *History of Japanese Pop Music* 日本流行歌史 , Shakai Shiso Sha 社会思想社 .

Kuwabara, Inetoshi 桑原稲敏 (1981) 'Occupying army and the arts' 進駐軍と戦後芸能 , *Art Review in Post-war Japan* 別冊新評戦後日本芸能史 , Shimpyosha, 新評社 .

Kwang, Hyok Bom 權赫範 (2001) 'Joining the world and knowing America' 世界化とアメリカ認識 , *Modern Thought 'Post-war East Asia and the Existence of America'* 現代 思想 「戦後東アジアとアメリカの存在」 , Seidosha, 青土社 : 30–43.

Lee, Jong Wong 李鍾元 (1996) *Cold War in East Asia and Japanese, Korean and American Relations* 東アジア冷戦と韓日米関係 , Tokyo Daigaku Shuppan Kai 東京大学出版会 .

Makino, Hirotaka 牧野浩隆 (1996) *Rethinking Okinawan Economy* 再考沖縄経済 , Okinawa Times Sha, 沖縄タイムス社 .

Matsuura, Souzou 松浦総三 (1969) *The Suppression of Speech During Occupation* 占領下の言論弾圧 , Gendai Janarizumu Shuppan Kai 現代ジャーナリズム出版会 .

Minamura, Takeichi 皆村武 (1995) *The Formation and Development of Post-war Japan* 戦後日本の形成と発展 , Nihon Keizai Hyoron Sha, 日本経済評論社 .

Mung, Bu Shuk 文富軾 (2001) '"Kwangju" 20 years later: the memories of history and men' 「光州」二〇年後：歴史の記憶と人間の記憶 , *Modern Thought 'Post-war East Asia and the Existence of America'* 現代思想 「戦後東アジアとアメリカの存在」 , Seidosha, 青土社 : 105–107.

Schaller, Michael (1985) *The American Occupation of Japan: The Origins of the Cold War in Asia*, Oxford University Press.

Tsuno, Kaitaro 津野海太郎 (1999) *Story, the Occupation of Japanese* 物語日本人の占 領 , Heibonsha 平凡社 .

Yamamoto, Taketoshi 山本武利 (1996) *Analysis of Media During Occupation* 占領期メ , Hosei Daigaku Shuppan Kyoku 法政大学出版局 .

Names

Kwang Hyok Bom 權赫範
Mung Bu Shuk 文富軾
Shin Jung Hyo 申重鉉

Chapter 12

Okinawa's 'postwar'

Some observations on the formation of American military bases in the aftermath of terrestrial warfare[1]

Toriyama Atsushi
(Translated by David Buist)

Introduction

Since 1995, the ongoing protestations emanating from Okinawa have served to remind Japanese society of the existence of the 'Okinawa Problem'. We must, however, ask ourselves what exactly this problem is. In the first five years following the beginning of the protests, a number of things have happened. First, it was announced that the American base at Futenma would be relocated to a new site within Okinawa Prefecture. A referendum was then held among the citizens of Nago (the site chosen for the relocation) in which the relocation plan was rejected by a bare majority, despite the efforts of the Japanese government. This was followed by the election of a new mayor of Nago, and also of a new governor of the Prefecture. Both the new mayor and the new governor accept the relocation programme. Thus, the relocation of Futenma base was 'decided'. In the process, Okinawan society became fractured along multiple lines of division, and the 'Okinawa Problem' appeared to have been reduced to an issue relating to Okinawa's ongoing struggle between 'ideals' and 'reality'.

In the resistance to this trend of events, this paper seeks to find ways of diffusing the explosive potential which the 'Okinawa Problem' must contain. My starting point is to seize the 'opportunity to begin re-imagining' through an account of 'how the present institutions of inequality and injustice came into being, and therefore, how we might be able to dismantle them' (Morris-Suzuki 2001: 91). To this end, I will attempt to weave together a number of threads relating to the historical period in which the framework of American bases in Okinawa took shape.

From terrestrial battlefield to 'Forgotten Island'

The 'snowy mountain' and the 'great road'

Okinawa came under American military occupation as the result of a land battle that began at the end of March 1945, and lasted for more than three months. Having pushed the Japanese army back to the southern tip of the Japanese mainland, the American military established bases on the island in preparation for its planned invasion of Japan proper. The inhabitants of Okinawa, now under occupation, were mostly confined in civilian concentration camps set up in the north of the main island (Hontou), leaving the American soldiers free reign over the abandoned villages and fields.

After his capture by the American military on the battlefield of southern Okinawa, Nakasone Seizen, who was then a teacher accompanying the 'Himeyuri Students Brigade', described the scene at the time of his transportation to a concentration camp in middle Okinawa as follows:

> On the way there, I saw for the first time the devastation of Shuri from the ruins of Naha. This really filled me with astonishment. It had become completely white, just like a snow-covered mountain. What was more, the hills had even been lowered. Wait! The very shape of the land had been altered. It was completely unrecognizable. Viewing that devastation, I had an acute sense of how tragic the battle for Okinawa had been. From there, a great road stretched out, and one could not see where it was going. Finally, I could see that the row of pine trees had withered, and realized that it was Futenma.
>
> (Arasaki 1982: 179)

The land blanketed white by the scattered dust of the coral rock; the very shape of the land altered by the ravages of war, and the American army's 'great road' whose destination one could not imagine – such scenes symbolized the transformation wrought on the island by the land battle and the construction of the bases. Amidst all this, the inhabitants confined in the camps began their postwar lives receiving rations from the American forces and carrying out collective labour under military supervision. The news of Japan's surrender came to them from the American military. On the evening of 10 August, from his bed in an American military hospital, Ikemiyagi Shuui heard the loud firing of guns and cheers of 'Jap surrender!', and saw the sky being lit up by tracer fire like fireworks. On that occasion, a certain deep sense of fear ran straight through the back of his mind: 'Are those shock troops? Are we finally to be killed by bullets from the Japanese army?' (Ikemiyagi 1970: 200–202).

In the process of setting up an administrative apparatus for the island's residents, the American military gathered together representatives from the concentration camps and held a meeting to establish the Okinawa Advisory Council, which surprisingly (but perhaps significantly) was held on 15 August. The declaration delivered at that meeting by the military government stated as follows: 'The prosecution of war necessitated the removal of most of the main island's land from agricultural production, and the relocation of most of the inhabitants to areas without residential facilities. These areas are too small for the number of people now living there. In the past they were sparsely populated, and the land is infertile. It is this situation which now presents the greatest problems for the military government and people' (Okinawaken Kyoiku Iinkai 1986: 13). This marked the starting point of Okinawa's very limited 'postwar' era – limited by the existence of military bases on its soil. Furthermore, this limitation was not removed by the surrender of Japan. Having found in Okinawa a place of strategic value, the Joint Chiefs of Staff began, in September of the same year, to consider officially the idea of making Okinawa into a permanent site for military bases. This became finalized as military policy on 23 October (Gabe 1996: 94–95). The Okinawa base plan formulated soon after Japan's surrender involved the continuous procurement of 11 airbases in total (among all branches of the armed forces). Therefore, even after people began returning to their homes from the camps in late October, land in and around military facilities was not released from occupation. The people from these areas, having lost the homes to which they should have returned, were forced to remain in crowded collective residential areas, waiting interminably for the release of their land (Toriyama 2001).

'Forgotten Island'

In January 1946, GHQ produced a 'Memorandum Concerning Governmental and Administrative Separation of Certain Outlaying Areas from Japan', in which Okinawa was clearly separated off from the occupation policies being pursued in the Japanese mainland. However, American policy in Okinawa remained undecided, due to the State Department's resistance to the military's plan and its insistence on returning Okinawa to a demilitarized Japan. As a result, the administration of the occupation in Okinawa, already suffering a shortage of personnel and funds, became confused, thus perpetuating the turmoil of Okinawan society. Despite the continued exclusion of the island's residents from large areas of land reserved for military use, the funding of the occupation forces in Okinawa was reduced by the US Congress. Temporary facilities built in order to economize funds were repeatedly ravaged by typhoons (Fisch 1988: 79–80). Among American soldiers, Okinawa came to be known as the 'Rock' ravaged by war, or as the 'Junk Yard' where disused military hardware was simply deposited (Miyagi 1982: 82). As the number of personnel dwindled, the efficiency of the military administration deteriorated. Daily life among the inhabitants thus continued to be chaotic, and recovery from the disaster of war was slow. The chronic shortage of goods was prolonged, due to the inadequate recovery of productive activity. Many residents resorted to stealing military goods, calling these the 'achievements of battle (*senka*)', and dismantled the scrap left on the battlefield for sale on the black-market or for smuggling. Popular jobs at the time were to work for the occupying military, such as drivers or mess-hall boys, but this was only because such occupations provided the greatest opportunity to obtain the 'achievements of battle', not because the conditions were good.

Later, a visiting American journalist called Okinawa the 'Forgotten Island' (Gibney 1949). This was a serious problem not only for the American soldiers stationed there, but also for the residents of the island living under occupation. They had been 'forgotten' by America. However, the difficulties suffered by the 'Forgotten Island' cannot be laid entirely at the feet of the American occupation. It must be borne in mind that the abandoned ruins of the land battle were the product of an all-out war between Japan and America. Furthermore, it was the Japanese Empire that had mobilized Okinawa for that war. At about this time, Okinawan newspapers carried editorials filled with a sense of despair, of which the following is an example:

> During the war Japan offered up Okinawa as its last and merciless sacrifice, but now it seems to have almost entirely lost any national feeling towards Okinawa. In parliamentary debate on the peace treaty Okinawa appears only by name. Those who have died fade further and further from memory by the day. For Okinawa in the present day, it is America by whom we cannot afford to be forgotten, rather than any of the other countries of the world with no connections to Okinawa. It

is America which now occupies Okinawa, and we will be in very severe difficulty unless we can gain the interest of the American people in Okinawa's salvation and recovery.

(*Okinawa Times*, 4 December 1949)

The gaze on Okinawa

How was 'Okinawa' viewed at the outset of postwar Japan? Having served as a Japanese soldier in the Battle of Okinawa, Furukawa Shigemi concludes his account of the war (published very soon after the war's end under the title *Okinawa no Saigo* [The Last Days of Okinawa]) with the following description of his evacuation from the island:

> The familiar Japanese ship stripped of all its guns, the Japanese crew. (Oh! To return to the motherland, the dear land of my parents.) . . . Farewell Okinawa. No-one uttered a word. Our hearts were rent by all the mixed emotions that pressed upon us, as we thought of the home country to which we would return and looked back over our time on that island we were about to leave. . . . Onwards and onwards towards Japan, that ship carrying so many feelings sped its way into the deep blue sea from where the islands could no longer be seen. Beyond the horizon where the white clouds gathered, there awaited Japan – the land of compatriots with whom we were to struggle together along the even longer road towards our ideals.
>
> (Furukawa 1947: 214)

Even for this survivor of the Battle of Okinawa, the 'home country to which we would return' and 'that island we were about to leave' were entirely separate places, and the 'compatriots with whom we were to struggle together' were the 'compatriots' of 'Japan'.

The fact that Okinawa had become a 'Forgotten Island' from the viewpoint of mainland Japan was a matter of great significance for American East Asia policy. In June 1947, General MacArthur made the following comment, in relation to the question of a peace treaty with Japan: 'The Okinawan people are not Japanese, and there does not seem to be any opposition by the Japanese government to America's occupation of Okinawa' (*Uruma Shimpo*, 4 July 1947). In September of the same year, GHQ received a 'message from the emperor' expressing the wish that the American military occupation of Okinawa be continued and proposing the 'fiction' of a loan spread out over several decades. Furthermore, MacArthur expounded his ideas on Okinawa to George Kennan, the Director of Policy Planning in the State Department, during the latter's visit to Tokyo at the end of February 1948. In this, MacArthur emphasized Okinawa's strategic importance, and its 'political' suitability as a military base. These were his words: 'The people were not Japanese, and had never been assimilated when they had come to the Japanese main islands. The Japanese looked down on them. . . . They were simple and good natured people, who would pick up a good deal of money and have a reasonably happy existence from an American base development in the Ryukyus' (Miyzato 1981: 222). Having already proposed the long-term occupation of Okinawa, and having taken note of the 'message from the Emperor', Kennan then prepared a report incorporating MacArthur's arguments urging the transformation of Okinawa into a permanent military base.

The construction of permanent bases and recovery

The sea of lights

Occupation policy changed abruptly following the State Department's adoption of the plan for long-term control of Okinawa. In October 1948, a plan for the construction of permanent bases received the approval of President Truman. This policy shift also marked the beginning of Okinawa's recovery from the destruction wrought by the land battle. In a document approved by the president in May 1949, it was stated as follows: 'The United States has determined that it is now in the United States' national interest to alleviate the burden now borne by those of the Ryukyu Islands south of latitude 29°N incident to their contribution to occupation costs, to the extent necessary to establish political and economic security' (Miyazato 1981: 211). In the fiscal year of 1950 (July 1949 to June 1950), economic aid for Ryukyu amounted to 49 million US dollars, which was double the amount allocated for the previous year. It was also the largest annual allocation ever made for this purpose in the entire 27-year history of American rule.

It was the policy pursued under Joseph R. Sheets, who became military governor in October 1949, that demonstrated most clearly to the people of Okinawa that the recovery effort had begun. The new governor made personal visits to the outlets where rationed goods were being sold, and inquired about the state of distribution. The supply of foodstuffs was immediately increased, and the governor returned to the retail outlets to view the results. Numerous measures were implemented to improve the lives of the inhabitants, including a moratorium on the levy of income tax in 1949, lowering the distribution price of foodstuffs, and abolition of the prohibition on building within one mile of military facilities. Along with these, the importation of goods from mainland Japan was begun and, at the end of 1949, the first bus truck for civilian use arrived at Naha port. In addition, the military government announced plans to reopen the old central district of Naha, which had been placed off limits as a place for the storage of American military material. Approval was also given for the construction of a 'business center' catering to American military personnel in the village of Goeku, close to Kadena Base, and a portion of the land reserved for the base was allowed to be used for this purpose.

What saved Okinawa from being the 'Forgotten Island' was America's East Asia strategy and the desire to maintain Okinawa as a permanent military base. As a matter of course, therefore, Okinawa's belated recovery began precisely at the same time as it was being converted into a fortress. In October 1949, a 58 million dollar budget for the construction of military bases in Okinawa was passed by the US Congress. Surveying in preparation for the building of housing, warehouses, power stations, port facilities and roads also got under way. In April of the following year, the first round of inter-national bidding for construction contracts was held, in which many Japanese mainland construction companies participated. Toubaru Kamerou, who was village chief of Ginowan at the time, wrote in his 'Diary' at the end of June 1949 as follows: 'When viewing the middle regions of the island, one has the sense more of a war not yet ended than of the aftermath of the wartime destruction. The prewar appearance of that area is nowhere to be seen' (Ginowanshi Kyoiku Iinkai 1997: 155). Those residents who had lived in the areas set aside for military use witnessed before their very eyes the onset of large-scale base construction, as if to remove all hope of their ever being able to return home.

The outbreak of the Korean War occurred just as Toubaru was penning these words about a 'war not yet ended'. On 27 June, the bombing corps stationed at Anderson Base in Guam was ordered to relocate immediately to Kadena with the aim of carrying out strikes on the Korean Peninsula. By the beginning of July, this relocation was almost complete. In a rush to meet the influx of reinforcements, runways were extended and repaired, night-time illumination was installed, hangars, arms dumps and oil storage facilities were built, and the temporary barracks were refurbished into more permanent housing (Okinawa Prefectual Archives: U90008134B).

The island that had experienced terrestrial warfare – especially the middle districts where military facilities were concentrated – was transformed into a giant fortress, without ever returning to its prewar appearance. This is illustrated by a verse published in a newspaper at the beginning of 1952:

> Stretching out into the evening mist
> a sea of shining lights
> just like the twilight of a foreign land
> In the darkness indeed is discerned
> the violent transformation of this isle
> in the middle district that has become a sea of lights[2]
> (*Ryukyu Shimpo*, 14 January 1952)

Residual sovereignty

In December 1950, the military government of Okinawa was reorganized as the 'United States Civil Administration of the Ryukyu Islands' (USCAR), and work went ahead on laying the foundations for long-term military occupation. In accordance with the terms of the peace treaty between the United States and Japan signed on 8 September 1951, Okinawa remained under American occupation. Article 3 of the treaty specified that Japan would give its consent to continued American control of Okinawa, pending approval of a trusteeship to be proposed to the United Nations. However, there was in reality no possibility that the US would propose a formal trusteeship to the UN. The continued occupation was therefore legitimized according to the strange logic of 'pending approval' of an impossible proposition.

In addition, the United States recognized Japan's 'residual sovereignty' with respect to Okinawa. Even within Okinawa, where there had initially been no clear movement on the question of sovereignty, an organized 'reversion movement *(fukki undou)*' demanding the restoration of Japanese rule had begun early in 1951. The recognition of 'residual sovereignty' gave some grounds for the faint hope that the occupation would end. However, the logic behind America's recognition of Japanese 'residual sovereignty' was neither a concession to the Okinawan people, nor to the Japanese government. This is clearly demonstrated by the argument used by John Foster Dulles, the Consultant to the Secretary, to persuade the military, which were demanding the implementation of trusteeship rule. Dulles stated as follows:

> If Japan renounces sovereignty in favor of no one, this would create a chaotic international situation, . . . It might then be claimed that sovereignty was vested

in the inhabitants, who could hereafter assert, perhaps with United Nations backing, a right to oust the United States.

(Miyazato 2000: 59)

For the United States, the unpredictable movements of the 'inhabitants' were a source of fear. Thus it was that the US required Japanese 'residual sovereignty' in order to head off any threat to the stability of its 'exclusive strategic management' of Okinawa by demands for self-determination from the inhabitants.

Nevertheless, the military feared that this might invite intervention from the Japanese government, and demanded that 'residual sovereignty' be purely nominal. When the Legislature of GRI (the Government of the Ryukyu Islands), formed in April 1952, passed a resolution calling for recovery aid from the Japanese government, USCAR rejected it on the grounds that Ryukyu had no need to receive aid from Japan because it was 'under the protective control of the United States' (*Ryukyu Shimpo*, 15 August 1952). Although the State Department had been considering the return of administrative control to Japan as a way of quelling residents' dissatisfaction, it finally gave in to the military's demands. One reason for this was the belief that continued American control of Okinawa would not harm US–Japan relations. Despite his earlier concerns that 'if the Okinawa issue is allowed to remain in its present condition, there is a high probability that a movement for national unification will emerge', the American ambassador to Japan installed in 1952, Robert Murphy, was surprised to find that there was no sign of a movement for the return of Okinawa to Japan, nor any demands from the Japanese government for the return of the territory (Miyazato 2000: 79). In the end, only the Amami Islands, which had few military installations, were returned at the end of 1953. In the president's new-year address of 1954, it was declared that the Okinawan bases would be maintained 'indefinitely'.

Dead-end recovery

The military's demands having been met, the militarization of Okinawa continued, and the place once known as the 'Forgotten Island' became the 'Keystone of the Pacific'. Tacit approval for American rule was extracted from the island's residents largely by continuing the input of economic aid for recovery. In April 1952, USCAR installed Higa Shuhei as the Chief Executive of the newly formed GRI. Higa was already on record for his view that 'a certain period of trusteeship rule is necessary and inevitable considering that there is no alternative but to rely on aid from the United States' (*Uruma Shimpo*, 21 June 1951). In response to the presidential new-year address of 1954, in which it was declared that the American bases would be maintained 'indefinitely', Higa made the following comment: 'This presidential declaration means that the United States will take responsibility and provide aid for the advancement of the welfare of the Okinawan people.' In reference to the movement for 'reversion' (*fukki*) to Japan, he declared that it was 'irresponsible to perpetuate in the people's minds an unrealizable and vain dream', and urged the need for 'deep reflection' (*Ryukyu Shimpo*, 13 January 1954). At this moment when Okinawan society was finally beginning its recovery from the devastation of the 'Forgotten Island', the most effective means of intimidation was to stress the 'reality' that recovery would be impossible without aid from the United States.

Nevertheless, the premise of 'recovery' underlying this intimidation was being eroded by the havoc militarization brought to residents' lives. Under the 'Land Acquisition Procedure' Ordinance promulgated in April 1953, the military expanded the land area under its control, in some cases even resorting to the use of armed troops to accomplish this. Furthermore, there was little compensation for the land lost, and those whose land had been taken became impoverished. Resistance to the land seizures was suppressed as the work of 'communist agitators'. In October 1954, leaders of the People's Party (*Jinmintou*), which advocated non-cooperation with the American military, were arrested and imprisoned. In 1955, there were successive land seizures by armed troops on the Island of Iejima and at Isahama in the middle area of the main island of Okinawa. This immediately raised the level of tension over the issue of military land use. The farmers of Iejima, now deprived of their means of livelihood, went on a 'Begging March' bearing placards inscribed with the words 'Begging is shameful. But, the American military who have stolen our land and forced us to beg is even more shameful' (Ahagon 1973: 123).

Two months previously, a negotiating party lead by Higa had been to Washington and presented its case before the House of Representatives Military Affairs Committee. They presented as the wishes of the Okinawa residents 'Four Principles' that had been passed by the Legislature of GRI – (1) Opposition to land purchase, perpetual use, and lump-sum payments; (2) Opposition to any new land acquisitions; (3) Demanding appropriate rents for military land use; (4) Demanding the payment of compensation. As a result, there was a preliminary suspension of lump-sum rent payments, and in October the Military Affairs Committee dispatched an investigation team (led by Melvin Price) to Okinawa. In response to this, Higa and the governing Liberal Party (*Minshutou*) adopted the stance of 'insistent trust in the good will of the American government, and seeking the expansion of self-rule, industrial economic recovery, and resolution of the military land use issue through a position of cooperation with the United States' (*Okinawa Times*, 26 February 1956). By that time, however, US troops had already carried out the forcible land seizure at Isahama.

Inherent to the demands placed before the American government in the form of the 'Four Principles' were the contradictions of a society reliant on military bases. At the time the Legislature approved the 'Four Principles' in April 1954, some members of the governing party had proposed the insertion of words to the effect that 'smooth resolution of the land issue is the most important issue in preventing the spread of communism'. This, it was proposed, would be effective as a way of extracting such things as 'economic support for residents' livelihood' and an 'increase in rent payments' (Gyoseishuseki Kanbo Bunshoka 1954: 55). In a publication of the Ryukyu Bank, it was also argued that obtaining appropriate rents for land under military use was not an issue for land-owners alone, but an 'issue of importance to all Ryukyu in view of the present unstable conditions of an economy totally reliant on the bases'. It was calculated that a 'constant average annual revenue of 700 million yen would be obtained' if rents were set at appropriate levels (Ryukyu Ginko: 1954). One can glimpse here the contradictions inherent to a situation in which recovery was being pursued through tacit acceptance of military occupation. The amount of economic aid fell from 49 million dollars in fiscal 1950, to a mere 1.74 million in 1954. The amount paid for construction work and other labour for the military reached a peak in 1952 to 1953, and then began to fall off. The political stance of accepting occupational rule in return for the promotion of economic recovery was undermined by the blind alley of the military base-dependent economy. 'Solving' the problem of military land use was seen as a way out of the deadlock.

In the legislative elections of March 1956, the Liberal Party retained its majority with a stance of cooperation with the United States. A resolution tabled by the opposition calling for reversion to Japan was rejected as 'futile and useless' (*Okinawa Times*, 1 April 1956). In the context of expectations towards the US Congress, tension raised by the protests of Iejima and Isahama seemed to have been contained by the 'reality' of a base-dependent society. Everything depended, however, on the recommendations to be concluded by the Price Commission.

The horizon of 'island-wide struggle'

Protest erupts

This occurred on 9 October 1956, when Okinawa learned of the outline of the 'Price Recommendation'. When it became clear that the report of the Price Commission almost completely ignored the 'Four Principles', Okinawan society erupted. Beginning with Higa himself, public officials at all levels, including members of the Legislature, town mayors and village chiefs, and members of local councils, one after another declared their intention to resign. Residents were called upon to 'maintain order independently and not allow society to become unstable' and to 'demonstrate now residents' capacity for self-government, and exercise powers of management in accordance with necessity, not allowing the functions of self-government to stop even in the absence of those in higher positions of responsibility' (*Ryukyu Shimpo*, 19 June 1956). Even the civilian police force put out a message saying, 'We too are residents of Okinawa. We carry out our duties as residents, and will not deviate at all from the battle line' (*Ryukyu Shimpo*, 20 June 1956). On 20 June, mass gatherings were held simultaneously in every locality, with more than 150,000 people participating in total. At the gatherings held on 25 June in Naha and Koza, 100,000 people participated. Statements made at this gathering appeared to break through the barriers: 'We Okinawans have been too restrained'; 'Having seen the newspapers for a long time, I think now the time has come'; 'We can't stand being trampled upon any longer' (*Ryukyu Shimpo*, 20 June 1956, *Okinawa Times*, 21 June 1956). This was a movement of unprecedented scale, and came to be known later as the 'Island-wide Struggle' (*Shimagurumi Tousou*).

A report presented to Washington from Naha expressed a sense of confusion at the sudden explosion of protest as follows:

> Though the United States has held requisitioned land in the Ryukyus for a number of years, satisfactory compensation has not yet been given (particularly in the eyes of the Ryukyuans – but also admitted by American authorities). Even though this failure by the United States has been compounded by inadequacies bearing on Ryukyuan welfare in other fields, the Ryukyuans have reacted almost docilely throughout. This attitude even obtained through last year when the villagers of Isahama were forcibly evacuated in the face of bulldozers while the village was surrounded by a cordon of soldiers. During that tense episode the GRI executive did not come out forcefully in defense of the villagers. . . . Why, then, did the

Ryukyuans, who are normally a good-natured, optimistic and even care-free people, with surprising suddenness pick this issue and this time as being propitious for taking a drastic and determined stand against the United States?
(Okinawa Prefectual Archives: U90006104B)

This was certainly a very serious turn of events. The reaction to the 'Price Recommendation' seemed to have broken through what had until then been an obstacle. The walls of 'reality' confining the base-dependent society seemed have been broken down. One young person told a journalist the following:

Once we demanded reversion or anything about our rights, we have been called 'communists'. When they threatened us, we shrank back. . . . But, then came the Price Recommendation. People were surprised at its unexpected contents, and everyone gathered together. When we came together and realized that we had all being thinking the same, those things that had been held back suddenly flowed out. Okinawans who had kept quiet finally started speaking out. The accumulated dissatisfactions built up over eleven years come out all at once. Everyone gave voice to their deep pent up feelings. That is why it was so intense, and anti-American. But, this is what everyone feels. We will no longer be afraid to be called 'communists' or anything by them. We have made up our minds.
(*Yomiuri Shinbun*, 30 June 1956, evening edn)

At that time, people had 'made up their minds' about something. This was no different in the areas where many residents' livelihoods were dependent on the bases. The leader of the women's association in the village of Chatan spoke thus: 'More than 90% of my village's land has been requisitioned for military use, and most of the households have people working for the American military. Even so, we all feel liberated from the gloomy atmosphere, and are relieved' (*Asahi Shinbun*, 4 July 1956, evening edn). Next to her, an old person from the village of Kadena, whose land had been kept from them ever since the war, replied as follows: 'That's right. My sons now work for the military. I know full well that we could not make a living without this work. But we are talking about something different here. Land is more important than life!' (*Asahi Shinbun*, 23 July 1956). On one hand, there was the 'reality' of livelihoods dependent on the American military. However, at that time when people rose up, they were 'talking about something different here'.

The scope of protest

Amid this groundswell, the aspiration for reversion was reawakened from its forced silence. The Price Recommendation's demand for land buy-out was criticized as a threat to Japanese territorial rights. It was claimed that one of the keys to reversion would be lost if land rights were yielded to the American military. Protecting the 'national territory' (*kokudo*) became a slogan. Above all, there was a growing sense that a fundamental resolution of the problem would have to involve negotiations between the United States and Japan, as the holder of 'residual sovereignty'. Since the negotiations between the US and Ryukyu governments had only yielded the flawed Price Recommendation, there was a need to break through the barrier confining the problem to an issue of American 'internal politics'. This went beyond simply demanding action on the part of the Japanese government. It went as far as calling for the 'rapid formation of a grass-roots organization to back up and lend strength to the weak stance of the Japanese government' (*Okinawa Shinbun*, 28 June 1956). This idea developed later into the key demand for the holding of three-party talks involving the Japanese government in addition to the US and Ryukyu governments.

However, there was more to the 'Island-wide Struggle' than simply the desire for reversion to Japanese rule. A photograph taken at the 'Naha Citizens' Rally for Implementation of the Four Principles' held on 20 June shows a placard bearing these words: 'Let us Protect our Land by Ourselves' (*Warera de Mamorou, Warera no Tochi wo*) (*Yomiuri Shinbun*, 23 June 1956). When the association of mayors and village chiefs were considering sending representatives to the Japanese mainland, some of those present at the meeting expressed objections such as the following: 'There is no need to go. The struggle should be pursued here now. We can stage strikes. Other methods could also be used. Anyway, we should carry on the struggle with our own strength alone.' Having recounted this episode, the mayor of Mawashi then stated that 'I think these words were representative of the voice of the Okinawan people at the time' (Asato *et al*. 1956: 104–105). Thus, even if only for a brief moment, there was a horizon going beyond the goal of reversion.

The containment of protest

USCAR took action to bring a conclusion to the affair. At the end of June, it declared its readiness to impose 'complete direct rule' in the event that the threatened mass resignations took place. In July, it announced a three- to five-fold increase in the ground rents paid on half of the land used by the military. At the same time, USCAR put pressure on Higa by approaching the then mayor of Naha, Toma Jugo, who was in favour of 'lump-sum' rent payments. Higa made an immediate about-turn and declared that 'mass resignation is not the aim', while Toma publicly announced his support for 'lump-sum' payments. At the residents' assembly held at the end of July, a motion was passed calling for the resignation of both Higa and Toma. This put a definitive seal on the divisions within Okinawan society. What put a final end to the movement was the indefinite 'off-limits' order enacted in the middle districts on 8 August. This forbade American military personnel from entering these areas, causing an immediate and serious economic decline in the vicinity of the bases. On the same day, a public gathering held mostly by students in Koza received a warning that 'members of the association of leisure and entertainment businesses will resort to their own powers to stop any demonstrations'. As a result, the demonstration was scheduled to be held after the meeting was called off. Higa immediately put out a statement in which he declared that Okinawa's economic dependence on the bases was a 'reality no-one can deny' and called upon residents to reflect on the 'excess' of such things as 'opposing the bases, seeking reversion, and non-cooperation with the United States' (*Ryukyu Shimpo*, 9 August 1956). The containment of the movement within the confines of 'reality' occurred very rapidly. In an attempt to have the 'off-limits' order lifted, the mayor of Koza refused permission for the holding of 'anti-American' rallies, and declared that he did not recognize the two individuals dispatched to the Japanese mainland (Senaga for the People's Party and Kaneshi of the Socialist Masses Party: *Shakaitaishuutou*) as 'representatives of the Okinawan people'. On 14 August, the 'off-limits' ban in Koza was lifted. Other mayors and village chiefs immediately followed suit with similar declarations, and on 17 August there was a general lifting of the 'off-limits' order.

Following the sudden death of Higa in November, Toma was appointed as his successor. Toma repeatedly made clear his support for 'lump-sum' land payments, and was backed up in this position by the Ryukyu Chamber of Commerce. At the Chamber's general conference, the following appeal was delivered by the chairman: 'There can be no hope of recovery in Ryukyu without a resolution of the land issue. There is therefore no alternative but to moderate the assertions made until now'. An official of USCAR attending the meeting expressed his belief that 'a situation will arise in which money will reach those who so far have not received any' (*Ryukyu Shimpo*, 7 November 1956). Thus, the 'Island-wide Struggle' was gradually contained by the 'reality' of base-dependency.

Relocation of the marine corps

Preparations for the relocation

The Okinawan 'Island-wide Struggle' gained considerable attention from public opinion in mainland Japan. Major newspapers covered the events extensively, and large rallies were held in support of the movement in Okinawa. One reason for this was the 'coincidence' with the rising intensity of struggle over American military facilities at Sunagawa and Uchinada on the mainland. At the end of July 1956, a 'Tokyo citizens' rally for the protection of Okinawa and Sunagawa' was held. The resolution adopted at this rally stated that it was to be 'understood as a nationwide struggle for the peace and independence of Japan' (Nakano 1969: 224).

However, the Japanese government took no real action. According to reports entering the US State Department, the Japanese Ministry of Foreign Affairs instructed its office in Naha to decline a petition from Okinawa in order to avert any involvement by the Japanese government. At a cabinet meeting held at the end of June, it was unanimously decided that the Japanese government would 'take no definite action' with respect to the Okinawa land issue (Miyazato 2000: 121–122). The Japanese government itself desired that 'residual sovereignty' remain frozen as a purely nominal entity.

There was more to this response by the Japanese government than simply tacit approval for the American occupation of Okinawa. This becomes clear when one looks at the matter in relation to the movements of the American military in mainland Japan at the time. In June 1955, the commander of the Third Marine Division made a visit to Okinawa, during which he announced that the Ninth Marine Corps was to be relocated there 'as soon as conditions are ready for its acceptance' (*Okinawa Times*, 3 June 1955). In accordance with military plans formulated in October, approximately 39,000 acres of land were to be requisitioned in addition to the existing 42,000 acres already reserved for military use (Ryukyu University Library: S312 UN12–5). At the end of March 1956, plans were announced for construction work on facilities for the marines beginning in autumn of the same year. From this, it became clear that extensive building work was to take place in Kim, Henoko, and Tengan (*Okinawa Times*, 1 April 1956).

Immediately after the publication of the 'Price Recommendation', Chairman Price himself made the following statement: 'As the American military gradually pulls out of mainland Japan, the importance of the bases in Okinawa becomes even greater for the maintenance of security in the Far East and Western Pacific. The Marine Corps has also been relocated to Okinawa' (*Ryukyu Shimpo*, 23 June 1956, evening edn). The Okinawa land issue was closely linked to the question of the American military pull-out from mainland Japan.

The marines' landing

At the close of 1956, the village of Kushi (later to be incorporated as part of the city of Nago) announced its acceptance of land requisitions and 'lump-sum' payments with respect to Henoko, which had been slated as the planned site for the construction of the new marine facility. This announcement was a significant moment in the decline of the 'Island-wide Struggle', marking the collapse of one of the key pillars of the 'Four Principles': opposition to new land acquisitions. The explanation given by the village chief was as follows: 'Notwithstanding the forced land acquisitions and loss of residents' rights such as occurred in Iejima and Isahama, support for cooperation [with the American military] gradually increased because of the expectation that the village economy would improve thanks to the existence of the base' (*Ryukyu Shimpo*, 22 December 1956). People became increasingly reticent as they came to believe that 'continued opposition would lead nowhere' and 'the majority accepted the situation with resignation' (*Ryukyu Shimpo*, 28 December 1956). Yet again, the 'Island-wide Struggle' was contained by 'reality', as expressed in statements such as the following:

> 'Our children will be able to continue their education further. Electricity and roads will be set up. Nothing could be better.'

> 'Electrical lighting and running water will be installed. In the future, our children will not have toil as farmers like we had to. This is the way we want things to go.'
> (*Ryukyu Shimpo*, 4 February 1957)

Thus the new base was built in Okinawa, and the marines began their preparations for arrival. In June 1957, immediately after the summit meeting between Japanese Prime Minister Kishi and American President Eisenhower, it was announced that all American ground forces would be withdrawn from the Japanese mainland by the end of the year. It was further announced that an advance party of marines from the Ninth Division stationed mostly at Camp Fuji would leave for Okinawa within a few days (*Mainichi Shinbun*, 8 August 1957). On 15 August, the advance party from Camp Fuji and Yokosuka Base disembarked at the military port of White Beach on the Katsuren Peninsula of Okinawa (*Mainichi Shinbun*, 9 August 1957, evening edn, and 13 August 1957, *Okinawa Times*, 16 August 1957). In October, the US Under Secretary for State was reported as saying, 'Now that American forces are withdrawing from Japan, we can even less afford to let go of Okinawa and Ogasawara' (*Okinawa Times*, 4 October 1957). The arrival of the main body of the marine corps took place quite literally in the form of a 'landing' as part of a military exercise, as described in the *Okinawa Times* as follows:

As part of the relocation of the Third Marine Corps from the mainland to Okinawa, 65 ships of various sizes, numerous fighter jets, 40 helicopters, and a tank division took part in the exercises. At 9 am, 2500 armed soldiers of the First Marine Regiment lead by Colonel Nelson began their landing in assault craft at Yonabaru and Kim from an LST escorted by the Seventh Fleet. At the same time, an armored division of 840 men carried out their landing at Henoko from helicopters. . . . As the landing began, support craft dived in continuously, and return fire from the marine side started. The whole area resounded with the sound of explosions, and it was just like a real war.

(*Okinawa Times*, 21 October 1957, evening edn)

In December of that year, it was announced that the Third Marine Corps had completed its withdrawal from mainland Japan (*Mainichi Shinbun*, 5 December 1957). A report from the Japanese government's Procurement Agency in June of the following year stated as follows:

As a result of Prime Minister Kishi's visit to the United States in June 1957, the complete withdrawal of US Army terrestrial combat divisions was announced as part of the 'Kishi-Eik Declaration', and the American Marine Corps was relocated to Okinawa. Progress was thus made towards resolution of the base issue in the mainland, but the problem of military land use in Okinawa consequently became even more serious.

(Suzuki 1958: 3)

In its manifesto for the elections held in February 1958, the Okinawa Socialist Masses Party continued its line (adopted in 1951) of advocating reversion with these words: 'The base expansion and reinforcement foisted upon Okinawa as a way of evading opposition to bases in mainland Japan must be opposed and redressed. . . . The military base issue will have to be resolved together with Japan and in conjunction with reversion to Japan' (*Okinawa Times*, 26 February 1958). Reversion was proposed at this time as the only remaining option in order to prevent the shifting of the base problem from the mainland to Okinawa. From 1952 to 1960, the size of US bases decreased from 33,000 acres to 8,000 acres in mainland Japan, while it increased from 42,000 acres to 75,000 acres in Okinawa. Nevertheless, as we shall see later, the terms agreed between the US and Japanese governments were such as to block the possibilities which the reversion could have opened up.

Futenma base

Here I would like to make a slight diversion and consider the issue of Futenma base, which is closely related to the movements of the Marine Corps. This base was established during the heat of the Battle of Okinawa in preparation for the planned strategy of invading mainland Japan. In the base plan formulated after Japan's surrender, it was marked out as one of the airfields to be maintained by the US Army. Nevertheless, use of this facility for the purpose thus indicated was not very great. A 1948 document describes the situation as follows:

Due perhaps to the fact that Futenma Airfield is not being used, there are those among the local residents who not only enter the off-limits zone but even live and engage in agriculture there. Aerial reconnaissance reveals that some people are even making use of the runways and have partially destroyed them. The military will henceforth keep a watch on these activities and clamp down on them.

(Okinawa Prefectural Archives: R00020584B)

A newspaper report from 1951, in the very midst of the Korean War, speaks of Futenma base as a 'good place for racing cars at high speed along that long runway, since fortunately it is not off-limits' (*Okinawa Times*, 1 April 1951). In the following year, the runway was extended and resurfaced, but even then it remained for a while as only a reserve airbase. The Price Recommendation said of Futenma base that 'it is used only in marginal fashion by the Air Force today but has a specific planned utilization for the future' (US Government Printing Office 1956: 7666). According to another newspaper report at the time, the ground around the runways had been dug up by scrap metal collectors, and therefore 'it would be awkward for the military to use' and 'there should be a clamp down on trespassing' (*Ryukyu Shimpo*, 4 April 1956, evening edn).

It was only in February 1958 that residents were told to vacate all properties within the limits of Futenma base (*Ryukyu Shimpo*, 11 February 1958, evening edn). In July 1959, the first squadron of the helicopter division arrived at the newly built marine base in Futenma (*Okinawa Times*, 10 July 1959, evening edn). Labour recruitment for the base began in 1960, and the ceremony marking the completion of the relocation and inauguration of the new barracks was held in May (*Ryukyu Shimpo*, 16 February 1960, evening edn and 8 May 1960). Having remained largely dysfunctional for a long time, Futenma airfield became fully operational as a base for the marine helicopter division. The marine base was thus readied for full action during the Vietnam War.

The policy shift and cooperation between Japan and the US

The 'red mayor'

At the end of 1956, at almost the same time as the American military and the village of Kushi reached agreement on the requisitioning of Henoko, a 'red mayor' (communist mayor) was elected in the city of Naha. Senaga Kamejiro had been arrested and imprisoned in October 1954. Soon after his release in April 1956, he was elected mayor of Naha representing the People's Party. This came unexpectedly to the Americans, who had gained a sense of security following the successful break up of the 'Island-wide Struggle'. Earlier in August 1956, in the immediate aftermath of the declarations by local government leaders of their non-recognition of Senaga as a representative of Okinawan residents, a report delivered from Naha to the State Department had offered the analysis that 'Senaga and his ideas promptly lost support as a result of his extreme statements'. However, after his election as mayor, the report changed completely to 'it must be recognized that his [Senaga's] anti-Americanism did not bring about any loss of trust [among electors]' (Okinawa Prefectural Archives: U90006094B; Miyazato 2000: 129).

Rather than taking the forceful measure of ordering Senaga's removal from office, USCAR attempted instead to 'persuade the electorate that American rule is important for Okinawa in terms of bread and butter issues' (Miyazato 2000: 129–130). In concrete terms, this meant suspending the flow of credit to Naha's economic recovery fund, and freezing the city's bank account. The city council then passed a no-confidence resolution against Senaga on the grounds that he was 'obstructing the recovery process'. The anti-Senaga factions united to form an 'Alliance for the Reconstruction of the Naha City Government' in order to fight the upcoming city council elections. However, supporters of Senaga (organized as the 'Liaison Conference for the Defense of Democracy') doubled their representation on the council as a result of those elections, making the passage of another no-confidence resolution impossible. Senaga's approach to city government had evidently begun to gain grassroots support, to the extent that even a member of the faction opposing him had to admit that 'credit has been cut off, but tax revenue is increasing. Farm roads here and there are being repaired with a little money' (*Okinawa Times*, 12 March 1957).

As is clear from a saying exchanged among Naha residents ('if Senaga falls the entire land of Okinawa will be lost') (*Okinawa Times*, 13 March 1957), the energy that had been released by the 'Island-wide Struggle' became focused on the figure of Senaga Kamejiro. An important medium for this public groundswell were speech meetings, such as the one described in the following passage:

> Adults became uniformly frenzied, as they moved in sympathy with the words of the speech and responded with shouts of '*yasa, yasa!*' (That is so, that is so!). The intonation of Senaga's speech grew higher and higher. . . . Words critical of America gushed out frequently, and every time the house rang with shouts and piercing whistles. People sent out cries of '*yu ichon*', meaning 'you said it well'. . . . Rarely does one see such luster on the faces of adults.
>
> (Miyazato Senri 2000: 55–56)

At the end of November 1957, USCAR resorted finally to a revision of the electoral law, and dismissed Senaga from his office. However, the following election held in January 1958 was won by Kaneshi Saichi, whom Senaga had designated as his own successor. Even the candidate who narrowly lost to Kaneshi, Taira Tatsuo, was an overt supporter of reversion to Japan. USCAR was forced to recognize that Kaneshi's victory was due to the fact that he had 'directly opposed cooperation with the United States', and that Taira Tatsuo was disadvantaged by the fact that he was supported by the 'pro-American conservative faction' (Miyazato 2000: 135). The United States was thus forced to make major changes to its policy in Okinawa.

The new dispensation

In the newspaper reports on Kaneshi's victory, two entirely opposing citizen responses were recorded. On one side, there were those who saw in it the 'strength of Okinawans finally rising up from centuries of oppression', while on the other side there were those who were 'surprised at the unrealizable nonsense' and wondered 'what is the point of resistance for the sake of resistance' (*Ryukyu Shimpo*, 14 January 1958). While this contention was going on Naha, moves were under way in the northern areas close to the marine base to find a way of stimulating the local economy through the military presence there. In July 1957, a gathering took place to celebrate the completion of electricity and water facilities in Henoko, where the new land requisitions had occurred at the end of 1956. At this gathering, a performance was staged in which the water supply was ceremonially switched on by the leader of the local women's association, and the electrical lighting activated by the American high commissioner (*Okinawa Times*, 5 July 1957). In order to harvest some of the dollars brought by the American troops, a new commercial district was set up in Henoko, leading to a significant growth in the population. The resulting economic liveliness in Henoko encouraged the formation of new aspirations in the surrounding areas. Some of the residents in the village of Kim overcame disquiet about the use of their land as a firing range, and began demanding the stationing of troops there (*Okinawa Times*, 7 September 1957). In November 1957, a plan was announced for the laying of an electrical power line from Kadena base to Henoko, and to supply the excess power from this line to local residents along the route (*Okinawa Times*, 2 November 1957). With the expansion of military bases in the north of the island, the 'benefits' of the presence of the bases began to penetrate local society in a visible manner.

Since his assumption of office in May 1958, it fell upon High Commissioner Donald Booth to spread these 'benefits' to the whole territory of Ryukyu. Having just taken office, he held a series of meetings with local leaders all over the island in late June, and announced numerous projects for electrification, land reclamation, and the construction of water works and roads. This lead to a widening impression that 'Lieutenant General Booth has an extraordinary enthusiasm for the development of industry in Ryukyu' (*Ryukyu Shimpo*, 26 June 1958). Furthermore, at the end of July, the abolition of lump-sum payments for the use of land by the military was announced, and the land issue seemed to be moving in the direction of a 'solution'. Opposition to new land acquisitions (another of the pillars of the 'Four Principles') ceased to be an issue on which people were united, as a result largely of the 'benefits' being handed down to local society. High Commissioner Booth went on to pay visits to the outlying islands as well, energetically carrying out inspections wherever he went. Beginning in 1959, he dispensed funds to all the regions, promoting schemes directly affecting the daily lives of local communities, including the construction of water works, irrigation facilities, bridges, and fire stations.

Along with this major shift in American policy, the Okinawa Liberal Democratic Party (OLDP: *Okinawa Jiyuuminshutou*) was formed in October 1959. At the inaugural meeting of the party's youth branch in February 1960, Chief Executive Ota declared the need to 'move from resistance to the politics of dialogue' (*Ryukyu Shimpo*, 20 February 1960). In the legislative elections held in November, the OLDP won a major victory by gaining 22 out of the 29 seats. Its electoral campaign was aided from the wings by funds from the high commissioner's developmental projects, to the extent that it was said, 'It was not just the OLDP that was campaigning, but also USCAR, in other words High Commissioner Booth. . . . One could say that the OLDP campaign was carried out by military and residents together' (*Ryukyu Shimpo*, 20 November 1960, evening edn). As if to overcome the havoc caused to daily life by the expansion of the bases, the newly dressed social 'benefits' of the bases began to envelope Okinawan society. Nevertheless, this apparently stable social 'reality' was always under threat from the energies released in the 'Island-wide Struggle'. In order to extract tacit acceptance of the bases from the island's inhabitants, the US was ultimately forced to invoke intervention by the Japanese government.

The policy of cooperation and the return of administrative control to Japan

In parallel with the input of funds into local communities, the United States altered the framework of its rule in Okinawa. In September 1958, the US dollar replaced the 'B-yen' as the currency, and the input of capital from outside Okinawa was encouraged. Beginning in the fiscal year of 1959, technological aid from the Japanese government was accepted, and in January 1960, a joint US–Japanese plan for the development of the Island of Iriomote was announced. This latter plan came to symbolize the whole policy of cooperation between the two governments. The OLDP adopted the slogan of 'Substantial Unification with the Fatherland' (*Sokoku to no Jisshitsuteki na Ittaika*). The basic policy of American rule thus shifted in the direction of cooperation with the Japanese government, as a means of securing political stability.

Nevertheless, the underlying aim of this cooperation was still the maintenance of American control in Okinawa. According to a report delivered to the State Department, Japanese Foreign Affairs Minister Kosaka promised during his talks with the American ambassador that Japan would not demand the return of administrative control so long as the United States provided an appropriate level of satisfaction to the Okinawan People. He also emphasized that there had to be cooperation on plans related to the economy and welfare in order that Japan would not demand the return of administrative control (Miyazato 2000: 195).

At this stage, Japan's role was actually extremely limited, and the overwhelming portion of economic aid to Okinawa came from the United States. Having fallen to a level of about 1 million dollars in 1957 and 1958, American aid grew to an amount almost three times as large in 1959. In July 1960, congressional authorization for aid to Okinawa was enacted through the president's signing of the 'Price Act' (a bill to provide for promotion of economic and social development in the Ryukyu Islands). The military still had misgivings about the possibility of intervention by the Japanese Government in the administration of Okinawa. USCAR insisted that it 'should maintain the bases in Okinawa by increasing the amount of aid we ourselves give' since 'aid from the Japanese government of itself threatens American rule in Okinawa' (Miyazato 2000: 207). Despite the 1962 'Kennedy Declaration' that anticipated the day of 'their restoration to full Japanese sovereignty' and directed actions 'to minimize the stresses that will accompany the anticipated eventual restoration of the Ryukyu Islands to Japanese administration' (Miyazato 2000: 217), the military rejected any involvement by the Japanese government, and negotiations between the two governments on economic aid to Okinawa were postponed. Furthermore, High Commissioner Paul W. Caraway, who took office in February 1961, adopted a firm line of 'separation from Japan'.

However, the military's policy of severely constraining Japanese government involvement had already reached its limits. In September 1962, the Kennedy administration made a request for an increase in the maximum amount of aid permitted according to the 'Price Act' to 25 million dollars. Congress reduced this maximum figure to only 12 million dollars, and the amount of aid actually allocated in the 1963 budget was a mere 6.9 million dollars (Miyazato 2000: 225). Meanwhile, in Okinawa, popular discontent grew in response to the 'separation from Japan' policy and the high commissioner's maximum exercise of his powers amounting to 'direct rule'. In August

1964, Caraway was removed from office, and a mechanism for bringing about cooperation between Japan and the Unites States began operating publicly. Even among the military, there was a growing perception that it would be inexpedient to continue opposing the return of administrative control to Japan. The instructions given by the Army Minister to Caraway's successor, High Commissioner Watson, were for 'slow progress', in other words to 'proceed cautiously, and slow the pace towards reversion' (Ryukyushimpo 1983: 385).

After 1965, the Vietnam War moved into full swing, and Okinawa played a full role as a base for bombing sorties. In order to maintain social stability in Okinawa and secure full functionality of the bases there, the policy of cooperation with the Japanese government was strengthened. In 1967, the Japanese contribution to economic aid exceeded that of the United States. In 1970, it grew to an amount 2.5 times greater than the US contribution, and the decision-making process as regards this aid was entrusted to direct consultations between Japan and Ryukyu. Finally, in November 1969, a joint declaration from the US and Japan laid the way for the return of administrative control to Japan, on the absolute condition that the bases would be maintained. Indeed, the marine corps facilities in Okinawa were actually strengthened in order to accommodate the forces then being withdrawn from Vietnam. Returning administrative control to Japan became a necessity precisely in order to retain the functionality of the bases. From the point of view of those inhabitants driven out of their homes by armed troops 30 years ago in Isahama, this 'return to Japan' occurred in such way as to render it irrelevant, as illustrated in the following passage:

> Is that the place where our homes used to be? Now it is nothing but barracks, armored vehicle motor pools, and military storage facilities. Now that we have been returned to the mother country, and are no longer starving, we will make our demands a lot stronger. We will get our land back under any circumstances, and desire our return to Isahama. The sooner we go back the better. When I look at the place where our homes used to be, the desire to go back there wells up so much that my chest aches.
>
> (Nihon Kyosyokuin Kumiai and Okinawa Kyoshokuin Kai 1968: 185)

Conclusions

In September 1995, protest once again erupted in Okinawa, in response to an incident in which a girl was raped by two Marines. The Japanese Government responded by expanding its policies for the promotion of economic activity in Okinawa, in order to 'provide support for Okinawa's development to catch up' (*Ryukyu Shimpo*, 11 October 1995, evening edn). In the following year, it was announced that Futenma base would be closed, and an alternative site for military facilities found within the Prefecture of Okinawa. The way this relocation plan was 'decided' illustrates very well the fact that cooperation between the US and Japan over the American bases in Okinawa has hardly changed at all in the 30 years since the return of administrative control to Japan. It is also highly significant that the site chosen for the construction of new military facilities to replace Futenma was none other than Henoko. Both Futenma and Henoko had started operating as bases at the end of the 1950s, at the time of the Marines' relocation to

Okinawa. The relocation from Futenma to Henoko is no more than a continuation of what happened 40 years ago. The 'Okinawa Problem' should therefore be discussed as an issue concerning postwar Japanese society as a whole, whereby the bases resulting from the American occupation of Japan were foisted upon Okinawa as a way of coping with anti-base protest on the mainland.

However, it is necessary to go even further. Further questions must be considered concerning the slogans of 'promotion' (*shinkou*) and 'development' (*kaihatsu*) enveloping Okinawa, beyond simply seeing them as part of a structure of placation and subordination. The historical prerequisites lying behind these slogans must also be considered. This involves looking at the whole 'postwar' history of Okinawa since it became a battlefield for terrestrial warfare towards the close of the Second World War. It needs to be remembered how Okinawa emerged from the neglected devastation of the 'Forgotten Island' and entered its 'postwar' phase as the periphery of a former empire.

When constructing an alternative vision for Okinawa, neither as a 'Forgotten Island' nor as the 'Keystone of the Pacific', aspects of the 'Problem' burdening Japan's postwar will perhaps become clear. This is what we must now consider.

Notes

1 Originally published in Japan: 地上戦の島の「戦後」：沖縄の米軍基地の成り立ち をめぐる断章 , *Gendai Shisou* 現代思想 . Vol. 29–9 (July 2001), 12–29.
2 The original lines go as, 夕もやに連なり点る灯の海はさながら異国の黄昏かとも，夜目まさに灯の海なせる中部地区 区にこの島の激しき変貌は知る .

References

Ahagon, Shoko 阿波根昌鴻 (1973) *US Troops and Farmers* 米軍と農民 , Tokyo: Iwanami Shoten 岩波書店 .

Arasaki, Moriteru (ed.) 新崎盛暉（編）(1982) *Oral Histories of Modern Okinawa (vol. 2)* 沖縄現代史への証言 (下), Naha: Okinawatimessha 沖縄タイムス社 .

Asato, Tsumichiyo, Onaga Josei, Nakaima Yaeko and Nakasone Satoru 安里積千代 ・ 翁長助静 ・ 仲井間八重子 ・ 仲宗根悟 (1956) 'Appeals to the fatherland'「座 談会 祖国への願い」, *SEKA* 世界 (September), 104–113.

Fisch, Arnold G. (1988) *Military Government in the Ryukyu Islands, 1945–1950*, Washington, DC: Center of Military History, United States Army.

Furukawa, Shigemi 古川成美 (1947) *The Last Days of Okinawa* 沖縄の最後 , Naha: Tyuosha 中央社 .

Gabe, Masaaki 我部政明 (1996) 'The decision-making process in Joint Chiefs of Staff regarding possession of Okinawa'「米統合参謀本部における沖縄保有の検 討 ・ 決定過程」, *Hougaku Kenkyu* 法学研究 67(7): 73–107.

Gibney, Frank (1949) 'Okinawa: Forgotten Island,' *Time* 28: 20–21.

Ginowanshi Kyoiku Iinkai 宜野湾市教育委員会 (1997) *The Early Postwar Years in Ginowan: Toubaru Kamero's diary* 戦後初期の宜野湾 桃原亀郎日記 , Ginowan: Ginowanshi Kyoiku Iinkai 宜野湾市教育委員会 .

Gyoseishuseki Kanbo Bunshoka 行政主席官房文書課 (1954) *Documents of the Legislature, the 4th session vol. 1–5* 立法院 会議録 第4回議会 (定例) 自第 1 号至第 5 号 , Naha.

Ikemiyagi, Shui 池宮城秀意 (1970) *My Life in Okinawa* 沖縄に生きて , Tokyo: Simul Shuppankai サイマル出版会 .

Miyagi, Etsujiro 宮城悦次郎 (1982) *The Eyes of Occupation Forces* 占領者の眼 , Naha: Nanashuppansha 那覇出版社 .

Miyazato, Seigen 宮里政玄 (1981) *The Decision-making Process of US Foreign Policies* アメリカの対外政策 決定過程 , Tokyo: Sanichishobo 三一書房 .

Miyazato, Seigen (2000) *The US–Japan Relations and Okinawa* 日米関係と沖縄 , Tokyo: Iwanami Shoten 岩波書店 .

Miyazato, Senri 宮里千里 (2000) *Umaku!* ウーマク , Tokyo: Shogakukan 小学館 .

Morris-Suzuki, Tessa (2001) 'The crisis for critical imaginations' 「批判的想像力の危機」, *SEKAI* January: 80–92.

Nakano, Yoshio 中野好夫 (ed.) (1969) *Documents of Postwar Okinawa* 編 , Tokyo: Nihon Hyoronsha 戦後資料 沖縄 .

Nihon Kyoshokuin Kumiai and Okinawa Kyoshokuin Kai (eds) 日本教職員組合 ・ 沖 縄教職員会 （ 共編 ） (1968) *Mothers in Okinawa* 沖縄の母親たち , Tokyo: Godoshuppan 合同出版 .

Okinawa Prefectual Archives 沖縄県公文書館 (R00020584B) 'On the off limits of the airbase to residents' 「飛行場内住民立入禁止について」 (GRI documents).

Okinawa Prefectual Archives (U90006094B) 'Naha to Secretary of State,' August 18, 1956 (copy documents).

Okinawa Prefectual Archives (U90006104B) 'Strategy and Tactics of Ryukyuans and US Authorities in dealing with Ryukyuan Land Problem,' 22 June 1956 (copy documents).

Okinawa Prefectual Archives (U90008134B) 'History of Twentieth Air Force, July–December 1950' (copy documents).

Okinawaken Kyoiku Iinkai 沖縄県教育委員会 (1986) *Documents of the Okinawa Advisory Council* 沖縄諮詢会記録 , Nana: Okinawaken Kyoiku Iinkai 沖縄県 教育委員会 .

Ryukyu Ginko 琉球銀行 (1954) *Finance and Economy* 金融経済 , November.

Ryukyu University Library 琉球大学附属図書館 (S312 UN12–5) 'Land Acquisition' October 7, *US Administration Materials XII, LAND 5, Land Problem* (copy documents).

Ryukyushimpo (ed.) 琉球新報 （編）(1983) *Informal Histories of Reversion* 世替わり裏 面史 , Naha: Ryukyushimposya 琉球新報社 .

Suzuki, Noboru 鈴木昇 (1958) 'Land problems and the Land Acquisition Procedure in Okinawa (part 1)' 「沖縄における土地問題と土地収用令（上）」, *Chousa Jihou* 調査時報 21: 1–7.

Toriyama, Atsushi 鳥山淳 (2001) 'Lands for military use and workers for US troops in early postwar years in Okinawa' 「軍用地と軍作業から見る戦後初期の沖縄 社会」, *Urasoe Shiritsu Toshokan Kiyo* 浦添市立図書館紀要 12: 67–82.

US Government Printing Office (1956) *Report of a Special Subcommittee of the Armed Services Committee, House of Representatives, Following an Inspection Tour October 14 to November 23, 1955,* Washington, DC: US Government Printing Office.

Title of the newspapers

Asahi Shinbun 朝日新聞

Mainichi Shinbun 毎日新聞

Okinawa Shinbun 沖縄新聞

Okinawa Times 沖縄タイムス

Ryukyu Shimpo 琉球新報

Uruma Shimpo 読売新聞

Yomiuri Shinbun うるま新報

Names

Higa Shuhei 兼次佐一

Kaneshi Saichi 比嘉秀平

Nakasone Seizen 仲宗根政善

Senaga Kamejiro 瀬長亀次郎

Taira Tatsuo 平良辰雄

Toma Jugo 当間重剛

Special terms

Chief Executive 行政主席

Four Principles 四原則

Futenma 普天間

Henoko 辺野古
High Commissioner 高等弁務官
Iejima 伊江島
Isahama 伊佐浜
Island-wide Struggle 島ぐるみ闘争
Land Acquisition Procedure 土地収用令
Legislature 立法院
Liberal Party 民主党
Lump-sum payments 一括払い
Okinawa Liberal Democratic Party (OLDP) 沖縄自由民主党
Okinawa Socialist Masses Party 沖縄社会大衆党
People's Party 人民党
Price Recommendation プライス勧告
Residual sovereignty 潜在主権
Reversion 復帰
The Government of the Ryukyu Islands (GRI) 琉球政府

Part IV

Feminism

Chapter 13

'You are entrapped in an imaginary well'[1]

The formation of subjectivity within compressed development – a feminist critique of modernity and Korean culture

Cho Han Hae-joang
(Translated by Michael Shin)

Introduction

> Thinking in terms of dichotomies
> and obsessed by a sense of victimization.
> Enjoying a mood of tragedy
> Drawn somehow to conspiracy theories.
> Distrusting local discussions
> and believing that macro-theories will explain all.
> These are the obstacles
> that the intellectuals of this land have to overcome.

One day in November 1997, South Koreans suddenly heard the news that their country needed a financial bailout by the International Monetary Fund (IMF). Up until the mid-1990s, South Korea's politicians, businessmen and the people themselves had all been in high spirits. Claiming that they had pioneered a new model of high-growth economic development, South Korea enjoyed its status as one of the 'four dragons' of East Asia. Many foreign students from South East Asia came to study the South Korean 'economic miracle', and scholarly discussions were held on the success of 'Confucian capitalism', which was considered to have rivalled the 'Protestant capitalism' of the West. Then came the news that South Korea was deeply in debt and needed a financial bailout.

As the extent of the economic crisis became clear, the various emerging responses have provided an opportunity to examine South Korea's ability to handle a crisis. At first, the IMF was viewed as a stand-in of the superpowers. Many perceived that the IMF was attempting to establish a 'trusteeship' over South Korea, referring to the crisis as a national disgrace. As the people somehow recovered from the initial state of panic, the general public's opinion that South Korea should accept reality and introduce free-market principles came to prevail. The powerful *chaebol* (conglomerates; in Japanese, *zaibatsu*) were the first targets of such criticism. People felt that state corruption, exacerbated by the inflexibility of the labour market and the *chaebol*'s monopolistic position, were the causes of the economic crisis. Accordingly, everyone generally shared the opinion that it was necessary to promote 'transparency' and 'fairness' since South Korea has to open its markets and increase its competitiveness. However, implementing solutions has not proved easy as the rapid economic growth of the past decades has left the people in an extreme state of both physical and mental exhaustion.

The potential for crisis has existed since the very incorporation of the South Korean economy into a world order dominated by transnational capital. Recognizing this fact will be helpful in organizing one's thoughts on the crisis. It would be a grave mistake to look at domestic factors alone and consider South Korea's situation to be unique. If there exist incentives to increase one's income, the people of any nation where a degree of popular education has been achieved, and where Hollywood movies have successfully spread dreams of a happy middle-class life, would work and sacrifice their own time and pleasure, especially if they were hungry and frustrated. Once people who are trying to escape from poverty begin to earn money, regardless of cultural differences, they gain the confidence that they can succeed, and their efforts enable the nation's economy to take off. Transnational financial capital flowed into South Korea when its 'hungry' people were willing to make sacrifices to rise out of poverty. Now that 'hungry' labour no longer exists, capital has left this country and moved to places where wages are cheaper. Prior to the onset of the crisis, the people had believed in the benefits of capital, had been engrossed in improving economic statistics, and had believed in the 'myth of success'. Now they are dazed and confused.

The current crisis is certainly also the responsibility of the domestic 'players' who were the leaders of South Korea's economic development. However, it is impossible to understand the current situation without knowledge of how the 'rules of the game' were determined. I agree with scholars who have argued that an explanation for South Korea's economic growth should be sought primarily in the favourable external conditions of the past 30 years (Cho, Hyiyon 1997; Kim, Hogi 1998). Explanations should be placed in the context of capitalist development in the East Asian region; in particular, South Korea should be examined as an example of an exportist regime of accumulation, a Listian warfare state, and as an authoritarian developmental mobilization structure. Simply put, conditions were favourable for rapid economic development in South Korea because of the fluidity of world capital in the 1960s, 1970s and 1980s, the cold war political situation in which the US was actively supporting capitalist economies, and South Korea's ability to follow the Japanese model of export-led industrialization.

In order to understand the dimensions of the crisis, it is necessary to avoid limiting the unit of analysis to that within the national boundary. It is also necessary to avoid falling into conspiracy theories, especially at a time when so many people feel victimized. If such pitfalls are avoided, a fruitful discussion can emerge regarding colonial modernization and the crisis. Over the past few decades, South Koreans have been able to create neither a way of life nor a rational labour system that is compatible with the economic changes they have experienced. Instead, a society has been created that is obsessed with 'miraculous statistics'. People have been pushed and shoved in the rush toward colonial modernization to the extent that it has been difficult to create any space for critical reflection or innovation. The realm of daily life has been severely affected.

In a sense, the current crisis was predictable, and so was 'our' passionate reaction to save 'our nation'. What is worrisome is that in increasing numbers, the younger generation feels that 'it is better to die than be stuck in a state of conflict'. I despair that the South Korean people have not been able to find a way to move beyond the dichotomy of a passionately defensive nationalism and passionless market principles. But, at the same time, as a cultural anthropologist, I cannot conceal my excitement at the un-precedented opportunity that the IMF crisis has brought about to conduct the 'native anthropology' of South Korean society. The work of intellectuals continues to be a delicate balancing act, between hope and despair, on the borders of transformation.

As the current crisis led me to think about the history of the world system, I began to reflect on the social impact of the 'compressed growth' of late-industrializing states, and such reflection led me to think about compressed time, the lack of databases and specialists, and the absence of a 'language' to discuss the quotidian world. My focus in this article is modernity and the formation of subjectivities. Discussion must begin with South Korea's 'abnormal' modernization and the extremely unbalanced form of 'development'.

Looking at 'my society' through the IMF crisis: a history of compressed economic growth and turbo capitalism

When the door finally opened,
I was not ready to leave.
> (Posted on the front page of the Chollian Internet
> Service Provider, 19 February)[2]

The book *The Global Trap*, which is virtually required reading for all 'thinking people' in South Korea these days, introduced the term 'turbo capitalism'. It refers to how capitalism has been able to develop without fetters, and with even greater speed after the fall of the Soviet Union and Eastern Europe in the late 1980s.[3] The authors of the book, Martin and Schumann (1997), have emphasized that 'turbo capitalism' destroys a society's basis for survival by rapidly undermining its traditional culture. In addition to this book, there have recently been many other books released that argue that a market-driven age of capitalism will cause humanity to suffer a tragic fate due to its relentless undermining of the foundations of any society.[4]

South Korean society represents a typical case of economic development through 'turbo capitalism'. Until the 1980s, the state ignored all demands made by various social groups, claiming that they should wait until the problems of basic survival had been solved. When South Koreans celebrated their ability to host the 1988 Olympics, issues of basic survival were somewhat less pressing. They were then able to turn their attention to other areas such as democratization or quality of life issues. Many people feel that the situation would have been better if the Olympics had been held four years later, if South Korea had joined the OECD a little later, or if the IMF bailout had come just five years later. However, the truth is that despite the great economic development, South Korea has been culturally destitute. Until per capita income reached ten thousand dollars, society operated under the principle that it was necessary to 'compete by cutting costs', and if wealth did accumulate, it was squandered on imperialist imitation. National leaders were so anxious to join the ranks of the 'superpowers', and the people always had something to catch up to.

I recently had a conversation with the architect Kim Jin-ae, who mentioned that a British architect who had worked for many years in Japan said that a building that took a year to build in England would take only six months in Japan. She added that the same house would probably take only three months to be built in South Korea.

Where has this speed and mobility come from? What price has had to be paid to make it possible? Although I may have generalized, I will attempt below to give a brief synopsis of South Korea's development/underdevelopment over the past 30 years.

Starting from a state of 'lack', modern South Korea has become more and more easily caught up in movements of capital that it was powerless to control from the very beginning. This malleability has been the strength of South Korean capitalism. However, 'turbo capitalism' has wreaked destruction in South Korea, leaving it with shoddy and unsafe buildings, superficial cultures, an ungrounded optimism and overwhelming individual adaptability to the status quo. At this moment, South Koreans seem to be divided into two groups. One group is made up of *kukmin*. The term '*kukmin*' is a combination of two Chinese characters meaning 'nation' and 'people'. Although it is sometimes translated as 'citizen' or 'people', there is no exact equivalent for this term in English. This group stubbornly believes that the IMF will be driven out in three years. The other group comprises 'non-*kukmin*', who wonder how they will sustain their lives until the end of the world. Lacking a mechanism for overall societal coordination, many 'non-*kukmin*' suffer from a sense of futility that nothing can be achieved, no matter how hard one works.

Although society lacks an overall coordinating mechanism, this does not mean that there is no underlying 'system'. The driving force of South Korea's turbo capitalism in the last century has been anxiety over survival and, in response, 'food chains' have been built. The term 'food chain' refers to a phenomenon which is often called 'crony capitalism' by scholars. 'Homo economicus' has been the dominant personality of South Korea, a person who secures food, shelter and wealth by building and managing 'food chains'. South Korean society has been structured around such chains and networks; it is centred on large-scale 'private profit associations' that are very different in nature from modern, rational organizations with a long-term perspective of collective community life. Formed in a time of quasi-war mobilization, 'private profit associations' operate according to 'well-known secrets' which are necessary to make dirty, backroom deals. People who are not aware of the 'well-known secret' and cannot join a 'food chain' become marginalized. Power and opportunities in society are determined according to one's position within quasi-personal networks disguised under the public ethic of '*inji sangjong*' (a natural feeling of well being for everyone).

Let me delve further into this history. During the colonial period 1910–1945, and the Korean War 1950–53, a social system was created in which the people were essentially reduced to a refugee status within an emergency state. Many people were unable to be concerned with anything but their day-to-day existence. This system was reinforced, not weakened, when the people of South Korea were then pushed to 'catch up' and pursue high-speed growth. Theoretically speaking, modern society is based on the principle that an individual can enjoy freedom as long as he or she does not infringe on the freedom of others. In a society built upon networks of 'food chains', the prevalent attitude is more one of intimidation: 'Why are you bothering me when I'm just trying to get ahead?' The South Korean elite constantly talk about 'essential' moral principles and logically consistent social theories. Everyday people's language, full of crude comforts, sentimentalism, or direct intimidation, is so different from the language of the elite. This duality is not the result of a failure in the process of implementation; rather, it is the very foundation which enables the 'private profit associations' to function properly.

Reformers have easily failed when they did not take this system into account. This is also the reason that many reforms by politicians and the government were, from the beginning, intended only to soothe popular discontent like 'giving a bottle to a crying baby' as a Seoul taxi driver once bluntly expressed it. Recently, a performance-based salary scale was introduced as part of the 'structural reforms' of the current, inefficient system. However, things reverted back to the same old system, while only paying lip service to a 'South Korean style' performance-based system. Until now, organizations have built and maintained a system where people were busy 'dividing the pie' amongst themselves, rather than creating a proper evaluation system for employees' performance in order to 'make a larger pie'. Thus, reforms will continue to fail.

The compressed time period of development and the intensity of that experience have had a tremendously destructive effect on society. Social scientists, who are already familiar with the concepts of modernity and compressed temporality, have noted that 'from the outset, modernity contained within itself the tragedy caused by compressed temporality'.[5] However, due to the unevenness and compressed time span of South Korea's economic growth, there is a great difference between the experiences of 'us' and 'them' who have pursued endogenous capitalist development.[6] In this sense, it is meaningless for the First World and the Third World to sit at the same negotiating table if the effects of such temporal compression are not fully understood. It will be difficult to talk about a global civil society without an understanding of the 'colonization of the image' and of the severe obliteration of subjectivity (Pieterse and Bhikhu 1997). There needs to be an analysis of why there are so many people in the Third World who are suffering from relative deprivation; why extremely conventional TV dramas revolving around issues like the nation, the family, and status reproduction are so popular; and why civil movements can do no more than merely run on the spot. Such phenomena are closely related to the fact that modernization has been pursued within an extremely 'compressed' period of time, leaving little time for reflection and modern system building.

Many social problems have arisen because society has not been prepared for certain reforms or policies. Let me give some examples. Despite the various difficulties, South Korea decided to implement reforms to increase autonomy in local administration. Unfortunately, it coincided with the national construction boom and the great success of construction brokers, most of whom were not the natives of the regions and who then emerged as a new power elite group in regional localities. The result is that, rather than working for the future of local areas, the local autonomy system serves the interests of ruthlessly profit–driven individuals.

The national policy for the information age that was pursued with such grand ambitions by the Kim Young Sam government is another example. Under the slogan 'Behind in manufacturing, but a leader in information', the government distributed expensive computers to middle and high schools. However, although hardware was distributed, it was done so without adequate software or the manpower that was able to utilize the hardware. Moreover, because of the high pressure of the 'college entrance examination hell', middle and high school students did not have the time to use these computers (Cho, Haejoang 1995). What students in this 'examination war' badly need is a quick way to relieve stress. Thus, when supplied by the government or bought by many parents who feel that computers are necessary for their children's education, computers are mainly used for playing games and enjoying worldwide pornography, if they are not abandoned in storage rooms.

What about the women's movement? As the anti-dictatorship social movements of the 1980s began to decline, feminists who were unable to establish their own voices within the major social movement circles felt that their time had come. They were excited to organize the 'revolutionary energy' that remained from the 1980's *minjung* (people's) movement. However, consumer capitalism, which arrived too rapidly as a result of 'compressed' growth, has drawn a new generation of women into fashion shows, department stores and fancy cafes. The feminist movement ended up losing the opportunity to advance into the next stage. Much energy was wasted because of such out-of-sync timing, and as a result, the gross inequities and unbalanced nature of society has become more severe.

What worries me most is that this compression and unevenness has brought about the destruction of the quotidian. When my students say that it is better to die than to be trapped in a situation of conflict, or that they are too exhausted to think, they are exposing the collapse of the capacity for mutual communication. People begin to feel that intentional acts only bring about unintended, disastrous consequences. So many people hesitate to pursue what they want to do. Living in such a society, people become powerless and lose the sense of how to talk about their discomfort or frustrations in order to improve their lives. Although much 'hardware' has been imported from other countries, there is little 'software' that can improve their everyday lives. The seriousness of the problem stems from the fact that many people have given up on creating information and software. If no one wants to make anything by oneself, there is no software; if no one thinks of creating software, there are no databases. Up to now, production in South Korea has followed the path of 'colonial' modernization, using software copied from other countries. As a result, it has been impossible to accumulate information and knowledge.

The distinguishing characteristic of South Korean development has been 'compressed growth through imitation', as there were model societies which had already developed to an advanced stage. It was only necessary to set a plan for development and urge people to work harder and faster without any reflection. As even a rough blueprint for the future was unnecessary, South Korea's intellectuals learned simply to mimic grand-sounding theories from the developed countries, and production line workers only had to imitate without thinking. Theoretical terminology became used to disguise reality, and harsh working conditions undermined the dimension of thought and reflection. Because the ultimate goal of development had already been decided upon, scepticism and doubt were considered to be subversive. What had to be performed was rapid and unthinking imitation. This tendency has been further reinforced by the Cold-war system. The Cold-war era had forced Koreans to think in terms of the extreme dichotomy of 'friends and enemies'. There was nothing in between.

A busy lifestyle, in itself, undermines people's capacity for thinking. The busier people are, the more convenient it is to think in terms of dichotomies. Men and women, adults and children, our people and your people, my alumni and those who went to other schools, my family and non-relatives, those who took piano lessons as a child and those who did not – by categorizing everyone into two groups, many things can be handled automatically. Many people feel that in a busy life, it is not necessary to waste any time on serious thinking. What needs to be determined is with whom will one make a connection. In a busy world where the ultimate objective is clear and there is a 'Big Brother' who decides the direction of society, all that is needed is strategic thinking.

So far, I have tried to emphasize that a 'compressed rush to development' creates a feeling of powerlessness. It draws people into a logic of dichotomies and deprives them of the capacity for self-reflection. The overwhelming speed and out-of-sync timing weakens the ability and will for mutual understanding by instrumentalizing others. However, I believe, and I hope, that in the current crisis, many residents in South Korea will begin to feel that it is now necessary to rectify the unevenness of development and to create a new, balanced society. Discussions have begun regarding the necessity of the insight to map out the future direction of society, to be able to analyse and interpret drastic changes, and to try to attain a social space through which to reduce the distances that exist between people. This is an essay by a student of mine reflecting on her life in the economic crisis.

One day on a radio talk show, I happened to hear that at an international conference, the South Korean development model which is characterized by miraculous economic growth and an entrenched system of corruption was brought up as the main issue. Despite the peculiar collusion of the government and the industry and their rationality of its bureaucratic culture, [the] South Korean economy consistently showed high growth rates. Some of the participants even seemed to propose that the system of corruption itself functioned as a positive variant for economic development. The Korean case seemed to be discussed as a counter example of established theories.

Hearing the discussion on the bus, and watching the scenery through the window, I was murmuring to myself that it would not end up in such an optimistic and happy way. This was before the IMF crisis. I was already sensing that the world had become more difficult to live in.

In this sudden economic crisis, I feel rather relieved. It seems that we have finally come to see the world through the right perspective. The pictorial history books of my primary school years always finished with the national flag surrounded by balloons and a picture of lots of smiling people with the rising sun in the background. We will now have to forgo our habit of vaguely drawing the future of Korea with these sort of images.

Whenever I would begin to talk about myself, there were always more important, more urgent problems to solve, which would stop me. For tomorrow, the me of today had to be subdued. And when tomorrow arrived, that tomorrow had to disappear to make way for the next day to come. In the end there was no happy me of today. I just kept being pushed toward tomorrow. Now I find myself at a cliff. I am rather comfortable now, knowing that the final happy days will not come.

I now want to get out of the car that I have been forced to ride in. I want to examine the car from a distance, and to check my map and compass to reassure myself of the direction. If I could, I would like to make some seat cushions for me and the others, so that we could have a more comfortable journey. Though the place I'm heading toward may not be a rose-colored dreamland, I would rather like to know where I am going before I take the journey.

(Chon Hye-jin)

It is comforting to know that students like Hye-jin are beginning to reflect upon the modernity of their own society. What can be done to end the vicious circle created by rapid growth and uneven development? What interventions are possible in order to break down the refugee-like 'private profit network' and to build a fairer public infrastructure? South Korean society is not entering a postmodern age; it is at a stage searching for an alternative modernity. This creation of an alternative modernity is a most urgent task, which can be made possible through fractal and 'postmodern' ways of thinking. I will examine the possibilities of such a transformation by focusing on the formation of subjectivities in South Korea's modern history.

'Nation' and 'Family': the history of the production of 'modern *kukmin*'

> Things in paintings seem to be actual,
> but they are not real.
> They resemble each other,
> but they are different.
> People seem to be free,
> but they just move according to the laws around them.[7]

'United we survive, divided we die' – this slogan, which probably came into public discourse during the nationalist resistance movement against Japanese rule, also expresses the mindset of compressed colonial growth through effective mass mobilization. In this section, I will try to examine in detail the hegemonic powers that are associated with the notions of the '*kukmin* – a member of the nation' and '*kajok* – family', two words that most vividly evoke such mobilization. These words are the two main signifiers that have exerted the most power in the constitution of modern life in South Korea. In a sense, South Korean society was able to achieve miraculous economic growth in such a short period of time due to its success in producing '*kukmin*'. This 'success' was possible by eliminating any space for civil society. As expressed in the quote above by an art critic, people appear to be free but are, in reality, behaving according to rules which make them nothing but nationalistic state subjects. The period of compressed growth produced a society with only grand state power and patriarchal families, but no citizens or autonomous individuals. Of course, in turn, the 'national persons' made compressed development possible.

In this process, people became highly instrumentalized. The social system worked efficiently to replicate 'identical-ness' among people, placing them in a state of non-differentiation. When a society is faced with a situation of total crisis, structural adjustment is unavoidable. I feel that the structural change necessary at present can be carried out effectively only through an effort to liberate the various subjectivities that have been completely suppressed by the signifiers of '*kukmin*' and the 'family'.

There is no civil society, only kukmin

When President Kim Dae Jung left to attend the ASEM meeting in 1999, he was reportedly asked the following question in an interview with a reporter from the British newspaper, *The Times*:

'South Koreans are known to be a proud people. What do they think about foreign investors?'

'They have a negative opinion of them. They think that foreign investment will turn South Korea into a colony. In 'town hall' televised meetings with *kukmin*, I have tried to persuade them that money has no nationality and that the important issue is which country it is invested in. If we are to succeed, we need to earn foreign currency by increasing exports, but, at the same time, we must also have significant investment from foreign companies. Recently, our people have begun to learn this. They are changing a lot.'

(Hangyoreh Newspaper, 4 April 1999)

In this interview, while acknowledging that the irrational group-centredness of South Koreans is a problem, President Kim urged foreign investors to wait as the problem of patriotism of South Koreans was being taken care of. If the president's intention implied in such statements becomes widely known, many of the South Korean *kukmin* would feel betrayed by him. Responses to the crisis have not much exceeded the bounds of nationalism. People have continued to assert that 'patriotism kept us in the black', even in the face of economic bankruptcy. They feel that tightening one's belt, the campaign for the collection of gold, promotions for the purchasing of only domestic products, increased money wires from overseas South Koreans, and reducing overseas travel, will all help to avoid the crisis (Pyon 2 February 1998). The foreign press has noted that South Korea's greatest strength is the patriotism of its people and praise South Korea's nationalistic character. Of course, it is important to take into account the standpoint and intentions of the Westerners who write such editorials. It is probable that they are right-wing nationalists and that they are praising South Korea's patriotism in order to advance their own country's socio-economic policies and their own interests.

In reality, the gold collection movement and displays of the national flag are more than just nationalistic displays. They were spectacles produced in times of crisis. Such spectacles are organized and staged by groups of patriotic *kukmin* who feel obliged to do something instantaneously to respond to the crisis. For example, some 'patriotic' schoolmasters and teachers in elementary schools told their students to bring in their family's receipts for the gold they contributed to the 'gold collection' movement. Other more diligent and nationalistic school principals suggested at morning assembly that students attach the national flag to their backpacks. Middle and high school students found this amusing and it became trendy among them to put the national flag on their backpacks.

In this way, young people became mobilized into displays of patriotic fervour in a society of the spectacle. Gift stores that target these students put away the flags of the world that they had stocked up when the talk of 'globalization' was picking up and replaced them with the national flag; these shopkeepers were able to become 'happy and good' *kukmin* who both made money and celebrated their patriotism. In public arenas, there are still many 'patriots' to the point that KBS announced in their evening news hour that seeing the movie *Titanic* would cost more in foreign currency than could be raised through the 'gold collection' campaign. Just as people who went to see *Titanic* were treated as criminals, South Korean society is pervaded with an atmosphere of terror in which it is not permissible to say anything that violates the sanctity of the 'nation'. Trained to be 'together' in times of crisis, *kukmin* felt proud to be doing their part to overcome the crisis by participating in the movement of 'saving the nation'. The mass media has always been at the forefront of promoting a 'nationwide' donation movement. In turn, the masses who participated in such rituals took comfort from the demonstrated wholesomeness of the *kukmin* through their virtually complete participation in such movements.

What I have been interested in is the people's automatic, Pavlovian reactions to catch phrases such as 'the nation' and 'unity'. This led me to analyse the roots of nationalist discourse. Nationalist discourse in South Korea is historically connected to the national liberation movements of the colonial period. However, rather than seeing it as a mere continuation from the colonial period, I regard today's nationalism as more of a reproduction of a similar but modified form of contemporary nationalism that has emerged in a time of rapid socio-economic transformation. Today's national discourse was newly constructed during the period of nation-building after liberation. Initially, the discursive power came from national security requirements and the related anti-communism. After the 1970s, the discourse of nationalism was directly connected with economy-first policies that sought the development of a powerful nation. When South Korea held the Olympics in 1988 and later joined the OECD, the mood became one of celebration of finally being included in the circle of the powerful. In the history of a world divided into developed and underdeveloped nations, South Korean *kukmin*'s pride has been severely hurt as members of an underdeveloped country. They could not miss the opportunity to join the ranks of the developed nations. This is the very reason why even the left-wing intellectuals who had been active in the *minjung* (people's democratic) movement in the 1980s did not really oppose the market-first policies. The elite, regardless of their ideological positions, ultimately all share the final goal of making the nation powerful. In a sense, nationalism and modernity have for the most part evolved together as two sides of the same coin.

Let me be more concrete about the process of producing modern *kukmin* in South Korean history. In the period right after liberation, anti-Japanese sentiment was an effective mechanism to provide unity for the state. President Lee Syngman most successfully mobilized this antagonistic sentiment. When the country was divided after the Korean War, pro (or anti)-Americanism was added to it. When President Park Chong-hee's regime normalized relations with Japan for the sake of economic cooperation in the 1960s, the state was successful in unifying the people through anti-communism rather than anti-Japanese sentiment. During the period of economic growth, the state successfully mobilized the people under slogans such as 'developing the fatherland'. Strictly speaking, South Korean nationalism was an exclusionist nationalism of resistance during the colonial period. After liberation, it combined with the imperatives of the state and served as the ideology for the production of *kukmin*, which enabled hyper-effective state mobilization. In a word, South Korean nationalism developed in conjunction and disjunction with anti-Japanese colonialism, anti-communism, pro-Americanism and now imperialism itself. Under the threat of communism, and through the goal of joining the ranks of the developed countries, the developmental authoritarian state was able to mobilize the people very effectively. The state was hardly concerned with the welfare of people or with anti-fascist democracy.

In the official discourse, the nation, the state and the people are one and the same. South Korean society was extremely successful in manufacturing a 'majority' consisting of middle-class, middle-aged male members of society. Until recently, the mass media frequently used expressions such as *kukminjokchongso* ('popular sentiment' or 'national sentiment') which functioned to block the emergence of alternative opinions and imagination, and these incantatory phrases contributed to producing the uniform subjectivity of the '*kukmin*'. The phrase *wihwagam chosong* ('promoting discord') has also played an important role in suppressing the emergence of any new voice. A president of a computer company has noted that the emphasis on 'becoming one' has not only repressed the people's freedom, but also obstructed economic development. He reminisced that although South Korea had developed its own colour television, the government initially did not permit its production for the reason that it would 'promote discord'.

Modern complex societies can only achieve unity through the institutionalization of diversity; thus, the effort of the South Korean state to create unity through the reproduction of the same is clearly counter to the goal of building a modern state. The reason that the far-right conservatives gain influence every time there is a crisis may not be because such groups have latent sources of power but rather because there are no alternative power groups or a radical new language to oppose them. Modernization through popular mobilization not only reduced the personal dimension of daily life, but also produced a totalitarian culture in which people were trained through discipline and surveillance, leaving no room for the emergence of civil society. It is a society in which it is dangerous for an individual to think or act from different subject positions other than that of one's national or familial identity.

Having lived in a such a uniform and totalitarian culture, *kukmin* have, for some time now, 'voluntarily' participated in reproducing their own alienation as they have become unable to create their own identities. For example, people read a comment made by a Japanese tourist that the South Korean people are an admirable people because they give up their seats on the bus to the elderly; then they began to assert their identity as a South Korean by diligently yielding their seats. What they are doing is participating in the process of producing 'admirable *kukmin*' of the Republic of Korea. If someone on the street asks, 'What is unique about Koreans?', the image of Koreans yielding their seats on a bus would automatically come to their minds.

I am not denying that differentiated subjects do exist. However, such differentiation has not been able to establish and express itself within the realm of official culture. Rapid economic growth and the myth that it will continue has not allowed these subjects to assert a 'difference', and the mass media, which has been a great promoter of the slogan 'united we survive', has not had the inclination to encompass such changes. Some managers of the mass media have still sought to unite the differentiated people into 'one grand mass' using phrases such as 'national sentiment', and '*wihwagam chosong*'.

How much longer can South Korea continue to reproduce such a *kukmin*? A student who went to the South Korea–Japan soccer match this spring told me of a scene which says something about the prospective change. The passionate soccer fans known as the 'Red Devils' were cheering, together with the 'Ultra Nippon' squad from Japan, creating a very amicable atmosphere in the stadium. The people who were taunting the Japanese fans were other spectators, not the 'Red Devils'. The student said that they seemed like people who have not been able to find a purpose in their lives. Maybe they are people who become energized only when they have an enemy, an object of hatred and when they can truly devote themselves to the 'imagined community' of the nation. There definitely are *kukmin* who are moved by phrases such as 'Let's beat Japan',

'Win or die', 'Save our country', and 'Korean residents in Japan, don't give up!'. Their own personal dreams become united with the nationalist ambitions of the nation to become a powerful country, and they desire a clear hierarchical order and achievements measurable in terms of strength and numbers. They are captivated by the beauty of unity, suffer from relative deprivation and are accustomed to thinking in terms of the dichotomy of 'centre' and 'periphery'. They want to overcome their own inferiority complexes by becoming citizens of a powerful country, so they turn all athletic contests into a matter of ego and pride. The miraculous strength to defeat Japan in soccer games is just one storyline within an ongoing drama about the preservation of national pride. Clearly, the word 'nation' still has the power to mobilize a certain population in South Korea.

At the same time, however, there are more and more people who no longer want to participate in such patriotic games. Because of the current crisis, the numbers of people who are becoming sceptical about the meaning of *kukmin* are increasing. The following is an excerpt from a report submitted for my class on 'Culture and Humanity' by Yi Chong'un, an undergraduate at Yonsei University:

> When the 'gold collection' movement caused such a big commotion, I felt uneasy for some reason. I am not sure what it was, but I was overrun by a bad feeling. Recently, that feeling became uncontrollable when there was that absurd controversy about the movie *'Titanic'*. Even if it was true [that actor Leonardo DiCaprio said negative things about South Korea], how should we (I) react to the suppression of the personal desire to see a movie through the circulation of such statements in society? People who do not see *'Titanic'* will feel an awkward patriotism that they did something good for the nation, and those who do will feel guilty. What can we do in a situation where cultural taste is determined by the demands of patriotism and where people are 'voluntarily' falling into such a trap? People should not get caught up in the incitement of a deceptive patriotism even for the sake of saving the country. Of course, I know that it is impossible to live in society purely as an individual, but at the very least, I do not want everything to be determined by the pressure of majority opinion. This society tries to suppress and deny the simple freedom of watching a movie; this society makes me sick . A little while ago, I saw a message posted on the Internet. Someone claimed that the meaning of 'EASTPAK', the name of the brand of knapsacks, is 'eliminate the east'. The person also expressed a desire for revenge, saying that 'we need to make a WESTPAK'. [When I saw it] I sighed and became frightened. How is such an abnormal patriotism created and maintained? How far can this go? There may be people who are moved by the words, 'South Koreans unite in times of difficulty', but these words sound scary to me. To me, such fabricated words are no more than wordplay, a deceit.

I can see individuals holding their breath under the shadows of rapid growth and the shadows of the singular subject, *kukmin*. I can see the emergence of reflexive 'non-*kukmin*', who wonder if they can trust any longer a state that insisted that there was no crisis up until the IMF announced its bailout, despite the fact that South Korea's financial bankruptcy was becoming evident prior to the announcement. Now it seems that the production of *kukmin* and the constitution of a single subjectivity can no longer be maintained, either through outside pressure or through internal divisions. The remaining task is how to deconstruct the *kukmin* and to accept and organize the internal differences.

Some time ago, I heard from a specialist on the labour movement that negotiation and compromise between classes could not be possible until consensus based on negotiation within a class is possible. The specialist noted that South Korea has experienced difficulty in establishing effective procedures for negotiation since negotiation within a class itself is hard to achieve. Workers can form a single group for a short period of time but, in reality, they are still divided by their private interests. Because agreement through negotiation has never been achieved within a class, or even within each occupational group, it will be difficult to achieve any kind of widespread overall agreement. A grand compromise and agreement is possible only when differences can be expressed fully, and when decentralization and flexibility are deemed valuable. South Koreans urgently need to acknowledge the existence of social differentiation and to learn to construct alternative flexible subjectivities that will enable them to coexist with various 'others'.

There are no individuals, only families

With the outbreak of the IMF crisis, one of the most urgent voices has been the cry of 'Save the family!'. The family has been the other sacred entity associated with the dreams of 'becoming a powerful nation'. Just as modernization has mass-produced *kukmin*, who had absolute faith in the notion of an 'eternal nation', it has also mass-produced patriarchs, who had a strong belief in the notion of an eternal family.

The current movements to 'encourage men' and to 'support and cheer up our fathers' who are depressed by the IMF crisis were actively led by the mass media. Worried that the unemployment of fathers will bring about the disintegration of the family, the mass media has once again been urging people to unite. While the mass media has been telling people to support the patriarch, it does not hesitate to blame women for ruining the country by their ignorance and over-consumption. Governmental support given to unemployed workers is also granted to male workers first. 'Fundamental restructuring' based on worker performance has been stalled because of the ideology of the family and the family wage system, which gives unconditional support to fathers as household providers. These various measures show clearly who are the core of *kukmin*. Men are considered to be the *kukmin* that should be protected first while women, the marginalized *kukmin*, are the first to be laid off.

The movements to 'save the head of the family' are further proof of the fact that fathers have been reduced to being moneymaking machines during the period of compressed economic growth. As the economic crisis has begun to undermine the patriarch's role as family provider, the movement to 'save the patriarch' has arisen from the fear that the whole family structure, which centres on the male head, will fall apart. The extremely instrumentalized family is in grave danger. Why are fathers now abandoning their families and committing suicide? Is it only because they lost their jobs? The family is supposed to be a shelter from an inhuman world of competition.

That the family itself is disintegrating because the patriarch, the pillar of the household, is laid off suggests that the family was already in a state of disintegration before the crisis began. Many fathers have no role other than to earn their family's living expenses, and many fathers have failed to perform their roles as a member of the family, particularly in making intimate relationships. During the period of compressed economic growth, many men did receive respect as financial providers, but at the same time the father has become the most instrumentalized and isolated member of the family.

Elsewhere I have written about how South Korea's modernization created modern gendered spaces: 'a public sphere where men dominate and a family sphere where women dominate'. I have also tried to show how there is an unseen war going on between men and women in those two spaces (Cho, Haejoang 1996). A significant difference exists between men and women's perceptions of the family. For men, the family is an extended family based on blood relations transmitted through the paternal line. However, for women, the family includes the family she was born into and her children, her 'uterine family'. The patriarch's conception of the family has generally been the official one, and the official version of the family has very much been a part of the ideology that has disguised reality.

When capitalist development reaches an advanced stage, the modern family naturally breaks down and gendered roles also have to be redefined. As television and video invade the living room, and as telephones and pagers connect the family with the outside world, change becomes unavoidable. Schools, the mass media and consumerism have easily undermined the authority of parents, and it has become harder and harder to maintain closeness and dialogue among members of the family. The collision of the ideology and the reality is inevitable in South Korea as society has undergone a drastic modernization process. However, the state still has a tight grip on family life.

The educational system in South Korea is a good example by which to demonstrate the extent of the state's intervention in the family. Centred on preparing students for the college entrance exam, the educational system has enabled an effective mobilization of the *kukmin*. The school has functioned as the place where people receive the training necessary to contribute to the nation's export-led, compressed growth. In this process, rather than being a space of care and affection, the home has been turned into a training ground for the battlefield of the college entrance exam. The mother–son relationship has changed to that of player and coach. Worried that their children might not be able to go to college, parents have willingly participated in the 'instrumentalization' of their children. Children had to become 'warriors' who fought for the sake of their 'private profit network' and for the reproduction of their family's social status. In return for becoming a warrior, children gained the right to become a consumer, who could use the money earned and saved by their parents. As consumers, children came to judge their parents according to their ability to provide materials, and parents even judged themselves according to their ability to provide tutoring fees and to satisfy the material wants of their children. While the cultural role of parents has become severely reduced in the process of compressed change, it was accompanied by a proportionate growth in their role as material providers.

When the reality of the family grows distant from its ideal, there are two possible reactions: people can either modify their conceptions of the ideal family, or they can cling even more to the existing ideal. The latter is the response of a society that has the ability to manage a crisis, and the former is the response of one that does not. What about the case of South Korea? Why don't the power elites or mass media say something about the 'restructuring of the family'?

A little while ago, when I went to the local government (*dong*) office, the female employee who had worked so quietly and efficiently had disappeared. In her place was a 'patriarch' who was slow and lazy in doing his job and chatted with his neighbouring officer. There are significant numbers of women who have to join the workforce in order to provide for their families because their husbands were laid off. However, it is difficult to find any mention of women in such a condition; the only thing that is emphasized is the efforts to find ways to keep husbands from becoming despondent. There are more than a few housewives who are the actual heads of households, and there are many who can earn money. Their only wish is to be treated as the equals of men in the workplace and for their husbands to stop their macho bluster and just manage their own affairs. Although times have changed, the mass media continues to focus on patriarchs and only thinks of structural reforms that can rescue them. The statistic that women comprise 16.8% of all household heads and the fact that women make up almost 40% of all workers has no meaning here (Cho Sun-kyung 1998).

I recently heard from a close friend that a newly appointed branch manager of a foreign bank established a policy of gender equality in hiring, saying that it was necessary to change the company's male-centred culture. Why do people not realize that if the *chaebol*-centred system is a source of problems, then the male-centred privilege system must also be harmful to the economy? Why is it still possible to indulge in the reckless notion that structural reform is possible without reform of existing gender relations that have divided men and women into 'the leaders of society' and 'the home'?

I think that the reason is connected to the problem discussed in the previous section; that is, the existence of 'private profit networks' of men which have prevented the creation of a healthy public space to mediate between the state, the family and individuals. During the period of compressed growth, members of society considered it normal to be mobilized and instrumentalized, and the same process also occurred within the family. The family even had to assume all the welfare functions that should have been the responsibility of the state. As the breakdown of the state system has accelerated, the family has also reached the verge of collapse. Up to now, the family has appeared to be successful at uniting family members into a single unit through the powerful emotions it elicits, based on the image of the bloodline and the tight survival unit.

In truth, the family did perform its central role of providing the basic necessities and meaning of life to its individual members during the Korean War and the following emergency state of the recent rush to development. However, in these economic crises, the reality of the contemporary family has emerged; it has become clear that paths of communication within the family have collapsed. While a welfare state has not yet developed to care for South Korea's *kukmin*, the family has also been unable to provide much of the caring and intimacy that its members need. Just as there are people who have become sceptical of the state, there are also more and more people who are questioning the value of the family. Many young people have begun to realize that the family is stifling; they argue that the family is no more than a mere survival unit in economic terms. Many young people now are ready to leave their families. But this time, the economy is not ready for them. It is another tragedy that out-of-synch timing has brought about, and which South Koreans must deal with.

What subjectivities should we seek, and with whom should we unite?

> There was a time when people instrumentalized and oppressed each other.
> An energy thrived by hurting others and
> an energy thrived by caring for others.
> Which one should we choose?

Now and then, I meet young students who ask me: 'How can a history be written, and a life be maintained, without the energy and passion that comes from the family and the nation?' I have been sometimes troubled by this very question. In this crisis, are there other kinds of energy and movements, besides those rooted in the love of the nation and the family? The backroom deals and collusion between politicians and businessmen that were made possible by familial, regional and alumni networks were the 'fuel' that powered the express train of South Korean economic development. Will it be possible to undo the linkages of the food chains? Can private profit networks and the bureaucratic authoritarianism that was firmly established during the period of abnormal economic development be dissolved?

Up to now, those who have not been able to earn a living have been able to survive on leftovers, thanks to the trickle-down effect of continual economic growth. Now, however, there will be a real struggle for survival. Changes in the outside environment are making it impossible to maintain the current system, and internal differentiation has also reached a critical stage. Meanwhile, people who feel trapped are getting more defensive and fearful. If the intensity of compressed time prevented civil society from nurturing its own consciousness, then how can South Koreans make a new beginning? Can they trust the new president who is said to be studying very diligently? No matter how skilled he is, and no matter how brilliant his advisors are, it will be difficult for him to free himself from the authoritarian culture of the politics of the 'Three Kims Era', from the essentialism of nationalism and from the 'culture of fear' created by the totalitarian politics of discipline and mass mobilization.

South Korean intellectuals must realize that the world they are living in is a closed circuit in which they are trapped. Compressed rush to growth has resulted in uneven development and created a distorted network of desire. In their crisis of identity, loved ones hurt each other through their obsessive desires and cultural absolutism. The bankruptcy of history has become apparent, a history in which various subjectivities were eliminated for the sake of creating a statist/nationalist subject. Society is rapidly losing its self-generating creative force.

South Korean society has now reached a crossroads; metaphorically speaking, South Koreans need to decide whether to repair the irrigation system in order to farm better or to just divide what has been harvested among the power elites and abandon any further production for this year. Will they continue to farm or will they let themselves fall into ruin? It is said that class structure is being reconstituted on a worldwide scale. Regardless of nationality, the population of the world is being polarized into a wealthy class and a poor class in the ratio of 20:80. Even though such facts have become quite clear, many South Korean power elites 'choose' to believe that the nation is eternal. What is the source of the patriotic psychology that resists all efforts to have a serious discussion on issues of class and capital, when the majority of a national population would fall into the marginalized category in the world-class system? Who, among South Koreans, join in changing the world-class system? Recently, multinational capital has established a firm foundation for world domination through ever more sophisticated methods. It has also begun to utilize nationalism to its advantage, and it is very likely that passionate nationalists and multinational capitalists will become allies, whether they realize it or not.

In the last three decades, South Koreans came to devote themselves to economic growth over an extremely short period of time. Now they must utilize all of their sensibilities and intellectual faculties to figure out quickly what sort of crisis they are facing. It is a time for a 'practical learning' of the act of deconstructing and constructing their own subjectivities. What perspective, what position, and with what groups, should one ally with? I feel that the great modern thinkers have already said much of what needs to be said. All that remains is for everyone to create one's own local space where the truths can be practised. I am suspicious of specialist scholars who are comfortable inside their 'well of knowledge'; they do not want to acknowledge change. The time has come for the concept of specialization to be redefined. The time has come when one begins to generate a language that can make sense of a local system that was made through compressed and colonial modernization. To accomplish this task, it will be necessary to grasp the complex interplay of political economy and cultural psychodrama to achieve an epistemologic break.

I have proposed that the notions of the nation, the state and the family should be re-examined (Cho, Haejoang 1997). There should be a more vigorous debate on issues of class, gender and capital only after those notions are successfully deconstructed. About South Korean nationalism, I agree with Kwon Hyokbom's statement that 'a system has [already] been made where things just move within an automatic closed circuit' (Kwon 1998). Nationalism has been the core of the discursive politics used by both conservative and radical domestic political groups to acquire power, and the system built around it is so well stabilized now that their language leaves little space for reflexivity.

A reflection on the nature of temporality is necessary in order to achieve the necessary 'epistemological' break. I see more and more people who want to restore the quotidian world that has been destroyed in the process of modernization. The restoration of the quotidian will be possible through the management of time. Nothing can be achieved without regulating and managing time. Beginning from the ontological recognition that all humans will someday die, there needs to be a philosophy and methodology that can slow down the pace of change until a system for regulating desire and for managing daily time can be discovered. People may become accustomed to living with pessimism rather than optimism. In this sense, the IMF can be seen as a turning point, offering an opportunity to move away from the tornado. Slowing the pace of change ultimately means that capital flows need to be regulated. There will be no change unless there is a comprehensive effort to regulate the system of monopoly capital and to expand the realm of the quotidian.

I/we need to acknowledge the differentiation of society and build a new system upon a foundation of differentiated subjects. Let me repeat that there no longer exists the beauty of national unity. There are no longer '*kukmin*' who can be mobilized under the threat of an 'emergency'. The higher social status that we try so hard to achieve only causes more anxiety. The instrumentalized family only perpetuates our misery by demanding sacrifice. For me/us, there are only various relationships and groups that have to be created and maintained at various levels in order to live in a world of globalization.

So, now, before discussing the nation, let us talk about the differences between men and women, the younger generation and the older generation, and the haves and the have-nots[8]. Before discussing the family, let us talk about individuals. I am now concerned about the lives of youth, not just as 'studying machines', but as active cultural agents and as frustrated unemployed young people. I am a resident of the South Korean peninsula, as well as an Asian, and global feminist. What determines me is what I choose from the various positions I have.

As an academic, I/we must stop thinking within established categories. I/we should view existing scholarly concepts with scepticism, overthrow the language I/we have been using, and change the boundaries of modern academia itself. The time has come for us to choose reality over the image and induction over deduction. It is time for us to do intensive fieldwork and participant observation just like an anthropologist in a strange world, travelling back and forth across borders, leaving time and space open to the imagination.

Conclusion

Milan Kundera (1995: 34) commented upon 'slowness' in his novel of the same name. 'There is a secret bond between slowness and memory, between speed and forgetting. Consider this utterly commonplace situation: a man is walking down the street. At a certain moment, he tries to recall something, but the recollection escapes him. Automatically, he slows down. Meanwhile, a person who wants to forget a disagreeable incident he has just lived through starts unconsciously to speed up his pace, as if he were trying to distance himself from a thing still too close to him in time.'

Have South Koreans been walking so quickly and mindlessly in order to forget the terrible experiences that they have had to go through? 'Don't talk about reality! Don't walk slowly!' The people of South Korea have been able to achieve an economic miracle by obeying these imperatives and have allowed their everyday existence to be regulated by those imperatives.

I do not think that these conditions are unique to South Korea. Rather, I think that this is a phenomenon common to many Third World nations, or even First or Second World nations that had to go through the compressed 'rush to' development; societies that underwent modernization while unable to make their own histories.

When I turned on the TV this morning, the news began with headlines about splits within political parties, announcing that 'this week is most critical'. I/we live in a society where every week is critical, a society where crisis is chronic, a society that makes crisis chronic. Confronting this harsh reality is often too hard for me to endure. Walter Benjamin provided some comfort on this point when he wrote, 'the state of emergency is not the exception but the rule'.

I am dreaming of the days when I will be able to manage my own time and space, when I will be more imaginative and caring. I wanted to open up a new space of reflection that breaks away from the closed circuit in which a sterile language is merely reproduced over and over again. I wanted to write a more dialogical text than this. Indeed, I want to know who are the time managers that make my life so hectic.

Acknowledgements

This work was financially assisted by the Institute for Modern Korean Studies. I am grateful to Michael Shin for his translation of this text, and to Sarah Ralston and Jeannie Martin for their comments and editorial assistance.

Notes

This essay was prepared for a workshop organised by the Graduate Student Association at Yonsei University, Seoul, and so was originally meant for a local audience only. It was written in anger and frustration at the silence of intellectuals in the current 'IMF crisis' in South Korea. Re-reading the text, I was somewhat embarrassed by its exaggerated expressions full of the 'spirit of enlightenment'. It has been translated without any major changes, partly because I am still unable to recover from the depressive mood of the economic slump. I have also been too busy taking action in the current 'state of emergency' as a consultant to the government and as a project manager dealing with the sudden unemployment crisis. Moreover, I did not see the point of rewriting it for an English speaking audience. In this world of 'globalization', it is crucial for the English speaking population to read 'locally produced texts' and train themselves to do it with sensitivity.

1 This title is borrowed from an art critic's, Yi Chuhon (19 February 1998: 13), essay on artistic thought which appeared in Hangyoreh Newspaper.
2 Chollian is one of the major computer network providers in South Korea.
3 Martin and Schumann (1997) note that it was American economist Edward Luttwak who first used the term 'turbo capitalism'.
4 There has been a rush of translations of books that discuss the dark future of global capitalism. These include those by Hans Peter Martin and Harold Schumann (1997), Jeremy Rifkin (1996) and Lester Thurow (1997).
5 Works that have treated compressed temporality include: Anthony Giddens (1991), David Harvey (1989) and Marshall Berman (1982). Interestingly, many books and articles have appeared lately discussing temporality and a busy lifestyle, such as Milan Kundera (1995), Bertrand Russell (1997), and Poul Lafarge (1997).
6 Of course, I am not asserting that the First and Third Worlds are fundamentally different societies. In fact, I have no intention of situating myself within a 'we/they' dichotomy of the world. I know quite well that there are great differences in people's experiences of time and space within a single state according to one's class or gender.
7 This passage is quoted from an article by art critic Yi Chuhon (19 February 1998: 13) on Rene Magritte and Michel Foucault. Published in the Hangyoreh Newspaper, this passage was originally meant to explain aspects of the postmodern condition, but it also contained something that captured the experience of those who live in an age where the feudal, the modern, and the postmodern, are intermixed.
8 Martin and Schumann (1997: 26–28) argue that in a '20: 80 society', where only 20% of the population performs labour, there will be no great problem in maintaining world capitalism. Regardless of nationality, this 20% are able to gain an occupation and actively participate in a life of production/consumption. According to them, the remaining 80% would either be faced with an extremely unstable situation of quasi-unemployment or have to live quietly, being satisfied with the little entertainment and nourishment provided by the ruling structure.

References

Berman, Marshall (1982) *All That is Solid Melts Into Air*, New York: Penguin Books.
Cho, Haejoang 조혜정 (1995) 'Children in the examination war in South Korea', in Sharon Stephens (ed.) *Children and the Politics of Culture*, Princeton, NJ: Princeton University Press.
Cho, Haejoang (1996) 'Marriage stories in a male-centered republic' 남성중심 공화국의 결혼 이야기, *Rewriting Marriage Stories 새로 쓰는 결혼 이야기 1 (2)*, Seoul: Tto hana ui munhwa: 도서 출판 또하나의 문화 .

Cho, Haejoang (1997) 'Feminist intervention in the rise of "Asian Discourse"', *Asian Journal of Women's Studies* 3 (3).

Cho, Hyiyon 조희연 (1997) 'Reexamination of the theory of Asian development: focused on the concept of the development state' 동아시아 성장론의 검토 : 발전 국가론을 중심으로 , *Economy and Society* 경제와 사회 36: 46–76. Seoul: Hanul 한울 .

Cho, Sun-kyung 조순경 (1998) 'A critique of democratic market economy and Confucian patriarchy' 민주적 시장 경 제와 유교적 가부장제 . A paper presented at the monthly forum of the Korean Women's Studies Association, 21 March (unpublished) 년 3 월 21 일 한국 여성학회 월례 발표 논문. 미간행 .

Giddens, Anthony (1991) *Postmodernity*, Hyoun-hee Yi 이현희 (trans. 1998), Seoul: Minyoungsa 민영사 .

Harvey, David (1989) *The Condition of Postmodernity*, Oxford: Basil Blackwell.

Kim, Elaine and Choi, Chinghoo (1998) *Dangerous Women: Gender and Korean Nationalism*, New York, Routledge.

Kim, Hogi 김호기 (1998) 'Sociology of the IMF era' 시대의 사회학 , *Report of the intellectuals* 시대의 사회학 , Seoul: Minumsa 민음사 .

Kundera, Milan (1995) *Slowness* 느림 , Byonwook Kim 김병욱 (trans.), Seoul: Minumsa 민음사 .

Kwon, Hyokbom 권혁범 (1998) 'Globalization and nationalism in the age of market/economy worship' 시장/경제' 숭배 시대의 민족주의와 세계화 . A paper presented at the monthly forum of the Korean Women's Studies Association, 18 April (unpublished) 4 월 18 일 한국 여성학회 월례 발표 논문 . 미간행 .

Lafarge, Poul (1997) *The Right to be Lazy*, Hyoung-jun Cho 조형준 (trans.), Seoul: Saemulgoyl 강수돌 .

Martin, Hans Peter and Schumann, Harold (1997) *The Global Trap: Globalization and the Assault on Prosperity and Democracy*, London: Zed Press; Kang Sudong 강수돌 (trans.), Seoul: Youngrim 영림 .

Pieterse, Jan Nederveen and Bhikhu, Parekj (1997) *The Colonization of Imagination*, Delhi: Oxford University Press.

Pyon, Yongsik 변용식 (1998) 'The patriotism of the Korean people' 한국인의 애국심 , *Choson Newspaper*, 9 February 조선일보 2 월 9 일 .

Rifkin, Jeremy (1996) *The End of Labor*, Young-ho Lee 이영호 (trans.), Seoul: Youngrim 영림 .

Russell, Bertrand (1997) *In Praise of Idleness*, Eun-gyong Song 송은경 (trans.), Seoul: Sahaepyongron 사회평론 .

Thurow, Lester (1997) *The Future of Capitalism*, Jae-hoon Yoo 유재훈 (trans.), Seoul: Koryowon 고려원 .

Yi, Chuhon (19 February 1998) 'Seeing the 20th century through art: Foucault and Magritte', *Hangyoreh Newspaper*.

Appendix

Special terms in Korean in Romanization–Korean–Chinese–English

chaebol 재벌 財閥 , conglomerates (zaibatsu in Japanese)

injisangjong 인지 상정 人之常情 , a natural feeling of common well-being for everyone

kajok 가족 家族 family

kukminjok chongso 국민적 정서 國民的 情緒 national sentiment, popular sentiment

minjok 민족 民族 , ethnic people, nation

minju 민주 民主 , democracy

minjung 민중 民衆 people, common people, oppressed people

wihwagam chosong 위화감 조성 危和感 造成 promoting discord

Chapter 14

Women and freedom

Firdous Azim

Feminist movements use many strategies and deploy various political and social theories for the attainment of their goals. In the new globalized order, 'third world' feminisms have taken recourse to a language of rights, seeking to bring in processes like the world conferences or conventions such as the Convention for the Elimination of all Forms of Discrimination against Women (CEDAW) for the framing of national agendas and demands. Whilst this has been an empowering strategy, what remains in the background is the notion of 'liberation'. Rights speak a language of equality and fair play, of entitlements and access. From within this arena of a rights-oriented movement, I would like to seek spaces where a redress of women's subordinated position translates not only into a movement for justice and equality, but also highlights the questions of freedom and liberation. These may be the spaces where women's problematic social positioning is highlighted, where the meaning of 'freedoms' as it pertains in a gender-discriminated world can be debated.

This paper will look at the way that notions of freedom enter into women's debates in their struggle for the formation of both personal and national identities or identities as citizens of nations. The paper is divided into two sections, which look at how women's voices were deployed to formulate notions of citizenship and statehood at the end of the nineteenth and twentieth centuries. The voices selected from these two eras are from different sources: literary sources from Bengal for the nineteenth and early twentieth centuries, and voices from a particular movement in Bangladesh for an illustration of the debate about women's citizenship in the late twentieth century. It is interesting to see how these very different spheres of struggle and articulation grapple with definitions of national spaces and debate the formation of public and private identities of women.

I would like to begin with a well-known essay by Cora Kaplan: 'Pandora's Box: Subjectivity, Class and Sexuality in Socialist Feminist Criticism' (1986). Analyzing the 'split' feminist field, the essay shows the different spaces ascribed to men and women in Enlightenment discourse. Based on an analysis of Mary Wollstonecraft's *A Vindication of the Rights of Woman* (1792), this essay traces the differences in gender to the differentiated terrain of post-revolutionary Europe in the eighteenth century, which had carved out different and more confined spaces for women in the aftermath of the French Revolution. The 'new' post-revolutionary woman could access the rights granted by the new state, only by curbing some freedoms and by bringing herself under the purview of reason and rationality. The freedoms to be sacrificed were psycho-sexual in nature and entailed a curbing of what the eighteenth century had called 'sensibilities' and that Wollstonecraft herself calls 'a romantic twist of the mind'. This 'sacrifice' of passion for reason creates a gender-differentiated position, and as Kaplan points out, men were carving out spaces that could incorporate both 'passion' and 'imagination'. Wordsworth's 'Preface to the Lyrical Ballads' written in 1800 is an impassioned document, which squarely puts passion, emotion and imagination at the centre of creative and artistic work.

Taking the *Vindication* as the document that spells out the position of women in the new era, we can easily see that the place of passion and emotion – of what was seen to lie at the other side of sense and reason – is problematic for women. Female sexuality, especially the expression of sexual and romantic desire, is construed as a problem. As Kaplan goes on to say:

> It is interesting and somewhat tragic that Wollstonecraft's paradigm of women's psychic economy still profoundly shapes modern feminist consciousness. How often are the maternal, romantic–sexual and intellectual capacity of women presented by feminism as in competition for a fixed psychic space.
>
> (Kaplan 1986: 159)

Translating these concerns into the language of rights and freedoms, the ease with which 'third world' feminisms deploy the language of rights can be contrasted with the ways in which demands for freedoms are cloaked. Freedom in this gendered construction refers to the larger space ('roomier' – as Kaplan says the male romantics had carved for themselves) where passions and emotions have a freer play.

In much of the world, the end of the nineteenth century witnessed a grappling with the issue of freedom from a colonial power. This process was accompanied by a process of self-definition, where nation-states that emerged out of anti-colonial struggles debated and constructed a discourse not just around a set of democratic rights, but around a notion of selfhood and identity. Hence independence meant not only a shaking off of colonial shackles, but coming into one's own – a return to self was seen as part of the process of gaining independence. A hundred years on from that moment, and in the case of the Indian sub-continent, fifty years after the departure of the British, and in the case of Bangladesh, after another war of liberation, it is interesting to look at how those founding concepts have weathered.

I will be looking specifically at the notions of independence and freedom as they apply to women. Women played a central role in this process, as both colonizer and colonized took recourse to notions of captured and debased womanhood as justifications of their position or struggles. Thus the colonialist justified his 'civilizing' mission as one that would 'liberate' women from the oppressions arising out of superstition and barbarity, and the colonized mounted their liberation struggles with an appeal to the mother nation, and saw their task as liberating the conquered motherland. The part that women played in this whole process has been highlighted, and it is interesting to see whether the discourse of freedom initiated by the colonized is different when women enter the field as active agents and actors. Women's voices are important in this context, as women are situated at the crossroads, as it were, between struggles for freedom and the definition of self.

I will be looking at literary writing in Bengal from the end of the last century to show how the issue of freedom entered women's writings. In contemporary Bangladesh

I will look at the struggle for freedom as a part of the women's movement which largely expresses itself as a struggle for rights. I will show how certain demands can be easily expressed and perhaps even hope to be met, whereas other forms of freedom are more difficult to bring into the public discursive arena. The nineteenth-century discourse will be examined through the area of literature, whereas the contemporary struggle will look at women's movements in Bangladesh as they struggle to voice demands for freedom. In both cases, the different sources show women's oblique positioning, and the transformative potential that their presence in any sphere of struggle or discourse contains.

Independence, freedom and a sense of home

One of the most striking literary portrayals of the independence struggle against the British is to be found in Rabindranath Tagore's *Ghare Baire* (1985a), translated as *Home and the World*. Written in 1905, this oft-read novel allies its heroine and her longings and desires to the longing and desire for freedom and independence as expressed through the various anti-British movements of the period. Bimala is shown in a typical scene, looking out of her window, at the landscape outside. Her eyes follow the little winding river, and she imagines the river as it finally meets the sea. She is like that tiny river, bound within its banks, with the ultimate desire of merging with the sea. This desire for freedom is also expressed as one of transgressing limitations and boundaries, of travelling vast expanses and of merging with a greater reality. The novel goes on to describe the pitfalls of this journey. Bimala and her desire for freedom are linked to India/Bengal and its struggle for independence and freedom, and the text serves as a warning of the dangers that stalk such desires.

While we struggle to understand what we are being warned against – women's desire or the struggle for national independence – we can only come to the conclusion that the two are linked. The notion of freedom itself is perhaps enough to open up a whole new horizon, where different constituencies clamouring for this democratic principle will force emerging nation-states to listen to different voices. Women's demand for freedom is highly significant in this context, linked as it is with the special space women are given within the discourse of independence and the formation of the nation-state.

Let us just pause for a moment and look at how women formed part of the debate around nationhood through the various movements of the nineteenth century. Partha Chatterjee's 1989 essay spells out for us the place of women in the definition of the nation, and the significant division of the colonial space into public and private, which is echoed in Tagore's novel. The place that women occupied was also perhaps a response to the colonial discourse, which measured the 'development' of a civilization according to the treatment it meted out to its women and the position it accorded them. In this response, a myth of a glorious Indian past was created, and a past that was evoked in order to place women within positions of dignity in an Indian situation.

We can then look at the way these issues are debated within women's writing. For my example, I have looked at the poetry of Toru Dutt, who was writing in English in the 1870s in Calcutta. Marginalized both by the fact that she was writing in English and also by being a woman, her poetry nevertheless can be seen as part of the project of defining the emerging nationalistic space through a concentration on the figure of the woman. 'Savitri', written in 1877 and published in 1882, is a poem that can be read as part of the reformulation of the figure of the woman as a literary/cultural symbol. It is a long poem that portrays this well-known figure from Indian mythology, a myth which is usually deployed to be the symbol of wifely devotion. Ironically enough, in Toru Dutt's rendition, 'Savitri' becomes a symbol of freedom, of freedoms that were once enjoyed by women in India, but which were now lost. Thus: 'In those far-off primeval days / Fair India's daughters were not pent / In closed zenanas ... ('Savitri', Part 1, lines 72–75).

The contrast between the inside and the outside is drawn as between the present and the past. It is in the present that Indian women are confined within their homes. Toru Dutt, however, seeks freedom not only in ancient India, but surprisingly enough, in modern Europe. Were we to read her poetry along with her letters, we would notice in both forms of writing an intense desire for freedom. Indrepal Grewal's *Home and Harem* (1996) has a very good reading of the desire for freedom expressed in Toru Dutt's letters to her English friend. 'Freedom' is not seen as political freedom here, but as freedom of movement, as freedom to wander and roam. Women's entry into this new sphere of writing poses the question of how the nationalistic discourse would accommodate these differing notions of freedom. Savitri wanders 'in boyish freedom', and one of her main freedoms was the choice of life partner. The contrast between an imagined and ancient India and the present sense of confinement finds expression in her letters as the contrast between her confined life in her family home in Baugmaree near Calcutta and the freedoms and friendships she had enjoyed during her sojourn in England. Ancient India is thus compared with contemporary England or Europe. The movement is both backwards in time – to the glories of the classical past – but also outwards – outside – for 'other' images of freedom. The notion of the comforts of the mother-nation is offset by the drawing of other sites and arenas where Indian daughters are more comfortable and crucially enjoy a sense of freedom.

If Toru Dutt can be seen as a marginalized literary figure in nineteenth-century Bengal, Swarnakumari Devi, sister of Rabindranath Tagore, is both a 'mainstream' as well as a marginalized figure. She is part of the mainstream that Tagore's literary output stands for in Bengali writing, but she is marginalized in that her personal reputation has always been subservient not only to her brother's, but also to the other literary 'greats' of Bengal, such as Bankim Chatterjee. In her novels, she also examines the concept of freedom via the concept of the new woman. Marriage and the creation of a home are perhaps the main themes in her writing. This home is geared towards the needs of this new woman, a site where all her desires and wishes could find expression. For example, the novel *Kahake* (1898), translated by herself as *The Unfinished Song*, contains long diatribes on the nature of love and whether marital love is qualitatively different from other kinds of domestic love, including that between parents and children. The debate is about women and choice in marriage, and hence hearkens to the definition of what constitutes a home, on how women's desires can be contained within the home. Devi follows the traditional nineteenth-century novelistic 'resolution' device, where personal desires and social realities need to harmonize into a neat ending, to avoid personal tragedy, but the irregularities in her writing – the long polemical speeches which disturb the narrative or the plot – are emblematic of this need to question the contours of the home and women's place within it. Greater rights and freedom of choice for women in marriage seem to be guiding her writing, even at the expense of artistic harmony and balance.

Another mainstream yet marginalized voice from the turn of the nineteenth century is that of Rokeya Sakhawat Hussain. Originally from provincial East Bengal, she established a school for Muslim girls in Calcutta, and her writings concentrate on the position of Bengali Muslim women. In 'Sultana's Dream' (1905), she adopts the 'literary' strategy of utopian writing, where she takes the notion of women's power and desire to the plane of fantasy, and through 'air-cars' and fountains etc an ideal world is imagined. This piece of fantasy takes recourse to the women's movement – flying across worlds – and contrasts strongly with her later work *Abaradh Bashini* or *Secluded Women*, which is a series of humorous essays, written between 1928–1930. These essays concentrate on women's confinement within the home, of the veiling of her body, and through humorous vignettes protest women's lack of freedom. Rokeya Sakhawat Hussein places women between this fantasy of freedom – of soaring to the sky – and the reality of women's confined bodies. Looking at her Calcutta school as the space she created for women, this oscillation between freedom and confinement becomes visible. The girls were transported to school in a horse-drawn carriage that was covered with a sheet according to purdah principles, while the education that they got was geared towards creating the first generation of free-thinking Muslim women in Bengal.

How are we to look at these women writers? For this essay, I have just touched on a few writings from women of the late nineteenth and early twentieth centuries, and I would really like to make the case that Bengali literary history needs to be re-read with a concentration on these marginalized literary voices. Such a re-reading would bring to the fore different dimensions of the terrain in which the nationalist ideal was being debated and formulated. Does this mean that there is a real change in the discourse when we include women writers? This takes us not to the question of the autonomy of women's voices, but to whether gendered readings can change the outlines of nationalist formations and discourses. Just by looking at the notion of home as expressed in Toru Dutt or Swarnakumari Devi, we see how definitions change. Toru Dutt opens the discourse wider and further afield, whereas Swarnakumari Devi makes an internal exploration to change the contours of the domestic sphere. A different kind of woman – a more assertive one in the case of Devi, and in Dutt's case, the expression of women's desire, serves to blur the boundaries between the private and the public and issues of freedom are brought into the private domain. Struggles for freedom do not pertain to the national struggle only, but enter into the home and struggle to redefine that sphere.

Thus, the blurring of the public/private through women's writings forces a public examination of the domestic terrain, and works towards a refashioning of that terrain. Women's writing and writing per se, as we know, in the late nineteenth and early twentieth centuries has to be considered within its class constraints, but even this very limited sphere of the emerging middle classes manages to bring out many issues. First, it shows how freedom and the concept of the home are contradictory, and how the woman, meant to be the centre of the home, traverses between her domestic status and her status as an independent citizen of the emerging nation-state. Significantly, it also highlights the transgressive nature of women's desires and opens up a special literary arena in which these desires can find artistic expression. Finally, it seeks to ascribe a kind of constrained freedom to women, a bonded freedom, as it were, in which certain demands can be addressed and others either ignored or suppressed. Women's writings are also interesting in the sense that they show us the emergence of women's voices and, in the period under consideration, the veiled and indirect expression of desires and demands.

The tone set by this late nineteenth-century nationalistic discourse persists, and we saw a complete re-emergence of it during the 1971 Bangladesh Liberation War. The nation was again imaged as a woman, and notions of freedom and independence were related to that figure. While doing so the 'real' position of women did not enter the liberation discourse at all, except in the case of rape cases during the war (and even here the discussion has been very weak and fragmentary). It is in the new context of Bangladesh that we now need to examine the way that women's demands are expressed, the notion of women's freedom brought into view and the various arenas and actors involved in this process.

The problematic and often oblique positioning of women that the nineteenth-century literary sphere delineated for women persists within the newly independent nations. How women were positioned in India, for example, in the aftermath of the partition and the division of the country has been very well recorded by Urvashi Butalia. Using first-person narratives and interviews, *The Other Side of Silence* (2000) is an account of the displacement of peoples across boundaries, which is the staple of partition studies in South Asia, but a concentration on the displacement of women brings along with it a re-questioning of the borders, a re-questioning of the contours of the newly formed states. Gender and citizenship – stock words of the rights discourse – acquire new meanings when viewed in this light. What are the parameters that define citizenship and how is the state to formulate and advocate for its gender-differentiated citizens? Though this section is not looking at literary renditions, it will be useful to look at Susie Tharu and K. Lalita's introduction to the second volume of their massive anthology of Indian women's writing, for an understanding of the ways in which women are written out of the national imaginary (Tharu and Lalita 1993).

Similarly, in the series of interviews put together under the title of *Ami Birangona Bolchi* (1998) by Nilima Ibrahim, the newly emerged nation of Bangladesh is made to look at the status of women victims of war rape. The word birangona (feminine for bir or hero) had been coined in 1972 to give the status of war heroes to the victims of Pakistani rape. The interviews reveal the very anomalous position that these women occupy within the nation for which it has been said they have 'sacrificed their honour'. Thus rights for women follow a sexed and gendered pattern, and movements for the rights of women have actually to grapple with those positions. At both moments of nation formation, in 1947 and 1971, women's sexual positioning ('vulnerability'/'honour'/'sacrifice') was central in determining their national identity, even their citizenship. Hence it is important to look at how the notion of women's sexuality is debated in women's struggles around citizenship rights and equality within the newly formed national spheres.

Here I will be concentrating on the women's movement in Bangladesh, which is manifested in a number of women's groups that seem to be acquiring greater visibility over the last 20 or so years. Without going into the various differences in approach, it can easily be said that the women's movement takes recourse to a discourse of rights and democracy. This seems to be the safest and most acceptable ground from which to operate, but it is interesting to see how even within this basically accepted democratic value, there are certain areas that are considered 'difficult'. The difficulty arises regarding what has already been seen as the psycho-sexual sphere, of the freedom to express desire. Control on women's sexuality at the personal and state levels are translated into a curbing of freedoms – of movement, of expression, of work and employment. The women's movement itself tends to mask its demands for greater freedoms, including sexual freedom, in issues such as violence against women or women's health issues instead of speaking directly of women's sexuality. This strategy is useful and often helps to 'smuggle in' a demand for greater sexual and emotional freedom, but it also has its flip side in that by containing demands for greater freedom, it keeps on curtailing freedoms.

Women's work, sexuality and freedom

The literary sphere continues to be the place from where women's desire especially for sexual freedom can be expressed. This is not only in the case of women's writing, but also in the strategies that women's groups adopt for themselves. I would like to take the case of Naripokkho, a woman's group in Bangladesh, which tried to bring the issue of women's desire to the political forefront first through its International Women's Day celebration in 1990. Using a late-nineteenth-century literary text – Rabindranath Tagore's dance-drama *Chitrangoda* (1985b) – notions of femininity and masculinity were highlighted as they played themselves out between the male and female protagonists of the play. Female sexual desire as it finds expression throughout the play is juxtaposed with an assertion of female identity and a demand for equality. However, the production had a limited impact. Though it could be viewed as an example of the way that literature could be brought to the service of women's liberation, it did not have the kind of larger social effect that women's movements need to make.

Finally, when the issue of sexuality and freedom did enter the public arena of the women's movement, it was not through these deliberate and subtle literary renditions, but through struggles of marginalized groups of women, whose living depended on sex work. Through a series of campaigns against brothel evictions (from 1993 onwards), Naripokkho, as well as other women's and human rights groups, brought to the public forefront the issues pertaining to women's sexuality, their status and position in society. A common platform, Shanghoti, comprising women's groups, human rights groups, NGOs, journalists, health workers and sex workers' groups, emerged out of these campaigns. Shanghati is an alliance of diverse groups and has been working formally since May 1999 to struggle for the recognition of the rights of sex workers. One of its most successful efforts was to win a court case against the eviction of a brothel in Narayanganj, where the judge in a historic ruling gave legal status to women residents of the brothel and to their trade.

The first change that the alliance brought about was perhaps the change in nomen-clature – from prostitution to sex work. Despite the problematic associated with the term sex work itself, this change in nomenclature helped to highlight the issues of women's right to work and also of what constituted women's work. Hence by combin-ing the words sex and work, the rights discourse could be brought into play with an emphasis on the right to work and also an opportunity arose which allowed us to debate the issue of sex. The rights agenda allowed the movement to spell out many demands that found an easy resonance in the larger political arena. The coalition, formed of many diverse organizations, can be seen as the way in which women's demands can be articulated through a diversity of groups, and can be used as an example of platform building, and what is gained and lost in the process. Many organizations in the alliance are lawyers and human rights groups, and maybe the emphasis on rights in the campaign was guided by this fact. However, this essay will look at how this emphasis on rights can be seen to modify the very arena of rights in which it is placed.

Despite the presence of multi-interest groups, one of the main strategies used was that of prioritizing women's voices. This had the effect of transforming political spaces, in that it brought voices of sex workers directly into the mainstream of political and social movement, and also gave us a space where again we can look at the 'autonomy' or otherwise of women's voices. Autonomous or not the transformatory effect of the inclusion of women's voices into the political discourse was again made clear. We may have come a long way from the time that Gandhi had expressed 'extreme resentment at the inclusion of prostitutes of Barisaal in the cause of the Congress party' because of their 'immorality' (Sangari and Vaid 1989: 22), but the inclusion of 'immoral' women's voices is still a struggle, and the political mainstream, including the feminist mainstream, is still wary of such an inclusion.

Let us now look at some of the main issues that came out of the campaigns. The first one to look at will be that of women's work, as we struggled to change the nomenclature from prostitution to sex work. The contention here was that this change in naming also highlighted the special nature of women's work, linking it to women's position in the job market in general. This pertained not only to lack of occupational options for women, but to how women's entry into the job market is reflective of the domestic roles assigned to her. Her entry into the public world can be seen as a continuum with her private and domestic roles. Prostitution also brings to the fore the notion of sexuality, based on presumed male predatoriness. What remains unexamined within the purview of prostitution is women's sexuality: she is merely a body to give pleasure. Just as women's pleasure is not at issue in prostitution, so is it not in the other sphere where women function as sexual beings – in marriage. Prostitution is work, not pleasure for women (and incidentally brings up the question of whether work and pleasure can mix), but the very feminized nature of the profession, of prostitution as women's work, showed us how women's sexual pleasure is not an issue, even where agency may be.

Women perform two major roles within the home – as wife and mother. Both refer to her reproductive functions and hence refer to the arena of sexuality, which includes sexual activity, desire, agency and so on. As women's sexuality is confined to or given legitimacy only within marriage, the question of how sex is organized within marriage remains crucial. Sex is a duty for women, performed to meet the husband's conjugal demands, and in order to produce children – it is sex work. Keeping the continuum between women's domestic duties and the work that is available to her in the job market, prostitution can easily be seen as sex work. Drawing a continuous line between women in public and private spheres helps us to see how women's subordination pertains to both spheres. So while we seek recognition for prostitution and call it sex work, we at the same time need to look at the positioning of women engaged in prostitution.

A question of rights

The main thrust of the campaign was on rights. This thrust as mentioned earlier was guided by strategic considerations and it was most helpful not only in keeping the coalition together, but in bringing certain other issues to the fore.

Let us look at what this emphasis on rights achieved. One of the main rights evoked, given that it was an anti-eviction campaign, was that to the right to dwelling and called on the sanctity of the home. This had the effect of redrawing the notion of home. Not only were brothels places of work, but homes, where domestic and affective roles were performed. Maternal functions and duties were performed here. Along with the recognition of brothels as homes was the fact that these homes were licensed workplaces.

Brothels are demarcated as red light areas by the government and the sexual trade that goes on here is given legal sanction by the laws of the land. Stressing legitimacy also helped to decriminalize the sex trade. Brothel residents emphasized the fact that they paid rent, even at exorbitant rates, and hence reiterated their absolute right to the spaces that they had been living in and working from.

Perhaps even more interesting was the demand for state protection. The law-enforcing agencies were blamed for failing to provide protection, as well as for joining hands with the criminal elements involved in the eviction. In this manner, it was the women now who were the legal occupants of these homes and spaces and their evictors the criminals. The government had to answer for their collusion with the evictors and their failure to provide protection. This is again a very significant dimension. The right to demand from government institutions the services and facilities that they are meant to provide is not a very established practice in countries like ours. One of the ways in which feminist groups have been working is to monitor service delivery systems, such as health, or law-enforcement agencies, point out the areas where citizens are not given the services that are their right, and work towards making these systems more effective. The demand for state protection and the institution of the court case are really a part of the same process. This campaign is an illustration of the way that the state and government are responsible for the protection of the rights of all its citizens and the ways in which diverse sections of the citizenry can place its demands.

Making the state responsive to women's demands may have a flip side in that it also allows the state to define and determine women's positions. The point that is being made here is one of demand and assertion – of incorporation and citizenship – and that of definition and control. Somehow women have to play between these poles. Even while they are placed at the centre of state control they have to 'prove' their status as citizens. Just as the post-enlightenment positions for women had called upon a redefinition of women as rational beings and hence fit citizen-subjects, so too the demand for state protection and services is based on a notion of 'deserving' citizens. The question whether by allowing state and law-enforcing functionaries entry into brothels and homes ensures greater security or whether it results in a greater state control (or coercion) is really emblematic of the very difficult positioning as citizens or subjects of the state. In a way we can see how these demands fluctuated between the personal and the public – the personal demands for home and the demand to the state for ensuring the security of that home. Again it is women, placed at the crossroads between the public and the personal, making the personal public, and demanding public recognition of duties and functions, who straddle both spheres. Using the rights discourse was a helpful and empowering strategy as far as the campaign was concerned, helping us to institute a court case for the rights of sex workers to their abode.

The incorporation of women's voices

The other and perhaps even more interesting strategic intervention was the active participation in leadership roles of evicted brothel residents and a direct voicing of their own concerns and needs.

Let us just spend a minute to look at these first-person voices and to examine a notion of truth or authenticity that may pertain to them. These voices did not function as conduits to the 'truth' of prostitution or sex work, but were strategically used to appeal to the audience. Brothel residents wielded the discourse to put forward their demands as they thought fit. The recourse to a notion of rights proved very useful and these rights were demanded on the basis of duties performed. The right to the home was justified through the fact that they paid rent, the right to state protection was demanded on the basis of the performance of civic duties, such as voting, paying taxes and being useful citizens of the state.

The definition of 'usefulness' was interesting. Brothel residents defined the use-value of their work in terms of a social 'safety valve' and even while they talked about eviction from brothels as a violation of their rights, they did not hesitate to use other arguments to bolster their demands. One strategy of course was the appeal to pity and sympathy – poor women driven out of their homes to walk the streets. The other was an appeal to social order, and the picture of poor women walking the streets was rendered in terms of a spectre that would not only haunt but corrupt social sexual morality. Thus there was no hesitation in using a conservative approach that appealed to the patriarchal status quo, to recover the brothels.

It was in the voicing of demands and organizing the campaign that a new form of political empowerment was experienced. This empowerment did not take the form of glorification of sex work as a site where alternative notions of female sexuality may surface, as some postmodernist feminist discourses seem to suggest. On the other hand, the organization of women's sexuality in prostitution rests upon a system of monogamy, and looks at itself as the flip side of marriage. It lays a premium on youth and beauty and old age appears as a dire fate to many prostitutes. Age sometimes brings its own compensations, and some women may acquire positions of power and decision-making within the brothel set-up. Female sexuality and female sexual desire, amongst prostitutes, seems to rely on a notion of monogamous and heterosexual sexuality. Very little emerges about female relationships, except that the hierarchy established by age and beauty is very palpable. It is difficult to look at prostitution as a site of female sexual emancipation, or even as a site where prevalent norms and rules are subverted. It indeed seems to be the other side of marriage – the other institution in which women function as sexual beings.

If we are looking for a 'different' voice within this campaign, it was to be found regarding the question of 'rehabilitation'. The stand normally taken is to 'rehabilitate' these 'unfortunate' women into the mainstream of society and a complete puzzlement ensues when these 'rehabilitated' women protest against the rehabilitation measures. The measures taken in the name of rehabilitation include (a) skill development in traditional female activities, such as sewing; (b) being given inputs, such as a sewing machine, to ease transition into another profession; and (c) marriage. Each of these measures has proved to be ineffective. As far as skill development and training are concerned, these skills do not give enough financial return in the job market. It is also unrealistic to feel that a sewing machine will suffice to set up a tailoring shop and finally, women who have been 'married off' find themselves being used as prostitutes by their new husbands, who now become their pimps. In each case, the special difficulty women who have been known to be sex workers may face are not taken into consideration. Employment in garment factories, for example, may even be protested by fellow workers, not to say of the fresh forms of sexual exploitation to which their past histories could expose these women. And of course it is facile to speak of rehabilitating women in prostitution into the job market, when we know of the limited opportunities available to all entrants into the job market and when we are speaking of a socially disabled group of women. As one brothel worker put it to the person recommending other jobs – 'Would it be all right for me to be working in your husband's office?' Women were sent into vagrant homes by the government, which they found very demeaning and where they were subjected to fresh forms of sexual exploitation.

The campaign of 1999 turned the notion of rehabilitation on its head, by demanding rehabilitation into brothels, by claiming rights over that space and by the demand that the women engaged in prostitution need to be recognized as citizens with the full rights of citizens. Earlier, sex workers had talked of 'social rehabilitation' and now we have had a demonstration of the full meaning of that term. Social rehabilitation, at one level, means the ability to hold up one's head; to be given dignity and recognition as a fellow member of society, regardless of who you are and what you do, but now the recognition is for the rights of women who are prostitutes, of recognition as workers, as women who are on their own and earning their own keep. One of the strongest statements to come out of the campaign was – 'We do not depend on anyone for food or lodging, so leave us alone'. This assertion of economic independence immediately places the sex worker in a position of dignity and does not allow the welfare approach that guides rehabilitation efforts to come into operation. The rehabilitation being asked for is recognition as citizens, as subjects of the state.

How are we to read these *fin-de-siècle* voices? One obvious way is to read them as an extension of the Enlightenment discourse, as an extension of the constituencies that are to be embraced within the democratic framework. At another level, we can also see these voices as disturbing, not merely clamouring for inclusion, but negotiating change and transformation. Be they the literary voices of the late nineteenth century, or the marginalized groups of today, women seem to be asking for a redefinition of the political and social body, of asking for a redefinition of the nation, so that different ways of inclusion can be envisioned. Ideas and definitions of home and nation are directly effected by the literary voices of the past. Today's women are actually seeking to change not only the private dimensions of what constitutes the 'home', but also asking for a public recognition of the variety of images and institutions that that word evokes. It seeks to force the body politic to take cognizance of the different ways of organizing life and sexuality and to make the nation and state respond to each of these changes.

What is also interesting is that in this age of privatization, where all services are being taken away from the state, we found women's groups in Bangladesh coalescing to demand services from the state. With all the prognostications of the demise of the nation-state, it seems that the state remains essential as a last recourse to marginalized groups. This is even true for inter-state situations – as is borne out in the case of migrant female labour and the response to their needs by various women's and human rights groups. It has been to lobby state and government bodies for better legislation and better protection. It is as though in this vast jungle of globalization, disempowered and marginalized groups can only turn to instruments of state for the protection of rights and freedoms. As the world 'opens up', individual states may yet be necessary for the guaranteeing of human rights and liberties, but the negotiations on which these rights are incorporated can be read to highlight the positional differences between citizens within national boundaries and which is then extended to the position that they may occupy in the globalized sphere where these boundaries do not have the same demarcating status.

References

Butalia, Urvashi (2000) *The Other Side of Silence: Voices from the Partition of India*, London: Hurst.

Chatterjee, Partha (1989) 'The nationalist resolution of the women's question' in K. Sangari and S. Vaid (eds) *Recasting Women: Essays in Colonial History*, New Delhi: Kali for Women, 233–253.

Dutt, Toru (1882) 'Savitri', *Ancient Ballads and Legends of Hindustan*, London: Kegan, Paul Trench, 3–45.

Grewal, Inderpal (1996) *Home and Harem: Nation, Gender Empire and the Cultures of Travel*, London: Leicester University Press.

Hussein, Rokeya Sakhawat (1985) *The Complete Works of Rokeya Sakhawat Hussein (Rokeya Rachanabali)*, Dhaka: Bangla Academy Press.

Ibrahim, Nilima (1998) *The Voices of War Heroines (Ami Birangana Bolchi)*, Dhaka: Jagrata Prakashani.

Kaplan, Cora (1986) 'Pandora's box: subjectivity, class and sexuality in socialist feminist criticism', *Sea Changes: Essays on Culture and Feminism*, London: Verso, 147–176.

Sangari, K. and Vaid, S. (eds) (1989) *Recasting Women: Essays in Colonial History*, New Delhi: Kali for Women.

Tagore, Rabindranath (1985a) 'Home and the World (Ghare Baire)' in *The Complete Works of Rabindranath Tagore (Rabindra Rachanabali)*, Calcutta: Viswabharati Press, Vol. 8, 137–334.

Tagore, Rabindranath (1985b) 'A dance-drama (Chitrangoda)' in *The Complete Works of Rabindranath Tagore (Rabindra Rachanabali)*, Calcutta: Viswabharati Press, Vol. 3, 157–200.

Tharu, Susie and Lalita, K. (eds) (1993) *Women Writing in India: 600 B.C. to the Present*, New York: The Feminist Press.

Chapter 15

Caught in the terrains

An inter-referential inquiry of trans-border stardom and fandom[1]

Eva Tsai

While stardom outside one's home country still holds an undeniable appeal for performers, it carries certain liabilities in the current global cultural economy. In a time of intense regional and global cultural traffic, transborder fame can transpire in unexpected temporalities and distant geographies. The same dynamic processes can result in an unpopular[2] mixture of celebrity and politics. Such situations present to us a timely opportunity to formulate an idea of stardom that goes beyond the naïve assumption that stardom is the result some kind of individual achievement or that it is merely the desired end product of culture industry manipulation. Stardom is better understood as a result of the compounding effect of media work, cultural formations, technological interfaces, and the flow of commodity and currency, and it is one of the primary constituents of public culture.

This paper juxtaposes two trans-Asian pop stars whose careers came to a grinding halt amid trans-border politics in 2004. Aboriginal-Taiwanese pop diva Chang Hui-Mei (hereafter A-Mei) faced 'patriotic' protesters in China just as politicians back home in Taiwan were claiming that she was unpatriotic. Song Seung-Heon, the leading man in the Korean Wave hit drama, *Autumn Fairytale*, admitted to draft-dodging and began his mandatory military service despite fans' efforts to keep him on as the star of a new, highly anticipated drama. These analogous cases both stirred up heated debates concerning national loyalty, and they are inter-referenced in this essay to reveal the complex borders and terrains in Asia that contextualize the public culture surrounding stardom and fandom. More than a validation of the fame of individual stars, the idea of transnational stardom in Asia is linked with participation in ordinary trans-Asia cultural traffic. Given celebrities' capacity to involve multiple publics in intimate ways, the twin engines of publicity/publicness across Asia emerge into a significant issue of inquiry.

A-Mei and Song are not the only Asian celebrities dealing with political issues such as cross-strait tensions and the morality of South Korea's conscription system. Their entanglement with patriotism and the subsequent affective responses of their fans are indications of the intimate relationship between politics and entertainment in Asia. The problem of stars being anything but seriously political has been identified by film scholar Richard Dyer: 'What the star does can *only* be posed in terms of the *star doing it*, the extraordinariness of difficulty of his/her doing it, rather than in terms of the ostensible political issues involved' (Dyer 1979: 79). Dyer's ideological criticism is well taken. But what if the 'political' does not reside so ostensibly in the star's action or will?

The 'uptake' of pop stars in Asia, for one thing, is their politicization in a region where nation-states still figure actively in the identities of people. The ideological changes and divides in the region have prompted some pop stars to cultivate a political career. For example, Kao Jin Su-mei, the female lead in Ang Lee's *Wedding Banquet* became a prominent legislator in Taiwan in 2001 and has been active in lending a decolonizing political voice in transnational situations. In 2006, Korean film stars initiated protests against the South Korean government's plan to weaken – under pressure from the US government – the existing film quota system. Despite the unflattering circumstances surrounding their reluctant entry into politics, A-Mei's and Song's sudden political enmeshment was no fluke. In fact, it is impossible to separate their stardom from the realm of politics. Doing so would inevitably mean returning to the assumption that stardom depends on individual will and action when it is clearly more about collective embodiment.

In this paper, stardom and fandom are mined to re-politicize the politically correct tone of popular culture. This could turn into a ruthless and hierarchical political game, preserving certain positions of substantiation – often more alternative, anti-establishment – while excluding other questionable 'political' practices. In 2006, the protests initiated by Korean film stars like Jang Dong-gun against the South Korean government's screen quota prompted a Hong Kong critic Ip Iam Chong (2006) to lament the political apathy of Hong Kong film directors and stars. Taiwanese critics have also cited American and European celebrities' involvement in agenda-based politics to criticize apolitical stars in Taiwan.[3] The place of fans as politicized publics seems to have been overlooked given their association with the 'depoliticized' stars.[4] But these problems with border-crossing are precisely what matters in the search for inter-Asia publics.

Doing inter-referential research in Asia

The year 2004 was a demoralizing year for A-Mei's and Song's fans. It was supposed to be a glorious year for both stars. A-Mei had planned a concert in China, which was the most anticipated event since her Beijing concert in 1999 and Shanghai concert in 2002. Song was riding high on the tide of Korean Wave (hallyu) owing to the popularity of Autumn Fairytale *and* Summer Scent. *All eyes were on his next starring role in* Sad Love Story, *a drama backed in part by Japanese and Taiwanese investors.*

But on June 12, 2004, A-Mei was forced to cancel her appearance in Hangzhou because of safety concerns. Outside the venue, a group of self-identified 'patriots' held a banner that read 'Pro-Taiwan Independence Greeners Not Welcome', apparently reacting to A-Mei's appearance on a 'green list' which was circulating online and which purported to identify the political leaning of Taiwanese entertainers. During the following month and a half leading up to A-Mei's scheduled solo concert in Beijing, tension loomed across the strait. That concert, at Capital Stadium on July 31, 2004, proved a success, but she had barely enough time to catch her breath before finding herself in hot water over another patriotic test. On a radio show, Taiwan's Vice President Annette Lu urged A-Mei to weigh her career prospects in China against the security of her fellow Taiwanese who are living in a 'quasi-war state' (Wang and Chang 2004: 1). A-Mei told the media that politics should be left in the hands of grown-ups/authorities (daren):[5] 'I am just a singer doing what I am meant to do. When I stand on the stage, I give my best to deliver a perfect performance. I don't have the capacity to join the world of the 'daren'. Let's leave the matter to 'daren' to handle since they know the best' (Yuan 2004: A3).

About a month after the public debate on A-Mei's dilemma quieted down in Taiwan, the South Korean police were conducting the largest draft-dodging investigation in the country's history. The arrest of ten baseball players and two brokers led the police to identify other athletes and entertainers who had attempted to get out of compulsory service. This included Song, who at the time was filming a music video for Sad Love Story *in Australia. In a public statement to the Korean press and his fans, Song admitted having manipulated medical records to dodge conscription. He expressed regret for his misconduct and his willingness to follow the government's order that he return to Korea to serve. 'I'd like to take this opportunity to be more mature,' he wrote in an open statement. Song returned to Seoul to cooperate with investigation after he finished shooting the music video. Support from his fan groups in Taiwan, China, Hong Kong, and Japan poured in to urge the Military Manpower Administration (MMA), the South Korean government, and related authorities to credit Song's contribution to the phenomenal* hallyu *and not conscript Song. Following a very public physical checkup and an international send-off, Song began a 24-month tour of service in the army on November 16, 2004.*

The above narrative weaves A-Mei's and Song's predicaments into a common coming-of-age story: both stars were subjected to public patriotic tests. The description juxtaposes the two entertainers whose dissimilar audiences and career paths become possible references for each other in our search for the elusive "public" among trans-Asian cultural traffic. This busy crossroads contains the materiality of what Kuan-hsing Chen (2001; 2002a; 2005b) called a not-yet-post-Cold-War Asia. A critical intellectual, Chen is committed to forming alliances with third-world cultural critics and turning to alternative, non-western-dominated frames of references to breathe new life into the practices of knowledge production. In 'Asia as Method', he further elaborates the potential gain in working toward a new Asian imagination, which makes it possible to own up to the historical legacies from the colonial, cold-war, and imperial structures of power in the region (Chen 2005a).[6]

Inspired by Chen's syncretic approach, this paper undertakes an inter-referencing experiment with the goal of enlarging the critical discursive space on Asia by interrogating the relations between the popular, political, and public. As several critical historians have pointed out (Ching 2000; Chun and Shamsul 2001; Sun 2000a; 2000b), the act of speaking or writing on Asia constitutes a political practice. Interventionist intellectual efforts such as the inter-Asia cultural studies movement[7] persistently complicate the meanings of Asia. But this practice is still often distant from popular experiences, discourses, and sites where other political definitions of Asia could just as well emerge.[8] Certainly, the 'public' has perpetually eluded the detection of academic discourses that speak in the name of the people. The 'deviant', the working class, and the truly marginalized are constantly excluded from the bourgeois elitist-produced 'public'. Ning Ying-bin even argues that despite their exploitativeness, low-brow variety shows on commercial TV channels demonstrate greater inclusiveness than public television by dint of their populist programming and notorious methods of publicity (Ning 2004).

Though not quite so subversive, the at-large 'public' in my research refers to various bodies (e.g., fans, academics, government) and styles (e.g., rational, affective) of interaction. Those who have studied cultural flows in Asia know how precarious it is to lay a claim on pan-Asian identity. Instead of hoping for an identity to emerge as a result of trans-Asian cultural traffic, I am more interested in locating the kinds of public spaces that accommodate it. Meaghan Morris has characterized trans-Asian cultural traffic as a 'new space of circulation that can tolerate, bear, and make use of relations of unlikeness, even while the liberating experiences of recognizing or constructing resemblances' (Morris 2004: 257). Could this new space be re-conceptualized as a public zone?

In this study, I bring in the personal – that is, the researcher's relationship, access, and sensitivity to the at-large public of inter-Asia. The public under question is not an undifferentiated public typically delimited by the nation-state (e.g., 'Chinese public', 'Korean public'). Informed by interpretive, ethnographic, reflexive, and empirical strategies of inquiry, my pursuit of publics in Asia led me to multiple issues of ir/reconciliation, by which I mean working out spaces of recognition and not doing away with the political or the popular. As Jing Wang suggests in her critique of the Chinese 'popular', the popular cannot be treated automatically in opposition to the state or to the high brow (Wang 2001). The recent rise of creative culture industries and the Korean popular culture, for example, are partly attributable to the influence of government authorities in the production of popular culture. Such non-fixed relations between the popular, public, and political may ultimately develop our capacity to handle and translate inter-Asian culture for each other.

Surviving patriotism in non-national zones

The rise of A-Mei is a classic Cinderella story in two senses. She lived out the promise of individual transcendence of the culture industry and that she – a Puyuma from Taitung – has also made it to the top in a society dominated by ethnic Han Chinese. The 'A-Mei phenomenon', coined after the release of two million-selling CDs in 1996, was said to symbolize the advent of new taste, the ascent of aboriginal culture, and the salvation of homesick urban audiences (Yang 1997; Lo 1998a; Lo 1998b; Wang 1998). No one ever doubted A-Mei's ability to sing, given her background as a television singing contest champion and seasoned pub singer. She also proved to be a true live diva, capable of moving her audience with a powerful and versatile voice and an unrestrained body language. In 1999, A-Mei held sold-out concerts throughout Southeast Asia. Her concert in Beijing, the first solo pop concert ever held at the fifty-thousand-seat Workers Stadium, nearly paralyzed the subway system. A veteran fan from Beijing, who walked two kilometers before she was able to hail a cab after the show, recalled the intoxicated feeling: 'I was sitting on the mezzanine, watching this tiny person perform on stage. But I was elated. My goodness, so many people were singing the same song with me' (Interview by author, 15 Oct. 2005).

If politics is narrowly defined as the power games played by wheeling and dealing bigwigs, then this seems to be the story before A-Mei became politicized. The year 2000 is often perceived as a watershed year for A-Mei, the end of her age of innocence. Censorship in mainland China followed A-Mei's performance of the Republic of China (ROC) anthem at President Chen Shui-Bian's inauguration. Rather than explaining away this 'political' problem as a simple tale of two nationalisms, the question inspired by A-Mei's resurgent predicament in 2004 is this: How does patriotism interweave with other modes of attachment enabled by the trans-Asian cultural traffic running alongside post-national and non-national feelings? The issue is in dialogue with Arjun Appadurai's observations about the global staying power of patriotism as well as discussions of 'new patriotism' (Appadurai 1993; Gavrilos 2003) – all of which recognize new forms of loyalty beyond the nation-state. In the following, I present an account of the complex ways A-Mei's fans in Taiwan and China negotiate loyalty amid cross-strait tensions and competing political discourses. Their 'being here' and 'being there' for A-Mei over the course of nine years was not simply a gesture of loyalty to their idol, but a period in which they created opportunities for cross-border understanding.

The specter of Teresa

Although A-Mei's reluctant brush with politics was often believed to have started in 2000, its 'anomaly' was shaped by a 'politically correct' reading of the relationship between entertainers and politics under a Cold War framework. In particular, A-Mei's multiple instances of 'politically incorrectness' were likened to the legacies of the first trans-Asian pop star and model patriotic entertainer: Teresa Teng. Born into a family of Kuomintang (KMT) nationalist soldiers, Teng started making records at the age of 14. In the 1970s, her sweet ballads soothed a variety of homesicknesses on the island, including those felt by resettled mainlanders as well as those caused by the loss of Taiwan's seat in the United Nations. Teng's music became popular in China in the 1980s via pirated tapes and CDs despite being officially denounced by the PRC government. Like many other 'patriotic entertainers' (e.g., dancers, musicians, film actresses, Beijing opera singers), Teng was involved in entertaining KMT troops on army bases and navy ships as well as performing for civilians in overseas Chinese communities. For these entertainers, performing was tantamount to performing patriotism – a virtue many even valued over fame and wealth.[9] Teng was not only formally recognized as being a 'patriotic entertainer' by the ROC Government of Information Office in 1981, but also remained politically active well into her career, as seen in her support of the Tiananman movement in Beijing in 1989. After she died of acute asthma in Thailand in 1995, she was given a national burial in Taiwan, which was also televised.

The emergence of categories such as a 'patriotic entertainer' requires a particular transnational context, one that in Teng's time was provided by the 'Free China vs. Red China' Cold War structure. As Asian and Chinese-language cultural markets merged under globalization, the idea of 'patriotic entertainer' seemed increasingly obsolete. Still, the specter of Teresa returned to remind us that it was possible to be patriotic without a nation because the legitimacy of the nation-state is never stable from within or outside.

As A-Mei's career began to cross-over to China, the Taiwanese press saw A-Mei and Teng's 'mainland penetration' as analogous since both occurred during times of heightened cross-strait tensions (Lee 2000). In A-Mei's case, it was shortly after former President Lee Teng-Hui enunciated the two-state formula, namely that Taiwan and the PRC are two different, but equal states. A magazine reporter describing A-Mei's influence wrote: 'Even at a low point in cross-strait relations a 'special harmony' existed. It showed the power of popular culture' (Shih 1999: 42). The familiar rhetoric that popular culture triumphs over politics underscores the persistence of patriotism since, for people living in different political realities, the meaning of patriotism pluralizes. Nancy Guy's research on the reactions to A-Mei's singing of the ROC anthem reveals just such political realities in Taiwan (Guy 2002).

The specter of Teresa refers not to the ghost nation imagined under the KMT regime or its presumed competitor, the state imagined as the end result of the Democratic Progressive Party's (DPP) nation-building project. Instead, the specter refers to the not-so-singularized and not-so-safe object of loyalty. President Chen Shui-Bian's attempt to help A-Mei by calling her a 'patriotic entertainer' after Vice President Lu's attack was completely ineffective (Liu 2004). The gesture also did nothing to address collective anxieties about prescript loyalty seen in the rising 'loving Taiwan' (aitaiwan) discourse and the uneasy position of Taiwanese business professionals in China.[10] Moreover, the aborigine voice that expressed a more chequered, post-national subjectivity clearly offered an alternative projection of political desire.

The protest in Hangzhou revealed that certain segments of the public who are typically not identified as fans could be mobilized for political action in response to popular symbols such as stars. Patriotism as a kind of structure of emotions is determined to intersect with the affective sensibility of fans. This is especially true in Asia where the political and historical entanglements in the region have long lacked sufficient public spaces for communication.[11]

Mattering map to mileage

Drawing on my fieldwork with twelve veteran fans living mostly in Taipei and Beijing, I want to explicate the power of affect, in particular the feelings generated from these fans' experiences with A-Mei's music, encounters with each other, and responses to A-Mei's suffering. Seminal to this discussion is the definition of affect developed by Lawrence Grossberg in his work on fandom. He argues that fans of any kind should be understood in relation to a sensibility clearly distinguishable from cultural critics' typical pursuit of 'meanings' or 'pleasure'.

> Affect is closely tied to what we often describe as the feeling of life. You can understand another person's life: You can share the same meanings and pleasure, but you cannot know how it feels . . . Affect is what gives 'color,' 'tone' or 'texture' to our experiences.
>
> (Grossberg 1991: 56, 57)

Grossberg's identification of the affective dimension locates a language that speaks to the realm of mattering – where things matter, where intensity of feeling takes precedence over the cognitive. What does it matter that it matters? Affect produces so-called 'mattering maps', which direct people's investments in the world and offer a place in the world for absorption (Grossberg 1991: 57). Suppose the notion of affect has found a place in fandom studies, we still need to account for how it is possible for the biographically situated researcher-body to write about such intensity which according to Brian Massumi occupies a different, much more excessive dimension than 'emotion' (Massumi 2002: 27).

I have come to see myself as a beneficiary of the affective investments made by A-Mei's fans in Taiwan and China, but not in the instrumentalized sense of 'rapport'. I was being let into an area of their mattering maps which yielded real mileage. My first trip to China, a research trip to meet A-Mei's fans in Beijing, was inspired by S1, a highly reflexive Taiwanese woman in her 30s who actively creates cultural and physical mileage by writing, traveling, and maintaining a website. In 2002 and 2004, the Taipei-based S1 traveled to Shanghai and Beijing to see A-Mei in concerts and meet the fans who have been reading her website. In very real ways, my visit to China was cared for by the fans because this affect had already been created by S1 and S1's friends. Once in Beijing, my journey with the fans to see an assorted (pinpan) concert in Tianjin further enfolded me into their mattering maps. S8 – a native of Beijing who brought his college schoolwork to study on the trip – said 'if it wasn't for A-Mei, I don't even know when I would get out of this town' (Interview by author, 16 Oct. 2005). The moments they spent waiting for A-Mei at the airport, talking about her while traveling together (and often finishing up each other's anecdotes), and seeing her perform were quite unlike their everyday lives at home, school, or work.

My embodiment in this highly affective care allowed me to experience affect as the 'encounter between the affected body and an affecting body' (Massumi, quoted in Shouse 2005). The 'hotness' of this research experience was precisely seen in the way the fans' mattering map registered on the researcher's mattering map. As Elspeth Probyn aptly put it: 'When affect becomes hot, it becomes untouchable and untouched by that wonder and by a necessary gratitude to the ideas that allow us to think and write. Writing affect should inspire awe and awe inspire modesty' (Probyn 2005: para. 14, 15).

The irrational forces of politics

The political implications of affect have been suggested by Van Zoonen in her discussion of 'affective intelligence', a quality resulting from mixing emotion and reason, which is central to the exercise of political citizenship among entertained constituencies in the West (Zoonen 2005). While she analyzes the convergence of the popular and the political, the political is often already a built-in aspect of the popular in her research (e.g., political celebrity, fictional representation of politics). On top of that, the idea that entertainment helps the development of political consciousness not only assumed a functionalist view, but also proved unhelpful where this happy marriage is rejected, such as in A-Mei's case. The following analysis takes the responses of A-Mei's cross-strait fans seriously as affect and recognizes its political significance.

The most salient response among A-Mei's cross-strait fans is a passionate, tragic sensibility that A-Mei has been innocently and repeatedly maligned by the irrational forces of politics. S10, a doctor in her mid 20s working in Shandong, found the accusation that A-Mei is pro-Taiwan independence 'nonsensical', especially when singing the ROC anthem could not have been her decision:

> A-Mei grew up in the mountains. How could she understand politics? She didn't mean anything by singing it. It was the politicians who did it. It's tragic.
> (Interview by author, 25 Oct. 2005)

S6, a petite woman in her 30s from Beijing who was drawn to A-Mei's invigorating quality that made her 'a contrast to the melodramatic soap world on television', simply asked: 'How strong must the hearts of her fans get?' (Interview by author, 16 Oct. 2005) The chain of events that set off since 2000 remained a difficult topic and created a progressively pessimistic world view for S6. When asked to compare, S6 said that 2004 was harder to bear because 'there's nothing you could do about it – even though it's unfolding right before your eyes' (Interview by author, 16 Oct. 2005). The fans felt helpless watching A-Mei being protested against in Hangzhou and besieged back in Taiwan. The weeks following the cancellation of her concert were described as disorienting and devastating.

This shared sentiment of tragicness is significant because it formed the affective reserves from which Chinese fans organized and expanded their mattering maps. In 2000, the prohibitive climate prompted her fans to take a more pro-active stance toward building networks, which included the setup of a large fan organization in China. In the absence of a promotions industry, the fans took up the task of promoting A-Mei themselves, including the staging of sales events for A-Mei outside the biggest record shops in town, during which they approached shoppers with self-made gifts. S12 was just an elementary school kid when he first heard A-Mei's song on the radio. Now 21 and a computer science major in college, he led a group of twenty-some fans to the concert in Tianjin and proudly recounted the sales event on the rented bus:

> We played some material provided from Warner. But I actually felt Warner didn't have to provide us with anything. The fans were plenty resourceful. We could handle it. Of course, if we were talking about getting her on TV or something, then we probably couldn't. But we will for sure build a good reputation for A-Mei. The vigor was very real.
>
> (Interview by author, 15 Oct. 2005)

The resourcefulness of the fans was evident in their collective effort to produce a song for A-Mei's birthday. In particular, S12 spent a week arranging a composition from A-Mei's repertoire, coordinating fans to record their individual singing from different locations, and editing these clips into a song.

While fans on both sides of the Taiwan Strait felt that A-Mei was catapulted into the throws of irrational politics during the second half of her career, the emotional experience was not uniform. A-Mei's performance at the 2000 presidential inauguration was a moment of pride for at least some ethnic Han Taiwanese. A fan in her late 20s who went swimming on the morning of the inauguration witnessed swimmers streaming out of the pool almost in unison just to watch A-Mei sing on TV (Interview by author, 23 Sept. 2005). The pride came not from trained respect for the ROC anthem, but from its being noticed as if for the *first time* because of A-Mei. In a way, the fans felt vindicated because their taste had been publicly justified.

But S5, a 20-year-old student who grew up both in her Taroko tribe and in the city of Hualien on the east coast of Taiwan, did not experience the same 'pride' or even the same 'tragicness' even though she empathized with A-Mei's repeated and reluctant entanglement with politics. Much more outspoken about her political views than the twenty something Taiwanese fans I met,[12] S5 situated A-Mei's plight in the history and media representation of aborigines in Taiwan rather than in relation to Taiwan–China tensions. As S5 became more actively engaged with aboriginal culture and politics, A-Mei's meaning for her changed from being a role model to a mainstreamed, co-opted star, a view that was deepened by her appreciation of other more 'authentic' aboriginal entertainers.

The emotional responses presented here were generated by people in different research circumstances, different generations, and with different perspectives on history and identity formation. Since the Taiwanese fans I met spanned four generations, their political experiences were expectedly more heterogeneous than the Chinese fan group, who had all been raised in post-socialist China. The Taiwanese fans, for instance, easily sensed the DDP–KMT divide among themselves and the limits of such political configurations. Despite its unifying pitch, cross-strait fans as a public is an idea that, if it is to be meaningful, must accommodate unshared experiences and political feelings together with a common reaction to politics as an irrational force.

Multiple border-crossings

I return to S1's story to acknowledge the historicized emotional structures behind strait-crossing, both idealized and feared. S1 situates herself in a Taiwanese (*bensheng*) generation that experienced political liberalization but for many lacks the freedom to abandon KMT ideological teachings and de-stereotype the mainland Chinese. She began associating with the mainland Chinese only after butting up against several other boundaries that caused her to relativize the prevailing statist agenda. The first boundary came from the marginal position of aboriginal cultures in Taiwan.

S1's job puts her in contact with two groups of teenagers with drastically different resources and value systems: privileged, middle-class, ethnic Han kids in Taipei on the one hand, and underprivileged, less-confident, aboriginal kids in the countryside on the other. A-Mei's debut came during a flurry of news reports about aborigine child prostitution and her proud announcement of her aborigine identity was a shock to S1: 'She's got to be the most secure aborigine in history, completely comfortable with her identity and family. This attitude is so different from the culture I was raised in. What's going on?' (Interview by author, 12 Aug. 2005).

To understand the nurturing environment that enabled A-Mei to come out and proudly announce her aboriginal identity, S1 began visiting A-Mei's tribe in Taitung regularly. Her purpose was ethnographic rather than star-chasing. She avoided the congested tourist festivals and documented her visits in special reports posted on her website. Despite her repeated visits and gradual familiarization with the area, S1 still felt uneasy with the inevitable tourist gaze. 'Save the trip', she tells fellow fans, 'if you go there expecting to meet Chang Hui-Mei!'. S1's practice of traveling and documenting have helped de-naturalize the stereotypical image of aborigines as optimistic and big-hearted.

Since it launched in 1999, S1's website has become an inviting forum of exchange. Her in-depth writing and multi-media presentations documenting A-Mei's performances drew comments and inspired similar practices from fans around the world. It is also how her interactions with several veteran Chinese fans began. S1 was affected by the passion and shared cultural knowledge of the mainland Chinese fans, who she saw as young and eager to introduce A-Mei's music to a broader audience. This purpose – or mattering map – was a little different from S1's former experience with a large fan organization in Taiwan which, in her opinion, failed to evolve into the open-minded network she had envisioned. In the same spirit of 'making a name for A-Mei' mentioned by S12, S1 runs her website according to an inclusive principle that makes A-Mei's performances accessible without requiring registration or membership. She said:

> I don't want money or anything like that. I just want you [A-Mei] to be good, to be known by everyone. I call this "doing reputation." If you want to get to know

her, you can get to know her. You don't need to pay because she is good. Good stuff. I have always thought this should be the way it is.

(Interview by author, 16 Sept. 2005)

The proud fan ethic embodied here by S1 positions the fan as a figure of cultural dissemination. Inspired by the diva, who has survived many injuries with kindness and dignity, the fan engages in any number of expansive sharing practices. Significantly, the fans on both sides of the strait used the phrase *mǔyítiānxià* – a classical Chinese expression describing exemplary wives of the ancient Chinese statesmen – to characterize how A-Mei 'tolerated' politics and rose into the limelight gracefully. In many ways, this still-expanding affective terrain was a dynamic source of heat which provided energy for fans to pursue their personal goals and identity projects.

However, as much as this alternative cosmos converges with the underlying family trope in fandom, the fans can only be 'family-like' because the world is composed of crisscrossing and multiplying borders that all require recognition. For S1, A-Mei is not only the one-and-only queen-diva, but also a transnational worker like many Taiwanese business professionals in China. Since studying and performing in America recently, A-Mei is now becoming known as a 'Chinese Girl', a song title on her 2006 album 'I Want Happiness'. And as A-Mei says on Discovery channel's program, *Taiwan Portrait*, she becomes just one of the many villagers in Taitung when she goes home for the New Year's celebration. A-Mei is constantly performing away from home. 'Home' hinges on feelings of attachment that may embrace new possibilities or just new questions. After a trip to the Orchid Island (Lan Yu), the island 49 miles off Taiwan's eastern shore that has become a permanent storage site of nuclear waste from the mainland (Taiwan), S1 remarked: 'Why doesn't Orchid Island go independent?!' The affective terrain from the popular culture has already altered the landscape of the homeland.

Feeling patriotism from a distance

Just as A-Mei's patriotic dilemma needs to be contextualized within the historical formation of 'patriotic entertainers' during the Cold War and Taiwan's growing economic dependence on China, the patriotic implications of Song Seung-Heon's draft scandal are rooted in the historical and emotional structures of South Korea's gendered citizenship and Korean Wave-engendered economies and discourses, all of which serve to complicate narrow conceptions of national loyalty. For our purposes here, I will focus on Song's stardom, the activities of his trans-Asian fans, and various culture-industry agents with eyes on the domestic and regional markets. I use all these contexts to grasp the gravity of draft-dodging in South Korea from a distance.[13] In particular, I probe the meanings of overseas fans' response to Song's draft-dodging scandal, particularly in relation to the cancellation of Song's starring role in the much anticipated television drama, *Sad Love Story*.[14] What is significant about Song's fans in relation to A-Mei's fans is that they share a similarly tragic, affective, and communicational experience in which the fans remake the meaning of the star in an adverse atmosphere. While the fans' actions were not in direct confrontation with the geopolitical problematic inscribed in South Korean conscription, their mobilization leading up to the spectacular send-off outside the boot camp in Chunchon, Kangwon Province, should be considered a crucial, feminized, transnational initiative which called into question a not-yet-post Cold-War Asia.

Anchoring conscription in globalization

From the start Song had been quick to admit publicly the mistake he made while at his career break. While in Australia filming the music video for the drama, he faxed the Korean press a handwritten letter of apology which also explained his pressing commitment in remorseful anguish. When he returned to Seoul on September 20, a thinner Song apologized in front of the press for 'having evaded conscription as a South Korean man' (Perfect SeungHeon 2004). The scandal involving Song and other celebrities[15] generated much public debate in the media. One Internet poll that drew intense participation from Taiwanese fans was posted on Central Daily (*Joongang Ilbo*). It asked netizens to determine 'what should happen to Song on the matter of military service?' Fans worried that the public opinion would tilt toward 'join immediately' and worked hard to encourage people to choose 'finish filming the drama before service'.

Despite the seemingly airtight stipulation in Article 3.1 of the ROK Military Service Law that all Korean men serve in the military, conscription as an institution in South Korea rests on something more fluid. The institution survives on mutual persuasion, co-optation, and constant negotiation between government authorities and different publics. It wasn't long ago that two public figures were implicated in draft-dodging scandals and both received very public punishments. One case was the defeat of the Grand National Party presidential candidate Lee Hoi-Chang (also written Yi Hoe-Chang), who was expected to have an easy win in the 1997 election until his two sons were found to have avoided military service by suspicious methods.

The second case was Yoo Seung-Jun, a pop teen idol who angered the Korean public after he became an American citizen in 2002. Earlier in his budding singing and dancing career, Yoo had announced that he would perform his military duty as a Korean citizen. This was a praiseworthy gesture for a 1.5 generation salmon (*yoen-uh-jok*) who had emigrated to the United States with his parents when he was only 14 years old. His American citizenship allows him to obtain a service waiver and Yoo went from a role-model citizen to an 'ugly American' whose English name – Steve Yoo – became sarcastically adopted by Korea's mainstream media (Lee D. 2003). His presence was considered such a corrupting force that the Ministry of Justice denied his entry into Korea several weeks later upon request from the Military Manpower Administration (MMA). These media stories of transgression suggest that the power that comes with the celebrity is not non-negotiable; it can be jeopardized and even denied when it conflicts with values central to the collective identities of a group. In this case, performing the military service not only builds one's character, but also sustains the ideology of patriarchy.

Nevertheless, patriotism in South Korea should not be viewed as an unchanging national characteristic. Ideological teachings in South Korea, from literature to war memorials, have championed different heroic male figures in a history narrated as a patriarchal lineage in continuous crisis (Jager 2003). According to Insook Kwon, conscription anchors in 1990s political culture because it is still serviceable to anti-communism and nationalism, a twin-engine driving the narrative of self-sacrifice for one's nation. As a result, not only has there been an absence of resistance to conscription in South Korea's rich protest history, popular support for conscription has only intensified in the post-Cold War period (Kwon 2001: 29). This is indicative in the newly amended (4 May 2005) Nationality Law which prohibits Korean males holding dual citizenship to give up their Korean citizenship until they have fulfilled their military service.

Perhaps the most powerful discovery in Kwon's feminist exploration of conscription is that the system has been the indispensable glue binding together some of the most crucial notions of being authentically Korean, such as masculinity, femininity, mother-hood, and fatherhood. Mothers become symbolically important during the men's conscription experiences; in the media they play a particular nurturing role that is con-nected to historical images of patriotic motherhood. *The Youth Report*, a weekly variety show that puts conscripts and celebrities together during prime-time hours, also exploits the culturally powerful mother-son bond by dressing the mother-guest in traditional garb as she waits for her chance to meet her conscripted son on the show (Moon 2005b: 79). For women who are not mothers, this entertaining show also unites selected couples and creates the expectation of heterosexual romance. The show personalizes conscription and contributes to the moral structure of feeling along with other accessible storytelling formats like news, television dramas, and films.

This historicized background aims to illuminate the indispensability of conscription as a legal, social, and ideological process. The gravity of draft-dodging in general must then confront the multiple subjectivities enabled by the military service and its discourses. It would also be necessary to observe how the associated patriotic morality gets reinvented in the infrastructure of South Korea's nationalist political culture.[16] Specific to Song's draft-dodging incident, however, is his embodiment of a different type of masculinity generated and celebrated by the Korean culture industry as evidence of Korea's own transnational cultural prowess. This development from the trans-Asian cultural traffic is reason enough to reframe South Korean conscription beyond the terms of domestic politics.

Conscription meets the constituencies in hallyu

> I was really shocked to see his picture from the airport. It wasn't so much that he looked disconcerted. I have never seen Song Seung-Heon like that. He was always dashing, with makeup and styled hair. But we all felt he looked like a prisoner in that photo taken at the airport. Not the typical dashing, spirited Song we are used to seeing.
>
> (A1, 8 Sept. 2005)

A veteran fan from Taiwan who has seen Song in person on many occasions conveyed her thoughts on pictures of Song returning from Australia to cooperate with the police investigation of his draft-dodging. A series of news photos had been posted on a major fan forum,[17] showing a very un-star-like Song in a white sweatshirt, blue jeans, and carrying his own bag while making a statement to the press. In another picture published on the day of his physical checkup, Song was shown wearing a blue medical gown and a metal name plate. He waited expressionlessly in a fluorescent-lit office with his hands folded on his abdomen, looking no different from two other actors – Chang Hyuk and Han Jae-suk – who were in the same boat. The rakish good looks of Song's character in *Sad Love Story*, images of which had begun to circulate around the same time, stood in stark contrast to these unfamiliar images of Song the citizen. He was well on his way to transforming into the idealized Foucauldian docile body – a soldier.

For his fans, talking about what Song went through was enormously difficult. It would not be an exaggeration to say that watching him go through the public criticism and speculation 'was like the end of the world'[18] for many of them. Even after a year had passed, the incident was an emotional trigger for a veteran Taiwanese fan (A4) who, representing a large fan organization, declined my interview request. Nonetheless, corresponding with her cued me to the fan's feelings, particularly their self-aware vulnerability and the low-key but determined way they tried to protect their star from unfavorable judgment. For instance, A4 did not see any point discussing Korean conscription. 'So what?' she asked me and cited the ineffectiveness of this line of criticism from Korea's most valued market – Japan. Even A1, who cordially shared her rich involvement in transnational fan networking, emphasized that Song's fans were not trying to appeal to the South Korean authorities to get any 'special treatment' like a service exemption. That is why the United Support Letter issued by five fan organizations from Taiwan, China, and Hong Kong prior to Song's return to Korea adopted a non-confrontational and non-imploring tone in their attempt to influence the resolution of the crisis. According to A1, respecting the decisions of the Korean government is also a measure to protect Song from sinking into deeper water.

The immediate question facing the overseas fans were indeed practical – that is, to drum up and lend support to Song. It seemed meaningless and groundless to directly criticize the South Korean conscription system. The lack of apparent justification is understandable. Kwon's interviews with Korean women activists during the student and democratization movements in the 1980s also revealed a curious lack of motivation to challenge conscription (Kwon 2001). So if the most anti-establishment women in Korea found it difficult to formulate a debate around mandatory military service in their own country, what could Asian women outside Korea – who are doubtless the constituencies of the Korean Wave – do tampering with issues concerning the 'boys' and a foreign government?[19] And what good does raising the agenda bring now that Song's 'heavenly body' has been squarely disciplined by the Korean MMA?

I bring up these points not to push for a politicized reading of the fans' experiences. Rather, I hope to use their responses to further articulate the interpenetration of trans-Asian cultural traffic and regional politics. Song's status as a red-hot *hallyu* star ensured that his draft-dodging would be no simple domestic affair. In fact, Steve Yoo's story had already illuminated the power of the transnational entertainment workings and the porousness of Korean national loyalty. As Hee-Eun Lee pointed out, the Korean pop music industry is the 'biggest habitat for salmons' like Yoo (Lee H. 2003). The hybridized reality of Korean popular culture has not prevented the invention of the 'other' category from within. Could a different mode of hybridity in *hallyu* – rendered in the realm of transnational fandom specifically – make a difference in the definition of Korean national loyalty? Following Shin Hyun-joon's suggestion to mine the under-represented cultural practices in intra-Asian cultural traffic (Shin 2005), I will turn to examine the communication practices engaged by Song's fans in Taiwan and China as a way to interject the 'Chinese-Asian' experience of Korean Wave.

To whom it may concern: without Song, Korean Wave is a sad love story[20]

The dramatic gathering of hundreds of female fans from Korea, Japan, Taiwan, and Hong Kong to send off Song outside the Chunchon preparatory camp on the morning of 16 November 2004 was a telling testament to Song's transnationalized stardom. It was the crystallization of fan mobilization and a media event with dramatic elements. According to a Taiwanese fan who provided her narrative account and 52 news photos from that day, Song inched his way to the camp entrance amidst an insistent and male-dominated press corps.[21] Close-up pictures from Yonhap News showed the mini dramas of Song looking down, frowning, biting his lower lips, and exhaling through his teeth during this supposedly short walk. This moment fraught with femininity and emotion resonates with many gendered themes in Korean conscription. But it also calls for a closer examination of the complexity of fan mobilization at the juncture of inter-Asian cultural traffic and market legitimation.

In particular, I would like to discuss two mobilization efforts that were not visible during the spectacular send-off: the United Support Letter issued by fans in China, Taiwan and Hong Kong and a letter-writing campaign launched by a large, China-based fan organization. Both efforts were organized during a worrisome period before anyone knew what would happen to Song. While drawing on the support of transnational Chinese fans, they deployed different strategies to create a speaking position to purposely communicate – or not communicate – with the authorities (*daren*) previously evoked in A-Mei's reluctant engagement with cross-strait politics. For Song's overseas fans, *daren* are the murky authority figures assumed to have influence over the fate of their icon. They range from cultural producers and capitalists (e.g., Song's management agency, broadcasting station, drama production agencies, overseas investors) to the equally image-conscious national governmental units (e.g., MMA, Tourism Bureau). Interestingly, these *daren* happen to have conflicting ideological and economic stakes in Song's participation in *Sad Love Story*, which ultimately led to divergent fan responses.

In our first mobilization case, the United Support Letter was carefully drafted to empathize first and foremost with Song's suffering. It then describes how encounters with Song's work in the Korean Wave had led the overseas fans to new experiences like traveling and taking interest in Korean culture. Praising his professional ethics and giving nature, the letter states the fans' unwavering support for his choice to tell the truth and closes with a warm and firm pledge to stand by him throughout this hardship. The open letter had no specific addressee – a strategy agreed upon by the heads of Taiwanese and Korean fan organizers (Interview A1). All in all, the tone of the letter was positive, yet when it later appeared in a Taiwanese news story, the role of the authors was misrepresented. Instead of being described as compassionate, grateful, or even strategically minded, the fans were immediately relegated to a humbled position from where they plead to the powerful Korean *daren*. The headline read, 'We beg you *daren*, don't conscript Song Seung-Heon' (Wu 2004: C4).

The fans quickly pointed out the press's misrepresentation, but our criticism needs to move beyond a critique of routinized conservative reporting decisions. The press has completely ignored the letter's self-aware strength as a form of dissemination that purposely was uninterested in holding any sort of direct communication with the Korean *daren* – be it pleading or demanding. This recognition is required for understanding the open letter as a moment at which the popular meets the political, but not in the reductive sense of rhetorical application as adopted by the *United Daily*. Critiquing the dialectical conundrum between the human desire for genuine connection and the reality of irreconciliation from unrequited love, an unanswered letter, or an unheard voice, John Peters writes:

> Dialogue ideology keeps us from seeing that expressive acts occurring over distances and without immediate assurance of reply can be desperate and daring acts of dignity. That I cannot engage in dialogue with Plato or the Beatles does not demean the contact I have with them.
>
> (Peters 1999: 152)

Judged within the pre-constructed fan–*daren* parameter, the open letter by the fans in Hong Kong, China, and Taiwan would seem almost inconsequential.[22] But if we understood it as a disseminational practice that acknowledged the divide between adoring Chinese-Asian female fans and Korean officialdom – a relation that also implies the gender hierarchy in Korean society, then the open letter was not a failure or a pathetic attempt on the part of the powerless fans. In fact, it is a revelation of trans-Asian politics, bodies, and language that have yet to transpire on equal and reciprocal terms.[23]

Your honorable nation: without Song, Korean Wave is a sad story

Informed by the reaction to the open letter, a second mobilization effort – a letter-writing campaign – not only directly implored the Korean authorities to postpone Song's conscription until he finishes filming *Sad Love Story*, but also spoke from a nationalized and feminized position.

> To all of our members, to support more effectively our beloved Seung-Heon, the management team would like to solicit open letters to relevant Korean governmental bodies that include the Ministry of Foreign Relations, the Ministry of Culture and Tourism, and the Military and Manpower Administration. Please leave messages here: Write down your love and support for Seung-Heon! Write down your hopes for him to carry on the promotion of Korean culture to China! The management team shall print out everyone's messages and send them to the relevant governmental bodies by international express mail. Sisters, let's take action! Let's use our love to protect our Seung-Heon!

These words, posted on 23 September 2004 on a large mainland Chinese fan site, tried to steer the public opinion climate in Korea toward favoring the postponing of Song's conscription. At that time, two online pollings in Korea already showed over 50 percent support for such a move.[24] The debate in the Korean press was weighing the cost of Song's contribution as a *hallyu* star against the gain of his immediate draft. A group of pro-government UriParty lawmakers even submitted a petition to the MMA to demand postponement of Song's draft date (Park 2004).

Still, the fans were worried. The 54[25] postings responding to the Team Management's solicitation from 23 September to 27 September seemed at first like melodramatic messages that amounted to little more than a mad essay contest, which in the Chinese context is taken to be a game of pure performance.[26] To illustrate, X20 began her letter by expressing her 'vehement impulse to shout and desire for release', which she finally put into writing to convince 'your honorable nation' of the 'significance of Mr. Song Seung-Heon to China's hundreds of millions of Chinese'. In the unlikely prospect of scrutiny, these messages knowingly deployed hyperbole to elaborate Song's virtues, calling him 'a real man for taking the fall for a more general social problem', and an 'exceptional cultural ambassador'.[27]

Furthermore, many letters adopted a diplomatic rhetoric, carefully addressing South Korea as 'your honorable country' and expressing their disinterest to interfere with another nation's domestic politics. This, however, is only a courteous overture before the unloading of forceful criticism directed at the Korean *daren*. Some fans admonished the South Korean government for their misjudgment of Song's national loyalty. X29 called into question the conflation between draft-dodging and a lack of patriotism. X9 wrote about Korea's double standards in allowing 'national' athletes shorter service terms while overlooking the fact that it was private interests that stood to gain most from the policy. She wrote: '[Song] brought in a handsome income and worked hard to promote the Korean culture around the world. Isn't this patriotic conduct? Why must conscription be the only patriotic embodiment?' Following this logic, many fans advised the South Korean government to be kind to their people (X30). Some fans threw down the gauntlet saying that should their advice be ignored, it would signal the end of friendly bilateral relations between China and South Korea.

The fans identified themselves as coming from a variety of backgrounds: an ordinary fan, a poor student, a middle-class office worker, a 60-year-old lady, a mother, a rational star chaser, a motivated fan-webmaster, a trend-setter in China, an overseas fan, and one of the 4,000 powerful Chinese fans of Song. Though the veracity of these fans' self-proclaimed identities remains uncertain, they spoke as Chinese citizens and addressed the Korean *daren* as equals. Many said haughtily that South Korea as a country did not exist in their mental map until Song made it stand out from the 'undifferentiated color mass' (X7).

Without jumping to conclusion that the imperial tone is inherently Chinese, I want to suggest that the fans' insolent attitude is an act of flouting rather than a desperate and ineffective attempt to engage the Korean *daren* in a bilateral relationship. This does not mean that the fans were not serious about having the message reach the Korean authorities, but their approach revealed the nationalist and gendered nature of *hallyu*. As Keehyeung Lee has written, various Korean *daren* – from local politicians, government agencies such as the Ministry of Culture and Tourism, to academics – all have made *hallyu* serviceable to the Korean national image (Lee 2005). While a softer, more economically inclined image of masculinity has been produced in the trans-Asian phenomenon of *hallyu*, its potential to undo the hegemony of militarized masculinity in South Korea remains to be seen.

Caught *Shiris*[28] in trans-Asian straits

A-Mei and Song Seung-Heon have been crucial agents of affect in the respective popular cultural fields where they were active: Mandarin pop and *hallyu*. Describing the characteristic of the 'Mei-style love ballads', veteran fan S1 said:

A-Mei achieves the coquettishness that a coquettish song needs. She achieves the giddiness that a giddy song needs. She can express [the color of a song] to its fullest. Her slow songs of late are already in colors more luminous than gold. They're white, the only color left after all pigments have faded out. We all love over-the-top songs because they are easy to sing, right? But how do you sing it not over-the-top but still make people shed tears? That's what she is capable of.

(Interview by author, 12 August 2005)

On 23 September 2006, it was reported that Song was voted in a South Korean pop vox as 'the No. 1 male star that most easily makes women shed tears' (Chuang 2006). Song beat out Bae Yong-Joon, the *hallyu* heartthrob who followed his hit TV drama, *Winter Sonata*, with two successful movies while Song was in the army. It is not coincidental that A-Mei (literally 'little sister') and Song (nicknamed 'obba', meaning brother) are both capable of moving people – large numbers of transnationally located people – to tears. Their affective and melodramatic charge was what ignited the interest of publics beyond the typically safe fan bases of their respective fields. As P. David Marshall suggested, celebrities bridge the individual and the public culture of the democratic age (Marshall 1997). 'Love for a star' and 'loyalty for a political-cultural affiliation' unleash and feed on similar reserves of emotions.

This paper juxtaposes two transborder stars in Asia who in different circumstances underwent an overwhelming test of patriotism. A-Mei's and Song's dilemmas provided opportunities to understand patriotism as a political and popular force in trans-Asian popular culture. At the same time, both cases call for a reconfiguration of the relationships between the popular, public, and the political. Out is the naïve assumption that the popular could 'overcome' the nastiness of politics by virtue of their assigned quality as cultural ambassadors. Stars bear important public experiences and morality. A-Mei bore the experience of the publics who found power in her inclusive representability as well as the experience of Taiwanese transborder workers in China. Song embodied the Korean national subjects who were perhaps still under the effect of militarized modernity (Moon 2005a).

If anything, it is not the star that 'affects' politics, but the fans. Embedded in various publics, some fans emerged as politicized bodies, speaking, as Song's Chinese fans did, as ambassadors representing Chinese citizens. Other fans, like the strategic coalition among fans in Taiwan, Hong Kong, and China, carved out a space neither occupied by national subjects nor by the entreating 'popular'. In fact, one conclusion that can be drawn from this inter-referential experiment is the inadequacy of *daren* as a political figure. The communication strategy adopted by Song's fans during the crisis already showed a lack of faith in the delivery of *daren*. Curiously, A-Mei's 2006 album contains a ballad called 'Unadult Like (*Bùxiàng ge Dàrén*)', which evokes the contemporary, individualist connotations of *daren* rather than the word's pre-democratic sense as 'authorities'. Was the song a response to the politician's castigation that she was not grown-up enough to recognize cross-strait political reality? Probably not. In fact, judging from A-Mei's attempts to engage with *daren* – whether it is her remark to 'leave the matter to the politicians' or her singing of 'Unadult Like', it's the politics that was not getting the popular, not the other way around.

In the world where narratives of stars, of fans, and of different publics intersect, the emotional structures of different groups of people need even more spaces for interaction and inter-referencing. Perhaps the way to enter and exist in Asian space is not through the trope of fluidity and mobility, but by being caught at the border or by some kind of terrain. It then becomes meaningful and necessary to seek out the configurations of the terrains under the currents.

Notes

1 This research was made possible thanks to collaborative funding from NHK under the project title: 'Publicness of TV Broadcasting in East Asia', which ran from April 2005–March 2006. An earlier draft was presented at the workshop, 'East Asian Pop Culture: Transnational Japanese and Korean TV Dramas', organized by the Asia Research Institute, National University of Singapore, on 8–9 December 2005. I would especially like to thank Chua Beng-huat, Kuan-hsing Chen, Iwabuchi Kōichi and Shin Hyun-joon for their insights and encouragement to pursue an inter-referential approach. I would like to thank Rong-Yu (Alice) Chi, Hae Rang (Philip) Noh, Jing-He (Michael) Chuang, and Jing-Hui Feng for their research assistance during different stages of the project. I thank the fans of Chang Hui-Mei in China and in Taiwan for their hospitality and their time. I also thank the Taiwanese fans of Song Seung-Heon for sharing their experiences and insights. I am solely responsible for any inaccuracies or other problems in this work.

2 This is a question of perspectives. It is unpopular for those who feel stars should be left alone by politicians. But even those who see this ideal division – like Chang's fans – expressed ambivalence. In reality, many entertainers have used political opportunities to boost their entertainment careers or even launch new political careers.

3 See, for instance, Chen Tsung-yi's magazine story about Western stars who have stood up against the human rights problem in China (Chen 2004a; 2004b). The story is followed by his reporting of Chang Hui-Mei's inability to call herself a Taiwanese while being interviewed on PRC's CCTV. But even the few examples that get mentioned converge with Taiwan's larger political, that is anti-communist and pro-American, stance. John Wayne's anti-Native American stance was never mentioned by the Taiwanese as a problem.

4 Rock 'n' roll, alternative, and hip-hop music all have been acknowledged to have the potential to challenge the political status quo. In contrast, popular music frequently receives dirty looks from more politicized performers. Shortly after A-Mei's Beijing concert in 2004, Taiwanese music critic Ho Tung-hung wrote an editorial in which he praised American singer Michelle Shocked for standing up against the commercial interests as well as Bush's politics (Ho T. 2004). In the same piece Ho pointed out that A-Mei has never intervened in public affairs of the aborigines. While I agree with his position that A-Mei's performance in China cannot escape political connotations, the criticism is really a blanket denunciation of all popular music for not being political enough (or at all).

5 Daren, literally 'big person', could mean grown-ups or adults. But it also refers to public officials or people holding important government positions in ancient China.

6 Drawing on Japanese historian Mizoguchi Yuzo's proposition of 'China as a method', Chen suggests that 'Asia as method' is a contemporary response to the inadequacy of nation-states. This inter-Asia project is linked up via heterogeneous movements and does not aim to prove Asia as different or unique from the West. It problematizes the northeast domination on the discourse of Asia and encourages diverse historical interpretations of the different linkages with the goal of making a new subjectivity (Chen 2005a: 200–201).

7 See, for instance, Iwabuchi (2003; 2004), Chua (2004), and Erni and Chua (2005).

8 An example I have in mind is the distance between Japanophiles in Taiwan and the critical dialogues between Taiwan and Japan's leftist critics.

9 Even after she retired from public performance, Teng still entertained the troops.

10 'Loving Taiwan' was originally invented as an election slogan aimed at mobilizing pan-green constituencies in Taiwan. The charge against Chang also needs to be situated in terms of the so-called Hsu Wen-long effect. Hsu, a rich industrialist once known for his vocal support of Taiwan independence, released an open letter in March 2004 in which he renounced the

pro-Taiwan independence position and announced his support for China's Anti-Secession Law. The change of position of this long-time DPP benefactor (who was even a character in Kobayashi Yoshinori's political manga, *Taiwan Ron*) shocked the pan-green leadership and revealed the political predicaments of Taiwanese business professionals (*taishang*) in China. An editorial in *Business Weekly* linked Chang to Hsu with the headline: "Don't Worry, A-Mei, but please take care, Hsu Wen-long" (Ho C. 2004: 18).

11 For example, even though Mizoguchi Yuzo, a Japanese historian of Chinese intellectual history, would like to respond to the question of Japanese war-time responsibility to the Chinese, it was simply impossible because there has been no discussion on historical memory in China 'at any level' (Chen 2002b: 242).

12 In fact, she felt it strange that I would be so cautious about getting political opinions from the fans. She asked, 'Why is that sensitive? I don't care about that. We've got freedom of speech. I am not afraid of being taken away by the police'.

13 I speak as a woman whose high school experience in the US in the early 1990s acquainted me with many male parachute kids who left Taiwan before they turned 16. For some of them, avoiding military was at least part — if not the goal — of studying abroad. Also, as a re-patriated Taiwanese in the early 2000s, I find it difficult to overlook the de-militarizing tendency in military service and the re-militarizing desire in the national defense budget. Currently the length of military service for Taiwanese men is one year and four months. I thank Shin Hyun-joon and Jungbong Choi for sharing their experience and views on the Korean military and masculinity.

14 The role was eventually filled by Yeon Jung Hoon.

15 Other implicated celebrities included actor Jang Hyuk, Han Jae-sok, and more than fifty former and active baseball players (Na 2004).

16 The Military Manpower Administration (MMA) of South Korea does seem to have more work to do to maintain the hegemony of militarized masculinity. In March 2005, it updated its communication platform to facilitate online applications from potential conscripts living abroad (Jung 2005). It has also been answering questions from abroad, in English, concerning qualifications, rights, and procedures through its user-friendly English website since 2004. Still, the patriotic bond can be fragile. Before the revised dual citizenship law went into effect on 1 June 2005, immigration offices were swarmed by applications to renounce their Korean nationality (Kim 2005; Seo 2005).

17 To protect the privacy of the fans, the name and URL of the fan website which I drew on substantially for this chapter will not be used. I collected postings of discussion during the critical one-month period from 16 September to 16 October 2004.

18 From A2's posting on 21 September 2004.

19 There was evidence that Song's Korean fans were in close contact with fans in Taiwan, Hong Kong, and Japan. International fans were called on to help with ballot-stuffing on Internet polls and were encouraged to write to Song's management company, GM Entertainment; his broadcasting station, MBC; and the MMA. Messages expressing gratitude in Korean were also translated into Chinese.

20 In addition to observing a Taiwanese fan site, I also collected past postings from a large Chinese fan site. The quote was posted on 23 September 2004 by fan X14 as part of a letter addressed to the Korean authorities. Accessed on 28 October 2005.

21 From the Taiwanese fan forum under the posting: 'Goodbye and Take Care, Seung-Heon . . . The Seeing-Off Day', posted on 16 November 2004. Accessed 5 September 2005.

22 A1 found it to be a success, for the publicity went beyond the circle of fans who participated.

23 Peters writes: 'Too often, "communication" misleads us from the task of building worlds together. It invites us into a world of unions without politics, understandings without language, and souls without bodies, only to make politics, language, and bodies reappear as obstacles rather than blessings' (Peters 1999: 30–31).

24 www.chosun.com (22 September 2004). I thank Noh Hae Rang for his assistance on the Korean-Chinese translation.

25 Of the 54 postings, thirty were addressed by different individuals to the Korean government authorities stated in the solicitation. The rest were supplementary comments, reactions to the call, and encouragement.

26 Right from the start, a fan with a science background called for help from the more literary-inclined 'sisters'. Some of the high-flying language by the fan included describing *Autumn Fairytale*'s effect on the Chinese cultural market as an 'atomic bomb' (X20).

27 A fan quickly remarked in between letters that 'To fight for all possibility, I have done all I could to praise the Koreans. Sigh . . . I don't know what else to say . . . Bless you!' (X18).

28 *Shiri*, South Korea's blockbuster film in 1999, refers to a species of fish that lives in the waters between North and South Korea.

References

Appadurai, Arjun (1993) 'Patriotism and its futures', *Public Culture* 5(3): 411–429.

Chen, Kuan-Hsing (2001) 'America in East Asia: The Club 51 syndrome', *New Left Review* 12 (November-December): 73–87.

Chen, Kuan-Hsing (2002a) 'Why is "great reconciliation" im/possible? de-Cold War/decolonization, or modernity and its tears (Part I)', *Inter-Asia Cultural Studies* 3(1): 77–99.

Chen, Kuan-Hsing (2002b) 'Why is "great reconciliation" im/possible? de-Cold War/decolonization, or modernity and its tears (Part II)', *Inter-Asia Cultural Studies* 3(2): 235–251.

Chen, Kuan-Hsing 陳光興 (2005a) 'Asia as method' '亞洲作為方法', *Taiwan: A Radical Quarterly in Social Studies* 台灣社會研究季刊 57: 139–218.

Chen, Kuan-Hsing (2005b) 'The question of Asia's independence (Yazhou duli de wenti)' '亞洲獨立的問題', *Dushu* 讀書 July: 38–46. Reprinted in Cultural Studies Monthly 文化 研究月報, hermes.hrc.ntu.edu.tw/csa/journal/48/journal_park370.html, accessed 1 August 2005.

Chen, Tsung Yi 陳宗逸 (2004a) 'The impact of the A-Mei incident on Taiwanese consciousness (A-Mei shijian chongji Taiwan yishi)' '阿妹事件衝擊台灣意識', *New Taiwan News Weekly* 14–20 August: 14–16.

Chen, Tsung Yi 陳宗逸 (2004b) 'Euro-American super stars defend their stances (Oumei jushing hanwei ziji zhuzhang)' '歐美巨星捍衛自己主張', *New Taiwan News Weekly* 14–20 August: 17–18.

Ching, Leo (2000) 'Globalizing the regional, regionalizing the global: Mass culture and Asianism in the age of late capital', *Public Culture* 12(1): 233–257.

Chua, Beng Huat (2004) 'Conceptualizing an East Asian popular culture', *Inter-Asia Cultural Studies* 5(2): 200–221.

Chuang, Wen-wu 莊玟敔 (2006) 'Song Seung-Heon beats out Yongsama for the tear-jerking king (Song Seung-Heon tsai yongya deng tsuileiwang)' '宋承憲踩勇樣 登催淚王', *Apple Daily* 23 September.

Chun, Allen and Shamsul, A. B (2001) 'Other "routes": the critical challenge for Asian academics', *Inter-Asia Cultural Studies* 2(2): 167–176.

Dyer, Richard (1979) *Stars*, London: BFI Publishing.

Erni, John Nguyet and Chua, Siew Keng (eds) (2005) *Asian Media Studies: Politics of Subjectivities*, Malden, MA: Blackwell.

Gavrilos, Dina (2003) 'Editor's introduction: Communicating the "new patriotism": What does it mean to be a citizen in a global context?', *Journal of Communication Inquiry* 27(4): 333–336.

Grossberg, Lawrence (1991) 'Is there a fan in the house?: The affective sensibility of fandom'. In Lisa A. Lewis (ed.) *The Adoring Audience: Fan Culture and Popular Media*, London and New York: Routledge, 50–65.

Guy, Nancy (2002) '"Republic of China national anthem" on Taiwan: one anthem, one performance, multiple realities', *Ethnomusicology* 46(1): 96–119.

Ho, Chang-Peng 何昶鵬 (2004) 'Don't worry A-Mei, but please take care Hsu Wen-long (A-Mei fanghsing, Hsu Wen-long ching paochong)' '阿妹放心，許文隆請保重', *Business Weekly* 商業週刊 21 June: 18.

Ho, Tung-Hung 何東洪 (2004) 'The sincerity and hypocricy of popular music (Liushing yinyue de zhengcheng yu xuwei)' '流行音樂的真誠與虛偽', *China Daily* 2 August.

Ip, Iam Chong 葉蔭聰 (2006) 'Why does Lee Young-ae support Korean farmers?' '為何李英愛簽名支持韓農', *Ming Pao* 20 February. Reprinted on Coolloud 苦勞網 http://www.coolloud.org.tw/news/database/Interface/Detailstander.asp?ID=110115.

Iwabuchi, Koichi (2003) *Recentering Globalization: Popular Culture and Japanese Transnationalism*, Durham and London: Duke University Press.

Iwabuchi, Koichi (ed.) (2004) *Feeling Asian Modernities: Transnational Consumption of Japanese TV Dramas*, Hong Kong: Hong Kong University Press.

Jager, Sheila Miyoshi (2003) *Narratives of Nation Building in Korea: A Genealogy of Patriotism*, New York: M.E. Sharpe.

Jung, Sung-Ki (2005) 'Conscripts abroad can apply for enrollment online', *The Korea Times* 31 March. Hankooki.com, accessed 12 September 2005.

Kim, Rahn (2005) 'Young Men Abandoning Nationality over New Law', *The Korea Times* 11 May. Hankooki.com, accessed 12 September 2005.

Kwon, Insook (2001) 'A feminist exploration of military conscription: The gendering of the connections between nationalism, militarism and citizenship in South Korea', *International Feminist Journal of Politics* 3(1): 26–54.

Lee, Coral (2000) 'From Little Teng to A-Mei: Marking Time in Music' '張惠妹現象的彼岸觀點', *Sinorama* 光華 Febuary: 34–44.

Lee, Dong-wook (2003) 'Let's forgive Yoo Seung-joon', *The Korea Times* 4 June Hankooki.com, accessed on 12 September 2005.

Lee, Hee-Eun (2003) 'Home is where you serve: Globalization and nationalism in Korean popular music', paper presented at the International Communication Association convention, San Diego, CA. 23–27 May 2003.

Lee, Keehyeung (2005) 'Assessing and situating the 'Korean Wave' (hanryu) through a cultural studies lens', paper presented at the workshop: 'East Asian Pop Culture: Transnational Japanese and Korean TV Dramas', organized by the Asia Research Institute, National University of Singapore, on 8–9 December 2005.

Liu, Pao-Jie 劉寶傑 (2004) 'A-Bian praises A-Mei: patriotic entertainer (Bianzan A-Mei: Aiguo yiren)' '扁讚阿妹：愛國藝人', *United Daily* 聯合報 7 August: A3.

Lo, Yi-Hsiou 羅儀修 (1998a) 'Discovering the new home of urbanites (Fashian duhuiren de shinyuanhsiang)' '發現都會人的新原鄉', *Global View Magazine* (Yuan Jian) 遠見雜誌 138: 85.

Lo, Yi-Hsiou 羅儀修 (1998b) 'Reading the A-Mei phenomenon (Jiedu A-Mei hsianhsiang)' '解讀阿妹現象', *Global View Magazine* (Yuan Jian) 遠見 140, 5 February: 118–122.

Marshall, David (1997) *Celebrity and Power: Fame in Contemporary Culture*, Minneapolis: University of Minnesota Press.

Massumi, Brian (2002) *Parables for the Virtual*, Durham and London: Duke University Press.

Moon, Seungsook (2005a) *Militarized Modernity and Gendered Citizenship in South Korea*, Durham and London: Duke University Press.

Moon, Seungsook (2005b) 'Trouble with conscription, entertaining soldiers: popular culture and the politics of militarized masculinity in South Korea', *Men and Masculinities* 8(1): 64–92.

Morris, Meaghan (2004) 'Participating from a distance'. In Koichi Iwabuchi, Stephen Muecke and Mandy Thomas (eds) *Rogue Flows: Trans-Asian Cultural Traffic*, Hong Kong: Hong Kong University Press, 249–261.

Na, Jeong-ju (2004) 'Pro-baseball players held for draft dodging', *The Korea Times* 5 September. Hankooki.com, accessed 12 September 2005.

Ning, Ying-Bing 甯應斌 (2004) 'Public television and publicity television (Gongguan dianshi yu gongguan dianshi)' '公關電視與公共電視'. In Ning Ying-Bing (ed.) *Body Politics and Media Criticism* 身體政治與媒體批評, Zhongli: Central University Sex Studies, 213–226.

Park, Chung-a (2004) 'Actor Song, Chang begin mandatory military military service', *The Korea Times* 16 November, Hankooki.com, accessed 12 September 2005.

Perfect SeungHeon (2004) '[News] 2004/09/20-Song SeungHeon returns', http://www.seungheon.net, accessed 5 September 2005.

Peters, John (1999) *Speaking into the Air: A History of the Idea of Communication*. Chicago and London: The Chicago University Press.

Probyn, Elspeth (2005) 'A-ffect: Let her RIP', *M/C Journal* 8(6), 1 March: 18 pars., http://journal.media-culture.org.au/0512/03-probyn.php.

Seo, Dong-Shin (2005) 'Lawmaker fuels controversy over dual citizenship law', *The Korea Times* 20 May. Hankooki.com, accessed 12 September 2005.

Shih, Chun (1999) 施群 'The Chang Hui-Mei phenomenon: Cultural exchange transcends cross-strait politics' '張惠妹現象：文化交流超越兩岸政治', *Exchange* 交流 47 October: 38–42.

Shin, Hyunjoon (2005) 'Cultural politics of K-Pop: Out of 'gayo' nationalism into pop Asianism', paper presented at the International Seminar on Asian Popular Culture, Seoul, South Korea, 22 February.

Shouse, Eric (2005) 'Feeling, emotion, affect', *M/C Journal* 8(6), 26 December: 15 pars., http://journal.media-culture.org.au/0512/03-shouse.php.

Sun, Ge (2002a) 'How does Asia mean? (Part 1)', *Inter-Asia Cultural Studies* 1(1): 13–47.

Sun, Ge (2002b) 'How does Asia mean? (Part 2)', *Inter-Asia Cultural Studies* 1(2): 319–341.

Wang, Hsiao-Wen and Chang, Yun-Pin (2004) 'A-Mei blasted for not taking a stand', *Taipei Times* August 7: 1.

Wang, Jing (2001) 'Guest editor's introduction', *Positions* 9(1): 1–27.

Wang, Shou-Hua 王守華 (1998) 'Radiating: A-Mei fires up Taipei (Mei-li fangsong: Chang Hui-Mei renshou Taibe)' '妹力放送：張惠妹燃燒台北', *Business Weekly* 商業週刊 19 January: 90–92.

Wu, Chi-Zong 吳啟綜 (2004) 'Please authorities, don't conscript Song Seung-Heon (Chiuchiu daren bierang Song Cheung-Hsian dangbing)' '求求大人別讓宋承憲當兵', *Mingsheng Pao* 民生報 20 September: C4.

Yang, Yi-Feng 楊一峰 (1997) 'Solving the puzzle of Chang Hui-Mei's fame (Chang Hui-Mei de chengming zhi mi)' '張惠妹的成名之謎', *The Journalist* 新新聞 530: 115–118.

Yuan, His-Pei 袁世珮 (2004) 'A-Mei just wants peace; let grown-ups resolve grown-up matters (A-Mei wunai: Zhiyao heping daren de shih daren jiejue)' '阿妹無奈：只要和平大人 的事大人解決', *United Daily* 聯合報 7 August: A3.

Zoonen, Liesbet Van (2005) *Entertaining the Citizen: When Politics and Popular Culture Merge*. Lanham, MD: Rowman and Littlefield.

Special terms

aiguo yiren 愛國藝人
aitaiwan 愛台灣
bensheng 本省
Chang Hui-Mei (A-Mei) 張惠妹（阿妹）
daren 大人
hallyu 韓流
muyitianshia 母儀天下
pinpan 拼盤
Sad Love Song 悲傷戀歌
Song Seung-Heon 宋承憲
taishang 台商

Part V

Sexuality

Chapter 16

Embodying gender

Transgender body/subject formations in Taiwan[1]

Josephine Ho

'A soul trapped in the wrong body' is a common description employed by trans subjects to explain their unusual condition.[2] This self-characterization includes two important premises: that the body and the soul (or identity, self-image, etc) are two separate and independent entities whose correct alignment makes up the effect of gender; and that the soul occupies a higher position than the body, to the extent that any mismatch between the two is to be resolved by modifying the body (through cross-dressing, hormonal therapy, SRS, or other procedures) to match the soul (differently known as identity, self-image, etc). Such a body–soul imagery has helped illustrate the awkward situation of trans subjects by graphically presenting the often contradictory feelings, perceptions, self-images, and social expectations that trans subjects have to negotiate as they move through social space. Yet the binary also tends to simplify trans subjectivity by slighting persistent/insistent trans investment in the transformation of the physical body and its image as well as obscuring the manifold differences (in sex, gender, age, socio-economic status, facial features, body shape, etc) among trans subjects, differences that may very well undermine the credibility of a claim to 'a soul trapped in the wrong body' in addition to creating different kinds of difficulties for differently positioned trans subjects in their efforts toward self-realization. Within any given social context, important aspects of contemporary socio-cultural life also add to the complexities of trans existence or even seriously hamper the logistics of their body/identity-construction. The present paper will attempt to demonstrate such specificities of Taiwanese trans-gender existence in relation to body and subject-formations for some trans subjects,[3] in the hope of not only shedding light on the actualities of trans efforts toward self-fashioning, but also illuminating the increasing entanglement between trans self-construction and the evolving gender culture that saturates it.

Limitations of the body–soul imagery have become increasingly apparent in Taiwan after two high-profile trans tragedies. The best-known MTF TS in Taiwan,[4] Lin Guo-Hua, committed suicide in a hotel room on May 7, 2003, five years after her transition. Her former psychiatrist said afterwards in a press interview that Lin was a victim of unrealistic dreams about becoming a female: she had been told by many that her quite plain looks and chubby body figure 'would not make a successful woman.' Still, the psychiatrist remarked, Lin insisted on going through SRS surgery and, as things turned out, had a hard time getting and holding jobs and ended up killing herself in desperation. The question of professional ethics aside, the psychiatrist's comments highlighted the grid of the body–soul imagery: trans subjects whose physical endowment (in facial features, body figure, height, etc) makes it difficult for them to exhibit normative gender image and gender performance in their adopted gender role will consistently encounter immense obstacles in the most mundane details of daily life, whether before or after transition. Another MTF TG, Tsai Yia-Ting, who was quite active in local Taiwanese trans causes, killed herself by throwing herself on the tracks of an oncoming train in December 2003 after a long period of unemployment and a futile romantic pursuit of a straight woman who considered it abhorrent that a trans woman could be a lesbian at the same time.[5] As it stands, frustration in employment and intimate relationships continues to produce devastating effects on the formation of Taiwanese trans subjects, especially those whose gender presentations do not fit, not to mention defy, the assumptions of normative sex-gender-sexuality alignment.

The difficulties facing trans existence span further beyond the pragmatics of daily life and deep into the basic fabric of personal character. Due to widespread ignorance about, and animosity toward, transgenderism, most transgender subjects – whether out of self-protection or resistance to misreadings by mainstream culture – try to maintain a certain degree of inscrutability, which makes it difficult for them to produce empowering knowledges about themselves as well as to produce resisting discourses against the totalization of medical sciences. As trans subjects move through social space, their body and performance often encounter gender policing in the form of curiosity, if not interrogation. In order to smooth over the impression of any possible gender incongruence, trans subjects have to learn to provide coherent stories to narrativize their trans identity and body presentation.[6] Writing about the way American transsexual Agnes constructed her body and narratives to manipulate the diagnosis of the medical community, Harold Garfinkel captures the continuous self-reflection and calculation that make trans identity into what Anthony Giddens would term 'a reflexive project of the modern self' (Giddens, 1991: 75):[7]

> Each of a great variety of structurally different instances required vigilance, resourcefulness, stamina, sustained motivation, preplanning that was accompanied continually by improvisation, and continually, sharpness, wit, knowledge, and very importantly her willingness to deal in 'good reasons' – i.e., to either furnish or be ready to furnish reasonable justifications (explanations) or to avoid situations where explanations would be required.
>
> (Garfinkel, 1967: 137)

Unfortunately, for trans subjects in Taiwan, the most basic information in self-narrativization that makes up the fabric of social interaction or friendship-building is also the most telltale information that may evoke further inquiries about the subject's life, inquiries that may expose the subject's trans identity. The kind of school you went to, the military unit you served in during compulsory military service, your major in college, your shopping favorites – all give out distinct gender-coded information and may very well jeopardize the narratives that trans subjects construct for their gender identity. To avoid social occasions where such information functions as a necessary lubricant, many trans subjects choose to adopt low profiles in their social existence, refraining from attending school class reunions or office mates' social gatherings, projecting images of coldness and aloofness rather than warm openness so as to preemptively frustrate the other party's urge for conversation, carefully keeping circles of acquaintances separate so that knowledges about their personal lives do not have any chance of being verified. This kind of defensive sensitivity that developed along with the subjects' self-fashioning necessarily impacts upon their character and personality, not to mention exacting a heavy toll on their social life by depriving them of the friendship and support that could have been enjoyed.

In a world that fails to see that all of us are involved in 'making and doing the work of bodies – of *becoming* a body in social space' (Turner, 1996/1997/1999: xiii, emphasis added), trans efforts in self-fashioning are often viewed with suspicion and, at best, described as 'passing' (Goffman, 1963: 73). As such, trans lives invoke serious ethical debates over the issue of deception, as the famous examples of trans persons Billy Tipton and Brandon Teena both demonstrate. In a similar case that hit the news in June 2002, Taiwanese aboriginal singer Xioulan-Maya was reported as having lived with her boyfriend for two months and even had wedding pictures taken with him without ever knowing that the boyfriend is actually a biological female. As the performer scrambled to eschew rumors and the stigma of being a lesbian, the transgender 'boyfriend' ended up being a target for serious allegations of fraud and deceit. The sensationalism of the media report only made it all the more horrifying that the deception could remain undetected for so long and through such intimacy. Set within a Taiwanese social context plagued with rampant phone scams and internet scams in recent years, the erosion of social trust cannot but worsen social perception and reception of trans-passing.

It is now clear that as useful as it may be in capturing the maneuvers of trans existence, the concept of 'passing' – along with its connotation of deception – entails profound knowledge/power maneuvers for trans subjects. For passing presupposes the unchallengeable 'naturalness' and 'truthfulness,' or the 'evidentiality' of the physical body, and affirms the meaning and status assigned to such a body by the social culture. The operation of such a truth regime thus serves to reduce/stigmatize the trans subjects' bodily self-realization as nothing but scams and deceit, not to mention creating a profound sense of shame and insecurity in the subjects in regard to the clear discrepancy between one's body (and assigned social gender) and one's chosen identity, a hard-to-explain discrepancy that haunts most trans subjects in their daily existence.

Struggling against social mistrust, discrimination, and humiliation, trans subjects' continued insistence on their self-identity and self-fashioning is in need of a concept that would help explain the close relationship between acts of doing gender, of embodiment, and trans subject formation, without necessarily invoking the gender binary. Here it may be helpful to look into FTM researcher Jay Prosser's adaptation of French psychoanalyst Didier Anzieu's concept of 'skin ego' into that of 'embodiment.' Prosser believes that 'Transsexuality reveals that extent to which embodiment forms an essential base to subjectivity; but it also reveals that embodiment is as much about feeling one inhabits material flesh as the flesh itself' (Prosser, 1998: 7).[8] In other words, neither self nor identity is merely a construction of mental cognition; on the contrary, cognition is quite materially rooted in the actual feelings of the body (especially those of the skin), all the more for trans subjects. At the same time, the skin of a body is no mere essential, physical, fixed *a priori* existence, but always mixed in with associated feelings and images that continue to form the self and identity. Within such a conception, both the self and the body can be understood as open, dynamic existences, constantly changing, adjusting, seeking/constructing different, inhabited, 'at home' feelings, feelings that are not necessarily in alignment with social expectations or prescriptions. Individual self-images, trans or not, far from being abstract imaginings or false consciousnesses, are deeply-rooted in and constitutive of this material body (especially its 'skin'). Similarly, our physical bodies are not given, fixed materials, nor are they the boundary of self-images; instead, bodies are the physical embodiment of self, and most importantly, both are constantly negotiated by all the desires, expectations, norms, and fantasies of daily life.[9] In that sense, trans subjects differ from other subjects only in that they have formed a very different feeling of 'at-homeness,' as their endowed body completely fails to provide that feeling.

Prosser's attention to the skin of the body as constitutive of the self and identity is not without precedent. Sigmund Freud had a similar materialist conception of the ego in relation to the body in which it is embedded. As Freud puts it, 'The ego is first and foremost a bodily ego; it is not merely a surface entity, but is itself the projection of a surface' (Freud, 1986/1991: 451). The ego is thus 'anaclitic' on the sensations and feelings of the body, and, above all, its surface. In that sense, Freud's conception situates the ego, its development, function and interpretation, squarely in the middle of the body and its materiality. Although Freud was probably referring to the material/physical sensations and feelings of the body surface, we can at this present moment extend the concept to include those sensations and feelings of inadequacy or satisfaction that accompany one's body surface/image as the body negotiates its course within a social context that imposes certain gender/sex values on all bodies. And as self-affirmation and self-contentedness are both rooted in the surface of the body, forged with feelings and emotions formulated within given social contexts and social interaction, it is little wonder that the body constitutes a vital site where trans subjectivity is constantly struggling to create itself.

Both Prosser and Freud are helpful in illuminating the importance of body and its valuation as constitutive of the self; their theories are also helpful in explaining trans insistence on non-normative body presentation. But in addition to the inexorable connection that has developed between body and self for the individual – in particular for trans subjects – there is a host of socially and culturally-specific forces that are both constitutive and transformative for such connection. As modernity marches on to produce a Taiwanese society increasingly filled with strangers, unfamiliar occasions, unforeseeable social interactions, and transient human encounters, traditional social markers are becoming increasingly irrelevant as the basis for mutual recognition. It is within such a social context that images of the body came to be loaded with increasing importance in the process of signification, thus becoming key markers for self-representation and other-recognition. Trans subjects, like other subjects, also feel an increasing urge to actively fashion their self-presentation. Unfortunately, in Taiwan, the cultural development that valorizes bodies and their 'readings' – readings that are always already saturated with, and arbitrated by, the sexual dimorphism that accompanies reproduction-oriented understanding of sexuality[10] – also flares up anxious concerns over gender presentations, which only exacerbates the delicate position of trans subjects and their self embodiment. It is also ironic that in an age that seems to have loosened gender barriers in body presentation,[11] there is a simultaneous, commercially-encouraged hyper-attention to exaggerated gender features in Taiwan, thus the popularity of big breasts for women and big muscles for men. The complexities of a seemingly diversifying gender culture eventually leave trans maneuvers vulnerable to unpredictable and often contradictory social interpretations. In addition, as sexual dimorphism continues to persist in Taiwan's public discourses, a relentless but over-simplified feminist critique of the pervasiveness of differential gender power and male malice only serves to imperil already difficult trans existence in Taiwan: within this highly sensitized gender atmosphere, FTM trans subjects tend to be understood as unfortunate souls who have succumbed to the lure of patriarchal values, and MTF trans subjects are read as conniving criminals who are crossing gender boundaries only to facilitate their criminal acts against women. In short, visible and obvious gender crossing is dismissed as either politically incorrect or psychotically criminal in intention, which greatly intensifies trans subjects' difficulties in practicing their embodiment.

Within this social context where gender non-conformity is looked upon with suspicion and body transformation procedures are both hard to come by and expensive to acquire, quite a number of trans subjects are forced to resort to various forms of entertainment work or sex-related work as their only viable source of income and the only site where their chosen embodiments and identities are at least applauded or appreciated as spectacles. As the sex workers' rights movement is still in its nascent stage of development in Taiwan, there is little support or understanding for so-called 'third-sex' sex workers. Worse, trans subjects who have found their only livelihood in the booming sex-related entertainment and recreation industry in Taiwan face increasing alienation from other trans subjects, as the latter, in their urgent quest for legitimacy, strive to resist any possible association with stigma or criminal elements.[12] This complex social atmosphere is further aggravated by the collusion between the police and the media, which guarantees that any news that involves gender-non-comforming trans subjects is sure to meet with sensationalized coverage and humiliating exposure,[13] which not only impinges on the basic human rights of the trans subject in question but also contributes to a reductive and inimical understanding of trans-genderism as a whole.

Many Taiwanese trans subjects have found some empowerment through the internet where they can locate otherwise inaccessible information and otherwise inaccessible friendship, as well as professional-sounding identity terms that could help with their self-representation. Unfamiliar with the historical and localized contextualization that had informed the meaning and connotation of western trans terms of identity,[14] Taiwanese trans subjects generally adopt western abbreviations (TV, TS, CD, and TG) to provide some identity intelligibility for themselves.[15] Unfortunately, divisions often convey a hierarchy of different degrees of authenticity (which each trans subject could lay claim to accordingly), or viewed from another angle, a hierarchy of different degrees of perverseness (which could be levied against trans subjects perceived as belonging to categories different from one's own). Each identity term also invokes a prescriptive life path to be followed by individual trans subjects who claim the identity category. Quite a few trans subjects thus hedge to settle into such categories, not only because existing trans categories do not adequately represent the diversity among trans subjects, but also because the terms never quite capture the tentative and transient state they find themselves in. After all, as Judith Halberstam aptly puts it: 'identity might best be described as process with multiple sites for becoming and being' (1998: 21). As a matter of fact, during the process of my research, several trans subjects whom I had interviewed completed their SRS procedure and moved into their new gender identity; others have entered different stages of the complicated transition process, thus making the gender of their bodies all the more indeterminate.[16] Still, public discourses surrounding trans subjects in Taiwan continue to be constructed on the simple dimorphic model.

Recent developments in Taiwan's gender culture and gender politics are also bringing forth new challenges for local trans subjects. Within the Taiwanese context, the rapid ascendancy and legitimation of the concept of 'gender' both as a social category and as a policy category have been helped and promoted most importantly by a nationalist project that aims to turn women into, more often than not, mere passive consumers of electoral politics. And increasingly, mainstream women's groups, inspired and led by the self-proclaimed 'state-feminists,' are acting as brokers in mediating women's votes so as to bring women into the public sphere en masse in an effort to feminize the state into its prescribed role of 'care-takers of its people.' The rise of the concept 'gender' is further propelled by a nationalist aspiration that aims to affirm Taiwan's nation-statehood by demonstrating its willingness to live up to international standards of performance in terms of paternalistic measures that claim to protect women and children against specifically sex-related travesties such as trafficking or pornography. The intersection between gender constructions of the nation as well as nationalist constructions of gender has thus led to a serious simplification or rarification of the concept of 'gender' that leans all the more toward the normative. Within this social context in which gender norms and gender rights have acquired policy status, other related developments further complicate trans existence. For example, an increasingly liberal view toward women's social role has created a social space somewhat hospitable toward women who choose to present themselves in gender-neutral embodiments. In the meantime, a burgeoning lesbian movement and accompanying lesbian consumption culture have also helped legitimate butch-looking gender presentations. Yet this liberal attitude toward gender crossing has only made more unintelligible, and thus unacceptable, trans subjects' insistence on body modification procedures. In other words, trans embodiment and trans quest for a sense of bodily at-homeness remain incomprehensible even to the liberalizing gender culture. Furthermore, several high-profile sex murders in 1996–97 and Taiwanese mainstream feminists' follow-up advocacy since have not only highlighted the hostility and danger against women in public spaces, but also widely propagated the idea and fear of 'sexual perversions.' This general and indiscriminate apprehension of sexual perversions is unlikely to stop at the door of trans subjects. More often than not, dubious gender performativity is conveniently read as expression of a dubious – i.e. perverse – sexuality. Consequently, gender non-conformity is easily collapsed into sexual perversion in the public eye, helped in no small way by mainstream feminists' reductive characterization of gender power differential as little more than sexual violence and sexual harassment against women. All in all, such recent developments in Taiwanese gender/sex culture are creating an increasingly complicated social space in which trans subjects and their embodiments are hard-pressed to navigate the treacherous waters.

It has already been established that the body–soul imagery beckons forth a simple and static juxtaposition of the body and its gender identity that further conceals 'the daily effort of "doing" gender in everyday interactions that all of us engage in' (Kessler and McKenna, 1978/1985: 126). After all, the imagery of a soul trapped in the wrong body addresses only the wrongness of the given body, while the subject's desired embodiment remains both unarticulated and unelaborated. This kind of silence has made it very difficult for underprivileged trans subjects to locate and acquire appropriate information and resources to build toward their desired embodiment. For if the subject inquires about such issues, it is considered discrediting to the subject's claim to gender authenticity; after all, gender embodiment and performance is still considered to be a natural endowment, even if 'wrongly' endowed. Many a trans subjects thus has to make special efforts to access the embodiment techniques that would help with their gender presentation, such as fashion choices, dressing styles, shopping tips, voice adjustment techniques, vocabulary choices, body part concealment accessories, etc, or else be forced to live with unsatisfactory embodiments that are sure to jeopardize their social existence.

The younger generation of trans subjects in Taiwan, mostly weak in economic resources, often live at home where privacy and mobility are both limited. While they have been encouraged by the democratizing/liberalizing Taiwanese society to start early and 'be themselves,' home is, ironically, where they feel least at home. Limited home space often results in siblings sharing the same room, thus making it all the more difficult to store trans materials for embodiment. Even if some secret corner – such as the top shelf of a closet or the far end behind drawers – could be found to store the clothes, shoes, or wigs; once found out, the result of exposure and humiliation is both direct and brutal. For familiarity among family members deprives trans subjects of any credibility to their fabricated excuses. In one family, one 19-year-old MTF TG has repeatedly lost precious clothing items on such occasions, leaving him distressed both in resources and family relations.[17] Some of the more mature trans subjects are forced to use their cars as key storage space as well as the site for other maintenance (make-up) purposes, which often leaves their outfit in much worse conditions than desired and thus quite damaging to their self-presentation. Still others resort to renting gender-crossing outfits only when needed, which greatly reduces the subject's cumulative experiences in embodiment in addition to significantly raising its cost.

Storage of materials for gender embodiment is but the first of the problems, for trans life and self-presentation are much more dynamic processes. To begin with, with the semi-tropical weather pattern of Taiwan, there is the necessity of frequent washing and drying of the clothing items when they become soiled through actual embodiment. It may not be too difficult to find private moments to schedule hand-washes, but as hanging to dry is still the general practice in Taiwan and may take up to a few hours to reach total dryness, trans subjects are faced with the problem of finding such airy places to renew the looks of their embodiment materials. Some are forced to risk hanging the clothing on the clothes lines of neighbors in the fragile hope of not being found out by their own family members or by their neighbors. All the time, trans subjects would have to be alert and watching, and have some kind of excuse or flat denial ready on hand in case things do not turn out the way they had been planned.[18] The horror of being found out, the humiliation of interrogation, the embarrassment of confrontation, the trouble of maintenance – all of these likely scenarios and difficulties leave young and dependent trans subjects constantly enmeshed in a keen sense of vulnerability that is bound to affect their self-identity as well as self-representation.

Even if trans subjects can overcome the difficulties of setting up a wardrobe, they may not have the luxury to utilize it fully, which can prove to be quite frustrating. As outward appearances of gender variance may provoke public interrogation and subsequent humiliation, many Taiwanese trans subjects are forced to create other kinds of 'personal privacy' to maintain their individual self-embodiment. Some of these are quite humble attempts: the many MTFs whose outward presentations may not survive the scrutiny of gender norms, or whose jobs may not tolerate any degree of gender deviation, are forced to reduce their gender embodiment to a mere set of female underwear underneath their male or neutral outfits, because, as one MTF puts it, 'I am a woman and I feel comfortable this way.' When the thin summer shirts or T-shirts make it too obvious to wear bras underneath, female panties became the last line of defense for the self-embodiment of many MTFs. Yet, even with such subdued and limited self-embodiment, trans subjects still run the risk of being found out and humiliated, as Taiwanese police often set up road blocks in the name of preventing crimes or drunk-driving and may conduct body searches if they deem it necessary. Once found out, the humble trans efforts can be easily read as another exemplary of fetishism if not an insidious performance of some unspeakable sexual perversion on the verge of committing sexual crimes. Even though there is no law prohibiting the donning of opposite-sex clothing, the collusion between the police and the tabloid media often work together to picture trans subjects as possible crime suspects.[19] Consequently, just as women had been deprived of access to public spaces after dark before they took back the night through activism, many trans subjects have also learned that their self-embodiment cannot share public space. The difference is: a woman may now demand a room of her own to pursue her self-actualization; trans subjects, in contrast, could hardly hold on to the bare minimum of their self-embodiment.

With trans subjects whose outer appearances may no longer arouse suspicion upon initial encounter, another important aspect of embodiment becomes a necessity. The voice uttered by such a body is still quite telling. MTF TS university professor Ah-Qi has some quite profound observations in this area:

> This is a learning process. You are in the process; you still have not managed the technique. You don't know how high you can go with the pitch of your voice. Many things take a lot of experimenting and you need to accumulate experiences. There are many cultural things, the adjectives that different genders use, the different vocabulary items, the voice, the pitch. Everything is different between the genders and needs learning.

As experienced as Ah-Qi is, trans embodiment is still a continuous process of becoming, the process of a highly reflexive self-fashioning that is constantly testing the limits of the body. FTM TS Xiau-Wei, on the other hand, has learned a quick way to change his pitch of voice through drinking and smoking. Interestingly, this comes as the side effect of a traditional socializing process for males. As Xiau-Wei puts it: 'Most of the guys I hang out with are smoking and drinking when we are together. If I don't, I won't feel that I belong anyway.' As he smoked and drank, his voice is also gradually tuned to the male pitch. The gendered body is truly a socially-induced body in this case.

Although the 21st century is already equipped with the chromosome, the hormone, the sex glands, and DNA to determine a person's gender, the scientific paradigm stubbornly hangs on to the genitals in gender assignment. The decades-old observation that 'Gender attribution is, for the most part, genital attribution' (Kessler and McKenna, 1978/1985: 153) seems to be alive and well. Such valorization of the genitals in gender determination – helped along in no little sense by recent Taiwanese mainstream feminist dramatization of the genitals as either the root of sexual evil (on the male body) or the site of most vulnerability (on the female body) – has created a social context in which the genitals have also become the focal points of concern for trans subjects. And it is here in the refashioning of the genitals that trans sense of embodiment demonstrates its most unusual operation. For as the body is recognized as a highly contested site in which trans subjects' self re-scripting is effected, the body and the self form an at once close yet alienated relationship: close because the body is demanded to mirror the self accurately and thoroughly so as to embody the transgendered self; alienated because the body is treated in this process as an objective, distant existence, to be subjected to manipulation and modification, but also equipped with feelings and concerns hard to explain by the norm. The body is thus a highly contested site: trans subjects' aggressive fashioning of their bodies is no less than a re-scripting of their bodies that announces their independence from a rigidified gender/sexuality regime.

The given body's resilience and failure to embody the transgender self often leads the subject to see the body itself as wrong, unsatisfactory, alienated, and desperately needing modification through SRS.[20] And when SRS procedures are still beyond the reach of trans subjects either because of a lack of funds to cover the huge surgery costs or difficulties in getting parental approval,[21] trans subjects often have to invent their own measures to reduce (or create) the visibility of protruding genitals. With increasingly accessible breast-binding techniques and commodities provided by a growing lesbian culture, FTMs can now concentrate on experimenting with techniques that help create the tubed look in the crotches. MTFs, on the other hand, are not so fortunate and have to resort to more dramatic measures to perform the disappearing act. While such dramatic measures are usually pathologized by the medical and counseling communities or the media as irrational behavior urged on by misguided desires or inverted identification; a whole generation of trans subjects, helped along with body modification technologies, endocrinological research, internet information, and gender/sexual liberation movements, are already forging aggressive ways to embody their selves. More importantly, these efforts of embodiment often challenge the fragile and shifting boundaries between self-management/self-mutilation, body-realignment/body-destruction, rational choice/blind impulse.

If actual physical transformation is still beyond the subject's means, it is at least feasible in fantasy. MTF TG graduate student Mei-Suei makes it a routine to dream herself into womanhood as she falls asleep every night:

> I am not sure when I began imagining its [penis] non-existence. I think it might have begun in the second or third grade. Everyday before falling asleep, I would make up a story . . . I would imagine an incident that would miraculously turn me into a girl. For example, maybe I got into a car accident or some other accident, and hurt my penis, then it became natural to get rid of it in the hospital.

Such fantasies may seem ridiculous and pathetic, yet when trans subjects recount such stories, they always sound quite nonchalant if not elated ('Wouldn't it be wonderful!' says Mei-Suei). The calm happiness is uttered in stark contrast to the many real obstacles in the lives of trans people as well as the seeming impossibility of ever reaching their goal.

Beyond the realm of fantasy, gradual changes in the Taiwanese social milieu have made it possible for many trans people to take actual steps to create their own gendered bodies. Contraceptive pills for women have long been recognized as effective for MTFs to change their contours as well as their skin tone. Thirty-year-old MTF TS Huei-Tze learned about the application of female hormones at the age of 12 while flipping through a dictionary of medicine in a doctor's waiting room. He also learned from the book that 'a complete woman would have to have female hormones and breasts besides a flat pubic area down there.' With Taiwan's rather loose regulation over the dispensing of medicine, Huei-Tze was able to purchase female hormones for himself from a neighborhood pharmacy, under the excuse of running his mother's errands. The early application of female hormones helped him through puberty without developing many of the expected secondary masculine sexual markers and happily with the welcomed growth of breasts. The easy accessibility of female hormones within a Taiwanese pharmaceutical system that is quite lenient in its dispensing practices has helped many MTFs as they seek to recreate their bodies. Recent public education on menopause issues, promoted by both medical professionals and feminists, has also made hormonal information even more easily accessible – especially for craving trans subjects. As more and more trans subjects begin their body modification process earlier and earlier, Taiwan's military draft system is now faced with an increasing number of gender-transposed draftees who have already developed obvious breasts and feminine traits through the use of female hormones, but still retain their penises. The increasing presence of such mixed-gender bodies in the all-male context of compulsory military services, along with demands from gender/sexuality rights groups, is forcing the Taiwanese military to review its drafting policies and to re-train its medical personnel to handle gender-related discharge evaluations.

Short of hormonal or surgical measures, many trans subjects can still make do with limited available resources to modify their bodies as they struggle to forge their own embodiment. While FTMs bind and flatten their breasts and stuff their groins to create a tubed look, it is now commonplace that MTFs try out pads, water balls, and other stuffing materials to create the look of breasts. The lower part of the MTF body calls for more ingenuity. As it turns out, the most gender-exclusive item may come to a surprising and creative application in the hands of the transgendered: 50-year-old MTF TG Ah-Mei had experimented with many different materials before settling down with none other than feminine napkins to create a flat and smooth look in the groin that would be held in place by the provided adhesives. Economically disadvantaged MTFs would fold toilet tissues or wear double under-panties to create the same smooth look. One MTF sex worker who always wears super mini-skirts at work was asked how she did it during her pre-op days. She proudly announced that she could tuck 'the whole thing' in the rear and still wear G-strings. The transformation was so successful that she would even lift her skirt to flirt with clients. I asked innocently whether it would feel uncomfortable to tuck away so much in so little space. The sex worker said nonchalantly: 'What does it matter? I don't want it anyway.' The light-hearted response demonstrates that, 'as a woman,' she has already effected a certain degree of aliena-tion from her male body and male organs to the extent that the value and feelings of such body parts are simply insignificant. In June 2001, she had her surgery done in Thailand and called me from overseas to tell me the good news. I again asked ignor-antly whether she felt anything missing from her body now. She answered: 'Missing? It has always been this way; it was never existent for me. The only difference is that I used to wear girdles to hold everything in, but now I don't have to do that anymore.' When I pursued this with a question about the possible feeling of 'empty-handedness' when she relieves herself now, she said as-matter-of-factly that she never felt any difference, for she had always relieved herself in the feminine sit-down posture and thus never developed any dependency on hands to hold or direct the penis. In fact, almost all of the MTF trans subjects I interviewed urinate in the feminine posture behind closed doors. Given bodies and organs obviously could not dictate the use to which the bodies and organs are put.

Still, no matter how trans subjects hide, conceal, fake, fabricate to create their gender embodiment, when interrogations and identity-checks became inevitable, the evidential presence of the gendered body poses such an undeniable reality that trans subjects feel hard-pressed to strive toward full embodiment.[22] After all, stuffing, pressing, binding, only succeed in temporarily getting those 'undesirable body parts' out of sight. When the undeniable and resilient presence of such body parts continues to haunt trans subjects, other futile measures emerge to deal with them. MTF TS Ah-qian has heard too many bloody trans stories to do anything drastic or stupidly harmful; still, she could not help but punch on the testicles when frustration rises. The MTF TS sex worker mentioned earlier had also tried the knife on the penis when she was in junior high school. The immense pain forced her to stop and let that 'piece of dead meat' hang there. Now that she has returned from Thailand with her ideal body, she no longer has to worry about it. Other trans subjects have resorted to more resolute steps to get rid of 'this thing that does not belong to me.' MTF TS Ru-Yuen hated the presence of 'such an ugly thing' so much that she tried many different ways to get it out of sight. She had tried to pull her panties all the way backward tightly so as to make the groins look flat. Once she soaked her genital in piping hot water until she could not bear it anymore, which did not seem to do much to it. Then she tried something else.

> I used rubber bands to tie them all up, cutting the blood flow so that they turned blue. That really hurt. I couldn't stand it but for half an hour. Then when you tried to remove the rubber bands, they were so tightly bound that you could not do it. Eventually I had to use scissors to cut them loose. The pain was so sharp that I lost all sensations for a while.

Other than rubber bands, trans subjects could be quite ingenious in using whatever is most conveniently at hand to create the look that matches their gender image. In the hope of creating a flat look in the groin, MTF TS Huei-Tze boldly used the sealing tapes sold in her family's grocery store and taped the unwanted organ down:

> It was very uncomfortable in summer time because the skin under the sealing tape would canker. But I felt very happy because at least temporarily I was a girl. I did that from third grade in the elementary school to second year in junior high. When I had to go to the bathroom, I would peel the tape off and press it back on afterwards. And my skin would canker all the time . . . I had done other crazy things. I would soak my organs in very hot water and I got burnt right away. I really hate this organ; it should not belong to me. I must do something to get rid of it.

Psychiatrists would probably view this kind of 'self-mutilating' behavior as an expression of 'self-hatred.' But the language and attitude of the trans subjects demonstrate clearly that it is not self-hatred, for the object of the hatred is by no means 'part of the self.' What the body should have, should not have; what is one's own, what is not – trans subjects have very definite ideas about these things. Their self-determination in the body is actually testing the bottom line of feminist position on 'our bodies, ourselves.'

The media or medical professionals tend to view such attitudes or acts as impulsive if not compulsive, saying that the trans subjects are doing those things because they are psychologically unbalanced. But many trans subjects are far from impulsive in the construction of their gender embodiment. SRS procedure is an important life choice, and trans subjects are not without their own calculations. Even when surgery is available and parental consent is in hand, some trans subjects still have their own considerations. The lack of relevant information and the imperfection of the medical procedure are most acutely felt by FTMs. FTM TS Tim had been waiting to go this way for 17 years. Now that everything seemed to be in place and he had gotten parental approval, he calmly deliberated and asked his psychiatrist not to rush him into the procedure even though he was fast approaching the surgery cut-off age of 40. Tim explains: 'I have not found out all there is to know about the surgery, and what I see today is still evolving and the techniques are improving.' He eventually received surgery in 2002, having 'learned everything about the procedure and evaluated all available doctors and hospitals.'[23]

As to the expensive cost of the transition, nobody knows it better than trans subjects themselves. Thirty-something FTM TS Wei-Wei has been living as a man since he was 15, has gone to all job interviews as a man, and has worked as a man with only a few people in the company personnel departments knowing anything about it. Such a long-term construction process derives its force from the deeply-rooted 'skin-ego' that insistently demands an embodiment different from the given one. When challenged about the importance of sex-change surgery to a life already acclimated to living in the opposite gender role, Wei-Wei says: 'You might think it is not important, but the important thing is how *I* feel in that body. My bodily senses about the need to change into the *right* body are too profound to be ignored.' Fragile-looking MTF TS Ru-Yuen says with a faint smile on the eve of her SRS:

> From the point of view of 'ordinary people,' such sacrifices are really terrible. Your lifespan will shorten, your body strength will worsen, you might not accomplish the dreams you have for your life. I don't know if my head is screwed on wrong or not, I just have to make myself into a true woman, a woman who does not have any worries. I think the price is well worth it. I don't mind not living too long. For somebody like me, I could never have children. I am not qualified to enjoy living-happily-ever-after. And if that is the case, I don't need to live too long.

The taking of hormones may damage the liver. Life span may be shortened because of that. SRS procedures do not offer reproductive capacities, nor do they guarantee finding a partner who would accept the newly constructed body and life.[24] Still, trans subjects are determined to charge forward. The road of gender embodiment is no smooth thoroughfare, yet their own life experiences have already proven that if they do not take this road, they will never feel at home in their bodies. The interrogations and humiliations of daily life are much more unbearable than whatever hazards accompany the embodiment measures.

In the thick woods of gender walked many trans subjects, covered with various scars and bruises. Some are still bleeding with pain; others have dried up into sophisticated scars. While existing gender stereotypes do exert strong pressures on trans subjects – either when they try to lead a regular and unobtrusive life in their chosen gender presentation, or when they are in the process of struggling to acquire the psychiatric evaluations needed to become eligible for SRS – trans subjects' chosen gender identities are not necessarily circumscribed by existing gender stereotypes. When I asked college freshman pre-op MTF TS Ah-Qian what kind of woman he pictures himself becoming, his answer came as a stark contrast to his soft and demure feminine appearance: 'A lewd, licentious woman. Very aggressive and enticing. I think many people look at me now and think I am a good girl, but I know that I have many different faces.' In fact, not every TS would like to remain low-profiled after transition. The MTF sex worker who eventually went to Thailand for her surgery said before her departure, 'If I had my SRS, I would be able to wear very sexy clothes, very tight clothes, and to become a very sexy enticing slut.' While many criticize trans subjects for giving in to gender stereotypes, the latter's conception of 'gender' may move beyond what is commonly assumed. After all, many members of the new generation of trans subjects were brought up in the post-1994 gender/sexuality liberation atmosphere of Taiwan, and in many ways they are exactly the ones whose lives carry and embody the ideals of that movement to its logical conclusion. MTF TG physics doctoral student Mei-Suei provides a self-description that may be considered confounded for the gender orthodox: 'I wish gender stereotypes did not exist. If I become a woman, I don't see anything improper if I act the way I do now as a man. I don't think I will ever be modest or demure; I will be confident, lively, and intellectual. I think I will become a feminist.' Pre-op FTM Hsu-Kuan may be anticipating her SRS very soon but also has very complicated thoughts about his future gender: 'If I lead a stereotypical man's life after the transition, I would hate that. Maybe after the surgery, I would not want to be referred to as a man, I don't know. I'm still thinking.' Such complicated gender formations are bound to bring unpredictable impact on existing gender culture.

Due to limitations in language and conceptualization, 'trans'-gender subjects are commonly perceived as merely trying to 'trans'-plant themselves so as to find their 'home' in the other sex/gender, to create a new at-home feeling in a self-fashioned body. Yet it is increasingly obvious that, as the contradictory and disharmonious body/identity of the transgender subjects struggles to assert itself despite existing gender stereotypes and prejudices, their self-reflexive project of doing gender is also constantly 'trans'-gressing/'trans'-forming existing gender/sexuality categories. As such, trans subjects are not only making/fashioning their bodies and selves but embodying new contents and possible meanings for gender imagination.

Notes

1 An earlier version of this paper was read at Sexualities, Gender, and Rights in Asia: 1st International Conference of Asian Queer Studies, Bangkok, Thailand, July 7–9, 2005; and subsequently at Inter-Asia Cultural Studies Conference on 'Emerging Subjectivities, Cultures and Movements,' Seoul, Korea, July 22–24, 2005. I want to thank the members of Taiwan TG Butterfly Garden for allowing me to share our group discussions and to conduct in-depth interviews with individual members when available. The group has been in existence since 2000 when my TG friend Winnie and I decided to create a regular meeting space for the transgendered

so as to promote support and education, and activism if possible. Since then, the group has seen more than 60 members come and go, and it is the only standing TG group in Taiwan that is meeting regularly and working in close alliance with other marginal gender/sexuality groups.

2   The term 'trans' is commonly used in the US context to refer only to transsexuals who have gone through SRS procedures. But in the Taiwanese context, gender-sexuality rights groups have created the term 'trans-gender' (*kuaxingbie*) in the year 2000 as an umbrella term that would cover all subjects of gender variance in an effort to rally unity and solidarity for a yet-to-develop transgender movement. The present paper will honor this spirit of solidarity in its non-essentialist use of terms.

3   Here I must emphasize the word 'some,' for the trans subjects reported in this paper do tend to be more articulate and resourceful in cultural-educational capital, though not necessarily so in financial capital. The 'other' trans subjects – who are large in number but mostly invisible, suffering from severe stigmatization and ostracization due to their marginal survival in various forms of sex-work-related occupation – can only be glimpsed in refraction.

4   As transition entails a long process during which the subject may continue to exist in various gender variant conditions, commonly used terms such as FTM (female to male) or MTF (male to female) are used in this paper not to denote the subject's eventual gender position but only to signal the subject's own description of their shift from a biological category (the former term) to an identity category (the latter term). Likewise, terms such as TS and TG are used not in any essentialist sense in this paper, but only to denote in the former case an active involvement in surgery-related transformation process (including psychiatrical evaluation in preparation for SRS procedure, hormonal treatment, and all forms of surgical procedure), and in the latter a nonchalance toward the surgery track of life (but not without occasional experimentation with hormonal or other body transformation technologies). The binary structure of FTM/MTF or TS/TG thus entails problems of identity intelligibility mixed in with the demands of gender authenticity.

5   Tsai became famous because she launched a personal campaign to demand that trans subjects, or for that matter all subjects, be allowed to use photos that reflect their chosen gender on their identity cards, instead of being required to pose for gender pictures that accord with their birth sex.

6   In that sense, gender embodiment is as much a narrative construction as it is a physical construction.

7   Although Anthony Giddens recognizes that tranvestism has become a lifestyle issue rather than a biological inevitability in late modernity (1992: 199), he never did include trans subjects' construction of their selves in his list of self-reflexive projects of the modern self. Garfinkel's description here, however, would situate trans existences squarely in the middle of the reflexive projects of the modern self.

8   Prosser may be limiting the discussion here only to transsexualism, but my experience with members of the Taiwan TG Butterfly Garden has been much more complicated. Whether those in their 50s for whom surgery is no longer viable, or those who are in their 20s for whom surgery is only one option in life, it is not always clear where to draw the line between a transsexual and a transgender. Entry into the SRS surgery process is likewise a problematic index, as many subjects would delay later stages of the transformation process indefinitely, which leaves them in a limbo stage of transition and gender designation, but accompanied by a more or less settled and pragmatic attitude toward life.

9   It needs to be stressed here that such adjusting/seeking/constructing is always done through continuous interaction with surrounding social forces (such as prevailing aesthetic values, suggestive fantasies conveyed in the ads, social discipline, etc). In that sense, embodiment, trans or not, is never an individual's willful act, nor purely dictated by fashion or fad, but a complicated process of negotiation between the self and the social. The discussion here also has profound implications for the Taiwanese orthodox feminist critique of body sculpturing and cosmetic surgery. Feminists who are against cosmetic surgery aim to expose the gender power behind such practices, yet the critical discourse they generate often reverts back to a biological point of view of the body, believing that women's imagination of their body images should not deviate from their given endowment and that women should be content with their 'real' (biologically endowed) conditions. Within this point of view, women who are devoted to body sculpturing or body shaping are seen as victims of false consciousness, as being duped into such dreams, or

as victims of patriarchal pressure, as being forced into living up to men's fantasies and expectations. Yet the concept of skin ego expresses that there are complicated relationships between desires of self-consciousness (self-identity) and existing body conditions that cannot be reduced to simplistic essentialism or political correctness.

10 Gilbert Herdt believes that 'dimorphism was an invention of modernism' and traces its theoretical origin to the Darwinian theory of natural selection, whereby the reproduction of species was taken to be the purpose of all existences (Herdt, 1993: 26). As sexual selection and reproduction became the foremost quality of species, the basic structure of sexual dimorphism also became the norm, consolidated by various religious doctrines and legal codes as well as by sexological discourses that began to develop in the 19th century. Of course, as the dimorphic model affirms itself and the function of reproduction dictates gender/sexual categories, a multiplicity of perverse/pathological subjects are also 'produced' (Foucault, 1978: 37–39).

11 Among multiplying body features, it is most unfortunate that trans presentations still attract the most alarmed gazes. I might offer here a personal observation made in June 2005. Even in London's Camden Town area, well-known for its subcultural bodies with their multiple and outrageous tattoos, piercing, Mohawk hairstyles, Gothic outfits, etc, it is still the transgender who stands out like a sore thumb, trailed by disapproving gazes.

12 Sex work is now completely outlawed in Taiwan, although in reality it prospers in many forms and sites. This contradictory existence often leaves sex workers, not to mention 'third-sex' sex workers, most vulnerable to various forms of exploitation. Here it may be also enlightening to examine another kind of alienation that has become quite visible in the Taiwanese gay community, where transgender gays (drag queens or sissy gays) are often treated with contempt even though they are the ones most directly facing the blunt force of homophobia and the ones most active in resisting the latter. Still, mainstreaming gays often go to great lengths to stand clear from those gays who may be considered promiscuous or sexually adventurous.

13 On the small island of Taiwan there are a total of eight around-the-clock cable news stations. The pressure of competition is so keen that a lot of effort is devoted to 'producing/creating' newsworthy reports, reports that tend to center upon sensational (aberrance-related) topics. The collaboration between the media and the police in Taiwan has been consistently criticized by marginal subject groups.

14 For one thing, in the context of the US in the 1970s, the term transgender had denoted 'living' in the opposite gender; in other words, trans status is a matter of the life activities of trans subjects rather than their identity. I met 89-year-old trans legend Virginia Prince in April 2002 at the annual convention held by the International Foundation for Gender Education, in Nashville, Tennessee. Prince reiterated time and again: 'The term "transgender" tells about what we "do," not what we "are."' The uneasiness she felt toward essentialistic identity politics was quite obvious, and her insistence on a praxis-oriented understanding of transgender was also quite firm.

15 Before the arrival of the trans identity terms, many trans subjects in Taiwan had at one time used 'Third Sex' to describe themselves as something that lies beyond the gender binary (Herdt, 1993: 20). Yet a shift in meaning has occurred in recent years: as booming tourism made transvestite song and dance shows in Thailand a regular stock in the expectations of Taiwanese tourists, 'the third sex' has come to denote those who perform in such shows. Consequently, Taiwanese trans subjects chose to shy away from this term and its association with a specific type of entertainment/sex work conducted mostly by trans subjects. The highly queer but trans-affirming Thai movie 'The Iron Ladies,' (webpage at http://www.pappayon.com/movies/ satreelek2/english/main/) has done a lot to mitigate the original negative connotations associated with the term. Still, most Taiwanese trans subjects would avoid 'The Third Sex' and its connections with stigmatized sex work.

16 Taiwan's only existing TG support group, the Taiwan TG Butterfly Garden, includes quite a few trans men who have had their breasts and female reproductive organs removed but are delaying the reconstructive surgery for penises due to various considerations, the least of which being a concern over the function of the reconstructed organ. Many trans women on the other hand are already into female hormones and growing breasts without going through surgery to remove any male sex organs. As things go, the trans identity labels in the present paper mark

only the moment of its writing, and that moment is always fast becoming the past as trans bodies continue their odyssey of embodiment.

17 The same youth also has to share a computer with his brother, which leaves him hard-pressed when the brother notices that Google searches have been performed on trans-related key words. At such critical and telling moments, a flat denial, a denial that violates the subject's sense of dignity, is the only and a very vulnerable response.

18 One trans youth jokingly tells me that he has developed a 'conniving/scheming personality' as a result of such constant necessity to come up with a variety of narratives to cover his tracks as a trans. The self-reflexivity demonstrated here speaks of a trans life that is much more dynamic and treacherous than conveyed by the body–soul misplacement imagery.

19 Many a trans subject has suffered the suspicion and threats by the police; the more unfortunate ones even scandals in the media. On May 19, 2002, actor Chen Juen-Sheng was found to be shopping, dressed like a woman, in a mall in Taipei. Mall security chased him down and had him arrested because the actor 'looked suspicious in women's clothing.' The huge scandal gave local trans group, Taiwan TG Butterfly Garden, its first opportunity to voice its defense of trans rights to alternative gender embodiment in public.

20 In that sense, what has been termed the 'transsexual ideology' that paints a rosy picture for trans subjects (MacKenzie, 1994: 57–102) only sets in relief the painful interrogations and embarrassment that make up their daily life, as well as the torturous process of getting the right medical procedure so that a new body and a new identity could be created.

21 As surgeons who perform body modification procedures could, under Taiwanese law, be sued by the patients' parents for malicious mutilation against their (even fully grown) children, no surgeon would perform SRS procedure without the patients first acquiring written approval from their parents. With age-old Chinese belief in family lineage and the traditional duty of bringing forth off-spring, parental approval has become a formidable obstacle for trans subjects.

22 In cases where such embodiment can no longer be realized, trans subjects can only harbor secret plans for their own final departure. Fifty-year-old MTF Ah-Mei says he is too old to do any actual body modification even when he can afford it now, but he hopes that he could be buried in women's clothing when he dies. Realizing that even such humble wishes probably will not be granted, he hopes that family members would at least incinerate all his female outfits for him to use in the other world. In 2004, when trans activist Tsai Yia-Ting threw herself in front of an oncoming train and was killed instantly, members of the Taiwan TG Butterfly Garden negotiated with her family and finally got them to agree to let Tsai be buried, according to her wish, in women's attire underneath a man's suit. The ancestral tablet that bore her name carried her given name as well as her adopted female name. It was a compromise won through persistent persuasion by gender/sexuality activists. For details, see 'The Woman Under the Burial Quilt – Death of a Trans Warrior' (Ho, 2005: 127–128).

23 As history would have it, Taiwan has now developed its fame in genital reconstructive surgery for FTMs. In fact, it was when the reconstructed genitals had proven to be fully functional that Tim finally decided to make the transition. He had said one year before the surgery: 'What good is the surgery if I end up with a limp organ that only highlights my inadequacy as a man?'

24 Again, gender makes a big difference here. It seems that in Taiwan FTMs enjoy more luck than MTFs in finding soul-mates after transition. Even in the small circle that I am familiar with, quite a few weddings have already taken place in the past few years for transitioned FTMs.

References

Foucault, Michel (1978) *The History of Sexuality, Vol. I: An Introduction,* translated by Robert Hurley, New York: Random House.

Freud, Sigmund (1986/1991) 'The Ego and the Id'. In *The Essentials of Psycho-analysis,* translated by James Strachey, London: Penguin, 439–483.

Garfinkel, Harold (1967/1984) *Studies in Ethnomethodology,* Cambridge: Polity.

Giddens, Anthony (1991) *Modernity and Self-Identity,* Oxford: Polity.

Giddens, Anthony (1992) *The Transformation of Intimacy: Sexuality, Love & Eroticism in Modern Societies*, London: Polity.

Goffman, Erving (1963) *Stigma: Notes on the Management of Spoiled Identity*, New York: Simon & Schuster.

Halberstam, Judith (1998) *Female Masculinity*, Durham, NC: Duke University Press.

Herdt, Gilbert (ed.) (1993) 'Introduction: Third Sexes and Third Genders'. In Gilbert Herdt (ed.) *Third Sex, Third Gender: Beyond Sexual Dimorphism in Culture and History*, New York: Zone Books, 21–84.

Ho, Josephine (2005) 'The Woman Under the Burial Quilt – Death of a Trans Warrior', *Left Curve* 29: 127–128.

Kessler, Suzanne J. and McKenna, Wendy (1978/1985) *Gender: An Ethnomethodological Approach*, Chicago: University of Chicago Press.

MacKenzie, Gordene Olga (1994) *Transgender Nation*, Bowling Green, OH: Bowling Green State University Popular Press.

Prosser, Jay (1998) *Second Skins: The Body Narratives of Transsexuality*, New York: Columbia University Press.

Turner, Bryan S. (1996/1997/1999) 'Introduction to the Second Edition: The Embodiment of Social Theory'. In Bryan Turner (ed.) *The Body and Society: Explorations in Social Theory*, 2nd edn, London: Sage, 1–36.

Special terms

kuaxingbie 跨性別
Iron Ladies 人妖打排球
third sex 第三性

Chapter 17

State power, prostitution and sexual order in Taiwan

Towards a genealogical critique of 'virtuous custom'[1]

Hans Tao-Ming Huang

Introduction: the Police Offence Law and the sage-king state

This paper concerns the state regulation of sexualities and the formation of gendered subjectivities in postwar Taiwan. It considers, by way of genealogical investigation, the policed culture of sex under the regulatory regime of 'virtuous custom' (*shanliang fengsu*) as sustained by the now defunct Police Offence Law. By analysing the police and journalistic discourse of sex between the 1950s and 1980s, it traces the process whereby *a particular segment-line* of contemporary Taiwan dominant social/sexual order came to be established through the state's banning of prostitution. As this genealogical project is motivated by an immediate political concern for the historical present, the paper will conclude by arguing against the current dominant anti-obscenity/prostitution state feminism and the new social/sexual order it ordains in Taiwan today.

The Police Offence Law, modelled on the pre-war Japanese Police Offence Law, was promulgated originally by the Qing government in 1906 (Li 1979: 24). Finalized after an overhaul in 1943, it remained *unconstitutionally* sustained by the Kuomingtang (KMT) or nationalist government in Taiwan until 1991 when it was abrogated and replaced by the Social Order Maintenance Law. This administrative law, which enabled the state actively to intervene in the course of social formations, played a pivotal role in nation-building in postwar Taiwan. Its regulatory realms encompassed virtually every aspect of public and, as this paper will show, private life. It conferred on the police the prerogative to discipline and punish the deviant individual: interrogation, jurisdiction, adjudication and the execution of punishment were all to be carried out within the police station. While the offender's true intent in the alleged crime did not preclude punishment, the police also had discretionary powers to impose harsher punishment on 'habitual' offenders. Penalties include confiscation, forced labour, admonition, detention of up to 14 days or a fine as well as the shutting down of a business either temporarily or permanently.[2]

To legitimize the operation of the Police Offence Law in Taiwan, the KMT government promulgated in 1953 the Police Law, enlisting 'redressing the customs' (*zhengsu*), among others, as part of police administration. While 'redressing the customs' included getting rid of 'backward' social practices such as foot-binding/breast-binding, it was the political management of sex that constituted the most significant part of this particular domain of police administration (Wang 1958: 242). Thus, in the name of maintaining 'virtuous custom', the police not only had the mission of rectifying individual sexual misconduct but also the task of administering the leisure/pleasure businesses associated with fostering sexual immorality in general and prostitution in particular in accordance with the Police Offence Law.

Of particular interest and significance here is the role assigned to the police by the architect of the modern police apparatus in China and Taiwan, Chiang Kai-shek, that of moral guardian of the population.[3] Maintaining that 'the aim of police administration is the practising of "the government of benevolence (*renzheng*)"' (Chiang, cited in Mei 1951: 4), Chiang upholds that the essential task of the police is to reform society and to 'enable all the people to become good national citizens (*guomin*)' (Chiang, cited in Feng 1958: 6).[4] To undertake such a task, the police must, as Chiang expounds in an admonitory speech he gave to students of the Central Police College, excel in their moral cultivation and assume the three governing positions of 'parent', 'teacher' and 'king' (*zuozhiqin, zuozhishi, zuozhijun*), with the last one construed as the agent of law:

> We have to first govern the people as their parents and teachers in guiding, teaching and disciplining them. It is only when you cannot govern them as their parents and teachers that you have to seek recourse to the law. Therefore, everybody must know that we should try our best to ensure that people do not offend the law. Try our best to make people listen to our admonishments and to be loved and cherished by us.
>
> (Chiang 1964: 149)

Here Chiang evokes the cultivation of a morally superior man – known as a man of noble character (*junzi*) – predicated upon what is generally called within the Confucian tradition practised by the intelligentsia the 'sage-king' (*shengwang*) paradigm. Schematically, the sage-king paradigm pertains to the art of government formulated in widening series of spheres, typified by the Confucian expression 'to cultivate the self, to regulate the household/family, to manage/rule the country, to pacify the world', with 'sage-king' being the impeccable moral subject. While every human being can in theory become a sage-king, the possibility of becoming or assuming the sage-king subject position is, as Jen-peng Liu has noted, in practice necessarily pre-determined by one's social status. In her important study of the late Qing and early republican discourse of women's rights, Liu employs the Dumontian notion of hierarchy and demonstrates how such a discourse pertaining to the modern notion of 'equality' came to be articulated through the 'sage-king' moral hierarchy, one that presupposes a pre-given totality naturalized in accordance with existing political/social relations such as the king/subject, father/son, husband/wife. Within this hierarchy, the morally inferior are proposed as contrary or subordinate to the morally superior and yet are entirely encompassed by the latter. Provided that the pre-given totality is not radically called into question, those assuming the sage-king speaking position are capable of acting benevolently towards the morally inferior (Liu 2000: 1–72). This paper will show how the *guomin* subject-position came into formation through the KMT government's forcible production of 'virtuous custom' premised on the sage-king moral hierarchy.

Before embarking on this investigation, it is essential first to look at the differences between the two main laws pertaining to the regulation of prostitution, namely, the criminal law and the Police Offence Law. Article 231 of the criminal law did not (and still does not) prohibit individuals from prostituting themselves. Rather, it outlawed those who made profits by encouraging and facilitating others to perform illicit sexual acts (categorized in juridical terms as 'carnal relations' (*jianyin*) designating extra-marital penis–vagina penetrative sex and 'indecency' (*weixie*), any sexual act other than 'carnal relations' such as same-sex genital relations). Of particular significance here is that, up to 1999, there existed in article 231 a legal category of women called 'woman of respectable family' (*liangjia funü*):[5]

> The so-called 'woman of respectable family' is not to be judged by her family background. Rather she is to be defined in accordance with whether she is accustomed to immoral sexual behaviour. If a prostitute has stopped plying her trade, she then can be called 'woman of respectable family'. On the other hand, if an illicit prostitute is prostituting herself, she cannot be said to be 'woman of respectable family.'
>
> (The Council of Grand Justices of the Judicial Yuan, Interpretation no. 718 [delivered in 1932], cited in Liu and Shi 1994: 579).

Thus, an individual running a brothel would not be prosecuted under the criminal law provided that his/her employee(s) could be proven to have been 'accustomed to immoral sexual behaviour'.

Article 64 of the Police Offence Law, on the other hand, outlawed the prostitute, the pimp (item 3) and the client (item 4). It should be noted that the illicit sexual act performed by the prostitute was defined in this article as *jiansu*, a compound which consists of 'illicit sexual relations' (*jian*) and 'sleep with someone' (*su*). In practice, the term had always been made to operate as a synonym of 'carnal relations' as defined in the criminal law. This meant that the Police Offence Law prohibited *only* heterosexual prostitution. However, male homosexual prostitution was, this paper will show, also outlawed under 'virtuous custom'.

To license or not? Prostitution policies in the 1950s

Prostitution was licensed under the Japanese colonial period (1895–1945) in Taiwan. All the registered courtesan/geisha houses and brothels were allowed to operate in the authorized red light districts. With the decline of courtesan/geisha house culture from the 1930s onwards, there emerged modern leisure/pleasure businesses, giving rise to the new profession of 'hostess'. By the mid 1940s, hostess culture had become a new social phenomenon and hostesses could be found in all the leisure/pleasure businesses, ranging from traditional wine houses and tea rooms to trendy coffee houses and dance halls (Lin 1997: 108–110). Although it was not until the promulgation of the Police Law in 1953 that the task of 'redressing the customs' was *formally* assigned to police administration, the police authority in Taiwan had already undertaken this task in the immediate aftermath of Taiwan's returning-to-China in 1945. Reasoning that 'our Taiwanese countrymen were allowed under the Japanese occupation to wallow in immorality which must be rectified' (*Taiwan Police Administration* 1946, cited in Lin 1997: 111), the new Chinese nationalist government launched in 1946 an island-wide police modus operandi to outlaw hostesses and prostitutes (Lin 1997: 112).[6]

Chiang Kai-shek's exiled government, having arrived in Taiwan in 1949, continued this de-colonizing/re-nationalizing schema. In its attempts to impose a war-time disciplinary lifestyle, the government ordered all existing wine houses and tea rooms to be renamed 'public canteens/tea rooms' and governed by local police as 'certain type of business'.[7] Officially renamed 'waitresses', hostesses of such establishments were strictly prohibited from accompanying customers 'drinking and singing' while dissolute behaviour was absolutely forbidden. They were required in addition to have regular venereal diseases check-ups in order to obtain work permits from the police (Wang 1958: 273–275). Implicit in this regulation was the presumption that all hostesses/waitresses were engaged in the practice of prostitution. Interestingly enough, it is precisely this same presumption that informed the government's 1951 pilot scheme, which tacitly allowed licensed prostitution to operate in the guise of the so-called 'certain type of wine house' (*tezhong jiujia*).[8] Meanwhile, it must be pointed out that the government also began to set up brothels island-wide to provide sexual services to its army population, an institution that came to be known as 'Military Paradise' (*junzhong leyuan*).[9] Beyond these somewhat covert measures, stamping-out prostitution remained the government's official policy.

Police observers in the early 1950s were generally of the opinion that the government should license prostitution. Broadly speaking, the police discourse on the subject of prostitution is predicated upon a political rationality that makes the distinction between two modes of governmental action – one negative, the other positive. The former, construed as bringing about a temporary solution to the problem, tends to seek recourse to the law, whereas the latter, figured as getting to the root of the problem, leans towards welfare policies. For instance, the police observer Yao Jishao argued that such a policy would enable the police to manage prostitutes, bringing them under control and gradually reducing the number of prostitutes by persuading them to 'gain respectability' (*congliang*). Meanwhile, he maintained that the government should try to raise money to build factories in order to encourage prostitutes into respectable employment (Yao 1949: 15). Another observer, Huang Yue, made his case for licensed prostitution by pointing out the impracticality of the positive approach. First, welfare policies, such as providing prostitutes with job training, education or financial relief, could not be implemented without first obtaining precise statistics of the prostitute population, Huang argued, yet obtaining such figures was difficult, if not impossible, for with prostitution being illegal, how could one expect prostitutes to come to the government asking for help? Moreover,

> in the province of Taiwan, apart from the typical kind of prostitute, wine house/tea room hostesses and even those lower class bondmaids cooking for the rich are all known to prostitute themselves for living. Tempted by money, these women often do not hesitate to sell their bodies and souls. With regard to these women, difficulties arise when one identifies them as prostitutes in order to rescue and help them out. However, one simply cannot adopt the laissez-faire attitude in dealing with these women who ply their trade in a covert way, because the harm they cause to 'social morality and the people's health' is no less than that caused by typical illicit prostitutes.
>
> (Huang 1949: 9)

Secondly, the government simply could not afford to pay the bill. Besides, given that the existence of prostitution was unavoidable as 'society has not reached the ideal stage whereby every man has a job and every woman has a husband', Huang maintained that licensed prostitution remained the only realistic option for the government, adding that it not only had the benefit of reducing sex crimes such as rape but also of 'protecting the health of *guomin* by stopping the spread of venereal diseases' (Huang 1949: 9).

There are three points to be made concerning Huang's advocacy of licensed prostitution. First, Huang rightly identifies the inherent contradiction within the positive mode of state intervention: any welfare policy for women prostitutes is doomed to failure from the outset if prostitution remains outlawed, yet the state's maintenance of virtuous custom is predicated upon the rooting-out of prostitution. Despite this, Huang's own stance on prostitution hinges upon this very contradiction which ambivalently construes the woman prostitute as at once victim (of sexual exploitation and therefore in need of rescue) and victimiser (of society), a dual figure whose construction Gail Hershatter has traced in the context of republican China (Hershatter 1997: 181–241). This explains why he would only go so far as to call for licensed prostitution rather than decriminalization of sex work. Second, his formulation of the utopia which licensed prostitution helps sustain is indicatively heterosexist and statist: marriage is paramount and women's sexuality must be sanctioned by the state. Thirdly, by virtue of her contagious body and depraved soul, the woman prostitute, even if licensed, is posited as the *guomin*'s sexual Other.

After a decade of outright banning of prostitution, the KMT government finally adopted the licensing policy, thus promulgating a regulation that prescribed the following four administrative procedures for local authorities:

(1) rooting-out illicit prostitutes completely: illicit prostitutes, once arrested, should be checked for venereal diseases.
(2) registering and managing: police were to be the authority in the matter of licensed brothels.
(3) rescuing (those forced into prostitution) and guiding the licensed prostitutes to regain respectability (by getting married).
(4) retaining and reforming: local governments should encourage the private sector to institute women's training/reform centres.[10]

These procedures, consisting of both the negative and positive modes of state intervention, represent what Foucault calls 'the marginalistic integration of individuals in the state's utility' (Foucault 2001: 409). As political technology of gendered/classed individuals, they aimed to reform prostitutes as either housewives or useful/productive labours for a rapidly industrializing society.

The reinstatement of the police outlawing illicit prostitution (Procedure 1) prompted the publication of two articles on the police offence of illicit prostitution in *Police and People Gazette* in 1960. Written with the intention of providing general guidance for the police handling of illicit prostitutes, the articles, authored by the police officers Zhang Yide and Zhang Wenjun respectively, reveal the police epistemology of the deviant female individual as well as the techniques employed to discipline and punish her. To begin with, when conducting 'unannounced inspection' (*linjian*),[11] the police should be alert if an unmarried couple is found sleeping in the same room:

> After interrogation, if one believes that they are not good friends or that there is
> a significant age difference between them, or that the woman is a bar girl, wine-
> house woman, that she works as waitress in a tearoom, or coffee house, or that she
> has a police record of plying her trade in the past, even if she categorically denies
> that she is prostituting herself, she should be seen as a prime suspect.
>
> (Zhang Yide 1960: 9)

This passage makes clear, once again, that women in the leisure/pleasure businesses are
regarded by the police as illicit prostitutes. It also suggests that once a woman becomes
a police offender, that identity will be hers forever. In addition, it demonstrates a
normative opposition to cross-generation relationships and casual sex. With regard to
the latter in particular, Zhang Wenjun, in his attempt to differentiate 'living illicitly
as husband and wife' (*pinju*) from sexual encounters, argued that a non-married woman
supported by male patrons can qualify as a prostitute if she intends to profit from her
relationship with a man and if she 'does not have the intent to "choose [carefully] the
man she serves" (*zeren er shi*)' (Zhang Wenjun 1960: 8).

With regard to adjudication, both authors maintained that the police must exercise
their power with extreme care and discretion in order to be 'just and reasonable':

> Although most of those who get involved in the pleasure businesses are the slothful
> kind who abandon themselves to vice, there are also some who are forced into
> doing it by difficult circumstances. Therefore, before a verdict is delivered, the
> police officer . . . should thoroughly investigate the offender's family background/
> upbringing, personality, motivation for becoming a prostitute, her manner toward
> the police, whether she expresses regret and whether she's a repeat offender. With
> regard to penalties, I reckon one should avoid a financial penalty as much as possible.
> This is because it is difficult to teach her a lesson by giving her a fine . . . Those
> who do not have evil nature can be given an admonition as punishment. On the
> other the other hand, those who have a bad attitude or who are repeat offenders
> should be given an austere punishment by doubling the length of detention. In so
> doing, the police officers can retain their dignity and the offender can be given a
> chance to repent for what she's done. Thus education can result from punishment.
>
> (Zhang Wenjun 1960: 8)

There are two points to be made here. First, the severity of penalty is graduated according
to the offender's personality, aptitude and attitude — attributes that cannot be known
without observation and verification. It follows that the police offender's sexual history
will come to determine her 'nature' (and consequently the severity of punishment
imposed on her). Secondly, the 'sage-king' style of benevolence and moral hierarchy is,
in Zhang's formulation, built into the economy of justice delivered within the purview
of the Police Offence Law. The police officer's assumption of the morally superior
subject-speaking position makes it possible for him to act benevolently towards the
prostitute when punishing her. Meanwhile, the prostitute is expected to be ashamed
of her sexual misconduct, a sense of shame which sustains the patriarchal sexual order
that the police help buttress. However, this style of benevolent justice meets its limitations when the prostitute refuses to play the game. And the only way for the police
officer to save face confronted by a prostitute 'with a bad attitude' (refusal to be

patronized, perhaps?) is, as Zhang made clear, to impose a severe penalty in order to teach her a lesson. The education of the woman prostitute indeed resides in punishment! However, in order further to mark out her subjugation, one must situate her labour within the general economy of the sex market, which expanded drastically in the 1960s.

The burgeoning of the sex industry in the 1960s

In 1962, the KMT government promulgated the 'Regulatory Procedures for Particular Businesses in the Province of Taiwan', which enlisted nine categories of businesses including wine houses/bars/tea rooms/coffee houses (category 3) to be governed by local police (Wang 1969: 119). What was loosely referred to in the 1950s within police administration as 'certain type of business' was now formally regulated as 'particular type of business' (PTB). While legalizing the profession of hostess, the regulation also made clear that category three businesses, along with hotels of category two, were strictly prohibited from running the 'prostitution/sex business' (yinye).

Of particular interest and significance here is the emergence of, and sharp increase in, the number of coffee-house and bar establishments within a leisure/pleasure business previously dominated by traditional establishments from the Japanese colonial period such as wine houses and tea rooms.[12] Two important historical factors brought about this transformation of the sex market in Taiwan in the 1960s. Prior to 1950, Taiwan was mainly an agrarian society. But under the KMT government's economic policy, known as 'cultivating industry on the basis of agriculture, using industry to develop agriculture', Taiwan quickly became an industrial country, with the total output value of industry outnumbering that of agriculture in 1963 (Chen and Zhu 1987: 107). This speedy industrializing process in turn gave rise to rapid urbanization. Between 1947 and 1966, the total population in Taipei virtually quadrupled as did that of Kaohsiung in south Taiwan (O'Hara 1973: 270). The huge influx of a young employable population into Taiwan's largest cities presented an invaluable opportunity for the leisure/ pleasure businesses, which grew within the expanding capitalist system.[13] The sharp rise of the coffee-house subculture in cities such as Taipei was a case in point. Similar to the traditional tea room in its function but with a trendy feel, the coffee house – nicknamed 'pitch-dark coffee house' – catered for the fast growing population of lower-middle-class young males. Its great appeal resided in the unconventional interior decor designed to create more 'privacy' within public space: small booths, high-backed seats, large potted plants, dim lighting (Zhang 1962: 10–11). The proliferation of the coffee house establishment also created many job opportunities for (mostly) working-class women, who could earn four to five times more as coffee house hostesses than as factory workers (Centre for Crime Prevention Studies, Judicial Yuan – CCPSJY 1967: 131–147).

On the other hand, the increase in bars was directly linked to the American contingent in Taiwan and the state's (tacit) promotion of (sex) tourism during the Cold War era. Following the enactment of the Mutual Defence Treaty in 1954, two US army bases were founded in Taiwan and the bar business was spawned to cater for the American military population (Ke 1991). In fact, the American contingent also gave rise to the dance hall/club business, which had been banned by the KMT government up to 1958. The biggest impact of American pressure on the leisure/pleasure businesses in Taiwan occurred at the height of the Vietnam War when the 'Rest and Relaxation Centre' was founded by the US government in Taipei in 1965: roughly 200,000 GIs took leave in Taiwan between 1965–1970 while yet another 200,000 were received by the Centre between 1970 and 1971.[14] If every GI spent US$5000 of his US$12,000 annual salary in Taiwan, it was once speculated, the influx of American GIs between 1970 and 1971 alone would have had brought into Taiwan the fortune of US$1000 million (Zhong 1988: 73). While this estimated figure may not be totally reliable, it is indisputable that Taiwan's sex industry became even more prosperous with the influx of the American capital during the Vietnam War. Significantly, after the departure of the Americans, came a new influx of Japanese sex tourists in the early 1970s.

The rapid growth of legal leisure/pleasure businesses in this period, however, was only half the story. A host of new establishments in the leisure/pleasure businesses arose, ones that were registered by law as of 'ordinary type' but skewed from their original purposes. Either as hybridized forms of category three PTB or as newly formed businesses, these new establishments proliferated all over Taiwan, particularly in urban areas. They include

(1) 'Tea-and-Only-Tea' cafés: the name 'tea-and-only-tea' was coined originally to distinguish both from the 'pitch-black' coffee house and the 'yellow' tea room (a colour which signifies locally the obscene and lasciviousness). However, the establishment, enormously popular among young people, had by the late 1960s been identified by the authorities as sleaze (*Great Chinese Evening News* 1968).

(2) Bathhouses and saunas (Liu 1973: 13): these establishments appeared to be the covert version of the licensed prostitution in the Beitou area – a hot-spring tourist resort in suburban Taipei, offering the so-called 'mandarin duck water-frolics bath' service.[15]

(3) Osteopathic/massage parlours: these establishments 'perverted' the conventional massage service, offering instead 'sexual therapy' (*China Evening News* 1969).

(4) Tourist guide agencies and craft shops: in some instances, customers purchasing items of a certain value or more were allowed to leave with one of the shop attendants (Huang and Wu 1971).

(5) Wine bars: because the KMT government stopped licensing category three PTB from 1968 onwards (see below), wine bar businesses began to proliferate, particularly during the Vietnam War (Hong 1973: 34–35).

(6) Catering businesses such as restaurants: any catering businesses using their staff as hostesses would become illegal. So-called 'Restaurants without Kitchens' were thriving businesses in Taipei in the early 1970s (*China Times* 1971).

(7) Underground dance halls/night clubs: as young people were priced out of the market due to the high license fees imposed on legal dance halls/night clubs, it became economically attractive for PTB and non-PTB to diversify into this business (Chen 1968).

(8) Apartment rooms for sex: a non-registered hotel whose primary purpose was the provision of rooms for sex trade. This was due to the rapid transformation of the urban landscape in cities like Taipei (*National Evening News* 1969).

(9) Tourist barber shops: luxuriously decorated salons designed to attract Japanese tourists, offering the additional massage service in a private space (often leading to sex) (Hong 1973).

Despite their diverse nature, the commodity all these businesses had in common was the provision, in one form or another, of sex. In addition, cinemas and theatres (also regulated as category one of PTB) across Taiwan (especially in the countryside and small towns) introduced a new form of entertainment, erotic dancing, in order to maintain a competitive edge over television, introduced in the 1960s.[16] By the mid 1960s, the erotic cultures stimulated by this burgeoning sex industry were flourishing to such an extent that the national culture predicated upon the Confucian sage-king morality was perceived to be under siege, thus prompting Chiang's government to implement a series of social reform programmes to police the crisis.

Defending society from the tidal wave of sex

As 1966 began, a new era of sexual control dawned in Taiwan. The press was excited about the new year's prospects as the government introduced new policing guidelines aimed at tightening control over sex businesses. 'If we are brave enough to face the reality', the *Evening Independent* reminded its readers in an editorial, 'we would be shocked to realise the extent to which this poisoned yellow tide has already risen in recent years':

> Obscene strip shows are everywhere . . . any performance, if not spiced up with a bit of yellow, would not appeal to the audience . . . In the cities, the number of night clubs, dance halls, wine houses, 'pitch-black' coffee houses are increasing rapidly day by day . . . In particular, the greatest development of all sex trade businesses in recent years has been the 'pitch-black' coffee house . . . There is a new pitch black coffee house every few yards in Taipei . . . Every type of immoral behaviour and shameless deed detrimental to virtuous custom is publicly performed under the cover of darkness in those tiny rooms. Countless young men and women who are not mature enough to withstand temptation . . . are being depraved by this type of sex-trade place. What is even more serious and worrying is that this type of place often attracts women of respectable families or runaway teddy girls, encouraging them onto the slippery slope . . .
>
> (*Evening Independent* 1966)

The new police guidelines included a 'three-strikes-and-you-are-out' penalty scheme made in accordance with the PTB regulations and the Police Offence Law, imposing in addition a strict dress and performance code and a decor code for tea rooms and coffee houses.[17] More state interventions ensued the following year, which saw the revision of the 1962 PTB regulation. Of particular significance here are two regulatory changes. First, a minimum age for women staff of 18 and a requirement for those between the ages of 18 and 20 to obtain permission from their guardians or husbands to work as hostesses were introduced, thus making it more difficult for teenage girls to work legally in pleasure/leisure businesses. Second, no new category three PTB were allowed within a distance of a 200 m radius of schools, hospitals, temples, churches, convents and residential areas. This represents the state's first systematic attempt in postwar Taiwan to zone sex out of the sight of respectable institutions (CCPSJY 1967: 178–182).[18]

At the end of 1967 there occurred an important incident whose discursive effects were to deepen the perceived crisis of national culture. An article entitled 'Rest and Recuperation for America's Fighting Men' – featuring a photo of two Taiwanese women accompanying an American GI taking a bath in a hotel in the Beitou red light district – appeared in the 22 December 1967 issue of the US *Time* magazine. Although the services provided in Beitou were no secret, the nation was nonetheless shocked by this revelation. Expressing moral outrage, the press saw this exposure to the world of Beitou prostitution culture as shaming a nation predicated upon Confucian propriety and morality. Responding to public moral outcry, the police managed to track down Yu Ruiqing, one of the women prostitutes in the photo, and charged her with offending public decency under the criminal law (He 1968). They were able to track down Yu because she was a licensed prostitute. Most importantly, what she had done was completely legal and the judge disallowed the case (*Taiwan Daily* 1968a). But throughout the late 1960s and early 1970s, the *Time* picture event continued to be cited by the press as evidence of national shame.[19]

In the immediate aftermath of the *Time* scandal, Chiang Kai-shek presided over the Sixth Annual Meeting of National Security held on 9 January 1968, laying down guidelines for social reform which aimed to 'get rid of the decadent trend affecting *guomin*, reinforce spiritual mobilisation and cultivate invisible form of military power' (Chiang, cited in Wang 1969: 190). Of the eight points mapped out in these guidelines, six pertained to the call for a lawful and ordered society in general, outlawing sexual immorality in particular, with the other two relating to the promotion of legitimate entertainment and the establishment of modern moral guidelines for *guomin*'s daily life conduct. Significantly, these guidelines were taken by the government as constituting an important part of its Cultural Renaissance Movement, a national campaign launched in 1966 to counteract Mao Zedong's Cultural Revolution which aimed at 'revitalizing' the Confucian ethic, namely, the moral tradition of the sage-king.

These guidelines led to yet more regulatory changes. While stopping the licensing of category three PTB (along with brothels and dance halls/night clubs), the government also decided to regulate the non-PTB *as* PTB by thoroughly inspecting all the leisure/pleasure businesses premises. Further, in addition to revising the criminal law to deter the inundation of pornography with stiffer penalties, it also attempted to ban government employees (including the military, civil servants and school teachers) and the youth population from patronizing the leisure/pleasure businesses, thus promulgating the 'Prohibiting Civil Servants From Loitering and Gambling Regulatory Procedures' and the 'Prohibiting Juveniles From Entering Places That Impair Body and Mind Regulatory Procedures' in 1968 and 1970 respectively (Yu 1972: 23–26). The former introduced a disciplinary penalty scheme to punish those frequenting immoral public spaces (*Business Daily* 1968) whereas the latter, which forbade students and youths under the age of 20 to set foot in sex businesses, included a naming and shaming penalty for those parents who were negligent of their duties (Xu 1972). Significantly, the implementation of both sets of procedures can be seen as the KMT government's endeavour to further regulate the private lives of the two populations over which it had most direct control, that is, the civil servant and the student populations. As such, it had the general effect of not only reinstating the moralistic injunction that sex was neither for fun nor for leisure but also stratifying the citizenry into moral and immoral populations, with those in sex businesses being further stigmatised.[20]

To carry out these new measures, Lo Yangbian, the newly appointed head of the police authority, issued an internal note to his subordinates, attempting to 'give a strict definition to the police's task in enforcing the moral order':

> This refers to blocking the inundation of sex *in society*. In other words, with regard to sex which occurs *outside society such as family and marital sex*, it is not within the police's remit to regulate this.
>
> (Lo, cited in Yu 1972: 22, emphasis added)

I have tried to preserve the flavour of Lo's remark in my translation, for his articulation of the kind of sex that needs to be policed is at once peculiar and specific. It is peculiar in that 'society' in this formulation appears to be a distinct entity demarcated from the institutions of family and marriage it encompasses. And yet it is specific in that it designates the type of sex performed beyond the boundary of family and marriage as that which must be outlawed. In other words, non-marital sex and non-familial sexuality must be strictly regulated for the greater good of the virtuous/sage-king *guomin* population.[21] Even when they are performed in non-public domains such as hotel rooms or private residences.

Over the years, by exercising 'unannounced inspection', the police could enter any hotel rooms on the grounds of suppressing the sex trade. In the 1960s and 1970s, many a heterosexual couple were woken up, usually at some unearthly hour in the morning, to be questioned about the nature of their relationship, such that the policing of hotel rooms became a huge public concern. Whether the police had the right to disregard personal privacy and indeed whether the hotel room constituted itself a public space was always a contentious issue. Nonetheless, when rights to privacy were raised in order to question such policing, the real issue was side-stepped. Liberals asserted that the intimate conduct of unmarried young couples in hotel rooms should not be conflated with sleaze. Provided that they did not have sex in public – on the street or in the park, young couples should be left alone in hotel rooms, *unless*, the liberals conceded, the woman turned out to be an unlicensed prostitute.[22] But this opposition to prostitution was the key issue in government policy. Debates over whether hotel rooms belonged to 'public space' were only meaningful in terms of legal prosecutions for 'public indecency'. And yet because the criminal offence of 'public indecency' was not so much about places accessible to the public as about the degree to which the behaviour in question was visible,[23] hotel room inspection was not directed at public indecency but rather at prostitution. Laborious attempts to draw the line between the public and private were futile as there was no privacy in the face of the Police Offence Law as far as sex was concerned.[24] And this was especially true in the case of women in the pleasure/leisure businesses. A police officer once proposed in a special forum on the policing technology of sex published in the *Police Torchlight* magazine that because some hostesses thought it was safer to take their customers home or to hotels rather than to have sex in their workplace, the police should take the opportunity of conducting a census, finding out where hostesses lived in order to raid their homes (Chen 1971: 22). The policing of sex was, in actual fact, turned into a witch hunt. The intensified police operation of the late 1960s and early 1970s, ostensibly to defend society from the inundation of sex, led to an increased surveillance over erotic practices in public spaces. Under this new regime of police control, students canoodling in the 'Tea-and-only-tea' cafés (*United Daily* 1968), hostesses kissing good-bye to American GIs returning to Vietnam (Weiyan 1968), 'nurses' wearing no underwear giving massages to customers in osteopathic parlours (*National Evening News* 1968), people watching licentious performances or pornography (*Central Daily* 1968) were all punished by the police and given penalties that varied from a fine to a seven-day detention for offending virtuous custom. The *Public Daily* even published a photo of a police operation rehearsal whereby an 'obscene facial expression' shown by a coffee house hostess and her patron was outlawed (Decai 1970). Of particular significance here is the police citation of item 11 of article 54 (disobeying government regulations of commerce and business, which could lead to temporary or permanent shutting down of any business) and item 1 of article 64 (misdemeanour) of the Police Offence Law. With their connotative power, both codes served as the most expedient tool for the political management of space and sex.[25]

The press played a crucial role in the incitement of public fear of commercial sex. Figuring commercial sex in terms of disease such as 'cancer' (*Evening Independent* 1971a), 'tumour' (*National Evening News* 1970a), 'epidemic' (*China Times* 1971), or as a natural disaster like 'flood' or 'tidal wave', it constantly urged the government to take the inundation of commercial sex more seriously, calling on the police to further curtail the sex businesses. Indeed, in an authoritarian state where freedom of speech was highly restricted, the domain of sexual morality remained the one area where the press was uncharacteristically critical about government actions. This is most clearly illustrated by the press response to the government's hesitation in abolishing licensed brothels and to its incompetence in dealing with the 'restaurants without kitchens' which mushroomed in downtown Taipei during this period.

In the first case, the press fully exposed the contradiction that lay at the heart of the government's policy on prostitution: vowing to outlaw any immoral activities, the government nevertheless continued to allow licensed brothels to exist. The *Evening Independent*, for instance, challenged in several editorials the rationale that sought to justify the existence of licensed prostitution. The institution of licensed prostitution, the paper argued, not only failed to curb the rampancy of illicit prostitution (which was its original purpose) but also implicitly helped promote the incorrect notion of '[people these days] laughing at the poor rather than at prostitutes', a traditional Chinese idiom (used here by the rising middle class) for lamenting the decline of sexual morality. Abolishing licensed prostitution was the least the government could do, the paper maintained, in preventing the tidal wave of sex from overwhelming society.[26] Similarly, the *Taiwan Daily* argued in two editorials that licensed prostitution, by virtue of its legal existence, not only washed away the sense of shame necessary to the cultivation of respectability but also gave rise to more illicit prostitutes.[27] Interestingly, while the government did come up with various welfare proposals, such as setting up introduction agencies to assist licensed prostitutes to get married, they could not even convince themselves that such proposals would work. 'What if those prostitutes, unable to get rid of their bad habits in such a short time, take advantage of the introduction agency and use it to continue to ply their trade?' An official was reported to express such a doubt (Fan 1968). Another reason that deterred the government from abolishing licensed prostitution was, according to the same report, that the government would have to abolish the institution of Military Paradise, which would mean the abolition of a welfare policy, in operation for the previous two decades, for its military population. In the end, the government got around this difficult question by, in 1973, amending its regulation for licensed prostitution: while the licensing of new brothels was frozen, the existing licenses were made non-transferrable, non-amendable, and non-inheritable (Yu 1972: 42).[28]

In the second case, the press forcefully expressed their disbelief and anger that the government should be turning a blind eye to such an extraordinary phenomenon: two hundred 'restaurants without kitchens' emerged in the Zhongshan North Road (where most established international tourist hotels in the 1970s were situated) within the space of two years (*China Times* 1971).[29] It blamed the government for leaving loopholes in its regulatory policies, such that evil businessmen could make ludicrous profits out of selling sex, holding the Construction Bureau of the Taipei city government (which was the governing body for licensing the non-PTB) and the police authority (which has the duty to inspect any business suspected of selling sex) accountable for negligence and lack of co-ordination.[30]

Such a criticism did, however, point to a new development in the sex market in the early 1970s. While the police considered the closing down of nearly one third of category three PTB by 1973 quite a remarkable achievement, they were also forced to acknowledge the fact that society continued to be plagued by sex, as a host of ordinary businesses – as mentioned in the previous section – had covertly 'metamorphosed' and taken over the sex market previously dominated by category three businesses (Liu 1973: 15). Indeed, the government's tougher stance on category three PTB was counter-productive in that it drove most of the sex businesses underground. Even though several sets of new regulations, such as the standard of equipment for catering businesses (for instance, the size of the kitchen)[31] were introduced in 1974, sex businesses continued to develop under such names as 'health centres' and 'beauty parlours'. Taiwanese society, as it continued to industrialize through the 1970s and 1980s, never stopped being inundated by commercial sex.

The implicit police regulation of male (homosexual) prostitution

In a society deeply preoccupied with the issue of female prostitution, male prostitution had long remained marginal in both official and journalistic discourses. The existence of male prostitution subculture in Taiwan, however, can be traced back at least to the 1950s and 1960s when a group of cross-dressed/transgender male prostitutes, called by the epithet 'human-spectre' (*renyao*), were reported as plying their trade in the brothels and tea rooms in Taipei's Wanhua red light district.[32] In addition, the New Park in Taipei – Taiwan's most infamous male homosexual hang-out – was also known to harbour male prostitution.[33] Significantly, even though the Police Offence Law did not contain any explicit code banning male (homosexual) prostitution, news reports showed that male prostitutes were subject to police control.[34] In 1978, when two Taipei gay bars were raided and exposed as 'hiring effeminate men to accompany men drinking, just like hostesses',[35] the incidence led the criminologist Xu Shenxi to identify the emergence of what he called 'the glass house (male prostitution)' [parentheses in original] as one of the latest metamorphosed forms of the sex trade businesses (Xu 1979: 87).[36]

The issue of male prostitution became highly profiled in the press in the early 1980s when a series of intensified police clean-up operations took place to root out what was perceived by the state to be the homosexual culture of prostitution, according to Li Jinzhen, the chief police officer stationed near New Park:

> The Prime Minster Sun Yunxuan read an article featured in an American magazine reporting: 'If you men are looking for excitement, please then go to New Park in Taipei, Taiwan. This place is Taiwan's male prostitute supply centre.' As [what was reported in] the article seriously contravened public morality, the Prime Minster issued an administrative order himself, demanding that the Taipei police authority root out the problem completely.
>
> (Li 1981: 96)

News reports of the policing activities in New Park followed. Significantly, they made little or even no distinction between so-called male prostitutes and homosexuals: all male homosexuals were seen and represented as prostitutes.

For instance, a special report from the *United Daily* stated that nearly 60 homosexuals had been arrested and punished by the police in New Park in less than a month in 1980, further citing the police as saying:

> Apart from New Park, homosexual male prostitutes are also scattered around the Youth Park, the Red Chamber cinema, and the Longshan district . . . There used to be only a few homosexuals plying their trade individually . . . But given their recent increase in numbers, they divide the market into different regions within which they ply their trade as a group.
>
> (Li 1980)

A year later, the *Taiwan Daily* serialized a special report entitled 'The Elegy of Homosexuals', revealing that over a hundred male homosexuals had been charged with 'misdemeanour' and detained by the police so far that year. To give the readers an in-depth knowledge about this rather hidden prostitution culture, the reporter interviewed the police officer Li Jinzhen, described as being 'very experienced in policing homosexuals (male prostitutes)'.[37] According to Li, male prostitutes fall into three categories, each using its own coded language for sex trade:

(1) secretive code 'No. 0': this kind of man lets other men treat him like a woman, and they usually charge from 600 to 800 NT dollars. Those who play no. 0 are usually young men with delicate features and a fine appearance.
(2) secretive code 'No. 1': *these men in the homosexual circle play 'the man' and are willing to pay.*
(3) secretive code 'No. 10': this type of man plays a double role. They can be men but are also willing to act/serve as 'women'. They first play with one another, and then see who invites whom, and the one who is invited gets paid between 200 to 400 NT dollars. This type of homosexual is in the majority.

These people who use different secretive codes have their own characteristics. For instance, those who hold a book, a handbag or newspaper, looking effeminate often serve/act as 'No. 0'. On the other hand, those men who are older and over forty often play 'No. 1'. However, the role they play can only be settled after the price is negotiated.

(Lin 1981, emphasis added)

What does the word 'prostitute' mean here when it refers to those who are willing to pay (as in the case of those categorized as 'No. 1' or those who don't necessarily charge (as in the case of those categorized as 'No. 10')? It is clear that in Li's formulation all homosexuals are prostitutes.[38]

Li's revelation to the *Taiwan Daily* is actually based on his article 'How to Outlaw Homosexuals-Male Prostitutes [hyphen original]' published in *the 45th Anniversary of the Central Police College Special Publication* in 1981. In that article, Li wrote of this briefing he gave to his subordinates:

Because it is not easy to find actual instances of indecency (*weixie*) or *jiansu* [illicit sexual relations/sleeping with someone] behaviour in the park . . . I want to reiterate our procedures in making arrests and getting convictions. Firstly, you must always conduct operations in pairs. When one of you succeeds in striking up a conversation with a male prostitute, the other must observe and follow from a distance. When chatting them up, you must pretend that you are actually going to do it. You should ask the other party if they are experienced and try to get examples, locations and dates, of this *jiansu* behaviour. Once you have an answer, then set off for the hotel or residence with the prostitute. As soon as you step out of New Park, pretend to be intimate and then grab him by the belt and reveal who you are and arrest him with the help of your partner before taking him back to the police station. Record all the *jiansu* details performed in the last three months to which he had previously admitted before passing sentence.

(Li 1981: 96, emphasis added)

Here, same-sex genital relations are taken as *jiansu*, even if those homosexuals-prostitutes were often charged with 'misdemeanour': just as that particular code was often cited to punish female prostitute suspects, it was equally convenient to punish male homosexual-prostitute suspects. Indeed, while homosexuality appeared to be absent from juridical codes in Taiwan, it was implicitly regulated by the state *through* prostitution.

The police operation in rooting out the homosexual culture of prostitution reached new heights in 1983 when the Golden Peacock Restaurant in Taipei was raided on suspicion of hiring a group of male youths aged between 15 and 18 as host(esse)s to covertly run a prostitution business (Zhang 1983: 98). Because the scale of the business was believed to be the largest of its kind to date, the raid was widely covered by the press, with sensational headlines featuring male homosexual epithets such as:

Men Serving as Hostesses in 'Golden Peacock'; 'Cut-Sleeves' Take to It Like Ducks to Water!

(*China Times* 1983)[39]

Called by the Name 'Officials' within the Glass Clique; Pleasures Provided Purely By and For Men. Homosexuals Ply Their Trade in Restaurant.

(*United Daily* 1983)[40]

Golden Peacock, the Headquarters of Homosexual Prostitution Business, Raided; Young Men Serve as 'Human-Spectres', Accompanying Men by Drinking and Sleeping with Them.

(Central Daily 1983)

After the Golden Peacock, another two gay restaurants/bars – the Dahan Club and the Tang Street Wine Bar – were also closed down by the police in April 1984 (Wu 1998). Thanks to the press's wide coverage of the series of police raids on New Park as well as other commercial premises, the cultural imaginary of the glass clique as a cesspool of promiscuous male homosexuals desperate for sex trade had, by the mid-1980s, been firmly established.[41]

The Social Order Maintenance Law

Public disquiet about the Police Offence Law began to emerge in the late 1970s. In the wake of increasing human rights agitation, liberals and legal scholars began to criticize the law from the viewpoint of jurisprudence, pointing out its dated/obscure regulatory codes and unevenly graduated penalties; the excessive para-juridical power it conferred on the police; and above all, its unconstitutional status (Lin 1979). The KMT government did not respond to this growing criticism until 1979 when a political crisis was caused by its severing of diplomatic ties with the US. As a political gesture to signal its willingness to reform, the government announced that it would replace it with a new law called 'the Social Order Maintenance Law' (Gui 1991). Nevertheless, it was not until 1991 that the Police Offence Law was finally abolished.

The regulatory regime of 'virtuous custom' as sustained now by the Social Order Maintenance Law continues to outlaw commercial sex: pimping, procuring and soliciting remain strictly prohibited (articles 80 and 81). Importantly, while the law decriminalizes the client, it decrees that prostitutes who offend the law three times within a year be sent to reform institutions for a period of between six and twelve months (article 80).[42] Of particular significance are the modes of sexual act by which prostitution is defined in item 1 of article 81, which prohibits 'a person having illicit sexual relations (*jian*) or sleeping with someone (*su*) for the purpose of gain'. Here, the compound *jiansu* as previously codified in the Police Offence Law is modified, with the words 'illicit sexual relations' (*jian*) and 'sleeping with someone' (*su*) separated by a comma (item 1, article 80). An interpretation offered by the juridical authority in reply to a question raised by a magistrates court (newly set up under the Social Order Maintenance Law) as to whether item 1 of article 80 is applicable to homosexual prostitution (apparently homosexuals had already been arrested and charged by the police) or to heterosexual prostitution involved with non penis-vaginal penetrative sex, should illuminate the meaning of this modification and its operation:

> The objective in implementing the Social Order Maintenance Law is to sustain public order and to ensure the security of society. Therefore one should take this objective into account when interpreting the law. Even if the behaviour of accompanying-sleeping (*peisu*) for the purpose of gain is not aimed at having carnal relations (*jianyin*), to the extent that such behaviour stems from illegitimate aims (such as sodomy or indecent acts), it is obvious that such behaviour is detrimental

to virtuous custom and public order: hence it is necessary to punish it. Accordingly, whether the behaviour of accompanying-sleeping for the purpose of gain occurs between the members of the same sex or members of the opposite sex *not* engaging in carnal relations (*jianyin*), to the extent that the behaviour in question is compelled by the illegitimate purpose detrimental to virtuous custom, it constitutes itself an offence against item 1 of article 80. On the other hand, if accompanying-sleeping has a legitimate purpose and is not detrimental to virtuous custom, then the law would not be applicable.

(Dept. of Criminal Affairs, Judicial Yuan 1993: 331–332)

The term *su* thus comes to be figured as a euphemism for 'having sex'. Although the juridical authority does not provide us with any example of what constitutes a legitimate act of 'accompanying-sleeping', it is clear that commercial sex, regardless of sexual object and aim, is illegitimate and hence must be outlawed so that the sexual order predicated upon the sage-king patriarchal family can be maintained. The only people who do not have to justify their act of 'accompany-sleeping' are those in marital relationships. All others – particularly non-married women and male homosexuals – must justify their private behaviour when it involves sleeping with someone. Through this tacit operation of the term *su*, all forms of non-marital sexual behaviour and erotic practices, including same-sex genital relations, continue to be policed, however implicitly, through the control of prostitution and the presumption of guilt in the post Police Offence Law era in Taiwan.

Conclusion: the rise of the sage-queen sexual morality

In this paper, I have sketched out a historical process whereby a dominant sexual order premised on the Confucian sage-king morality came to be established in postwar Taiwan through the workings of state power. By examining the official and journalistic discourse of sex, I have demonstrated that the disciplinary regime of 'virtuous custom' as sustained by the Police Offence Law operated as a norm of sex whose boundary was secured through the policing of commercial sex and non-familial/marital sexualities. In particular, I have shown how the making of the sage-king nationalist/*guomin* subject-position was deeply imbricated within the KMT government's forcible production of 'virtuous custom'. Within such a gender/sexuality system, unmarried women and other marginal sexual minorities such as transgenders and male homosexuals came to be treated as sexual suspects and policed *as* prostitutes: female sexuality and male homosexuality have both been historically regulated by the state *through* its banning of prostitution in postwar Taiwan.

A progressive sexual and gender politics must therefore challenge the social/sexual order based upon the state's maintenance of 'virtuous custom'. Significantly, the political imperative to contest 'virtuous custom' is made all the more urgent as its regulatory regime has greatly expanded in recent years due to the rise of anti-obscenity/prostitution state feminism and its intervention in legal reforms. While it lies beyond the scope of the present paper to trace such a transformation, I do want briefly to make a case against anti-prostitution feminist politics, thereby establishing the link between the genealogy traced above and the present situation in Taiwan.

Josephine Ho has traced a hegemonic process whereby an anti-trafficking campaign, launched shortly before the lifting of martial law in 1987 by a coalition of nascent NGOs to rescue aborigine teenage girls forced into prostitution, gradually reconfigured itself into an anti-prostitution/obscenity bloc, lobbying for a new law (endowed with more punitive and preventive measures than existing regulations), which was to become the Law to Suppress Sexual Transaction Involving Children and Juveniles (hereafter referred to as LSSTICJ). In particular, Ho draws out the instrumental role that the women's NGOs played in that process, further showing their continual involvements in transforming the law (passed by parliament in 1995) into 'an intricate web of social discipline' through which teenage sexuality and especially cyber sex came to be increasingly regulated (Ho 2004). Meanwhile, with the onset of the prostitute rights movement in 1997 (triggered by the Taipei city government's sudden decision to abolish licensed prostitution) which split the women's movement over the issues of sexuality and sex work, some self-proclaimed 'gender politics' and 'state feminists' made it clear that they were only interested in working with the new state on 'gender issues' that related to the family (Lin 1998). With housewives placed at the centre of such a women's movement, the goal of state feminism was not only to transform the state into a carer, but also for 'all' women to take over the state and rule the country (starting with mobilizing housewives to take part in running local communities before getting into mainstream electoral politics). In a forceful critique of such a 'state feminism' as elaborated and theorized by feminists such as Lin Fang-mei and Liu Yu-xiu, Naifei Ding acutely observes the state feminists' exclusion of the issue of sexuality and their adherence to domestic morality prescribed by Confucian doxa of sage-king moral cultivation. Moreover, Ding notes a certain 'reticence' at work in the state feminists' claim to include 'all' women as the subjects of these campaigns, due to their uncritical appropriation of Confucian moralistic doctrine. Such a position rules out those who fail or refuse to assume Confucian familial norms, such as prostitutes and queers (Ding 2003: 315).[43]

In line with Ho and Ding's critique of mainstream feminist politics, I want to show how a certain kind of gender politics as enacted by the state feminists, or rather, the sage-queen state feminists, which seeks to transcend non-familial sexuality, is complicit with the nation-state in buttressing the heteronormative regime of 'virtuous custom'. I shall do this by looking at the state feminists' recent campaigns to amend the two major sex laws; namely, the Social Order Maintenance Law and the Criminal Law.

In 1998, several women's NGOs, including the Women Rescue Foundation, the Garden of Hope Foundation (both of which had been axiomatic in giving birth to the LSSTICJ), the Taipei Women's Rights Association and the Taiwan Feminist Scholar Association, proposed to a cross-party coalition of women legislators a bill to amend the Social Order Maintenance Law. The bill purported to criminalize the (male) client who patronizes the (woman) prostitute. These women's NGOs argued that the current regulation was discriminatory because it punished only the prostitute, not the client. Not only should the client be criminalized but he should also be given a heavier penalty than the prostitute. Apart from 'naming and shaming' the client, the women's groups also demanded that the (male) client be given mandatory sex education about gender equality and be checked for venereal diseases. However, punishment for those who were not married, they added, could be reduced. Lighter penalties such as admonition should also be given to first-time offender prostitutes. Furthermore, the bill not only called for greater punishment of pimps and sex business owners but also the penalizing of landlords of places where prostitution took place. Finally, heavier penalties would be given to those commercial places found to be in the vicinity of kindergartens, nurseries and all types of schools within a distance of a 500 m radius (Liang 1998).

The social/sexual order as envisioned in this bill 'with a feminine and tender touch', as Liu Yu-xiu reportedly put it, is no different from the existing one maintained by the sage-king state, except that it is even more punitive and puritanical. The sage-queen feminists' outrage at the discriminatory stance of the law against women prostitutes did not lead them to question radically the justice of the law which penalized the prostitute in the first place: instead, they wanted the client to be penalized as well. In addition, the client should be re-educated to learn how to behave like a gentleman who treats women politely. Interestingly, it is in the state femin(in)ists' benevolence and lenience towards the novice woman prostitute and the unmarried adult male client that the heterosexist and sage-king style of benevolent justice (delivered previously by the police officer under the Police Offence Law) is replicated.[44] In the case of the novice woman prostitute, the sage-queen state femin(in)ist appears to be saying, 'OK, I'll just tell you off this time for the sake of our sisterhood, but if you don't try to better yourself and offend again, expect harsher punishment next time.' In the case of the unmarried client, the sage-queen femin(in)ist re-imposes, however tacitly, the norm of marital sex to the regulatory neglect of non-familial sexual suspects such as unmarried women who patronize men and the wide range of sexual practices offered in the sex industry.

Paradoxically, while the sage-queen femin(in)ists were proposing a bill for a new social order that would keep prostitutes/hostesses out of sight so that 'their children' could be brought up in a *more* respectable environment (sex is further zoned out in their proposal [within a distance of a 500 m radius] than in the 1967 revision of the PTB regulation [within a distance of a 200 m radius]), they were at the same time lobbying parliament to delete the category of 'woman of respectable family' from the criminal law. With this legal category in operation, those sex business owners employing *not* first-time prostitutes had long been exempted from criminal prosecution. Thus, it is no surprise that the anti-prostitution feminists had always wanted this legal category to be abrogated for it was not only a product of patriarchal thinking which, they argued, divided women into the virtuous (women of respectable families) and the non-virtuous (prostitutes) but also encouraged the development of the sex industry wherein women were conceived as universally victimised. However, there lies a paradox at the heart of this anti-sex feminist argument and this can be seen in a revealing slip made by the liberal feminist Shen Meizhen in her influential *Victimised Women Prostitutes and Prostitution Policies in Taiwan*.[45] Campaigning for the abolition of the category of 'woman of respectable family', Shen wrote, in a section of her book depicting the sex businesses in 1980 Taiwan and the harm it caused to society, that '[these days] Taiwan is inundated with sex barbershops, so much so that makes it very difficult for *the paternal elders of respectable families* to find a place to have a simple haircut' (Shen 1990: 63, emphasis added). Despite her avowal to eliminate the *sexual* difference between women, Shen identifies herself totally as a 'woman of respectable family' and with the feminine virtue ordained by the sage-king patriarch.

To the delight of state/anti-prostitution femin(in)ists, 'woman of respectable family' was finally deleted by parliament on 14 January 1999, and replaced by the phrase 'man and woman'. This effectively means that, since 1999, prostitution has – except for those licensed brothels remaining – been completely outlawed. Naifei Ding and Jen-peng Liu have acutely observed the significance of this legal change:

> Strangely enough, as 'woman of respectable family' is being deleted, 'she' becomes omnipresent. (Because no one can say that I am 'accustomed to immoral behaviour' anymore.) As far as the article is concerned, the term 'man and woman' has replaced 'woman of respectable family'. What scarcely changes is the victimhood of 'woman of respectable family', that is, her being induced and retained by the baddies to have sex with others. After the deletion of 'woman of respectable family', man and woman, that is, everyone, is forced to become 'woman of respectable family'. Everyone, as far as the matter of sex or 'immoral behaviour' is concerned, all ought to be taken as 'woman of respectable family', such that they could become the pure object of a victimiser. All the sexual subjects and sexual behaviour other than [that of] 'woman of respectable family' have come to be targeted as the objects of deletion and exclusion.
>
> (Ding and Liu 1999: 441)

The anti-prostitution/obscenity bloc's most recent moral crusade against the sex industry will reveal, as I hope to show, just how that 'woman of respectable family' subject-position is enabled and encompassed by the sage-queen femin(in)ist and how citizens of Taiwan are now all compelled to cite that gendered norm of sex to live out their desires.[46]

In January 2004, the Taiwanese government, having belatedly consulted the recommendations of a specially commissioned report on the sex industry, announced its proposal to decriminalize the prostitute and to work gradually towards the decriminalization of the sex industry in the long run. Terrified by the news, the anti-prostitution/obscenity women NGOs (including the Women Rescue Foundation, Garden of Hope, P-W-R Foundation, ECPAT Taiwan, Taiwan Good Shepherd Sisters and Taiwan Women's Link) quickly formed a coalition called the Policy-Pusher Alliance for the Downsizing of the Sex Industry (hereafter referred to as PPADSI) and staged a protest in the following month. 'Not punishing the prostitute by no means amounts to the decriminalization of the sex industry', insisted the PPADSI. Given 'the manifold bad influences of the sex industry on gender relations, family and society', the PPADSI demanded that the government: (1) implement effective welfare and regulatory policies to downsize the sex industry; (2) 'not punish' individuals selling sex; (3) penalize the client, with the imposition of fines to pay for the huge social risk and cost of prostitution; (4) punish the third party profiting from the sex trade; (5) enable, through state promotion, 'everyone including young blue collar workers, the mentally disabled, the elders and homosexuals to enjoy good sexual relation that is equal and non-transactional' (PPADSI 2004).

Compared with her previous stance, the sage-queen femin(in)ist appears now to be even more benevolent towards the prostitute, this time urging the government not to punish her since it is the demand side who 'commands and benefits from the prostitute-client relation' that should be penalized. Meanwhile, she continues to chastise the client, holding him accountable for not only corrupting the teenage girls of Taiwan by enticing them into sex work but also attracting huge influxes of illegal migrant sex workers (from China and south East Asia) to Taiwan, which puts the sexual health of society in peril. Thus, the client, as an active consumer of sex, home and abroad, should be punished for making Taiwan a high risk area for the spread of 'dangerous trans-national diseases such as AIDS' [sic] as well as be made to pay for the huge increases in public spending on the policing of sex (such as teenage prostitution prevention and human trafficking) and VD prevention, the cost of which is being unjustly paid for by the tax payer (Huang 2004).

So, the sage-queen proposal to 'decriminalize the prostitute/penalize the client' in effect amounts to more policing: a harsher (albeit appearing to be more benevolent) regime of police state is being called for, ironically in the post Police Offence Law era. The general effect of attributing un-harnessed male lust as the sole driving motor of the sex industry means that more police (wo)men are required to prevent would-be 'daughters of Formosa' from 'sliding onto the slippery slope',[47] and more police surveillance is required to protect the Taiwanese nationals of respectable families from coming into contact with the contagious body of illegal sex migrant workers. A recent article co-authored by Liu Yu-xiu and Huang Shuling – two leading figures of the PPADSI – demonstrates just that fear of Taiwanese society being swamped by migrant sex workers being played out. In that article, Liu and Huang set out to dispel the 'myth' concerning the decriminalization of the sex trade in countries such as the Netherlands and Germany. Such a policy not only fails to achieve its original goal – namely, better (state) management of the sex industry and de-stigmatization of the prostitute – but also, Liu and Huang contend, disastrously gives rise to huge influxes of illegal foreign sex workers into both countries. Interestingly enough, they give a list of instances whereby sex workers in Germany are still being unfairly treated by the German state to show the continual exploitation and stigmatization of the sex workers under the new policy, noting in particular the plight of immigrant sex workers there. These instances mainly concern the German system's strident regulatory and registration procedures through which prostitutes and brothels are obliged to comply, as well its institutionalized discrimination, which prevents sex workers from being fully protected by labour law. Liu and Huang then go on to argue that the only country where the policy of legalizing the sex trade has been more successful is Australia because it is 'pre-conditioned/well-disposed':

> racially pure/simple, [hence] immigration control made easier, good welfare system and very small population working in the sex industry. Neither Taiwan nor Germany, not even Holland has that disposition.
>
> (Liu and Huang 2004)

Having used this argument to make their point, Liu and Huang then move on to recommend the Swedish model – on which the PPADSI campaign is based – further urging the Taiwanese government 'not to recognize the rights of sex workers, lest it encourages sex work'. Only a moment ago these two women professors were telling us of the maltreatment of the sex workers by the German government and yet here they are attempting to dissuade the Taiwanese government from working on the very socio-legal domain (that they identify through the German experience) that constitutes the very exploitation and stigmatization of sex workers. How is one to make sense of the fault-line that runs through their argument? Or could it be that terms such as 'de-stigmatization' mean something else to them?

Perhaps Huang Shuling's own articulation of 'the whore stigma' in her previous work 'Women in Sex Industries: Victims, Agents or Deviants?' might yield a clue. In that essay, Huang argues, on the basis of her socio-anthropological study of the sex industry in contemporary Taiwan, neither decriminalization nor legalisation of sex trade can eradicate the whore stigma, as 'the one essence that characterizes the trade is social disdain' (Huang 1996: 141). Moreover,

> [I]n a patriarchal society, the relationship between the woman prostitute and her male client is by no means equal. Because prostitutes are paid a high price by men to transgress the 'woman of respectable family' stipulation that is made by men, they cannot escape from male discrimination. Men's contempt towards them is not only shown during sex trade, it is also reflected in the marriage market from which prostitutes are excluded. As far as their social status is concerned, they can by no means be the pioneers who can subvert male-female sexual relation. On the contrary, they are regarded by men as female sexual other (*nüxing yilei*).
>
> (Huang 1996: 142)

Thus, the whore stigma exists and will continue to exist in so far as the woman prostitute is disqualified from entering the marriage market within the patriarchal system. In other words, it is her failing to cite/assume the normative position of the housewife within such a system that renders her as, to use Huang's own wording, the 'female sexual other' that is despised by the male-dominated society. Significantly, by essentializing the social disdain of the 'female sexual other', Huang in effect posits a patriarchy impervious to any social changes that feminism as a political force purportedly seeks to instigate. In other words, patriarchy is presumed here as a pre-existent totality into which the whore stigma is structurally built, a totality premised on the sage-king moral hierarchy wherein the woman prostitute must know her proper place as the encompassed 'female sexual other', therefore shameful to herself, and indeed shameful 'to all women in the new nation, and the nation itself', as Naifei Ding notes in her insightful analysis of the state feminists' profound sense of hierarchical gender shame on behalf of the Taipei ex-licensed prostitutes (Ding 2002: 446). Thus, by identifying herself as 'woman of respectable family' subject-position as prescribed by the sage-king, the sage-queen comes to maintain the distinction between her and the 'female sexual other'. And it is only by repudiating that very stigma which never was, and shall never be, hers that the sage-queens can safely assume the moral high ground while remaining indifferent to her (abjectified) sexual other's daily struggles against social inequalities.

The sage-queen femin(in)ist is that omnipresent figure of 'woman of respectable family'. She controls the sexual life of teenage girls and boys through the LSSTICJ. Normative notions of 'sexuality' are to be inculcated into youth so that they learn to respect members of the opposite sex, to shame those who sell their bodies for money, and so know that only marital sex is legitimate. Further, to teach boys especially how to practice 'egalitarian, joyful and responsible sex', she proposes an improved sex/gender education which allows teenagers to 'moderately' explore their bodies in an especially designed space that is 'somewhat hidden and yet not too much hidden at the same time' (Liu 1998), thus giving her the panoptic view to ensure the decency of the classroom.[48] She wanted to train adult women to conform to domestic sexual morality by introducing a graduated scheme of penalties for women prostitutes. Even when she changes her mind and decides not to punish adult women sex workers, she wants to incriminate all the people around them (lest someone, their friends or lovers, lives off their immoral earnings), forcing them to work on their own and, in doing so, disempowering them and putting them in a more vulnerable position in the face of real abuse and exploitation.[49] Meanwhile, she also calls for more punishment to be given to married male clients so that her housewife status can be better secured, which in turn provides her with a stable family life to bring up normal children together with her equally virtuous husband. Even if her children grow up to be the non-marrying type, she can tolerate this as long as s/he remains respectable by cautiously maintaining his/her own bodily autonomy over erotic life, living out his/her slightly unconventional desires in a segregated social environment free of commercial sex.[50] In the name of preventing supposedly innocent children, youth and adults of both genders from being preyed upon by the evil 'sex wolf' as well protecting Taiwanese society from the diseased bodies of migrant sex workers, the sage-queen femin(in)ist righteously takes on the role of policewoman, working with and for the sage-king state to not only maintain but also expand the heteronormative regime of 'virtuous custom'.

This is the new sexual order ordained by the sage-queen femin(in)ists in 21st-century Taiwan. It is also the normative condition that one must take into account if one wants to ask what it means to be a sexual dissident in Taiwan today. As every citizen of the nation is being forced to become a 'woman of respectable family' under the new legal-disciplinary regime that has become even more sex-punitive, recent developments in Taiwan attest to the fact that sexual freedom is increasingly under siege. While the anti-prostitution/obscenity bloc has impeached the feminist sex radical Josephine Ho for her longstanding outspoken sexual dissidence by bringing a criminal case against her (for disseminating pornographic bestiality material through a hyperlink on the website dedicated to the study of sexualities), Taiwan's only gay bookshop Gin Gin is also being prosecuted by the state for importing 'pornographic' gay magazines that can be legally bought everywhere else in the country. Just as sex workers have been hounded by the police on a daily basis and forced to undergo HIV screening tests, the state continues to police its gay population through prostitution and AIDS, raiding gay venues on suspicion of sex trade or drug abuse that is then linked to 'the spread of AIDS'. Directly involved or not, the sage-queens are deeply complicit with all this anti-sex state culture and the violence it exerts. Contesting this new social/sexual order on the grounds of its ideological operations and practices thus represents the most challenging task for the articulation of dissident sexual citizenship in Taiwan today.

Notes

1   An earlier version of this paper was presented at 'By Culture: the 2004 Taiwan Cultural Studies Association Annual Conference' held at Soochow University, 3–4 January 2004, Taipei, Taiwan. I would like to thank my discussant Fang Xiaoding for his critical responses. Many thanks to Chris Berry, Tim Buckfield, Kuan-Hsing Chen, Naifei Ding, Nick Downing, Harriet Evans, Mandy Merck and Jen-peng Liu for their comments and support. I'd also like to extend my

gratitude to the *IACS* reviewers for their invaluable suggestions. Needless to say, I am responsible for all shortcomings. All the translations of the Chinese sources, unless otherwise noted, are mine.

2 'The Police Offence Law' in Lin (1989: 813–820).

3 Chiang Kai-shek founded the Central Police Officer College in Nanking, China, in 1936, serving as its principal for the following 12 years while he was also the leader of the republican government in China. The college was reconstituted in Taiwan in 1955.

4 The term *guomin* is compounded by 'nation' (*guo*) and 'people/citizen' (*min*). Like its rendition in Korean (*kukmin*), there is no exact English translation for it. I retain the linguistic specificity of this term in this paper. See Cho (2000) for the formation of the *kukmin* subjectivity in postwar South Korea.

5 In the 1999 amendment of criminal law, this legal category was deleted and replaced by the phrase 'man and woman'. See the Conclusion for the ramifications of this legal change.

6 Observing the trope of 'cultural morality' as predicated on Confucian ethic within the context of film censorship in martial Taiwan, Chao (2000: 235) has noted how sexual immorality in its various manifestations is represented as essentially 'anti-Chinese' and as such comes to signify as the Other of the Chinese nationalist subject.

7 A police jargon rather than a legal term, 'certain type of business' referred to a wide range of businesses deemed as posing potential danger to 'social order' or 'public health'. See Lu (1958).

8 See Deputy Reporter (1954). This pilot scheme came to an end in 1956 when the government decided to implement licensed prostitution.

9 See Deputy Reporter (1955a). This particular institution was abolished in 1992.

10 'Women Prostitutes Administrative Procedures for the Local Governments in the Province of Taiwan' in Wang (1969: 195–196).

11 This practice amounts to surveillance, which enables the police to inspect anyone at any place at any time. I thank the human rights lawyer Ken Chiu for bringing this practice to my attention in our private conversation.

12 According to *A Study on the Problems of Offences Against Morale in Taiwan* published by Centre for Crime Prevention Studies, Judicial Yuan (hereafter referred to as CCPSJY), between 1962 and 1966 the total number of coffee houses increased by 129% while that of bars increased by 93%. Meanwhile, the total number of the registered hostesses in 1966 was 2.25 times more than in 1962 (CCPSJY 1967: 15–16).

13 I am indebted to Ho (1997) on this point.

14 Upon the request of the US government, Taiwan set up its first medical institution specializing in the prevention and treatment of venereal diseases in 1969 (Chen 1992).

15 Licensed prostitutes in the Beitou red light district were regulated in accordance with an administrative procedure specially made for this hot-spring resort near Taipei in 1951. Licensed prostitutes could not ply their trade in the brothels that accommodated them but were only 'delivered' upon request to hotels (Deputy Reporter 1955b). This special institution was abolished in 1979.

16 Strip shows would often be staged in the middle of film screening in the cinema, see Cui (1968).

17 Dancers were prohibited from wearing Bikini swimwear, showing breasts and buttocks in their naked display and acting out any sexually suggestive performance. With regard to the decor of tea rooms and coffee houses, standardized lighting no less than five 5 W light bulbs per 5 m^2; only one single switch allowed; no screen or other object allowed to block off vision; small rooms cannot be built within; staff bedrooms should be segregated; couches no more than 110 cm above the ground, armchairs no more than 75 cm (CCPSJY 1967: 21–26).

18 See the Conclusion for mainstream feminists' attempt to zone sex in 1990s Taiwan.

19 See for instance *Evening Independent* (1971b).

20 The civil servant population constituted a class of its own under the wing of the KMT government, which rewarded the loyalty of its employees with welfare schemes (such as an 18% interest rate for pensions) unavailable to the rest of the population. Importantly, they were further prohibited from marrying prostitutes and ex-prostitutes (who were qualified as 'women of respectable families' under the definition given by the judicial system). On the last point, see Peng (1968: 12).

21 Cf. Foucault (1990: 23–26).

22 See for instance Lin (1974).

23 See Liu and Shi (1994: 595–598).

24 On the press's mild criticism of the police's practice of hotel room inspection, see *Business Daily* 1969; *United Daily* 1969).

25 Diverse modes of sexual misbehaviour such as 'three men and one woman sleeping in one bed', 'loitering at night with aphrodisiacs', 'men hiring prostitutes stripping at table to accompany them drinking', 'waitresses accompanying customers drinking in ordinary restaurants' had been outlawed as 'misdemeanours', according to Xie Ruizhi (1979: 19–20), former principal of the Central Police Officer College. In addition, other sources reveal the code had also been used to punish female prostitute suspects (Mu 1974) as well as male (homosexual) prostitute suspects (see below).

26 See *Evening Independent* (1968a; 1968b; 1968c).

27 See *Taiwan Daily* (1968b; 1968c).

28. As this new regulation did not undergo any further revision after 1973, this effectively means that licensed brothels will become extinct in years to come.

29 On the human geography of this particular road and its significance in relation to the formation of sexual subjectivities and nation-building since postwar Taiwan, see Yin (2000).

30 See *China Times* (1971); *Evening Independent* (1971a, 1971b, 1973).

31 On this new regulation, see Ding (1994: 172–174).

32 See *United Daily* (1951); Yang (1961); Liao (1962); Hu (1985: 67).

33 See *United Daily* (1959); *Public Daily* (1971). Pai Hsien-yung's (1990) *Crystal Boys* is a fictional representation of the male prostitution subculture in 1970s New Park. For a discussion of the significance of the novel in relation to contemporary queer politics in Taiwan, see Martin (2003), Huang (forthcoming b).

34 For the police arrest of a 'human-spectre' at the Wanhua red light district, see *National Evening News* (1970b); for the policing activities in New Park, see *Public Daily* (1971).

35 See *Evening Independent* (1978).

36 A gangster slang term from the 1960s, 'glass' alluded originally to the 'buttock' or 'bottom' and was circulated throughout the 1970s as an epithet for male homosexuals. By the 1980s, it was firmly established as *the* name for the imagined homosexual community, known as the 'glass clique' (*boliquan*).

37 The bracket is used here in the original Chinese text. Here, homosexuals and male prostitutes appear to be made synonymous.

38 It is of interest here to mention a *Central Daily* report whereby the practice of homosexuality was understood as a mode of prostitution, *even if it was figured as an act of sex without payment*: 'According to the police investigation, there are two types of homosexuals/homosexuality (*tongxinglian*). One looks for love while the other for excitement. Trading for the former costs nothing. It's purely about emotion while for the latter they first talk about how much it costs. But both are abnormal behaviour; they belong to serious psychological perversion.' (Xie 1982)

39 The idiomatic expression 'cut-sleeve', which comes to designate male-to-male genital relations, is derived from the famous love story between the Han Emperor Ai (r. 6–1 BC) and Dong Xian, his beloved subject. The Emperor was in bed sleeping with Dong Xian stretched out across the sleeve of his garment. Not wanting to disturb his beloved when rising, the emperor chose instead to cut his sleeve. See Hinsch (1992: 53).

40 Traditionally a respectable social term for the scholar-literati or literati-bureaucrat, the term '*xianggong*' came to be appropriated by cross-dressed Peking opera actors in the Qing dynasty as an identity-name. Because of the prominent prostitution culture that developed around the Peking opera, it later came to refer to male prostitutes.

41 The equation of male homosexuality with prostitution continued to be configured within the eroto-homophobic discourse of AIDS in the late 1980s. See Huang (forthcoming a).

42 'The Social Order Maintenance Law', in Liu and Shi (1994: 1277–1287). See the Conclusion for the ramifications of this legal change within the context of contemporary feminist politics.

43 See also Ding (2002) for an excellent discussion on the bifurcation of domestic and sex work in relation to the formation of base femininity and its implications for feminist sexual/class politics in the context of contemporary Taiwan.

44 I use the term femin(in)ist to underline Liu Yu-xiu's stress on their feminine mode of legal intervention.

45 Founder of the Women Rescue Foundation, Shen was a practising lawyer heavily involved in the drafting of the LSSTICJ (Ho 2004).
46 Here I am employing the notions of citationality and gender performativity as expounded by Judith Butler (1993).
47 'Daughter of Formosa' is the title of the Garden of Hope's latest model girl award.
48 The rationale in this policing of space is reminiscent of the KMT government's 1966 regulatory specification of the tea room/coffee house décor. See note 17.
49 This is exactly what happens in Sweden. See the prostitute right activist Petra Ostergren's account of the current legal situation in Sweden in Xia (2000: 193–202).
50 The sage-queen appears to be more liberal in her attitude towards homosexuality than the sage-king. For instance, Liu Yu-xiu (1997) uses the example of the Swedish mainstream sex education's promotion of gay rights to advance her argument that the Swedish form of egalitarian, non-transactional form of gender justice is the most progressive type of modernity to be willed for.

References

Business Daily 商工日報 (1968) 'On the 'Prohibiting civil servants from loitering and gambling regulatory procedures'' 從「禁止公務人員冶遊賭博」說起 , 28 November.
Business Daily (1969) 'Hotel room inspection' 查房間 , 7 June.
Butler, Judith (1993) *Bodies that Matter: On the Discursive Limits of 'Sex'*, London: Routledge.
Centre for Crime Prevention Studies, Judicial Yuan (CCPSJY) 司法行政部犯罪問題研究中心 (1967) *A Study on the Problem of Offences Against Morals in Taiwan* 妨害風化罪問題之研究 , Taipei: Judicial Yuan 司法院 .
Central Daily 中央日報 (1968) 'Watching licentious performances will be punished by the police offence law' 觀看色情表演將受違警罰法處罰 , 13 September.
Central Daily (1983) 'Golden Peacock, the headquarters of homosexual prostitution business, tracked down by the police' 同性戀色情營業大本營 , 金孔雀酒店被查獲 , 10 April.
Chao, Antonia (2000) 'So, who is the stripper? State power, pornography and the cultural logic of representability in post-martial-law Taiwan', *Inter-Asia Cultural Studies* 1(2): 233–248.
Chen, Guoxiang and Zhu Ping 陳國祥、祝萍 (1987) *Forty years of the press development in Taiwan* 台灣報業演進四十年 , Taipei: Evening Independent 自立晚報 .
Chen, Rongsheng 陳榮生 (1968) 'The many problems within small night clubs' 小型夜總會弊竇叢生, *Business Daily* 商工日報 , 11 July.
Chen, Peizhou (1992) 'From syphilis and gonorrhoea to AIDS: the history of venereal diseases in Taiwan' 陳佩周: 從梅毒、淋病到愛滋:走過台灣性病史 , *United Daily* 聯合報 , 13 December.
Chen, Wenfu 陳文福 (1971) 'Familiarising with the law and environment such that one can successfully carry out the task' 熟悉法令對象環境,才能做到百舉百發 , *Police Torchlight Magazine* 警光雜誌 146: 15.
Chiang, Kai-shek 蔣介石 (1964) 'Everything has to be done from ground-up' 一切工作須從基層做起 . In Central Police College (ed.) 中央警官學校 (編) *An Anthology of President Chiang's Admonitory Talks to the Police* 總統對警察人員訓辭選集 , Taipei: Central Police Officer College 中央警官學校 , 104–109.
China Times 中國時報 (1971) 'Please act fast to outlaw sleazy grottos and gambling dens' 請速取締淫窩賭窟 , 15 June.
China Times (1983) 'Men serving as hostesses in 'Golden Peacock'; 'cut-sleeves' take to it like ducks to water!' 金孔雀有男陪酒,斷袖人趨之若鶩 , 10 April.
China Evening News (1969) 'Osteopathic/massage parlours' 理療院 , 25 June.
Cho, Han Haejoang (2000) '"You are entrapped in an imaginary well": the formation of subjectivity within compressed development – a feminist critique of modernity and Korean culture', *Inter-Asia Cultural Studies* 1(1): 49–69.
Cui, Guiqing 崔桂清 (1968) 'Cleansing the sleaze, redressing the social custom 滌淫穢 , 正民風 , *Police Torchlight Magazine* 警光雜誌 84: 20–22.

Decai 德才 (1970) 'Police outlaw obscene facial expressions' 警察取締猥褻表情 , *Public Daily* 大眾日報 , 19 March.

Dept. of Criminal Affairs, Judicial Yuan 司法院刑事廳 (1993) (ed.) *Anthology of Legal Problems in the Application of the Social Order Maintenance Law* 社會秩序維護法法規函令法律問題文書例稿彙編 , Taipei: Judicial Yuan 司法院 .

Deputy Reporter 本刊記者 (1954) 'Where on earth do the pitiful wine house women belong? A visit to certain type of wine house' 可憐酒家女天涯歸何處？ 特種酒家訪問記 , *Woman's Companion* 婦友 2: 14–19.

Deputy Reporter (1955a) 'Military Paradise at a glance' 軍中樂園一瞥 , *Woman's Companion* 婦友 10: 15–16.

Deputy Reporter (1955b) 'A group of fallen women in the Fire Pit: a visit to the Beitou licensed brothels' 一群墮落在火坑的婦女 — 北投公娼訪問記 , *Woman's Companion* 婦友 9: 12–14.

Ding, Naifei and Jen-peng Liu 丁乃非、劉人鵬 (1999) 'New Taiwanese are (good) women "unaccustomed to immoral sexual behaviour"?' 新台灣人是不習於淫行的女人 ?, *Working Papers in Gender/Sexuality Studies* 性/別研究 5&6: 438–443.

Ding, Naifei (2000) 'Prostitutes, parasites, and the house of state feminism', *Inter-Asia Cultural Studies* 1(2): 305–318.

Ding, Naifei (2002) 'Feminist knots: sex and domestic work in the shadow of the bondmaid-concubine', *Inter-Asia Cultural Studies* 3(3): 449–467.

Ding, Weixin 丁維新 (1994) *Police Administration* 行政警察業務 3rd edn, Taipei: Central Police Officer College 中央警官學校 .

Evening Independent 自立晚報 (1966) 'Do not support and boost yellow businesses' 勿為黃色交易張目 , 16 January.

Evening Independent (1968a) 'What's so difficult about abolishing licensed prostitution?' 廢除公娼的困難在哪裡 , 14 June.

Evening Independent (1968b) 'The institution of licensed prostitution should be abolished' 公娼制度應廢止 , 16 June.

Evening Independent (1968c) 'The will to ban prostitution must be firm and determined' 禁娼態度必須堅決 , 17 October.

Evening Independent (1971a) 'The obstacles and gaps in the government's mopping up of sex' 掃蕩色情的阻力與漏洞 , 13 January.

Evening Independent (1971b) 'Cutting out the cancer of commercial sex from Taipei city' 割除台北市色情之癌 , 13 February.

Evening Independent (1973) 'On the elimination of commercial sex' 再論消彌色情 , 28 April.

Evening Independent (1978) 'Men serving as hostesses, utterly perverse; looking into their minds, this can only be perversion' 男士陪酒 , 不倫不類 ; 探其心理 , 莫非變態 , 21 June.

Fan, Qiaoke 范喬可 (1968) 'Inside stories about the prostitution problem – how the authorities are trying hard to solve the problem' — 當前娼妓問題內幕重重如何整頓當局煞費苦心 , *Taiwan Daily* 台灣日報 18 October.

Feng, Yukun 酆裕坤 (1958) 'President Chiang's contribution to and influence on the police in China' 總統對我國警察之貢獻及其影響 , *Police and People Gazette* 警民導報 321: 3–6.

Foucault, Michel (1990) *The History of Sexuality. Volume I: An Introduction*, London: Penguin.

Foucault, Michel (2001) 'The political technology of individuals' in James Faubion (ed.) *Michel Foucault: Power, the Essential Works*, Three, London: Penguin, 403–417.

Great Chinese Evening News 大華晚報 (1968) 'Tea turns sour' 茶變了質 , 23 May.

Gui, Jingshan 桂京山 (1991) 'On the difference between the Social Order Maintenance Law and the Police Offence Law' 剖析社會秩序維護法與違警罰法的異同 , *Police Science Quarterly* 警學叢刊 22(2): 66–69.

He, Zhenfen 何振奮 (1968) 'Are hotel rooms public or private spaces once rented out?' 旅館出租應屬公有亦私用 , *United Daily* 聯合報 , 20 January.

Hershatter, Gail (1997) *Dangerous Pleasures: Prostitution and Modernity in Twentieth-Century Shanghai*, Berkeley: University of California Press.

Hinsch, Bret (1992) *Passions of the Cut Sleeve: The Male Homosexual Tradition in China*, Berkeley: University of California Press.

Ho, Josephine 何春蕤 (1997) 'Sexual revolution: a Marxist perspective on one-hundred years of American history of sexualities' 性革命：一個馬克思主義觀點的美國百年性史. In Josephine Ho (ed.) *Visionary Essays in Sexuality/Gender Studies: Proceedings of the First International Conference On Sexuality Education, Sexology, Trans/Gender Studies and LesBiGay Studies* 性/別研究的新視野：第一屆四性研，討會論集, Taipei: Yuanzun 元尊文化, 33–99.

Ho, Josephine (2004) 'From anti-trafficking to social discipline (or, the changing role of 'women's' NGOs in Taiwan', in Kamala Kempadoo *et al.* (eds) *Shifting the Debate: New Approaches to Trafficking, Migration, and Sex Work in Asia*, London: Routledge.

Hong, Fuqin 洪復琴 (1973) 'Sleazy hairdressing business on the rise' 滋蔓中的色情理髮業, *Police Science Quarterly* 警學叢刊 4(1): 34–39.

Hu, Yiyun 胡亦云 (1985) *Looking Through the Secret of the Glass Circle* 透視玻璃圈的秘密, Taipei: Longchuan 隆泉書局.

Huang, Haipeng and Wu Ping 黃海鵬、吳平 (1971) 'Counting up the sex businesses, looking at new aspect of tourism' 數都市色情業，看新觀光面, *Taiwan Daily* 台灣日報, 20 September.

Huang, Hans Tao-Ming 黃道明 (forthcoming a) 'Glass clique and its Secret Trade: The discursive production of male homosexuality in Taiwan, 1950s–1980s.'

Huang, Hans Tao-Ming (forthcoming b) 'From glass clique to *Tongzhi* Nation: identity formation and politics of sexual shame – an articulation by way of *Crystal Boys*.'

Huang, Shuling 黃淑玲 (1996) 'Women in sex industries: victims? agents or deviants? 台灣特種行業婦女：受害者？行動者？偏差者？*Taiwan: A Radical Quarterly in Social Studies* 台灣社會研究季刊 22: 103–151.

Huang, Shuying 黃淑英 (2004) 'The social cost of the client' 嫖客的社會成本, http://twl.ngo.org.tw/other13.htm, accessed 28 February 2004.

Huang, Yue 黃樾 (1949) 'Can illicit prostitutes be wiped out completely?' 私娼能禁絕嗎, *Police and People Gazette* 警民導報 4: 9–10.

Ke, Ruiming 柯瑞明 (1991) *Prostitution Culture in Taiwan* 台灣風月, Taipei: *Evening Independent* 自立晚報.

Li, Hongxi 李鴻禧 (1979) 'On the revision and abolition of the Police Offence Law' 違警罰法修廢之商榷, *China Tribune* 中國論壇 8(8): 22–28.

Li, Jinzhen 李錦珍 (1981) 'How to outlaw homosexuals-male prostitutes' 如何取締同性戀—男娼, *The 45th Anniversary of the Central Police College Special Publication* 中警四十五週年校慶特刊: 96.

Li, Wenbang 李文邦 (1980) 'Police clean up cut-sleeve quirks; 60 people arrested within a month', 警方掃蕩斷袖癖，月來查獲六十幾, *United Daily* 聯合報, 23 April.

Liang, Yufang 梁玉芳 (1998) 'Punishing both the prostitute and the client, women organisations propose an amendment bill for the Social Order Maintenance Law' 罰娼也罰嫖，婦女團體提出修正社違法, *United Daily* 聯合報, 19 September.

Liao, Yuwen 廖毓文 (1962) 'The filthy business in Taipei's Sanshui Street' 台北市三水街的職業, *Taiwan Folkways* 台灣風物 1(12): 5–9.

Lin, Fang-mei 林芳玫 (1998) 'Identity politics and women's movement in Taiwan' 當代婦運的認同政治：以公娼廢存為例, *Chung-Wai Literary Monthly* 中外文學 27(1): 56–87.

Lin, Hongdong 林弘東 (1989) (ed.) *The Latest Edition of the Six Major Legal Categories* 新編基本六法全書, Taipei: Wunan 五南圖書.

Lin, Jiongren 林炯仁 (1981) 'The elegy of homosexuals' 閒同性戀者的悲歌, *Taiwan Daily* 台灣日報, 12–14 September.

Lin, Hongxun 林弘勳 (1997) 'Taipei city's abolition of licensed prostitution and the history of prostitution in Taiwan' 台北市廢娼與台灣娼妓史, *Contemporary Journal* 當代 122: 106–115.

Lin, Shantian 林山田 (1979) 'Promulgating an administrative law to replace the Police Offence Law' 訂立行政罰法以代違警罰法 , *China Tribune* 中國論壇 8(8): 12–17.

Lin, Xingyi 林信義 (1974) 'Are hotel rooms public spaces?' 旅館房間是否為公共場所 *Evening Independent* 自立晚報 , 7 August.

Liu, Jen-peng 劉人鵬 (2000) *Modern Chinese Feminist Discourses: Nation, Translation, and Sexual Politics* 近代中國女權論述－國族、翻譯與性別政治 , Taipei: Student Books 學生書局 .

Liu, Mingshi 劉明詩 (1973) 'On the straightening things out in the regulation of morality' 談風化之整頓 , *Police Science Quarterly* 警學叢刊 4(1): 11–18.

Liu, Qingjing and Shi Maolin 劉清景、施茂林 (ed.) (1994) *An Anthology of Six Major Laws* 最新詳明六法全書 , Taipei: Dawei 大為書局 .

Liu, Yu-xiu 劉毓秀 (1997) 'Sex education movement in Sweden' 瑞典性教育運動 , *United Daily* 聯合報 , 30 September.

Liu, Yu-xiu (1998) 'De-commoditisation, integration of public and private, and egalitarian, joyful, responsible sex and familial intimacy' 去商品化、公私融合及平等歡愉負責的性愛與親情 , http://taiwan.yam.org.tw/nwc/nwc3/papers/forum313.htm, accessed 24 February 2004.

Liu, Yu-xiu and Huang Shuling 劉毓秀、黃淑玲 (2004) 'Prostitute career is nothing but a dream' 神女生涯原是夢 , *China Times* 中國時報 , 8 February.

Lu, Qing 魯青 (1958) 'On the management of certain type of business' 談特種營業 的管理 , *Police and People Gazette* 警民導報 327: 4–5.

Martin, Fran (2003) *Situating Sexualities: Queer Representation in Taiwanese Fiction, Film and Public culture*, Hong Kong: Hong Kong University Press.

Mei, Kewang 梅可望 (1951) 'President Chiang, the Father of Chinese Police' 總統：中國警察之父 , *Police and People Gazette* 警民導報 67: 4.

Mu, Ming 慕銘 (1974) 'On whether rented hotel rooms belong to public space and on the intervention in lovers on secret dates' 論旅館出租房間是否為公共場所及干涉情侶幽會的問題 , *Police Torchlight Magazine* 警光雜誌 212: 38–40.

National Evening News 民族晚報 (1968) 'Sex hidden covertly in bath houses, wine houses, flowery tea rooms and osteopath parlours' 浴室、酒家、花茶室、理療院裡暗藏春色 , 13 April.

National Evening News (1969) 'Hotels? Apartments?' 旅館？公寓？, 16 December.

National Evening News (1970a) 'A big tumour in society that urgently needs to be cut out' 現社會一個大毒瘤急需割除 , 27 July.

National Evening News (1970b) 'Human-spectre importuning in a seedy alley arrested' 陋巷人妖 , 招蜂引蝶被捕 , 4 December.

O'Hara, Albert (1973) *Social Problems: Focus on Taiwan*, Taipei: Meiya Publication.

Pai, Hsien-yung (1990) *Crystal Boys*, Howard Goldblatt (trans.), San Francisco: Gay Sunshine Press.

Peng, Kuan 彭寬 (1968) 'Propagating morality; revising the regulation on particular type of businesses' 宣導倫理道德的觀念,重訂特定營業管理法 , *Police Torchlight Magazine* 警光雜誌 88: 11–12.

Policy-Pusher Alliance for the Downsizing of the Sex Industry (PPADSI) 推動縮減性產業政策聯盟 (2004) 'Against the decriminalisation of the sex industry' 反性產業除罪化 , http://www.twrf.org.tw/news8.htm, accessed 4 March 2004.

Public Daily 大眾日報 (1971) 'Shadowy human-spectre haunts New Park' 新公園‧人妖幢幢 , 14 August.

Shen, Meizhen 沈美真 (1990) *Victimised Women Prostitutes and Prostitution Policies in Taiwan* 台灣被害娼妓與娼妓政策 , Taipei: Qianwei 前衛 .

Taiwan Daily 台灣日報 (1968a) 'The backward custom of bath-taking company' 陪浴陋習 , 5 February.

Taiwan Daily (1968b) 'Abolishing the institution of licensed prostitution is unquestionable' 廢止公娼制度之必要無可商量 , 18 June.

Taiwan Daily (1968c) 'Try to do well with the task of abolishing licensed prostitution' 做好廢止公娼的工作 , 16 October.

United Daily (1951) 'Teddy boy steals money from a male prostitute after having paid him a visit' 太保狎男妓 , 事後竊款而去 , 18 November.

United Daily (1959) 'New Park turns into male brothel; the authorities should install street lamps and send police to patrol the area' 新公園變成男娼館，應速裝燈派警巡邏, 22 January.

United Daily (1968) 'A he and a she: two school students behaving dissolutely in the 'tea-and-only-tea' café' 補習學生純喫茶，行為放蕩他和她, 30 December.

United Daily (1969) 'Proposing solutions for the conflict between the hotel customer/business and the police' 為解決旅客旅館業與警察的矛盾提建議, 4 May.

United Daily (1983) 'Called Officials within the Glass Clique; Pleasure provided purely by and for men' 玻璃圈內稱相公，吃喝玩樂全男人, 10 April.

Wang, Lieming 王烈民 (1958) *Security Police* 保安警察, Taipei: Central Police Officer College 中央警官學校.

Wang, Lieming (1969) *The Science of Security Policing* 保安警察學, Taipei: Central Police Officer College 中央警官學校.

Weiyan 微言 (1968) 'Unfairly punished' 罰得不公, *Evening Independent* 自立晚報, 29 March.

Wu, Ryan Jui-yuan 吳瑞元 (1998) *As a 'Bad' Son: The Emergence of Modern 'Homosexuals' in Taiwan, 1970–1990* 孽子的印記 - 台灣近代男性「同性戀」的浮現 (1970–1990), MA Thesis, Institute of History, National Central University, Taiwan.

Xia, Lingqing 夏林清 (ed.) (2000) *1998 World Action Forum for Sex Work Rights* 公娼與妓權運動：第一屆性工作權利與性產業國際行動論壇會議實錄, Taipei: Collective Of Sex Workers and Supporters 日日春關懷互助協會.

Xie, Ruizhi 謝瑞智 (1979) 'On the ways the Police Offence Law might be revised' 違警罰法修正方向之探討, *China Tribune* 中國論壇 8(8): 18–21.

Xie, Wencong 謝文聰 (1982) 'Taking the problem of homosexuality seriously' 正視同性戀問題, *Central Daily* 中央日報, 29 July.

Xu, Shengxi 徐聖熙 (1972) 'On "the prohibiting juveniles from entering places that impair body and mind regulatory procedures"' 談「禁止青少年涉足妨害身心健康場所辦法」, *Chinese Police Volunteer* 中國義警 41: 7–9.

Xu, Shengxi (1979) 'On the investigation of sex crimes' 色情案件之偵查, *Jurisprudence Quarterly* 法學叢刊 24(4): 84–89.

Yang, Wei 楊蔚 (1961) 'Appalling, filthy, base, despicable . . .: Sanshui Street's male prostitutes' 駭俗、骯髒、卑劣和不堪入耳 . . . 三水街的男妓, *Detective News* 徵信新聞報, 26 July.

Yao, Jishao 姚季韶 (1949) 'On the question of licensed prostitution' 論娼妓廢存問題, *Police and People Gazette* 警民導報 2: 15–16.

Yin, Baoning 殷寶寧 (2000) '"Zhongshan North Road": the construction of sexual subjectivities and national identification in the course of landscape transformations' 「中山北路」：地景變遷歷程中之情慾主體與國族認同建構, Ph.D. Dissertation, National Taiwan University.

Yu, Junliang 余俊亮 (1972) 'Regulations of Sex' 風化管制. In Yu Junliang (ed.) *Lectures in Police Administration* 行政警察幹部講習班講習錄, Taipei: Central Police Officer College 中央警管學校, 21–45.

Zhang, Wenjun 張文軍 (1960) 'A discussion on how to deal with the police offence of illicit prostitution' 處理姦宿暗娼違警之商榷, *Police and People Gazette* 警民導報 392: 7–8.

Zhang, Yide 張義德 (1960) 'A study on the police offence of illicit prostitution' 意圖得利與人姦宿違警處理之研究, *Police and People Gazette* 警民導報 376: 9–10.

Zhang, Xiongchao 張雄潮 (1962) 'Taiwan's immoral sexual trend and the female prostitution problem' 台灣之色情風氣與妓女問題, *Taiwan Folkways* 台灣風物 12(3): 19–24.

Zhang, Minzhong 張民忠 (1983) 'Police raid on the *Golden Peacock* restaurant running prostitution business' 孔雀多男飛：警方破獲金孔雀餐廳色情營業, *China Times Express* 時報週刊 268: 98–99.

Zhong, Junsheng 鍾俊陞 (1988) 'Taiwan's prostitution economy: war and sex trade and their contribution to the economic development in Taiwan' 台灣的娼婦經濟：戰爭色情與貿易色情對台灣經濟的貢獻 *Human World* 人間 37: 73–76.

Special terms

Beitou 北投
congliang 從良
guomin 國民
jiansu 姦宿
junzhong leyuan 君子
linjian 良家婦女
pinju 女性異類
renyao 人妖
shanliang fengsu 善良風俗
tezhong jiujia 特種酒家
xianggong 相公
zeren er shi 擇人而侍
zuozhiqin, zuozhishi, zhozhijun 作之親，作之師，作之君

boliquan 玻璃圈
duanxiu 斷袖
jianyin 姦淫
junzi 君子
liangjia funu 軍中樂園
nüxing yilei 臨檢
peisu 陪宿
renzheng 仁政
Shengwang 聖王
weixie 猥褻
yinye 淫業
zhengsu 正俗

Chapter 18

Reticent poetics, queer politics

Liu Jen-peng and Ding Naifei[1]

How is it that silent tolerance (*moyan kuanrong*) turns 'coming out' (*xianshen*) into 'becoming invisible' (*yinshen*)?

The attitude of the Chinese tradition towards sexual matters between the same sex is to silently tolerate rather than to openly accept.

(Chou 1997: 384)[2]

Ever since [I] have had something to do with the subject of 'tongzhi', the three characters, 'same sex love', has like a curse been tattooed to my face, with the rest of my body rendered invisible [. . .]. In any situation, this 'tattoo' will follow me like a shadow its form. My colleagues say, 'hey, there's a guy waiting for you in the office'. My old schoolmates will insinuate, 'don't underestimate [your] mother, maybe you can just be honest and tell her'. My mother says, 'if you continue to communicate with Beijing tongzhi after 1997, then you cannot stay on in this home'. Before that, she said, 'if you are gay/homosexual, you are not my son'.

(Chou 1997: 34)

In the final pages of Chou Wah-Shan's latest influential book *Postcolonial Gay*, he notes the following 'three characteristics' of 'the more successful cases of coming out in China, Hong Kong, and Taiwan':

(1) non-conflictual harmonious relationships
(2) non-declarative practical everyday acts
(3) a healthy personality that is not centred on sex(uality)

Yet, when mirrored against western gay and lesbian movements' assertive and self-confident 'coming out' postures, it seems arguable whether, with such exhaustive demands for perfection [in managing and maintaining one's familial relationships] at the most technical level, one can still count these cases as 'coming out.' One wonders whether this is not an excessive appropriation of a canonical mould-model, and whether we have not come right up to the cusp of a need for a new mould-model.

(Chu 1998: 53)

Can it be that in Taiwan only orphans can 'come out'? It is often said that families are happy, that families are places that provide warmth, but it seems that actually [to gay/lesbian/bisexual/queer persons] only orphans can 'come out', because the politics of the family is too terrible.

(Ni 1997: 201)

There is a paradox at the heart of recent formulations of the question of 'coming out' in Taiwan (and possibly in various Chinese speaking worlds). That paradox is symptomatically expressed in the first two quotations above, taken from the recent *Post-Colonial Tongzhi*, written by one of the most frequently published and read writers in the region, Chou Wah-Shan (Hong Kong).

In his writings, Chou seems to have stepped out of line. In his preface, he notes how the mere fact of writing on the subject of gay and lesbian and queer politics in the Chinese social context has marked him as if with a permanent tattoo on the face. This stigma gives him a face without a body (only the stigmatized face is left, or so he is made to feel).

Paradoxically, this situation has led him to write of an 'essentially' non-homophobic Chinese culture. This culture has always treated its persons with same-sex tendencies with silent tolerance rather than outright violence (as happens in the West). On the one hand, Chou insists on a 'Chinese traditional culture' as a continuous entity nearly 2000 years old, wherein there is no such thing as homosexuality or homophobia, but only same-sex erotic acts and roles. There are no homosexual persons and therefore certainly no such identities in the modern (i.e. Western) sense (Chou 1997: 327). Homosexuality is a Western construct and, as an identity, entered the Chinese cultural worlds along with Western colonial forces and languages in the 19th century. Homophobia and its more virulent or violent manifestations are entirely Western and therefore colonial, and have no relation at all to a 'Chinese traditional cultural' that emphasizes harmony (*he*) and tolerance (*kuanrong*). Hence, the first quotation, 'The attitude of Chinese tradition towards same-sex sexual matters is one of silence and tolerance, rather than official-public-rhetorical tolerance.'[3]

Chou Wah-Shan furthermore notes the intensely creative and convoluted strategies for (not) coming out to one's parents/family invented by gays and lesbians and bisexuals often living at home, resisting marriage or married, in present-day Taiwan, Hong Kong and China. Chou's explanation for what can only be termed a peculiar expansiveness of familial power, in terms of the situation in Hong Kong, is that a pseudo-extended familial network (Chou 1997: 375) has taken the place of the old 'extended familial' (or clan) logic. Thus, despite Hong Kong's apparent 'Westernization', most people in Hong Kong, including gays, lesbians and bisexuals, live out their lives inextricably entangled within a network of primarily familial relational associations. Chou's interviews in his book and his preface concur with what Ni Jiazhen had said at a panel discussion on queer politics in Taiwan in 1995: in this particular time and place, only orphans can (afford to) come out.

In the contemporary cultural and movement discourses in Taiwan surrounding the issue of coming out, there is a recurring anxiety about the great difficulties presented by an 'American-style' 'coming out' for queers in Taiwan. These difficulties allegedly revolve around the site of the family. The thinking through of this issue includes attempting to forge alternatives for an individual-based coming out in a collective coming-out, as well as questioning to what extent this 'American-style' model has in practice already been exceeded. This last point is made in the last quotation that begins this section by Wei-cheng R. Chu. The question we would like to ask is, in what ways might the residual and reconfigured ideology of reticent tolerance actually enable or facilitate the workings of an unfamiliar 'gentle' homophobia, or constitute homophobia as effect? What and who are preserved in the full perfectibility of their face in the transmission and circulation of these value-laden concepts and terms? How come it's all right for others to be homosexual, but if it's my son/daughter, then he/she is no longer my son/daughter? How come this can sometimes amount to a matter of life and death – as when the mother threatens suicide as prevention and the child threatens suicide in retaliation?

What forces keep those persons whose sexual and desiring practices have already gone beyond the acceptable, or are plainly dissident? What keeps these persons in the shadowy ghostly spaces of the socio-familial continuum? This ghostly position demands of shadow beings the responsibility (at their expense) for the upkeep of the wholeness and harmony of the very continuum wherein they do not have a place. We will not try here to answer the question of whether an alternative (to) 'coming out' might be proposed. Instead, we are concerned to delineate and describe the workings of the forces that continuously rework themselves, reconfiguring silent tolerance to '*keep us in place*'. These are forces that keep lesbians, gays, bisexuals and transgender peoples in the realm of ghosts – without a proper place – vis-à-vis the socio-familial continuum. It is as various forms of shadows and shades that we are conceded survival space, only to have these liminal spaces taken away at the merest hint of infraction or disturbance of the existing order of persons and things. This is one way in which an effective homophobia works, very much like the fear and patronizing placation of 'lone spirits and wild ghosts' (*guhun yegui*). The erstwhile dominant, still in place but now residual thinking goes like this: although they cannot be made to disappear for good, they can be made to cooperate in their own invisibility and quiescence; to that extent they must continuously be guarded against with containment and preventive measures in the guise of appeasement. At the same time, the very sense of having to appease and guard against infringement or retaliation marks the powers of 'ghosts' and *wangliang* non-persons in relation to institutional persons.

We propose that, in the time-space of present day Taiwan at least, it is too simplistic to think of pre-Western traditional 'tolerance' and (post) colonial or Western epistemic, Judeo-Christian homophobia as mutually exclusive and diametrically clear-cut attitudes and ways of knowing or ignoring. We would further claim that such a distinction, although claiming to enlarge the space of survival for queer persons in the present by invoking a homophobic-free site in some idealized pre-colonial past, instead too easily slips into the service of residual disciplinary forces. For one thing, the discretionary use of tolerance rhetoric and reticent strategies (*moyan kuanrong*) by both the Taiwan state and certain sectors of the new social movements have recently and effectively policed the boundaries of sexual acts *and* persons, as well as tried to punish transgressors, offenders *and* their associates, friends and families.

What we object to in Chou's account then, are these assumptions. (1) The simplified binarism of past versus present, Chinese tolerance versus Western homophobia, in what purports to be a historical narrative of homosexuality and homophobia; (2) the idealization and reification of 'tolerance' in such a historical narrative as a sign of a benevolent albeit class-fractured yet somehow authentic Chinese past; and (3) an effective, culturally essentialist move that separates a positive tolerance of the past from contemporary 'modern' forces of oppression, repression and homophobia in the family or at work. We suggest that just as person-hood is – in Taiwan if not in other Chinese-language worlds – inextricably entangled, intensely cathected to parental/familial relations in impure 'modern' forms, so too have the rhetoric and politics of tolerance and reticence retained powers while articulating new disciplinary and rhetorical forces, always deformed and deforming, *especially* in the field of sexuality in/around the family. We would like to attempt then a preliminary rethinking, through readings of certain texts in and of Taiwan, of the interface of tolerance and reticence (as dominant aesthetic-ethical value) with the maintaining of 'proper' sexual relations and the keeping of deviant sex(ualities) in the realm of ghosts. This will yield, we hope, the beginnings of a descriptive analysis of certain effects of homophobia as the latter is re-figured through 'silent words and reticent tolerance', passing, as it were, for the most 'traditional' of virtues in modern 'democratic' guise.

Our preliminary claim is that there is a 'reticent' politics that is deployed in Chinese-speaking places such as Taiwan and Hong Kong. This reticence is not (and perhaps never was) merely a poetics and a rhetoric, but constitutes ever-refigured socio-familial force and power. It circulates in everyday practices along pathways that maintain the 'normal order' of persons and things as well as of actions and behaviour. However, this force may also be activated to work in reverse, against that 'normal order', disturbing or harassing it, in the form of querying penumbrae and other uninvited guests. Significantly, if we do not or cannot describe that normally circulating reticent force (which could also be termed a dominant reticence[4]) so that its deployment is recognized, then the reversal of that reticent force, its subversive counter-usage will remain buried or less effectively activated in the shadow world of rumours.

The poetics and politics of reticence: a finely deployed force

Reticence is one among various 'traditional' poetics-aesthetics. Not only does reticence produce shadows, but there is also the nearly indiscernible shadow of a shadow, which is a 'shade' (*wangliang*, also rendered 'penumbrae'). All of these forms of the unspeakable/unspoken/unrecognizable/unrecognized are difficult to discern. In this essay, we aim particularly to focus on the relevance and relations of reticent forces, their shadows and shades, to contemporary queer politics in Taiwan, especially insofar as such a politics can and does travel in the guise of how 'the Chinese traditionally reticently tolerate homosexual or same-sex persons, feelings and acts'. We hope to explore how reticence deploys its peculiar force as rhetoric, narrative deployment and aesthetic ideal, as well as model behaviour and as a mode of speech. In these various forms, reticence simultaneously hides yet displays and deploys an ineradicable force and effects.

We will not broach here 'tolerance' (*kuanrong*) as a virtue, and its discussion in ethics. In this paper our focus is on 'tolerance' as an unthinking rhetorical ploy. In everyday language, the meanings expressed in 'tolerance' are reticent. Once spoken explicitly, it signifies that which can no longer be tolerated, or the limits of tolerance, as for example in 'I have been tolerant enough as regards him/his behaviour', or as in 'as for this issue, I have always shown the greatest tolerance'. These phrases would not appear in relations that are 'good' or where there is still 'true' tolerance. In this paper, we are rather discussing how reticent homophobic forces might be embedded within conditions of 'tolerance', and the cultural myths that make up 'silent tolerance' (Tsai 1986: 105–107).

Our notion of reticence, and our inspiration for thinking through various forms of reticence that contain sexually deviant and dissident bodies and persons, come primarily from Tsai Ying-chun's paper, 'The poetics of reticence in classical Chinese thought'. After a period of gestation and further discussion and writing, however, Tsai's reticence has become, perhaps in our essay as well as in the texts we examine, transfigured and alien (to itself) turning into a plethora of reticences (major and minor), even though our main focus remains the queer texts and discourses in Taiwan and their relations to gay and lesbian and queer movements. Tsai's formulation of a reticent poetics has been a matrix for our engagement with the politics of reticence from a queer standpoint and angle. It has also been a productive historical, rhetorical and epistemological resource. We do not believe in some non-transformational cultural unity that transcends time and space, or history and place. At the same time, we hope to provide in our reading of certain texts of the present an alternative language and attendant resources that work somewhat like the reversal techniques of a dissident reticence. Our reading of how reticences (always plural) work – how hegemonic reticence represses and disciplines, as well as how minor 'improper' reticences (such as that of Angel's mother's in *The Unfilial Daughter*) make place for alternative agencies – has been useful most recently in the classroom, providing occasion for non-habitual and counter-intuitive thought-work against major deployments and articulations of reticence and hierarchy.[5]

According to Tsai Ying-chun (1998),[6] the poetics of reticence as one of the aesthetic ideals of a Chinese literary tradition is a mode of writing wherein 'the real message tends to go beyond the actual words of the text'. Reticence (*hanxu*) literally means both 'holding back' (*han*) and 'storing up' (*xu*), and has been variously translated as 'conservation', 'reserve', and 'potentiality'.[7] Tsai traces the literary, historical, and socio-political contexts wherein the poetics of reticence evolved, and suggestively notes its relation to, on the one hand, the lyric poetic tradition's emphasis on poetry's affective expression, and the philosophic notion of the ultimate inadequacy of language. On the other hand, the poetics of reticence was aligned to Chou dynasty's quasi-ritualistic exchanges (*fushi yanzhi*) at court gatherings, wherein the recitation of fragments from the *Book of Songs* allowed for the indirect expression of ministers' and courtiers' inclinations and opinions. Yet, such uses of poetic fragments did not demand adherence to their textual context; rather, this was considered to be a form of general usage that gave precedence to the situation wherein the fragment was quoted, as well as to the ritual and political demands of the occasion and the speakers concerned. More significant is the demand that such quotations of poetic fragments obey the rules of a communal harmonious order, wherein it could then gently and indirectly work its persuasive powers. The disciplinary forces of such a communal harmony are registered in the phrase 'to recite poems [one] must be like, or, of the [same] kind' (*geshi bilei*). The *Zuo Zhuan* records an anecdote wherein the one at a court gathering who does not recite in a recognizably 'like' manner is declared as dangerously harbouring 'differing/different tendencies' (*you yizhi*) (Tsai 1997: 285).

As a form of indirect expression of subjective affect and mood, the poetics of reticence came to acquire ethico-political weight and directives with the establishment of Confucianism as state ideology by the early second century BC. The notion of poetic rhetoric as a guide for personal morality, as a means to 'encourage good and guard against evil', came to be seen as a moral orthodoxy (Tsai 1998: 4).[8] According to Confucius, the *Book of Songs* is the backbone, the classic whereupon moral orthodoxy rests.[9] The long-term effects on classical literary criticism may be seen in the orthodox belief that poetry and writing are best used in providing 'ethical lessons or to regulate one's emotions in accordance with ethical or political propriety' (Tsai 1997: 5). Under the influence of Confucianism, classic Chinese literary criticism insists on how poetry can provide ethical teaching and/or discipline emotions and relations in accordance with moral and political propriety (imperatives). The extant Han period exegeses of the *Book of Songs* systematically read part of the *Book of Songs* as applauding the Empress's virtues in not showing jealousy and abilities in woman's needlework, etc. Because emotions (*qing*) are not entirely good, one has constantly to revisit and examine one's emotions, and control, manage, discipline these in accordance with the teachings of the sages (*yi shengwang zhi jiao yi zhiqing*). Thus, in the *Book of Songs* we find, 'that which arises from emotions, [is] the people's nature, that which stops at propriety and ritual, [is] the blessings of the sages'.[10] Whereas in the *Book of the Means*, we note that '[b]efore the feelings of happiness, anger, melancholy and joy are aroused, it is called equilibrium (centrality, mean). When these feelings are aroused and each and all attain due measure and degree, it is called harmony. Equilibrium is the great foundation of the world, and harmony its universal path. When equilibrium and harmony are realized to the highest degree, heaven and earth will attain their proper order and all things will flourish'.[11] It is within such a matrix of discourse and thought and ritual acts that has arisen the famous notion of 'gentle generosity' (*wenrou dunhou*).

Tsai notes how this particular praxis of the poetics of reticence might have led to its articulation with 'self-discipline or even self-preservation when one happened to live in a society where all forms of intellectual activity had been incorporated into the political program' (Tsai 1998). That is to say, the poetics of reticence might very well, in later imperial regimes, have evolved into and in support of strategies of personal and communal self-preservation as much as those of self-discipline. Self-preservation and self-discipline together would then constitute a two-pronged mechanism for maintaining a purportedly orthodox order. Within such a context, 'self-discipline' and 'self-preservation' are no longer mere matters of how one might regard and maintain the proper self, but extend to how one must attend to socio-familial and personal-political relations at large. That is to say, they extend to how one feels and acts towards others. Those who feel and act in line with the given socio-familial order, in accordance with their proper-official position (government official, teacher, parent, etc), wield reticence most often in self-discipline. While those who tend toward feelings, acts and words *out of line*, not befitting their place and role in the received order of persons and things, are commanded to a self-disciplining reticence. The recitation of poetry is, in such cases, a game with rules in a public or political position. The rules of this game are articulated to each player's effect, each person's loyalty. Reticent and indirect speech and ritual acts reinforce the restraining power of such a field and postulate a 'like' heart for all players within that game field. This then is how a reigning order (a force-field) might be preserved through the circulation of reticent forces of self(other)-discipline and self(other)-preservation: those bodies occupying the liminal sites of this force-field immediately become shades or ghosts, deprived of the resources for life or action.

The centripetal disciplining and preserving force deployed upon such ghostly liminality might be gauged in the number of reticent recalcitrant suicides. These rules of reticent feeling and behaviour have left discursive and textual records at certain points in history. Given the interests of this paper, we will not be able to give a genealogy of reticence, nor analyse exactly which forms have come to produce such residual effects in the present. We do note, however, a strange yet familiar confluence of reticent values and proprieties with the suicide (an active and aggressive, but above all, an untimely because of not waiting for death) of persons not conforming to orthodox bipolar and reproductive-familial gender roles and sexual desires. We aim to describe analytically the novelistic representation of a silent, often speechless force so great that it can kill or push to suicide. Those who have died by suicide in the recent past and present of Taiwan too often include homosexual children and adolescents of both sexes. We contend that this disciplinary, sometimes even murderous, force works to the greatest effect when woven into the rich textures of reticent everyday rhetoric and strategies. Contemporary novelistic representation, even in the case of an acclaimed novel of 'queer' desire (our example is *The Unfilial Daughter*) may be seen as both representing and complicit with precisely such reticent aesthetic and political powers.

We are also concerned with how new regimes of progressive knowledge-production in the fields of gender and queer theorizing and historical analyses can be inadvertently complicit with precisely these same reticent and shadowy homophobic forces. Complicity in these new fields of knowledge production takes the form of a paradoxical claim to cultural specificity (e.g. tolerance as a quintessentially Chinese value) and cultural purity (tolerance as pure and innocent of any workings of power). Pure and particular Chinese values (of tolerance, for example) are then deemed to operate entirely separately from and free from modern 'Western' homosexual and homophobic categories. Such claims are further supposed to authorise and instantiate some form of epistemological purity (untainted by colonial Western modes of knowledge), or an epistemological alternative (some traditional, non-homophobic way of practising and knowing same-sex desire). Ironically, this is precisely when they most easily slip toward the interests that include the very forces that (in our reading) kill homosexual teenagers by forcing them to commit suicide – alone, in pairs, in threesomes.

Our aim in this paper is twofold. We will first read the ways in which specific cultural essentialist gestures of reading and analysis, circulating in recent gender studies and queer theories, in fact support the reticent structures of homophobic forces in present-day Taiwan. This critique contends that there is no essential, trans-historical or trans-cultural way in which same-sex desire, love or acts can be claimed or isolated outside specific political-historical formations. A gender studies that seeks to privilege pre-modern categories and concepts of gender over and against both 'Western' modern gender relations and 'Western' feminism is just as problematic as a queer theory that seeks to claim the absence of homophobia and homosexuality in a would-be post-colonial decolonized present. The women of some pre-Modern China were not uniformly happy, nor did they all live in gender-equal relations in a way unattainable by women in present-day 'Chinese' societies. Homosexuals and queers in present-day Taiwan do not have less, but rather differently, difficult lives because homophobic forces do not operate as overtly and violently but rather to protect everyone else's face (read: the faces of those who conform). 'Chinese' values must not and cannot become yet another transcendental repository of a state perfect and good, implying that if only realities and representations could be made to conform to such a state now lost, all would be fine.

We will then follow with a close reading of a mid-1990s non-reticent realist narrative so as to describe the familial strategies that kill a young lesbian, as well as the reticent strategies of the narrative itself in revenge against an abusive, non-reticent, maternal figure debased in class and ethnicity. Such a reading is only possible against the grain, not just of the narrative, but of many of its critics and readers, as well as of the unspoken aesthetics and politics of reticence 'in the very air we breathe'. We propose that the incidental (not central) representation of teenage lesbian suicide in *The Unfilial Daughter* be read in relation to media representations of several teenage (lesbian) suicides in recent years. These representations all too often deploy a logic according to which lesbianism can only be incidental to suicide rather than a possible pressure towards it. Consequently, the suicides themselves are presented as unjustifiable, possibly even inexplicable and somehow a shameful waste. Such a reticently 'generous' rhetoric refuses to consider that lesbian desire can play a central role in how one values life and death, and therefore feels that lesbianism cannot possibly be implicated in one's decision to commit suicide and that there necessarily must be a better reason for that action. Such logic only confirms that there cannot possibly be a 'place for us' that is configured on our terms. There may indeed by a space now, but it is one that allows gay and lesbian and queer feelings to occupy only the liminal space and time of ghosts and shades.[12]

Chinese tradition is reticent and tolerant concerning same-sex acts and feelings?

We suggest that to consider a 'traditional Chinese' 'tolerance' as attitudes and/or ways of (not) knowing that are radically different from a (post)colonial or 'Western' homophobia is too simple. Yet, this marks not just the writings of Chou Wah-Shan, but is an effect also found in recent writings in the field of Chinese literary and historical studies of gender.

In recent writings in Taiwan introducing new trends in local gender studies, especially those concerning 'traditional' women and 'homosexuality', many evoke a 'Chinese' historical experience or mode of thought different from 'the West' by way of resisting a Western hegemonic gender politics. Interestingly, such supposedly different 'historical experiences' show a certain unified tendency in adhering to very old received ideas concerning the differences between 'East' and 'West', for instance, that the 'West' emphasizes dualistic opposition and struggle, whereas 'Chinese' emphasizes peace, tolerance and yin-yang harmony. This indisputable and fundamental difference has not only become the presupposition and result of Chinese studies in the field of gender and sexuality. It has also come to adjudicate whether a certain research or study topic is 'Chinese' (enough) or not, or, 'excellent' or not. When the object of study is 'minoritarian', then the methodological and stylistic demand is that the study foregoes the dualist category of 'oppression/resistance' because these are simplistic, pre-Foucauldian, 'Western' feminist modes of operation. Rather, these studies are commanded to write on 'minoritarian' subjects in terms of inclusive 'negotiated resistances' the better to render historical 'complexities' and 'minoritarian' agencies.[13] Needless to say, gender and sexual formations are contextually formed and materially marked in specific and differential time/space configurations. The study of gender and sexual historical formations and feelings and acts will then, of course, be likewise differently marked and valenced. However, just as it is important to trace how gender and sexualities are differently discursively constituted, relationally mapped and relayed, felt, acted upon and talked about in different temporalities and geopolitical sites, so it is just as important not to reify 'difference' into trans-historical categories that would seem primarily to shore up authenticity (truth) and superiority (value) in any mode of specific time-space gender representation. In effect, 'difference' becomes rhetorically limited to difference from a so-called 'West', and allows one to safely tally that difference to the 'traditional China' or 'Chinese tradition' in one's heart, as if identifying some correct answer. The reticent narrative and aesthetic ideals herein preserved warrant careful consideration and further analysis.

When such questions are raised in the hope of tracing a 'China' that is different from 'the West' due to some sort of (post)colonial resistance, the answer is always already in the question, and one slips into a tautological discourse. There must certainly be a 'Chinese-ness' different from 'the West' that is then found to reside in Taiwan, Hong Kong, China, Malaysia, in Chinese America, even in Taiwan queers and licensed prostitutes. In such discourses, 'Chinese/Western' differences become a trope whereby feminism, the gay and lesbian movement, or the study of (dissident) sexualities are seen to have originated in 'the West'. In relation to which, 'China' and 'Chinese-ness' provide an idealized and romanticized contrast, or, take on the attributes of a 'student' working hard to progress in the face of the challenges from 'the West'. When such discourses take effect in the contemporary space of social movements, the former attitude affirms how 'we' have a different tolerant and gentle tradition and therefore do not need certain modes of struggle, resistance and change. The latter, on the other hand, states that a certain formation is 'native', and therefore implies how strident calls for change and struggle must then be externally-derived and non-necessary or contingent. Both are reticent discourses that by implication deny or refuse to face minoritarian or subaltern subjects and their necessarily non-reticent, sometimes even violent, struggles. Only those minoritarian or subaltern subjects that possess adequate resources to allow for travel in the interstices of the prevailing order and routes of power can afford simultaneously resistant and tolerant postures. Their resistances, minimally disturbing the reigning order of things, will nonetheless add to its 'modern' variety and 'democratic' multiplicity. These minoritarian subjects are the ones most gently treated and tolerated.

Even Foucault has referred to, in passing, what can only be termed a truly romantic view of 'Chinese' sexuality. Foucault has noted how, in contrast to 'our civilization's' positivistic science of sex(uality), societies such as those of China, Japan and India have an art of sex(uality), where truth comes from a pleasure that has nothing to do with taboos and functions. An idealized and neatly bipolarized view of 'the West as science' and 'the East as art' are the presuppositions of studies in 'Chinese' homosexuality, where homophobia and the fear of, and exclusionary practices against, different or dissident sexualities come to be seen as limited to 'the West'. In sharp contrast, 'the East' or 'traditional China' is a haven for sexual arts, a line of thinking that is affiliated to the equally mythical idea of China as loving peace, China as gently and generously tolerant. Or, 'the Chinese view of life is one that is based on life in harmony with the natural forces' (Gulik 1974: 350) etc.

Recent work in the field of sinology has expressly sought to resist and work against 'orientalism'. Yet, with a clearly projected 'orientalist' other, such studies have sometimes produced an equally fixed 'oriental', perpetuating a differently positioned orientalism. Dorothy Ko, for example, criticizes the orientalism of historical studies that represent

Chinese women as slaves or victims, while portraying a 'traditional' feminine cultural sphere that is almost without any trace of gender discrimination. This can be understood as producing a kind of self-orientalizing effect. Yet another 'orientalism' that is often critiqued is that of Van Gulik, best known for his studies of the ancient Chinese sex life. His portrayal of the Chinese ancient sex life as healthy (without perversions) and variegated has been critiqued as 'orientalist' by, for example, Charlotte Furth (1994b). Furth points to how Van Gulik's representation of ancient Chinese sex life is entirely healthy – with neither repression or perversion, turning China into a repository of what is lacking in 'the West': sensual freedom and variegated pleasures. Furth discusses how, in traditional Chinese medical discourse, sexuality has been gendered, pointing specifically to how sexuality has been construed in the service of biological reproduction, with woman's (avoidance of) orgasm being assigned great value in terms of fertility and birth. In another article on Ming and Qing medical discourse, Furth (1994a) states that the body is a gendered body, although not strictly in a bipolar way. Furth's primary concern throughout is on gender. As for sexuality and sexual desire, she noted how in traditional or classic medical tracts no single sexual act or object or desire is considered sick or perverted, the only significant aspect being whether or not it fits with reproductive functions. Furth avers that this has to do with yin-yang cosmological beliefs; since male and female are both comprised of yin and yang forces in constant complementary flux, there will be within this framework a greater tolerance for sexual acts and persons who are different or strange. Yet again, we seem to have returned to a reliance on the notion of a singular Chinese tradition of generosity and tolerance.

Van Gulik has noted of Chinese sex life, 'lesbians are quite common and tolerated by most people, so long as these do not go overboard in their [sexual?] acts. People think that lesbianism is what necessarily happens to girls in the custom of enforced domesticity, to the extent where if there should occur self-sacrificial acts of love, people will even eulogize such acts.' In his study of Chinese male homosexuality, Bret Hinsch has also emphasized a Chinese traditional tolerance different from 'the West' (Hinsch 1990).

Pan Guangdan's work in the 1940s gave many examples from the Shang and Zhou dynasties ('Not only did the phenomenon exist, it was quite popular') and also from the Wei Jing period ('Homosexuality at that time was actually a common tendency among high society and the elite'). Pan Guangdan concludes that according to the sources, Chinese society always had a markedly different attitude toward perversions (male homosexuality), and that it is 'solely because of such a tolerant and generous attitude that homosexuals could have become during certain periods the fashion that it was'. As for lesbians, Pan writes that women were rarely seen outside their homes, even less were such women noted in historical records and writings. Yet, Pan could still write: 'In the past, women rarely ventured outdoors, did not commune with society at large and even less with the other sex. That is why lesbian tendencies were very easily developed. Relations with the so-called "intimate friend in one's private rooms" are often marked by some taint of lesbianism' (Pan 1987: 517, 531, 539).

The terms 'generosity' and 'tolerance' are mobilized each time there is mention of non-reproductive or non-heterosexual sex in such Chinese historical studies, whether in English or Chinese, as if these terms could explain homosexuality in the past. We note how this seems a habit peculiar to Chinese classical or historical research when it takes homosexuality as its object of study. However, even though there is ample record of wars in historical texts, none will state from such evidence that 'traditional Chinese society was especially tolerant of war'. Nor for that matter will scholars conclude that Chinese society in the past was especially tolerant just because there are records of, for example, romance between talented literati and beauties, literati and prostitutes, the drowning of female children at birth, the binding of feet, etc. In these instances, few researchers invoke 'tolerance' as some sort of explanation, nor do they resort to a nostalgia for the past. We concede that the intention of some of these historical studies may be to enlarge the spaces for homosexual and queer survival in the present. But the 'historical' construction of some pre-colonial generous, tolerant, yin-yang balanced, non-homophobic utopia in the past might inadvertently veil as it facilitates residual modes of feeling and discourse that pass under the name of either traditional virtues (old tolerance/generosity) or new civic virtues (new tolerance/respect). Such a tolerant world-view reticently presupposes and demands a harmonious order that is an absolute priority just as it is a generalized good.

We propose that, in the contemporary gay and lesbian and queer discourses, to construct or to contribute to the construction of an allegedly healthy, liberated, diverse and non-homophobic, traditional Chinese utopian space and time can have the following problematic effects. First, in such narratives, 'China' and 'the West', the present and the past, all become reified entities, with very little relevance to the hybrid complexities of the time-spaces and modes of feelings of contemporary Taiwan, to give but one example. Secondly, the idealization and reification of 'tolerance' in such a historical schema reinforces the suggestion that the imagined tolerance extends from the past into the present. Positing a tradition of tolerance thus demands allegiance and debt-return. Such a demand emanates from a symbolically superior or normative position and is aimed at all those in inferior but especially in dissident or different positions. Thirdly, the invocation of a utopian space refuses to acknowledge that a reticent politics of 'tolerance' is a definite part of everyday public/private life and is a structuring pressure in everyday speech, acts and feelings. These need to be further analysed, especially in terms of how 'tolerance' has become a primary rhetoric in the deployment of reticent power techniques, conveniently awarded an a priori ethical value. In Taiwan, at least, tolerance and reticence as rhetoric and politics are very much in effect, albeit in new 'democratic' guise, and this is so especially for sexual matters, persons and feelings in the family-social continuum.

Lesbian suicide in/as *The Unfilial Daughter*

We will now turn to specific forms of rhetorical and narrative homophobia in Taiwan with an analysis of a recent 'lesbian' novel awarded a major fiction prize. The novel has been seen as part of the 1990s 'fad' in queer cultural objects, and has been denigrated and dismissed for its patently unliterary elements (elements that are too melodramatic and hence fail to measure up to the poetics of reticence).

The Unfilial Daughter (*Ni Nü*) was awarded the best novel prize by the foremost popular press (Huangguan Literary Publishing) in 1996. The novel is a realist *bildungs-roman* in the first person. Its protagonist, literally named Angel (*Tianshi*) grows up in a severely dysfunctional family amidst abject Taipei suburban poverty. Despite the author's disclaimer in her preface, where she warns that she does not mean the novel to be read as a statement to the effect that dysfunctional families in general and abusive mothers in particular will produce a rebel, an unfilial, a lesbian (quasi-T, or butch) daughter; the novel could nonetheless very well be read as an allegory of precisely such a trajectory. It could also be read as rehearsing a dominant narrative logic whereby the wronged daughter's accusation against an abusive mother/family is authorized by her eventual, tragically fated death (albeit 'innocent' death of cancer, not AIDS). Angel's short life is filled with, on the one hand, her silent shame of, resistance to, and attempts to get away from her Holo[14] mother's torrential vocal abuse and performances of victimized motherhood in front of an audience of avidly interested neighbours. The family's primary income derives from the neighbourhood store that Angel's mother manages after her father's retirement. On the other hand, Angel experiences a penchant for tender quiet girls (explicitly stated in the novel as incarnating the antithesis of her mother), and finally falls in love with two girls – one in junior high and one in high school. Later, in college, Angel moves in with her lover, an older woman, and begins hanging out with several other older women in T-bars. At the end of the novel, she dies of cancer, at first suspecting it to be AIDS, unforgiving of the mother who never loved her, surrounded by her lover and friends; that is to say, by her alternative family. In this section, we will focus on just two episodes early in the novel strongly resonant of the reticent homophobia we wish to describe and analyse. In the first episode, Angel and Zhan Qingqing have been caught fully dressed in bed together in their school dorm. The woman disciplinary officer, upon opening the door and seeing them in bed together, immediately orders them to put their clothes on. Their parents are summoned by the disciplinary officers who teach invalid care in girls' schools, but who are also responsible for the student's daily behaviour and appearance.

> Ma came in and immediately pinched me hard on the arm, 'I told you not to live at school but you insisted, now look at what's happened! Your damn father, never takes care of anything, all he knows is to encourage you to live at school, he'd be happiest if you were all to die.' With Ma's moves, everybody knew who she was without need of introduction, *Mr. Zhan's expression clearly said, look at that! With such a perverted family, no wonder the child is abnormal.* The Zhan family on purpose sat far away from us, while the school authorities said that we would both be on surveillance, we would not be allowed to stay in the dorms, and because the semester was almost over, the dorm fees would not be returned either. *Ma did not say much to this, but Mrs. Zhan insisted that I be expelled, so that I would not continue on at school and influence her daughter.* This angered Ma: 'Why insist that my daughter be expelled; as for sleeping, both of them slept, not to mention it was your daughter who came to sleep on my daughter's bed.' *Ma's saying all this nakedly made me feel once again as if I had been stripped of all clothing and exposed in front of everyone. What little self-respect left now entirely gone, I wished I could immediately shrink so small I would completely disappear, and everyone would then forget this humiliatingly disgusting (wuocuo) memory.*
> (Du 1996: 113–114, italics added)

Note how the narrative represents Mr. Zhan's appraisal at a glance of Angel's mother's improper, non-motherly words and behaviour. Mr. Zhan's gaze notes Angel's mother's words and behaviour, which are distinguished by their vulgar non-reticence in terms of class and gender. This non-reticence (its lower-class feminine coding) is one source of Angel's shame of her mother and herself. Sexual perversion is immediately adduced in Mr. Zhan's vision as part of that non-standard class-gender makeup. Secondly, Mrs. Zhan tries to distinguish between the actively perverting Angel, and her own 'innocent' daughter. Mrs. Zhan wants Angel punished so that her daughter may be protected from Angel's contaminating presence. Angel's mother immediately answers with how the two girls are both implicated in having slept together and that since it was Angel's bed they were caught in, then Zhan Qingqing must have been the one who came to Angel's bed. At this point, the narrator writes of wishing to disappear from shame – shame that her mother had actually said the unspeakable (that the two girls had been caught in bed and then, further specifying in whose bed).

For Angel, there is clearly in this scene the double shame of being exposed in homosexual acts, and having her mother exposed as coarsely non-reticent concerning such acts. However, it is precisely her mother's non-reticence that Angel is subsequently able to interpret as ignorance and thus it allows Angel to deny her homosexuality:

> I was silent on the way home. Ma, uncharacteristically, said very little. Perhaps she had never seen me with so severe an expression? On the train, Ma suddenly asked me: 'What is homosexual(ity)? Why do they say that you are a homosexual?' I was taken aback. The word homosexual reverberated like an incessant echo in the empty car with its few occupants. I lifted my eyes and looked around. Fortunately no one had paid attention to Ma's words. Now I understood why Ma's reactions had not been as violent as those of Zhan Qingqing's parents. She did not even understand what exactly homosexuality was, nor its meaning in society. My heart stabilized, and I found myself lying: 'The school doesn't know what it is saying! We were only tired and had slipped back to the dorm for a nap.' 'That simple? Then why is your school so strict as to have us come and take you back home for such a little thing?' Ma didn't seem to quite believe me, and after a moment of silence, she suddenly asked, 'You – should know that what's her name, Qing, is a girl? Or – you wouldn't ignore that you're a girl, would you? Ah?', 'Ma . . .' I said impatiently, 'I've been wearing skirts all these years. Of course I know I'm a girl.' Since Ma didn't seem to know too clearly what she was talking about, I would deny it to the death.
>
> (Du 1996: 116)

Angel's mother's uncharacteristic silence and her final hesitant question suggest the opposite of Angel's conclusion in the novel. Her mother seemed to know what was at issue: gender roles and whether these conform and align with given social demands, and the playing out of those roles 'in bed', that is, in sexual acts and desire. On the other hand, what she seemed not to know, or at least seemed willing to pretend not to know, was how and when to speak and act on such knowledge, especially since, at the school, she had already defended her daughter against the accusations of Zhan Qingqing's mother; they had been on the same side, against class-marked attacks. But Angel is able to turn her mother's hesitation into support for her own silence and denial of any intimacy with Zhan Qingqing.

Zhan Qingqing is not so lucky. The novel does not narrate what happens in her family. However, it is clear that her parents and family conform to middle-class economic and social standards (and Angel's ideal of the beautiful, clean, happy, warm family). At school, in front of outsiders, in accordance with the image projected by their family,

Zhan Qingqing's parents wished to insist on their daughter's innocence and even claimed that their daughter was seduced and influenced by bad elements. Yet, Zhan Qingqing finally commits suicide. In the novel, Angel decides one day to visit Zhan Qingqing's home in order to pay her last respects to her portrait hanging in the hallway with incense burning before it, and to learn why Zhan Qingqing had committed suicide.

> 'If you've finished, please leave. My mother's coming back soon. If she sees you, she'd be really mad.' Zhan Jiaming [Zhan Qingqing's younger brother] opened the door wide, with hand on the knob, and stood very straight, looking as if he was sending off a guest. I wanted to smell a bit more of Zhan Qingqing, to know a bit more of how it was for her before she died: 'Did she say anything?' 'You better go I don't want to hit a girl, if you can count as one. But if you don't leave, I can't promise I won't.' He opened the door wide, and leaned his entire person on it, clearly wanting me to get out immediately. 'Why did Zhan Qingqing do this? Did you force her to do anything?' I insisted on getting an answer, even if I got beaten up. '. . . *No one forced her to do anything, my father told her to go to school, she wouldn't, my mother helped her get into her school uniform and dragged her out of the house. She hadn't yet reached the front door, she'd already undressed naked and wouldn't go out the door*; we all tried to persuade her: she was about to graduate, and must then take the joint entrance exams for college, she should finish her studies. But she wouldn't listen and used a pair of scissors to cut up her uniform. We carried her into the car. Halfway to school she jumped out. We really didn't force her to do anything. We only wanted her to go to school.' 'Didn't force her?' My heart had broken to pieces for the hardship Zhan Qingqing had gone through. '*No! We didn't force her. It's you who killed her!*' Zhan Qingqing's brother insisted.
>
> (Du 1996: 125, italics added)

The reticent mother does not say anything, nor does the daughter. But the normative family wants the daughter to act out her normality by going back to school and reverting to the good student role she had always played so well. It is this, donning the uniform and going back to school, that Zhan Qingqing cannot and will not do – to the extent of pulling off the uniform and cutting it to pieces. The episode represents the silent struggle between parents who would enforce the 'normal order' at all costs, and their daughter, who refuses to conform to their demands formulated as expectations. Suicide is the ultimate and final act of resistance. But even this does not release the family's claim on her; her room is left as if she still inhabited it, and her portrait is put up in remembrance of the beloved daughter. Moreover, the bad element (the outsider, intruder) allegedly responsible for their daughter's 'difference' is allowed in only when the parents are not there, threatened with a beating and finally directly accused of murder. We would like to suggest that, in this case, it is precisely the family's reticence and silent tolerance (*moyan kuanrong*) of Zhan Qingqing's lesbian acts and sentiment, a benevolence and tolerance that is nonetheless forcefully, even violently expressed in making her go back to school for her own sake and for her future good (as if those lesbian acts and sentiments had never happened or been found out), that pushes Zhan Qingqing to just as absolutely reticent a resistance – suicide. We note how Angel's mother acts in direct contrast and reversal of the Zhan family's attitude. Whereas Angel's mother is not loath to admit to the crime in order to protect her daughter from being the only one accused, she is also willing to nominally or rhetorically give her daughter space, for silence and denial if need be. Angel's mother thus shows improper reticence, or non-reticence in public and reticence (silent tolerance) vis-à-vis her daughter; that is, she allows for the maintenance of Angel's 'face' rather than either her own (and by extension the family's) or everyone's (the family-school continuum) good face in the scene at school.

Alternatively, a reading inspired by Eve Sedgwick's (1998) talk on 'Queer Shame' might propose that the Zhan family's very ideal qualities and the appearance of perfect benevolence and tolerance, especially in the face of what happens (the exposure), constitutes the terrible force (of shame) that finally breaks Zhan Qingqing. She is not only responsible for her entire family's efforts at covering up her shame, she must herself play into those efforts by getting into that uniform and going to school as if nothing had happened. Zhan Qingqing's skin, habituated as it is to being admired as the appearance of perfection itself (just as her family seems to be), cannot withstand such a weight of shame; unlike Angel, who has always lived under constant abrasive shaming by her mother, as well as with the constant shame of her mother's non-reticent vulgarities.

Proper or disciplining reticence, the kind enforced in the Zhan family against their daughter, is a kind of force that can bring on unbearable, unliveable shame. Reticence judges and holds responsible, silently demanding a return in kind only by way of indirect speech, with actions and not words. Shame is the lining to reticent textures, and the shade of its shadow. On the other hand, in her direct abusiveness and rare moments of reticence toward her daughter, Angel's mother produces a counter-disciplinary reticence. Angel's mother's ethnic-class and gender attributes do not measure up to what is proper. As a 'native Taiwanese' (Holo) wife to a veteran 'Mainlander' (*waisheng*, literally, outside-province) husband, she is represented in the novel as imprisoned in the political nightmare of an eventual 'return to the Mainland', convinced that she would immediately be left then in the most solitary and absolute destitution. The mother's only outlet is a continuous hysterical demand for 'filiality' in order to ensure the security she can never feel. She does not seem to understand the rules of reticence (perhaps fully knowing how these can never work to her advantage), nor does she have the cultural resources to play that game. She is thus caricatured in the novel in the farcical and despicable role of someone who insists on disturbing the quiet order of things (Angel's family, the scene at school). At the same time, she is portrayed as pitiable and ultimately tolerated but despised for having produced, through her very ineptness and unrestraint, a lesbian daughter (veritably and literally in the novel, her own special form of punishment). This may partially explain the suicide of Zhan Qingqing, a lesbian from a 'model' family. Angel, on the other hand, seems to withstand the humiliation of being found out and, later, of going back to school. On the thematic level, the novel seems to represent how a family not versed in the game and rules of reticence might inadvertently provide the necessary gaps and holes for survival of the improper kids with non-orthodox tendencies, while the non-reticent conflicts and fights that occur in Angel's family paradoxically allow for differences to sprout and strengthen. Yet, as we have earlier shown, one instance of Angel's agential 'denial' of homosexuality is produced through the base mother's uncharacteristic and improper reticent tolerance of Angel's homosexuality. Angel's lesbianism as we shall see in the next section is partially transposed at the level of narrative reticence into punishment as well as ultimately authorizing Angel as the narrator's unfilial accusation of the 'bad mother'. This might be seen to constitute the penumbric status of Angel's role and function in the narrative.

If the Zhan family's ideal 'reticent' mode of upbringing constitutes precisely that force onto the surface of which is limned a most virulent homophobic effect, the narrative itself and its implicit reader-critic likewise are afforded the possibility of avoiding any form of direct censure or repression of homosexuality. Yet, the narrative and its implied reader-critic participate in an implicit narrative erasure, censure and de-valorization tantamount, we would claim, to a gentle homophobia.

Narrative reticence and class-ethnic-sexual vileness

In contrast to Zhan Qingqing's story, Angel's story is the novel's main narrative focus. Her story is also the implied reader's primary site of investment and concern. Such an implied reader might be seen as exemplified in Zhang Man Juan's preface to the novel.[15] In her symptomatic reading, (Zhan Qingqing and Angel's) homosexuality is accorded a certain sideline 'place', a by-the-way value and the particularly gentle homophobic force of that place and that value (in the hierarchy of things and values narrated). We are not saying that Zhang Man Juan is homophobic, but rather, that the coincidence of her reading together with the novel's own narrative logic constitute the novel's complex, conflict-ridden thematic/subjective sensibility. This coincidence rehearses homosexuality as incidental to the narrative, a by-product of a class-ethnic-gender vileness (baseness) residing in and motivating the daughter Angel's reticent narrative revenge: Angel's own death by cancer outside of the story proper, eaten away with a class-ethnic-gender hatred and shame directed at her mother, the 'vile' (base) libidinal centre of the story.

The novel's narrative voice is very close to the point of sometimes becoming one with the narrator's (Angel's) voice. This accounts for Zhang Man Juan's reading of the novel as 'almost approximating the reading of a biographical record in its ability to startle the heart'. What we would like to pursue here, however, is what exactly is the relation posited in such a reading between 'being a homosexual' and 'being in a dysfunctional family'? How does the representation of Angel's lesbianism both nurture and serve the narrative's positing of an either perfect or dysfunctional familial sentiment? What does the repetitive detail of Angel's 'sense of vileness' (*wuocuo gan*) have to do with the politics of desire within a family mired in poverty and whose libidinal centre is a mother whose class/ethnicity is marked as the source and motor of all vileness and is simultaneously held accountable for the formation of her daughter's homosexual desire? How is an arguably class/ethnically shaded 'sense of dirt' or vileness transformed into yet another matrix for a narrative homosexual contingency and/or homophobic displacement?

In a very short preface at the beginning of her narrative, the narrator recalls a translated (foreign) story in a newspaper,

> The novel was about an aristocratic European woman whose relation to her husband was not intimate, whereupon she became dependent upon her son as if he was her lover, I was shocked mute by such a relation within the family, and felt that it was so vile . . .

I forgot the ending of the story, but *that paradoxical sense of vileness has miraculously stayed with me, and influenced my whole life.*

(Du 1996: 9, italics added)

The narrative of *The Unfilial Daughter* begins with recalling the memory of an ineradicable familial-incestuous (mother-son) vileness. It is then the representation of the continuing recurrence of this sense of vileness that allows the narrator finally to become freed or cleansed, and the same process seems to hold for the 'implied reader' according to Zhang Man Juan's preface: 'Because the writer's writing is of such a degree of accuracy, its power to startle our heart is like that of a biographical record. And because of the writer's generosity and tolerance in the denouement of her novel, the reader's soul is cleansed in the {narrator's} tragedy, and is left soft and bright' (Du 1996: 125). How might we then understand this 'sense of vileness' that so disturbs, that forecloses (for the narrator, but also for the reader) a settled, stable place in the world, that it must be evoked repeatedly?

One of the sites where vileness marks the narrative is Angel's memory of the grocery store; the grocery store that feels much more like the property and domain of her mother than of her emasculated father. Another site of vileness lies in memories of her mother's and her own femininity: puberty, bras and the onset of menstruation.

I looked around at the crowded and dirty grocery store, with all the merchandise chaotically piled one on top of the other up to the ceiling, and rows and rows of merchandise with only room enough for one person in between. The space beneath these rows and rows of goods was filled with empty bottles, soda bottles, juice bottles . . . The soured smell of these things combined with the smell of various marinated vegetables and beans, one couldn't tell what kind of smell exactly, one could only feel the intense thickness of the atmosphere, so thick and damp that one could feel its obstruction as one tried to walk through it. An indescribable pressure would suddenly descend upon me, making me feel frustrated and suffocated. Especially after I had been to Qiao Mengling's home, and seen that home could be so wonderful, with this comparison in mind, my own home became even more awful and unbearable. I was suddenly overwhelmed by anger, 'the food at other people's is better. When I visit my classmates, her mother even makes coffee for me!'

(Du 1996: 46)

The client had walked away, but Ma was still angry and, stamping her feet, said: '*Has your spirit flown to the mainland?* You stupid not-willing-to-die old thing!' Ma stopped for a moment, I thought she'd finished, but she went on: 'Useless is useless, useless outside, useless at home . . . useless even in bed . . .' That last phrase Ma said in a very low voice, almost like she was complaining. I wondered at that time what being useful in bed might mean. Dad just lowered his head, as if nothing had happened, and began to sort out the string that would tie the empty bottles together. Ma spit another mouthful, and finally went into the kitchen. I could not bear to watch Dad's expression, and returned to the toilet, but this time I could no longer shit a thing.

(Du 1996: 18, italics added)

I opened the bag and saw two bras and one menstruation underpants. I lifted my eyes and saw Ma's high breasts and fat hips as she squatted at the doorway picking vegetable leaves. Suddenly I realized that Ma and I were both women. Before this she was only a mother and me only a kid; that last time she said something about 'useless even in bed,' that phrase suddenly seemed to rise in my mind hot and scalding my cheeks red. I was so ashamed for Ma. I felt that a mother should really not say such improper things.

(Du 1996: 74)

From the above quotes, it is clear that the grocery in its mixture of smells and constriction of space is a vile place. Vile is the mother as well, especially when in frustration and anger she speaks of (even if with a lowered voice) the father's sexual impotence. The vileness of these persons and time-space are what Angel is fated to carry with her, unable to escape, as if she were haunted. In the last quote, when Angel's mother is once (twice in the narrative) uncharacteristically reticent, and shows attentiveness toward Angel (third quotation), she gives Angel two bras and one pair of menstruation underpants. Angel again feels ashamed, this time at her mother's ugly feminine body: her bad-looking figure, improper posture. This is a strange, queer section. All we can be sure of are the gaps left in Angel's narrative: her escape, the narrative's ducking, and how her memory acts much the way it did that time she narrates her ride home with her mother when she was caught in bed with Zhan Qingqing in high school. On both occasions, her mother speaks to her with care, uncharacteristically reticent, something that never happens anywhere else in the novel. Both times, her mother speaks barely at all, of things having to do with sex (sleeping with girls, signs of puberty).

These passages contain a distillation of the complicated, contradictory vileness Angel carries with her through her short life: disgust-desire for her class-ethnically debased mother and sympathy for and empathy with her father (in his economic failure and sexual impotence vis-à-vis his wife?). The narrative does not finally resolve this bundle of vile feeling. Angel merely writes of hoping to take it all away with her, unto death, thereby cleansing herself, the narrative, even the reader (if correctly positioned). In Angel's narrative and in her memories, her homosexual desire seems not to be a major part of this abiding vileness that lies just beneath her skin. Only when Maggie, one of Angel's lovers, transforms into her mother, does Angel look at her with disgust. In a similar move, homosexual feelings and acts seem finally not the novel's most pressing concern. Early in the novel, Angel comments retrospectively on the mores of the town in which she grew up:

In comparison with homosexuals, perhaps it is heterosexuals who are so incredible and strange in ways one cannot understand at all? Or is it that the human ability to compromise with reality has developed to unforeseen lengths?

(Du 1996: 19)

The phrase 'in comparison with homosexuals' might shock orthodox, straight-minded readers. Yet this phrase, ostensibly reversing the hierarchy of seeing and judging, merely makes homosexuality into a corrective mirror for misbehaving heterosexuals. In one kind of reading, this would be more or less how homosexuality figures in and as *The*

Unfilial Daughter. Angel would thus serve, like cancer (and AIDS), to carry an even more unspeakable, because more hierarchically valued, indictment of Angel's resentment of, and revenge against, her class-ethnic-gender debased mother.

In such a reading, vileness and baseness derive primarily from economic-ethnic and gender impropriety and humiliation, while gender humiliation would subsume Angel's homosexual desiring formation. That is, the humiliation of gender and homosexuality occupy the same site, with differentiated density and valuation. In the narrative's latter part especially, homosexuality and cancer both serve to 'prove' Angel's tragic fate as an unfortunate 'quirk' of heredity. According to such a narrative hierarchical logic, although both homosexuality and cancer may lead to death, both need to be 'tolerantly understood' rather than blamed, since neither is at fault. Rather, the family and the mother are what must be faulted and made responsible (while at the same time occupying the most time and space in terms of narrative economy and narrative desire).

> Angel is on the brink of death, yet she insists on going back home to see the mother who had brought her up and yet was like an enemy to her. This is the entire story's most shattering moment.
>
> *A mother still possessed by evil, a daughter physically destroyed breathing her last thin breath finally pass each other by without recognition.*
>
> Perhaps they have never known each other.
>
> 'I now realize that I am fundamentally someone who absolutely loves the home/family, because of too much love; its pain makes me all the more brokenhearted; desperate, hopeless, I finally left home, and yet I have never been able to shed its shadow.'
>
> Because the author's descriptive powers are so accurate, the reader experiences the shock of reading a [historical] record; and *because the author's arrangement for the denouement is so tolerant and understanding, the reader's heart is left soft and smooth, having been cleansed in the tragedy.*
>
> (Du 1996: 4–5, italics added)

In the above quotation from her preface to Du Xioulan's *The Unfilial Daughter*, the famous romance writer Zhang Man Juan notes the most memorable, touching, shattering moment in the whole novel as occurring at the very end. Angel is near death, and asks her friends to take her back for a last meeting and possible reconciliation with her mother. She arrives only to overhear from the car her mother angry and bitter as ever, saying to neighbours passing by: '*Talking about that dead-waisheng {mainlander} –pig {her father}, he sure won't get a good death, that one, you don't know how he hooked up with that daughter of mine and, together, kept me crushed under their feet*, only this low-down doesn't-want-a-face man would give birth to that not-even-an-animal-or-a-pig-or-a-dog kind of daughter [. . .] People would laugh so if only they knew, [how she is] living with a group of girl-vamps[16] doing unspeakable things, how people would laugh! Even got together with those girl-vamps to force me, her old mother, away.' At this point Angel immediately decides to leave, without even getting out of the car.

One of the uses of a preface is to indicate how the novel might best (most literarily) be read, or conversely and more rarely, how novels might not measure up, but have redeeming features nevertheless (Genette 1987). To read, as Zhang Man Juan does in her preface to this prize-winning novel, its most touching moment as that of its closure, when Angel wants to but finally cannot forgive or reconcile with her mother, is to make a number of claims for the novel. First, that for the novel, and for the 'correct' reader and reading, the relations between Angel and her mother constitute the central subject of the narrative. Secondly, and following on from that, the novel is then about the doubly unspeakable possibility, in the familial ethical and generational order as well as in contemporary class-ethnic politics, that the mother has done the family and the daughter irreparable harm; with the daughter transposing onto the mother everything vile about poverty and class-ethnic-gender/sexual shame. Thirdly, the narrative is not reticent about these supposed wrongdoings of the mother (the mother's vulgar abusiveness and lack of all proper restraint in manner and speech); however, it is reticently certain, as is its model reader-critic, how these wrongdoings are punished and the wrongdoer exposed. The wrongdoer being the mother, she can only be indicted (in perfect reticent mode) most effectively and finally through the bodies and actions of her children. The daughter who, as Zhang quotes, 'absolutely loves the home/family', is yet prevented *by her mother* from ever returning home, or from ever forming a satisfactory alternative home in the form of lesbian relationships. (The pop psychology explanation given by the narrative throughout the novel is that Angel seeks her mother's opposite yet substitute figure in all of her girlfriends, resenting them at the same time for motherly possessiveness). Zhang Man Juan affirms the lasting (shock) value of this novel by reading it as a narrative indictment of a mother's devastating impact on a daughter's life. It is as if Zhang Man Juan were affirming a narrative logic that constitutes the daughter's tragedy (lesbian loves and death-dealing cancer in the body) as directly caused by the lack of a properly reticent family (i.e. maternal) love and intimacy. Poverty and class, intra-familial ethnic and gender-sexual conditions and injustices are simultaneously erased, from both narrative and its concomitant reticent readings.

There is in such a reading the reversed finger-pointing and assigning of sole responsibility (for harm and hurt to some previously imagined ideal familial/social order) that in the narrative itself effectively pushes Zhan Qingqing to reticent retaliation in the form of suicide. Just as Zhan Qingqing is accused by the school and by her family of somehow being responsible for disorder and thus in need of rehabilitation, so too, Zhang Man Juan and the narrative together 'accuse' the Holo mother of failure correctly to nurture her children into productive adulthood and proper (middle-class heterosexual) emotional as well as physical lives. All three of her children are monsters of some sort, though at the same time, their monstrosity *serves primarily the narrative's ethical logic of indicting that mother who cannot be called monstrous, and whose supposed monstrosity cannot be specified or can only be hinted at in its class-ethnic formation.* Angel does not, cannot forgive her mother at the end, but she has once again proven and shown her mother's 'evil' in speech overheard (by Angel, by the readers). Having shown this, she *must* die of cancer, so as to prove herself innocent of simply wanting revenge by recording such a story. Only thus, when the daughter is so good as not even to want revenge after abuse, can the critic-reader assure us that our hearts will be left cleansed and smooth. Angel's hurts have been avenged, better yet, simultaneously vindicated, justified.

The problem, of course, is that in vindicating Angel's narrative revenge via self-punishment (an improbable and homophobic AIDS that turns into terminal cancer), the critic-reader simultaneously upholds the reticent strategies of familial power that killed Zhan Qingqing. If we concur with the narrative in feeling that the mother is to blame for Angel's cancer, then Zhan Qingqing too must die. But whereas Angel's death (withheld in the novel, but nevertheless certain) is tragic, Zhan Qingqing's is merely pitiful (and somehow weak), her death is insufficient if not wrongly motivated. In short, in the most damning of judgements, her death is denied value. The narrative's detailing of certain of Zhan Qingqing's actions as told to Angel by Zhan Qingqing's brother already hint at Zhan Qingqing's own mental disorder: she takes off all her clothing, she jumps out of the car, she kills herself. She is deranged; therefore her suicide is somehow on a continuum with abnormal actions, from her lesbianism to her silent refusal to rejoin the world of the normal (put on her uniform, go back to school). It is *not* her family's fault, for they have been ever so gentle with her all along; except perhaps in wanting her to keep up appearances almost at any cost (eventually, even at the cost of her life). Thus, the fault or weakness that leads to death by suicide must lie in Zhan Qingqing herself, or so the narrative implies. Only Angel knows different: Angel knows Zhan Qingqing was pushed to madness and death by the same reticence that makes her brother refrain from beating Angel up. This is after all a well-behaved family.

Angel's own death is similarly (despite her mother and her upbringing) well behaved or proper: it is not narrated in the novel. It ensures the critic-reader's (and most readers') empathy with Angel's tragic life. Importantly, it agrees with Angel's incrimination of her mother's class-ethnically marked non-reticent behaviour. In facilitating such a reticent allegorical reading, Angel's terminal cancer becomes the material *implantation* of improper and insufficient maternal nurture. In this sense, her implied narrative death is fully and sufficiently, even ethically, motivated. It allows for a reticent punishing of an 'empowered' culprit (parents are never wrong; so goes a received Confucian saying; something that has had to be reformulated to accommodate the realities of modern-day child abuse) from a position of lesser power. At the same time it absolves the lesser-powered accuser of any infraction of the familial order, since she too must die.

No such narrative absolution is available in reading Zhan Qingqing's death. Zhan Qingqing's suicide is shamefully not reticent (apart from its displacement of speech with action): it is sudden, bloody (Angel notes the traces of blood on the ceiling when she visits), and forces those who are intimate or associated with her to seek for and give explanations. All are implicated; suicide is disorder. The brother and family are sure that Angel killed her (by falling in love with her and having a relationship with her: the beginning of Zhan Qingqing's going astray). Angel knows that it is the family that has killed her (by accepting Zhan Qingqing's going astray only to the extent that she will be making up for it ever after). Zhan Qingqing's last heard voice in the novel is a piercing goodbye to Angel, while being dragged away by her parents after they are caught at school. Two days after hearing of Zhan Qingqing's suicide, Angel receives a letter from her. 'We do not hurt other people, why do they hurt us? I am leaving [this world, before you].'

For Zhan Qingqing's death to be read as tragic and actively accusatory would need a reading *against the grain of reticence*: the novel's own, as well as its prefacer's reticence, that is, their joint valorization of precisely those familial values that effortlessly kill Zhan Qingqing. 'They' are indeed out to maim 'us', only in such a way that will at best leave not even a trace of shame, excepting the shame of unexplained, unjustified and unjustifiable death. But then, that can always be contained, explained away as merely a weakness of, and in, the already dead. The wording of Zhan Qingqing's letter, on the other hand, could be read as precisely shaming, as accusing those who have hurt her (without word or blow) for the reticent discipline that has forced her to leave before her time. The wording of her reproach recalls that of a real life letter left by two high school seniors from the best girls' high school in Taiwan. This letter was found after the two had committed suicide (by inhaling poisonous gases) on 26 July 1994 in the bathroom of a (love) hotel in Yilan.[17] 'Society's nature does not suit us', says the letter. This phrase aroused a furore of controversy and interpretation in the media. We would rephrase it as, 'society's *order* does not suit us' and thereby mark both the reticent discipline and the reticent countering of that discipline in their joint suicide and in that cryptic sentence.

We now return to Chou Wah-Shan, partly because his most recent book directly connects historical interpretation and contemporary movement strategies and discourses. In an anecdote showing how, despite (post) colonialism, Hong Kong homophobia cannot but be gentler and nicer than its counterpart in more violently repressed and repressive western societies, Chou Wah-Shan writes of how very few gays and lesbians lose their jobs because of their sexual orientation. For 'even if the boss is very homophobic, he will understand (enough) to fire his gay employee for "unsatisfactory work", and as there is no need at all to broach [the issue of] gay identity', therefore the employee will not have been outed (Chou 1997: 383).

The giveaway line of course is how '[the employer] too will understand enough' (*ye dong de*), or more accurately, 'be understanding enough' to fire the employee in such a way as to 'keep' the latter's homosexuality invisible. In fact, what is happening in the very writing of this little story, is how Chou Wah-Shan interprets the boss's homophobic firing in the gentler, nicer light of silent words and reticent tolerance! What is maintained in such reticence is the very social order that can, without having to resort to overt violence, 'repress' its homosexual members. Order is preserved by (1) the magnanimity of a reticent firing, and (2) the warning it serves to the person concerned that he/she is already potentially vulnerable to becoming 'visible', and therefore must make more effort to tow the line (of invisibility) in the future. What actually already amounts to an act of sexual discrimination (the firing) is discreetly deferred: a threatened homophobic firing is forestalled by way of a preventive dismissal that then becomes (is recalled as) an act of generous, gentle tolerance on the part of the employer who understands 'enough' not to fire his employee for homosexuality. Strangely, in order to prove the gentleness of Hong Kong homophobia, Chou's narrative will go so far as to entirely concur with the well-meaning of the preventive reticence that has occurred and whose effect is homophobic insofar as it works to preserve the social order as is.[18]

We note here two levels of a reticent deployment of homophobic repression. The first is that of the employer who 'understands enough' not to fire his employee for homosexuality, but rather for unsatisfactory work. We suggest that what this employer understands are precisely the invisibility and unspeakability of anything having to do with homosexuality. The second level is Chou's reading of the episode. In one sentence, Chou registers the reticence of the employer in the act of firing a sexually improper employee and his own approbation of such reticence as evidence of a uniquely 'Chinese' virtue.

We suggest that reticence in this case allows for the reigning proper order in speech and action (at work, at home, in the socius) to sustain the notion of an untouched, unsullied, harmonious whole. Nothing as it should be has been changed or disturbed; at least not on the surface. The employee alone bears the warning that has been given *in silence*, through the very fact of a firing that only he/she and the employer know to have other reasons besides the speakable ones. The order of things whereby some things are more speakable than others and therefore allow those unspeakable things to remain in the shadow 'where they belong' – *this* order is what is preserved.

We further suggest that cooperating in the preservation of such an order has itself homophobic effects to the extent that its very preservation in a narrative as influential as Chou's will allow for the continued spawning of just this sort of benevolence and reticent good will, with its especial containing force in the areas of personal sexual and affective behaviour. Chou writes as if containment itself (*baorong*) were not in this particular 'Chinese' space/time a sufficiently effective form of homophobia and discrimination.

It may, and no doubt will, be objected that such a reading gives neither credit nor place to the space-making effects of the employer's reticent ploys, not to mention the very possibly well-intended commitment to 'traditional' tolerance in his sentimental make-up.[19] We are nonetheless interested in forcing such a reading precisely in order to prize open and peel away the very finely tuned socio-ethical practices that effectively turn a discriminatory homophobia into a morally valorized rhetoric of reticent tolerance. It is in the face of such a strategy of social containment, relegating social-familial shades to their proper non-places in the micro-politics of everyday life that Ni Jiazhen passionately can ask: 'Can only orphans consider coming out here?' What is it in the famous 'traditional' tolerance and reticence of everyday life in/with the family that makes it impossible, that silently creates no room, no space, for gays and lesbians and bisexuals and transgendered people to be heard and seen? How is it that in one of the main ways to fight back at these reticent containment techniques, one apparently has to adopt equally, albeit differently, reticent tactics, to the extent that Wei-cheng R. Chu has asked whether these convoluted techniques of 'successfully coming out to one's family' can be termed 'coming out' at all? Isn't it time to forge another paradigm, other models of thinking, acting and feeling enabling and empowering non-reticent acts and feelings, allowing non-reticent lives to articulate the challenging legitimacy of their spaces?

Penumbrae query shadow

Penumbra said to Shadow, 'A little while ago you were walking and now you're standing still; a little while ago you were sitting and now you're standing up. Why this lack of independent action [*tecao*]?'

Shadow said, 'Do I have to wait for something before I can be like this? Does what I wait for also have to wait for something before it can be like this? Am I waiting for the scales of a snake or the wings of a cicada? How do I know why it is so? How do I know why it isn't so?'

Penumbrae once asked Shadow, 'A little while ago you were looking down and now you're looking up, a little while ago your hair was bound up and now it's hanging loose, a little while ago you were sitting and now you're standing up, a little while ago you were walking and now you're still – why is this?'

Shadow said, 'Quibble, quibble! Why bother asking about such things? I have them but I don't know how. I'm the shell of the cicada, the cast-off skin of the snake – like them and yet not like them. In firelight or sunlight I draw together, in darkness or night I fade away. Am I not dependent on the substance from which I am thrown? And that substance is itself dependent on something else! When it comes, I come with it; when it goes, I go with it. When it comes under the influence of the strong Yang, I come under the same. Since we are both produced by that strong Yang, what occasion is there for you to question me?'[20]

This well-known fable from Zhuangzi appears in 'Making All Things Equal' and 'Fables' in the above two slightly different versions. In the exegetical traditions, Guo Xiang has annotated *wangliang* (shade, penumbrae) as 'the slight shade outlining a shadow'. The character *ying* is in some ancient sources *ying*, what today is termed *yingzi*, that is, shadow.

According to ancient exegeses, this is a fable that explicates a philosophical thought by way of the question-answer between penumbrae and shadow. We will here forget for the moment any ancient or mystic philosophy and return to this staging of a question and answer between penumbrae and shadow. As subjects of speech in everyday life in the present moment, we have become used to listening to 'form-substance' (*xing*) speak, while shadow which follows substance is usually thought of as less than subject. Shadow is the darkness that follows or attends upon form-substance when and where there is light. Shadow comes together and changes following substance and light. Not only does shadow not have self-autonomy, she lacks constancy and loyalty. Time, space, light, direction, distance and speed can all make her change, like the rudder of a boat in strong wind. Yet, should one want to get rid of shadow in the manner of throwing away an old shoe, one will find that she cannot be trampled into disappearance. As long as there is light, shadow is that silent darkness that cannot be shed. When substance runs from shadow in the light of day, substance can run to the death, shadow would still be there, unless substance were to enter into darkness, too. Penumbra, that slight shade outlining shadow, the shadow of a shadow, is that nothing or no-matter that everyone had almost forgotten. Penumbra is too far away from substance to be seen or discerned. Penumbra, or *wangliang*, is not a common usage; it has nothing to do with the language of the everyday. We need a dictionary, an exegetical text, to understand what it means; many have come to know the term first, and then turned to examine their shadow. Besides the shadow, which is without subjectivity, there is penumbra that is even less a subject. If penumbra's existence is hard to detect, then, penumbra's followings, its attendances or lack of independence, its transformations, its lack of integrity, all of these are even more difficult to know. All blurred indeterminacies that cannot be named are termed 'penumbrae' in the plural (*zhong wangliang*). Penumbra, or *wangliang* are seen as not having character(istics) while their form-substance cannot be outlined. They remain in the margin of shadow where people cannot see them, stealing a life (*gouqie tousheng*).

And yet, this story has it so that *wangliang* should ask a question!

Has shadow answered her question? If shadow represents the voice of Zhuangzi in the fable, then, she speaks of the Zhuangzi philosophy of non-dependence or non-attendance (*wudai*) and self-transformation (*duhua*). But whose or what question has shadow answered? Has shadow heard penumbra, can shadow understand penumbra's questions?

Substance never appears in this fable, yet s/he is everywhere (addressed), in the text, in the readings and exegeses, but also in the answer given by shadow. Shadow's thought, her speech, are all addressed to substance. In relation to substance, perhaps shadow is speaking of another inter-subjective mode of thought. But does this mode of thought answer penumbra's question? Penumbra's conditions of existence are different from that of shadow. Perhaps penumbra admires how shadow constantly transforms; or penumbra is curious about shadow's changing postures and hairdo. Penumbra may well have its own particular mode of 'independent action' (*tecao*, 'hold onto')[21] and wants to share this with shadow. Perhaps the dependency or attendance that shadow speaks of is a familiar story or condition of existence or irrelevant philosophy for penumbra. Penumbra's question, on the other hand, is about 'independent action'. Shadow cannot see this and does not understand. Yet, in being questioned and in shadow's answer and rethinking of the question, penumbra's questions inspire and incite shadow while completing shadow's alternative (to substance's) subjectivity.

Penumbra continues to question, again and again.

The many effects of homophobic forces, like shadow in Zhuangzi's fable, must be questioned. But the answers must also be read anew, rethought, so that that which is reticent might be formulated and spoken. Reticence of course has its own reversal and resistant forces. Whether or not the latter can take effect as a counter-directional form of reticence, awaits continued publicizing of that initial reticent force. In the past, to speak up against dominant reticent techniques of power was invariably to risk accusation of resorting to despised and inferior tactics. Such would be the case of fictional femme fatale Pan Jinlian, the adulteress-murderer, who is extremely adept at mimicking her foes and revealing their machinations in fantastic stories, thus 'stealing a life' for as long as possible. Figures such as Pan Jinlian will not commit suicide in proper self-regarding shame (*zhichi*). In the story that is said to be hers, she is eventually literally carved up by a hero loyal to the Chinese masculine code of brotherly honour so that he can examine whether the adulteress has the heart and liver of an animal. Zhan Qingqing is no less agentially desiring than Pan Jinlian but Zhan Qingqing is born into a model nuclear family (Pan Jinlian is sold into domestic bondservice as a child to a wealthy merchant). Moreover, Zhan Qingqing is well brought up, has thinner face-skin, and is represented as 'holding onto' proper self-regard and shame, only finally to commit suicide. Her action counters as much as it completes the Zhan family, from which she disappears in the body but at the same time, from which she will never be quite released as ghost.[22] How reticently counter-reticent: to complete the model family, return it to wholeness, and simultaneously enact the most injurious mode of accusation, one that shames the entire family and holds it accountable to all.

Notes

1 This paper grew out of the Crossroads in Cultural Studies Conference Panel (June 1998) that we attended with funding from the National Science Research Council of Taiwan. An earlier Chinese version of this paper appeared in *Working Papers in Gender/Sexuality Studies*, Nos. 3 & 4, pp. 109–155, October 1998. The work of Tsai Ying-chun has inspired a large part of the paper. We are deeply grateful to Amie Parry, David Barton, Chen Kuan-hsing, Waiter, Mei Chia-ling, Wang Ping, Cindy Patton, Anne Cheng, Tejaswini Niranjana, Ashish Rajadhyaksha, Vivek Dhareshwar, Teri Silvio, Lin Wen-ling, Yang Fangchi and Yau Ching, all of whom have commented on versions of the paper. Finally, we thank the anonymous reviewers for IACS for meticulous corrections and invaluable criticism. All errors remain our own.

2 Our readings in this paper and all references are to this Chinese edition. For Chou Wah-Shan's work in English, please see Chou (2000).

3 Samshasha's 1984 *Zhongguo Tongxingai Shilu* is probably the first response to the early 1980s discourse of 'Homosexuality is this evil colonial thing' in Hong Kong. 'My book was a response to all that. In my book I argued that homophobia, not homosexuality, had been imported to Hong Kong by the colonialists! Although now I don't have that view and have revised it in the new edition. But at that time I used this argument a lot as a kind of political weapon against all those Chinese who were saying homosexuality was this foreign vice.' (59) 'In the [revised] new book [1997] I show that yes, we Chinese did already have homophobic attitudes *but not so obvious and not so severe* as in the Western world because we don't have Christianity [. . .]. The source of Chinese homophobia is different. In Chinese society your body has to be a procreation tool to continue the family line. It's a totally different situation from the modern West where "gay is gay", you know, full stop. In China, Japan, Korea and even in Thailand, there is this idea that "OK you're gay – so what? *You still have to produce children*"' (72, italics added). Our essay takes up from that last statement: 'You still have to produce children' and how it demands non-difference and conformity. From 'Interview with Samshasha, Hong Kong's First Gay Rights Activist and Author' conducted and presented by Mark McLelland, http://wwwsshe.murdoch. edu.au/intersections/issue4/ interview_mclelland.html (download 16 July 2004).

4 As suggested by Amie Parry at the Crossroads Conference in Finland.

5 In January 2004, the Center for the Study of Sexuality held a workshop in Guangzhou, China, where DNF presented this essay. In the spring and fall semesters of 2004, LJP used this essay in a gender and sexuality theories course at Tsing-Hua University, Hsinchu, Taiwan.

6 See also Tsai (1997), especially Chapter Five.

7 By Herbert A. Giles, Wai-lim Yip and Pauline Yu respectively. See Tsai (1997: 307).

8 See also Note 5.

9 As to Confucius on the ethics and uses of poetry, see especially Holzman (1978: 29–38). According to Tsai (1997), Holzman holds that one of the reasons China did not have a literary criticism in the style of the 'West' is because Confucius was not a good critic. This roused great anger on the part of C. H. Yang who retorted in a book review of Holzman's book that such a pronouncement is neither here nor there because 'Confucius never wanted to be a literary critic'.

10 'Great Preface (Daxu)' to the *Mao Text of the Book of Songs*.

11 The *Doctrine of the Means*, p. 98.

12 This is from the title of a talk and book by D.A. Miller (1998), *Place for Us: Essay on the Broadway Musical*.

13 Such a trend in recent Chinese gender research is best exemplified in the works of Sun Kang-Yi (1998), who has emphasized a Chinese traditional female and feminine world that is more 'equal' than 'Western' gender equality. Even more paradoxical is how a position ostensibly stressing the agency of minoritarian subjects in the past (in research and writing) will often refuse to concede that same agency to (certain) minoritarian subjects in the present (as in the case of Taipei's licensed prostitutes movement, for example).

14 In 'The Mirror and The Window of Taiwan History,' (*Taiwan News*, 5 March 2001; Taiwan's bilingual news website, http://www.etaiwannews.com/Viewpoint/), historian Tai Pao-tsun writes:

> The Han people all immigrated to Taiwan from mainland China, but immigration is divided into different stages. In the seventeenth century, waves of poverty-stricken people from Fujian and Guangdong, continued to brave the Taiwan Strait to come to Taiwan, and because they came from different hometowns, and spoke different languages and practiced different customs, there was a distinction between Holo and Hakka. Holo speakers currently make up around 70% of the population, while Hakka speakers make up around 15%. Hakka speakers are concentrated around Taoyuan, Hsinchu, Miaoli, Pingtung and Hualien. The Holo and Hakka languages are mutually unintelligible, and their speakers have different beliefs and customs. Even within the Holo and Hakka languages, there are different accents and dialects, and so we have this complex phenomenon of Taiwan ethnic groups based on language. In 1949, the government of the Republic of China moved to Taiwan and proceeded to govern it, bringing over around 1.5 million people from every province in China, mainly

from the professional (i.e. military, civil service or teaching professions) population. [These people speak Mandarin Chinese with a variety of accents and varying degrees of fluency]. This later period of immigrants are known as 'Waisheng Ren,' literally, 'people from out of province,' and they have had a very deep influence on politics and society in modern-day Taiwan. The 'Waisheng Ren' [rendered Mainlanders in this essay] and the 'Bensheng Ren' (literally, 'people from this province') had very different languages, lifestyles, customs and political and social activities. Bensheng Ren often call themselves 'yams,' and use the name 'taro' for the Waisheng Ren. Now, after several decades of social interaction, it's no exaggeration to say that Taiwan has countless numbers of 'yam-taros' born to Bensheng Ren and Waisheng Ren parents. As a result, Taiwan society has developed the special characteristics of an immigrant society, with its multiculturalism and constant interaction between ethnic groups (http://www.twcenter.org.tw/e02/20010305.htm, download October 19, 2004).

The Unfilial Daughter represents Angel as one of these 'yam-taros' with a lower-class Mainlander or Waisheng veteran father and Holo mother while marking the cultural and class stigmatization of Holo language and people under KMT rule through the narrative's (and the narrator's) debasing of Angel's mother's class and ethnic traits as well as the latter's translation into undesirable femininity and sexuality.

15 Zhang Man Juan is one of Taiwan's best-known and most popular romance writers; she also teaches Chinese literature at Soochow University, Taiwan.

16 The term used here is yao jing, as in monstrous-essence. For this term's specifically denigrating and gay connotations, we are indebted to Hans Tao-ming Huang, unpublished paper, 1997.

17 For a fine reading of this incident and the media's subsequent effective erasure of even the possibility of a romantic (i.e. lesbian) suicide and how such a notion itself would constitute shame and smirching of the 'innocence' of two of the best and most intelligent of Taiwan's high-school students, see Lee Heuy-ling's unpublished essay. Note especially the reticent rhetorical techniques whereby the lovers' suicide is accorded a more elevated and valorized interpretation than mere romance: we are granting them the greater wisdom of a philosophically motivated death, how ungenerous of you to translate that into mere homophobia.

18 This is not the first time, nor the single instance of otherwise progressive persons and politics resorting to the reticent rhetoric of tolerance in the face of, and to veil over, actions with homophobic effect if not intent. An example too close to home is the firing in November 1997 of two lesbian-queer full-time staff from a feminist organization in Taipei, and the subsequent organization newsletter devoting an entire issue (February 1998) to this scandalous affair, appropriately entitled 'If Only [We] Could Choose Silence' wherein one of the board members writes: 'To this day, I still feel that whether in terms of the discussion of issues or in interpersonal relations, the Awakening Foundation has shown the greatest [possible] sincerity and tolerance' (Awakening Foundation Newsletter [Funu Xinzhi Tongxun], Issue 186, February 1998).

19 It is important to note how the active construction of 'reticent tolerance' in this case by Chou Wah-Shan's discourse as 'essentially' 'Chinese' produces a particular 'reticent tolerance' as 'Chinese', whereas it could also be recognized as being articulated to other kinds of homophobic strategies and effects elsewhere, as represented, for example, in the Hollywood film Philadelphia. One difference would be where a heightened political sense gained from anti-homophobic LGBT movement and public discourses would obstruct the voicing of protests against a reading such as ours. Few would publicly commend such a boss for his reticent tolerance while shaming the employee for ingratitude. Thanks to Teri Silvio for this reminder.

20 This translation has combined the translations of Burton Watson (1968), The Complete Works of Chuang-Tzu, and Juliette Chung (1998: 78), 'Comparative rhetoric, intersubjectivity, and cross-cultural studies – an alternative comparativism'.

21 According to Wang Shu-Min (1988) Zhuangzi Jiaoquan, tecao [independent action] should be chicao, or 'hold onto' as in bachi.

22 Ghosts and penumbra are not the same, yet might sometimes have overlapping semantic fields, such as in the homophonic term wangliang, with the ghost radical. We are unable to trace the relations between ghosts and wangliang in this paper but wish to thank Teri Silvio for the thought.

References

Chou, Wah-Shan 周華山 (1997) *Post-Colonial Tongzhi* 後殖民同志 , Hong Kong: Hong Kong Queer Press 香港同志研究社 .

Chou, Wah-Shan (2000) *Tongzhi: Politics of Same-Sex Eroticism in Chinese Societies*, Binghamton: Haworth Press.

Chu, Wei-cheng R. 朱偉誠 (1998) 'Coming out or not: postcolonial autonomy and gay/activism in Taiwan' '台灣同志運動的後殖民思考： 論'現身'問題' ' *Taiwan: A Radical Quarterly in Social Studies* 台灣社會研究 季刊 30(June): 35–62.

Chung, Juliette 鐘月岑 (1998) 'Comparative rhetoric, intersubjectivity, and cross-cultural studies – an alternative comparativism' 比較分析措詞、, 相互主體性與出入異文化 － 錢新祖先生對比較研究的另類選擇 *Taiwan: A Radical Quarterly in Social Studies* 29: 78.

Du, Xioulan 杜修蘭 (1996) *The Unfilial Daughter* 逆女 Taipei: Huangguan 皇冠 .

Foucault, Michel (1980/1976) *The History of Sexuality*, Vol. 1, translated by Robert Hurley, New York: Vintage Books.

Furth, Charlotte (1988) 'Androgynous males and deficient females: biology and gender boundaries in sixteenth- and seventeenth-century China', *Late Imperial China* 9(2) December: 1–31.

Furth, Charlotte (1994a) 'Ming-Qing medicine and the construction of gender', *Research on Women in Modern Chinese History* 2: 229–250.

Furth, Charlotte (1994b) 'Rethinking Van Gulik: sexuality and reproduction in traditional Chinese medicine'. In Christina K. Gilmartin, Gail Hershatter, Lisa Rofel and Tyrene White (eds) *Engendering China: Women, Culture, and the State,* Cambridge: Harvard University Press, 125–146.

Genette, Gerard (1987) 'Les fonctions de la preface originale'. In *Seuils,* Paris: Editions du Seuil.

Gulik, R. H. Van (1974) *Sexual Life in Ancient China: A Preliminary Survey of Chinese Sex and Society from ca. 1500 B.C. till 1644 A.D,* Leiden, Netherlands: E. J. Brill.

Hinsch, Bret (1990) *Passions of the Cut Sleeve,* Berkeley and Los Angeles: University of California Press.

Holzman, Donald (1978) 'Confucius and ancient Chinese literary criticism'. In Adele Austin Rickett (ed.) *Chinese Approaches to Literature from Confucius to Liang Ch'i-ch'ao,* Princeton: Princeton University Press.

Ko, Dorothy (1994) *Teachers of the Inner Chambers: Women and Culture in Seventeenth-Century China*, Stanford: Stanford University Press.

Miller, D.A. (1998) *Place for Us: Essay on the Broadway Musical*, Cambridge: Harvard University Press.

Ni, Chia-Chen 倪家珍 (1997) '"Queer Politics" symposium' '「同性戀的政治」座談會 '. In Josephine Ho Chuen-juei' (ed.) *Visionary Essays in Sexuality/Gender Studies: Proceedings of the First International Conference on Sexuality Education, Sexology, Gender Studies and LesBiGay Studies,* Taipei: Yuanzun, 201.

Pan, Guang-Dan 潘光旦 (1987 [1933]) 'Examples of homosexuality in Chinese textual sources or: examples of homosexuality in Chinese archival sources' '中國文獻中的同性戀舉例 ', appendix to Havelock Ellis *Psychology of Sex: a Manual for Students* 性心理學 , Pan (trans.), Beijing: Sanlian Shudian 三聯書店 .

Sedgwick, Eve (1998) 'Affect and performativity,' *Taiwan Lecture,* October 4, Center for the Study of Sexuality and Difference, National Central University, Chung-li, Taiwan.

Sun, Kang-Yi 孫康宜 (1998) 'Defining and explaining "woman" in imperial and modern times' 古典與現代的 女性闡釋 Taipei: Lianhe Wenxue 聯合文學 .

Tsai, Ying-chun 蔡英俊 (1986) 'An Interpretation of "Wenrou Dunhou"' '溫柔敦厚釋義 '. In *Bixing Wuse and Qingjing Jiaorong 比興物色與情景交融* Taipei: Daan Publisher 大安出版社 .

Tsai, Ying-chun (1997) 'Text, meaning, and interpretation: a comparative study of Western and Chinese literary theories', Centre for British and Comparative Cultural Studies, The University of Warwick.

Tsai, Ying-chun (1998) 'The poetics of reticence in classical Chinese literary thought', paper presented at the Crossroads in Cultural Studies Conference, Tampere, Finland, June.

Wang, Shu-Min 王叔岷 (1988) *Collation and Interpretation of Zhuangzi* 莊子校詮 Taipei: The Institute of History and Philology Academia Sinica 中央研究院歷史與哲學研究所.

Watson, Burton (1968) *The Complete Works of Chuang-Tzu*, New York: Columbia.

Special terms

baorong 包容
chicao 持操
Ding Tianshi (Angel Ding) 丁天使
Duhua 獨化
fushi yanzhi 賦詩言志
geshi bilei 歌詩必類
gouqie tousheng 苟且偷生
guhun yegui 孤魂野鬼
han 含
hanxu 含蓄
he 和
kuanrong 寬容
moyan kuanrong 默言寬容
bachi 把持
Pan Jinlian 潘金蓮
Qing 情
tecao 特操
wangliang 罔兩
wangliang wenying 罔兩問景

wenrou dunhou 溫柔敦厚
wuochuo 齷齪
wuochuo gan 齷齪感
wudai 無待
xianshen 現身
xu 蓄
ye dong de 也懂得
yi shengwang zhi jiao yi zhiqing 依聖王之教以制情
yinshen 隱身
ying 景
ying 影
yingzi 影子
you yizhi 有異志
Zhan Qingqing 詹青青
Zhang Man Juan 張曼娟
zhezhongshi kuoda jiating 折衷式擴大家庭
zhichi 知恥
zhong wangliang 眾罔兩
Zhuangzi Jiaoquan 莊子校詮

Part VI

Cinema

Chapter 19

Transnational imagination in action cinema

Hong Kong and the making of a global popular culture

Meaghan Morris

Total is a strong word. There are different degrees of totality.

James Cameron's *True Lies* (1994)

In contrast with [the self-consciousness of a slave], when the worker knows himself as a commodity his knowledge is practical. *That is to say, this knowledge brings about an objective structural change in the object of knowledge.*

Lukács (1968: 169)

How do we *imagine* the 'transnational' flows and movements in culture so often invoked in critical rhetoric today? Acts of imagining enable as well as shape our research projects, and in cultural domains of enquiry (as distinct from, say, the study of capital or population movements), the imaginings we work with are often surprisingly thin – a blurry wash of rhetoric about movement, speed and space, spread through a critique of national or 'bounded' categories and affects as though the transnational can be imagined only in terms of what it is not. The term *transnational* itself is heavily spatialized today, carrying an insistent flow of images about 'global' forces rolling round 'borderless' worlds. Yet this was not always the case: in what Connery (2002) calls the 'global Maoist' 1960s and early 1970s, 'transnational' led by association to 'capitalism' and thence to 'historical' (and 'dialectical') analysis. What makes the difference between then and now is a historical question. However, what 'history' means to people now is a *critical* question. Studying the history of action cinema and its 'spatializations' is a good way to think about both these problems. Theories of globalization abound these days, but empirical work is needed to advance our understanding of how globalizing forces are working, or *not* working, in culture (Morris 2000). Action cinema is a useful case for study because it has well-developed aesthetic and industrial traditions – its transnationalism is not new, and the genre has already gone through several cycles of rising and declining popularity – and because 'action' so clearly dramatizes the conflict-ridden conditions of its own circulation and globally popular status. In an inter-Asian context, it also allows us to reflect historically on transnational industrial as well as aesthetic imaginings, which do not solely derive from the West and which 'flow', as it were, towards and through Western cinemas as well as around the region itself.

Let me develop these claims with reference to a French situationist film from 1973, *La Dialectique peut-elle casser les briques?* (*Can Dialectics Break Bricks?*) directed by René Viénet. (Viénet reportedly lives or has lived in Taiwan and now disavows this film, although I do not know if that is true). Made as the ferment of cultural radicalism after the 'May 68' events in Paris was fading and some of the French Far Left were contemplating a 'Common Program' with the Communist and Socialist parties to win government at the ballot box, this film has never stopped circulating as an underground classic. Viénet's group took an existing Hong Kong film, removed the soundtrack, and hilariously substituted for it an anarcho-Marxist reading in French of the entire image-track as though the film were an allegory of class struggle between 'proletarians' and 'bureaucrats'. This technique was called *détournement* – twisting or diverting a text away from its presumed original meaning and making the second text do something different from, or antagonistic to, the first text's project. Treating one text in this way as raw material for the production of another, politically critical text was a powerful gesture; arguably, this surrealism-based 'situationist' practice helped to shape philosophical deconstruction, and it has certainly influenced the weaker tradition of 'subversive' or 'transgressive' reading in literary and cultural studies.

However, particular instances of *détournement* can date very quickly. While *Can Dialectics Break Bricks?* is still delightful, the joke does wear thin over the duration of a full-length film (unless you have a fondness for the ranting political rhetoric of those days, which I do not). It can also be faintly embarrassing in the beginning, although the image-track soon asserts its power; the story is exciting and easy to follow, the new dialogue brilliantly consistent with all we see on screen. But today I want to see or rather *hear* the first, Chinese, film, and it's gone – erased by these know-all French voices blasting out of the past. I'm embarrassed because I remember what it was like to see a 'Hong Kong film', *any* Hong Kong film, in that blankly Orientalist way – unable to distinguish one film from another let alone kung fu from swordplay (or, indeed, from karate and then from *chambara*), wholly ignorant of Chinese genres, and believing in response to the famously bad English dubbing that the films were uniformly so terrible they were funny – a camp reception of Hong Kong films that survives in some Western fan subcultures today. It is embarrassing, too, to remember a time when the idea that other cultures' stories might be taken seriously was of interest only in relation to 'my own' Australian culture as it differed from those of Britain and the US.

But there is another way to look at this. I'm interested in the uptake in many different cinemas of the 'two rival schools' narrative that structures innumerable Hong Kong films, and the film *underneath* the French Situationist film was evidently one of those.[1] The evil bureaucrats are visibly Japanese swordsmen, while the proletarians are Chinese masters of unarmed combat – in essence, Wang Yu's *The Chinese Boxer* (1970) and Lo Wei's *Fist of Fury* (a.k.a. *The Chinese Connection*, 1972) replayed all over again. Apparently the first film was *Crush*, a.k.a. *Crush Karate* (1972) directed by Tu Guangqi ('Doo Kwang Gee' on the tape I have of the film). According to Teo (1997: 14, 23–24), Tu (1914–1980) came after World War Two from Shanghai to Hong Kong, where he made cultural nationalist Mandarin-language films; a right-winger who worked for the Asia Film Company, established in 1953 with American money, Tu helped remake and reinterpret – indeed, *détourner* – successful *left-wing* dramas and themes from a right-wing nationalist perspective. If that is so, there is a definite poetic justice in the French fate of *Crush*.

However, while allegorical of my point about the uses of historical work to critical interpretation across 'transnational space', this is petty stuff. How can we do such work on a larger scale, and with significant stakes? Method is the hard part, and in cultural studies reflections on method are much more common than innovations *in* method. The 'how' of any kind of historical work in cultural studies is a complex problem. Several essays have argued that such work *ought* to be done, but then do readings of theories instead; Michael Pickering's (1997) *History, Experience and Cultural Studies* is a recent example. Many critiques of representation have temporal depth or a period focus, and most work in cultural studies alludes to world-historical forces – imperialism, patriarchy, capitalism, racism – as these structure specific events. Yet relatively few historically substantive works have so far appeared in English beside those written by sympathetic historians such as Carolyn Steedman (1995) and Catherine Hall (2002). Paul Gilroy's (1993) *The Black Atlantic* and Ann McClintock's (1995) *Imperial Leather: Race, Gender and Sexuality in the Colonial Context* are models more admired than imitated at this stage, although Ding Naifei's (2001) *Obscene Things: Intimate Politics in Jin Ping Mei* and Dai Jinhua's (2002) *Cinema and Desire: Feminist Marxism and Cultural Politics in the Work of Dai Jinhua* have the innovative force that I'm looking for in literary and cinema studies respectively.

This is a small group of texts after so many years of discipline-building debate. Disciplinary borders are institutional as well as conceptual *barriers*, and they render extremely difficult the emergence of a genuinely transnational scholarship as distinct from the internationally distributed products of the Anglo-American publishing industry. It is very difficult not to re-inscribe national boundaries in scholarly discourse on culture, not only as we formulate objects of study but in our enunciative practice. What Pickering (1997: 12) casually calls 'geo-political discontinuities' in cultural studies are real-world gaps between us that are gaps not only in knowledge and intellectual formation but in feeling and *desire* to know, and they entail real difficulties for historical work within cultural studies fields. The familiar figure of a 'borderless world' is both a sign and a symptom of that difficulty, as Yau (2001: 25) notes in the Introduction to her collection, *At Full Speed: Hong Kong Cinema in a Borderless World*. Too often, we simply do not *know* enough to discuss cinema historically *in* a transnational register, even on a regional scale – as distinct from talking with cultural compatriots 'about' transnational cinema.

So I proceed in a broken sort of way. In the next part of this essay I sketch a historical case *about* 'transnational imagination' taken from a research project I share with my colleagues at Lingnan University, Stephen Chan Ching-kiu and Li Siu-leung.[2] The problems I have mentioned inevitably structure this project. My Chinese colleagues are focused on Hong Kong and its cinema, and therefore have interests much wider than 'action films'. I am focused on Australian culture in particular and action-adventure generally, and while I certainly do not conflate action with Hong Kong cinema (a complaint commonly heard in Hong Kong about Western critics), I am not especially interested *as a scholar* in 'Hong Kong cinema'. The national cinema model ('national' is hardly the right word for Hong Kong, but let it stand for the moment) remains a powerful and pertinent framework for analysis in cinema studies (Willemen, 1994: 206–219).[3] I am subject to its attractions and limitations as much as anyone else, but I think it has to be exceeded if Hollywood is not to define the norms for discussing cinema itself. So in the second half of the essay I look at some aspects of the generic uptake *of* Hong Kong action cinema in Western contexts.

Hong Kong and the making of a global popular culture

Here is a simple historical proposition: Hong Kong has played a *formative* rather than a marginal role in shaping action cinema as it circulates globally today. Most accounts of the genre in English focus on Hollywood, limiting Hong Kong's influence to the 1970s' 'kung fu craze' associated with Bruce Lee, and the impact of a few famous figures (Jackie Chan, John Woo, Tsui Hark, Chow Yun-fat, Yuen Woo-Ping) in Hollywood today. However, action cinema has long had a complex economy in which Hollywood not only trades film styles and narratives with the hybrid culture of Hong Kong cinema itself but draws both formally and industrially on a vast 'direct to video' industry significantly based in Asia, with Hong Kong as its creative centre.

By 'Hong Kong', I mean a location in which filmmakers from many places – notably Japan, the Philippines, Australia, the US, Taiwan and the Chinese mainland – have interacted with the local industry to produce a new transnational genre. In multiple forms and languages, from the Hollywood blockbuster playing in a multiplex wherever there's a shopping mall, to outdoor screenings of tapes in remote communities with only one video-player, action cinema circulates scenarios of 'contact' between rival ways of life to diverse audiences worldwide. In doing so it borrows deeply from Hong Kong cinema, which has long addressed local concerns in cosmopolitan cultural forms. Shaped largely by Japanese and Filipino models in the 1960s,[4] as well as memories and experiences brought to Hong Kong by émigré filmmakers from the mainland, the kung fu tradition popularized worldwide by Bruce Lee in the 1970s gave more than a new fighting style to action cinema. Just as consequentially, *contact* between different 'ways' of being and acting was a key theme of this tradition: along with *The Chinese Boxer* and *Fist of Fury* – both 'kung fu vs. karate' stories of an attack by a rival school – a wonderful example is Lau Kar Leung's *Shaolin Challenges Ninja* (1978), in which a contest for supremacy between multiple Chinese and Japanese styles seriously strains a marriage. It is worth noting that while most of the Shaw Bros. films from the 1970s are only now becoming available again in Chinese languages in Hong Kong, grubby video-tapes dubbed in English and many other languages have never stopped circulating in the decades since the films were made. (I once paid a lot of money over the Internet for a very poor copy of *Shaolin Challenges Ninja* subtitled in Dutch.) Meanwhile the story is still being updated today: *Shaolin Soccer* is a Shanghai-based, pre-World Cup remake of Stephen Chiau's own sublime revision of the 'rival ways' tradition, *The God of Cookery* (1996), an ethics of cooking and eating.

A couple of points here about the value of a transnational historical study of globally popular forms. First, a Hong Kong-*based* study can (if it is not only Hong Kong focused) provide a model of how to understand *global* cinema from a non-American but cosmopolitan local context. In order to be convincing such a study would need, second, to focus on film production as well as the reception issues that have recently preoccupied studies of what During (1992) calls the 'global popular'. It also needs to be multi-lingually sensitive, not least because the English-language version of Hong Kong films is the one which usually initiates the widest circle of distribution, and it may tend to heighten or accentuate the 'two schools/two styles' narrative of rivalry. For example, the Chinese title of a film made in 1990 by Taylor Wong Tai-loi translates literally into English as 'Modern Buddha Magic Palm', a title placing the film in a tradition of elaborately imagined fictitious martial techniques; generically it is a Cantonese 'warrior out of time' comedy, following the success of Clarence Fok Yiu Leung's *Iceman Cometh* (1989). In Hong Kong English, however, the title became *Kung Fu vs. Acrobatic* – an impossible phrase, a noun contesting an adjective, the evocatively fuzzy semantics of which serves primarily to highlight the syntax of a 'two ways' story: *X vs. Y*.

For the sake of argument, let us imagine that a history of the development of contemporary action cinema could look like the following.

1973–85: the international film, or the era of co-productions

Where Hollywood-based accounts begin with the 'disaster movie' (*The Towering Inferno*, 1974) and the inventive marketing of *Jaws* (1975), an East Asian-based study could begin with the co-productions, location shoots, talent exchanges and other fly-by-night collaborations proliferating in the region by the 1950s. From a Hong Kong base, the regional adventures of Shaw Brothers would be central: for example, in 1955 SB and Daiei Co. co-produced *Empress Yang Kwei Fei*, 'the first picture to bear the common brand name of a "Hong Kong-Japan co-production"' (Law Kar 2000: 105), while in 1957 *Love with an Alien* was the first joint production between SB and a Korean company, Shen Films, using a Japanese director (Wakasugi Mitsuo) as well as a Korean (Kim Cheong Gen) and, from the Chinese side, none other than Tu Guangqi. The imaginative calculation involved at Shaws appears to have been developmental as well as a matter of creative marketing; Korean directors were thought to be efficient and knowledgeable about American films as well as good at melodrama (popular at the time), while the Japanese were admired for their daring use of technology and the budget benefits that followed (Law Kar 2000: 140).

However, a fine symbolic starting point for a genealogy of today's globally marketed blockbusters could be Kimoyoshi Yasuda's *Zatoichi and the One-Armed Swordsman*, Japan/HK, 1970, which pitted Zatoichi, the popular 'blind swordsman' of Japanese cinema, against Wang Yu's famous maimed and disabled Chinese hero from Chang's Che's *The One-Armed Swordsman* (HK, 1967). The interesting thing about this production is that two endings were made: for Japanese distribution Zatoichi wins and for Chinese markets the One-Armed Swordsman wins. The West then comes into the picture with the Warner–Golden Harvest co-production of *Enter the Dragon* (1973), starring Bruce Lee, Angela Mao, John Saxon and Jim Kelly. Note that this now legendary film mixed kung fu elements with a scenario taken from *You Only Live Twice* (1967), the James Bond film that introduced ninjas to a global public and borrowed in turn from a popular Japanese TV series screened as *The Samurai* by the Australian Broadcasting Commission (ABC-TV) – a series that did more to 'Asianise' my own imagination when I was in my early teens than a decade of government policy would do in the 1986–1996 period.[5]

The global kung fu craze that followed *Enter the Dragon* is well known (see Desser 2000). Just as influential as the fight scenes – in some ways the least interesting aspect of this history, though the choreography, staging and later the editing of fights would become a key element of an internationally influential 'Hong Kong style' (Martin 2005) – was *Enter the Dragon*'s hybrid form and its mode of address. It found a way of pitching an elemental story of good against evil in such a spectacle-saturated way that diverse audiences could happily laugh at and enjoy whatever they did not understand. This may also have involved coaching Westerners in the blank Orientalizing gaze I noted in *Can Dialectics Break Bricks?*, but in the same moment it instituted a 'gaze', as it were, there where *no* gaze was before – for example, amongst white working-class audiences and surf subcultures in Australia (I speak from experience here). *Enter the Dragon* also fostered adaptations for all kinds of 'minor' purposes. The experiments it shaped include *Black Belt Jones* (1974), which took the 'rival schools' story via Hong Kong from Japan and Akira Kurosawa's first film, *Sugata Sanshiro*, (1943), transposing it to an African-American context where a karate school teaching self-esteem to black kids is threatened by real estate developers and the Mafia; *The Man From Hong Kong* (1975), an Australian film, which brought Wang Yu to Sydney to satirize xenophobia and police corruption in that city (Morris 2004); and Corey Yuen Kwai's *No Retreat, No Surrender* (1985), which took the story into the heart of white American suburbia. Made by a bunch of now very eminent Hong Kong filmmakers (including Ng See Yuen as well as Yuen Kwai himself), *No Retreat, No Surrender* is considered an American martial arts classic (Morris 2001).

1985–93: a 'direct-to-video' industry

From the mid-1980s, the rapid spread of home video technology enabled a new form of production in which Western stars with real martial arts expertise and often experience in Hong Kong cinema – Chuck Norris, Jean-Claude van Damme, Cynthia Rothrock and the Australian martial artist Richard Norton are good cases for study – made films that might have an American director, Israeli producers, finance from Luxembourg, an assistant director, crew, and supporting cast from whatever country in Asia (including Australia) the film could be cheaply and quickly made, sometimes a specialist choreographer from Hong Kong and a 'two ways' story foregrounding a cultural or ethical conflict.

Most of these films were rarely or never screened in theatres. An early video classic that did receive theatrical release was Mark DiSalle's and David Worth's *Kickboxer* (1988), which remade, as a tale of American hubris and re-education, an intensely nationalistic 1971 Chang Che film about Chinese brothers in Thailand, *Duel of Fists*. Remade by Worth for Rapi Films in Indonesia as *Lady Dragon* (1990), featuring Cynthia Rothrock in a 'bereaved spouse' version of the story (with Bella Esperance as the 'local' star and Ackyl Anwary as Associate Director), this 'pan-Asian' revenge-driven story of a cross-cultural *Bildung* (education or 'formation') in which two brothers or a couple go to a foreign place, one dies, and the other slowly transforms or 'assimilates', was recently remade for the umpteenth time, in a Thai setting, as *A Fighter's Blues* starring Andy Lau with Takiko Tokiwo.

The production companies churning out large quantities of action films that would be released direct to video in Western countries during this period would repay further study, particularly as they interacted in often hostile ways with the institutions, creative talent and film critics devoted to developing national cinemas. Fortunately, I have no space to trace any details here (research in this area is extremely difficult) so let me briefly follow a textual trail. The 'minor' cinema these companies created cheaply distributed around the world not only the narrative of rivalry (two schools, two styles, two 'ways') but also a model of learning based on *emulation*. That this model assumes a hierarchical relation between teacher and student is unremarkable; more significant for my purposes is that the way to 'empowerment' for the student in kung fu pedagogy films goes through a particular form or practice of mimesis – a specific art of imitation involving an ethical as well as bodily effort of learning to become *like* the ideal embodied by the teacher.

Likeness is not 'identity' and unlikeness is not the same as 'difference'. Action cinema generally is fascinated with both 'like' and 'unlike' doubles (in *Double Impact* the short-statured Jean-Claude van Damme plays his own twin, while *Double Team* combines him with the black American basketball player Dennis Rodman). Correspondingly, action cinema is also fascinated by 'sameness', and by the difference of sameness from 'similarity': 'we're the same, you and I!' is the appeal of villain to hero in films as diverse as *Eye for an Eye*, *Good Guys Wear Black*, *Bloodmatch*, *Tiger Claws*, *Eve of Destruction*, *Perfect Weapon*, *The Hard Truth*, *No Retreat No Surrender 3* and *The Expert*, to cite a few in the minor mode, and *The Year of Living Dangerously*, *The Specialist*, *Under Siege* and *Judge Dredd* in the blockbuster mode. In kung fu pedagogy films, however, the one who yearns to become identical with or *be* the master is usually a villain, typically a deviant abbot who has killed or betrayed his own master in the past and now uses his powers for evil. In Western settings, this figure becomes a crazed martial artist or a fascist gym teacher: examples are *The Karate Kid* (1984), *Tiger Claws* (1991) and, from Australia, *Watch the Shadows Dance* (1987), starring a very young Nicole Kidman.

Identity is the achievement of villainy, but *similarity* is the aspiration of heroism. In contrast to the villain's trajectory towards Being, one that consumes or annihilates the model, the hero follows a line of emulatory becoming that approaches its model ever more closely while leaving its aura and its otherness intact. In Deleuze and Guattari's (1987) model, a becoming is a process with three terms in which A becomes B while B becomes X, and the Master in pedagogy films is appropriately often busy becoming drunk, or asleep, or withdrawn. The distance between the hero and the hero's hero is never finally closed and this 'gap' functions temporally; it consists of the *history* between teacher and student, which villainy betrays or denies.

A sophisticated play upon this principle occurs between strangers in *Shaolin Challenges Ninja* when the aristocratic Chinese boxer (Lau Kar-fai), knowing that he must face the most accomplished fighter from Japan, searches the inns for the Drunken Master, played by Lau Kar-leung himself. Prodding the latter half-out of his stupor, the 'student' in the foreground of the shot mimics the movements of the master in the background, literalizing a chain of emulation that not only extends back through time and in film history (Lau Kar-fai 'learns' from his older adopted brother Lau Kar-leung, who famously learned from men who learned from men who learned kung fu from Wong Fei-hung) but also has the potential to extend forward in time – even into the space of the viewer who may imitate the moves on screen. This, of course, is what radical idealists hope and social protectors fear that we audiences will do in response to images (a proposition that has been nonetheless consequential in film and social history for being debatable). It is also exactly what millions of people in the West really would begin to do with home aerobics, exercise and 'teach yourself' martial arts videos soon after Lau's film appeared.

1993–94 was a peak season for direct-to-video action, soon to be challenged by the Internet, DVDs and, above all, a flood of re-released and 'quick' movies on VCD, and in Hong Kong by a growing sense of industry crisis; *Jurassic Park* was the first Hollywood blockbuster to outdo Hong Kong cinema on its home box-office turf, and piracy became a financially significant problem along with triad pressure on the industry itself. The creative story can be followed further, however, as new tendencies renewed the action genre. As Hollywood became more cosmopolitan, with Hong Kong stars and directors going there to work – in part because of the pressure of 1997 and rising costs at home, but also within a wider influx of foreign talent to Hollywood (half of the Australian film industry migrated around the same time) – more action blockbusters began to *address* a diverse global audience on the *Enter the Dragon* model: *Blade*, *Rush Hour*, *Dark City*, *The Matrix*, *Crouching Tiger Hidden Dragon*, *Gladiator*. Stanley Tong had a hit on US television with the series *Martial Law*, starring Sammo Hung and Arsenio Hall. At the same time, new forces emerged in Hong Kong cinema itself to create, on the one hand, ambitiously pan-Asian transnational films (Jingle Ma's *Tokyo Raiders*, for example) and, on the other, intensely local reworkings of Hong Kong traditions (Johnny To's *The Mission*).[6] Somewhere in between is Andrew Lau's incredible romantic saga of triad life and gangster globalization, the *Young and Dangerous* films and their spin-offs and prequels, which meticulously map an internally diverse Hong Kong localism within a regional network of connections linking Taiwan, the Chinese mainland, Macau, Japan, Britain and even Tuen Mun (home to Lingnan University) in Hong Kong itself.

Of necessity, I have largely left Hollywood out of this account; it would take a large volume to trace those connections too. In the remainder of this essay, I want to discuss just two features of the second period outlined above, in which a largely non-theatrical 'cinema' emerged on a global scale. One of these is the capacity of direct-to-video action to address Western working-class viewers in complex ways. The other is how it projects the principle of heroic emulation taken from Hong Kong cinema on to a socially as well as culturally diversified narrative plane.

History and class-consciousness on video

In action cinema, as in many societies today, transnational historical issues are often raised in the form of an emotional discourse on 'heritage'. Following the introduction of significant black, Hispanic and Chinese characters to the landscape of the Western genre, in Sergio Leone's and now Clint Eastwood's films (*Unforgiven*), Asian-American identity sagas with a 'family history' dimension have emerged, such as *Rising Son* [sic] and *Dragon*, Rob Cohen's fictionalized life of Bruce Lee (which briefly includes the figure of a shipboard Chinese 'history teacher' guiding the young Lee on his passage to America). There are also blurry but emotionally laden allusions to communal histories of discrimination and displacement in countless 'migrant' and 'minority' versions of the kung fu pedagogy film, from *Black Belt Jones* to *Bounty Tracker* (featuring a US 'Indonesian' dojo), *Perfect Weapon* (Koreans) or *Only the Strong* (Brazilians). Related to this is the marking of history as a haunting of the present by the past in white guilt films such as *The Shining*, where the vast hotel in which Jack Nicholson's insanity takes murderous form rests on a Native American burial ground, and the 'white panic' of the *Mad Max* trilogy, which reworks the colonizing past of white Australians as an apocalyptic vision of the global human future (Morris 1998).

There are many ways of thinking broadly about history in action cinema (see Morris 1998, 2004). I want to focus here on a more specialized notion, deriving from critical theory in the strict sense of the term, of history as a process globally driven by class struggle, and posing to analysis questions about contending modes or 'positions' of knowledge. Class analysis is not my preferred mode of criticism. Nevertheless, critical theory provides a way in to thinking about one of the most insistent yet critically neglected categories of direct-to-video action: economically defined social *class*.

Class *matters* in action films and, as Kleinhans (1996: 251) points out in a fine essay on Steven Seagal, many revolve around ethical wish-fulfilment fantasies ('in which one does the right thing without having to calculate economic hardship') which make a strong and explicit appeal to working-class audiences. For an example of such explicitness in 'appeal' – that is, an address or interpellation as well as an imputed attractiveness – consider the opening sequence of Bob Radler's classic *Best of the Best* (1989) starring Eric Roberts, James Earl Jones and the Korean-American martial arts star Philip Rhee.[7] The sequence is composed of a succession of three lovingly realized cinematic clichés, to each of which is consecrated a separate scene.

(1)   The film opens at dawn with credits rolling over a high, panoramic shot of a wide, flat *field* where a school or perhaps a private army of black-belted men identically dressed in white practices a martial arts routine in tightly choreographed unison. This is a portrait of disciplined collectivity, with one medium shot but no individualizing close-ups; only a goal-post in the distance tells sharp-eyed viewers that this is a modern sports-ground rather than a medieval plain. Lifted direct from Hong Kong cinema, globally familiar from *Enter the Dragon* (and a version opens the action in *Crush/Can Dialectics Break Bricks?*), this scene announces the genre of the film ('martial arts') and, given the 'cult' status of martial arts cinema in the West, welcomes an ideal audience of fans.

(2)   Abruptly, with the credits still rolling we cut inside to a *factory*. Here the disciplined moves are those of a car assembly-line tended by stressed human body parts. The set is visually crowded, colourful with the sparks and fires of industry, loud with the clanging of tools and the driving beat of a rock song. One anonymous human removes a helmet to reveal the sweating, warmly-lit and intensely individualized face of Eric Roberts; visibly, a hero emerges. Recalling the opening of Paul Schrader's *Blue Collar* (invoked again in *Flashdance*, a Reagan-era romance about a woman welder who dances erotically in a club by night while nursing 'high art' dreams of ballet), this pounding industrial scene can be called a 'white proletarian cliché', and it brings a wider social content into the 'field' of the 'martial arts' cliché. An excursus outside the factory emphasizes this by taking us briefly to the streets of suburbia, where Alex Grady (Roberts) is teaching his son to ride a bicycle.

(3)   Another cut returns us to a martial arts setting. This one is, like the factory, indoors, in a crisp white gymnasium featuring a huge American flag. In a logical flow from the bicycle scene, here the bodies unstably attempting 'disciplined moves' are those of children. No army, this gathering is definitely a *school* – and, the camera quickly reveals, an ethnically diverse martial arts school with a good-looking, clean-cut Asian-American teacher (Rhee). Enter the 'Bruce Lee' cliché. Like the field and the factory, the 'martial arts class' under the flag is a generic marker (this will be an *American* martial arts movie) while adding two qualifications: coming after the white proletarian moment, the individualized figure of Rhee announces a story of race and cultural identity in the US, while an emphasis on his pastoral care for other people's children (as he prevents two boys from fighting) prepares for a 'formation' story of tolerance, learning and personal self-esteem.

The Bruce Lee cliché retroactively organizes the field/factory, collective/individual, Asian/American oppositions along a tradition/modernity axis. The martial field opens up from within the vaguely feudal world of classic 'Hong Kong' cinema, the factory blasts in from contemporary American cinema, and the disciplined but individualizing, video-oriented Asian-American space synthesizes the energies of both – while marking its own hybridity in such a way as to introduce the problem of *national* belonging that will drive much of the narrative. For, as it turns out, the 'army' practising in the open field is in fact auditioning for the Korean national 'karate' team, while both the white factory worker, Alex Grady (Roberts) and the Korean-American teacher, Tommy Lee (Rhee) will receive letters inviting them to try out for the US national team.

Interestingly, national belonging as a *problem* is posed most acutely in this film to the 'white proletarian' and not to the 'Bruce Lee' figure. Rhee's character Tommy has to deal with racial prejudice from his team-mate, Travis (Christopher Penn), but at a narrative level he is removed from the site of national anxiety by a 'dead brother' sub-plot; the top Korean champion, Dae Han (Simon Rhee), has killed Tommy's brother in the tournament ring. It follows that the Korean-American's commitment to his adopted land is underwritten by his longing for revenge against a Korean fighter; thanks to this plot device, blood loyalty and American patriotism will coincide for Tommy. In contrast, while the white worker is a patriot at the sporting level ('representing his country'), Alex Grady is a far more alienated figure than Tommy Lee at the level of everyday life. Bored and unhappy at work, he primarily seeks personal fulfilment in playing a national role and his deepest commitment is to his own fractured family; forced at one stage to choose between his son and the national team, he does not hesitate to choose his son. In this respect, *Best of the Best* is an unusually complex expression of the white working-class sense of displacement that would become such a powerful factor in American (and Australian) domestic politics throughout the 1990s, and it also works hard to deflect the 'angry white male' reaction against migrants and minorities that would be explored three years later by Joel Schumacher's *Falling Down* (1992).

I will return to this articulation of class with race, gender and nationality in *Best of the Best*. First, I need to give my claim that action cinema is conscious of class a more solid foundation.

Major and minor economies

Let me complicate the term 'action cinema' by dividing it heuristically into 'major' and 'minor' modes. Loosely following Deleuze's usage, this distinction is not a binary opposition and it does not contrast two essences; as in music, it distinguishes two practices, two different 'ways' of handling the same material.[8] A major mode of action cinema would be the Hollywood blockbuster, instances of which may be less or more cosmopolitan in composition and mode of address. An instance of a minor mode would be what I've called 'direct-to-video' cinema, which is transnational in industrial composition and highly variable in mode of address as the image track is dubbed (rather than subtitled) in different languages by unrelated distributors in diverse markets world-wide.[9]

Table 1 roughly sketches some ways to contrast two modes of action cinema. Incoherent and incomplete, the table reflects the complexity and *porousness* of the processes it tries to organize. Nevertheless, the difference between the 'big business' blockbuster economy and the 'small business' of direct-to-tape is no less real for being negotiable.

Most of these categories and descriptions are self-explanatory, but let me highlight a couple. First of all, *casting*: while it is common now for Hollywood to calculate precisely the proportion of on-screen 'representation' to be allocated to relevant American racial minorities ('affirmative action'), even allowing black male stars (Denzel Washington, Wesley Snipes), imported Asian male stars (Jackie Chan, Chow Yun-fat, Jet Li), and recently the New York-born Lucy Liu to play a hero's role, the direct-to-tape production is more likely to have a white star wandering around a poverty-stricken, exotic location for some vaguely justified reason (he/she is a spy, a soldier, a mercenary, a bereaved spouse of one of these, or a martial arts devotee), accompanied by a local sidekick and threatened by a local villain. The 'locals' are played by actors hired wherever the film is shot, and some are well-known stars of their national or native cinema. The white star is there to pull Western audiences (not all of whom, of course, are white), and the local stars – who often get more screen time than 'ethnic representatives' do under Hollywood affirmative action – help sell the film into diverse non-Western or, in fan contexts, Western 'minority' markets. There are some variations on these formulae. Hollywood films addressing a global market sometimes relegate 'white' representation to a modest proportion of the cast (*Blade* is a good example), while a whole range exists of dubbed or cheaply re-made action movies produced for non-Western local or national markets – for example, Telugu remakes of Hong Kong action films, my minuscule knowledge of which I owe to S. V. Srinivas (2005) – and these are rarely seen in the West outside migrant communities.

Casting issues help to shape the address or *pitch* of a film. In *True Lies*, a twist on the 'affirmative' approach ensures that one sidekick of the white American hero Harry Tasker (Arnold Schwarzenegger) is an Arab-American, 'Fast Faisal' (Grant Heslov); his role is to delink the quality of 'Arabness' from the *foreign* (Arab) terrorists, detaching ethnic/racial affinity from national/cultural loyalty. At the same time, the cosmo-politanism of the group globally ensuring the US's 'last line of defence' is secured by Harry's fictive fluency in half a dozen languages (including, an emphatic and otherwise gratuitous subtitle tells us, 'perfect Arabic') and by Arnie's thickly foreign accent in English. This is a *globally* patriotic American action-comedy; Schwarzenegger will save the world and only 'bad guys' are not on his side. Hollywood blockbusters with a less overtly political agenda offer a spectacular acting-out of a very simple story of humanity's salvation in a struggle of good against evil – whether vampires (*Blade*), viruses (*Outbreak*), mad science (*Jurassic Park*), natural disasters (*Volcano*, *Armageddon*) or hostile extra-terrestrials (*Alien*, *Species*), to mention some usual suspects. The important thing about these stories today, in my view, is less their potential to transmit American national paranoia (on the pattern of the 'commie bugs from outer space' sci-fi stories popular in 1950s Hollywood), than their capacity to draw on multiple sources in resonance with widely dispersed cultural traditions (a 'global folkloric' address). In both groups of films, however, an elite with special capacities and skills – physical, technical, mental, spiritual or, like the death-defying hero of Rob Cohen's *XXX*, just plain attitudinal – has the duty and privilege of preventing global disaster.

In contrast, the vagaries of *casting* in the minor action mode nudge frictions of migrancy and displacement into the foreground while the struggle of good against evil works to *achieve* a state of security that is not initially taken for granted as it is in the

Table 1 Major and minor modes of action cinema

	Major	*Minor*
Budget	Big: upscale producers, established companies; long shooting schedule, high production values	Small: specialist producer, fly-by-night companies; fast schedule, cost-cutting values, 'sleazy' look
Promotion and release	Instant global saturation: plus product tie-ins (computer games, CD, DVD, VCD, toys, clothes), long profit chain; franchise structure	Erratic global spread: local stores, rental and lending, word of mouth, chat rooms, fan spaces (e.g. gyms), martial arts magazines, niche markets
Exhibition	Multiplex, then multiple formats and places (including planes)	Informal consumption spaces: homes, clubs, halls (not usually planes)
Casting	'All American affirmative action', or Hollywood global	'All local/national', or, transnational (Western star, local sidekick and villain, imported director, local technical crew)
Location	Expensive second-rank cities near exotic scenery; digital laboratory	Anywhere cheap. 'Third World', sometimes fourth world and former Second; urban slums in the West.
Generic settings	'Non-places': hotel, airport, resort, military installation, transport and communications hub, yacht, skyscraper	'Any-space-whatever': motel, bus, train, factory, wharf, container depot, shed, warehouse, kitchen, disused buildings
Temporal mode	Emergency: apocalyptic privilege, 'saving the world'	Aftermath: chronic dereliction and loss, 'distressed futures'
Design	Big screen; rectangle	Small screen; square
Pitch (mode of address)	US patriotic or global folkloric	Community building or 'long-distance' nationalist
Ethic	'Shit happens' (special effects)	Authenticity (emulation)

major mode (in order to be placed 'under threat'). Whether the minor hero is a 'white man/woman stranded in the tropics', a proletarian with suppressed or unrecognized talents, or a member of a social minority dealing with discrimination and prejudice, a problem of bonding with a wider community is high on his or her narrative agenda. Like many training and tournament films, *Best of the Best* makes this problem explicit as its assortment of American male stereotypes – white working-class family man, white redneck 'cowboy', sensitive New Age white Buddhist, Italian-American and Korean-American – must forge a common national spirit not only in the face of a formidable adversary (the culturally homogeneous, tradition-saturated and life-long trained Korean team) but under the tutelage of a stern African-American man, Coach Couzo (James Earl Jones), and, in the silliest scenes of a generally well-made film, a white female spiritual adviser, Wade (Sally Kirkland), who 'grew up in East Asia'.

Minor action heroes face dilemmas of divided or suspended loyalty. Whether they resolve these in favour of a deeper patriotic identity than state officials reveal (a common solution in Stephen Seagal and Chuck Norris films), or whether they work through their 'issues' at a family or personal-ethical level (Don 'the Dragon' Wilson, Cynthia Rothrock, Lorenzo Lamas, Jean-Claude van Damme), the pitch of these films is broadly to a mobile and self-selecting 'community' rather than to state-based modes of affective mobilization, and for all their hybridity they lend themselves easily to an uptake in the register of identification that Anderson (1998) calls 'long-distance nationalist'. Rob Cohen's *Dragon* explores the poetics of Bruce Lee's Chinese cultural nationalism in just this long-distance register, connecting his return to Hong Kong near the end of his life with the rejection he experienced in Hollywood.

Minor heroes tend to be humourless. Not for them the wise-cracking one-liners that evoke the 'Arnie' effect ('*Hasta la vista*, baby'; 'I'll be back'), or the cool, cruel ruling-class irony that epitomizes 'James Bond'. With some exceptions (Chuck Norris, for one), the minor hero is more likely to cry than crack jokes; the final fight in *Best of the Best* concludes not with a bloodbath (that is the penultimate phase) but with the two teams embracing and weeping all over each other. In his glory days of the mid-1990s, Jean-Claude van Damme was notorious for flashing his thighs and buttocks for a presumed 'gay male gaze', but an equally distinctive feature of his iconography was the lingering close-up on his large, soft eyes, long lashes moist with tears (*Cyborg*, *Wrong Bet*, *No Place to Hide*). Minor heroes *live with* grief and loss. Harry Tasker is so oblivious to the problems afflicting his nice suburban family that it takes a nuclear attack on Florida to wake him up to his wife and child, but Alex Grady has, from the outset, lost a wife, his son has lost a mother, and Alex's mother has lost a husband (no explanation of *her* bereavement is offered or required) – while Tommy Lee has been traumatized since childhood by seeing his brother's death.

Trauma and disruption is the premise of minor action rather than the product of its central crisis. Where otherness *erupts* in many Hollywood films, shattering a sunny normality (the terrorist's bomb, the sniper's shot, the fire, the crack in the earth, the scream and the blood in the water; the opening of *Jaws* is canonical here), minor action *begins and ends abruptly* with trouble all around – and in this respect, too, it borrows from the budget-conscious style and capacious mythological scale of older Hong Kong cinema, in which there are always more stories to tell about much the same bunch of heroes. Otherness in minor action is always already embedded in the midst of things, *in medias res*. The hero is ever watchful, sad, bereaved, in hiding or on the run, and the 'central' crisis of a film will be but a moody episode in a life that presumes no ultimate happy ending.

Whether it results from a cheap, fly-by-night mode of production or some deeper aesthetic imperative, this banalization of trauma and disruption favours an imaginary of socio-economic dereliction: peopled by bodyguards, bouncers, street fighters, deserters, mercenaries, prostitutes, club dancers, ex-spies, drug dealers, underpaid cops, renegade cyborgs and self-employed martial artists or *ronin*, the world of minor action is 'post-industrial' in that its conflicts are shaped in the ruined spaces and times of industrial-colonial capitalism (*Mad Max*, *Johnny Mnemonic*, *Surviving the Game*) and its characters are sustained by black economies that survive the Brave New World by inhabiting the shell of the Old. Its favoured *settings* for action are not the luxury hotels, resorts and hi-tech communications command centres ('Bondspace') defining Harry Tasker's sphere

– the transit spaces of 'supermodernity' that Augé (1992) calls 'non-places' – but the abandoned or recycled industrial and underclass spaces: the wharves, factories, slums, container depots, fight clubs, mean streets and brothels that Deleuze (1986) calls *any-space-whatever* – marshalling yard, disused warehouse, the undifferentiated fabric of the city':

> . . . we ask ourselves what maintains a set [*ensemble*] in this world without totality or linkage. The answer is simple: what forms the set are clichés and nothing else. Nothing but clichés, clichés everywhere . . . They are these floating images, these anonymous clichés, which circulate in the external world, but also penetrate each one of us and constitute his internal world, so that everyone possesses only psychic clichés by which he thinks and feels, is thought and is felt, being himself a cliché among others in the world which surrounds him.
>
> (Deleuze 1986: 208)

Deleuze has in mind here a compositional principle, not merely a bleak and mournful critique of a contemporary Western cine-psychic reality; in French, the word 'cliché' still refers strongly to the photographic negative, i.e. the matter from which multiple copies of images can be *generated*. Arguably, action heroes *perform* this compositional function of cliché, by the modelling over time of their very bodies after ideal athletic, beefcake or 'Bruce Lee' images and, in the case of 'major' heroes, by the enhancing of their bodies' potential by expensive 'special effects'. This constitutive relation to the cliché is in part why 'Arnie', 'Sly' (Sylvester Stallone) and 'Keanu' (Reeves) are at once so recognizable and so limited in their acting repertoire by our demand for recognition – we will not easily *allow* that they can act, or might be able to act, in other genres and other ways. However, minor action stars such as Seagal, Norris, Rothrock, Norton and van Damme have no 'repertoire' to speak of; abject as actors and yet models for emulation to untold numbers of fans (see Chuck Norris in *Sidekicks*, an apologia for martial arts cinema in terms of the benefits emulation can bring to physically disabled children), the minor stars are *authentic* clichés – 'real life martial artists' – and they know it. Kelly Makin's *Tiger Claws* is an explicit send-up of their burden of authenticity; here, the 'real' martial artist (Bolo Yeung) is an iconophobic psychopath who kills his master while the hero is played by the unconvincing and narcissistic Jalal Merhi, with the thoroughly authentic Cynthia Rothrock fluttering on the sidelines.

With this in mind, let me return to *Best of the Best* and the sequence that flows out of the opening predication of cliché-spaces for action (the field, the factory, the martial arts school). The rivalry narrative emerges in the third space when Tommy is handed his letter of invitation to try out for the US team. The rest of the sequence renders the other two spaces intelligible in terms of this narrative and further defines their protagonists, as Alex discusses his letter with his mother and son and then a barking, unsmiling leader now identifiable as Korean announces the results of what is now evidently a competition.

I want to examine more closely the longest section of the sequence, the one focused on Alex, for its consciousness of class (which is not the same thing as 'class consciousness' in a more exact sense). The white worker is territorialized on to the family within this sequence in a way that demarcates him (at this stage of events) from, on the one hand, the single but socially responsible Asian-American individual, and, on the other, the anonymous solidarity of 'the Koreans', who are given names and characteristics only much later in the film (when the Americans watch videos of their future opponents at work) and who are endowed with individuality only in the final scene of reconciliation when it turns out they can all speak English. In between these masculine extremes of Asian-American singularity and Korean collectivity, Alex is positioned as a white Family Man.

From a shot of Tommy pumping his fist in delight in response to his letter, we cut to a family tea-table and an argument between mother and son. Dialogue matters here, as it does in TV drama. In a few seconds of testy remarks between mother and son we learn that Alex is a white, Western version of the Hong Kong 'one-armed' hero; injured badly in a previous fight, he has plastic cartilage ('junk', his mother calls it) and a steel pin in his shoulder. Emotionally, too, he is maimed, if by industrialism rather than colonial occupation: 'Ma – I got *nothing* here. Nothing. Competing was the only thing that made me feel . . .'. Too moist-eyed and emotional to finish his sentence, Alex quivers the fingers of one hand upwards in a twisted, fragile gesture that echoes and contrasts with Tommy's conventional pumping fist, and softly adds, 'You saw me.' Mother and son share a tender moment of remembered pride, then she begins a new line of attack: 'what about your son?' So we learn that Alex is a single father, and watch him lovingly read his son a story of battle and male friendship from the medieval legend of King Arthur, the mythical 'Hero' of early Britain.

What kind of working-class consciousness is this?

Georg Lukács: the legend

The most influential and least read cultural theorist in the world these days is a Hungarian Marxist and Communist more than 30 years dead. The early work of Georg Lukács (1885–1971) is influential wherever students learn to recite that bourgeois culture converts history into nature; I picked that up from Barthes (1957), and Australian high school students still rehearse it today as they fluently decode advertisements. Lukács is influential wherever critics seek out the 'structuring absences' of a text, construing those things that it does not or 'cannot' say as more significant than its manifest content or surface. I learned to do this from Goldmann (1964) and from the 'symptomatic reading' of Althusser's collaborator, Macherey (1978). Reinforced and rendered personal by psychoanalysis, it is now a reproductive tactic of political correctness: 'You didn't talk about [my interests] and I find this symptomatic of your [political error]'. Above all, Lukács is influential wherever his major populariser, Fredric Jameson, is read,[10] and most pervasively in cultural studies through two of Jameson's revisions of Lukács. One of these is Jameson's (1991) thesis that 'late capitalist culture' from the 1960s is characterized by a loss of real historical consciousness; in *The Historical Novel* Lukács (1962) wrote exactly this about bourgeois decadence in Europe after 1848. Jameson's other revision of Lukács is earlier but, I believe, more consequential: the core cultural studies doctrine that in the most 'degraded' modes of art, the most commodified of cultural practices, there is a utopian energy reaching for a future moment of reconciliation or redemption. This comes to us through Raymond Williams and Stuart Hall, as well as from Jameson's wonderful 1979 essay on 'Reification and Utopia' (reprinted in Jameson 1992).

In emphasizing Lukács's barely acknowledged legacy in cultural studies, in particular that of *History and Class Consciousness* (published in 1923), I am not calling for a 'return' to his work.[11] There are serious reasons why Lukács's principles are, however much they varied over the course of his life, at odds with the kind of feminist and, in his terms, undoubtedly 'bourgeois' cultural studies that I practice. However, these are not the caricatural and reductive reasons that prevail in cultural studies *doxa*: for example, that because Lukács writes of 'false consciousness' he believes that ordinary people are 'cultural dopes' (or 'dupes'); or, because Lukács invoked 'totality', he must believe that there is a single transcendent position from which 'the truth' can be seen and mapped. Lukács did not think either of these foolish things, although he did want to distance what he called 'genuine historical analysis' from 'the naïve description of what men *in fact* thought, felt and wanted at any moment in history and from any given point in the class structure' (Lukács 1968: 50–51). Cultural studies is committed to examining people's diverse thinkings, feelings and desires, from as many given points as possible for a specific context of analysis and discussion to form, but it does not have to be devoted to 'naïve description'; like sociology (a mode of thought that Lukács despised), it can be very bad when it succumbs to this devotion.

Totality is a tricky issue for cultural studies practitioners; for many of us, totality is the name of a lofty dream of seeing the whole, or a 'lust to be a viewpoint' (de Certeau 1984: 92) projected by a Western tradition of masculinist and difference-denying intellectual desire. But for Lukács, totality (that is, the concrete totality of real relations under capitalism) never was a vista to be 'viewed' from a detached position; in the 1920s he explicitly criticized this illusion and the flattering but self-deluding role it accorded to intellectuals (see Jay 1984: 125–127). The argument of *History and Class Consciousness* is rather that totality could only be grasped in 'immanence', and only from one standpoint emergent in the heat and dust of capitalism: the proletariat. As a shortcut to why this idea does not work for most of us today, consider the moment in *True Lies* when Harry Trasker, Fast Faisal and Albert (Tom Arnold) are blasted by their CIA boss (played by the granddaddy of patriotic, gun-toting American action heroes, Charlton Heston): 'Please tell me how I can see this as anything but a total disaster?' Arnie replies in a 'shit happens' mode ('Total is a strong word . . .'), while Albert stammers defensively: '*yeah . . . there are different degrees of totality*'. This is a mild joke, a non-sense or logical transgression, but its low-power humour captures very precisely the dry refusal of epistemological ambition that forms a routine, working ideology for many intellectuals and service workers today: it is a realistic articulation of common sense perceptions about the ultimately ungraspable and uncontrollable nature of our world.

Lukács would have had no problem diagnosing this 'common sense' as profoundly petty-bourgeois. But for cultural studies as for feminist, postcolonial, or queer scholarship today, the real trouble with *History and Class Consciousness* is precisely its theory of class. Lukács wrote out of a Marxism that had multiple class categories at its disposal but for him (in this phase of his thinking) only two mattered: the bourgeoisie and the proletariat, 'the only pure classes in bourgeois society' (Lukács 1968: 59). Theirs was the struggle for the future; only their class interests were concentrated on 'the construction of society as a whole'. The aristocracy, the petty-bourgeoisie, the peasantry, the lumpen-proletariat could be regarded as 'vestigial', left-over from feudal society, and/or 'transitional', trying to effect (like Albert's joke) 'adjustments' to the capitalist order – as the chivalric personal pedagogy of Alex does in *Best of the Best*. The problem today is not only that this stripped-down theory cannot recognize gender, sexuality, race or coloniality as operative categories for 'genuine historical analysis', but also that the marginalization of peasants, the petty-bourgeoisie and the underclass was a wrong move on its own turf, that of class analysis itself, as these categories have come into focus as immensely important and *consequential* in the globalizing struggle between capital and labour in our time.

These three class figures are in fact the key 'social heroes' of the global action cinema that has emerged over the past 20 years, and this is most clearly visible if we allow Hong Kong cinema a formative role along with Hollywood in shaping the genre. Most Western action films, 'major' or 'minor' in mode, are all about 'petty-bourgeois' people, whether aspirational workers like Alex Grady, or those on the sleazy end of the corporate-managerial class, the foot soldiers and mercenaries of finance capitalism (Harry Tasker, the spy disguised as a computer salesman). Hong Kong cinema has plenty of these, but significantly also lots of peasants or former peasants on the make, seeking upward mobility through rural to urban migration (a scenario incipient in most of the adult Bruce Lee's Hong Kong films) – diasporics drifting from city to city, caught up in criminal or gangster activity. Hollywood and Hong Kong films alike are full of lumpen-proletarians, all those street-fighters, bodyguards, hired muscle, hitmen, prostitutes and self-employed 'martial artists' trying to survive with the only assets they have, their bodies, their beliefs and their street-smarts.

Now, for Lukács proletarian class consciousness was special because it transformed the world: 'in contrast with [the self-consciousness of a slave], when the worker knows himself as a commodity his knowledge is practical. *That is to say, this knowledge brings about an objective structural change in the object of knowledge*' (Lukács 1968: 169). If a slave becomes aware that he is a 'slave' (says Lukács), this changes nothing because slavery is an accident that befalls an individual in a certain type of society. But when a worker in the key structural position of producing commodities – that is, reified forms of a relation between people, not between people and things – comes to know that he *himself* is a commodity, this transforms the 'object of knowledge', i.e. the worker 'himself'. He is in a position to apprehend the totality of concrete relations under capitalism and he is also (Lukács argues) in a position to do something about it.

Suppose that, in a petty-bourgeois spirit of affirming 'different degrees of totality', we bring to bear the knowledge of other key worker-commodities in contemporary capitalism, such as: sex workers; soldiers (on soldier-commodities, see *Soldier* with Kurt Russell and *Universal Soldier* with van Damme and Lundgren); sportsmen and professional fighters, martial artists for hire; indeed, super-models. What do sex workers, super-models or super-soldiers *know* when they know themselves as commodities, and what kind of change does this knowledge bring about, or have the potential to bring about? For Lukács (for whom it was doubtful that peasants, petty-bourgeois and lumpens could claim 'class' status at all), they could only learn 'the hopelessness of their particularist strivings in the face of the inevitable course of events' (Lukács 1968: 61). In cultural studies, a comparably automatic answer might be, 'there's no single answer to that question'. A better response would be: 'it depends on where, what and *who* else, she might be or be becoming'; we produce (rather than 'arrive at') useful understanding of the transformative value of knowledge by articulating responses from *different* places in the concrete totality.

A spatializing answer will miss the mark here if it rests content with a potentially endless listing of ever more minutely defined *positions* in relations of exploitation and oppression. As with 'apprehension' for Lukács, articulation is an *event*; it takes work, and it unfolds in time. So, too, does the famous 'body' of the action star; bodily *knowledge* in action cinema generally has to be a paying activity. In action cinema, the body may be many things – object, spectacle, prosthesis, site of desire, commodity, product of labour – but it is first and foremost *a way of making a living* and sometimes, as in Cynthia Rothrock's films, the body is a means of access to wider kinds of independence. This is why the contrasting, Hong Kong-derived figure of the pure, ethically-driven martial artist who does not 'sell' his skills has utopian force in Western cinema, however, tacky or 'Orientalist' its rendition. Underpinned by the DIY, 'teach yourself' exercise culture I mentioned earlier, the 'artistically' trained, lovingly shaped, and spiritualized martial body functions – in the very midst of a multi-million dollar 'self-improvement' industry – as an emblem of unalienated labour.

Yet these are Lukácsian claims that need to be supplemented. One way to develop (on another occasion) a more nuanced understanding of knowledge issues in action cinema is modelled in Eve Sedgwick's analysis in *The Epistemology of the Closet* of Herman Melville's novel *Billy Budd*. Discussing the juncture of same-sex desire with homophobia in the violent figure of Claggart, Sedgwick writes:

> The projective mutual accusation of two mirror-image men, drawn together in a bond that renders desire indistinguishable from predation, is the typifying gesture of paranoid knowledge. 'It takes one to know one' is its epistemological principle, for it is able, in Melville's phrase, to form no conception of an unreciprocated emotion . . . And its disciplinary processes are all tuned to the note of police entrapment.
>
> (Sedgwick 1990: 100)

Two mirror-image men: think of all the bonded male 'double'-couples that inhabit the hybridizing space between Hong Kong and Hollywood cinema: *Iceman Cometh*, *Demolition Man*, *Face Off*. However, Sedgwick's text is most helpful for its stress on the *problem* of reciprocity, on the violence of ways of knowing that admit 'no conception of an unreciprocated emotion' and the difficulty of thinking *with* such a conception. As I noted earlier, the major action hero's model of learning – 'paranoid knowledge' – is such that his central problem is, 'are you like me, or *not* like me?' There is no place for a third possibility, the unreciprocal or unresponsive. Action heroes often come to self-consciousness *as* heroes in Hollywood cinema when they decide that they are *not* 'like' the villain: 'you're just like me', says the neo-Nazi to the angry-white-male-on-a rampage in *Falling Down*, and the latter is bemused before rejecting the appeal: 'I'm an American and you're a sick fuck'. Two deviant copies of heroism argue about their relation to each other and the scene explodes with rape and murder. However, the tragedy of Michael Douglas' 'American' is in fact that he is *becoming* the 'sick fuck', a laid-off worker and a family man gone astray, becoming his mirror-image, 'the bad guy' – but he will be the last one to know.

In the canon of minor cinema, however, there is at least one scene in which an action heroine discovers unreciprocated emotion. David Worth's *Angel of Fury*, a.k.a *Lady Dragon 2* (Rapi Films, Indonesia, 1991), allows into its narrative sentiments between women which undermine what Spivak (1988) famously called the rescue fantasy: 'white men are saving brown women from brown men'. Expatriate martial arts star Susan (Cynthia Rothrock) sallies forth in Jakarta to save her servant, Sari (Bella Esperance), from white and brown men alike.[12] As the scene begins Sari is in the classic 'woman-to-be-rescued' position, tied up on the edge of the action while Susan takes out all the men, but as the 'Angel of Fury' strides confidently towards her ('C'mon Sari, let's get you out of here'), Sari pulls a gun. Various threads lead up to this surprise, but Sari's interruption of her own rescue gives over an inordinately long time *in dialogue* for a race- as well as class-intensive commodity rebellion to erupt. The exchange is too long to quote in its entirety, but as the white woman and the 'brown' woman circle each other giddily, full face to the camera, framed by the airy massiveness of the depot and wedged in by the vivid colours of sleek, motionless trains, the no-longer subaltern Sari expounds her social philosophy:

> In this world there are two kinds of people, those who buy and those who are sold. Well I'm tired of being sold! . . . I don't ever want to serve, or cook, or clean, or fetch for anyone ever again!

Susan can't believe her ears and appeals to Sari to conform to her 'true' model, the virtuous servant ('This doesn't sound like you!'), a demand for correct emulation that drives Sari into a rage: 'Doesn't sound like me? Not like me! God! You don't know me! You don't even notice me . . .'. Susan's feeble liberal response ('I treated you as my friend . . . as an equal') underlines that Sari's reproaches are just.

Alas, Sari's commodity self-knowledge is insufficient to save her. A creature of melodrama with a low *gender* consciousness, she converts her rebellion into another rescue fantasy – that the bad guy will take her away ('to Rio!') in reward for her treachery to Susan. Susan's scornful response is pragmatic, as befits an action heroine ('Get real! Diego doesn't want you, he wants the diamonds!') and with an unanswerable 'fuck you' she terminates their dispute – a genre dispute, about what kind of film this will be, action or romance. Sadly, Susan is correct about what kind of film this is; Diego does want the diamonds, and Sari the treacherous servant is shot a few moments later. However, the memory of her aberrant outburst – barely motivated by the narrative, intensely filmed – lingers powerfully over the routine ending.

Films such as *Angel of Fury* are arguably bad for the development of a national film industry, as companies like Rapi use up resources, funding and talent to make international quickies in 'cheap' locations (Sen 1994). A cultural studies approach, however, might want to research the 'uptake' of the scene I have just described – how is it received as the film circulates in different exhibition contexts and spaces? What varying uptakes of Sari's outburst might there be in, for example, Hong Kong, where large numbers of Chinese families employ Filipina and Indonesian maids? More widely, we need to think transnationally about the generic mixing involved in an aesthetically 'rough' film like *Angel of Fury*. The contrast in style between Rothrock's 'no-acting' acting and the high formal melodrama of Esperance's performance may be 'only' a contingency of production, but it is striking; such economically conjoined *aesthetic* contingencies and the way they work disjunctively, for diverse audience contexts, would be a good place (I like to imagine) for a transnational study of action cinema to begin.

Notes

1 One of the earliest versions of this story still available today is Akira Kurosawa's influential *Sugata Sanshiro* (Japan, 1943).
2 'Transnational Imagination in Action Cinema: Hong Kong and the Making of a Global Popular Culture", Research Grants Council Competitive Earmarked Research Grant, Hong Kong, 2001–03.
3 My point here bears on Western criticism in English that unreflectively approaches Hong Kong cinema *as though it were* a 'national cinema'. In criticism written in Hong Kong, the term 'national' now usually designates the Hong Kong Special Administrative Region's complex relations with, and position within, the People's Republic of China. On the complexities of this issue, see the Introduction to Cheung and Chu (2004).
4 Mr Law Kar of the Hong Kong Film Archive drew our attention in a conversation to the popularity of films from the Philippines in Hong Kong during this period.
5 For copious information about this series see 'Nikki White's Samurai Page', http:// www. webone.com.au?_nikkiw/
6 I owe this observation to Li Siu-leung.
7 The last time I looked there were four films in the series; Rhee himself directed *Best of the Best 3*, which was duly promoted as 'the first film by a Korean-American'.
8 See Deleuze and Guattari (1987), especially chapter 4, 'Postulates of Linguistics'. My use of their distinction is loose indeed, since for them it corresponds to 'two different treatments of language, one of which consists in extracting constants from it, the other in placing it in continuous variation' (Deleuze and Guattari 1987: 106). In these terms it would make no sense to claim that all direct-to-tape action cinema places cinematic materials 'in continuous variation', although a particular director or a film text might.
9 Following this definition, any Hollywood film might become 'minor' as it is dubbed into local languages. In a developed analysis it also would be important to consider such developments as the 'Korean blockbuster', arguably a 'minor' mode of big-screen action cinema itself.
10 For Jameson's clearest statement of his debt to Lukács, see 'The Case for Georg Lukács' in Jameson (1971).
11 I am inclined to agree with Lichtheim's (1967: 245–255) assessment of Lukács's career as 'an intellectual disaster'. Given the extent of Lukács's impact on cultural studies, it is for this very reason that I believe we should re-read his work carefully.
12 This is a partial reversal of the roles the two women played in *Lady Dragon*, where Rothrock *masquerades* as a servant for a rich Indonesian woman (Esperance).

References

Anderson, Benedict (1998) *The Spectre of Comparisons: Nationalism, Southeast Asia and the World*, London: Verso.
Augé, Marc (1992) *Non-Places: Introduction to an Anthropology of Supermodernity*, John Howe (trans.) London: Verso.
Barthes, Roland (1957) *Mythologies*, Paris: Seuil.
Cheung, Esther M.K. and Chu Yiu-wah (2004) *Between Home and World: A Reader In Hong Kong Cinema*, Hong Kong: Oxford University Press.
Connery, Christopher (2002) 'Maoism: China's Globalism', paper delivered at *Higher Education and the Humanities* co-organised by *Boundary 2* and the English Department of Nanjing University with the English Department, University of Hong Kong, 3–4 May. Forthcoming, *South Atlantic Quarterly*.
Dai, Jinhua (2002) *Cinema and Desire: Feminist Marxism and Cultural Politics*. In Jing Wang and Tani E. Barlow (eds) *The Work of Dai Jinhua*, London: Verso.
de Certeau, Michel (1984) *The Practice of Everyday Life*, Steven F. Rendall (trans.), Berkeley and Los Angeles: University of California Press.
Deleuze, Gilles (1986) *Cinema 1: The Movement-Image*, High Tomlinson and Barbara Habberjam (trans.), Minneapolis: University of Minnesota Press.

Deleuze, Gilles and Guattari, Félix (1987) *A Thousand Plateaus: Capitalism and Schizophrenia*, Brian Massumi (trans.), Minneapolis: University of Minnesota Press.

Desser, David (2000) 'The kung fu craze: Hong Kong cinema's first American reception'. In Fu Poshek and David Desser (eds) *The Cinema of Hong Kong: History, Arts, Identity*, Cambridge: Cambridge University Press, 19–43.

Ding Naifei (2001) *Obscene Things: Intimate Politics in Jin Ping Mei*, Durham: Duke University Press.

During, Simon (1992) 'Postcolonialism and globalization', *Meanjin* 51(2): 339–353.

Gilroy, Paul (1993) *The Black Atlantic: Modernity and Double Consciousness*, Cambridge, MA: Harvard University Press.

Goldmann, Lucien (1964) *The Hidden God: A Study of Tragic Vision in the Pensées of Pascal and the Tragedies of Racine*, Phillip Thody (trans.), London: Routledge and Kegan Paul. First published in French 1956.

Hall, Catherine (2002) *Civilising Subjects: Colony and Metropole in the English Imagination, 1830–1867*, Chicago: University of Chicago Press.

Jameson, Fredric (1971) *Marxism and Form*, Princeton NJ: Princeton University Press.

Jameson, Fredric (1991) *Postmodernism, or, The Cultural Logic of Late Capitalism*, Durham: Duke University Press.

Jameson, Fredric (1992) *Signatures of the Visible*, New York and London: Routledge.

Jay, Martin (1984) *Marxism and Totality: The Adventures of a Concept from Lukács To Habermas*, Berkeley and Los Angeles: University of California Press.

Kleinhans, Chuck (1996) 'Class in action', in David E. James and Rick Berg (eds) *The Hidden Foundation: Cinema and the Question of Class*, Minneapolis: Minnesota University Press, 240–263.

Law Kar (ed.) (2000) *Border Crossings in Hong Kong Cinema*, The 24th Hong Kong International Film Festival, Hong Kong: Leisure and Cultural Services Department.

Lichtheim, George (1967) *The Concept of Ideology and Other Essays*, New York: Vintage Books.

Lukács, Georg (1962) *The Historical Novel*, Hannah and Stanley Mitchell (trans.), Lincoln and London: University of Nebraska Press. First published in German 1955.

Lukács, Georg (1968) *History and Class Consciousness*, Rodney Livingstone (trans.), London: Merlin Press. First published in German 1923.

Macherey, Pierre (1978) *A Theory of Literary Production*, Geoff Wall (trans.), London: Routledge. First published in French 1966.

Martin, Adrian (2005) 'At the edge of the cut: the "Hong Kong Style" in contemporary world cinema'. In Meaghan Morris, Siu-leung Li and Stephen Chan Ching-kiu (eds) *Hong Kong Connections. Transnational Imagination in Action Cinema*, Hong Kong, Durham and London: Hong Kong University Press and Duke University Press, 175–188.

McClintock, Ann (1995) *Imperial Leather: Race, Gender and Sexuality in the Colonial Context*, London and New York: Routledge.

Morris, Meaghan (1998) 'White panic, or Mad Max and the sublime', in Kuan-Hsing Chen (ed.) *Trajectories: Inter-Asia Cultural Studies*, London and New York: Routledge, 239–262.

Morris, Meaghan (2000) 'Globalisation and its discontents', *Meridian* 17(2): 17–29; also in *Sekai* 686 (2001), 266–278 [Japanese].

Morris, Meaghan (2001) 'Learning from Bruce Lee: pedagogy and political correctness in martial arts cinema', in Matthew Tinckcom and Amy Villarejo (eds) *Keyframes: Popular Film and Cultural Studies*, London and New York: Routledge, 171–186.

Morris, Meaghan (2004) 'The man from Hong Kong in Sydney, 1975'. In Judith Ryan and Chris Wallace-Crabbe (eds) *Imagining Australia: Literature and Culture in the New New World*, Cambridge, MA: Harvard University Press, 235–266.

Pickering, Michael (1997) *History, Experience and Cultural Studies*, London: Macmillan.

Sedgwick, Eve Kosofsky (1990) *Epistemology of the Closet*, Berkeley and Los Angeles: University of California Press.

Sen, Krishna (1994) *Indonesian Cinema*, London and New Jersey: Zed Books.

Spivak, Gayatri Chakravorty (1988) 'Can the subaltern speak?' In Cary Nelson and Lawrence Grossberg (eds) *Marxism and the Interpretation of Culture*, Urbana: University of Illinois Press, 271–313.

Srinivas, S. V. (2005) 'Hong Kong action film and the career of the Telugu mass hero'. In Meaghan Morris, Siu-leung Li and Stephen Chan Ching-kiu (eds) *Hong Kong Connections. Transnational Imagination in Action Cinema*, Hong Kong, Durham and London: Hong Kong University Press and Duke University Press, 111–124.

Steedman, Carolyn (1995) *Strange Dislocations: Childhood and the Idea of Human Inferiority, 1780–1930*, Cambridge, MA: Harvard University Press.

Teo, Stephen (1997) *Hong Kong Cinema: The Extra Dimensions*, London: British Film Institute.

Willemen, Paul (1994) *Looks and Frictions: Essays in Cultural Studies and Film Theory*, Bloomington and London: Indiana University Press and British Film Institute.

Yau, Esther (ed.) (2001) *At Full Speed: Hong Kong Cinema in a Borderless World*, Minneapolis: Minnesota University Press.

Chapter 20

The 'Bollywoodization' of the Indian cinema

Cultural nationalism in a global arena

Ashish Rajadhyaksha

I Rajnikant in Japan

> The West may have the biggest stalls in the world's media bazaar, but it is not the only player. Globalization isn't merely another word for Americanization – and the recent expansion of the Indian entertainment industry proves it. For hundreds of millions of fans around the world, it is Bollywood – India's film industry – not Hollywood, that spins their screen fantasies. Bollywood, based in Mumbai, has become a global industry. India's entertainment moguls don't merely target the billion South Asians, or desis, at home: they make slick movies, songs and TV shows for export. Attracted by a growing middle class and a more welcoming investment environment, foreign companies are flocking to Bollywood, funding films and musicians. The foreign money is already helping India's pop culture to reach even greater audiences. And it may have a benign side-effect in cleaning up an Indian movie industry business long haunted by links to the underworld.
>
> ('Bollywood Goes International', *Newsweek International*,
> February 28, 2000)

Let us keep aside for a moment the gross misrepresentations in *Newsweek*: that the Indian film industry is not solely based in Bombay, that 'foreign money' is still hardly available for film *productions* even though it would like to cream off non-local *distribution* profits; that such money is not necessarily distinguishable from the 'underworld' and is, therefore, not exactly what you would describe as 'benign'; that *Newsweek*'s assumptions about good and bad money are unsustainable and pernicious.

Let us concentrate instead on just what this literature claims is happening. For something like the past decade, leading up to *Newsweek*'s final consecration, a range of print and television media have been claiming some rather dramatic developments in the Indian cinema. Practically every newspaper has commented, usually in the same breathless prose as *Newsweek*, on the phenomenon: there is a craze for 'Bollywood' masala that quite exceeds anything we've ever seen before; from Tokyo to Timbuktu people are dancing to Indipop, names such as Shah Rukh Khan are circulating in places where people may never have heard of Indira Gandhi, and there seems to be an opportunity, there is apparently money to be made. Everyone, it seems, is scrambling – new Bollywood websites continue to emerge, new distributors and intermediaries rise with new ideas of how to exploit this development, new television channels are seen, satellite technology is projected with an unprecedented ability to overcome distribution inefficiencies – and every one of these is powered by entrepreneurs and their venture-capitalist backers, and their unique idea about what will earn money.

On what is this hype based? Interestingly, in the past year, the box office of an Indian cinema made indigenously was itself less central to the phenomenon than a range of ancillary industries, mostly based in London, including theatre (the much-hyped London stage musical *Bombay Dreams*, a collaboration between Indian composer A. R. Rehman and Andrew Lloyd Webber), the music industry, advertising[1] and even fashion (the month-long 'Bollywood' festival of food, furniture and fashion marketing in Selfridges, London), all of which culminated in the extraordinary marketing exercise known as *Indian Summer*, in July 2002 (see http:// www.bbc.co.uk/asianlife/film/indian summer/index.shtml).

All of this began, it is usually said, with the four films that *Newsweek* also mentions as having made distribution history, three of them directly or indirectly Yash Chopra productions: *Dilwale Dulhania Le Jayenge* (*DDLJ*, 1995), the film which in some ways started it all, *Dil To Pagal Hai* (*DTPH*, 1997) and Karan Johar's *Kuch Kuch Hota Hai* (*KKHH*, 1998), and Subhash Ghai's *Taal* (1998). Before all these, there is of course the original box-office hit *Hum Aapke Hain Kaun?* (1994). Of *Taal*, for example, producer and noted 'showman' of Hindi cinema Ghai said,

> There'll be 125 prints of *Taal* only for the foreign market. This is almost a three-fold increase since *Pardes*, for which I'd made 45 prints, and five times that of *Khalnayak*. Hindi films now have a significant market in the US, Canada, UK and the Middle East. It is making inroads into South Africa and Australia. And it is also popular in Japan, Hong Kong, South East Asia and, of course, Mauritius. In most if not all these countries, Hindi films are no longer weekend events, they are showing three shows everyday wherever they're released. Now, beginning with *Taal*, there will be vinyl banner hoardings advertising the films on the roads of the Western cities. Everybody, including the Westerners, will now see what films are on! The whole world will take note, because we will also be on the net.
>
> (Ratnottama Sengupta, 'Taalis for the Showman',
> *The Times of India*, 8 July 1999)

How much did these films collectively earn? That's difficult to say, but *The Economic Times* reported that 'The first big success of the new Bollywood is *Who Am I to You?* (*Hum Aapke Hain Koun?* dubbed), a musical that focuses on two weddings. Thanks to its untraditional [sic] plot and effective marketing, it's India's biggest hit ever. Playing for nearly a year, the film grossed more than $30 million, a phenomenal amount in a country where the average moviegoer pays 65 per cent admission and the average movie makes about $3 million – barely what an arthouse film makes in the US' (Sharon Moshavi, 'Bollywood breaks into the big time', *The Economic Times*, 3 October 1995). Of *Taal*, the same paper reports that it was

> released around the world on August 13 (and) grossed the highest average collection per cinema hall (per screen average) for movies released in North America on the August 13–15 weekend. According to Weekend Box-Office figures, the first three-day collections were $591,280. Released simultaneously on 44 theatres in North

America, *Taal* has set a record for Bollywood releases abroad by notching the highest first three-day collections with $13,438 per screen. Though there is no independent verification, a press release by Eros Entertainment Inc, the distributor of the film abroad, claimed that *Taal*'s initial collections have even surpassed that of Hollywood blockbusters like *Haunting*, *The Blair Witch Project* and *Eyes Wide Shut*.

('US Box Office Sways to the Rhythm of *Taal*',
The Economic Times, 21 August 1999)

All these are undoubted marketing successes, and the releases – in particular of *Kuch Kuch* in South Africa, *Dil to Pagal Hai* in Israel and the brief weekend when *Taal* made it to the top 10 in the US domestic market – are now the stuff of marketing legend. On the other hand, here is a salutary fact: *Newsweek* claims that 'India's movie exports jumped from $10 million a decade ago to $100 million last year, and may top $250 million in 2000'.

Contrast these figures with the brief dotcom boom when every Indian internet portal, such as satyam online, rediff-on-the-net and planetasia, marketed itself with Bollywood paraphernalia. Following the unprecedented sale of just one portal, indiainfo.com, for Rs500 crore (or over $100 million), it would have been a safe argument that just ten of the top websites of the time (as computed by a *Businessworld* issue, 'Hot New Dot.coms', 24 January 2000) were, in that period, collectively worth more than the total box-office earnings of the Indian film industry.

There was, and continues to be, a real discrepancy involved. Contrary to *Newsweek*'s statement that Bollywood is 'India's film industry . . . based in Mumbai', perhaps we could argue instead precisely that, at least in one sense, this is not so: that Bollywood is *not* the Indian film industry, or at least not the film industry alone. Bollywood admittedly occupies a space analogous to the film industry, but might best be seen as a more diffuse cultural conglomeration involving a range of distribution and con-sumption activities from websites to music cassettes, from cable to radio. If so, the film industry itself – determined here solely in terms of its box office turnover and sales of print and music rights, all that actually comes back to the producer – can by definition constitute only a part, and perhaps even an *alarmingly small* part, of the overall culture industry that is currently being created and marketed.

If this is so, then at the back of it all is a real difficulty, one that, for all its unprecedentedness, has a disarmingly familiar tone. The fact is that nobody responsible for the production of the film narrative, if we include in this the producers, directors and stars responsible for the nuts-and-bolts assembly of the cinematic product that goes into these markets, actually knows what is going on. How do they make sense of these developments? Why is *Dil To Pagal Hai* popular in Tel Aviv, and why now? How would they convert all this hoopla into a stable market that would guarantee their next product an audience? Nobody quite knows the overall picture, and it is worth exploring some of the literature that's emerged on these developments to speculate on just why that is so.

Amitabh Bachchan, for example, was one of the iconic stars of the 1970s and early 1980s, before his career nosedived following the 'first-ever' effort to corporatize the film industry with the lame-duck ABCL, which most critics say was 'an idea before its time'. Despite not having a substantial hit for over a decade, Bachchan is India's most famous 'film personality', mainly through a Bollywoodized makeover that owes itself to television (he hosted the Hindi version of *Who Wants to be a Millionaire* for Star TV), and he has this to say:

> Evidently, our film personalities have begun to matter in world fora. Hindi cinema is gaining worldwide recognition and I don't mean only those films which make it to Berlin or Cannes. Once, I was walking down London's Piccadilly Circus and I saw this group of Kurds running towards me. (Laughs) I thought they wanted to assassinate me. But they stopped right there and started singing songs from *Amar Akbar Anthony* and *Muqaddar Ka Sikandar*. Rajnikant is tremendously popular in Japan. And I'm told that our stars are known even in Fiji, Bali and Chile. Amazing! But we're not marketing ourselves properly. Someone out there is making pots of money at our expense.
>
> (Interview, '*Netvamsham!*', *The Times of India*, 18 July 1999)

Who is this mysterious 'someone' making money and how come Bachchan doesn't know? Let us explore this further with the instance that Bachchan himself provides, perhaps the most bizarre instance in this whole new development: the sudden, inexplicable, popularity of Rajnikant in Japan.

Rajnikant is, of course, well known as perhaps the biggest Tamil film star ever, after the legendary M. G. Ramachandran, but it is also important to say that his career has largely been restricted to that language, despite several efforts to get into Hindi film, where he has often played subsidiary parts in Bachchan films (*Andha Kanoon*, 1983, *Giraftaar*, 1985, *Hum*, 1991) and one marginal effort in a Hollywood production (*Bloodstone*, 1989). Within Tamil Nadu where he reigns supreme, on the other hand, he has demonstrated all the hallmarks of a major star who knows his audience and his market: he has carefully constructed his screen persona, built a team around him that understands how to work it, has even tested out his popularity politically when he campaigned on behalf of the DMK and was at least partially responsible for its victory in the 1996 elections.

And then came his Japanese success. Here is *The New Indian Express* on this phenomenon:

> An entire generation of recession-hit Japanese have discovered a new hero: Rajnikant. Jayalalitha's bête noire and the man with that unflagging swagger and oh-so-cool wrist flicks has emerged there as the hippest craze after Leonardo DiCaprio and *Muthu*, his 150th film, is the biggest grosser in Japan after *Titanic*. So far the film has been seen by over 127,000 Japanese in a 23-week run at Tokyo's Cinema Rise alone, netting as much as $1.7 million and premieres on satellite television in June.
>
> ('Rajnikant bowls over Japanese youth', *The New Indian Express*, 10 June 1999)

So how does one explain this success? B. Kandaswamy Bharathan, executive producer at Kavithalaya, credited with having masterminded the Japanese marketing of this film, offers a typically 'Bollywoodist-culturalist' explanation:

The movie carries an important message – that money is not everything in life. Instead, it propagates human values, highlighted in the first song itself – and this philosophy appealed to the Japanese audience. This is especially significant for a youth that's been talked down about for not being as hardworking as the post-war generation.

('Rajnikant bowls over Japanese youth', The New Indian Express, 10 June 1999)

Indeed. Keeping aside the distortions by which the producer of Muthu represents his own production, in fact a violent feudal drama addressing caste differences, I am reasonably sure that if one were to ask Bharathan why this film proved a hit and no other, and how he suggests that Rajnikant capitalize on this sudden popularity to stabilize a Japanese market for his next film and his future career, we may perhaps get an honest answer, that he has no idea why Muthu did well in Tokyo.

2 Cinema versus the Bollywood culture industry

Says Ft. Lauderdale housewife Sameera Biswas, 'We go to the movies to keep our culture alive'.

('Bollywood Goes International', Newsweek International, 28 February 2000)

'Kids in Bombay go to night clubs to become Western. Here (i.e. in Brisbane) we go to assert our Eastern identity. The basic difference lies there' – Fiji Indian enthusiast of Indipop.

(Ray 2000)

The main contention of this paper seeks to separate out the Bollywood industry from the Indian cinema. It suggests that while the cinema has been in existence as a national industry of sorts for the past 50 years (the Indian cinema, of course, has celebrated its centenary, but the industry, in the current sense of the term, might be most usefully traced to the post-Second World War boom in production), Bollywood has been around for only about a decade now. The term today refers to a reasonably specific narrative and a mode of presentation: the Newsweek essay, for example, quotes Plus Channel's Amit Khanna as saying that 'Indian movies are feel-good, all-happy-in-the-end, tender love stories with lots of songs and dances . . . That's what attracts non-Indian audiences across the world' and to this we could add 'family values' and their palpable, if not entirely self-evident, investment in 'our culture'. To such content we would need also to add a distinctive mode of presentation, couched in the post-Information Technology claims that Indian enterprise has been making in the past few years of global competitiveness, and by language such as:

Spurred by competition from dubbed versions of such flashy Western hits as Jurassic Park and Speed, Bollywood is rushing to enter the era of high tech films. Producers are founding new companies, boosting their marketing, and seeking new sources of financing . . . [C]ameras are rolling for the first Bollywood high-tech films. CMM

Ltd, an 18-month-old special-effects company backed by such stalwarts as State Bank of India, has bought more than $1 million worth of software and hardware from Silicon Graphics Inc, the Mountain View (California) computer company whose special-effects equipment is used by nearly every Hollywood studio. The technology is key to a still untitled film featuring Indian megastar Shah Rukh Khan in a double role, allowing him to appear with himself in the same scene. Silicon Graphics is lining up other clients in India as well.

(Sharon Moshavi, 'Bollywood breaks into the big time', The Economic Times, 3 October 1995)

There are further distinctions to be made: while Bollywood exists for, and prominently caters to, a diasporic audience of Indians, and sometimes (as, for example, with Bhangra-rap) exports *into* India, the Indian cinema – much as it would wish to tap this 'non-resident' audience – is only occasionally successful in doing so, and is in almost every instance able to do so only when it, so to say, *Bollywoodizes* itself, a transition that very few films in Hindi, and hardly any in other languages, are actually able to do.

Speaking historically, ever since the film industry in India assumed something like its current form – the period roughly between 1946 and 1975 – the export market of films has been a relatively minor, disorganized and chaotic, but at the same time familiar, field. Few films were made with a non-Indian audience in mind, and the 'foreign market' (usually a single territory) remained small, and entirely controlled by the government of India's Indian Motion Picture Export Corporation, which in its initial years was accountable to the Reserve Bank of India and later merged with the National Film Development Corporation. Film was dominated by state policy on export and remained, until 1992 when the area was de-controlled and opened out to private enterprise, subsidiary to the policy of exporting 'art' films within the film festival circuit. It was generally assumed in this time that Indian mainstream films, to the extent to which they had an offshore audience at all, addressed émigré Indians or their descendants. In 1975–77, for example, statistics show that Indian films were exported to Africa, the Arab states, Trinidad, Guyana and Barbados, Burma, Hong Kong, Indonesia, Iran, Malaysia, Singapore, Sri Lanka and Thailand.[2] Perhaps the most visible form of export in this time was the 'gulf boom', of workers (domestic, industrial, white-collar) exported to the Middle East becoming an audience for Malayalam films through the 1970s. Apart from this kind of market, the only other that existed was the one related to bilateral trade arrangements with the Socialist bloc, as part of what came to be called Nehruite internationalism, but which nevertheless did yield some spectacular marketing successes, such as Raj Kapoor's films, and later Mithun Chakraborty's, in the former USSR.

Such audiences, and such modes of marketing, could hardly resemble what we are trying here to identify as the Bollywood culture industry of the 1990s. The term itself, Bollywood, has been around most notably in film trade journals – it was probably invented in a slightly jokey self-deprecating way by the journal *Screen* in Bombay and by its page 'Bollywood Beat', with the companion words Tollywood for the Calcutta film industry based in Tollygunge and even, for a while, Mollywood for the Madras industry, neither of which are of course used these days. It is probable that its current usage is a British one, associated with Channel 4's ethnic programming as we see in

Kabir (2001), and came into circulation via literary speculations on film as mass culture by writers such as Shashi Tharoor or Farrukh Dhondy on Indian film to mean what it does today: an expression of the outsider's fascination with a slightly surreal practice that nevertheless appears to possess the claim to be a genuine popular art form. So Tharoor, for example, says:

> The way in which different communities have come together for simply secular ends whether in ecological movements like the Himalayan agitations against deforestation, or in the social work of Baba Amte, or in the cinema industry of Bollywood – points to the potential for co-operative rather than divisive mobilisation. It is when groups have stayed apart, and failed to interact in secular activities, that their communal identities prevail; the lack of brotherhood guarantees their 'other' hood. And then conflict, hatred and violence can erupt.
>   Not surprisingly, this idea of India is one that is sustained by our popular culture. Some readers might think my reference to Bollywood out of place. One of my novels deals with the trashy world of commercial cinema – because to me, Indian films, with all their limitations and outright idiocies, represent part of the hope for India's future. In a country that is still 50 per cent illiterate, films represent the prime vehicle for the transmission of popular culture and values.
>
> ('Make Bollywood's India a Reality', *The Indian Express*,
> 19 April 1998)

Today, as Tharoor shows (or rather unwittingly demonstrates), the term comes with its own narrative, one that we could perhaps call techno-nostalgia, and is clearly not restricted any more solely to the cinema but informs a range of products and practices. It would certainly have informed the displays around the Swaminarayan Sanstha's Cultural Festival of India in Edison, New Jersey, in 1991, when one apparently entered through large gates signifying traditional temple entrances which were named Mayur Dwar (Peacock Gate) and Gaja Dwar (Elephant Gate), and saw traditional artisans making handicrafts sharing their space with entrepreneurs from Jackson Heights selling electronic products, with sponsorship from AT&T. Of this form, most directly demonstrated in recent cinematic memory by the foreign-returned Rani Mukherjee in *KKHH* suddenly bursting into the bhajan *Om jai jagdish hare*, Sandhya Shukla has this to say:

> Emerging as it did out of a constellation of interests – Indian, Indian-American and otherwise American – the Cultural Festival generated questions about common ground: where was it and how did it function? [T]he Cultural Festival deliberately intertwined culture, nation and identity in its production of metaphors and myths. *With the synchronous developments of international capital and diasporic nationalism, we see infinitely complex realms of cultural production.*
>
> (Shukla 1997)

The 'our culture' argument, of which Bollywood forms an admittedly prime exemplar, clearly then also informs a range of productions, all combining the insatiable taste for nostalgia with the felt need to keep 'our (national) culture alive': from websites to chat shows, from Ismail Merchant and Madhur Jaffrey cookery programmes to advertising, soap operas to music video, niche marketing of various products, satellite channels, journalism, the Indipop 'remix' audio cassette and CD industry.

If then, we see Bollywood as a culture industry, and see the Indian cinema as only a part, even if culturally a significant one, of that industry, then it is also likely that we are speaking of an industry whose financial turnover could be many times larger than what the cinema itself can claim. This would be almost certainly true of the export market, but – if we include the extraordinary 'dotcom' boom being witnessed in India right now – it may even be already true within India itself.

The transition, or crossover in marketing terms, from a domestic film product that has comparatively fewer options for merchandising its products to one that more successfully gears itself for exploiting the new marketing opportunities that Bollywood now presents, are now palpably evident, certainly to any clued-in filmgoer. The difference between the 'Bollywood' movie and the rest of the Hindi and other language films being made would be, say, the difference between Karan Johar and David Dhawan, between Shah Rukh Khan and Govinda, between *Phir Bhi Dil Hai Hindustani* and *Anari Number 1* (see for example, Banker 2001). While *Hum Aapke Hain Koun?* was perhaps the first Indian film to recognize and then systematically exploit a marketing opportunity here, it has since been most visibly Shah Rukh Khan who has been committed to the Bollywood mode, mainly as an actor (*DDLJ, Pardes, DTPH, KKHH*) but this year with *Phir Bhi Dil Hai Hindustani* having personally taken charge over its global marketing.

I want to drive a further wedge into the difference, by pointing to two crucial consequences of making this a distinction between the cinema and the more generalised Bollywood culture industry. In one obvious sense, Bollywood is of course identical to the Hindi (if not Indian) cinema: film continues to remain the most prominent presence figureheading the global 'Indian' culture industry. However, in ironic contrast, whereas practically every other ancillary industry seems to have by now defined an audience, a market, and a means of sustained production for that market, the cinema continues to suffer from its old difficulties of defining a generic production line and thus of defining a stable channel of capital inflow.

Let us see the problem as one of *defining culture economically*. If one were to extrapolate a larger theoretical question from all this, it would be: what are the circumstances under which cultural self-definitions *resist* economic or (we could now add) political resolution? And why does the cinema suffer from this problem in India, when other forms from television to radio to the music industry and, of course these days, the internet, seem to have no problem here?

To ask the question in these terms is, I suggest, to get to the very basis of why the Indian cinema exists at all. It is the further contention of this paper that since the Second World War, when the Indian cinema first defined itself as a mass-culture industry, the very reason for why it occupied so crucial and prominent a space in the emerging post-war and – more crucially, post-Partition – public sphere has actively forced it to resist capitalist organization. The globalization of this duality in the past decade under the aegis of Bollywood, I finally suggest, leads us to important insights into the phenomenon that I shall argue is also, and among other things, the globalization of a crucial set of conflicts bred into Indian *nationalism*.

3 The resistance to industrialization

On 10 May 1998, the former Information & Broadcasting Minister, Sushma Swaraj, declared, at a national conference on 'Challenges before Indian Cinema', that she would shortly pass a Government Order declaring 'industry status' to the film industry in India. This was a direct response to perhaps the most intense lobbying the film industry had yet done to achieve what Hollywood, for instance, achieved in the 1930s and what the Indian cinema has been denied since its inception. K. D. Shorey, the General Secretary of the Film Federation of India, had already, in 1996, sought to include this declaration into the Ninth Five-Year Economic Plan, saying that

> the situation in the film industry is very alarming. While the cost of production is on the increase, the revenue at the box-office is dwindling because of the rampant piracy of feature films on the cable and satellite networks. India should have more than a lakh of theatres, considering its population and according to an UNESCO report. But unfortunately, there is a declining trend in cinema houses from 13,000 and odd to 12,000 . . . .What is worrying us, producers, is that the entertainment tax, which was started by the British as a war-time measure, has been increased to such large proportions by various state governments that it is eating into the revenue of films. Nowhere in the world is entertainment tax levied, barring in countries like India, Pakistan and Sri Lanka . . . What is Rs800 crore to the Government? The Planning Commission can ask state govts to abolish the entertainment tax and the Central Govt can easily allocate that much of reimbursement. As far as the other central duties are concerned, they hardly work out to Rs35 crore . . . If only financial institutions lend money for the construction of theatres and institutional finance for film production (is made available) as it is prevalent in western countries . . . the film industry can survive in a healthy atmosphere.
> (*The Indian Express*, 3 October 1996)

Shorey was of course not talking about Bollywood here: the problems to which *he* refers are the old ones, the ones that the film industry still continues to face on the ground, problems we have heard since at least the 1960s. However, for independent and more contemporary reasons, this seemed an appropriate time for the government to make the move of declaring film as an industry capable of attracting institutional finance.

By the early 1990s, the growing economic power of the non-resident Indian or NRI, people of Indian origin who were domiciled abroad – whom the Indian government was actively wooing with attractive investment schemes that already formed a substantial part of the Reserve Bank of India's foreign exchange reserves – had already announced the arrival of a new culture industry that we have here named Bollywood. The failure of the Broadcast Bill by the previous government had placed growing pressure upon the Bharatiya Janata Party (BJP)-led coalition to come up with some kind of consolidated media bill that would address in an integrated fashion the merger of satellite communications with cable, television and the internet, all of which featured film prominently in their output, and all of which stood at the threshold of attracting serious financial investment from a range of international investors. Already, Rupert Murdoch's entry into the satellite television market with his STAR-TV had transformed the field, and it appeared as though film production would be the next target as Murdoch's 20th Century-Fox acquired a majority stake in the Bombay-based UTI-TV production house.

This was then not merely a matter of abolishing entertainment tax or making local institutional finance available for production alone, as K. D. Shorey seemed to think. The reform of the film industry through corporatization – signalled most directly by the formation of the Amitabh Bachchan Corporation and indirectly by a range of films, from Shekhar Kapur's *Mr. India* (1987), Mani Rathnam's *Roja* (1992) or Vinod Chopra's *1942 A Love Story* (1994), all addressing the theme of techno-nationalism that was on its way to being incarnated as *the* Bollywood thematic – had made it a prime candidate for international, including NRI, investor support.[3]

At the back of it all there was also the more complex political issue involved, of the Indian state itself negotiating a transition from an earlier era of decolonization and 'high nationalism' and into the newer times of globalization and finance capital. The BJP's own investment into the concept of a 'cultural nationalism' – a rather freer form of civilizational belonging explicitly delinked from the political rights of citizenship, indeed delinked even from the state itself, replaced by the rampant proliferation of phrases like 'Phir Bhi Dil Hai Hindustani' and 'Yeh mera India/I love my India' – has clearly taken the lead in resuscitating the concept of nation from the very real threats that the state faces as an institution of legitimation, particularly following its policy of widespread disinvestment in a range of functions. The significance of the cultural turn has been well documented, as has the unexpected support that such a brand of cultural definition – and the ensuing industry that, to quote the Fort Lauderdale housewife mentioned earlier, functions to keep 'our culture alive' – extended to the form of 1990s Hindutva governance in which Sushma Swaraj has been, of course, a prominent presence.

It was for both economic as well as political reasons that the cinema had to feature prominently in all this, if for no other reason than simply by virtue of its presence as *the* most prominent culture industry in modern India. There are however deeper issues involved, as well as a few problems, which involve an investigation into just why the cinema occupies such a prominent location in India in the first place. We may need to digress here slightly, to revisit a situation in the late 1940s, which I want to suggest bears both direct relevance to, and helps illuminate, the 'Indian cinema versus Bollywood' divide that I am trying to map.

The period to which I refer is between 1945 and 1951, when film production in India suddenly more than doubled (from 99 films in 1945 to 221 in 1951). This is usually seen as a low moment in Indian film history, when a whole range of independent financiers and producers jumped into the fray, effectively ending the more stable studio systems of the pre-war period, whom the Film Enquiry Committee Report of 1951 – the most elaborate and authentic record of this crucial time – castigates in no uncertain language as 'leading stars, exacting financiers and calculating distributors' who 'forged ahead' at the 'cost of the industry and the taste of the public'.[4]

It was nevertheless an extraordinary achievement, perhaps unparalleled in the history of world cinema, that in this period the film industry set itself up as a national industry in the sense of assembling a national market, even devising a narrative mode that has since been extensively analysed as nationalist melodrama[5] in ways that actually *precede* and even anticipate institutionalized state functioning in this field. Film theory has repeatedly demonstrated the crucial role that nationalist-political constructions play in determining narrative and spectatorial practices. Even in the instance of American film, it has been demonstrated that it was only around 1939 when the notion of 'American unity', informed by the pre-war situation that 'both necessitated and enabled national cohesion', and that saw the 'unified, national subject – the paradigmatic American viewer' – being put in place, did Hollywood actually deploy several of the technical and narrative conventions for which it is today renowned (Cormack 1994: 140–142) and for which *Gone With The Wind* (1939) remains so crucial an event in American film history.

This departure from the more usual condition of a decolonizing nation-state was a source of some embarrassment to the Nehru government, as the Film Enquiry Committee report consistently shows. Unlike any other comparable instance – where, much more conventionally, newly formed 'third world' nations established national film industries from scratch, usually by reducing or eliminating their financial and infrastructural dependence on the erstwhile colonial power, and where, from North Africa to Latin America to large parts of East Asia, the founding of a local film industry has almost always been a culturally prominent part of national reconstruction – India in contrast inherited an already established, even if chaotic, production and exhibition infrastructure for a cinema industry that was poised, even then, to become the largest in the world.

The Enquiry Committee report's main thrust is in startling contrast to the stand taken by film organizations in other countries with whom India, in fact, had exchange links, like FEPACI (the Federation of Pan-African Cineastes, affiliated to the Organization of African Unity, OAU), who believed their 'prophetic mission was to unite and to use film as a tool for the liberation of the colonized countries' (Diawara 1992: 39). The Indian government wanted to keep the film industry in check, to regulate it in some way, to reform its dubious credentials as a national form and also thereby to address cultural nationalism's discomfort at having to depend on such inauthentic resources; eventually to replace it with something better, something that more authentically represented the modernist aspirations of India's newly enfranchised civil society (Rajadhyaksha 1993).

Some of these perceptions of the industry would seem quaint today, and were even then controversial. Critic Chidananda Das Gupta, India's leading theorist of precisely the kind of cinema that the government of India tried to launch after the 1950s with the direct involvement of state agencies, for instance tried to re-integrate the difficulties posed by the typically modernist divide between 'good' and 'bad' culture. He attributed to the mainstream cinema a specifically, even consciously, nationalist function. Coining the term 'All India film', he suggested that India had evolved an idiom, and industry, that appropriated aspects both from indigenous popular film and theatre genres and from Hollywood, subordinating them to an all-encompassing entertainment formula designed to overcome regional and linguistic boundaries, providing in the process 'cultural leadership [that reinforces] some of the unifying tendencies in our social and economic changes [a]nd provides an inferior alternative [to a leadership that] has not emerged because of the hiatus between the intelligentsia, to which the leaders belong, and the masses' (Das Gupta 1968). The contention that the All India film performed by default an integrating nationalist function similar to the consciously stated aim of, say, All India Radio (whose name Das Gupta clearly evokes in his term All India film) and, more recently, Doordarshan, went on to have an important influence on India's national film industry policies after the Enquiry Committee report. The industry's inability to be financially self-sustaining thereafter often came to be counterbalanced by its alleged ability to foster a unified contemporary 'indigenous' culture.

The claim of the mainstream cinema as a repository of national-cultural value in one sense has its origin in these times. The claim by itself does not, however, explain how the cinema industry pulled together a national market or national audience even before national independence, and consequently without state support. How, to return to our earlier question, did the cinema pull this off and how did it come to occupy its crucial presence as a 'cultural unifier' and a keeper of the flame in the sense in which that Fort Lauderdale housewife sees the ritual of cultural bonding involved in going to the movies?

I suggest that the answer would need to be sought in the very categories of national culture that India invoked in the 1940s and early 1950s, and identify something of a zone, a domain of some sort, a blind spot, in the role that this *national culture* had to play *politically*, a zone into which the cinema came to ensconce itself. Partha Chatterjee offers here a larger argument around the 'hiatus' that contextualizes Das Gupta's move, for what was going on at the time.

> [W]hereas the legal-bureaucratic apparatus of the state had been able, by the late colonial and certainly in the post-colonial period, to reach as the target of many of its activities virtually all of the population that inhabits its territory, the domain of civil social institutions as conceived above is still restricted to a fairly small section of 'citizens'. The hiatus is extremely significant because it is the mark of non-Western modernity as an always-incomplete project of modernisation[.]
>
> (Chatterjee 1997)

Given a corresponding analytical problem posed by the usual ways of working through this hiatus – that we either 'regard the domain of the civil as a depoliticized domain in contrast with the political domain of the state' or blur all distinctions by claiming that everything is political, neither of which helps us get very far – Chatterjee posits the existence of an intermediary domain of some kind: a 'domain of *mediating institutions between civil society and the state*' (emphasis added). He names this 'political society'.

It is not the purpose of this essay to go into the complex nature of the political manoeuvres that ensued within state functioning and within the domain of private capital at this time (the late 1940s–1950s) in India. Suffice it to say that if part of Indian nationalism defined itself in terms of a modern 'national' culture, and instituted a whole paraphernalia of activities defining the identity of the 'modern citizen', then there was another part of the national state functioning at another level altogether, the level for example of population control, welfarism, democracy, and finally, there was a 'domain' of something in between, something that enabled the protagonists of national culture, its civil society, to talk to, negotiate with, the state, something that we more commonly refer to as the sphere of 'politics'.

It is mainly the concept of 'mediating institutions' that I shall briefly explore here, and their relevance to the cinema of this time. Let me trace back into this era yet another familiar characteristic of the 1990s Bollywood movie, one incarnated by its first big manifestation *Hum Aapke Hai Kaun?*, that this cinema addresses a 'family' audience and deals with 'family values', as against another kind of film, the non-Bollywood variety, that did not and maybe still does not know how to do this. In this time, says Chatterjee, there was a move by the dominant state to name its people as 'citizens' of some kind, and this move was a displacement away 'from the idea of society as constituted by the elementary units of homogeneous families to that of a population, differentiated but classifiable, describable and enumerable'.

It is possible to see the cinema as the suturing agency par excellence of such displacement and mediation. The cultural role of the neighbourhood movie theatre as a prominent institution of the new public sphere in this time is crucially accounted for by the fact that a ticket-buying spectator automatically assumed certain rights that were symbolically pretty crucial to the emerging state of the 1940s–1950s. (In some ways the contentious aspect of 'entertainment tax' – effectively equating the spectator with the price of his ticket, extended into equating the film solely with its box office income, all the problems to which K. D. Shorey refers above – is a legacy of these times.) These rights – the right to enter a movie theatre, to act as its privileged addressee, to further assert that right through, for example, various kinds of fan activity both inside and outside the movie theatre (Srinivas 1996) – went alongside a host of political rights that defined the 'describable and enumerable' aspects of the population, like, for example, the right to vote, the right to receive welfare, the right to have a postal address and a bank account. Film historians through this period repeatedly assert how, for example, in many parts of India the cinema was perhaps the first instance in Indian civilization where the 'national public' could gather in one place that was not divided along caste difference (Sivathamby 1981).

It is not important that these rights were not necessarily enforced on the ground. It is important instead to recognize that spectators were, and continue to be, *symbolically* and *narratively* aware of these rights, aware of their political underpinnings, and do various things – things that constitute the famous 'active' and vocal Indian film spectator – that we must understand as a further assertion of these rights in the movie theatre. I am suggesting here that, first, the many characteristics of film viewing in India – as well known as its masala and songs – of vocal audiences, throwing money at the screen, going into trances during devotional films and so forth, were in turn characteristic of *spectators identifying themselves* through identifying the film's address. And secondly, that this entire process of identification and counter-identification narratively spans precisely the divide that Chatterjee's 'domain of mediating institutions' would play in the world outside the movie theatre. It now appears that the aspect of 'identification' that film theorist Christian Metz, for instance, once defined when he answered the question, who does the film spectator 'identify' with?, by suggesting that the spectator identifies with '*himself* . . . as a pure act of perception' (Metz 1982) this reasonably well known aspect of film theory developed a distinctly political meaning in the India of the 1940s and early 1950s.

There now developed a serious contradiction, from which the Indian cinema never really recovered: one as glaring today in the Bollywood versus film industry divide as it has ever been. In one sense, the film industry was able to manoeuvre itself into a certain position that made it indispensable to the state. As, in many ways, the most prominent independent cultural exemplar of the national market and the provider of leisure activity to the 'people' in the larger populational sense to which Chatterjee gestures in his more encompassing definition of the citizen, the cinema demanded the right to exist and receive some kind of industrial sustenance. It did, for example, win certain regulatory concessions in the form of the various State Film Chambers of

Commerce, a certain limited amount of infrastructural support, such as a subsidy for imported film stock (via the public sector Hindustan Photo Film); and in turn it also chose to view disciplinary institutions such as the Censor Board as not merely capable of punitive action, but also, and more positively, as agencies underscoring and validating the objects of its spectatorial address.

On the other hand, the very space that the film industry came to occupy disqualified it by definition from the range of *new* concessions and supports that the Film Enquiry Committee recommended, including, most crucially, institutional finance. Indeed, all these concessions, then and ever since, were meant for precisely a kind of cinema that the film industry was *not*. They were meant for a different cinema that the state hoped to encourage, one that would fit better into what Chatterjee calls the 'pedagogical mission' of civil society and its agendas of modernization: a 'different' cinema that we could today see as the direct ancestor of the Bollywood mode.

Indeed, in the barely concealed claims to some sort of reformism that Bollywood so often presents these days in its biggest successes – the claims of commitment to family values, to the 'feel-good-happy-ending' romance that carries the tag of 'our culture' – one can see the ghosts of past trends going pretty far back into time. The problem of the cinema's legitimacy has, since the pre-war years, consistently produced version after version of what was claimed as culturally authentic cinema: authentic because it was *authenticated* by the national culture. One long distance ancestor to, say *HAHK*, would be the pre-war 'Swadeshi' movie: the devotionals and socials emphasizing *indigenism* of story and production. Post-war and in the early years of Independence, there was the first descendant of this indigenism: the cinema that the state repeatedly anointed as 'authentically national'. The process of authentication in this time was more palpable than the films that benefited by various declarations of recommended viewing – and continues to be so, if we see, for example, the extraordinary premium that the film industry continues to place upon the government's national film awards and its tax exemption criteria. One could safely say, however, that among the candidates vying for this kind of accreditation were Devika Rani and Ashok Kumar socials from the Bombay Talkies studios, reformist musicals such as some of Raj Kapoor's work or some of Dev Anand's Navketan production house (both of which often hired ex-practitioners from the Indian People's Theatre Association movements of the 1940s) and realist-internationalist films by directors from Satyajit Ray to Bimal Roy to the early Merchant–Ivory (Rajadhyaksha 1993).

This then was the situation. The film industry had won for itself a distinct, even unique, space of spectatorial address and spectatorial attention that is even today not shared by any of its other ancillary industries – not, for example, by television, despite all the many programmes seeking to evoke the excitement of the filmgoing experience with its coverage of the industry, its 'behind the scenes' programmes and its efforts to get stars to endorse televised versions of the Indian cinema. It has extended this spectatorial space into some kind of peripheral, perennially unstable and yet functioning economy with a rough-and-ready system of funding for its productions. It has also weathered a divide within its production processes, between those who control infrastructure – licensed stockists of film stock, lab owners and owners of dubbing theatres, editing suites, sound studios and other post-production facilities, all of whom routinely get banking and corporate-institutional support – and those who invest in *production*, bear the entrepreneurial risks of a film doing well or badly, and *never* receive institutionalised funding support. They do not receive support because they cannot, for to do so would be to certainly threaten the very *raison d'être* of why the cinema is so popular, the space the industry occupies.

This is the situation – an evidently backdated, relentlessly modernist, even statist, situation, wedded to governmental support while at the same time aware of its peculiar illegitimacy – to which K. D. Shorey refers, when he enumerates the problems that film producers continue to face. This is self-evidently not the situation that Bollywood faces. The old movie spectator, the member of Chatterjee's political society, would – and does – feel distinctly uncomfortable in plush new foyers with Pepsi soda fountains. And Bollywood, in its turn, quite explicitly qualifies for a range of corporate funding support systems.

Bollywood does however manage something else in its turn, it seems, something that none of its cinematic predecessors could quite achieve. It succeeds, on the whole, in mediating the transition into the new category of citizen-as-family-member while maintaining intact the cultural insiderism of film spectatorship. Few films being locally made in Bombay, Chennai or Calcutta can aspire to such a transition. Few films, ergo, can claim international venture capital support.

4 Exporting the spectator: new sites for modernism

'There is a near unanimity that the right kind of recognition would eventually lower the cost of an industry, where expenses and price of funds are mindboggling. Thanks to the well accepted practice of tapping undisclosed money, particularly the mega-budget ones, the string of financiers (mostly operating through fronts) extract a rate of return which is three to four times the interest a commercial bank would possibly charge . . . This unpredictability has become inseparable with films. Immediately, I can't think of an evaluation procedure by which I can call a production viable,' said a senior PSU bank official. Bringing the activity within the banking parlance of 'productive purpose' appears to be the crux of the matter. 'Is it an income generating asset? This is neither manufacturing nor trading nor agriculture nor self-employment,' said a private bank official . . . 'We may consider the track record of a producer, personal investments and net worth and ability to repay if the production flops and then take a short-term loan backed by sound collaterals. But will this attract the filmwallas? They might get a better deal from sources they have been tapping so far,' said an official of one of the older private banks.

('Industry status: Cinema may find itself going round trees',
Sugata Ghosh, *The Economic Times*, 12 May 1998).

Sushma Swaraj, then, was clearly making an intervention more complex than what the Film Federation of India necessarily saw as the issues, when she offered 'industry status' to the cinema. The problem was old, even tediously familiar; the circumstances however brand new.

There is one crucially important sense, perhaps, in which the new international market opening up for Indian film could be continuing its old symbolic-political adherences. It is possible that the Indian cinema's modes of address have opened up a new category for spectatorial address that appears not to be accounted for by, say, the

American cinema after it discovered the storytelling mode for itself and after numerous critics and theorists went on to assume that this mode was globally relevant and that 'we all internalize at an early age as a *reading competence* thanks to an exposure of films . . . which is universal among the young in industrial societies' (Burch 1990). If this is so, then in several places, like Nigeria, whose distinctive reception of Indian cinema has been analysed so remarkably by Brian Larkin (2001), or among the Fijian Indians in Australia who even make their own Hindi films on video, as examined by Manas Ray (Ray 2000), or for that matter among audiences who still flock to Indian films in Trinidad and South Africa, there could be people still going to these films precisely for what Hollywood cannot be seen to offer. It is possible that the cinema's addresses are entering complex realms of identification in these places, which would definitely further argument around the nature of the cultural-political mediation that the Indian, or possibly the Hong Kong, cinemas continue to allow.

Evidently, *this* was not the market that was pressuring Swaraj to define a law offering industrial status to film. Nor was this the market that has film distributors and producers in Bombay in a tizzy, wondering how they can rake in their megabucks or go corporate. In fact, a recent news item about Burma and how popular Hindi films are there, speaks of print rights of *Taal* being sold for $10,000, a 'relatively high amount by Burmese standards' ('Mania for Hindi movies sweeps Myanmar', Lalit K. Jha, *The Hindu*, 29 February 2000).

In the Bollywood sense of the export of the Indian spectator to distant lands, I want to suggest another kind of export: the export of Indian nationalism itself, now commodified and globalized into a 'feel good' version of 'our culture'. If so, then what we are also seeing is a globalization of the conflict, the divide, central to nationalism itself: the divide of *democracy* versus *modernity*, now playing itself out on a wider, more surreal, canvas than ever before.[6]

We do not know too much about this right now, but in conclusion, I would like to state the following issues that could be of relevance.

First, the question of *modernism*. If the civil- and political-society divide means anything at all, it shows how prevalent, foundational, and indeed how virtually unbridgeable the divides in India have been across the chasm of modernity. It is true that *something* has happened recently, which seemingly wipes them away as though they have never existed, and different people have tried to explain this erasure differently. Arjun Appadurai's famous formulation of 'modernity at large', modernity cleansed of the mechanics of geographical belonging by the diaspora and the cyber-neighbourhood, certainly offers the *terrain* on which this insiderism is acted out (Appadurai 1997). There do nevertheless seem to be larger, and still unanswered questions, which might be asked both of the theorist but even more directly of the practitioner of Bollywood culture. For example, why now? The transition of cultural insiderism away from its heartland, away then from its historic political function of creating a certain category of citizen, and into something that informs the feelings of the visitor to the Brisbane night club, quoted earlier, who wants to go there to 'assert her Eastern identity' – this transition would clearly have something basic to offer in its rewriting the *very trajectories of modernism* that have historically linked places such as India to the 'West'. Why does it seem so simple to pull off today when the Indian cinema has sought this transition to national legitimacy since at least the 1960s, without success?

A second question deals with the area of cultures resisting economic and political resolution. Bollywood clearly is reconfiguring the field of the cinema in important ways. What does it pick as translatable into the new corporate economy, what is it that this economy leaves behind? This would be as important a cultural question as an economic one.

For example, I believe it is demonstrable that practically all the new money flowing into the cinema right now is concentrating on the ancillary sector of film production. On one side, software giants such as Pentafour and Silicon Graphics use film in order to demonstrate their products, so that it is unclear as to whether, say Shankar's *Jeans* (1998), noted for all its digitized camerawork and produced by Hollywood's Ashok Amritraj, was more an independent feature film surviving on a pay-per-view basis or more a three-hour demo for Pentafour's special effects. On the other hand, the range of consumables increasingly visible on film screens – Stroh's beer in *DDLJ*, Coca-Cola in *Taal*, Swatch watches in *Phir Bhi Dil Hai Hindustani* – are symptomatic of the nature of funding that the cinema increasingly depends upon.

If so, it would be the final irony of the Bollywoodization of the Indian cinema that the very demand that the industry has sought for from the government for so many decades could be the reason for its demise. The arrival of corporate-industrial-finance capital could reasonably lead to the final triumph of Bollywood, even as the cinema itself gets reduced only to a memory, a part of the nostalgia industry.

Author's note: All references in this essay have been drawn from the Media & Culture Archive of the Centre for the Study of Culture & Society. I am grateful to Tejaswini Niranjana and to S. V. Srinivas for their comments, as well as to the conference participants of the 'Bollywood Unlimited' conference in the University of Iowa 1998, and to Philip Lutgendorf, Corey Creekmur and Rick Altman, for their responses to an earlier version of this paper, as well as to the 'Representations of Metropolitan Life in Contemporary Indian Film: Bombay, Calcutta, Madras' workshop in Copenhagen, 1999. An earlier version was published in Preben Kaarsholm (ed.) (2002) *City Flicks: Cinema, Urban Worlds and Modernities in India and Beyond*, Roskilde University Occasional Paper No. 22.

Notes

1 So *The New Indian Express* (29 October 1999) reports that 'The opening titles of Sooraj Barjatya's forthcoming film *Hum Saath Saath Hain*, billed as the most cracking release this Diwali, will feature an important new player in Bollywood: Coca-Cola. The cola giant, in its bid to scramble to the very top of the Rs3500 crore soft drinks market, has spent a comparatively smaller amount, Rs1.5 crore, on branding Barjatya's family film and ensuring its release as *Coca-Cola Hum Saath Saath Hain*.

2 *Statistics on Film and Cinema 1975–77*, Paris: Office of Statistics, UNESCO, 1981.

3 Tejaswini Niranjana defines this newly forged relationship, in *Roja*, of a 'techno-aesthetic' with a new category of the 'national' subject: see Niranjana (1994).

4 Report of the Film Enquiry Committee (S. K. Patil, Chairman), New Delhi, Government of India Press (1951).

5 See especially Prasad (1998) and Chakravarty (1993).

6 Chatterjee elaborates his 'civil' versus 'political' society argument by suggesting that while modernity was the main agenda for the former, democracy could be seen as the main issue addressing the latter. So, in effect, the entire debate around modernism, around high and low art, around a religious secularism versus theories of caste and religion, could be mapped around this often unbridgeable divide between modernity and democracy (Chatterjee 1997).

References

Appadurai, Arjun (1997) *Modernity At Large: Cultural Dimensions of Globalization*, New Delhi: Oxford University Press.

Banker, Ashok (2001) *Bollywood*, New Delhi: Penguin Books.

Burch, Noel (1990) *Life to those Shadows*, Ben Brewster (trans.), Berkeley: University of California Press.

Chakravarty, Sumita (1993) *National Identity in Indian Popular Cinema 1947–87*, Austin: University of Texas Press.

Chatterjee, Partha (1997) 'Beyond the Nation? Or Within?', *Economic & Political Weekly*, xxxii, nos 1–2.

Cormack, Mike (1994) *Ideology and Cinematography in Hollywood, 1930–39*, New York: St. Martin's Press.

Das Gupta, Chidananda (1968) 'The Cultural Basis of Indian Cinema', *Talking About Films*, New Delhi: Orient Longman.

Diawara, Manthia (1992) *African Cinema: Politics & Culture*, Bloomington: Indiana University Press.

Larkin, Brian (2001) 'Indian films, Nigerian lovers: media and the creation of parallel modernities', *Africa* 67(3): 406–440.

Kabir, Nasreen Munni (2001) *Bollywood: The Indian Cinema Story*, London: Channel 4 Books.

Metz, Christian (1982) *The Imaginary Signifier: Psychoanalysis and the Cinema*, Bloomington: Indiana University Press.

Niranjana, Tejaswini (1994) 'Integrating whose nation? Tourists and terrorists in *Roja*', *Economic & Political Weekly* 29(3): 79–81.

Prasad, Madhava (1998) *Ideology of the Hindi Film: a Historical Construction*, New Delhi: Oxford University Press.

Rajadhyaksha, Ashish (1993) 'The epic melodrama: themes of nationality in Indian cinema', *Journal of Arts & Ideas* 25–26: 55–70.

Ray, Manas (2000) 'Bollywood down under: Fiji Indian cultural history and popular assertion'. In Stuart Cunningham and John Sinclair (eds) *Floating Lives: The Media and Asian Diaspora*, University of Queensland Press, 136–184.

Sivathamby, K. (1981) *The Tamil Film as a Medium of Political Communication*, Madras: New Century Book House.

Srinivas, S. V. (1996) 'Devotion and defiance in fan activity', *Journal of Arts & Ideas* 29 (January): 67–83.

Shukla, Sandhya (1997) 'Building diaspora and nation: the 1991 "Cultural Festival of India", *Cultural Studies* 11(2) (July): 296–315.

Chapter 21

Detouring through Korean cinema

Paul Willemen

Prelims

The discipline of comparative literature and its emphasis on ethno-linguistic units 'to be compared' seems quite inappropriate as a model for approaching the study of a thoroughly industrialized cultural form such as cinema. There is no need even to recall the complicity between comparative literature and comparative religion and that Goethe's notion of 'world literature' gestured towards the alleged universality of Western-Christian values as the yardstick with which to measure the degree of a particular, 'regional' literary work's adherence to a norm deemed to be universal.[1] Nevertheless, it is precisely the whiff of clerical thinking that attaches to comparative literature that provides a clue as to why the notion of comparative film studies may be worth considering, *mutatis mutandis*. In the West, the shift from religion and its professionals as the legitimators and enforcers of particular regimes of social power to a more secular notion of 'universal values' – a shift accompanied by the gradual transformation of clerics into intellectuals and, now, media practitioners – is the history of the emergence of the 'public sphere' challenging and eventually supplanting the court as the legitimate site for the discussion of issues of governance. That is the history underpinning the designation of the peculiar mix of moral philosophy and aesthetics known as 'literature' – 'lit and its crit', as Tom Nairn once put it – as the training ground for 'modern' state legitimators (enforcement duties have been passed on to the military and the police). Given that the force driving this change is the one identified by Karl Marx, that is to say, the gradual elaboration and spread of the capitalist mode of production that set about its triumphal globalization in the second half of the twentieth century, and given that the history of cinema coincides with the industrialization of culture enforced in the West since the closing years of the nineteenth century, it must follow that there is indeed a kind of 'universalism' that informs cinema as a cultural form.[2]

The universalism at issue is not to be defined or conceived in terms of a particular set of values, the presence or absence of which would determine a film's place in the domain of 'world cinema', even though many if not most histories and theories of cinema proceed as if that were the case. The universalism at stake that enables 'comparisons' to be made is the universal encounter with capitalism, a process that has massively accelerated since the 1950s. Georges Sadoul's *Histoire générale du cinéma* started covering 'world cinema' from 1946 onwards, but the first major 'world cinema' chronology, Philippe Esnault's *Chronologie du cinéma mondial* was published in Paris in

1963, followed by a Belgian publication in Dutch in 1976, edited by Dirk Lauwaert, *83 Jaren Filmgeschiedenis – Een Tijdstabel* (1893–1975). Since then, the notion of 'world cinema' has become generally accepted, unfortunately. Screening venues attached to film archives now regularly advertise seasons of national cinemas by resorting to the language of 'discovery' familiar from colonial expeditions as much as from tourist brochures. Alongside this notion of world cinema, as its inevitable companion piece, we are treated to histories of national cinemas elaborated according to the very same nationalist assumptions that govern the formulation of romantically nationalist histories of literature by way of appeals to some mysteriously unifying 'spirit' of the nation, mostly located in the 'spirit' of whatever language was imposed as the national language by some governing group.

That is the unsavoury context within which the notion of comparative film studies begins to make some sort of sense. If we jettison the inherited framework of film history that locates a film at the intersection between 'universal values' and 'nationalist' specificity, and if we also refuse to credit the nationalist mystifications invoking 'blood and soil' to explain why it is possible – even necessary – to differentiate between one state's industrial production of cultural commodities and that of another,[3] it becomes possible to reflect on the ways in which 'national' histories and the capitalist-industrial production of culture intersect, generating specific ways of 'discoursing'. It is worth repeating here that the 'universality' underpinning comparisons between such discursive constellations (marked by the particular institutional networks that orchestrate the way social–historical tensions between groups contending for power are to be narrativized) is first and foremost the universality provided by the pervasive capitalist mode of production. Notoriously, capitalism thrives on its ability to advance and advocate very different sets of values as appropriate for different regions, people and sectors of the economy, which is why the encounter with capitalism cannot be treated in the same way as an encounter with, say, Christian values: an encounter with forces reducing every thing and every body to their exchange value is quite different from a confrontation with the codified equation between the good, the true and the beautiful, an equation propagated by people and institutions that are none of the three and seek to counter the equalizing tendencies within capitalism in favour of even more oppressively anti-democratic, 'traditional' regimes of power.

Given that film history and film theory were elaborated within the particular forcefield constituted by the twin poles of Europe and the USA, the former clinging to its clerical–intellectual models of culture and the latter functioning as the locomotive (fuelled also by state subsidies and the power of its military–industrial complex) of the industrialization of culture, it should not come as a surprise that it is the Euro–American model of cinema that constitutes the frame for the existing paradigm of film studies. It is equally unsurprising that the model(s) elaborated to understand the functioning of *that* cinema – film theory – should present difficulties to whoever tries to understand the workings of non-Euro–American cinemas. In that respect, comparative film studies does constitute, not an alternative discipline, but a detour in order to re-arrive at a better model of cinematic functioning. Comparative film studies is concerned with the elaboration of a better film theory by paying attention to the differential encounters with capitalism and the consequent modulations of cinematic 'speech' or discourse.

What this essay attempts to offer is a set of suggestions, some more tentatively advanced than others, for ways of going about understanding what the 'corrective' might be and how to identify the discursive knots where the particularities of the encounter with capitalism (with 'production' and the economic–ideological apparatuses designed to advance, resist or negotiate with capitalism) may be traced.

Setting out

In the first issue of the revamped *New Left Review*, Franco Moretti (Moretti 2000) outlines a hypothesis for the reformulation of comparative literature as a discipline. His starting point is an extrapolation of a remark by Fredric Jameson which Moretti formulates as a law: 'When a culture starts moving towards the modern novel, it's *always* as a compromise between foreign form and local materials', later specified further as a triangular relationship between 'foreign form, local material – *and local form*. Simplifying somewhat: foreign *plot*, local *characters*, and then, local *narrative* voice'. The first question that presents itself follows from the Jameson–Moretti *law*'s very formulation: 'when a culture starts moving towards the modern novel . . .'. This phrase begs a host of questions: What propels the culture in question? Why would it invariably move towards 'the modern novel' (however defined)? Why should this movement immediately be conceptualized in terms of a problem around 'narrative voice'?[4] Is this problem of narrative voice to be found only in literature? Is literature necessarily always the best place to study narrative voice? All these issues revolve around one basic problem: What is at stake in 'cultural dynamics' that it should manifest itself so crucially in the deployment (inscription, orchestration) of subjective discourse, or, the discourse of subjectivity, which is precisely what the 'narrator's voice' enacts in the telling of a story, any story, regardless of whether it is narrated in verbal language or in the heterogeneous mix of codes that is cinema.

The second question then must address the central position attributed to the individuated voice as the measure of a culture's move towards 'modernity'. The notion that an Enlightenment-derived notion of subjectivity can function as such a yardstick is, to say the least, controversial. The discomfort that may be generated with such a way of measuring a culture's move towards 'the modern' does not, however, constitute an argument against it. Especially not when we realize that such a way of moving towards the modern implies the recognition that capitalist commodification as a global phenomenon also and inevitably harbours, for worse but also for better,[5] equalizing tendencies (the formal atomization and equalization of 'subjects' as units of labour power) and that these tendencies also are a fundamental force propelling cultural dynamics. Indeed, the often heard jeremiads about the ravages of alienation or anomie merely signal regret at the passing of the pre-modern and actively seek to discredit the advance of an individuated subjectivity as it forges a space whence it can speak as 'narrative voice', displacing the previous, pre-modern 'narrative voices' underpinning and providing the coherence of the acts of storytelling in societies pinning 'subjects' to status identities.

Admittedly, Moretti does not specify that his notion of narrative voice is always that of an individuated subjectivity. Indeed, it may be a voice that speaks animatedly against anomie and extols the virtues of collective speaking voices (a caste voice, a class voice, a voice advocating reliance and dependence on a – mostly religiously legitimated – authority, and so on). But all his examples from the various national literatures speak of the narrator in terms of a move towards 'the modern' in terms of the increasing prominence of an inscription of individuation in relation to the narratorial voice.

On the other hand, Moretti never acknowledges the problems that Adorno and Horkheimer signalled in their account of *The Dialectic of Enlightenment* first published in 1947. They wrote: 'The principle of individuality was always full of contradiction . . . the individual who supports society bears its disfiguring mark; seemingly free, he is actually the product of its economic and social apparatus . . . . The only reason why the culture industry can deal so successfully with individuality is that the latter has always reproduced the fragility of society.' (Adorno and Horkheimer 1973: 155) This remark suggests that the process of individuation manifested in the relations between narratorial and other enunciations in that corridor of voices called 'a text' bears an indexical relation to the social relations within which the text is articulated. It presumably has such an indexical relation to history because the sense one has of a 'self' is always shaped, given form and endowed with a spurious kind of impression of coherence in the interplay between what Freud called the psychic apparatus and the historically developing social-economic conditions with and within which that 'self' necessarily has to be produced. The problematic of subjectivity is, therefore, always one of vectoriality: the many grammatical subjects superimposed onto each other in any statement[6] produce a 'subject' of the enunciation similar to the way in which, for instance, a survey may produce 'the typical English family' as having 2.3 children, condensing a great many variables and differences into a kind of hieroglyph of social relations. When Adorno, noting how in television 'the will of those in charge enters that language of images' (Adorno 1984: 21–22), resorts to a notion of 'image-writing' that is akin to his earlier suggestion of 'hieroglyphic writing', he is also gesturing towards that aspect of the text 'in which producer and consumer meet' as the site where the orchestration and management of 'speaking positions' generates a complex, multi-voiced subjectivity-constellation that allows the fragility of social relations to be read.

The questions raised by the Jameson–Moretti law of cultural dynamics are important and difficult ones, but I agree with Moretti that it is sometimes necessary to make 'a leap, a wager – a hypothesis, to get started', and that the best (the only?) way of moving forward is to rely on corroborative evidence. I also agree with him that the way forward in literature is extremely difficult since no scholar can hope to encompass the necessary linguistic competencies and, besides, the quantity of the material together with the problems caused by having to rely on translation, compound the difficulties. I would like to draw attention to an alternative route that, although originating primarily in the study of literature, has branched off into the domain of cinematic narration where it joined up with (found corroboration from) some aspects of art history and from other disciplines as well. In that context, the question of narrative voice and subjectivity is discussed in terms of regimes of looking, that is to say, the inscription of a narratorial 'voice' which manifests itself and can be tracked in, among other aspects of the cinematic text, the orchestration of looks and the articulation of spaces in cinema.[7]

More specifically, I want to open up this question in relation to the alleged in-built perspectival modernity of the cinematic apparatus. Following on from literary studies that show the multiplicity of 'voices' contending with each other and which it is the task of the 'narratorial voice' to orchestrate, it is safe to assume that films also operate with more than one regime of subjectivation simultaneously, which should lead us, at least, to reconsider much of what has been written these last 30 years or so on questions of looking and subjectivity. A new look, so to speak, is required at the study of the cinematic institution, the relations between audiences and films and a number of other questions pertaining to theories of cinematic functioning. The Jameson–Moretti *law* pertaining to 'world literature' prompts us to explore the issues involved in the recognition that the scopic regime Western intellectuals currently rely on, the perspectival regime, is a composite apparatus that combines both pre-capitalist and individuating modes of looking. Consequently, it inevitably marshals more than one 'speaking-looking' subject position, either of which may be pushed to the fore depending on the overall direction – modernizing, archaicizing or some compromise between the two that nevertheless leans towards one or the other – in which the discursive constellation seeks to move 'us', the reader-viewers. As such, the scopic-discursive regime that orchestrates a text is never the expression of some singular, unified 'point of view', some singular 'subjectivity' or even less of some identity (given that an identity is a politically truncated version of a person's concatenation of subject positions), but always a process, an invitation to the viewer-reader to 'move' to a new 'setting' somewhere between the dissolution of the human into the cosmos of analogical magic and the horizon of an individuated subjectivity emotionally and intellectually capable of acting in the 'common good'. In other words, the issue of a text's mode of address necessarily poses the problem of subjectivity itself: how is that concept to be understood and how or to what extent can or should it be deployed? A text's mode of address enacts the posing and the always-provisional solution to a suggested way of conceiving of subjectivity. In that sense, it is true, as Stephen Heath once put it, that a text presents 'the drama of the subject', but only on condition of understanding 'the' subject as a kind of orchestral performance. Moreover, it is not 'the' subject posited by psychoanalysis or by philosophies of subjectivity such as phenomenology. It is, as Adorno and Horkheimer noted, a subjective constellation that bears the marks of 'the fragility of society' in the sense that a social formation is also always an unstable concatenation of contending 'interests' and positions.

In addition, the assertion that one key dimension of any text is necessarily the particular regime of subjectivity it enacts, does not imply that this dimension must always be regarded as its dominant dimension. Whether it is or isn't will depend on how a text is activated through reading. The conditions in which and the purposes for which one encounters a text are historical variables capable of rearranging the hierarchical relations that obtain within and between the varied, complexly intertwined discursive strands lumped together under the unifying label provided by the very notion of 'a' text. In other words, as the film scholar Ashish Rajadhyaksha once put it in conversation, my identification of a text's mode of address as a key to the study of how texts are caught in the long-term dynamics of cultural change, is overdetermined by my particular Western context's 300-year habit of individuation. But then, not all habits are bad ones.

Nevertheless, studying the problem of modes of address in cinema allows us to circumvent, to a significant degree, the limitations inherent in the literary reference of the Jameson–Moretti law. Not because the study of the cinematic mode of address can dispense with verbal language, but because a film's verbal language, whether manifest or latent, is never more than one component of the strategies of address deployed. It is that wide and complex range of strategies of address that would form the core of a comparative film studies approach. The formulation of a new starting point, a new hypothesis functioning as a basic law, might then be a more elegantly phrased version of the following: When a culture starts exploring the modalities of 'modern' enunciative forms, it is *always* as a compromise between contending archaicizing and modernizing forces, determining both the nature and the scope of the deployment of both 'foreign form' and 'local materials'. That is what generates *local form* characterized by 'local *narrative* voice',[8] and that is what makes the narratorial voice into a field profiling the most directly identifiable and available options and problems for 'modernization' in any given social–historical constellation. Tensions manifested in relation to the (in)coherence of the narratorial voice thus come to function as the indices of the social 'field' presiding over and shaping the speaking positions it is possible for subjects to occupy in a particular place/time, given the extra constraints and determinations embedded in the forms of expression deployed (cinema, painting, literature, music and so on), which have been the focus of so-called formalist approaches.

Passing through Korea

When early in 1997 I was able to spend some time in Seoul in a film studies milieu, the fraught problems of modernization and modernity in cultural practices such as cinema, and the narrative as well as the compositional peculiarities these tensions appeared to generate in films offered a way in to dialogues that enabled my interlocutors and me to test our models of understanding cinema. Especially since in Korea at the time just before the IMF crisis, it appeared that cinema occupied a crucially important political space precisely because of the way cinema invites a negotiation of issues of subjectivity and identity as part of its narrative as well as visual, that is to say, its attenuated verbal mode of address.[9]

Refusing the notion that Western film criticism and theory have elaborated a universal standard against which all cinemas are to be measured, and starting from the position that films are shaped by the cultural and historical constellations within which and for which they are made, my superficial acquaintance with Korean cinema and even more scanty knowledge of Korean history and culture left me in a difficult position to try and read why and how subjectivity and modernization seemed to occupy such a crucial place in the films I saw.[10]

In a recent essay first delivered as a paper at the Kwangju Biennale in 1997, Kim Soyoung (1998: 174–187) argued that the current wave of cinemania and the spate of film festivals in South Korea addressed the tensions that arose in the post-dictatorial period between ideological–cultural tendencies that she summarized by invoking the complex concepts of *shintopuli* and *saegaewha*: 'The notion of national identity has re-emerged in the nineties under the slogan of *shintopuli*, meaning the non-differentiated sameness of the body and the native soil. This essentialised notion conflating the nation, the body and nature has arisen as a complicit counter-narrative to the anxiety generated by the allegedly post-modern discourse of *saegaewha*.' Elsewhere in the essay, Kim Soyoung characterizes *saegaewha* as the official Korean version of globalization and economic liberalization launched by the establishment of civil government in 1991. She goes on to note that somewhere in between those two sloganized notions, 'the notion of the modern remains somewhat abstract', opening up a space within which the questions of identity and subjectivity can be rehearsed and negotiated. She also argues that the recently initiated film festivals in Seoul, Pusan, Puchon and Chongju locate themselves squarely within that space and provide an institutional context for dealing with those questions of subjectivity and identity, thus perhaps offering what could be described as an emergent public sphere, taking, in a sense, the relay of the directly political contestations on the streets and in the factories of the earlier decade.

Picking up on the statement that 'the notion of the modern remains somewhat abstract' in contemporary Korean culture, and that one of the most frequently mentioned terms when discussing Korean cinema's place on the global culture-market at the time was the term 'blockage', my reading of Korean films concentrated on the many dimensions of cinema that could be summarized as 'the mode(s) of address'. When one applies the insights of Western film theory, with its emphases on realism and subjectivity, to Korean films, it quickly becomes clear that Western film theory is not capable of dealing adequately with the peculiarities of that cinema: demarcations between the sacred and the profane, that is to say, between the real and the supernatural, are marked differently, for instance, in the films deploying 'shamanist' themes. Consequently, the Western category of realism, itself a compromise formation between declining aristocratic and rising bourgeois cultures at a time when the organized working class first made its appearance on the political map in Europe, cannot operate quite in the same way Euro–American cultural histories assume realism to function: for instance, the antagonistic relation between realism and naturalism is not in play. Moreover, examples from Hindi and other Indian films that are described as realist, but retain the melodrama's notion of character would amply confirm that lack of fit even more blatantly.

Second, the assumptions underpinning Western cinema's notion of spatial and psychological coherence do not apply or, at least, do not apply in the same way, so that spatial relations in a scene operate differently, with the narrator and the viewer being inscribed into a scene in ways that the dominant Euro–American conventions of realist cinema were designed to displace.[11] An instance of this can be found in the acting style and the accompanying mise en scène. The best but by no means the only example I saw came in a rather tacky sexploitation film where in a moment of great intimacy and privacy, the actors seemed constantly to turn towards an imaginary audience and to launch their facial grimaces as well as their contorted body language emphatically towards the spectators. The 'realistic' notion of a couple being discretely overlooked by an invisible camera was replaced by an acting style and a mode of presentation that emphasized the sense of the scene being 'in public'. Consequently, the modes of behaviour and the attendant emotions were presented, by the mise en scène, as subject to a 'public' kind of scrutiny prominently activating social norms represented by the imaginary onlookers. Incidentally, Madhava Prasad noted a similar mechanism at play in Indian cinema that he deployed to explain the taboo on kissing in that cinema (Prasad 1993) and especially his telling analysis of the mode of address in Shyam Benegal's film *Nishant* (1975) (Prasad 1997: 51–54). Similarly, Lee Jang-ho's *Nageuneneun gilesedo swiji anheunda* (*The Man with Three Coffins*, 1987), a thriller that eventually invoked shamanist themes, appeared to have considerable trouble sorting out its narratorial strategy at the start of the film, taking some time and risking a number of confusions before allowing the narrator to settle into a more consistent position.

The film that struck me as offering a direct and systematic address of precisely the 'problem' of the modernization of subjectivity that Kim Soyoung identified in between *shintopuli* and *saegaewha*, was Yu Hyonmok's extraordinary *Obaltan* (*The Aimless Bullet*,

1961), demonstrating that the problem had been brewing for a considerable time in films prior to the current cinemaniacs' way of mobilizing cinema to revisit and reformulate the notion of subjectivity. *Obaltan* presents the problem in an arresting fashion in its opening sequence. The first shot of a bar taken from the street through the modernist designs of the bar's glass-panelled doors, reminiscent of the Russian Eccentrics' notion of modernism as exemplified by the work of Kozintsev and Trauberg in the 1920s, locates the space of modernity 'beyond' the obstructing doors. The glass in the doors is promptly shattered towards the camera and three ex-soldiers in 'modern' urban clothes emerge, one of them soon afterwards meeting a woman in 'traditional' dress. As they walk and converse, she remains a few paces behind him as the camera tracks laterally to keep the couple in frame. Here we have the theme of the film outlined in condensed form: modernity is undesirable (the drunken and violent space from which the soldiers emerge, on the other side of modernist designs) from the narrator's point of view in the street, yet the space of 'tradition' is no longer unproblematically available, as is made clear in the scene with the couple shortly afterwards.

The two terms that, as a result of viewing films as well as dialogues with colleagues and students, imposed themselves as themes for reflection on my encounter with Korean cinema were thus: subjectivity and blockage. The term blockage recurred mainly as referring to a blockage of Korean cinema (difficulties of export, international recognition, competition with Hollywood, etc). My response, in the light of the internationalism of the art cinema, was to consider the possibility that Korean cinema had difficulties inserting itself in the art cinemas of the world because of a blockage *within* Korean cinema, perhaps mainly due to a large and complex set of currents and tensions that make it very difficult to find a way out of what seems and feels to many like a 'no-way-out' situation, which may relate to the unusual number of freeze-frame endings I noticed in the films I was able to see of the 1970s and 1980s (see also note 17). If the blockage was to be located within the Korean films, making them difficult or too unfamiliar for global art cinema distributors to think they can be profitably distributed and exhibited, this would require the identification of factors that could account for the 'impossibility' of Korean films to reach a global market. These 'impossible' tension areas might be found in a number of dynamics at work not only in Korean films, but also in Korean cultural constellations generally.

A cursory listing of such tensions would include positions that may be described, perhaps too crudely and polemically, as follows:

1   Modernity is desirable but it came with Japanese colonial rule. Moreover, that particular version of modernity was already highly suspect in the light of the way Japanese culture refunctioned and adapted modernity issues for its own feudal–capitalist compromise when seeking to extend through 'modernization' the Emperor system into the modern era, inspiring itself from Absolutist German legal ideologies. An example of the way this modernity arrived in Korea and the complexities it engendered is the fact that left activists in South Korea in the 1980s had to study Marxism via a Japanese writer's account of what Marxism was supposed to be about.

2   Tradition is desirable *but* in so far as it can be mobilized to oppose South Korean notions of dictatorially imposed modernization, it is in danger of producing North Korea as the authentic, *real* Korea, since opposition to the Southern regime is

automatically regarded as sympathy for the North. Consequently, notions of a 'traditional' Korea necessarily are contaminated by the dictatorial, paranoid anti-communist Cold War ideology and end up supporting what they set out to oppose: southern style modernity represented by the governmental slogans of national pride, strength and development (in competition with the North's slogan about self-reliance, *juche*, which mobilizes a greater sense of continuity with an equally fictitious 'authentic' past).

3   If Japanese modernity is rejected, an alternative notion of modernity is available: Western modernity that arrived in the shape of Christianity and its missionaries. *But* Christianity, as an ideology, whether Catholic or Protestant, is itself a profoundly anti-modern and obscurantist, feudal-oriented ideology. Although it bears the imprint of its accommodations with notions of individualism (especially in its Protestant versions), it more importantly is grounded in notions, not of subjectivity, but of subjection and authority (in Protestantism, this is subjection to a plethora of 'regional' authorities claiming to possess the 'truth' of 'the' text – in Catholicism it is more a subjection to a centralized institutional authority). So, both Japanese and the Western notions of modernity have a historical baggage grounded in profoundly anti-modern ideologies: Japanese efforts to perpetuate the Emperor system into the modern era and the West's main ideology and institutional framework used for the retardation of modernity, Christianity, which was and is still the principal way in which Western feudalism seeks to salvage as much as it can from the pre-capitalist era. As the always-interesting writer, Régis Debray, quipped: 'In this perspective and sticking with clichés, religion is no longer the opium of the people but the vitamin pills of the feeble' (Debray 1996: 4).

4   Since the end of the 1940s (i.e. within living memory), a third notion of modernity has become available in South Korea: US modernity via its intervention in Korean elections and its subsequent stimulation of a civil war. The US made Korea the terrain of its first major demonstration of world hegemony after World War II, ostentatiously subordinating the UN and NATO, set up as Cold-War institutions, to its foreign policy. This modernity is inextricably tainted by its local Korean version: the military dictatorship set up and maintained by the US, leading to Korea's peculiar version of state capitalism in a close alliance between the military (and its machinery of violent oppression, surveillance and censorship) and the big conglomerate enterprises, a symbiosis that led to the corruption largely responsible for the virulence of the economic crisis currently besetting South Korea. US modernity is further tainted by the cultural effects of occupation: military prostitution, which is particularly notable because it bears on the most sensitive area where popular culture and popular ideologies register and negotiate the transition from Tradition to Modernity: the control of female sexuality, mostly dramatized in terms of the control of lineage and the generational transmission of values.

Western modernity US-style arrived exactly at the moment when Korea finally was on the point of addressing its own road to modernity after the liberation from Japanese rule. Typically, this means that the arrival of Western modernity finds representation either in US soldiers' raping or otherwise corrupting Korean womanhood (e.g. Chang Kil-su's *Silver Stallion*, 1991), or an American-accented (female) missionary, as in *The Daughters of Pharmacist Kim* (Yu Hyonmok, 1963). This made prostitution into a particularly potent metaphor for modernity and corrupted it from the outset. In this respect, the public emergence in the 1990s of the issue of the comfort women provides a significant shift in the way it is now possible to negotiate the question of individual subjectivity. Because the issue relates to Japanese occupation and thus no longer implies criticism of the US occupation and its kind of modernization, a space has become available in which to address not only the effects of Japan's nefarious impact on Korean society, but also, and perhaps more importantly, a space in which to address the status of women in directly Korean terms, with the opposition between tradition (the woman as symbol of the nation and the debatable 'five thousand years' of homogeneous ethnic continuity) and a modernity in which women through individual acts of extreme courage reject the 'shame' of sexual exploitation and subordination which, traditionally, they are to suffer in silence. In this respect, the comfort women issue raises the question of contemporary Korean attitude towards women.

Because of the way modernity, and its inevitable shadow, tradition, arrived in Korea, one should expect that Korea's confrontation and negotiations with Western-style modernity will assume various and complex forms, including (at least):

(a) A repressed component in the aspects of modernity imported by the Japanese colonial occupation (urbanization, industrialization – including some industrialization of culture such as the beginning of cinema). Japanese modernity brought with it a new mix of oppression and 'equalization' (the disturbance of existing, domestic status hierarchies) in Korea, but at the same time it was a profoundly flawed, not to say bogus kind of modernity derived from Japan's efforts, via the Meiji Restoration, to prolong a pre-modern form of imperial governance by adapting it to pressures created by the rise of capitalism in the second half of the nineteenth century.[12]

(b) A regressive anti-modern tendency inherent in the associations with Christianity (see, for instance, *Nabi and the Butterfly*, Moon Seong-Wook, 2001);[13]

(c) A corrupting sexual component represented initially by US soldiers and later aggravated by the issue of state-sponsored prostitution, both elements condensing with the emergence of the comfort women issue in the 1980s, bundling feudal Korean patriarchy together with US and Japanese modernities into a particularly sensitive knot on the site of female sexuality;[14]

(d) An association with a militarily 'modernizing' dictatorship by way of the US connections with the regime and the constant presence and involvement of military bases right in the heart of Seoul; however, the dictatorship is also associated, and associated itself, with a pre-capitalist status hierarchy founding its legitimacy in an alleged continuity with pre-colonial Korean dynastic rule. Moreover, the Northern regime, in its quasi-deification of the ruling family, also strengthens this link between dictatorship and dynastic feudal rule.[15] Hence, Korea's modernizing dictatorships are deeply feudal, both North and South.

As a result, both the way back to tradition and the way forward to modernity are blocked, as both directions appear to open out onto anti-modern, absolutist and corrupting social organizations. Individualist solutions/critiques are censored as well as experienced as inappropriate (too dangerous for physical safety as well as politically futile and ineffective when facing issues such as regimes of sexual violence), while collectivist solutions are either hi-jacked by the prevailing dictatorships (and party organizations) or mired in feudal submission residues (demands for total obedience, the dissolution of individuality into a rigid, collective and hierarchically enforced discipline), a dimension that probably extends into the waves of fashion and other 'manias' judging by teenage group behaviour on a Saturday morning in the Myong Dong district among the fashion boutiques, not to mention the phenomenon of cinemania itself.

In view of the fact that notions of subjectivity, especially as represented in the orchestration of narrative voices into the process of narration, are inextricably connected with the way modernity negotiates notions of individuality in cultural production, this blockage within Korean film culture is likely to be manifested in 'troubles' concerning the manipulation and inscription of the narrative voice, typically in the form of difficulties around the problems of 'who speaks?' (as in Lee Jang-ho's *The Man with Three Coffins*) and 'how to narrate events-in-spaces', that is to say: how to handle the spatio-temporal aspects of cinema pivoting around the axis of the narratorial voice.

In the Korean films I have seen, these problems manifested themselves in rhetorical figures (also often called 'mistakes' when tested against the rules of 'classical' Western cinema) such as:

- Narratives with multiple foci (group narratives with characters relaying each other; which may be what Ashish Rajadhyaksha observed when he suggested in a discussion that Korean cinema has no central protagonist). Central characters in such relay-narratives seem both collective/representative and individual, thus allowing for tensions between the two alternatives to be dramatized;
- Repeated difficulties with spatial coherence in dialogue scenes (breaking the 180 degree rule, making characters appear in different, spatially 'illogical' positions on the screen, looking in different directions from previous shots, etc);
- Problems with coherence in time/space signalled by inappropriate dress (e.g. 1950s costume in a movie set in the 1930s, as in *Kim the Pharmacist*) as if historicity in dress and self-presentation is not really important in the face of the 'eternal' themes.

A further symptom of the hypothesis that Korean cinema is deeply preoccupied with its own very specific and 'impossible' modernization can be found in the kinds of solutions that individual film makers appear to advocate:

- Im Kwon-taek's work is often described as humanist, even though his films are also associated with the *minjung* cultural moment and endowed with 'green grass' connotations: *minjung* thus in its very name evokes a notion of eternal nature and recurrence. 'Renewal' becomes associated with 'tradition' and is represented in terms of associations with 'nature'. However, this humanism is a very abstract, an allegedly universal norm liable to be incarnated by the state's self-presentation as benevolent patriarch, and it is an abstract humanism because it is notional and aspirational, to be equated with human nature, thus draining history out of its notion of the 'human'. Such humanism can never proclaim its values radically or militantly.

It cannot proclaim its individualist and anti-state values, in the sense that humanism also must refuse the state the right to define the 'human'. This aspect of humanism is clearly visible in the fact that there are unending conflicts between the UN/Human Rights discourses and absolutely all existing states, a conflict noticeable, e.g. in the conflicts between Amnesty International's reports and the states to which they apply. All states gathered under the United Nations umbrella have officially subscribed to Human Rights,[16] but none approves of the reports about its own violations of those rights. Consequently, the only humanist ideology that can be mobilized in Korea is one that lacks its radical dimensions of individualism, making it into a humanism that can be and is mobilized by the very state it is supposed to be able to oppose;

- A second solution is sought in a strategy of rendering things imprecise, i.e. deliberate vagueness and irresolution, of which the various freeze-frame endings may also be a symptom. Vagueness is discernible, for instance, in the way in which notions of Christianity are represented, leaving it unclear what variety of religious institution or practice is being invoked: *Obaltan* has Protestant songs, but the procession of religious people it features is left unspecified as to its denomination, allowing a general and rather confused notion of Christianity to insinuate itself. Religious matters of the Christian kind, because implicated in both the modern and the anti-modern/traditional (although not the Korean Traditional), cannot be represented in their specific dimensions since that would require some engagement with the historicity of the religious forms involved. In other words, avoidance of a consideration of the conflicting tendencies within religious references dictates the representation of a vague notion of religiosity;

- A third route is the resort to paranoid realism, presenting the trappings of realism (psychological motivations; urban or poor rural settings with accuracy of costume and furnishings, lower class protagonists, regional speech rhythms and accents, the incorporation of references to current events, etc), but riddling realism with representations of madness and hysteria. It is here that the unevenly modernized types of acting and make-up can become significant, as well as the flashy formal conceits (tilted camera angles, obsessive repetitions of events and shots or framings, perhaps helping to explain the popularity of Wong Kar-wei's films and their imitations, such as the adolescent voyeurism focusing on women's legs in *Holiday in Seoul*, 1997). The pre-modern acting style that allows actors to signal to the audience that they are 'on show' may have inspired Brecht and Eisenstein, but it is not Brechtian in the Korean films because it is not deployed as a critique of hegemonic notions of individual subjectivity. A fascinating discussion of these 'hysterical' aspects of Korean cinema has been provided by Kim Soyoung's essay on the work of Kim Kiyoung, *Modernity in Suspense: The Logic of Fetishism in Korean Cinema* (Kim Soyoung 2001).[17] Paranoid realism, with its hysterical overtones, also evokes aspects of the quasi-religious dimensions of socialist realism (i.e. Exemplary Lives of the Saints transposed into industrializing dictatorships) suggesting that paranoid realism may well be the reverse of the socialist realist coin. What remains to be explored (and is being explored in Korean cinema) is the connection between paranoid realism, socialist realism and the market realism currently dominating Western industrial cinema: glossy imagery and editing styles and rhythms recalling advertising; the framing of consumer items such as shoes, clothing or glamorized gadgetry interrupting the narrative; endless walks and drives through apparently or allegedly 'Post-modern' environments; special effects suggesting a reality reeking of computers, and so on);

- A fourth avenue is presented by various traditional forms of irrationalism, such as fortune-telling and sorcery/shamanism. However, these irrationalisms are presented as possessing, obscurely, an enlightening core, a forever inaccessible, 'unspeakable' core of Truth possessed by whomever one wants to install into the position of authority. This results in highly ambiguous representations mixing laughter/irony with a sense of the sacred/frightening aspect of irrationalisms such as shamanism, as if it is both real and absurd at the same time. References to mandalas and other forms of pre-capitalist mysticisms are grounded in 'nature' and induce historical amnesia. However, it is precisely in this area that some interesting new strategies of representation are being tried, as Choi Chungmoo noted (Choi 1995) when she suggested that radical theatre in the 1980s was able to mobilize representations of shamanism in an allegorizing manner. She argued that shamanism was mobilized in the plays precisely to reintroduce a dimension of historicity when direct critical representations of contemporary history were not allowed. Moreover, Kim Soyoung's account of the tension between *shintopuli* and *saegaewha* also seems to have a bearing on this renewed topicalization of shamanism in the sense of a renewed negotiation of the drastically 'ancient' pre-modern notion of a subjectivity (if the term can be applied at all in this context) in which self and nature constitute a magical continuum: one way of opposing 'tradition' and the hierarchical social formations that invented 'tradition', is to recall pre-traditional forms. All this suggests that one cannot simply speak of shamanism in contemporary Korean cinema and that further differentiations are required, for instance, between neo-shamanism and revisionist shamanism. Neo-shamanism would then be a version of shamanism adapted to contemporary situations but harking back to an ahistorical 'state of things', eternal and traditional, or rather: a particular version of the traditional presented as eternal and even universal; revisionist shamanism would be a version of shamanism mobilizable for the purposes of standing in for representations of contemporary historical processes, that is to say, without pushing that representation back into the realms of the eternal and universal.

The upshot of these reflections on Korean cinema is that a consideration of modes of address in cinema leads directly to one of the central issues in cultural theory: the question of exactly how, through which textual mechanisms, the social/cultural dimensions of a historical experience are 'readable' in a text. To solve that question, nothing less is required than a way of conceiving the dialectics between text and history in a manner that both respects the formal aspects of a text and the complexities of specific historical constellations. It would appear that an investigation of modes of address could provide insights into this process provided the conventional notions of subjectivity, that is to say, notions of subjectivity that assume a monadic structure of the subject as a result of the West's 300-year-habit of negotiating individuation, be abandoned or, at least, reconfigured in order to allow for the synchronous co-deployment of a number of different, historically rooted modalities of subjectivity. At present, film theory does not allow for such an approach, although some scholars are experimenting with the emerging paradigm, such as Valentina Vitali's detailed analysis, an as yet unpublished doctoral thesis presented at the University of Ulster in 2001, of the complexities in modes of address deployed in Hindi films of the 1950s.

Packing

For a Western cultural theorist, these issues confirm the need to rethink a number of points. First of all, it is a mistake, although widely practised, to locate the specificity of, say, Korean, Indian or Japanese cinema precisely in the 'blind spots' of Western cultural theory: Korean or any other cinema cannot be reduced to those aspects of it that do not fit or fit only awkwardly into the frame(s) of Western aesthetic theories. Instead of positively valuing, in principle, the areas of Korean cinema that escape or resist Western theory, it is necessary to question the adequacy of Western film theories as such. If those theories cannot deal with the historical and cultural dimensions of Korean cinema without 'blocking' them, how much confidence can one have in their ability to deal with the historical and cultural aspects of the films made in Europe or in the USA?

Second, the habit of 300 years of individualist philosophy cannot be taken for granted. Western notions of aesthetics and storytelling presuppose and uncritically deploy the notion of individual subjectivity introduced during the Renaissance with the invention of perspective and given a philosophical formulation in the subsequent centuries by Descartes, Spinoza and others. The American cultural theorist Martin Jay even coined the phrase Cartesian Perspectivalism to describe the link between the aesthetic and the philosophical movements over a 200-year period from the Italian Renaissance to seventeenth-century philosophy when capitalism and the bourgeoisie were increasingly challenging the political as well as the cultural–ideological rule of the feudal aristocracy (resulting in the eventual triumph of the bourgeoisie and capitalism in the middle of the twentieth century at the price of two world wars), a period that resulted in the programme enounced by 'the enlightenment', a programme still awaiting its realization.

Korean cinema – and, therefore, any 'national' cinema whatsoever – would then best be seen as a cultural practice in which the pre-capitalist and the (in Korea's case, colonially induced) capitalist cultural formations continue to coexist in different measures, the tensions between these formations being negotiated in different ways depending on the prevailing historical situation and the forces contending within it.[18] Briefly, paraphrasing McKeon's work, pre-Renaissance aesthetics in the West assumed that the order of things, the world, had been designed by God and was revealed in the sacred texts as known and interpreted by the professional guardians of ideology: the clergy. Moreover, the social order was rigorously stratified into status divisions, and to each caste-estate, a number of essential characteristics were attributed: the king, at the top of the status hierarchy, was deemed also to be the richest, the wisest, the most beautiful, the strongest, and so on. The nobility, the clergy and the other castes were equally rigidly defined down to the non-people called 'villains' (i.e. ordinary people who, in pre-capitalist times, were peasants or serfs). Legitimate identity was bestowed by people from a higher caste on those of the lower orders. Contrary to the innovation introduced by perspective of identifying a unique point of view structure occupied by the individual (in a mirroring relationship with the vanishing point which still remained identified as God's point of view), in feudal society legitimacy was bestowed upon individuals when they appeared in the field of vision of an authority: the ritual of the 'audience' granted by authorities through the practice of appearing as petitioners before noblemen. In addition, as is demonstrated by the contemporary relevance of the Korean concept of *shintopuli* as well as in various aspects of Hebrew culture (e.g. the golem myth) and poetry, not to mention the popularity of astrology and other kinds of magical thinking throughout the West, there is ample evidence to accept that even pre-antiquity modes of thought in which body/self and the natural world are regarded as being moments within a continuum, have persisted and are available, if the occasion arises, to be mobilized.

Many of the pre-capitalist and even pre-historical ideological elements, predating the emergence of the problem of representation itself, all supposedly having been displaced by the Renaissance and the Enlightenment, have in fact remained very much a part of our own cultures and can be seen to operate not only in films, but also in social rituals (the public appearances of royalty, star worship, governmental practices, art exhibitions, etc). The reliance on and the belief in a revealed world, a belief underpinning the valuation of realist representations, along with the assumption that the resonance of magic formulas or incantations has the power to change history and the value-frameworks associated with status hierarchies or castes, have persisted alongside the modernizing emphasis on the notion of individuality as required by capitalist legality and political aspirations and strategies.

The signifiers of the presence of the pre-capitalist aesthetic or conception of social organization can be found in a whole range of aspects of a film, from the delineation of a character to an actor's body language, from spatial dislocations between one shot and another (when spatial co-ordination or continuity are implied) to editing decisions contradicting the laws of verisimilitude (e.g. in Guru Dutt's *Pyaasa* [1957], there is a point of view shot which *includes* the character whose point of view the camera follows; at another moment of the film, the camera follows the look of a character and the movement ends by cutting back to the perceiving character which has its eyes firmly shut). Similarly, discrepant sound-perspectives may strengthen or undermine, depending on the circumstances, the regime of belief solicited by a film. In addition, the pressures exerted by the pre-modern may inflect the way reality is distinguished from the supernatural or from fantasy (as in India's mythologicals), the amount of time a leading actor is allowed to hog the frame overriding considerations of narrative economy and rhythm or the way sequence shots in the films of Amos Gitai often obsessively scrutinize landscapes as if the contours of some ancestral 'identity' could be traced there (an assumption also criticized in his films, e.g. in the re-burial scene in his *Field Diary*, 1982).

Returning home to Baron Frankenstein, Count Dracula and Karl Marx

As far as the West is concerned, two brief examples may clarify the point that the tensions between the modernizing and the archaicizing forces orchestrated in modes of address are not peculiar to non-Western cultural practices. The persistence of films telling the stories of Frankenstein and Dracula (often made in the same period of a film industry's development, as is demonstrated by the Universal horror films of the early

1930s and the Hammer films of the late 1950s) suggests that they negotiate a similar set of tensions. However, they do so from opposite sides of an imaginary line: whereas the Frankenstein story tells of the threat posed by a rational-scientific future to a religiously modelled world (the Baron tampers with God's prerogatives), the Dracula story tells of a religiously modelled world that should have passed but is not dead yet (the Count and his world have no place in the era of scientific rationalism, but there he is . . .). The films are about the same issue: the transition from a religiously legitimated status society to the world of Cartesian (or should one say, Spinozan) reason.

The second example of the continued relevance of the 'old corruption' in the 'modern' world, is the evolution of the melodrama. Initially, the kind of melodrama elaborated during the French Revolution – a significant marker in itself – concerned itself with, among other things, the drama of lineage: noblemen who betrayed the values of their status and 'ordinary heroes' who often turned out to be of noble descent. The problem put on the agenda by these dramas and the novelistic forms that flowed from them, was that it was no longer sufficient to know a person's social status (family line) to be able to tell what kind of person one was dealing with, but the values associated with 'status' did not change: the aspiration remained that of being 'noble'. In narrative terms, this took the form of stories of 'status inconsistency'. More recent melodrama, especially as produced in Hollywood, dramatizes the same conflict, but in slightly modified terms, also focusing on the figure of those who are supposed to 'reproduce' people as well as the social order, women. In the Hollywood melodrama, the problem has become a generational conflict: the parents 'know' who is an appropriate mate for their daughter because they can tell by 'traditional' means, that is to say, they understand the importance of 'social identities' as embodied by the status and reputation of a family. However, sons and daughters, already more individualized, transgress the rules of status societies and insist on picking a 'wrong' mate. The solution to this drama may be presented in favour of individual choice or, on the other hand, individual choice may be presented as the source of tragedy. In either case, what is at stake is a negotiation between two sets of cultural–historical social forms, understood as alternative options. This kind of conflict is given a further turn of the screw in contemporary comedy romances, usually set in New York or Los Angeles: two individuals who know rigorously nothing about each other except that they are potential mates, meet. Here, the frenetic comedy barely hides the sense of underlying panic at the absence of 'traditional knowledge'. Implicitly, the horrors of parental interference and oppression have turned into a regretted absence as the lovers embark upon a nightmarish journey of mutual discovery, threatened at each turn by yet another unsuspected bit of information about their partner's history and characteristics. The medieval, lineage-dominated world organized according to a status hierarchy may seem distant from *When Harry Met Sally* (Rob Reiner, 1989) or *Pretty Woman* (Garry Marshall, 1990), but without its shadowy presence, the films simply could not exist. In effect, these comedies are modulations of melodramas, rehearsing and negotiating the coexistence of (at least) two conflicting ideologies belonging to radically different historical epochs.

Modernization can then be measured according to the way a cultural text (a film, a book, a festival, an exhibition and so on) orchestrates the tensions between identity (fixed by institutional arrangements and pressures) and subjectivity (the individual's complex ways of relating to the social environment and which always exceeds the boundaries imposed by institutionally defined notions of identity). Not that I am arguing for 'good', liberating subjectivity against 'bad', oppressive identity. It would take too long to provide all the reasons why 'identity', however limiting and oppressive, is not only inescapable, because institutions will impose some form of it regardless of our wishes, but necessary: without some administerable 'identity' defining us as part of an interest group enmeshed in shared social institutions, political management and change would be unthinkable, which is one argument against the absurdity of the more radical kinds of anarchist utopias. The point I am making is that the tension between subjectivity and identity is, at present, a defining aspect (not more, but at least *that*) of our lives and that identity considerations should never be allowed to impose a straitjacket on our subjectivity: if subjectivity is not allowed to transgress the boundaries imposed by identity, totalitarianism rules.

Different societies will narrate differently these tensions and conflicts between, on the one hand, 'the old', 'traditional' order of things and its 'moral' values, and, on the other hand, the 'new', modernizing framework operating with notions of individual subjectivity. Modernization can be measured by the yardstick of a cultural text's commitment to individual subjectivity as against the requirements of submission to status (caste, class, gender and so on) identities. This yardstick which is the baton conducting the orchestration of a film's mode of address, in turn appears to be an index of the relations between contending 'speaking positions' within the encompassing social-historical constellation (or 'society'). In addition, for instance in a society such as India, the very shift from caste to class identities generates an extra set of complexities within the problems attached to status identities.

It is not only in Korean cinema that these problems are writ large and generate specific narrative and representational strategies. The realization that Korean films are shaped by the need to negotiate these tensions in ever evolving historical and economic circumstances, made it clear that so-called advanced, modern societies are just as caught up in such negotiations between tradition and modernity, except that these negotiations necessarily take on different forms, as the examples of horror films or melodramas and crazy comedies indicate. Consequently, the notion of modernization applies just as much to Hollywood and to European films as it does to Korean, Indian or Chinese cultural practices. It is a mistake to attribute a linear chronology to Western societies suggesting that, with the Renaissance and the Enlightenment, the 'old' traditions were definitively replaced by the modern notions of individual subjectivity. It is just that the Korean etc films have to negotiate *different* sets of complexities in the struggle between the old and the new. Western films are just as riddled with feudal and older, even prehistoric ideologies, with political/ideological institutions fixing at any given moment the appropriate (for the ruling power bloc) definitions of identity, except that we have to look for them in different ways. Both the Korean and the Western films are equally involved in the very same questions of modernization and subjectivity, but because the histories are different, the narrative and representational forms organized by way of a film's mode of address must and will also be different.

It may be useful to remind ourselves of Marx's question regarding the works of art produced by Greek civilization: how is it possible, given that texts are deeply embedded in their histories, for a late-twentieth-century Western intellectual to 'read' films from another cultural constellation? Marx wondered, given that cultural forms are shaped by the histories that give rise to them, why the art of classic antiquity appeared to transcend the boundaries of its time and place. In other words, he raised the question of an artwork's apparent universality: 'The difficulty we are confronted with is not that of understanding how Greek art and epic poetry are associated with certain forms of social development. The difficulty is that they still give us aesthetic pleasure and are in certain respects regarded as a standard and unattainable ideal' (Marx 1971: 217). Marx tried to solve the problem by assuming that cultures go through periods of maturation in the same way that human beings grow from children into adults: 'Why should not the historical childhood of humanity, where it attained its most beautiful form, exert an eternal charm because it is a stage that will never recur?'

These were not among Marx's most insightful comments. Strangely, he under-estimated the difficulties involved in discerning the connections between artworks and 'forms of social development'. Returning to the notion of realism touched on earlier in this essay, assumptions have been made about the way realism somehow 'reflected' the power and the world of the rising bourgeoisie. Yet, there are many aspects of nineteenth-century realist works of art that relate far more to the persistent domination of patrician values stemming from medieval state formations and their ideological–religious justifications. The evil aristocrats of nineteenth-century European novels and melodramas do not convey a rejection of aristocratic values. On the contrary, they betray a middle-class submission to those very same values, including the obscene idealization of religious values, and the bitter realization that aristocrats do not necessarily embody aristocratic values. Similarly, the narrative system deployed in realist novels, with, for instance, the figure of the omniscient narrator, betrays the presence of a scarcely secular-ized version of a God-like figure who is omnipresent and from whom not even a character's innermost thoughts can be hidden. Moreover, both Roland Barthes and Michel Foucault have argued, persuasively, that the very notion of the author, commodified and individualized as that figure may have been by capitalist relations of production, derives from a medieval religious way of thinking. So, the very least one can say about an apparently 'transcendental' and 'universal' art form such as the realist novel, is that things are a great deal more complicated than any straight reference to its contemporary 'forms of social development' or to some general 'move towards the modern novel' might suggest. In the years since 1859, when Marx's text was first published, it has become clear that works of art cannot be understood in terms of a simple reference to the relations of production that pertained at the time the work was made. Similarly, the notion that civilizations 'mature' in stages analogous to the maturation of a human being, with Greek art belonging to humanity's childhood, is an untenable proposition.

Nevertheless, Marx's question remains: how is it possible for cultural productions that are formed within one set of social–historical conditions to be 'appreciated' in other social–historical configurations? Or, in different terms: how is it possible for a twenty-first-century European to appreciate Korean cinema, or any other non-European cinema, for that matter? The question deserves a book-length attempt to answer it. That an 'other' culture's art can indeed be appreciated beyond that culture's boundaries is undeniable. The difficulty is to explain how this is possible, and in order to resolve that particular difficulty, it is necessary to return to the very point Marx assumed to be easily understood: exactly how do texts register the histories within which they arise? To my knowledge, no theory of artistic production to date has produced even a halfway satisfactory answer to that question. On the other hand, slipping rapidly to the conclusion that there must be something universal in works of art that is appreciated internationally and in different cultural epochs, is, to say the least, premature. To what extent can it be said that, say, a Hollywood film such as David Lynch's *Lost Highway* (1997) or a Scottish film such as *Trainspotting* (1995) is 'understood' by North Americans or by Scots? There are plenty of examples, especially in modern (and even more in Modernist) art that show that 'locals' and 'contemporaries' are not always the ones who best understand or appreciate 'their own' works of art.

What then do we mean by 'understanding' a cultural production, a text, or, indeed, what are we appreciating when we say we 'appreciate' something such as, say, an Indian film and do Indians necessarily understand these films better?

For the time being, my own answer to such questions is twofold. It is true that a Korean film of whatever sort is thoroughly irrigated by the currents that shape Korean history, and a familiarity with, to extend the metaphor, the appropriate navigational charts is essential if we are to make sense of what we see and experience. However, the way we construct such charts, the factors we take into account or discard, depend on the mode of analysis we deploy. In other words, and returning to the issue of cinema, if we accept that a film is a cultural product generated by a specific historical constellation of forces, one of the key issues is also the way we understand history itself: the way we understand the 'workings' of history is a constituent part of the way we read the presence of history, that is to say, the way we read social-cultural specificity in films. To give a concrete example: I find the Indian film maker Kumar Shahani's films easier to understand, as soon as someone has explained some of the 'special knowledges' involved about, for instance, the different kinds of music deployed in it, than I do the latest James Bond film, mainly because I can detect that Shahani's film works with assumptions about the workings of history that I share. In that sense, Kumar Shahani's work, though thoroughly 'Indian', addresses all those who ask themselves similar questions about cultural dynamics and developments. If I realize that individuality is not a universal but a historical concept, I can relate to the way Shahani poses the questions of individuality and subjectivity in an Indian context, which is as 'historical' as my own conceptual world and implicated in similar forces (industrialization, urbanization, conflicts between religious and rational modes of thought, and so on). The same can be said, except more so, for Korean films, in spite of my lack of familiarity with Korean history both past and present. As was explained to me, much of Korean contemporary culture has been shaped in struggles between political positions and notions of subjectivity with which I am relatively familiar: feminism, Marxism etc (of whatever brand). Consequently, some of the terms and the way they are deployed will be both familiar and strange to me, giving me a way in to the historical constellation that, on the one hand, considered those terms relevant and, on the other hand, changed their meaning to suit local requirements. In that 'translation', a gap opens up that gives me, as a reader, access to the set of problems involved, access to a way of registering and assessing the importance of the changes implicated in those translations. Until other avenues have been more adequately identified, that 'access portal' is to be found by addressing a text's mode of address.

Postscript

Having read the helpful comments on my attempt to argue the need for a comparative cinema studies approach, I agree that the problems raised are, as yet, far from resolved to anyone's satisfaction, including mine. Some of the points raised by my Korean interlocutor have resulted in a few clarifications being inserted into my essay. However, an engagement with the more substantial points he makes can only take place on the terrain of specific film analyses and debates about the trajectories of Korean cinema's possible histories. I look forward to the results of the research currently pursued by a number of Korean scholars and I gladly acknowledge that, in the light of that research, the reflections that marked my Korean detour may well have to be reassessed as far as the specificities of Korean cinemas are concerned.

My Indian interlocutor raises more theoretically formulated points that I should be able to answer satisfactorily, but cannot, mainly because I agree with the reservations voiced. The 'slight confusion' he notes in my double use of the term 'subject' is unfortunately endemic in the English language, where it may denote both the grammatical subject of a sentence and the (psychologized) notion of the 'individual subject', also sometimes described as a sense of 'the self'. The gesture performed in my essay is to suggest that what we regard as a 'human subject', a personalized agency identifiable as a narrator or even an author, is indeed a concatenation of multiple grammatical subjects folded into and over each other. The 'coherence' of the apparently 'directive' voice designated as 'the narrator', the subject of a film's enunciation, is indeed an 'as if' coherence, an imaginary coherence assumed by a personal subject (a narrator conceived as a person analogous to you or me as individuals). How the slippage from the grammatical to the individual subject is achieved 'in and by texts' is a complex debate in itself requiring the mobilization of many disciplines including psychoanalysis, poetics, theories of history as well as of historiography and so on. Nevertheless, I think it is worth running the risk of that confusion, for the time being.

The more intractable difficulties emerge regarding the problem, noted by both interlocutors, of the separation between the modern and the pre-modern that I also gesture towards 'as if' it were a 'real' distinction. Of course, I acknowledge that 'we' can only speak from within modernity, and that there is no pre or post outside of it, only, to adapt Derrida's phraseology, spectres of possible pre- or post-modernities. The latter, incidentally, are beginning to look more and more like the former, making distinctions between the directionalities of vectorial change in contemporary societies increasingly difficult to discern, which, no doubt, is the reason why the post-modern spectre is so frequently trotted out nowadays in what passes for cultural analysis. Nevertheless, my distinction between the modern and whatever 'went before', even though produced from within (invented by) modernity, gestures towards two things that I have found no other, better way of designating. One is the question of directionality: the 'archaicizing or modernizing' vectors that result from any particular orchestration of the many 'voices' that are discernible in the 'corridor of voices' dramatized by texts. The second, even more intractable problem, is that of the baggage that comes with the mobilization of a 'before' that is always already preformatted, so to speak. To resist what needs to be resisted in some particular version of 'modernity' (say: the modernity which imperial Britain claimed to incarnate), it may be useful, even necessary, to mobilize some aspects of a 'before'. In that sense, the version of the pre-modern mobilized may well be itself a form of modernization that seeks to go 'beyond' the dominant version of modernity on offer by those in power. However, I remain uneasy with such a theoretical possibility if it involves, as I think almost any invocation of a 'before' does, the repudiation of the equalizing tendencies represented by the notions of individuation and subjectivity. However, I cannot fully answer the objections raised because I am not clear enough, as yet, about the merits – or dangers – of deploying a 'future anterior' tense to re-narrativize selected aspects of a 'before' against 'what is'. Directors such as Ritwik Ghatak or Kumar Shahani seem to me to deploy a cinematic equivalent of the future anterior by mobilizing selected aspects of a (constructed) 'tradition' to suggest ways of going beyond the limits of the 'modernity' they face and suffer, but I am the first to admit that a great deal more analytical and critical as well as theoretical work is required before I can claim to see my way through that particular thicket of political–cultural–temporal twists and knots.

Notes

1 The notes for this paper were first prepared for a conference on Korean cinema organized by Kim Soyoung and Choi Chungmoo at the University of California – Irvine. For the development of comparative literature, see René Etiemble's contribution to Dufrenne (1979: 83–92).

2 For the background to this line of argumentation, see Harvey (1999), Arrighi (1994), Hohendahl (1995), Eagleton (1984) and Ohmann (1996).

3 Briefly, my argument is that the specific network of linked institutions that form the state (such as the judicial, legislative, military, educational, syndical, political institutions and more) address individuals living within the state's boundaries in particular ways and oblige people to address 'it' in equally specific ways, producing what we have come to know as 'national cultures'. For a fuller exposition of the argument, see 'The National' in Willemen (1994).

4 Moretti's footnotes, especially on pp. 62–63, provide extremely telling corroborative evidence culled from a wide variety of analyses of national literatures to substantiate the argument that it is indeed narrative voice and subjectivity which mark the sites of 'modernization' in aesthetic discourse. Additional, persuasive evidence is provided in McKeon (1987), Fujii (1993), Godzich (1994), Godzich and Kittay (1987). Crary (1994) further confirms the literary studies.

5 For the 'worse' aspects of individuation, see Adorno and Horkheimer (1973), especially their chapter on 'The Culture Industry: Enlightenment as Mass Deception'. For some remarks on the 'better' aspects of individuation, see Adorno (1984: esp. 21–22).

6 It may be worth recalling that a statement consists of the weaving together of many discursive, including semantic, chains invoking diverse knowledges, abbreviations for memories and associations/connotations and so on, each of them positing a speaker, an 'I', and that in any given enunciation, the overall 'subject' of the enunciation consists of a bound-together bundle of such discursive chains. For instance, in the simple statement 'I am homeward bound', there is one subject signalling the intention to go somewhere; a second subject is signifying its ability to speak English, a third one conveys its familiarity with a somewhat rural and old-fashioned American vernacular possibly derived from country and western or folk music; depending on the context, a fourth could be signalling its ironic distance from the phrase's 'Western' or 'hobo' connotations; in the context of this footnote, there is a fifth subject positioning itself as the donor of an example addressed to readers capable of reading and understanding English, and so on. A more sophisticated example is provided by Adorno (1998: 281–283) where he shows how a pre-modern voice resounds alongside the eminently modernizing voices enunciating the main philosophical works of Kant and Hegel.

7 'Other aspects' probably include editing strategies and the deployment of devices that ostentatiously perform the act of narration, such as the zoom. For a more detailed discussion of the zoom and narratorial performance, see Willemen (2001: 6–13). For a discussion of the way the orchestration of looking relates to the inscription of contending notions of 'the subject' within a given text, see Willemen (1995: 101–129).

8 At this stage, a preliminary warning may be in order. Although there are likely to be as many regimes of subjectivity as there are social–historical formations (plus transitional and negotiated forms within them), I am working with an initial, rather simple opposition between capitalism and whatever went before, which I call, loosely, feudal or pre-capitalist. The suggestion that

there are two main regimes is merely a necessary methodological fiction for the purposes of this exploration. The specification of other regimes of looking, of subjectivity, and, therefore, of narratorial inscription, will have to emerge from the study of how exactly the join between the construction of a sense of 'self' operates in social–historical conditions marked – I would say 'energized' – by the dynamic interplay (struggle for domination and/or advantage) of 'subject positions' anchored in and committed to specific arrangements of social relations, specific kinds of 'society'.

9   The phrase 'attenuated verbal mode of address' is used to recall the fact that in cinema, the visual cannot bypass verbal language, which persists as a structuring force, even if only at the level of 'inner speech'.

10   I wish to record here my thanks to the film students and the staff at the Korean National University of the Arts for their assistance in my efforts to read Korean films as well as the critical debates surrounding them. Special thanks are due to Kim Soyoung for her particularly generous and insightful help in this regard.

11   For the most useful discussion of realism, see Jakobson (1978: 38–46), 'On Realism in Art' [1921]. For the intellectual framework underpinning my discussion of modes of address, see Jakobson (1960: 350–77).

12   In this respect, it cannot be repeated often enough that the 'modernities' exported by colonial regimes such as Japan and Britain were, in fact, 'modernizing' rather than 'modern'. Both in Britain and in Japan, the 'old corruption' was still in power and whatever measure of modernization had been achieved in these countries consisted of the minimum concessions the ruling caste had been forced to yield in order to prolong their hold on political and ideological power. As to when 'modernity' will eventually be achieved and the residues of the former status hierarchy will have been decisively marginalized, that remains an open question. It is a programme that remains to be implemented in post-colonial as well as in post-Imperial societies.

13   This anti-modern aspect of an apparently 'modernized' kind of religion may help to explain why the Moonies became such a force in Korea: it represented a fusion of Korean feudal elements with notions of modernity suggesting in a perverted and corrupt manner the possibility of a non-communist authentically Korean modernization.

14   A factor that must present an extra complication for Korean feminism in that the whole notion of individual human rights, for men as well as for women, is knotted together in the area of the representation of female sexuality, making it a focus for progressive (i.e. modernizing) men as well as for women, regardless of whether the women are inclined towards modernization or some form of neo-traditionalism.

15   The best book-length study of Korean cinema in English, Lee Hyangjin (2000), notes the intriguing fact that the only head of state ever to have written a book on film theory is Kim Jongil (1987). It is a work explicitly enjoining filmmakers to deploy a cinematic mode of address designed to bolster the Kim family's dynastic ambitions.

16   For an enlightening and challenging account of the Human Rights discourse enshrined in the International Bill of Rights to which all members of the UN have agreed, see the publication of The Human Rights Council of Australia's *The Rights Way to Development: A Human Rights Approach to Development Assistance – Policy and Practice*, 1995 (obtainable from PO Box L23, Maroubra, NSW, Australia 2035) and with a website at www.ozemail.com.au/hrca.

17   In this essay, Kim Soyoung also proposes a more positive reading of the freeze-frame endings unusually frequent in the Korean films of that era.

18   For a discussion of what a pre-capitalist or a pre-Renaissance aesthetic might look like, see McKeon (1987).

References

Adorno, Theodore (1984) *Aesthetic Theory*, London: RKP.
Adorno, Theodore (1998) *Critical Models: Inventions and Catchwords*, Henry W. Pickford (trans.), New York: University of Columbia Press.
Adorno, Theodore and Horkheimer, Max (1973) *Dialectic of Enlightenment*, John Cumming (trans.), London: Verso.

Arrighi, Giovanni (1994) *The Long Twentieth Century*, London: Verso.

Choi, Chungmoo (1995) 'Transnational capitalism, national imaginary and the protest theatre in South Korea', *Boundary2* 22(1): 235–261.

Crary, Jonathan (1994) *Techniques of the Observer*, Cambridge, MA: MIT Press.

Debray, Régis (1996) *Media Manifestos: On the Technological Transmission of Cultural Forms*, Eric Rauth (trans.), London: Verso.

Dufrenne, Mikel (1979) *Main Trends in Aesthetics and the Sciences of Art*, New York: Holmes & Meier.

Eagleton, Terry (1984), *The Function of Criticism*, London: Verso.

Fujii, James (1993) *Complicit Fictions*, Berkeley: University of California Press.

Godzich, Wlad (1994) *The Culture of Literacy*, Cambridge, MA: Harvard University Press.

Godzich, Wlad and Kittay, Jeffrey (1987) *The Emergence of Prose*, Minneapolis: University of Minnesota Press.

Harvey, David (1999) *The Limits to Capital*, London: Verso.

Hohendahl, Peter Uwe (1995) 'Recasting the public sphere', *October* 73: 27–54.

Jakobson, Roman (1960) 'Linguistics and poetics'. In T.A. Sebeok (ed.) *Style in Language*, Cambridge, MA: MIT Press, 350–377.

Jakobson, Roman (1978) 'On realism in art' [1921]. In L. Matejka and K. Pomorska (eds) *Readings in Russian Poetics: Formalist and structuralist views*, Ann Arbor: University of Michigan, 38–46.

Kim Jongil (1987) *The Theory of Cinematic Art*, Pyongyang: Korean Workers' Party Publishing House.

Kim Soyoung (1998) 'Cine-mania or cinephilia: film festivals and the identity question', *UTS Review* 4(2): 174–187.

Kim Soyoung (2001) 'Modernity in suspense: the logic of fetishism in Korean cinema', *Traces* 1 301–317.

Lee Hyangjin (2000) *Contemporary Korean Cinema: Identity, culture, politics*, Manchester: Manchester University Press.

Marx, Karl (1971) *A Contribution to the Critique of Political Economy*, London: Lawrence & Wishart.

McKeon, Michael (1987) *The Origins of the English Novel*, Baltimore, MD: Johns Hopkins University Press.

Moretti, Franco (2000) 'Conjectures on world literature', *New Left Review* II(1): 54–68, 174–187.

Ohmann, Richard (1996) *Selling Culture: Magazines, markets and class at the turn of the century*, London: Verso.

Prasad, Madhava (1993) 'Cinema and the desire for modernity', *The Journal of Arts and Ideas* (New Delhi) 25–26: 87–104.

Prasad, Madhava (1997) 'From speech to voice', *Deep Focus* 7(3–4): 51–54.

Willemen, Paul (1994) *Looks and Frictions*, London: British Film Institute.

Willemen, Paul (1995) 'Regimes of subjectivity and looking', *The UTS Review* 1(2): 101–129.

Willemen, Paul (2001) 'The zoom in popular cinema', *New Cinemas: Journal of Contemporary Film* 6–13.

Chapter 22

The birth of the local feminist sphere in the global era

'Trans-cinema' and *Yosongjang*

Kim Soyoung

I 'Yosongjang' (women's sphere or funeral)

The emphasis in this essay's title – *Yosongjang* – is an attempt to mark a flash-forward vision of a feminist public sphere, a portrayal of an imagined future rather than an account of the present.

In one sense, this essay responds to a marked proliferation of disparate forms of feminist production in South Korea, a production that might well make feminism in the early 21st century an unprecedented period. Amongst such production, feminist websites in particular provide an interesting case of activism, in the way they are linked to both existing and newly formed feminist publishing houses, street protests, performances and women's film festivals. All of these comprise, in a word, *yosongjang*.

I propose *yosongjang* as a term borrowed from a recent incident. On 29 January 2002, 14 sex workers were killed by fire in the city of Kunsan. Confined as they were to a workplace of enslaved prostitution, without an exit, they died helplessly when the fire broke out. On 8 February, women's groups held a ritual funeral on the site of the tragic accident in Kunsan. On the same day, women's groups and their supporters in the capital city of Seoul joined the ritual by organizing a 'street funeral' protest in front of the police station headquarters. The funeral became known as the first *yosong-jang* (women's funeral). 'Jang' meaning funeral corresponds to 'Jang' connoting space and sphere. So *Yosongjang* in Korean becomes a homonym with a doubly coded significance. It is both women's funeral and women's sphere. A woman's public funeral entitled *Yosongjang* is now a space open to both semiotic experiment and feminist politics.

It is the public ritual evoking abject figures such as sex workers that I now wish to incorporate into a discussion about the public sphere. My discontent with a historically gendered and Eurocentric notion of the public sphere propels me to move towards *yosongjang*, a concept that I suggest is closer to the notion of *political society* than that of the public sphere. Hence, I evoke the tearful scenes of the women's public funeral. To contextualize *yosongjang* within profoundly local scenes penetrated by elements of globalization, I now turn to another dimension of its manifestation, that of blockbuster culture and net activism.

2 Blockbusters and net documentaries

As a Korean version of a blockbuster hits the box office, both domestic and in some Asian film markets, a certain desire brews at the heart of a Korean film industry that has been bombarded by venture capital. Reclaiming its position as something in-between the Hollywood, the Asian and the Korean cinema industries, South Korean blockbusters desperately seek ways in which an internal cultural incommensurability makes its peace within the optical and aural unconscious of its imagined audience. In one sense, it is not a surprise that the existence of such an audience largely depends on the technological mobilization of digital effects, on promotion and marketing systems and on saturation booking. But this aspect alone cannot sustain the larger *cultural* ambitions of the blockbuster movie industry that aspires to square its Asian aspirations and global markets with the excess of a guarded nationalism.

Obviously, the South Korean blockbuster is a compromise between foreign forms and local materials, a compromise itself often staged on a grand scale. This blockbuster offers both a voluntary mimicry of, as well as imagined resistance to, large Hollywood productions, playing off various logics of both identity and difference in the global culture industry. Backed by the Korean nation-state and its national culture, the South Korean blockbuster presents itself as the cultural difference opposing the homogenizing tendencies of Hollywood. But it is an opposition between what Jameson once called 'the Identity of identity and nonidentity' (Jameson 1998: 76) and, as such, the blockbuster in the South Korean mode involves a contradiction.

In a recent book entitled *Blockbuster in Korean Mode: America or Atlantis* (Kim 2001), film critics and scholars noted the huge impact of such recent popular cinema on society. This impact ranges from redefinitions of the very role of cultural nationalism and globalization to the new configurations of morality, desire and 'everydayness'. The local film weekly *Cine-21* sums up the phenomenal success of local blockbusters in the following way:

> *As Good as It Gets.* It succinctly describes the phenomenal success of recent Korean movies. *Chingu (Friends)* occupied 38.3 percentage of the domestic market by drawing an eight million audience. During the summer season, local films like *Shillaui Talbam* (The Moonlight on Shilla) and *Yopkichoguin Kuyo* (Sassy Girl) would be competing at the box office. There has been a speculation that local movies would dominate 40% of the domestic market. It is not a slogan anymore, but a reality.
>
> (*Cine-21* 2001: 10)

The key issue that local blockbusters bring to the fore lies not so much in the actual amounts of real profit they generate as the investments they show of national cultural value. These investments go alongside a consistent emphasis on the virtues of the movie industry itself as something of an exemplary smog-free, post-industrial sector by the government since the 1990s, which sits well with its new purpose in the popular imagination. Notwithstanding the often outrageous marketing fees and ticket sales, the film industry as a whole in the year of 2001 made profits that were only equivalent to those of a medium-size corporation. Nevertheless, what the film industry in its blockbuster mode displays and informs are the popular imaginings of the working of finance capital and mass investment culture. The 'Netizen Fund' set up on the internet by film companies finds enthusiastic investors, often with such volume of usage that people complain about accessibility. However, the blockbuster movies and the related dissemination of blockbuster culture appear to announce a cultural era of investment that clearly plays a critical role in strengthening the hegemonic dominance of finance capital. This cultural intervention links the perceived interests of tens of millions of workers to its own by embedding 'investor practices' into their everyday lives and by offering them the appearance of a stake within a neo-liberal order (Harmes 2001).

Alongside the blockbuster mode housed in multiplexes, there has been the parallel proliferation of film festivals. Apart from the three international film festivals of Pusan, Puchon and Jeonju, we now see a range of other alternative festival forms – women, queer, labour and human rights – all managing to carve out a distinct audience. The cinephiliac culture of 1990s continues even after the IMF crisis of 1997. The issues that now define the global and the local, gender and class, in dialogue with cinematic specificity, manifest themselves within the new public sphere known as the film festival. This is indeed both a cinematic society and societal cinema. The cinema provides a privileged site from where to read Korean society, and vice versa.

Paralleling the emphasis among activists and intellectuals on the internet as an alternative public sphere, some filmmakers turn to digital video, easily transferable to streaming technology on the net. Access to a DSL service is both easy and cheap (approximately $15.00 per month per household) both at home and outside (less than one dollar per hour at PC lounges). This kind of public access has literally introduced two independent but related phenomena into the home. On the one hand we see a popularization of cyber trading and stock investment, and on the other, the formation of a new kind of public sphere sometimes claimed, perhaps hastily, as cyber democracy (http://soback.kornet.nm.kr/~wipaik/). Both activities, of mass investment culture and of cyber democracy, have become the *mise-en-abyme* of the era of globalization and of what is also claimed as the network society.

Glimpsing the possibilities of constructing a new critical space, most militant independent film and video groups, many of whom were connected to, and have grown out of, the 1980s labour and people's movements, have created their websites on which both demo versions and full length documentaries are freely available. Recently, the female workers' network (http://www.kwwnet.org/) has been showing a documentary on the issue of how irregular employment was expedited after the IMF crisis. It claims that seven out of ten female workers are now employed as irregular and flexible labour without any benefits. *Patriotic Games* (www.redsnowman.com) comes as a forceful attack on nationalism, a taboo area even among the progressive intellectuals of the 1980s, not only because of the National Security Law but also because of the way it reflects on the post-colonial and neo-imperial impact of Japan and America. The makers of *Patriotic Games* declare the net as a distinctive space for their counter-cinema. They refuse to sell their works on video and have very limited public screenings outside the net.

3 Trans-cinema

Taking a cue from the proliferation of digital cinema vis-à-vis new modes of activism, I would like to propose a notion of *trans-cinema*, or a cinema that should, I suggest, be attentive to the transformation of its production, distribution and reception modes, as shown by independent digital filmmaking and its availability on the net. Trans-cinema proposes that digital and net cinema, LCD screens (installed in subways, taxis and buses) and gigantic electrified display boards (*chonkwangpan* in Korean) should be seen as spaces into which cinema theories and criticism should intervene. The gigantic screens in downtown Seoul exist as a phantasmatic space, permeating and simultaneously constructing the everydayness of the city.

By conceptually framing this new space as trans-cinema, one could further claim that these spaces should not be used or taken solely as advertisement space, and indeed that such spaces should be opened up to issues concerning the public. Unlike individual or family viewing that marks TV viewers, the big monitors installed on the walls of tall buildings inevitably involve collective and temporary watching. People in transit get a glimpse of electric displays showing movie trailers, advertisements and news. Gigantic images looming on the walls of buildings certainly create *Blade Runner*-type effects that bring differing registers of temporality and spatiality to existing urban space. In a word, a heterotopia is being constantly invented in such space.

Media City Seoul 2000 used these electric display boards to present experimental images by 25 media artists including Paik Namjun. It was entitled the 'Clip City' project under the section of City Vision. It was an eye-opening experience to watch a one-minute clip of experimental images in the midst of the usual commercials. The tone of festivity around the project was, however, suddenly changed when Song Ilkon's video entitled *Flush* was found among abstract and experimental images on 43 monumental electric boards (available at http://www.nkino.com/moviedom/online sig.asp). This one-minute video captured a sequence where a teenage girl delivered and flushed a baby down a toilet. Soon *Flush* disappeared from the Clip City project. But this was an event that used the electric display boards as a space for public art.

To cite another, contrasting, example, I evoke scenes of catastrophe. It was almost an apocalyptic experience to watch the collapse of Songsu bridge and the Sampung department store (both icons of successful modernity), which claimed thousands of lives. The social disaster looms larger in the *Chonkwangpan*. The female body in *Flush* and the fractured modernity epitomized by the fall of modern monuments, challenged viewers around *Chonkwangpan*. As an exemplary icon of Marc Augé's super modern non-place (Augé 1995) or of Manuel Castells' post-industrial space in flow (Castells 2000), *Chonkwangpan* disrupts the demarcations between cinema, TV and billboards. It also blurs the line between public art, commercials and public announcements. In terms of collective spectatorship, *Chonkwangpan* is closer to cinema but it is akin to the content of television (composed of commercials, news and public announcements). The City Vision/Clip City project shows both a communicative and artistic dimension articulated within the public space. *Chonkwangpan* is trans-cinema and public TV that expands existing notions of both cinema and television.

The 2002 World Cup, in particular, showed a marked transformation in the way people perceived these mushrooming electrified billboards. The electrified billboard in front of the City Hall momentarily served as public cinema and a street TV contingent upon a collective spectatorship. The supporters of the Korean football team, known as the 'Red Devils', mobilized almost a whole nation to 'be the reds'. Whereas in Japan public gatherings were disallowed around electrified billboards, it was the other way round in South Korea. The City Hall square was turned into a public space that was virtually a liberation zone where millions flocked together to watch the World Cup games. Many were reminded of the massive people's protests in the late 1980s in this very space. This memory brought forth an uncanny superimposition of the political upon the mass gatherings of the World Cup. The layers of events and historical memories inscribed in *Chonkwangpan* await a name other than that of pure advertising. So I suggest trans-cinema. Rather than a premature and sensational celebration of the 'death of cinema' into its high-tech corporate versions, trans-cinema is an endeavour to locate and theorize an emergent spectatorship and mode of production. Trans-cinema is a form that can potentially unsettle the dominant interpellation of cinemas either as national or transnational. It is:

> a critique of transnational cinema and a transformative, reflexive practice, in which production of films and critical discourses are firmly intertwined. It produces a multiplicity of cinematic practices and a critical framework, which are not reducible either to the false universality of Hollywood as a new transnational standard or to its mirror image, the particularity of identity embraced by multiculturalism and transnational capitalism.
>
> (Yoshimoto 2000: 7)

The construction of a critical constellation of trans-cinema can contribute to the effort to stimulate new comparative work in film studies. Ironically, here, by one argument, 'the universalism which enables "comparison" to be made is the universal encounter with capitalism, a process that has massively accelerated since the 1950s' (Willemen 2002: 167). By that argument, the Korean blockbuster, which could be seen both as a response to Hollywood and as a translation of universality into a spectral dimension, provides an instance where the fraught problems of the universal and the particular, as well as global dominance and local resistance and gender politics, can be examined in the age of global finance capitalism. As the theoretical construction of the alternative public sphere in early cinema was proposed within the modes of *industrial* capitalism by Miriam Hansen (Hansen 1991: 5–20), so today there seems to be a need to conceive and imagine the (cinematic) alternative public sphere within the era of *transnational* capitalism. This, I suggest, should be an ongoing effort, for 'even if there were no empirical traces of autonomous public formations, they could be inferred from the force of negation, from hegemonic efforts to suppress or assimilate any conditions that might allow for an alternative (self-regulated, locally, and socially specific) organization of experience' (Hansen 1991: 91).

Yet, trans-cinema is a curious entity, an unstable mixture. It cuts across film and digital technology and challenges the normative process of spectatorship that followed the institutionalization of cinema. As a critique of, and successor to, the pairing of world cinema with national cinemas, it proposes the need to re-think the constellations of the local cinemas in the era of transnational capitalism. As such, trans-cinema, unlike trans*national* cinema, is also a recognition of, and a response to, the increasing rate of, for instance, inter-Asia cultural traffics that include local blockbuster movies (Hong Kong, China, India and South Korea) and art-house cinema (Taiwanese and Iranian cinema). Inter-Asian blockbusters, in particular, should provide an instance of re-visiting the Hollywood-type global culture industry formations, and allow a re-thinking of the way in which local or sub-global (regional) circuits get simultaneously de-articulated and re-articulated. The genealogy of the cinematic apparatus as we know it is embedded in the culture of industrial capitalism. One might need to redefine this apparatus in relation to a shifting political economy and its transformation into a global space. In order to articulate the cinematic apparatus in relation to a public sphere that encounters radically shifting socio-economic, political and cultural conditions, it becomes very clear that one should note both the persistence of diverse constituencies as well as the emergence of new ones in cinematically aided 'public spheres'.

4 The image of transparency and trans-nationalizing women in the blockbuster culture

Given that the structure and function of the liberal model of the bourgeois public sphere envisioned by Jurgen Habermas was both historically and sociologically specific to late 17th-century Great Britain and 18th-century France, as stated in the preface of *The Structural Transformation of the Public Sphere* (Habermas 1991: xvii), it is worth asking what one might expect to gain by bringing up this notion in a neo-liberal era, when the classical model of the public sphere in a developing market economy is no longer feasible and the nation-state can no longer provide the unity and boundedness conceived by Habermas.

The ideal of transparency haunts the liberal model of the bourgeois public sphere, where the state's role is stated as no more than that of a nightwatchman, even as its role serves the interest of the bourgeoisie. Critiquing this rhetoric of transparency, Seyla Benhabib evokes the salon in the Varnhagen biography where the play of identities in the form of self-revelation and self-concealment disrupts the public sphere's ideal of transparency (Dean 2001: 245). Transparency is, again, an intriguing term when located within the global socio-economic context, especially given its seeming connection with the regime of looking (of being transparent to someone's gaze). In the neo-liberal era, the trope of transparency stalks the post-IMF South Korea. The IMF and the World Bank repeatedly used the trope of transparency (*tumyongsong* in Korean) when they tried to restructure the political economy of the state. Now, the thinly disguised nightwatchman is overseen by an all-seeing disciplinary gaze of the neo-liberal man. Effectively, the demand is to make South Korea expose itself as a transparent or hollow being under neo-liberal global eyes. Given the prevailing tropes of transparency, it is worth contrasting these with Immanuel Wallerstein's warning of the *opacity* of the world system under finance capital (Wallerstein 1998: 32–33).

Where 'seeing man', seeing with imperial eyes, was accompanied with the countervailing narrative of 'anti-conquest' (Pratt 1992), today the administrator of global capital employs the trope of transparency. As the discourse of transparency prevails over and creeps into the political, as well as optical, unconscious of the popular, the working of global capital becomes more opaque and impenetrable to local eyes. Along with it, restructuring has brought job insecurity, low real wages, extended working hours and increasing inequality. Critiques of the failure of local public intellectuals in the era of globalization have flooded the mass media, especially the critique that accuses local intellectuals of not prophesying the impending IMF crisis. It used to be the case that it was only within the territorial framework of the nation-state that the critical discourse of public intellectuals was contested. Once the boundary gets re-drawn, they are blamed for being blind to the opacity of global capital. Indeed, the public intellectuals' intervention is confined to the point where a group of young venture capitalist and blockbuster movie producers are elevated to New Intellectuals (*shin jishikin*) by the present government. The Brain Korea project, aimed at churning out functionaries for the 'post-industrial' mode of production, has been rapidly changing the mode of knowledge production at universities.

The image of transparency clearly also involves a regime of looking. To the powerful, it is designed to be transparent, but to the powerless, impenetrable. Of course, the rhetoric usually presents the situation to be exactly the reverse. As social anxiety prevails over economic restructuring, the presumed and mainly male-centred memories of collective identity sustained by the nation and the *chaebol*, now disintegrate. The nostalgia industries sustained by the dotcom business, such as *I Love School* (http://www.iloveschool. co.kr/alumni associations), gain an enormous popularity due to their allusions to past bonding.

As South Korea is exposed to the gaze of the powerful global, and in turn mimics this gaze with its desire to be a player in Asia, the dynamics of anxiety and desire as these explode upon the blockbusters in the Korean mode take unexpected forms. Paralleling the rise of a local popular culture known as the Korean Wave (*hanryu*, composed mainly of TV drama, music and fashion) now hitting other parts of Asia, blockbusters turn to a strategy of multi-nationalizing their women characters. *Shiri* has a North Korean woman as an espionage agent (code name Hydra). *JSA (Joint Security Area)* employs a Swiss-Korean woman as an inspector to resolve a murder mystery at the JSA. *Failan* casts a Hong Kong actress to play a Chinese migrant worker in Korea. Zhang Ziyi (a heroine of *Crouching Tiger, Hidden Dragon*) plays Ming Princess Musa (*Warrior*). The heroine of *Pichonmu (Flying Heaven Martial Arts)* is cast as a Mongolian.

Such characterization is quite unprecedented. From the mid-1950s, South Korean films sustained themselves largely through representing women as tropes of traumas concerning modernity and the post-colonial condition. These ranged from *Madame Freedom* (1955), *Bitter But Once Again* (1968), *Petal* (1996), *Sopyonjae* (1993). When the blockbusters have South Korean women in central roles, these are usually associated with gangsters and monsters – recent examples being *A Wife of Organized Gangster* (*Chopok Manura*), *The Moonlight in Shilla* (*Shillaui Dalbam*) and *Soul Guardians* (*Toimarok*).

Now, the disappearance of South Korean women from the films and their displacement into these new characters is problematic, especially in circumstances where the identity of a fraternal collective is being re-constituted around notions of a global citizenship. At the representational level, it appears that such a global citizenship now excludes South Korean women. The films mentioned above reveal a newly forming nationalism in conjunction with globalization. To have a global façade, these films appear to suggest that one needs to make their local women invisible. Predictably, the vanishing of South Korean women characters is offset by a new consolidation of homo-social bonding among men. And when Chinese migrant female labour is invoked in *Failan* (2001), she bears the archetypal role of an innocent and sacrificing woman that appeared both in the film and in the literature of the period of condensed industrialization of the 1970s. The presumed virtue, now allegedly lost, of South Korean women of the recent past, is projected upon a woman from a less globalized sector. As South Korean women disappear, other women are summoned to enable the purposes of nostalgia.

Relegating women to the invisible, the blockbusters mobilize the male dominant groups, such as the army, the Korean Central Intelligence Agency, and organized gangsters, to foreground homo-social relations. The relationship, recognizable to male members in the group, simply becomes opaque to female characters. The Swiss-Korean heroine in *JSA* (Sophie Chang) is dispatched by the Neutral Nations Supervisory Commission as an investigator to unravel the mystery around the murders of South Korean and North Korean soldiers at the North Korean camp located in the DMZ. The situation becomes impenetrable to Sophie. Her investigator's 'look' is constantly denied agency, presumably because the murder and its concealment is provoked, sustained and empowered by a brotherhood based on ethnic nationalism that transcends the different ideologies along the lines of the cold war. Sophie, in desperation, tries to connect to this situation via her deceased father who had served in the Korean War but had defected to Switzerland after being detained in the war prisoners' camp.

Her father's photograph now alludes to the complexities of modern history ravaged by the Cold War, division and migration. But it does not really enable her to look at the cover up of the murders among North and South Korean soldiers. Neither does her expertise in international law (Zurich law school graduate) help, nor her half 'ethnicity' as Korean.

What the impenetrability and opacity of male bonding suggests is quite evident. However, the brotherhood of nationalism is not destined to find a secure space of its own under the global gaze that demands transparency. This sense of the impossibility of reconstructing a nationalist male space must be both a cause and a consequence of the endless remaking of blockbusters, amongst other reasons. The disappearance of local women constitutes the structuring absence and a symptom in a new globalized national discourse. The orchestration of transparency and impenetrability bitterly resounding in the global and the national arena increasingly stages an orchestra without women players. A retreat of gender politics, indeed. And this retreat does not stop at the level of representation. Along with the official declaration of the collapse of public intellectuals and their replacement with twenty or thirty-something young venture capitalists as the 'new intellectuals', the feminist intervention in the public sphere attuned to a globalized national is doubly denied.

The feminist journal *Yo/Song I-lon* (*Feminist Theory* 2001) declares the present government of South Korea to be a zombie that incorporates the remnants of an earlier military regime that took pride in presenting itself as an authoritarian father. As the dominant media and blockbusters register the absence of local women and the mobilization of other Asian women for reasons of both economy and nostalgia, there arises a dire need to cope with this situation on the grounds of feminist cultural politics. In conditions where both the transnational and the national are structured within the relations of competitive dominance, even as they equally often function in complicity, conditions that debilitate liminal subject positions whose everydayness simply cannot share the abstract promises of triumphal globalization, then neither international nor local feminism is yet ready to provide a sufficient analysis for such a conjuncture. Without taking a position similar either to statist or liberal feminism, an emergent feminist articulation needs be attentive to locally specific but globally resistant issues.

5 Film festivals and local female labour

Towards the late 1990s, facing the need for a new direction in a social movement that no longer appears grounded on the proletarian class perspective of the 1980s' labour movement in alliance with student protests, groups composed of feminists, gay and lesbian activists, some members of youth sub-cultures and civil activists, have all initiated film festivals as public platforms to address their rights and concerns. The desire to be represented or recognized in public prevails in many such festival modes. It seems that diverse festivals have become not only a space of negotiation among different forces but also form a cultural practice that links audiences to the specific agendas raised by new identities, subject positions and newly proliferating NGOs.

Generally speaking, the film festivals can be classified into three categories. First, there are those derived from a coalition of the state, local governments, corporations and specialists equipped with film expertise, as exemplified by the Pusan International Film Festival, the Puchon International Fantastic Film Festival and the Jeonju International Film Festival. Secondly, there are corporate-sponsored festivals such as the Q Channel Documentary Film and Video Festival and Nices Short Film Festival (which closed in 1999). Thirdly, there are festivals organized by both new and old activist groups. The third kind of festival is relatively autonomous from the state and the corporate sector. Therefore, it provides an interesting example of how the new social movement of the 1990s is taking tentative steps away from the preceding 1980s social movement, which was pivoted on the labour movement.

In this third category, the discourses of the 1980s and the 1990s are simultaneously operative. Both the similarities and continuities as well as the differences and ruptures between the two periods become visible when the different film festivals are examined closely. In addition, through the politics of these festivals, the notion of identity politics and the possible formation of alternative public spheres may be tested against the civil society claims put forth by the Kim Yongsam and Kim Daejung governments and the mainstream media. So far, the third category has included the Women's Film Festival in Seoul, the Queer Film Festival, and the Human Rights Watch Festival (organized by an ex-political prisoner previously jailed for violation of the National Security Law), and the Independent Film Festival (held by young filmmakers), as well as various other small scale and perennial festivals that take place on college campuses, in cinemas, videotheques and so forth.

The way the three categories of film festival operate may be viewed as an index to the new contours of cultural specificity in the 1990s. The notion of the public sphere and the alternative public spheres within which each film festival is located (or dislocated) has to be taken into consideration vis-à-vis the inauguration of the civil government, the retreat of the labour movement as the privileged force of social change, and the concomitant endeavour to find new agencies for social change. Around the same period, the discourse on nationalism has been re-mobilized, both with and against the official discourse of *Saegaehwa* (globalization in Korean in the late 1990s). The international scale film festivals in particular thrive on the manifold manifestations of the global and the local and the national and the local. The film festival provides a condensed space where different interests and ideologies all come into play at the contested intersection of residual authoritarian and emergent democratic modes. The negotiations and compromises between the state, the corporations, the intellectuals and the audiences reveal how the different societies are in contest with one another in this historical location.

The various film festivals are indeed public spaces working through a complex structure of articulation. They tend to operate in a strategic way so as to render the festival occasion a cultural and political site of ongoing recognition, negotiation and contest.

The banning of festivals such as the Queer Film Festival and the Human Rights Watch Film Festival explicitly throws up the pressure points in the hegemonic order. The whole process of organizing, exhibiting and banning film festivals reveals blockages and points of compromises, as well as possible directions towards alternative or oppositional platforms (Kim 1998).

As the official ban on the above festivals was withdrawn in 1998, the festivals seem to continue taking up the issues they initially raised. But there was one deeply problematic incident. This issue concerned internalized censorship and female local labour in the global era. The documentary entitled *Pab, Ggot, Yang* (*Food, Flower and Scapegoat*) dealt with the protest of female workers at the Hyundai car factory in the city of Ulsan after the IMF provoked restructuring. The female workers were mostly cooks and kitchen aids at the canteen. What made the situation worse was that they were the first group laid off after a strike. Nevertheless, during the strike, male workers described their female colleagues as 'flowers' since they provided food. But the labour union did not give substantive support when the female workers lost their jobs. They became the scapegoats. This is a story rarely told, even by the progressive media. The documentary was made by a woman filmmaker, IM, Inae with her group, Labour Reporters' Network. During the process of release, the work met problem. Ulsan is a heavy-industry city and a home of Hyundai. In the 1980s, the labour struggle at Hyundai was often depicted as a David-and-Goliath fight. After the IMF crisis, as with other *chaebols*, there was a demand made that Hyundai restructure its system. The multinational corporate, heavily backed by the state, was to see its disintegration under global capital. The documentary was made in the immediate post-IMF period. As the Human Rights Watch Film Festival made an impact in Seoul in 1998, the film soon began to tour the country. The city of Ulsan Human Rights Watch Film Festival was also established. But it refused to include *Pab, Ggot, Yang* in the programme, saying that it would provoke antagonism among the people of Ulsan. This incident led to protests on the net. *jinbo.net* (Progressive Net) and others took this censorship not only to be a violation of freedom of expression but obvious repression on the female labour issue.

These incidents burst open the long-overdue gender-and-class related problems within the allegedly progressive movement sector. What this incident shows quite clearly is that control of female labour continues to be an issue. Both the labour union and the festival committee, which was composed of local activists and intellectuals in Ulsan, refused to take the female labour issue as crucial to their agenda. One of the labour activists in Ulsan noted that the public screening of this kind of documentary would put the upcoming labour–capital negotiation in jeopardy. The fact that the emergent underclass group is heavily marked by gender – the gendered underclass in short – causes a situation that is not dissimilar to the problematic vanishing of South Korean women in some blockbusters, and this upsets festival and net communities.

Intriguingly, the filmmaker of *Pab, Ggot, Yang* declares to its audiences that hers is not a film. She obviously seeks to deny to her work the ways in which 'film' is made, viewed and served. She expressed her reservation about showing this work in existing exhibition venues including film festivals. In the end, she preferred to show its segments on the net (http://larnet.jinbo.net/movie.html). But the question remains – if it cannot be named as a film and if it cannot be circulated in the usual film exhibition venues, what then is it?

6 Links: formation of feminist sphere

Since the late 1990s, there have been increasing numbers of feminist publications and activities centred on the net. If one enters 'feminism' on a search engine, one gets many inviting sites. These range from lesbian sites to female labour organization sites. In feminist cultural politics, they exist along with feminist presses such as *Ttohanui Munhwa* (*Alternative Culture*), *Yoyon* (*Women's Studies*), Asian Women Studies, Feminism Studies and webzines – notably *Onninae* (*Sisters*), *Dalnara Ttalsepo* (*Moon Daughter Cell*). It appears that a relatively autonomous and radical (virtual) space is in the process of being formed, which (in)voluntarily puts a distance between itself and the state and the economy. Anyway, is it not a truism now that, even as critique, the notion of public sphere is deeply entrenched in the idealization and the rationalization of the bourgeois? And that, among the list of feminist critiques of the Habermasian public sphere, it notoriously excludes women's dissident subjectivities and non-normative sexualities. Here is one example:

> Modern normative reason and its political expression in the idea of the civic public, then, has unity and coherence by its expulsion and confinement of everything that would threaten to invade the polity with differentiation: the specificity of women's bodies and desires, the difference of race and culture, the variability of heterogeneity of the needs, the goals and desires of each individual, the ambiguity and changeability of feelings.
>
> (Young 1987: 67)

Not dissimilar to the ideas of modernity and the universal and so on, the public sphere continues to be a quite contentious term, especially when it shifts its locale to the non-West, or to the 'rest of the world'. Once the notion is evoked in the non-Western context, it immediately invites controversy. For instance, Korean historian Choi Kapsu argues that Europe, in comparison with China, lags behind in the formation of the state. In the midst of a relatively delayed political process, the European notion of public sphere emerged as a mediator between the civil society and the state. Hence, the European idea of a public sphere betrays itself as a particular case rather than an universal one, contrary to its own claim as universal (Choi 2001).

The Chinese scholar Wang Hui emphatically separates the public sphere from civil society in conversation with Korean scholar Paik Seunguk on the issue of the *Paradox of Modernity – China, Modernity and Globalization* (Wang and Paik 2000). He rightly points out that civil society is a product of Europe dating back to Greek society, and it is closely tied to an emergence of the bourgeois class, the self-regulated market theory of Adam Smith and the Hegelian spirit. He further argues, however, that the public sphere *can* exist without a formation of the bourgeois class. He contends that it can come into existence even inside the state and, hence, that the formation of a public sphere can be relatively independent from civil society. The historical process of China indicates that the collapse of civil society with the public sphere causes a hazardous misunderstanding. And then he writes,

> Who would represent the civil society in present China in terms of proprietorship? The power transforms itself into the capital, which again transforms into the

economic power in the social. It becomes a representative of the civil society. They monopolize the public media with the power. They could monopolize the media and the public opinion. They might be considered as the bourgeois class. But they pose only non-democratic demands. This kind of condition raises a necessity of distinguishing the civil society from the public sphere.

(Wang and Paik 2000)

Elsewhere, Wang Hui goes further. He reminds us of the vision of Lu Xun, whose critique of the nation-state and industrialization is inspired by the world of ghosts in folklore, which contains both affection as well as horror. The perspective of ghosts allowed Lu Xun to see the modern in an entirely new mode. Instead of evoking Confucian civilization in East Asia, Lu Xun suggests the world of ghosts. What Lu Xun sees through the ghostly vision is the persistence of the living world of the subaltern class, despite the violence of the modern state. The world of ghosts refuses to be reducible. It is the realm of affect, which defies the logic of modernization. Wang Hui's evocation of Lu Xun's world of ghosts as the repressed but, nevertheless, persistent vision of the subaltern is an intriguing one. Instead of expelling it to the realm of superstition, one can learn something from defining the world of ghosts alongside a subaltern class rendered invisible and inarticulate by the ruling elite. In other writing, Wang Hui evokes the last days of Lu Xun to illustrate the scene where Lu Xun envisions himself as a female ghost (Nu Diao) in red (Wang 1999: 18–38).[1]

The male author's identification with, and affective investment in, the female ghost is illuminating in the sense that Nu Diao belongs to the penumbrae, the possible place of a 'non-subject', which is positioned in the hierarchized modes of existence such as 'substance', 'shadow' and 'penumbrae' (Liu 2001: 71–72). In this schema, subject positions such as the courtesan, the maid and the concubine belong to the penumbrae, the shadow of a shadow.[2] Lu Xun's Nu Diao also slips into the penumbrae with her vengeance and bitterness. The theoretical re-reading of hierarchized living space of 'substance', 'shadow' and 'penumbrae' renders visible what the notion of public sphere excludes.[3]

Lu Xun's storytelling of the disenchanted world of ghosts in the midst of modernization has some resonance with a mode of storytelling that Partha Chatterjee calls for when he quotes the instance of an epitaph written by Urdu writer Saadat Hassan Manto for himself. Chatterjee reads into it the desire for a storytelling mode that deals with the complicated relationship of modernity to democracy, and the role of the violence of the modern state. And this storytelling renders political society legible, where the spectre of pure politics haunts, and thereby the certainties of civil social norms and constitutional proprieties are put under challenge.[4] Thus, 'those who dream of building the new democratic society must aspire to be greater storywriters than god', as Manto writes. (Chatterjee 2001: 20)

Taking up the constellation of political society, Kuan-Hsing Chen throws it into relief by criticizing the binary framework of state and civil society. As a transient mediating space between state and civil society, political society provides a space of rethinking the notion of the political for the subaltern. In the Taiwanese case, it is the popular democracy line that shares a sort of elective affinity with political society. Translating Partha Chatterjee's influential proposition of political society into an East Asian context, and one addressing Taiwan in particular, Chen suggests that political society not only mediates the state and civil society, but also *min-jian* (roughly, a folk, people or commoners society, *jian* means in-between and space). Here *min-jian* is the space that has allowed the commoners to survive, so that no radical break could be brought about by the violence of the modernizing state and civil society (Chen 2002).[5]

Turning back to the issues concerning non-unionized female casual labour, sex workers and the public memorial ceremony named as a women's funeral (*yosongjang*), all of these certainly demand to be re-viewed within a perspective that is distinct from the trinity of state, civil society and public sphere. Female casual labour was dismissed as 'illegitimate' even by the labour unions in the beginning, as is vividly captured in the documentary *Pab, Ggot, Yang*. And issues concerning sex work do not enter the realm of civil society and public sphere in the South Korean context unless it is the US military-related sex industry. These are issues and subject positions that require a theorization of an uncertain zone of political society, *min-jian* and *yosongjang*. But just like the forked tongue used in the post-colonial context, one needs to be strategically dextrous with the use and promise of the public sphere. It has constantly, historically, made gestures towards including the sector of the excluded. Because of its hopelessly unattainable ideal, it accidentally redraws a map even though there is a limit. Being wary of a contingent opening, in its true sense of *Öffentlichkeit* but certainly not being dependent upon it, one needs to make an 'event' out of the contingent and accidental opening of an episodic public sphere. Film festivals such as the Women's Film Festival in Seoul, the Queer Film Festival, the Labour Film Festival, the Human Rights Film Festival are instances. At the same time, however, attention must be drawn to the way in which normative notions of the public sphere cannot deal with the persistence and transformation of political society, *min-jian* and *yosonjang*. Thus it is that one needs such frameworks as are attentive to the in-between and emergent movement.

As I noted at the beginning of this paper, there has been a women's funeral (*yosongjang*) organized by different groups of women. Recently, a public funeral of 14 sex workers was held on the streets in the name of *yosongjang* in this way by women's organizations. These organizers argue that the history of *yosongjang* in fact dates back to the YH incident in 1979, recorded as one of the crucial labour movements against multinational corporations. Female workers went naked during the strike in defence against the police and the privately hired gangsters by the YH company. Their leader, Kim Kyongsuk, was found dead in the midst of violent suppression of the strike. The funeral of the female labour activist Kim Kyongsuk was held by her fellow workers in secret, and now the organizer of *Yosongjang* for sex workers has chosen to trace its origin to the funeral ritual for Kim Kyongsuk by her fellow workers.

Coincidentally, the women's public sphere (one of the Korean translations for the public sphere is *Kongkaejang*) in Korean can also be named *yosongjang*. Two concepts of *yosongjang*, related to death, friendship and resistance, betray the accidental coming together of the female public sphere. The public ritual for sex workers in the streets marks a new chapter in the women's movement in South Korea, as the Women's Weekly News (*yosongshinmun*) reported. First, it implicitly challenges a dominant form of ritual conducted in the Confucian way, which excludes women as key participants in the process. Second, it is an open acknowledgement to a certain sector of sex workers who are largely made invisible in the public sphere.

This event can, however, take a different turn afterwards. The organizer (the women's association group) has to take recourse to the state and to the legal system to tackle the law concerning reparation and the establishment of the law governing the prostitution. Is it a move similar to liberal reformism such as NOW (National Organization for Women) in the US? Or, is it connected to a specificity, a conjuncture of South Korea?

Finally, in response to the statement by the filmmaker of *Pab, Ggot, Yang*, I am very tempted to describe it as trans-cinema. Trans-cinema is a cinema in *translation* and in *transition*. What the work is able to have is an after-life even after it has been rejected from entering the progressive public space, and this is something that has much to do with its dissemination on the net and with the support garnered from it. However, the critical constellation of trans-cinema, I think, is yet to come.

Acknowledgements

This paper was initially read at the UC Berkeley Conference entitled as *Look Who's Talking: Media and Public Sphere*, and a revised version was delivered at the Asian Women's Forum at the Fourth Seoul International Women's Film Festival and the ICA Pre-Conference at Tokyo University. I thank Chris Berry, Kim Eunshil, Kang Myung-Koo and Yoshimi Shunya for their kind invitations. Because of their encouragement, this paper itself becomes a trans-Asia project. My thanks also go to Naifei Ding, Kuan-Hsing Chen and Ashish Rajadhyaksha for their suggestions.

Notes

1 I thank Wang Hui for alerting me to this book. My thanks also go to Lee Jung-Koo for translating this passage in Chinese to Korean for me.
2 For further readings on the penumbrae and its significance in feminism and the women's movement, refer to Ding and Liu (2000).
3 I am particularly interested in Lu Xun's perspective since it illuminates my reading of horror cinema with female ghosts in 1960s South Korea when state-led modernization took place with full force. In relation to horror cinema, modernization and female ghosts, please refer to my book *Specters of Modernity: Fantastic Korean Cinema* (2000), which tries a diagnostic reading of modernity and gender.
4 For an articulation of cinema and political society, see Ashish Rajadhyaksha's essay in this volume.
5 This paper was revised and delivered at Pre-ICA conference in Tokyo, July 2002 organized by Yoshimi Shunya and Kang Myung-Koo.

References

Augé, Marc (1995) *Non-Places: Introduction to an Anthropology of Supermodernity*, John Howe (trans.), London: Verso.
Castells, Manuel (2000) *The Rise of the Network Society*, London: Blackwell.
Chatterjee, Partha (2001) 'Democracy and the violence of the state: a political negotiation of death', *Inter-Asia Cultural Studies* 2(1): 7–21.
Chen, Kuan-Hsing (2002) 'Civil society and Min Jian: on political society and popular democracy', unpublished paper.
Choi, Kapsu 최갑수 (2001) 'The public-ness and public sphere in the West', *The Radical Review* 진보평론 Vol. 9.
Cine 21 (2001) August 17: 10–15.
Dean, Jodi (2001) 'Cyber salons and civil society: rethinking the public sphere in transnational technoculture', *Public Culture* 13(2): 256–257.

Ding, Naifei and Liu Jen-Peng (2000) 'Penumbrae ask shadow (II): Crocodile Skin, Lesbian Stuffing, Qiu Mialjin's Half-man Half-horse', presented at the Third International Crossroads in Cultural Studies Conference, 21–25 June, Birmingham, UK.

Habermas, Jurgen (1991) *The Structural Transformation of the Public Sphere*, Cambridge: MIT Press.

Hansen, Miriam (1991) *Babel and Babylon*, Cambridge: Harvard University Press.

Harmes, Adam (2001) 'Mass investment culture', *New Left Review*, No. 9, May–June.

Jameson, Frederic (1998) 'Notes on globalization as a philosophical issue'. In Fredric Jameson and Masao Miyoshi (eds) *The Cultures of Globalization*, Durham: Duke University Press, 54–77.

Kim, Soyoung 김소영 (1998) 'Cinemania, cinephilia and identity question', *The UTS Review* 4(2): 174–187

Kim, Soyoung 김소영 (2000) *Specters of Modernity: Fantastic Korean Cinema* 근대성의 유령들 : 판타스틱 한국 영화 , Seoul: Ssiat Publishing 씨앗을 뿌리는 사람들 .

Kim, Soyoung 김소영 (2001) *Korean Blockbusters* 한국형 블록버스터 , Seoul: Hyunshil Munhwa Yongu Publishing 현실문화연구 .

Liu, Jen Peng (2001) 'The disposition of hierarchy and the late Qing discourse of gender equality', *Inter-Asia Cultural Studies* 2(1): 69–79.

Pratt, Mary Louise (1992) *Imperial Eyes*, London: Routledge Young, Iris Marion (1987) 'Impartiality and the civic public'. In Seyla Benhabib (ed.) *Feminism as Critique*, Minneapolis: University of Minnesota Press, 56–76.

Yoshimoto, Mitsuhiro (2000) 'Trans-Asian cinema', an unpublished paper presented at Jeonju International Film Festival Forum.

Wallerstein, Emmanuel (1998) *Utopistics*, New York: New Press.

Wang, Hui (1999) *Resistance and Despair: The Literary World of Lu Xun* 反抗絶望 , Beijing: 河北教育出版社 .

Wang, Hui and Paik Seunguk (2000) 'Paradox of modernity – China, modernity and globalization', *Radical Review* 진보평론 Vol. 6.

Willemen, Paul (2002) 'Detouring through Korean cinema', *Inter-Asia Cultural Studies* 3(2): 167–186.

Part VII

Other popular cultures

Discourse of cultural identity in Indonesia during the 1997–1998 monetary crisis

Melani Budianta

Introduction

As a result of increased global flow of goods, people, images, technology and information, especially from more prominent countries to the rest of the world, imagined boundaries of national cultures have become more permeable than ever. As shown in the latest Asian economic crisis, the global expansion of economic activities has had a significant yet different impact on the internal condition of nation-states – depending on the ways the political regimes that govern the respective nation-states respond to the crisis. In the case of Indonesia, the 1997–1998 financial crisis led to the downfall of the Soeharto regime, followed by prolonged social unrest that threatened national unity.

The economic crisis has also led to a serious cultural identity crisis, as boundaries that separate the 'imagined community' of a nation-state from the external global forces, as well as the internal cohesion of the plural ethnic and regional communities that makes up the nation-state are disintegrating. In public discourse, the issues of globalization versus nationalism and nationalism versus ethnic and regional communalism have surfaced, especially as the country is torn by secessionist and inter-group conflicts. The triangular relationship of the global-national-local (multicultural) interests became more complicated as 'internal' regional issues such as East Timor and Aceh prompted global or international intervention.

To understand the complex relations of global-national-local in the 1997–1998 crisis we need a conceptual framework that positions the (nation-)State as a double agent 'broker' that mediates the impact of the global flow internally. This paper will analyse a selection from public discourse on cultural identity and globalization in Indonesia during the 1997–1998 financial crisis. It illustrates how the New Order cultural politics informs its (mis)management of the global and local cultural exchange, and how cultural politics as well as its mismanagement of global-local exchange results in the identity and cultural crisis. Through the analysis of public discourse, the paper examines the interrogation of the imagined community of Indonesia during the economic crisis, and envisions what the future is likely to be.

The paper begins with the context of the Indonesian monetary crisis and the position of the New Order regime *vis-à-vis* global financial order. Discussion of the arts and culture campaign in an Indonesian newspaper in the third section gives an example of how the New Order cultural policy follows the logic of capitalism in treating culture as a commodity or as an unchanging token of traditional values, while at the same time masking or denying its ideological and political features. The repression or denial of the ideological orientation of the state's cultural policy, which centralizes one cultural identity (Javanese) and marginalizes others, would be the seed of ethnic and racial problems. As the authoritarian state, eroded by the economic crises, started to crumble, the cultural crisis – the root of which has been planted in history and later nurtured and repressed simultaneously by the cultural politics of the regime – exploded unchecked. In response to these internal insurgencies, the state evokes the global forces as threatening the dignity of the nation (section four).

The paper concludes that, in the case of Indonesia, the rise of sectarianism is more closely linked to the racial and cultural politics of the New Order as it appropriates economic globalization for its own purposes. The global, it argues, is very much intertwined with local power struggles. The cultural crisis marks the turning point for Indonesians, whether to lapse into an essentialist and nativist imagining of national identity or to construct a concept of nationhood that is more inclusive and open to heterogeneity.

As Appadurai (1993: 331) suggests, the global-local dynamics are expressed in specific cultural and ideological idioms and enunciated in a particular historical and cultural juncture that needs to be contextualized. Behind these representations is an 'institutionalized system for the production of knowledge in regulated language' (Bove 1990: 54).

Some of the discourses analysed in this paper are of the nature of propaganda. Its very strategy is to convert the reader unconsciously, by constructing imagined objects that mask its ideological, political, economic or cultural messages or purposes. Others are more sophisticated, verbal configurations of ideology supported by practices, systems and institutions. Constructed within the discourse of a particular system, some group or individual statements reflect the unconscious subscription to the dominant ideology, while simultaneously expressing hopes, dreams, anxiety, confusion and ambiguities about the subject of its discourse.

Monetary crisis and the crisis of cultural identity

1998 was a crucial time in the history of Indonesia as a nation-state, as it witnessed the downfall of a political regime, which had held on to power for 32 years. The fall of the New Order highlights the peculiar relations of this regime with the forces of economic globalization, on which it cashed in and by which it was cashed out. It is not a coincidence that the end of the regime is linked with the onslaught of the worst economic crisis in Asia since the great depression.

The New Order, established by Soeharto in 1965 after toppling Soekarno, Indonesia's first president, began with the promise of an economic difference: internally, from a nation wrecked by political turmoil to a nation which can feed its people; externally, from a 'go to hell with your aid' policy to an open door policy. Preoccupied with the processes of nation building, the earlier government had been a failure in improving the national economy. Externally, Soekarno's obsession with national sovereignty and an 'anti-imperialist, neocolonialist' campaign resulted in more or less antagonist relations with the West.[1]

In contrast to his predecessor, right after his ascendancy, Soeharto opened the door, which was formerly closed, to foreign investment. In 1967, Freeport McMoran Copper and Gold Inc. was the first American multinational company to obtain a permit to mine copper and gold in the virgin forest of Irian, later named Tembagapura. Soeharto's bow to economic globalization and his 'politically correct' anti-communist stand won him full support from international funding agencies, such as the World Bank, The IMF[2] and their influential nation-state members, including the USA.[3] It is an irony that the regime that made global economy its major capital was to collapse because of its very susceptibility to the global sway of economic crisis.

The neo-patrimonial, authoritarian state of the New Order had been highly dependent on transnational investment, and had used the economic opportunities arising from the network of global relations to establish what has been called 'crony capitalism' under the guise of developmentalism.[4] In Soeharto's era, 'development' was a sacred cow. In the name of development, rice fields were turned into real estate and golf courses, rainforests into monoculture palm-oil plantations to increase national income, fishing shores into five-star world-class resorts all funded by foreign debt. In his 32-year rule, Indonesia's metropolis capital became a consumer culture paradise, with gigantic retail outlet and shopping centres. But this haven for consumer culture also produced a great social gap among the rich and the poor.

The complex interaction of global and local political and economic forces, which lay the foundation of the Indonesian economy in the last three decades, requires elaboration. It is sufficient to say that the external–internal dichotomy is a misleading construction of the processes of globalization. Even for the layperson unfamiliar with economic terms, it is quite obvious that the New Order's investment in global markets has become a profitable source not only for increasing national income, but also the filling the pockets of its official supporters. Banking industries gain more in giving credit facilities of internationally credible joint ventures and multinational projects, than do local investors with dubious credit records. This partiality to big business provides more space for the participation of the elite (including the relatives of the ruling officials), the powerful (government officials, many of them consisting of retired military officials) and the rich (hardworking Chinese entrepreneurs), than the rest of the society, making the social and economic gap unbridgeable. The encouragement of conglomerations in the Indonesian economic system since the 1980s has further motivated the collusion of these three power elites, most prominently the collusion between the sons and daughters of the first family with Chinese tycoons.

Criticism and protest of the practices that give monopolies, tax exemption and other extra facilities to Soeharto's children (who soon joined the richest elite in the country) were not only unheeded but also repressed. While stressing 'Asian family values' as a jargon to inculcate the people's obedience and respect to rulers as one would to one's own 'father', this regime managed to build a safety network to secure the welfare of the ruling elite and their families. The engineering of polls and election systems helped this New Order to maintain the status quo, by making the single majority party, Golkar, as solid as ever. By the same means, the President and the ruling party that supported him managed to put in the house of representative and people's consultative assembly as many of his relatives and supporters as possible, including the sons, daughters and in-laws of government officials, governors, and the children of the president himself. All of them managed to pamper and shelter the President from being exposed to people's dissatisfaction and criticism.

The New Order developmentalism brought Indonesia, or more specifically President Soeharto, to international recognition. These positive images had been used by the State to boost national pride. Before the onslaught of the economic crisis, the New Order government had prided itself for its success in ruling the country, a claim that was often confirmed by external sources. In the 'Asian miracle' discourse, Indonesia was even predicted to be one of the top five leading economies in the Pacific Rim. The key to this achievement in the eyes of the government was political stability guarded by the armed forces, and by the politics of repression that were cloaked under the guise of harmony and tolerance. Pancasila, or the five basic principles, was thought to be the recipe of this success in maintaining social cohesion and peace in a nation that consisted of more than 300 languages and ethnic groups.

The regional crisis, however, exposed the exceedingly weak fundamentals of the economy that was otherwise covered by the success stories of the New Order, inviting waves of internal dissatisfaction as the public learnt how the ruling elites benefited from the global exchanges for their own interests rather than for the common good. The good self-image that was portrayed by government officials in their yearly exhibition of the successes of development could no longer hide its dark sides. External surveys helped to further highlight these. Indonesia was ranked amongst the lowest in both the Corruption Index and the UNDP Human Development Index in 1996. This hurt the national pride, and some Indonesian experts questioned the validity and biases of the surveys. However 1996 and 1997 witnessed natural and man-made disasters, which overshadowed the importance of any surveys. Among the most serious tragedies was a large forest fire, which was due to mismanagement of environment, weak legal implementation and collusion between big businesses, which owned the licence for deforestation, and government officials.[5] Neighbouring countries, which felt the impact of the forest fire's smoke, lent their hands to curbing the fire, thus pushing the Indonesian self-esteem even lower. From October 1996 to February 1997, Indonesia also saw social unrest which caused the burning of 15 churches and the destruction of 25 others in Situbondo (10 October 1996); the burning and looting of shops, hotels, police headquarters and churches in Tasikmalaya (30 December and 18 February), which killed around 300 people; and the burning of Chinese shops and houses in Rengasdengklok on 30 January 1997. By the time the monetary crisis hit Indonesia in mid 1997 dissatisfaction with the whole system that regulated life in the country had steadily mounted, and was ready to erupt.

What occurred internally within one year, starting in June 1997, when the US dollar to rupiah exchange rate climbed slowly from Rp2.200 to more than eight times this rate in mid June 1998, was more complicated than the subsequent fall of the New Order. Public discourse – official as well as popular – during that critical period reflects a psychological tension of a nation in crisis. On one hand, there was a heightened awareness of the twofold global dependence – first in seeing how generalized market behaviour could affect the national economy, and secondly in expecting other nations and international funding agencies to relieve the blow. On the other hand, there was a mixed feeling of shame, anger and uneasiness at this dependence. The feeling of national inferiority at this critical time often found its expression in a heightened need to defend the nation from global or external powers. Simultaneously, the crisis could not but disclose the internal flaws of the nation that had been suppressed by the political authorities: weak economic fundamentals caused by corruption, collusion and nepotism, mismanagement of human natural resources, weakness in the implementation of law, unpreparedness in facing natural and man-made tragedies. The discourse of cultural identity in Indonesia during the monetary crisis consists of this heterogeneous outward–inward assessment of self and other, forgetting and foregrounding the intricate power structure, which bonds or blurs the division.

The discourse of cultural identity

Globalization and the traffic of cultural commodities

It so happens that 1998 was officially declared to be the year of Arts and Culture. Midway into the crisis, beginning in the first month of 1998, advertising companies in cooperation with the mass media started a national campaign in newspapers, television and radio. One example of such advertisements is the one published in Indonesia's leading national newspaper, *Kompas*. The *Kompas Year of Arts and Culture* campaign was designed in two strands. The first strand compares two shadow images, one representing a 'foreign' popular culture icon, the other one supposedly representing the 'Indonesian' cultural heritage.

In one, the question below the two icons (one of Mickey Mouse's ears and the other a *wayang* figure), reads: 'Ask your children, who is this?' It is obvious that the purpose of this advert is to warn the reader against the impact of cultural globalization, especially on the young generation, and to awaken the impulse to return to or preserve the forgotten or marginalized local culture. The sentence, which runs across the two shadows in another picture reads as follows: 'He [Michael Jackson] is rich in style. We [*wayang* shadow puppet] are rich in culture.' The sentences remind the reader that Indonesian culture is so rich that Indonesians do not need to worship cultures that are not their own. Ironically, however, the pose of the *wayang* puppet figure is actually imitating the characteristic pose of Jackson, one hand on top of the head, another one covering the crotch, an unusual pose in the strict rules of *wayang* shadow puppet performance.[6]

Theses two advertising examples capture what Arjun Appadurai (1993: 326) calls the 'ironies and resistance [of the emerging global cultural system], some camouflaged as a bottomless appetite in the Asian world for things Western'. They resist, while implying and admitting, the intolerable rate of cultural globalization (read: *Americanization*). From the two advertisements, it is clear which culture the advertisers think Indonesian people are actually worshipping. The presence of America in Indonesia is not only evident in popular culture industries (music, film, television serials), but also in franchising of retail centres (Tops, Sears, Seven-Eleven, Disney's shops, Woolworth's), and fast food industries (McDonald's, Kentucky Fried Chicken, Pizza Hut, Sizzler, T.G.I. Fridays). The popularity of things American, especially among the young generation, has been on the rise, and parallels the acceleration of consumer culture in the last decade. American theme-food chains, the Hard Rock Café and Planet Hollywood in Jakarta, are the most trendy places for yuppies, upper- and middle-class youngsters to gather. Likewise, private television stations do not only show reruns of American films, television serials and soap operas, but also successfully popularize imitations of American game shows and talk shows. Ariel Heryanto (1999) notes that this opening up to 'Western influences' has increasingly been tolerated.

The *Kompas* public advertisements, if we were to follow Heryanto's logic, construct a fictional image of 'we' and 'they', which should not have resonated strongly in the age of global consumerism; that is, in the time before the crisis. Published exactly when people felt the negative impact of the global market, the advert struck a chord. If one were to examine it carefully, however, the construction of the foreign and the native here, however, is questionable. First, the *wayang* puppet is only native in degrees. Historically it is another synchreticization of a foreign, Indian culture. It is worth noting that this very symbol of difference, the *wayang* shadow puppet, is often used by a local franchiser of an American fast food chain to represent the stylishness of their stores. Achieving the status symbol of upper-middle-class culture, what was originally a cheap fast food chain has changed its stature in the host country to be semi-luxurious consumption. This cultural construct of 'self' and 'other', however, is not pure fiction. The indigenization of the American cultural icon can never be complete, nor can it achieve its synchretic form as in the case of *wayang* in Javanese or Sundanese culture, because its appeal and exchange value rests on its being American.

The second strand of *Kompas*'s public advertisement for the year of arts and culture is more verbal, consisting of an appeal to reflect on the richness of Indonesian cultural heritage, its local languages, dances, music and literatures, with background pictures of one or more of these local cultures. One of these adverts depicts a scene in a Javanese *wayang orang* theatre, in which the protagonist hero Gatotkaca overpowers a giant monster. The big caption reads: 'One day our cultural heritage can save the dignity of our nation'. The lines underneath explain what that means. 'The pressure of globalization and business competition is increasing, and the impact of the monetary crisis is hard on the people. One of our national assets which can be sold to increase national income is our arts and culture, our pride and priceless cultural ambassadors.'

The globalization referred to in the text and the giant monster figure are both monsters to be defeated. There is anxiety here and acknowledgement of a problem. What is at stake is the dignity of a nation. At the same time, there is a reassurance, because in the fixed plot of a *wayang orang* play, the protagonist hero always eventually wins over the giant. However, the two have to be presented interlocked in this battle position in order for them to be 'priceless cultural ambassadors', i.e. arts that have an exchange value. Globalization, thus, is not to be shunned but to be overcome by joining in the competition prepared with quality goods for sale.

Underlying this advertisement is a certain conception about arts and culture familiar in the discourse of the New Order. The first is the glorification of cultural heritage, based on an essentialist notion of culture as ideal values to be excavated from the archaeological past and to be sanctified and preserved as a normative structure. Within the sanctification of ideal norms is the preservation of traditional art forms as the highest artistic expressions of the nation. The second is the commodification of arts and culture with an additional bonus. By reducing arts and culture to marketable goods, it represses the function of art to voice social criticism, to be the conscience of the nation, that is, its 'subversive' potentials. The New Order has a history of censorship, of banning books, of imprisoning writers who do not share its ideological view or agree with its political practices. At the same time, the other definition of arts and culture as fixed ideal norms functions to legitimize the particular ideologies of the status quo.

Internal hegemony: Soeharto as a (Javanese) King

The choice of the *wayang* shadow puppet, considered the high art of the Javanese traditional elite, to represent 'we', the natives, further betrays an internal colonial structure within the plural arts communities in Indonesia. The overtly Javanese make-up of the New-Order culture was conspicuous in the heavy Javanese diction of President Soeharto, which was further imitated by hierarchies of state officials all over Indonesia.

In the realm of culture, Soeharto managed to create a new set of idioms and symbols, mostly from Javanese culture, which worked to strengthen his status quo. For example, the President misused the Javanese culture of politeness and harmony to instil obedience. The mimicry and Javanese bias went so far until Javanese dialect became the unofficial state idioms and jargon. The appointment of Javanese military officials as local administrative and military rulers throughout Indonesia was another example of internal colonialization, gossiped about in whispers and jokes, but never in published discourse. (That these adverts are made by private organizations shows how this colonial ideology has been widely internalized.) In the New Order culture, unity and uniformity is stressed over pluralism, conformity over difference, with a strong favour for ritualistic performance. The New Order culture is basically paternalistic, with the power centralized in the metropolis, and more specifically in the hands of the president, who behaves in the manner of a Javanese King.

It should therefore come as no surprise that the escalating voices of discontent at the peak of the crisis were directed at the centre of the hegemonic power. For students who were marching in the street for total reform, it is clear that no serious change can be done without removing the most powerful person in the country who was deemed responsible for engineering and establishing it in the first place: Soeharto. Criticism against the president who had ruled for 32 years was not uncommon before. Among other examples was the student revolt of 1974, which prompted the government to issue the policy called NKK (the Normalization of Campus Life), which prohibits students from forming independent student organizations, and prevents students from 'engaging in practical politics'. Another example of Soeharto's repressive measures was the banning of *Tempo* magazine in 1996. As a result of the long history of censorship, published criticism of the hegemonic order tended to be voiced in subtle, disguised ways.

With the worsening of the crisis, however, the mass media became more daring and straightforward. In March 1997 a news magazine called *D&R*, which employed many of the journalists of the banned *Tempo* magazine, appeared with the cover depicting President Soeharto as the King of Spades, with the letter K changed to P for President. This event invited angry responses from the President's inner circles, which threatened to bring the magazine to trial. The *D&R* cover clearly illustrated a growing weariness towards the rule of the New Order Javanese self-made patriarch.

In contrast, there was the significance of the symbolic gesture of the young Sultan of Yogya, the most important Javanese feudal figure, to offer his palace as a setting for a peaceful rally that demanded total political reform, on 20 May 1998, one day before Soeharto announced his retirement,[7] with the Sultan leading the rally himself (Kompas 1998d). This gesture symbolically revoked the King's support and blessing for the national leadership, something that was historically significant (the King's father was a stout and important defender of the young republic against the Dutch colonial power).

The Sultan's move must have hurt the president, who had been known to be eagerly anxious to bestow upon himself any forms of connections to Royal lineage.

Interrogating the cultural boundaries of the imagined community

The events that follow the financial crisis in June 1997 show not only the dismantling of Soeharto, but also the confused, often violent, reconfiguring of the national identity. This section of this paper will examine the discourse and processes, in which the various aspects of the national image are re-evaluated. These processes, which include scapegoating, the purging the unwanted elements in society, are unfortunately often accompanied by much violence.

The post-Soeharto era witnessed the re-surfacing of a plethora of group identities, of ethnic, religious, ideological and interest groups. One day after the fall of Soeharto, a group of students showing emblems of Moslem identities went to confront the remaining students who occupied the building of the People's Consultative Assembly. This group demanded that the students stop their campaign to refuse the election of Habibie as the new president. Habibie was the former vice president and also the leader of ICMI, a Moslem organization that is favoured by the government. The confrontation nearly sparked conflict, but was mediated by the military and ended in the removal of all parties from the place. This marked the volatility of the common goal of the reform movement and a beginning of identity politics.

The May riots turned out to be only the beginning of a series of violent mass incidents that continuously disrupted reform movements in Indonesia after the fall of Soeharto. In various parts of the country, individual disputes spread into bloody conflict between ethnic or religious groups. The myth of the harmonious *Bhineka Tunggal Ika* (the Indonesian version of *E Pluribus Unum*) fell apart to expose repressed prejudice and jealousy between classes, ethnic and religious groups.

Soon to follow was the eruption of new political parties and organizations, some bearing group (ethnic/gender/racial/religious) identities, like the Chinese party, the women's party and the various Moslem parties. Some, in contrast, come with emblems stressing solidarity, nationalism or inter-group coalition like the Assimilation Party, Madya or the society for religious dialogue. Others are based on ideological frameworks, like the liberal Gema Madani (Echo of Civil Society) and the leftist PRD (Party of People's Democracy), while representatives of the East Timorese people started their campaign for freedom and the rights of self-determination (SiaR News Service 1998b). In the same mood, the press opened up the old cases of internal colonialization of marginal cultures in Irian Jaya (SiaR News Service 1998c) and Aceh (*Kompas*, 5 June 1998f).

The pendulum, it seemed, has swung from homogeneity to heterogeneity, from unity to diversity. At the same time, this fracturing of communities into sectarian and primordial groups can be seen as the result of the racial politics of the New Order that not only overstressed unity over diversity, but was also ambivalent and contradictory.

The Chinese element

On 19 May, rioting and looting by angry mobs occurred at the same time, all over Jakarta.[8] The targets of the violence were mostly Chinese-owned shops and other places of wealthy consumption such as department stores, retail centres, shopping malls, police headquarters, and Soeharto's children's affiliated businesses (including Soeharto's Chinese business ally, the conglomerate Liem Sioe Liong).[9] The number of casualties of this incident totalled more than 1000 deaths, most of the victims, the authority claimed, were shoplifters and looters burned together with the very department stalls and shopping centres they were assaulting.

A few weeks after the incidents, witnesses and victims revealed another atrocity, i.e. the mass rape, molestation, killing and harassment of dozens of Chinese women and girls,[10] evoking anger especially from women's groups and Indonesian Chinese intellectuals. However, most of the society refused to believe that these incidents really happened. This incident sadly indicated that the Chinese remain an unwanted part of the Indonesian racial/cultural make-up. Below is a report written by a foreign journalist based on her interview with Fadli Zon, a young member of an extreme right religious group:

> Fadli Zon had a vision. The former student activist imagines his countrymen cycling down Jakarta's Jalan Thamrin. . . . Instead of Western clothes, everyone will be wearing sarongs made of rough cloth. 'If necessary, we'll go backward 10 or 15 years', he said fervently. 'The Muslim majority is ready to face any challenge, as long as there is economic justice. We can start to develop our country without them.'
>
> To Fadli, a rising young thinker and editor, 'them' refers to Indonesia's tiny ethnic-Chinese minority, which he holds responsible for the country's deepening economic crisis. If 'they' don't return their wealth parked overseas, he warns, it's payback time. Time for the 87% Muslim majority to seize the reins of an economy from a community that accounts for a mere 3% of the country's 200 million people. . . . Time, too for the military to help assert the rights of the nation's Muslims.
>
> (Cohen 1998: 16)

These distinctions of 'us' and 'them' were made obvious during the riots, as mobs let buildings bearing signs 'Belonging to a Muslim', 'Owned by native Hajji so and so', 'Pure Betawian' untouched, while unmarked buildings were burned. These signs strengthen the construction of a cultural self that differentiates between what is considered as the 'indigenous' self, and the self that is of 'foreign origin', a construction of a colonial origin that was sustained after the independence.

The discourse of Chinese bashing was not merely an example of the psychology of scapegoating in the time of crisis. The Chinese problem, which had its roots in colonial practice that used the Chinese as tax collector, a colonial buffer, was aggravated by the contradictory practice of the New Order racial policy regarding the Chinese minority. After the civil war against communism in 1965, in an effort to sever the ties between overseas Chinese in Indonesia and the Chinese in Mainland China, the government made several policies to assimilate the Chinese into the 'native' communities. In 1968, the government issued a regulation that ordered the Chinese to drop their Chinese names. The use of Chinese characters was also forbidden, including the publication and use of any Chinese books. Chinese rituals and tradition were likewise not permitted. As communism in the public discourse is associated with atheism, since 1996 every Indonesian citizen had to profess a religion, but Confucianism is not among the five religions acknowledged by the State. Many Chinese then chose Buddhism and Christianity. The efforts in erasing from the Chinese marks of their identity can be seen as an effort to blend the Chinese with the larger communities. At the same time, however, there were discriminatory practices against the Chinese, e.g. marking their identity cards, requiring them to obtain special kinds of papers for identification, etc. To prevent the possible return of communism to the political sphere, the Chinese were not encouraged to enter politics, the military or the state institutions. One result was the concentration of the Chinese in business sectors, further affirming the binary opposition that is constructed in the public imagination. The rich are the Christian and the Chinese; the poor are the Moslem and the native.

The practice of collusion, by which government and military officials took money or business facilities from the Chinese and in turn gave them protection, administrative leeway or special treatment, increased jealousy and hatred against the latter. As social gaps widened, chances for conflict increased, and in 1987 the Commander for Security and Order, Soedomo, issued censorship on four touchy issues, i.e. ethnic, religious, racial and group or class conflicts, abbreviated in Indonesian as SARA. This censorship again worked as a blanket of repression that gave the appearance of harmony and unity, while actually repressing unvoiced hurts and resentments. The inconsistency of the SARA policy was revealing as the government, while asking people to keep their eyes shut with regard to any ethnic, class and religious conflicts, introduced various verbal markers of difference in the society, including the term 'native' and 'non-native', and routinely practised official discriminations.

After the repressive blanket of harmony and unity is lifted in the demise of the New Order government, in its wake ethnic and sectarian politics bolted, unchecked. These diverse groups, whose existence was historically construed, came forward to claim their participation in the new configuration of power. However, whether this new configuration of power challenges or reconfirms the New Order cultural politics remains to be seen. The feudal cultural heritage of the New Order, the ethnic and religious conflicts, are the many burdens of history that Indonesians will have to deal with in coming up with a new definition of selfhood in the post-Soeharto era.

The global saviour or the neo-colonial threat: the IMF and the USA

In an effort to defend its weakened legitimacy, the official discourse of the New Order attempted subtly to awaken public sentiments towards the neo-colonial aggression of the West. The strategy of creating an external enemy to strengthen national cohesion and to divert attention from internal problems was not an uncommon political practice, in Indonesia as elsewhere.[11] Indeed, the final years of Soekarno's era in the 1960s were also filled with isolationist and anti-Western sentiments. Soekarno considered the establishment of Malaysia as a neo-colonialist project of the British Empire, and preferred to have Indonesia quit the UN in 1965 rather than accept the UN's decision to include Malaysia in the Security Council. In the public discourse of the 1960s anti-Anglo jingles were memorized by school children ('*Amerika kita seterika, Inggris kita linggis*' or 'Let's burn the Americans, let's crush the British'). Compared with the Old Order's rhetoric, however, the New Order's depiction of the West was ambiguous and contradictory. The New Order could not afford to dispense with the West as Soekarno did, as its very foundation was built by global investments. Such ambiguities could be seen in the IMF–Soeharto psychological battle in the last days of his reign.

Thanks to modern photography and audiovisual technology, the image of Michel Camdessus, the IMF managing director, standing erect, folding his arms, watching President Soeharto as the latter bent to sign the Indonesian agreement with the IMF in January 1998, will remain a public memory.

The controversy over that scene as the image was printed next to headlines in newspapers, magazines, tabloids, and broadcast by television stations indicates that the damage had been done. Critics and defenders of Mr Soeharto alike read Camdessus's pose as a show of power, and the president's, a humiliation. This image has helped to strengthen the association of the IMF with colonial power, external pressure or global threat. Like the giant monster of the year of arts and culture advert, he has somehow hurt the dignity of the nation.

The New York Times quoted Dewi Fortuna Anwar, a leading political scientist, as she summarized people's comments about the picture. 'How could our president be humiliated that way? Indonesia is a proud country. We have been known to choose to go hungry rather than to give in to outside pressure' (Mydans 10 March 1998). The *Australian Financial Review* interviewed Syarifuddin Harahap, the chairman of the Islamic Universities Association, who claimed that he was changed by the picture and decided to start an anti-IMF and anti-globalization campaign. For Harahap as well as many other public leaders and intellectuals, the IMF, globalization and the United States are the same things in different veils (Hartcher 26 February 1998).

The direct association of this global, colonial pressure with the USA was manifested in the demonstration organized by right-wing Moslem student groups, which picketed the American embassy in Jakarta and American consulate in Surabaya. The tearing of the American flag in Surabaya on 4 June 1998 served as a symbolic protest against this supposedly colonial intervention by the USA (Kompas 1998e).

In his Padang Bulan series of talks, its written version distributed via list-server, the moderate Islam leader and popular preacher, Emha Ainun Najib bitterly regretted the condition that forced Indonesia to accept the IMF package. 'The only way to survive is to fulfill all requirements so that debts can be disbursed. This means we are entering the new colonial pattern of the Allies, led by the United States' (Najib 1998b). For this poet popularly called Emha, who once obtained a three-month fellowship in the International Writing Program in Iowa, globalization is a 'grand design' of neo-colonial forces to enslave the nation. This neo-colonial force comes 'not only through the global free trade that will start in the twentieth century, but it actually enters directly into our bedrooms' (Najib 1998a).

Mentioning no names, Emha does admit, however, that these external forces operate with the cooperative help of the 'national players' of this grand design of globalization. He does not elaborate, for example, how the internal ruling elites invite these global economic forces to invade the market for their own profit, especially through the practice of collusion, the corruption of the bureaucracies and nepotism. These unhealthy economic practices had come under attack by reform activists, especially among the student groups, with these prime targets: the President, his families and his cronies.

Soeharto then changed his attitude towards the IMF after the first signing of the agreement, on 16 January. Four days later, responding to the rising anti-IMF sentiment, he assured that 'the IMF is not an economic colonizer' (*Kompas* 20 January 1998a). But in February, he shifted his attention to another option, that of the currency board system, simultaneously proclaiming the IMF agreement to be unconstitutional. His strategies of backing off from the agreement, proclaiming it to be incongruent with the Indonesian constitution, of flirting with the currency board system as an alternative to the solution offered by the IMF, signalled indirectly that the Javanese leader was actually fighting back. Reproached by local economic experts as a bad delay and a distraction that further worsened the economic condition, Soeharto's move in fact won him some sympathy. Emha Ainun Najib seemed to read the signals in that line, saying that compared with his successor, Habibie, 'Pak Harto is more hardheaded and defiant' in his nerve against the IMF and the United States (Najib 1998a).

Besides the negative accusations, however, there were different representations and uses of the IMF. For mainstream local economists, the IMF is an external hand to help overcome the economic crisis. One week after the historic signing of the first IMF agreement, an advertising agency and the *Kompas* newspaper put up a public advertisement supporting the founding of the Board for Strengthening Economic and Financial Security. The advert compares life with a battlefield. In that scene, Indonesia was depicted to be 'fighting against the storms of monetary crisis', helped 'by the IMF and Indonesia's friends'.

For students and other reformist groups whose immediate aim was to oust Soeharto from power, the IMF was considered as an influential external pressure. While the IMF's delay in its second disbursement of $3 million angered the establishment, it was hailed by students, who put up banners in their campus, urging the IMF not to disburse any more funds to 'corrupt leaders', as the burden of the debts will be on the shoulders of the young generations.

A neutral attitude towards the IMF can be seen in the statement by the 19 LIPI researchers. If for some anti-IMF economists like Didi Rachbini, the IMF is 'Indonesia's second problem', for these 19 young researchers the problem lies in the government, not in the IMF. But their representation of the IMF supports the binary opposition of foreign and local, 'us' and 'them'. The researchers blame government authority for trusting and relying on 'foreign insights', neglecting the nation's own thinking. The most significant reform programmes suggested by the IMF have long been pointed out by various local experts. The government authorities have closed their eyes and conscience. They have ignored the people's sovereignty (LIPI 1998).

These diverse representations of the IMF illustrate the complex relations of the outside and the inside. The construction of the IMF as a benevolent other, colonial aggressor or foreigner, depends on the particular purposes of the speakers and their specific usage of these constructions in their own battlefields.

Conclusions

In the heterogeneous discourses of cultural identity discussed above, we see heightened efforts in redefining the boundaries of the imagined community called Indonesia during a critical period when global forces sapped its foundation (Sudarman 1999).[12] One way to affirm the fragile boundary is to contrast the national culture *vis-à-vis* globalization. Globalization in the Arts and Culture year advertisement is American popular culture (versus local traditional culture), high technology (versus simple creative manipulation of nature); luxury (versus simplicity); foreign (versus local) products; foreign consultants (versus local experts); what you buy (versus what you made yourself). The question remains, however, how effective is this kind of propaganda? Ariel Heryanto (1999:

41–45) has noted that this kind of back to tradition, nature and simple life campaign never had a wide appeal, especially in the age that celebrates global consumerism. Published in the crucial moment of crisis, however, this campaign resonated. This difficult period seems to have awakened mixed feelings of fear, anxieties and ambiguities toward the boundaries of self and others. Intellectuals, community leaders in e-group discussions, talk shows, interviews and public statements later voiced similar concern, using the same binary opposition. Thus, while the construction is based on a simplistic binary opposition, it also carries with it real concerns that were intensified during the time of crisis.

The discussion of the discourse of Indonesian cultural identity during the 1997–1998 monetary crisis above affirms the established theory that the quest for cultural identity is heightened in response to the rising awareness of a global threat (Featherstone 1995: 91; Giddens 1993: 182). Unlike what is usually alleged, however, the rise of sectarianism and traditionalism does not seem to be directly caused or related to the speeding of globalization, but rather to the particular contextual and internal processes and power structures. In the case of Indonesia, the rise of sectarianism is more closely linked to the racial and cultural politics of the New Order as it appropriates economic globalization for its own purposes.

The discourse of Indonesian cultural identity in this particular time of crisis evokes not only an interrogation of the boundary between what is inside and outside, but also the repressed feelings against the most sensitive, problematic sides of the national self: the Chinese, the New Order version of national identity, the military, the racial-ethnic-religious-gender configurations. The discourse consists of heterogeneous voices, often in conflict with one another, but what is similar is the tone of dissatisfaction, the urgency for reform and change.

On the other hand, the global, as we see, is very much intertwined with local power struggles. During the May riot in 1998, a local franchise owner of the Jakarta-based McDonald's store attempted to save the restaurant from looting and rioting by covering the M sign with a green cloth and putting up a sign that said: 'owned by a Moslem native' written both in Arabic and Indonesian. (It was not the sign alone that saved the building, but the rows of military personnel that guarded the capital's main boulevard where the restaurant was located.) The 'Islamization' of the McDonald's store in Jakarta during the 1998 riot is a telling illustration of the interlacing of the global and the local. Here, the global signifier is masked beneath a nativist symbol of identity in a shameless display of ironic contradiction.

Needless to say, words only could not bring about political changes that had occurred in Indonesia, which were due to very complex and complicated processes. Without the pressure of the economic crisis, no one could imagine that this strong regime could ever be shaken. However, Camdessus's rigid pose, the students' occupation of the building of the people's consultative assembly, the tearing of the flag, all of these actions and events are also discursively charged with symbolic and metaphoric dimensions. The events that unfolded in Indonesia show that we are not trapped within the closed system of signifiers without any access to reality. Discursive representation not only helps boost the courage to fight, but in fact constitutes the fight itself. On the other hand, the change that is brought about further affects the nature of the discursive practices (more direct, open and daring expressions of protest).

The discursive battle waged by Indonesians also affirms the primacy of readers, the importance of situating texts in the very context and act of reading, as shown by many cultural studies. The uses and readings of the famous photograph of Camdessus and Soeharto signing the IMF contract are the best example. The fact that Michel Camdessus stood that way because his mother always taught him to fold his hands in that manner, or that the protocol staff failed to provide a chair for him, as Camdessus later explained, is irrelevant. What matters is not how this picture reflects reality, or records the actual thoughts and feelings of the characters in it, but how it is read and used by many Indonesians for different ends (affecting anti-IMF sentiments, evoking patriotic emotion or satisfying the need to humiliate a strong enemy).

Another strategic force in the discursive battle is the media, popular as well as official, licensed as well as underground, foreign as well as domestic. The report published in *The Economist* of 31 October 1994, which predicted Indonesia to be one of the future's top five leading economies, as well as the CNN repeated images of the angry mob, serve as an external mirror that helps construct (or misconstrue) the self image of the nation. The domestic media, which compete with one another for the best coverage of this dramatic moment in Indonesian history, help to fasten as well as to complicate the processes of change. President Soeharto's exasperated retort to the Indonesian media during the crisis, implying that it is the media that lead the people to a crisis, misleading as it is, shows how powerful the media is in the eye of this ruler.

This paper has not seen the end of the discursive battle, nor the end of the crisis. Is this period of crisis a mere abnormal, temporary phase? Will Indonesians return to the comfortable ride of economic and cultural globalization, and forget these moments of doubts and anxiety once the economic crisis is over? Or will this crisis lead to a redefinition and a significant remake of Indonesian cultural identity? What new cultural identity would that be?

By the end of 1998, with the rising demands of regional autonomy or secession, and the continuous inter-group conflicts, Indonesians have to deal with even more basic questions regarding the future of Indonesia as a nation-state. An extreme view (which no Indonesians are yet ready to visualize) is that Indonesia would prove the theory that predicts the beginning of a global system and the end of nation-states. A less drastic one would be to imagine the return of a military and repressive regime. There are other dreams that are shared by different groups. Extreme right-wing groups wish for a country ruled and characterized by a culture of the religious majority, with a stronger and firmer bargaining position *vis-à-vis* a global (read Western) culture.[13] The optimistic liberal dreams of, and strives for, a new equilibrium of balanced global and local exchange, and new pluralist, democratic relations among Indonesian peoples.[14] The stake of this battlefield of the imagination is the extent to which you can convince others of your dream and move others to realize it. Or, seen as propaganda, the key is how to use these imagined pictures of the nation as a means to power. Now that Pandora's box is open, and the crisis is or is not over, the discursive battle over cultural identity will continue. Indonesians, as individuals or in groups, as intellectuals, artists, activists, women or men, members of religious communities, solid members of an ethnic group or as hybrids with plural identities, come to a point where they have to stop and decide what they mean by 'Indonesia', especially as they grapple to shape the nation's fate in the context of a globalized future.[15]

Notes

1 Soekarno's plan in founding the Conference of the New Emerging Forces, his own version of New World alliances, prompted him to withdraw Indonesia from its membership in the United Nations in 1963.

2 For discussion on the differences between Soekarno and Soeharto's economic policies and the IMF relationship with the New Order, see *D&R* (28 March 1998a: 57).

3 Soeharto's success in achieving self-sufficiency in rice production was recognized by the FAO. His efforts in slowing down the fast growth of population earned him worldwide reputation.

4 For a discussion on the neo-patrimonial character of the New Order regime, see Brown (1994: 114–121).

5 Other national disasters include the epidemic of dengue fever, drought and the attack of insects on rice fields.

6 I am indebted to students of the Introduction to Cultural Studies seminar of 1999 for observing this ironic mimicry.

7 On 20 May, which happened to be the National Awakening day, the Sultan invited students and the people of Yogya to do a peaceful demonstration in his courtyard.

8 The killing of the students occurred on 13 May, and the riot started that day and lasted until 15 May.

9 Also burned was the house of the leader of the People's Consultative Assembly, who then happened also to be the head of Golkar, the strongest party and the main supporter of the New Order regime.

10 Documentation of data was difficult, since many victims declined to report the case, let alone testify. Humanitarian groups that investigated the case and helped the victims were later accused of making the incidents up because they refused to disclose the identities of the victims.

11 This kind of psychological defence mechanism manifests itself again later during the Indonesian–Australian conflicts over East Timor (especially with the establishment of the International Peacekeeping force led by Australia).

12 Sudarman (1999) summarizes Benedict Anderson's theory on the ironic relationship between global capitalism which helped bring nation-states into being, but will sap its foundation in its later stages.

13 Such a version of national make-up of power is proposed by the leading Moslem newspaper, *Republika*, to the newly elected President Habibie (SiaR News Service 1998a).

14 This stand is voiced by the Echo of Civil Society (*Gema Madani*), a short lived non-governmental organization led by one leading statesman and economist Emil Salim, who had onceserved as Minister of Finance during Soeharto's regime. (See his agenda for National Awakening 12 February 1998.) But a similar kind of jargon is also used in the campaigns of the 'New' Golkar, the party associated with the New Order, which tried to remake itself in order to suit the reform demands.

15 See public statements issued by various groups regarding what changes they believe should take place. The artists have a specific concern about cultural and artistic reform (Tarman 1998), while some women's groups press the issue of solidarity and humanitarianism ('Seruan Perempuan Indonesia'). During 1997–1998, various organizations were founded with the objectives of achieving inter-ethnic and inter-religious solidarity.

References

Appadurai, Arjun (1993) 'Disjuncture and difference in the global cultural economy'. In P.Williams and L. Chrisman (eds) *Colonial Discourse and Postcolonial Theory, a Reader*, New York: Harvester/Wheatsheaf.

Bove, Paul A. (1990) 'Discourse'. In F. Lentricchia and T. McLaughlin (eds) *Critical Terms for Literary Study*, Chicago: The University of Chicago Press.

Brown, David (1994) *The State and Ethnic Politics in South-east Asia*, London: Routledge.

Cohen, Margot (1998) '"Us" and "Them"', *Far Eastern Economic Review*, 12 February.

D & R (1998a) 'IMF is not the Old One' (IMF bukan Yang Dulu Lagi?), 28 March: 57.

D & R (1998b) 'If the IMF package is inconstitutional, what next?' (Jika Paket IMF In konstitusional, Lalu?), 21 March: 57.

D & R (1998c) 'If CBS is postponed, will we be bankrupt?' (CBS Ditunda, Akan Bangkrutkah Kita?), 28 February: 55.

Featherstone, Mike (1995) *Undoing Culture: Globalization, Postmodernism and Identity*, London: Sage.

Giddens, Anthony (1993) 'The consequences of modernity'. In P. Williams and L. Chrisman (eds) *Colonial Discourse and Postcolonial Theory, a Reader*, New York: Harvester/Wheatsheaf.

Hartcher, Peter (1998) 'Indonesia campaign sows hatred for US', *Australian Financial Review*, 26 February.

Heryanto, Ariel (1999). 'The years of living luxuriously; identity politics of Indonesia's new rich'. In M. Pinches (ed.) *The Culture of the New Rich in Asia*, London: Routledge.

Kompas (1998a) 'Tutut exchanged US Dollar' (Tutut Tukarkan Dollar AS), 10 January: 1.

Kompas (1998b) 'Camdessus: Indonesia Serious', 16 January: 1.

Kompas (1998c) 'President: IMF is not an economic colonizer' (Presiden: IMF Bukan Penjajah Ekonomi), 20 January: 1.

Kompas (1998d) 'His Majesty HB X: the throne for reform' (HB X: Takhta untuk Reformasi), 20 May: 16

Kompas (1998e) 'Department of Foreign Affairs regretted the tearing of US flag' (Deplu Sesalkan Penyobekan Bendera AS), 5 June.

Kompas (1998f) 'NGO forum demanded military operation in Aceh stopped forum' (LSM Minta Operasi Militer Aceh Dihentikan), 5 June.

LIPI (1998) 'Statement of Concern from 19 LIPI Researchers' (Pernyataan Keprihatinan 19 Peneliti LIPI'), Public Statement, 20 January.

Mydans, Seth (1998) 'Crisis aside, what pains Indonesia is the humiliation', *New York Times*, 10 March.

Najib, Emha Ainwa (1998a) 'Welcome new oppressor' (Selamat Datang Penjajah Baru), Padang Bulan Series of Lectures no 21, Diskusi@ypb.or.id, 9 June.

Ramage, Douglas (1995) *Politics in Indonesia, Democracy, Islam and the Ideology of Tolerance*, London: Routledge.

SiaR News Service (1998a) 'Proposal for the reform order, from 'Republika' to B.J. Habibie' (Usulan Orde Reformasi Versi 'Republika' Untuk B.J.Habibie), qmail@minihub.org& number 152, 12 June.

SiaR News Service (1998b) 'The Timor Leste youth ask for freedom at the Department of Foreign Affairs' (Pemuda Timor Leste Minta Kemerdekaan di Deplu), qmail@minihub. org&number 151, 12 June.

SiaR News Service (1998c) 'Hundreds of students in Jayapura demonstrating', qmail@minihub. org&number 143, 12 June.

Sudarman, Suzie (1999) 'Untangling the knotted cord: studies of nationalism in a global era', unpublished paper.

Wallerstein, I. (1991) 'The ideological tensions of capitalism: universalism versus racism and sexism' in E. Balibar and I. Wallerstein (eds) *Race, Nation, Class: Ambiguous Identities*, London: Verso.

Chapter 24

Emotional energy and sub-cultural politics

Alternative bands in post-1997 Hong Kong

Eric Ma

This ethnographic study tries to capture the moment of post-1997 sub-cultural formation in Hong Kong. The particular case of Hong Kong sub-culture is exploited to demonstrate the general theoretical question of how sub-cultural forms resist and collaborate with popular discourses. Sub-cultural researchers have taken the analytic tracks along the elite/popular and domination/resistance binaries (e.g. Cohen, Phil 1972, Fiske 1989, Hebdige 1979, Hall and Tom 1976, Willis 1978). In this paper, I try to experiment with a different approach by focusing on the emotionality of sub-cultural politics. The focus of analysis is not on semiotics or ideologies that have dominated sub-culture studies. Instead, I will examine the 'emotional energies' produced in everyday interactions within sub-cultural groups and between these groups and mainstream society (mainstream here is more a discursive or imagined than a descriptive term). These emotional energies are produced by discursive processes such as the inversion of ethno-methods, the oppositional impression management of self-stigmatization, the tactics of bodily control, and de-commodified forms of emotion production. This subverted emotionality differentiates sub-cultural from mainstream solidarity. However, at particular historical junctures, as in post-1997 Hong Kong, sub-cultural emotional energies may form an affective alliance with public unrest and consumerist populism. This socio-emotive approach is an attempt to de-particularize sub-culture studies by bridging sub-cultural and general cultural politics. In this case study, sub-cultural groups produce particularized emotional energies, but these emotional energies exhibit comparable socio-cultural configurations with those of the larger society.

This initial theoretical speculation was in fact triggered by the contextual question of why there is a sudden 'uprising' of alternative bands in post-1997 Hong Kong. Local bands have a long history of more then a few decades (Chu 2001). Why is it that their voices have been so distinctive and discernable in the mainstream media since 1998? Critical to mainstream middle-class ideologies, these bands and their music serve as symbolic resources for cultural differentiation and popular resistance among teenagers. They generate strong 'emotional energies', which have been mixing with populist anti-government sentiments of the larger society. This socio-emotive web of sub-cultural politics has become a conspicuous display that marks the particular historical juncture of post-1997 Hong Kong.

Sub-cultural politics

Instead of explaining the musical by the social, I want to trace the capillary networks between the sub-cultural and the social by first providing a contextual grounding for this ethnographic study. In the 1980s and 1990s, sub-cultural voices in Hong Kong were quite difficult to surface and develop into wider collective forms. When Hong Kong was a colony without a nation, both the Chinese and British governments refrained from imposing strong nationalistic imperatives. This meant, for many years, Hong Kong people did not have a strong historical or national narrative against which they could negotiate or situate their own subjectivity. Colonial politics was mysteriously disguised by administrative diversion (Law 1998) and sub-cultural energies had been absorbed by Hong Kong's upward mobile economy and non-interventionist polity.

Hong Kong has been an immigrant society for many years. As an immigrant society, the cultural make-up of Hong Kong did not privilege an elite culture (Luk 1995). To put it in another way, elitist/traditional Chinese culture was recognized as a remote cultural authority and did not have a dominant discursive power in the everyday life of Hong Kong people. Without the productive discipline of a nationalistic narrative and a dominant high culture, Hong Kong's post-war cultural formation had arguably been the mainstreaming of different sub-cultures to form a secular and energetic local culture. In fact, popular culture cut across grassroots and elite classes to become the cradle of a collective local identity in the 1970s and the 1980s (Ma 1999, Sinn 1995). The painstaking valorization of popular culture against the hegemony of the state and high culture in some of the now classic Birmingham projects seem not readily relevant in colonial Hong Kong.

However, these contextual factors have been undergoing gradual changes since the sovereignty reversion in 1997 (Ma 2000). Here I am not offering a socio-political analysis of post-1997 Hong Kong; suffice it to generalize a few discursive formations, which tend to bridge sub-cultural emotional energies with the public sentiments of the larger society. Most obviously, the economic crisis in 1997 and its after effects have triggered a series of chain reactions. The discourse of unfailing capitalism can no longer serve as a stable base from which local identity was built. The widening gap between the rich and poor breeds despair and unrest. At the same time, the myth of upward mobility, which was a dominant discourse in the colonial years, has failed to absorb and dissipate the emotional energies of the underprivileged as it did in the past.

Since 1997, there has been a discursive crash between progressive political desire and regressive political infrastructure. During the decolonization and democratization programmes in the 1990s, proposals of political reforms had encouraged the development of high expectations on democratic politics. In the final years of the British rule, Hong Kong developed a dual power structure in which the British and the Chinese were fighting for political control over the colony. This political duality provided a contingent space for participation of the general public. Exploiting this political space, Hong Kong people had voiced out their demands for more progressive democratic reform. However, after 1997, the dual power structure has regressed to the conservative local government of Hong Kong Special Administrative Region (HKSAR). HKSAR government is backed up by an autonomy licensed by the central government but not legitimized by democratic election. Unfulfilled political expectation crashes with regressive political reality that turns into frequent protest and opposition mediated by the populist media. Since the reversion of sovereignty, the government has been installing a nationalistic discourse at school, in public ritual, the media and the education system. Programmes of re-nationalization have left an impression of central political imposition from the mainland Chinese Government. The disciplinary discourse of re-nationalization produces nationalistic as well as oppositional discourses. However, the local Hong Kong government, which is not legitimized by a democratic polity, has not been able to re-negotiate new ideological consent.

These changes have generated strong emotions, which have over-spilled to different walks of life. Workers are disappointed with structural unemployment, new immigrants from mainland China are tangled in the controversial issue of the right to abode, middle-class families have been struck by the collapse of the property market, lawyers are protesting against the erosion of the rule of law, and doctors against the deteriorating working conditions in the medical field. At the same time, the Hong Kong government was accusing the general public and the media of spilling out too much bitterness and acridity. These negative energies dilute social solidarity and encourage dissolution and oppositions. The discourses of re-nationalization, downward mobility, failed market economy and weak local governance have cultivated a discursive context for sub-cultural formation. Although it is not the case that there are simple and direct articulations between the social and the sub-cultural, but macro political economic discourses are in fact compatible with the sub-cultural politics of local alternative bands. In this paper, I will present the most prominent of such bands, LMF, to examine the socio-emotive networks within sub-cultural communities and their possible connections with the larger social context of Hong Kong.

LMF and friends

At the time of writing, LMF has been commercially the most successful among local alternative bands since 1999. LMF first appeared in 1992 when members from various bands came together to jam songs in a musical style that they would not usually do in their own bands. They called this ad-hoc group LMF, a name referring to one vocalist Ah Wah, who is, in their words, a 'lazy mother-fucker', doing nothing except fooling around. Most of these groups were alternative bands that did not engage in mainstream commercial operations. After that one-off performance, there was no LMF for a few years since it was actually not a group in the first place. However, core members of the group produced four CDs in the mid-1990s under the name Anodize. Among these alternative bands, group boundaries are quite fluid and members from different groups join each other's performances at different points of time. In 1999, Anodize and friends regrouped into LMF and produced their independent debut album *LazyMuthaFucka*. The six songs in this album are mostly about grassroots youth and their everyday life in public housing estates. The album was enthusiastically received among alternative bands and music lovers but later picked up by the mainstream, especially focusing on the issue of swearing, indecency and 'bad' effects on teenagers. 18 000 CDs were independently distributed and sold. Because of this initial success, LMF has been signed up by Warner Music. LMF's first Warner distributed album sold more than 70 000 copies in the summer of 2000.

In this case study, I interviewed the 12 members of LMF, their friends and five other independent bands. I also befriended some concertgoers in mini concerts. In a later stage of the research, I was able to participate in their daily activities and attended recording sessions and stage performances. Thus my target community included LMF members, fans, concertgoers and a few independent bands. Half a dozen postgraduate students also took part in field research and reception studies by attending concerts and interviewing more than 60 people from all walks of life. As a group, we have published two non-academic books in Chinese (Ma 2001, Ng *et al.* 2001) with the aim of opening up more flexible interpretative possibilities in Hong Kong. A postgraduate student has written an MPhil thesis focusing on textual and reception analyses (Chan 2002). In another paper, I discuss the spatial practices of alternative bands and the spatial configurations of their band rooms (Ma 2002). While in this paper, I will mainly focus on examining the emotive dimension of their life-worlds, I should emphasize that it is somewhat misleading to label these semi-open communities as 'underground'. The activities within their life-worlds can fall into a spectrum, with one end relatively restrictive and the other end extended into 'normal' public life. Except for some illegal activities (such as drawing graffiti and taking drugs), which can be considered as underground, most of their activities, music related or otherwise, are pretty 'normal'. They are not doing something radically subversive. Yet, their lifestyles and aspirations are quite alternative, in the sense that they are usually discredited or condemned by mainstream institutions such as schools and the media.

Emotional energies

As a 'regular' guy with rather mainstream musical taste and minimal musical knowledge, I experienced a series of surprises and uneasiness during my field study. These ethnographic adjustments are exploited to serve as the raw resources for this interpretative essay. I first encountered this type of music at a concert where the band was screaming unintelligible lyrics on stage. As a researcher with a strong desire to 'collect data', my attention in my fieldwork has always been directed towards the conceptual and the analyzable. At the very beginning, I was inclined to look for cogni-tively analyzable data such as lyrics, visuals and conversations. However, as I became more involved, my encounters were more emotive, bodily and spatial. Band sound is more than lyrics. Indeed, screaming on stage is 'unintelligible', but a strong emotive power is clearly presented on stage through heavy musical rhythms, violent body movements and techno-electronic noises.

Adapting Collins' (1990) sociology of emotions, these bands can be seen as active producers of what he calls 'emotional energies'. They discursively mobilize oppressive energies of social stigmas thrown upon them, turn them around and use these stigmas as their own identity resources for drawing boundaries of inclusion and exclusion. These free-flowing emotional energies are charged and re-charged in concerts, stored in CDs, pregnant with self-produced signs and saturated in their own private underground spaces. Life history interviews of band members indicate that most of them were 'failures' by elitist standards. They dropped out from school, some had serious problems with their parents, and others had taken up freelance jobs in CD shops, construction sites and delivery companies. Of course there are a few who obtained university degrees, but as a whole, many of them can hardly be considered academic achievers. They do not integrate well into the mainstream. Durkheim asked a funda-mental question of sociology: what holds society together? His answer is the mechanisms that produce moral solidarity. Collins (1990) suggests that these mechanisms do so by producing emotions. Yet emotions work both ways. My informants are stigmatized by the general public, but at the same time they exclude themselves from an imagined mainstream society by self-stigmatization. Antagonisms generate negative emotions, which build up barriers between these bands and the society at large. Yet these negative emotional energies are used positively to mobilize in-group solidarity.

In classic social theories, the role of emotionality in social formation is suggested but not explicitly discussed. These theoretical inclinations are quite compatible with the modernity project, which often calls for the taming of irrationality (or emotionality). However, there has recently been an upsurge of academic interest in emotions. Factors underpinning this interest, as suggested by Williams (2001), include the challenge to rationality in high-modernity, a return to the body in social theory, the growth of consumer culture and emotional products and the serialization and sensationalization of emotions in mediascapic society. In this paper, I try to use the case of alternative bands to explore the emotionality of sub-cultural formation. With emotional energy, I refer to routine as well as dramatic emotions generated, maintained, dissipated and re-charged in interactive rituals within and between communities. It is somewhat similar to the psychological concept of drive. However, emotional energy is more than personal and biographical, it is collective, bodily, interactive, and thus social and structural. I draw heavily on theories of ethnomethodology, which conceptualize and analyze the skills and methods deployed by ordinary people in daily interactions (Garfinkel 1967, Sacks 1992). Ordinary people reflexively deploy these 'people's methods', or ethno-methods, to accomplished social interactions in their everyday life. These are rules and categorization devices mutually agreed by members within a community.

As the following analysis will illustrate, sub-cultural formation can be seen as an on-going construction of alternative ethno-methods by subverting and reworking emotional energies of the larger society. When mainstream ethno-methods are challenged and inverted, intense emotional energies are generated (Garfinkel 1967). These emotional energies are the glue and repellent for stabilizing mainstream and differentiating sub-cultural communities. This emotive and ethno-methodological approach to sub-culture has the strength of bridging psychological drive with collective desire, connecting micro-personal action with macro-social interaction and articulating the cultural with the structural. It can also bypass the binary of domination and resistance in sub-culture studies by seeing the connection between the wild and tamed emotional energies running though different dominant and subordinate social groups. Emotional energy is polymorphous. It can serve as resistive energy and at the same time be absorbed by the market and the elite to re-energize economic and cultural formation. In the following, I will apply this socio-emotive framework to delineate some discursive tactics of emotion production and management used by sub-cultural groups.

Fears and spatial frictions

Many sub-culture studies examine the ways in which sub-cultural groups distinguish themselves from the general public by dressing styles and esoteric rituals (c.f. Gelder and Thornton 1997). I would like to add a socio-emotive dimension to this sub-cultural differentiation. During my 4 months of intensive fieldwork, casual conversations with outsiders (those initially not familiar with LMF and their music) indicated that their first reaction to LMF and other imagined alternative bands ranged from curiosity to anxiety and sometimes fear. Outsiders' perceptions are often clouded with the cultural imaginations of criminality, violence and aggressiveness.

In fact, LMF and their affiliates often use signs of danger to mark off boundary and territory. They inscribe onto their body and their life-world conspicuous signs of trouble such as tattoos, metallic accessories, long hair and leather boots. Devilish posters, fierce looking figures, machine guns and a seemingly chaotic array of equipment and gear fill their band rooms. These are not necessarily signs of danger; interpretations depend on the set of ethno-methods one is deploying. Already, some of these sub-cultural signs, such as tattoos, have become symbols of being hip and trendy and have been appropriated by youth groups. I will come back to this at a later stage. However, the conspicuous display of dramatic signs inhibits easy psychological and interpersonal access. In their words, they like things that are 'a bit evil'. Although none of my informants is a member of a triad gang, many of them have permanent tattoos that make them look like gangsters. One informant recalled: 'In the past, when we went to concerts, we didn't have to queue. Those poor people were scared and they stayed away from us. We just walked in.' Some of them told me that, 10 years ago, when they started to take on their conspicuous 'bad boy' appearances, police officers always spot checked them at night. Members of bands have always been easy targets for the police. When they go out in groups, the police read it as a sign of trouble and interrogate them in the streets.

From an ethno-methodological point of view, people 'above ground' are used to a set of ethno-methods, which will facilitate effective everyday encounters by providing hints and cues concerning appropriateness, normality and dangers. Following the rules of mutually agreed ethno-methods, people accomplish socially acceptable behaviour such as holding friendly conversations and having proper dress codes. These ethno-accomplishments maintain a routine level of 'cool' emotional energy, which builds solidarity. People will display dramatic or 'hot' emotional energies when they are forced to face conflicting ethno-methods from their ritual partners.

A fieldwork incident is relevant here. One night, I went out biking with LMF and their friends. We formed a gang of about 12 people. We speeded through empty streets and parks from 2 a.m. until 7 a.m. Sometimes, we stopped for a while and let graffiti artist Ah Yan spray his paints on the walls. This is illegal. We had to look out for him. In one quite amusing moment, we spotted a foreigner with a heavy build jogging towards us. It was 6 a.m. Some suggested the approaching man might be a retired police officer, and we told Yan to hurry up. '100 meters, 90 meters . . .' we whispered as Yan was giving his final touches. The big man perceived that in front of him was a gang of 'trouble-makers' with heavy-duty bicycles idling in the street. He avoided us by slowing down quietly, pretending to take a rest and facing away from us. We were not a violent gang at all, but our appearances set up what Harvey (1989) calls 'spatial friction' that separates in-group and out-group space by physical, semiotic and emotional barriers. My experience is that once this spatial friction has been overcome, this group of people is in fact quite friendly. To build up boundaries and scare off outsiders, they deploy signs that are usually considered evil and aberrant. These markers, as inverted ethno-methods, are effective because they are loaded with negative emotional energy, but signs that are 'a bit evil' are inverted to become sacred anchors of collective pride and solidarity.

DIY: in and out of control

If you look at these bands from a mainstream middle-class ideology, generally defined, their disdain of work, indulgences in different kinds of games, 'hysterical' shaking and dancing on stage, and their 'chaotic' lifestyle all lead to a common-sense conclusion that their lives are pretty out of control. However, in their own world, they are controlling their own body movements in dance halls and in performances (Frith 1983; Straw 2001). Using Elias and Dunning's phrasing, they display a controlled de-controlling of emotional controls (Elias and Dunning 1986). They are also experts in remodelling, re-assembling and re-mixing of all kinds of given resources available to them. Their band rooms were designed and refurnished by themselves and have been continuously renovated and upgraded. Ah Wah, the laziest among the LazyMuthaFucka, told me that he did most of the renovations when they first rented the band room in 1993. The wires, pipes and sockets were all installed on the spot. However, everything was mixed up. A friend who was a technician visited the place and told him he had installed it incorrectly. Now posters, wallpaper and sound-absorbent materials have covered up those technical mistakes. The band room is now saturated with homemade do-it-yourself (DIY) decorations.

LMF members build toy models. They rebuild their bicycles. They re-assemble legal CO_2 guns, increasing muzzle energy to an illegal and lethal level. Another band group has built a hawker cart. They sold meatballs on the street for a while. Yet another group publishes a music magazine on bands and skateboarding. The magazine, which is called *Start from Scratch*, is produced and distributed by the group itself, without the help of a commercial publisher or distributors. Of course, the most prestigious attempt among bands is the independent production of their own CD albums. There are many stories of how CDs are produced by borrowing money from friends and parents, of shared studios and equipment, and exchanging drummers and guitarists to finish recordings. This DIY style is compatible with the 'scratch aesthetic' of hip-hop culture, which has been incorporated by some local bands. They inscribe graffiti upon the decaying infrastructures of city walls, build their disc-scratching music from existing old vinyl records and mix different computer generated noises with instruments to foster their own music culture (Potter 2001).

Their flexible re-creation of resources is empowered by technologies. Skilled in managing sound technologies, they overcome unexpected malfunctions and technical limitations by skilful improvisation during performances. In concerts, a substantial portion of emotional energy is generated by electronic guitars, high-power amplifiers, gigantic drum sets and sophisticated mixers (Theberge 2001). Emotions would be flattened if concerts are cut off from the power of modern techno-electronic sound systems. Electronics are the technical core of band sound. On stage, we can see wires snaking everywhere. Drummers are submerged in their drum sets that make them look larger than life. Electronic guitars are amplifying their ability to produce heart-throbbing rhythms. Guitarists shake and jump when they plug into the 'electric energy' of the systems. Performer and fans can both experience this techno-power when the sound waves are beating across the concert halls. Machines and men are one.

DIY improvisations are 'energy consuming' in a work-and-spend consumer culture. Ready-made products, user-friendly services and instant-consumer goods can increase turnover, boost sales, save time, strengthen production and enable precise marketing control. To rehabilitate assembly-line monotony, post-Fordist mechanisms ensure an easy but exciting life for consumers by providing a constant flow of ready-made but individualized niche products. In fact, DIY products have been appropriated into another line of niche products, giving consumers a small part of carefully programmed DIY autonomy and flexibility.

Instant goods are time saving, so consumers can have more time to work and more time to spend. On the contrary, it is energy consuming to improvise because we are not accustomed to re-creation. Consumerist ethno-methods have been 'McDonaldized', sliding into the ready-made track of niche marketing (Ritzer 2000). However, DIY improvisations are the survival tactic of the underprivileged. With limited resources, they make do by the arts of breaking and mixing whatever is available to them. These energy-consuming ethno-methods can generate alternative emotional energies of self-confidence, autonomy, freedom and a sense of active agency. DIY is emotionally satisfying. DIY rituals of alternative bands are charging up energy for members to construct their own sense of confidence and self-worth.

Dramatized masculinity

There are more men than women in local bands. Most bands are all male. In the local community of bands, there are signs of dramatized masculinity everywhere, erect penises and naked women are among the most obvious. These signs are displayed on posters, in graffiti and band-room decoration and articulated in daily conversation. It is not uncommon for vocalists to hold their penises while singing and dancing on stage. While backstage during a concert, I overheard a story told by concert organizers saying that a group masturbated and ejaculated while they performed. Whether this story is true is not the point, what is interesting is that it was retold as if it had a legendary aura attached to it. All these suggest the valorization of sexual power and transgression.

Inside band rooms, there are images of sexy and naked women mixed with images of machine guns, weapons and military figures. They talked about how exciting it was to fire at rats, frogs, tin cans and old CDs. 'Senior' LMF members said they could not write songs about love because most of them are fooling around. 'We have 3 to 4 "pieces" with us. How can we talk about (romantic) love?' I was quite surprised when one of them said he ought to have children because he is the only child; he has the responsibility to marry and have a son to bear his family name. Some others said that obedience is the most important criterion for girls who want to 'follow' them. In my field study, I saw girlfriends waiting backstage, preparing for examinations inside a very noisy band room, or tenderly taking care of their boyfriends after a performance. Females in these groups are displaced to a marginal, supporting and sexually pleasing position. Although many male band members have resisted mainstream ideologies on various fronts, they seem to take for granted those mediated representations of obedient, sexy and exploitable women and dramatize their masculinity through explicit reproduction of sexist signs and practices.

I am not suggesting mysogynist ideology of a specific group or person. There are a few of my informants who do not take up such a macho posture. Yet it is quite easy to spot male-centred values through inscribed signs and casual conversations. In the case of black American hip-hop, the circulation of some women-hating songs suggests that part of the reason can be related to the emotional conflict between unsuccessful black men and successful black women (George 1998). In the case of Hong Kong, dramatized masculinity among bands has not been developed into a situation that breeds the production of women-hating songs. However, among my informants, their deficiencies in socio-economic and educational terms can indeed be compensated by dramatizing their masculinity in physical and musical terms. Besides, the desire to express oneself through transgression, sensuality, sexuality, physicality and emotionality may have also contributed to the uninhibited subscription to a mysogynist ideology. As Cohen argues from a case study, gender is 'musically constructed not only through performance texts, images and styles but also through the relations, events and contexts that shape their form and meaning' (Cohen, Sara 2001: 240).

Shepherd's socio-musicological approach (Shepherd 1991) is highly relevant here. He argues that the internal logic (voice, timbre, etc) of a music genre and its socio-cultural condition are having a mutually structuring relation. The male dominating culture in band communities are structuring the lyrics of songs and the timbre of band sound, and vice versa. As noted by Frith and McRobbie, 'Cock' rock performers tend to be 'aggressive, dominating, boastful and constantly seeking to remind their audience of their powers, their control' (Frith and McRobbie 1979: 5) They also suggest that the strong and macho sound and style of hard rock are a mix of power and self-doubt, confidence and aggression. These descriptions are applicable to local bands like LMF. These band members are bound together by a feeling of brotherhood. Male bonding is mediated, expressed, reinforced and extended into their musical and sub-cultural life-world. It is the source of power and security. As one LMF member says: 'Chicks stay with you for days or perhaps months, (male) buddies are for life.'

Transgression

Outsiders often associate alternative bands with various forms of 'deviant' behaviour, which, in turn, have frequently been associated with the discursive category of 'youth'. These may be merely imaginative or induced by self-stigmatization (e.g. the association of tattoo with violence). Some other deviancies are legal (drug abuse and illegal graffiti) and cultural (e.g. swearing, smoking and casual sex). Whether these practices are genuinely deviant is arguable. Alternative bands often transgress these social norms and stimulate disputes, which subsequently reinforce disapproval and stigmatization. In this section, I am more interested in relating these acts of transgression to the subverted emotional energies they generate.

There has always been high-profile media coverage on drug abuse among teenagers at discos and parties in Hong Kong. Government officials, social workers and the general public articulate a powerful consensus condemning drug abuse, which is causally associated with grave personal, family and social problems. Most of my informants are quite sensitive to the powerful discourse on drugs. Since some have a public face and are not completely underground, they are conscious of the need to overcome these public discourses and at the same time stick to their own rebellious impulses. However, most are direct in talking about their habit of smoking marijuana. During my first life history interviews with LMF members, some smoked marijuana with glass pipes inside the bandroom. The leaders of the band told me frankly that they have been smoking it for more than 10 years. Most of them try to differentiate between different types of drug abuse. They are all against heroin, cocaine and other popular chemical drugs, which they think are addictive and may cause permanent bodily damage, but some admit taking them anyway. They smoke marijuana for relaxation, socializing and boosting up sensitivity and creativity. However, there are also 'straight edges' among band groups. Straight edges are those who take no drugs, no alcohol and do not have casual sex. Both drug users and straight edges are quite tolerant of each other.

Another illegal activity is drawing graffiti. Since graffiti is rather new to Hong Kong, it is not widely considered as vandalism. Graffiti appears on T-shirts, in band rooms and band shows, and on the walls in various parts of the city. Ah Yan started to draw graffiti in Hong Kong some years ago. Since then he has been drawing illegal graffiti, training 'disciples' and hired to paint legally in specific sites. The public and the police are ambivalent. One night when Yan was painting with a foreign graffiti artist, both of them were spotted by a police officer. Yan just stopped right there because he knew Hong Kong police officers were not quite sure of what he was doing. However, the foreign graffiti artist, fully aware of the legal consequence, tried to run away. The police officer called for a chase not because he thought graffiti spraying was vandalism, but because he sensed trouble when he saw a man running at midnight. Several police cars rushed to the scene. The police later discovered that they were just 'painting' and thought it was not a serious crime, yet they could not call off the chase because police cars had been summoned and a report had to be written. Both graffiti artists were caught and charged. Similar stories have been circulated among teenagers and amplified by the media. Illegality 'charges up' sub-culture by conferring on the transgressors an aura of bravery and rebellion.

Drawing graffiti can be seen as a spatial subversion by reclaiming city space symbolically. Against macro-spatial practices by property developers, advertisers and city planners, graffiti artists mark their presence by conspicuous symbolic display. They earn prestige among underground graffiti artists by putting their nametags, throw-ups (large patches of paint on a wall) and masterpieces on walls (Phillips 1999). The more difficult the graffiti and the more dangerous the circumstances, the more emotional energy they will acquire by achieving it. The emotional energy they gained is derived from how far they have transgressed legal and spatial restrictions.

From these brief descriptive accounts, we can articulate transgression and sub-cultural emotional energies. For the general public, transgression generates negative emotions because it challenges moral consensus and legal power. However, for sub-cultural groups, transgression generates positive emotions, which confer emotive power and status to the transgressor. Emotional energies work reciprocally and dialectically with social taboos. As Bataille argues, transgression does not deny taboos but transcends and completes them (Bataille 1987). Local band members recognize all sorts of social taboos, but transgress them and generate emotional energies when they do so. The emotional friction is there only when the taboo is hot and active. Underground communities negotiate their own lines of transgression according to the desire of how far they want to distance themselves from normality. As discussed earlier, alternative bands differentiate themselves by dramatizing masculinity and inverting symbolic emotions of fear and anxiety. They 'complete' the taboos by confirming the popular prediction that they are really the bad seeds of the community. They 'transcend' them by self-stigmatization, absorbing the emotional energies of transgression and turning them into identity resources.

Re-enchanting consumption

At this point, I would like to borrow from Grossberg (1992), who uses the term 'affective alliance' to relate social reality and emotionality of popular music. An affective alliance is the organization of concrete material practices, cultural forms and social experience that both opens up and structures the space of affective investments of the youth. The previous analysis has already partly demonstrated the affective alliance of Hong Kong bands in their everyday material and bodily practices. Here I want to extend Grossberg's argument by connecting sub-cultural emotional energies with the larger political economy, highlighting the affective alliance between micro sub-cultural interaction and macro contextual discourses. In the following, I will respectively connect sub-culture with the market and the polity of post-1997 Hong Kong.

Alternative bands share an ambivalent attitude towards mainstream commercial media. Although the fame conferred by media exposure seems hard to resist, there is still a rough consensus that discourages a close relationship with the media. To them, going commercial and entering the mainstream is a sign of weakness and compromise. Recently, LMF members have appeared in commercials, interviews and at various promotional activities. They have attracted sporadic criticism from other independent bands. To maintain a critical posture, LMF has been tactically utilizing the media to negotiate their own financial survival but at the same time continue to defy social norms and the rules of the media.

These seemingly contradictory processes are in fact complementary. Here I want to insert two relevant incidents of my field studies. In one promotional activity, a local beer company sponsored a rave party and hired LMF for a brief performance. The admission ticket was HK$250 per person. Instead of taking up an onlooker's role, I joined the crowd on the lowered dance floor. Those on the dance floor had to actually 'look up' to the surrounding stages, where there were more then 30 photographers. They were all armed with king-sized professional cameras pointing at the dance floor and the front stage where LMF was performing. It was quite an awesome scene watching from below: cameras above were pointing down at us, aggressively capturing frantic facial expressions and body movements of sexy girls 'dancing out of their minds'. 'Fuck the media', LMF screamed on stage; 'Fuck the media', shouted back the financially secure audience on the dance floor. Ironically, the media was tapping into this energy-producing ritual in order to re-charge their pages with the exotic images of stigmatized youth. In the near climax of the performance, a couple representing the sponsor jumped in for a lucky draw. Of course, LMF members were fully aware of their role as cultural intermediary in all these processes of stigmatization and commodification.

Another story was at a band performance organized by the Polytechnic University. One of the sponsors was a new fashion magazine called *Cool*. Before the show, I noticed that the promoter was asking the lighting technician to project their logo onto the background of the stage, thus mixing LMF's very energetic performance with the logo of the magazine. The cover story of the magazine is about LMF: *The Trendiest Group in Town*, headlined the cover of the first issue. The inside story has portraits of all 12 LMF members in stylistic close-ups, with captions telling what kind of fashion each wears. The magazine is tapping onto LMF's energetic stage performance, exploiting LMF's 'bad boy' image, reframing LMF members as trendsetters and capturing their emotional energies to become the aura embedded in the consumerist ideology of the magazine.

Market developers constantly need to tap into all forms of emotional energies to re-charge cultural products and material goods. Market-driven dynamics have led to what Ritzer (1999) calls product disenchantment: a Fordist mode of production erases whatever is fresh and special along the assembly line, while the post-Fordist mode seeks to re-enchant products by constantly adding in exotic elements. Alternative bands, with their excessive signs and overflowing emotional energies, become ideal resources for re-enchanting the disenchanted world. Since sub-cultures have highly inflated markers of differences, they are easy targets of stigmatization. The stronger the stigmatization, the more emotional energies are pumped into these sub-cultural forms. These emotional energies can be deployed by sub-cultural groups to foster solidarity; they can also be absorbed and appropriated by the mainstream to recreate fashion-able commodities. Emotional energy is a wild card for many situations. It can serve as resistive energy and at the same time absorbed by the market and the elite to re-energize dominant economic and cultural formations. Sub-culture studies have long been tracing the reciprocity and convertibility between sub-cultural forms, the media representations, and commodities (Hebdige 1979, Thornton 1995). Here, I just want to add a dimension of emotionality into the discussion. As I have argued in this section, the seemingly de-commodified forms of emotionality generated by sub-cultural groups is ironically a highly sought-after commodity in high modernity (Williams 2001).

Socio-emotive articulation

The previous section is on market absorption. In this concluding section, I would like to connect the above ethnographic case back to the contextual question raised at the very beginning of this paper: why is there a sudden 'uprising' of alternative bands in post-1997 Hong Kong? The sub-cultural lifestyles and practices discussed in the above have been here for many years. In fact, they are not unique to LMF but are common features of alternative band culture, local and elsewhere. For a long time, local under-ground communities have been producing alternative emotional energies to differentiate with the mainstream and maintain a strong in-group emotional solidarity. However, as I have discussed at the beginning of this paper, there were very few bridges between the sub-cultural and the mainstream in the colonial Hong Kong. For instance, LMF and friends have been practising a way of life that is pretty 'out of control'. If we judge them from a middle-class ideology that emphasizes education and academic achievement, most of them are complete losers and failures. In the 1980s and the 1990s, the myths of upward mobility and unfailing market were still very dominant in Hong Kong. The subterranean values of LMF were highly incompatible with these mainstream ideologies. If they did get through, they could only appear as an occasional outbreak of liminal pleasures.

However, the prolonged economic downturn after 1997 has tarnished the myth of Hong Kong's unfailing capitalism to such an extend that teenagers and adults in general no longer have strong faith in the middle-class success formula of educational investment and upward mobility. In this post-1997 context, the alternative emotional energy generated by the hedonistic and DIY mode of existence has struck a chord in the larger society. One of the LMF greatest hits is the song 'Lazy Clan' which sells a lazy lifestyle. Its lyrics say: 'Slacker getting up late at 3 p.m. in the afternoon. Tangled hair. Blab all the day. Poorly dressed. With nothing to do and nothing to care about.' This philosophy of non-action is not as unacceptable in the early 2000s as it was in the 1990s. It is even attractive to students who increasingly find their parents' working ethics driving to a dead end.

These alternative bands can mobilize strong emotional energies that are generated by their social semiotics of fear and transgression. For instance, LMF uses swear words as weapons in their provocative song *Hum-ga-ling* (*uknuwudafuckimsayin*) to criticize mainstream media. Heavy drums and hardcore rhymes articulate a very angry and unique oppositional posture. In another co-performed song, *Hong Kong for Sure*, LMF and singer Paul Wong voice out a very angry satire against the impotency of the HKSAR government. Other teenage bands I visited are also fluent in anti-establishment discourses. One teenage band even posts the picture of the SAR Chief on their drum set so that they can hit him whenever they jam their music. Another upcoming band, Lam Ke, won the Asian Independent Band Contest in 2000. They believed that the reason why they stood out among hundreds of veteran bands from all over Asia was that, on stage, they had delivered something distinctively Hong Kong, and it was rage. 'That (award winning) song is a song of extreme rage', they said. Interestingly, after 1997, when the HKSAR government has been suffering from legitimacy and administration crises, these highly critical underground voices are quite compatible, in fact popular, among the general public of Hong Kong. The general public and the sub-cultural are standing together on the same political and emotive front, despite the fact that LMF has been heavily criticized by the public in cultural and moral terms.

A note of caution is that micro ethno-energies are not related directly to the macro political contexts. As a researcher, I have a strong desire to look for active resistance to socio-political discourses among bands. However, my informants are not interested in advancing explicit political critique. LMF members said they are not good at talking about politics in their songs. They know little about it. What they really care about are those trivial things in their daily lives. They seem to have developed a resistant mode by refusing macro-narratives and have constructed micro-narratives of everyday practices of rebellion.

These everyday rebellions are biographical. Most informants have experienced different kinds of conflict with the establishment throughout their life. When they were in their teenage years, they found that the formula for their improvement offered to them by teachers, parents and mainstream media could not solve their own problems of growing up, or they simply just did not want to study in school. The sub-cultural style of the alternative bands is class-based. Some members of the group are restricted to a lower social stratum, deprived by the education system, and are categorized as academic losers. However, their talents have been re-directed into music. Together they have fostered an alternative lifestyle, which is not necessarily subversive, but is different from those options offered by the mainstream. They have established alternative ethno-methods of survival by challenging and inverting established ethno-methods of the larger society. They are reversing seemingly negative emotions of fear, rage, shame and inferiority into positive emotions of solidarity and rebellion. In the particular historical juncture of post-1997 Hong Kong, the emotional energies they generated transpire through sub-cultural boundaries and articulate with public acridity and disappointment. These energies have been amplified and re-charged by media stigmatization and commercial absorption, and subsequently articulate into a messy web of antagonistic discourses, which has marked the sub-cultural politics of post-1997 Hong Kong.

Concluding remarks

From a socio-emotive approach, this paper argues that sub-cultural groups generate a pool of alternative emotional energies for socio-cultural differentiation. They differentiate themselves by inverting ethno-methods, producing spatial friction of fear and anxiety, dramatizing masculinity and transgressing acceptable moral boundaries. They inflict upon themselves the stigmas forced upon them by the mainstream. In return, they stigmatize themselves by inflating and inscribing signs of troubles into their life-worlds. The irony is that they have inflated these stigmas and at the same time attack the stupidity of stigmatization. They are recognizing and at the same time denying these stigmas. These involve the de-skilling and re-skilling of mainstream ethno-methods, which generate particularized emotional energies, but these subcultural emotional energies exhibit comparable socio-cultural configurations with those of the larger society. They form an emotive web that connects or disengages with different social formations, bridging or subverting micro ethno-methods and social habitus in macro socio-historical contexts. This socio-emotive web is comparable to Grossberg's 'affective alliance', but is more extensive, networking micro interactions with social, economic and political dynamics. As illustrated in this case study, the emotional energies generated by Hong Kong alternative bands are polymorphous. They are partly fuelled by the rebellious spirit of independent music incorporated translocally (Ma 2002); they can be charged by personal frustrations in schools, families and the workplaces (Ng et al. 2001); their production can be a tactic of differentiating a youth identity in contrast with the adult and the established world; they can be exploited by some privileged group members to serve as fashionable identity labels (Ma 2001, Chan 2002). Emotional energies can also be political. In the particular juncture of the post-1997 Hong Kong, sub-cultural energies have articulated and channelled into popular anti-establishment discourses. There are obvious thematic parallels between alternative music and public sentiments on the widespread dissatisfaction with the tabloid media, the education system and the conservative polity. Intense emotional energies generated by sub-cultural groups may sometime be seen as uncontrollable emotional outbreaks. However, as illustrated in this case study, sub-cultural emotional energies have traceable configurations, serving multiple discursive purposes and connecting with different social, cultural, commercial and political forms of emotionality.

Acknowledgements

Very special thanks are due to the two reviewers for their sharp observations. They have pointed out the 'Westernizing' tendency of the original version of this paper, which conformed to the formality of placing academic jargon at the very beginning of the paper. I have revised the paper in a data-driven approach and find this version more engaging. The paper was first presented at the conference 'After the end: Hong Kong culture after 1997', UCLA. Kindest thanks are due to Professor Shu-mei Shih for her invitation and valuable comments. Thanks also go to team members Anthony Fung, Ducky Tse, Ka Yan Chan, Wincy Ng, Frankie Cheung, Christine Cheng, Ka Yee Wong and Natalie Ma for making the project a joyful and rewarding research experience.

References

Bataille, George (1987) *Eroticism*, M. Dalwood (trans.), London: Boyars.

Chan, Ka Yan (2002) *Exploring Youth Subculture in Hong Kong: A case study on the local band LazyMuthaFucka (LMF)*, MPhil Thesis, Chinese University of Hong Kong.

Chu, Stephen 朱耀偉 (2001) *Glorious Days: a study of Hong Kong popular bands (1984–1990)* 光輝歲月：香港流行樂隊組合研究 *(1984–1990)*, Hong Kong: Hui zhi 匯智出版 .

Cohen, Phil (1972) 'Subcultural conflict, working class community'. In *Working Papers in Cultural Studies 2*, Birmingham: Centre for Contemporary Cultural Studies, University of Birmingham.

Cohen, Sara (2001) 'Popular music, gender and sexuality'. In Simon Frith *et al.* (eds) *The Cambridge Companion to Pop and Rock*, Cambridge: Cambridge University Press, 226–242.

Collins, Randall (1990) 'Stratification, emotional energy, and the transient emotions'. In Theodore Kemper (ed.) *Research Agendas in the Sociology of Emotions*, New York: State University of New York Press, 41–60.

Elias, Norbert and Dunning, Eric (1986) *Quest for Excitement: sport and leisure in the civilizing process*, Oxford: Basil Blackwell.

Fiske, John (1989) *Reading the Popular*, London: Routledge.

Frith, Simon (1983) *Sound Effects: Youth, leisure, and the politics of rock*, London: Constable.

Frith, Simon and McRobbie, Angela (1979) 'Rock and sexuality', *Screen Education* 29: 3–19.

Garfinkel, Harold (1967) *Studies in Ethnomethodology*, Englewood Cliffs, NJ: Prentice Hall.

Gelder, Ken and Thornton, Sarah (eds) (1997) *The Subcultures Reader*, London: Routledge.

George, Nelson (1998) *Hip Hop America*, New York: Viking.

Grossberg, Lawrence (1992) *We Gotta Get Out of This place: Popular conservatism and postmodern culture*, New York: Routledge, 1992.

Hall, Stuart and Tom, Jefferson (eds) (1976) *Resistance Through Ritual*, London: Routledge.

Harvey, David (1989) *The Condition of Postmodernity*, Oxford: Blackwell.

Hebdige, Dick (1979) *Subculture: The meaning of style*, London: Routledge.

Law, Wing-sang (1998) 'Managerializing colonialism'. In Kuan-Hsing Chen (ed.) *Trajectories: Inter-Asia cultural studies*, London: Routledge, 109–121.

Luk, Bernard 陸鴻基 (1995) 'Hong Kong history and Hong Kong culture' 香港歷史與香港文化. In Elizabeth Sinn 冼玉儀 (ed.) *Culture and Society in Hong Kong* 香港文化與社會, Hong Kong: The Centre of Asian Studies 香港大學亞洲研究中心, 64–79.

Ma, Eric Kit-wai 馬傑偉 (1999) *Culture, Politics and Television in Hong Kong*, London: Routledge.

Ma, Eric Kit-wai (2000) 'Re-nationalization and me: my Hong Kong story after 1997', *Inter-Asia Cultural Studies* 1(1): 173–179.

Ma, Kit Wai (2001) *Underground Radicals* 地下狂野分子 , Hong Kong: Ming Pao 明窗出版社 .

Ma, Eric Kit-wai (2002) 'Translocal spatiality', *International Journal of Cultural Studies*, 5(2): 131–151.

Ng, Wincy *et al.* 伍詠詩等 (2001) *Selling LMF* 出賣 LMF: 粗口音樂檔案 Hong Kong: Ming Pao.

Phillips, Susan (1999) *Wallbangin': Graffiti and gangs in L.A.*, Chicago: University of Chicago Press.

Potter, Russell (2001) 'Soul into hip-hop'. In Simon Frith *et al.* (eds) *The Cambridge Companion to Pop and Rock*, Cambridge: Cambridge University Press, 143–157.

Ritzer, George (1999) *Enchanting a Disenchanted World: Revolutionizing the means of consumption*, Thousand Oaks, CA: Pine Forge Press.

Ritzer, George (2000) *The McDonaldization of Society*, rev edn, Thousand Oaks, CA: Pine Forge Press.

Sacks, Harvey (1992) *Lectures on Conversation*, Oxford: Blackwell.

Shepherd, John (1991) *Music as Social Text*, Cambridge: Polity

Sinn, Elizabeth 冼玉儀 (ed.) (1995) *Culture and Society in Hong Kong* 香港文化與社會 , Hong Kong: The Centre of Asian Studies 香港大學亞洲研究中心 .

Straw, Will (2001) 'Dance music'. In Simon Frith *et al.* (eds) *The Cambridge Companion to Pop and Rock*, Cambridge: Cambridge University Press, 158–175.

Theberge, Paul (2001) 'Plugged in: technology and popular music'. In Simon Frith *et al.* (eds) *The Cambridge Companion to Pop and Rock*, Cambridge: Cambridge University Press, 3–25.

Thornton, Sarah (1995) *Club Cultures: Music, Media and Subcultural Capital,* Cambridge: Polity Press.

Williams, Simon (2001) *Emotion and Social Theory*, London: Sage.

Willis, Paul (1978) *Profane Culture*, London: Routledge and Kegan Paul.

Chapter 25

Feminization of the 2002 World Cup and women's fandom[1]

Kim Hyun Mee
(Translated by Hong Sung Hee)

'Feminization' of the 2002 World Cup

The history of soccer shows a happy union of masculinity and nationalism. In the case of the 2002 World Cup games, however, at least in Korean society, soccer seems to have become a feminized event, with the main 'masculine' symbols associated with soccer losing their powers. This claim that the World Cup hosted in Korea was 'feminized', is based on the following two factors. First, Korean women participated in the games in unprecedented numbers, as the majority of consumers and active supporters. It is said that half or two thirds of those cheering the games were women.[2] The participation of women pushed out the 'soju (cheap and popular Korean liquor) packs', 'bad language under the pretence of cheering' and the 'hooligans' who romanticized collective violence. Instead, they filled the stadium and the streets with style, vibrance and energy. Second, women transformed the soccer games into a space where they could project their 'sexual desires', hence breaking the linkage of harsh solidarity and tension between the macho male players and the equally macho male supporters. The cheerleaders, who had been the only women shared between those two groups of men, disappeared, while women in stadiums, on the streets, and in front of the TV screens enjoyed imaginary and direct 'heterosexual' romance with the male soccer players. In short, women brought soccer, which had been the symbol of men's exclusive homosocial solidarity, out into the 'open world' of romance and fantasy.

It was due to their outstanding activities that Korean women, previously known to hate 'boring stories about soccer games played by men, especially those in the army', came to decorate the media with headlines such as 'wind of women', 'women's power' and 'cheering women warriors'. Stripping the Korean national flag of its heavy solemnity and nationalism, they brought change with their white, red, blue and black sports bras, scarves, tank tops and skirts. Young Korean women who had been the target of criticism by the media every summer for their 'excessive spending' and 'oversexed outfits' were praised for being original and attractive fashion leaders at the soccer scenes. As participation by the new generation of women in soccer scenes increased considerably, the 'ajummas (a popular term indicating older, married women), who had waited for their husbands while setting the table with beers, set out for 'Gwanghwamoon Square (main street in front of City Hall)' with their kids. Foreigners of different skin colours joined in the street festivals, free from fears of unpredictable group violence. Women, as the majority of the street supporters, had saved the stadium and the streets from madness and violence and instead enlivened them as an open space of cultural festivities. In the midst of this, women's soccer teams started to be formed around the country and suggestions that women's soccer should be developed grew rapidly.

The appearance of women as the biggest 'unexpected event' of the 2002 World Cup signalled the points of negotiations that were to be formed between the World Cup as a global event and the local women in Korea. Although soccer is a game, the FIFA World Cup is a global cultural product created by the global media and the various multinational commercial advertisements. The 2002 World Cup was geared toward satisfying the cultural taste of the new generation of Koreans who have come to dictate consumer patterns since the 1990s. It successfully reconstructed an audience comprising women and the young generation with varied inventions of visual imageries of soccer stars, rock and roll bands and music, cheering, and fashion. As indicated by Martinez in her analysis of pop culture in Japan (1998), the 2002 World Cup could also be seen as a space of negotiation where tradition, the present, future, national identity, gender identity and class identity are reflected, coerced, created, disintegrated and re-created. It therefore follows that people watching the games on the big screens on the streets or on TV at home 'consume' the World Cup each in their own way. There is a multitude of heterogeneous consumptions and appropriations in this process. Some women may watch the game with a keen interest in the teams' strategies while other women may project their emotions and desires as if they were watching a music video.

The fervour of these women over this World Cup series in Korea was, on the one hand, the manifestation of women's characteristic fandom in the 'public space' and, on the other hand, a new collective experience of pleasure by women as viewers of men's bodies and not as objects of men's gaze. In this respect, a reading of the World Cup from a gender perspective is an attempt to expose the contradictions between young women's newly emerging desires and their structural positioning, as well as to expand the historical imagination regarding Korea's gender politics in the global era. This World Cup was an opportunity for Korean society, previously accustomed to the evaluation of women as asexual, fixed gender role-fulfilling beings, to acutely realize the historical moment of 'gender instability' (Stivens 1998) of Korean society. The feminization of the 2002 World Cup should be understood in the context of what has been defined as 'private' – such as the issue of sexualities and intimacy – has been increasingly politicized in the form of social movements in Korea. Through this paper, I wish to give meaning to the changes affected by women and intervene in the discursive politics of the post-World Cup period.

'Oppa Budae' (a squad of teenage female fans)[3] and 'trained' fandom[4]

The world media had expressed curiosity about why there were no hooligans at the soccer scenes in Korea. The Korean media had announced with pride that the Korean people became the people who could incorporate passion with 'order'. It was the 'Red Devils', Korea's cheering team, who received the most attention from the world's media in the 2002 World Cup. The 'Red Devils' were given the title of the '12th player' of the Korean team for their contribution to helping Korea reach the quarter-finals. This 'Red Devils phenomenon', Hong Sung-Tae (2002: 40) wrote, 'is the "fandom culture", which appeared 10 years ago with Seo Tae-Ji [a famous Korean singer leading a most well-known boy band, Seo Tae-Ji and His Friends], being manifested in soccer, which is indeed a true national sport'. Soccer supporters, the Red Devils are an autonomous new generation cheering team who shy away from both national mobilization and too much commercialism.[5] As the Red Devils are a product of expansion through PC communications and the Internet, they are a result of the social environment and value system of the 'Net' generation. The cheering practices and game watching are mostly mediated through the Red Devils Internet homepage, and their members are constituted of various groups ranging from elementary school kids to the elderly (Ko 2002: 18), illustrating their flexibility and openness. Women account for 40% of the Red Devils' members. However, even if one cheers just as much for soccer and raves just as much about the players, depending on who one is, woman, man, 20s or 40s, one's actions are to be interpreted differently. If the supporter is male, he is most likely to be taken as 'liking soccer itself' and to be displaying 'a paranoia as a Korean that our country has to win', while a female gender supporter is taken as 'not even knowing the rules but just liking the players'. A woman that I know has told me that she likes soccer so much that she went to the stadium to watch a game and cheered for the Italian team which had better skills than the Korean team. It is said that many of the women who participate in soccer gatherings through the Internet have enjoyed soccer for a long time. Notwithstanding the diverse reasons for individual women's enthusiasm for it, the 'feminization' of this World Cup is a phenomenon that begs interpretation.

Numerous interpretations have been offered for why two-thirds of those cheering on the street were women, the majority of whom were in their mid-teens and early 20s. There were such comments as 'it came out of the characteristic of the new generation's women who are faithful to their own needs', 'the deviant energy of women who are oppressed in their daily lives had broken out', and that 'the rules of soccer being simple, women could easily follow the games'. The dominant opinion, however, has been that women's enthusiasm over the World Cup is due to the male stars. Owing to this view, female soccer fans were easily looked down on as *ppasun-is* (Oppa Girls) just like the *oppa budae* chasing after male entertainers. The young women of the *oppa budae* are often denounced by the media as 'being subordinate to the stars and used for the commercial strategy of the management companies', but this is an oversimplification of the relationship between the consciousness of these women and their expressed actions. Just because these women go fanatical over the male entertainers, it does not mean that they are blind followers, and the power relations between many of the women fans and the male stars are not fixed, but rather multivocal and dynamic. Looking at only the images represented in Korean media with no information about the politics of fandom, these women in their teens and 20s seem like reckless followers. But this World Cup provided a momentum for a new interpretation of the experiences of *oppa budae*'s women who are condescendingly referred to as *ppasun-is*. Actually, to the women fans, heterosexual desire and social activism are not separate. In the fan club for the singer Seo Tae-ji, there is a feminist group, and the fan club for the singer Lee Seung-Hwan carries out activities with NGO organizations to abolish Korean pop ranking shows. The women fans of the male hip-hop/R&B group GOD are leading a large-scale movement to protect their 'stars' from the tyranny of the management company and to ensure their position within the cultural industry system. As such, consumers of mass culture and followers of stars are carrying out 'civil movements' within their social conditions through efforts such as fan club activities. Even if they may have initially become fans because they were attracted to the images and appearances of the soccer players, the women fans create regulations and change the culture in the process of forming their identities as fans.

Usually, fans of a popular star wield a collective 'power', which helps the pop star to climb the ladder from being an 'entertainer' to being a 'star', and this power is formed through certain rules and negotiations. To have an identity as a fan is thus to consciously learn specific behaviours. For an *oppa budae* to demonstrate its power as a *'budae* (squad)', individual fans must train for their actions and languages to be organized in systematic ways. They must wear the same clothes, shout the same slogans and show contained passion. Therefore, 'fandom', which signifies the identity as a fan of a star, is not something that is formed suddenly or practised abruptly. Fans build placards, buy group T-shirts, make character products such as head scarves, towels and raincoats, and train themselves in moderate 'codes of action' to fight fans of other stars in open broadcasts. They learn fans' codes of action that cannot be actualized without 'collective and organized' efforts, such as singing along certain words of songs and shouting 'slogans' together. Being conscious of other fan clubs, they must show their moral superiority as much as they can. They try to maintain 'grace' as fans that are worthy of the star's status by abstaining from talking back or cursing when attacked by rival fan clubs, upholding order and calm, and cleaning up after events. It is through such process that they believe they can construct true fandom.

Not a small number of women of the Red Devils and street supporters have had this experience of fandom as teenagers and twenty-somethings and have imitated and practised basic actions that are required to root for and support stars. By devoting themselves to such efforts that demand time and money, fans not only consume images of stars, but also become acquainted with a certain 'civil spirit' in the process of embodying fandom. That members of the Red Devils 'checked and set up instruments and equipment needed for street cheers the night before a game and arranged seats around *Dong-a Ilbo* company building's electric board early in the morning' (Lee Dong-Yeon 2002: 53), mobilized a variety of cheering methods and cleaned the trash off the streets, is all owing to such experiences of practice and imitation.

The codes of action trained and familiarized by women fans in their teens and 20s were grafted onto the cheering culture of the Red Devils, and were the underlying power for embracing heterogeneous groups. Whether their reasons for loving soccer were because of the players or the game of soccer itself, women's 'fan culture', which had so far been treated as a sub-culture, has emerged as a mainstream culture by contributing to making a 'sophisticated country'. My analysis is that the diverse fan club experiences of women in their teens and 20s had contributed to achieving the 'Red Devils' a global standing of 'order' and 'civil spirit'.

Sexualization of soccer

Where did the strength and desire of women who mediated in the process of the approximately one month period in which a Korean soccer player of a yearly income of 24 million won became a 'global sports star' of hundreds of millions of won per year[6] come from? The bonuses allotted to the Korean soccer team with each victory and the price on the players' bodies of 'hundreds of millions of won' since the World Cup were not enough for them to become 'stars'. What was the background power that raised the sports players who depend on their bodies and sports technique up to the level of 21st-century cultural stars, selling images and desires? In order for a soccer player running on the field to create a cultural image that is traded as style and taste, a buyer who discovers his 'star quality' and improves upon it is needed. When Korean soccer players are beautified and visualized through repeated life stories of their families and upgraded bonuses, the enthusiasm of fans is also increased. However, women's powers, which propel 'star making', are more active than that. While their fandom is a result of heterosexual desires, it does not follow an archetype of patriarchy. Ehrenreich *et al.* (1986) explain that the craze of girl fans over the stars provides a rich opportunity for them to openly display their enormous sexual energy. It is indeed difficult for women of Korea in their teens and 20s who have been defined as 'asexual beings' despite their physical growth, and having been under constant surveillance, to realize their heterosexual desires naturally, in everyday life. To these women, showing their enthusiasm for male stars is a 'safe' way to express their socially oppressed desires. It is an 'exciting' experience for young women to project their burgeoning sexual fantasies on male objects.

In her article entitled 'World Cup cute guys shock, waking up women's basic instincts,' reporter Yang Sung-Hee (2002: 27) points out that the image of soccer as 'a "simple and ignorant", unrefined sport, where players with faces burnt from the sun chase the ball around like crazy' has been completely changed by the world's cute soccer players and that this has put a spur on Korean women finding pleasure in their hitherto oppressed sexual fantasies. She adds that, in the respect that the fans are not one-sidedly subordinate to the stars for they scrutinize the players and 'judge the quality of' their attractiveness, this is a 'subversive stardom'. In this sense, the World Cup has been a show performed by various types of men in front of women so that their potential attractiveness may be bought. Rather than boy bands comprising similar-looking men, the soccer games in which around a hundred different men were displayed were more than adequate to arouse Korean women. From Beckham, with a quality of a bisexual multi-breed, to innocent Ronaldino, austere and cold Kahn, and the ever-so-shy Song Jong-Guk, women evaluated the soccer players' bodies and projected their own desires upon them, as if they were potential buyers looking through an exhibit and, for a limited amount of time, they experienced 'visual' pleasures. It is a quite disconcerting experience for Korean men that Korean women are expressing their thoughts on men's bodily shapes and faces in elaborate and detailed words. Next to men who are being praised as 'sexy' and 'attractive', the 'men of reality' who exist with ordinary appearances wish to laugh at women's desires as shallow in order to restore their pride. This is somewhat of a revenge on men who have judged and derided the physical appearances of 'women of reality' with a standard of beauty that most women cannot attain. As women's sexual desires became a part of 'public discourse', they gained a rapid infectious effect, and Korean women, regardless of marital status, age or region, came to share an experience of collective sexualization. The emergence of women as the 'viewers' of male bodies, outside of their familiar position as 'the viewed', was a momentum for a rupture in the power relationship between women and men through the gaze.

Women's preferred images of men are not fixed, and this World Cup has shown that the scope of women's preferences for male images is expanding. The liking of 'cute guys' also demands a new reading. Ho (2001: 63–86), a feminist from Taiwan, points out that most of the recent idols of teenage girls are no longer buff and tough men but rather 'feminine men' who evoke a sense of sympathy, saying that there is a 'clear contrast between teenage girls of enormous strength and their idols of somewhat weak images'. This illustrates that women in their teens are breaking away from the typical framework of heterosexual romance in which women long for men who will devote themselves to, and take care of, them, and have started to express their sexuality in an active manner. The preference for men with the capability and personality of the breadwinner as the 'most attractive' is being undermined.

A reporter of Korean Weekly Journal, *Hankyoreh 21*, Kim Eun-Hyung (2002: 24–27), who analysed the recent Korean soccer player, Kim Nam-Il syndrome in her article, provocatively titled 'Kim Nam-Il, raw as is!' claims that the physicality of Kim Nam-Il 'differentiates' itself from the genealogy of the 'right-doing cute boy', popular since the late 1990s. According to her, women relish the 'image of the raw thing, not fooled around with or smoothened' (of Kim) and feel the pleasure of seeing his 'bare face' and 'undressed body' in the unconstrained movements of his muscular body. This is in contrast with Song Jong-Guk's 'soft-skinned, right-doing boy of good and humble behavior image'. It is because Kim is seen as the 'familiar party boy' that women can dare such bold and crude seductions as 'Turn off the lights, Nam-Il' or 'Let's make just three children, Nam-Il', without self-censorship. This World Cup was an opportunity for women to let out their sexual energy in a 'healthy way', and this demonstrated that women's zeal for male stars should not be treated as a fantasy of romance or a kind of group madness.

Soccer players such as Kim Nam-Il, Ahn Jeong-Hwan and Song Jong-Guk, underwent the typical process of that experienced by a 'star' of enthusiastic women fans' support. They started appearing in broadcast shows and various events, as well as commercial advertisements, and held fan autograph conventions. Photo books of their fabulous bodies were published, and a variety of cultural products based on the players' character images were created. Followers of different soccer players, hitherto dispersed, began to organize fan meetings through the Internet and set off on their practice of diverse strategies to make sure that their 'star' stays in 'stardom' for a long time. With the 'organization' of fans, star discourses created and circulated by them were absorbed by the media, generating more fans. The 'Kim Nam-Il' syndrome, which has recently swept over the Korean soccer world, is one such example. Currently, there are more than 1000 of his fan club websites, and members of the Daum Internet Café, 'Best MF Kim Nam-Il' are as many as 470,000. In addition, an original fanfiction series with Kim as the main character is said to be upgraded every day (Kim Eun-Hyung 2002: 24). Pictures of Kim from his unknown days are sold on the Internet at 700 won a piece, and knitted hats similar to the one worn by him are in such high demand that there are not enough to be sold (Sohn 2002: 45). The heterosexual energy shown by the women surrounded ordinary Korean sporting players with resources and a support system comparable to those of 'global stars'. That the post-World Cup is not desolate is probably due to the continuous generation of cultural phenomena around these stars.

The happy union of women's sexual desires and 'new patriotism'

Ahn Min-Seok (2002: 6–7) emphasizes that Korean sports have been ruled by the 'elite sport paradigm', rather than a paradigm of everyday sport. In other words, sports have been supported and nurtured by the South Korean state to be used as a means for improving the state's image and unifying the people to raise the country's status, as well as to prove its systematic superiority in its competition with North Korea. This was the reason behind the achievement-oriented policy geared toward making 'results' in a short amount of time and thus was the foundation of the elite-centred sports formed. The Korean soccer players who achieved far better results than expected in the 2002 World Cup were an outcome of that system, and they faithfully carried out their role of *taegeuk* (the Great Absolute) warriors'. The national identities of the women who cheered for them were not monolithic. Nevertheless, I see women's fandom as an outcome of the happy union of sexual desire and new patriotism. For the Korean women to accept fully a global identity, Korea's ethnocentricism seems still to have too much of a strong hold over them.

During the modernization process of the past 30 years, Koreans were not allowed any individual identity apart from that of a Korean national. But now that the 'Korean people making' project of the state's mobilization tactics has lost its effect, nationalism and patriotism are less Koreans' primary identity than a part of each individual's identity that is constructed and changed according to circumstance. Hosting the World Cup, a soccer battle of the nations, in our own backyard, was a chance for us to test out our skills in negotiating with the international society's racial, ethnic and class diversity. As a matter of fact, Koreans enjoyed the month of June as an extraordinary time of festivities, but were utterly indifferent to the historical experience of the 'Others' who 'bestowed meaning' to the World Cup as a global cultural festival. During the World Cup period, the official 2002 World Cup song, said to have been made with a big budget, could rarely be heard, and the mascot, 'Atmo', quickly vanished from our memories. Korean TV broadcasts of games held in Japan, the co-host of the World Cup, were exceedingly few, as with games of the Japanese team. This situation was aggravated as the Korean team kept up its winning streak and all the broadcasting stations continued sending out reruns of games won by the Korean team. Koreans spent one month listening to Yun Do-Hyun Band's '*Oh! Pil-Seung* (Must Win) Korea' and 'Arirang', along with Jo Su-Mee's 'Victory'. At the moment when the win of the Korean team was confirmed, Koreans completely forgot about the composure we should keep as the hosting country. With every increase of street 'cheerers', from 500,000 for the game against Poland, 770,000 for the US, 2,790,000 for Portugal, 4,200,000 for Italy, 5,000,000 for Spain, and 7,000,000 for Germany, and still 2,100,000 for Turkey, the Korean media's ethnocentric narrowness was reinforced and, as one pours one's love over one's own children, Korean people's love for their own team seemed to know no limits. This 2002 World Cup was historically an unfamiliar experience in that there was a tremendously large amount of spontaneous participation, not mobilized by the state. But even then, the old habit of the country, of executing collective performance in national unison based on narcissism, was repeated, tainting the newness of the experience.

President Shin In-cheol of the Red Devils, when asked what was the reason Koreans loved soccer so much, answered that '(soccer) has a strong nationalistic tendency and maybe that fits the Korean people well' (Kwon and Kim 2002: 8). Just like the rest of the country, Korean women did not hesitate to be united with symbols such as 'nation' and 'state'. Their insatiable heterosexual hollers for the Korean soccer team, changing stadiums with each game, were readily 'translated' into 'patriotism' and 'love for the country'. These women did not have to worry about how their enthusiasm might be viewed by the men of their country, or by strict feminists. No one was going to blame them as being vulgar or foolish for screaming, shouting out that the soccer players were 'hot', or that they 'loved them'. The women who had been constantly forced into feelings of moral inferiority for admiring and idolizing stars, were accepted by society in their union with symbols of 'patriotism'. Shouting *Dae-Han Min Guk* (which means the Republic of Korea, Note of Cheering)', feeling the energy rush and tears come to their eyes, they were in the process of acknowledging themselves as bonded with the state.

In Korea's long history of male-centric nationalism, women have been viewed as having strong individual aspirations but lacking national consciousness. In the elitist historical view of Korean men, nationalism or patriotism has been only recognized when displayed within the public sphere, through political and organized activities. Women naturally accepted the concepts of the nation, state and nationalism as the only, and all-encompassing, way to 'loving the country'. As long as nationalism and patriotism were defined as male concepts, women's experiences could not but take extraneous or discontinuous forms. Women who showed wild enthusiasm for the male soccer players in the World Cup might draw contempt after all for their individual, bourgeois, temporary and extravagant way of practising patriotism. But the new patriotism by the new generation is, unlike the exclusive and collective ethnocentrism, an expression of their national identity without feelings of inferiority. Instead of being tied up in highbrow nationalistic images, they advocate the 'ism' while being mindful of 'style'. The compassion shown by the cheering crowd toward players in the Korea–Turkey quarter-final was an expression of this new patriotism. Called 'open-minded patriotic spirit and flexible nationalism' (Kim Chan-Hee 2002: 8), new patriotism was the framework for the relationship women forged with the state in the 2002 World Cup.

But if Korean women's enthusiasm had mostly been directed at handsome Western soccer players, such as England's Beckham or Owen, Portugal's Figu, Italy's Toti or Spain's Morientes, the situation would have been drastically different. That they zealously applauded Hiddinck, a Dutch male and the director of the Korean team, seemingly too much of a 'father' for them to desire sexual union with, and the familiar handsome guys of Korea such as Ahn Jeong-Hwan, Kim Nam-Il and Song Jong-Guk, must have been the chief reason for the positive response the Korean women fans got from the rest of the society. The story that they came to like Kim Nam-Il because he 'stood his ground', one on nine against American players, is commended as a healthy response of indigenous Koreans who are no longer scared of, or feel small next to, the West. The attitude of the Korean media that looks down on Japanese women for expressing their love for Beckham and treats them as '*ppasun-is*', clearly shows what line the Korean women should not dare cross. This World Cup, which ended up as a worshipping of the 23 *taegeuk* warriors, delineates the limitations as Korean women rose up as the subjects of their own sexual desires. This is a society in which there is still a strong belief in the sexual union of the full bloods: for the women to collectively root for Ronaldo or Morientes, there is too much at stake. It is so much easier to shout out that they want the 'yellow bodies' of our own race rather than 'white and black bodies'. Hence, the happy union of women's sexual desires and new patriotism in the 2002 World Cup.

The symbol of 'women' in the global era

After one month of temporary leave during which the old barriers of 'discriminations of gender, region and age' were suspended, Korean society still calls the soccer players '*taegeuk* warriors'. Should the women of Korea, who have no chance of reaching the status of the Great Absolute warriors, be content to go on living as the 'hot blooded cheering warriors'? What women actually want is a society where they are given recognition and acknowledgement as their individual selves, not as 'daughters of the Great Korea', nor as followers of '*taegeuk* warriors'. In fact, discourses about the World Cup and women illustrate well how this era is mediating in the formation of women's subjectivity.

The global era is one in which images and desires incessantly moving across boundaries are being circulated and consumed, creating diverse meanings. The World Cup is no longer a competition for victory between nations, but a prominent global cultural product. Women are consumers and active buyers of this product, who construct specific 'gendered experiences'. Women acquire global identities and incorporate new opportunities and images, getting beyond the local parochialism, which restricts the basis of their lives. In this World Cup, women demonstrated their passions and desires collectively, outside of the self-censorship and supervision they have grown accustomed to in the patriarchy-regulated system.

This World Cup created a 'Dynamic Korea', replacing Korea's internationally established image of rigidity with those of liveliness and passion. Some scholars and opinion-makers are lending full support to this trend, claiming that utilization of women's labour force should be raised to the global level, to reach the goal of 'quarter-finalist for gender equality' (Lee In-Shil 2002: 7). Bitter self-criticisms ensue about the low ranking of Korea in the GEM (Gender Empowerment Measures), a widely accepted criterion of a state's development level. As such, it is recognized that despite women's sufficient strengths and aspirations for equality, they are not able to claim their place as subjects of society, for they do not have the political and economic power (Kim Ji-Young 2002: 6). A government official has recently claimed that he will support 'women labour force' development through policy measures to ensure that the zeal and potential manifested by women in the cheers find an adequate space for utilization (Kim Dong-Ho 2002: 25).

All this provides an answer to the question of 'why did the young women's potential and abilities have to be let out as "sexual energy"?' Who were the countless women who poured out onto the streets of City Hall, Gwanghwamoon, and JamShil? Had there been workplaces for them to go back to? When gender discrimination in public areas such as the labour market and politics is still powerfully all-pervasive, Korean women often feel helpless in thinking that change won't come easily. Their sense of devastation leads to displays of resistance and subversiveness in 'private areas' such as sexuality. Sexuality and intimacy lend themselves to being viewed as the only arena where the women can affect a measure of change through their will or emotions. In this respect, Korean women's rapid sexual subjectification demonstrates, on the one hand, the power to transform and, on the other, a collective sense of powerlessness. In Korean society, which has achieved economic growth at an incredible speed – to the extent of becoming the first Asian country to host the World Cup – women are under structural conditions to express their subjectivity only through channels of physical exercise, zeal for education, and experimenting with their sexualization. This situation of women attests to the emptiness of their country's modernization 'revolution'. As long as Korean society fails to come up with measures for recognizing each woman's individuality, the women's sexual progressiveness is a source of transformation as well as just another repetition of historical habit.

If Korea made full use of the vitality and civil consciousness of its women in this 2002 World Cup to raise its state image, what can it do as a state for women in return? Will women always be used and mobilized just as 'symbols' and 'images'? Before we take complacent satisfaction in the fact that the whole world has been applauding Korea's non-violent, non-hooligan-filled World Cup, should we not lend sufficient evaluation and reflective interpretation to efforts made by women in the whole process of this festival? The 2002 World Cup should not stop at being a past case of temporary and suspended space of liberation for women and youth. It should be brought into the construction of a global civil society where women and the young generation may become the main agents both in their workplaces and life spaces.

Notes

1 The original version of this paper was published in Korean by *Contemporary Criticism* 당대비평 , Vol. 20, 2002.
2 Numerous newspaper articles reported this as follows; *Jung-Ang Ilbo* 중앙일보 , 3 July 2002: 25; *Segye Ilbo* 세계일보 , 21 June, 2002: 6; *Chosun Ilbo* 조선일보 , 3 July, 2002: 11 and etc.
3 This term of '*Oppa* (Older Brother) *Budae* (Squad),' widely used in Korea, refers to teenage girls who form a kind of fan club in their pursuit of male idol stars. These girls follow their male idols wherever they may perform or to whichever shows they may appear in, calling them *Oppa* and rooting for them with all their might. This phenomenon of collective women's fandom first appeared in the 1980s with devoted women fans of the Korean male singer, Cho Yong-Pil.
4 I use the term 'fandom' defined by John Fiske (1996) which indicates a certain group of people who actively incorporate into their own subculture the specific genre, artists, performers that they like.
5 The name, Red Devils, was decided one and half years after the organizing of the soccer club. The original name is said to have been 'Great *Hankuk* Supporters Club' (Ko 2002: 17, 31).
6 Song Jong-Guk, a Korean soccer player who was particularly popular among women, had been an ordinary player of the Busan ICONS team within the Korean league, receiving only 24 million won per year. After the World Cup, he was scouted by a Netherlands pro team, becoming a world star of considerable yearly pay.

References

Ahn, Min-Seok 안민석 (2002) 'Succession of the World Cup achievements as a civil society: building a new ground and large framework through sports clubs' 시민사회 체육적 관점에서 본 월드컵 평가 , *What has the World Cup Left Us* 월드컵은 우리 사회에 무엇을 남겼나 , World Cup Evaluations Forum hosted by Policy Research Institute for Democratic Society, Citizens Association for Cultural Reform, and Citizens Association for Sports.

Ehrenreich, Barbara, Hess, Elizabeth, and Jacobs, Gloria (1986) *Re-Making Love: The Feminization of Sex*, New York: Archor Books, Doubleday.

Fiske, John (1996) 'The cultural economy of fandom'. In Lisa A. Lewis (ed.) *The Adoring Audience-Fan Culture and Popular Media*, London & New York: Routledge, 187–209.

Ho, Josephine (2001) 'From "Spice Girls" to "compensated dating" – sexualization of Taiwanese teenage girls', *Yonsei Women's Journal* 7: 63–86.

Hong, Sung-Tae 홍성태 (2002) 'The social formation and significance of the "Red Devils phenomenon"' "붉은악마" 현상의 사회적 형성과 의미, *What has the World Cup Left Us* 월드컵은 우리 사회에 무엇을 남겼나, World Cup Evaluations Forum hosted by Policy Research Institute for Democratic Society, Citizens Association for Cultural Reform, and Citizens Association for Sports, 40.

Kim, Chan-Hee 김찬희 (2002) 'Post-World Cup – Korean power goes global' 포스트-월드컵-한국의 힘, 세계로 간다, *Kuk-Min Ilbo* 국민일보, 4 July: 8.

Kim, Dong-Ho 김동호 (2002) 'Women's potential confirmed through street cheers, says Hyeon Jeong-Taek, Vice Minister of Gender Equality' 거리응원통해 여성 잠재력 확인-현정택 여성부 차관, *Jung-Ang Ilbo* 중앙일보, 3 July: 25.

Kim, Eun-Hyung 김은형 (2002) 'Kim Nam-Il, raw as is!' 김남일, *Hankyoreh 21* 날것 그대로21 419 (August): 24–27.

Kim, Ji-Young 한겨레 (2002) 'World Cup's women: subjects or crowd?' 월드컵 여성 주체 또는 군중, *Kyeong-Hyang Shinmun* 경향신문, 23 July: 6.

Ko, Yu-Soo 구유수 (2002) *Red Devils* 붉은 악마들, Seoul: Leaders.

Kwon, Tae-Ho and Kim Yang-Joong 권태호, 김양중 (2002) 'Restricted communality recovered through street cheering' 거리 응원 통해 억눌렸던 공동체성 회복, *Hankyoreh Shinmun* 한겨레 신문, 2 July 2: 28.

Lee, Dong-Yeon 이동연 (2002) 'Carnival culture and the task of civil movement' 카니발 문화와 시민운동의 과제, *What has the World Cup Left Us* 월드컵은 우리 사회에 무엇을 남겼나, World Cup Evaluations Forum hosted by Policy Research Institute for Democratic Society, Citizens Association for Cultural Reform, and Citizens Association for Sports, 9 July: 53.

Lee, In-Shil 이인실 (2002) 'Let gender equality go "4th finalists" as well!' 남녀평등도, *Mun-Hwa Ilbo* 강 가자, 27 July: 7.

Martinez, Dolores (1998) 'Gender, shifting boundaries and global cultures', in D. P. Martinez (ed.) *The Worlds of Japanese Popular Culture*, Cambridge, UK: Cambridge University Press, 1–18.

Sohn, Min-Ho 문화일보 (2002) 'Cute badness, the "I love Kim Nam-Il" phenomenon' 손민호, "I love 귀여운 불량기" 현상, *Joong-Ang Ilbo* 중앙일보, 26 July 26: 45.

Stivens, Maila (1998), 'Theorising gender, power and modernity in affluent Asia', in Krishna Sen and Maila Stivens (eds) *Gender and Power in Affluent Asia*, London & New York: Routledge, 1–34.

Yang, Sung-Hee 양성희 (2002) 'World Cup "cute guys shock"/waking up women's "basic instincts"' 월드컵, 꽃미남 쇼크/여성의 원초적 본능을 깨우다, *Mun-Hwa Ilbo* 문화일보, 21 June 21: 27.

Chapter 26

The power of circulation

Digital technologies and the online Chinese fans of Japanese TV drama

Kelly Hu

The wave of Japanese TV dramas in the mid-to-late 1990s covered the whole of the Southeast Asian region, with the greatest influence in societies with a Chinese population.[1] The main appeals of Japanese TV 'trendy' dramas to Asian audiences are the young people's stories of love, work, friendship and consumerism in the metropolis, which operates in the cognitive frames of the cultural proximity between Japan and other Asian countries (Iwabuchi 2005: 23–26). In addition, Asian modernity is 'synchronously and contemporaneously' experienced by Asian audiences through the viewing of Japanese TV dramas (Iwabuchi 2004: 15). From other perspectives, Japanese TV drama in general symbolizes the high-quality scripts and expensive TV production that also demonstrate the greater advance of Japanese modernity and consumerism (Ko 2004: 420–424; Lee 2004: 135–144). As early as 1993, Taiwan pioneered the fever for Japanese TV dramas whether in legal or pirated form and Hong Kong, China, Singapore and Malaysia have followed in its footsteps. In addition, it is not surprising to find that some Chinese fans may live in Western countries, such as the US, Canada, Britain and Australia. Up to the present (2004), the steady demand for Japanese TV dramas has created a niche market catering for a certain Chinese audience that is consistently interested in watching Japanese TV dramas.

Here, let me mainly focus on a brief review of the way in which Taiwan established itself in the legal and illegal reproduction base of Japanese TV dramas, since Taiwan is acknowledged as possessing the richest sources for distributing Japanese TV drama, and has taken the strongest lead in the enthusiastic pirating of Japanese TV dramas of all the Asian societies. The release of Japanese TV dramas in Taiwan began with the authorized channels, including satellite TV and Cable TV.[2] Gradually, unlicensed videos of some Japanese TV dramas became available in video rental shops and CD stores. However, in the mid-to-late 1990s, VCD (Video CD), a popular digital technology, which has swept across most Asian countries apart from Japan, became the dominant format, displacing video because of its lightness, miniaturization, relatively low price and ease of duplication and pirating.[3] As the most widespread media technology, VCD has prompted the pirating and wider circulation of Japanese TV dramas among Chinese communities worldwide. So far, Taiwan has been the world's biggest centre for the reproduction of Chinese titles in Japanese TV dramas, in particular as regards pirated versions of Japanese TV dramas in VCD format.

Several points can suggest why the legal system of broadcasting Japanese TV dramas in Taiwan cannot prevent the boom in pirated Japanese VCDs (Hu 2004: 214–215). They may be summarized as follows: first, Japanese TV dramas usually take a long time to be released. The delay before they are broadcast in Taiwan ranges from several months, or half a year, to several years. Secondly, there is not enough Japanese TV drama to meet the demand. Thirdly, since Japanese TV companies have made ample profits from the domestic market, their concern with complicated issues about copyright makes them appear aloof from the overseas markets. It is not uncommon for Japanese copyright owners to refuse to issue copyrights altogether. In addition, some copyright fees may simply be too high for local Taiwanese distributors to pay. Consequently, Taiwanese businessmen must take the initiative in importing and marketing these dramas (Iwabuchi 2001: 59).

Fourthly, the lax state of the copyright agreement between Taiwan and Japan gives Taiwan the privilege of manufacturing a so-called 'B copy' of any Japanese product after 30 days if no other legal Taiwanese agencies secure the right of distribution (Wong 2002). In fact, a 'B copy' literally signifies a 'pirated copy', since the Japanese VCD businessmen can automatically reproduce versions of Japanese TV dramas subtitled in Chinese without having to pay any fees to the Japanese copyright owners. The underground guerrilla, medium/small-size nature of VCD retailer businesses controlled by ethnic Chinese successfully challenges the authority of the Japanese TV marketing strategy.

Even though authorities from Japanese TV stations have sometimes protested against the rampant piracy of Japanese TV dramas in Taiwan, they are rarely determined enough to cope with copyright problems. The Taiwanese government once made a short-lived attempt to smash the piracy, but did not maintain it. Thus, it may be fair to assume that the piracy of Japanese TV drama will continue, since neither the Japanese side nor the Taiwanese side seems to be concerned about it. The original VCDs of Japanese TV dramas are only made in small numbers compared with the massive production of pirated VCDs. The whole set of a Japanese TV drama costs about US$15, while the pirated ones cost from US$5 to US$7. The copyrighted Japanese VCDs are more expensive, with very few options and very delayed supplies. In such a situation, it is no wonder that the consumption of pirated VCDs is so popular among Chinese people.

In this paper, not restricting myself to the topic of pirate capitalist production, I want to go further and to consider how to map the digitalized consumption, distribution and circulation of Japanese TV dramas among Chinese fans online. It will explore the way in which the new digital technologies, including the Internet fan forum, VCDs and the newly developing websites for exchanging audio-visual products such as Japanese TV dramas, open up new possibilities for resistance and flight. This paper seeks to show how online Chinese fans build up enough strength via transnational activities in connection with the audio-visual pirate culture and fan's autonomous production to combat the ineffectiveness of the Japanese distribution system in Southeast Asian countries.

By making a case study of alternative practices in the consumption of Japanese TV dramas by online Chinese fans, we may gain a better understanding of the way in which the Chinese audience, as a 'minority' audience, which is not the one targeted by Japanese capitalists, is forming a global digitalized network based on self-help and sharing. It will reveal how the online Chinese fans create 'subcultural immediacy' centering around 'the flows of information' and use 'the Internet as an environment that supports their attempts to gain and provide access to information' and will also show the sort of audio-visual content presented by Japanese TV dramas, which exists 'beyond the means of control' of the legitimate culture of corporate Japanese TV broadcasting (Kahn and Kellner 2003: 300).

Japan has much powerful capital invested in audio-visual industrial production, which most other Asian countries cannot compete with. It concerns the power relationship between Japan and the Asian societies in the distribution and release of Japanese TV dramas. The present study of online Chinese fans' practices seeks to show that the important issue is less one of straight exploitation and domination; for instance, it is not concerned with Japan's imperialistic exertion of cultural influence on Asia. Nor is it an attempt by online Chinese fans to resist the spread of cultural colonization. Instead, a reverse logic would see the situation as merely the resistance of online Chinese fans to the hierarchic stagnation and exclusion dictated by Japan's apathetic overseas distribution system. That is, we should not be too credulous of the assumption of cultural imperialism, which certainly ignores the complicated issues aroused by globalization.

Globalization has opened up to Chinese fans new possibilities for getting in touch with foreign culture. In the realm of consumption, globalization also reinforces the desire for the other, such as Japanese TV dramas. Hollywood motion picture industries exemplify the global cultural hegemony all over the rest of the world. However, aside from the irresistible blandishments of Hollywood, the audio-visual industries elsewhere in the world may not be so globally ambitious and capable. Exposed to intercultural exchange of information about various audio-visual products from countries other than America, the global audiences may not be able to use products unless they are wrapped up as globally marketable commodities. Under such conditions, 'minority' audiences, such as the online Chinese devotees of Japanese TV dramas, object to passively playing the games set up by capitalist interests. Driven by dissatisfaction with the power of time–space/geographical/institutional limitations, online Chinese fans make immense efforts to claim their equal need to have quick and efficient access to Japanese TV drama. Thus, the present study of online Chinese fans is an attempt to capture and illustrate how people in modernity struggle 'between the conditions' they 'find themselves in and those they both desire and recognize as possibilities' (Tomlinson 1999: 62).

Moreover, I would hope in this paper to bring some new perspectives into studies of the classical fan subculture by emphasizing mostly an analysis of the fans' textual excursions/reinvention, their cult fandom and the meaning-makings of interpretative communities (Ang 1985; Jenkins 1992; Radway 1991). However, studies of the ways in which digital technologies are incorporated into the fan cultures and generate new transnational practices of digital consumption are still ongoing projects, which call for yet more research investment.

My mapping strategy of the transcultural space focuses on two websites – one based in Taiwan and the other in Hong Kong – both of which are supported by Chinese fans of Japanese TV dramas. I shall provide detailed description of these two websites in later sections. The emergence of websites backed by Chinese fans cannot be separated from the popularity of the PC and the Internet in Chinese societies among the digital generation – now ranging in age from the late teens to the 20s and 30s, in particular students and those who need a computer at work. The young digital generation in Asian societies corresponds to the survey finding that Asian audiences of Japanese TV dramas are mostly young people who live in modern urban settings (Iwabuchi 2004:

11). It signifies that the consumption of Japanese TV dramas can be digitalized and grasped through virtual ethnography. Such a technological revolution has allowed Chinese fans to diversify the means and broaden the spaces of their worship of Japanese TV dramas.

'Dorama': resistance, self-help and Chinese transnational networking

From late 2001, I began to observe a Taiwanese fan website 'Dorama', established on 8 January 1999.[4] The website maintainer is a 20-something Taiwanese fan of Japanese TV drama with a major in computing. By 12 January 2005, the record indicated that there had been 5,303,500 hits on the website since 3 February 2001.

This is a website with multiple functions, providing systematic files of Japanese TV dramas, actors/actresses and scriptwriters, free listening to Japanese TV midi music, wallpapers and different sections to allow open interaction for the Internet participants who are interested in Japanese TV dramas.

'Dorama' can be regarded as a virtual space for the social gathering of Chinese fans of Japanese TV dramas from all over the world, even though it is based in Taiwan. The language used in 'Dorama' is mainly Chinese – although it can be further differentiated as follows. Most fans from Taiwan and Hong Kong communicate in traditional Chinese. Sometimes the way in which they write can be perceived as either the Taiwanese or the Hong Kong version of Cantonese oral expression. Fans from China, Singapore or Malaysia may use simplified Chinese writing. Some fans write in English – in some cases perhaps they live in Western countries or they are from Malaysia and Singapore. The Japanese language is also used in some of the topics, conversations and drama documents, or Japanese-language news reports about TV stars and TV dramas may even be posted.

'Dorama' reflects the spontaneity of fandom. The maintainer always keeps up with the documentation of the latest Japanese TV dramas/stars and the weekly schedule of Japanese TV dramas broadcast on Japanese-language cable TV in Taiwan. In addition, the 'just-in-time' feedback to the viewing echoes the simultaneity generated by online interactivity. The development of a cyberspace online fan club significantly reinforces the audience's eager pursuit of time-space compression and speed so as to catch up with Japan. The instant circulation of information among fans on the website about the latest Japanese TV dramas in a sense substitutes for the lack of powerful capitalist motivation from the Japanese distributors. In most circumstances, fans' mutual exchanges of updated Japanese TV drama news in cyberspace can spread faster and more efficiently than any commercialized marketing from Cable TV channels broadcasting Japanese programmes or even from Japanese VCD business pirates. In addition, the release of pirated Japanese VCDs is mostly quicker than any legal broadcasting. The main problems are that the advertising of both the legal and illegal distribution of Japanese TV dramas is always lagging behind Japan's. Moreover, it is impossible for underground pirated VCDs to be openly promoted through official channels. It is thus necessary for fans to actively keep up with the pirate market. Interestingly, online fans are found to be the best promoters of the information released about pirated VCDs, through the wide interconnectivity of the Internet.

In 'Dorama', among the most frequently asked questions are where and how to get VCDs of Japanese TV dramas. 'Dorama' has specified a hyperlink entitled 'shopping', which lists online VCD shops and VCD markets in different cities in Taiwan and Hong Kong. Some other questions on VCDs concern the places to shop for them in countries such as Malaysia, Singapore and Canada. In addition, online VCD stores and Yahoo auction websites are much patronized since they are convenient access points for Chinese fans worldwide. The Internet as a digital technology of global information flows thus corresponds with VCD as a miniaturized and portable consumer digital technology – both are dedicated to the availability and flexibility so much desired by the Chinese fans of Japanese TV dramas. VCD and the Internet enable the restructuring of time–space, in terms of distributing, circulating and consuming Japanese TV dramas, in forms that can be appropriated by online Chinese fans for their own logic and convenience.

As stated earlier, Taiwan is a fearless pirating kingdom for the production of Chinese-subtitled Japanese TV dramas. However, this situation was imperilled once Taiwan was 'upgraded' to membership of the WTO (the World Trade Organization) in 2002. Since then, copyright problems have become a sensitive area. According to the WTO's official website, it is 'the only global international organization dealing with the rules of trade between nations. At its heart are the WTO agreements, negotiated and signed by the bulk of the world's trading nations and ratified in their parliaments. The goal is to help producers of goods and services, exporters and importers conduct their business.'[5] Thus, after joining the WTO, Taiwan would need to have fair trade practices with Japan and all Japanese products would be under legal protection in Taiwan.

The Taiwanese government had been lax about piracy before joining the WTO but in 2002 it started to crackdown occasionally on factories and shops dealing in pirated VCDs. The efforts invested in cleaning up piracy were in the nature of a demonstration on the part of the Taiwanese government – to show the whole world that it had done its best to eradicate piracy and carry out self-regulation. According to my observations between 2002 and 2004, however, Taiwan still has a leading position in the pirated Japanese VCD trade, even though it retreated for several months in 2002. The Taiwan-based pirated VCD companies were indeed under threat and they gradually cut the level of VCD production.

In early 2002, the Japanese VCD companies in Taiwan announced that they would no longer release the latest season's Chinese-subtitled Japanese TV dramas. This was shocking and sad news to most of their Chinese fans. They became panic-stricken at the prospect of the Taiwanese VCD production collapsing,[6] since they would lose the privilege of having quick and convenient access to Japanese TV dramas at the least cost, which no legal distributor could match. 'The most powerful impact of Taiwan's involvement with the WTO is that there would not be any new Japanese TV dramas', a fan said (Xiao–Yu 2002). Another fan complained, 'There are few legal copies of Japanese TV dramas in VCD format available, even if I wanted to support copyrighted products' (Miller 2001).

In June 2004, 'Dorama' focused on questions about whether the marketing of pirated Japanese VCDs could survive in Taiwan under the intimidating new law. The two years from 2002 to June 2004 were a cushioning time to allow both businessmen and consumers to reconcile themselves to the fact that Japanese VCDs were illegal. On the forum of 'Dorama', one fan protests that it is indeed painful for people like him to wait for 1 or 2 years, or even longer, to watch Japanese TV dramas under copyright (Salt 2004). Since June 2004, other fans have begun to discuss what would they do if pirated Japanese VCDs disappeared. If the price of legal VCDs was fair, they would be able to afford them. However, if the price were too high, the alternative would be to form alliances – that is, for fans to club together to buy Japanese VCDs and then to burn copies for private circulation (Ah-Xian 2004). All of those signs show that there has been a steady resistance to the unavailability of Japanese TV dramas, a resistance that might continue.

In late April 2002 there was the unexpected news that V-BOX, a Malaysia-based company, had started to distribute Japanese TV dramas.[7] Consequently, Malaysian Chinese fans who had noticed this turning of the tide began to recommend commercial websites where Japanese VCDs could be bought. Following the intense discussions on 'Dorama' by fans from different countries, a new geography for the distribution and circulation of the latest Japanese VCDs can be vaguely mapped in the processes of deterritorialization and reterritorialization. Apparently, these processes occurred during Taiwan's retreat when Malaysia leaped to the forefront in distributing Japanese VCDs. Based on the information exchanged among online fans on 'Dorama', those Japanese VCDs released in Malaysia flowed into the pirate markets of the nearest countries – Singapore, Hong Kong and even cities with a high Chinese population in Canada such as Vancouver.[8]

Although it is not certain whether the mysterious production bases have actually moved to Malaysia or elsewhere, at least it is clear that the sudden and temporary shifting of dominance in the pirate markets from Taiwan to Malaysia has made the Malaysian Chinese fans more visible in 'Dorama' than they used to be and further intensifies their sense of belonging to a community. The emergence of Malaysia as a site from which to obtain Japanese TV dramas somehow undermined the overriding status of Taiwan and injected fresh energy into 'Dorama' from these new transnational interactions. Several Malaysian Chinese fans started to chat online regularly in order to pick up local information, such as where they could buy Japanese VCDs in Kuala Lumpur. A discussion forum, 'Japanese TV dramas, good!', originally set up by a Malaysian Chinese fan, has attracted fans from Malaysia, Singapore, Hong Kong, Taiwan, Canada and America and has lasted from late April 2002 until the present (2005).

Messages were posted, either looking for new Japanese VCDs or asking for exchange offers.[9] Through online negotiations, fans reached agreement over VCD exchanges. Some fans in Hong Kong and Taiwan ordered new Japanese VCDs from the cyber VCD shops in Malaysia at a much higher price than they had been paying, because of the additional postal fees. In the case of 'Dorama', fans in Singapore or Malaysia got new Japanese TV dramas in exchange for old Japanese TV dramas that Taiwanese fans could already get in Taiwan. Another arrangement was that fans from different countries owning different new Japanese VCD dramas would burn copies of their own VCDs and send them to each other by post.

The drop in the costs of CD/VCD recording and DVD recording technology has encouraged the private burning and circulation of VCDs. Fans who receive copies of updated Japanese VCDs from abroad may pass them around to their friends and increase their chances of reproducing even more Japanese VCDs. The following related cheap and flexible digital technologies – PC, VCD, VCD players, DVD/VCD compatible players, VCD/DVD computer software for viewing on PC and CD or DVD rewriters – are popular among Chinese young people living in a number of Asian societies.

As shown in above examples, the ardent fans instantly spread the news of where these discs could be bought, through the global interconnections of the Internet and the common practice of VCD reduplication. Because of the shortage of Japanese TV drama in Taiwan, one way to deal with the problem is for online Chinese fans, as an 'interpretative community', to invent 'their own internal dynamics' in the circulation of Japanese TV dramas, which would be different from the local viewing culture in Japan (Lee and LiPuma 2002: 192). Online Chinese fans have experimented vigorously in exploring the fluidity and potentiality of transnational trading in the original products via various approaches and even various production locations and travelling trajectories. They have become investigators, tracking down the underground routes of the global pirate links. They have also channelled their emotional frustrations and affection for Japanese TV dramas into a kind of anonymous collective action through self-help, transnational networking and the mediation of digital technologies.

The 'BitTorrent' phenomenon: sharing and autonomous production

In early 2004, on the discussion board of 'Dorama', a topic entitled 'Takuya's latest drama: very good!' activated a new way of access to Japanese TV dramas. Kimura Takuya is one of the most famous TV stars in Japan. *Pride*, a drama in which he stars, has been running since 12 January 2004, and is scheduled to be broadcast in Japan on Fuji TV for 3 months. The main concerns of the discussion in 'Dorama' do not lie only on the story, the actor and performance, but also on getting information about the quickest way of obtaining episodes of *Pride* – downloading from a connecting platform offered by a Hong Kong-based newsgroup website.[10] Newsgroup.com.hk was set up in June 2001 and its goals are to provide a free newsgroup service for Hong Kong citizens and to develop new newsgroup technology.[11] This website is officially in the Chinese language and is free to everyone on the Internet. Inevitably, it has been used by Chinese people all round the world. But from 1 July 2004, Newsgroup.com.hk will begin to charge a fee to people living outside Hong Kong. Newsgroup.com.hk established another newsgroup server, bt.newsgroup.com.hk, in October 2003. Bt.newsgroup.com.hk invites people to post their requests for any audio-visual products over a wide range of categories, including TV dramas from Japan, Korea, Hong Kong/Taiwan/Mainland China, TV commercials, soccer TV documentaries and even technical discussions on the problems of BitTorrent.[12] What is special about this newsgroup is that digital files can only be circulated by a transfer protocol named BitTorrent. BitTorrent was invented in 2003 by Bram Cohen, an American living in California.[13]

> BitTorrent is a protocol designed for transferring files. It is peer-to-peer in nature, as users connect to each other directly to send and receive portions of the file. However, there is a central server (called a tracker) which coordinates the action of all such peers. The tracker only manages connections, it does not have any knowledge of the contents of the files being distributed and therefore a large number of users can be supported with relatively limited tracker bandwidth. The key

philosophy of BitTorrent is that users should upload (transmit outbound) at the same time they are downloading (receiving inbound). In this manner, network bandwidth is utilized as efficiently as possible. BitTorrent is designed to work better as the number of people interested in a certain file increases, in contrast to other file transfer protocols.[14]

According to this description of BitTorrent, it is quite efficient for many people to share files at the same time, which solves the problem of busy servers. BitTorrent is based on the logic of generosity and sharing in order to benefit others by quick and easy distribution and circulation. The more peers there are online to use BitTorrent, the quicker each peer can have his/her files successfully downloaded. Downloading time can be as quick as 3 minutes or as long as several hours or even a day or more, depending on how many peers and seeders there are online. Usually the purveyors provide the BT tracker for the requesters to click into, letting this tracker begin to connect with other peers online. It is important for someone to be the seeder – that is, either the person who is the one who provides the file or those who download the file to 'seed' the files by keeping their computers open. Otherwise, if there were no seeds at all it would be impossible for requesters to download files. Of course, the more seeds there are, the faster the downloading. Peers' 'contribution grows at the same rate as their demand, creating *limitless scalability* for a fixed cost'.[15] It appears that the application of BitTorrent in cheap file distribution certainly encouraged collective downloading, as well as friendly online fan fellowship, which enhances the acts of giving and supplying.

A P2P technology like this has enabled the fans of Japanese TV dramas to explore and practise new types of distribution and consumption through fans' technological support and sympathy in understanding the needs of other fans to follow Japanese TV dramas and even investing in translating the subtitles. In January 2004, a Hong Kong fan, R, who is a skilled Japanese speakers did the Chinese subtitling for *Pride*. The subtitling work is done on a weekly basis as other fans supply each new episode of *Pride* a few days after the original broadcast in Japan. Pirate businessmen cannot compete with such immediacy – since they usually make a Japanese TV drama into a complete set ('package') of VCDs instead of selling each episode at a time.

Attention should be paid to the stylistic injection of R's personal enthusiasm in her Chinese translation. Her subtitling is an individual display of her mastery of language in articulation with her love for the drama. Unlike the pirated version, which hides the translator behind the scenes, R makes it clear that she did the subtitling by giving her name and email contact address. She thanks T and A for their supplies of the raw material, and online fans for their support and suggestions by constructing herself a fan persona, which interacts with those of other fans. Even when she made a mistake in the subtitling, she took care to insert a correction by thanking another fan for pointing out the mistake. The colours in which the subtitles are printed sometimes change according to the situation of the TV text. For example, blue is the normal colour for subtitles, but sometimes it turns into red, when the atmosphere is that of a love scene. R is also a canny and prudent fan for she includes the following statement: 'This version is only for the purpose of friendly exchange. The copyright remains the property of Fuji TV station in Japan. Those who attempt to illegally market this product for commercial purposes must be responsible for possible outcomes.'

The version of R's Chinese subtitling of *Pride* was extremely popular in the Hong Kong newsgroup through its online circulation by means of BitTorrent. As I learned from R, the marketing of another version of *Pride* produced by a Taiwanese-based leading pirated Japanese VCD company seems to be threatened, because R's version has already been so widely circulated among Chinese fans through the Internet.[16] R's achievement has consequently encouraged N, the super fan of Japanese actor Naohito Fujiki, to do the subtitling for another Japanese TV drama *Ito shi kimi he*, which is scheduled to be broadcast from 19 April 2004. As a close friend of N, R persuaded her to make the Chinese translation for the Hong Kong newsgroup and to provide her with technological support in subtitling.

R and N's initiative in subtitling *Pride* in Chinese has been a great success among Chinese fans. Many thanks to them from fans are posted online. The inner passions for drama, fan friendship and performance/self-expression are displayed in the context of this Chinese translation/subtitling; being 'acknowledged by a community of the like-minded is a characteristically romantic structure of feeling' (Streeter 2003: 649). R and N's Chinese subtitling can be regarded as a kind of creative and self-expressive practice in fan subculture, which cannot be regulated and confined by the commercial mechanism. For example, it has never before been the case that a translator of a VCD version of an official release or a pirated version has exposed him/herself by giving a nickname and an email address or by investing emotion as R and N did when they identified themselves as fan translators.

Based on my observation so far in January 2005, there has been consistent and regular online circulation of Chinese subtitled Japanese TV drama made by Chinese fans.[17] Whether this trend of autonomous production in the Chinese subtitling of Japanese TV dramas will continue has yet to be observed. However, it has become an alternative way of viewing Japanese TV dramas, which goes beyond such forms of transmission as legal TV channels or the pirate trading of VCDs. The autonomous production of Japanese TV dramas with Chinese subtitles has emerged as a new sub-cultural practice demonstrating the spirit of DIY and of precious non-commercial sharing through widespread networking.

A student of mine in Taiwan also saw R's version of *Pride*, as some of her friends obtained the files through BitTorrent and put them on an FTP to share with acquaintances. In consequence, either people can view these files on computers, as most university/college students in Taiwan tend to do, or the files can be reproduced as VCD duplications, which can be viewed on TV. A Japanese TV drama can be contained in various digital file formats, such as the 'avi', 'dat' or 'rmvb' formats, etc.

The circulation of most digital files on the Hong Kong newsgroup website must depend on the conversion of pirated Japanese VCDs into digital files so that they can be uploaded and downloaded through the channelling of BitTorrent. That is, the existence of the pirated VCD industry still plays an important role in supplying Chinese subtitled versions, since they can be re-circulated online in the form of digital files. The BitTorrent mechanism of file sharing reinforces the speed of downloading, but also the quick comings and goings of the seeders. As an audio-visual file uses up a great deal of most hard disks, the audience has to consume or preserve them soon, for example, by turning them into VCDs and quickly deleting them from the computer. In the case of the Hong Kong newsgroup, there are many dozens of postings for requests and supplies. Such online circulation is unfocused and instant with sporadic flows of file sharing. For example, a week is perhaps long enough for a helpful fan to act as a seeder. The survival of BitTorrent files containing TV dramas in the Hong Kong newsgroup is normally based on immediacy. Fans have to be keen and sensitive enough to keep tracking down the latest offers.

The BitTorrent method of distributing and circulating Japanese TV drama on cyberspace certainly does not fit into commercial parameters, but is rather supported by the enthusiasm and decisions of fandom. The same distinction is made by Matt Hills: 'to perceive information technology only as a technology of information flow (Jenkins 1995) is to neglect the affective flow and intensification which accompany the process' (Hills 2002: 181). The Hong Kong newsgroup is surrounded by an atmosphere of fandom, active exchange and even heroic fans acting as sources. Some fans are particularly committed in providing BitTorrent trackers with a supply of seeds. They not only respond to the requesting fans, but also volunteer to do so in the spirit of sharing good things without asking anything in return. A few fans with their cyberspace nicknames have become famous, as they can always supply abundant first-hand files.

The online sharing of Japanese TV dramas in audio-visual files has resulted in connections being made between suppliers and recipients. The Internet exchange 'incorporates opportunities for messaging and chat that allow reconfiguration to new forms of connection between consumers (and purveyors)' (Jones 2002: 222). A certain form of fan community ethos is displayed here – it becomes a ritual for recipients to politely/sincerely request and express thanks to suppliers and consequently the suppliers win recognition from other fans. In addition, the constant logging on to the Hong Kong newsgroup by people either providing or searching for Japanese TV dramas may be regarded as a kind of routinized 'ritual' performed by Chinese fans on cyberspace. As it appears, the online sharing of digital files of Japanese TV dramas constitutes an interactive virtual fan community network and multidimensional reception and feedback.

Indeed, the rise of the BitTorrent phenomenon in the circulation of Japanese TV drama signifies the importance of computer literacy for various kinds of software uses. Chinese fans surfing on the Hong Kong newsgroup certainly belong to the 'class' that is at least capable of learning to manage the technical problems with basic technological facilities. The technological class made up mostly of students or people at work who are familiar with computers may be distinguished from other fans who may be poor in terms of cultural and material capital by their use of technology, even though PCs and the Internet are popular tools for information consumption in both households and worksites generally in Hong Kong and Taiwan and the richer regions of China.

In the case of online fans joining the Hong Kong newsgroup, the love for Japanese TV dramas may create an extra incentive for them to learn to apply technological knowledge, such as the main functions of BitTorrent, its technical terms, how to upload and download Japanese TV dramas via the BitTorrent tracker, or even how to convert VCD into digital files with different formats or how to convert different formats of digital files into VCD. These are the basic concepts for fans to grasp in order to participate in the virtual exchange community, to get the sources they want and to understand the conversational content that mixes information about Japanese TV dramas with technological questions. That is, fans are compelled to learn more about computer software and the mechanism of technological operations.

Apart from the Hong Kong newsgroup, which carves out multiple spaces for the circulation of audio-visual files, some other China-based BitTorrent websites have similar audio-visual exchanges, which also include Japanese TV dramas. For example, several websites claim that they want to reach Chinese people worldwide and can provide ample amounts of audio-visual products.[18] They have wanted very much to recruit people who have good, strong technological capacity in offering FTP, recording TV programmes from Hong Kong, Taiwan, China, Japan, America and Europe, supplying TV programmes that can be transferred into VCDs and DVDs and even works to be subtitled in Chinese. Like what happened in the Hong Kong newsgroup, more and more Japanese TV dramas with Chinese subtitles are made without any commercial purpose; they originated from these China-based websites with BitTorrent functions and are circulated to other websites. Bold as it may seem, these China-based websites have the global ambition to burst through any territorial bondage, with an idealistic notion of autonomous production and self-help through Internet networking.

My updated observations indicate that so far (January 2005), several China-based BitTorrent websites have emerged as the new and powerful suppliers of Chinese-subtitled Japanese TV dramas online.[19] For example, there is 'tvbt.com', one of the most popular websites, which is sophisticated in setting up a division of labour specializing in the Chinese subtitling of Japanese TV dramas – it has even expanded to produce traditional Chinese subtitles since, in the past, only simplified Chinese subtitles were available.[20] It can be supposed that there might be trans-border collaborations between online fans of Japanese TV dramas from China and Hong Kong/Taiwan to produce both simplified and traditional Chinese subtitles, since I saw a Chinese fan C travelling between Hong Kong newsgroups and 'tvbt.com'. C has been always enthusiastic about transferring original 'rmvb' format into 'meg' format, as 'rmvb' files can only be seen on computer, while 'meg' files can be compatible to VCD burning.

This is a sign that China is intimately connected with the frequent and broad uses of BitTorrent. The windows for the legal broadcasting of Japanese TV dramas do not seem to be widely opened up in China. From the evidence of this study, it seems to be the case that the DIY practices in the Chinese subtitling of Japanese TV dramas involved with Chinese transnationalism have been very considerably empowered by BitTorrent, a P2P technology. At the moment, China's access to Japanese TV drama, which is very much marginalized as regards legal channels compared to Taiwan, has now escalated, facilitated by digital technologies, to a level which can become a non-commercial alternative/counterpart to Taiwan, the present dominant pirate capital in Japanese VCD productions.

The BitTorrent phenomenon among Chinese communities reveals the significance of transnational technological cultural reshaping, digital circulation and the globalizing impulse. That is, receiving audio-visual programmes from various countries does not have to be attached, as it traditionally was, to fixed TV schedules and VCR recording. Undoubtedly, new P2P protocols such as BitTorrent, in correlation with the digital technologies, have radically transformed the structural oppressions/exclusions from TV or theatre, cinema and distributors' marketing strategies with the result that audio-visual contents can be multiplied and can move more smoothly and freely across various geographical boundaries, to be consumed by audiences at low cost and sooner than before.

New spaces in circulation, distribution and consumption

Thanks to the convergence of digital technologies – VCD, CD-R/DVD-R burners, PC and the Internet – the fans of Japanese TV dramas have consolidated Chinese trans-national networking, which was established on the basis of self-help and mutual trust. Piracy, online VCD stores, cyber fan clubs, BitTorrent-based websites, informal inter-connection and private VCD burning channelled through multiple digital technologies offer resistance both to uncaring Japanese TV stations and attacks on pirated Japanese VCDs by the Taiwanese government. As it appears, the culture of circulating Japanese TV dramas has linked together the endless circles of digitalized production/consumption.

Timothy D. Taylor maintains that 'flexibility' is 'what made the difference historic-ally', as testified in the historical development of cassette and MP3 (Taylor 2001: 23). Both cassettes and MP3, despite their inferior sound, are extremely popular because of their flexibility. Unlike the situation in Japan, the adaptation of Japanese TV dramas into pirated VCDs and unauthorized online downloads can also be seen as the operation of flexibility in the digitalization, distribution and circulation of audio-visual products in the contexts of Chinese societies.

Steve Jones well argues in his observations on the online distribution of music that:

> Developments in digital audio and of the Internet have meant that the placement of a musical commodity into the hands of the consumer or the media is at least for the time being no longer exclusively under the control of, or even in the realm of, the music industry, whether retail or wholesale.
>
> (Jones 2002: 220)

Jones' statement may bring us to reflect on the online exchange of audio-visual products. Audio-visual products, although they may appear to be less easy to circulate online than audio music, since they may require much more time and more computer capacity to download, have the potential to develop along similar lines to the digitalized transformation of music. The network technologies associated with the distribution of Japanese TV dramas can be seen as 'technologies of *geography* and, in turn, of *audiences*' and fans (Jones 2002: 214). That is, these technologies are concerned with the breaking down of the geographical borders that once restrained cultural imports and exports according to the decisions of media controllers.

In Shinobu Price's survey of the cross-cultural phenomenon of American fans' reception and consumption of Japanese anime, she also discovered American fans' alternative practices, which are somewhat similar to what has been observed in Chinese fan communities. 'Strangely enough, anime basically owes much of its popularity in the US to "illegal" transactions such as bootlegging, pirating and unauthorized distrib-ution' (Price 2001: 161). Perhaps it is not so strange; if unauthorized products are not easily attainable or they are not satisfactory enough in term of distribution speed or the content of the translation, inevitably they become the object of pirating or auton-omous production, in the form of underground marketing or exchange.

From pirated VCDs in real life to the online circulation of digital files converted from pirated VCDs, we may say that, to a certain degree, the Chinese fans of Japanese TV dramas and pirate capitalism live through one another. For good or ill, pirated Japanese VCD capitalism is still the most powerful centre of efficiently produced Chinese-subtitled Japanese TV dramas. The dominant Chinese subtitling operations of the pirate organization tighten the connection between the fans and the pirate market. Fans, although they seem to have capitulated to the pirate market, have begun to connect with each other in the online circulation of converted VCD versions, which can further lead to the burning of private VCDs. Even though the online circulation of digital files still depends heavily on pirated VCDs, paradoxically the innumerable personal duplications of downloaded versions of pirated VCDs may in a sense jeopardize the profits of pirating and prevent the total manipulation of the pirate industry.

In a different transnational context from Japan, online Chinese fans' alternative modes of consumption and distribution draw our attention to the restructuring of the modes of circulation of Japanese TV dramas when mediated by different digital technologies. The power of circulation does exist, although it may be fragmented, dispersed and mobile. The majority of online fans use nicknames instead of real names. It is a way of avoiding public disclosure and of securing a sense of privacy, although such characteristics of the online community are not restricted to the online fan community only. The actions of online Chinese fans and their use of virtual identities may easily escape the law and allow them to remain hidden with a sense of security behind borderless cyberspace.

The uncertainty generated by the characteristics of cyberspace impels us to think about how to define the sort of fan activities portrayed in this study. Several factors should be taken into consideration: digital technology, globalization and the cyber fan community, Chinese ethnicity and resistance. As Mark Poster argues, 'the conditions of globalization' 'include the linking of human and machine'. 'The new "community" will not be a replica of the agora but it will be mediated by information machines' (Poster 2002: 4). Echoing the importance of understanding the human/machine interface which plays a role in the shaping of the new global communities, I also want to reframe the questions proposed by Poster: 'Can the new media promote the construction of new political forms not tied to historical, territorial powers?' and 'What are the characteristics of new media that promote new political relations and new political subjects?' (Poster 2002: 6). Here I would like to reflect on an implicit question posed by this study: are those fans 'political subjects' who have invented new forms of political action?

We may say that the practices of online fans construct a kind of Chinese transnationalism. The Chinese transnationalism portrayed in this study is not the version that celebrates capitalist Chinese modernities (Ong and Nonini 1997), but rather something which signifies the capacity of Chinese subjects to link up with one another through consumerism and circulation. Chinese ethnicity does play a part in Chinese transnationalism – it refers to the fact that the sharing of the Chinese language and a similar taste for popular culture mobilizes online Chinese fans to set in motion transnational practices. In this case study, such a creation on the part of Chinese ethnicity is not predestined but is 'a moment of self-construction' through cyberspace and pirate networking and 'a sort of practice fitting with a thickening global landscape' (Poster 2001: 149).

Castells precisely points out the new types of social movement in a network society as follows:

> *They are actual producers and distributors, of cultural codes.* Not only over the Net, but in their multiple forms of exchange and interaction. Their impact on the society rarely stems from a concerted strategy and masterminded by a center.
>
> (Castells 1997: 362)

The efforts of online Chinese fans may fit awkwardly into the model of social movement. However, the above remarks by Castells can inspire us to think again about fans' online practices, as illustrated in this study. Admittedly, neither clear political claims nor a call for collective Chinese identity were put forward in the activities of the online Chinese fans in this study. In Alberto Melucci's theorization on new social movement, he notes that 'the actors' own beliefs will not provide a sufficient ground for an account of their actions, for such beliefs always depend on the broader relations in which the actors are involved' (Melucci 1996: 15). This study is not intended to draw precise answers from online Chinese fans of Japanese TV drama about how they are politically aware of their actions, which are apparent violations justified by how little the legal channels could offer. Through regular online observations, I will argue that the resistance of Chinese fans can be seen as 'political' since they have "unwittingly" achieved a "political" outcome, regardless of whether this was their intention or not.

As pointed out earlier, some online fans have complained of the inaccessibility of Japanese TV drama and show us their self-help networking in overcoming the restrictions. Moreover, online Chinese fans identify themselves as BitTorrent users who are engaged with circulating and transferring the digital files either for the sake of convenience/low-cost consumption or because they cannot bear to be left behind. From the wider perspective, online Chinese fans are involved – whatever their individual reasons for consuming pirated VCDs and exchanging downloaded files – and their behaviours have certainly disregarded and challenged the legitimate sources.

Such actions 'are consisted on behalf of autonomous sources of meaning' (Castells 1997: 65) – these Chinese people exist as fans who are able to act to obtain what they desire instead of being trapped in helplessness and at the mercy of legal distributors. It is hard to predict if such fan actions could be consistent per se, or consistent for the same group of people on the Internet. Perhaps this exactly corresponds to the issues of the new media technologies addressed by Mark Poster: Internet activity may launch new forms of political struggle. The characteristics of such struggles could be more or less decentralized and anonymous without any certain direction.

Online Chinese fans hanging on in the unidentified flows could be identified as the promoters and inventors of an alternative subculture, which integrates fan culture with digital culture and includes human/machine interactivity, transnational links and the spirit of autonomous production. As shown above, the fan activities signify that the capitalist production-based modes of capitalism should be re-examined.

> The contemporary processes of globalization demonstrate that capitalism, in its cycles of creative destruction and resurrection, has again reinvented itself. It is in transition from a production-centric system to one whose primary dynamic is circulation. The process is occurring with unprecedented speed – an acceleration that is intrinsic to this reinvention.
>
> (Lee and LiPuma 2002: 191–213)

This study indicates that the circulation of Japanese TV dramas in its various forms is unquestionably out of control and dislocated from its original standardized TV production and distribution. The power of circulation excites an endless desire to go beyond the boundary and to carve out new spaces of consumption. Online Chinese fans are engaged in multiple ways of transforming unauthorized audio-visual products into diversified versions of technological consumer products. They attempt to overcome and master new cultural/consumer technological space through competing means of circulation, connection and mapping. Such a tendency can be characterized as 'the production of space' and a 'force working towards the simultaneous transcendence and disruption of immobility and coherence' (Morley and Robins 1995: 30). This case study testifies that the expansion of space and the yearning for simultaneity/mobility in globalization are not the privileges restricted to capitalist forms of production, but are also turning into the ways for audiences/consumers to empower themselves.

Some of the fan activities in this study appear as a response to the impossibility of joining the authentic Japanese audience and a wish to reach a timeless region in which they are not excluded from the latest trends of Japanese TV dramas. In Koichi Iwabuchi's study of the Taiwanese audience's reception of Japanese TV dramas, his main point is that the Taiwanese have the feeling that they 'share a modern temporality with Japan' (Iwabuchi 2002: 122). This reflects the fact that Taiwanese audiences long for a kind of modernity that is based on the 'cultural proximity' represented in Japanese TV dramas (Iwabuchi 2002: 132). The yearning for being simultaneous with Japan is also evidence of the Chinese fans' desire for the immediate and unlimited access to Japanese TV dramas. However, my case study of online Chinese fans implies that based on the legitimate rules in broadcasting, it would be an illusion to equate Japanese modernity with Asian forms of modernities, in as much as Chinese fans have to struggle desperately to get what they want, compared with Japanese audiences who can relax in an abundance of Japanese TV dramas. The desire to find 'freedom from time' and space is 'decisively facilitated by new information technologies and embedded in the structure of the network society' (Castells 1996: 433).

'Time . . . a form through which we define the content of relations between the Self and the Other. Moreover, Time may give form to relations of power and inequality under the conditions of capitalist industrial production' (Fabian 1983: x). In Brian Larkin's research on Nigerian video and piracy, he also argues that 'instead of being marginalized by official distribution networks', video piracy 'has made available to Nigerians a vast array of world media at a speed they could never imagine' and connected them with global cultural flows (Larkin 2004: 297). Apparently, online Chinese fans' technological practices, very much like the video pirate culture with which Nigerians are complicit, are directed at dismantling the spatial constraints imposed by the legalized order of time. To a certain degree, piracy and fan activities activate the politics of time.

This research on the online Chinese fans of Japanese TV dramas serves as an example of something new; it begins to shed light on the new possibilities for audio-visual products being digitally circulated and consumed. That is, it is an emerging scenario not only for Chinese fans of Japanese TV dramas, but also for other Chinese audiences/ fans, who may have different interests in different audio-visual materials. The pervasiveness of BitTorrent, in particular, reinforces and envisions the energetic DIY digital productions with Chinese subtitling of various foreign audio-visual products that could be widely circulated online. Japanese TV drama is not an exceptional case. According to the experiences of my university students, Hollywood movies without subtitles are also often widely available throughout the Internet while plug-in Chinese subtitles devised by enthusiastic fans hang on certain websites. Thus, the online movie files and the Chinese texts originate separately. Most of the Chinese subtitles come from China, Hong Kong and Taiwan.

The recent trend in the use of BitTorrent indicates that China, with its growing technological human assets and technological capital, loose legal restriction on piracy, and its rather restrained markets for films and TV programmes, has turned itself into an empowered site of sources from which Chinese communities can be supplied with the online versions of audio-visual files. Apparently, there are various versions of Chinese subtitles competing with each other – including the copyrighted version, the version from pirate businessmen and different versions made by fans. We are witnessing a digital age which has made individual self-fulfilment possible – Chinese fans circulate works with Chinese subtitles but not for the purpose of profit – more out of a kind of affection for their favourite foreign audio-visual products and pride in their language/technological capability, together with the impulse to transcend the bonds of time–space.

The Chinese fan phenomenon in the DIY digital production and circulation of Chinese subtitled works constitutes an ambivalent zone that prompts us to reconsider the issues surrounding the online circulation of non-profit files and the power of Chinese fan subculture, which invests in the remaking of Chinese subtitles so as to construct a kind of 'digitalized'/'virtual' Chinese transnationalism. As this study indicates, Chinese fans of Japanese TV drama seek alternative ways, assisted by digital technologies, to transcend the traditional pattern of standardized and legalized distribution. Playing the role of both audience and user of digital technologies, these people do not constitute a clearly organized body with a single stable and collective identity; they are guerrilla fighters in the 'network' and 'autonomy' politics of geography, time, fan practice and digital technology in the uncertain age of late modernity.

Author's note

This paper was sponsored by the National Science Council in Taiwan. The topic of this project is "Japanese TV and Chinese fans' transnational cultural production: the significance of reflexivity and narrative of the self". The project number is: NSC 92–2412-H-194–011-, August 2003 – July 2004. The author especially thanks her research assistant, Gingwen Cheung, for help in collecting fan website materials and Japanese language translations.

Notes

1 Japanese TV drama indicated here is generally known as Japanese 'trendy' TV drama, which features stories about the struggles and happiness of love, friendship and work in a metropolitan setting.
2 At present, Taiwan has three cable TV channels which specialize in Japanese TV programmes. Jet TV was established in 1996, Videoland TV in 1995 and GoldSun TV in 1993.
3 VCD is a digital format, first released in 1993 by transnational electronics corporations including Sony, Panasonic, Philips and Matsushita, etc. VCD is not popular in countries other than Asia.
4 'Dorama', http://www.dorama.info, 8 January 1999.
5 http://www.wto.org/english/thewto_e/whatis_e/whatis_e.htm, 23 July 2004.
6 See 'Dorama'. In the topic 'Suggestions', fans expressed upset about the unavailability of the latest Japanese TV dramas, 13 April 2002. Another Singaporean fan was unhappy about the impact of the WTO on Japanese VCDs in the topic 'I hate WTO', 13 April 2002.
7 See 'Dorama', Xiao-yi from Malaysia who was a high school student in Singapore told the news in a topic: 'Japanese TV dramas, good!', 30 April 2002.

8 See 'Dorama'. Taiki initiated a topic for discussion: 'You can order Japanese TV dramas at http://www.sensasian.com', 7 May 2002.

9 See 'Dorama'. In the topic of 'First Love VCDs', Salin from Hong Kong talked about the experience of ordering Japanese VCDs online and consequently some fans asked for an exchange, 30 May–10 June 2002. In another topic, Serene from Singapore asked if anyone could buy her an old Japanese TV drama. Eventually she and a Taiwanese fan promised to exchange, 6–12 June 2002.

10 http://bt.newsgroup.com.hk/, 20 February 2004.

11 http://www.newsgroup.com.hk/about.asp, 25 June 2004.

12 For the website for Japanese TV drama exchanges, please see the following: http://bt.newsgroup.com.hk/?newsgroup=bt.tv.jp, 28 February 2004.

13 http://bitconjurer.org/BitTorrent/donate.html, 8 June 2004.

14 http://www.dessent.net/btfaq/#what, 17 March 2004, Brian's BitTorrent FAQ and guide.

15 http://bitconjurer.org/BitTorrent/introduction.html, 29 June 2004.

16 R's personal email to me, 12 April 2004.

17 For example, some latest Japanese TV dramas released in July 2004 were Chinese subtitled by Chinese fans, including *Orange Days* (2004), *Home Drama* (2004), *Sekai no Chushin de Ai o Sakebu* (2004) and *Nan Minamikun no koibito* (2004), and more.

18 For example, http://bbs.btpig/com/forumdisplay.php?fid=175, 12 June 2004; http://www.newmov.com/, 12 June 2004; http://www.ydy.com/, 12 June 2004; http://bbs.tvbt.com/index.php, 11 January 2005. All BitTorrent websites listed are established in China.

19 http://bbs.tvbt.com/index.php, 11 January 2005.

20 http://bbs.tvbt.com/index.php, 11 January 2005.

References

Ah-Xian 阿祥 (2004) 'Reply to 'What price would acceptable for copyright Japanese TV dramas in the future?'' 以後正版日劇價錢多少你能接受 ?, 3May, http://www.dorama.info.

Ang, Ien (1985) *Watching Dallas: Soap Opera and the Melodramatic Imagination,* London: Routledge.

Castells, Manuel (1996) *The Rise of the Network Society: The Information Age – Economy, Society and Culture (Volume 1),* Cambridge and Massachusetts: Blackwell Publishers.

Castells, Manuel (1997) *The Power of Identity: The Information Age – Economy, Society and Culture (Volume 2),* Cambridge and Massachusetts: Blackwell Publishers.

Fabian, Johannes (1983) *Time and the Other: How Anthropology Makes its Object,* New York: Columbia University Press.

Hills, Matt (2002) *Fan Cultures,* London and New York: Routledge.

Hu, Kelly (2004) 'Chinese re-makings of pirated VCDs of Japanese TV dramas'. In Koichi Iwabuchi (ed.) *Feeling Asian Modernities: Transnational Consumption of Japanese TV dramas,* Hong Kong: Hong Kong University Press, 205–226.

Iwabuchi, Koichi (2001) 'Becoming "cultural proximate": the A/Scent of Japanese Idol dramas in Taiwan'. In Brian Morean (ed.) *Asian Media Productions,* London: Curzon Press, 54–74.

Iwabuchi, Koichi (2002) *Recentering Globalization: Popular Culture and Japanese Transnationalism,* Durham and London: Duke University Press.

Iwabuchi, Koichi (2004) 'Introduction: cultural globalization and Asian media connections'. In Koichi Iwabuchi (ed.) *Feeling Asian Modernities: Transnational Consumption of Japanese TV dramas,* Hong Kong: Hong Kong University Press, 1–22.

Iwabuchi, Koichi (2005) 'Discrepant intimacy: popular culture flows in East Asia'. In John Erni and Siew Keng Chua (eds) *Asia Media Studies,* Oxford: Blackwell Publishing, 19–36.

Jenkins, Henry (1992) *Textual Poachers: Television Fans & Participatory Culture,* New York and London: Routledge.

Jones, Steve (2002) 'Music that moves: popular music, distribution and network technologies', *Cultural Studies* 16(2): 213–232.

Kahn, Richard and Douglas, Kellner (2003) 'Internet subcultures and oppositional politics'. In David Muggleton and Rupert Weinzierl (eds) *The Post-subcultures Reader,* New York: Berg, 299–313.

Ko, Yu-fen (2004) 'The desired form: Japanese Idol dramas in Taiwan'. In Koichi Iwabuchi (ed.) *Feeling Asian Modernities: Transnational Consumption of Japanese TV dramas,* Hong Kong: Hong Kong University Press, 107–128.

Larkin, Brian (2004) 'Degraded images, distorted sounds: Nigerian video and the infrastructure of piracy', *Public Culture* 16(2): 289–314.

Lee, Benjamin and LiPuma, Edward (2002) 'Cultures of circulation: The imaginations of modernity', *Public Culture* 14(1): 191–213.

Lee, Ming-tsung (2004) 'Travelling with Japanese TV dramas: cross-cultural orientation and flowing identification of contemporary Taiwanese youth'. In Koichi Iwabuchi (ed.) *Feeling Asian Modernities: Transnational Consumption of Japanese TV dramas,* Hong Kong: Hong Kong University Press, 129–154.

Miller (2001) 'Reply to "Thinking of establishing an exchange center of Japanese TV dramas"' 想要建立交換日劇中心, 8 June, http://www.dorama.info.

Morley, David and Robins, Kevin (1995) *Spaces of Identity: Global Media, Electronic Landscapes and Cultural Boundaries,* London: Routledge.

Ong, Aihwa and Nonini, Donald (1997) *Ungrounded Empire: the Cultural Politics of Modern Chinese Transnationalism,* New York: Routledge.

Poster, Mark (2001) *What's the matter with the Internet?* Minneapolis: University of Minnesota Press.

Poster, Mark (2002) 'Citizens, digital media and globalization', *Mots Pluriels* 18, http:// www. arts.uwa.edu.au/MotsPluriels/MP1801mp.html.

Price, Shibono (2001) 'Cartoons from another planet: Japanese animation as cross-cultural communication', *Journal of American & Comparative Cultures,* 24(1/2): 153–169.

Radway, Janice A. (1991) *Reading the Romance: Women, Patriarchy, and Popular literature,* Chapel Hill: University of North Carolina Press.

Salt (2004) 'Reply to "From June 2004 marketing pirated VCDs of Japanese TV dramas is illegal"' 盗版日劇 VCD 開始抓了本月起不得販售 2002 年前日本出版品亦違法, 2 June, http://www.dorama.info.

Streeter, Thomas (2003) 'The Romantic self and the politics of Internet commercialization', *Cultural Studies* 17(5): 648–668.

Taylor, Timothy D. (2001) *Strange Sounds: Music, Technology & Culture,* New York and London: Routledge.

Tomlinson, John (1999) *Globalization and Culture,* Cambridge: Polity Press and Blackwell Publishers.

Wong, Pei-hua 王珮華 (2002) 'Japanese businessmen act on tracking down pirated video game discs' 查緝盗版遊戲光碟, 日商展開行動, January 2, http://www.libertytimes.com.tw/2002/new/jian/2/today-e2.htm.

Xiao-Yu (2002) 'Reply to "Slowing down your steps to watch Japanese TV dramas . . ."' 放慢腳步看日劇, 10 April, http://www.dorama.info.

Special terms

Dorama 日本偶像劇場
GoldSun TV 國興衛視
Home Drama ホームドラマ
Ito shi kimi he 愛し君へ
Kimura Takuya 木村拓哉
Minamikun no Koibito 南くんの恋人（阿南的小情人）

Naohito Fujiki 藤木直人
Orange Days オレンジデイズ
Pride プライド
Sekai no Chushin de Ai o Sakebu 世界の中心で愛を叫ぶ
Videoland TV 緯來日本台

Part VIII

Movements

Chapter 27

Asian peace movements and empire

Muto Ichiyo

American war and its impacts

It started in a small way. In October 2001, we – a score of Asian social action groups, their coalitions, and NGOs – met in Hong Kong and agreed to establish an Asian regional peace network entitled the Asian Peace Alliance (APA).[1] We scrambled reacting to the massive US military invasion of Afghanistan. We were enraged by the showering of bombs on the Afghan people by the world's richest and strongest military power. To this situation, we wanted to crystallize Asian people's concerted response.

There was a keen sense of crisis shared by all of us over the US military attack on Afghanistan. Generally we were all indignant against the American arrogance to call it a war to defend civilization, disgusted with the conceit and hypocrisy of dropping 'humanitarian aid' packages together with lethal bombs. We all strongly disapproved the 11 September attacks, but we concurred that the most serious danger to peace and lives of the people came from the way the United States was reacting to 'terrorism'.

However, at that time it was also felt that organizing effective peace action in Asia vis-à-vis the US war was not an easy task.

In countries with overwhelmingly Islamic populations, such as Indonesia and Pakistan, it was Islamic fundamentalists who had promptly and visibly taken to the street shouting anti-American slogans and carrying Bin Ladin portraits. Friends from Indonesia reported that it was difficult to stage independent civic peace action without falling into the Bush trap, 'with us or with the terrorists'. Certainly the Islamist demonstration was more forceful and photogenic. The media would either identify any peace action with the Islamists or simply ignore it.

War had been brought into a series of Asian countries. Pakistani friends were then reporting that under the Musharaf regime that pledged to support Bush, the rule of law had been obliterated. American FBI agents were running rampant, arresting any persons as terrorist suspects, including tenant farmers protesting about landlords.

By that time, the war had already spread to the Philippines, opening the 'second front' of the American 'war on terrorism'. The United States had sent its special military units to Mindanao and Basyylan islands allegedly for joint exercises with the Philippine military for the purpose of wiping out a small band of Islamists-turned-bandits, who the US branded as Al Qaeda-connected terrorists. The whole locale was overwhelmed by the massive presence of the US–Filipino military, shrouding the local communities with the climate of terror. This situation created serious obstacles to the peace processes with Muslim forces promoted patiently by local voluntary groups. Yet, in the fall of

2001, opinion polls showed that public opinion in Manila was still overwhelmingly supportive of Bush and his 'war on terror'.

The nuclear confrontation between India and Pakistan over the Kashmir issue was already serious and peace movements were preoccupied with it. In East Asia, the keenest social movement concern of South Korea was with national reunification, hopes for which, raised with the 2000 North–South summit, were eclipsed as Bush shifted the American North Korea policy from normalization to hostility. In Japan, the hottest issue was the wartime legislation pushed forward by the centre-right government to break the constraints of the pacifist Constitution riding on the Bush 'crusade'.

Situations, concerns, histories and cultures were widely different country by country and subregion by subregion in this vast continent. Movement groups were already fully preoccupied with their respective national issues. Given this diversity of concerns and issues, what could it mean to bring into being an Asian people's peace alliance rooted in the diverse Asian realities that is capable of confronting the imperial war of global pacification? What is the new context into which Asian people, and peoples, can emerge as forceful peacemakers effectively exercising their influence on the global centres of power? Answering these questions was a challenge faced and taken by all of us.

Peace redefined

By the time APA held its founding assembly in August–September 2002, however, we began to understand what it meant to take this challenge. The contours of the imperial project in the meantime were fully shown as Bush's state of the union address early in the year made the real imperial agenda clear to all. No longer in the guise of retaliatory war against terrorism, the United States was now claiming its right to rule the world as it pleased, feeling free to name sovereign states it handpicked as members of an 'axis of evil' which the US had the right to pre-emptively attack and destroy.

Entitled 'Kalinaw – Asian People Speak up for Peace!', the APA assembly was convened at this stage of the Bush war. Held in the University of the Philippines campus in Quezon city, in the northern part of greater Manila, Philippines (29 August–1 September) it drew 140 activists from 17 countries and 95 organizations. It was not a conference held in a vacuum. For months prior to its opening, the Philippines host committee worked hard to make it an event rooted in the local movements, and succeeded. In the Philippines, two major peace coalitions had already been set up, and including them almost all major movement trends came together not only to host it but also to participate actively.

The assembly was a real activists' workshop not delimited by any institutional interests, all participants speaking up freely on an equal footing. The prevailing atmosphere was an intense urge for action in response to actual people's needs and concerns. As the assembly proceeded, it proved to be an arena into which all the real problems Asian people suffered from were brought into, shared and thrashed out. We experienced a process in which national and local pieces fell into a full picture of an Asia placed under the US Empire and its war scheme.

The assembly had three agenda items: (I) the World under the War on Terrorism; (II) Overcoming Conflicts and Violence among People; and (III) Hopes and Strategies. Workshops (called sub-plenaries), prepared and conducted with the full participation of local host organizations, examined a whole gamut of our problems: under topic I, (1) militarization, nuclearization and the role of the US; (2) war and the economy, (3) the erosion of international standards; (4) media and public discourse; under topic II, (1) internal conflicts and peace processes; (2) gender and violence in multi-ethnic communities; (3) religion, ethnicity and the search for peace; (4) amidst a world at war: the role of social movements.

I am not going into details of the discussion, but one thing that struck me was that we were spending very much of our time and energy, say 60%, discussing our own – meaning Asia's own – problems and issues. In other words, the second agenda item had to absorb much of our attention. This does not mean that we did not discuss the American war. The assembly did discuss it and did take a clear position on the Bush war itself. All the speakers, analysing the post-9/11 situation from different angles, concurred that the Bush war was the attempt to establish imperial rule over the world. We also agreed that violence wielded against civilian populations, such as the 9/11 attacks, had nothing to do with any people's cause and will only be conveniently used by the imperial centre to justify its global pacification scheme. Another perception shared by all was that Bush's global war was integral to the neo-liberal globalization processes that are creating social, economic, cultural and environmental havocs on the world community, hitting its most vulnerable segments.

But there was more to it. Listening to, and participating in, the discussion, I began to ask myself, and imagine, what the scene would be if a peace conference of this kind were being held in Canada, or Australia, or somewhere in the west. Then the basis and premise of discussion – in fact the implication of the very word, peace – would be significantly, if not totally, different. There the reasoning would be much simpler. Probably we would be discussing the American policy and 'terrorism' more straight-forwardly. We would criticize them against our shared criteria and values and come up with a short resolution and plan of action. There we would be grasping the war situation as external to us and responding to it to remove it. Differences of views would certainly exist but they would be resolved using the same, shared frame of reference, and the frame would stay intact. I said that the whole process would be much simpler because we would not be discussing ourselves so much as we did in Manila. We would be discussing peace, but – to simplify – peace largely would mean a return to the status quo ante.

Things did not go on like that in Manila. For us who came from the vast expanse of South Asia, Southeast Asia and East Asia, a different procedure was necessary to discuss the Bush war. We had to discuss ourselves as much as we discussed Bush. We had to go through the painful realities of the India–Pakistan nuclear confrontation, the rampancy of Hindu, Muslim and other fundamentalisms, and other sectarian violence destroying communities, the Gujarat massacre, military repression on separatist movements, constant human rights violations by the military, police and private agencies, economic violence wielded on the large bulk of population in the name of neo-liberal globalization, refugees of all kinds, and, notably, patriarchy underlying all these cruelties. In many Asian settings, vast numbers of people are deprived of peace and security. For them, peace is what they badly need to create here and now and not a state that existed before but is now disturbed by what has befallen. In other words, peace means creating new relationships and situations out of the almost hopeless realities.

I know that essentially peace should be understood as building new relationships. Peace should not be a simple going back to the status quo ante but creation of new social, human and cultural relationships, and this is so in societies of the North as it is in third-world Asia. In fact, the difference between them is a matter of degree. But in actual terms the degree matters and the degree makes the approaches asymmetrical. The situation where peace should be emphatically understood as a change of the status quo is certainly a negative situation for the people captive in it. But peace in our sense at once can carry a positive significance, if we take its challenge, because it involves radical transformation of societies and cultures. This, I felt, is a crucial dimension of peace often missed in the northern peace movement.

The point is that the Bush war has been grafted on to this already peaceless structural setting, transfiguring it, making it more violent and repressive, and multiplying the suffering of the already suffering people. Reflecting this overdetermined complexity of Asia, the founding declaration of the APA assembly had to be a long statement. It points out the relationship between the Bush war and Asia as follows:

> In the past year, the peoples of Asia have experienced a significant rise in their already high levels of insecurity. From Korea in the East to Palestine in the West, from Central Asia in the North to Indonesia in the South, wars, conflicts, and rising tensions have been our shared reality. The common source of our heightened insecurity is unmistakable: the winds of war unleashed by the United States in its pursuit of the so-called campaign against terror. This is based on a militarism that links physical coercion and patriarchy as the currency of power.

The Bush war has joined with the local fabrics to make more vicious the 'already high levels of insecurity' accelerating militarization and reinforcing anti-democratic forces all over Asia. The declaration gives a glimpse into what I might call the 'nexus of evil' after Bush, being organized between the global war machinery and the local nodes of power. Let me quote in part:

> Confident of Washington's backing Pakistani dictator Musharraf flouts rising demands for democracy, consolidates his repressive regime, and massacres unarmed landless peasants and fisherfolk. Taking advantage of Washington's rhetoric, the Hindu chauvinist government in New Delhi labels the Pakistani government 'terrorist' in order to close off any peaceful resolution of the Kashmir issue and cover up culpability in the barbaric pogroms that its own followers have carried out against Muslims.
>
> George W Bush's naming of North Korea as part of the 'axis of evil' has effectively scuttled the move towards rapprochement between the two Koreas and set back their eventual reunification.
>
> The US push to enlist Japan in the anti-terror coalition has resulted in the Koizumi government compounding the violation by previous governments of the Japanese constitution by sending Japanese Self Defence forces to the Indian Ocean to support Washington's war on Afghanistan. In addition, the emergency military bill has been promoted. These moves have stoked legitimate fears of Japan's remilitarization.

In the Philippines, President Gloria Macapagal-Arroyo has effectively overturned the Filipino people's decision a decade ago to kick out the US military bases by allowing US troops to return in force via the Visiting Forces Agreement. In the name of the war against terror, the Pentagon has renewed its aid to the Indonesian military, an institution notorious for its violation of human rights. In Malaysia, Mahathir has been emboldened to carry out more repression under the draconian ISA (Internal Security Act).

Let me cite another case of the nexus of evil and escalation of violence under the global war on terrorism. An urgent letter from an Indonesian activist/scholar to her Asian friends tells us about the aftermath of the bomb explosions in Bali in October 2002:

> ... This terrible incident occurred when President Bush is persuading many countries to join him to launch a 'holy' war against Iraq, and unfortunately, the Bali event became food for his campaign. This event happened during the time when the US and the neighboring countries under US influence, had just been pressuring Indonesia to tighten its control over the radical Muslim elements in the country.
>
> Does stopping terrorism mean increasing state repressive power? Politically there is global pressure on the Indonesian government to be more repressive. The government has hurriedly issued an anti-terrorist bill. Internationally this is considered an important requirement to make Indonesia a safer place for entry. The Urban Poor Consortium is now starting to mobilize a movement against this bill. What many pro-democracy activists fear is that the bill will increase 'State terrorism' instead.

Peace building

Building a peace movement in Asia in the midst of this reality is a difficult but extremely challenging task. For a peace movement as a permanent category that directly addresses global peace as exists in the West does not exist in most part of Asia (with the exception of Japan with a long postwar history of the anti-nuclear bomb movement). On the other hand, there is great potential of the power of the people in Asia, whose occasional explosions from South Korea to Indonesia have brought about regime changes in the past couple of decades.

As was earlier hinted, Asian people's response to the war-making Empire would inevitably come as a comprehensive movement, transforming the local and national repressive, exploitative, patriarchal and violence-ridden relationships and at once resisting and undermining the global imperial regime. In urbanized parts of Asia with a growing middle-class population, the traditional peace movement will emerge, directly addressing world peace issues, and that will play an important role in broadening the vistas of national movements. But generally, if peace is to be redefined as the remaking of the status quo and not as the return to some better old days, the challenge is to let emerge comprehensive Asian people's alliances resolving their issues autonomously and confronting and ultimately liquidating the global-to-local imperial meshes of power.

Why then is it a peace movement, instead of a general people's movement against the global regime? Because, although the naming does not matter much, it represents intense efforts to bring into the various social movements, communities, families and societies as a whole as well as global relations distinct elements and cultures of peace and justice – demilitarization of society, non-violent ways of resolving conflicts, and elimination of exploitative, repressive, patriarchal and exclusivist power relationships. The APA founding declaration thus stated:

> The dominant militarist statist and masculinist theory and regime of 'national security' and 'international security,' in short, must be replaced by one that is de-militarised, peace loving, feminist, universal, and people-centred.

People's alliances for peace

For the Asian peace movement to emerge, we are faced by the problematic well ex-pounded by Hardt and Negri, that of incommunicability and lack of a common language. Or rather we would note that the excesses and exclusivity of national political languages, or the national perceptual frames, entrenched in Asian countries, while reflecting the historical rootedness of social movements, also can serve to narrow our vistas and prevent us from taking a whole view of the landscape unless they are encouraged to interact with one another. As some of the fixed frames I have in mind, the notions of national reunification for Korea, the peace constitution for Japan, and national democracy for the Philippines. In the same vein, the Indian understanding of themselves as the world's largest democratic country, though nothing wrong in itself, seems sometimes to serve as an obstacle to imagining the world beyond the South Asian borders. These are the particular movement values and assets established through years of struggles and should not be cast away or replaced by a simple, cosmopolitan language. But it should also be recognized that these, in themselves, do not provide us with the basis of transborder alliances. Besides, these can keep us confined to the bilateral interpretation of events that the United States has been conveniently manipulating to maximize its strategic benefits.

The Asian Peace Alliance will play its role in letting a new common language emerge through joint action, interaction and exchanges as do the World and Asian Social Forum movement.

We are at the beginning of a long and challenging process of formation of global people's alliances, focusing our efforts on Asia. Under the impact of the American war, with all its direct and dire consequences befalling us, we have stepped into this dynamic process. Asian social movements participated actively in the unprecedented 15 February international anti-Iraq war mobilization by holding street demonstrations in a number of cities. Compared with mobilization in the West, the sizes of Asian demonstrations were still small, but as the global situation develops, we will see fresh swells of a new type of peace movement arise throughout Asia.

Note

1   The convenors of the Hong Kong consultation were the Asian Exchange for New Alternatives (ARENA) in Hong Kong and Focus on the Global South in Bangkok. The Tokyo-based People's

Security Forum, which had convened in 2000 together with Focus and Okinawan groups, and the Okinawa International Forum on People's Security in Okinawa were also active in promoting the idea.

In March 2002, a 14-member Focus-APA fact-finding mission visited the war-affected areas of Basyylan and Mindanao. A full report of its findings is available from www.focusweb.org.

The full documentation of the APA assembly and its activities, including the Founding Declaration, is available from www.yonip.com/YONIP/APA.

Chapter 28

Revitalizing the Bandung spirit

Hee-Yeon Cho

Preface

The year 2005 was the 50th anniversary of the 'birth' of the Third World.[1] How can the spirit of Bandung, expressed in 1955 and inherited by the non-aligned movement, be revived in the contemporary period? This is our question.

When we talk about the Third World, many think that the Third World continued to be the same entity. However, as soon as the momentum of the emergence of the Third World was given by the Bandung conference, and it started as an official movement of many non-Western weak countries on the international political scene, it began to show a huge difference in terms of the internal composition and political orientations of its members. Tracing such a change, this paper tries to respond to such a question as whether the Bandung spirit is still valid in a new context.

In this paper, I define the Bandung spirit as a non-aligned self-helped organization against the predominance of the powerful, especially the Western advanced, countries, and analyze in what kind of domestic conditions this spirit was born, how these initial conditions changed in the process of authoritarianization of the Third World, how should the Third World revive its original spirit in democratization of the authoritarian Third World, and then consider what kind of tasks are ahead in order to revive the Bandung spirit.

The birth of the Third World and its 'death' under authoritarianism and the Cold War

The Bandung conference and subsequent Belgrade conference were signs of the emergence of a non-aligned block from the two giants that were the US and the USSR. In my opinion, the Bandung spirit is not 'detachment' from the powerful Western countries but a non-aligned self-helped 'organization against' the powerful countries. In this sense, the Bandung spirit has to be interpreted as one of 'anti-predominance'. The traditional non-alignment meant isolation, while this 'new' non-alignment meant positive action for protecting the interests of the weak and achieving positive aims, including peace and public regulation of the international regime, on the basis of active alliance and formation of 'trans-border' solidarity.

Although the meaningfulness of this positive non-alignment is that it has been expressed on the scene of international politics or global politics, the non-aligned self-helped organization against predominance of the powerful countries could emerge on the basis of the following domestic orientation and realities. We can say that the outer declaration of non-alignment against predominance was an expression of the special inner configuration.

(1) Internal characteristics of the Third World in its early stage

First, there was a strong orientation and consensus towards a self-reliant 'national' economy in the economic aspect. People thought that the former colonialism had been reproduced by economic dependence on a suzerain state and, in that sense, economic self-reliance should be achieved in order to overcome this dependence. The local capital, especially middle and small ones, which has been restrained in its growth, has also shared this orientation, because such a self-reliance was expected to bring an expanded possibility for more accumulation. Of course, at that time, there was no other positive perspective except such a self-reliant national economy, because the former imperialism-connected development policy could not be accepted by people who had just escaped from colonialism.

Second, on the political aspect, there was a strong orientation and consensus towards a kind of 'nationally integrated democracy', which meant the least exclusive political regime in which unlimited participation was guaranteed to different political forces, in terms of ethnicity, religion, ideology and so on. The political regime was expected to be comprehensively inclusive and inter-tolerant among diverse forces, although such extremist trends as ultra-rightism and ultra-leftism have had to be constrained.

Third, the non-aligned self-helped organization against predominance of the Western advanced countries meant that the anti-colonial ethos in the civil society was represented by the state action. The Bandung principle was not only the decision of the state leaders. It has also been possible by a strong existence of the ethos eager for political and economic independence. The governments of the Third World wanted to respond to this civil consensus and aspiration, and manufacture further social consensus and political stability by combining this domestic consensus with outward non-aligned policy. In this sense, the outward non-aligned anti-predominance has been the state project and civil society project as well. We see convergence of such state and civil society projects in the Bandung principle.

In the emergent stage, the Third World stood on such domestic orientations as economic self-reliance, a nationally integrated political regime, and convergence of the state and civil society around anti-colonialism, which means that the non-aligned organization against predominance was not only the state project and but also a joint project among politics, economy and civil society in the Third World countries. In this sense, I can say it is 'consensual' emergence of the Third World in its early stage.

(2) Change in the Third World in the authoritarian period

This early Third World changes to a 'new' Third World, although it has existed as a 'formal' block, on the international political level, to counter the capitalist First World and socialist Second World and has wielded a strong voting power in the UN. The domestic configuration of the early Third World has changed. This change was coerced by intensification of the Cold War confrontation on the international level. The international politics has been bi-polarized into an America-centered or Russia-centered block, capitalism or communism, ultra-rightism and ultra-leftism and so on. The formation of the Third World on the basis of non-alignment meant that centripetal force towards a self-helped organization was stronger than the centrifugal force of the powerful countries. However, the centrifugal force of the Cold War has overwhelmed the centripetal one in the 1960s and 1970s. The Third World countries moved to an 'aligned' position to get economic and political-military subsidies from America or Russia. The Third World countries thought that they needed the 'umbrella' of the Cold War in the intensified confrontation between capitalism and communism (Arrighi 1996).[2] The Third World countries rushed competitively to become one part of a bi-polarized Cold-War block and to get fragmented in a competitive pursuit of 'individual' economic interest coming from affiliation with the powerful.

Under this outside influence, the domestic configuration of the early Third World changed to the opposite of what it once was. First, the orientation of economic self-reliance has been replaced by that of dependent developmentalism. In the economic aspect, the Third World turned to dependent capitalist modernization or socialist 'modernization' strategies. For example, South Korea adopted the development policy of dependent capitalist modernization, especially export-oriented development. This kind of dependent developmentalism was representing the interest of big capital, rather than middle and small capital, which wanted to make a further accumulation in alliance with foreign capital. In this authoritarian period, the dependent developmentalism continued to be mostly protectionist and state-centered.[3]

Secondly, a nationally integrated political regime changed to be an authoritarian one – ideologically extremist right-wing or left-wing. The inclusiveness of the regime was rapidly marginalized. Instead of the former inclusive regime, a new authoritarian – mostly military – one tried to repress and exclude other political and social forces, which were opposed to the dominant one, through the legal political arena. This change to a new authoritarian Third World was signified by, for example, withdrawal of leaders of its early stage, such as Nasser, who enforced the famous nationalization of the Suez canal; Sukarno, who was stripped of his title of president for life in 1966 and remained under house arrest until his death; and so on.

In the capitalist-oriented Third World countries, dependent developmentalism was combined with an authoritarian political regime. Its form of combination has been diverse. The 'bureaucratic authoritarianism', which was developed to conceptualize the Latin American developmental political regime, is an example to show such diversity. We could say that there has been, at this stage, a kind of developmentalist alliance of an authoritarian state and big capital with the orientation of dependent developmentalism.

Third, the authoritarian state has repressed the civil society while supporting big capital's accumulation and market growth. Furthermore, the state tried to mobilize the civil society with the modernization ideology, while repressing it in the authoritarian way. The combination of the non-alignment policy of anti-predominance on the international politics level and the economic self-reliance policy of the Third World state at the early stage made room for a relatively friendly relation between the state and civil society. However, the authoritarian character and dependent developmentalist economic policies have been confronted with oppositional response from civil society. The state responded to this opposition with harsh repression armed by the military coercive measures.

The Third World in this stage could be characterized by an exclusive authoritarian political regime, dependent developmentalist economic orientation and coercively repressed and mobilized, in the top-down way, civil society. In this sense, transition to authoritarianism did not mean change in the form of the political regime. It did mean change in economic development strategies, the state-civil society relation, international policy including marginalization of the non-alignment policy and so on. The Third World at the authoritarian stage was not what it used to be at the emergent stage.

Democratization of the Third World in the context of the neo-liberal globalization

This 'authoritarian' Third World came to crisis by the oppositional activation of the civil society in response to the contradiction of the authoritarianism and dependent development.

(1) Crisis in the 'authoritarian Third World' and transition to democracy

The crisis in some of the authoritarian Third World countries has been caused by success in development, while in other countries it has been caused by its failure. Most authoritarian states could not escape from crisis coming from this contradiction. The modernization pushed by the authoritarian state brought with it a diversified civil society in terms of class inequality. Diverse classes, especially the working class and urban poor, have been mobilized into opposition. The main beneficiary class, the urban middle class, has been a faithful supporter of the dependent development under the authoritarian state. However, it turned increasingly critical of the authoritarianism in the process of modernization. The working class changed itself from that in obedience to that in struggle, and increasingly from the economic struggle to the political one. The Third World, characterized by authoritarianism, dependent development and a repressed civil society, became confronted with strong demands and a struggle from the bottom for democratization. Although the retreat of the authoritarian regime has been pushed by the opposing mobilized civil society, the driving force also came from the capital, which has been financially supported by the authoritarian state. The capital, which has grown under the support of authoritarianism, in turn demanded former government-centered development, i.e. the dirigiste method of government initiative, and the former hierarchical relation between the government and business, to change to a market-centered one and a horizontal and consultatively cooperative one (Cho and Kim 1998).[4] They demanded autonomy rather than state control, market-initiative rather than state-initiative. In this sense, the driving force for democratization came from the repressed civil society unprivileged by the authoritarian state, on the one hand, and ironically from the capital and market sector privileged by dependent developmentalism of it, on the other hand. As a result, the 'authoritarian' Third World began to change to a 'democratic' one, which means that the authoritarian Third World came to be confronted with dual challenges for democratization. One challenge is demands for political liberalization (overcoming of the repressive control of the civil society by the state) and the other is an economic one (overcoming of dirigiste control of the economy by the state).

However, if we look at the economic character of the democratic struggle, we can see that dual – also contradictory – demands have been given to the state. One is demands for progressive forces in civil society for a 'radical' reversal of a dependent development policy, which biased mostly big business. The other came from the capital and market sector to demand more autonomy of the economy from the government's control (i.e. a demand for economic liberalization). In this sense, we can say that two opposing forces are competing in the democratic stage: civil society, liberated from the state control, demanded social regulation of the market and democratic reform of the state, while the capital demanded autonomy from the state and a market-friendly state's role in promoting international competitiveness.

The outcome brought by democratization is determined by the qualitative character of democratization, the conservative democratization from above or the radical democratization from below. The former means that the transition to democracy and the retreat of the former authoritarian regime proceeds under the initiative of the authoritarian forces, while the latter means that they proceed under the initiative of radical forces in the anti-authoritarian movement and, as a result, the former authoritarian regime becomes dismantled in a discontinuous way. In most cases, the conservative democratization became dominant and economic liberalization policies also became dominant rather than a radical reversal of the former dependent development policies of the authoritarian state, which is strengthened by the global condition of neo-liberal globalization, as described below.

One other important thing for understanding change in the Third World is that democratization proceeded in the context of the neo-liberal globalization. The strong stream of neo-liberal globalization influenced the characteristics of democratization of the Third World and drove the post-authoritarian regime into the neo-liberal policy line.

(2) New tasks of the 'democratic' Third World

Here we have to meet such questions as 'what kind of tasks are ahead of the "democratic" Third World?' Or 'in what direction do the Third World countries have to go in order to substantiate the democracy in the context of neo-liberal globalization?'

Democratization means basically a change of the political regime to democracy. However, the kind of 'substantive' change that will be realized in such a 'formal' change might be different depending on practical intervention. In other words, whether or not transition to a 'democratic' Third World could bring with it a revival of the original spirit of the Bandung communiqué and a non-aligned Third World is not predetermined. As aforementioned, a change from the initial Third World to an authoritarian one did not mean only a change in the political form. It also meant changes in the international non-alignment policy, economic development strategies, state–civil society relation and so on. Considering this, we have to think about how to make the transition to a democratic Third World a process revival of the initial Bandung spirit.

In order for democratization of the Third World to result in its true revival, attention should be paid to the following tasks.

Recovery of countervailing power

First, transition to democracy should bring with it recovery of the central principle of the Bandung spirit, that is self-helped organization against the predominance of the powerful in the new globalization context. The anti-predominance spirit should be revived in the new spirit against neo-liberal globalization. In the early stage of the Third World, the predominance of the powerful advanced countries has been expressed in the form of political-military power based on economic dominance. However, such predominance is now being expressed in the form of economic predominance of the transnational capital, especially a financial one. There is no countervailing power against it on the contemporary global scene. I think that the revived Third World should function as a countervailing collective power against this economic predominance.

The violent result coming from the movement of transnational financial capital, such as in the economic crisis in East Asia in 1997, shows that the current economic order without any public regulatory mechanism (Cho 2000a) can result in disastrous outcomes to people's lives in the Third World. The democratic Third World can be a great driving force for the institutionalization of the transnational public regulatory mechanism, whether a Tobin Tax regime, democratic reform or dismantling IMF liquidation of the foreign debt and so on.

Struggles against the neo-liberal globalization are happening in the form of an anti-globalization demonstration. However, it is the struggle of the 'non-state' civil society level. If the democratic Third World countries could do some kind of action against neo-liberal globalization, it could mean the actions of the 'state' actors. If we look back on the history of capitalism in the one nation, we find that diverse public regulatory mechanisms have been instituted in the name of substantiation of democracy. If we were to revive the Bandung spirit, we could do a new self-helped organization of the weak countries and the victim countries against the current predominant political and economic powers, which would give some momentum for constructing a certain regulatory mechanism against economic predominance of transnational capital. It will be a great step towards a global democracy (Young 2000; Held 1996; 2004).[5]

Beyond the dependent developmentalism

Second, the democratic transition of the Third World countries should go together with a change in the former dependent developmentalism. Under the strong influence of the global neo-liberalism, the democratic Third World countries are adopting 'transformed' – not changed – dependent development strategies (Cho 2000b).[6] The former protectionist and state-centered dependent developmentalism changes to an open-door oriented and market-centered one. We could define the economic policies of the democratic Third World countries as those of 'dependent neo-liberalism' (Lee 1999).

In particular, this dominance of dependent neo-liberalism is more apparent in those Third World countries on the road to conservative democratization. Most of the democratic new governments adopt transformed dependent development strategies, without any fundamental change in the former dependent developmentalism. We can find a good example in the Kim Dae-Jung government in South Korea. The Kim Dae-Jung government is an opposition party government for nearly 50 years, having a great political legitimacy. However, based on such a political legitimacy, it has driven a strongly open-door oriented and market-centered economic policy line, including privatization of many public enterprises, including electricity, gas and so on, opened the capital market, stock market and so on to a very high level without instituting countervailing regulatory mechanisms to keep the macroeconomic stability of the national economy. It is ironic that the political legitimacy kept by the new democratic government is playing the role of a political facilitator of neo-liberal economic policies. The Kim Dae-Jung government considered privatization as a typical economic reform. Removing the entry barrier that limits the introduction of foreign capital has been given a top priority in policy in order to exit from the economic crisis.

In that the transition to democracy brought with it more freedom and autonomy in political and social activities in the civil society, the democratization has given the 'blessing' of political liberalization to the people. However, in that the democratization brought with it more freedom and autonomy of the capital movement and more privatization of the public enterprises, resulting in economic bi-polarization on the domestic and global levels (Chossudovsky 1997) and the so-called '20:80 society',[7] democratization has given the 'disaster' of economic liberalization to the people. We can find a good example of duality of democratization in the Kim Dae-Jung government in South Korea.

For more inclusiveness and openness of the state and political society

Third, democratization should go along with recovery of political inclusiveness and openness of the state to civil society's demands. The reformulation of collective countervailing power of the Third World against neo-liberal globalization should presuppose the constructive effort of this positive domestic relation, the reconstruction of a democratically open relation between the state and civil society, and democratically integrated 'political society'.

Under the authoritarianism, dominant ethnic, religious, ideological forces have repressed and excluded others by coercion. In some cases, ultra-right forces, while in other cases, ultra-left forces, disclosed this kind of exclusiveness. Democratization should endorse political inclusiveness and openness to diversity in terms of ethnicity, religion, ideology and so on, which is an ideal value to be promoted in this globalization period. The effort to overcome the predominance of one force on the domestic scene can go together with that to form a counter-force against the predominance on the international scene.

In addition, democratization should bring with it an open attitude of the state to civil society's demands. As previously mentioned, the civil society has been diversified in terms of class, ideology, economic property and so on. After the start of democratization, civil and class dynamism and activism spread to various issues and areas. If the civil society has been oppositely activated under the authoritarianism, the civil society in the democratic transition is being activated in this way for the formerly voiceless to make their voices heard and for voluntary organizations to look after their interests. This kind of activation will increase in the process of increasing deterioration of the livelihood under the global neo-liberalism. If the 'democratic' state after the breakdown of the authoritarian regime should not be open to these diversified demands and voices, it would not be a truly democratic one, only one disguising its economic and social content. To make the state open to diverse social demands and voices is to transform the 'democratic' state to be a 'social' state or socially democratic regime in the Third World way.

In conclusion, based on the analysis done until now, democratization should not be narrowed only to political 'form' change but should be a comprehensive project to make 'substantive' change in the state–civil society relation, inclusive of the political society, dependent development policies and international solidarity strategies, and in this way revive the Bandung spirit.

Nationalist Bandung or globalist Bandung?

Here, I mainly discuss the domestic tasks in front of the Third World countries. I want to discuss the trans-national struggle and its relation to the Bandung spirit.

The Bandung spirit in the current globalization

Given such understanding of the change in the Third World, how is the Bandung spirit valid in the current context, in which globalization is being problematized? In the context of a struggle against the so-called neo-liberal globalization, how can the Bandung spirit be revived?

It is not enough for us to pay a verbal tribute of praise to the Bandung conference and argue for revival of it despite such a long gap. It might be a simple retrospective revival. In order to say that the Bandung spirit is still meaningful to us and that the Third World is not dead, we have to look at how it is related to the current globalization context. We can say that the Third World has been imagined and constructed in the conjuncture of the mid-1950s by diverse actors in reality, not given from the heaven. If we have to remember it, it should be reconstructed by us in the current context. The issue of whether and how the Bandung spirit is meaningful in the current globalization is deeply related to whether and how the resistance based on the nation-state order is valid in the globalized context (Hardt and Negri 2000).[8]

There are two views and approaches to confrontation with the current globalization. One is laying stress on strengthening national sovereignty, in the way of recovering the maneuvering power of the nation-state and emphasizing that nation-state-centered strategy is still basic and important. The other is a globalist approach, which regards such a strategy as out-of-date and pursues a kind of 'non-national alternative globalization'.

One emphasizes that the main task of movement in the contemporary context is to oppose the globalization itself and the sovereign power should be recovered as 'a defensive barrier against the control of foreign capital and global capital'. The other emphasizes that, because of the transnational global integration of the reality, the strategy to strengthen the sovereign power is needed, and, in that sense, nationalist struggles have already become out-of-date (Hardt 2002; Mertes 2002).[9]

Apparently, the first view seems easily to be friendly to the position of emphasizing the Third World nationalism and reviving the Bandung spirit as such. If we stand on the first view, we can endorse the effort to revitalize the Bandung spirit without any logical mediation.

However, if someone adopts the second view, he/she is confronted with some logical tensions. Some argue that the Bandung spirit based on nationalist ethos should be dismissed in the current globalization context. Is it right? Cannot we stay as a globalist, while advocating the current meaning of Bandung? In order to say the affirmative, we have to discuss, as a stepping stone, the relation between the contextual difference and similarity between mid-1950s and mid-2000s and the validity of the Bandung spirit over the time difference of 50 years.

In this regard, there is a quite simple identification that is 'nationalist position = strategy of strengthening the nation-state = Bandung as an exemplary case, globalist position = supra-national global strategy = Bandung as an out-of-date example'. In order to talk about the meaningfulness of Bandung, even if we adopt the globalist view, we have to consider the following two points.

Imperialist and imperial globalization

The first point is the continuity in discontinuity between the contexts of the mid-1950s and the mid-2000s or the similarity and difference between the domination order in the mid-1950s, which the historical Bandung confronted, and that we confront now. I would say that, if the Bandung conference tried to confront the 'newly emerging' repressive global order and meant a collective effort of the powerless to confront it, the people in the current context are also confronted with a 'newly emerging' repressive order, called the neo-liberal globalization, and are provided with momentum by the breakdown of the socialist regime and the information society.

The Bandung conference meant a collective critique from the oppressed could be expressed against the new dominant order of the powerful Northern nations. As is well known, the mid-1950s were the transitional period when the pre-World War II dominant order was changing to the new East–West Cold-War dominant order, although many countries of Asia and Africa could enjoy an independence through their anti-imperialist struggles. The Bandung effort meant a collective will against 'incomplete liberation', which was not going towards a 'complete liberation' but a new repressive order to be overcome by a new struggle from below.

Although the newly fixed dominant order has taken a form of the East–West Cold War, it was the South–North order in substance, in which the South has been given the worse status. In this sense, the Bandung conference meant problematizing not only the new Cold-War order but also the newly engulfing gap between the South and the North as a real economic substance, which meant that the latter continued to keep its economically dominant status just as in the pre-War period.

This kind of effort to problematize the South–North substantial gap in the form of the East–West conflict has resulted in securing 'a niche of the Cold War', which gives non-aligned countries a manoeuvering space between two opposing powerful countries. Taking advantage of this niche space, non-aligned countries wanted to try to pursue alternative political and economic trajectories.

However, there are similarities and differences between such a situation and the current one. I want to interpret the current globalization in a different way from the recent common-sense. I think that we do not have to see the globalization process just as an after-1990s phenomenon. In fact, the modern imperialism has been one process of globalization. In this sense, the context of liberation, which Bandung confronted, was *imperialist* globalization, while the current one is *imperial* globalization. While the former, imperialist, globalization means that globalization proceeded in the way of one dominant nation colonizing the other weak nations, the current, imperial, globalization means that globalization proceeds in the way of making a trans-border global homogenized market and marginalizing and relativizing the nation-state's sovereign status. Despite such a difference, the two phenomena are two expressions of the same globalization process.

In a sense, we are put in the worse situation of globalization: in the conflict between the capitalist First World and socialist Second World, the former has beaten the latter. In addition, with the help of this victory, the movement of capital, constrained in by the existence of the Second and Third Worlds, is rapidly going forwards, making a unitary global market and reconstructing the globe according to its own logic. The period in which the theory of dependency has had a strong intellectual impact has been, ironically, the period in which the global movement of capital has been impossible due to several factors, such as resistance from below, the existence of anti-colonial state actors and so on. However, now we are in the worse situation, in which the powers of capital and the US as a dominant power are stronger. While we can say that the opposition against the incomplete condition of liberation in the mid-1950s was oriented towards a full condition of liberation, now the incomplete condition of liberation is getting worse by imperial globalization. In addition, the niche of the Cold War has gone away and a horrible global order of unitary dominance is now in place. Considering that, we have to say that there *is* still the Third World in reality and there is still the validity of it as an analytical category if we don't want to purposely try to nullify the real internal hierarchy of inequality of the current global order.

In this sense, the Bandung spirit of a collective self-helped organization against the newly emerging dominant order should be revived in this worse imperial globalization context.

A nationalist resistance as one of the multiple resistances in the current globalization

The second point is the relation between the nationalist resistance and the transnational globalist one, both of which are expressed in struggles against the current imperial globalization.

Behind the declaration of the state leaders of non-aligned countries, there have been people's strong voices for post-colonial autonomy, which have been awakened through a long period of anti-imperialist opposition. Of course, the voice demanded a new trajectory of their countries, not following the model of former imperialist countries. In this sense, the Bandung principle meant an escape from the shadow of the former imperialist countries, which has dominated them, and a new effort to try to find an alternative way of development. In this sense, the Bandung spirit can be defined as a new spirit to try to find an alternative way not to comply with the current domination.

However, such a Bandung spirit for pursuing an alternative from below has been sure to be based on the nation-state order and nationalist ethos. Here, some argue that such a struggle based on nationalism became out-of-date. But I think that, considering the multiplicity of resistance in the globalization process, we don't have to say that trans-national struggles are only meaningful and other struggles based on nationalism in one aspect are meaningless. We have to admit that people's struggles are expressed in a very complex form, and in diverse forms, even to be contradictory with each other.

As we have seen in the process of capitalist modernization, the struggles against the horrible and vulgar monster that is the early stage of capitalism have been expressed in diverse forms from the Luddite Movement to the revolutionary movement, from reactionary orientation to the so-called orientation of 'scientific communism'. It has been the same in the struggles against colonialism.

The multiplicity of resistance (Hardt and Negri 2000; 2004) against imperial global-ization is being expressed already: from Islamic fundamentalist to anti-globalization transborder struggles, from nationalist to transborder struggles, from reactionary to anarchist or communitarian and so on. This diversity itself is the characteristic of resist-ance in this imperial globalization context. In this sense, we do not have to define a specific form of transborder struggle as its proper form in the imperial globalization context. If we see in this way, although we were to adopt the globalist view, we can escape from the fallacy that the nationalism-based struggle in the globalization is not a proper form and should be dismissed. Just as the current imperial globalization itself is complex, the struggle against it is expressed in a complex and diversified form, including the nationalist struggle and others. This is the right admittance of the diversity of struggle in this globalization context.

However, we have to indicate that the diverse struggles have a diverse differentiated status. It means that nationalism-based struggles against the current globalization cannot keep their dominant position as in the pre-World War II period and the mid-1950s, a position that is being delivered to globalism-based struggles. We have to accept that the status of the struggle based on nationalist ethos and one based on globalist ethos came to have different positions.

In relation to this issue, we have to pay attention to specificities of different struggles, while we admit the multiplicity of struggles against the current globalization. For example, struggles against the current globalization in the Western countries and those in the Third World countries are different. They have different statuses in the hierarchical structure of the current imperial system. The Bandung conference teaches us about the different specificity of the repressed in the increasingly globalized system of inequality.

When we emphasize the global struggle against globalization of domination, we should not come to think that all the hybrid oppositions are the same, although we do not have to admit the traditional view of a hierarchical relation of diverse oppositions. What the Bandung conference aimed at problematizing in the imperialist globalization context is that specificity of status of Asia and Africa in the global structure of inequality, and the self-helped collective voice against it.

In addition, we want to say that the Bandung principle was not declared as a one nation-state declaration but a collective declaration of many nation-states, which means that the perception of limitation of the nation-state was implied in the Bandung principle as a trans-national collective self-helped organization. We have to find a trans-national commonality and transnational common solidarity based on it in the Bandung principle. This is also what we have to revive in the Bandung declaration.

Here, I have tried a globalist re-interpretation of the Bandung spirit, rather than the nationalist one. The Bandung spirit can be revived in the form of not only a national-ist Bandung but also a globalist Bandung.

Second death of the Third World or revival? Summary and concluding remarks

As a critical scholar of South Korea, who was not invited to the 1955 conference and followed the dependent development strategy under the authoritarian regime, now in the process of conflict over democratic reform, I wanted to analyze the historical change in the Third World in its emergent stage, in the authoritarian stage and in the current democratic stage in terms of its international policy and domestic relations among the state, the political regime, development strategy and civil society. The analytical content of this paper is summarized as follows.

The Bandung conference in 1955 and subsequent Belgrade conference in 1961 were signs of the start of the emergence of a non-aligned block from the two giant blocks. I defined 'non-aligned self-helped "organization against" the dominant powerful countries'; that is the spirit of 'anti-predominance'. This non-aligned self-helped organization against predominance of the powerful countries has emerged on the base of such domestic orientation and realities as economic self-reliance, nationally integrated political regime, convergence of the state and civil society around anti-colonialism. In this sense, we can say there was 'consensual' emergence of the Third World in its early stage.

However, according to the intensification of the Cold War confrontation on the international level and its centrifugal influence, the early Third World changed to a 'new' authoritarian Third World. The Third World in this stage could be characterized by an exclusive authoritarian political regime, a dependent developmentalist economic orientation and a coercively repressed and mobilized, in the top-down way, civil society. The Third World at the authoritarian stage was not what it used to be at the emergent stage.

The Third World, characterized by authoritarianism, dependent development and repressed civil society, became confronted with a strong struggle from the bottom for democratization. Although the retreat of the authoritarian regime has been pushed by oppositely mobilized civil society, the driving force came also from the capital which has been financially supported and controlled by the authoritarian state. The former demanded change in the repressive control of the civil society by the state (political liberalization), while the latter demanded former government-centered development, i.e. the dirigiste way of government control of the economy (economic liberalization).

Under the overlapping processes of democratization and globalization, the strong stream of neo-liberal globalization influenced the characteristics of democratization of the Third World and drove the post-authoritarian regime into the neo-liberal policy line. If democratization means, basically, a change of the political regime to democracy, it does not automatically mean socio-economic democracy. Whether transition to a 'democratic' Third World could bring with it revival of the original spirit of the Bandung communiqué and a non-aligned Third World or not is not predetermined. In this sense, in order for democratization of the Third World to become its true revival, the following tasks should be considered. First, transition to democracy should bring with it recovery of the central principle of the Bandung spirit, that is a self-helped organization against the predominance of the powerful. The revived Third World should be a countervailing collective power against this economic predominance. In addition, the democratic Third World can be a great driving force for the institutionalization of the transnational public regulatory mechanism. Second, democratic transition of the

Third World countries should go together with a change in the former dependent developmentalism. Under the strong influence of global neo-liberalism, the democratic Third World countries are adopting 'transformed' dependent development strategies. Third, democratization should go along with recovery of political inclusiveness and openness of the state to civil society's demands.

Thereafter, I tried a kind of globalist reinterpretation of Bandung. Concerning the strategy of struggle against globalization, one view emphasizes national sovereignty and the other emphasizes a new effort to go beyond the national horizon. I wanted to argue that the Bandung spirit can be emphasized and revived in the globalist view of the current globalization, by way of conceptualizing the current globalization as imperial globalization, unlike the imperialist globalization, which the historical Bandung wanted to confront. I argued that the Bandung spirit of collective self-helped organization against the newly emerging dominant order should be revived in this worse imperial globalization context. In addition, I argued that the resistance with an emphasis on the boundary of the nation-state or with an aim of strengthening it against the transnational capital is also one important component of the multiple resistances in the current imperial globalization.

As a concluding remark, the Third World is now confronted with two options, the second death or revival. If it could be revived, the Bandung spirit, which is oriented to non-aligned self-helped organizations against the predominance of the powerful, should be revived as an egalitarian countervailing collective power against the contemporary global neo-liberalism, and truly democratic orientation tolerating and accepting diverse differences in ethnicity, religion, ideology and so on. Is it my dream that the 'democratic' Third World will be reviving the Bandung spirit in the way to form a collective countervailing power against the current inhumane globalization? Borrowing George Monbiot's expression, I would say that 'it depends on your preparedness to abandon your attachment to the old world and start thinking like a citizen of the new; to exchange your security for liberty, your comfort for elation. It depends on your willingness to act' (Monbiot 2003: 261).

Notes

1 As is well known, the so-called Third World was symbolically born in the Asia-Africa Conference in Bandung in Indonesia in 1955 and officially born in the first Conference of the Non-Aligned Heads of State, which counted 25, at Belgrade in September 1961. The declaration of the '10 Principles of Bandung', released at the former meeting, included anti-imperialism, resolution of conflicts via the UN, non-violence, etc, which has comprised a guiding spirit for the non-aligned movement in 1961. Countries such as South Africa, Israel, Taiwan, South Korea and North Korea were not invited to this conference.

2 Northeast Asian countries such as Taiwan and South Korea have been most highly incorporated into the Cold-War confrontation and had the most dependent relations with America. As a result, they enjoyed the most favour from America. This can be called the 'contradiction of the Cold War'.

3 Dependent developmentalism can be divided into protectionist developmentalism and an open-door oriented one, and state-centered developmentalism and a market-centered one.

4 Hee-Yeon Cho and Eun Mee Kim (1998) describe this change as change from 'hierarchical symbiosis' to 'collaborative symbiosis' between the state and bourgeoisie.

5 For more information on the global democracy, which aims at extending the democratic principle onto the global level and making a supranational democratic mechanism to regulate the state and market actors, refer to Young (2000) and Held (1996).

6 Hee-Yeon Cho described this phenomenon as a change from the old developmental regime to 'a new developmental regime'.

7 Under the Kim Dae-Jung government, the first opposition party government in 50 years, economic inequality and the ratio of irregular employment has increased greatly. For example, the ratio of the income of the upper 20% versus that of the lower 20% was 4.81 in one quarter of 1997 but changed to be 5.40 in one quarter of 2002 (*Hankyorye Daily Newspaper*, 18 May 2002). The ratio of irregular employment was 42% in 1995. However, it increased sharply to 58.4% in August 2000 (Kim 2001). This inequality and poverty situation has not improved, being reproduced in a changed form (Chang 2005).

8 Polemically, Antonio Negri and Michael Hardt are saying that 'Third Worldist perspectives – were now completely useless' (Hardt and Negri 2000: 264, 332–336). The special issue of the journal, *Rethinking Marxism*, 18(34) Fall/ Winter, deals with diverse kinds of critiques on Hardt and Negri's *Empire*. In there, they are responding to such critiques (Hardt and Negri 2001).

9 I think that the Bandung spirit can be re-interpreted and revived in a different sense from the nationalist view or globalist view.

References

Arrighi, G. (1996) 'The rise of East Asia: world systemic and regional aspects', *International Journal of Sociology and Social Policy* 16(7): 6–44.

Chang, Se-Hoon (2005) 'The continuity and change of the recent urban poverty: a study on 'new poverty' phenomenon', *Economy and Society* 경제와사회 66: 95–125.

Cho, Hee-Yeon and Kim, Eun-Mee 조희연 김은미 (1998) 'State autonomy and its social conditions for economic development in South Korea and Taiwan'. In Eun-Mee Kim (ed.) *The Four Asian Tigers: Economic Development and the Global Political Economy,* San Diego: Academic Press, 125–158.

Cho, Hee-Yeon 조희연 (2000a) 'Civic action for global democracy: a response to neo-liberal globalization', *Inter-Asia Cultural Studies* 1(1): 163–167.

Cho, Hee-Yeon (2000b) 'The structure of the South Korean developmental regime and its transformation', *Inter-Asia Cultural Studies* 1(3): 408–426.

Chossudovsky, M. (1997) *The Globalization of Poverty: Impacts on IMF and World Bank Reforms,* Ontario: Agora Publishing Consortium.

Hardt, Michael (2002) 'Today's Bandung?', *New Left Review* 14 (March–April): 1112–1118.

Hardt, Michael and Negri, Antonio (2000) *Empire,* Cambridge, MA: Harvard University Press.

Hardt, Michael and Negri, Antonio (2001) 'Adventures of the multitude: response of the authors', *Rethinking Marxism* 13(34) Fall/Winter: 190–198.

Hardt, Michael and Negri, Antonio (2004) *Multitude: War and Democracy in the Age of Empire,* New York: The Penguin Press.

Held, David (1996) *Democracy and the Global Order: From the Modern State to Cosmopolitan Governance,* Stanford: Stanford University Press.

Held, David (2004) *Global Covenant: The Social Democratic Alternative to the Washington Consensus,* Cambridge: Polity Press.

Kim, Yoo-Seon 김유선 (2001) 'The amount and situation of irregular employment', Seminar on the Irregular Laborers and Labor Movement hosted by Korean Association for Industry and Labor Studies, May 26, Hangulhakwhe Hall.

Lee, Byeong-Chon 이병천 (1999) 'Korean economic crisis and IMF bailout regime: risk of dependent neoliberalism', *Socio-Economic Review* 사회경제평론 13: 117–165.

Mertes, Tom (2002) 'Grass-roots globalism: reply to Michael Hardt', *New Left Review* 17 (September–October): 101–110.

Monbiot, George (2003) *The Age of Consent: A Manifesto for a New World Order,* New Delhi: Harper Collins.

Young, Iris M. (2000) *Inclusion and Democracy,* New York: Oxford University Press.

Chapter 29

Rethinking social movements through retranslating the economy

Po-keung Hui

> Usually – Heidegger reminds us – we think of the possible as an unrealized actual. However,
> to see the present as radically not-one and thus plural is to see its 'now' as a state of partial
> disclosedness, without the suggestion or promise of any principles – such as dharma, capital,
> or citizenship – that can or will override this heterogeneity and incompleteness and eventually
> constitute a totality . . . To think of the 'not yet,' of the 'now,' as a form of 'unrealized actual'
> would be to remain trapped entirely within historism. For a possibility to be neither that
> which is waiting to become actual nor that which is merely incomplete, the possible has to
> be thought of as that which already actually is but is present only as the 'not yet' of the
> actual.
>
> (Chakrabarty 2000: 249–250)

Chakrabarty argues that the process of the so-called "transition to capitalism" is in fact
also a "process of translation of diverse life-worlds and conceptual horizons about being
human into the categories of Enlightenment thought that inhere in the logic of capital."
(Chakrabarty 2000: 71) For instance, and of concern to this paper, diverse experiences
are translated into economic terms like "private property rights," "free trade," "profit
and money seeking" and "management" that are further translated into exclusion,
privilege, accumulation, control and a linear logic of maximizing material gains.[1]
These translations depict "capitalism" and its related economic concepts as homogenously
materialistic and hence limit our understanding of the economy. However, they are by
no means the only possible translations, and are certainly not very pleasurable ones for
the people that are excluded, exploited, managed and controlled in capitalist societies.
A critique of capitalism, therefore, inexorably involves an alternative translation process
that could transcend the "poverty of economic language" and create new languages that
are able to frame a better understanding of the economy.[2]

Provoked by, and hence reacting to, such homogenized and essentialized notions
of the economy, radical social and cultural criticisms in Hong Kong have always
gone astray. Although economism – concerned exclusively with material gains – is not
an unfair description of some social movements (particularly labor movements) in
Hong Kong, "hardcore economic issues" such as patterns and modes of trade, business
development, money and finance have not been a major concern even for the most
materialistic social activists and cultural critics. When these economic issues were
mentioned, they were largely the targets of criticism. This is perhaps the result of an
essentialist understanding of capitalism – that capitalism is a homogenous economic
system of "free market," "free trade," "private property," and the logic of "profit

maximization," which produces the wicked consequences of exploitation, inequality, and alienation. This essentialized version of capitalism, which originated in the 19th century, appears to be further reinforced by the neo-liberal translation project. It is particularly interesting to note that in a highly commercialized city like Hong Kong radical social activists and cultural critics are extremely reluctant to engage in economic affairs, except by passively responding to selected economic policies that concern material gains for the workers and other marginal groups – minimum wage, unemployment benefits and so forth. As such, the conservative political forces – the advocates of neo-liberalism and the pragmatic populists – have largely dominated the discourse on the economy, a domain about which most Hong Kong people are very much concerned.

Discourses on co-operatives and community economies

A case in point is the discussion of co-operatives and community economies in the second half of the 1990s and the early 2000s. The later part of the 1990s witnessed a high unemployment rate in Hong Kong, especially after the financial crisis in 1998 that signaled the end of several decades of rapid economic expansion. In 1998, the Hong Kong government made a proposal to dramatically reduce Comprehensive Social Security Assistance (CSSA) by utilizing a strategy of "blaming the victim." This was condensed in the slogan: "CSSA feeds lazy bones."[3] In an environment lacking employment opportunities and of shrinking social welfare, workers had no other choice and were forced to accept appalling working conditions and unacceptably low wages. In response to this demoralizing context, trade unionists, local NGOs and even political parties are now increasingly interested in finding ways to deal with unemployment problems. In addition to targeting conventional struggles such as minimum wage legislation, trade unions, local NGOs and political parties are directly committed to providing retraining courses for unemployed workers.[4] However, not many graduates from these retraining programs could find decent jobs. In fact, the retraining practices themselves are criticized as merely helping the government defer the serious problem of unemployment. For NGOs working on labor issues and critical of conventional trade unionism, retraining programs, if at all successful, are nothing more than a means to push workers back to a "capitalist hell." For these NGOs, forming co-operatives (and other community economic projects of a similar nature) is therefore a preferred proposal, because co-operatives and community economies are believed to be able not only to create employment opportunities, but also to engender patterns of living alternative to existing capitalism. Yet directly engaging in the creation of (alternative) business activities that they had rarely dealt with before becomes an imperative challenge to these NGOs. Starting from scratch, they need both the intellectual resources and practical frames of reference. Several critical journals, with a limited circulation, were published in the 1990s and immediately filled this gap by introducing foreign experiences and local experiments with co-operative practices. These short-lived journals, such as *Alternative Discourses* and *Co-operative Bi-Monthly*, were the main advocates of co-operative movements in Hong Kong in the late 1990s and the early 2000s.

The most enthusiastic and articulate writers for these journals are university graduates from the 1980s and 1990s, who have committed themselves to social movements and critical cultural works for many years. As mediators between marginal groups (such as manual workers, single mothers, prostitutes, etc.) and intellectuals/NGO organizers, some of these advocates of co-operatives share three common enemies – "party politics," "statist social welfarism" and "mainstream trade unionism" – that are criticized as either elitist or orthodox Leninist, and that suppress the diversity and plurality of grassroots cultures and needs into narrow economic considerations (Ha 2000: 88; Ah So 1996: 2). Basically what these co-operative advocates propose is calling for the liberation of marginal people – unemployed, poor single mothers, new immigrant workers and the like – by getting rid of all forms of bureaucratic and economistic institutions. In order to prove the feasibility of this kind of non-bureaucratic and non-economistic co-operatives they have created a small typing co-operative based primarily on anarchical principles.[5] The purpose of this co-operative, according to one of the founders, is to promote "members' participation on a *completely voluntary basis, mutual caring and understanding*, and trying not to turn into an instrument of routine organizational work, or a chip serving elites' aspiration for money and power." This small co-operative is designed not to turn into a mere income-generating machine, but a place in which *members' interactions* can take place." (Chui 1998: 89, my translation and emphasis added) One of the central themes of their discourse and practice is, as expected, a complete rejection of "capitalist practices," that is, bureaucracy, management, profit making, market exchange and economic rationality. At the same time, "voluntary participation," "mutual caring" and "members' interaction" are presented as non-capitalist or even anti-capitalist practices. As such, the discussion of co-operatives, which supposedly addresses economic issues more directly and critically, ironically turns into a total rejection of seriously engaging in economic practices and business knowledge.[6]

In a context where labor and social movements have long been dominated by trade unionism, conventional party politics and social work perspectives, taking this radical position is not unreasonable. In fact, we might even argue that this kind of radical critique of the single-mindedness of the dominant discourse – state welfarism – on how to improve the situation of the marginal groups is a timely intervention. Yet adopting a strategy that simply dichotomizes (and essentializes) capitalist practices and "non-capitalist" values, and glorifies the latter while rejecting the former, significantly weakens the effectiveness of the radical critique. The case of the newly established Community Investment and Inclusion Fund (CIIF) illustrates how such a radical critique could be easily appropriated by conservative forces and rendered ineffective.

In his 2001 Policy Address, Mr Tung Chee Hwa, the Chief Executive of the HKSAR, proposed the setting up of a HK$300 million CIIF. The Fund is operated under the Health, Welfare and Food Bureau, and "will provide seed money to support the collaborative efforts of community organizations and the private sector." The CIIF was subsequently set up in April 2002 and started to accept the first batch of applications in August 2002. By October 2002, there were 227 applications submitted for funding, and eventually 12 projects were funded with a total amount of HK$8.9 million.

From the CIIF documents and related speeches, it is not hard to see that the language used by the government is not particularly different from that of social activists advocating co-operatives (or community economies). The CIIF aims to encourage "mutual concern, support and assistance," and the ultimate goal is to rebuild "social capital," a magical term that underscores the CIIF. According to Dr Raymond Wu, the Chairperson of the CIIF Committee, social capital "refers to the strength of our *community support networks*, the *links and respect between people*, the *sense of cohesion* and *willingness to sacrifice self-interest* for *our common good*, the commitments we have for Hong

Kong and the sense of belonging in being a member of the community." (http://www.hwfb.gov.hk/ciif/en/index.htm, emphasis added) Likewise, the focus of the 12 funded projects, according to the spokesperson of the CIIF, "will be on *empowering* and building up the capacities of marginalized service recipients and into contributors to the Society, forming *self-help co-operatives*, strengthening *support networks* or becoming helpers to others in need." (Government press release, 14–1–2003, http://www.info.gov.hk/gia/general/200301/14/0114193.htm, emphasis added). "Mutual concern, support and assistance," "empowering," "self-help co-operatives," "links and respect between people" and "willingness to sacrifice self-interest" are terms widely circulating among social activists and trade unionists in Hong Kong, even among the radical co-operative advocates as discussed above, although they certainly reject the notions of "our common good" and "sense of cohesion."

At a first glance it seems contradictory that the HKSAR government, a capitalist state that fervently advocates neo-liberalism, is willing to promote "non-capitalist" (or even "anti-capitalist") values such as "mutual concern, support and assistance," "co-operatives," "links and respect between people" and "willingness to sacrifice self-interest." Yet when we take a closer look at the CIIF and its funded projects, it is understandable why such "non-capitalist" (or community) language is employed.

Mr Tung Chee Hwa's 2001 Policy Address makes it clear that:

> The objective of the Fund is to encourage mutual concern and aid among people, and to promote community participation in district and cross-sector programmes. This will enhance the function of different communities and foster their development. *We do not believe that money alone can solve our problems. We* also *rely on the community's motivation and dedication to help each other.* These efforts enhance social cohesion, strengthen community networks, support families more effectively and provide services to improve the health and well being of youth and women. We emphasize *the importance of self-initiative* by individual members of the community . . . . The Fund should not be seen as a kind of social welfare. Rather, *it is a social investment . . .*
>
> (*Policy Address 2001*, item 127, http://www.info.gov.hk/ce/
> speech/cesp-c.htm, emphasis added)

From the government's perspective, the Fund is a "social investment," not "social welfare."[7] Of course, "money alone" is surely not enough to "solve our problem," yet Tung's emphasis on "self-initiatives" and "community's motivation" may better be understood as a way to shift the government's financial burden to the community. This perhaps is more clearly revealed in his speech on February 26, 2002 at a briefing and consultation session on the proposed operational arrangements of the CIIF. He said, "we do not believe government efforts alone can build a caring community, particularly in face of such *sizable deficits*. We also *rely on the community's motivation and dedication* to foster social cohesion and a spirit of mutual care and aid." (Government *Press Release* on February 26, 2002, http://www.hwfb.gov.hk/ciif/en/ speech press/press020226.htm, emphasis added) And Mr. Tung is not the only government official who holds this view,[8] and the CIIF is not the only government fund that aims at shifting the government's responsibility to the community.[9]

The first batch of funded projects provides some clues to understand the government's criteria in directing the CIIF. A common feature of almost all the 12 funded projects is to aim at establishing networks of *voluntary workers* consisting of the retired, the young, housewives and new immigrants. Most of these projects are in fact a continuation of the host organizations' (mainly NGOs and religious organizations) previous social services, such as counseling, providing training courses, sharing sessions, household visits, job seeking, and family services. The only differences seem to lie in two areas. The first is the change from conventional social work frameworks to a language of community economy – from "welfare," "servicing the clients," "caring" and the likes to "social investment," "social capital," and "self-help co-operatives" etc. The second change lies in the way of securing financial resources – from direct government subsidies to indirect subsidies, plus the expansion of voluntary work.[10] From the government's point of view, the shift from direct to indirect subsidies and the emphasis on voluntary work are obviously in line with the current tight-budget situation, and also in line with the neo-liberal doctrine that aims at transforming the government's role from a redistributor to a regulator. From an NGO perspective, receiving money from the CIIF, though less stable and less certain than previous direct government subsidies, is still a second best option in the context of "a sizable budget deficit." This explains why the CIIF can attract more than 200 applications in less than two months,[11] and why this new language of community economy is pragmatically and promptly picked up by many NGOs without any reservation.

Besides the government and the NGOs, other political forces also try to take advantage of the CIIF. According to a CIIF committee member, many political parties want to secure financial resources from the CIIF for their daily operation and for mobilization and organization for elections. They prefer to work at the community level, where most of their votes come from. As a result, these political parties have recently set up satellite organizations to apply for the CIIF (*Sing Pao*, 9–29–2002, A14).[12] In order to be selected for funding, these political parties, following the NGOs, have also pragmatically taken up the "social capital" language. The active participation of the NGOs and political parties has effectively advanced the circulation of the language of community economy and thus help translate these "non-capitalist" terms into conservative politics.

The case of CIIF clearly reveals the limits of creating and sticking to "non-capitalist" (community) language. Working within the binary oppositional framework – organization/bureaucracy, management, profit, market, efficiency (or in short the capitalist economy) are bad; whereas openness, self-determination, voluntary, reciprocity, equality (or in short community) are good[13] – will not guarantee that radical social movement is on the right track. Advocating co-operatives or other community economic projects can be easily and pragmatically translated into conservative politics by various political forces, including the NGOs themselves.

To be fair, being the initiator of the discourses on alternative economic practices, the radical advocates of co-operatives do understand well the danger that their discourse could be hijacked by the government and other conservative political forces. However, their deliberate attempt to detach from the state (and all forms of bureaucracy), and to avoid "capitalist" practices, cannot prevent the government and other political forces from effectively articulating co-operatives and community economic language to conservative politics. This, I would argue, is largely a result of radical social activists' reluctance to seriously engage in any form of bureaucratic and business practices, which are indispensable for meaningful and sustainable alternative economic projects, thus rendering themselves unable to address the material and cultural needs of the populace. In fact, some grassroots members of the aforementioned small typing co-operative are concerned more with the material interests, such as income, productivity and competitiveness, than with the abstract principles as advocated by the radicals. (Lam & So 1998) Unable to establish a solid and sustainable model of alternative economy in which people benefit both materially and culturally, it would be ineffective to counter the appropriation of "community" language by conservative forces for their own advantage.

In short, criticizing the labor and social movements that have long been dominated by state welfarism and economism is of course justifiable and timely. However, if this anti-economist and anti-capitalist stance has foreclosed an understanding of existing capitalism as constituted by heterogeneous and non-essentializing processes, and if it has resulted in a complete rejection of all capitalist aspects (including material gains) that are indispensable even in alternative ways of life, then it could backfire and project a negative image, not only to the parties involved, but also to the entire field of alternative practice – the image of an unrealizable utopia.[14]

The "Go West" campaign

Another interesting case is the discussion of the "Go West" campaign in Hong Kong. In May 2001, a Hong Kong Special Administrative Region (HKSAR) delegation, made up of a group of the richest tycoons in Hong Kong and senior government officials led by Mr Donald Tsang, the Chief Secretary for Administration of the HKSAR, visited several cities in the western part of China. The official aim was to explore business opportunities and to help develop the "poor and underdeveloped" northwest areas of China. The two TV stations in Hong Kong produced accompanying programs that were entirely uncritical of this event, which understandably provoked criticism from local social and cultural activists. The critics pointed out the potentially devastating impact of the "Go West" campaign, such as environmental destruction, a detrimental cultural impact on ethnic and religious minorities, and "internal colonization" or exploitation of the western inland by southeast coastal capitalists. However, the TV programs by and large did not represent the populist view in Hong Kong. Instead of celebrating the "Go West" campaign, the three best-selling newspapers in Hong Kong consistently criticized the government's involvement in the project. What these newspaper editorials and columnists advocated was a populist view of "saving the local economy first." This is not incompatible with the populist mentality of keeping out Mainland Chinese new immigrants. By attacking the submissiveness of the Hong Kong government to the Beijing regime and its inability to help local people survive through economic difficulties, and by arguing that investments in the west of China would diminish monetary resources available for local development, these newspaper editorials and columnists interpellated a local subject position that was selfishly centered on the well-being of Hong Kong people. In other words, the criticism of radical social activists, though indeed pointing to some of the blind spots of the mainstream discourses on the "Go West" campaign, for example, on the possible harmful impact to the region, are largely misplaced in a local context.

Local populist politics obviously had no interest in advocating the "Go West" campaign. Instead, they took this opportunity to articulate the event on a populist political agenda, such as anti-communism (and the assumed counter-thesis is neo-liberalism). They tried to demonstrate that the "Go West" campaign was another form of mismanagement by the HKSAR government, which is increasingly regarded as a disciple of the Beijing regime. In fact, building on the Cold War legacy, most of the populist newspapers have long utilized anti-"leftist," or more precisely anti-Chinese Communist Party (CCP) rhetoric, because "left" in Hong Kong means the political forces affiliated with the CCP. This stance appeals to Hong Kong readers, who have been nurtured on anti-communist ideology all their lives.

For the "Go West" advocates, the whole issue was linked with nationalism and patriotism. Not only was the "Go West" campaign connected to the metaphor of family members helping each other (in this case, Hong Kong helping to develop other parts of the motherland), but it was further argued that by improving the economy of the northwestern region, the tension between the ethnic/religious minorities and the *Han* people (read central government) would eventually be alleviated. Needless to say, this whole idea was built on the notion of "comparative advantages," not surprisingly matched with a neo-liberal ideology.

The difficulty of the situation that the "Go West" critics encountered in Hong Kong was that they were trapped between the two above-mentioned discursive positions that almost exhausted all other discursive spaces for alternative voices. In this difficult context, merely criticizing the "Go West" campaign by pointing out its damaging impact was not particularly effective because it was very easily co-opted by irrational populist political forces. For instance, in pursuit of its political goal of "developing the Hong Kong economy first" and defending the neo-liberal doctrines of "non-government intervention," the editorial of *Oriental Daily*, a local populist, anti-Marxist newspaper, did not hesitate to adopt Marxist jargon to condemn the "Go West" campaign: ". . . Investing in the Great North West will bring about various capitalist crimes such as environmental destruction and labor exploitation. It would be similar to what happened in 1984 in Bhopal, India, for example, where a chemical factory emitted poisonous waste killing several thousand people and leading to over ten thousand poor people being blinded. This was precisely the result of the cruel robbery of backward regions by imperial transnational corporations in the name of 'development'." (*Oriental Daily*, May 24, 2001, A23, my translation) This sounds like what might come out of the mouth of a Marxist![15] The problem perhaps lies in the fact that these radical critics are unable to articulate the anti-"Go West" campaign to a wider discourse and to everyday practices as the irrational populists have done. By merely condemning the "Go West" campaign, the critics have failed to address the concerns of local people and to mobilize their emotional and affective energies to more constructive projects that are connected with their material life. This is also the problem for the advocates of co-operatives. If the critics are not able to find ways to re-articulate people's material (and cultural) needs to constructive social projects without falling back to economism and populist politics that selfishly focus on the well-being of "local" people and on the survival of NGOs and political parties, the interpretation and representation of the economy will simply be left in the hands of the neo-liberals and the pragmatic populists. Although social activists and cultural critics do not need to go as far as Bourdieu who claims that "the *only* effective way of fighting against national and international technocracy is by confronting it on its own preferred terrain, in particular that of economics" (Bourdieu 1998a: 27, emphasis added), recapturing the economic domain is certainly an extremely important direction in which to go. Instead of kicking all the "capitalist" or "economic" "evils" out of social movements, is it possible to find a way to re-articulate the economy and economic languages to a radical project that moves people?

If there is no inherent connection between "bourgeois concepts" and "capitalist reality," as well as between "community language" and "progressive politics," counter-capitalist practices, such as community/alternative economic projects, could perhaps adopt a more open attitude and pragmatic approach to retranslate economic language and to transform the capitalist economy. Since the 1980s, and especially after the 1997 Handover, the "Left"[16] in Hong Kong has been translated and represented as a conservative force closely affiliated with the CCP regime, while "Liberal" is in fact another name for conservatives. Similar to the CCP in mainland China that started to invite capitalists to become members of the Party, the "Left" in Hong Kong also do not hesitate to speak for and to collaborate with the capitalists. It is rare, if at all, that one hears the "Left" in Hong Kong criticize the capitalist system as fundamentally unacceptable. For the "Liberals," what they basically ask for is minimal government intervention that in fact means nothing substantial should be changed. In such a confused political context, accompanied by the dominance of pragmatic populism and a business mentality, it is perhaps not particularly effective to merely repeat conventional leftist language disparaging capitalism and exalting co-operatives and community economic practices. Instead, taking economic/business language and practices seriously may better serve the endeavor of anti-capitalist social movements.

Unsettling the myths of capitalism

Radical critics have often ignored the contingency of the relationship between main-stream economic concepts/language and the capitalist exclusive and exploitative reality. Social activists and cultural critics in Hong Kong always try to avoid using economic concepts such as profit, market, rational calculation, free trade and management in a positive manner. In their critiques of globalization,[17] for example, some Hong Kong radicals are ironically locked into the language of the conservatives and very often take at face value, terms like "privatization" and "free trade," as really representing the reality of the capitalist economy and then subsequently launch moralistic attacks on them (see *Globalisation Monitor* 2000, particularly Wong 2000). To be fair, as some of these critics point out, in real politics, "privatization" and "free trade" under the World Trade Organization (WTO) regulations do need to be condemned, and in fact, some of the critics of "globalization" have focused on more concrete contexts in which International Monetary Fund (IMF) policies or WTO regulations have indeed produced a devastating impact on social life in Hong Kong (see for instance, Kong 2000 and Yuen 2000). Yet these depressing consequences may have nothing to do with the "evil nature" of "private properties" or "market exchanges." To confuse what these terms represent with the reality of capitalism is self-defeating for the radicals. In so doing, the radicals inevitably speak through the framework and agenda set by the neo-liberals or irrational populists (such as endorsing the inevitability of 'globalization'), thus essentializing "Capitalism" and also its other – the subaltern, marginal groups, and various NGOs. Consequently, social activists and cultural critics in Hong Kong have disappointingly tolerated the conservative socio-political forces, which have monopolized the representation and translation of the (capitalist) economy.

However, capitalism is not as its advocates, and subsequently its critics, portray. Capitalism is not a system of "free market" and "private property." It is neither homogenous, nor merely economic. (See Braudel 1982 and 1984; Gibson-Graham 1996.) Rather, as anthropologists and geographers demonstrate, the so-called capitalist economy is filled with diverse socio-cultural practices, in which durable personal relationships, "animal spirits" (*à la* Keynes), rituals, superstition and emotion play significant roles in all economic practices in the capitalist worlds. (See Carrier 1995 and 1998; Thrift 1997 and 1998; Chapman and Buckley 1997.)

A brief review of the history of the Hong Kong economy, which is widely believed to be "capitalist paradise," suffices to show the irrelevance of the "free market" and "private property." In Hong Kong, the markets that significantly affect people's every-day life, such as land, money, public utilities, transportation, food and other daily consumption items, are certainly not as free as commonly perceived. One could argue that centralization and monopolization, rather than privatisation and liberalization, describe more accurately the historical development of these markets in Hong Kong. Land supply has been completely controlled in the hands of the government ever since the beginning of the colonial period when all "private land" was turned into Crown Land. The post-War period, especially in the 1980s and 1990s, has witnessed the centralization of the property market in the hands of a few property developers (Consumer Council 1996). The money markets have also been highly regulated in the post-War period. Interest rates had been determined by the Interest Rate Agreement among members of the Hong Kong Association of Banks since 1964, and this Agreement was abolished only in 2001. Likewise, it is hard to regard the foreign exchange market as completely free. The Hong Kong dollar was pegged with sterling from 1935 to 1972 and foreign exchange control had been in place until 1959. Since 1972, the Hong Kong dollar has been pegged with the US currency. (Feng 2002; Consumer Council 1994a) Similarly, public utilities and transportation have also been monopolized by a few British (and recently Chinese) firms – the Hong Kong and China Gas Co., Ltd. (established in 1862), Hong Kong Electric Co., Ltd. (1889), China Light & Power Co., Ltd. (1901), the Peak Tramways Co., Ltd. (1888), Hong Kong Star Ferry (1872), Cable and Wireless Ltd. (1936), as well as tunnels and buses companies (Feng 1996). The markets for food and other daily consumption items are no exception. Since the 1930s, the Hong Kong government has restricted street hawking because of concern with unfair competition to formal retail outlets. (McGee 1973: 39) This policy of eliminating competition between street hawkers and formal retailing outlets continues in the contemporary period, as was manifested in the 1983 Hong Kong Housing Authority's Hawker Report which suggested that mobile hawkers should be banned "on the estate for the purpose both of *eliminating competition* between the hawkers and the commercial tenants and of providing an acceptable living environment to the tenants." (cited in Smart 1989: 38, emphasis added) As a result, the two giant supermarkets, Park'N and Wellcome, have increasingly monopolized the markets for food and other daily consumption items, thanks to the policy that eliminates competition (Consumer Council 1994b).[18]

If capitalism is not equivalent to a homogenous economic entity governed by a system of "free market" and "private property" as the neo-liberals suggest, its Other –

the subaltern, marginal groups and non-profit making organizations (including NGOs and trade unions) – is also not entirely free from "capitalist" practices and self-interested motivations. In fact, a primary concern of many of the subaltern and marginal groups in Hong Kong is still material advancement, and numerous NGOs in Hong Kong have engaged in various business-like practices, such as fund-raising, marketing and advertising (through advocacy campaigns) as well as networking (through attending conferences and other social activities). The NGOs today have turned into big businesses that have served as government contractors, and hence are beneficiaries of "privatization" (or contracting out) in many areas, such as providing welfare services and engaging in activities that governments no longer care to do.[19] Bourdieu rightly reminds us that altruism, idealism and independence are not necessarily the only characteristics of charity and non-profit organizations. Wholly disinterested activities appear to be very rare (Bourdieu 1998b: 75–91).

Likewise, as illustrated in the cases of the CIIF and the "Go West" campaign, conservative forces could easily assemble "non-(anti-)capitalist" terms widely circulated among NGOs. "Empowerment," "self-reliance," "community," "mutual concern, support and assistance," "capitalist crimes" and "imperial transnational corporations" are now rather dubious terms that could mean something very different from how they were originally understood. Businesses are also willing to take up the language of ecological and human ethics because this language may help to advance their business interests in particular geo-historical contexts.[20] Furthermore, advocating "difference" and "diversity" is not necessarily anti-capitalist by nature because, as Grossberg (1992: 371) argues, "[i]f the new individualities and communities are the product of changing economic relations, if capitalism itself is largely responsible for the proliferation of differences, then it seems rather odd to assume that they precede those economic relations or that they are a response to some other development."

Pressing the neo-liberal rhetoric to live up to its promises

David Harvey argues that instead of taking the stance of criticizing the Universal Declaration [of Human Rights] as a "bourgeois institution" or a legacy of Eurocentric "Enlightenment thought," one could easily cast neo-liberalism "as a gross violation of human rights" since "almost all countries that were signatories to the Universal Declaration [of Human Rights] are in gross violation of these articles."[21] Following this logic and what we have discussed above, it appears that there is no reason why we cannot bring free trade/private property/free market/management in contest with capitalism and look for alternatives by seriously integrating economic practices that are often contingently – and sometimes without ground – associated with capitalism.

For instance, although neo-liberal ideologists often utilize the strategy of blaming the victim by propagating the notion of "no free lunch," and in particular of advocating the *yongzhe zifu* (user pays) policy in pushing through the "privatization" of the medical services, when coming to their turn, they do not wholeheartedly endorse this neo-liberal principle. Lam Hang-chi, the founder of the newspaper *Hong Kong Economic Journal* and one of the most prominent advocates of neo-liberal economics in Hong Kong, ironically argues against the *yongzhe zifu* policy. His reason is very simple: not all government services are apt for taking on the *yongzhe zifu* principle. He argues that it is ridiculous to ask the victim, say a bank that has been robbed, to pay for the cost of the police forces. Likewise, to ask real estate owners to pay firemen's salaries and to ask industrial and commercial firms to pay the expenditures of trade delegations that help these firms to negotiate better terms in the international business environment, as well as to ask "protection services receivers" to pay for national defense equally makes no sense. According to Lam, all these services should be offered by the government and financed by taxation. (*Xin Bao – Hong Kong Economic Journal*, April 27, 2000, 9). It appears that Lam understands well those who gain the most from government services. Social activists tend to take a defensive position when faced with an attack on social services from the Right that uses the "no free lunch" rhetoric. What I propose here is another option: an offensive strategy, which takes the "no free lunch" concept and turns it into an attack on the Right by pointing out the fact that a large share of government expenditure has been channeled to subsidize giant corporations, and that TNCs have externalized costs of production and reproduction to nature and society.[22]

In fact, if one takes the neo-liberal rhetoric seriously enough, it could easily be turned into an anti-capitalist weapon. In many instances, the quasi-governmental organization, the Hong Kong Consumer Council, staffed with mainly mainstream economists, ironically stands in opposition to giant corporations in Hong Kong. Their support of fair trade legislation and their studies of the degree of monopolization of the real estate market, the banking market and the largest supermarket chain stores (Consumer Council 1996, 1994a, 1994b) reveal the "not-so-free" nature of these markets in Hong Kong and hence cast doubt on the workings of giant corporations and contest their monopolistic tendency.

Similarly, instead of completely dumping the notion of competitiveness simply because it is advocated by the World Economic Forum which produces the World Competitiveness Report, social activists and cultural critics may struggle to redefine the meaning of world competitiveness, so much so that it comes to include ecological considerations (cleaner air and water), humanistic working conditions (such as job-sharing, minimum wage, and healthy working environment), cutting salaries of high/middle-income executives and professionals (with shorter working hours as compensation), preserving indigenous livelihood and cultural products, etc. in order to increase the distinctiveness of the environment and quality of workers, and consequently the competitiveness of the economy.

Obviously, finding ways to articulate "free-market" and "free-trade" to anti-monopolistic forces will undoubtedly help critical discourse and social movements to fortify their influence on the populace. In contrast, regarding these neo-liberal terms as totally incompatible with social justice, equality, diversity and difference will very likely leave spaces for the expansion of "irrationalism of populisms of all kinds."[23]

Retranslating the economy

Unsettling the myths of capitalism and pressing the neo-liberal rhetoric to live up to its promises are not the only strategies open to social activists. Another approach is to rearticulate "mainstream economic concepts" in alternative contexts and thereby transform their meanings. Gibson-Graham suggests a project that cultivates alternative "economic" subjectivities by re-defining and re-articulating economic languages and economic processes. They argue that many of the diverse everyday activities of ordinary people can be viewed as different "economic" practices that are represented as "non-economic" activities by mainstream economic languages. Within the mainstream economic languages, community and ecological services, household management, voluntary and religious works are not regarded as proper economic activities and are thus marginalized as secondary or insignificant. In order to claim back their centrality in the economy, Gibson-Graham develops a new language that represents these practices as economic (but not capitalist) activities, and "to cultivate an unconscious in which dreams, fantasies and desires for non-capitalist forms of economic organization might take shape and circulate."[24] Supplementing their views, I suggest that these new economic languages should also include the "old ones" – profit, market, management and so forth – and to rearticulate them in new contexts.

These new contexts include various alternative economic practices that have flourished in the last decades, such as the alternative currency and trade movements in North and South America, Europe and Asia, and the co-operative movements all over the world. In Hong Kong in the last few years, there have also been a number of alternative economic initiatives. These include several production co-operatives, barter trade of service and secondary goods in three communities, a community currency project, three convenient retailing co-ops in universities, three household service networks, a credit union, a consumer (green) co-operative, a community cultural commodity production project, community women mutual aid networks and a "fair trade goods" shop (I thank Billy Hung for providing this list of alternative practices).

The alterative/community economic projects/experiments advanced in Hong Kong over the last few years are very small in scale and their social impact has yet to be felt. Yet they are undeniably creating new spaces that could facilitate the emergence of new economic subjectivities. How to articulate these practices to a wider cultural and social movement that may contest the thinning of economic meanings and consequently create a new language of economics becomes an important task to be undertaken by critical intellectuals in Hong Kong.

To differentiate from the CIIF statist project as discussed above, and to rearticulate these community projects to a progressive politics, relying on the old leftist and NGOs' language is obviously not enough. Instead of playing with the NGOs' jargon, the criticalness of which has been diminishing, actively reincorporating the mainstream (economic) language could be an alternative. For instance, if activists who advocate co-operatives[25] as an alternative to capitalism focus on more than the "non-economic" aspects of these projects, there is greater room for re-linking the "economic aspects" of co-operatives to alternative livelihoods and to mainstream economic language, thereby transforming their meanings. In the history of co-operative movements, it is not difficult to find that many successful co-operatives, in the sense of lasting for a significant period of time, have taken management, technical efficiency, product quality, profits or earnings for expansion, property rights (a combination of private and collective ownership), as well as market exchange and pricing very seriously. Mondragon, the icon of successful co-operatives for half a century, is a case in point. Established in the Basque area in Spain in 1956 with only 24 members, the Mondragon Co-operative Corporation now employs more than 50,000 people, with offices and production plants in four continents. In terms of mainstream economic indicators, the Mondragon group has outperformed many private companies (Thomas and Logan 1982: Chapter 5), although recently they have been criticized for detaching themselves from the lives of workers and focusing too much on managerial practices, rather than real workers' participation and democracy (see for instance, Kasmir 1996. As discussed above, this criticism is echoed by one radical advocate of co-operatives in Hong Kong, see So 2000: 90–96). For more than 40 years the Mondragon co-operative groups have, to a significant extent, advanced and maintained important principles of a co-operative movement, including democratic participation, at least formally and institutionally, equality in terms of incomes and job security. The Mondragon groups have also been able to transform the economic and cultural ecology of the Basque areas, as well as to inspire the development of inter-national co-operative movements in the post-war era. Interestingly, although many members that were interviewed by researchers revealed their dissatisfaction with the increasing manageralism, when asked whether or not they would prefer to work in a private company or to privatize the co-operatives, their answers were a unanimous "NO"! (Kasmir 1996: 165–166)

In the course of its development, management,[26] training, including technical knowledge as well as co-operative education, research and development, efficiency and competitiveness, accounting and financial arrangements, including pricing policies, have to a significant extent been articulated with ethical considerations such as equality, fairness, solidarity and mutual respect (Thomas and Logan 1982). The extent of the success of the Mondragon experience is subject to further debate, but at least it has established a viable, sustainable, and significant (both in terms of scale and scope) exemplar of alternative economic practices, which cannot come into existence without taking both business practices and alternative values seriously. The success and limitations of Mondragon should be understood in its own specific historical context.[27] Co-operative movements in general, and the Mondragon group in particular, can be regarded as incomplete only if measured by a utopian yardstick.

Professionalizing cultural mediation

In Hong Kong, there is a tradition for radical student leaders to assume posts in grassroots organizations and trade unions. They are the *de facto* mediators or translators between the grassroots and the intellectuals. Perhaps too strongly identified with the subaltern that they work for and with, some of these mediators have a tendency to detach themselves from radical intellectual works and may even go to the extreme and advance an anti-intellectual position. For those who take intellectual works seriously, they are tightly constrained by too much work and too few resources.[28] On the other hand, many intellectual works by academics in Hong Kong are even worse than what Edward Said described as "professionalism" in his little book *Representations of the Intellectuals* (Said 1996). This is because Hong Kong academic production mainly aims at the international (read the US) academic market and is almost completely detached from local concerns. We also know too well that academic language often alienates social activists.

In response to academic "professionalism" or, to use a better term "careerism" (a term I think that more accurately describes what Said really means), Said advocates intellectual amateurism – "an activity that is fueled by care and affection rather than by profit and selfish, narrow specialization" – and argues that intellectuals today should be able to "raise moral issues at the heart of even the most technical and professionalized activity" (Said 1996: 82–83). Said's warning and recommendation are certainly timely ones, but posting "professionalism" as opposite to "amateurism" runs the risk of downplaying the importance of serious intellectual (and even technical) works, especially in the context of Hong Kong social movements and cultural critiques. If professionalism, and not careerism, also means serious, specialized and good quality technical intellectual work, then it is important to encourage the production of such works in order to balance the already too heavy moral considerations in social movement circles in Hong Kong.

To effectively bridge the gap between the worlds of intellectuals (professionals) and social activists, one should simultaneously pursue at least two levels of articulation: linking technical and professional knowledge to critical and moral ideas and translating technical and professional intellectual knowledge to enhance the material conditions for new discourses or new languages (of economics, in our case) to emerge. In other words, it is important to connect different specialized professionals and professional knowledge with social movements, and in that process cultural activists (or amateur intellectuals) may play the role of translators between professional knowledge and social activism. In our case of rethinking the economy, specialized professionals such as businessmen, accountants, lawyers and production technicians, and professional knowledge such as that of financial, market and management issues, need to be incorporated into ethical-political considerations for advancing alternative economies. Only by seriously articulating this kind of "professional" knowledge and human resources (as a consultant or even participant) does amateurism that makes "connections across lines and barriers, in refusing to be tied down to a specialty, in caring for ideas and values despite the restrictions of a profession" (Said 1996; 76) become a feasible choice.

Concluding remarks

It is not hard to realize the difficulty of creating discursive conditions that facilitate the liberation of new imaginations and the opening up of new possibilities. And it is not easy to change established values by merely criticizing commonly accepted values or re-articulating them as something more critical and imaginative at the discursive level. In fact, as Grossberg observes, "the Right does actively seek to articulate issues into larger structures, even hierarchically organized structures, of commitment." (Grossberg 1992: 382) It is therefore not particularly effective to just create new concepts without articulating these concepts into larger discursive fields and structures. The strategy of creating completely new concepts and languages has been tried in various ways and has advanced to a certain extent.[29] However, it also has its limits. As discussed above, many "progressive languages" have already been re-articulated by mainstream organizations and the media into something extremely conservative.

Hijacked by conservative political forces, the language of the economy is not particularly easily re-articulated to the everyday desire of common people in the Hong Kong context, in which the "Left" stands for conservative (or pro-government) forces, while "Liberals" is another name for conservatives (suggesting that nothing substantial should be changed under the rhetoric of *laissez faire*). In such a confused context, the predominant political forces are pragmatic populism and neo-liberal conservatism. Hence, instead of criticizing the negative sides of capitalism by merely repeating conventional leftist and NGOs' language, the strategy of re-articulating mainstream economic language in alternative projects may be more effective in Hong Kong where, in addition to the confused political context, a strong business mentality dominates. This discursive strategy could be perceived as a battle on several fronts. The first step is to unsettle the myths of capitalism that are perpetuated by the existing articulation of economic language. As demonstrated above, an effective way to do so is to point out that these myths are not grounded on empirical facts. Then we may re-link the language that is conventionally affiliated with capitalist ideology to anti-capitalist forces, such as taking "no free lunch" and "*yongzhe zifu*" back and use them to the disadvantage of the capitalist power blocs. After disrupting the established connections between mainstream economic languages and capitalist reality, one can go further to reconnect the new economic languages (including the old languages in a new context) with the material contexts of alternative economies, through either a reinterpretation of the existing "capitalist" practices or linking up the language with the processes of creating alternative economies, such as co-operatives. The effectiveness of this last strategy heavily depends on the viability and sustainability of these various alternative economic practices, which in turn rely on taking the economic/technical aspects seriously.

By confusing the rhetoric with the reality, radical social activists and cultural critics in Hong Kong leave the domain of the economy and economic/business knowledge to the advocates of neo-liberalism and pragmatic populists, leading to the "transition" and "translation" of capitalism. Hence, to counter this trend, a critical intellectual project that seeks to represent the economy and capitalism differently is urgently required. This critical intellectual project needs to re-articulate every important aspect of material life to alternative structures and practices, and to connect popular economic concepts to existing and historical alternative experiences. The role of critical intellectuals as translators/mediators in this process is precisely to find effective ways to link technical/business/economic issues to ethical-political considerations.[30] This is certainly a vital challenge for intellectuals engaging in critical cultural studies.

Acknowledgements

The author would like to thank Lau kin-chi, Meaghan Morris, Pun Ngai and two anonymous reviewers for their valuable comments.

Notes

1 Foucault similarly describes the transition/translation process of the emergence of a modern disciplinary society. When talking about the formation of the disciplinary police forces that served as "an instrument for the political supervision of plots, opposition movements or revolts" in 18th-century France, Foucault argues that this disciplinary force "was a complex function since it linked the absolute power of the monarch to the lowest levels of power disseminated in society; since, between these different, enclosed institutions of discipline (workshops, armies, schools), *it extended an intermediary network, acting where they could not intervene, disciplining the non-disciplinary spaces; but it filled in the gaps, linked them together, guaranteed with its armed force an interstitial discipline and a meta-discipline*." See Foucault (1979: 215, emphasis added).

2 As Michel Callon argues, "economics, in the broad sense of the term, performs, shapes, and formats the economy, rather than observing how it functions." Cited from Gibson-Graham (2002).

3 In fact, the retreat of government from social welfare has been a worldwide phenomenon since the 1980s. To borrow the terms from Jeannie Martin (2002), the government has changed its role from a "redistributor" to a "regulator."

4 These retraining courses are heavily subsidized by the HKSAR government as a kind of "positive welfare," a key component of the "Third Way" social policies as advocated by Giddens (1998).

5 This is clearly presented in Ah So's (1996: 2) description of his Grassroots (non-)Organization: "From the very beginning, Grassroots Organization operates according to an 'anti-organization' principle – no membership, no vertical division of labour, no voting, (non-)members can freely participate or not participate in any work, (non-)membership fee is determined by each (non-)member." Moreover, the co-operative has never required a common will and goal (Chui 1998: 89). It is not surprising that this co-operative was rather short-lived.

6 See, for instance, the two symposiums on co-operatives published in *Alternative Discourses*, No. 2 (July 1998) and No. 5 (March 2000). Almost all these discussions on co-operatives are unrelated to the concrete operation of the co-operative as a business that strives to survive in the sea of capitalism. An illuminating case is the discussion of the Mondragon experiences. The advocates of co-operatives were among the first who introduced the Mondragon model to Hong Kong with great enthusiasm. Yet when the managerial nature of the Mondragon was brought up by international and local critics, the local advocates of Mondragon not only abandoned the model but also heavily criticized its bureaucratic tendency (So 2000). For a more detailed discussion of the Mondragon experiences, see the section "Retranslating the Economy" below.

7 Ironically, despite the government's intention of building up a "positive welfare" system through the CIIF "social investments," it seems impossible that the 12 funded projects are able to be sustainable because, except for one project, there is no income-generating mechanism in place.

8 Other senior government officials or consultants maintain similar views. For instance, Mr Yeoh Eng Kiong, the Head of the Health, Welfare and Food Bureau, complains that Hong Kong people are getting used to relying on the government to solve all their individual problems because the welfare services have expanded significantly in the past 5 to 10 years. He argues that this trend is not acceptable and "social problems have to be resolved by society, not the government" (*Hong Kong Economic Times*, 22–8–2002, P07). Dr Edgar W K Cheng, the former Chief Consultant of the Central Policy Unit (CPU), goes further to argue that "past experiences" of various countries have proved that even if the governments were willing to spend huge resources on a range of social projects, social problems may still not be resolved. In contrast, the "Third Sector" could be a feasible and effective alternative (Information Services Department, HKSAR Government, 19–10–2001). Similarly, Dr Nelson Chow Wing Sang, a conservative social work professor, argues that the government should reverse its social welfare policy in the last two decades and go back to the earlier (colonial) period in which voluntary organizations, such as the Tung Wah Group of Hospitals and *Kai Fong* associations, had taken care of the social welfare of the Chinese communities in Hong Kong without relying on government subsidies (*Ta Kung Pao*, 11–10–2001, A14).

9 The government also subcontracts many of its direct services to the NGO sector in the 1990s. One of the most notable examples is adult education.

10 According to Mrs Carrie Yau, the Secretary of the Health, Welfare and Food Bureau, 90% of the social welfare services in Hong Kong are provided by NGOs, which received HK$7 billion government subsidies in the fiscal year 2002. Aside from subcontracting out social services, the government has also systemically promoted voluntary work since 1999 by setting up a committee within the Social Welfare Department to encourage and monitor voluntary work (http://www.hwfb.gov.hk/ch/ speech/sp020914.htm).

11 Perhaps this also explains why only 12 out of a total of 227 proposals are funded. As a CIIF committee member complains, many applications submitted by local NGOs and social workers are "unqualified" and "they just think it is very easy to share a part of the pie" (*Apple Daily*, 15–01–2003, A04, my translation).

12 For instance, the largest pro-PRC trade union – the Hong Kong Federation of Trade Unions (FTU) – has recently set up an NGO – the Lok Kwan social service center. Under this center, several co-operatives are set up. According to Cheng Yiu Tong, the Chairman of the FTU, Lok Kwan would certainly apply for funding from the CIIF (*Oriental Daily* 8–22–2002: A23).

13 For instance, Lau Chin Shek, one of the most prominent independent trade union leaders in Hong Kong, explicitly argues that the market is by nature evil whereas social capital is humanistic (*Oriental Daily* 12–1–2002, B16).

14 At worst, this may turn into a politics of anger and resentment and "may even translate into a desire for Capitalism, the antagonist without which self-recognition is difficult and emotional energy diffuse." See J.K. Gibson-Graham, Stephen A. Resnick and Richard D. Wolff (2000: 14).

15 Similarly, "ATV Review," a conservative pro-Beijing news review program in Hong Kong, did not hesitate to support the anti-globalization demonstration in Genoa by equating the anti-G8 event in June to the anti-US (the West) discourse in order to emphasize the righteousness of the Chinese regime. This kind of pragmatic attitude from the Right is not special to Hong Kong. In Australia, for instance, the rural and regional areas were "portrayed in the popular media as an economic and social disaster area and in this context a new political party (One Nation led by Pauline Hanson) emerged to mobilize economic nationalist, anti-immigration and racist resentments within the Australian electorate" Gibson-Graham (2002: 21). Likewise, in Europe and North America, Sakai (n.d.) has shown that the revival of the Fascist movements has a close connection with anti-globalization movements. With its long-term investments on "affective commonalities" in all directions, the Right has been able to direct the energy of the anti-globalization movements to the support of the new Fascist regimes. See Grossberg (1992: 393) for a similar argument. In other words, without an extensive material basis and effective discursive strategies that could articulate the anti-globalization demonstrations to alternative projects, the new radical social movements have ironically paved the way for the revival of the Fascist movements in Europe and in the USA. I think we should take Sakia's warning seriously.

16 The most notable "Leftist" forces include the political party Democratic Alliance for Betterment of Hong Kong, the Hong Kong Federation of Trade Unions, and the newspapers *Ta Kung Pao* and *Wen Wei Po*.

17 Despite many having already pointed out that globalization is at best a tendency of economic and socio-cultural change, and by no means having succeeded in shaping a homogeneous world, it is increasingly popularized by enemies and supporters alike as something which results in a disempowering impact on social movements. I tend to agree with Touraine that "[t]he idea of globalization has in fact been popularized by the ultra-left rather than the right." See Touraine (2001: 17).

18 In this respect, Hong Kong is not alone. The Reagan and Thatcher "neo-liberal" governments never sincerely promoted "free market" and "free trade" either. In contrast, as Chomsky (1999) notes, despite their rhetoric of liberalism, both the Reagan and Thatcher governments adopted the most protective trade measures in the US and Britain in the last few decades. Likewise, international "capitalist agents" such as the WTO have never whole-heartedly promoted "free trade." What these organizations have been doing is setting up regulations that benefit the privileged giant transnational corporations the most (Hui 2000). As Alain Touraine (2001: 14) argues, "[f]ree trade in goods and the unrestricted movement of capital are two very different things." Similarly, in contrast to popular belief, not many chief executive officers (CEOs) of transnational corporations (TNCs) take management and accounting seriously as a rational means to improve their firms' technical efficiency. Nor do they necessarily have a keen interest in maximizing profit for stockholders. Instead, many of them are more willing to spend time and energy in seeking their personal benefits, which are not entirely material – such as self-esteem, respect, security, reducing pressure and responsibility (Goux 1997; Thrift 1997, 1998). In fact, accounting and management strategies are more often used as rhetorical devices to present healthy images of the firm to the public than as a rational means for organizing businesses (Thompson 1994; Montagna 1990).

19 For example, "[b]etween 1990 to 1994, the proportion of the EU's relief aid channelled through NGOs rose from 47% to 67%. The Red Cross reckons that NGOs now disburse more money than the World Bank . . . In 1995 non-profit groups (including, but not only, NGOs) provided over 12% of all jobs in the Netherlands, 8% in America and 6% in Britain" (*The Economist* January 29, 2000: 26–27). In Hong Kong, the funding decisions of the CIIF are illustrative. As discussed above, almost all the 12 first batch funded proposals are old wine in new bottles, i.e., providing conventional social services by establishing networks of voluntary workers but in the name of promoting social capital, the magic word that the CIIF advocates.

20 For instance, since 1973, corporations such as Toyota, GM, and IBM have increasingly adopted team concepts, employee-ownership programs and participatory management as new managerial strategies aimed at increasing work incentives and productivity. Under Reagan and Thatcher,

many corporations in the USA and UK promoted the "worker ownership" scheme by giving tax breaks to firms that gave stocks to their workers. In 1991, more than 9,000 US firms had established employee stock option programs. See Kasmir (1996: 3–7, 19).

21 See Harvey (2000: 90). In fact, Harvey's recommendation that the "[s]trict enforcement of such rights would entail massive and in some senses revolutionary transformations in the political-economy of capitalism" (Harvey 2000: 90) has already been suggested earlier by E.P. Thompson, who maintains that law, which could be used by capitalists, could also be turned into constructive and productive forces for dominated people. It is because "[i]f the law is evidently partial and unjust, then it will mask nothing, legitimize nothing, contribute nothing to any class's hegemony . . . It cannot seem to be so without upholding its own logic and criteria of equity; indeed, on occasion, by actually being just . . . And the rulers were, in serious senses, whether willingly or unwillingly the prisoners of their own rhetoric; they played the games of power according to rules which suited them, but they could not break those rules or the whole game would be thrown away" (Thompson 1975: 263).

22 One of the most obvious examples is the construction of various infrastructures (such as highways, airports and railways) that are not regarded as government subsidies by dominant economic discourses. Yet taking a closer look at these constructions, it is not difficult to illustrate that for the most part they are used by the business community and its employees, thus significantly lowering the production and reproduction costs of these corporations.

23 See Touraine (2001: 18–19). Touraine points out that, while in France neo-liberalism and social welfare are seen as incompatible, in Italy, Denmark, the Netherlands and Portugal, economic neo-liberalism has been reconciled with social welfare. See Touraine (2001: 8).

24 See Gibson-Graham (2002: 23). Gibson-Graham also tries to facilitate the development of various kinds of alternative economic practices, some of which have already existed in the sea of capitalisms in various forms. In their own words, their project is "cultivating new ways of being, that created new languages, discourses and representations, that built organizations" (Gibson-Graham 2002: 34).

25 Another interesting example of retranslating the economy is the community money project. By looking back to these heterogeneous historical experiences of money and markets, that were un-related to what we call capitalism today, it certainly opens up our imagination about the possibility of alternative economies that in turn provide new contexts for redefining economic concepts. For a detailed discussion on this possibility in the Hong Hong context, see Hui (2004).

26 Father Arizmendi, the founder of the Mondragon co-operative, had a very clear idea of the importance of management in operating the co-operative. He wrote: "Human work must be subjected to discipline and its performance as a team effort requires order and thus authority. The members of this co-operative, once they have elected those most suitable for government, must show spontaneous and rigorous respect for the order of those who hold positions of command within their internal structure." Cited from Lutz (1997: 1410).

27 Kasmir (1996) has provided an interesting analysis of the political context of the development and transformation of the Mondragon experience.

28 One of the reasons for local activists' and groups' reluctance to engage in international or regional exchanges (including exchanges with academics) is the lack of intellectual resources. For instance, in responding to the question of why social movements should engage in inter-Asian exchanges, Wuo Young-yi, the coordinator of Committees for Actions for Labor Legislation in Taiwan, complains that "if we prioritize local work, then perhaps these exchanges would have a low priority on our list" because only a handful of organizers can master a foreign language and they do not even have the time to check e-mails. In such discouraging conditions, it is no surprise to hear local activists remark "I'd rather sleep at home than go to a conference and speak English." See Wuo (2001: 133 and 136).

29 In particular, in 1994, some Hong Kong cultural activists already pointed out that institutionalized and sometimes abused terms such as "exploitation," "unfairness," and inequality in resources" have long lost their communicative functions that express people's emotion. Even worse, these dead languages may alienate people and reduce their desire to participate in social movements. They therefore advocate the reconstruction of symbols that originated from real life and feelings, i.e. symbols that can better facilitate the communication between people. And the languages they advocate are mainly expressions through the body (as in drama and dancing). Mok, Tang, and Hung (1994: 71–83).

30 However, one has to be very cautious about this mediation process. Merely bringing people of different sites together to talk to each other is not necessary useful. Communication is a long-term process and involves much ground work before it can be effectively conducted. The ethics of translators and mediators is also the ethic of "parasites," that requires a sensitivity to the politics of dirty work, such as administrative and secretarial work.

References

Ah So 亞蘇 (1996) "A Story of the Grassroots Association" 基層社傳奇, *Co-operative Bi-Monthly* 合作社雙月刊 No. 1 (Dec.): 2–17.

Bourdieu, Pierre (1998a) *Acts of Resistance: against the new myths of our time*, Richard Nice (trans.) Cambridge: Polity Press.

Bourdieu, Pierre (1998b) *Practical Reason*, Oxford: Polity Press.

Braudel, Fernand (1982) *Civilization and Capitalism 15th-18th Century Vol. II – The Wheels of Commerce*, New York: Harper & Row.

Braudel, Fernand (1984) *Civilization and Capitalism 15th-18th Century Vol. III – The Perspective of the World*, New York: Harper & Row.

Carrier, James (1995) *Gifts and Commodities – Exchange and Western Capitalism since 1700*, London and New York: Routledge.

Carrier, James (1998) "Abstraction in Western Economic Practice." In James Carrier and Daniel Miller (eds) *Virtualism – A New Political Economy*, Oxford and New York: Berg, 25–47.

Chakrabarty, Dipesh (2000) *Provincializing Europe – Postcolonial Thought and Historical Difference*, Princeton and Oxford: Princeton University Press.

Chapman, Malcolm and Peter J. Buckley (1997) "Markets, Transaction Costs, Economists and Social Anthropologists." In James Carrier (ed.) *Meaning of the Market – The Free Market in Western Culture*, Oxford and New York: Berg, 225–250.

Chomsky, Noam (1999) *Profit over People: Neoliberalism and Global Order*, New York: Seven Stories Press.

Chui, Lo Tau 崔老頭 (1998) "A Story of Cooperative Typists Association" 合作打字社傳奇, *Alternative Discourses* 基進論壇 No. 2: 87–89.

Consumer Council (1994a) *Are Hong Kong Depositors Fairly Treated?* HK: Consumer Council.

Consumer Council (1994b) *Report on the Supermarket Industry in Hong Kong*, Hong Kong: Consumer Council.

Consumer Council (1996) *How Competitive is the Private Residential Property Market?* Hong Kong: Consumer Council.

Feng, Bang Yen 馮邦彥 (1996) *British Conglomerates in Hong Kong 1841–1996* 香港英資財團, Hong Kong: Joint Publishing Co.

Feng, Bang Yen (2002) *A Century of Hong Kong Financial Development* 香港金融業百年, Hong Kong: Joint Publishing Co.

Foucault, Michel (1979) *Discipline and Punish – The Birth of the Prison*, New York: Vintage Books.

Gibson-Graham, J.K. (1996) *The End of Capitalism (As We Knew It) – A Feminist Critique of Political Economy*, Cambridge, Mass.: Blackwell Publishers.

Gibson-Graham, J.K., Stephen A. Resnick and Richard D. Wolff (2000) "Introduction: Class in a Poststructuralist Frame." In J.K. Gibson-Graham, Stephen A. Resnick and Richard D. Wolff (eds) *Class and Its Others*, Minneapolis and London: University of Minnesota Press, 1–22.

Gibson-Graham, J.K. (2002) "Beyond Global vs. Local: Economic Politics Outside the Binary Frame." Forthcoming in A. Herod and M. Wright (eds) *The Geography of Scale*, Oxford: Blackwell.

Giddens, Anthony (1998) *The Third Way – the Renewal of Social Democracy*, Cambridge, UK: Polity Press.

Globalisation Monitor 全球監察 (2000) No.2, November 1999 and No. 5, May.

Goux, Jean-Joseph (1997) "Values and Speculations: The Stock Exchange Paradigm," *Cultural Values* 1(2): 159–177.

Grossberg, Lawrence (1992) *We Gotta Get Out of this Place – Popular Conservatism and Postmodern Culture*, New York and London: Routledge.

Ha Suk 夏菽 (2000) "An Investigation of Hong Kong Cooperative Movements" 香港合作社運動考察, *Alternative Discourses* 基進論壇 No.5: 79–89.

Harvey, David (2000) *Spaces of Hope*, Berkeley and Los Angeles: University of California Press.

Hui, Po-keung 許寶強 (2000) "Rescuing Free Trade From the WTO," *Asian Exchange* 16(1): 86–97.

Hui, Po-keung (2002) *What Capitalism is Not* 資本主義不是什么, Hong Kong: Oxford University Press 香港：牛津大學出版社.

Hui, Po-keung (2004) "In Search of a Communal Economic Subject – Reflections on the Community Currency Project in Hong Kong." In Agnes Ku and Pun Ngai (eds) *Remaking Citizenship in Hong Kong*, London and New York: Routledge, 215–234.

Kasmir, Sharryn (1996) *The Myth of Mondragon – Cooperatives, Politics, and Working-Class Life in a Basque Town*, Albany, New York: State University of New York Press.

Kong San (2000) 崗山 "The Defects of Privatizing Water Services" 水務私營的害處, *Globalization Monitor* 全球化監察, No.5, May, http://globalmon.uhome.net/.

Lam, Pui Kei 林培基 and So Yiu-Cheong 蘇耀昌 (1998) "Tuen Wandragon – A Symposium on Co-operatives" 荃灣拉貢 – 合作社專輯, *Alternative Discourses* 基進論壇 No.2 (July): 75–99.

Lutz, Mark A. (1997) "The Mondragon Co-operative Complex: An Application of Kantian Ethics to Social Economics," *International Journal of Social Economics* 24(12): 1404–1421.

Martin, Jeannie with P. O'Loughlin (2002) *Women and sustainability in regional Australia*, Final report to the Minister, Department of Women, New South Wales Government, *Partnership Project 2000*.

McGee, T.G. (1973) *Hawkers in Hong Kong*, HK: Centre of Asian Studies, University of Hong Kong.

Mok Chiu Yu, Tang Wing Mui, Hung Fan Keung 莫昭如、鄧詠梅、孔繁強 (1994) "Personal Growth, Social Organizations, and Hong Kong People's Drama" 個人成長，社區 組織與香港民眾戲劇, *Hong Kong Grassroots Movements – Non-mainstream Perspectives* 香港基層運動 – 非主流角度, Hong Kong: Radical Publisher 香港：基進出版社, 71–83.

Montagna, Paul (1990) "Accounting Rationality and Financial Legitimation." In Sharon Zukin and Paul DiMaggio (eds) *Structures of Capital*, Cambridge and New York: Cambridge University Press, 227–260.

Said, Edward W. (1996) *Representations of the Intellectual*, New York: Vintage Books.

Sakia, J. (n.d.) "Aryan Politics & Fighting the W.T.O.," from www.nologo.org.

Smart, Josephine (1989) *The Political Economy of Street Hawkers in Hong Kong*, HK: Centre of Asian Studies, University of Hong Kong.

So, Yiu Cheong 蘇耀昌 (2000) "Mondragon in Hong Kong" 蒙德拉貢模式在香港, *Alternative Discourses* 基進論壇 No.5: 90–96.

Thomas, Henk and Chris Logan (1982) *Mondragon: An Economic Analysis*, London: George Allen & Unwin.

Thompson, E. P. (1975) *Whigs and Hunters – The Origin of the Black Act*, London: Allen Lane.

Thompson, Grahame (1994) "Early Double-Entry Bookkeeping and the Rhetoric of Accounting Calculation." In A.G. Hopwood and P. Miller (eds) *Accounting as Social and Institutional Practice*, Cambridge and New York: Cambridge University Press, 40–66.

Thrift, Nigel (1997) "The Rise of Soft Capitalism," *Cultural Values* 1(1): 29–57.

Thrift, Nigel (1998) "Virtual Capitalism: The Globalisation of Reflexive Business Knowledge." In James Carrier and Daniel Miller (eds) *Virtualism – A New Political Economy*, Oxford and New York: Berg, 161–186.

Touraine, Alain (2001) *Beyond Neoliberalism*, David Macey (trans.) Malden, Mass.: Polity Press.

Wong, Ying Yu 王英瑜 (2000) "Privatization, WTO, and Chinese Workers" 私有化、世貿與中國工人, *Globalization Monitor* 全球化監察 No.5, May, http://globalmon.uhome.net/.

Wuo, Young-ie (2001) "Why Inter-Asia? Labour movement," Petrus Liu (trans.) *Inter-Asia Cultural Studies* 2(1): 133–136.

Yuen, Wai Ching 阮惠晴 (2000) "Protecting Established Interests or Anti-Privatization Movement?" 是「既得利益保衛戰」還是「反私有化運動」 *Globalization Monitor* 全球化監察 No.5, May, http://globalmon.uhome.net/.

Names and special terms

Alternative Discourses 基進論壇
Apple Daily 蘋果日報
ATV Review 亞視評論
Carrie Yau 尤曾家麗
Cheng Yiu Tong 鄭耀棠
Co-operative Bi-Monthly 合作社雙月刊
CSSA feeds lazy bones 綜援養懶人
Democratic Alliance for Betterment of Hong Kong 民建聯
Donald Tsang 曾蔭權
Edgar W K Cheng 鄭維健
Hong Kong Economic Times 經濟日報
Hong Kong Federation of Trade Unions 工聯會
Kai Fong Associations 街坊會
Lam Hang-chi 林行止
Lau Chin Shek 劉千石
Lok Kwan 樂群
Nelson Chow Wing Sang 周永新
Oriental Daily 東方日報
PTU 工聯會
Raymond Wu 鄔維庸
Sing Pao 成報
Ta Kung Pao 大公報
Tung Chee Hwa 董建華
Tung Wah Group of Hospitals 東華三院
Wen Wei Po 文匯報
Xin Bao – Hong Kong Economic Journal 信報
Yeoh Eng Kiong 楊永強
yongzhe zifu 用者自付 user pays

Index

4.3 Incident *see* Cheju April Third Incident
'4.3 Speaks' 196, 197

Abaradh Bashini (*Secluded Women*) (Hussein) 315
academic professionalism 604–5
action cinema 427–48; class and 434–6, 440–1, 442–3, 445; Georg Lukács 441–4; major and minor modes of 436–41; role of Hong Kong in shaping global popular culture 430–4
activists: female labour 499, 502; film festivals organized by 498; gender/sexuality 362n22; Hong Kong 604; Indonesian 215, 221n9, 513–14, 517, 518; intellectuals and 605, 609n28; Japanese 255–6; Korean 490; Malaysian 156; peace 571–7; women fans 541; *see also* movements
address in cinema, modes of 471, 473, 479, 485, 488n9
Adorno, Theodore 470
affect 328–9
affective alliance 533, 536
Africa 109–10
alternative bands in Hong Kong 523–38; emotional energies produced by 526–7, 533–6; LMF 525–6, 528–30; masculinity of 530–1; sub-cultural politics in Hong Kong 523–5; transgression of 531–2
alternative economic practices 603, 606, 609nn24, 25; *see also* cooperatives and community economies
alternative frames of reference 111–12
A-Mei 135, 323, 324, 326–32, 339, 340n3
Americanism 225, 247, 259–65, 511; *see also* Japan, Americanization in postwar; Korea, Americanism in; military bases on Okinawa, US
Anderson, Benedict 264–5
Anderson, Perry 71
Angel of Fury (Worth) 444–5
anthropology 108–9, 148
anti-capitalism 594, 597, 599, 601, 606; *see also* capitalism
anti-globalization 517, 588, 608n15; *see also* globalization

Appadurai, Arjun 263, 464, 508, 511
appearances 228, 233–6, 528; *see also* transgender subjects, Taiwanese
Appiah, Kwame 110
area studies 145, 148
arts and culture, Indonesian 511–13
'Asia is one' 11, 16–17
Asianism 25–7, 37, 45, 51, 53–4; *see also* Great Asianism
Asianism (Takeuchi) 25–7
Asian Peace Alliance (APA) 571, 572–6
Asian Perspectives 43–56, 60n23; China 49–50; Hamashita Takeshi 44–5, 51–2; idea of Asia 55–6; Kawakatsu Heita 47–9; Mizoguchi Yuzo 43–4, 45
Asian Women's Fund (AWF) 181–2
Asia question 9–11, 21–3, 51, 78, 98; *see also* *Asian Perspectives*; intellectual history of modern Japan
audiences 127–32, 146–9; *see also* fans
Australian cinema 432, 433, 434
authoritarianism, third world 580–1, 584, 589
Azim, Firdous 311–22; Bengali women's writing 313–17; women sex workers in Bangladesh 317–21

Bachchan, Amitabh 451–2
Bandung spirit 578, 582–3, 585–8, 589–90, 590n1
Bangladesh 316–21
beauty 134, 233–5, 261
Bengal, literature of 312–17
Benjamin, Walter 238, 308
Best of the Best (Radler) 435–6, 438, 439, 440–1, 443
Bicol 261–3
'BitTorrent' 556–60, 565
blockage 474
blockbusters, Korean 490–2, 494, 496
body: in action cinema 444; emotional energies and 526–7; modernization of 225, 227–8, 233–40; transgender subjects and 347, 349–50, 354–7